UNIVERSITY CASEBOOK SERIES®

CONSTITUTIONAL LAW

CASES AND MATERIALS

CONCISE FIFTEENTH EDITION

JONATHAN D. VARAT

Professor of Law Emeritus and Former Dean
University of California, Los Angeles

VIKRAM D. AMAR

Dean and Iwan Foundation Professor of Law
University of Illinois College of Law

FOUNDATION
PRESS

University Casebook Series is a trademark registered in the U.S. Patent and Trademark Office.

© 2006, 2009 THOMSON REUTERS/FOUNDATION PRESS
© 2013 LEG, Inc. d/b/a/ West Academic Publishing
© 2017 LEG, Inc. d/b/a West Academic
    444 Cedar Street, Suite 700
    St. Paul, MN 55101
    1-877-888-1330

Printed in the United States of America

ISBN: 978-1-63460-326-3

For Our Families, Who Sustain Us

PREFACE

Since our last edition, the sole vacancy on the Supreme Court occurred when Justice Antonin Scalia died on February 13, 2016. The second of President Ronald Reagan's three appointments to the Court, Justice Scalia had joined the Court on September 26, 1986, and during his almost 30-year service considered himself an ardent "originalist." The day Justice Scalia's death became public, Senate Majority Leader Mitch McConnell (R-KY) issued a public statement declaring that the Republican Senate majority would not consider any nominee put forth by President Barack Obama, then less than a year away from finishing his second term, and that the vacancy should be left to the next President to fill. President Obama responded that he intended to "fulfill [his] constitutional duty to appoint a judge to our highest court," and that, notwithstanding contrary intimations by Republicans, there was no "well established tradition" that a President could not fill a Court vacancy during the last year of a presidential administration. About a month later, on March 16, 2016, President Obama nominated Merrick Garland, who had served as a Judge on the United States Court of Appeals for the DC Circuit since 1997 and at the time of his nomination was the Chief Judge of that Circuit, to fill the vacancy created by Justice Scalia's death. The Senate Republicans made good on their commitment not to hold hearings or vote on Chief Judge Garland, and his nomination lapsed on January 3, 2017—the end of the 114th Congress—after 293 days.

President Donald J. Trump won the election in November 2016 with a majority of the Electoral College (though he lost the popular vote), and on January 31, 2017, he nominated 49-year-old Neil Gorsuch, a Judge on the United States Court of Appeals for the Tenth Circuit since 2006, to fill the vacancy. Judge Gorsuch had been one of 21 people whose names then-Candidate Trump had released in September 2016, during the presidential campaign, as potential Supreme Court picks. After Judge Gorsuch was nominated, and after hearings were held, Democrats in the Senate mounted a filibuster, prompting the slight Republican majority in the Senate to adopt what has variously been called the "constitutional option" or (less charitably) the "nuclear option," a majoritarian parliamentary procedure designed to eliminate the filibuster device as to Supreme Court appointments. (A Democratic majority of Senators in November 2013 had already invoked the constitutional option to eliminate the filibuster for all federal judicial appointments other than Supreme Court appointments.) On April 7, 2017, Judge Gorsuch's nomination came to a floor vote, where his confirmation prevailed 54–45 (with three Democrats joining all the Republicans in attendance.) Justice Gorsuch received his commission on April 8, 2017, and took the oath of office two days later, on Monday, April 10, 2017.

It is of course difficult to predict—based on his prior writings and the limited information that Supreme Court confirmation hearings of recent decades tend to generate—how Justice Gorsuch's voting patterns on the Court might diverge from those of his predecessor, Justice Scalia. It may be worth noting, however, that, like Justice Scalia, Justice Gorsuch is a public proponent of originalism. Most analysts thus do not expect dramatic changes in the Court's directions on account of Justice Scalia having been replaced by Justice Gorsuch, although any subsequent vacancy during the Trump Administration could have that effect. Most striking for the Court at this point is that the Republicans having won the White House and the Senate in the fall of 2016, the Democrats lost a substantial chance to have a Supreme Court with a majority of its members appointed by Democratic Presidents. The Court has not had a majority of Justices appointed by Democratic Presidents since Republican President Richard Nixon appointed Justice Harry Blackmun to the Court to replace Justice Abe Fortas in May of 1970.

With respect to the Court's opinions during the past four years since the last edition of this book, perhaps the most notable development—one that was highlighted in both presidential campaigns' treatment of the future of the Court, and one that receives prominent treatment in this new edition of the casebook—was the Court's recognition of a constitutional right to marriage equality for gays and lesbians in *Obergefell v. Hodges*, perhaps the most significant case in a generation concerning constitutional equality and dignity rights. Yet *Obergefell* was far from the only major ruling in the last four years. In this, the 15th Concise Edition, we have included a number of other significant doctrinal developments across the constitutional range, incorporating substantial treatment of major separation of powers rulings (especially *Zivotofsky v. Kerry* and *National Labor Relations Board v. Noel Canning*), and cases concerning congressional power over the States pursuant to the Reconstruction Amendments (*Shelby County v. Holder*). Important but more fact-intensive rulings in abortion rights (*Whole Woman's Health v. Hellerstedt*) and affirmative action (*Fisher v. University of Texas*) are treated in depth as well. As for the First Amendment, an important case concerning public fora (*McCullen v. Coakley)* is presented in full.. Finally, this Edition contains developments in religious liberty and equality, including the important if incremental Establishment Clause ruling in *Town of Greece v. Galloway*.

Although many of its cases are new, the goal and approach of the book remain unchanged: to offer deep and wide coverage of almost all major areas of constitutional doctrine by focusing—more than any other major casebook—on the text of Supreme Court opinions and other primary documents. For several decades the distinctive pedagogical approach reflected in the book—its commitment to providing as much of the raw decisional, statutory and historical background material as is practical—has allowed teachers to structure constitutional law courses as they see fit, and has encouraged students to formulate their own generalizations directly from the materials. The book covers all major traditional constitutional topics, including the role of the federal judiciary, separation of powers, federalism, the non-criminal provisions of the Bill of Rights, and the Reconstruction Amendments.

To make room for the important new developments mentioned above (among others), we necessarily consolidated, condensed and trimmed other, less vital, sections in the book so that, even with all the new materials, the 15th Edition is not appreciably longer than the 14th. One simply cannot offer comprehensive coverage of major areas of constitutional doctrine in a lightweight book, but we have done our best to keep the book's size manageable.

In keeping with our past practice, we have included in this 15th Edition cases decided by the Court though the October 2015 Term; a 2017 softbound supplement will be published this summer and will address decisions handed down during the October 2016 Term.

Notes on style: As we have done in previous editions, we have indicated our restatement of the facts or other passages in principal cases by square brackets around our descriptions; we have omitted footnotes of the Court without specifically indicating that fact; footnotes that we have kept retain their original numbering used by the Court; and footnotes we have added to cases are indicated by letters.

JONATHAN DAVID VARAT
VIKRAM DAVID AMAR

Los Angeles, California
Champaign, Illinois
April 2017

SUMMARY OF CONTENTS

TABLE OF CONTENTS

PART 2. ALLOCATION OF GOVERNMENTAL POWERS: THE NATION AND THE STATES; THE PRESIDENT, THE CONGRESS, AND THE COURTS

PART 3. GOVERNMENT AND THE INDIVIDUAL: THE PROTECTION OF LIBERTY AND PROPERTY UNDER THE DUE PROCESS AND EQUAL PROTECTION CLAUSES

PART 4. CONSTITUTIONAL PROTECTION OF EXPRESSION AND CONSCIENCE

TABLE OF CASES

The principal cases are in bold type.

UNIVERSITY CASEBOOK SERIES®

CONSTITUTIONAL LAW

CASES AND MATERIALS

CONCISE FIFTEENTH EDITION

PART 1

THE CONSTITUTION AND THE COURTS: THE JUDICIAL FUNCTION IN CONSTITUTIONAL CASES

CHAPTER 1

THE CONSTITUTION

1. THE CONSTITUTION OF THE UNITED STATES OF AMERICA

We the People of the United States, in Order to form a more perfect Union, establish Justice, insure domestic Tranquility, provide for the common defence, promote the general Welfare, and secure the Blessings of Liberty to ourselves and our Posterity, do ordain and establish this Constitution for the United States of America.

ARTICLE I

Section 1. All legislative Powers herein granted shall be vested in a Congress of the United States, which shall consist of a Senate and House of Representatives.

Section 2. [1] The House of Representatives shall be composed of Members chosen every second Year by the People of the several States, and the Electors in each State shall have the Qualifications requisite for Electors of the most numerous Branch of the State Legislature.

[2] No Person shall be a Representative who shall not have attained to the Age of twenty five Years, and been seven Years a Citizen of the United States, and who shall not, when elected, be an Inhabitant of that State in which he shall be chosen.

[3] Representatives and direct Taxes shall be apportioned among the several States which may be included within this Union, according to their respective Numbers, which shall be determined by adding to the whole Number of free Persons, including those bound to Service for a Term of Years, and excluding Indians not taxed, three fifths of all other Persons. The actual Enumeration shall be made within three Years after the first Meeting of the Congress of the United States, and within every subsequent Term of ten Years, in such Manner as they shall by Law direct. The Number of Representatives shall not exceed one for every thirty Thousand, but each State shall have at Least one Representative; and until such enumeration shall be made, the State of New Hampshire shall be entitled to chuse three, Massachusetts eight, Rhode Island and Providence Plantations one, Connecticut five, New York six, New Jersey four, Pennsylvania eight, Delaware one, Maryland six, Virginia ten, North Carolina five, South Carolina five, and Georgia three.

[4] When vacancies happen in the Representation from any State, the Executive Authority thereof shall issue Writs of Election to fill such Vacancies.

[5] The House of Representatives shall chuse their Speaker and other Officers; and shall have the sole Power of Impeachment.

Section 3. [1] The Senate of the United States shall be composed of two Senators from each State, chosen by the Legislature thereof, for six Years; and each Senator shall have one Vote.

[2] Immediately after they shall be assembled in Consequence of the first Election, they shall be divided as equally as may be into three Classes. The Seats of the Senators of the first Class shall be vacated at the Expiration of the Second Year, of the second Class at the Expiration of the fourth Year, and of the third Class at the Expiration of the sixth Year, so that one third may be chosen every second Year; and if Vacancies happen by Resignation, or otherwise, during the Recess of the Legislature of any State, the Executive thereof may make temporary Appointments until the next Meeting of the Legislature, which shall then fill such Vacancies.

[3]   No Person shall be a Senator who shall not have attained to the Age of thirty Years, and been nine Years a Citizen of the United States, and who shall not, when elected, be an Inhabitant of that State for which he shall be chosen.

[4]   The Vice President of the United States shall be President of the Senate, but shall have no Vote, unless they be equally divided.

[5]   The Senate shall chuse their other Officers, and also a President pro tempore, in the Absence of the Vice President, or when he shall exercise the Office of President of the United States.

[6]   The Senate shall have the sole Power to try all Impeachments. When sitting for that Purpose, they shall be on Oath or Affirmation. When the President of the United States is tried, the Chief Justice shall preside: And no Person shall be convicted without the Concurrence of two thirds of the Members present.

[7]   Judgment in Cases of Impeachment shall not extend further than to removal from Office, and disqualification to hold and enjoy any Office of honor, Trust, or Profit under the United States: but the Party convicted shall nevertheless be liable and subject to Indictment, Trial, Judgment, and Punishment, according to Law.

Section 4 [1] The Times, Places and Manner of holding Elections for Senators and Representatives, shall be prescribed in each State by the Legislature thereof; but the Congress may at any time by Law make or alter such Regulations, except as to the Places of chusing Senators.

[2]   The Congress shall assemble at least once in every Year, and such Meeting shall be on the first Monday in December, unless they shall by Law appoint a different Day.

Section 5.   [1] Each House shall be the Judge of the Elections, Returns, and Qualifications of its own Members, and a Majority of each shall constitute a Quorum to do Business; but a smaller Number may adjourn from day to day, and may be authorized to compel the Attendance of absent Members, in such Manner, and under such Penalties as each House may provide.

[2]   Each House may determine the Rules of its Proceedings, punish its Members for disorderly Behavior, and, with the Concurrence of two thirds, expel a Member.

[3]   Each House shall keep a Journal of its Proceedings, and from time to time publish the same, excepting such Parts as may in their Judgment require Secrecy; and the Yeas and Nays of the Members of either House on any question shall, at the Desire of one fifth of those Present, be entered on the Journal.

[4]   Neither House, during the Session of Congress, shall, without the Consent of the other, adjourn for more than three days, nor to any other Place than that in which the two Houses shall be sitting.

Section 6. [1] The Senators and Representatives shall receive a Compensation for their Services, to be ascertained by Law, and paid out of the Treasury of the United States. They shall in all Cases, except Treason, Felony and Breach of the Peace, be privileged from Arrest during their Attendance at the Session of their respective Houses, and in going to and returning from the same; and for any Speech or Debate in either House, they shall not be questioned in any other Place.

[2]   No Senator or Representative shall, during the Time for which he was elected, be appointed to any civil Office under the Authority of the United States, which shall have been created, or the Emoluments whereof shall have been increased during such time; and no Person holding any Office under the United States, shall be a Member of either House during his Continuance in Office.

Section 7. [1] All Bills for raising Revenue shall originate in the House of Representatives; but the Senate may propose or concur with Amendments as on other Bills.

[2] Every Bill which shall have passed the House of Representatives and the Senate, shall, before it become a Law, be presented to the President of the United States; If he approve he shall sign it, but if not he shall return it, with his Objections to the House in which it shall have originated, who shall enter the Objections at large on their Journal, and proceed to reconsider it. If after such Reconsideration two thirds of that House shall agree to pass the Bill, it shall be sent together with the Objections, to the other House, by which it shall likewise be reconsidered, and if approved by two thirds of that House, it shall become a Law. But in all such Cases the Votes of both Houses shall be determined by yeas and Nays, and the Names of the Persons voting for and against the Bill shall be entered on the Journal of each House respectively. If any Bill shall not be returned by the President within ten Days (Sundays excepted) after it shall have been presented to him, the Same shall be a Law, in like Manner as if he had signed it, unless the Congress by their Adjournment prevent its Return in which Case it shall not be a Law.

[3] Every Order, Resolution, or Vote, to Which the Concurrence of the Senate and House of Representatives may be necessary (except on a question of Adjournment) shall be presented to the President of the United States; and before the Same shall take Effect, shall be approved by him, or being disapproved by him, shall be repassed by two thirds of the Senate and House of Representatives, according to the Rules and Limitations prescribed in the Case of a Bill.

Section 8. [1] The Congress shall have Power To lay and collect Taxes, Duties, Imposts and Excises, to pay the Debts and provide for the common Defence and general Welfare of the United States; but all Duties, Imposts and Excises shall be uniform throughout the United States;

[2] To borrow money on the credit of the United States;

[3] To regulate Commerce with foreign Nations, and among the several States, and with the Indian Tribes; *commerce eaob clause*

[4] To establish an uniform Rule of Naturalization, and uniform Laws on the subject of Bankruptcies throughout the United States;

[5] To coin Money, regulate the Value thereof, and of foreign Coin, and fix the Standard of Weights and Measures;

[6] To provide for the Punishment of counterfeiting the Securities and current Coin of the United States;

[7] To Establish Post Offices and Post Roads;

[8] To promote the Progress of Science and useful Arts, by securing for limited Times to Authors and Inventors the exclusive Right to their respective Writings and Discoveries;

[9] To constitute Tribunals inferior to the supreme Court;

[10] To define and punish Piracies and Felonies committed on the high Seas, and Offenses against the Law of Nations;

[11] To declare War, grant Letters of Marque and Reprisal, and make Rules concerning Captures on Land and Water;

[12] To raise and support Armies, but no Appropriation of Money to that Use shall be for a longer Term than two Years;

[13] To provide and maintain a Navy;

[14] To make Rules for the Government and Regulation of the land and naval Forces;

[15] To provide for calling forth the Militia to execute the Laws of the Union, suppress Insurrections and repel Invasions;

[16] To provide for organizing, arming, and disciplining, the Militia, and for governing such Part of them as may be employed in the Service of the United States, reserving to the States respectively, the Appointment of the Officers, and the Authority of training the Militia according to the discipline prescribed by Congress;

[17] To exercise exclusive Legislation in all Cases whatsoever, over such District (not exceeding ten Miles square) as may, by Cession of particular States, and the Acceptance of Congress, become the Seat of the Government of the United States, and to exercise like Authority over all Places purchased by the Consent of the Legislature of the State in which the Same shall be, for the Erection of Forts, Magazines, Arsenals, dock-Yards, and other needful Buildings;—And

[18] To make all Laws which shall be necessary and proper for carrying into Execution the foregoing Powers, and all other Powers vested by this Constitution in the Government of the United States, or in any Department or Officer thereof.

Section 9. [1] The Migration or Importation of Such Persons as any of the States now existing shall think proper to admit, shall not be prohibited by the Congress prior to the Year one thousand eight hundred and eight, but a Tax or duty may be imposed on such Importation, not exceeding ten dollars for each Person.

[2]   The privilege of the Writ of Habeas Corpus shall not be suspended, unless when in Cases of Rebellion or Invasion the public Safety may require it.

[3]   No Bill of Attainder or ex post facto Law shall be passed.

[4]   No Capitation, or other direct, Tax shall be laid, unless in Proportion to the Census or Enumeration herein before directed to be taken.

[5]   No Tax or Duty shall be laid on Articles exported from any State.

[6]   No Preference shall be given by any Regulation of Commerce or Revenue to the Ports of one State over those of another: nor shall Vessels bound to, or from, one State be obliged to enter, clear, or pay Duties in another.

[7]   No money shall be drawn from the Treasury, but in Consequence of Appropriations made by Law; and a regular Statement and Account of the Receipts and Expenditures of all public Money shall be published from time to time.

[8]   No Title of Nobility shall be granted by the United States: And no Person holding any Office of Profit or Trust under them, shall, without the Consent of the Congress, accept of any present, Emolument, Office or Title, of any kind whatever, from any King, Prince, or foreign State.

Section 10. [1] No State shall enter into any Treaty, Alliance, or Confederation; grant Letters of Marque and Reprisal; coin Money; emit Bills of Credit; make any Thing but gold and silver Coin a Tender in Payment of Debts; pass any Bill of Attainder, ex post facto Law, or Law impairing the Obligation of Contracts, or grant any Title of Nobility.

[2]   No State shall, without the Consent of the Congress, lay any Imposts or Duties on Imports or Exports, except what may be absolutely necessary for executing its inspection Laws: and the net Produce of all Duties and Imposts, laid by any State on Imports or Exports, shall be for the Use of the Treasury of the United States; and all such Laws shall be subject to the Revision and Controul of the Congress.

[3]   No State shall, without the Consent of Congress, lay any Duty of Tonnage, keep Troops, or Ships of War in time of Peace, enter into any Agreement or Compact with another State, or with a foreign Power, or engage in War, unless actually invaded, or in such imminent Danger as will not admit of delay.

ARTICLE II

Section 1. [1] The executive Power shall be vested in a President of the United States of America. He shall hold his Office during the Term of four Years, and, together with the Vice President, chosen for the same Term, be elected, as follows:

[2]   Each State shall appoint, in such Manner as the Legislature thereof may direct, a Number of Electors, equal to the whole Number of Senators and Representatives to which the State may be entitled in the Congress; but no Senator or Representative, or Person holding an Office of Trust or Profit under the United States, shall be appointed an Elector.

[3]   The Electors shall meet in their respective States, and vote by Ballot for two Persons, of whom one at least shall not be an Inhabitant of the same State with themselves. And they shall make a List of all the Persons voted for, and of the Number of Votes for each; which List they shall sign and certify, and transmit sealed to the Seat of the Government of the United States, directed to the President of the Senate. The President of the Senate shall, in the Presence of the Senate and House of Representatives, open all the Certificates, and the Votes shall then be counted. The Person having the greatest Number of Votes shall be the President, if such Number be a Majority of the whole Number of Electors appointed; and if there be more than one who have such Majority, and have an equal Number of Votes, then the House of Representatives shall immediately chuse by Ballot one of them for President; and if no Person have a Majority, then from the five highest on the List the said House shall in like Manner chuse the President. But in chusing the President, the Votes shall be taken by States, the Representation from each State having one Vote; A quorum for this Purpose shall consist of a Member or Members from two thirds of the States, and a Majority of all the States shall be necessary to a Choice. In every Case, after the Choice of the President, the Person having the greater Number of Votes of the Electors shall be the Vice President. But if there should remain two or more who have equal Votes, the Senate shall chuse from them by Ballot the Vice President.

[4]   The Congress may determine the Time of chusing the Electors, and the Day on which they shall give their Votes; which Day shall be the same throughout the United States.

[5]   No person except a natural born Citizen, or a Citizen of the United States, at the time of the Adoption of this Constitution, shall be eligible to the Office of President; neither shall any Person be eligible to that Office who shall not have attained to the Age of thirty five Years, and been fourteen Years a Resident within the United States.

[6]   In case of the removal of the President from Office, or of his Death, Resignation or Inability to discharge the Powers and Duties of the said Office, the Same shall devolve on the Vice President, and the Congress may by Law provide for the Case of Removal, Death, Resignation or Inability, both of the President and Vice President, declaring what Officer shall then act as President, and such Officer shall act accordingly, until the Disability be removed, or a President shall be elected.

[7]   The President shall, at stated Times, receive for his Services, a Compensation, which shall neither be increased nor diminished during the Period for which he shall have been elected, and he shall not receive within that Period any other Emolument from the United States, or any of them.

[8]   Before he enter on the Execution of his Office, he shall take the following Oath or Affirmation: "I do solemnly swear (or affirm) that I will faithfully execute the Office of President of the United States, and will to the best of my Ability, preserve, protect and defend the Constitution of the United States."

Section 2. [1] The President shall be Commander in Chief of the Army and Navy of the United States, and of the militia of the several States, when called into the actual Service of the United States; he may require the Opinion, in writing, of the principal Officer in each of the executive Departments, upon any Subject relating to the Duties of their respective Offices, and he shall have Power to grant Reprieves and Pardons for Offenses against the United States, except in Cases of Impeachment.

[2]   He shall have Power, by and with the Advice and Consent of the Senate, to make Treaties, provided two thirds of the Senators present concur; and he shall nominate, and by and with the Advice and Consent of the Senate, shall appoint Ambassadors, other public Ministers and Consuls, Judges of the supreme Court, and all other Officers of the United States, whose Appointments are not herein otherwise provided for, and which shall be established by Law: but the Congress may by Law vest the Appointment of such inferior Officers, as they think proper, in the President alone, in the Courts of Law, or in the Heads of Departments.

[3]   The President shall have Power to fill up all Vacancies that may happen during the Recess of the Senate, by granting Commissions which shall expire at the End of their next Session.

Section 3.   He shall from time to time give to the Congress Information of the State of the Union, and recommend to their Consideration such Measures as he shall judge necessary and expedient; he may, on extraordinary Occasions, convene both Houses, or either of them, and in Case of Disagreement between them, with Respect to the Time of Adjournment, he may adjourn them to such Time as he shall think proper; he shall receive Ambassadors and other public Ministers; he shall take Care that the Laws be faithfully executed, and shall Commission all the Officers of the United States.

Section 4.   The President, Vice President and all civil Officers of the United States, shall be removed from Office on Impeachment for, and Conviction of, Treason, Bribery, or other high Crimes and Misdemeanors.

ARTICLE III

Section 1.   The judicial Power of the United States, shall be vested in one supreme Court, and in such inferior Courts as the Congress may from time to time ordain and establish. The Judges, both of the supreme and inferior Courts, shall hold their Offices during good Behaviour, and shall, at stated Times, receive for their Services a Compensation, which shall not be diminished during their Continuance in Office.

Section 2. [1] The judicial Power shall extend to all Cases, in Law and Equity, arising under this Constitution, the Laws of the United States, and Treaties made, or which shall be made, under their Authority;—to all Cases affecting Ambassadors, other public Ministers and Consuls;—to all Cases of admiralty and maritime Jurisdiction,—to Controversies to which the United States shall be a Party;—to Controversies between two or more States;—between a State and Citizens of another State;—between Citizens of different States;—between Citizens of the same State claiming Lands under the Grants of different States, and between a State, or the Citizens thereof, and foreign States, Citizens or Subjects.

[2]   In all Cases affecting Ambassadors, other public Ministers and Consuls, and those in which a State shall be a Party, the supreme Court shall have original

Jurisdiction. In all the other Cases before mentioned, the supreme Court shall have appellate Jurisdiction, both as to Law and Fact, with such Exceptions, and under such Regulations as the Congress shall make.

[3]   The trial of all Crimes, except in Cases of Impeachment, shall be by Jury; and such Trial shall be held in the State where the said Crimes shall have been committed; but when not committed within any State, the Trial shall be at such Place or Places as the Congress may by Law have directed.

Section 3. [1] Treason against the United States, shall consist only in levying War against them, or, in adhering to their Enemies, giving them Aid and Comfort. No Person shall be convicted of Treason unless on the Testimony of two Witnesses to the same overt Act, or on Confession in open Court.

[2]   The Congress shall have Power to declare the Punishment of Treason, but no Attainder of Treason shall work Corruption of Blood, or Forfeiture except during the Life of the Person attainted.

ARTICLE IV

Section 1.   Full Faith and Credit shall be given in each State to the public Acts, Records, and judicial Proceedings of every other State. And the Congress may by general Laws prescribe the Manner in which such Acts, Records and Proceedings shall be proved, and the Effect thereof.

Section 2.   [1] The Citizens of each State shall be entitled to all Privileges and Immunities of Citizens in the several States.

[2]   A Person charged in any State with Treason, Felony, or other Crime, who shall flee from Justice, and be found in another State, shall on demand of the executive Authority of the State from which he fled, be delivered up, to be removed to the State having Jurisdiction of the Crime.

[3]   No Person held to Service or Labour in one State, under the Laws thereof, escaping into another, shall, in Consequence of any Law or Regulation therein, be discharged from such Service or Labour, but shall be delivered up on Claim of the Party to whom such Service or Labour may be due.

Section 3. [1] New States may be admitted by the Congress into this Union; but no new State shall be formed or erected within the Jurisdiction of any other State; nor any State be formed by the Junction of two or more States, or Parts of States, without the Consent of the Legislatures of the States concerned as well as of the Congress.

[2]   The Congress shall have Power to dispose of and make all needful Rules and Regulations respecting the Territory or other Property belonging to the United States; and nothing in this Constitution shall be so construed as to Prejudice any Claims of the United States, or of any particular State.

Section 4.   The United States shall guarantee to every State in this Union a Republican Form of Government, and shall protect each of them against Invasion; and on Application of the Legislature, or of the Executive (when the Legislature cannot be convened) against domestic Violence.

ARTICLE V

The Congress, whenever two thirds of both Houses shall deem it necessary, shall propose Amendments to this Constitution, or, on the Application of the Legislatures of two thirds of the several States, shall call a Convention for proposing Amendments, which, in either Case, shall be valid to all Intents and Purposes, as part of this Constitution, when ratified by the Legislatures of three fourths of the several States, or by Conventions in three fourths thereof, as the one or the other Mode of Ratification may be proposed by the Congress; Provided that no Amendment which may be made prior to the Year One thousand eight hundred and eight shall in any Manner affect the first and fourth Clauses in the Ninth Section of the first Article; and that no State, without its Consent, shall be deprived of its equal Suffrage in the Senate.

ARTICLE VI

[1] All Debts contracted and Engagements entered into, before the Adoption of this Constitution shall be as valid against the United States under this Constitution, as under the Confederation.

[2] This Constitution, and the Laws of the United States which shall be made in Pursuance thereof; and all Treaties made, or which shall be made, under the Authority of the United States, shall be the supreme Law of the Land; and the Judges in every State shall be bound thereby, any Thing in the Constitution or Laws of any State to the Contrary notwithstanding.

[3] The Senators and Representatives before mentioned, and the Members of the several State Legislatures, and all executive and judicial Officers, both of the United States and of the several States, shall be bound by Oath or Affirmation, to support this Constitution; but no religious Test shall ever be required as a Qualification to any Office or public Trust under the United States.

ARTICLE VII

The Ratification of the Conventions of nine States shall be sufficient for the Establishment of this Constitution between the States so ratifying the Same.

Done in Convention by the Unanimous Consent of the States present the Seventeenth Day of September in the Year of our Lord one thousand seven hundred and Eighty seven and of the Independence of the United States of America the Twelfth.

ARTICLES IN ADDITION TO, AND AMENDMENT OF, THE CONSTITUTION OF THE UNITED STATES OF AMERICA, PROPOSED BY CONGRESS, AND RATIFIED BY THE LEGISLATURES OF THE SEVERAL STATES PURSUANT TO THE FIFTH ARTICLE OF THE ORIGINAL CONSTITUTION.

AMENDMENT I [1791]

Congress shall make no law respecting an establishment of religion, or prohibiting the free exercise thereof; or abridging the freedom of speech, or of the press; or the right of the people peaceably to assemble, and to petition the Government for a redress of grievances.

AMENDMENT II [1791]

A well regulated Militia, being necessary to the security of a free State, the right of the people to keep and bear Arms, shall not be infringed.

AMENDMENT III [1791]

No Soldier shall, in time of peace be quartered in any house, without the consent of the Owner, nor in time of war, but in a manner to be prescribed by law.

AMENDMENT IV [1791]

The right of the people to be secure in their persons, houses, papers, and effects, against unreasonable searches and seizures, shall not be violated, and no Warrants shall issue, but upon probable cause, supported by Oath or affirmation, and particularly describing the place to be searched, and the persons or things to be seized.

AMENDMENT V [1791]

No person shall be held to answer for a capital, or otherwise infamous crime, unless on a presentment or indictment of a Grand Jury, except in cases arising in the land or naval forces, or in the Militia, when in actual service in time of War or public danger; nor shall any person be subject for the same offense to be twice put in jeopardy of life or limb; nor shall be compelled in any criminal case to be a witness against himself, nor be deprived of life, liberty, or property, without due process of law; nor shall private property be taken for public use, without just compensation.

AMENDMENT VI [1791]

In all criminal prosecutions, the accused shall enjoy the right to a speedy and public trial, by an impartial jury of the State and district wherein the crime shall have been committed, which district shall have been previously ascertained by law, and to be informed of the nature and cause of the accusation; to be confronted with the witnesses against him; to have compulsory process for obtaining witnesses in his favor, and to have the Assistance of Counsel for his defence.

AMENDMENT VII [1791]

In Suits at common law, where the value in controversy shall exceed twenty dollars, the right of trial by jury shall be preserved, and no fact tried by jury, shall be otherwise re-examined in any Court of the United States, than according to the rules of the common law.

AMENDMENT VIII [1791]

Excessive bail shall not be required, nor excessive fines imposed, nor cruel and unusual punishments inflicted.

AMENDMENT IX [1791]

The enumeration in the Constitution, of certain rights, shall not be construed to deny or disparage others retained by the people.

AMENDMENT X [1791]

The powers not delegated to the United States by the Constitution, nor prohibited by it to the States, are reserved to the States respectively, or to the people.

AMENDMENT XI [1798]

The Judicial power of the United States shall not be construed to extend to any suit in law or equity, commenced or prosecuted against one of the United States by Citizens of another State, or by Citizens or Subjects of any Foreign State.

AMENDMENT XII [1804]

The Electors shall meet in their respective states and vote by ballot for President and Vice-President, one of whom, at least, shall not be an inhabitant of the same state with themselves; they shall name in their ballots the person voted for as President, and in distinct ballots the person voted for as Vice-President, and they shall make distinct lists of all persons voted for as President, and of all persons voted for as Vice-President, and of the number of votes for each, which lists they shall sign and certify, and transmit sealed to the seat of the government of the United States, directed to the President of the Senate;—The President of the Senate shall, in the presence of the Senate and House of Representatives, open all the certificates and the votes shall then be counted;—The person having the greatest number of votes for President, shall be the President, if such number be a majority of the whole number of Electors appointed; and if no person have such majority, then from the persons having the highest numbers not exceeding three on the list of those voted for as President, the House of Representatives shall choose immediately, by ballot, the President. But in choosing the

President, the votes shall be taken by states, the representation from each state having one vote; a quorum for this purpose shall consist of a member or members from two-thirds of the states, and a majority of all the states shall be necessary to a choice. And if the House of Representatives shall not choose a President whenever the right of choice shall devolve upon them before the fourth day of March next following, then the Vice-President shall act as President, as in the case of the death or other constitutional disability of the President.—The person having the greatest number of votes as Vice-President, shall be the Vice-President, if such number be a majority of the whole number of Electors appointed, and if no person have a majority, then from the two highest numbers on the list, the Senate shall choose the Vice-President; a quorum for the purpose shall consist of two-thirds of the whole number of Senators, and a majority of the whole number shall be necessary to a choice. But no person constitutionally ineligible to the office of President shall be eligible to that of Vice-President of the United States.

AMENDMENT XIII [1865]

Section 1. Neither slavery nor involuntary servitude, except as a punishment for crime whereof the party shall have been duly convicted, shall exist within the United States, or any place subject to their jurisdiction.

Section 2.   Congress shall have power to enforce this article by appropriate legislation.

AMENDMENT XIV [1868]

Section 1. All persons born or naturalized in the United States, and subject to the jurisdiction thereof, are citizens of the United States and of the State wherein they reside. No State shall make or enforce any law which shall abridge the privileges or immunities of citizens of the United States; nor shall any State deprive any person of life, liberty, or property, without due process of law; nor deny to any person within its jurisdiction the equal protection of the laws.

Section 2.   Representatives shall be apportioned among the several States according to their respective numbers, counting the whole number of persons in each State, excluding Indians not taxed. But when the right to vote at any election for the choice of electors for President and Vice President of the United States, Representatives in Congress, the Executive and Judicial officers of a State, or the members of the Legislature thereof, is denied to any of the male inhabitants of such State, being twenty-one years of age, and citizens of the United States, or in any way abridged, except for participation in rebellion, or other crime, the basis of representation therein shall be reduced in the proportion which the number of such male citizens shall bear to the whole number of male citizens twenty-one years of age in such State.

Section 3. No person shall be a Senator or Representative in Congress, or elector of President and Vice President, or hold any office, civil or military, under the United States, or under any State, who having previously taken an oath, as a member of Congress, or as an officer of the United States, or as a member of any State legislature, or as an executive or judicial officer of any State, to support the Constitution of the United States, shall have engaged in insurrection or rebellion against the same, or given aid or comfort to the enemies thereof. But Congress may by a vote of two-thirds of each House, remove such disability.

Section 4. The validity of the public debt of the United States, authorized by law, including debts incurred for payment of pensions and bounties for services in suppressing insurrection or rebellion, shall not be questioned. But neither the United States nor any State shall assume or pay any debt or obligation incurred in aid of insurrection or rebellion against the United States, or any claim for the loss or emancipation of any slave; but all such debts, obligations and claims shall be held illegal and void.

Section 5. The Congress shall have power to enforce, by appropriate legislation, the provisions of this article.

AMENDMENT XV [1870]

Section 1. The right of citizens of the United States to vote shall not be denied or abridged by the United States or by any State on account of race, color, or previous condition of servitude.

Section 2. The Congress shall have power to enforce this article by appropriate legislation.

AMENDMENT XVI [1913]

The Congress shall have power to lay and collect taxes on incomes, from whatever source derived, without apportionment among the several States, and without regard to any census or enumeration.

AMENDMENT XVII [1913]

[1]   The Senate of the United States shall be composed of two Senators from each State, elected by the people thereof, for six years; and each Senator shall have one vote. The electors in each State shall have the qualifications requisite for electors of the most numerous branch of the State legislatures.

[2]   When vacancies happen in the representation of any State in the Senate, the executive authority of such State shall issue writs of election to fill such vacancies: *Provided,* That the legislature of any State may empower the executive thereof to make temporary appointments until the people fill the vacancies by election as the legislature may direct.

[3]   This amendment shall not be so construed as to affect the election or term of any Senator chosen before it becomes valid as part of the Constitution.

AMENDMENT XVIII [1919]

Section 1. After one year from the ratification of this article the manufacture, sale, or transportation of intoxicating liquors within, the importation thereof into, or the exportation thereof from the United States and all territory subject to the jurisdiction thereof for beverage purposes is hereby prohibited.

Section 2. The Congress and the several States shall have concurrent power to enforce this article by appropriate legislation.

Section 3. This article shall be inoperative unless it shall have been ratified as an amendment to the Constitution by the legislatures of the several States, as provided in the Constitution, within seven years from the date of the submission hereof to the States by the Congress.

AMENDMENT XIX [1920]

[1]   The right of citizens of the United States to vote shall not be denied or abridged by the United States or by any State on account of sex.

[2]   Congress shall have power to enforce this article by appropriate legislation.

AMENDMENT XX [1933]

Section 1. The terms of the President and Vice President shall end at noon on the 20th day of January, and the terms of Senators and Representatives at noon on the 3d day of January, of the years in which such terms would have ended if this article had not been ratified; and the terms of their successors shall then begin.

Section 2.   The Congress shall assemble at least once in every year, and such meeting shall begin at noon on the 3d day of January, unless they shall by law appoint a different day.

Section 3.   If, at the time fixed for the beginning of the term of the President, the President elect shall have died, the Vice President elect shall become President. If the President shall not have been chosen before the time fixed for the beginning of his term, or if the President elect shall have failed to qualify, then the Vice President elect shall act as President until a President shall have qualified; and the Congress may by law provide for the case wherein neither a President elect nor a Vice President elect shall have qualified, declaring who shall then act as President, or the manner in which one who is to act shall be selected, and such person shall act accordingly until a President or Vice President shall have qualified.

Section 4.   The Congress may by law provide for the case of the death of any of the persons from whom the House of Representatives may choose a President whenever the right of choice shall have devolved upon them, and for the case of the death of any of the persons from whom the Senate may choose a Vice President whenever the right of choice shall have devolved upon them.

Section 5.   Sections 1 and 2 shall take effect on the 15th day of October following the ratification of this article.

Section 6.   This article shall be inoperative unless it shall have been ratified as an amendment to the Constitution by the legislatures of three-fourths of the several States within seven years from the date of its submission.

AMENDMENT XXI [1933]

Section 1.   The eighteenth article of amendment to the Constitution of the United States is hereby repealed.

Section 2.   The transportation or importation into any State, Territory, or possession of the United States for delivery or use therein of intoxicating liquors, in violation of the laws thereof, is hereby prohibited.

Section 3.   This article shall be inoperative unless it shall have been ratified as an amendment to the Constitution by conventions in the several States, as provided in the Constitution, within seven years from the date of the submission hereof to the States by the Congress.

AMENDMENT XXII [1951]

Section 1.   No person shall be elected to the office of the President more than twice, and no person who has held the office of President, or acted as President, for more than two years of a term to which some other person was elected President shall be elected to the office of President more than once. But this Article shall not apply to any person holding the office of President when this Article was proposed by the Congress, and shall not prevent any person who may be holding the office of President, or acting as President, during the term within which this Article becomes operative from holding the office of President or acting as President during the remainder of such term.

Section 2.   This article shall be inoperative unless it shall have been ratified as an amendment to the Constitution by the legislatures of three-fourths of the several States within seven years from the date of its submission to the States by the Congress.

AMENDMENT XXIII [1961]

Section 1.   The District constituting the seat of Government of the United States shall appoint in such manner as the Congress may direct:

A number of electors of President and Vice President equal to the whole number of Senators and Representatives in Congress to which the District would be entitled if it were a State, but in no event more than the least populous state; they shall be in addition to those appointed by the states, but they shall be considered, for the purposes of the election of President and Vice President, to be electors appointed by a state; and they shall meet in the District and perform such duties as provided by the twelfth article of amendment.

Section 2. The Congress shall have power to enforce this article by appropriate legislation.

AMENDMENT XXIV [1964]

Section 1. The right of citizens of the United States to vote in any primary or other election for President or Vice President, for electors for President or Vice President, or for Senator or Representative in Congress, shall not be denied or abridged by the United States or any State by reason of failure to pay any poll tax or other tax.

Section 2. The Congress shall have power to enforce this article by appropriate legislation.

AMENDMENT XXV [1967]

Section 1. In case of the removal of the President from office or of his death or resignation, the Vice President shall become President.

Section 2. Whenever there is a vacancy in the office of the Vice President, the President shall nominate a Vice President who shall take office upon confirmation by a majority vote of both Houses of Congress.

Section 3. Whenever the President transmits to the President pro tempore of the Senate and the Speaker of the House of Representatives his written declaration that he is unable to discharge the powers and duties of his office, and until he transmits to them a written declaration to the contrary, such powers and duties shall be discharged by the Vice President as Acting President.

Section 4. Whenever the Vice President and a majority of either the principal officers of the executive departments or of such other body as Congress may by law provide, transmit to the President pro tempore of the Senate and the Speaker of the House of Representatives their written declaration that the President is unable to discharge the powers and duties of his office, the Vice President shall immediately assume the powers and duties of the office as Acting President.

Thereafter, when the President transmits to the President pro tempore of the Senate and the Speaker of the House of Representatives his written declaration that no inability exists, he shall resume the powers and duties of his office unless the Vice President and a majority of either the principal officers of the executive departments or of such other body as Congress may by law provide, transmit within four days to the President pro tempore of the Senate and the Speaker of the House of Representatives their written declaration that the President is unable to discharge the powers and duties of his office. Thereupon Congress shall decide the issue, assembling within forty-eight hours for that purpose if not in session. If the Congress, within twenty-one days after receipt of the latter written declaration, or, if Congress is not in session, within twenty-one days after Congress is required to assemble, determines by two-thirds vote of both Houses that the President is unable to discharge the powers and duties of his office, the Vice President shall continue to discharge the same as Acting President; otherwise, the President shall resume the powers and duties of his office.

AMENDMENT XXVI [1971]

Section 1. The right of citizens of the United States, who are eighteen years of age or older, to vote shall not be denied or abridged by the United States or by any State on account of age.

Section 2. The Congress shall have power to enforce this article by appropriate legislation.

AMENDMENT XXVII [1992][1]

No law, varying the compensation for the services of Senators and Representatives, shall take effect, until an election for Representatives shall have intervened.

2. HISTORY OF THE ADOPTION OF THE CONSTITUTION AND ITS MOST SIGNIFICANT AMENDMENTS

A. THE ARTICLES OF CONFEDERATION AND THE ORIGINAL CONSTITUTION

The Constitutional Convention, which met in Philadelphia in May, 1787, resulted from a growing belief that the federal government set up by the Articles of Confederation was inadequate. Under the Confederation, the United States were governed by Congress, a unicameral body in which each state had one vote. Nine votes were required for any significant action, and, more restrictively, "alteration" of the Articles required unanimity.[2] There was no national executive, and no significant federal judiciary. Congress lacked the power to tax and, since states were often delinquent in responding to Congress' requisitions, Congress was perpetually hampered by lack of funds. Congress lacked the power to regulate interstate commerce, leading to commercial wars between the states.[3]

Agreement at the Constitutional Convention that a new federal government should be established, with power to act directly on individuals and not just upon the

---

[1]   The twenty-seventh amendment was one of twelve amendments proposed by Congress in 1789. Ten of those twelve amendments were ratified by 1791 and became the first ten amendments to the Constitution. After more than two centuries, interest in the amendment was revived and the 38th State ratified it in 1992. In the intervening years it had never been resubmitted for ratification by Congress.

[2]   This mandate of unanimity for alterations has led some to question the "legality" of the Constitution itself, insofar as Article VII of the Constitution states that it would take effect upon the ratification of 9—not all—the states. For opposing views on this "legality" question, see Ackerman, *The Storrs Lectures: Discovering the Constitution*, 93 Yale L.J. 1013 (1984) and Akhil Amar, *Popular Sovereignty and Constitutional Amendment*, in *Responding to Imperfection: The Theory and Practice of Constitutional Amendment* 92–95 (Levinson ed. 1995).

In addition to requiring unanimous consent for all amendments in Article XIII, the Articles of Confederation, in Article II, stated that "[e]ach state retains its sovereignty, freedom and independence, and every power, jurisdiction, and right, which is not by this Confederation expressly delegated to the United States, in Congress assembled." When you read Marbury v. Madison, 5 U.S. (1 Cranch) 137 (1803) in Chapter 2 and McCulloch v. Maryland, 17 U.S. (4 Wheat.) 316 (1819) in Chapter 4, compare Chief Justice Marshall's descriptions of the essence of the United States Constitution to the character of the Articles of Confederation that emerges from the sovereignty language of Article II.

[3]   While a number of the features of the Constitution that emerged from the Convention can be traced to perceived inadequacies in the Articles of Confederation, other provisions reflect provisions contained in the Articles. Under the Articles, Congress controlled war, peace and foreign policy; a number of lesser powers described in Art. I, § 8, of the Constitution appeared in the Articles; the concepts of privileges and immunities of state citizens, extradition of fugitives, and full faith and credit were contained in Article IV of the Articles of Confederation.

member states, masked considerable disagreement as to the extent of the powers of that new government. It took four months of debate and compromise before the final draft of the Constitution was approved on September 17, 1787. To protect free debate, the Convention adopted a secrecy rule, and no contemporary accounts were available of the debates and decisions at the Convention. A sketchy journal was kept by William Jackson, secretary of the Convention. The journal remained in the archives of the Department of State until published in 1818 under the editorship of John Quincy Adams. More comprehensive information about the Convention's deliberations is contained in James Madison's account. Madison's notes, however, were not published until 1840, four years after his death, and more than half a century after ratification.

Ratification of the Constitution by the necessary nine states was completed in 1788. The ratification controversy was intense. The Federalist Papers, produced in the debate over ratification, are an important source of information as to contemporary views of the meaning of the Constitution. They are a series of 85 letters published in the New York papers from October, 1787 to April, 1788, under the pseudonym "Publius." The Federalist Papers were, in fact, written by Alexander Hamilton, James Madison and John Jay. One should keep in mind that the Federalist Papers, despite their high quality and the prominence of their authors, were intended as partisan debate on the side of ratification and not as dispassionate analysis of the meaning of the Constitution. Historical treatments of the Confederation period and of the drafting and ratification of the Constitution include: G. Bancroft, *History of the Formation of the Constitution of the United States of America* (1893); J. Fiske, *The Critical Period of American History* (1888); M. Jensen, *The Articles of Confederation: An Interpretation of the Social-Constitutional History of the American Revolution, 1774–1781* (1940); A. McLaughlin, *The Confederation and the Constitution: 1783–1789* (1905); J. Rakove, *Original Meanings: Politics and Ideas in the Making of the Constitution* (1996); C. Rossiter, *1787: The Grand Convention* (1966); C. Van Doren, *The Great Rehearsal: The Story of the Making and Ratification of the Constitution of the United States* (1948); C. Warren, *The Making of the Constitution* (1928); B. Wright, *Consensus and Continuity, 1776–1787* (1958). The Federalist is available in a number of editions. Documentary collections include: H. Commager (ed.), *Documents of American History* (9th ed. 1973); J. Elliott (ed.), *The Debates of the Several State Conventions on the Adoption of the Federal Constitution* (1836); M. Farrand (ed.), *The Records of the Federal Convention of 1787* (1911, 1937); P. Kurland and R. Lerner (ed.), *The Founders' Constitution* (1987).

B. THE BILL OF RIGHTS

Protection of Freedom in the Constitution of 1787

The emphasis that must be placed upon the Bill of Rights and other amendments to the Constitution, Professor Chafee reminds us, should not lead one to ignore the protections for individual liberty which were built into the original document; perhaps the most important of these is the limitation on suspension by the national government of the writ of *habeas corpus*.[1] Professor Chafee adds:

"Among the affirmative rights in Article I are the immunity of debates in Congress; the Interstate Commerce Clause which, without expressly mentioning any human right, has in fact been invoked to protect freedom of movement across state lines; . . . and the prohibition of bills of attainder and *ex post facto* laws in the nation or the states. . . . Article III on the judiciary obliges criminal cases to be tried by a jury of the neighborhood. It also contains the definition of treason. . . . Finally, the

---

[1] Art. I, § 9. Chafee, *How Human Rights Got Into the Constitution* (1952) 51.

miscellaneous provisions found in Article IV entitle citizens of one state to enjoy in another state 'all the Privileges and Immunities' of its own citizens, and empower the United States to preserve in every state a 'Republican Form of Government' and to protect the right to life 'against domestic violence.' "[2]

Professor Chafee's brief summary does not purport to be complete. For example, the protection of economic (and even intellectual) liberty was possible under the prohibition in Article I, Section 10, against state laws impairing the obligation of contracts. But in spite of the importance of these and other guaranties established by the original document, federal constitutional protection for individual liberty must be derived, for the most part, from two groups of amendments separated in time by almost eighty years: the Bill of Rights and the three post–Civil War amendments. The objectives of these two groups of amendments and the relationship between them raise questions that are as important as they are difficult.

The Bill of Rights

The importance of a written declaration of the rights of the individual loomed large in the minds of early Americans. This tradition had grown out of struggles against royal prerogative, and was reflected in written guaranties of Magna Carta (1215),[3] the Petition of Right (1628)[4] and the Bill of Rights (1689).[5]

This tradition was carried to the New World. Many of the early Colonial Charters offered important assurances to the settlers of "all Liberties and Immunities of free and natural Subjects."[6] But the most direct antecedents of modern guarantees of individual rights appeared in the constitutions that the colonists framed for themselves at the outbreak of the Revolution. In eight state constitutions, these guarantees were gathered into separate provisions called a Bill of Rights or Declaration of Rights; three states wove them into the fabric of the document.[7] Probably the most influential of these early bills of rights was that of Virginia.

Since the Articles of Confederation (1777) did not grant significant legislative power to the central government, the absence of a bill of rights is understandable. It is more surprising that proposals for a Bill of Rights made in the Constitutional

---

[2]   Id. at 5–6 (Footnotes omitted.) See also: *The Federalist No. 84* (Hamilton); Story, *Commentaries on the Constitution of the United States* (4th ed. 1873) § 1859.

[3]   Magna Carta exacted from King John numerous limitations on his prerogative. Chapter 39 read: "No freeman shall be seized or imprisoned or disseised or outlawed or in any way destroyed nor will we go against him or send against him except by the lawful judgment of his peers, or by the law of the land."

[4]   The Petition of Right directed to Charles I contained the prayer that further military commissions for proceedings by martial law should not issue "lest by colour of them any of your majesty's subjects be destroyed or put to death, contrary to the laws and franchise of the land. . . ."

[5]   The Bill of Rights was designed to limit the power of William of Orange. It proclaimed ". . . that it is the right of the subjects to petition the king and all commitments and prosecutions for such petitioning are illegal . . . that the subjects which are Protestants may have arms for their defense suitable for their conditions and as allowed by law; that election of members of parliament ought to be free; that the freedom of speech and debates or proceedings in parliament ought not to be impeached or questioned in any court or place out of parliament; that excessive bail ought not to be required, nor excessive fines imposed, nor cruel and unusual punishment inflicted; that jurors ought to be duly impanelled and returned, and jurors which pass upon men in trials for high treason ought to be freeholders. . . ."

[6]   Charter of Connecticut, 1662, in 1 Thorpe, *American Charters, Constitutions and Organic Laws,* 529, 533 (1909). Similar provisions occur in other colonial charters. See Chafee, *How Human Rights Got into the Constitution* 36 (1952). Several of the charters also had guarantees of religious freedom. Id. at 40–42. Cf. Rutland, *The Birth of the Bill of Rights* (1955).

[7]   Connecticut and Rhode Island retained their colonial charters. Chafee, op. cit. supra, at pp. 18–19.

Convention of 1787 were rejected. No single explanation is compelling. There is some evidence of concern lest prohibiting Congress from intruding into enumerated areas of individual rights might suggest that Congress possessed power to invade other rights not specifically protected. Another deterrent appears to have been the fear that disagreement over the definition of individual rights might jeopardize the Convention's completion of the Constitution and the launching of the new government.[8] Finally, there is evidence that the delegates were persuaded to avoid the problem by the supposition that the limited powers of Congress made a Bill of Rights unnecessary.[9]

One of the few records of the debates on this question in the constitutional convention is as follows:[10]

"Mr. Pinckney & Mr. Gerry, moved to insert a declaration 'that the liberty of the Press should be inviolably observed—'

"Mr. Sherman—It is unnecessary—The power of Congress does not extend to the Press. On the question, (it passed in the negative)."

The reasons that impelled the Constitutional Convention to omit a federal bill of rights proved unsatisfactory in crucial state ratification conventions. After relatively smooth sailing in Delaware, Pennsylvania, New Jersey, Georgia and Connecticut, the storm broke in Massachusetts. Opposition was quieted in part by the proposal that ratification be coupled with suggestions for amendments to the Constitution that would protect individual liberty; the Federalists tendered a gentleman's agreement to give them favorable consideration. Many of the subsequent state conventions suggested amendments[11] that included proposals for a bill of rights.[12]

To keep faith with these states, James Madison compiled a set of proposed amendments based on the state bills of rights and the amendments proposed by the state conventions. His conception of the role of a bill of rights is summarized in a letter to Jefferson dated October 17, 1788:[13]

"My own opinion has always been in favor of a bill of rights; providing it be so framed as not to imply powers not meant to be included in the enumeration. At the same time I have never thought the omission a material defect, nor been anxious to supply it even by *subsequent* amendment, for any other reason than that it is anxiously desired by others. I favored it because I have supposed it might be of use, and if properly

---

[8] On September 12 a motion for a committee to prepare a bill of rights was defeated by a vote of 10–0; the only recorded objection to the motion was in connection with a proposed guaranty of jury trial in civil cases. "Mr. Gorham. It is not possible to discriminate equity cases from those in which juries are proper. The Representatives of the people may be safely trusted in this matter," 2 Farrand, *Records of the Federal Convention* (1911) 587, 588.

Speaking in the South Carolina House of Representatives, C.C. Pinckney summarized the reasons listed above and added the further point that bills of rights "generally begin with declaring that all men are by nature born free. Now, we should make that declaration with a very bad grace, when a large part of our property consists in men who are actually born slaves." 3 Id. at 256.

[9] This and other arguments against the adoption of a Bill of Rights were reviewed and answered at length by Madison in his proposals to the House of Representatives. 1 *Annals of Congress* 438–439 (1834).

[10] 2 Farrand, op. cit. supra 617–618 (Madison's notes for September 14).

[11] Bloom, *History of the Formation of the Union under the Constitution* (1941) 24–27, 280 et seq.; Hart, *Formation of the Union* (1892) 130–31; 1 Nichols & Nichols, *The Republic of the United States* (1942) 262.

[12] Madison believed that the chief basis of popular opposition to ratification of the Constitution to be its omission of such guarantees, 1 *Annals of Congress* 433 (1834).

[13] *Writings of James Madison* 269, 271–274 (Hunt ed. 1904); see further 1 *Annals of Congress* 436–44 (1834). For Jefferson's prodding of Madison see Bowers, *Jefferson and the Bill of Rights,* 41 Va.L.Rev. 709, 712–714 (1955).

executed could not be of disservice. I have not viewed it in an important light 1. because I conceive that in a certain degree, though not in the extent argued by Mr. Wilson, the rights in question are reserved by the manner in which the federal powers are granted, 2. because there is great reason to fear that a positive declaration of some of the most essential rights could not be obtained in the requisite latitude ... 3. because the limited powers of the federal Government and the jealousy of the subordinate Governments, afford a security which has not existed in the case of the State Governments, and exists in no other, 4. because experience proves the inefficacy of a bill of rights on those occasions when its control is most needed. ... What use then it may be asked can a bill of rights serve in popular Governments? ... 1. The political truths declared in that solemn manner acquire by degrees the character of fundamental maxims of free Government, and as they become incorporated with the national sentiment, counteract the impulses of interest and passion. 2. Altho[ugh] it be generally true ... that the danger of oppression lies in the interested majorities of the people rather than in usurped acts of the Government, yet there may be occasions on which the evil may spring from the latter source; and on such, a bill of rights will be a good ground for an appeal to the sense of the community ... *absolute* restrictions in cases that are doubtful, or where emergencies may overrule them, ought to be avoided."

In the First Congress, Madison proposed detailed amendments to the text of the Constitution which, after material modification, led to the Bill of Rights.[14]

The original Constitution contained relatively few express limitations on state power. (The most important of these are in Section 10 of Article I, and Sections 1 and 2 of Article IV.) The addition of the Bill of Rights left state power unchanged. Forty-two years after their ratification, Chief Justice Marshall confirmed that the provisions of the Bill of Rights were limitations only on the power of the federal government. Barron v. Baltimore, 32 U.S. (7 Pet.) 243 (1833). Until after the Civil War, state constitutions—interpreted by state courts—were the source of most constitutional limitations on state government.

C. THE ADOPTION OF THE CIVIL WAR AMENDMENTS

Appomattox marked the end of the struggle over the constitutional issue of secession but it precipitated the country's most serious social problem: the future status of the four million individuals who had been held in slavery. This transition to freedom posed an acute problem of assimilation reflected in grave problems of constitutional law.

Slavery and the Thirteenth Amendment. By language only thinly veiled, the Constitution of 1787 recognized and sanctioned slavery.[1] Thus, although Lincoln's Emancipation Proclamation[2] declared an end to slavery in the Confederacy, firm legal support for the eradication of slavery required constitutional change. This support was

---

[14] Madison's initial proposals called for amendments that were to be worked into the body of the Constitution, rather than supplements added to the original text. Thus, Madison's proposals included ten new provisions to be added to Article I, Section 9. 1 *Annals of Congress* 434–35 (1834). These correspond, for the most part, to the first ten amendments which finally received approval. Madison's proposals also included the following addition to Article I, Section 10: "No state shall violate the equal rights of conscience, or the freedom of the press, or the trial by jury in criminal cases." 1 Id. at 435. He further proposed to rewrite Article III, Section 2 to require, inter alia, that "in all crimes punishable with loss of life or member, presentment or indictment by a grand jury shall be an essential preliminary ... " and that "In suits at common law, between man and man, the trial by jury, as one of the best securities to the rights of the people, ought to remain inviolate" Ibid.

[1]   Art. I, § 2, ¶ 3; Art. I, § 9, ¶ 1; Art. IV, § 2, ¶ 3.

[2]   12 Stat. 1268 (1863).

provided in 1865 by the Thirteenth Amendment.[3] The original proposition for the Amendment was introduced in Congress in December, 1863, achieving final passage in January, 1865. It was declared ratified and in force on December 18, 1865.

The 1866 Civil Rights Acts and the Fourteenth and Fifteenth Amendments. The Civil Rights Act of 1866 was before Congress at the same time as the Fourteenth Amendment. In large part, the Amendment was designed to assure the constitutionality of the Act.

The Act was Congress's response to the so-called "Black Codes" enacted in several states. Mississippi enactments of 1865, for example, provided:

". . . Every civil officer shall, and every person may, arrest and carry back to his or her legal employer any freedman, free negro, or mulatto who shall have quit the service of his or her employer before the expiration of his or her term of service without good cause. . . .

". . . If any freedman, free negro or mulatto, convicted of any of the misdemeanors provided against in this act, shall fail or refuse for the space of five days after conviction, to pay the fine and costs imposed, such person shall be hired out by the sheriff or other officer, at the public outcry, to any white person who will pay said fine and all costs, and take the convict for the shortest time."[4]

Other provisions of some of the Black Codes barred Blacks from any business except "husbandry" without obtaining a special license, or forbade them from renting or leasing land except in towns and cities.[5]

The Civil Rights Act,[6] which was introduced in January 1866, passed in March, vetoed by President Johnson, and passed over his veto in early April, was designed to put an end to these laws. The two opening sections provided:

"Sec. 1. . . . all persons born in the United States and not subject to any foreign power, excluding Indians not taxed, are hereby declared to be citizens of the United States; and such citizens, of every race and color, without regard to any previous condition of slavery or involuntary servitude, except as a punishment for crime whereof the party shall have been duly convicted, shall have the same right, in every State and Territory in the United States, to make and enforce contracts, to sue, be parties, and give evidence, to inherit, purchase, lease, sell, hold, and convey real and personal property, and to full and equal benefit of all laws and proceedings for the security of person and property, as is enjoyed by white citizens, and shall be subject to like punishment, pains, and penalties, and to none other, any law, statute, ordinance, regulation, or custom, to the contrary notwithstanding.

"Sec. 2. *And be it further enacted,* That any person who, under color of any law, statute, ordinance, regulation, or custom, shall subject, or cause to be subjected, any inhabitant of any State or Territory to the deprivation of any right secured or protected by this act, or to different punishment, pains, or penalties on account of such person having at any time been held in a condition of slavery or involuntary servitude, except as a punishment for crime whereof the party shall have been duly convicted, or by reason of his color or race, than is prescribed for the punishment of white persons,

---

[3] See tenBroek, *Thirteenth Amendment to the Constitution of the United States—Consummation to Abolition and Key to the Fourteenth Amendment,* 39 Cal.L.Rev. 171 (1951).

[4] Laws of Mississippi, 1865, 82, 84, 166–167. See also Laws of Mississippi, 1865, 86–96; Acts of the General Assembly of Louisiana Regulating Labor. Extra Session, 1865, 3 et seq.; 2 Commager, *Documents of American History,* 2–7 (5th ed. 1949).

[5] Stephenson, *Race Distinctions in American Law* 41–43 (1910); Maslow and Robison, *Civil Rights Legislation and the Fight for Equality,* 20 U.Chi.L.Rev. 363, 367 (1953).

[6] Act of April 9, 1866, 14 Stat. 27.

shall be deemed guilty of a misdemeanor, and, on conviction, shall be punished by fine not exceeding one thousand dollars, or imprisonment not exceeding one year, or both, in the discretion of the court."

The question arose: was there constitutional support for this Act? Did the racial discrimination in question reach the level of "involuntary servitude" encompassed by the Thirteenth Amendment? If not, where else could constitutional support be found? This difficulty was one of President Johnson's grounds for vetoing the bill. He said:[7]

"Hitherto every subject embraced in the enumeration of rights contained in this bill has been considered as exclusively belonging to the States. They all relate to the internal police and economy of the States. They are matters which in each State concern the domestic condition of its people, varying in each according to its own peculiar circumstances, and the safety and well-being of its own citizens. I do not mean to say that upon all these subjects there are not Federal restraints, as for instance, in the State power of legislation over contracts, there is a Federal limitation that no State shall pass a law impairing the obligations of contracts; and, as to crimes, that no State shall pass an *ex post facto* law; and, as to money that no State shall make anything but gold and silver a legal tender. But where can we find a Federal prohibition against the power of any state to discriminate, as do most of them, between aliens and citizens, between artificial persons called corporations, and natural persons, in the right to hold real estate?

"If it be granted that Congress can repeal all State laws discriminating between whites and blacks in the subjects covered by this bill, why, it may be asked, may not Congress repeal in the same way all State laws discriminating between the two races on the subjects of suffrage and office? If Congress can declare by law who shall hold lands, who shall testify, who shall have capacity to make a contract in a State, then Congress can by law also declare who, without regard to color or race, shall have the right to sit as a juror or as a judge, to hold any office, and, finally, to vote 'in every State and Territory of the United States.'"

Concurrently with the early debates on the Civil Rights Bill Congress was also considering drafts of a constitutional amendment. The Joint Committee on Reconstruction referred to Congress on February 10, 1866 a draft of an amendment designed to grant Congress general power to legislate for the protection of civil rights.[8] The draft was promptly tabled in the Senate. On February 26–28 it was debated in the House but action was postponed and it was never taken up.

Although Congress had overridden the President's veto of the Civil Rights Act, the challenge to the constitutionality was not resolved. So in April the Joint Committee on Reconstruction returned to the problem of constitutional amendment, reporting a new version to Congress on April 28. This version was debated in May and June and finally adopted with amendments on June 13. By March, 1867, the Amendment had been ratified by 20 states and rejected by 11. Also in March Congress passed over the President's veto a bill setting the conditions under which the Rebel States would be entitled to representation in Congress. One of those conditions for readmission was that the state should have ratified the Fourteenth Amendment and

---

[7]   Cong.Globe, 39th Cong., 1st Sess., 1680 (1866).

[8]   Unlike Section 1 of the final draft, these earlier versions of the Fourteenth Amendment were, in form, grants to Congress of a general power to legislate for the protection of civil rights. The first draft reported by the committee considering the amendment read: "Congress shall have power to make all laws necessary and proper to secure to all citizens of the United States, in every State, the same political rights and privileges; and to all persons in every State equal protection in the enjoyment of life, liberty and property." See Fairman, *Does the Fourteenth Amendment Incorporate the Bill of Rights: The Original Understanding*, 2 Stan.L.Rev. 5, 20–21 (1949); Flack, *The Adoption of the Fourteenth Amendment* (1908); Akhil Amar, *The Bill of Rights* (1999).

that the Amendment should have become part of the Constitution. By July, 1868, 9 more states had ratified, including 7 of the southern states seeking readmission pursuant to the 1867 statute, and the Amendment was declared adopted on July 28.

One of the conditions imposed for the readmission of the Rebel States was that their constitutions guarantee the continuance of the suffrage provisions adopted during the period of federal control through the Reconstruction Acts. These constitutions guaranteed Negro suffrage and disenfranchised large elements of the white population. Texas, Mississippi, and Virginia were delayed in readmission because of opposition to the franchise provisions. In 1869 a bargain was struck under which these states were not required to accept the rigor of the original franchise provisions but were required to ratify a constitutional amendment then being proposed to guarantee the franchise to Negroes. The three states complied, were readmitted in early 1870, and the Fifteenth Amendment was finally ratified in March, 1870.[9]

---

[9]   For background on and analysis of the Reconstruction Amendments, particularly the Fifteenth, see Vikram Amar, *Jury Service as Political Participation Akin to Voting*, 80 Cornell L.Rev. 203 (1995).

CHAPTER 2

JUDICIAL REVIEW

1. THE LEGITIMACY OF JUDICIAL REVIEW

The Constitutional Convention

In the Constitutional Convention of 1787 the Virginia Plan proposed to the Convention by Mr. Randolph (Va.) on May 29 served as the basis for the ensuing discussion and action of the delegates.

The sixth resolution in the Virginia Plan contained the provision that the national legislature be empowered "to negative all laws passed by the several States, contravening in the opinion of the National Legislature the articles of Union. . . ." This provision was ultimately rejected, in part because of the adoption of the Supremacy Clause, Art. VI, cl. 2.

The eighth resolution provided "that the Executive and a convenient number of the National Judiciary, ought to compose a council of revision with authority to examine every act of the National Legislature before it shall operate, & every act of a particular Legislature before a Negative thereon shall be final; and that the dissent of the said Council shall amount to a rejection, unless the Act of the National Legislature be again passed, or that of a particular Legislature be again negatived by _____[1] of the members of each branch." The Convention ultimately rejected the participation of the judiciary in the veto process and adopted the executive veto. Art. I, § 7, cl. 2.

The following excerpts from the debate on the eighth resolution will give a little of the flavor of the discussion that led to its rejection. They are taken from Madison's Notes of the proceedings on July 21, 1787, 2 Farrand, *The Records of the Federal Convention of 1787* (1911) 74, 76, 78:

"Mr. [Madison]—considered the object of the motion as of great importance to the meditated Constitution. It would be useful to the Judiciary department. by giving it an additional opportunity of defending itself agst: Legislative encroachments; It would be useful to the Executive, by inspiring additional confidence & firmness in exerting the revisionary power: It would be useful to the Legislature by the valuable assistance it would give in preserving a consistency, conciseness, perspicuity & technical propriety in the laws, qualities peculiarly necessary; & yet shamefully wanting in our republican Codes. It would moreover be useful to the Community at large as an additional check agst. a pursuit of those unwise & unjust measures which constituted so great a portion of our calamities. If any solid objection could be urged agst. the motion, it must be on the supposition that it tended to give too much strength either to the Executive or Judiciary. He did not think there was the least ground for this apprehension. It was much more to be apprehended that notwithstanding this cooperation of the two departments, the Legislature would still be an overmatch for them. Experience in all the States had evinced a powerful tendency in the Legislature to absorb all power into its vortex. This was the real source of danger to the American Constitutions; & suggested the necessity of giving every defensive authority to the other departments that was consistent with republican principles. . . .

---

[1] Blank left in original.

"Mr. L. Martin. considered the association of the Judges with the Executive as a dangerous innovation; as well as one which, could not produce the particular advantage expected from it. A knowledge of mankind, and of Legislative affairs cannot be presumed to belong in a higher degree to the Judges than to the Legislature. And as to the Constitutionality of laws, that point will come before the Judges in their proper official character. In this character they have a negative on the laws. Join them with the Executive in the Revision and they will have a double negative. It is necessary that the Supreme Judiciary should have the confidence of the people. This will soon be lost, if they are employed in the task of remonstrating agst. popular measures of the Legislature. Besides in what mode & proportion are they to vote in the Council of Revision? . . .

"Col Mason Observed that the defence of the Executive was not the sole object of the Revisionary power. He expected even greater advantages from it. Notwithstanding the precautions taken in the Constitution of the Legislature, it would so much resemble that of the individual States, that it must be expected frequently to pass unjust and pernicious laws. This restraining power was therefore essentially necessary. It would have the effect not only of hindering the final passage of such laws; but would discourage demagogues from attempting to get them passed. It had been said (by Mr. L. Martin) that if the Judges were joined in this check on the laws, they would have a double negative, since in their expository capacity of Judges they would have one negative. He would reply that in this capacity they could impede in one case only, the operation of laws. They could declare an unconstitutional law void. But with regard to every law however unjust oppressive or pernicious, which did not come plainly under this description, they would be under the necessity as Judges to give it a free course. He wished the further use to be made of the Judges, of giving aid in preventing every improper law. Their aid will be the more valuable as they are in the habit and practice of considering laws in their true principles, and in all their consequences."

Marbury v. Madison

5 U.S. (1 Cranch) 137, 2 L.Ed. 60 (1803).

[John Marshall was Secretary of State in the Adams administration when he took office as Chief Justice on January 31, 1801. He continued as Acting Secretary of State until the last day of the Adams administration, March 3, 1801. William Marbury was one of a number of persons who were appointed justices of the peace in the District of Columbia and who were confirmed by the Senate on March 3. His commission remained in Marshall's office undelivered when the new administration took over. President Jefferson directed his Secretary of State, James Madison, to withhold several commissions, including that of Marbury. Marbury then brought this suit against Madison, taking the unusual step of starting the action in the Supreme Court, invoking its original jurisdiction.[a]]

■ MR. CHIEF JUSTICE MARSHALL delivered the opinion of the Court.

At the last term on the affidavits then read and filed with the clerk, a rule was granted in this case, requiring the secretary of state to shew cause why a mandamus

---

[a]   For accounts of the background of the case, see Burton, *The Cornerstone of Constitutional Law: The Extraordinary Case of Marbury v. Madison,* 36 A.B.A.J. 805 (1950); Van Alstyne, *A Critical Guide to Marbury v. Madison,* 1969 Duke L.J. 1. Two good symposia collection of essays commemorating the bicentennial anniversary of *Marbury* can be found in Volume 101 of the Michigan Law Review (2003), and Volume 20 of Constitutional Commentary (2003).

For an interesting discussion of the last minute appointment of judges by President Adams, see Turner, *The Midnight Judges,* 109 U.Pa.L.Rev. 494 (1961).

should not issue, directing him to deliver to William Marbury his commission as a justice of the peace for the county of Washington, in the district of Columbia.

No cause has been shewn, and the present motion is for a mandamus. The peculiar delicacy of this case, the novelty of some of its circumstances, and the real difficulty attending the points which occur in it, require a complete exposition of the principles, on which the opinion to be given by the court, is founded.

These principles have been, on the side of the applicant, very ably argued at the bar. In rendering the opinion of the court, there will be some departure in form, though not in substance, from the points stated in that argument.

In the order in which the court has viewed this subject, the following questions have been considered and decided.

1st. Has the applicant a right to the commission he demands?

2dly. If he has a right, and that right has been violated, do the laws of his country afford him a remedy?

3dly. If they do afford him a remedy, is it a *mandamus* issuing from this court?

The first object of enquiry is,

1st. Has the applicant a right to the commission he demands?

His right originates in an act of congress passed in February 1801, concerning the district of Columbia.

After dividing the district into two counties, the 11th section of this law enacts, "that there shall be appointed in and for each of the said counties, such number of discreet persons to be justices of the peace as the president of the United States shall, from time to time, think expedient, to continue in office for five years."

It appears, from the affidavits, that in compliance with this law, a commission for William Marbury as a justice of peace for the county of Washington, was signed by John Adams, then president of the United States; after which the seal of the United States was affixed to it; but the commission has never reached the person for whom it was made out.

In order to determine whether he is entitled to this commission, it becomes necessary to enquire whether he has been appointed to the office. For if he has been appointed, the law continues him in office for five years, and he is entitled to the possession of those evidences of office, which, being completed, became his property.

The 2d section of the 2d article of the constitution, declares, that, "the president shall nominate, and, by and with the advice and consent of the senate, shall appoint ambassadors, other public ministers and consuls, and all other officers of the United States, whose appointments are not otherwise provided for."

The third section declares, that "he shall commission all the officers of the United States." . . .

It is therefore decidedly the opinion of the court, that when a commission has been signed by the President, the appointment is made; and that the commission is complete, when the seal of the United States has been affixed to it by the secretary of state. . . .

To withhold his commission, therefore, is an act deemed by the court not warranted by law, but violative of a vested legal right.

This brings us to the second enquiry; which is,

2dly. If he has a right, and that right has been violated, do the laws of his country afford him a remedy?

The very essence of civil liberty certainly consists in the right of every individual to claim the protection of the laws, whenever he receives an injury. One of the first duties of government is to afford that protection. In Great Britain the king himself is sued in the respectful form of a petition, and he never fails to comply with the judgment of his court. . . .

The government of the United States has been emphatically termed a government of laws, and not of men. It will certainly cease to deserve this high appellation, if the laws furnish no remedy for the violation of a vested legal right.

If this obloquy is to be cast on the jurisprudence of our country, it must arise from the peculiar character of the case. . . .

It follows then that the question, whether the legality of an act of the head of a department be examinable in a court of justice or not, must always depend on the nature of that act. . . .

By the constitution of the United States, the President is invested with certain important political powers, in the exercise of which he is to use his own discretion, and is accountable only to his country in his political character, and to his own conscience. To aid him in the performance of these duties, he is authorized to appoint certain officers, who act by his authority and in conformity with his orders.

In such cases, their acts are his acts; and whatever opinion may be entertained of the manner in which executive discretion may be used, still there exists, and can exist, no power to control that discretion. The subjects are political. They respect the nation, not individual rights, and being entrusted to the executive, the decision of the executive is conclusive. The application of this remark will be perceived by adverting to the act of congress for establishing the department of foreign affairs. This officer, as his duties were prescribed by that act, is to conform precisely to the will of the President. He is the mere organ by whom that will is communicated. The acts of such an officer, as an officer, can never be examinable by the courts.

But when the legislature proceeds to impose on that officer other duties; when he is directed peremptorily to perform certain acts; when the rights of individuals are dependent on the performance of those acts; he is so far the officer of the law; is amenable to the laws for his conduct; and cannot at his discretion sport away the vested rights of others.

The conclusion from this reasoning is, that where the heads of departments are the political or confidential agents of the executive, merely to execute the will of the President, or rather to act in cases in which the executive possesses a constitutional or legal discretion nothing can be more perfectly clear than that their acts are only politically examinable. But where a specific duty is assigned by law, and individual rights depend upon the performance of that duty, it seems equally clear that the individual who considers himself injured, has a right to resort to the laws of his country for a remedy. . . .

It remains to be enquired whether,

3dly. He is entitled to the remedy for which he applies. This depends on,

1st. The nature of the writ applied for, and,

2dly. The power of this court.

1st. The nature of the writ. . . .

This writ, if awarded, would be directed to an officer of government, and its mandate to him would be, to use the words of Blackstone, "to do a particular thing therein specified, which appertains to his office and duty and which the court has previously determined, or at least supposes, to be consonant to right and justice." Or, in the words of Lord Mansfield, the applicant, in this case, has a right to execute an office of public concern, and is kept out of possession of that right.

These circumstances certainly concur in this case.

Still, to render the mandamus a proper remedy, the officer to whom it is to be directed, must be one to whom, on legal principles, such writ may be directed; and the person applying for it must be without any other specific and legal remedy.

1st. With respect to the officer to whom it would be directed. The intimate political relation, subsisting between the president of the United States and the heads of departments, necessarily renders any legal investigation of the acts of one of those high officers peculiarly irksome, as well as delicate; and excites some hesitation with respect to the propriety of entering into such investigation. Impressions are often received without much reflection or examination, and it is not wonderful that in such a case as this, the assertion, by an individual, of his legal claims in a court of justice, to which claims it is the duty of that court to attend; should at first view be considered by some, as an attempt to intrude into the cabinet, and to intermeddle with the prerogatives of the executive.

It is scarcely necessary for the court to disclaim all pretensions to such a jurisdiction. An extravagance, so absurd and excessive, could not have been entertained for a moment. The province of the court is, solely, to decide on the rights of individuals, not to enquire how the executive, or executive officers, perform duties in which they have a discretion. Questions, in their nature political, or which are, by the constitution and laws, submitted to the executive, can never be made in this court.

But, if this be not such a question; if so far from being an intrusion into the secrets of the cabinet, it respects a paper, which according to law, is upon record, and to a copy of which the law gives a right, on the payment of ten cents; if it be no intermeddling with a subject, over which the executive can be considered as having exercised any control; what is there in the exalted station of the officer, which shall bar a citizen from asserting, in a court of justice, his legal rights, or shall forbid a court to listen to the claim; or to issue a mandamus, directing the performance of a duty, not depending on executive discretion, but on particular acts of congress and the general principles of law? . . .

This, then, is a plain case for a mandamus, either to deliver the commission, or a copy of it from the record; and it only remains to be enquired,

Whether it can issue from this court.

The act to establish the judicial courts of the United States authorizes the supreme court "to issue writs of mandamus, in cases warranted by the principles and usages of law, to any courts appointed, or persons holding office, under the authority of the United States."[b]

The Secretary of State, being a person holding an office under the authority of the United States, is precisely within the letter of the description; and if this court is not authorized to issue a writ of mandamus to such an officer, it must be because the law is unconstitutional, and therefore absolutely incapable of conferring the authority, and assigning the duties which its words purport to confer and assign.

---

[b] The full sentence, a part of Section 13 of the Judiciary Act of 1789, read: "The Supreme Court shall also have appellate jurisdiction from the circuit courts and courts of the several states, in the cases herein after specially provided for; and shall have power to issue writs of prohibition to the district courts, when proceeding as courts of admiralty and maritime jurisdiction, and writs of mandamus, in cases warranted by the principles and usages of law, to any courts appointed, or persons holding office, under the authority of the United States."

The constitution vests the whole judicial power of the United States in one supreme court, and such inferior courts as congress shall, from time to time, ordain and establish. This power is expressly extended to all cases arising under the laws of the United States; and consequently, in some form, may be exercised over the present case; because the right claimed is given by a law of the United States.

In the distribution of this power it is declared that "the supreme court shall have original jurisdiction in all cases affecting ambassadors, other public ministers and consuls, and those in which a state shall be a party. In all other cases, the supreme court shall have appellate jurisdiction."

It has been insisted, at the bar, that as the original grant of jurisdiction to the supreme and inferior courts, is general, and the clause, assigning original jurisdiction to the supreme court, contains no negative or restrictive words; the power remains to the legislature, to assign original jurisdiction to that court in other cases than those specified in the article which has been recited; provided those cases belong to the judicial power of the United States.

If it had been intended to leave it in the discretion of the legislature to apportion the judicial power between the supreme and inferior courts according to the will of that body, it would certainly have been useless to have proceeded further than to have defined the judicial power, and the tribunals in which it should be vested. The subsequent part of the section is mere surplusage, is entirely without meaning, if such is to be the construction. If congress remains at liberty to give this court appellate jurisdiction, where the constitution has declared their jurisdiction shall be original; and original jurisdiction where the constitution has declared it shall be appellate; the distribution of jurisdiction, made in the constitution, is form without substance.

Affirmative words are often, in their operation, negative of other objects than those affirmed; and in this case a negative or exclusive sense must be given to them or they have no operation at all.

It cannot be presumed that any clause in the constitution is intended to be without effect; and therefore such a construction is inadmissible, unless the words require it.

. . .

To enable this court then to issue a mandamus, it must be shewn to be an exercise of appellate jurisdiction, or to be necessary to enable them to exercise appellate jurisdiction.

. . .

It is the essential criterion of appellate jurisdiction, that it revises and corrects the proceedings in a cause already instituted, and does not create that cause. Although, therefore, a mandamus may be directed to courts, yet to issue such a writ to an officer for the delivery of a paper, is in effect the same as to sustain an original action for that paper, and therefore seems not to belong to appellate, but to original jurisdiction. . .

The authority, therefore, given to the supreme court by the act establishing the judicial courts of the United States, to issue writs of mandamus to public officers, appears not to be warranted by the constitution; and it becomes necessary to enquire whether a jurisdiction, so conferred, can be exercised.

The question, whether an act, repugnant to the constitution, can become the law of the land, is a question deeply interesting to the United States; but, happily, not of an intricacy proportioned to its interest. It seems only necessary to recognize certain principles, supposed to have been long and well established, to decide it.

That the people have an original right to establish, for their future government, such principles as, in their opinion, shall most conduce to their own happiness, is the basis, on which the whole American fabric has been erected. The exercise of this original right is a very great exertion; nor can it, nor ought it to be frequently repeated. The principles, therefore, so established, are deemed fundamental. And as the authority, from which they proceed, is supreme, and can seldom act, they are designed to be permanent.

This original and supreme will organizes the government, and assigns, to different departments, their respective powers. It may either stop here; or establish certain limits not to be transcended by those departments.

The government of the United States is of the latter description. The powers of the legislature are defined, and limited; and that those limits may not be mistaken, or forgotten, the constitution is written. To what purpose are powers limited, and to what purpose is that limitation committed to writing, if these limits may, at any time, be passed by those intended to be restrained? The distinction, between a government with limited and unlimited powers, is abolished, if those limits do not confine the persons on whom they are imposed, and if acts prohibited and acts allowed, are of equal obligation. It is a proposition too plain to be contested, that the constitution controls any legislative act repugnant to it; or, that the legislature may alter the constitution by an ordinary act.

Between these alternatives there is no middle ground. The constitution is either a superior, paramount law, unchangeable by ordinary means, or it is on a level with ordinary legislative acts, and like other acts, is alterable when the legislature shall please to alter it.

If the former part of the alternative be true, then a legislative act contrary to the constitution is not law: if the latter part be true, then written constitutions are absurd attempts, on the part of the people, to limit a power, in its own nature illimitable.

Certainly all those who have framed written constitutions contemplate them as forming the fundamental and paramount law of the nation, and consequently the theory of every such government must be, that an act of the legislature, repugnant to the constitution, is void.

This theory is essentially attached to a written constitution, and is consequently to be considered, by this court, as one of the fundamental principles of our society. It is not therefore to be lost sight of in the further consideration of this subject.

2 (If an act of the legislature, repugnant to the constitution, is void, does it, notwithstanding its invalidity, bind the courts, and oblige them to give it effect? Or, in other words, though it be not law, does it constitute a rule as operative as if it was a law?]This would be to overthrow in fact what was established in theory; and would seem, at first view, an absurdity too gross to be insisted on. It shall, however, receive a more attentive consideration.

It is emphatically the province and duty of the judicial department to say what the law is. Those who apply the rule to particular cases, must of necessity expound and interpret that rule. If two laws conflict with each other, the courts must decide on the operation of each.

So if a law be in opposition to the constitution; if both the law and the constitution apply to a particular case, so that the court must either decide that case conformably to the law disregarding the constitution, or conformably to the constitution disregarding the law; the court must determine which of these conflicting rules governs the case. This is of the very essence of judicial duty.

If then the courts are to regard the constitution, and the constitution is superior to any ordinary act of the legislature, the constitution, and not such ordinary act, must govern the case to which they both apply.

Those then who controvert the principle that the constitution is to be considered, in court, as a paramount law, are reduced to the necessity of maintaining that courts must close their eyes on the constitution, and see only the law.

This doctrine would subvert the very foundation of all written constitutions. . . . It would be giving to the legislature a practical and real omnipotence, with the same breath which professes to restrict their powers within narrow limits. It is prescribing limits, and declaring that those limits may be passed at pleasure.

That it thus reduces to nothing what we have deemed the greatest improvement on political institutions—a written constitution—would of itself be sufficient, in America, where written constitutions have been viewed with so much reverence, for rejecting the construction. But the peculiar expressions of the constitution of the United States furnish additional arguments in favour of its rejection.

The judicial power of the United States is extended to all cases arising under the constitution.

Could it be the intention of those who gave this power, to say that, in using it, the constitution should not be looked into? That a case arising under the constitution should be decided without examining the instrument under which it arises?

This is too extravagant to be maintained.

In some cases then, the constitution must be looked into by the judges. And if they can open it at all, what part of it are they forbidden to read, or to obey?

There are many other parts of the constitution which serve to illustrate this subject.

It is declared that "no tax or duty shall be laid on articles exported from any state." Suppose a duty on the export of cotton, of tobacco or of flour; and a suit instituted to recover it. Ought judgment to be rendered in such a case? ought the judges to close their eyes on the constitution, and only see the law?

The constitution declares that "no bill of attainder or *ex post facto* law shall be passed."

If, however such a bill should be passed and a person should be prosecuted under it; must the court condemn to death those victims whom the constitution endeavours to preserve?

"No person," says the constitution, "shall be convicted of treason unless on the testimony of two witnesses to the same overt act, or on confession in open court."

Here the language of the constitution is addressed especially to the courts. It prescribes, directly for them, a rule of evidence not to be departed from. If the legislature should change that rule, and declare one witness, or a confession out of court, sufficient for conviction, must the constitutional principle yield to the legislative act?

From these, and many other selections which might be made, it is apparent, that the framers of the constitution contemplated that instrument, as a rule for the government of courts, as well as of the legislature.

Why otherwise does it direct the judges to take an oath to support it? This oath certainly applies, in an especial manner, to their conduct in their official character. How immoral to impose it on them, if they were to be used as the instruments, and the knowing instruments, for violating what they swear to support.

The oath of office, too, imposed by the legislature, is completely demonstrative of the legislative opinion on this subject. It is in these words, "I do solemnly swear, that I will administer justice without respect to persons, and do equal right to the poor and to the rich; and that I will faithfully and impartially discharge all the duties incumbent on me as _____ according to the best of my abilities and understanding, agreeably to the constitution, and laws of the United States."

Why does a judge swear to discharge his duties agreeably to the constitution of the United States, if that constitution forms no rule for his government? if it is closed upon him, and cannot be inspected by him?

If such be the real state of things, this is worse than solemn mockery. To prescribe, or to take this oath, becomes equally a crime.

It is also not entirely unworthy of observation, that in declaring what shall be the supreme law of the land, the constitution itself is first mentioned; and not the laws of the United States generally, but those only which shall be made in pursuance of the constitution, have that rank.

Thus, the particular phraseology of the constitution of the United States confirms and strengthens the principle, supposed to be essential to all written constitutions, that a law repugnant to the constitution is void; and that courts, as well as other departments, are bound by that instrument.

The rule must be discharged.[c]

Legitimacy of Judicial Review: Some Comments

(1) Gibson, J., dissenting, in Eakin v. Raub, 12 S. & R. 330, 344–358 (Pa.1825) considered the question of the legitimacy of judicial review of the constitutionality of legislation. The following excerpts will illustrate the course of his argument:

"The constitution and the *right* of the legislature to pass the act, may be in collision; but is that a legitimate subject for judicial determination? If it be, the judiciary must be a peculiar organ, to revise the proceedings of the legislature, and to correct its mistakes; and in what part of the constitution are we to look for this proud preeminence? Viewing the matter in the opposite direction, what would be thought of an act of assembly in which it should be declared that the supreme court had in a particular case, put a wrong construction on the constitution of the *United States,* and that the judgment should therefore be reversed? It would, doubtless, be thought a usurpation of judicial power. But it is by no means clear, that to declare a law void, which has been enacted according to the forms prescribed in the constitution, is not a usurpation of legislative power. It is an act of sovereignty; and sovereignty and

---

[c]   During the tenure of Marshall as Chief Justice, the only other case holding an Act of Congress unconstitutional was the obscure decision in Hodgson v. Bowerbank, 9 U.S. (5 Cranch) 303 (1809). In a brief opinion, Marshall held a provision of the Judiciary Act of 1789 unconstitutional in conferring jurisdiction on federal courts to try suits between aliens. (For a strong argument that Marshall interpreted the statute and did not declare it to be unconstitutional, see Mahoney, *A Historical Note on Hodgson v. Bowerbank,* 49 U.Chi.L.Rev. 725 (1982)). The next Act of Congress to be declared unconstitutional was the Missouri Compromise in Dred Scott v. Sandford, 60 U.S. (19 How.) 393 (1857), overruled by the Civil War. The first Act of Congress of general applicability to be declared unconstitutional was the Legal Tender Act in Hepburn v. Griswold, 75 U.S. (8 Wall.) 603 (1870). This decision was promptly overruled by the Court itself in Knox v. Lee, 79 U.S. (12 Wall.) 457 (1871).

The modern Court, because the modern Congress has enacted a much larger volume of legislation and for other reasons as well, has been much more active in striking down federal statutes. During the years 1995 to 2000, for instance, the Court invalidated at least twenty-four congressional enactments. See Akhil Amar, *The Document and the Doctrine*, 114 Harv.L.Rev. 26, 84 n.194 (2000); Vikram Amar, How Much Protection Do Injunctions Against Enforcement of Allegedly Unconstitutional Statutes Provide?, 31 Ford.Urb.L.J. 657, 660 n.17 (2004).

legislative power are said by Sir William *Blackstone* to be convertible terms. It is the business of the judiciary, to interpret the laws, not scan the authority of the lawgiver; and without the latter, it cannot take cognisance of a collision between a law and the constitution. So that, to affirm that the judiciary has a right to judge of the existence of such collision, is to take for granted the very thing to be proved; and that a very cogent argument may be made in this way, I am not disposed to deny; for no conclusions are so strong as those that are drawn from the *petitio principii. . . .*

"But the judges are sworn to support the constitution, and are they not bound by it as the law of the land? In some respects they are. In the very few cases in which the judiciary, and not the legislature, is the immediate organ to execute its provisions, they are bound by it, in preference to any act of assembly to the contrary; in such cases, the constitution is a rule to the courts. But what I have in view in this inquiry, is, the supposed right of the judiciary, to interfere, in cases where the constitution is to be carried into effect through the instrumentality of the legislature, and where that organ must necessarily first decide on the constitutionality of its own act. The oath to support the constitution is not peculiar to the judges, but is taken indiscriminately by every officer of the government, and is designed rather as a test of the political principles of the man, than to bind the officer in the discharge of his duty: otherwise, it were difficult to determine, what operation it is to have in the case of a recorder of deeds, for instance, who in the execution of his office, has nothing to do with the constitution. But granting it to relate to the official conduct of the judge, as well as every other officer, and not to his political principles, still, it must be understood in reference to supporting the constitution, *only as far as that may be involved in his official duty;* and consequently, if his official duty does not comprehend an inquiry into the authority of the legislature, neither does his oath.

"It is worthy of remark here, that the foundation of every argument in favor of the right of the judiciary, is found, at last, to be an assumption of the whole ground in dispute. Granting that the object of the oath is to secure a support of the constitution in the discharge of official duty, its terms may be satisfied by restraining it to official duty in the exercise of the *ordinary* judicial powers. Thus, the constitution may furnish a rule of construction, where a particular interpretation of a law would conflict with some constitutional principle; and such interpretation, where it may, is always to be avoided. But the oath was more probably designed to secure the powers of each of the different branches from being usurped by any of the rest; for instance, to prevent the house of representatives from erecting itself into a court of judicature, or the supreme court from attempting to control the legislature; and in this view, the oath furnishes an argument equally plausible *against* the right of the judiciary. But if it require a support of the constitution in anything beside official duty, it is, in fact, an oath of allegiance to a particular form of government; and considered as such, it is not easy to see, why it should not be taken by the citizens at large, as well as by the officers of the government. It has never been thought, that an officer is under greater restraint as to measures which have for their avowed end a total change of the constitution, than a citizen who has taken no oath at all. The official oath, then, relates only to the official conduct of the officer, and does not prove that he ought to stray from the path of his ordinary business, to search for violations of duty in the business of others; nor does it, as supposed, define the powers of the officer.

"But do not the judges do a *positive* act in violation of the constitution, when they give effect to an unconstitutional law? Not if the law has been passed according to the forms established in the constitution. The fallacy of the question is, in supposing that the judiciary adopts the acts of the legislature as its own; whereas, the enactment of a law and the interpretation of it are not concurrent acts, and as the judiciary is not required to concur in the enactment, neither is it in the breach of the constitution which may be the consequence of the enactment; the fault is imputable to the legislature, and on it the responsibility exclusively rests. . . ."

(2) Abraham Lincoln, First Inaugural Address, March 4, 1861, in 4 Basler, *The Collected Works of Abraham Lincoln* 262, 268 (1953): "I do not forget the position assumed by some, that constitutional questions are to be decided by the Supreme Court; nor do I deny that such decisions must be binding in any case, upon the parties to a suit, as to the object of that suit, while they are also entitled to very high respect and consideration, in all parallel cases by all other departments of the government. And while it is obviously possible that such decision may be erroneous in any given case, still the evil effect following it, being limited to that particular case, with the chance that it may be overruled and never become a precedent for other cases, can better be borne than could the evils of a different practice. At the same time the candid citizen must confess that if the policy of the government upon vital questions affecting the whole people, is to be irrevocably fixed by decisions of the Supreme Court, the instant they are made, in ordinary litigation between parties in personal actions, the people will have ceased, to be their own rulers, having, to that extent, practically resigned their government, into the hands of that eminent tribunal. Nor is there, in this view, any assault upon the court, or the judges. It is a duty, from which they may not shrink, to decide cases properly brought before them; and it is no fault of theirs if others seek to turn their decisions to political purposes."

Consider also the words of President Andrew Jackson in 1832, when he vetoed a bill to continue the Bank of the United States, an institution whose constitutionality was upheld by the Court 13 years earlier in McCulloch v. Maryland, 17 U.S. (4 Wheat.) 316 (1819): "It is maintained by the advocates of the bank that its constitutionality in all its features ought to be considered as settled by precedent and by the decision of the Supreme Court. To this conclusion I can not assent. Mere precedent is a dangerous source of authority, and should not be regarded as deciding questions of constitutional power except where the acquiescence of the people and the States can be considered as well settled. . . . [Even] [i]f the opinion of the Supreme Court covered the whole ground of this act, it ought not to control the coordinate authorities of this Government. The Congress, the Executive, and the Court must each for itself be guided by its own opinion of the Constitution. Each public officer who takes an oath to support the Constitution swears that he will support it as he understands it, and not as it is understood by others. It is as much the duty of the House of Representatives, of the Senate, and of the President to decide upon the constitutionality of any bill or resolution which may be presented to them for passage or approval as it is of the supreme judges when it may be brought before them for judicial decision. . . ."

(3) In Cooper v. Aaron, 358 U.S. 1, 17 (1958) the Court made the following statements in answer to an argument that the Governor and the Legislature of Arkansas were not bound by the holding of the Court in the case of Brown v. Board of Educ., 347 U.S. 483 (1954):

"It is necessary only to recall some basic constitutional propositions which are settled doctrine.

"Article VI of the Constitution makes the Constitution the 'supreme Law of the Land'. In 1803, Chief Justice Marshall, speaking for a unanimous Court, referring to the Constitution as 'the fundamental and paramount law of the nation,' declared in the notable case of Marbury v. Madison, 1 Cranch 137, 177, that 'It is emphatically the province and duty of the judicial department to say what the law is.' This decision declared the basic principle that the federal judiciary is supreme in the exposition of the law of the Constitution, and that principle has ever since been respected by this Court and the Country as a permanent and indispensable feature of our constitutional system. It follows that the interpretation of the Fourteenth Amendment enunciated by this Court in the *Brown* case is the supreme law of the land, and Art. VI of the Constitution makes it of binding effect on the States 'any Thing in the Constitution or Laws of any State to the Contrary notwithstanding.'"

(4)   For more than a century after *Marbury v. Madison,* judicial review of legislation was largely an American phenomenon. The Twentieth Century, particularly the years following World War II, saw an explosion of the concept both on the national and international levels. A comparison of judicial review in the United States and in Western Europe is particularly instructive. Austria, Italy and Germany have specialized constitutional courts to determine the constitutional validity of legislation. Ordinary courts cannot decide whether laws are constitutional or not, although they can refer those questions for decision to the constitutional courts. This system of "centralized" judicial review is often contrasted with the "decentralized" system represented by *Marbury v. Madison.* Nearly all of the decisions in this volume are by the Supreme Court of the United States, and most attention centers on the function of judicial review as performed by that court. The theory of *Marbury,* however, requires every court, even the most inferior, to decide whether laws are constitutional. Does it also require that executive officials determine whether their official actions are consistent with the Constitution? Compare the view of President Lincoln, in note 2 above, with that of the Court in *Cooper v. Aaron,* note 3. For an analysis and description of judicial review systems outside the United States, see Cappelletti and Cohen, *Comparative Constitutional Law: Cases and Materials* 1–196 (1979).

(5)   In 1994, Walter Dellinger, then-Assistant Attorney General heading up the Office of Legal Counsel, authored a memorandum entitled "Presidential Authority to Decline to Execute Unconstitutional Statutes." In it he said that there is "significant judicial approval of [the] proposition" that "there are circumstances in which the President may appropriately decline to enforce a statute that he views as unconstitutional." He also noted, however, that the "Supreme Court plays a special role in resolving disputes about the constitutionality of enactments. As a general matter, if the President believes that the Court would sustain a particular provision as constitutional, the President should execute the statute, notwithstanding his own beliefs about the constitutional issue." Is this blending of the views of Presidents Lincoln and Jackson on the one hand, and of the Court itself in Cooper v. Aaron on the other hand, coherent?

(6)   The dispute over the legitimacy of judicial review of legislation has long raged among legal scholars. However, Bator, Meltzer, Mishkin and Shapiro, *Hart and Wechsler's The Federal Courts and the Federal System* 9 (3d ed. 1988) [hereinafter cited as Hart and Wechsler, *Federal Courts* (3d ed. 1988)], after a modern reappraisal of the dispute conclude: "The grant of judicial power was to include the power, where necessary in the decision of cases, to disregard state or federal statutes found to be unconstitutional. Despite the curiously persisting myth of usurpation, the Convention's understanding on this point emerged from its records with singular clarity." See also Wechsler, *Principles, Politics, and Fundamental Law* 4 (1961): "Let me begin by saying that I have not the slightest doubt respecting the legitimacy of judicial review, whether the action called in question in a case which otherwise is proper for adjudication is legislative or executive, federal or state."

(7)   One particularly influential observer, Alexander Bickel, identified the crux of the problem as the "counter-majoritarian" quality of judicial review. In his famous work *The Least Dangerous Branch—The Supreme Court at the Bar of Politics* 16–18 (1962), Bickel observed: "The root difficulty is that judicial review is a counter-majoritarian force in our society. There are various ways of sliding over this ineluctable reality. . . . Most assuredly, no democracy operates by taking continuous

nose counts on the broad range of daily government activities. . . . Nevertheless, although democracy does not mean constant reconsideration of decisions once made, it does mean that a representative majority has the power to accomplish a reversal [of policy]. This power is of the essence, and no less so because it is often merely held in reserve. . . . [There is] nothing in the further complexities and perplexities of the system [that] can alter the essential reality that judicial review is a deviant institution in the American democracy." Are there easy answers to the difficulty Bickel identifies? For more discussions of judicial review and the role of the Supreme Court, consult Bickel, *The Supreme Court and the Idea of Progress* (1970); Gunther, *The Subtle Vices of the "Passive Virtues"—A Comment on Principle and Expediency in Judicial Review,* 64 Colum.L.Rev. 1 (1964); Tribe, *American Constitutional Law, Volume 1* (3d ed. 2000); Ely, *Democracy and Distrust: A Theory of Judicial Review* (1980).

Students interested in the general historical background of judicial review should examine, in addition to the works cited above, 1 *Selected Essays on Constitutional Law* 1–173 (1938), hereinafter cited as *Selected Essays* (1938).

2. CONGRESSIONAL CONTROL OF JUDICIAL REVIEW BY THE FEDERAL COURTS

The Scope of Congressional Power over the Jurisdiction of Lower Federal Courts

While Article III of the Constitution created the Supreme Court, it deliberately gave Congress the option to create "such inferior Courts as the Congress may from time to time ordain and establish." Since inferior federal courts, in theory, exist at the pleasure of Congress, it has always been clear that Article III does not require that any single lower federal court exercise all, or any particular part, of the judicial power described by that Article. Indeed, the current general jurisdiction of the inferior federal courts in civil cases arising under federal law was not conferred until after the Civil War. What has been an issue, however, is whether all of the judicial power must be lodged somewhere in the federal judicial system—either originally in a lower federal court, or on appeal of state court decisions to the Supreme Court.

Justice Story, in dicta in Martin v. Hunter's Lessee, 14 U.S. (1 Wheat.) 304 (1816), stressed the mandatory language of Article III ("The judicial power of the United States shall be vested. . . ." "The judicial power shall extend. . . .") He concluded that Congress had an obligation to vest the entire judicial power somewhere within the federal judicial system. Later, in his writings, he argued that any contrary conclusion would mean that "the judiciary, as a co-ordinate department of the government, may, at the will of Congress, be annihilated, or stripped of all its important jurisdiction." 2 *Commentaries on the Constitution of the United States* 395 (4th ed. 1873). Story's position was authoritatively rejected in Sheldon v. Sill, 49 U.S. (8 How.) 441 (1850). In upholding a restriction on the diversity jurisdiction, the Court concluded that since Congress had the option to create inferior federal courts it also had the power to create them as courts of limited jurisdiction. "[H]aving a right to prescribe, Congress may withhold from any court of its creation jurisdiction of any of the enumerated controversies. Courts created by statute can have no jurisdiction but such as the statute confers." Id. at 449. Notice that the Supreme Court, which was created by the Constitution, has never had power to review state court decisions on the basis that the parties are of diverse citizenship. The result in Sheldon v. Sill was thus to deny all federal courts a portion of the judicial power. If Congress must create a supreme court, must Congress vest in that Court the judicial power not lodged somewhere else in the federal judicial system?

Ex parte McCardle

74 U.S. (7 Wall.) 506, 19 L.Ed. 264 (1868).

Appeal from the Circuit Court for the Southern District of Mississippi.

The case was this:

The Constitution of the United States ordains as follows:

"§ 1. The judicial power of the United States shall be vested *in one Supreme Court,* and in such inferior courts as the Congress may from time to time ordain and establish."

"§ 2. The judicial power shall extend to all cases in law or equity arising *under this Constitution, the laws of the United States,*" & c.

And in these last cases the Constitution ordains that,

"The Supreme Court shall have appellate jurisdiction, both as to law and fact, *with such exceptions, and under such regulations, as the Congress shall make.*"

With these constitutional provisions in existence, Congress, on the 5th February, 1867, by "An act to amend an act to establish the judicial courts of the United States, approved September 24, 1789," provided that the several courts of the United States, and the several justices and judges of such courts, within their respective jurisdiction, in addition to the authority already conferred by law, should have power to grant writs of *habeas corpus* in all cases where any person may be restrained of his or her liberty in violation of the Constitution, or of any treaty or law of the United States. And that, from the final decision of any judge, justice, or court inferior to the Circuit Court, appeal might be taken to the Circuit Court of the United States for the district in which the cause was heard, and *from the judgment of the said Circuit Court to the Supreme Court of the United States.*

This statute being in force, one McCardle, alleging unlawful restraint by military force, preferred a petition in the court below, for the writ of *habeas corpus.*

The writ was issued, and a return was made by the military commander, admitting the restraint, but denying that it was unlawful.

It appeared that the petitioner was not in the military service of the United States, but was held in custody by military authority for trial before a military commission, upon charges founded upon the publication of articles alleged to be incendiary and libellous, in a newspaper of which he was editor. The custody was alleged to be under the authority of certain acts of Congress.

Upon the hearing, the petitioner was remanded to the military custody; but, upon his prayer, an appeal was allowed him to this court, and upon filing the usual appeal-bond, for costs, he was admitted to bail upon recognizance, with sureties, conditioned for his future appearance in the Circuit Court, to abide by and perform the final judgment of this court. The appeal was taken under the above-mentioned act of February 5, 1867.

A motion to dismiss this appeal was made at the last term, and, after argument, was denied.

Subsequently, on the 2d, 3d, 4th, and 9th March, the case was argued very thoroughly and ably upon the merits, and was taken under advisement. While it was thus held, and before conference in regard to the decision proper to be made, an act was passed by Congress, returned with objections by the President, and, on the 27th March, repassed by the constitutional majority, the second section of which was as follows:

"*And be it further enacted,* That so much of the act approved February 5, 1867, entitled 'An act to amend an act to establish the judicial courts of the United States, approved September 24, 1789', as authorized an appeal from the judgment of the Circuit Court to the Supreme Court of the United States, or the exercise of any such jurisdiction by said Supreme Court, on appeals which have been, or may hereafter be taken, be, and the same is hereby repealed."

The attention of the court was directed to this statute at the last term, but counsel having expressed a desire to be heard in argument upon its effect, and the Chief Justice being detained from his place here, by his duties in the Court of Impeachment, the cause was continued under advisement. Argument was now heard upon the effect of the repealing act. . . .

■ THE CHIEF JUSTICE delivered the opinion of the Court.

The first question necessarily is that of jurisdiction; for, if the act of March, 1868, takes away the jurisdiction defined by the act of February, 1867, it is useless, if not improper, to enter into any discussion of other questions.

It is quite true, as was argued by the counsel for the petitioner, that the appellate jurisdiction of this court is not derived from acts of Congress. It is strictly speaking, conferred by the Constitution. But it is conferred "with such exceptions and under such regulations as Congress shall make."

It is unnecessary to consider whether, if Congress had made no exceptions and no regulations, this court might not have exercised general appellate jurisdiction under rules prescribed by itself. For among the earliest acts of the first Congress, at its first session, was the act of September 24th, 1789, to establish the judicial courts of the United States. That act provided for the organization of this court, and prescribed regulations for the exercise of its jurisdiction.

The source of that jurisdiction, and the limitations of it by the Constitution and by statute, have been on several occasions subjects of consideration here. In the case of Durousseau v. The United States [6 Cranch 307 (1810)], particularly, the whole matter was carefully examined, and the court held, that while "the appellate powers of this court are not given by the judicial act, but are given by the Constitution," they are, nevertheless, "limited and regulated by that act, and by such other acts as have been passed on the subject." The court said, further, that the judicial act was an exercise of the power given by the Constitution to Congress "of making exceptions to the appellate jurisdiction of the Supreme Court." "They have described affirmatively," said the court, "its jurisdiction, and this affirmative description has been understood to imply a negation of the exercise of such appellate power as is not comprehended within it."

The principle that the affirmation of appellate jurisdiction implies the negation of all such jurisdiction not affirmed having been thus established, it was an almost necessary consequence that acts of Congress, providing for the exercise of jurisdiction, should come to be spoken of as acts granting jurisdiction, and not as acts making exceptions to the constitutional grant of it.

The exception to appellate jurisdiction in the case before us, however, is not an inference from the affirmation of other appellate jurisdiction. It is made in terms. The provision of the act of 1867, affirming the appellate jurisdiction of this court in cases of *habeas corpus* is expressly repealed. It is hardly possible to imagine a plainer instance of positive exception.

We are not at liberty to inquire into the motives of the legislature. We can only examine into its power under the Constitution; and the power to make exceptions to the appellate jurisdiction of this court is given by express words.

What, then, is the effect of the repealing act upon the case before us? We cannot doubt as to this. Without jurisdiction the court cannot proceed at all in any cause. Jurisdiction is power to declare the law, and when it ceases to exist, the only function remaining to the court is that of announcing the fact and dismissing the cause. And this is not less clear upon authority than upon principle.

. . .

It is quite clear, therefore, that this court cannot proceed to pronounce judgment in this case, for it has no longer jurisdiction of the appeal; and judicial duty is not less fitly performed by declining ungranted jurisdiction than in exercising firmly that which the Constitution and the laws confer.

Counsel seem to have supposed, if effect be given to the repealing act in question, that the whole appellate power of the court, in cases of *habeas corpus,* is denied. But this is an error. The act of 1868 does not except from that jurisdiction any cases but appeals from Circuit Courts under the act of 1867. It does not affect the jurisdiction which was previously exercised.

The appeal of the petitioner in this case must be dismissed for want of jurisdiction.

United States v. Klein
80 U.S. (13 WALL.) 128 (1871).

An 1863 Statute provided for seizure and sale of captured or abandoned property in areas of rebellion, and for payment of the proceeds into the united states treasury. The statute further provided that loyal owners, upon proof that they had not given aid or comfort to the rebellion, could recover those proceeds by suit in the court of claims. In United States v. Padelford, 76 U.S. (9 Wall.) 531 (1870), the statute was construed to permit recovery by a claimant who had not been loyal in fact, but who had been given a presidential pardon. Radical Republicans in Congress were outraged with the Court's decision and promptly passed a statute providing that a Presidential pardon was not proof of loyalty, but was proof that the claimant had given aid to the rebellion. The 1870 statute provided further that, upon proof of a pardon, either in the court of claims or the Supreme Court, "the court shall forthwith dismiss the suit of such claimant." Klein's case was similar to Padelford's. At the time the 1870 Act was passed, the court of claims had given judgment for the claimant, and the government's appeal was pending in the Supreme Court. The government moved in the Supreme Court that Klein's suit be dismissed as required by the act. the court denied the motion, and affirmed the judgment of the court of claims.

Chief Justice Chase's opinion concluded that the 1870 statute was unconstitutional in two respects—in prescribing how a court should decide an issue of fact, and in denying effect to a Presidential pardon. Since the law was unconstitutional, the Court could not constitutionally be required to dismiss Klein's case. "We must think that Congress has inadvertently passed the limit which separates the legislative from the judicial power. . . . Congress has already provided that the Supreme Court shall have jurisdiction of the judgments of the Court of Claims on appeal. Can it prescribe a rule in conformity with which the court must deny to itself its jurisdiction thus conferred, because and only because the decision, in accordance with settled law, must be adverse to the government and favorable to the suitor?"

The Scope of Congressional Power over Supreme Court Jurisdiction Under the Exceptions Clause

(1)   For full accounts of the background of the *McCardle* case see Fairman, 433–514, and 2 Warren, *Supreme Court in United States History* 464–484 (Rev. ed. 1926).

(2)   In his plurality opinion in Glidden Co. v. Zdanok, 370 U.S. 530, 567–568 (1962), Justice Harlan suggested this distinction between the *McCardle* and *Klein* cases: *McCardle* sustained Congressional power to withdraw jurisdiction to proceed with a case then *sub judice; Klein* was an unconstitutional restriction of judicial power because it prescribed an unconstitutional rule of decision in a pending case. (In dissent, Justice Douglas implied that the two cases were inconsistent, and doubted whether the principle of *McCardle* could command a modern majority. Id. at 605, n. 11.) Is it significant that McCardle had lost his case below and Congress directed dismissing his *appeal,* while Klein had won in the court below and Congress directed dismissing his suit? (The Congressional direction to the Supreme Court to dismiss claimants' suits, rather than simply dismiss appeals, was not "inadvertent." Sponsors of the legislation wanted to overturn the results in the cases of claimants who had obtained judgment in the court of claims where the government's appeal was pending in the Supreme Court.)

(3)   The *McCardle* case is the only example of a result-oriented restriction on the Supreme Court's appellate jurisdiction sustained by the Supreme Court. Is it significant that it *was* sustained, even as applied to a case which had been argued and submitted for decision? Less than a year after *McCardle,* another newspaper editor in military custody, who had been denied habeas corpus by a lower federal court, successfully invoked the Supreme Court's jurisdiction to issue an "original" writ of habeas corpus under Section 14 of the Judiciary Act of 1789. Ex parte Yerger, 75 U.S. (8 Wall.) 85 (1868). (The government avoided a constitutional test of the powers of military reconstruction governments by releasing Yerger from military custody, mooting the case.) Can the *McCardle* case then be explained as a narrow decision that one route of Supreme Court review can always be closed so long as another remains open? See Van Alstyne, *A Critical Guide to Ex Parte McCardle,* 15 Ariz.L.Rev. 229, 244–254 (1973).

(4)   Some proposals to restrict the jurisdiction of inferior federal courts in constitutional cases would leave undisturbed the appellate jurisdiction of the Supreme Court. Does that kind of legislation present lesser constitutional problems than legislation that closes the door to the Supreme Court? Consider, for example, the "Human Life Statute," introduced in 1981 in both the Senate and House of Representatives.[1] Section 2[2] provided:

"Notwithstanding any other provision of law, no inferior Federal court ordained and established by Congress under article III of the Constitution of the United States shall have jurisdiction to issue any restraining order, temporary or permanent injunction, or declaratory judgment in any case involving or arising from any State law or municipal ordinance that (1) protects the rights of human persons between conception and birth, or (2) prohibits, limits, or regulates (a) the performance of abortions, or (b) the provision at public expense of funds, facilities, personnel, or other assistance for the performance of abortions."

Notice that the proposed statute would leave intact the authority of the Supreme Court to review state court decisions, including both abortion convictions and state

---

[1]   97th Cong., 1st Sess., H.R. 900 (Hyde and Mazzoli) and S. 158 (Helms and D'Amato).

[2]   Section 1 of the Human Life Statute was a substantive provision attempting to change the result in the Supreme Court's abortion decisions by ordinary legislation.

court actions for injunctions and declaratory judgments. Also undisturbed would be the lower courts' jurisdiction in habeas corpus to review state abortion convictions.

Most troublesome of all are proposals that both deny the lower federal courts' jurisdiction to entertain actions, and the Supreme Court's jurisdiction to review state court decisions, concerning particular constitutional issues. Consider the examples in the next three notes.

(5)   The Omnibus Crime Control and Safe Streets Act of 1968 as it was reported to the Senate by the Senate Judiciary Committee contained the following provision which was eliminated on the floor prior to final passage of the bill: "Neither the Supreme Court nor any inferior court ordained and established by Congress under article III of the Constitution of the United States shall have jurisdiction to review or to reverse, vacate, modify, or disturb in any way, a ruling of any trial court of any State in any criminal prosecution admitting in evidence as voluntarily made an admission or confession of an accused if such ruling has been affirmed or otherwise upheld by the highest court of the State having appellate jurisdiction of the cause." See U.S.Code Cong. and Adm.News, 90th Cong.Sec.Sess.1968, p. 2138. This provision was designed to "revise" the holding in Miranda v. Arizona, 384 U.S. 436 (1966). Would it have been constitutional?

(6)   In 1962 and 1963, the Court held that prayers and Bible readings in public schools were unconstitutional, whether or not objecting pupils were excused. Engel v. Vitale, 370 U.S. 421 (1962); Abington School Dist. v. Schempp and Murray v. Curlett, 374 U.S. 203 (1963). Public furor created by the decisions led to proposals for constitutional amendments, on which the House Judiciary Committee held hearings in 1964.

On April 9, 1979, the Senate passed, as a rider to a bill on Supreme Court jurisdiction, an amendment originally proposed by Senator Jesse Helms, which would have added the following two new sections to 28 U.S.C.:

§ 1259.   Notwithstanding the provisions of sections 1253, 1254 and 1257 of this chapter the Supreme Court shall not have jurisdiction to review, by appeal, writ or certiorari, or otherwise, any case arising out of any State statute . . . which relates to voluntary prayers in public school and public buildings.

§ 1364.   Notwithstanding any other provision of law, the district courts shall not have jurisdiction of any case or question which the Supreme Court does not have jurisdiction to review under Section 1259. . . .

If the Helms Amendment were to be enacted, and were to be sustained by the federal courts, what would be the impact of the Supreme Court's earlier decisions concerning school prayers when cases were litigated in state courts?

(7)   In 2004, the House of Representatives passed two bills that would have stripped all federal courts of jurisdiction over certain federal questions. The first, the so-called Marriage Protection Act, purported to build upon the Defense of Marriage Act (DOMA), 28 U.S.C. § 1738C, which was passed by Congress and signed into law in 1996. The DOMA attempts to permit each state to refuse to recognize same-sex marriages entered into in other states, notwithstanding the requirement in Article IV of the Constitution that each state give "full faith and credit" to the judgments of other states. The Marriage Protection bill passed by the House was seemingly the result of a fear that federal courts might strike down the DOMA as unconstitutional. The bill provided that: "No court created by Act of Congress shall have any jurisdiction, and the Supreme Court shall have no appellate jurisdiction, to hear or decide any question pertaining to the interpretation of, or the validity under the Constitution of, section 1738C [that is, DOMA] or this section."

The second jurisdiction-stripping bill passed by the House, about two months later, concerned the Pledge of Allegiance. Apparently worried that the federal courts, including the Supreme Court, might invalidate the inclusion of the words "one nation under God" in the Pledge as it is recited in public schools and other public institutions—a question raised, but not decided by the Court, in Elk Grove Unified School Dist. v. Newdow, 542 U.S. 1 (2004), the House passed a measure that would have deprived all federal courts of any "jurisdiction[ ] to hear or decide any question pertaining to the interpretation of, or the validity under the Constitution of, the Pledge of Allegiance . . . or its recitation."

(8)   For discussion of the limits of Congressional power to control jurisdiction of the lower federal courts, and a summary of the enormous literature on that question, see Gunther, *Congressional Power to Curtail Federal Court Jurisdiction: An Opinionated Guide to an Ongoing Debate,* 36 Stan.L.Rev. 895 (1984); Akhil Amar, *A Neo-Federalist View of Article III: Separating the Two Tiers of Federal Jurisdiction*, 65 B.U.L.Rev. 205 (1985).

CHAPTER 3

THE JURISDICTION OF FEDERAL COURTS IN CONSTITUTIONAL CASES

Judicial review can be understood only in the context of constitutional litigation. Minimum familiarity with jurisdictional boundaries and the special rules devised for constitutional cases is necessary to understanding the substantive doctrines. This chapter is designed to present a brief introduction to a very complicated set of related doctrines that govern both Supreme Court review and the conduct of the lower federal courts. Those doctrines concern the definition of "cases" and "controversies" and the extent to which issues of constitutional interpretation are justiciable.

1. INTRODUCTION

The limitations explored below arose initially from the Court's early rejection of an advisory opinion role for the federal courts and from the theory of *Marbury v. Madison* that judicial review is simply a function of deciding ordinary litigation between adverse parties in which it becomes necessary to determine the constitutional validity of legislation to resolve the disputes.

The doctrines involved in this section are characteristically "soft" in the sense that it is difficult to define the rules with precision and in the sense that they do not appear to be consistent in their application. The imprecision and inconsistency result in part from the fact that these doctrines are used by the Court to regulate the extent of its impact An "activist" Court seeking to expand the application of certain constitutional doctrines is more likely to construe justiciability limitations narrowly in order to reach the merits of cases; a Court interested in "retrenchment and consolidation" is more likely to construe justiciability limitations broadly in order to avoid reaching the merits of cases.

Advisory Opinions

In 1793 President Washington over the objection of Hamilton, who thought the matter was not within the province of the judiciary, submitted to the Justices 29 questions relating to international law, neutrality, and the construction of the French and British treaties. Secretary of State Jefferson wrote as follows to Chief Justice Jay:

"The war which has taken place among the powers of Europe produces frequent transactions within our ports and limits, on which questions arise of considerable difficulty, and of greater importance to the peace of the United States. These questions depend for their solution on the construction of our treaties, on the laws of nature and nations, and on the law of the land, and are often presented under circumstances which do not give a cognizance of them to the tribunals of the country. Yet their decision is so little analogous to the ordinary functions of the Executive as to occasion much embarrassment and difficulty to them. The President would, therefore, be much relieved if he found himself free to refer questions of this description to the opinions of the Judges of the Supreme Court of the United States, whose knowledge of the subject would secure us as against errors dangerous to the peace of the United States, and their authority ensure the respect of all parties. He has therefore asked the attendance of such of the Judges as could be collected in time for the occasion, to know, in the first place, their opinion, whether the public may, with propriety, be availed of their advice on these questions. And if they may, to present, for their advice, the abstract questions which have already occurred, or may soon occur, from which they will themselves strike out such as any circumstances might, in their opinion, forbid them to pronounce on."

After considering the matter for a few weeks the Justices replied as follows:

"We have considered the previous question stated in a letter written by your direction to us by the Secretary of State, on the 18th of last month regarding the lines of separation, drawn by the Constitution between the three departments of the government. These being in certain respects checks upon each other, and our being Judges of a Court in the last resort, are considerations which afford strong arguments against the propriety of our extra-judicially deciding the questions alluded to, especially as the power given by the Constitution to the President, of calling on the heads of departments for opinions, seems to have been *purposely* as well as expressly united to the *Executive* departments. We exceedingly regret every event that may cause embarrassment to your Administration, but we derive consolation from the reflection that your judgment will discern what is right, and that your usual prudence, decision and firmness will surmount every obstacle to the preservation of the rights, peace, and dignity of the United States."

Hayburn's Case

2 U.S. 409 (1792).

A dispute arose about whether federal courts could be required by Congress to perform claim-processing functions that would then be subject to review by an Executive Branch officer and Congress. A 1792 congressional Act directed federal Circuit Courts to entertain petitions by disabled Revolutionary War veterans for pension benefits. Under the Act, decisions by the Circuit Courts were subject to being blocked by the Secretary of War, pending further congressional action. A number of Circuit Court judges, including five of the six members of the U.S. Supreme Court sitting individually in their capacity as Circuit judges, declared the law unconstitutional insofar as it imposed non-judicial duties on them and subjected their decisions to revision by the other branches of government. The Attorney General, on behalf of a pension claimant, asked the Supreme Court to issue a writ of mandamus requiring the lower federal courts to implement the Act; while the case was pending in the Supreme Court, Congress revised the Act so as to relieve Circuit judges of their obligation to hear the pension applications, so the Supreme Court itself never issued a ruling on the merits of the mandamus request.

Flast v. Cohen Summary

■ WARREN, C.J., for the Court in Flast v. Cohen, 392 U.S. 83, 94–97 (1968):

"The jurisdiction of federal courts is defined and limited by Article III of the Constitution. In terms relevant to the question for decision in this case, the judicial power of federal courts is constitutionally restricted to 'cases' and 'controversies.' As is so often the situation in constitutional adjudication, those two words have an iceberg quality, containing beneath their surface simplicity submerged complexities which go to the very heart of our constitutional form of government. Embodied in the words 'cases' and 'controversies' are two complementary but somewhat different limitations. In part those words limit the business of federal courts to questions presented in an adversary context and in a form historically viewed as capable of resolution through the judicial process. And in part those words define the role assigned to the judiciary in a tripartite allocation of power to assure that the federal courts will not intrude into areas committed to the other branches of government. Justiciability is the term of art employed to give expression to this dual limitation placed upon federal courts by the case and controversy doctrine.

"Justiciability is itself a concept of uncertain meaning and scope. Its reach is illustrated by the various grounds upon which questions sought to be adjudicated in federal courts have been held not to be justiciable. Thus, no justiciable controversy is presented when the parties seek adjudication of only a political question, when the parties are asking for an advisory opinion, when the question sought to be adjudicated has been mooted by subsequent developments, and when there is no standing to maintain the action. Yet it remains true that '[j]usticiability is . . . not a legal concept with a fixed content of susceptible or scientific verification. Its utilization is the resultant of many subtle pressures. . . .' Poe v. Ullman, 367 U.S. 497, 508 (1961).

"Part of the difficulty in giving precise meaning and form to the concept of justiciability stems from the uncertain historical antecedents of the case and controversy doctrine. . . . [I]t is quite clear that 'the oldest and most consistent thread in the federal law of justiciability is that federal courts will not give advisory opinions.' Wright, Federal Courts 34 (1963). Thus, the implicit policies embodied in Article III, and not history alone, impose the rule against advisory opinions on federal courts. When the federal judicial power is invoked to pass upon the validity of actions by the Legislative and Executive Branches of the Government, the rule against advisory opinions implements the separation of powers prescribed by the Constitution and confines federal courts to the role assigned them by Article III. . . . However, the rule against advisory opinions also recognizes that such suits often 'are not pressed before the Court with that clear concreteness provided when a question emerges precisely framed and necessary for decision from a clash of adversary argument exploring every aspect of a multifaced situation embracing conflicting and demanding interests.' United States v. Fruehauf, 365 U.S. 146, 157 (1961). Consequently, the Article III prohibition against advisory opinions reflects the complementary constitutional considerations expressed by the justiciability doctrine: Federal judicial power is limited to those disputes which confine federal courts to a role consistent with a system of separated powers and which are traditionally thought to be capable of resolution through the judicial process.

"Additional uncertainty exists in the doctrine of justiciability because that doctrine has become a blend of constitutional requirements and policy considerations. And a policy limitation is 'not always clearly distinguished from the constitutional limitation.' Barrows v. Jackson, 346 U.S. 249, 255 (1953). For example, in his concurring opinion in Ashwander v. Tennessee Valley Authority, 297 U.S. 288, 345–348 (1936), Mr. Justice Brandeis listed seven rules developed by this Court 'for its own governance' to avoid passing prematurely on constitutional questions. Because the rules operate in 'cases confessedly within [the Court's] jurisdiction,' id., at 346, they find their source in policy, rather than purely constitutional, considerations. However, several of the cases cited by Mr. Justice Brandeis in illustrating the rules of self-governance articulated purely constitutional grounds for decision. See, e.g., Massachusetts v. Mellon, 262 U.S. 447 (1923); Fairchild v. Hughes, 258 U.S. 126 (1922); Chicago & Grand Trunk R. Co. v. Wellman, 143 U.S. 339 (1892). The 'many subtle pressures' which cause policy considerations to blend into the constitutional limitations of Article III make the justiciability doctrine one of uncertain and shifting contours."

Justiciability and the Form of the Litigation—Raising Constitutional Issues

Raising Constitutional Issues. How do persons go about getting an adjudication concerning the constitutionality of statutes (or other governmental actions) which affect them? In any individual case one or more of the following methods may be available:

(1) If the statute is made the basis of claim or defense in a suit between private individuals, the constitutional issue can be litigated. For an important constitutional law case which arose in this manner, see Gibbons v. Ogden, 22 U.S. (9 Wheat.) 1 (1824), set out infra p. 98.

(2) If the government (federal or state) brings a civil suit based on the statute, the claim of unconstitutionality can be raised in defense. For a leading constitutional case which arose in this matter, see McCulloch v. Maryland, 17 U.S. (4 Wheat.) 316 (1819), set out infra p. 82.

(3) If the government institutes criminal proceedings based on the statute, unconstitutionality of the statute is a defense. For cases in which important issues of state and federal taxing power were raised in this fashion, see Brown v. Maryland, 25 U.S. (12 Wheat.) 419 (1827); United States v. Kahriger, 345 U.S. 22 (1953).

(4) One damaged by governmental action claimed to be unconstitutional may be able to raise the issue in a suit for damages. For a case where a plaintiff succeeded in such a suit see United States v. Causby, 328 U.S. 256 (1946).

(5) Persons held in official custody may challenge the constitutionality of their detention by writ of habeas corpus (or a statutory substitute for the writ such as 28 U.S.C. § 2255). See, e.g., Fay v. Noia, 372 U.S. 391 (1963).

(6) One may bring a suit seeking an injunction or a declaratory judgment as to the constitutionality of a statute. Frequently such an action is brought in order to challenge constitutionality without taking the risk of civil or criminal liability involved in acting in disregard of the statute. A large portion of constitutional litigation takes this form.

(7) The Supreme Court has suggested that a governmental official sued for damages for violating the Constitution, who wins in the lower court on the ground of qualified immunity, may nonetheless seek review in the Supreme Court of a ruling by the lower court that the official violated the Constitution, provided the official desires to continue to engage in the allegedly unconstitutional conduct as part of the performance of her job in the future, and provided that the plaintiff in the damage action remains someone who is affected by the way the official performs her public duties. See Camreta v. Greene, 131 S.Ct. 2020 (2011).

Relevance of Form of Litigation to Justiciability. Few issues of justiciability arise where constitutional issues are determined in suits taking the first five forms described above. The litigation involves adverse parties in traditional forms. The constitutional issue is posed in a way quite compatible with the theory of Marbury v. Madison. However, when suits are brought seeking to enjoin the enforcement of statutes on the ground of unconstitutionality or seeking judgments declaring statutes unconstitutional, problems of case and controversy and justiciability frequently arise. The student will notice that most of the cases in this section involve such suits.

2. STANDING

Warth v. Seldin

422 U.S. 490, 95 S.Ct. 2197, 45 L.Ed.2d 343 (1975).

■ MR. JUSTICE POWELL delivered the opinion of the Court.

Petitioners, various organizations and individuals resident in the Rochester, New York, metropolitan area, brought this action in the District Court for the Western District of New York against the Town of Penfield, an incorporated municipality adjacent to Rochester, and against members of Penfield's Zoning, Planning, and Town Boards. Petitioners claimed that the town's zoning ordinance, by its terms and as enforced by the defendant board members, respondents here, effectively excluded persons of low and moderate income from living in the town, in contravention of petitioners' First, Ninth, and Fourteenth Amendment rights and in violation of 42 U.S.C. §§ 1981, 1982, and 1983. . . . [The lower courts found no standing for plaintiffs.]

. . .

II

We address first the principles of standing relevant to the claims asserted by the several categories of petitioners in this case. In essence the question of standing is whether the litigant is entitled to have the court decide the merits of the dispute or of particular issues. This inquiry involves both constitutional limitations on federal court jurisdiction and prudential limitations on its exercise. . . . In both dimensions it is founded in concern about the proper—and properly limited—role of the courts in a democratic society. . . .

In its constitutional dimension, standing imports justiciability: whether the plaintiff has made out a "case or controversy" between himself and the defendant within the meaning of Art. III. This is the threshold question in every federal case, determining the power of the court to entertain the suit. As an aspect of justiciability, the standing question is whether the plaintiff has "alleged such a personal stake in the outcome of the controversy" as to warrant *his* invocation of federal-court jurisdiction and to justify exercise of the court's remedial powers on his behalf. . . . The Art. III judicial power exists only to redress or otherwise to protect against injury to the complaining party, even though the court's judgment may benefit others collaterally. A federal court's jurisdiction therefore can be invoked only when the plaintiff himself has suffered "some threatened or actual injury resulting from the putatively illegal action. . . ." . . .

Apart from this minimum constitutional mandate, this Court has recognized other limits on the class of persons who may invoke the courts' decisional and remedial powers. First, the Court has held that when the asserted harm is a "generalized grievance" shared in substantially equal measure by all or a large class of citizens, that harm alone normally does not warrant exercise of jurisdiction. . . . Second, even when the plaintiff has alleged injury sufficient to meet the "case or controversy" requirement, this Court has held that the plaintiff generally must assert his own legal rights and interests, and cannot rest his claim to relief on the legal rights or interests of third parties. . . . Without such limitations—closely related to Art. III concerns but essentially matters of judicial self-governance—the courts would be called upon to decide abstract questions of wide public significance even though other governmental institutions may be more competent to address the questions and even though judicial intervention may be unnecessary to protect individual rights. . . .

Although standing in no way depends on the merits of the plaintiff's contention that particular conduct is illegal, . . . it often turns on the nature and source of the claim asserted. The actual or threatened injury required by Art. III may exist solely by virtue of "statutes creating legal rights, the invasion of which creates standing. . . ." . . . Moreover, Congress may grant an express right of action to persons who otherwise would be barred by prudential standing rules. Of course, Art. III's requirement remains: the plaintiff still must allege a distinct and palpable injury to himself, even if it is an injury shared by a large class of other possible litigants. . . . But so long as this requirement is satisfied, persons to whom Congress has granted a right of action, either expressly or by clear implication, may have standing to seek relief on the basis of the legal rights and interests of others, and, indeed, may invoke the general public interest in support of their claim. . . .

One further preliminary matter requires discussion. For purposes of ruling on a motion to dismiss for want of standing, both the trial and reviewing courts must accept as true all material allegations of the complaint, and must construe the complaint in favor of the complaining party. . . . At the same time, it is within the trial court's power to allow or to require the plaintiff to supply, by amendment to the complaint or by affidavits, further particularized allegations of fact deemed supportive of plaintiff's standing. If, after this opportunity, the plaintiff's standing does not adequately appear from all materials of record, the complaint must be dismissed.

III

With these general considerations in mind, we turn first to the claims of petitioners Ortiz, Reyes, Sinkler, and Broadnax, each of whom asserts standing as a person of low or moderate income and, coincidentally, as a member of a minority racial or ethnic group. We must assume, taking the allegations of the complaint as true, that Penfield's zoning ordinance and the pattern of enforcement by respondent officials have had the purpose and effect of excluding persons of low and moderate income, many of whom are members of racial or ethnic minority groups. We also assume, for purposes here, that such intentional exclusionary practices, if proved in a proper case, would be adjudged violative of the constitutional and statutory rights of the persons excluded.

But the fact that these petitioners share attributes common to persons who may have been excluded from residence in the town is an insufficient predicate for the conclusion that petitioners themselves have been excluded, or that the respondents' assertedly illegal actions have violated their rights. Petitioners must allege and show that they personally have been injured, not that injury has been suffered by other, unidentified members of the class to which they belong and which they purport to represent. . . .

In their complaint, petitioners Ortiz, Reyes, Sinkler, and Broadnax alleged in conclusory terms that they are among the persons excluded by respondents' actions. None of them has ever resided in Penfield; each claims at least implicitly that he desires, or has desired, to do so. Each asserts, moreover, that he made some effort, at some time, to locate housing in Penfield that was at once within his means and adequate for his family's needs. Each claims that his efforts proved fruitless. We may assume, as petitioners allege, that respondents' actions have contributed, perhaps substantially, to the cost of housing in Penfield. But there remains the question whether petitioners' inability to locate suitable housing in Penfield reasonably can be said to have resulted, in any concretely demonstrable way, from respondents' alleged constitutional and statutory infractions. Petitioners must allege facts from which it reasonably could be inferred that, absent the respondents' restrictive zoning practices, there is a substantial probability that they would have been able to purchase or lease in Penfield and that, if the court affords the relief requested, the asserted inability of petitioners will be removed. . . .

We find the record devoid of the necessary allegations. As the Court of Appeals noted, none of these petitioners has a present interest in any Penfield property; none is himself subject to the ordinance's strictures; and none has ever been denied a variance or permit by respondent officials. Instead, petitioners claim that respondents' enforcement of the ordinance against third parties—developers, builders, and the like—has had the consequence of precluding the construction of housing suitable to their needs at prices they might be able to afford. The fact that the harm to petitioners may have resulted indirectly does not in itself preclude standing. When a governmental prohibition or restriction imposed on one party causes specific harm to a third party, harm that a constitutional provision or statute was intended to prevent, the indirectness of the injury does not necessarily deprive the person harmed of standing to vindicate his rights. E.g., Roe v. Wade, 410 U.S. 113, 124, 147 (1973). But it may make it substantially more difficult to meet the minimum requirement of Art. III: to establish that, in fact, the asserted injury was the consequence of the defendants' actions, or that prospective relief will remove the harm.

Here, by their own admission, realization of petitioners' desire to live in Penfield always has depended on the efforts and willingness of third parties to build low-and moderate-cost housing. The record specifically refers to only two such efforts: that of Penfield Better Homes Corp., in late 1969, to obtain the rezoning of certain land in Penfield to allow the construction of subsidized cooperative townhouses that could be purchased by persons of moderate income; and a similar effort by O'Brien Homes, Inc., in late 1971. But the record is devoid of any indication that these projects, or other like projects, would have satisfied petitioners' needs at prices they could afford, or that, were the court to remove the obstructions attributable to respondents, such relief would benefit petitioners. Indeed, petitioners' descriptions of their individual financial situations and housing needs suggest precisely the contrary—that their inability to reside in Penfield is the consequence of the economics of the area housing market, rather than of respondents' assertedly illegal acts. In short, the facts alleged fail to support an actionable causal relationship between Penfield's zoning practices and petitioners' asserted injury.

. . .

IV

The petitioners who assert standing on the basis of their status as taxpayers of the city of Rochester present a different set of problems. These "taxpayer-petitioners" claim that they are suffering economic injury consequent to Penfield's allegedly discriminatory and exclusionary zoning practices. Their argument, in brief, is that Penfield's persistent refusal to allow or to facilitate construction of low-and moderate-cost housing forces the city of Rochester to provide more such housing than it otherwise would do; that to provide such housing, Rochester must allow certain tax abatements; and that as the amount of tax-abated property increases, Rochester taxpayers are forced to assume an increased tax burden in order to finance essential public services.

. . .

. . . In short the claim of these petitioners falls squarely within the prudential standing rule that normally bars litigants from asserting the rights or legal interests of others in order to obtain relief from injury to themselves. As we have observed above, this rule of judicial self-governance is subject to exceptions, the most prominent of which is that Congress may remove it by statute. Here, however, no statute expressly or by clear implication grants a right of action, and thus standing to seek relief, to persons in petitioners' position. In several cases, this Court has allowed standing to litigate the rights of third parties when enforcement of the challenged restriction against the litigant would result indirectly in the violation of third parties' rights. . . . But the taxpayer-petitioners are not themselves subject to Penfield's zoning practices. Nor do they allege that the challenged zoning ordinance and practices preclude or otherwise adversely affect a relationship existing between them and the persons whose rights assertedly are violated. . . .

V

We turn next to the standing problems presented by the petitioner associations— Metro-Act of Rochester, Inc., one of the original plaintiffs; Housing Council in the Monroe County Area, Inc., which the original plaintiffs sought to join as a party-plaintiff; and Rochester Home Builders Association, Inc., which moved in the District Court for leave to intervene as plaintiff. There is no question that an association may have standing in its own right to seek judicial relief from injury to itself and to vindicate whatever rights and immunities the association itself may enjoy. Moreover, in attempting to secure relief from injury to itself the association may assert the rights of its members, at least so long as the challenged infractions adversely affect its members' associational ties. . . . With the limited exception of Metro-Act, however, none of the associational petitioners here has asserted injury to itself.

Even in the absence of injury to itself, an association may have standing solely as the representative of its members. . . . The possibility of such representational standing, however, does not eliminate or attenuate the constitutional requirement of a case or controversy. . . . The association must allege that its members, or any one of them, are suffering immediate or threatened injury as a result of the challenged action of the sort that would make out a justiciable case had the members themselves brought suit. . . . So long as this can be established, and so long as the nature of the claim and of the relief sought does not make the individual participation of each injured party indispensable to proper resolution of the cause, the association may be an appropriate representative of its members, entitled to invoke the court's jurisdiction.

A

Petitioner Metro-Act's claims to standing on its own behalf as a Rochester taxpayer, and on behalf of its members who are Rochester taxpayers or persons of low or moderate income, are precluded by our holdings in Parts III and IV, supra, as to the individual petitioners, and require no further discussion. . . .

. . .

B

Petitioner Home Builders, in its intervenor-complaint, asserted standing to represent its member firms engaged in the development and construction of residential housing in the Rochester area, including Penfield. . . .

. . .

Home Builders' prayer for prospective relief fails. . . . It can have standing as the representative of its members only if it has alleged facts sufficient to make out a case or controversy had the members themselves brought suit. No such allegations were made. The complaint refers to no specific project of any of its members that is currently precluded either by the ordinance or by respondents' action in enforcing it. There is no averment that any member has applied to respondents for a building permit or a variance with respect to any current project. Indeed, there is no indication that respondents have delayed or thwarted any project currently proposed by Home Builders' members, or that any of its members has taken advantage of the remedial processes available under the ordinance. In short, insofar as the complaint seeks prospective relief, Home Builders has failed to show the existence of any injury to its members of sufficient immediacy and ripeness to warrant judicial intervention.

. . .

VI

The rules of standing, whether as aspects of the Art. III case-or-controversy requirement or as reflections of prudential considerations defining and limiting the role of the courts, are threshold determinants of the propriety of judicial intervention. It is the responsibility of the complainant clearly to allege facts demonstrating that he is a proper party to invoke judicial resolution of the dispute and the exercise of the court's remedial powers. We agree with the District Court and the Court of Appeals that none of the petitioners here has met this threshold requirement. Accordingly, the judgment of the Court of Appeals is

Affirmed.

■ MR. JUSTICE DOUGLAS, dissenting.

. . .

Standing has become a barrier to access to the federal courts, just as "the political question" was in earlier decades. The mounting caseload of federal courts is well known. But cases such as this one reflect festering sores in our society; and the American dream teaches that if one reaches high enough and persists there is a forum where justice is dispensed. I would lower the technical barriers and let the courts serve that ancient need. . . .

. . .

. . . I would let the case go to trial and have all the facts brought out. Indeed, it would be better practice to decide the question of standing only when the merits have been developed.

I would reverse the Court of Appeals.

■ MR. JUSTICE BRENNAN, with whom MR. JUSTICE WHITE and MR. JUSTICE MARSHALL join, dissenting.

In this case, a wide range of plaintiffs, alleging various kinds of injuries, claimed to have been affected by the Penfield zoning ordinance, on its face and as applied, and by other practices of the defendant officials of Penfield. Alleging that as a result of these laws and practices low-and moderate-income and minority people have been excluded from Penfield, and that this exclusion is unconstitutional, plaintiffs sought injunctive, declaratory, and monetary relief. The Court today, in an opinion that purports to be a "standing" opinion but that actually, I believe, has overtones of outmoded notions of pleading and of justiciability, refuses to find that any of the variously situated plaintiffs can clear numerous hurdles, some constructed here for the first time, necessary to establish "standing." While the Court gives lip service to the principle, oft repeated in recent years, that "standing in no way depends on the merits of the plaintiff's contention that particular conduct is illegal," in fact the opinion, which tosses out of court almost every conceivable kind of plaintiff who could be injured by the activity claimed to be unconstitutional, can be explained only by an indefensible hostility to the claim on the merits. I can appreciate the Court's reluctance to adjudicate the complex and difficult legal questions involved in determining the constitutionality of practices which assertedly limit residence in a particular municipality to those who are white and relatively well off, and I also understand that the merits of this case could involve grave sociological and political ramifications. But courts cannot refuse to hear a case on the merits merely because they would prefer not to, and it is quite clear, when the record is viewed with dispassion, that at least three of the groups of plaintiffs have made allegations, and supported them with affidavits and documentary evidence, sufficient to survive a motion to dismiss for lack of standing.

. . .

II

Low-Income and Minority Plaintiffs

. . .

. . . [T]he Court's real holding is not that these petitioners have not *alleged* an injury resulting from respondents' action, but that they are not to be allowed to prove one, because "realization of petitioners' desire to live in Penfield always has depended on the efforts and willingness of third parties to build low and moderate-cost housing," and "the record is devoid of any indication that . . . [any] projects, would have satisfied petitioners' needs at prices they could afford."

Certainly, this is not the sort of demonstration that can or should be required of petitioners at this preliminary stage. . . .

Here, the very fact that, as the Court stresses, these petitioners' claim rests in part upon proving the intentions and capabilities of third parties to build in Penfield suitable housing which they can afford, coupled with the exclusionary character of the claim on the merits, makes it particularly inappropriate to assume that these petitioners' lack of specificity reflects a fatal weakness in their theory of causation. Obviously they cannot be expected, prior to discovery and trial, to know the future plans of building companies, the precise details of the housing market in Penfield, or everything which has transpired in 15 years of application of the Penfield zoning ordinance, including every housing plan suggested and refused. To require them to allege such facts is to require them to prove their case on paper in order to get into court at all. . . .

III

Associations Including Building Concerns

. . .

Again, the Court ignores the thrust of the complaints and asks petitioners to allege the impossible. According to the allegations, the building concerns' experience in the past with Penfield officials has shown any plans for low-and moderate-income housing to be futile for, again according to the allegations, the respondents are engaged in a purposeful, conscious scheme to exclude such housing. Particularly with regard to a low-or moderate-income project, the cost of litigating, with respect to any particular project, the legality of a refusal to approve it may well be prohibitive. And the merits of the exclusion of this or that project is not at the heart of the complaint; the claim is that respondents will not approve *any* project which will provide residences for low and moderate-income people.

. . .

I would reverse the judgment of the Court of Appeals.

Village of Arlington Heights v. Metropolitan Housing Development Corp.
429 U.S. 252 (1977).

Metropolitan Housing Development Corporation (MHDC), a builder of low and moderate income housing in the Chicago area, contracted to purchase a 15-acre site in the Village of Arlington Heights. The contract was contingent upon MHDC securing zoning clearances from the Village and Federal approval to build a 190-unit project with subsidies under § 236 of the National Housing Act. MHDC submitted detailed plans for the project to the Village which refused to rezone the property to permit construction of multiple-family housing. MHDC and three individuals brought suit in the federal district court seeking an injunction and declaratory relief, alleging that the denial was racially discriminatory. The Supreme Court, in an opinion by Justice Powell, held that the plaintiffs had standing, saying in part:

"Clearly MHDC has met the constitutional requirements and it therefore has standing to assert its own rights. Foremost among them is MHDC's right to be free of arbitrary or irrational zoning actions. . . . [T]he heart of this litigation . . . has been the claim that the Village's refusal to rezone discriminates against racial minorities in violation of the Fourteenth Amendment. As a corporation, MHDC has no racial identity and cannot be the direct target of the petitioners' alleged discrimination. In the ordinary case, a party is denied standing to assert the rights of third persons. Warth v. Seldin, 422 U.S., at 499. But we need not decide whether the circumstances of this case would justify departure from that prudential limitation and permit MHDC to assert the constitutional rights of its prospective minority tenants. . . . For we have at least one individual plaintiff who has demonstrated standing to assert these rights as his own.

"Respondent Ransom, a Negro, works at the Honeywell factory in Arlington Heights and lives approximately 20 miles away in Evanston in a 5-room house with his mother and his son. The complaint alleged that he seeks and would qualify for the housing MHDC wants to build in Arlington Heights. Ransom testified at trial that if Lincoln Green were built he would probably move there, since it is closer to his job.

"The injury Ransom asserts is that his quest for housing nearer his employment has been thwarted by official action that is racially discriminatory. If a court grants the relief he seeks, there is at least a 'substantial probability,' that the Lincoln Green project will materialize, affording Ransom the housing opportunity he desires in Arlington Heights. His is not a generalized grievance. Instead, . . . it focuses on a particular project and is not dependent on speculation about the possible actions of third parties not before the court. . . . Unlike the individual plaintiffs in *Warth,* Ransom has adequately averred an 'actionable causal relationship' between Arlington Heights' zoning practices and his asserted injury. . . . We therefore proceed to the merits."[a]

Consider the following cases dealing with the issue whether plaintiffs had shown the requisite injury in fact to establish standing. Are they consistent?

Sierra Club v. Morton, 405 U.S. 727 (1972). The Court held that an environmental group lacked standing to challenge the construction of a recreation area in a national forest. The fact that the Sierra Club—which did not allege that any of its members were affected by the proposed development—had an interest in the problem of maintaining the environment did not confer standing.

United States v. SCRAP, 412 U.S. 669 (1973). An environmental group had standing to challenge a railroad rate structure of the Interstate Commerce Commission claimed to discourage the shipment, and use, of recycled materials and promote the use of raw materials. Plaintiff alleged that its members (five law students): were caused to pay more for finished products; used the forests, rivers, mountains and other natural resources in the vicinity of Washington, D.C. and those recreational uses had been affected by increased littering; breathed the air in the Washington metropolitan area, which had suffered increased air pollution. All of these

---

^a   For the decision on the merits, see infra p. 553.

effects were alleged to be caused by the ICC rate structure which caused the increased use of raw materials and decreased recycling. (In *Sierra Club* the plaintiff had alleged only a "public interest" and not the injury to its members.)

SCRAP, like *Sierra Club,* was an action based on a provision of the Administrative Procedure Act, conferring standing to sue on persons "adversely affected" or "aggrieved" by an agency's decision. The Court concluded that standing, under that provision, was neither confined to those who suffer economic harm nor denied to many people who suffer the same injury. Otherwise, the most injurious and widespread government actions could be questioned by nobody. (On the merits, the Court reversed the lower court's decision enjoining the Commission's rate structure.)

Simon v. Eastern Kentucky Welfare Rights Organization, 426 U.S. 26 (1976). Indigent persons lacked standing to challenge Internal Revenue Service rulings granting favorable tax treatment to nonprofit hospitals providing inadequate hospital services to indigents. Allegations that the rulings "encouraged" hospitals to deny services were speculative. It was just as plausible that the relevant hospitals would forego favorable tax treatment rather than expend substantial funds for increased hospital services to indigents. Thus, plaintiffs' complaint did not demonstrate a substantial likelihood that declaring the rulings invalid would result in their receiving the hospital services they desire.

Allen v. Wright, 468 U.S. 737 (1984). Parents of black children attending public schools did not have standing to challenge IRS practices concerning denial of tax exemptions to racially discriminatory private schools. Plaintiffs' allegations that the IRS practices inhibited the process of desegregation in their children's public schools did not show injury traceable to the challenged government policy. It was speculative whether denial of tax exemption to any private school would induce it to change its policies and whether children would be transferred to public schools if their private schools were threatened with loss of tax exemption.

Lujan v. Defenders of Wildlife, 504 U.S. 555 (1992). The Endangered Species Act of 1973 requires the Secretary of Interior to promulgate a list of endangered species, and requires all federal agencies to insure that any action by them is not likely to threaten their continued existence. The Interior Department issued a regulation interpreting the Act to be inapplicable to projects undertaken outside the United States. Two scientists claimed they would be affected by overseas projects: one had observed in the past, and intended to observe in the future, crocodiles that would be endangered by rehabilitation of the Aswan Dam in Egypt; another had observed in the past, and intended to observe in the future, elephants and leopards endangered by a project in Sri Lanka. Plaintiffs lacked standing because their injury was speculative, since they alleged only that they intended to return to the overseas sites "some day," without specifying a definite date.

Associated General Contractors v. City of Jacksonville, 508 U.S. 656 (1993). Non-minority contractors who alleged that they would have bid on construction work set aside for minority contractors had standing to challenge the requirement that 10% of city contracts be awarded to minority-owned businesses. It was not necessary that plaintiffs allege or prove that they would have been awarded contracts but for the challenged program. In equal protection cases, the injury in fact is not the denial of the benefit itself but the denial of equal treatment imposed by a barrier to obtaining a benefit—here the inability to compete on an equal footing in the bidding process.

United States v. Hays, 515 U.S. 737 (1995). Voters attacking an alleged racial gerrymander lack standing unless they show that they, personally, have been subject to racial discrimination. White voters who neither resided in the challenged predominantly-Black district, nor were excluded from that district because they were White, had only a "generalized grievance" and had not suffered "individualized harm."

Texas v. Lesage, 528 U.S. 18 (1999). An applicant for admission to a graduate program in a state university who challenges an ongoing race-conscious program and seeks forward-looking relief need not establish that he or she would have been admitted to the program if race were not considered. The relevant injury is "the inability to compete on an equal footing." The rejected applicant's claim for damages, however, is defeated by the university's demonstration that it would have made the same decision absent the alleged discrimination. If the government would have made the same decision regardless, there is no cognizable injury justifying the award of damages.

Clapper v. Amnesty International, 570 U.S. ___, 133 S.Ct. 1138 (2013). A group of American attorneys and human rights, labor, legal and media organizations lacked standing to challenge the FISA Amendments Act of 2008, which permits the U.S. Attorney General and the Director of National Intelligence to seek approval from the Foreign Intelligence Surveillance Court (FISC) to obtain foreign intelligence information through surveillance of individuals who are not "United States persons." The plaintiffs' allegations that they engage in sensitive international communications with foreign individuals who, plaintiffs believe, are likely targets of federal surveillance were inadequate, because there was not a strong enough likelihood that: (1) the federal government would imminently target persons with whom plaintiffs communicated; (2) even if such persons were targeted, the federal government would make use of the FISA Amendments Act rather than other surveillance methods; (3) even if FISC permission were sought, it would be granted; and (4) even if FISC permission were sought and obtained, the federal government would successfully intercept particular communications to which plaintiffs were parties.

Lujan v. Defenders of Wildlife
504 U.S. 555, 112 S.Ct. 2130, 119 L.Ed.2d 351 (1992).

■ JUSTICE SCALIA delivered the opinion of the Court with respect to Parts I, II, III-A, and IV, and an opinion with respect to Part III-B in which THE CHIEF JUSTICE, JUSTICE WHITE, and JUSTICE THOMAS join.

This case involves a challenge to a rule promulgated by the Secretary of the Interior interpreting § 7 of the Endangered Species Act of 1973 (ESA), 87 Stat. 892, as amended, 16 U.S.C. § 1536, in such fashion as to render it applicable only to actions within the United States or on the high seas. The preliminary issue, and the only one we reach, is whether the respondents here, plaintiffs below, have standing to seek judicial review of the rule.

I

The ESA ... seeks to protect species of animals against threats to their continuing existence caused by man.... The ESA instructs the Secretary of the Interior to promulgate by regulation a list of those species which are either endangered or threatened under enumerated criteria, and to define the critical habitat of these species.... Section 7(a)(2) of the Act then provides, in pertinent part: "Each Federal agency shall, in consultation with and with the assistance of the Secretary [of the Interior], insure that any action authorized, funded, or carried out by such agency ... is not likely to jeopardize the continued existence of any endangered species or threatened species or result in the destruction or adverse modification of habitat of such species which is determined by the Secretary, after consultation as appropriate with affected States, to be critical." ...

In 1978, the Fish and Wildlife Service (FWS) and the National Marine Fisheries Service (NMFS), on behalf of the Secretary of the Interior and the Secretary of Commerce respectively, promulgated a joint regulation stating that the obligations imposed by § 7(a)(2) extend to actions taken in foreign nations. . . . The next year, however, the Interior Department began to reexamine its position. . . . A revised joint regulation, reinterpreting § 7(a)(2) to require consultation only for actions taken in the United States or on the high seas, was proposed in 1983. . . .

Shortly thereafter, respondents, organizations dedicated to wildlife conservation and other environmental causes, filed this action against the Secretary of the Interior, seeking a declaratory judgment that the new regulation is in error as to the geographic scope of § 7(a)(2), and an injunction requiring the Secretary to promulgate a new regulation restoring the initial interpretation. . . . [T]he Secretary moved for summary judgment on the standing issue, and respondents moved for summary judgment on the merits. The District Court denied the Secretary's motion, . . . and ordered the Secretary to publish a revised regulation. The Eighth Circuit affirmed. . . .

. . .

[The court held that two members of the organization who alleged, without adequate specificity, that they intended to observe animals endangered by specific projects had not suffered an "injury in fact."]

IV

The Court of Appeals found that respondents had standing for an additional reason: because they had suffered a "procedural injury." The so-called "citizen-suit" provision of the ESA provides, in pertinent part, that "any person may commence a civil suit on his own behalf (A) to enjoin any person, including the United States and any other governmental instrumentality or agency . . . who is alleged to be in violation of any provision of this chapter." 16 U.S.C. § 1540(g). The court held that, because § 7(a)(2) requires interagency consultation, the citizen-suit provision creates a "procedural righ[t]" to consultation in all "persons"—so that anyone can file suit in federal court to challenge the Secretary's (or presumably any other official's) failure to follow the assertedly correct consultative procedure, notwithstanding their inability to allege any discrete injury flowing from that failure. To understand the remarkable nature of this holding one must be clear about what it does not rest upon: This is not a case where plaintiffs are seeking to enforce a procedural requirement the disregard of which could impair a separate concrete interest of theirs (e.g., the procedural requirement for a hearing prior to denial of their license application, or the procedural requirement for an environmental impact statement before a federal facility is constructed next door to them). Nor is it simply a case where concrete injury has been suffered by many persons, as in mass fraud or mass tort situations. Nor, finally, is it the unusual case in which Congress has created a concrete private interest in the outcome of a suit against a private party for the government's benefit, by providing a cash bounty for the victorious plaintiff. Rather, the court held that the injury-in-fact requirement had been satisfied by congressional conferral upon all persons of an abstract, self-contained, noninstrumental "right" to have the Executive observe the procedures required by law. We reject this view.

We have consistently held that a plaintiff raising only a generally available grievance about government—claiming only harm to his and every citizen's interest in proper application of the Constitution and laws, and seeking relief that no more directly and tangibly benefits him than it does the public at large—does not state an Article III case or controversy. . . .

. . .

To be sure, our generalized-grievance cases have typically involved Government violation of procedures assertedly ordained by the Constitution rather than the Congress. But there is absolutely no basis for making the Article III inquiry turn on the source of the asserted right. Whether the courts were to act on their own, or at the invitation of Congress, in ignoring the concrete injury requirement described in our cases, they would be discarding a principle fundamental to the separate and distinct constitutional role of the Third Branch—one of the essential elements that identifies those "Cases" and "Controversies" that are the business of the courts rather than of the political branches. "The province of the court," as Chief Justice Marshall said in Marbury v. Madison, 1 Cranch 137, 170 (1803) "is, solely, to decide on the rights of individuals." Vindicating the public interest (including the public interest in government observance of the Constitution and laws) is the function of Congress and the Chief Executive. The question presented here is whether the public interest in proper administration of the laws (specifically, in agencies' observance of a particular, statutorily prescribed procedure) can be converted into an individual right by a statute that denominates it as such, and that permits all citizens (or, for that matter, a subclass of citizens who suffer no distinctive concrete harm) to sue. If the concrete injury requirement has the separation-of-powers significance we have always said, the answer must be obvious: To permit Congress to convert the undifferentiated public interest in executive officers' compliance with the law into an "individual right" vindicable in the courts is to permit Congress to transfer from the President to the courts the Chief Executive's most important constitutional duty, to "take Care that the Laws be faithfully executed," Art. II, § 3. It would enable the courts, with the permission of Congress, "to assume a position of authority over the governmental acts of another and co-equal department," Frothingham v. Mellon, 262 U.S., at 489 . . . We have always rejected that vision of our role. . . .

. . .

. . . The opinion of the Court of Appeals is hereby reversed, and the cause remanded for proceedings consistent with this opinion.

It is so ordered.[a]

■ JUSTICE KENNEDY, with whom JUSTICE SOUTER joins, concurring in part and concurring in the judgment.

. . .

I . . . join Part IV of the Court's opinion with the following observations. As government programs and policies become more complex and far-reaching, we must be sensitive to the articulation of new rights of action that do not have clear analogs in our common-law tradition. Modern litigation has progressed far from the paradigm of Marbury suing Madison to get his commission, Marbury v. Madison, 1 Cranch 137 (1803), or Ogden seeking an injunction to halt Gibbons' steamboat operations. Gibbons v. Ogden, 9 Wheat. 1 (1824). In my view, Congress has the power to define injuries and articulate chains of causation that will give rise to a case or controversy where none existed before, and I do not read the Court's opinion to suggest a contrary view. . . . In exercising this power, however, Congress must at the very least identify the injury it seeks to vindicate and relate the injury to the class of persons entitled to bring suit. The citizen-suit provision of the Endangered Species Act does not meet these minimal requirements, because while the statute purports to confer a right on "any person . . . to enjoin . . . the United States and any other governmental instrumentality or agency

<hr>

[a]　Justice Scalia's position in *Lujan* was originally propounded in Scalia, *The Doctrine of Standing as an Essential Element of the Separation of Powers*, 17 SUFFOLK U. L. REV. 831 (1983). For a critique, see Sunstein, *What's Standing After Lujan? Of Citizen Suits, "Injuries," and Article III*, 91 MICH. L. REV. 163 (1992).

. . . who is alleged to be in violation of any provision of this chapter," it does not of its own force establish that there is an injury in "any person" by virtue of any "violation." 16 U.S.C. § 1540(g)(1)(A).

The Court's holding that there is an outer limit to the power of Congress to confer rights of action is a direct and necessary consequence of the case and controversy limitations found in Article III. . . .[b]

. . .

Massachusetts v. Environmental Protection Agency

549 U.S. 497 (2007).

The Court ruled 5–4 that the State of Massachusetts had standing to challenge the Federal Environmental Protection Agency's decision not to regulate four particular "greenhouse" gases under section 202(1)(a) of the Clean Air Act. Writing for the majority, Justice Stevens observed that "[w]hen a State enters the Union, it surrenders certain sovereign prerogatives. Massachusetts cannot invade Rhode Island to force reductions in greenhouse gas emissions, it cannot negotiate an emissions treaty with China or India, and in some circumstances the exercise of its police powers to reduce in-state motor-vehicle emissions might well be pre-empted. . . . These sovereign prerogatives are now lodged in the Federal Government, and Congress has ordered EPA to protect Massachusetts (among others) by prescribing standards applicable to the 'emission of any air pollutant from any class or classes of new motor vehicle engines, which in [the Administrator's] judgment cause, or contribute to, air pollution which may reasonably be anticipated to endanger public health or welfare.' 42 U.S.C. § 7251(a)(1). Congress has moreover recognized a concomitant procedural right to challenge the rejection of its rulemaking petition as arbitrary and capricious. § 7606(b)(1). Given that procedural right and Massachusetts' stake in protecting its quasi-sovereign interests, the Commonwealth is entitled to special solicitude in our standing analysis."

The majority went on to find the elements of standing satisfied because "EPA's steadfast refusal to regulate greenhouse gas emissions presents a risk of harm to Massachusetts that is both 'actual' and 'imminent'. . . . There is, moreover, a 'substantial likelihood that the judicial relief requested' will prompt EPA to take steps to reduce that risk." As to actual injury, the Court noted that the "widely-shared" nature of climate-change risks "does not minimize Massachusetts' interest in the outcome of this litigation." As for causation, the majority rejected EPA's argument that because the effect of any regulation on the global warming problem would be incremental, the agency's contributions to Massachusetts' injuries are so "insignificant[ ] . . . that the agency cannot be haled into court to answer for them": this "argument rests on the erroneous assumption that a small incremental step, because it is incremental, can never be attacked in a federal judicial forum. Yet accepting that premise would doom most challenges to regulatory action."

Finally, and relatedly, as to the effectiveness of any remedy to redress Massachusetts' injury, the majority reasoned: "While it may be true that regulating motor-vehicle emissions will not by itself reverse global warming, it by no means follows that we lack jurisdiction to decide whether EPA has a duty to take steps to slow or reduce it. . . . Because of the enormity of the potential consequences associated with man-made climate change, the fact that the effectiveness of a remedy might be delayed during the (relatively short) time it takes for a new motor-vehicle fleet to

---

[b]   Justice Stevens concurred in the judgment, and Justice Blackmun, joined by Justice O'Connor, filed a dissenting opinion.

replace an older one is essentially irrelevant. Nor is it dispositive that developing countries such as China and India are poised to increase greenhouse gas emissions substantially over the next century: A reduction in domestic emissions would slow the pace of global emissions increases, no matter what happens elsewhere."

The Chief Justice, with Justices Scalia, Thomas and Alito, dissented.

3. POLITICAL QUESTIONS

Baker v. Carr

369 U.S. 186 (1962).

The court held that a suit by voters seeking reapportionment because the apportionment of a state legislature denied them equal protection of the laws did not involve a nonjusticiable political question. Justice Brennan's opinion for the court contained this summary of political question doctrine:

"We have said that 'in determining whether a question falls within [the political question] category, the appropriateness under our system of government of attributing finality to the action of the political departments and also the lack of satisfactory criteria for a judicial determination are dominant considerations.' ... The nonjusticiability of a political question is primarily a function of the separation of powers. Much confusion results from the capacity of the 'political question' label to obscure the need for case-by-case inquiry. Deciding whether a matter has in any measure been committed by the Constitution to another branch of government, or whether the action of that branch exceeds whatever authority has been committed, is itself a delicate exercise in constitutional interpretation, and is a responsibility of this Court as ultimate interpreter of the Constitution. To demonstrate this requires no less than to analyze representative cases and to infer from them analytical threads that make up the political question doctrine. We shall then show that none of those threads catches this case.

"*Foreign Relations.* There are sweeping statements to the effect that all questions touching foreign relations are political questions. Not only does resolution of such issues frequently turn on standards that defy judicial application, or involve the exercise of a discretion demonstrably committed to the executive or legislature; but many such questions uniquely demand single-voiced statement of the Government's views. Yet it is error to suppose that every case or controversy which touches foreign relations lies beyond judicial cognizance. Our cases in this field seem invariably to show a discriminating analysis of the particular question posed, in terms of the history of its management by the political branches, of its susceptibility to judicial handling in the light of its nature and posture in the specific case, and of the possible consequences of judicial action. For example, though a court will not ordinarily inquire whether a treaty has been terminated, since on that question 'governmental action ... must be regarded as of controlling importance,' if there has been no conclusive 'governmental action' then a court can construe a treaty and may find it provides the answer. Compare Terlinden v. Ames, 184 U.S. 270, 285, with Society for the Propagation of the Gospel in Foreign Parts v. New Haven, 8 Wheat. 464, 492–495. Though a court will not undertake to construe a treaty in a manner inconsistent with a subsequent federal statute, no similar hesitancy obtains if the asserted clash is with state law. Compare Whitney v. Robertson, 124 U.S. 190, with Kolovrat v. Oregon, 366 U.S. 187. ...

"*Dates of Duration of Hostilities.* Though it has been stated broadly that 'the power which declared the necessity is the power to declare its cessation, and what the cessation requires,' Commercial Trust Co. v. Miller, 262 U.S. 51, 57, here too analysis reveals isolable reasons for the presence of political questions, underlying this Court's refusal to review the political departments' determination of when or whether a war has ended. Dominant is the need for finality in the political determination, for emergency's nature demands 'a prompt and unhesitating obedience,' Martin v. Mott, 12 Wheat. 19, 30 (calling up of militia). . . .

"*Validity of Enactments.* In *Coleman v. Miller,* . . . , this Court held that the questions of how long a proposed amendment to the Federal Constitution remained open to ratification and what effect a prior rejection had on a subsequent ratification, were committed to congressional resolution and involved criteria of decision that necessarily escaped the judicial grasp. Similar considerations apply to the enacting process: 'the respect due to coequal and independent departments,' and the need for finality and certainty about the status of a statute contribute to judicial reluctance to inquire whether, as passed, it complied with all requisite formalities. Field v. Clark, 143 U.S. 649, 672, 676–677; see Leser v. Garnett, 258 U.S. 130, 137. But it is not true that courts will never delve into a legislature's records upon such a quest: If the enrolled statute lacks an effective date, a court will not hesitate to seek it in the legislative journals in order to preserve the enactment. Gardner v. Collector, 6 Wall. 499. The political question doctrine, a tool for maintenance of governmental order, will not be so applied as to promote only disorder. . . .

"It is apparent that several formulations which vary slightly according to the settings in which the questions arise may describe a political question, although each has one or more elements which identifies it as essentially a function of the separation of powers. Prominent on the surface of any case held to involve a political question is found a textually demonstrable constitutional commitment of the issue to a coordinate political department; or a lack of judicially discoverable and manageable standards for resolving it; or the impossibility of deciding without an initial policy determination of a kind clearly for nonjudicial discretion; or the impossibility of a court's undertaking independent resolution without expressing lack of the respect due coordinate branches of government; or an unusual need for unquestioning adherence to a political decision already made; or the potentiality of embarrassment from multifarious pronouncements by various departments on one question.

"Unless one of these formulations is inextricable from the case at bar, there should be no dismissal for non-justiciability on the ground of a political question's presence. The doctrine of which we treat is one of 'political questions,' not one of 'political cases.' The courts cannot reject as 'no law suit' a bona fide controversy as to whether some action denominated 'political' exceeds constitutional authority. The cases we have reviewed show the necessity for discriminating inquiry into the precise facts and posture of the particular case, and the impossibility of resolution by any semantic cataloguing.

"But it is argued that this case shares the characteristics of decisions that constitute a category not yet considered, cases concerning the Constitution's guaranty, in Art. IV, § 4, of a republican form of government. A conclusion as to whether the case at bar does present a political question cannot be confidently reached until we have considered those cases with special care. We shall discover that Guaranty Clause claims involve those elements which define a 'political question,' and for that reason and no other, they are nonjusticiable. In particular, we shall discover that the nonjusticiability of such claims has nothing to do with their touching upon matters of state governmental organization.

"*Republican Form of Government.* Luther v. Borden, 7 How. 1, 48 U.S. 1, though in form simply an action for damages for trespass was, as Daniel Webster said in opening the argument for the defense, 'an unusual case.' The defendants, admitting an otherwise tortious breaking and entering, sought to justify their action on the ground that they were agents of the established lawful government of Rhode Island, which State was then under martial law to defend itself from active insurrection; that the plaintiff was engaged in that insurrection; and that they entered under orders to arrest the plaintiff. The case arose 'out of the unfortunate political differences which agitated the people of Rhode Island in 1841 and 1842,' 7 How. at 34, which had resulted in a situation wherein two groups laid competing claims to recognition as the lawful government. The plaintiff's right to recover depended upon which of the two groups was entitled to such recognition; but the lower court's refusal to receive evidence or hear argument on that issue, its charge to the jury that the earlier established or 'charter' government was lawful, and the verdict for the defendants, were affirmed upon appeal to this Court. . . .

"Clearly, several factors were thought by the Court in Luther to make the question there 'political': the commitment to the other branches of the decision as to which is the lawful state government; the unambiguous action by the President, in recognizing the charter government as the lawful authority; the need for finality in the executive's decision; and the lack of criteria by which a court could determine which form of government was republican."

Powell v. McCormack

395 U.S. 486, 89 S.Ct. 1944, 23 L.Ed.2d 491 (1969).

■ MR. CHIEF JUSTICE WARREN delivered the opinion of the Court.

In November 1966, Petitioner Adam Clayton Powell, Jr., was duly elected from the 18th Congressional District of New York to serve in the United States House of Representatives for the 90th Congress. However, pursuant to a House resolution, he was not permitted to take his seat. Powell (and some of the voters of his district) then filed suit in Federal District Court claiming that the House could exclude him only if it found he failed to meet the standing requirements of age, citizenship, and residence contained in Art. I, § 2, of the Constitution—requirements the House specifically found Powell met—and thus had excluded him unconstitutionally. The District Court dismissed petitioners' complaint "for want of jurisdiction of the subject matter." The Court of Appeals affirmed the dismissal, although on somewhat different grounds, each judge filing a separate opinion. We have determined that it was error to dismiss the complaint and that Petitioner Powell is entitled to a declaratory judgment that he was unlawfully excluded from the 90th Congress.

. . .

[At the organization of the 90th Congress in January, 1967, Powell was asked to step aside while the oath was administered to the other members. A Select Committee was then appointed which reported that Powell met the standing qualifications but that he had asserted an unwarranted privilege and immunity from the processes of the courts of New York; that he had wrongfully diverted House funds for the use of others and himself; and that he had made false reports on expenditures of foreign currency to a House committee. After a ruling by the Speaker that only a majority vote would be needed to exclude Powell and declare the seat vacant, the House adopted such a resolution of exclusion. By the time the case got to the Supreme Court Powell had been elected again and was seated in the 91st Congress. The Court held that the case was not moot because Powell had asked for damages. The Court also held that the vote by the House could not be treated as a vote to expel even though the actual vote exceeded a two-thirds majority. The Court's discussion of the political question objection to ruling on the validity of the action of the House follows.]

. . .

1.   *Textually demonstrable constitutional commitment*

Respondents maintain that even if this case is otherwise justiciable, it presents only a political question. . . .

Respondents' first contention is that this case presents a political question because under Art. I, § 5, there has been a "textually demonstrable constitutional commitment" to the House of the "adjudicatory power" to determine Powell's qualifications. Thus it is argued that the House, and the House alone, has power to determine who is qualified to be a member.

In order to determine whether there has been a textual commitment to a co-ordinate department of the Government, we must interpret the Constitution. In other words, we must first determine what power the Constitution confers upon the House through Art. I, § 5, before we can determine to what extent, if any, the exercise of that power is subject to judicial review. Respondents maintain that the House has broad power under § 5, and, they argue, the House may determine which are the qualifications necessary for membership. On the other hand, petitioners allege that the Constitution provides that an elected representative may be denied his seat only if the House finds he does not meet one of the standing qualifications expressly prescribed by the Constitution.

If examination of § 5 disclosed that the Constitution gives the House judicially unreviewable power to set qualifications for membership and to judge whether prospective members meet those qualifications, further review of the House determination might well be barred by the political question doctrine. On the other hand, if the Constitution gives the House power to judge only whether elected members possess the three standing qualifications set forth in the Constitution; further consideration would be necessary to determine whether any of the other formulations of the political question doctrine are "inextricable from the case at bar."[42] Baker v. Carr, supra, at 217.

. . .

In order to determine the scope of any "textual commitment" under Art. I, § 5, we necessarily must determine the meaning of the phrase "be the judge of the qualifications of its own members." . . . Our examination of the relevant historical materials leads us to the conclusion that petitioners are correct and that the Constitution leaves the House without authority to *exclude* any person, duly elected by his constituents, who meets all the requirements for membership expressly prescribed in the Constitution.

[A long review of the historical precedents is omitted.]

Had the intent of the Framers emerged from these materials with less clarity, we would nevertheless have been compelled to resolve any ambiguity in favor of a narrow construction of the scope of Congress' power to exclude members-elect. A fundamental principle of our representative democracy is, in Hamilton's words, "that the people should choose whom they please to govern them." 2 Elliot's Debates 257. . . . Moreover, it would effectively nullify the Convention's decision to require a two-third vote for expulsion. Unquestionably, Congress has an interest in preserving its institutional integrity, but in most cases that interest can be sufficiently safeguarded by the exercise of its power to punish its members for disorderly behavior and, in extreme cases, to expel a member with the concurrence of two-thirds. In short, both the

---

[42] Consistent with this interpretation, federal courts might still be barred by the political question doctrine from reviewing the House's factual determination that a member did not meet one of the standing qualifications. This is an issue not presented in this case and we express no view as to its resolution.

intention of the Framers, to the extent it can be determined, and an examination of the basic principles of our democratic system persuade us that the Constitution does not vest in the Congress a discretionary power to deny membership by a majority vote.

For these reasons, we have concluded that Art. I, § 5, is at most a "textually demonstrable commitment" to Congress to judge only the qualifications expressly set forth in the Constitution. Therefore, the "textual commitment" formulation of the political question doctrine does not bar federal courts from adjudicating petitioners' claims.

2. *Other considerations*

Respondents' alternate contention is that the case presents a political question because judicial resolution of petitioners' claim would produce a "potentially embarrassing confrontation between coordinate branches" of the Federal Government. But, as our interpretation of Art. I, § 5, discloses, a determination of Petitioner Powell's right to sit would require no more than an interpretation of the Constitution. Such a determination falls within the traditional role accorded courts to interpret the law, and does not involve a "lack of respect due [a] coordinate [branch] of government," nor does it involve an "initial policy determination of a kind clearly for nonjudicial discretion." Baker v. Carr, supra, at 217. Our system of government requires that federal courts on occasion interpret the Constitution in a manner at variance with the construction given the document by another branch. The alleged conflict that such an adjudication may cause cannot justify the courts' avoiding their constitutional responsibility. . . .

Nor are any of the other formulations of a political question "inextricable from the case at bar." Baker v. Carr, supra, at 217. Petitioners seek a determination that the House was without power to exclude Powell from the 90th Congress, which, we have seen, requires an interpretation of the Constitution—a determination for which clearly there are "judicially . . . manageable standards." Finally, a judicial resolution of petitioners' claim will not result in "multifarious pronouncements by various departments on one question." For, as we noted in Baker v. Carr, supra, at 211, it is the responsibility of this Court to act as the ultimate interpreter of the Constitution. Marbury v. Madison, 5 U.S. (1 Cranch) 137 (1803). Thus, we conclude that petitioners' claim is not barred by the political question doctrine, and having determined that the claim is otherwise generally justiciable, we hold that the case is justiciable.

. . .

Nixon v. United States

506 U.S. 224, 113 S.Ct. 732, 122 L.Ed.2d 1 (1993).

■ CHIEF JUSTICE REHNQUIST delivered the opinion of the Court.

Petitioner Walter L. Nixon, Jr., asks this court to decide whether Senate Rule XI, which allows a committee of Senators to hear evidence against an individual who has been impeached and to report that evidence to the full Senate, violates the Impeachment Trial Clause, Art. I, § 3, cl. 6. That Clause provides that the "Senate shall have the sole Power to try all Impeachments." But before we reach the merits of such a claim, we must decide whether it is "justiciable," that is, whether it is a claim that may be resolved by the courts. We conclude that it is not.

Nixon, a former Chief Judge of the United States District Court for the Southern District of Mississippi, was convicted by a jury of two counts of making false statements before a federal grand jury and sentenced to prison. . . .

On May 10, 1989, the House of Representatives adopted three articles of impeachment for high crimes and misdemeanors. . . .

After the House presented the articles to the Senate, the Senate voted to invoke its own Impeachment Rule XI, under which the presiding officer appoints a committee of Senators to "receive evidence and take testimony." . . . The Senate committee held four days of hearings. . . . Pursuant to Rule XI, the committee presented the full Senate with a complete transcript of the proceeding and a report stating the uncontested facts and summarizing the evidence on the contested facts. Nixon and the House impeachment managers submitted extensive final briefs to the full Senate and delivered arguments from the Senate floor during the three hours set aside for oral argument in front of that body. Nixon himself gave a personal appeal, and several Senators posed questions directly to both parties. . . . The Senate voted by more than the constitutionally required two-thirds majority to convict Nixon on the first two articles. . . . The presiding officer then entered judgment removing Nixon from his office as United States District Judge.

Nixon thereafter commenced the present suit, arguing that Senate Rule XI violates the constitutional grant of authority to the Senate to "try" all impeachments because it prohibits the whole Senate from taking part in the evidentiary hearings. . . . The District Court held that his claim was nonjusticiable, and the Court of Appeals for the District of Columbia Circuit agreed.

A controversy is nonjusticiable—i.e., involves a political question—where there is "a textually demonstrable constitutional commitment of the issue to a coordinate political department; or a lack of judicially discoverable and manageable standards for resolving it. . . ." Baker v. Carr, 369 U.S. 186, 217 (1962). But the courts must, in the first instance, interpret the text in question and determine whether and to what extent the issue is textually committed. . . . As the discussion that follows makes clear, the concept of a textual commitment to a coordinate political department is not completely separate from the concept of a lack of judicially discoverable and manageable standards for resolving it; the lack of judicially manageable standards may strengthen the conclusion that there is a textually demonstrable commitment to a coordinate branch.

In this case, we must examine Art. I, § 3, cl. 6, to determine the scope of authority conferred upon the Senate by the Framers regarding impeachment. It provides:

"The Senate shall have the sole Power to try all Impeachments. When sitting for that Purpose, they shall be on Oath or Affirmation. When the President of the United States is tried, the Chief Justice shall preside: And no Person shall be convicted without the Concurrence of two thirds of the Members present."

The language and structure of this Clause are revealing. The first sentence is a grant of authority to the Senate, and the word "sole" indicates that this authority is reposed in the Senate and nowhere else. The next two sentences specify requirements to which the Senate proceedings shall conform: the Senate shall be on oath or affirmation, a two-thirds vote is required to convict, and when the President is tried the Chief Justice shall preside.

Petitioner argues that the word "try" in the first sentence imposes by implication an additional requirement on the Senate in that the proceedings must be in the nature of a judicial trial. From there petitioner goes on to argue that this limitation precludes the Senate from delegating to a select committee the task of hearing the testimony of witnesses, as was done pursuant to Senate Rule XI. . . .

There are several difficulties with this position which lead us ultimately to reject it. The word "try," both in 1787 and later, has considerably broader meanings than those to which petitioner would limit it. . . . [W]e cannot say that the Framers used the word "try" as an implied limitation on the method by which the Senate might proceed in trying impeachments. "As a rule the Constitution speaks in general terms, leaving Congress to deal with subsidiary matters of detail as the public interests and changing conditions may require. . . ." Dillon v. Gloss, 256 U.S. 368, 376 (1921).

The conclusion that the use of the word "try" in the first sentence of the Impeachment Trial Clause lacks sufficient precision to afford any judicially manageable standard of review of the Senate's actions is fortified by the existence of the three very specific requirements that the Constitution does impose on the Senate when trying impeachments: the members must be under oath, a two-thirds vote is required to convict, and the Chief Justice presides when the President is tried. These limitations are quite precise, and their nature suggests that the Framers did not intend to impose additional limitations on the form of the Senate proceedings by the use of the word "try" in the first sentence.

. . . [The first sentence of Clause 6] provides that "[t]he Senate shall have the sole Power to try all Impeachments." We think that the word "sole" is of considerable significance. Indeed, the word "sole" appears only one other time in the Constitution—with respect to the House of Representatives' "*sole* Power of Impeachment." Art. I, § 2, cl. 5 (emphasis added). The common sense meaning of the word "sole" is that the Senate alone shall have authority to determine whether an individual should be acquitted or convicted. . . .

. . .

Petitioner . . . argues that even if significance be attributed to the word "sole" in the first sentence of the clause, the authority granted is to the Senate, and this means that "the Senate—not the courts, not a lay jury, not a Senate Committee—shall try impeachments." It would be possible to read the first sentence of the Clause this way, but it is not a natural reading. Petitioner's interpretation would bring into judicial purview not merely the sort of claim made by petitioner, but other similar claims based on the conclusion that the word "Senate" has imposed by implication limitations on procedures which the Senate might adopt. . . .

. . .

The Framers labored over the question of where the impeachment power should lie. Significantly, in at least two considered scenarios the power was placed with the Federal Judiciary. See 1 Farrand 21–22 (Virginia Plan); id., at 244 (New Jersey Plan). Indeed, Madison and the Committee of Detail proposed that the Supreme Court should have the power to determine impeachments. See 2 id., at 551 (Madison); id., at 178–179, 186 (Committee of Detail). Despite these proposals, the Convention ultimately decided that the Senate would have "the sole Power to Try all Impeachments." Art. I, § 3, cl. 6. . . .

. . .

. . . [The framers concluded that] judicial review would be inconsistent with the Framers' insistence that our system be one of checks and balances. In our constitutional system, impeachment was designed to be the only check on the Judicial Branch by the Legislature. . . . Judicial involvement in impeachment proceedings, even if only for purposes of judicial review, is counterintuitive because it would eviscerate the "important constitutional check" placed on the Judiciary by the Framers. . . . Nixon's argument would place final reviewing authority with respect to impeachments in the hands of the same body that the impeachment process is meant to regulate.

. . .

In addition to the textual commitment argument, we are persuaded that the lack of finality and the difficulty of fashioning relief counsel against justiciability. See

Baker v. Carr, 369 U.S., at 210. . . . This lack of finality would manifest itself most dramatically if the President were impeached. The legitimacy of any successor, and hence his effectiveness, would be impaired severely, not merely while the judicial process was running its course, but during any retrial that a differently constituted Senate might conduct if its first judgment of conviction were invalidated. Equally uncertain is the question of what relief a court may give other than simply setting aside the judgment of conviction. Could it order the reinstatement of a convicted federal judge, or order Congress to create an additional judgeship if the seat had been filled in the interim?

. . .

Affirmed.

■ JUSTICE STEVENS, concurring.

For me, the debate about the strength of the inferences to be drawn from the use of the words "sole" and "try" is far less significant than the central fact that the Framers decided to assign the impeachment power to the Legislative Branch. . . .

■ JUSTICE WHITE, with whom JUSTICE BLACKMUN joins, concurring in the judgment.

Petitioner contends that the method by which the Senate convicted him on two articles of impeachment violates Art. I, § 3, cl. 6 of the Constitution. . . . The Court is of the view that the Constitution forbids us even to consider his contention. I find no such prohibition and would therefore reach the merits of the claim. I concur in the judgment because the Senate fulfilled its constitutional obligation to "try" petitioner.

. . .

II

. . .

Of course the issue in the political question doctrine is not whether the Constitutional text commits exclusive responsibility for a particular governmental function to one of the political branches. There are numerous instances of this sort of textual commitment, e.g., Art. I, § 8, and it is not thought that disputes implicating these provisions are nonjusticiable. Rather, the issue is whether the Constitution has given one of the political branches final responsibility for interpreting the scope and nature of such a power.

. . .

■ JUSTICE SOUTER, concurring in the judgment.

I agree with the Court that this case presents a nonjusticiable political question. Because my analysis differs somewhat from the Court's, however, I concur in its judgment by this separate opinion.

. . .

. . . As the Court observes, judicial review of an impeachment trial would under the best of circumstances entail significant disruption of government.

One can, nevertheless, envision different and unusual circumstances that might justify a more searching review of impeachment proceedings. If the Senate were to act in a manner seriously threatening the integrity of its results, convicting, say, upon a coin-toss, or upon a summary determination that an officer of the United States was simply "a bad guy," . . . judicial interference might well be appropriate. . . .

Zivotofsky v. Clinton

566 U.S. 189 (2012).

Plaintiff sued the *Secretary of State, invoking a Congressional statute "providing that Americans born in Jerusalem may elect to have 'Israel' listed as the place of birth on their passports. The State Department declined to follow that law, citing its longstanding policy of not taking a position on the political status of Jerusalem. . . . [T]he Secretary of State argued that the courts lacked authority to decide the case because it presented a political question." The lower courts agreed, and the Supreme Court reversed. Chief Justice Roberts's majority opinion explained:

"The lower courts ruled that this case involves a political question because deciding [plaintiff]'s claim would force the Judicial Branch to interfere with the President's exercise of constitutional power committed to him alone. The District Court understood [plaintiff to be asking] the courts to 'decide the political status of Jerusalem.' . . . This misunderstands the issue presented. [Plaintiff] does not ask the courts to determine whether Jerusalem is the capital of Israel. He instead seeks to determine whether he may vindicate his statutory right . . . to choose to have Israel recorded on his passport as his place of birth.

"For its part, the D. C. Circuit treated the two questions as one and the same. . . . Indeed, the D. C. Circuit's opinion does not even mention [the statute being invoked] until the fifth of its six paragraphs of analysis, and then only to dismiss it as irrelevant: 'That Congress took a position on the status of Jerusalem and gave [plaintiff] a statutory cause of action . . . is of no moment to whether the judiciary has [the] authority to resolve this dispute. . . .' . . .

"The existence of a statutory right, however, is certainly relevant to the Judiciary's power to decide [plaintiff]'s claim. The federal courts are not being asked to supplant a foreign policy decision of the political branches with the courts' own unmoored determination of what United States policy toward Jerusalem should be. Instead, [plaintiff] requests that the courts enforce a specific statutory right. To resolve his claim, the Judiciary must decide if [plaintiff]'s interpretation of the statute is correct, and whether the statute is constitutional. This is a familiar judicial exercise.

"Moreover, because the parties do not dispute the interpretation of [the statute], the only real question for the courts is whether the statute is constitutional. At least since Marbury v. Madison, 1 Cranch 137 (1803), we have recognized that when an Act of Congress is alleged to conflict with the Constitution, '[i]t is emphatically the province and duty of the judicial department to say what the law is.' *Id.*, at 177. That duty will sometimes involve the '[r]esolution of litigation challenging the constitutional authority of one of the three branches,' but courts cannot avoid their responsibility merely 'because the issues have political implications.' INS v. Chadha, 462 U.S. 919, 943 (1983).

"In this case, determining the constitutionality of [the statute] involves deciding whether the statute impermissibly intrudes upon Presidential powers under the Constitution. If so, the law must be invalidated and [plaintiff]'s case should be dismissed for failure to state a claim. If, on the other hand, the statute does not trench on the President's powers, then the Secretary must be ordered to issue [plaintiff] a passport that complies with [the statute]. Either way, the political question doctrine is not implicated. 'no policy underlying the political question doctrine suggests that Congress or the Executive . . . can decide the constitutionality of a statute; that is a decision for the courts.' *Id.*, at 941–942.

"The Secretary contends that 'there is "a textually demonstrable constitutional commitment" ' to the President of the sole power to recognize foreign sovereigns and, as a corollary, to determine whether an American born in Jerusalem may choose to have Israel listed as his place of birth on his passport. . . . Perhaps. But there is, of course, no exclusive commitment to the Executive of the power to determine the constitutionality of a statute. The Judicial Branch appropriately exercises that authority, including in a case such as this, where the question is whether Congress or the Executive is 'aggrandizing its power at the expense of another branch'. . . .

"Our precedents have also found the political question doctrine implicated when there is 'a lack of judicially discoverable and manageable standards for resolving' the question before the court. Framing the issue as the lower courts did, in terms of whether the Judiciary may decide the political status of Jerusalem, certainly raises those concerns. They dissipate, however, when the issue is recognized to be the more focused one of the constitutionality of [the statute]. Indeed, both sides offer detailed legal arguments regarding whether [the statute] is constitutional in light of powers committed to the Executive, and whether Congress's own powers with respect to passports must be weighed in analyzing this question.

". . .

". . . Having determined that this case is justiciable, we leave it to the lower courts to consider the merits in the first instance."

Justice Sotomayor filed an opinion concurring in part and concurring in the judgment (in which Justice Breyer partially joined). Justice Alito filed an opinion concurring in the judgment, and Justice Breyer filed a dissenting opinion.

Political Questions

(1) That aspect of the political question doctrine relying on "a textually demonstrable commitment of the issue to a coordinate political department" is, as the Court noted in Baker v. Carr, "primarily a function of the separation of powers." The issue will be raised again in Chapter 7—see especially United States v. Nixon, infra p. 291. One question concerning "textually demonstrable commitments" is alluded to by Justice White's concurrence in the case involving Judge Nixon, see supra p. 68: What is distinctive about some text in the Constitution that creates a "commitment" of an issue to a branch other than the courts? For example, the Constitution in Article I empowers Congress to pass laws that are "necessary and proper" but does not exclude the judiciary from visiting the question whether specific congressional enactments are "necessary and proper." Is there something particular about certain language in the Constitution, e.g., the impeachment provisions or the provisions enabling each house to judge qualifications and discipline itself, that reflects a distinct kind of textual commitment?

(2) In Baker v. Carr, the Court noted that a case might be held to involve a political question because of "a lack of judicially discoverable and manageable standards for resolving it." The Court held that reapportionment cases did not require "the Court to enter upon policy determinations for which judicially manageable standards are lacking. Judicial standards under the Equal Protection Clause are well developed and familiar, and it has been open to courts since the enactment of the Fourteenth Amendment to determine, if on the particular facts they must, that a discrimination reflects *no* policy, but simply arbitrary and capricious action." When studying the subsequent reapportionment cases, including those involving the use of race by those who draw district lines, infra Chapter 10, the student should ask whether the Court's prediction as to the manageability of the standards proved to be true.

The Supreme Court found a lack of judicially manageable standards for resolving a claim that Pennsylvania's legislature had violated the Constitution by taking partisan considerations into account too much in the drawing of district lines. Rejecting the analogy to the racial redistricting cases, where the Court has held that race may not "predominate" over other districting criteria, the Justices held, 5–4, in Vieth v. Jubelirer, 541 U.S. 267 (2004) that claims in that case that one political party had used districting unfairly to ensure that party's success in too many legislative districts were not amenable to federal adjudication. Importantly, Justice Kennedy, who provided the fifth vote and concurred in the judgment only, wrote separately to emphasize the possibility that manageable standards not present today may be developed over time.

(3) Consider the suggestion in Justice Powell's concurrence in Goldwater v. Carter, 444 U.S. 996 (1979), that when adjudication would "compel[ ] this Court to oversee the very constitutional process used to reverse Supreme Court decisions" judicial discretion is particularly important. While Justice Powell was referring to cases involving the validity of constitutional amendments, which are discussed below, are there other constitutional processes "used to reverse Supreme Court decisions" in which the Court should tread lightly? In this regard, consider the Court's controversial decision to enter into the 2000 Presidential election dispute in Florida and the Bush v. Gore, 531 U.S. 98 (2000), decision described at p. 97 and 676 infra.

(4) Professor Henkin suggests that there is no separate political question doctrine:

"The thesis I offer for discussion is that there may be no doctrine requiring abstention from judicial review of 'political questions.' The cases which are supposed to have established the political question doctrine required no such extra-ordinary abstention from judicial review; they called only for the ordinary respect by the courts for the political domain. Having reviewed, the Court refused to invalidate the challenged actions because they were within the constitutional authority of President or Congress. In no case did the Court have to use the phrase 'political question'. . . ."

Henkin, *Is There a "Political Question" Doctrine?,* 85 Yale L.J. 597, 600 (1976).

In connection with Professor Henkin's thesis, consider U.S. Department of Commerce v. Montana, 503 U.S. 442 (1992). Following the apportionment method dictated by a 1941 federal statute, Congressional reapportionment pursuant to the 1990 census reduced Montana's delegation from two representatives to one. Montana claimed that the federal statute was unconstitutional insofar as it caused Montana to be represented by a single district 231,189 persons larger than an average district. The Court rejected the argument that Congressional selection of an apportionment method was a political question not subject to judicial review. Article I, § 2, places substantive limitations on Congress' apportionment power, including a requirement that representatives be apportioned to the states "according to their respective numbers." Violation of that limitation would present a justiciable controversy. The Court concluded, however, that the apportionment method mandated by the 1941 statute was not unconstitutional. Since Congressional districts cannot cross State lines, it is impossible for all districts to be the same size.

"The constitutional framework . . . must . . . delegate to Congress a measure of discretion that is broader than that accorded to the States in the much easier task of determining district sizes within State borders. . . . Its apparently good-faith choice of a method of apportionment of Representatives among the several States 'according to their respective numbers' commands far more deference than a state districting decision that is capable of being reviewed under a relatively rigid mathematical standard."

PART 2

Allocation of Governmental Powers: The Nation and the States; The President, the Congress, and the Courts

CHAPTER 4

THE SCOPE OF NATIONAL POWER

1. THE CONSTITUTIONAL CONVENTION AND THE ESTABLISHMENT OF A NATIONAL GOVERNMENT

Introduction. The following excerpts from the records of the Constitutional Convention of 1787 are designed to afford an intimate glimpse into the process of deliberation and compromise that produced the Constitution and also to provide a sample of the materials available for an examination of the historical setting and meaning of provisions of the Constitution.

A thorough examination of the historical setting and "legislative history" of constitutional provisions requires the weighing of voluminous material; there is room here for only a small sample. But the excerpts that follow can provide a basis for hypotheses, to be checked against the full record, concerning: (1) The weaknesses of the Articles of Confederation that the framers sought to avoid in their new constitution; (2) The choice (or compromise) between conflicting views concerning the power to be given the national government; (3) The nature and scope of the national power over commerce contemplated by the draftsmen.

Proceedings in the Federal Convention: May 29, 1787

Madison's Notes; I Farrand, Records of the Federal Convention of 1787 (1911) 18–19
(Hereafter Cited as "Farrand").[1]

Mr. Randolph [Va.] opened the main business. He expressed his regret, that it should fall to him, rather than those, who were of longer standing in life and political experience, to open the great subject of their mission. But, as the convention had originated from Virginia, and his colleagues supposed, that some proposition was expected from them, they had imposed this task on him.

He then commented on the difficulty of the crisis, and the necessity of preventing the fulfillment of the prophecies of the American downfall.

He observed that in revising the federal system we ought to inquire (1) into the properties, which such a government ought to possess, (2) the defects of the confederation, (3) the danger of our situation and (4) the remedy.

1. The character of such a governme[nt] ought to secure (1) against foreign invasion: (2) against dissentions between members of the Union, or seditions in particular states: (3) to p[ro] cure to the several states various blessings, of which an isolated situation was i[n] capable: (4) to be able to defend itself against encroachment: and (5) to be paramount to the state constitutions.

2. In speaking of the defects of the confederation he professed a high respect for its authors, and considered them as having done all that patriots could do, in the then infancy of the science, of constitutions, and of confederacies,—when the inefficiency of requisitions was unknown—no commercial discord had arisen among any states—no rebellion had appeared as in Massachusetts—foreign debts had not become urgent—

---

[1] This and the following excerpts are copied by permission of the Yale University Press. [Bracketed references to the states from which the delegates came have been added by the editors.]

the havoc of paper money had not been foreseen—treaties had not been violated—and perhaps nothing better could be obtained from the jealousy of the states with regard to their sovereignty.

He then proceeded to enumerate the defects:[2] (1) that the confederation produced no security agai[nst] foreign invasion; congress not being permitted to prevent a war nor to support it by th[eir] own authority—of this he cited many examples; most of whi[ch] tended to show that they could not cause infractions of treaties or of the law of nations, to be punished; that particular states might by their conduct provoke war without control; and that neither militia nor draughts being fit for defense on such occasions, enlistments only could be successful, and these could not be executed without money.

(2)   that the federal government could not check the quarrels between states, nor a rebellion in any not having constitutional power Nor means to interpose according to the exigency:

(3)   That there were many advantages, which the U.S. might acquire, which were not attainable under the confederation—such as a productive impost—counteraction of the commercial regulations of other nations—pushing of commerce ad libitum—& c & c.

(4)   that the federal government could not defend itself against the incroachments from the states:

(5)   that it was not even paramount to the state constitutions, ratified as it was in [many] of the states.

3.   He next reviewed the danger of our situation appealed to the sense of the best friends of the U.S.—the prospect of anarchy from the laxity of government everywhere; and to other considerations.

4.   He then proceeded to the remedy; the basis of which he said, must be the republican principle.

He proposed as conformable to his ideas the following resolutions, which he explained one by one.

Note. The "resolutions" to which Randolph referred at the close of this excerpt constituted the "Virginia Plan"—probably developed by James Madison. See Warren, *The Making of the Constitution* 139–141 (1928). These resolutions formed the basis for discussion and action by the Convention in the days that followed. Thus the proposition debated in the following excerpt from the proceedings of May 31 was the second part of the sixth "resolution" which Randolph proposed.

Proceedings in the Federal Convention: May 31, 1787

Madison's Notes; I Farrand 53.

On the proposition for giving "Legislative power in all cases to which the State Legislatures were individually incompetent".

Mr. Pinckney [S.Car.] & Mr. Rutledge [S.Car.] objected to the vagueness of the term *incompetent,* and said they could not well decide how to vote until they should see an exact enumeration of the powers comprehended by this definition.

---

[2]   Reasons for the failure of the Articles of Confederation and the need for a stronger national union were eloquently expounded by Alexander Hamilton in The Federalist, Nos. 15 and 22. See also Kelly & Harbison, *The American Constitution* 108–110 (1970). On the influence of Hamilton, *see:* Morris, *Alexander Hamilton and the Founding of the Nation* (1957); Dietze, *Hamilton's Federalist, Treatise for Free Government,* 42 Corn.L.Q. 307, 501 (1957).

Mr. Butler [S.Car.] repeated his fears that we were running into an extreme in taking away the powers of the States, and called on Mr. Randolph for the extent of his meaning.

Mr. Randolph [Va.] disclaimed any intention to give indefinite powers to the national Legislature, declaring that he was entirely opposed to such an inroad of the State jurisdictions, and that he did not think any considerations whatever could ever change his determination. His opinion was fixed on this point.

Mr. Madison [Va.] said that he had brought with him into the Convention a strong bias in favor of an enumeration and definition of the powers necessary to be exercised by the national Legislature; but had also brought doubts concerning its practicability. His wishes remained unaltered; but his doubts had become stronger. What his opinion might ultimately be he could not yet tell. But he should shrink from nothing which should be found essential to such a form of Govt. as would provide for the safety, liberty and happiness of the Community. This being the end of all our deliberations, all the necessary means for attaining it must, however reluctantly be submitted to.

On the question for giving powers, in cases to which the States are not competent,

Massts. ay. Cont. divd. (Sherman no Ellsworth ay) N.Y. ay. N.J. ay. Pa. ay. Del. ay. Va. ay. N.C. ay. S.Carolina ay. Georgia. ay. [Ayes-9; noes-0; divided-1].

Proceedings in the Federal Convention: July 17, 1787

(a) Journal; II Farrand 21.

It was moved and seconded to postpone the consid[eration] of the second clause of the Sixth resolution[3] reported from the Committee of the whole House in order to take up the following:

"To make laws binding on the People of the United States in all cases which may concern the common interests of the Union: but not to interfere with the government of the individual States in any matters of internal police, which respect the government of such States only, and wherein the general welfare of the United States is not concerned."

which passed in the negative [Ayes-2; noes-8.]

It was moved and seconded to alter the second clause of the 6th resolution so as to read as follows, namely

"and moreover to legislate in all cases for the general interests of the Union, and also in those to which the States are separately incompetent, or in which the harmony of the United States may be interrupted by the exercise of individual legislation."

which passed in the affirmative [Ayes-6; noes-4.]

[To agree to the second clause of the 6. resolution as amended. Ayes-8; noes-2.]

(b) The same proceedings are reported more fully in Madison's Notes;

---

[3] The Sixth Resolution, based on Randolph's propositions, as adopted by the Committee of the Whole House on May 31, 1787 (see the excerpt from Madison's notes quoted supra), provided in part: "That the national legislature ought to be empowered to enjoy the legislative rights vested in Congress by the Confederation; and moreover To legislate in all cases, to which the separate States are incompetent or in which the harmony of the United States may be interrupted by the exercise of individual legislation." See 1 Farrand 47 (Journal, May 31, 1787).

II FARRAND 25–27

The 6th Resoln. in the Report of the Comm. of the whole relating to the powers, which had been postponed in order to consider the 7 & 8th, relating to the Constitution of the Natl. Legislature, was now resumed—

Mr. Sherman [Conn.] observed that it would be difficult to draw the line between the powers of the Genl. Legislatures, and those to be left with the States; that he did not like the definition contained in the Resolution, and proposed in place of the words "of individual legislation" line 4 inclusive, to insert "to make laws binding on the people of the (United) States in all cases (which may concern the common interests of the Union); but not to interfere with (the Government of the individual States in any matters of internal police which respect the Govt. of such States only, and wherein the General) welfare of the U. States is not concerned."

Mr. Wilson [Pa.] 2ded. the amendment as better expressing the general principle.

Mr. Govr. Morris [Pa.] opposed it. The internal police, as it would be called & understood by the States ought to be infringed in many cases, as in the case of paper money & other tricks by which Citizens of other states may be affected.

Mr. Sherman, in explanation of his ideas read an enumeration of powers, including the power of levying taxes on trade, but not the power of *direct taxation.*

Mr. Govr. Morris remarked the omission, and inferred that for the deficiencies of taxes on consumption, it must have been the meaning of Mr. Sherman, that the Genl. Govt. should recur to quotas & requisitions, which are subversive of the idea of Govt.

Mr. Sherman acknowledged that his enumeration did not include direct taxation. Some provision he supposed must be made for supplying the deficiency of other taxation, but he had not formed any.

On Question on Mr. Sherman's motion, (it passed in the negative)

Mas. no. Cont. ay. N.J. no. Pa. no. Del. no. Md. ay. Va. no. N.C. no. S.C. no. Geo. no. [Ayes-2; noes-8].

Mr. Bedford [Del.] moved that the (2d. number of Resolution 6.) be so altered as to read "(and moreover) to legislate in all cases for the general interests of the Union, and also in those to which the States are 'separately incompetent,' (or in which the harmony of the U. States may be interrupted by the exercise of individual Legislation".)

Mr. Govr. Morris 2ds. (the motion.)

Mr. Randolph. This is a formidable idea indeed. It involves the power of violating all the laws and constitutions of the States, and of intermeddling with their police. The last member of the sentence is (also) superfluous, being included in the first.

Mr. Bedford. It is not more extensive or formidable than the clause as it stands: *no State* being *separately* competent to legislate for the *general interest* of the Union.

On question for agreeing to Mr. Bedford's motion (it passed in the affirmative).

Mas. ay. Cont. no. N.J. ay. Pa. ay. Del. ay. Md. ay. Va. no. N.C. ay. S.C. no. Geo. no. [Ayes-6; noes-4].

On the sentence as amended (it passed in the affirmative).

Mas. ay. Cont. ay. N.J. ay. Pa. ay. Del. ay. Md. ay. Va. ay. N.C. ay. S.C. no. Geo. no. [Ayes-8; noes-2].

Report of the Committee of Detail: August 6, 1787

II Farrand 181–182.

[On July 24, 1787, the Convention appointed a Committee of Detail[4] "to report a Constitution conformable to the Resolutions passed by the Convention" (II Farrand 106). The Report of the Committee on August 6, 1787 defined as follows the powers of the National Government:]

Art. VII, [erroneously numbered as VI by printer's error].

Sect. I. The Legislature of the United States shall have the power to lay and collect taxes, duties, imposts and excises;

To regulate commerce with foreign nations, and among the several States;

To establish an uniform rule of naturalization throughout the United States;

To coin money;

To regulate the value of foreign coin;

To fix the standard of weights and measures;

To establish Post-offices;

To borrow money, and emit bills on the credit of the United States;

To appoint a Treasurer by ballot;

To constitute tribunals inferior to the Supreme Court;

To make rules concerning captures on land and water;

To declare the law and punishment of piracies and felonies committed on the high seas, and the punishment of counterfeiting the coin of the United States, and of offences against the law of nations;

To subdue a rebellion in any State, on the application of its legislature;

To make war;

To raise armies;

To build and equip fleets;

To call forth the aid of the militia, in order to execute the laws of the Union, enforce treaties, suppress insurrections, and repel invasions;

And to make all laws that shall be necessary and proper for carrying into execution the foregoing powers, and all other powers vested, by this Constitution, in the government of the United States, or in any department or officer thereof.

NOTE

It is evident from the foregoing excerpts that questions of large import are presented by the shift from a general and loosely-phrased grant of power to the national government, which the Convention initially approved on May 31 and July 17, to the itemized list of national powers embodied in the August 6 report of the Committee of Detail. Consideration should be given to two conflicting interpretations: (a) The enumeration by the Committee of Detail, which the Convention employed as a basis for final action, should be construed to reach towards the same generalized grant of power to the national government which the Convention had earlier approved; (b)

---

[4] The members of the Committee of Detail were John Rutledge (So.Car.), Edmund Randolph (Va.), Nathaniel Gorham (Mass.), Oliver Ellsworth (Conn.), and James Wilson (Pa.).

The decision to enumerate the powers of Congress reflects a decision sharply to circumscribe national power.[1]

With respect to the commerce clause in particular, the proposal submitted on August 6 by the Committee of Detail was unanimously approved on August 16, 1787. (II Farrand 308). After this vote, however, strong Southern opposition to this commercial power developed out of fear that commercial regulations in the interest of Northern shipping might restrict free access for Southern staples to foreign shipping and foreign markets. This opposition was in part placated by an agreement by Northern delegates to prohibit the taxation of exports (Art. I, Sec. 9, cl. 1). See II Farrand 305–308 (Aug. 16), 359–363 (Aug. 21), 414–417 (Aug. 25); Warren, *The Making of the Constitution* 567–589 (1928); 2 Curtis, *History of the United States Constitution* 279–308 (1858).

On August 29, 1787, Charles Pinckney of South Carolina proposed requiring a ⅔ vote of each House for federal regulation of commerce. The deliberation preceding the Convention's rejection of this proposal (II Farrand 449–53) included these remarks of James Madison:

"Mr. Madison [Va.] went into a pretty full view of the subject. He observed that the disadvantage to the S. States from a navigation act, lay chiefly in a temporary rise of freight, attended however with an increase of Southn. as well as Northern Shipping—with the emigration of Northern seamen & merchants to the Southern States—& with a removal of the existing & injurious retaliations among the States (on each other). The power of foreign nations to obstruct our retaliating measures on them by a corrupt influence would also be less if a majority shd be made competent than if ⅔ of each House shd. be required to legislative acts in this case. An abuse of the power would be qualified with all these good effects. But he thought an abuse was rendered improbable by the provision of 2 branches—by the independence of the Senate, by the negative of the Executive, by the interest of Connecticut & N. Jersey which were agricultural, not commercial States; by the interior interest which was also agricultural in the most commercial States—by the accession of Western States which wd. be altogether agricultural. He added that the Southern States would derive an essential advantage in the general security afforded by the increase of our maritime strength. He stated the vulnerable situation of them all, and of Virginia in particular. The increase of the Coasting trade, and of seamen, would also be favorable to the S. States, by increasing, the consumption of their produce. If the Wealth of the Eastern should in a still greater proportion be augmented, that wealth wd. contribute the more to the public wants, and be otherwise a national benefit."

2. SOURCES OF NATIONAL POWER: EARLY DEVELOPMENTS AND THE MARSHALL COURT'S VIEW

Introduction. The allocation of powers between the nation and the states in the Constitution has given rise to a number of major sets of issues, which arose early after the Constitution's adoption and which remain with us today:

(1) What is the scope of the power of the federal government to regulate the private realm? Are the specifically-granted powers to be construed narrowly or

---

[1] See Abel, *The Commerce Clause in the Constitutional Convention and in Contemporary Comment,* 25 Minn.L.Rev. 432 (1941). For general studies, see Warren, *The Making of the Constitution* (1928); Farrand, *The Framing of the Constitution of the United States* (1913). Cf. Brown, *Charles Beard and the Constitution* (1956).

broadly? What is the significance of the clause conferring on Congress the power to make all laws which shall be "necessary and proper" for executing the powers granted to it and the other federal branches?

(2)   What are the limits imposed on the powers of the states to regulate and to tax the private realm? When does the mere grant of a power to the federal government imply the exclusion of the states from exercising the same power? When does the exercise of a granted power by the federal government imply the exclusion of the states from exercising the same power?

(3)   Does the Constitution impose any special limitations when the regulations or taxes of the national government impinge on the state governments? To what extent may the states impose regulations or collect taxes from the federal government or its instrumentalities? In short, what intergovernmental immunities are created by the Constitution?

(4)   What immunities do states and their subdivisions enjoy from lawsuits brought against them designed to enforce national or federal norms? Where does any sovereign immunity states enjoy come from?

The first three of these issues came before the Court in a set of great cases between 1819 and 1851. The major cases—*McCulloch v. Maryland, and Gibbons v. Ogden*—are set out in this section. They provide a useful introduction to the various doctrinal threads pursued in this chapter and in Chapters 5, 6 and 12, which also take up the fourth question, that of state sovereign immunity. The early decisions are also relevant to modern concerns since they are often discussed and applied in current Supreme Court cases. When you read each of these Nineteenth century cases, try to discern the theory or theories of federalism—the relationship between the federal and state governments—on which the Court appears to be acting. What values does the division of power between the national and state governments promote?

For modern collections of good introductory essays on the meaning of federalism historically and today, readers may wish to consult various law review symposia published on the general subject, including *Federalism's Future*, 47 Vand. L.Rev. 1205 (1994) and *Major Issues in Federalism*, 38 Az. L.Rev. 793 (1996).

The Bank of the United States

The Bank of the United States moved into the legal arena only after a quarter-century of political controversy. The plan for the Bank was developed by Alexander Hamilton promptly upon the establishment of the new government and led to a bill enacted by Congress in 1791. This First Bank, like the Second Bank involved in *McCulloch*, was operated primarily on the basis of privately invested capital and through private control. The national government subscribed to seven million dollars of the Second Bank's total capitalization of thirty-five million; the President appointed five of the twenty-five directors. The Act that established the Bank, however, imposed upon it certain public obligations such as providing for free transfer of government deposits and making frequent statements to the Secretary of the Treasury.

Disputes in President Washington's cabinet over the constitutionality of the First Bank shed some light on the issues at stake in *McCulloch*. When in 1791 the bill to establish the bank reached the President, he called upon three members of his cabinet for their opinions. Attorney General Edmund Randolph submitted two opinions, one negative and the other noncommittal. Secretary of the Treasury Alexander Hamilton prepared an opinion that Daniel Webster closely followed in his argument for the bank and which in turn was reflected in Marshall's opinion. The opinion of the Secretary of State, Thomas Jefferson, presented a sharply narrower view of the basic powers of the national government.

Washington followed the advice of Hamilton rather than of Jefferson, and signed the bill. During the next twenty years the Bank became unpopular; attempts in 1811 to renew the charter failed. However, the disorganization of the nation's business and fiscal structure during and following the War of 1812 led to support, even among Jefferson's Republican party which then was in power, for a central banking institution to stabilize the economy; in 1816 Congress adopted a plan for a second Bank of the United States that President Madison approved. This new Bank soon encountered hostility from those who believed that its policies were contributing to the financial distress of the state banks. Several states passed legislation to curb the Bank;[1] one of these laws led to the following case.

McCulloch v. Maryland

17 U.S. (4 Wheat.) 316, 4 L.Ed. 579 (1819).

[The State of Maryland brought an action for debt against McCulloch, cashier of the Baltimore branch of the Bank of the United States. It was admitted that the Bank had issued bank notes which were not on stamped paper as required by the following statute:

"An act to impose a tax on all banks or branches thereof in the state of Maryland, not chartered by the legislature.

"Be it enacted by the General Assembly of Maryland. That if any bank has established, or shall without authority from the State first had and obtained, establish any branch, office of discount and deposit, or office of pay and receipt, in any part of this state, it shall not be lawful for the said branch, office of discount and deposit, or office of pay and receipt, to issue notes in any manner, of any other denomination than five, ten, twenty, fifty, one hundred, five hundred and one thousand dollars, and no note shall be issued except upon stamped paper of the following denominations; that is to say, every five dollar note shall be upon a stamp of ten cents; every ten dollar note upon a stamp of twenty cents; every twenty dollar note, upon a stamp of thirty cents; every fifty dollar note, upon a stamp of fifty cents; every one hundred dollar note, upon a stamp of one dollar; every five hundred dollar note, upon a stamp of ten dollars; and every thousand dollar note, upon a stamp of twenty dollars; which paper shall be furnished by the Treasurer of the Western Shore, under the direction of the Governor and Council, to be paid for upon delivery. Provided always, That any institution of the above description may relieve itself from the operation of the provisions aforesaid, by paying annually, in advance, to the Treasurer of the Western Shore, for the use of the State, the sum of fifteen thousand dollars.

"And be it enacted, That the President, Cashier, each of the Directors and officers of every institution established, or to be established as aforesaid, offending against the provisions aforesaid, shall forfeit a sum of five hundred dollars for each and every offence . . . "

The Court of Appeals of the State of Maryland affirmed a judgment for the plaintiff.]

---

[1] See Warren, *The Supreme Court in United States History* (Rev. ed. 1932) 505–06. The Constitutions of Indiana and Illinois prohibited establishment of banks chartered outside the state. Five states, other than Maryland, resorted to taxation to accomplish the same result; Tennessee and Ohio, $50,000 per branch, North Carolina, $5,000 per branch, and Kentucky, $60,000 per branch. Georgia laid a tax of 31¼% on bank stock employed within the state which on its face appeared nondiscriminatory; the following year the legislature declared that the intent was to tax the Bank of the United States only.

■ MR. CHIEF JUSTICE MARSHALL delivered the opinion of the Court:

In the case now to be determined, the defendant [in error], a sovereign state, denies the obligation of a law enacted by the legislature of the Union, and the plaintiff [in error], on his part, contests the validity of an act which has been passed by the legislature of that state. The constitution of our country, in its most interesting and vital parts, is to be considered; the conflicting powers of the government of the Union and of its members, as marked in that constitution, are to be discussed; and an opinion given, which may essentially influence the great operations of the government. No tribunal can approach such a question without a deep sense of its importance, and of the awful responsibility involved in its decision. But it must be decided peacefully, or remain a source of hostile legislation, perhaps of hostility of a still more serious nature; and if it is to be so decided, by this tribunal alone can the decision be made. On the Supreme Court of the United States has the constitution of our country devolved this important duty.

The first question made in the cause is, has Congress power to incorporate a bank?[a]

. . .

The power now contested was exercised by the first Congress elected under the present constitution. The bill for incorporating the bank of the United States did not steal upon an unsuspecting legislature, and pass unobserved. Its principle was completely understood, and was opposed with equal zeal and ability. After being resisted, first in the fair and open field of debate, and afterwards in the executive cabinet, with as much persevering talent as any measure has ever experienced, and being supported by arguments which convinced minds as pure and as intelligent as this country can boast, it became a law. The original act was permitted to expire; but a short experience of the embarrassments to which the refusal to revive it exposed the government, convinced those who were most prejudiced against the measure of its necessity and induced the passage of the present law. It would require no ordinary share of intrepidity to assert that a measure adopted under these circumstances was a bold and plain usurpation, to which the constitution gave no countenance.

These observations belong to the cause; but they are not made under the impression that, were the question entirely new, the law would be found irreconcilable with the constitution.

In discussing this question, the counsel for the state of Maryland have deemed it of some importance, in the construction of the constitution, to consider that instrument not as emanating from the people, but as the act of sovereign and independent states. The powers of the general government, it has been said, are delegated by the states, who alone are truly sovereign; and must be exercised in subordination to the states who alone possess supreme dominion. . . .

The government of the Union, . . . (whatever may be the influence of this fact on the case), is, emphatically, and truly, a government of the people. In form and in substance it emanates from them. Its powers are granted by them, and are to be exercised directly on them, and for their benefit.

This government is acknowledged by all to be one of enumerated powers. The principle, that it can exercise only the powers granted to it, would seem too apparent to have required to be enforced by all those arguments which its enlightened friends, while it was depending before the people, found it necessary to urge. That principle is now universally admitted. But the question respecting the extent of the powers

---

[a] What is the relationship between the constitutionality of the act of Congress creating the bank and the constitutionality of the Maryland tax?

actually granted, is perpetually arising, and will probably continue to arise, as long as our system shall exist.

In discussing these questions, the conflicting powers of the general and state governments must be brought into view, and the supremacy of their respective laws, when they are in opposition, must be settled.

If any one proposition could command the universal assent of mankind, we might expect it would be this—that the government of the Union, though limited in its powers, is supreme within its sphere of action. This would seem to result necessarily from its nature. It is the government of all; its powers are delegated by all; it represents all, and acts for all. Though any one state may be willing to control its operations, no state is willing to allow others to control them. The nation, on those subjects on which it can act, must necessarily bind its component parts. But this question is not left to mere reason; the people have, in express terms, decided it by saying, "this constitution, and the laws of the United States, which shall be made in pursuance thereof," "shall be the supreme law of the land," and by requiring that the members of the state legislatures, and the officers of the executive and judicial departments of the states shall take the oath of fidelity to it.

The government of the United States, then, though limited in its powers, is supreme; and its laws, when made in pursuance of the constitution, form the supreme law of the land, "anything in the constitution or laws of any state to the contrary notwithstanding."

Among the enumerated powers, we do not find that of establishing a bank or creating a corporation. But there is no phrase in the instrument which, like the articles of confederation, excludes incidental or implied powers,[b] and which requires that everything granted shall be expressly and minutely described. Even the 10th amendment, which was framed for the purpose of quieting the excessive jealousies which had been excited, omits the word "expressly," and declares only that the powers "not delegated to the United States, nor prohibited to the states, are reserved to the states or to the people;" thus leaving the question, whether the particular power which may become the subject of contest has been delegated to the one government, or prohibited to the other, to depend on a fair construction of the whole instrument. The men who drew and adopted this amendment had experienced the embarrassments resulting from the insertion of this word in the articles of confederation, and probably omitted it to avoid those embarrassments. A constitution, to contain an accurate detail of all the subdivisions of which its great powers will admit, and of all the means by which they may be carried into execution, would partake of a prolixity of a legal code, and could scarcely be embraced by the human mind. It would probably never be understood by the public. Its nature, therefore, requires, that only its great outlines should be marked, its important objects designated, and the minor ingredients which compose those objects be deduced from the nature of the objects themselves. That this idea was entertained by the framers of the American constitution, is not only to be inferred from the nature of the instrument but from the language. Why else were some of the limitations, found in the ninth section of the 1st article, introduced? It is also, in some degree, warranted by their having omitted to use any restrictive term which might prevent its receiving a fair and just interpretation. In considering this question, then, we must never forget that it is a constitution we are expounding.

Although, among the enumerated powers of government, we do not find the word "bank" or "incorporation," we find the great powers to lay and collect taxes; to borrow

---

[b]   The Articles of Confederation (1777) provided in Article II: "Each State retains its sovereignty, freedom and independence, and every power, jurisdiction and right, which is not by this confederation expressly delegated to the United States, in Congress assembled."

money; to regulate commerce; to declare and conduct a war; and to raise and support armies and navies. The sword and the purse, all the external relations, and no inconsiderable portion of the industry of the nation, are entrusted to its government. It can never be pretended that these vast powers draw after them others of inferior importance, merely because they are inferior. Such an idea can never be advanced. But it may with great reason be contended, that a government, entrusted with such ample powers, on the due execution of which the happiness and prosperity of the nation so vitally depends, must also be entrusted with ample means for their execution. The power being given, it is the interest of the nation to facilitate its execution. It can never be their interest, and cannot be presumed to have been their intention, to clog and embarrass its execution by withholding the most appropriate means. Throughout this vast republic, from the St. Croix to the Gulf of Mexico, from the Atlantic to the Pacific, revenue is to be collected and expended, armies are to be marched and supported. The exigencies of the nation may require that the treasure raised in the north should be transported to the south, that raised in the east conveyed to the west, or that this order should be reversed. Is that construction of the constitution to be preferred which would render these operations difficult, hazardous, and expensive? Can we adopt that construction (unless the words, imperiously require it) which would impute to the framers of that instrument, when granting these powers for the public good, the intention of impeding their exercise by withholding a choice of means? If, indeed, such be the mandate of the constitution, we have only to obey; but that instrument does not profess to enumerate the means by which the powers it confers may be executed; nor does it prohibit the creation of a corporation, if the existence of such a being be essential to the beneficial exercise of those powers. It is, then, the subject of fair inquiry, how far such means may be employed. . . .

But the constitution of the United States has not left the right of Congress to employ the necessary means for the execution of the powers conferred on the government to general reasoning. To its enumeration of powers is added that of making "all laws which shall be necessary and proper, for carrying into execution the foregoing powers, and all other powers vested by this constitution, in the government of the United States, or in any department thereof."

The counsel for the State of Maryland have urged various arguments, to prove that this clause, though in terms a grant of power, is not so in effect; but is really restrictive of the general right, which might otherwise be implied, of selecting means for executing the enumerated powers.

In support of this proposition, they have found it necessary to contend, that this clause was inserted for the purpose of conferring upon Congress the power of making laws. That, without it, doubts might be entertained, whether Congress could exercise its powers in the form of legislation. . . .

But the argument on which most reliance is placed, is drawn from the peculiar language of this clause. Congress is not empowered by it to make all laws, which may have relation to the powers conferred on the government, but such only as may be "necessary and proper" for carrying them into execution. The word "necessary" is considered as controlling the whole sentence, and as limiting the right to pass laws for the execution of the granted powers, to such as are indispensable, and without which the power would be nugatory. That it excludes the choice of means, and leaves to Congress, in each case, that only which is most direct and simple.

Is it true that this is the sense in which the word "necessary" is always used? Does it always import an absolute physical necessity, so strong that one thing, to which another may be termed necessary, cannot exist without that other? We think it does not. If reference be had to its use, in the common affairs of the world, or in approved authors, we find that it frequently imports no more than that one thing is convenient, or useful, or essential to another. To employ the means necessary to an end, is generally understood as employing any means calculated to produce the end, and not as being confined to those single means, without which the end would be entirely unattainable. Such is the character of human language, that no word conveys to the mind, in all situations, one single definite idea; . . . The word "necessary" is of this description. It has not a fixed character peculiar to itself. It admits of all degrees of comparison; and is often connected with other words. . . . A thing may be necessary, very necessary, absolutely or indispensably necessary. . . . This comment on the word is well illustrated, by the passage cited at the bar, from the 10th section of the 1st article of the constitution. It is, we think, impossible to compare the sentence which prohibits a State from laying "imposts, or duties on imports or exports, except what may be *absolutely* necessary for executing its inspection laws," with that which authorizes Congress "to make all laws which shall be necessary and proper for carrying into execution" the powers of the general government, without feeling a conviction that the convention understood itself to change materially the meaning of the word "necessary," by prefixing the word "absolutely." This word, then, like others, is used in various senses; and, in its construction, the subject, the context, the intention of the person using them, are all to be taken into view.

Let this be done in the case under consideration. The subject is the execution of those great powers on which the welfare of a nation essentially depends. It must have been the intention of those who gave these powers, to insure, as far as human prudence could insure, their beneficial execution. This could not be done by confining the choice of means to such narrow limits as not to leave it in the power of Congress to adopt any which might be appropriate, and which were conducive to the end. This provision is made in a constitution intended to endure for ages to come, and, consequently, to be adapted to the various crises of human affairs. To have prescribed the means by which government should, in all future time, execute its powers, would have been to change, entirely, the character of the instrument, and give it the properties of a legal code. . . .

. . .

In ascertaining the sense in which the word "necessary" is used in this clause of the constitution, we may derive some aid from that with which it is associated. . . . This clause, as construed by the State of Maryland, would abridge, and almost annihilate this useful and necessary right of the legislature to select its means. . . . [T]his could not be intended . . . for the following reasons.

1st. The clause is placed among the powers of Congress, not among the limitation on those powers.

2nd. Its terms purport to enlarge, not to diminish the powers vested in the government. . . . No reason has been, or can be assigned for thus concealing an intention to narrow the discretion of the national legislature under words which purport to enlarge it. The framers of the constitution wished its adoption, and well knew that it would be endangered by its strength, not its weakness. . . . If, then, their intention had been, by this clause, to restrain the free use of means which might otherwise have been implied, that intention would have been inserted in another place, and would have been expressed in terms resembling these. "In carrying into execution the foregoing powers, and all others, & c. 'no laws shall be passed but such as are necessary and proper.'" Had the intention been to make this clause restrictive, it would unquestionably have been so in form as well as effect.

The result of the most careful and attentive consideration bestowed upon this clause is, that if it does not enlarge, it cannot be construed to restrain the powers of Congress, or to impair the right of the legislature to exercise its best judgment in the selection of measures to carry into execution the constitutional powers of the government. If no other motive for its insertion can be suggested, a sufficient one is found in the desire to remove all doubts respecting the right to legislate on that vast mass of incidental powers which must be involved in the constitution, if that instrument be not a splendid bauble.

We admit, as all must admit, that the powers of the government are limited, and that its limits are not to be transcended. But we think the sound construction of the constitution must allow to the national legislature that discretion, with respect to the means by which the powers it confers are to be carried into execution, which will enable that body to perform the high duties assigned to it, in the manner most beneficial to the people. Let the end be legitimate, let it be within the scope of the constitution, and all means which are appropriate, which are plainly adapted to that end, which are not prohibited, but consist with the letter and spirit of the constitution, are constitutional. . . .

If a corporation may be employed indiscriminately with other means to carry into execution the powers of the government, no particular reason can be assigned for excluding the use of a bank, if required for its fiscal operations. . . .

But, were its necessity less apparent, none can deny its being an appropriate measure; and if it is, the degree of its necessity, as has been very justly observed, is to be discussed in another place. Should Congress, in the execution of its powers, adopt measures which are prohibited by the constitution; or should Congress, under the pretext of executing its powers, pass laws for the accomplishment of objects not entrusted to the government, it would become the painful duty of this tribunal, should a case requiring such a decision come before it, to say that such an act was not the law of the land. But where the law is not prohibited, and is really calculated to effect any of the objects entrusted to the government, to undertake here to inquire into the degree of its necessity, would be to pass the line which circumscribes the judicial department, and to tread on legislative ground. This court disclaims all pretensions to such a power. . . .

After the most deliberate consideration, it is the unanimous and decided opinion of this court that the act to incorporate the bank of the United States is a law made in pursuance of the constitution, and is a part of the supreme law of the land. . . .

It being the opinion of the court that the act incorporating the bank is constitutional, and that the power of establishing a branch in the state of Maryland might be properly exercised by the bank itself, we proceed to inquire:

2.   Whether the state of Maryland may, without violating the constitution, tax that branch?

That the power of taxation is one of vital importance; that it is retained by the states; that it is not abridged by the grant of a similar power to the government of the Union; that it is to be concurrently exercised by the two governments: are truths which have never been denied. But, such is the paramount character of the constitution that its capacity to withdraw any subject from the action of even this power, is admitted. The states are expressly forbidden to lay any duties on imports or exports, except what may be absolutely necessary for executing their inspection laws. If the obligation of this prohibition must be conceded—if it may restrain a state from the exercise of its taxing power on imports and exports—the same paramount character would seem to restrain, as it certainly may restrain, a state from such other exercise of this power, as is in its nature incompatible with, and repugnant to, the constitutional laws of the Union. A law, absolutely repugnant to another, as entirely repeals that other as if express terms of repeal were used.

On this ground the counsel for the bank place its claim to be exempted from the power of a state to tax its operations. There is no express provision for the case, but the claim has been sustained on a principle which so entirely pervades the constitution, is so intermixed with the materials which compose it, so interwoven with its web, so blended with its texture, as to be incapable of being separated from it without rending it into shreds.

This great principle is, that the constitution and the laws made in pursuance thereof are supreme; that they control the constitution and laws of the respective states, and cannot be controlled by them. . . .

. . .

That the power to tax involves the power to destroy; that the power to destroy may defeat and render useless the power to create; that there is a plain repugnance, in conferring on one government a power to control the constitutional measures of another, which other, with respect to those very measures, is declared to be supreme over that which exerts the control, are propositions not to be denied. But all inconsistencies are to be reconciled by the magic of the word CONFIDENCE. Taxation, it is said, does not necessarily and unavoidably destroy. To carry it to the excess of destruction would be an abuse, to presume which, would banish that confidence which is essential to all government.

But is this a case of confidence? Would the people of any one state trust those of another with a power to control the most insignificant operations of their state government? We know they would not. Why, then, should we suppose that the people of any one state should be willing to trust those of another with a power to control the operations of a government to which they have confided the most important and most valuable interests? In the legislature of the Union alone, are all represented. The legislature of the Union alone, therefore, can be trusted by the people with the power of controlling measures which concern all, in the confidence that it will not be abused. This, then, is not a case of confidence, and we must consider it as it really is. . . .

If the states may tax one instrument, employed by the government in the execution of its powers, they may tax any and every other instrument. They may tax the mail; they may tax the mint; they may tax patent-rights; they may tax the papers of the custom-house; they may tax judicial process; they may tax all the means employed by the government, to an excess which would defeat all the ends of government. This was not intended by the American people. They did not design to make their government dependent on the states. . . .

It has also been insisted, that, as the power of taxation in the general and state governments is acknowledged to be concurrent, every argument which would sustain the right of the general government to tax banks chartered by the states, will equally sustain the right of the states to tax banks chartered by the general government.

But the two cases are not on the same reason. The people of all the states have created the general government, and have conferred upon it the general power of taxation. The people of all the states, and the states themselves, are represented in Congress, and, by their representatives, exercise this power. When they tax the chartered institutions of the states, they tax their constituents; and these taxes must be uniform. But, when a state taxes the operations of the government of the United States, it acts upon institutions created, not by their own constituents, but by people over whom they claim no control. It acts upon the measures of a government created by others as well as themselves, for the benefit of others in common with themselves. The difference is that which always exists, and always must exist, between the action of the whole on a part, and the action of a part on the whole—between the laws of a government declared to be supreme, and those of a government which, when in opposition to those laws, is not supreme.

But if the full application of this argument could be admitted, it might bring into question the right of Congress to tax the state banks, and could not prove the right of the states to tax the Bank of the United States.

The court has bestowed on this subject its most deliberate consideration. The result is a conviction that the states have no power, by taxation or otherwise, to retard, impede, burden, or in any manner control the operations of the constitutional laws enacted by Congress to carry into execution the powers vested in the general government. This is, we think, the unavoidable consequence of that supremacy which the constitution has declared.

We are unanimously of opinion that the law passed by the legislature of Maryland, imposing a tax on the Bank of the United States, is unconstitutional and void.

This opinion does not deprive the states of any resources which they originally possessed. It does not extend to a tax paid by the real property of the bank, in common with the other real property within the state, nor to a tax imposed on the interest which the citizens of Maryland may hold in this institution, in common with other property of the same description throughout the state. But this is a tax on the operations of the bank, and is, consequently, a tax on the operation of an instrument employed by the government of the Union to carry its powers into execution. Such a tax must be unconstitutional.

. . . It is, therefore, adjudged and ordered, that the said judgment of the said Court of Appeals of the state of Maryland in this case, be, and the same hereby is, reversed and annulled. And this court, proceeding to render such judgment as the said Court of Appeals should have rendered; it is further adjudged and ordered, that the judgment of the said Baltimore County Court be reversed and annulled, and that judgment be entered in the said Baltimore County Court for the said James W. M'Culloch.

McCulloch *and the Scope of Federal Power*

(1) Marshall rejected the argument that the powers of the federal government were delegated to it by the sovereign states. The government of the Union, he said, is a government of the people, it "emanates from them. Its powers are granted by them, and are to be exercised directly on them, and for their benefit." What is the significance of this reasoning by Marshall? If powers were granted by the states, could the states insist upon their own interpretation of the powers granted? Could a state legally secede from the Union? These questions assumed importance from the beginning of the country. Examples include the Kentucky-Virginia Resolutions of 1798, the New England resistance to the War of 1812, Calhoun's doctrine of nullification as reflected in the South Carolina Exposition of 1828 and the Statute of Nullification of 1832. The ultimate test took place in the Civil War where the right of secession was rejected on the battlefield. For an account of these early episodes and others, see Reference Note, *Interposition vs. Judicial Power,* 1 Race Rel.L.Rep. 465 (1956). The issue recurred in the middle 1950s when state legislatures passed resolutions seeking to nullify the enforcement of Brown v. Board of Educ., 347 U.S. 483 (1954). The Alabama Resolution, e.g., commenced as follows:

"WHEREAS the Constitution of the United States was formed by the sanction of the several states, given by each in its sovereign capacity; and

"WHEREAS the States, being the parties to the constitutional compact, it follows of necessity that there can be no tribunal above their authority to decide, in the last resort, whether the compact made by them be violated; and, consequently, they must decide themselves, in the last resort, such questions as may be of sufficient magnitude to require their interposition; . . . " Act No. 42, Spec.Sess., 1956, Feb. 2, 1956, set out 1 Race Rel.L.Rptr. 437 (1956). Other resolutions of the time are set out id. 438–447.

The Supreme Court gave its answer to these latter-day nullifiers in Cooper v. Aaron, 358 U.S. 1 (1958).

(2)   The Constitution did not contain an express power to create banks. Did Marshall rely primarily upon the "necessary and proper" clause as the basis for inferring such a power from other powers expressly granted? Or is Professor Black correct in suggesting that Marshall "does not place principal reliance on this clause as a ground of decision; that before he reaches it he has already decided, on the basis of far more general implications . . . ; that he addresses himself to the . . . clause only in response to counsel's arguing its *restrictive* force; and that he never really commits himself to the proposition that the necessary and proper clause enlarges governmental power. . . ." Black, *Structure and Relationship in Constitutional Law* 14 (1969). For an elaborate exegesis of the necessary and proper clause, see Engdahl, *Constitutional Federalism* 16–73 (2d ed. 1987).

(3)   **United States v. Comstock,** 560 U.S. 126 (2010). The Court, by a 7–2 vote, relied directly on the "necessary and proper" clause, and on *McCulloch*, to permit Congress to authorize detention of mentally ill, sexually dangerous federal prisoners beyond the date the prisoners would otherwise be released.

The statute in question allows a district court to order the civil commitment of an individual currently in the custody of the Federal Bureau of Prisons if the Department of Justice certifies and then establishes by clear and convincing evidence that the individual (1) has previously engaged or attempted to engage in sexually violent conduct or child molestation, (2) currently suffers from a serious mental illness, abnormality, or disorder, and (3) as a result of that mental illness, abnormality, or disorder is sexually dangerous. If the requirements of the statute are met, the court will order the prisoner's continued commitment in the custody of the Attorney General, who must attempt to get the State where that person was tried, or the State where he is domiciled, to assume responsibility for his custody, care, and treatment. If, notwithstanding such efforts, neither such State will assume such responsibility, then the person is confined in a suitable federal facility until either (1) the person's mental condition improves to the point where he is no longer dangerous, in which case he will be released; or (2) a State assumes responsibility for his custody, care, and treatment, in which case he will be transferred to the custody of that State.

Justice Breyer's majority opinion, joined in full by Chief Justice Roberts and Justices Stevens, Ginsburg and Sotomayor, framed the issue as follows: "The question *presented* is whether the Necessary and Proper Clause . . . grants Congress authority sufficient to enact the statute before us. In resolving that question, we assume, but we do not decide, that other provisions of the Constitution—such as the Due Process Clause—do not prohibit civil commitment in these circumstances. . . ." The Court found federal power did exist, basing its conclusion on five considerations, taken together:

"*First,* the Necessary and Proper Clause grants Congress broad authority to enact federal legislation. Nearly 200 years ago, this Court stated that the Federal '[G]overnment is acknowledged by all to be one of enumerated powers,' *McCulloch,* . . . which means that '[e]very law enacted by Congress must be based on one or more of' those powers, United States v. Morrison, 529 U.S. 598, 607 (2000). But, at the same time, 'a government, entrusted with such' powers 'must also be entrusted with ample means for their execution.' *McCulloch,*. . . . Accordingly, the Necessary and Proper Clause makes clear that the Constitution's grants of specific federal legislative authority are accompanied by broad power to enact laws that are 'convenient, or useful' or 'conducive' to the authority's 'beneficial exercise.' *Id.,* . . . ; see also *id.,* at 421 ('[Congress can] legislate on that vast mass of incidental powers which must be involved in the constitution . . . '). . . .

"We have since made clear that, in determining whether the Necessary and Proper Clause grants Congress the legislative authority to enact a particular federal statute, we look to see whether the statute constitutes a means that is rationally related to the implementation of a constitutionally enumerated power. . . .

"We have also recognized that the Constitution 'addresse[s]' the 'choice of means' 'primarily . . . to the judgment of Congress. If it can be seen that the means adopted are really calculated to attain the end, the degree of their necessity, the extent to which they conduce to the end, the closeness of the relationship between the means adopted and the end to be attained, are matters for congressional determination alone.' *Burroughs v. United States,* 290 U.S. 534, 547–548, 54 S.Ct. 287, 78 L.Ed. 484 (1934). . . .

"Thus, the Constitution, which nowhere speaks explicitly about the creation of federal crimes beyond those related to 'counterfeiting,' 'treason,' or 'Piracies and Felonies committed on the high Seas' or 'against the Law of Nations,' Art. I, § 8, cls. 6, 10; Art. III, § 3, nonetheless grants Congress broad authority to create such crimes. . . .

"Similarly, Congress, in order to help ensure the enforcement of federal criminal laws enacted in furtherance of its enumerated powers, 'can cause a prison to be erected at any place within the jurisdiction of the United States, and direct that all persons sentenced to imprisonment under the laws of the United States shall be confined there.' *Ex parte Karstendick,* 93 U.S. 396, 400 (1876). Moreover, Congress, having established a prison system, can enact laws that seek to ensure that system's safe and responsible administration by, for example, requiring prisoners to receive medical care and educational training, see, *e.g.,* 18 U.S.C. §§ 4005–4006; § 4042(a)(3), and can also ensure the safety of the prisoners, prison workers and visitors, and those in surrounding communities by, for example, creating further criminal laws governing entry, exit, and smuggling, and by employing prison guards to ensure discipline and security. . . .

"Neither Congress' power to criminalize conduct, nor its power to imprison individuals who engage in that conduct, nor its power to enact laws governing prisons and prisoners, is explicitly mentioned in the Constitution. But Congress nonetheless possesses broad authority to do each of those things in the course of 'carrying into Execution' the enumerated powers 'vested by' the 'Constitution in the Government of the United States,' Art. I, § 8, cl. 18—authority granted by the Necessary and Proper Clause.

"*Second,* the civil-commitment statute before us constitutes a modest addition to a set of federal prison-related mental-health statutes that have existed for many decades. We recognize that even a longstanding history of related federal action does not demonstrate a statute's constitutionality. . . . A history of involvement, however, can nonetheless be 'helpful in reviewing the substance of a congressional statutory scheme,' . . . and, in particular, the reasonableness of the relation between the new statute and pre-existing federal interests. . . .

"*Third,* Congress reasonably extended its longstanding civil-commitment system to cover mentally ill and sexually dangerous persons who are already in federal custody, even if doing so detains them beyond the termination of their criminal sentence. For one thing, the Federal Government is the custodian of its prisoners. As federal custodian, it has the constitutional power to act in order to protect nearby (and other) communities from the danger federal prisoners may pose. . . . Indeed, at common law, one 'who takes charge of a third person' is 'under a duty to exercise reasonable care to control' that person to prevent him from causing reasonably foreseeable 'bodily harm to others.' Restatement (Second) of Torts § 319, p. 129 (1963– 1964); . . . If a federal prisoner is infected with a communicable disease that threatens others, surely it would be 'necessary and proper' for the Federal Government to take action, pursuant to its role as federal custodian, to refuse (at least until the threat diminishes) to release that individual among the general public, where he might infect others (even if not threatening an interstate epidemic, cf. Art. I, § 8, cl. 3). And if confinement of such an individual is a 'necessary and proper' thing to do, then how could it not be similarly 'necessary and proper' to confine an individual whose mental illness threatens others to the same degree?

"[Moreover the statute in question is] 'reasonably adapted,' *Darby,* 312 U.S., at 121, to Congress' power to act as a responsible federal custodian (a power that rests, in turn, upon federal criminal statutes that legitimately seek to implement constitutionally enumerated authority). Congress could have reasonably concluded that federal inmates who suffer from a mental illness that causes them to 'have serious difficulty in refraining from sexually violent conduct,' . . . would pose an especially high danger to the public if released. Cf. H.R.Rep. No. 109–218, at 22–23. And Congress could also have reasonably concluded (as detailed in the Judicial Conference's report) that a reasonable number of such individuals would likely *not* be detained by the States if released from federal custody, in part because the Federal Government itself severed their claim to legal residence in any State' by incarcerating them in remote federal prisons. . . .

"*Fourth,* the statute properly accounts for state interests. Respondent [challengers] and the dissent contend that [the statute] violates the Tenth Amendment because it 'invades the province of state sovereignty' in an area typically left to state control. *New York v. United States,* 505 U.S. 144, 155 (1992) . . . But the Tenth Amendment's text is clear: 'The powers *not delegated to the United States* by the Constitution, nor prohibited by it to the States, are reserved to the States respectively, or to the people.' (Emphasis added.) The powers 'delegated to the United States by the Constitution' include those specifically enumerated powers listed in Article I along with the implementation authority granted by the Necessary and Proper Clause. Virtually by definition, these powers are not powers that the Constitution 'reserved to the States.' . . .

"[Relatedly, the statute] requires *accommodation* of state interests: The Attorney General must inform the State in which the federal prisoner 'is domiciled or was tried' that he is detaining someone with respect to whom those States may wish to assert their authority, and he must encourage those States to assume custody of the individual. . . .

"*Fifth,* the links between [the statute] and an enumerated Article I power are not too attenuated. Neither is the statutory provision too sweeping in its scope. Invoking the cautionary instruction that we may not 'pile inference upon inference' in order to sustain congressional action under Article I, *Lopez,* 514 U.S., at 567, respondents argue that, when legislating pursuant to the Necessary and Proper Clause, Congress' authority can be no more than one step removed from a specifically enumerated power. . . . But this argument is irreconcilable with our precedents. [In Greenwood v. United States, 350 U.S. 366 (1956), for example], we upheld the (likely indefinite) civil commitment of a mentally incompetent federal defendant who was accused of robbing a United States Post Office. . . . The underlying enumerated Article I power was the power to 'Establish Post Offices and Post Roads.' Art. I, § 8, cl. 7. But, as Chief Justice Marshall recognized in *McCulloch*, the power 'to establish post offices and post roads' . . . is executed by the single act of *making* the establishment. . . . [F]rom this has been inferred the power and duty of *carrying* the mail along the post road, from one post office to another. And, from this *implied* power, has *again* been inferred the right to *punish* those who steal letters from the post office, or rob the mail. . . . (emphasis added).

". . .

"Our necessary and proper jurisprudence contains multiple examples of similar reasoning. For example, in *Sabri* [v. United States, 541 U.S. 600 (2004)] we observed that 'Congress has authority under the Spending Clause to appropriate federal moneys' and that it therefore 'has corresponding authority under the Necessary and Proper Clause to see to it that taxpayer dollars' are not 'siphoned off' by 'corrupt public officers.' . . . We then further held that, in aid of that implied power to criminalize graft of 'taxpayer dollars,' Congress has the *additional* prophylactic power to criminalize bribes or kickbacks even when the stolen funds have not been 'traceably skimmed from specific federal payments.'. . . .

". . .

Justice Kennedy and Justice Alito each wrote a concurring opinion, and Justice Thomas wrote a dissent, in which Justice Scalia joined.

(4)   Near the end of the Constitutional Convention, Benjamin Franklin moved that Congress be given "a power to provide for cutting canals where deemed necessary." Madison then suggested enlarging Franklin's motion to add the power "to grant charters of incorporation where the interest of the U.S. might require & the legislative provisions of individual States may be incompetent." The Convention rejected these proposals. II Farrand, 615–616. Consider the possible relevance of that rejection to the preceding question of federal power to charter the Bank of the United States and the following question of federal power to build roads and canals.

Federal Power to Build Roads and Canals

Proposals for the building of national roads and canals generated substantial debates over the scope of national legislative power. A bill appropriating funds for such "internal improvements" was passed in 1817, but was vetoed by President Madison as not "among the enumerated powers; or . . . , by any just interpretation, within the power to make laws necessary and proper for carrying into execution those or other powers vested by the Constitution in the Government of the United States." II Messages and Papers of the Presidents 569, 570 (1897). The commerce power did not reach that far "without a latitude of construction departing from the ordinary import of the terms," and to construe the power "to provide for the common defence and general welfare" to do so "would be contrary to the established and consistent rules of interpretation, as rendering the special and careful enumeration of powers, which follow the clause, nugatory and improper. Such a view of the Constitution would have the effect of giving to Congress a general power of legislation, instead of the defined and limited one hitherto understood to belong to them. . . ." Id.

On similar strict construction grounds, President Monroe vetoed "with great regret" an appropriation passed in 1822 for the preservation and repair of the Cumberland Road. He suggested that Congress propose a constitutional amendment authorizing the necessary federal power.

McCulloch *and State Power to Control the Selection of Members of Congress*

McCulloch concluded "that the states have no power, by taxation or otherwise, to retard, impede, burden, or in any manner control the operations of the constitutional laws enacted by Congress. . . ." Powell v. McCormack, 395 U.S. 486 (1969), held that Congress could not alter the qualifications set forth in the Constitution for election to Congress. Where Congress lacks power to act and the Constitution is silent regarding state power, does *McCulloch* bear on state power to control who may be elected to Congress to exercise federal power?

In U.S. Term Limits, Inc. v. Thornton, 514 U.S. 779 (1995), the Court concluded that the States, like Congress, lack the power to add to the "exclusive qualifications" of age, citizenship and residency the Constitution prescribes for members of Congress. It invalidated a voter-adopted Arkansas constitutional amendment that prohibited the name of an otherwise-eligible candidate for Congress from appearing on the general election ballot if that candidate had already served three terms in the House or two terms in the Senate.

Justice Stevens' opinion for the Court relied on *McCulloch* in two respects to reject the argument that the State's voters possessed "reserved power" to impose term limit qualifications on candidates for Congress from their State. First, "the power to add qualifications is not within the 'original power' of the States, and thus is not reserved to the States by the Tenth Amendment. . . . [E]lecting representatives to the National Legislature was a new right, arising from the Constitution itself[,] . . . [and] any state power to set the qualifications for membership in Congress must derive not from the reserved powers of state sovereignty, but rather from the delegated powers of national sovereignty."

Second, even if the States' original power embraced some control over congressional qualifications, "the Qualifications Clauses were intended to preclude the States from exercising any such power." Recognizing state power to add qualifications would violate the "fundamental principle of our representative democracy" that "the people should choose whom they please to govern them." That right "belongs not to the States, but to the people"—a proposition supported by *McCulloch*:

"Permitting individual States to formulate diverse qualifications for their representatives would result in a patchwork of state qualifications, undermining the uniformity and the national character that the Framers envisioned and sought to ensure. Cf. McCulloch v. Maryland, 4 Wheat., at 428–429 (1819) ('Those means are not given by the people of a particular State, not given by the constituents of the legislature, . . . but by the people of all the States. They are given by all, for the benefit of all—and upon theory should be subjected to that government only which belongs to all'). Such a patchwork would also sever the direct link that the Framers found so critical between the National Government and the people of the United States."

Concurring separately, Justice Kennedy also emphasized *McCulloch* in support of his view that "the National Government . . . owes its existence to the act of the whole people who created it" and that there "can be no doubt, if we are to respect the republican origins of the Nation and preserve its federal character, that there exists a federal right of citizenship, a relationship between the people of the Nation and their National Government, with which the States may not interfere." Insisting "that the people of the United States . . . have a political identity . . . independent of, though consistent with, their identity as citizens of the State of their residence[,]" Justice Kennedy stated:

"It might be objected that because the States ratified the Constitution, the people can delegate power only through the States or by acting in their capacities as citizens of particular States. But in *McCulloch v. Maryland*, the Court set forth its authoritative rejection of this idea: 'The . . . constitution . . . was submitted to the people. . . . It is true, they . . . act in their States. But the measures they adopt do not, on that account, cease to be the measures of the people themselves, or become the measures of the State governments.' . . .

"The political identity of the entire people of the Union is reinforced by the proposition . . . that, though limited as to its objects, the National Government is and must be controlled by the people without collateral interference by the States. *McCulloch* affirmed this proposition as well, when the Court rejected the suggestion that States could interfere with federal powers. . . . The States have no power, reserved or otherwise, over the exercise of federal authority within its proper sphere. . . ."

Justice Thomas, joined by Chief Justice Rehnquist and Justices O'Connor and Scalia, dissented. Stressing that the "ultimate source of the Constitution's authority is the consent of the people of each individual State, not the consent of the undifferentiated people of the Nation as a whole[,]" he found nothing in *McCulloch* that denied "*the people* of the States" a reserved power under the Tenth Amendment to prescribe eligibility requirements for the candidates who seek to represent them in Congress, given the Constitution's silence on the question. The majority misunderstood *McCulloch*, he argued:

"For the past 175 years, *McCulloch* has been understood to rest on the proposition that the Constitution affirmatively barred Maryland from imposing its tax on the Bank's operations. . . . For the majority, however, *McCulloch* apparently turned on the fact that before the Constitution was adopted, the States had possessed no power to tax the instrumentalities of the governmental institutions that the Constitution created. This understanding of *McCulloch* makes most of Chief Justice Marshall's opinion irrelevant; according to the majority, there was no need to inquire into whether federal law deprived Maryland of the power in question, because the power could not fall into the category of 'reserved' powers anyway."

Justice Thomas also found "perfectly consistent with my position" *McCulloch*'s argument "that the people of a single State may not tax the instrumentalities employed by the people of all the States through the National Government, because such taxation would effectively subject the people of the several States to the taxing power of a single State":

"This sort of argument proves that the people of a single State may not prescribe qualifications for the President of the United States; the selection of the President, like the operation of the Bank of the United States, is not up to the people of any single State. . . . It does not follow, however, that the people of a single State may not prescribe qualifications for their own representatives in Congress."

Following similar reasoning, the Court later invalidated another state attempt to influence congressional elections in favor of candidates who supported congressional term limits. Cook v. Gralike, 531 U.S. 510 (2001). A state constitutional amendment adopted by Missouri voters attempted to "instruct" the members of Missouri's congressional delegation, and nonincumbent congressional candidates who might win election, to support a particular form of Congressional Term Limits Amendment to the United States Constitution. Incumbents who did not comply were to have "DISREGARDED VOTERS' INSTRUCTION ON TERM LIMITS" placed next to their names on all primary and general ballots; nonincumbents who refused to pledge support were to have "DECLINED TO PLEDGE TO SUPPORT TERM LIMITS" placed next to their names on all such ballots.

Because the adverse ballot designations were intended to "handicap candidates for the United States Congress" just at the crucial time when votes were cast, they constituted attempts to "dictate electoral outcomes" rather than regulations of "the procedural mechanisms of elections," explained Justice Stevens' majority opinion, and thus the state law did not fall within the power delegated to the State by the Elections Clause, Article I, section 4.

It bears noting that neither *Thornton* nor *Gralike* involved the power of a state people to exert control and/or pressure on state, as opposed to federal, legislators in the drive for federal term limits. On the power of a state people to control their own state legislators in the federal term limits context, see Vikram Amar, *The People Made Me Do It: Can the People of the State Instruct and Coerce Their State Legislatures in the Article V Constitutional Amendment Process?*, 41 Wm. & Mary L.Rev. 1037 (2000).

Arizona State Legislature v. Arizona Independent Redistricting Commission
576 U.S. ___, 135 S.Ct. 2652 (2015).

In 2000 the voters of Arizona enacted Proposition 106, an initiative creating the Arizona Independent Redistricting Commission (AIRC) and giving it the exclusive power to draw congressional district lines in the State, a function previously exercised by the elected state legislature. In early 2012, based on the 2010 census, the AIRC formulated redistricting maps to be used in federal elections. The elected state legislature then filed suit in federal court, alleging that Proposition 106 impermissibly divested authority from the elected representative body in violation of the so-called Elections Clause, Article I § 4, which provides: "The Times, Places and Manner of holding Elections for Senators and Representatives shall be prescribed in each State by the Legislature thereof; but Congress may at any time by Law make or alter such Regulations." A three-judge district court rejected the challenge on the merits, and the Supreme Court affirmed on appeal by a 5–4 vote.

Justice Ginsburg's opinion for the Court, joined by Justices Kennedy, Breyer, Sotomayor and Kagan, held that the term "legislature" in Article I § 4 does not require that federal redistricting be done by a state's representative body, but instead permits the people of a state to provide for redistricting by an independent commission. The Court, recognizing that the framers may not have envisioned the full scope of the initiative process in place in many states today, relied on the general history and purpose of the Clause, and also on prior cases in which the Court had upheld, respectively, the use of the referendum process and the gubernatorial veto in rejecting the districts drawn by elected state legislatures. Ohio ex rel. Davis v. Hildebrant, 241 U.S. 565 (1916); Smiley v. Holm, 285 U.S. 355 (1932). The Court also relied on a federal statute, 2 U.S.C. § 2(a(c), which the Court interpreted as expressing Congress' desire that so long as a state has redistricted in a manner consistent with its own state laws, the resulting districting plan should become the presumptively governing map. Noting that "there can be no dispute that Congress itself may draw a State's congressional-district boundaries" and has "plenary authority to 'make or alter' [a] State's plan," the majority rejected as "wooden" the idea, advanced by the elected Arizona legislature, that Congress is "preclude[d] from allowing a State to redistrict without the involvement of its representative body, even if Congress could enact the same redistricting plan" itself. But any uncertainty about the "import" of the Congressional authorization was "resolved" by the Court's clear holding that the

Elections Clause itself, even in the absence of Congressional authorization, "permits regulation of congressional districts by initiative."

Chief Justice Roberts wrote a dissent, joined by Justices Scalia, Thomas and Alito, arguing that the text of the Elections Clause, and that of other provisions of the Constitution that refer to the "Legislature" of a state, along with the history underlying and the cases interpreting these provisions, cut against the constitutionality of Proposition 106.

State Power to Administer Presidential Elections

Even though *Thornton* and *Gralike* make clear that states may not impose qualifications for members of Congress (and presumably the President), other cases make note of the ways in which the Constitution, especially before the Seventeenth Amendment, involves states in the process of constituting federal offices. For example, writing for the Court in Garcia v. San Antonio Metropolitan Transit Authority, 469 U.S. 528, 551 (1985), Justice Blackmun observed that:

"The Framers . . . gave the States a role in the selection both of the Executive and the Legislative Branches of the Federal Government. The States were vested with indirect influence over the House of Representatives and the Presidency by their control of electoral qualifications and their role in presidential elections. U.S. Const., Art. I, § 2, and Art. II, § 1. They were given more direct influence in the Senate, where each State received equal representation and each Senator was to be selected by the legislature of his State. Art. I, § 3."

The role of the states, and in particular the interplay between state legislatures and state courts, in Presidential selection prompted Chief Justice Rehnquist, joined by Justices Scalia and Thomas, to write a concurring opinion in Bush v. Gore, 531 U.S. 98, 112 (2000), in which he remarked:

"In most cases, comity and respect for federalism compel us to defer to the decisions of state courts on issues of state law. That practice reflects our understanding that the decisions of state courts are definitive pronouncements of the will of the States as sovereigns. . . . But there are a few exceptional cases in which the Constitution imposes a duty or confers a power on a particular branch of a State's government. This is one of them. Article II, § 1. cl. 2, provides that '[e]ach State shall appoint, in such Manner as the Legislature thereof may direct,' electors for President and Vice President. Thus, the text of the election law itself, and not just its interpretation by the courts of the States, takes on independent significance.

In McPherson v. Blacker, 146 U.S. 1 (1892), we explained that Article II, § 1, cl. 2, 'convey[s] the broadest power of determination' and 'leaves it to the legislature exclusively to define the method' of appointment."[a]

In essence, the concurring opinion in Bush v. Gore argues that the phrase "legislature [ ]of" "each State" in Article II essentially insulates state legislative decisions in the Presidential selection realm from state judicial revision, even if state law principles might otherwise justify state judicial involvement. The phrase "legislature of each state," or something very similar to it, appears in the Constitution outside of Article II as well, for example in Article V's amendment provisions, in Article I's congressional election provisions, and Article IV's provisions concerning the creation of new states. For a discussion of the meaning of these terms, and one that differs from the concurring opinion in Bush v. Gore, see Vikram Amar and Alan

---

[a]   Factual background on Bush v. Gore, and the reliance by the majority opinion in that case on federal equal protection principles, is discussed infra, at p. 676.

Brownstein, Bush v. Gore *and Article II: Pressured Judgment Makes Dubious Law*, 48 Fed. Lawyer 27 (2001).

Gibbons v. Ogden

22 U.S. (9 Wheat.) 1, 6 L.Ed. 23 (1824).

[Ogden obtained an injunction from the Court of Chancery of New York ordering Gibbons to stop operating his ferry-boats in the waters of the State of New York. In 1803 the New York legislature had granted to Robert Livingston and Robert Fulton the exclusive right for twenty years to operate ships powered by fire or steam in New York waters; in 1808, on proof that Livingston and Fulton had built a steamboat that could operate at more than four miles per hour, the grant was extended until 1838. Ogden alleged that he held an assignment from these grantees of the exclusive right to run a steamboat between Elizabethtown, New Jersey, and New York City, and that the defendant, Gibbons, was running two boats between these points. Gibbons alleged that his boats, the *Stoudinger* and *Bellana,* had been duly enrolled and licensed under the laws of the United States for carrying on the coasting trade.

Chancellor Kent sustained the injunction prohibiting the operation of Gibbons' boats. 4 Johns. Ch. 150 (1819). The Chancellor rejected the defendant's contention that plaintiff's monopoly was inconsistent with the United States coasting license; Chancellor Kent concluded that the coasting license was designed merely to relieve American ships of the burdens imposed upon foreign shipping. In an earlier case involving the steamboat monopoly the Chancellor had further rejected the contention that this state law, in regulating interstate commerce, fell within an area exclusively reserved to Congress. On the contrary, Chancellor Kent held that the states could regulate interstate commerce unless Congress had enacted inconsistent legislation. Livingston v. Van Ingen, 9 Johns. 507 (1812).

The New York Court for the Correction of Errors affirmed the order sustaining Ogden's injunction. 17 Johns. 488 (1820).]

■ MR. CHIEF JUSTICE MARSHALL delivered the opinion of the Court, . . .

The appellant contends that this decree is erroneous, because the laws which purport to give the exclusive privilege it sustains, are repugnant to the constitution and laws of the United States.

They are said to be repugnant:

1st. To that clause in the constitution which authorizes Congress to regulate commerce. . . .

The words are: "Congress shall have power to regulate commerce with foreign nations, and among the several states, and with the Indian tribes."

The subject to be regulated is commerce; and our constitution being, as was aptly said at the bar, one of enumeration, and not of definition, to ascertain the extent of the power it becomes necessary to settle the meaning of the word. The counsel for the appellee would limit it to traffic, to buying and selling, or the interchange of commodities, and do not admit that it comprehends navigation. This would restrict a general term, applicable to many objects, to one of its significations. Commerce, undoubtedly is traffic, but it is something more; it is intercourse. It describes the commercial intercourse between nations, and parts of nations, in all its branches, and is regulated by prescribing rules for carrying on that intercourse. The mind can scarcely conceive a system for regulating commerce between nations, which shall exclude all laws concerning navigation, which shall be silent on the admission of the vessels of the one nation into the ports of the other, and be confined to prescribing rules for the conduct of individuals, in the actual employment of buying and selling, or of barter.

If commerce does not include navigation, the government of the Union has no direct power over that subject, and can make no law prescribing what shall constitute American vessels, or requiring that they shall be navigated by American seamen. Yet this power has been exercised from the commencement of the government, has been exercised with the consent of all, and has been understood by all to be a commercial regulation. All America understands, and has uniformly understood, the word "commerce" to comprehend navigation. It was so understood, and must have been so understood, when the constitution was framed. The power over commerce, including navigation, was one of the primary objects for which the people of America adopted their government, and must have been contemplated in forming it. . . .

. . .

To what commerce does this power extend? The constitution informs us, to commerce "with foreign nations, and among the several states, and with the Indian tribes."

It has, we believe, been universally admitted that these words comprehend every species of commercial intercourse between the United States and foreign nations. No sort of trade can be carried on between this country and any other, to which this power does not extend. It has been truly said, that commerce, as the word is used in the constitution, is a unit, every part of which is indicated by the term.

If this be the admitted meaning of the word, in its application to foreign nations, it must carry the same meaning throughout the sentence, and remain a unit, unless there be some plain intelligible cause which alters it.

The subject to which the power is next applied, is to commerce "among the several states." The word "among" means intermingled with. A thing which is among others, is intermingled with them. Commerce among the states cannot stop at the external boundary line of each state, but may be introduced into the interior.

It is not intended to say that these words comprehend that commerce which is completely internal, which is carried on between man and man in a state, or between different parts of the same state, and which does not extend to or affect other states. Such a power would be inconvenient, and is certainly unnecessary.

Comprehensive as the word "among" is, it may very properly be restricted to that commerce which concerns more states than one. The phrase is not one which would probably have been selected to indicate the completely interior traffic of a state, because it is not an apt phrase for that purpose. . . . The genius and character of the whole government seem to be, that its action is to be applied to all the external concerns of the nation, and to those internal concerns which affect the states generally; but not to those which are completely within a particular state, which do not affect other states, and with which it is not necessary to interfere, for the purpose of executing some of the general powers of the government. The completely internal commerce of a state, then, may be considered as reserved for the state itself.

But, in regulating commerce with foreign nations, the power of Congress does not stop at the jurisdictional lines of the several states. It would be a very useless power if it could not pass those lines. The commerce of the United States with foreign nations, is that of the whole United States. Every district has a right to participate in it. The deep streams which penetrate our country in every direction, pass through the interior of almost every state in the Union, and furnish the means of exercising this right. If Congress has the power to regulate it, that power must be exercised whenever the subject exists. If it exists within the states, if a foreign voyage may commence or terminate at a port within a state, then the power of Congress may be exercised within a state.

This principle is, if possible, still more clear, when applied to commerce "among the several states." They either join each other, in which case they are separated by a mathematical line, or they are remote from each other, in which case other states lie between them. What is commerce "among" them; and how is it to be conducted? Can a trading expedition between two adjoining states commence and terminate outside of each? And if the trading intercourse be between two states remote from each other, must it not commence in one, terminate in the other, and probably pass through a third? Commerce among the states must, of necessity, be commerce with the states. In the regulation of trade with the Indian tribes, the action of the law, especially when the constitution was made, was chiefly within a state. The power of Congress, then, whatever it may be, must be exercised within the territorial jurisdiction of the several states. The sense of the nation, on this subject, is unequivocally manifested by the provisions made in the laws for transporting goods, by land, between Baltimore and Providence, between New York and Philadelphia, and between Philadelphia and Baltimore.

We are now arrived at the inquiry, What is this power?

It is the power to regulate; that is, to prescribe the rule by which commerce is to be governed. This power, like all others vested in Congress, is complete in itself, may be exercised to its utmost extent, and acknowledges no limitations, other than are prescribed in the constitution. These are expressed in plain terms, and do not affect the questions which arise in this case, or which have been discussed at the bar. If, as has always been understood, the sovereignty of Congress, though limited to specified objects, is plenary as to those objects, the power over commerce with foreign nations, and among the several States, is vested in Congress as absolutely as it would be in a single government, having in its constitution the same restrictions on the exercise of the power as are found in the constitution of the United States. The wisdom and the discretion of Congress, their identity with the people, and the influence which their constituents possess at elections, are, in this, as in many other instances, as that, for example, of declaring war, the sole restraints on which they have relied, to secure them from its abuse. They are the restraints on which the people must often rely solely, in all representative governments. . . .

But it has been urged, with great earnestness, that although the power of Congress to regulate commerce with foreign nations, and among the several states, be co-extensive with the subject itself, and have no other limits than are prescribed in the constitution, yet the states may severally exercise the same power within their respective jurisdictions. In support of this argument, it is said that they possessed it as an inseparable attribute of sovereignty, before the formation of the constitution, and still retain it, except so far as they have surrendered it by that instrument; that this principle results from the nature of the government, and is secured by the tenth amendment; that an affirmative grant of power is not exclusive, unless in its own nature it be such that the continued exercise of it by the former possessor is inconsistent with the grant, and that this is not of that description.

The appellant, conceding these postulates, except the last, contends that full power to regulate a particular subject, implies the whole power, and leaves no residuum; that a grant of the whole is incompatible with the existence of a right in another to any part of it.

Both parties have appealed to the constitution, to legislative acts, and judicial decisions; and have drawn arguments from all these sources to support and illustrate the propositions they respectively maintain.

The grant of the power to lay and collect taxes is, like the power to regulate commerce, made in general terms, and has never been understood to interfere with the exercise of the same power by the states; and hence has been drawn an argument which has been applied to the question under consideration. But the two grants are not, it is conceived, similar in their terms or their nature. Although many of the powers formerly exercised by the states, are transferred to the government of the Union, yet the state governments remain, and constitute a most important part of our system. The power of taxation is indispensable to their existence, and is a power which, in its own nature, is capable of residing in, and being exercised by, different authorities at the same time. We are accustomed to see it placed, for different purposes, in different hands. . . . When, then, each government exercises the power of taxation, neither is exercising the power of the other. But, when a State proceeds to regulate commerce with foreign nations, or among the several States, it is exercising the very power that is granted to Congress, and is doing the very thing which Congress is authorized to do. There is no analogy, then, between the power of taxation and the power of regulating commerce. . . .

But, the inspection laws are said to be regulations of commerce, and are certainly recognized in the constitution, as being passed in the exercise of a power remaining with the States.

That inspection laws may have a remote and considerable influence on commerce, will not be denied; but that a power to regulate commerce is the source from which the right to pass them is derived, cannot be admitted. The object of inspection laws, is to improve the quality of articles produced by the labour of a country; to fit them for exportation; or, it may be, for domestic use. They act upon the subject before it becomes an article of foreign commerce, or of commerce among the States, and prepare it for that purpose. They form a portion of that immense mass of legislation, which embraces everything within the territory of a State, not surrendered to the general government: all which can be most advantageously exercised by the States themselves. Inspection laws, quarantine laws, health laws of every description, as well as laws for regulating the internal commerce of a State, and those which respect turnpike roads, ferries, & c., are component parts of this mass.

No direct general power over these objects is granted to Congress; and, consequently, they remain subject to State legislation. . . .

It has been contended by the counsel for the appellant, that, as the word "to regulate" implies in its nature full power over the thing to be regulated, it excludes, necessarily, the action of all others that would perform the same operation on the same thing. That regulation is designed for the entire result, applying to those parts which remain as they were, as well as to those which are altered. It produces a uniform whole, which is as much disturbed and deranged by changing what the regulating power designs to leave untouched, as that on which it has operated.

There is great force in this argument, and the Court is not satisfied that it has been refuted.

Since, however, in exercising the power or regulating their own purely internal affairs, whether of trading or police, the States may sometimes enact laws, the validity of which depends on their interfering with, and being contrary to, an act of Congress passed in pursuance of the constitution, the Court will enter upon the inquiry, whether the laws of New York, as expounded by the highest tribunal of that State, have, in their application to this case, come into collision with an act of Congress, and deprived a citizen of a right to which that act entitles him. Should this collision exist, it will be immaterial whether those laws were passed in virtue of a concurrent power "to regulate commerce with foreign nations and among the several States," or in virtue of a power to regulate their domestic trade and police. In one case and the other, the acts of New York must yield to the law of Congress; and the decision sustaining the privilege they confer, against a right given by a law of the Union, must be erroneous. . . .

. . .

. . . [Federal law] declares . . . that vessels enrolled by virtue of a previous law, and certain other vessels, enrolled as described in that act, and having a license in force, as is by the act required, "and no others, shall be deemed ships or vessels of the United States, entitled to the privileges of ships or vessels employed in the coasting trade."

This section seems to the Court to contain a positive enactment, that the vessels it describes shall be entitled to the privileges of ships or vessels employed in the coasting trade. These privileges cannot be separated from the trade, and cannot be enjoyed, unless the trade may be prosecuted. The grant of the privilege is an idle, empty form, conveying nothing, unless it convey the right to which the privilege is attached, and in the exercise of which its whole value consists. To construe these words otherwise than as entitling the ships or vessels described, to carry on the coasting trade, would be, we think to disregard the apparent intent of the act.

. . .

But if the license be a permit to carry on the coasting trade, the respondent denies that these boats were engaged in that trade, or that the decree under consideration has restrained them from prosecuting it. The boats of the appellant were, we are told, employed in the transportation of passengers; and this is no part of that commerce which Congress may regulate.

If, as our whole course of legislation on this subject shows, the power of Congress has been universally understood in America, to comprehend navigation, it is a very persuasive, if not a conclusive argument, to prove that the construction is correct; and, if it be correct, no clear distinction is perceived between the power to regulate vessels employed in transporting men for hire, and property for hire. . . .

. . .

■ MR. JUSTICE JOHNSON.[a] . . .

I cannot overcome the conviction, that if the licensing act was repealed tomorrow, the rights of the appellant to a reversal of the decision complained of, would be as strong as it is under this license. One half the doubts in life arise from the defects of language, and if this instrument had been called an exemption instead of a license, it would have given a better idea of its character. . . .

Decree. . . . [T]his Court is of opinion, that the several licenses to the steam boats, the Stoudinger and the Bellona, to carry on the coasting trade . . . which were granted under an act of congress, passed in pursuance of the constitution of the United States, gave full authority to those vessels to navigate the waters of the United States, by steam or otherwise, for the purpose of carrying on the coasting trade, any law of the State of New York to the contrary notwithstanding; and that so much of the several laws of the State of New York, as prohibits vessels, licensed according to the laws of

---

[a]   Justice William Johnson, of South Carolina, was appointed to the Supreme Court in 1804 by Jefferson with the hope that the new justice would provide an antidote to Marshall and his Federalism. See Morgan, Justice William Johnson, The First Dissenter (1954). Was this hope realized in the *Gibbons* case?

the United States, from navigating the waters of the State of New York, by means of fire or steam, is repugnant to the said constitution, and void [Reversed.][b]

NOTE

The Chief Justice regarded "inspection laws, quarantine laws, health laws of every description, as well as laws for regulating the internal commerce of a State, and those which respect turnpike roads, ferries, etc." as component parts of "that immense mass of legislation, which embraces everything within the territory of a State, not surrendered to the general government." According to Justice Story, such laws "are not so much regulations of commerce as of police" and the powers exercised in their enactment "are entirely distinct in their nature from that to regulate commerce". Story on the Constitution (1833), § 1066. In what sense these powers, when applied to interstate or foreign commerce, are entirely distinct from the power to regulate such commerce was not made clear, but doctrinal foundations were thus laid which could enable the Court to sustain certain state laws affecting commerce while asserting that the power to regulate such commerce was vested exclusively in the national government. Marshall actually applied the "police power" view in only one case, which follows.

Willson v. Black-Bird Creek Marsh Co.

27 U.S. (2 Pet.) 245 (1829).

The legislature of Delaware authorized a company owning marshy lands along Black Bird Creek to dam and bank the creek with a view to improving their lands. The creek, which was navigable, flowed into the Delaware, but was described by counsel for the company as "one of those sluggish, reptile streams, that do not run but creep, and which wherever it passes, spreads its venom, and destroys the health of all those who inhabit its marshes." The owners of a sloop, licensed and enrolled under the navigation laws of the United States, broke the dam in order to secure passage for their vessel. The company sued for the resulting damage and defendants claimed that since the dam obstructed navigation, the state law authorizing it was in violation of the commerce clause.

Chief Justice Marshall wrote a brief unanimous opinion for the Court containing the following observations: "The act of assembly by which the plaintiffs were authorized to construct their dam, shows plainly that this is one of those many creeks, passing through a deep, level marsh adjoining the Delaware, up which the tide flows for some distance. The value of the property on its banks must be enhanced by excluding the water from the marsh, and the health of the inhabitants probably improved. Measures calculated to produce these objects, provided they do not come into collision with the powers of the general government, are undoubtedly within those which are reserved to the States. . . . If congress had passed any act which bore upon the case; any act in execution of the power to regulate commerce, the object of which was to control State legislation over those small navigable creeks into which the tide

---

[b] The arguments to the Court drove home the fact that the *Gibbons* case involved more than the run between Elizabethtown and New York. In the preceding decade, navigation by steam had developed at a rapid pace. Monopolies for the development of this modern means of travel, similar to that conferred on Fulton by New York, had been granted by New Jersey, Connecticut, Ohio, Massachusetts, New Hampshire, Vermont and Georgia; a particularly significant monopoly by Louisiana covered the mouth of the Mississippi. The legislation of New Jersey and Connecticut was designed to retaliate against New York. William Wirt's peroration enlarged on the theme that these "three states are almost on the verge of war". 9 Wheat. 184. For popular response to the *Gibbons* decision see: 1 Warren, *The Supreme Court in United States History* 615.

flows, and which abound throughout the lower country of the middle and southern States; we should feel not much difficulty in saying that a state law coming in conflict with such act would be void. But congress has passed no such act. The repugnancy of the law of Delaware to the Constitution is placed entirely on its repugnancy to the power to regulate commerce with foreign nations and among the several States; a power which has not been so exercised as to affect the question. We do not think that the act [authorizing the dam] can, under all the circumstances of the case, be considered as repugnant to the power to regulate commerce in its dormant state, or as being in conflict with any law passed on the subject."

3. THE SCOPE OF NATIONAL POWER TODAY

A. THE COMMERCE POWER

Introduction. An evil genius choosing a time for a new constitution that would tax its capacity for adaptability could hardly have selected a more trying time than 1789. Though some foresaw that the coastal settlements might expand across the continent, the framers had no inkling of the impact of the industrial revolution. The power of steam was soon harnessed for steamships and for railroads, which by 1869 spanned the continent. This new source of power also led to undreamed expansion of industrial production. The new Constitution thus was established on the eve of the great transition from an economy based on agriculture and handicraft to an economy based on power, machines and factories. The new forms of production were accompanied by the development of legal devices to organize and concentrate wealth: the business corporation and their combination through "trusts."

Correlated with this account, Congress did not often exercise its commerce power during most of the nineteenth century, but began to do so in significant ways starting with railroad regulation in the 1887 Interstate Commerce Act, followed closely by the Sherman Antitrust Act in 1890. The quantity of congressional commerce regulation jumped sharply beginning with Franklin Roosevelt's New Deal responses to the Great Depression and has continued at high levels. In response, the Supreme Court's commerce clause decisions after Gibbons v. Ogden, supra p. 98, have fallen into three roughly 50-year periods. Until the late 1800's the Court primarily addressed, not Congress' power to legislate, but state power to regulate where Congress might have. Then, from the beginning of significant congressional regulation of the incidents of nationwide transportation systems and industrial production until 1936, the Court adopted a variety of approaches simultaneously to limit perceived excesses of the commerce power and approve perceived needful uses. Finally, from 1937 until at least the 1995 decision in United States v. Lopez, the Court largely abandoned the attempt to restrain congressional power to regulate the economy.

In lieu of more extensive treatment of these developments, the following summary tracing the Court's precedents is drawn from a portion of Justice Kennedy's concurring opinion in United States v. Lopez, 514 U.S. 549, 568–73 (1995), augmented with footnote annotations by the editors:

"Chief Justice Marshall announced that the national authority reaches 'that commerce which concerns more States than one' and that the commerce power 'is complete in itself, may be exercised to its utmost extent, and acknowledges no limitations, other than are prescribed in the constitution.' Gibbons v. Ogden, 22 U.S. (9 Wheat.) 1, 194, 196, 6 L.Ed. 23 (1824). His statements can be understood now as an early and authoritative recognition that the Commerce Clause grants Congress extensive power and ample discretion to determine its appropriate exercise. The progression of our Commerce Clause cases from *Gibbons* to the present was not marked, however, by a coherent or consistent course of interpretation; for neither the course of technological advance nor the foundational principles for the jurisprudence itself were self-evident to the courts that sought to resolve contemporary disputes by enduring principles.

"Furthermore, for almost a century after the adoption of the Constitution, the Court's Commerce Clause decisions did not concern the authority of Congress to legislate. Rather, the Court faced the related but quite distinct question of the authority of the States to regulate matters that would be within the commerce power had Congress chosen to act. The simple fact was that in the early years of the Republic, Congress seldom perceived the necessity to exercise its power in circumstances where its authority would be called into question. . . .

. . .

"One approach the Court used to inquire into the lawfulness of state authority was to draw content-based or subject-matter distinctions, thus defining by semantic or formalistic categories those activities that were commerce and those that were not. For instance, in deciding that a State could prohibit the in-state manufacture of liquor intended for out-of-state shipment, it distinguished between manufacture and commerce. . . . Kidd v. Pearson, 128 U.S. 1, 20 (1888). Though that approach likely would not have survived even if confined to the question of a State's authority to enact legislation, it was not at all propitious when applied to the quite different question of what subjects were within the reach of the national power when Congress chose to exercise it.

"This became evident when the Court began to confront federal economic regulation enacted in response to the rapid industrial development in the late 19th century. Thus, it relied upon the manufacture-commerce dichotomy in United States v. E.C. Knight Co., 156 U.S. 1 (1895), where a manufacturers' combination controlling some 98% of the Nation's domestic sugar refining capacity was held to be outside the reach of the Sherman Act. Conspiracies to control manufacture, agriculture, mining, production, wages, or prices, the Court explained, had too 'indirect' an effect on interstate commerce.[a] Id., at 16. And in Adair v. United States, 208 U.S. 161 (1908), the Court rejected the view that the commerce power might extend to activities that, although local in the sense of having originated within a single state, nevertheless had a practical effect on interstate commercial activity. The Court concluded that there was not a 'legal or logical connection . . . between an employee's membership in a labor organization and the carrying on of interstate commerce,' id., at 178, and struck down a federal statute forbidding the discharge of an employee because of his membership in a labor organization. . . .

"Even before the Court committed itself to sustaining federal legislation on broad principles of economic practicality, it found it necessary to depart from these decisions. The Court disavowed *E.C. Knight*'s reliance on the manufacturing-commerce distinction in Standard Oil Co. of New Jersey v. United States, 221 U.S. 1 (1911),

---

[a] The Court worried "that, if the national power extends to all contracts and combinations in manufacture, agriculture, mining, and other productive industries, whose ultimate result may affect external commerce, comparatively little of business operations and affairs would be left for state control." In Addyston Pipe & Steel Co. v. United States, 175 U.S. 211 (1899), however, the Court held that the Sherman Act could apply to a conspiracy among companies engaged in the manufacture, sale, and transportation of iron pipe to divide sales territory and arrange for noncompetitive bidding, because, unlike *Knight*, the agreement directly restrained not only the manufacture but also the purchase, sale or exchange of the manufactured commodity among the states. And in Northern Securities Co. v. United States, 193 U.S. 197 (1904), the Court held that the Act could be applied to break up joint control of competing railroads by a holding company, because this directly embraced interstate commerce.

declaring that approach 'unsound.' The Court likewise rejected the rationale of *Adair* when it decided, in Texas & New Orleans R. Co. v. Railway Clerks, 281 U.S. 548, 570–571 (1930), that Congress had the power to regulate matters pertaining to the organization of railroad workers.

"In another line of cases, the Court addressed Congress' efforts to impede local activities it considered undesirable by prohibiting the interstate movement of some essential element. In the Lottery Case, 188 U.S. 321 (1903), the Court rejected the argument that Congress lacked power to prohibit the interstate movement of lottery tickets because it had power only to regulate, not to prohibit. See also Hipolite Egg Co. v. United States, 220 U.S. 45 (1911); Hoke v. United States, 227 U.S. 308 (1913). In Hammer v. Dagenhart, 247 U.S. 251 (1918), however, the Court insisted that the power to regulate commerce 'is directly the contrary of the assumed right to forbid commerce from moving,' id., at 269–270, and struck down a prohibition on the interstate transportation of goods manufactured in violation of child labor laws.[b]

"Even while it was experiencing difficulties in finding satisfactory principles in these cases, the Court was pursuing a more sustainable and practical approach in other lines of decisions, particularly those involving the regulation of railroad rates. In the Minnesota Rate Cases, 230 U.S. 352 (1913), the Court upheld a state rate order, but observed that Congress might be empowered to regulate in this area if 'by reason of the interblending of the interstate and intrastate operations of interstate carriers'

---

[b]   The Court distinguished the cases involving interstate transport of lottery tickets, impure food and drugs (*Hipolite Egg*), women for purposes of prostitution and debauchery (*Hoke*), and liquor (Clark Distilling Co. v. Western Maryland R. Co., 242 U.S. 311 (1917)), as "instances . . . of interstate transportation . . . necessary to the accomplishment of harmful results[,]" whereas in *Hammer* "[t]he act in its effect does not regulate transportation among the states, but aims to standardize the ages at which children may be employed in mining and manufacturing within the states. The goods shipped are of themselves harmless. . . ." The Court also rejected the argument that the act was a valid attempt to protect business in states with high labor standards from unfair interstate competition resulting from production in those states permitting child labor conditions:

"The commerce clause was not intended to give to Congress a general authority to equalize such conditions. In some of the states laws have been passed fixing minimum wages for women, in others the local law regulates the hours of labor of women in various employments. Business done in such states may be at an economic disadvantage when compared with states which have no such regulations; surely this fact does not give Congress the power to deny transportation in interstate commerce to those who carry on business where the hours of labor and the rate of compensation for women have not been fixed by a standard in use in other states and approved by Congress. . . ."

The act was held unconstitutional as invading the reserved powers of the states.

Justice Holmes (with McKenna, Brandeis and Clarke, JJ.) dissented, saying:

"The notion that prohibition is any less prohibition when applied to things now thought evil I do not understand. But if there is any matter upon which civilized countries have agreed—far more unanimously than they have with reference to intoxicants . . . —it is the evil of premature and excessive child labor. . . .

"But I had thought that the propriety of the exercise of a power admitted to exist in some cases was for the consideration of Congress alone and that this Court always had disavowed the right to intrude its judgment upon questions of policy or morals. It is not for this Court to pronounce when prohibition is necessary to regulation if it ever may be necessary—to say that it is permissible as against strong drink but not as against the product of ruined lives.

"The Act does not meddle with anything belonging to the States. They may regulate their internal affairs and their domestic commerce as they like. But when they seek to send their products across the State line they are no longer within their rights. If there were no Constitution and no Congress their power to cross the line would depend upon their neighbors. Under the Constitution such commerce belongs not to the States but to Congress to regulate. It may carry out its views of public policy whatever indirect effect they may have upon the activities of the States. . . ."

After *Hammer*, Congress imposed a 10% tax on net profits of factories employing child labor, which the Court invalidated as being palpably prohibitory and regulatory in a manner indistinguishable from *Hammer*, rather than being a valid tax. The Child Labor Tax Case, 259 U.S. 20 (1922).

the regulation of interstate rates could not be maintained without restrictions on 'intrastate rates which substantially affect the former.' Id., at 432–433. And in the Shreveport Rate Cases, 234 U.S. 342 (1914), the Court upheld an ICC order fixing railroad rates with the explanation that congressional authority, 'extending to these interstate carriers as instruments of interstate commerce, necessarily embraces the right to control their operations in all matters having such a close and substantial relation to interstate traffic that the control is essential or appropriate to the security of that traffic, to the efficiency of the interstate service, and to the maintenance of conditions under which interstate commerce may be conducted upon fair terms and without molestation or hindrance.' "c Id., at 351.

"Even the most confined interpretation of 'commerce' would embrace transportation between the States, so the rate cases posed much less difficulty for the Court than cases involving manufacture or production. Nevertheless, the Court's recognition of the importance of a practical conception of the commerce power was not altogether confined to the rate cases. In Swift & Co. v. United States, 196 U.S. 375 (1905), the Court upheld the application of federal antitrust law to a combination of meat dealers that occurred in one State but that restrained trade in cattle 'sent for sale from a place in one State, with the expectation that they will end their transit . . . in another.' Id., at 398. The Court explained that 'commerce among the States is not a technical legal conception, but a practical one, drawn from the course of business.' Id., at 398. Chief Justice Taft followed the same approach in upholding federal regulation of stockyards in Stafford v. Wallace, 258 U.S. 495 (1922). Speaking for the Court, he rejected a 'nice and technical inquiry,' id., at 519, when the local transactions at issue could not 'be separated from the movement to which they contribute,' id., at 516.

"Reluctance of the Court to adopt that approach in all of its cases caused inconsistencies in doctrine to persist, however. In addressing New Deal legislation the Court resuscitated the abandoned abstract distinction between direct and indirect effects on interstate commerce. See Carter v. Carter Coal Co., 298 U.S. 238, 309 (1936) (Act regulating price of coal and wages and hours for miners held to have only 'secondary and indirect' effect on interstate commerce);d Railroad Retirement Bd. v.

---

c　In order to end rate discrimination, the ICC order effectively required railroads engaged in both interstate and intrastate traffic to raise rates on intrastate hauls because proportionately higher rates it had approved were in effect for interstate hauls. The Court also said: "Wherever the interstate and intrastate transactions of carriers are so related that the government of the one involves the control of the other, it is Congress, and not the state, that is entitled to prescribe the final and dominant rule, for otherwise Congress would be denied the exercise of its constitutional authority, and the state, and not the nation, would be supreme within the national field."

d　The Carter case arose in the middle of the Depression at the end of the Court's most active period of assault on congressional control of the economy. It held unconstitutional the Guffey Coal Act, which sought to regulate minimum coal prices and minimum wages and maximum hours for mine workers, and in which Congress declared "that the production and distribution by producers of such coal bear upon and directly affect interstate commerce, and render regulation of production and distribution imperative for the protection of such commerce. . . ." Justice Sutherland, for the majority, said in part:

"The proposition, often advanced and as often discredited, that the power of the federal government inherently extends to purposes affecting the nation as a whole with which the states severally cannot deal or cannot adequately deal, and the related notion that Congress, entirely apart from those powers delegated by the Constitution, may enact laws to promote the general welfare, have never been accepted but always definitely rejected by this court. . . .

"A consideration of [many cases, including Knight] renders inescapable the conclusion that the effect of the labor provisions of the act, including those in respect of minimum wages, wage agreements, collective bargaining, and the Labor Board and its powers, primarily falls upon production and not upon commerce; and confirms the further resulting conclusion that production is a purely local activity. It follows that none of these essential antecedents of production constitutes a transaction in or forms any part of interstate commerce. . . .

Alton R. Co., 295 U.S. 330 (1935) (compulsory retirement and pension plan for railroad carrier employees too 'remote from any regulation of commerce as such'); A.L.A. Schechter Poultry Corp. v. United States, 295 U.S. 495 (1935) (wage and hour law provision of National Industrial Recovery Act had 'no direct relation to interstate commerce').[e]

. . .

"The case that seems to mark the Court's definitive commitment to the practical conception of the commerce power is NLRB v. Jones & Laughlin Steel Corp., 301 U.S. 1 (1937), where the Court sustained labor laws that applied to manufacturing facilities, making no real attempt to distinguish *Carter* . . . and *Schechter*. . . . 301 U.S., at 40–41.[f] The deference given to Congress has since been confirmed. United States v.

"Whether the effect of a given activity or condition is direct or indirect is not always easy to determine. . . . And the extent of the effect bears no logical relation to its character. The distinction between a direct and an indirect effect turns, not upon the magnitude of either the cause or the effect, but entirely upon the manner in which the effect has been brought about. . . . It is quite true that rules of law are sometimes qualified by considerations of degree, as the government argues. But the matter of degree has no bearing upon the question here, since that question is not—What is the *extent* of the local activity or condition, or the *extent* of the effect produced upon interstate commerce? but—What is the *relation* between the activity or condition and the effect? . . ."

[e]   The NIRA was perhaps the most widely heralded New Deal measure designed to stimulate recovery from the Great Depression. Schechter Poultry, a Brooklyn business that bought poultry at markets or railroad terminals within New York City and slaughtered and distributed poultry wholesale to New York dealers who resold to New York consumers, was convicted of code violations "in any transaction in or affecting foreign or interstate commerce." The evidence indicated that ninety-six per cent of the live poultry marketed in New York came from other states. The Supreme Court reversed the conviction, first, because the act had attempted an unconstitutional delegation of power to the President, and second, because as applied it exceeded the commerce power. For a unanimous Court, Chief Justice Hughes concluded that the poultry transactions involved were not "in" interstate commerce: "The poultry had come to a permanent rest within the State. It was not held, used, or sold by defendants in relation to any further transactions in interstate commerce and was not destined for transportation to other states. Hence, decisions which deal with a stream of interstate commerce— where goods come to rest within a state temporarily and are later to go forward in interstate commerce—and with the regulations of transactions involved in that practical continuity of movement, are not applicable here. See Swift & Co. v. United States, 196 U.S. 375, 387, 388; . . . Stafford v. Wallace, 258 U.S. 495, 519. . . ." Defendant's transactions did not "directly 'affect' interstate commerce so as to be subject to federal regulation. . . . In determining how far the federal government may go in controlling intrastate transactions upon the ground that they 'affect' interstate commerce, there is a necessary and well-established distinction between direct and indirect effects. The precise line can be drawn only as individual cases arise, but the distinction is clear in principle. . . . If the commerce clause were construed to reach all enterprises and transactions which could be said to have an indirect effect upon interstate commerce, the federal authority would embrace practically all the activities of the people and the authority of the state over its domestic concerns would exist only by sufferance of the federal government. . . ." Concurring, Justice Cardozo stated: "The law is not indifferent to considerations of degree. Activities local in their immediacy do not become interstate and national because of distant repercussions. What is near and what is distant may at times be uncertain. . . . There is no penumbra of uncertainty obscuring judgment here. To find immediacy or directness here is to find it almost everywhere. If centrifugal forces are to be isolated to the exclusion of the forces that oppose and counteract them, there will be an end to our federal system."

[f]   Under the National Labor Relations Act, enacted in 1935, the newly created National Labor Relations Board ordered Jones & Laughlin to cease and desist from interfering with the right of its employees at a steel and iron manufacturing plant to organize and bargain collectively. The Court upheld the NLRB's order under the commerce power, relying in part on the notion of the Shreveport Rate Case, supra, that "intrastate activities, by reason of close and intimate relation to interstate commerce, may fall within federal control. . . ." The Court now said that the "question is necessarily one of degree" and "the fact that the employees here concerned were engaged in production is not determinative. The question remains as to the effect upon interstate commerce of the labor practice involved." As to that, the Court said:

"[T]he stoppage of [respondent's manufacturing] operations by industrial strife would have a most serious effect upon interstate commerce. In view of respondent's far-flung activities, it is idle to say

Darby, 312 U.S. 100, 116–117 (1941), overruled Hammer v. Dagenhart, supra. And in Wickard v. Filburn, 317 U.S. 111 (1942), the Court disapproved *E.C. Knight* and the entire line of direct-indirect and manufacture-production cases, explaining that 'broader interpretations of the Commerce Clause [were] destined to supersede the earlier ones,' id., at 122, and 'whatever terminology is used, the criterion is necessarily one of degree and must be so defined . . . ', id., at 123, n. 24. . . ."

The Roosevelt Court Plan

The initial New Deal program had been shattered by the series of major judicial defeats suffered in the Supreme Court. Stricken down in succession were the Railroad Retirement Act of 1934, the National Industrial Recovery Act of 1933, the Agricultural Adjustment Act of 1933, and the Bituminous Coal Conservation Act of 1935. By the time of the *Carter Coal* decision of May 18, 1936, a feeling was growing within the administration that something had to be done about the Supreme Court. Actual steps awaited the election of November 1936, which returned Roosevelt to the presidency by an overwhelming majority. On February 7, 1937, the President sent to Congress a message calling for legislation to "reorganize the judicial branch"—a proposal commonly known as the court-packing plan. After dealing at some length with other less controversial problems of judicial organization, the message turned to "the question of aged or infirm judges—a subject of delicacy and yet one which requires frank discussion." The message stressed the difficulty for older men to keep up with the work of the courts, and also stated: "A lowered mental or physical vigor leads men to avoid an examination of complicated and changed conditions. Little by little, new facts become blurred through old glasses fitted, as it were, for the needs of another generation; older men, assuming that the scene is the same as it was in the past, cease to explore or inquire into the present or the future." The message then recommended that legislation provide for "the appointment of additional judges, in all Federal Courts, without exception, where there are incumbent judges of retirement age who do not choose to retire or resign." At that time six members of the Supreme Court had passed the voluntary retirement age of 70: Hughes (75), Sutherland (75), Butler (71), Brandeis (81), McReynolds (75), and Van Devanter (78).

---

that the effect would be indirect or remote. It is obvious that it would be immediate and might be catastrophic. We are asked to shut our eyes to the plainest facts of our national life and to deal with the question of direct and indirect effects in an intellectual vacuum. Because there may be but indirect and remote effects upon interstate commerce in connection with a host of local enterprises throughout the country, it does not follow that other industrial activities do not have such a close and intimate relation to interstate commerce as to make the presence of industrial strife a matter of the most urgent national concern. When industries organize themselves on a national scale making their relation to interstate commerce the dominant factor in their activities, how can it be maintained that their industrial labor relations constitute a forbidden field into which Congress may not enter when it is necessary to protect interstate commerce from the paralyzing consequences of industrial war?"

After *Jones & Laughlin* the Court sustained the application of the NLRA to a variety of smaller industrial enterprises. In National Labor Relations Board v. Fainblatt, 306 U.S. 601 (1939), involving a manufacturer who processed materials into about a thousand dozen garments a month shipped in interstate commerce, the Court said that it was not important "that the volume of the commerce here involved though substantial, was relatively small as compared with that in the cases arising under the National Labor Relations Act which have hitherto engaged our attention. The power of Congress to regulate interstate commerce is plenary and extends to all such commerce be it great or small." The Court went on to note that the garment industry was one in which relatively small units contributed in the aggregate to a vast volume of commerce and that strikes in the industry would have a substantial effect on interstate commerce.

The proposal produced a hurricane of controversy which lasted for months.[a] Opposition mounted as it became increasingly clear that the President's object was to change the judicial philosophy of the Supreme Court; on June 14, 1937, the Senate Judiciary Committee recommended rejection of the proposed legislation "as a needless, futile, and utterly dangerous abandonment of constitutional principle," Report No. 711, 75th Cong., 1st Sess. (1937). On July 22, the bill was killed by recommitment to the Judiciary Committee. During this interval, there were before the Supreme Court cases involving the constitutionality of the National Labor Relations Act and the Social Security Act, which had been enacted along with the Bituminous Coal Act in the summer of 1935; National Labor Relations Board v. Jones & Laughlin Steel Corp., supra, was argued February 10, 11, 1937, and decided April 12; Charles C. Steward Machine Co. v. Davis, 301 U.S. 548, was argued April 8, 9, 1937, and decided May 24.

In both cases the legislation was held valid by votes of 5 to 4.

President Roosevelt lost the battle but won the war. Within four years he was given the opportunity to replace seven members of the Court. In 1937 Justice Van Devanter retired and was succeeded by Senator Hugo Black. The following year Justice Sutherland retired, to be succeeded by Solicitor General Stanley Reed. In 1939, Justice Cardozo was succeeded by Professor Felix Frankfurter, Justice Brandeis by William O. Douglas, Chairman of the Securities and Exchange Commission, and Justice Butler by Attorney General Frank Murphy. In 1941, Justice McReynolds resigned and was succeeded by Senator James Byrnes. Later in 1941, Chief Justice Hughes resigned, Justice Stone was made Chief Justice, and Attorney General Robert H. Jackson was added to the Court.

By 1942 the Court had dramatically reversed itself, sustaining in their broadest applications the National Labor Relations Act, the Fair Labor Standards Act, and the Agricultural Adjustment Act. As we will see in later chapters, the Court also changed its interpretation of the due process and equal protection clauses so as to increase substantially governmental regulatory powers over economic matters.

The Post-Depression Commerce Power

As Justice Kennedy hints in his survey, United States v. Darby, 312 U.S. 100 (1941), and Wickard v. Filburn, 317 U.S. 111 (1942), confirmed a sweepingly deferential approach to Congress' exercise of its commerce power. The way these twin pillars of modern commerce clause doctrine did so is noteworthy.

Darby sustained application of the Fair Labor Standards Act of 1938, first, in § 15(a)(1), to prohibit the shipment in interstate commerce of lumber manufactured by employees whose wages were less than a prescribed minimum or whose weekly hours of labor at that wage were greater than a prescribed maximum, and, second, in § 15(a)(2), to prohibit employment in the production of goods "for interstate commerce" at other than the prescribed wages and hours. As to § 15(a)(1), the Court rejected the contention "that while the prohibition is nominally a regulation of [interstate] commerce its motive or purpose is regulation of wages and hours of persons engaged in

---

[a] For subsequent developments, and especially the generalship of Chief Justice Hughes in meeting this challenge, see Pusey, *Charles Evans Hughes* (1951). Cf. Robert H. Jackson, *The Struggle for Judicial Supremacy,* 176 et seq. (1941); Leuchtenburg, *The Origins of Franklin D. Roosevelt's "Court-Packing" Plan,* 1966 Supreme Court Review 347 (1966). In answer to the charge that this proposal produced a "switch in time that saved nine", Justice Roberts left a paper with Justice Frankfurter for posthumous publication, which shows that Justice Roberts's vote to sustain state minimum wage legislation in West Coast Hotel Co. v. Parrish, 300 U.S. 379 (1937), although announced on March 29, 1937, reflected a vote taken in conference on December 19, 1936. See Frankfurter, Mr. Justice Roberts, 104 U.Pa.L.Rev. 311, 314, 315 (1955). This memorandum does not deal with the relationship between the *Carter* case, supra, and the *Jones & Laughlin* case, supra.

manufacture, the control of which has been reserved to the states"—that "under the guise of a regulation of interstate commerce, it undertakes to regulate wages and hours within the state contrary to the policy of the state which has elected to leave them unregulated." Justice Stone's opinion for the Court responded:

"The motive and purpose of the present regulation are plainly to make effective the Congressional conception of public policy that interstate commerce should not be made the instrument of competition in the distribution of goods produced under substandard labor conditions, which competition is injurious to the commerce and to the states from and to which the commerce flows. The motive and purpose of a regulation of interstate commerce are matters for the legislative judgment upon the exercise of which the Constitution places no restriction and over which the courts are given no control. McCray v. United States, 195 U.S. 27; Sonzinsky v. United States, 300 U.S. 506, 513, and cases cited. . . ."

Since the "reasoning and conclusion of the Court's opinion [in Hammer v. Dagenhart] cannot be reconciled with the conclusion which we have reached, that the power of Congress under the Commerce Clause is plenary to exclude any article from interstate commerce subject only to the specific prohibitions of the Constitution[,] . . . it should be and now is overruled."

As to § 15(a)(2), "the validity of the prohibition turns on . . . whether the employment, under other than the prescribed labor standards, of employees engaged in the production of goods for interstate commerce is so related to the commerce and so affects it as to be within the reach of the power of Congress to regulate it." Justice Stone gave two answers. First, "Congress, having by the present Act adopted the policy of excluding from interstate commerce all goods produced for the commerce which do not conform to the specified labor standards, it may choose the means reasonably adapted to the attainment of the permitted end, even though they involve control of intrastate activities." Second,

". . . § 15(a)(2) . . . is sustainable independently of § 15(a)(1). . . . [T]he evils aimed at by the Act are the spread of substandard labor conditions through the use of the facilities of interstate commerce for competition by the goods so produced with those produced under the prescribed or better labor conditions; and the consequent dislocation of the commerce itself caused by the impairment or destruction of local businesses by competition made effective through interstate commerce. The Act is thus directed at the suppression of a method or kind of competition in interstate commerce which it has in effect condemned as 'unfair'. . . .

"The means adopted by § 15(a)(2) . . . is so related to the commerce and so affects it as to be within the reach of the commerce power. . . . Congress . . . has made no distinction as to the volume or amount of shipments in the commerce or of production for commerce by any particular shipper or producer. It recognized that in present day industry, competition by a small part may affect the whole and that the total effect of the competition of many small producers may be great. See H.Rept. No. 2182, 75th Cong. 1st Sess., p. 7. The legislation aimed at a whole embraces all its parts. . . .

. . .

"Our conclusion is unaffected by the Tenth Amendment which provides: 'The powers not delegated to the United States by the Constitution, nor prohibited by it to the States, are reserved to the States respectively, or to the people'. The amendment states but a truism that all is retained which has not been surrendered. . . ."

The decision in Wickard v. Filburn, a suit to enjoin the marketing penalty imposed by the Agricultural Adjustment Act of 1938 upon that part of Filburn's 1941 wheat crop that was available for marketing in excess of the marketing quota established for his farm, went further. As Justice Jackson's opinion for the Court said, the commerce power challenge raised "would merit little consideration since our decision in United States v. Darby, 312 U.S. 100, sustaining the federal power to regulate production of goods for commerce except for the fact that this Act extends federal regulation to production not intended in any part for commerce but wholly for consumption on the farm." The opinion contained these observations:

"The Court's recognition of the relevance of the economic effects in the application of the Commerce Clause . . . has made the mechanical application of legal formulas no longer feasible. Once an economic measure of the reach of the power granted to Congress in the Commerce Clause is accepted, questions of federal power cannot be decided simply by finding the activity in question to be 'production' nor can consideration of its economic effects be foreclosed by calling them 'indirect.' . . .

". . . [E]ven if appellee's activity be local and though it may not be regarded as commerce, it may still, whatever its nature, be reached by Congress if it exerts a substantial economic effect on interstate commerce and this irrespective of whether such effect is what might at some earlier time have been defined as 'direct' or 'indirect.' "

The Court noted that "[c]ommerce among the states in wheat is large and important[,]" that the "wheat industry has been a problem industry for some years[,]" and that "[t]he effect of consumption of homegrown wheat on interstate commerce is due to the fact that it constitutes the most variable factor in the disappearance of the wheat crop." The Court continued:

". . . The effect of the statute before us is to restrict the amount which may be produced for market and the extent as well to which one may forestall resort to the market by producing to meet his own needs. That appellee's own contribution to the demand for wheat may be trivial by itself is not enough to remove him from the scope of federal regulation where, as here, his contribution, taken together with that of many others similarly situated, is far from trivial. . . .

". . . One of the primary purposes of the Act . . . was to increase the market price of wheat and to that end to limit the volume thereof that could affect the market. It can hardly be denied that a factor of such volume and variability as home-consumed wheat would have a substantial influence on price and market conditions. This may arise because being in marketable condition such wheat overhangs the market and if induced by rising prices tends to flow into the market and check price increases. But if we assume that it is never marketed, it supplies a need of the man who grew it which would otherwise be reflected by purchases in the open market. Home-grown wheat in this sense competes with wheat in commerce. The stimulation of commerce is a use of the regulatory function quite as definitely as prohibitions or restrictions thereon. This record leaves us in no doubt that Congress may properly have considered that wheat consumed on the farm where grown if wholly outside the scheme of regulation would have a substantial effect in defeating and obstructing its purpose to stimulate trade therein at increased prices."[a]

---

[a]   United States v. South-Eastern Underwriters Ass'n, 322 U.S. 533 (1944), sustained the applicability of the Sherman Anti-Trust Act to the insurance business, overturning a district court decision based on Paul v. Virginia, 75 U.S. 168 (1868), that "a policy of insurance is not a transaction of commerce" and insurance contracts "are not interstate transactions, although the parties are domiciled in different states". The opinion, by Justice Black, emphasized the size of the insurance business and the extent to which companies located in one part of the country write insurance contracts for persons in other states. The opinion also stated:

"We may grant that a contract of insurance, considered as a thing apart from negotiation and execution, does not itself constitute interstate commerce. . . . But . . . a nationwide business is not deprived of its interstate character merely because it is built upon sales contracts which are local in

Heart of Atlanta Motel, Inc. v. United States

379 U.S. 241, 85 S.Ct. 348, 13 L.Ed.2d 258 (1964).

[The owner of the Motel brought a declaratory judgment action, attacking the constitutionality of Title II of the Civil Rights Act of 1964. A three-judge court sustained the Act and enjoined its further violation by the Motel. An appeal was taken to the Supreme Court.]

■ MR. JUSTICE CLARK delivered the opinion of the Court.

. . .

1.   THE FACTUAL BACKGROUND AND CONTENTIONS OF THE PARTIES

. . . Appellant owns and operates the Heart of Atlanta Motel which has 216 rooms available to transient guests. The motel is located on Courtland Street, two blocks from downtown Peachtree Street. It is readily accessible to interstate highways 75 and 85 and state highways 23 and 41. Appellant solicits patronage from outside the State of Georgia through various national advertising media, including magazines of national circulation; it maintains over 50 billboards and highway signs within the State, soliciting patronage for the motel; it accepts convention trade from outside Georgia and approximately 75% of its registered guests are from out of State. Prior to passage of the Act the motel had followed a practice of refusing to rent rooms to Negroes, and it alleged that it intended to continue to do so. In an effort to perpetuate that policy this suit was filed.

. . .

Since Title II is the only portion under attack here, we confine our consideration to those public accommodation provisions.

3.   TITLE II OF THE ACT

This Title is divided into seven sections beginning with § 201(a) which provides that:

"All persons shall be entitled to the full and equal enjoyment of the goods, services, facilities, privileges, advantages, and accommodations of any place of public accommodation, as defined in this section, without discrimination or segregation on the ground of race, color, religion, or national origin."

There are listed in § 201(b) four classes of business establishments, each of which "serves the public" and "is a place of public accommodation" within the meaning of § 201(a) "if its operations affect commerce, or if discrimination or segregation by it is supported by State action." The covered establishments are:

"(1) any inn, hotel, motel, or other establishment which provides lodging to transient guests, other than an establishment located within a building which contains not more than five rooms for rent or hire and which is actually occupied by the proprietor of such establishment as his residence; . . . ."

Section 201(c) defines the phrase "affect commerce" as applied to the above establishments. It first declares that "any inn, hotel, motel, or other establishment which provides lodging to transient guests" affects commerce *per se*. . . .

---

nature. Were the rule otherwise, few businesses could be said to be engaged in interstate commerce. . . .

"The power granted Congress . . . is the power to legislate concerning transactions which, reaching across state boundaries, affect the people of more states than one;—to govern affairs which the individual states, with their limited territorial jurisdictions, are not fully capable of governing."

4. APPLICATION OF TITLE II TO HEART OF ATLANTA MOTEL

It is admitted that the operation of the motel brings it within the provisions of § 201(a) of the Act and that appellant refused to provide lodging for transient Negroes because of their race or color and that it intends to continue that policy unless restrained.

The sole question posed is, therefore, the constitutionality of the Civil Rights Act of 1964 as applied to these facts. The legislative history of the Act indicates that Congress based the Act on § 5 and the Equal Protection Clause of the Fourteenth Amendment as well as its power to regulate interstate commerce. . . .

The Senate Commerce Committee made it quite clear that the fundamental object of Title II was to vindicate "the deprivation of personal dignity that surely accompanies denials of equal access to public establishments." At the same time, however, it noted that such an objective has been and could be readily achieved "by congressional action based on the commerce power of the Constitution." S.Rep. No. 872, supra, at 16–17. Our study of the legislative record, made in the light of prior cases, has brought us to the conclusion that Congress possessed ample power in this regard, and we have therefore not considered the other grounds relied upon. . . .

. . .

6. THE BASIS OF CONGRESSIONAL ACTION

While the Act as adopted carried no congressional findings the record of its passage through each house is replete with evidence of the burdens that discrimination by race or color places upon interstate commerce. . . . This testimony included the fact that our people have become increasingly mobile with millions of people of all races traveling from State to State; that Negroes in particular have been the subject of discrimination in transient accommodations, having to travel great distances to secure the same; that often they have been unable to obtain accommodations and have had to call upon friends to put them up overnight, . . . ; and that these conditions had become so acute as to require the listing of available lodging for Negroes in a special guidebook which was itself "dramatic testimony to the difficulties" Negroes encounter in travel. . . . We shall not burden this opinion with further details since the voluminous testimony presents overwhelming evidence that discrimination by hotels and motels impedes interstate travel.

7. THE POWER OF CONGRESS OVER INTERSTATE TRAVEL

. . .

[T]he determinative test of the exercise of power by the Congress under the Commerce Clause is simply whether the activity sought to be regulated is "commerce which concerns more States than one" and has a real and substantial relation to the national interest. Let us now turn to this facet of the problem.

That the "intercourse" of which the Chief Justice [Marshall] spoke [in Gibbons v. Ogden] included the movement of persons through more States than one was settled as early as 1849. . . . Nor does it make any difference whether the transportation is commercial in character. . . .

The same interest in protecting interstate commerce which led Congress to deal with segregation in interstate carriers and the white-slave traffic has prompted it to extend the exercise of its power to gambling, Lottery Case, 188 U.S. 321 (1903) . . . and to racial discrimination by owners and managers of terminal restaurants, Boynton v. Virginia, 364 U.S. 454 (1960).

That Congress was legislating against moral wrongs in many of these areas rendered its enactments no less valid. In framing Title II of this Act Congress was also dealing with what it considered a moral problem. But that fact does not detract from the overwhelming evidence of the disruptive effect that racial discrimination has had on commercial intercourse. It was this burden which empowered Congress to enact appropriate legislation, and, given this basis for the exercise of its power, Congress was not restricted by the fact that the particular obstruction to interstate commerce with which it was dealing was also deemed a moral and social wrong.

It is said that the operation of the motel here is of a purely local character. But, assuming this to be true, "[i]f it is interstate commerce that feels the pinch, it does not matter how local the operation which applies the squeeze." United States v. Women's Sportswear Mfrs. Assn., 336 U.S. 460, 464 (1949). . . .

. . .

We, therefore, conclude that the action of the Congress in the adoption of the Act as applied here to a motel which concededly serves interstate travelers is within the power granted it by the Commerce Clause of the Constitution, as interpreted by this Court for 140 years. . . .

Affirmed.

[Justice Douglas's opinion stated that although he agreed with the Court's opinion, he was reluctant to rest solely on the commerce clause because of his belief that the right of people to be free of state action that discriminates against them because of race "occupies a more protected position in our constitutional system than does the movement of cattle, fruit, steel and coal across state lines." Black and Goldberg, JJ., filed concurring opinions. All of these opinions also applied to the following case.]

Katzenbach v. McClung
379 U.S. 294 (1964).

This case was argued and decided with Heart of Atlanta Motel v. United States. McClung, as an owner of Ollie's Barbecue restaurant, sued to contest the constitutionality of Title II of the Civil Rights Act of 1964, the relevant sections of which prohibit race discrimination by any "restaurant . . . principally engaged in selling food for consumption on the premises," if "it serves or offers to serve interstate travelers or a substantial portion of the food which it serves . . . has moved in commerce." A three-judge court enjoined Attorney General Katzenbach from enforcing the Act against the restaurant and an appeal was taken. The Supreme Court reversed, upholding the Act in the context of Ollie's Barbeque, "a family-owned restaurant in Birmingham, Alabama, specializing in barbecued meats and homemade pies, with a seating capacity of 220" patrons, "located on a state highway 11 blocks from an interstate one and a somewhat greater distance from railroad and bus stations."

The Court's opinion upholding the Act, authored by Justice Clark, identified the "sole question" as being "whether Title II, as applied to a restaurant receiving about $70,000 worth of food which has moved in commerce, is a valid exercise of the power of Congress." The Court said yes, finding that Congressional "testimony afforded ample basis for the conclusion that established restaurants in such areas sold less interstate goods because of the discrimination, that interstate travel was obstructed directly by it, that business in general suffered and that many new businesses refrained from establishing there as a result of it." The Court echoed and cited Wickard v. Filburn, 317 U.S. 111 (1942), for the proposition that what was significant was not "the volume of food purchased by Ollie's Barbecue from sources supplied from out of state" viewed in isolation, but rather the aggregated effect on commerce resulting from discrimination among all similarly situated restaurants. Responding to the restaurant's arguments of federal overreaching, the Court asserted: "Much is said about a restaurant business being local but 'even if appellee's activity be local and though it may not be regarded as commerce, it may still, whatever its nature, be reached by Congress if it exerts a substantial economic effect on interstate commerce. . .'"

Justices Black, Douglas and Golberg concurred.

The "New" Federalism

Beginning in the late 1980s/early 1990s, the Supreme Court has revisited, and to some extent revised, its thinking on the four sets of questions discussed at the beginning of this chapter, supra pp. 80–81. The Court has redefined the scope of federal powers and state immunities in a number of decisions: cases involving Congress' power to regulate the private sector under the Commerce Clause (discussed in this chapter below); cases involving Congress' power to regulate state entities in order to implement federal legislative goals (discussed in Chapter 5); cases addressing the question when states can be subject to suit by private citizens in federal court (also discussed in Chapter 5 and Chapter 12); and cases involving the limits on Congress' authority to regulate private and public sectors under Section 5 of the Fourteenth Amendment (discussed in Chapter 12). While each of these groups of cases is complex and distinct, they are all also related. As you read the recently-decided decisions in the balance of this chapter, as well as those presented in Chapters 5, 6 and 12, consider what the animating spirit or theory of the Court's current attitude toward the division of power between the federal and state governments appears to be. Are decisions to rule in favor of state power grounded primarily in the benefits of state public policy experimentation and diversity? Are states worthy of protection from federal overreaching so that they can act as counterbalances to the federal government, and if so, why are counterbalances needed and precisely how can states perform this function? Are states simply entitled to respect as a matter of constitutional etiquette? Consider also how the particular doctrinal devices the Court has employed in each of these lines of cases—the requirements and limits various cases have imposed on the federal government—correlate with any particular explanation for why federalism remains a vital idea. Finally, consider what other kinds of cases the Court might address in the intermediate future if the "new" federalism is to be meaningful.

The recent federalism decisions have given rise to a host of scholarly works. For additional background discussion and analysis, students may want to consult Todd Pettys, *Competing for the People's Affection: Federalism's Forgotten Marketplace*, 56 Vand. L.Rev. 329 (2003); Vikram Amar, *The New 'new Federalism,'* 6 Green Bag 2d 349 (2003); Vikram Amar and Samuel Estreicher, *Conduct Unbecoming a Coordinate Branch*, 4 Green Bag 2d 351 (2001); Akhil Amar, *Of Sovereignty and Federalism*, 96 Yale L.J. 1425 (1987).

United States v. Morrison

529 U.S. 598, 120 S.Ct. 1740, 146 L.Ed.2d 658 (2000).

■ CHIEF JUSTICE REHNQUIST delivered the opinion of the Court.

. . . 42 U.S.C. § 13981 . . . provides a federal civil remedy for the victims of gender-motivated violence. The . . . Fourth Circuit, sitting en banc, struck down § 13981 because it concluded that Congress lacked constitutional authority to enact the section's civil remedy. . . . [W]e affirm.

I

[Petitioner Christy Brzonkala alleged that shortly after she enrolled at Virginia Tech in 1994 two members of the varsity football team, Morrison and Crawford, assaulted and repeatedly raped her, and that both then and later Morrison made shockingly vulgar remarks about women. She left the university and brought an action alleging that their attack violated § 13981.]

The District Court . . . held that Brzonkala's complaint stated a claim against Morrison and Crawford under § 13981, but . . . that Congress lacked authority to enact the section under either the Commerce Clause or § 5 of the Fourteenth Amendment. . . .

[The en banc Court of Appeals affirmed both] the District Court's conclusion that Brzonkala stated a claim under § 13981 . . . [and,] by a divided vote . . . that Congress lacked constitutional authority to enact § 13981's civil remedy. . . .

Section 13981 was part of the Violence Against Women Act of 1994 . . . It states that "[a]ll persons within the United States shall have the right to be free from crimes of violence motivated by gender." 42 U.S.C. § 13981(b). To enforce that right, subsection (c) declares:

"A person (including a person who acts under color of any statute, ordinance, regulation, custom, or usage of any State) who commits a crime of violence motivated by gender and thus deprives another of the right declared in subsection (b) of this section shall be liable to the party injured, in an action for the recovery of compensatory and punitive damages, injunctive and declaratory relief, and such other relief as a court may deem appropriate."

. . .

. . . Congress explicitly identified the sources of federal authority on which it relied in enacting § 13981. It said that a "federal civil rights cause of action" is established "[p]ursuant to the affirmative power of Congress . . . under section 5 of the Fourteenth Amendment to the Constitution,[a] as well as under section 8 of Article I of the Constitution." 42 U.S.C. § 13981(a). . . .

II

Due respect for the decisions of a coordinate branch of Government demands that we invalidate a congressional enactment only upon a plain showing that Congress has exceeded its constitutional bounds. See United States v. Lopez, 514 U.S., at 568, 577–578 (Kennedy, J., concurring). . . .

As we discussed at length in *Lopez*, our interpretation of the Commerce Clause has changed as our Nation has developed. . . . We need not repeat that detailed review of the Commerce Clause's history here; it suffices to say that, in the years since NLRB v. Jones & Laughlin Steel Corp., 301 U.S. 1 (1937), Congress has had considerably greater latitude in regulating conduct and transactions under the Commerce Clause than our previous case law permitted. . . .

Lopez emphasized, however, that even under our modern, expansive interpretation of the Commerce Clause, Congress' regulatory authority is not without effective bounds. Id., at 557.

"[E]ven [our] modern-era precedents which have expanded congressional power under the Commerce Clause confirm that this power is subject to outer limits. *In Jones & Laughlin Steel*, the Court warned that the scope of the interstate commerce power

---

[a]　That portion of the opinion concluding that § 13981 was invalid under § 5 of the fourteenth amendment appears infra, page 820.

'must be considered in the light of our dual system of government and may not be extended so as to embrace effects upon interstate commerce so indirect and remote that to embrace them, in view of our complex society, would effectually obliterate the distinction between what is national and what is local and create a completely centralized government.'" Id., at 556–557 (quoting *Jones & Laughlin Steel, supra,* at 37).

As we observed in *Lopez,* modern Commerce Clause jurisprudence has "identified three broad categories of activity that Congress may regulate under its commerce power." 514 U.S., at 558. . . ."First, Congress may regulate the use of the channels of interstate commerce." 514 U.S., at 558 (citing Heart of Atlanta Motel, Inc. v. United States, 379 U.S. 241, 256 (1964)); United States v. Darby, 312 U.S. 100, 114 (1941)). "Second, Congress is empowered to regulate and protect the instrumentalities of interstate commerce, or persons or things in interstate commerce, even though the threat may come only from intrastate activities." 514 U.S., at 558 (citing Shreveport Rate Cases, 234 U.S. 342 (1914)); Southern R. Co. v. United States, 222 U.S. 20 (1911). . . ." Finally, Congress' commerce authority includes the power to regulate those activities having a substantial relation to interstate commerce, . . . i.e., those activities that substantially affect interstate commerce." 514 U.S., at 558–559 (citing *Jones & Laughlin Steel, supra,* at 37).

Petitioners do not contend that these cases fall within either of the first two of these categories of Commerce Clause regulation. They seek to sustain § 13981 as a regulation of activity that substantially affects interstate commerce. Given § 13981's focus on gender-motivated violence wherever it occurs (rather than violence directed at the instrumentalities of interstate commerce, interstate markets, or things or persons in interstate commerce), we agree that this is the proper inquiry.

Since *Lopez* most recently canvassed and clarified our case law governing this third category of Commerce Clause regulation, it provides the proper framework for conducting the required analysis of § 13981. In *Lopez,* we held that the Gun-Free School Zones Act of 1990, 18 U.S.C. § 922(q)(1)(A), which made it a federal crime to knowingly possess a firearm in a school zone, exceeded Congress' authority under the Commerce Clause. . . . Several significant considerations contributed to our decision.

First, we observed that § 922(q) was "a criminal statute that by its terms has nothing to do with 'commerce' or any sort of economic enterprise, however broadly one might define those terms." . . . Reviewing our case law, we noted that "we have upheld a wide variety of congressional Acts regulating intrastate economic activity where we have concluded that the activity substantially affected interstate commerce." . . . Although we cited only a few examples, including Wickard v. Filburn, 317 U.S. 111 (1942); Hodel, supra; Perez, supra; Katzenbach v. McClung, 379 U.S. 294 (1964); and Heart of Atlanta Motel, supra, we stated that the pattern of analysis is clear. . . ."Where economic activity substantially affects interstate commerce, legislation regulating that activity will be sustained." . . .

Both petitioners and Justice Souter's dissent downplay the role that the economic nature of the regulated activity plays in our Commerce Clause analysis. But a fair reading of *Lopez* shows that the noneconomic, criminal nature of the conduct at issue was central to our decision in that case. See, e.g., id., at 551 ("The Act [does not] regulat[e] a commercial activity"), 560 ("Even *Wickard,* which is perhaps the most far reaching example of Commerce Clause authority over intrastate activity, involved economic activity in a way that the possession of a gun in a school zone does not"). . . . *Lopez*'s review of Commerce Clause case law demonstrates that in those cases where we have sustained federal regulation of intrastate activity based upon the activity's substantial effects on interstate commerce, the activity in question has been some sort of economic endeavor. . . .[4]

[S]econd[,] . . . the statute contained "no express jurisdictional element which might limit its reach to a discrete set of firearm possessions that additionally have an explicit connection with or effect on interstate commerce." Id., at 562. Such a jurisdictional element may establish that the enactment is in pursuance of Congress' regulation of interstate commerce.

Third, we noted that neither § 922(q) " 'nor its legislative history contain[s] express congressional findings regarding the effects upon interstate commerce of gun possession in a school zone.' ". . . While "Congress normally is not required to make formal findings as to the substantial burdens that an activity has on interstate commerce," 514 U.S., at 562 . . . the existence of such findings may "enable us to evaluate the legislative judgment that the activity in question substantially affect[s] interstate commerce, even though no such substantial effect [is] visible to the naked eye." . . .

Finally, our decision in *Lopez* rested in part on the fact that the link between gun possession and a substantial effect on interstate commerce was attenuated. . . . The United States argued that the possession of guns may lead to violent crime, and that violent crime "can be expected to affect the functioning of the national economy in two ways. First, the costs of violent crime are substantial, and, through the mechanism of insurance, those costs are spread throughout the population. Second, violent crime reduces the willingness of individuals to travel to areas within the country that are perceived to be unsafe." . . . The Government also argued that the presence of guns at schools poses a threat to the educational process, which in turn threatens to produce a less efficient and productive workforce, which will negatively affect national productivity and thus interstate commerce. . . .

We rejected these "costs of crime" and "national productivity" arguments because they would permit Congress to "regulate not only all violent crime, but all activities that might lead to violent crime, regardless of how tenuously they relate to interstate commerce." . . . We noted that, under this but-for reasoning:

"Congress could regulate any activity that it found was related to the economic productivity of individual citizens: family law (including marriage, divorce, and child custody), for example. Under the[se] theories . . . , it is difficult to perceive any limitation on federal power, even in areas such as criminal law enforcement or education where States historically have been sovereign. Thus, if we were to accept the Government's arguments, we are hard pressed to posit any activity by an individual that Congress is without power to regulate." . . .

With these principles underlying our Commerce Clause jurisprudence as reference points, the proper resolution of the present cases is clear. Gender-motivated crimes of violence are not, in any sense of the phrase, economic activity. While we need not adopt a categorical rule against aggregating the effects of any noneconomic activity in order to decide these cases, thus far in our Nation's history our cases have upheld Commerce Clause regulation of intrastate activity only where that activity is economic in nature. . . .

Like the Gun-Free School Zones Act at issue in *Lopez*, § 13981 contains no jurisdictional element establishing that the federal cause of action is in pursuance of Congress' power to regulate interstate commerce. Although *Lopez* makes clear that

---

[4]   Justice Souter's dissent . . . cannot persuasively contradict *Lopez*'s conclusion that, in every case where we have sustained federal regulation under *Wickard*'s aggregation principle, the regulated activity was of an apparent commercial character. . . .

such a jurisdictional element would lend support to the argument that § 13981 is sufficiently tied to interstate commerce, Congress elected to cast § 13981's remedy over a wider, and more purely intrastate, body of violent crime.[5]

In contrast with the lack of congressional findings that we faced in *Lopez*, § 13981 is supported by numerous findings regarding the serious impact that gender-motivated violence has on victims and their families. . . . But the existence of congressional findings is not sufficient, by itself, to sustain the constitutionality of Commerce Clause legislation. As we stated in *Lopez*, " '[S]imply because Congress may conclude that a particular activity substantially affects interstate commerce does not necessarily make it so.' " . . . Rather, " '[w]hether particular operations affect interstate commerce sufficiently to come under the constitutional power of Congress to regulate them is ultimately a judicial rather than a legislative question, and can be settled finally only by this Court.' " . . .

In these cases, Congress' findings are substantially weakened by the fact that they rely so heavily on a method of reasoning that we have already rejected as unworkable if we are to maintain the Constitution's enumeration of powers. Congress found that gender-motivated violence affects interstate commerce

"by deterring potential victims from traveling interstate, from engaging in employment in interstate business, and from transacting with business, and in places involved in interstate commerce; . . . by diminishing national productivity, increasing medical and other costs, and decreasing the supply of and the demand for interstate products." H.R. Conf. Rep. No. 103–711, at 385, U.S.Code Cong. & Admin.News 1994, pp. 1803, 1853.

Accord, S.Rep. No. 103–138, at 54. Given these findings and petitioners' arguments, the concern that we expressed in *Lopez* that Congress might use the Commerce Clause to completely obliterate the Constitution's distinction between national and local authority seems well founded. . . . The reasoning that petitioners advance seeks to follow the but-for causal chain from the initial occurrence of violent crime (the suppression of which has always been the prime object of the States' police power) to every attenuated effect upon interstate commerce. If accepted, petitioners' reasoning would allow Congress to regulate any crime as long as the nationwide, aggregated impact of that crime has substantial effects on employment, production, transit, or consumption. Indeed, if Congress may regulate gender-motivated violence, it would be able to regulate murder or any other type of violence since gender-motivated violence, as a subset of all violent crime, is certain to have lesser economic impacts than the larger class of which it is a part.

Petitioners' reasoning, moreover, will not limit Congress to regulating violence but may, as we suggested in *Lopez*, be applied equally as well to family law and other

---

[5]   . . . § 13981 is not the sole provision of the Violence Against Women Act of 1994 to provide a federal remedy for gender-motivated crime. Section 40221(a) of the Act creates a federal criminal remedy to punish "interstate crimes of abuse including crimes committed against spouses or intimate partners during interstate travel and crimes committed by spouses or intimate partners who cross State lines to continue the abuse." S.Rep. No. 103–138, p. 43 (1993). That criminal provision has been codified at 18 U.S.C. § 2261(a)(1), which states:

"A person who travels across a State line or enters or leaves Indian country with the intent to injure, harass, or intimidate that person's spouse or intimate partner, and who, in the course of or as a result of such travel, intentionally commits a crime of violence and thereby causes bodily injury to such spouse or intimate partner, shall be punished as provided in subsection (b)."

The Courts of Appeals have uniformly upheld this criminal sanction as an appropriate exercise of Congress' Commerce Clause authority, reasoning that "[t]he provision properly falls within the first of *Lopez*'s categories as it regulates the use of channels of interstate commerce—i.e., the use of the interstate transportation routes through which persons and goods move." United States v. Lankford, 196 F.3d 563, 571–572 (C.A.5 1999) (collecting cases) (internal quotation marks omitted).

areas of traditional state regulation since the aggregate effect of marriage, divorce, and childrearing on the national economy is undoubtedly significant. Congress may have recognized this specter when it expressly precluded § 13981 from being used in the family law context. See 42 U.S.C. § 13981(e)(4). Under our written Constitution, however, the limitation of congressional authority is not solely a matter of legislative grace.[7] . . .

We accordingly reject the argument that Congress may regulate noneconomic, violent criminal conduct based solely on that conduct's aggregate effect on interstate commerce. The Constitution requires a distinction between what is truly national and what is truly local. . . . In recognizing this fact we preserve one of the few principles that has been consistent since the Clause was adopted. The regulation and punishment of intrastate violence that is not directed at the instrumentalities, channels, or goods involved in interstate commerce has always been the province of the States. See, e.g., Cohens v. Virginia, 6 Wheat. 264, 426, 428 (1821) (Marshall, C.J.) (stating that Congress "has no general right to punish murder committed within any of the States," and that it is "clear . . . that congress cannot punish felonies generally"). Indeed, we can think of no better example of the police power, which the Founders denied the National Government and reposed in the States, than the suppression of violent crime and vindication of its victims. . . .

. . .

Affirmed.

■ JUSTICE THOMAS, concurring.

The majority opinion correctly applies our decision in United States v. Lopez, 514 U.S. 549 (1995), and I join it in full. I write separately only to express my view that the very notion of a "substantial effects" test under the Commerce Clause is inconsistent with the original understanding of Congress' powers and with this Court's early Commerce Clause cases. By continuing to apply this rootless and malleable standard, however circumscribed, the Court has encouraged the Federal Government to persist in its view that the Commerce Clause has virtually no limits. Until this Court replaces its existing Commerce Clause jurisprudence with a standard more consistent with the original understanding, we will continue to see Congress appropriating state police powers under the guise of regulating commerce.

■ JUSTICE SOUTER, with whom JUSTICE STEVENS, JUSTICE GINSBURG, and JUSTICE BREYER join, dissenting.

. . .

I

Our cases, which remain at least nominally undisturbed, stand for the following propositions. Congress has the power to legislate with regard to activity that, in the

---

[7]   Justice Souter's dissent theory that Gibbons v. Ogden, 9 Wheat. 1 (1824), Garcia v. San Antonio Metropolitan Transit Authority, 469 U.S. 528 (1985), and the Seventeenth Amendment provide the answer to these cases is remarkable because it undermines this central principle of our constitutional system. As we have repeatedly noted, the Framers crafted the federal system of government so that the people's rights would be secured by the division of power. . . .

No doubt the political branches have a role in interpreting and applying the Constitution, but ever since *Marbury* this Court has remained the ultimate expositor of the constitutional text. . . . Contrary to Justice Souter's suggestion, *Gibbons* did not exempt the commerce power from this cardinal rule of constitutional law. His assertion that, from *Gibbons* on, public opinion has been the only restraint on the congressional exercise of the commerce power is true only insofar as it contends that political accountability is and has been the only limit on Congress' exercise of the commerce power *within that power's outer bounds*. As the language surrounding that relied upon by Justice Souter makes clear, *Gibbons* did not remove from this Court the authority to define that boundary. . . .

aggregate, has a substantial effect on interstate commerce. See Wickard v. Filburn, 317 U.S. 111, 124–128 (1942); Hodel v. Virginia Surface Mining & Reclamation Assn., 452 U.S. 264, 277 (1981). The fact of such a substantial effect is not an issue for the courts in the first instance, ibid., but for the Congress, whose institutional capacity for gathering evidence and taking testimony far exceeds ours. By passing legislation, Congress indicates its conclusion, whether explicitly or not, that facts support its exercise of the commerce power. The business of the courts is to review the congressional assessment, not for soundness but simply for the rationality of concluding that a jurisdictional basis exists in fact. . . . Any explicit findings that Congress chooses to make, though not dispositive of the question of rationality, may advance judicial review by identifying factual authority on which Congress relied. Applying those propositions in these cases can lead to only one conclusion.

One obvious difference from United States v. Lopez, 514 U.S. 549 (1995), is the mountain of data assembled by Congress, here showing the effects of violence against women on interstate commerce. Passage of the Act in 1994 was preceded by four years of hearings, . . . and we have the benefit of specific factual findings in the eight separate Reports issued by Congress and its committees over the long course leading to enactment. . . .

. . . Is its conclusion irrational in view of the data amassed? . . . [T]he sufficiency of the evidence before Congress to provide a rational basis for the finding cannot seriously be questioned. . . .

. . .

While Congress did not, to my knowledge, calculate aggregate dollar values for the nationwide effects of racial discrimination in 1964, in 1994 it did rely on evidence of the harms caused by domestic violence and sexual assault, citing annual costs of $3 billion in 1990, see S. Rep. 101–545, and $5 to $10 billion in 1993, see S.Rep. No. 103–138, at 41. . . .

. . . In *Wickard*, we upheld the application of the Agricultural Adjustment Act to the planting and consumption of homegrown wheat. The effect on interstate commerce in that case followed from the possibility that wheat grown at home for personal consumption could either be drawn into the market by rising prices, or relieve its grower of any need to purchase wheat in the market. . . . The Commerce Clause predicate was simply the effect of the production of wheat for home consumption on supply and demand in interstate commerce. Supply and demand for goods in interstate commerce will also be affected by the deaths of 2,000 to 4,000 women annually at the hands of domestic abusers, see S.Rep. No. 101–545, at 36, and by the reduction in the work force by the 100,000 or more rape victims who lose their jobs each year or are forced to quit, see id., at 56, H.R.Rep. No. 103–395, at 25–26. Violence against women may be found to affect interstate commerce and affect it substantially.[10]

II

The Act would have passed muster at any time between *Wickard* in 1942 and *Lopez* in 1995, a period in which the law enjoyed a stable understanding that congressional power under the Commerce Clause, complemented by the authority of the Necessary and Proper Clause, Art. I. § 8 cl. 18, extended to all activity that, when aggregated, has a substantial effect on interstate commerce. . . .

---

[10] It should go without saying that my view of the limit of the congressional commerce power carries no implication about the wisdom of exercising it to the limit. I and other Members of this Court appearing before Congress have repeatedly argued against the federalization of traditional state crimes and the extension of federal remedies to problems for which the States have historically taken responsibility and may deal with today if they have the will to do so. . . .

. . .

. . . [T]he majority is . . . moving toward [a] new system of congressional deference subject to selective discounts . . . on the basis of characteristics other than their commercial effects. Such exclusions come into sight when the activity regulated is not itself commercial or when the States have traditionally addressed it in the exercise of the general police power. . . .

. . . My disagreement with the majority is not, however, confined to logic, for history has shown that categorical exclusions have proven as unworkable in practice as they are unsupportable in theory.

A

. . .

. . . [The] revival of a distinction between commercial and noncommercial conduct is at odds with *Wickard*, which repudiated that analysis, and the enquiry into commercial purpose, first intimated by the *Lopez* concurrence, see *Lopez*, supra, at 580 (opinion of Kennedy, J.), is cousin to the intent-based analysis employed in *Hammer*, . . . but rejected for Commerce Clause purposes in *Heart of Atlanta* . . . and *Darby*. . . .

Why is the majority tempted to reject the lesson so painfully learned in 1937? . . . It was obvious in *Wickard* that growing wheat for consumption right on the farm was not "commerce" in the common vocabulary,[13] but that did not matter constitutionally so long as the aggregated activity of domestic wheat growing affected commerce substantially. . . .

If we now ask why the formalistic economic/noneconomic distinction might matter today, after its rejection in *Wickard*, the answer is not that the majority fails to see causal connections in an integrated economic world. The answer is that in the minds of the majority there is a new animating theory that makes categorical formalism seem useful again. Just as the old formalism had value in the service of an economic conception, the new one is useful in serving a conception of federalism. It is the instrument by which assertions of national power are to be limited in favor of preserving a supposedly discernible, proper sphere of state autonomy to legislate or refrain from legislating as the individual States see fit. . . .

B

. . . [T]he theory of traditional state concern as grounding a limiting principle has been rejected previously, and more than once. . . .

The objection to reviving traditional state spheres of action as a consideration in commerce analysis . . . is compounded by . . . the majority's rejection of the Founders' considered judgment that politics, not judicial review, should mediate between state and national interests as the strength and legislative jurisdiction of the National Government inevitably increased through the expected growth of the national economy. . . .

---

[13] Contrary to the Court's suggestion, *Wickard* applied the substantial effects test to domestic agricultural production for domestic consumption, an activity that cannot fairly be described as commercial, despite its commercial consequences in affecting or being affected by the demand for agricultural products in the commercial market. The *Wickard* Court admitted that Filburn's activity "may not be regarded as commerce" but insisted that "it may still, whatever its nature, be reached by Congress if it exerts a substantial economic effect on interstate commerce. . . ." 317 U.S., at 125. The characterization of home wheat production as "commerce" or not is, however, ultimately beside the point. For if substantial effects on commerce are proper subjects of concern under the Commerce Clause, what difference should it make whether the causes of those effects are themselves commercial? . . . The Court's answer is that it makes a difference to federalism, and the legitimacy of the Court's new judicially derived federalism is the crux of our disagreement.

... Madison ... took care ... to hedge his argument for limited power by explaining the importance of national politics in protecting the States' interests. The National Government "will partake sufficiently of the spirit [of the States], to be disinclined to invade the rights of the individual States, or the prerogatives of their governments." The Federalist No. 46, at 319. ... In any case, this Court recognized the political component of federalism in the seminal *Gibbons* opinion. ...

Politics as the moderator of the congressional employment of the commerce power was the theme many years later in *Wickard*, for after the Court acknowledged the breadth of the *Gibbons* formulation it invoked Chief Justice Marshall yet again in adding that "[h]e made emphatic the embracing and penetrating nature of this power by warning that effective restraints on its exercise must proceed from political rather than judicial processes." ... Hence, "conflicts of economic interest ... are wisely left under our system to resolution by Congress under its more flexible and responsible legislative process. Such conflicts rarely lend themselves to judicial determination. And with the wisdom, workability, or fairness, of the plan of regulation we have nothing to do." ...

As with "conflicts of economic interest," so with supposed conflicts of sovereign political interests implicated by the Commerce Clause: the Constitution remits them to politics. ... [In Garcia v. San Antonio Metropolitan Transit Authority, 469 U.S. 528, 552, the Court] concluded that

"the Framers chose to rely on a federal system in which special restraints on federal power over the States inhered principally in the workings of the National Government itself, rather than in discrete limitations on the objects of federal authority. State sovereign interests, then, are more properly protected by procedural safeguards inherent in the structure of the federal system than by judicially created limitations on federal power." ...

The *Garcia* Court's rejection of "judicially created limitations" in favor of the intended reliance on national politics was all the more powerful owing to the Court's explicit recognition that in the centuries since the framing the relative powers of the two sovereign systems have markedly changed. Nationwide economic integration is the norm, the national political power has been augmented by its vast revenues, and the power of the States has been drawn down by the Seventeenth Amendment, eliminating selection of senators by state legislatures in favor of direct election.

... The significance for state political power of ending state legislative selection of senators was no secret in 1913, and the amendment was approved despite public comment on that very issue. ...

Amendments that alter the balance of power between the National and State Governments, like the Fourteenth, or that change the way the States are represented within the Federal Government, like the Seventeenth, are not rips in the fabric of the Framers' Constitution, inviting judicial repairs. The Seventeenth Amendment may indeed have lessened the enthusiasm of the Senate to represent the States as discrete sovereignties, but the Amendment did not convert the judiciary into an alternate shield against the commerce power.

C

... Today's majority ... finds no significance whatever in the state support for the Act based upon the States' acknowledged failure to deal adequately with gender-based violence in state courts, and the belief of their own law enforcement agencies that national action is essential.

The National Association of Attorneys General supported the Act unanimously, ... and Attorneys General from 38 States urged Congress to enact the Civil Rights

Remedy, representing that "the current system for dealing with violence against women is inadequate,". . . .

. . .

III

All of this convinces me that today's ebb of the commerce power rests on error, and at the same time leads me to doubt that the majority's view will prove to be enduring law. . . .

■ JUSTICE BREYER, with whom JUSTICE STEVENS joins, and with whom JUSTICE SOUTER and JUSTICE GINSBURG join as to Part I-A, dissenting.

No one denies the importance of the Constitution's federalist principles. . . . The question is how the judiciary can best implement that original federalist understanding where the Commerce Clause is at issue.

I

. . . [T]he majority's holding illustrates the difficulty of finding a workable judicial Commerce Clause touchstone—a set of comprehensible interpretive rules that courts might use to impose some meaningful limit, but not too great a limit, upon the scope of the legislative authority that the Commerce Clause delegates to Congress.

A

Consider the problems. The "economic/noneconomic" distinction is not easy to apply. Does the local street corner mugger engage in "economic" activity or "noneconomic" activity when he mugs for money? See Perez v. United States, 402 U.S. 146 (1971) (aggregating local "loan sharking" instances); United States v. Lopez, 514 U.S. 549, 559 (1995) (loan sharking is economic because it consists of "intrastate extortionate credit transactions"). Would evidence that desire for economic domination underlies many brutal crimes against women save the present statute? . . .

The line becomes yet harder to draw given the need for exceptions. The Court itself would permit Congress to aggregate, hence regulate, "noneconomic" activity taking place at economic establishments. See Heart of Atlanta Motel, Inc. v. United States, 379 U.S. 241 (1964) (upholding civil rights laws forbidding discrimination at local motels); Katzenbach v. McClung, 379 U.S. 294 (1964) (same for restaurants); Lopez, supra, at 559 (recognizing congressional power to aggregate, hence forbid, noneconomically motivated discrimination at public accommodations). And it would permit Congress to regulate where that regulation is "an essential part of a larger regulation of economic activity, in which the regulatory scheme could be undercut unless the intrastate activity were regulated." Lopez, supra, at 561; cf. Controlled Substances Act, 21 U.S.C. § 801 et seq. (regulating drugs produced for home consumption). Given the former exception, can Congress simply rewrite the present law and limit its application to restaurants, hotels, perhaps universities, and other places of public accommodation? Given the latter exception, can Congress save the present law by including it, or much of it, in a broader "Safe Transport" or "Workplace Safety" act?

More important, why should we give critical constitutional importance to the economic, or noneconomic, nature of an interstate-commerce-affecting cause? If chemical emanations through indirect environmental change cause identical, severe commercial harm outside a State, why should it matter whether local factories or home fireplaces release them? The Constitution itself refers only to Congress' power to "regulate Commerce . . . among the several States," and to make laws "necessary and proper" to implement that power. Art. I, § 8, cls. 3, 18. The language says nothing about either the local nature, or the economic nature, of an interstate-commerce-affecting cause.

. . . Nothing in the Constitution's language, or that of earlier cases prior to *Lopez*, explains why the Court should ignore one highly relevant characteristic of an interstate-commerce-affecting cause (how "local" it is), while placing critical constitutional weight upon a different, less obviously relevant, feature (how "economic" it is).

Most important, the Court's complex rules seem unlikely to help secure the very object that they seek, namely, the protection of "areas of traditional state regulation" from federal intrusion. The Court's rules, even if broadly interpreted, are underinclusive. The local pickpocket is no less a traditional subject of state regulation than is the local gender-motivated assault. Regardless, the Court reaffirms, as it should, Congress' well-established and frequently exercised power to enact laws that satisfy a commerce-related jurisdictional prerequisite—for example, that some item relevant to the federally regulated activity has at some time crossed a state line. . . .

And in a world where most everyday products or their component parts cross interstate boundaries, Congress will frequently find it possible to redraft a statute using language that ties the regulation to the interstate movement of some relevant object, thereby regulating local criminal activity or, for that matter, family affairs. . . .

The majority, aware of these difficulties, is nonetheless concerned with what it sees as an important contrary consideration. To determine the lawfulness of statutes simply by asking whether Congress could reasonably have found that aggregated local instances significantly affect interstate commerce will allow Congress to regulate almost anything. Virtually all local activity, when instances are aggregated, can have "substantial effects on employment, production, transit, or consumption." . . .

This consideration, however, while serious, does not reflect a jurisprudential defect, so much as it reflects a practical reality. We live in a Nation knit together by two centuries of scientific, technological, commercial, and environmental change. Those changes, taken together, mean that virtually every kind of activity, no matter how local, genuinely can affect commerce, or its conditions, outside the State—at least when considered in the aggregate. . . . And that fact makes it close to impossible for courts to develop meaningful subject-matter categories that would exclude some kinds of local activities from ordinary Commerce Clause "aggregation" rules without, at the same time, depriving Congress of the power to regulate activities that have a genuine and important effect upon interstate commerce.

Since judges cannot change the world, the "defect" means that, within the bounds of the rational, Congress, not the courts, must remain primarily responsible for striking the appropriate state/federal balance. . . . Moreover, Congress often can better reflect state concerns for autonomy in the details of sophisticated statutory schemes than can the judiciary, which cannot easily gather the relevant facts and which must apply more general legal rules and categories. . . .

. . .

For these reasons, as well as those set forth by Justice Souter, this statute falls well within Congress's Commerce Clause authority, and I dissent from the Court's contrary conclusion.[a]

. . .

---

[a] For earlier commentary on the issues raised by *Lopez*, see the contributions to Symposium, *Reflections on United States v. Lopez,* 94 Michigan Law Review 533–831 (1995).

NOTE ON THE LEVEL OF GENERALITY AT WHICH CHALLENGES TO CONGRESSIONAL POWER ARE FRAMED

In *Morrison* and *Lopez*, the Court evaluated each of the two federal statutes in question on its face—without regard to whether the defendants' particular conduct was the kind that Congress could reach. In Sabri v. United States, 541 U.S. 600 (2004), excerpts of which appear infra p. 163, a defendant indicted under a federal statute that makes it a crime to bribe an official of a state or local governmental entity that receives at least $10,000 in federal funds challenged the statute on its face as beyond Congress' regulatory powers because the statute does not require the government to prove in each case that the bribery involved any of the programs for which federal funds were received. After pointing out that the defendant's alleged acts of bribery did involve federally-funded programs, and after holding that Congress can, under its Spending Clause powers, prohibit bribery of officials who receive federal funding whether or not the bribery involves federally-funded programs, the Court in an opinion by Justice Souter had this to say about facial attacks against Congressional laws challenging Congress' enumerated authority to regulate:

"Although passing on the validity of a law wholesale may be efficient in the abstract, any gain is often offset by losing the lessons taught by the particular, to which common law method normally looks. Facial adjudication carries too much promise of [decisionmaking] on the basis of factually bare-bones records. . . . [It is] obvious that the acts charged against Sabri himself were well within the limits of legitimate congressional concern. . . . [T]he most he could say was that the statute could not be enforced against him, because it could not be enforced against someone else whose behavior would be outside the scope of Congress's Article I authority to legislate. Facial challenges of this sort are especially to be discouraged. . . . We have recognized the validity of facial attacks alleging overbreadth (though not necessarily using that term) in relatively few settings. . . . Outside of these limited settings, and absent a good reason, we do not extend an invitation to bring overbreadth claims."

This discussion prompted Justice Kennedy, with whom Justice Scalia concurred, to write separately to say that the Court's overbreadth observations "do[ ] not specifically question the practice we have followed in cases such as United States v. Lopez . . . and United States v. Morrison . . . , [where] the Court did resolve the basic question whether Congress, in enacting the statutes challenged there, had exceeded its legislative power under the Constitution." A similar facial/as-applied issue arose in the context of a challenge to Congress' power under Section 5 of the Fourteenth Amendment in Tennessee v. Lane, 541 U.S. 509 (2004), which appears infra on p. 864.

Gonzales v. Raich

545 U.S. 1, 125 S.Ct. 2195, 162 L.Ed.2d 1 (2005).

■ JUSTICE STEVENS delivered the opinion of the Court.

California is one of at least nine States that authorize the use of marijuana for medicinal purposes. The question presented in this case is whether the power vested in Congress by Article I, § 8, of the Constitution "[t]o make all Laws which shall be necessary and proper for carrying into Execution" its authority to "regulate Commerce with foreign Nations, and among the several States" includes the power to prohibit the local cultivation and use of marijuana in compliance with California law.

I

... In 1996, California voters passed Proposition 215, now codified as the Compassionate Use Act of 1996. The proposition was designed to ensure that "seriously ill" residents of the State have access to marijuana for medical purposes, and to encourage Federal and State Governments to take steps towards ensuring the safe and affordable distribution of the drug to patients in need. The Act creates an exemption from criminal prosecution for physicians, as well as for patients and primary caregivers who possess or cultivate marijuana for medicinal purposes with the recommendation or approval of a physician. ...

Respondents Angel Raich and Diane Monson are ... being treated by licensed, board-certified family practitioners, who have concluded, after prescribing a host of conventional medicines to treat respondents' conditions and to alleviate their associated symptoms, that marijuana is the only drug available that provides effective treatment. Both women have been using marijuana as a medication for several years pursuant to their doctors' recommendation, and both rely heavily on cannabis to function on a daily basis. ...

Respondent Monson cultivates her own marijuana, and ingests the drug in a variety of ways including smoking and using a vaporizer. Respondent Raich, by contrast, is unable to cultivate her own, and thus relies on two caregivers. ...

On August 15, 2002, county deputy sheriffs and agents from the federal Drug Enforcement Administration (DEA) came to Monson's home. After a thorough investigation, the county officials concluded that her use of marijuana was entirely lawful as a matter of California law. Nevertheless, after a 3-hour standoff, the federal agents seized and destroyed all six of her cannabis plants.

Respondents thereafter brought this action against the Attorney General of the United States and the head of the DEA seeking injunctive and declaratory relief prohibiting the enforcement of the federal Controlled Substances Act (CSA) [21 U.S.C. § 801 *et seq.*] ... to the extent it prevents them from possessing, obtaining, or manufacturing cannabis for their personal medical use. ... Respondents claimed [among other things] that enforcing the CSA against them would violate the Commerce Clause. ...

. . .

[The Ninth Circuit reversed the district court's denial of respondents' motion for a preliminary injunction.] The Court of Appeals distinguished prior Circuit cases upholding the CSA in the face of Commerce Clause challenges by focusing on what it deemed to be the "*separate and distinct class of activities*" at issue in this case: "the intrastate, noncommercial cultivation and possession of cannabis for personal medical purposes as recommended by a patient's physician pursuant to valid California state law." ...

. . .

The obvious importance of the case prompted our grant of certiorari. ... Well-settled law controls our ... [resolution of this case]. The CSA is a valid exercise of federal power, even as applied to the troubling facts of this case. We accordingly vacate the judgment of the Court of Appeals.

II

. . .

... [A]s early as 1906 Congress enacted federal legislation imposing labeling regulations on medications and prohibiting the manufacture or shipment of any adulterated or misbranded drug traveling in interstate commerce. ...

Marijuana itself was not significantly regulated by the Federal Government until 1937 when accounts of marijuana's addictive qualities and physiological effects, paired with dissatisfaction with enforcement efforts at state and local levels, prompted Congress to pass the Marihuana Tax Act . . . [which] did not outlaw the possession or sale of marijuana outright. Rather, it imposed registration and reporting requirements for all individuals importing, producing, selling, or dealing in marijuana, and required the payment of annual taxes in addition to transfer taxes whenever the drug changed hands. . . .

. . . [I]n 1970, after declaration of the national "war on drugs," federal drug policy underwent a significant transformation. . . . [Ultimately, that year] . . . , prompted by a perceived need to consolidate the growing number of piecemeal drug laws and to enhance federal drug enforcement powers, Congress enacted the Comprehensive Drug Abuse Prevention and Control Act.

Title II of that Act, the CSA, repealed most of the earlier antidrug laws in favor of a comprehensive regime to combat the international and interstate traffic in illicit drugs. The main objectives of the CSA were to conquer drug abuse and to control the legitimate and illegitimate traffic in controlled substances.[20] Congress was particularly concerned with the need to prevent the diversion of drugs from legitimate to illicit channels.

To effectuate these goals, Congress devised a closed regulatory system making it unlawful to manufacture, distribute, dispense, or possess any controlled substance except in a manner authorized by the CSA. 21 U.S.C. §§ 841(a)(1), 844(a). The CSA categorizes all controlled substances into five schedules. § 812. The drugs are grouped together based on their accepted medical uses, the potential for abuse, and their psychological and physical effects on the body. . . . Each schedule is associated with a distinct set of controls regarding the manufacture, distribution, and use of the substances listed therein. . . . The CSA and its implementing regulations set forth strict requirements regarding registration, labeling and packaging, production quotas, drug security, and recordkeeping. . . .

---

[20] In particular, Congress made the following findings:

"(1) Many of the drugs included within this subchapter have a useful and legitimate medical purpose and are necessary to maintain the health and general welfare of the American people.

"(2) The illegal importation, manufacture, distribution, and possession and improper use of controlled substances have a substantial and detrimental effect on the health and general welfare of the American people.

"(3) A major portion of the traffic in controlled substances flows through interstate and foreign commerce. Incidents of the traffic which are not an integral part of the interstate or foreign flow, such as manufacture, local distribution, and possession, nonetheless have a substantial and direct effect upon interstate commerce because—

"(A) after manufacture, many controlled substances are transported in interstate commerce,

"(B) controlled substances distributed locally usually have been transported in interstate commerce immediately before their distribution, and

"(C) controlled substances possessed commonly flow through interstate commerce immediately prior to such possession.

"(4) Local distribution and possession of controlled substances contribute to swelling the interstate traffic in such substances.

"(5) Controlled substances manufactured and distributed intrastate cannot be differentiated from controlled substances manufactured and distributed interstate. Thus, it is not feasible to distinguish, in terms of controls, between controlled substances manufactured and distributed interstate and controlled substances manufactured and distributed intrastate.

"(6) Federal control of the intrastate incidents of the traffic in controlled substances is essential to the effective control of the interstate incidents of such traffic." 21 U.S.C. §§ 801(1)–(6).

In enacting the CSA, Congress classified marijuana as a Schedule I drug. 21 U.S.C. § 812(c). . . . Schedule I drugs are categorized as such because of their high potential for abuse, lack of any accepted medical use, and absence of any accepted safety for use in medically supervised treatment. § 812(b)(1). . . . By classifying marijuana as a Schedule I drug, as opposed to listing it on a lesser schedule, the manufacture, distribution, or possession of marijuana became a criminal offense, with the sole exception being use of the drug as part of a Food and Drug Administration pre-approved research study. §§ 823(f), 841(a)(1), 844(a); see also United States v. Oakland Cannabis Buyers' Cooperative, 532 U.S. 483, 490 (2001).

. . . Despite considerable efforts to reschedule marijuana, it remains a Schedule I drug.

III

Respondents . . . do not dispute that passage of the CSA, as part of the Comprehensive Drug Abuse Prevention and Control Act, was well within Congress' commerce power. . . . Nor do they contend that any provision or section of the CSA amounts to an unconstitutional exercise of congressional authority. Rather, respondents' challenge is actually quite limited; they argue that the CSA's categorical prohibition of the manufacture and possession of marijuana as applied to the intrastate manufacture and possession of marijuana for medical purposes pursuant to California law exceeds Congress' authority under the Commerce Clause.

In assessing the validity of congressional regulation, none of our Commerce Clause cases can be viewed in isolation. As charted in considerable detail in United States v. Lopez [514 U.S. 549 (1995)], our understanding of the reach of the Commerce Clause, as well as Congress' assertion of authority thereunder, has evolved over time. . . .

. . .

Our case law firmly establishes Congress' power to regulate purely local activities that are part of an economic "class of activities" that have a substantial effect on interstate commerce. . . . As we stated in [Wickard v. Filburn, 317 U.S. 111, 125], "even if appellee's activity be local and though it may not be regarded as commerce, it may still, whatever its nature, be reached by Congress if it exerts a substantial economic effect on interstate commerce." . . . We have never required Congress to legislate with scientific exactitude. When Congress decides that the " 'total incidence' " of a practice poses a threat to a national market, it may regulate the entire class. . . . In this vein, we have reiterated that when " 'a general regulatory statute bears a substantial relation to commerce, the *de minimis* character of individual instances arising under that statute is of no consequence.' " . . .

Our decision in *Wickard* . . . is of particular relevance. In *Wickard*, we upheld the application of regulations promulgated under the Agricultural Adjustment Act [AAA] of 1938 . . . which were designed to control the volume of wheat moving in interstate and foreign commerce in order to avoid surpluses and consequent abnormally low prices. The regulations established an allotment of 11.1 acres for Filburn's 1941 wheat crop, but he sowed 23 acres, intending to use the excess by consuming it on his own farm. Filburn argued that even though we had sustained Congress' power to regulate the production of goods for commerce, that power did not authorize "federal regulation [of] production not intended in any part for commerce but wholly for consumption on the farm." *Wickard*, 317 U.S. at 188. Justice Jackson's opinion for a unanimous Court rejected this submission. He wrote:

"The effect of the statute before us is to restrict the amount which may be produced for market and the extent as well to which one may forestall resort to the market by producing to meet his own needs. That appellee's own contribution to the demand for wheat may be trivial by itself is not enough to remove him from the scope of federal regulation where, as here, his contribution, taken together with that of many others similarly situated, is far from trivial." *Id.*, at 127–128.

Wickard thus establishes that Congress can regulate purely intrastate activity that is not itself "commercial," in that it is not produced for sale, if it concludes that failure to regulate that class of activity would undercut the regulation of the interstate market in that commodity.

The similarities between this case and *Wickard* are striking. Like the farmer in *Wickard*, respondents are cultivating, for home consumption, a fungible commodity for which there is an established, albeit illegal, interstate market. Just as the Agricultural Adjustment Act was designed "to control the volume [of wheat] moving in interstate and foreign commerce in order to avoid surpluses . . . " and consequently control the market price . . . a primary purpose of the CSA is to control the supply and demand of controlled substances in both lawful and unlawful drug markets. See [n. 20] *supra*. In *Wickard*, we had no difficulty concluding that Congress had a rational basis for believing that, when viewed in the aggregate, leaving home-consumed wheat outside the regulatory scheme would have a substantial influence on price and market conditions. Here too, Congress had a rational basis for concluding that leaving home-consumed marijuana outside federal control would similarly affect price and market conditions.

More concretely, one concern prompting inclusion of wheat grown for home consumption in the 1938 Act was that rising market prices could draw such wheat into the interstate market, resulting in lower market prices. . . . The parallel concern making it appropriate to include marijuana grown for home consumption in the CSA is the likelihood that the high demand in the interstate market will draw such marijuana into that market. . . . In both cases, the regulation is squarely within Congress' commerce power because production of the commodity meant for home consumption, be it wheat or marijuana, has a substantial effect on supply and demand in the national market for that commodity.[29]

Nonetheless, respondents suggest that *Wickard* differs from this case in three respects: (1) the Agricultural Adjustment Act, unlike the CSA, exempted small farming operations; (2) *Wickard* involved a "quintessential economic activity"—a commercial farm—whereas respondents do not sell marijuana; and (3) the *Wickard* record made it clear that the aggregate production of wheat for use on farms had a significant impact on market prices. Those differences, though factually accurate, do not diminish the precedential force of this Court's reasoning.

The fact that . . . [Filburn's] own impact on the market was "trivial by itself" was not a sufficient reason for removing him from the scope of federal regulation. . . . That the Secretary of Agriculture elected to exempt even smaller farms from regulation does not speak to his power to regulate all those whose aggregated production was significant, nor did that fact play any role in the Court's analysis. Moreover, even though . . . [Filburn] was indeed a commercial farmer, the activity he was engaged in—the cultivation of wheat for home consumption—was not treated by the Court as part of his commercial farming operation. And while it is true that the record in the *Wickard* case itself established the causal connection between the production for local use and the national market, we have before us findings by Congress to the same effect.

---

[29] To be sure, the wheat market is a lawful market that Congress sought to protect and stabilize, whereas the marijuana market is a unlawful market that Congress sought to eradicate. This difference, however, is of no constitutional import. It has long been settled that Congress' power to regulate commerce includes the power to prohibit commerce in a particular commodity. . . .

Findings in the introductory sections of the CSA explain why Congress deemed it appropriate to encompass local activities within the scope of the CSA. See n. 20, *supra*. . . . Respondents nonetheless insist that the CSA cannot be constitutionally applied to their activities because Congress did not make a specific finding that the intrastate cultivation and possession of marijuana for medical purposes based on the recommendation of a physician would substantially affect the larger interstate marijuana market. Be that as it may, we have never required Congress to make particularized findings in order to legislate, see *Lopez*, 514 U.S. at 562, Perez [v. United States], 402 U.S. at 156, absent a special concern such as the protection of free speech. . . . While congressional findings are certainly helpful in reviewing the substance of a congressional statutory scheme, particularly when the connection to commerce is not self-evident, and while we will consider congressional findings in our analysis when they are available, the absence of particularized findings does not call into question Congress' authority to legislate.

In assessing the scope of Congress' authority under the Commerce Clause, we stress that the task before us is a modest one. We need not determine whether respondents' activities, taken in the aggregate, substantially affect interstate commerce in fact, but only whether a "rational basis" exists for so concluding. *Lopez*, 514 U.S. at 557. . . . Given the enforcement difficulties that attend distinguishing between marijuana cultivated locally and marijuana grown elsewhere . . . and concerns about diversion into illicit channels, . . . we have no difficulty concluding that Congress had a rational basis for believing that failure to regulate the intrastate manufacture and possession of marijuana would leave a gaping hole in the CSA. Thus, as in *Wickard*, when it enacted comprehensive legislation to regulate the interstate market in a fungible commodity, Congress was acting well within its authority to "make all Laws which shall be necessary and proper" to "regulate Commerce . . . among the several States." U.S. Const., Art. I, § 8. That the regulation ensnares some purely intrastate activity is of no moment. As we have done many times before, we refuse to excise individual components of that larger scheme.

IV

To support their contrary submission, respondents rely heavily on two of our more recent Commerce Clause cases. In their myopic focus, they overlook the larger context of modern-era Commerce Clause jurisprudence preserved by those cases. Moreover, even in the narrow prism of respondents' creation, they read those cases far too broadly.

Those two cases, of course, are *Lopez* . . . and [United States v. Morrison, 529 U.S 598 (2000)]. As an initial matter, the statutory challenges at issue in those cases were markedly different from the challenge respondents pursue in the case at hand. Here, respondents ask us to excise individual applications of a concededly valid statutory scheme. In contrast, in both *Lopez* and *Morrison*, the parties asserted that a particular statute or provision fell outside Congress' commerce power in its entirety. This distinction is pivotal for we have often reiterated that "[w]here the class of activities is regulated and that class is within the reach of federal power, the courts have no power 'to excise, as trivial, individual instances' of the class." . . .

At issue in *Lopez* . . . was the validity of the Gun-Free School Zones Act of 1990, which was a brief, single-subject statute making it a crime for an individual to possess a gun in a school zone. . . . Distinguishing our earlier cases holding that comprehensive regulatory statutes may be validly applied to local conduct that does not, when viewed in isolation, have a significant impact on interstate commerce, we held the statute invalid. We explained:

"Section 922(q) [, the Act,] is a criminal statute that by its terms has nothing to do with 'commerce' or any sort of economic enterprise, however broadly one might define those terms. Section 922(q) is not an essential part of a larger regulation of economic activity, in which the regulatory scheme could be undercut unless the intrastate activity were regulated. It cannot, therefore, be sustained under our cases upholding regulations of activities that arise out of or are connected with a commercial transaction, which viewed in the aggregate, substantially affects interstate commerce." 514 U.S. at 561.

The statutory scheme [here] is at the opposite end of the regulatory spectrum. [T]he CSA . . . was a lengthy and detailed statute creating a comprehensive framework for regulating the production, distribution, and possession of five classes of "controlled substances." . . .

. . . [The] classification [of marijuana as a Schedule I substance], unlike the discrete prohibition established by the Gun-Free School Zones Act of 1990, was merely one of many "essential part[s] of a larger regulation of economic activity, in which the regulatory scheme could be undercut unless the intrastate activity were regulated." *Lopez*, 514 U.S. at 561.[34] Our opinion in *Lopez* casts no doubt on the validity of such a program.

Nor does this Court's holding in *Morrison*. . . . The Violence Against Women Act of 1994 . . . created a federal civil remedy for the victims of gender-motivated crimes of violence. . . . The remedy was enforceable in both state and federal courts, and generally depended on proof of the violation of a state law. Despite congressional findings that such crimes had an adverse impact on interstate commerce, we held the statute unconstitutional because, like the statute in *Lopez*, it did not regulate economic activity. We concluded that "the noneconomic, criminal nature of the conduct at issue was central to our decision" in *Lopez*, and that our prior cases had identified a clear pattern of analysis: " 'Where economic activity substantially affects interstate commerce, legislation regulating that activity will be sustained. ' ". . .

Unlike those at issue in *Lopez* and *Morrison*, the activities regulated by the CSA are quintessentially economic. "Economics" refers to "the production, distribution, and consumption of commodities." Webster's Third New International Dictionary 720 (1966). The CSA is a statute that regulates the production, distribution, and consumption of commodities for which there is an established, and lucrative, interstate market. Prohibiting the intrastate possession or manufacture of an article of commerce is a rational (and commonly utilized) means of regulating commerce in that product. . . .

. . .

. . . [I]f, as the principal dissent contends, the personal cultivation, possession, and use of marijuana for medicinal purposes is beyond the " 'outer limits' of Congress' Commerce Clause authority," . . . it must also be true that such personal use of marijuana (or any other homegrown drug) for recreational purposes is also beyond those " 'outer limits,' " whether or not a State elects to authorize or even regulate such use. . . . One need not have a degree in economics to understand why a nationwide exemption for the vast quantity of marijuana (or other drugs) locally cultivated for personal use (which presumably would include use by friends, neighbors, and family

---

34 The principal dissent asserts that by "[s]eizing upon our language in *Lopez*", i.e., giving effect to our well-established case law, Congress will now have an incentive to legislate broadly. Even putting aside the political checks that would generally curb Congress' power to enact a broad and comprehensive scheme for the purpose of targeting purely local activity, there is no suggestion that the CSA constitutes the type of "evasive" legislation the dissent fears, nor could such an argument plausibly be made. . . .

members) may have a substantial impact on the interstate market for this extraordinarily popular substance. . . .

Second, limiting the activity to marijuana possession and cultivation "in accordance with state law" cannot serve to place respondents' activities beyond congressional reach. The Supremacy Clause unambiguously provides that if there is any conflict between federal and state law, federal law shall prevail. . . .

. . .

V

. . . The case is remanded for further proceedings consistent with this opinion. . . .

■ JUSTICE SCALIA, concurring in the judgment.

I agree with the Court's holding that the Controlled Substances Act (CSA) may validly be applied to respondents' cultivation, distribution, and possession of marijuana for personal, medicinal use. I write separately because my understanding of the doctrinal foundation on which that holding rests is, if not inconsistent with that of the Court, at least more nuanced.

. . .

I

. . .

As we implicitly acknowledged in *Lopez* . . . , Congress's authority to enact laws necessary and proper for the regulation of interstate commerce is not limited to laws directed against economic activities that have a substantial effect on interstate commerce. Though the conduct in *Lopez* was not economic, the Court nevertheless recognized that it could be regulated as "an essential part of a larger regulation of economic activity, in which the regulatory scheme could be undercut unless the intrastate activity were regulated." . . . This statement referred to those cases permitting the regulation of intrastate activities "which in a substantial way interfere with or obstruct the exercise of the granted power." . . .

. . . The regulation of an intrastate activity may be essential to a comprehensive regulation of interstate commerce even though the intrastate activity does not itself "substantially affect" interstate commerce. Moreover, as the passage from *Lopez* quoted above suggests, Congress may regulate even noneconomic local activity if that regulation is a necessary part of a more general regulation of interstate commerce. . . . The relevant question is simply whether the means chosen are "reasonably adapted" to the attainment of a legitimate end under the commerce power. . . .

. . .

III

The application of these principles to the case before us is straightforward. In the CSA, Congress has undertaken to extinguish the interstate market in Schedule I controlled substances, including marijuana. The Commerce Clause unquestionably permits this. The power to regulate interstate commerce "extends not only to those regulations which aid, foster and protect the commerce, but embraces those which prohibit it." . . . To effectuate its objective, Congress has prohibited almost all intrastate activities related to Schedule I substances—both economic activities (manufacture, distribution, possession with the intent to distribute) and noneconomic activities (simple possession). . . . That simple possession is a noneconomic activity is immaterial to whether it can be prohibited as a necessary part of a larger regulation. . . .

. . . Not only is it impossible to distinguish "controlled substances manufactured and distributed intrastate" from "controlled substances manufactured and distributed interstate," but it hardly makes sense to speak in such terms. Drugs like marijuana are fungible commodities. As the Court explains, marijuana that is grown at home and possessed for personal use is never more than an instant from the interstate market—and this is so whether or not the possession is for medicinal use or lawful use under the laws of a particular State.[3] . . . Congress need not accept on faith that state law will be effective in maintaining a strict division between a lawful market for "medical" marijuana and the more general marijuana market. . . ."To impose on [Congress] the necessity of resorting to means which it cannot control, which another government may furnish or withhold, would render its course precarious, the result of its measures uncertain, and create a dependence on other governments, which might disappoint its most important designs, and is incompatible with the language of the constitution." *McCulloch*. . . .

. . .

■ JUSTICE O'CONNOR, with whom THE CHIEF JUSTICE and JUSTICE THOMAS join as to all but Part III, dissenting.

. . .

This case exemplifies the role of States as laboratories. The States' core police powers have always included authority to define criminal law and to protect the health, safety, and welfare of their citizens. . . . Today the Court sanctions an application of the federal Controlled Substances Act that extinguishes . . . [California's] experiment, without any proof that the personal cultivation, possession, and use of marijuana for medicinal purposes, if economic activity in the first place, has a substantial effect on interstate commerce and is therefore an appropriate subject of federal regulation. In so doing, the Court announces a rule that gives Congress a perverse incentive to legislate broadly pursuant to the Commerce Clause—nestling questionable assertions of its authority into comprehensive regulatory schemes—rather than with precision. That rule and the result it produces in this case are irreconcilable with our decisions in [*Lopez* and *Morrison*]. Accordingly I dissent.

. . .

II

A

What is the relevant conduct subject to Commerce Clause analysis in this case? The Court takes its cues from Congress. . . . The Court's decision rests on two facts about the CSA: (1) Congress chose to enact a single statute providing a comprehensive prohibition on the production, distribution, and possession of all controlled substances, and (2) Congress did not distinguish between various forms of intrastate noncommercial cultivation, possession, and use of marijuana. . . . Today's decision suggests that the federal regulation of local activity is immune to Commerce Clause

---

[3]   The principal dissent claims that, if this is sufficient to sustain the regulation at issue in this case, then it should also have been sufficient to sustain the regulation at issue in [*Lopez*]. . . . This claim founders upon the shoals of *Lopez* itself, which made clear that the statute there at issue was "not an essential part of a larger regulation of economic activity." . . . On the dissent's view of things, that statement is inexplicable. Of course it is in addition difficult to imagine what intelligible scheme of regulation of the interstate market in guns could have as an appropriate means of effectuation the prohibition of guns within 1000 feet of schools (and nowhere else). The dissent [mentions] a federal law . . . barring licensed dealers from selling guns to minors, . . . but the relationship between the regulatory scheme of which [that statute] is a part (requiring all dealers in firearms that have traveled in interstate commerce to be licensed . . .) and the statute at issue in *Lopez* approaches the nonexistent—which is doubtless why the Government did not attempt to justify the statute on the basis of that relationship.

challenge because Congress chose to act with an ambitious, all-encompassing statute, rather than piecemeal. In my view, allowing Congress to set the terms of the constitutional debate in this way, i.e., by packaging regulation of local activity in broader schemes, is tantamount to removing meaningful limits on the Commerce Clause.

The Court's principal means of distinguishing *Lopez* from this case is to observe that the Gun-Free School Zones Act of 1990 was a "brief, single-subject statute," . . . whereas the CSA is "a lengthy and detailed statute creating a comprehensive framework for regulating the production, distribution, and possession of five classes of 'controlled substances,' ". . . . Thus, according to the Court, it was possible in *Lopez* to evaluate in isolation the constitutionality of criminalizing local activity (there gun possession in school zones), whereas the local activity that the CSA targets (in this case cultivation and possession of marijuana for personal medicinal use) cannot be separated from the general drug control scheme of which it is a part.

Today's decision allows Congress to regulate intrastate activity without check, so long as there is some implication by legislative design that regulating intrastate activity is essential (and the Court appears to equate "essential" with "necessary") to the interstate regulatory scheme. Seizing upon our language in *Lopez* that the statute prohibiting gun possession in school zones was "not an essential part of a larger regulation of economic activity, in which the regulatory scheme could be undercut unless the intrastate activity were regulated," . . . the Court appears to reason that the placement of local activity in a comprehensive scheme confirms that it is essential to that scheme. . . . If the Court is right, then *Lopez* stands for nothing more than a drafting guide: Congress should have described the relevant crime as "transfer or possession of a firearm anywhere in the nation"—thus including commercial and noncommercial activity, and clearly encompassing some activity with assuredly substantial effect on interstate commerce. Had it done so, the majority hints, we would have sustained its authority to regulate possession of firearms in school zones. . . .

    . . .

The hard work for courts . . . is to identify objective markers for confining the analysis in Commerce Clause cases. Here, respondents challenge the constitutionality of the CSA as applied to them and those similarly situated. I agree with the Court that we must look beyond respondents' own activities. Otherwise, individual litigants could always exempt themselves from Commerce Clause regulation merely by pointing to the obvious—that their personal activities do not have a substantial effect on interstate commerce. . . . The task is to identify a mode of analysis that allows Congress to regulate more than nothing (by declining to reduce each case to its litigants) and less than everything (by declining to let Congress set the terms of analysis). The analysis may not be the same in every case, for it depends on the regulatory scheme at issue and the federalism concerns implicated. . . .

A number of objective markers are available to confine the scope of constitutional review here. Both federal and state legislation—including the CSA itself, the California Compassionate Use Act, and other state medical marijuana legislation—recognize that medical and nonmedical (i.e., recreational) uses of drugs are realistically distinct and can be segregated, and regulate them differently. . . . Moreover, because fundamental structural concerns about dual sovereignty animate our Commerce Clause cases, it is relevant that this case involves the interplay of federal and state regulation in areas of criminal law and social policy, where "States lay claim by right of history and expertise." . . . California, like other States, has drawn on its reserved powers to distinguish the regulation of medicinal marijuana. To ascertain whether Congress' encroachment is constitutionally justified in this case, then, I would focus here on the personal cultivation, possession, and use of marijuana for medicinal purposes.

B

Having thus defined the relevant conduct, we must determine whether, under our precedents, the conduct is economic and, in the aggregate, substantially affects interstate commerce. Even if intrastate cultivation and possession of marijuana for one's own medicinal use can properly be characterized as economic, and I question whether it can, it has not been shown that such activity substantially affects interstate commerce. Similarly, it is neither self-evident nor demonstrated that regulating such activity is necessary to the interstate drug control scheme.

The Court's definition of economic activity is breathtaking. It defines as economic any activity involving the production, distribution, and consumption of commodities. And it appears to reason that when an interstate market for a commodity exists, regulating the intrastate manufacture or possession of that commodity is constitutional either because that intrastate activity is itself economic, or because regulating it is a rational part of regulating its market. Putting to one side the problem endemic to the Court's opinion—the shift in focus from the activity at issue in this case to the entirety of what the CSA regulates, see *Lopez* . . . ("depending on the level of generality, any activity can be looked upon as commercial")—the Court's definition of economic activity for purposes of Commerce Clause jurisprudence threatens to sweep all of productive human activity into federal regulatory reach.

. . . It will not do to say that Congress may regulate noncommercial activity simply because it may have an effect on the demand for commercial goods, or because the noncommercial endeavor can, in some sense, substitute for commercial activity. Most commercial goods or services have some sort of privately producible analogue. Home care substitutes for daycare. Charades games substitute for movie tickets. Backyard or windowsill gardening substitutes for going to the supermarket. To draw the line wherever private activity affects the demand for market goods is to draw no line at all, and to declare everything economic. We have already [explicitly] rejected [in *Lopez*] the result that would follow—a federal police power. . . .

In *Lopez* and *Morrison*, we suggested that economic activity usually relates directly to commercial activity. . . . The homegrown cultivation and personal possession and use of marijuana for medicinal purposes has no apparent commercial character. Everyone agrees that the marijuana at issue in this case was never in the stream of commerce, and neither were the supplies for growing it. (Marijuana is highly unusual among the substances subject to the CSA in that it can be cultivated without any materials that have traveled in interstate commerce.) *Lopez* makes clear that possession is not itself commercial activity. . . . And respondents have not come into possession by means of any commercial transaction; they have simply grown, in their own homes, marijuana for their own use, without acquiring, buying, selling, or bartering a thing of value. . . .

The Court suggests that *Wickard*, which we have identified as "perhaps the most far reaching example of Commerce Clause authority over intrastate activity," . . . established federal regulatory power over any home consumption of a commodity for which a national market exists. I disagree. In contrast to the CSA's limitless assertion of power, Congress provided an exemption within the AAA for small producers [in *Wickard*]. . . . *Wickard*, then, did not extend Commerce Clause authority to something as modest as the home cook's herb garden. This is not to say that Congress may never regulate small quantities of commodities possessed or produced for personal use, or to deny that it sometimes needs to enact a zero tolerance regime for such commodities. It is merely to say that *Wickard* did not hold or imply that small-scale production of commodities is always economic, and automatically within Congress' reach.

Even assuming that economic activity is at issue in this case, the Government has made no showing in fact that the possession and use of homegrown marijuana for medical purposes, in California or elsewhere, has a substantial effect on interstate commerce. Similarly, the Government has not shown that regulating such activity is necessary to an interstate regulatory scheme. . . .

. . .

III

. . . If I were a California citizen, I would not have voted for the medical marijuana ballot initiative; if I were a California legislator I would not have supported the Compassionate Use Act. But whatever the wisdom of California's experiment with medical marijuana, the federalism principles that have driven our Commerce Clause cases require that room for experiment be protected in this case. For these reasons I dissent.

■ JUSTICE THOMAS, dissenting.

. . . If Congress can regulate this under the Commerce Clause, then it can regulate virtually anything—and the Federal Government is no longer one of limited and enumerated powers.

. . .

II

B

. . .

. . . [I]t is implausible that this Court could set aside entire portions of the United States Code as outside Congress' power in *Lopez* and *Morrison*, but it cannot engage in the more restrained practice of invalidating particular applications of the CSA that are beyond Congress' power. This Court has regularly entertained as-applied challenges under constitutional provisions. . . . There is no reason why, when Congress exceeds the scope of commerce power, courts may not invalidate Congress' overreaching on a case-by-case basis. . . .

. . . [a]

---

[a]   In Taylor v. United States, 577 U.S. ___, 136 S.Ct. 2074 (2016), a 7–1 majority of the Court invoked *Raich* to resolve a criminal dispute under the Hobbs Act, which makes it a federal crime to use robbery to affect, or attempt to affect, "commerce"—a term defined broadly as interstate commerce "and all other commerce over which the United States has jurisdiction." Taylor was accused of targeting for robbery a marijuana dealer's drugs or drug proceeds, and the Court had little difficulty in concluding that such a robbery fell within the Hobbs Act because under *Raich* "the Commerce Clause gives Congress authority to regulate the national market for marijuana, including the authority to proscribe the purely intrastate production, possession, and sale of this controlled substance. Because Congress may regulate these intrastate activities based on their aggregate effect on interstate commerce, it follows that Congress may [as it has chosen to in the Hobbs Act] also regulate intrastate drug *theft*." Justice Thomas dissented.

National Federation of Independent Business v. Sebelius

567 U.S. 519, 132 S.Ct. 2566, 183 L.Ed.2d 450 (2012).

■ CHIEF JUSTICE ROBERTS announced the judgment of the Court and delivered . . . an opinion with respect to Part[ ] III-A [addressing the Commerce Clause and Necessary and Proper Clause issues].

Today we resolve constitutional challenges to . . . provisions of the Patient Protection and Affordable Care Act of 2010 [,including] the individual mandate, which requires individuals to purchase a health insurance policy providing a minimum level of coverage. . . . We do not consider whether the Act embodies sound policies. That judgment is entrusted to the Nation's elected leaders. We ask only whether Congress has the power under the Constitution to enact the challenged provisions.

. . .

The Federal Government "is acknowledged by all to be one of enumerated powers." *Ibid.* That is, rather than granting general authority to perform all the conceivable functions of government, the Constitution lists, or enumerates, the Federal Government's powers. Congress may, for example, "coin Money," "establish Post Offices," and "raise and support Armies." Art. I, § 8, cls. 5, 7, 12. The enumeration of powers is also a limitation of powers, because "[t]he enumeration presupposes something not enumerated." Gibbons v. Ogden, 9 Wheat. 1, 195 (1824). The Constitution's express conferral of some powers makes clear that it does not grant others. Government "can exercise only the powers granted to it." *McCulloch, supra,* at 405.

. . .

Indeed, the Constitution did not initially include a Bill of Rights at least partly because the Framers felt the enumeration of powers sufficed to restrain the Government. As Alexander Hamilton put it, "the Constitution is itself, in every rational sense, and to every useful purpose, A BILL OF RIGHTS." The Federalist No. 84, p. 515 (C. Rossiter ed. 1961). And when the Bill of Rights was ratified, it made express what the enumeration of powers necessarily implied: "The powers not delegated to the United States by the Constitution . . . are reserved to the States respectively, or to the people." U. S. Const., Amdt. 10. The Federal Government has expanded dramatically over the past two centuries, but it still must show that a constitutional grant of power authorizes each of its actions. See, *e.g.,* United States v. Comstock, 560 U. S. ___ (2010).

The same does not apply to the States, because the Constitution is not the source of their power. . . .The States thus can and do perform many of the vital functions of modern government—punishing street crime, running public schools, and zoning property for development, to name but a few—even though the Constitution's text does not authorize any government to do so. Our cases refer to this general power of governing, possessed by the States but not by the Federal Government, as the "police power." See, *e.g.,* United States v. Morrison, 529 U. S. 598, 618–619 (2000).

"State sovereignty is not just an end in itself: Rather, federalism secures to citizens the liberties that derive from the diffusion of sovereign power." New York v. United States, 505 U. S. 144, 181 (1992). Because the police power is controlled by 50 different States instead of one national sovereign, the facets of governing that touch on citizens' daily lives are normally administered by smaller governments closer to the governed. . . . The independent power of the States also serves as a check on the power of the Federal Government: "By denying any one government complete jurisdiction over all the concerns of public life, federalism protects the liberty of the individual from arbitrary power." Bond v. United States, 564 U. S. ___, ___ (2011) (slip op., at 9–10).

This case concerns ... powers that the Constitution does grant the Federal Government, but which must be read carefully to avoid creating a general federal authority akin to the police power. The Constitution authorizes Congress to "regulate Commerce with foreign Nations, and among the several States, and with the Indian Tribes." Art. I, § 8, cl. 3. Our precedents read that to mean that Congress may regulate "the channels of interstate commerce," "persons or things in interstate commerce," and "those activities that substantially affect interstate commerce." *Morrison, supra,* at 609. The power over activities that substantially affect interstate commerce can be expansive. That power has been held to authorize federal regulation of such seemingly local matters as a farmer's decision to grow wheat for himself and his livestock, and a loan shark's extortionate collections from a neighborhood butcher shop. See Wickard v. Filburn, 317 U. S. 111 (1942); Perez v. United States, 402 U. S. 146 (1971).

. . .

The reach of the Federal Government's enumerated powers is broader still because the Constitution authorizes Congress to "make all Laws which shall be necessary and proper for carrying into Execution the foregoing Powers." Art. I, § 8, cl. 18. We have long read this provision to give Congress great latitude in exercising its powers: "Let the end be legitimate, let it be within the scope of the constitution, and all means which are appropriate, which are plainly adapted to that end, which are not prohibited, but consist with the letter and spirit of the constitution, are constitutional." *McCulloch,* 4 Wheat., at 421.

Our permissive reading of these powers is explained in part by a general reticence to invalidate the acts of the Nation's elected leaders. "Proper respect for a co-ordinate branch of the government" requires that we strike down an Act of Congress only if "the lack of constitutional authority to pass [the] act in question is clearly demonstrated." United States v. Harris, 106 U. S. 629, 635 (1883). Members of this Court are vested with the authority to interpret the law; we possess neither the expertise nor the prerogative to make policy judgments. Those decisions are entrusted to our Nation's elected leaders, who can be thrown out of office if the people disagree with them. It is not our job to protect the people from the consequences of their political choices.

Our deference in matters of policy cannot, however, become abdication in matters of law. . . . Our respect for Congress's policy judgments thus can never extend so far as to disavow restraints on federal power that the Constitution carefully constructed. . . .

. . .

I

In 2010, Congress enacted the Patient Protection and Affordable Care Act, 124 Stat. 119. The Act aims to increase the number of Americans covered by health insurance and decrease the cost of health care. The Act's 10 titles stretch over 900 pages and contain hundreds of provisions. This case concerns constitutional challenges to[, in addition to another key provision, the provision] commonly referred to as the individual mandate. . . . The individual mandate requires most Americans to maintain "minimum essential" health insurance coverage. 26 U. S. C. § 5000A. The mandate does not apply to some individuals, such as prisoners and undocumented aliens. § 5000A(d). Many individuals will receive the required coverage through their employer, or from a government program such as Medicaid or Medicare. See § 5000A(f). But for individuals who are not exempt and do not receive health insurance through a third party, the means of satisfying the requirement is to purchase insurance from a private company. Beginning in 2014, those who do not comply with the mandate must make a "[s]hared responsibility payment" to the Federal Government. § 5000A(b)(1). That payment, which the Act describes as a "penalty," is calculated as a percentage of household income, subject to a floor based on a specified dollar amount and a ceiling based on the average annual premium the individual would have to pay for qualifying private health insurance. § 5000A(c). In 2016, for example, the penalty will be 2.5 percent of an individual's household income, but no less than $695 and no more than the average yearly premium for insurance that covers 60 percent of the cost of 10 specified services (*e.g.*, prescription drugs and hospitalization). *Ibid.*; 42 U. S. C. § 18022. The Act provides that the penalty will be paid to the Internal Revenue Service with an individual's taxes, and "shall be assessed and collected in the same manner" as tax penalties, such as the penalty for claiming too large an income tax refund. 26 U. S. C. § 5000A(g)(1). The Act, however, bars the IRS from using several of its normal enforcement tools, such as criminal prosecutions and levies. § 5000A(g)(2). And some individuals who are subject to the mandate are nonetheless exempt from the penalty—for example, those with income below a certain threshold and members of Indian tribes. § 5000A(e).

On the day the President signed the Act into law, Florida and 12 other States filed a complaint in the Federal District Court for the Northern District of Florida. Those plaintiffs . . . were subsequently joined by 13 more States, several individuals, and the National Federation of Independent Business. . . .

The Court of Appeals for the Eleventh Circuit . . . [held] that the individual mandate exceeds Congress's power. . . . [finding] that the individual mandate was not supported by Congress's power to "regulate Commerce . . . among the several States." . . . According to the majority, the Commerce Clause does not empower the Federal Government to order individuals to engage in commerce. . . .

. . .

Other Courts of Appeals have also heard challenges to the individual mandate. . . . The Sixth Circuit and the D.C. Circuit upheld the mandate as a valid exercise of Congress' commerce power. . . .

. . .

We granted certiorari to review the judgment of the . . . Eleventh Circuit. . . .

. . .

III

The Government . . . argues that Congress had the power to enact the mandate under the Commerce Clause. Under that theory, Congress may order individuals to buy health insurance because the failure to do so affects interstate commerce, and could undercut the Affordable Care Act's other reforms. . . .

A

The Government's first argument is that the individual mandate is a valid exercise of Congress's power under the Commerce Clause and the Necessary and Proper Clause. According to the Government, the health care market is characterized by a significant cost-shifting problem. Everyone will eventually need health care at a time and to an extent they cannot predict, but if they do not have insurance, they often will not be able to pay for it. Because state and federal laws nonetheless require hospitals to provide a certain degree of care to individuals without regard to their ability to pay, see, *e.g.*, 42 U. S. C. § 1395dd; Fla. Stat. Ann. § 395.1041, hospitals end up receiving compensation for only a portion of the services they provide. To recoup the losses, hospitals pass on the cost to insurers through higher rates, and insurers, in turn, pass on the cost to policy holders in the form of higher premiums. Congress estimated that the cost of uncompensated care raises family health insurance premiums, on average, by over $1,000 per year. 42 U. S. C. § 18091(2)(F).

In the Affordable Care Act, Congress addressed the problem of those who cannot obtain insurance coverage because of preexisting conditions or other health issues. It did so through the Act's "guaranteed-issue" and "community-rating" provisions. These provisions together prohibit insurance companies from denying coverage to those with such conditions or charging unhealthy individuals higher premiums than healthy individuals. See §§ 300gg, 300gg–1, 300gg–3, 300gg–4.

The guaranteed-issue and community-rating reforms do not, however, address the issue of healthy individuals who choose not to purchase insurance to cover potential healthcare needs. In fact, the reforms sharply exacerbate that problem, by providing an incentive for individuals to delay purchasing health insurance until they become sick, relying on the promise of guaranteed and affordable coverage. The reforms also threaten to impose massive new costs on insurers, who are required to accept unhealthy individuals but prohibited from charging them rates necessary to pay for their coverage. This will lead insurers to significantly increase premiums on everyone. See Brief for America's Health Insurance Plans et al. as *Amici Curiae* . . . 8–9.

The individual mandate was Congress's solution to these problems. By requiring that individuals purchase health insurance, the mandate prevents cost-shifting by those who would otherwise go without it. In addition, the mandate forces into the insurance risk pool more healthy individuals, whose premiums on average will be higher than their health care expenses. This allows insurers to subsidize the costs of covering the unhealthy individuals the reforms require them to accept. The Government claims that Congress has power under the Commerce and Necessary and Proper Clauses to enact this solution.

1

The Government contends that the individual mandate is within Congress's power because the failure to purchase insurance "has a substantial and deleterious effect on interstate commerce" by creating the cost-shifting problem. . . . The path of our Commerce Clause decisions has not always run smooth, see United States v. Lopez, 514 U. S. 549, 552–559 (1995), but it is now well established that Congress has broad authority under the Clause. . . . Congress's power, moreover, is not limited to regulation of an activity that by itself substantially affects interstate commerce, but also extends to activities that do so only when aggregated with similar activities of others. See *Wickard*, 317 U. S., at 127–128.

Given its expansive scope, it is no surprise that Congress has employed the commerce power in a wide variety of ways to address the pressing needs of the time. But Congress has never attempted to rely on that power to compel individuals not engaged in commerce to purchase an unwanted product[3]. Legislative novelty is not necessarily fatal; there is a first time for everything. But sometimes "the most telling indication of [a] severe constitutional problem . . . is the lack of historical precedent" for Congress's action. Free Enterprise Fund v. Public Company Accounting Oversight Bd., 561 U. S. ___, ___ (2010) (slip op., at 25). . . .

---

[3] The examples of other congressional mandates cited by Justice Ginsburg . . . (opinion concurring in part, concurring in judgment in part, and dissenting in part), are not to the contrary. Each of those mandates—to report for jury duty, to register for the draft, to purchase firearms in anticipation of militia service, to exchange gold currency for paper currency, and to file a tax return— are based on constitutional provisions other than the Commerce Clause. See Art. I, § 8, cl. 9 (to "constitute Tribunals inferior to the supreme Court"); *id.*, cl. 12 (to "raise and support Armies"); *id.*, cl. 16 (to "provide for organizing, arming, and disciplining, the Militia"); *id.*, cl. 5 (to "coin Money"); *id.*, cl. 1 (to "lay and collect Taxes").

The Constitution grants Congress the power to "*regulate* Commerce." Art. I, § 8, cl. 3 (emphasis added). The power to *regulate* commerce presupposes the existence of commercial activity to be regulated. If the power to "regulate" something included the power to create it, many of the provisions in the Constitution would be superfluous. For example, the Constitution gives Congress the power to "coin Money," in addition to the power to "regulate the Value thereof." *Id.,* cl. 5. And it gives Congress the power to "raise and support Armies" and to "provide and maintain a Navy," in addition to the power to "make Rules for the Government and Regulation of the land and naval Forces." *Id.,* cls. 12–14. If the power to regulate the armed forces or the value of money included the power to bring the subject of the regulation into existence, the specific grant of such powers would have been unnecessary. The language of the Constitution reflects the natural understanding that the power to regulate assumes there is already something to be regulated. . . .

Our precedent also reflects this understanding. As expansive as our cases construing the scope of the commerce power have been, they all have one thing in common: They uniformly describe the power as reaching "activity." It is nearly impossible to avoid the word when quoting them. See, *e.g., Lopez, supra,* at 560 ("Where economic activity substantially affects interstate commerce, legislation regulating that activity will be sustained"); *Perez,* 402 U. S., at 154 ("Where the *class of activities* is regulated and that *class* is within the reach of federal power, the courts have no power to excise, as trivial, individual instances of the class" (emphasis in original; internal quotation marks omitted)); *Wickard, supra,* at 125 ("[E]ven if appellee's activity be local and though it may not be regarded as commerce, it may still, whatever its nature, be reached by Congress if it exerts a substantial economic effect on interstate commerce"); NLRB v. Jones & Laughlin Steel Corp., 301 U. S. 1, 37 (1937) ("Although activities may be intrastate in character when separately considered, if they have such a close and substantial relation to interstate commerce that their control is essential or appropriate to protect that commerce from burdens and obstructions, Congress cannot be denied the power to exercise that control"). . . .

The individual mandate, however, does not regulate existing commercial activity. It instead compels individuals to *become* active in commerce by purchasing a product, on the ground that their failure to do so affects interstate commerce. Construing the Commerce Clause to permit Congress to regulate individuals precisely *because* they are doing nothing would open a new and potentially vast domain to congressional authority. Every day individuals do not do an infinite number of things. In some cases they decide not to do something; in others they simply fail to do it. Allowing Congress to justify federal regulation by pointing to the effect of inaction on commerce would bring countless decisions an individual could *potentially* make within the scope of federal regulation, and—under the Government's theory—empower Congress to make those decisions for him.

. . .

Wickard has long been regarded as "perhaps the most far reaching example of Commerce Clause authority over intrastate activity," *Lopez,* . . . but the Government's theory in this case would go much further. Under *Wickard* it is within Congress's power to regulate the market for wheat by supporting its price. But price can be supported by increasing demand as well as by decreasing supply. The aggregated decisions of some consumers not to purchase wheat have a substantial effect on the price of wheat, just as decisions not to purchase health insurance have on the price of insurance. Congress can therefore command that those not buying wheat do so, just as it argues here that it may command that those not buying health insurance do so. The farmer in *Wickard* was at least actively engaged in the production of wheat, and the Government could regulate that activity because of its effect on commerce. The

Government's theory here would effectively override that limitation, by establishing that individuals may be regulated under the Commerce Clause whenever enough of them are not doing something the Government would have them do.

Indeed, the Government's logic would justify a mandatory purchase to solve almost any problem. . . . To consider a different example in the health care market, many Americans do not eat a balanced diet. That group makes up a larger percentage of the total population than those without health insurance. . . . The failure of that group to have a healthy diet increases health care costs, to a greater extent than the failure of the uninsured to purchase insurance. . . . Those increased costs are borne in part by other Americans who must pay more, just as the uninsured shift costs to the insured. . . . Congress addressed the insurance problem by ordering everyone to buy insurance. Under the Government's theory, Congress could address the diet problem by ordering everyone to buy vegetables. . . .

. . .

To an economist, perhaps, there is no difference between activity and inactivity; both have measurable economic effects on commerce. But the distinction between doing something and doing nothing would not have been lost on the Framers, who were "practical statesmen," not metaphysical philosophers. Industrial Union Dept., AFL-CIO v. American Petroleum Institute, 448 U. S. 607, 673 (1980) (Rehnquist, J., concurring in judgment). . . . The Framers gave Congress the power to *regulate* commerce, not to *compel* it, and for over 200 years both our decisions and Congress's actions have reflected this understanding. There is no reason to depart from that understanding now.

. . .

2

The Government next contends that Congress has the power under the Necessary and Proper Clause to enact the individual mandate because the mandate is an "integral part of a comprehensive scheme of economic regulation"—the guaranteed-issue and community-rating insurance reforms. . . . Under this argument, it is not necessary to consider the effect that an individual's inactivity may have on interstate commerce; it is enough that Congress regulate commercial activity in a way that requires regulation of inactivity to be effective.

The power to "make all Laws which shall be necessary and proper for carrying into Execution" the powers enumerated in the Constitution, Art. I, § 8, cl. 18, vests Congress with authority to enact provisions "incidental to the [enumerated] power, and conducive to its beneficial exercise," *McCulloch*, 4 Wheat., at 418. Although the Clause gives Congress authority to "legislate on that vast mass of incidental powers which must be involved in the constitution," it does not license the exercise of any "great substantive and independent power[s]" beyond those specifically enumerated. *Id.*, at 411, 421. Instead, the Clause is " 'merely a declaration, for the removal of all uncertainty, that the means of carrying into execution those [powers] otherwise granted are included in the grant.' " Kinsella v. United States ex rel. Singleton, 361 U. S. 234, 247 (1960) (quoting VI Writings of James Madison 383 (G. Hunt ed.1906)).

. . .

Applying these principles, the individual mandate cannot be sustained under the Necessary and Proper Clause as an essential component of the insurance reforms. Each of our prior cases upholding laws under that Clause involved exercises of authority derivative of, and in service to, a granted power. . . . The individual mandate, by contrast, vests Congress with the extraordinary ability to create the necessary predicate to the exercise of an enumerated power.

. . .

[A separate part of Chief Justice Roberts's opinion for the Court, joined by Justices Ginsburg, Breyer, Sotomayor, and Kagan, upheld the mandate as within Congress' constitutional power to "lay and collect Taxes, Duties, Imposts and Excises, to pay the Debts and provide for the common Defence and general Welfare of the United States," U. S. Const., Art. I, § 8, cl. 1., and is reported at p. 154, infra.]

■ JUSTICE SCALIA, JUSTICE KENNEDY, JUSTICE THOMAS, and JUSTICE ALITO, dissenting [from the judgment upholding the mandate, but agreeing with the Chief Justice's resolution of (though not joining his opinion on) the Commerce Clause and Necessary and Proper Clause issues].

. . .

This case is in one respect difficult: it presents . . . questions of first impression. The first of those is whether failure to engage in economic activity (the purchase of health insurance) is subject to regulation under the Commerce Clause. . . .

The case is easy and straightforward, however, in another respect. What is absolutely clear, affirmed by the text of the 1789 Constitution, by the Tenth Amendment ratified in 1791, and by innumerable cases of ours in the 220 years since, is that there are structural limits upon federal power—upon what it can prescribe with respect to private conduct, and upon what it can impose upon the sovereign States. . . .

. . . The striking case of Wickard v. Filburn, 317 U. S. 111 (1942), which held that the economic activity of growing wheat, even for one's own consumption, affected commerce sufficiently that it could be regulated, always has been regarded as the *ne plus ultra* of expansive Commerce Clause jurisprudence. To go beyond that, and to say the *failure* to grow wheat (which is *not* an economic activity, or any activity at all) nonetheless affects commerce and therefore can be federally regulated, is to make mere breathing in and out the basis for federal prescription and to extend federal power to virtually all human activity.

. . .

I

The Individual Mandate

. . .

A

. . .

The case upon which the Government principally relies to sustain the Individual Mandate under the Necessary and Proper Clause is Gonzales v. Raich, 545 U. S. 1 (2005). That case held that Congress could, in an effort to restrain the interstate market in marijuana, ban the local cultivation and possession of that drug. . . . *Raich* is no precedent for what Congress has done here. That case's prohibition of growing (cf. *Wickard*, 317 U. S. 111), and of possession (cf. innumerable federal statutes) did not represent the expansion of the federal power to direct into a broad new field. The mandating of economic activity does, and since it is a field so limitless that it converts the Commerce Clause into a general authority to direct the economy, that mandating is not "consist[ent] with the letter and spirit of the constitution." *McCulloch* v. *Maryland*. . . .

Moreover, *Raich* is far different from the Individual Mandate in another respect. The Court's opinion in *Raich* pointed out that the growing and possession prohibitions were the only practicable way of enabling the prohibition of interstate traffic in marijuana to be effectively enforced. . . . Intrastate marijuana could no more be distinguished from interstate marijuana than, for example, endangered-species trophies obtained before the species was federally protected can be distinguished from trophies obtained afterwards—which made it necessary and proper to prohibit the sale of all such trophies. . . .

With the present statute, by contrast, there are many ways other than this unprecedented Individual Mandate by which the regulatory scheme's goals of reducing insurance premiums and ensuring the profitability of insurers could be achieved. For instance, those who did not purchase insurance could be subjected to a surcharge when they do enter the health insurance system. Or they could be denied a full income tax credit given to those who do purchase the insurance.

The Government was invited, at oral argument, to suggest what federal controls over private conduct (other than those explicitly prohibited by the Bill of Rights or other constitutional controls) could *not* be justified as necessary and proper for the carrying out of a general regulatory scheme. . . . It was unable to name any. . . .

C

A few respectful responses to Justice Ginsburg's dissent on the issue of the Mandate are in order. That dissent duly recites the test of Commerce Clause power that our opinions have applied, but disregards the premise the test contains. It is true enough that Congress needs only a " 'rational basis' for concluding that the *regulated activity* substantially affects interstate commerce". . . . But it must be *activity* affecting commerce that is regulated, and not merely the failure to engage in commerce. And one is not now purchasing the health care covered by the insurance mandate simply because one is likely to be purchasing it in the future. Our test's premise of regulated activity is not invented out of whole cloth, but rests upon the Constitution's requirement that it be commerce which is regulated. If all inactivity affecting commerce is commerce, commerce is everything. Ultimately the dissent is driven to saying that there is really no difference between action and inaction, . . . a proposition that has never recommended itself, neither to the law nor to common sense. . . .

The dissent claims that we "fai[l] to explain why the individual mandate threatens our constitutional order." . . . But we have done so. It threatens that order because it gives such an expansive meaning to the Commerce Clause that *all* private conduct (including failure to act) becomes subject to federal control, effectively destroying the Constitution's division of governmental powers. Thus the dissent, on the theories proposed for the validity of the Mandate, would alter the accepted constitutional relation between the individual and the National Government. . . .

. . .

■ JUSTICE GINSBURG, [joined by JUSTICES BREYER, SOTOMAYOR and KAGAN, agreed with THE CHIEF JUSTICE "that the minimum coverage provision is a proper exercise of the taxing power[,]" but dissented from his and the joint dissent's Commerce Clause conclusion.]

. . . I would hold . . . that the Commerce Clause authorizes Congress to enact the minimum coverage provision. . . .

I

C

States cannot resolve the problem of the uninsured on their own. Like Social Security benefits, a universal health-care system, if adopted by an individual State, would be "bait to the needy and dependent elsewhere, encouraging them to migrate and seek a haven of repose." Helvering v. Davis, 301 U. S. 619, 644 (1937). See also Brief for Commonwealth of Massachusetts as *Amicus Curiae* in No. 11–398, p. 15 (noting that, in 2009, Massachusetts' emergency rooms served thousands of uninsured, out-of-state residents). An influx of unhealthy individuals into a State with universal health care would result in increased spending on medical services. To cover the increased costs, a State would have to raise taxes, and private health-insurance companies would have to increase premiums. Higher taxes and increased insurance costs would, in turn, encourage businesses and healthy individuals to leave the State.

States that undertake health-care reforms on their own thus risk "placing themselves in a position of economic disadvantage as compared with neighbors or competitors." *Davis*, 301 U. S., at 644. See also Brief for Health Care for All, Inc., et al. as *Amici Curiae* in No. 11–398, p. 4 ("[O]utof-state residents continue to seek and receive millions of dollars in uncompensated care in Massachusetts hospitals, limiting the State's efforts to improve its health care system through the elimination of uncompensated care."). Facing that risk, individual States are unlikely to take the initiative in addressing the problem of the uninsured, even though solving that problem is in all States' best interests. Congress' intervention was needed to overcome this collective action impasse.

D

Aware that a national solution was required, Congress could have taken over the health-insurance market by establishing a tax-and-spend federal program like Social Security. Such a program, commonly referred to as a single-payer system (where the sole payer is the Federal Government), would have left little, if any, room for private enterprise or the States. Instead of going this route, Congress enacted the ACA, a solution that retains a robust role for private insurers and state governments. To make its chosen approach work, however, Congress had to use some new tools, including a requirement that most individuals obtain private health insurance coverage. . . .

. . .

To ensure that individuals with medical histories have access to affordable insurance, Congress devised a three part solution. First, Congress imposed a "guaranteed issue" requirement, which bars insurers from denying coverage to any person on account of that person's medical condition or history. See 42 U. S. C. §§ 300gg–1, 300gg–3, 300gg–4(a) (2006 ed., Supp. IV). Second, Congress required insurers to use "community rating" to price their insurance policies. See § 300gg. Community rating, in effect, bars insurance companies from charging higher premiums to those with preexisting conditions.

But these two provisions, Congress comprehended, could not work effectively unless individuals were given a powerful incentive to obtain insurance. See Hearings before the House Ways and Means Committee, 111th Cong., 1st Sess., 10, 13 (2009) (statement of Uwe Reinhardt) ("[I]mposition of *community-rated premiums* and *guaranteed* issue on a market of competing private health insurers will inexorably drive that market into extinction, unless these two features are coupled with . . . *a mandate on individual[s] to be insured.*" (emphasis in original)).

. . .

* * *

In sum, Congress passed the minimum coverage provision as a key component of the ACA to address an economic and social problem that has plagued the Nation for decades: the large number of U. S. residents who are unable or unwilling to obtain health insurance. Whatever one thinks of the policy decision Congress made, it was Congress' prerogative to make it. Reviewed with appropriate deference, the minimum coverage provision, allied to the guaranteed-issue and community-rating prescriptions, should survive measurement under the Commerce and Necessary and Proper Clauses.

II

A

The Commerce Clause, it is widely acknowledged, "was the Framers' response to the central problem that gave rise to the Constitution itself." EEOC v. Wyoming, 460 U. S. 226, 244, 245, n. 1 (1983) (Stevens, J., concurring). Under the Articles of Confederation, the Constitution's precursor, the regulation of commerce was left to the States. This scheme proved unworkable, because the individual States, understandably focused on their own economic interests, often failed to take actions critical to the success of the Nation as a whole. . . .

What was needed was a "national Government . . . armed with a positive & compleat authority in all cases where uniform measures are necessary." See Letter from James Madison to Edmund Randolph (Apr. 8, 1787), in 9 Papers of James Madison 368, 370 (R. Rutland ed. 1975). See also Letter from George Washington to James Madison (Nov. 30, 1785), in 8 *id.,* at 428, 429 ("We are either a United people, or we are not. If the former, let us, in all matters of general concern act as a nation, which ha[s] national objects to promote, and a national character to support."). The Framers' solution was the Commerce Clause, which, as they perceived it, granted Congress the authority to enact economic legislation "in all Cases for the general Interests of the Union, and also in those Cases to which the States are separately incompetent." 2 Records of the Federal Convention of 1787, pp. 131–132, ¶ 8 (M. Farrand rev. 1966). See also North American Co. v. SEC, 327 U. S. 686, 705 (1946) ("[The commerce power] is an affirmative power commensurate with the national needs.").

The Framers understood that the "general Interests of the Union" would change over time, in ways they could not anticipate. Accordingly, they recognized that the Constitution was of necessity a "great outlin[e]," not a detailed blueprint, see McCulloch v. Maryland, 4 Wheat. 316, 407 (1819), and that its provisions included broad concepts, to be "explained by the context or by the facts of the case," Letter from James Madison to N. P. Trist (Dec. 1831) . . . ."Nothing . . . can be more fallacious," Alexander Hamilton emphasized, "than to infer the extent of any power, proper to be lodged in the national government, from . . . its immediate necessities. There ought to be a CAPACITY to provide for future contingencies[,] as they may happen; and as these are illimitable in their nature, it is impossible safely to limit that capacity." The Federalist No. 34, pp. 205, 206 (John Harvard Library ed. 2009). See also *McCulloch,* 4 Wheat., at 415 (The Necessary and Proper Clause is lodged "in a constitution[,] intended to endure for ages to come, and consequently, to be adapted to the various *crises* of human affairs.").

B

Consistent with the Framers' intent, we have repeatedly emphasized that Congress' authority under the Commerce Clause is dependent upon "practical" considerations, including "actual experience." *Jones & Laughlin Steel Corp.,* 301 U. S., at 41–42; see Wickard v. Filburn, 317 U. S. 111, 122 (1942); United States v. Lopez, 514 U. S. 549, 573 (1995) (Kennedy, J., concurring) (emphasizing "the Court's definitive commitment to the practical conception of the commerce power"). See also *North American Co.,* 327 U. S., at 705 ("Commerce itself is an intensely practical matter. To deal with it effectively, Congress must be able to act in terms of economic and financial realities."). . . . We afford Congress the leeway "to undertake to solve national problems directly and realistically." American Power & Light Co. v. SEC, 329 U. S. 90, 103 (1946).

Until today, this Court's pragmatic approach to judging whether Congress validly exercised its commerce power was guided by two familiar principles. First, Congress has the power to regulate economic activities "that substantially affect interstate commerce." Gonzales v. Raich, 545 U. S. 1, 17 (2005). This capacious power extends even to local activities that, viewed in the aggregate, have a substantial impact on interstate commerce. See *ibid.* See also *Wickard*, 317 U. S., at 125 ("[E]ven if appellee's activity be local and though it may not be regarded as commerce, it may still, *whatever its nature*, be reached by Congress if it exerts a substantial economic effect on interstate commerce." (emphasis added)); *Jones & Laughlin Steel Corp.*, 301 U. S., at 37.

Second, we owe a large measure of respect to Congress when it frames and enacts economic and social legislation. See *Raich*, 545 U. S., at 17. See also Pension Benefit Guaranty Corporation v. R. A. Gray & Co., 467 U. S. 717, 729 (1984) ("[S]trong deference [is] accorded legislation in the field of national economic policy."); Hodel v. Indiana, 452 U. S. 314, 326 (1981) ("This [C]ourt will certainly not substitute its judgment for that of Congress unless the relation of the subject to interstate commerce and its effect upon it are clearly non-existent." . . .). When appraising such legislation, we ask only (1) whether Congress had a "rational basis" for concluding that the regulated activity substantially affects interstate commerce, and (2) whether there is a "reasonable connection between the regulatory means selected and the asserted ends." *Id.*, at 323–324. See also *Raich*, 545 U. S., at 22; *Lopez*, 514 U. S., at 557; . . . In answering these questions, we presume the statute under review is constitutional and may strike it down only on a "plain showing" that Congress acted irrationally. *United States* v. *Morrison*,. . . .

C

Straightforward application of these principles would require the Court to hold that the minimum coverage provision is proper Commerce Clause legislation. Beyond dispute, Congress had a rational basis for concluding that the uninsured, as a class, substantially affect interstate commerce. Those without insurance consume billions of dollars of health-care products and services each year. . . . Those goods are produced, sold, and delivered largely by national and regional companies who routinely transact business across state lines. The uninsured also cross state lines to receive care. Some have medical emergencies while away from home. Others, when sick, go to a neighboring State that provides better care for those who have not prepaid for care. . . .

Not only do those without insurance consume a large amount of health care each year; critically, as earlier explained, their inability to pay for a significant portion of that consumption drives up market prices, foists costs on other consumers, and reduces market efficiency and stability. . . . Given these far-reaching effects on interstate commerce, the decision to forgo insurance is hardly inconsequential or equivalent to "doing nothing"; it is, instead, an economic decision Congress has the authority to address under the Commerce Clause. . . .

The minimum coverage provision, furthermore, bears a "reasonable connection" to Congress' goal of protecting the health-care market from the disruption caused by individuals who fail to obtain insurance. By requiring those who do not carry insurance to pay a toll, the minimum coverage provision gives individuals a strong incentive to insure. This incentive, Congress had good reason to believe, would reduce the number of uninsured and, correspondingly, mitigate the adverse impact the uninsured have on the national health-care market.

Congress also acted reasonably in requiring uninsured individuals, whether sick or healthy, either to obtain insurance or to pay the specified penalty. As earlier observed, because every person is at risk of needing care at any moment, all those who lack insurance, regardless of their current health status, adversely affect the price of health care and health insurance. . . . Moreover, an insurance-purchase requirement limited to those in need of immediate care simply could not work. Insurance companies would either charge these individuals prohibitively expensive premiums, or, if community rating regulations were in place, close up shop. . . .

"[W]here we find that the legislators . . . have a rational basis for finding a chosen regulatory scheme necessary to the protection of commerce, our investigation is at an end." *Katzenbach*,. . . . Congress' enactment of the minimum coverage provision, which addresses a specific interstate problem in a practical, experience informed manner, easily meets this criterion.

D

Rather than evaluating the constitutionality of the minimum coverage provision in the manner established by our precedents, the Chief Justice relies on a newly minted constitutional doctrine. The commerce power does not, the Chief Justice announces, permit Congress to "compe[l] individuals to become active in commerce by purchasing a product." . . .

1

a

The Chief Justice's novel constraint on Congress' commerce power gains no force from our precedent and for that reason alone warrants disapprobation. . . . But even assuming . . . that Congress lacks authority under the Commerce Clause to "compel individuals not engaged in commerce to purchase an unwanted product," . . . such a limitation would be inapplicable here. Everyone will, at some point, consume health-care products and services. . . . Thus, if the Chief Justice is correct that an insurance purchase requirement can be applied only to those who "actively" consume health care, the minimum coverage provision fits the bill.

. . .

Maintaining that the uninsured are not active in the health-care market, the Chief Justice draws an analogy to the car market. An individual "is not 'active in the car market,'" the Chief Justice observes, simply because he or she may someday buy a car. . . . The analogy is inapt. The inevitable yet unpredictable need for medical care and the guarantee that emergency care will be provided when required are conditions nonexistent in other markets. That is so of the market for cars, and of the market for broccoli as well. Although an individual *might* buy a car or a crown of broccoli one day, there is no certainty she will ever do so. And if she eventually wants a car or has a craving for broccoli, she will be obliged to pay at the counter before receiving the vehicle or nourishment. She will get no free ride or food, at the expense of another consumer forced to pay an inflated price. See Thomas More Law Center v. Obama, 651 F. 3d 529, 565 (CA6 2011) (Sutton, J., concurring in part) ("Regulating how citizens pay for what they already receive (health care), never quite know when they will need, and in the case of severe illnesses or emergencies generally will not be able to afford, has few (if any) parallels in modern life."). Upholding the minimum coverage provision on the ground that all are participants or will be participants in the health-care market would therefore carry no implication that Congress may justify under the Commerce Clause a mandate to buy other products and services.

. . . Virtually everyone, I reiterate, consumes health care at some point in his or her life. . . . Health insurance is a means of paying for this care, nothing more. In requiring individuals to obtain insurance, Congress is therefore not mandating the purchase of a discrete, unwanted product. Rather, Congress is merely defining the terms on which individuals pay for an interstate good they consume: Persons subject to the mandate must now pay for medical care in advance (instead of at the point of service) and through insurance (instead of out of pocket). Establishing payment terms for goods in or affecting interstate commerce is quintessential economic regulation well within Congress' domain. . . .

 . . .

b

In any event, the Chief Justice's limitation of the commerce power to the regulation of those actively engaged in commerce finds no home in the text of the Constitution or our decisions. Article I, § 8, of the Constitution grants Congress the power "[t]o regulate Commerce . . . among the several States." Nothing in this language implies that Congress' commerce power is limited to regulating those actively engaged in commercial transactions. Indeed, as the D. C. Circuit observed, "[a]t the time the Constitution was [framed], to 'regulate' meant," among other things, "to require action." . . . Arguing to the contrary, the Chief Justice notes that "the Constitution gives Congress the power to 'coin Money,' in addition to the power to 'regulate the Value thereof,'" and similarly "gives Congress the power to 'raise and support Armies' and to 'provide and maintain a Navy,' in addition to the power to 'make Rules for the Government and Regulation of the land and naval Forces.'". . . . In separating the power to regulate from the power to bring the subject of the regulation into existence, the Chief Justice asserts, "[t]he language of the Constitution reflects the natural understanding that the power to regulate assumes there is already something to be regulated.". . . .

This argument is difficult to fathom. Requiring individuals to obtain insurance unquestionably regulates the interstate health-insurance and health-care markets, both of them in existence well before the enactment of the ACA. See *Wickard*, 317 U. S., at 128 ("The stimulation of commerce is a use of the regulatory function quite as definitely as prohibitions or restrictions thereon."). Thus, the "something to be regulated" was surely there when Congress created the minimum coverage provision.

Nor does our case law toe the activity versus inactivity line. In *Wickard*, for example, we upheld the penalty imposed on a farmer who grew too much wheat, even though the regulation had the effect of compelling farmers to purchase wheat in the open market. . . ."[F]orcing some farmers into the market to buy what they could provide for themselves" was, the Court held, a valid means of regulating commerce. . . . In another context, this Court similarly upheld Congress' authority under the commerce power to compel an "inactive" landholder to submit to an unwanted sale. See Monongahela Nav. Co. v. United States, 148 U. S. 312, 335–337 (1893) ("[U]pon *the [great] power to regulate commerce*[,]" Congress has the authority to mandate the sale of real property to the Government, where the sale is essential to the improvement of a navigable waterway (emphasis added)); Cherokee Nation v. Southern Kansas R. Co., 135 U. S. 641, 657–659 (1890) (similar reliance on the commerce power regarding mandated sale of private property for railroad construction).

In concluding that the Commerce Clause does not permit Congress to regulate commercial "inactivity," and therefore does not allow Congress to adopt the practical solution it devised for the health-care problem, the Chief Justice views the Clause as a "technical legal conception," precisely what our case law tells us not to do. . . . This Court's former endeavors to impose categorical limits on the commerce power have not fared well. In several pre–New Deal cases, the Court attempted to cabin Congress' Commerce Clause authority by distinguishing "commerce" from activity once conceived to be noncommercial, notably, "production," "mining," and "manufacturing." See, *e.g.,* United States v. E. C. Knight Co., 156 U. S. 1, 12 (1895) ("Commerce succeeds to manufacture, and is not a part of it."); Carter v. Carter Coal Co., 298 U. S. 238, 304 (1936) ("Mining brings the subject matter of commerce into existence. Commerce disposes of it."). The Court also sought to distinguish activities having a "direct" effect on interstate commerce, and for that reason, subject to federal regulation, from those having only an "indirect" effect, and therefore not amenable to federal control. See, *e.g.,* A. L. A. Schechter Poultry Corp. v. United States, 295 U. S. 495, 548 (1935) ("[T]he distinction between direct and indirect effects of intrastate transactions upon interstate commerce must be recognized as a fundamental one.").

These line-drawing exercises were untenable, and the Court long ago abandoned them. . . .

. . .

At bottom, the Chief Justice's and the joint dissenters' "view that an individual cannot be subject to Commerce Clause regulation absent voluntary, affirmative acts that enter him or her into, or affect, the interstate market expresses a concern for individual liberty that [is] more redolent of Due Process Clause arguments." *Seven-Sky,* 661 F. 3d, at 19. See also Troxel v. Granville, 530 U. S. 57, 65 (2000) (plurality opinion) ("The [Due Process]Clause also includes a substantive component that provides heightened protection against government interference with certain fundamental rights and liberty interests.") . . . Plaintiffs have abandoned any argument pinned to substantive due process, however, . . . and now concede that the provisions here at issue do not offend the Due Process Clause. . . .

2

Underlying the Chief Justice's view that the Commerce Clause must be confined to the regulation of active participants in a commercial market is a fear that the commerce power would otherwise know no limits. . . . The joint dissenters express a similar apprehension. . . . This concern is unfounded.

First, the Chief Justice could certainly uphold the individual mandate without giving Congress *carte blanche* to enact any and all purchase mandates. As several times noted, the unique attributes of the health-care market render everyone active in that market and give rise to a significant free-riding problem that does not occur in other markets. . . .

Nor would the commerce power be unbridled, absent [the] "activity" limitation. Congress would remain unable to regulate noneconomic conduct that has only an attenuated effect on interstate commerce and is traditionally left to state law. See *Lopez,* . . . ; *Morrison,* . . . .

An individual's decision to self-insure, I have explained, is an economic act with the requisite connection to interstate commerce. . . . As an example of the type of regulation he fears, the Chief Justice cites a Government mandate to purchase green vegetables. . . . One could call this concern "the broccoli horrible." Congress, the Chief Justice posits, might adopt such a mandate, reasoning that an individual's failure to eat a healthy diet, like the failure to purchase health insurance, imposes costs on others. . . .

Consider the chain of inferences the Court would have to accept to conclude that a vegetable-purchase mandate was likely to have a substantial effect on the health-care costs borne by lithe Americans. The Court would have to believe that individuals forced to buy vegetables would then eat them (instead of throwing or giving them away), would prepare the vegetables in a healthy way (steamed or raw, not deep-fried), would cut back on unhealthy foods, and would not allow other factors (such as lack of exercise or little sleep) to trump the improved diet. Such "pil[ingof] inference upon inference" is just what the Court refused to do in *Lopez* and *Morrison.*

Other provisions of the Constitution also check congressional overreaching. A mandate to purchase a particular product would be unconstitutional if, for example, the edict impermissibly abridged the freedom of speech, interfered with the free exercise of religion, or infringed on a liberty interest protected by the Due Process Clause.

Supplementing these legal restraints is a formidable check on congressional power: the democratic process. . . . As the controversy surrounding the passage of the Affordable Care Act attests, purchase mandates are likely to engender political resistance. This prospect is borne out by the behavior of state legislators. Despite their possession of unquestioned authority to impose mandates, state governments have rarely done so. . . .

When contemplated in its extreme, almost any power looks dangerous. The commerce power, hypothetically, would enable Congress to prohibit the purchase and home production of all meat, fish, and dairy goods, effectively compelling Americans to eat only vegetables. Cf. *Raich*, . . . ; *Wickard*, ... Yet no one would offer the "hypothetical and unreal possibilit[y]," . . . of a vegetarian state as a credible reason to deny Congress the authority ever to ban the possession and sale of goods. The Chief Justice accepts just such specious logic when he cites the broccoli horrible as a reason to deny Congress the power to pass the individual mandate. Cf. R. Bork, The Tempting of America 169 (1990) ("Judges and lawyers live on the slippery slope of analogies; they are not supposed to ski it to the bottom."). But see, *e.g., post* (joint opinion of Scalia, Kennedy, Thomas and Alito, JJ.) (asserting, outlandishly, that if the minimum coverage provision is sustained, then Congress could make "breathing in and out the basis for federal prescription").

3

To bolster his argument that the minimum coverage provision is not valid Commerce Clause legislation, the Chief Justice emphasizes the provision's novelty. . . . While an insurance-purchase mandate may be novel, the Chief Justice's argument certainly is not. . . . For decades, the Court has declined to override legislation because of its novelty, and for good reason. As our national economy grows and changes, we have recognized, Congress must adapt to the changing "economic and financial realities." . . . Hindering Congress' ability to do so is shortsighted; if history is any guide, today's constriction of the Commerce Clause will not endure. . . .

. . .

Pierce County v. Guillen

537 U.S. 129 (2003).

To receive funding to improve dangerous public road conditions under the federal Hazard Elimination Program, states and localities must identify hazardous locations, 23 U.S.C. § 152. To overcome state fears that doing so without the protection of confidentiality would subject them to increased liability risks at hazardous locations before improvements could be made, Congress provided state and local agencies with a federal privilege to decline to disclose information compiled or collected for purposes of the Program only, 23 U.S.C. § 409. In a suit to extract such information brought under a state public disclosure law, the Court unanimously rejected a challenge to the commerce power of Congress to provide the federal privilege, saying: ". . . Congress could reasonably believe that adopting a measure eliminating an unforeseen side effect of the information-gathering requirement of § 152 would result in more diligent efforts to collect the relevant information, more candid discussions of hazardous locations, better informed decisionmaking, and, ultimately, greater safety on our Nation's roads. Consequently, [§ 409 and its 1995 amendment] can be viewed as legislation aimed at improving safety in the channels of commerce and increasing protection for the instrumentalities of interstate commerce. As such, they fall within Congress' Commerce Clause power."

Reno v. Condon
528 U.S. 141 (2000).

The Driver's Privacy Protection Act of 1994 (DPPA) limits both disclosure by state motor vehicle departments of drivers' personal information without their consent and disclosure by private persons who have obtained drivers' personal information from a state DMV. The Court's unanimous rejection of South Carolina's contention that the DPPA violates principles of federalism began by observing that the Act fell within Congress' commerce power based "on the fact that the personal, identifying information that the DPPA regulates is a 'thin[g] in interstate commerce,' and that the sale or release of that information in interstate commerce is therefore a proper subject of congressional regulation. United States v. Lopez, 514 U.S. 549, 558–559 (1995). . . . The motor vehicle information which the states have historically sold is used by insurers, manufacturers, direct marketers, and others engaged in interstate commerce to contact drivers with customized solicitations. The information is also used in the stream of interstate commerce by various public and private entities for matters related to interstate motoring. Because drivers' information is, in this context, an article of commerce, its sale or release into the interstate stream of business is sufficient to support congressional regulation. We therefore need not address the Government's alternative argument that the states' individual, intrastate activities in gathering, maintaining, and distributing drivers' personal information has a sufficiently substantial impact on interstate commerce to create a constitutional base for federal legislation."

B. THE TAXING POWER

National Federation of Independent Business v. Sebelius
567 U.S. 519 (2012).

By a 5–4 vote, the Court upheld the so-called individual mandate provision of the Patient Protection and Affordable Care Act of 2010 under Congress's power to "lay and collect Taxes." U. S. Const., Art. I, § 8, cl. 1. The individual mandate requires most Americans to procure "minimum essential" health insurance coverage. 26 U. S. C. § 5000A. Some individuals, such as prisoners and undocumented aliens, are exempt from the procurement requirement. § 5000A(d). And many individuals will receive the required coverage through their employer, or from a government program such as Medicaid or Medicare. See § 5000A(f). Individuals who are not exempt and do not receive health insurance through a third party can satisfy the requirement by purchasing insurance from a private company. Beginning in 2014, those who do not maintain the coverage required by the mandate must make a "[s]hared responsibility payment" to the Federal Government. § 5000A(b)(1). A fuller description of the operation of the payment is set out in the part of the case that appears at pp. 141–141, supra.

Chief Justice Roberts, writing for himself and Justices Ginsburg, Breyer, Sotomayor and Kagan, explained that the mandate fell within Congress's taxing powers. Before turning to the constitutional issue, the Court addressed a separate "taxation" question: whether the Anti-Injunction Act, which provides that "no suit for the purpose of restraining the assessment or collection of any tax shall be maintained in any court by any person . . . ", 26 U. S. C. § 7421(a), foreclosed the Court's jurisdiction to consider the merits of the case. The Court, per the Chief Justice, held that there was no jurisdictional bar because Congress did not intend the Anti-Injunction Act to apply to challenges to the shared responsibility payment provisions of the Affordable Care Act.

Turning to the merits, the Chief Justice wrote first for himself only:

"The Government's tax power argument asks us to view the statute differently than we did in considering its commerce power theory. In making its Commerce Clause argument, the Government defended the mandate as a regulation requiring individuals to purchase health insurance. The Government does not claim that the taxing power allows Congress to issue such a command. Instead, the Government asks us to read the mandate not as ordering individuals to buy insurance, but rather as imposing a tax on those who do not buy that product.

"The text of a statute can sometimes have more than one possible meaning. To take a familiar example, a law that reads 'no vehicles in the park' might, or might not, ban bicycles in the park. And it is well established that if a statute has two possible meanings, one of which violates the Constitution, courts should adopt the meaning that does not do so. Justice Story said that 180 years ago: 'no court ought, unless the terms of an act rendered it unavoidable, to give a construction to it which should involve a violation, however unintentional, of the constitution.' *Parsons* v. *Bedford*, 3 Pet. 433, 448–449 (1830). Justice Holmes made the same point a century later: '[T]he rule is settled that as between two possible interpretations of a statute, by one of which it would be unconstitutional and by the other valid, our plain duty is to adopt that which will save the Act.' Blodgett v. Holden, 275 U.S. 142, 148 (1927) (concurring opinion). . . .

"...

"Under the mandate, if an individual does not maintain health insurance, the only consequence is that he must make an additional payment to the IRS when he pays his taxes. See § 5000A(b). That, according to the Government, means the mandate can be regarded as establishing a condition—not owning health insurance—that triggers a tax—the required payment to the IRS. Under that theory, the mandate is not a legal command to buy insurance. Rather, it makes going without insurance just another thing the Government taxes, like buying gasoline or earning income. And if the mandate is in effect just a tax hike on certain taxpayers who do not have health insurance, it may be within Congress's constitutional power to tax.

"The question is not whether that is the most natural interpretation of the mandate, but only whether it is a 'fairly possible' one. Crowell v. Benson, 285 U.S. 22, 62 (1932). As we have explained, 'every reasonable construction must be resorted to, in order to save a statute from unconstitutionality.' Hooper v. California, 155 U.S. 648, 657 (1895). The Government asks us to interpret the mandate as imposing a tax, if it would otherwise violate the Constitution. Granting the Act the full measure of deference owed to federal statutes, it can be so read, for the reasons set forth below."

Chief Justice Roberts then continued, this time joined by Justices Ginsburg, Breyer, Sotomayor and Kagan:

"The exaction the Affordable Care Act imposes on those without health insurance looks like a tax in many respects. The '[s]hared responsibility payment,' as the statute entitles it, is paid into the Treasury by 'taxpayer[s]' when they file their tax returns. 26 U. S. C. § 5000A(b). It does not apply to individuals who do not pay federal income taxes because their household income is less than the filing threshold in the Internal Revenue Code. § 5000A(e)(2). For taxpayers who do owe the payment, its amount is determined by such familiar factors as taxable income, number of dependents, and joint filing status. §§ 5000A(b)(3), (c)(2), (c)(4). The requirement to pay is found in the

Internal Revenue Code and enforced by the IRS, which—as we previously explained—must assess and collect it 'in the same manner as taxes.' This process yields the essential feature of any tax: it produces at least some revenue for the Government. United States v. Kahriger, 345 U.S. 22, 28, n. 4 (1953). Indeed, the payment is expected to raise about $4 billion per year by 2017. . . . It is of course true that the Act describes the payment as a 'penalty,' not a 'tax.' But while that label is fatal to the application of the Anti-Injunction Act, . . . it does not determine whether the payment may be viewed as an exercise of Congress's taxing power. It is up to Congress whether to apply the Anti-Injunction Act to any particular statute, so it makes sense to be guided by Congress's choice of label on that question. That choice does not, however, control whether an exaction is within Congress's constitutional power to tax. Our precedent reflects this: In 1922, we decided two challenges to the 'Child Labor Tax' on the same day. In the first, we held that a suit to enjoin collection of the so called tax was barred by the Anti-Injunction Act. George,. . . . Congress knew that suits to obstruct taxes had to await payment under the Anti-Injunction Act; Congress called the child labor tax a tax; Congress therefore intended the Anti-Injunction Act to apply. In the second case, however, we held that the same exaction, although labeled a tax, was not in fact authorized by Congress's taxing power. Drexel Furniture,. . . . That constitutional question was not controlled by Congress's choice of label.

"We have similarly held that exactions not labeled taxes nonetheless were authorized by Congress's power to tax. In the License Tax Cases, for example, we held that federal licenses to sell liquor and lottery tickets—for which the licensee had to pay a fee—could be sustained as exercises of the taxing power. 5 Wall., at 471. And in New York v. United States we upheld as a tax a 'surcharge' on out-of-state nuclear waste shipments, a portion of which was paid to the Federal Treasury. 505 U. S., at 171. We thus ask whether the shared responsibility payment falls within Congress's taxing power, '[d]isregarding the designation of the exaction, and viewing its substance and application.' United States v. Constantine, 296 U.S. 287, 294 (1935); cf. Quill Corp. v. North Dakota, 504 U.S. 298, 310 (1992) ('[M]agic words or labels' should not 'disable an otherwise constitutional levy' . . . ; Nelson v. Sears, Roebuck & Co., 312 U.S. 359, 363 (1941) ('In passing on the constitutionality of a tax law, we are concerned only with its practical operation, not its definition or the precise form of descriptive words which may be applied to it' . . . ; United States v. Sotelo, 436 U.S. 268, 275 (1978) ('That the funds due are referred to as a "penalty" . . . does not alter their essential character as taxes').

"Our cases confirm this functional approach. For example, in Drexel Furniture, we focused on three practical characteristics of the so-called tax on employing child laborers that convinced us the 'tax' was actually a penalty. First, the tax imposed an exceedingly heavy burden—10 percent of a company's net income—on those who employed children, no matter how small their infraction. Second, it imposed that exaction only on those who knowingly employed underage laborers. Such scienter requirements are typical of punitive statutes, because Congress often wishes to punish only those who intentionally break the law. Third, this 'tax' was enforced in part by the Department of Labor, an agency responsible for punishing violations of labor laws, not collecting revenue. . . .

"The same analysis here suggests that the shared responsibility payment may for constitutional purposes be considered a tax, not a penalty: First, for most Americans the amount due will be far less than the price of insurance, and, by statute, it can never be more. It may often be a reasonable financial decision to make the payment rather than purchase insurance, unlike the 'prohibitory' financial punishment in Drexel Furniture. . . . Second, the individual mandate contains no scienter requirement. Third, the payment is collected solely by the IRS through the normal means of taxation—except that the Service is *not* allowed to use those means most suggestive of a punitive sanction, such as criminal prosecution. See § 5000A(g)(2). The reasons the Court in *Drexel Furniture* held that what was called a 'tax' there was a penalty support the conclusion that what is called a 'penalty' here may be viewed as a tax.

"None of this is to say that the payment is not intended to affect individual conduct. Although the payment will raise considerable revenue, it is plainly designed to expand health insurance coverage. But taxes that seek to influence conduct are nothing new. Some of our earliest federal taxes sought to deter the purchase of imported manufactured goods in order to foster the growth of domestic industry. . . . Today, federal and state taxes can compose more than half the retail price of cigarettes, not just to raise more money, but to encourage people to quit smoking. And we have upheld such obviously regulatory measures as taxes on selling marijuana and sawed-off shotguns. See United States v. Sanchez, 340 U.S. 42, 44–45 (1950); Sonzinsky v. United States, 300 U.S. 506, 513 (1937). Indeed, '[e]very tax is in some measure regulatory. To some extent it interposes an economic impediment to the activity taxed as compared with others not taxed.' *Sonzinsky,*. . . . That § 5000A seeks to shape decisions about whether to buy health insurance does not mean that it cannot be a valid exercise of the taxing power.

"In distinguishing penalties from taxes, this Court has explained that 'if the concept of penalty means anything, it means punishment for an unlawful act or omission.' United States v. Reorganized CF & I Fabricators of Utah, Inc., 518 U.S. 213, 224 (1996); see also United States v. La Franca, 282 U.S. 568, 572 (1931) ('[A] penalty, as the word is here used, is an exaction imposed by statute as punishment for an unlawful act'). While the individual mandate clearly aims to induce the purchase of health insurance, it need not be read to declare that failing to do so is unlawful. Neither the Act nor any other law attaches negative legal consequences to not buying health insurance, beyond requiring a payment to the IRS. The Government agrees with that reading, confirming that if someone chooses to pay rather than obtain health insurance, they have fully complied with the law. . . .

" . . .

"The joint dissenters argue that we cannot uphold § 5000A as a tax because Congress did not 'frame' it as such. . . . In effect, they contend that even if the Constitution permits Congress to do exactly what we interpret this statute to do, the law must be struck down because Congress used the wrong labels. An example may help illustrate why labels should not control here. Suppose Congress enacted a statute providing that every taxpayer who owns a house without energy efficient windows must pay $50 to the IRS. The amount due is adjusted based on factors such as taxable income and joint filing status, and is paid along with the taxpayer's income tax return. Those whose income is below the filing threshold need not pay. The required payment is not called a 'tax,' a 'penalty,' or anything else. No one would doubt that this law imposed a tax, and was within Congress's power to tax. That conclusion should not change simply because Congress used the word 'penalty' to describe the payment. Interpreting such a law to be a tax would hardly '[i]mpos[e] a tax through judicial legislation.' . . . Rather, it would give practical effect to the Legislature's enactment.

". . . The 'question of the constitutionality of action taken by Congress does not depend on recitals of the power which it undertakes to exercise.' Woods v. Cloyd W. Miller Co., 333 U.S. 138, 144 (1948).

"Even if the taxing power enables Congress to impose a tax on not obtaining health insurance, any tax must still comply with other requirements in the Constitution. Plaintiffs argue that the shared responsibility payment does not do so, citing Article I, § 9, clause 4. That clause provides: 'no Capitation, or other direct, Tax shall be laid, unless in Proportion to the Census or Enumeration herein before directed to be taken.' This requirement means that any 'direct Tax' must be apportioned so that each State pays in proportion to its population. According to the plaintiffs, if the individual mandate imposes a tax, it is a direct tax, and it is unconstitutional because Congress made no effort to apportion it among the States.

"Even when the Direct Tax Clause was written it was unclear what else, other than a capitation (also known as a 'head tax' or a 'poll tax'), might be a direct tax. See Springer v. United States, 102 U.S. 586, 596–598 (1881). Soon after the framing, Congress passed a tax on ownership of carriages, over James Madison's objection that it was an unapportioned direct tax. . . . This Court upheld the tax, in part reasoning that apportioning such a tax would make little sense, because it would have required taxing carriage owners at dramatically different rates depending on how many carriages were in their home State. See Hylton v. United States, 3 Dall. 171, 174 (1796) (opinion of Chase, J.). The Court was unanimous, and those Justices who wrote opinions either directly asserted or strongly suggested that only two forms of taxation were direct: capitations and land taxes. See . . . (opinion of Paterson, J.); . . . (opinion of Iredell, J.).

"That narrow view of what a direct tax might be persisted for a century. In 1880, for example, we explained that '*direct taxes*, within the meaning of the Constitution, are only capitation taxes, as expressed in that instrument, and taxes on real estate.' *Springer*,. . . . In 1895, we expanded our interpretation to include taxes on personal property and income from personal property, in the course of striking down aspects of the federal income tax. Pollock v. Farmers' Loan & Trust Co., 158 U.S. 601, 618 (1895). That result was overturned by the Sixteenth Amendment, although we continued to consider taxes on personal property to be direct taxes. See Eisner v. Macomber, 252 U.S. 189, 218–219 (1920).

"A tax on going without health insurance does not fall within any recognized category of direct tax. It is not a capitation. Capitations are taxes paid by every person, 'without regard to property, profession, or *any other circumstance*.' *Hylton*, . . . (opinion of Chase, J.) (emphasis altered). The whole point of the shared responsibility payment is that it is triggered by specific circumstances—earning a certain amount of income but not obtaining health insurance. The payment is also plainly not a tax on the ownership of land or personal property. The shared responsibility payment is thus not a direct tax that must be apportioned among the several States.

"There may, however, be a more fundamental objection to a tax on those who lack health insurance. Even if only a tax, the payment under § 5000A(b) remains a burden that the Federal Government imposes for an omission, not an act. If it is troubling to interpret the Commerce Clause as authorizing Congress to regulate those who abstain from commerce, perhaps it should be similarly troubling to permit Congress to impose a tax for not doing something.

"Three considerations allay this concern. First, and most importantly, it is abundantly clear the Constitution does not guarantee that individuals may avoid taxation through inactivity. A capitation, after all, is a tax that everyone must pay simply for existing, and capitations are expressly contemplated by the Constitution. . . .

     ". . .

"Second, Congress's ability to use its taxing power to influence conduct is not without limits. A few of our cases policed these limits aggressively, invalidating punitive exactions obviously designed to regulate behavior otherwise regarded at the time as beyond federal authority. . . .

"...

"Third, although the breadth of Congress's power to tax is greater than its power to regulate commerce, the taxing power does not give Congress the same degree of control over individual behavior. Once we recognize that Congress may regulate a particular decision under the Commerce Clause, the Federal Government can bring its full weight to bear. Congress may simply command individuals to do as it directs. An individual who disobeys may be subjected to criminal sanctions. Those sanctions can include not only fines and imprisonment, but all the attendant consequences of being branded a criminal: deprivation of otherwise protected civil rights, such as the right to bear arms or vote in elections; loss of employment opportunities; social stigma; and severe disabilities in other controversies, such as custody or immigration disputes.

"By contrast, Congress's authority under the taxing power is limited to requiring an individual to pay money into the Federal Treasury, no more. If a tax is properly paid, the Government has no power to compel or punish individuals subject to it. . . .

"...

Justices Scalia, Kennedy, Thomas and Alito dissented in a joint opinion, arguing in part:

"So the question is, quite simply, whether the exaction here is imposed for violation of the law. It unquestionably is. The minimum-coverage provision is found in 26 U. S. C. § 5000A, entitled '*Requirement* to maintain minimum essential coverage.' (Emphasis added.) It commands that every 'applicable individual *shall* . . . ensure that the individual . . . is covered under minimum essential coverage.' *Ibid.* (emphasis added). And the immediately following provision states that, '[i]f . . . an applicable individual . . . fails to meet the *requirement* of subsection (a) . . . there is hereby imposed . . . a *penalty.*' § 5000A(b)(emphasis added). . . .

"...

". . . [T]o say that the Individual Mandate merely imposes a tax is not to interpret the statute but to rewrite it. Judicial tax-writing is particularly troubling. . . .

C. THE SPENDING POWER

United States v. Butler

297 U.S. 1 (1936).

One of the major measures of the "new deal", in combating the great depression, was the Agriculture Adjustment Act of 1933. It was designed to raise farm prices and reduce the farm surplus of certain crops through curtailment of production and a tax upon the first processing of these crops. The Secretary of Agriculture was authorized to enter into agreements with individual farmers to reduce acreage in exchange for benefit payments computed on the basis of the reduction. Funds for the payments were derived from a tax levied upon the processor of the commodity involved, the total revenue from the tax being devoted to crop control and no part of it available for general governmental use. The secretary entered into agreements for the reduction of acreage devoted to cotton (as well as certain other crops) and a processing tax was imposed upon the processors, including Hoosac Mills for which Butler was receiver. Suit was brought to recover the tax on the ground that it was invalid as an integral part of an unconstitutional program to control agricultural production.

The act did not purport to be a regulation of interstate or foreign commerce and the government did not attempt to uphold it on the basis of the commerce clause. The court of appeals held the tax unconstitutional and the Supreme Court affirmed.

Justice Roberts, speaking for the Court, said:

"The clause thought to authorize the legislation . . . confers upon the Congress power 'to lay and collect taxes, duties, imposts and excises to pay the debts and provide for the common defence and general welfare of the United States'. . . . It is not contended that this provision grants power to regulate agricultural production upon the theory that such legislation would promote the general welfare. . . . The true construction undoubtedly is that the only thing granted is the power to tax for the purpose of providing funds for payment of the nation's debts and making provision for the general welfare. . . .

"Since the foundation of the nation, sharp differences of opinion have persisted as to the true interpretation of the phrase [to provide for the general welfare]. Madison asserted it amounted to no more than a reference to the other powers enumerated in the subsequent clauses of the same section; that, as the United States is a government of limited and enumerated powers, the grant of power to tax and spend for the general national welfare must be confined to the enumerated legislative fields committed to the Congress. In this view the phrase is mere tautology, for taxation and appropriation are or may be necessary incidents of the exercise of any of the enumerated legislative powers. Hamilton, on the other hand, maintained the clause confers a power separate and distinct from those later enumerated, is not restricted in meaning by the grant of them, and Congress consequently has a substantive power to tax and to appropriate, limited only by the requirement that it shall be exercised to provide for the general welfare of the United States. Each contention has had the support of those whose views are entitled to weight. This court has noticed the question, but has never found it necessary to decide which is the true construction. Mr. Justice Story, in his Commentaries, espouses the Hamiltonian position. We shall not review the writings of public men and commentators or discuss the legislative practice. Study of all these leads us to conclude that the reading advocated by Mr. Justice Story is the correct one. While, therefore, the power to tax is not unlimited, its confines are set in the clause which confers it, and not in those of section 8 which bestow and define the legislative powers of the Congress. It results that the power of Congress to authorize expenditure of public moneys for public purposes is not limited by the direct grants of legislative power found in the Constitution.

"But the adoption of the broader construction leaves the power to spend subject to limitations. . . .

"We are not now required to ascertain the scope of the phrase 'general welfare of the United States' or to determine whether an appropriation in aid of agriculture falls within it. Wholly apart from that question, another principle embedded in our Constitution prohibits the enforcement of the Agricultural Adjustment Act." [The Court went on to find that the act "invades the reserved rights of the states by reaching a matter that was not intended to be within federal control.]

Stone, J. (joined by Brandeis and Cardozo, JJ.) dissented, stating in part:

"The Constitution requires that public funds shall be spent for a defined purpose, the promotion of the general welfare. Their expenditure usually involves payment on terms which will insure use by the selected recipients within the limits of the constitutional purpose. Expenditures would fail of their purpose and thus lose their constitutional sanction if the terms of payment were not such that by their influence on the action of the recipients the permitted end would be attained. The power of Congress to spend is inseparable from persuasion to action over which Congress has no legislative control. Congress may not command that the science of agriculture be taught in state universities. But if it would aid the teaching of that science by grants to state institutions, it is appropriate, if not necessary, that the grant be on the condition, incorporated in the Morrill Act [July 2, 1862], 12 Stat. at L. 503, chap. 130, U.S.C. title 7, § 301, August 30, 1890, 26 Stat. at L. 417, chap. 841, U.S.C. title 7, § 322, that it be used for the intended purpose. Similarly it would seem to be compliance with the Constitution, not violation of it, for the government to take and the university to give a contract that the grant would be so used. It makes no difference that there is a promise to do an act which the condition is calculated to induce. Condition and promise are alike valid since both are in furtherance of the national purpose for which the money is appropriated."

He added: "It is a contradiction in terms to say that there is power to spend for the national welfare, while rejecting the power to impose conditions reasonably adapted to the attainment of the end which alone would justify the expenditure."

Chas. C. Steward Machine Co. v. Davis
301 U.S. 548 (1937).

Plaintiff employer presented a challenge to Title IX of the Social Security Act of 1935 relating to unemployment compensation. A tax was imposed on employers of eight or more persons; the proceeds were not earmarked, but went into the general funds of the treasury. If the taxpayer made contributions to a state unemployment compensation fund created by state law certified by the Social Security Board as meeting certain minimum standards, he was entitled to credit such contributions against his federal tax up to 90% of the tax. In order to assure proper administration of the state compensation system, it was required that contributions to the state fund be paid over to the Secretary of the Treasury to the credit of the Unemployment Trust Fund, the Secretary then being required to pay back to the authorized state agency the sums requisitioned by it. Federal machinery for the administration of the Social Security Act was quickly provided and most states immediately enacted legislation making possible their participation in the program. Steward Machine Company sued Davis, a Collector of Internal Revenue, to recover payroll taxes paid, claiming that the law, particularly the 90% credit provisions, resulted in "coercion of the states" in violation of the Tenth Amendment or of restrictions implicit in our federal system.

In a 5–4 decision the Court sustained the statute. In rejecting the coercion argument, the Court referred to the widespread unemployment during the Great Depression and continued:

". . . The fact developed quickly that the states were unable to give the requisite relief. The problem had become national in area and dimensions. There was need of help from the nation if the people were not to starve. It is too late today for the argument to be heard with tolerance that in a crisis so extreme the use of the moneys of the nation to relieve the unemployed and their dependents is a use for any purpose narrower than the promotion of the general welfare. Cf. United States v. Butler, 297 U.S. 1, 65, 66. . . . The Social Security Act is an attempt to find a method by which all these public agencies may work together to a common end. Every dollar of the new taxes will continue in all likelihood to be used and needed by the nation as long as states are unwilling, whether through timidity or for other motives, to do what can be done at home. At least the inference is permissible that Congress so believed, though retaining undiminished freedom to spend the money as it pleased. On the other hand, fulfillment of the home duty will be lightened and encouraged by crediting the taxpayer upon his account with the Treasury of the nation to the extent that his contributions under the laws of the locality have simplified or diminished the problem of relief and the probable demand upon the resources of the fisc. . . . The difficulty with the petitioner's contention is that it confuses motive with coercion. 'Every tax is in some measure regulatory. To some extent it interposes an economic impediment to the activity taxed as compared with others not taxed.' Sonzinsky v. United States, 300 U.S. 506. In like manner every rebate from a tax when conditioned upon conduct is in some measure a temptation. But to hold that motive or temptation is equivalent to coercion is to plunge the law in endless difficulties. . . .

"In ruling as we do, we leave many questions open. We do not say that a tax is valid, when imposed by act of Congress, if it is laid upon the condition that a state may escape its operation through the adoption of a statute unrelated in subject-matter to activities fairly within the scope of national policy and power. No such question is before us. In the tender of this credit Congress does not intrude upon fields foreign to its function. The purpose of its intervention, as we have shown, is to safeguard its own treasury and as an incident to that protection to place the states upon a footing of equal opportunity. Drains upon its own resources are to be checked; obstructions to the freedom of the states are to be leveled. It is one thing to impose a tax dependent upon the conduct of the taxpayers, or of the state in which they live, where the conduct to be stimulated or discouraged is unrelated to the fiscal need subserved by the tax in its normal operation, or to any other end legitimately national. The Child Labor Tax Case, 259 U.S. 20, and Hill v. Wallace, 259 U.S. 44, were decided in the belief that the statutes there condemned were exposed to that reproach. Cf. United States v. Constantine, 296 U.S. 287. It is quite another thing to say that a tax will be abated upon the doing of an act that will satisfy the fiscal need, the tax and the alternative being approximate equivalents. In such circumstances, if in no others, inducement or persuasion does not go beyond the bounds of power. We do not fix the outermost line. Enough for present purposes that wherever the line may be, this statute is within it. Definition more precise must abide the wisdom of the future. . . .

"United States v. Butler, supra, is cited by petitioner as a decision to the contrary. . . . The decision was by a divided court, a minority taking the view that the objections were untenable. None of them is applicable to the situation here developed.

"(a) The proceeds of the tax in controversy are not earmarked for a special group.

"(b) The unemployment compensation law which is a condition of the credit has had the approval of the state and could not be a law without it.

"(c) The condition is not linked to an irrevocable agreement, for the state at its pleasure may repeal its unemployment law, § 903(a)(6), terminate the credit, and place itself where it was before the credit was accepted.

"(d) The condition is not directed to the attainment of an unlawful end, but to an end, the relief of unemployment, for which nation and state may lawfully cooperate. . . ."

The Court also concluded that the statute did not call "for a surrender by the states of powers essential to their quasi-sovereign existence."

". . . A credit to taxpayers for payments made to a state under a state unemployment law will be manifestly futile in the absence of some assurance that the law leading to the credit is in truth what it professes to be. An unemployment law framed in such a way that the unemployed who look to it will be deprived of reasonable protection is one in name and nothing more. What is basic and essential may be assured by suitable conditions. The terms embodied in these sections are directed to that end. A wide range of judgment is given to the several states as to the particular type of statute to be spread upon their books. . . . What they may not do if they would earn the credit, is to depart from those standards which in the judgment of Congress are to be ranked as fundamental. Even if opinion may differ as to the fundamental quality of one or more of the conditions, the difference will not avail to vitiate the statute. In determining essentials, Congress must have the benefit of a fair margin of discretion. . . ."

Justices McReynolds, Sutherland, Van Devanter and Butler dissented.

Helvering v. Davis

301 U.S. 619 (1937).

This case involved the old age benefit provisions (Titles II and VIII) of the Social Security Act. In meeting the contention that the program for paying old age benefits was not authorized by the general welfare clause, the Court reviewed evidence of the widespread economic plight of the aged and added:

"The problem is plainly national in area and dimensions. Moreover, laws of the separate states cannot deal with it effectively. Congress, at least, had a basis for that belief. States and local governments are often lacking in the resources that are necessary to finance an adequate program of security for the aged. This is brought out with a wealth of illustration in recent studies of the problem. Apart from the failure of resources, states and local governments are at times reluctant to increase so heavily the burden of taxation to be borne by their residents for fear of placing themselves in a position of economic disadvantage as compared with neighbors or competitors.

"We have seen this in our study of the problem of unemployment compensation. Steward Machine Co. v. Davis, supra. A system of old age pensions has special dangers of its own, if put in force in one state and rejected in another. The existence of such a system is a bait to the needy and dependent elsewhere, encouraging them to migrate and seek a haven of repose. Only a power that is national can serve the interests of all.

"Whether wisdom or unwisdom resides in the scheme of benefits set forth in Title II, it is not for us to say. The answer to such inquiries must come from Congress, not the courts. Our concern here, as often, is with power, not with wisdom. Counsel for respondent has recalled to us the virtues of self-reliance and frugality. There is a possibility, he says, that aid from a paternal government may sap those sturdy virtues and breed a race of weaklings. If Massachusetts so believes and shapes her laws in that conviction, must her breed of sons be changed, he asks, because some other philosophy of government finds favor in the halls of Congress? But the answer is not doubtful. One might ask with equal reason whether the system of protective tariffs is to be set aside at will in one state or another whenever local policy prefers the rule of laissez faire. The issue is a closed one. It was fought out long ago. When money is spent to promote the general welfare, the concept of welfare or the opposite is shaped by Congress, not the states. So the concept be not arbitrary, the locality must yield. Constitution, Art. VI, Par. 2. . . ."

Sabri v. United States

541 U.S. 600 (2004).

The Court upheld under Congress' Spending Clause powers 18 U.S.C. § 666(a)(2), which criminally proscribes bribery of state or local officials of entities that receive at least $10,000 in federal funds. Defendant, who was accused of offering three separate bribes to a Minneapolis councilman, "raises what he calls a facial challenge to § 666(a)(2): the law can never be applied constitutionally because it fails to require proof of any connection between a bribe or kickback and some federal money. It is fatal, as he sees it, that the statute does not make the link an element of the crime. . . . We can readily dispose of this position that, to qualify as a valid exercise of Article I power, the statute must require proof of connection with federal money as an element of the offense. . . . Congress has authority under the Spending Clause to appropriate federal monies to promote the general welfare, Art. I. § 8, cl. 1, and it has corresponding authority under the Necessary and Proper Clause, Art. I, § 8, cl. 18, to see to it that taxpayer dollars appropriated under that power are in fact spent for the general welfare, and not frittered away in graft or on projects undermined when funds are siphoned off or corrupt public officers are derelict about demanding value for dollars. . . . Congress does not have to sit by and accept the risk of operations thwarted by local and state improbity. . . . Section 666(a)(2) addresses the problem at the sources of bribes, by rational means, to safeguard the integrity of the state [and] local recipients of federal dollars. It is true, as Sabri says, that not every bribe or kickback offered or paid to agents of governments covered by § 666(b) will be traceably skimmed from specific federal payments. . . . But . . . corruption does not have to be that limited to affect the federal interest. Money is fungible, bribed officials are untrustworthy stewards of federal funds, and corrupt contractors do not deliver dollar-for-dollar value. . . . It is certainly enough that the statutes condition the offense on a threshold amount of federal dollars defining the federal interest, such as that provided here, and on a bribe that goes well beyond liquor and cigars."

The Impact of Federal Grants to the States

Federal grants to the states and local governments have increased rapidly in recent years. Total federal grants-in-aid and shared revenue increased from just under 11 billion dollars in 1965 to an estimated total of 228 billion in 1995. *Statistical Abstract* 1995, p. 302. The percentage of state and local government budgets received from the federal government was 23% in 1994, id.

South Dakota v. Dole

483 U.S. 203 (1987).

South Dakota challenged a federal statute that instructed the Secretary of Transportation to withhold a percentage of federal highway funds to which a state would otherwise be entitled if the state permitted anyone under the age of 21 to purchase or possess in public alcohol. Writing for himself and six other Justices, Chief Justice Rehnquist upheld the condition on the receipt of federal funds. Even assuming the Constitution, in particular the Twenty-First Amendment, prohibited Congress from directly enacting a national minimum drinking age, Congress could legislate under its spending power to encourage uniformity in the States' drinking ages. The Court laid out a four-part test to judge Congress' exercises of spending clause authority. First, "the exercise of the spending power must be in pursuit of 'the general welfare,' "—a question on which Congress is entitled to considerable deference. Second, Congress' conditions on the receipt of federal funds must be imposed "unambiguously" so that the States are able to " 'exercise their choice knowingly, cognizant of the consequences of their participation.' " Third, the condition on federal funding must be related to " 'the federal interest in particular national projects or programs.' " Last, other constitutional provisions may provide "an independent bar" to the conditions imposed. Applying this test, the Court upheld the highway funding statute. In particular, the Court found that Congress' goal of safe highways was one that explained the existence of federal funding in the first place, and that explained the drinking age limitation. Justice O'Connor dissented, complaining that the Court's "application of the requirement that the condition imposed be reasonably related to the purpose for which the funds are expended, is cursory and unconvincing." She objected to the Court's "attenuated" linkage between the goals for which spending was provided, and the conditions imposed on states. Under such a relaxed inquiry, she said, Congress could "regulate almost any area of a State's social, political or economic life. . . ."

National Federation of Independent Business v. Sebelius

567 U.S. 519 (2012).

Seven members of the Court voted to strike down portions of the Patient Protection and Affordable Care Act of 2010 that required States to accept significant expansion of the Medicaid program to previously uncovered persons, or else lose all federal funding for Medicaid, even funding that was available to cover persons who were eligible for Medicaid before the 2010 Act's expansion. Chief Justice Roberts wrote an opinion for himself and Justices Breyer and Kagan, in which he said:

"The States . . . contend that the Medicaid expansion exceeds Congress's authority under the Spending Clause. They claim that Congress is coercing the States to adopt the changes it wants by threatening to withhold all of a State's Medicaid grants, unless the State accepts the new expanded funding and complies with the conditions that come with it. This, they argue, violates the basic principle that the 'Federal Government may not compel the States to enact or administer a federal regulatory program.' *New York v. United States*, 505 U. S., at 188.

"There is no doubt that the Act dramatically increases state obligations under Medicaid. The current Medicaid program requires States to cover only certain discrete categories of needy individuals—pregnant women, children, needy families, the blind, the elderly, and the disabled. 42 U. S. C. § 1396a(a)(10). There is no mandatory coverage for most childless adults, and the States typically do not offer any such coverage. The States also enjoy considerable flexibility with respect to the coverage levels for parents of needy families. § 1396a(a)(10)(A)(ii). On average States cover only those unemployed parents who make less than 37 percent of the federal poverty level, and only those employed parents who make less than 63 percent of the poverty line. . . .

"The Medicaid provisions of the Affordable Care Act, in contrast, require States to expand their Medicaid programs by 2014 to cover *all* individuals under the age of 65 with incomes below 133 percent of the federal poverty line. § 1396a(a)(10)(A)(i)(VIII). The Act also establishes a new '[e]ssential health benefits' package, which States must provide to all new Medicaid recipients—a level sufficient to satisfy a recipient's obligations under the individual mandate. §§ 1396a(k)(1), 1396u–7(b)(5), 18022(b). The Affordable Care Act provides that the Federal Government will pay 100 percent of the costs of covering these newly eligible individuals through 2016. § 1396d(y)(1). In the following years, the federal payment level gradually decreases, to a minimum of 90 percent. *Ibid.* In light of the expansion in coverage mandated by the Act, the Federal Government estimates that its Medicaid spending will increase by approximately $100 billion per year, nearly 40 percent above current levels. . . .

"The Spending Clause grants Congress the power 'to pay the Debts and provide for the . . . general Welfare of the United States.' U. S. Const., Art. I, § 8, cl. 1. We have long recognized that Congress may use this power to grant federal funds to the States, and may condition such a grant upon the States' 'taking certain actions that Congress could not require them to take.' . . . Such measures 'encourage a State to regulate in a particular way, [and] influenc[e] a State's policy choices.' *New York*, ... The conditions imposed by Congress ensure that the funds are used by the States to 'provide for the . . . general Welfare' in the manner Congress intended.

"At the same time, our cases have recognized limits on Congress's power under the Spending Clause to secure state compliance with federal objectives. 'We have repeatedly characterized . . . Spending Clause legislation as "much in the nature of a *contract*." ' Barnes v. Gorman, 536 U.S. 181, 186 (2002). The legitimacy of Congress's exercise of the spending power 'thus rests on whether the State voluntarily and knowingly accepts the terms of the "contract." ' . . . Respecting this limitation is critical to ensuring that Spending Clause legislation does not undermine the status of the States as independent sovereigns in our federal system. That system 'rests on what might at first seem a counterintuitive insight, that "freedom is enhanced by the creation of two governments, not one." ' . . . For this reason, 'the Constitution has never been understood to confer upon Congress the ability to require the States to govern according to Congress' instructions.' *New York,*. . . . Otherwise the two-government system established by the Framers would give way to a system that vests power in one central government, and individual liberty would suffer.

"That insight has led this Court to strike down federal legislation that commandeers a State's legislative or administrative apparatus for federal purposes. . . . It has also led us to scrutinize Spending Clause legislation to ensure that Congress is not using financial inducements to exert a 'power akin to undue influence.' *Steward Machine Co.* v. *Davis,* . . . (1937). Congress may use its spending power to create incentives for States to act in accordance with federal policies. But when 'pressure turns into compulsion,' . . . the legislation runs contrary to our system of federalism. '[T]he Constitution simply does not give Congress the authority to require the States to regulate.' . . . That is true whether Congress directly commands a State to regulate or indirectly coerces a State to adopt a federal regulatory system as its own.

"Permitting the Federal Government to force the States to implement a federal program would threaten the political accountability key to our federal system. '[W]here the Federal Government directs the States to regulate, it maybe state officials who will bear the brunt of public disapproval, while the federal officials who devised the regulatory program may remain insulated from the electoral ramifications of their decision.' . . . Spending Clause programs do not pose this danger when a State has a legitimate choice whether to accept the federal conditions in exchange for federal funds. In such a situation, state officials can fairly be held politically accountable for choosing to accept or refuse the federal offer. But when the State has no choice, the Federal Government can achieve its objectives without accountability, just as in *New York.* . . . Indeed, this danger is heightened when Congress acts under the Spending Clause, because Congress can use that power to implement federal policy it could not impose directly under its enumerated powers.

"We addressed such concerns in *Steward Machine.* That case involved a federal tax on employers that was abated if the businesses paid into a state unemployment plan that met certain federally specified conditions. An employer sued, alleging that the tax was impermissibly 'driv[ing] the state legislatures under the whip of economic pressure into the enactment of unemployment compensation laws at the bidding of the central government.' . . . We acknowledged the danger that the Federal Government might employ its taxing power to exert a 'power akin to undue influence' upon the States. . . . But we observed that Congress adopted the challenged tax and abatement program to channel money to the States that would otherwise have gone into the Federal Treasury for use in providing national unemployment services. Congress was willing to direct businesses to instead pay the money into state programs only on the condition that the money be used for the same purposes. Predicating tax abatement on a State's adoption of a particular type of unemployment legislation was therefore a means to 'safeguard [the Federal Government's] own treasury.' . . . We held that '[i]n such circumstances, if in no others, inducement or persuasion does not go beyond the bounds of power.' . . .

"   . . .

"The States, however, argue that the Medicaid expansion is far from the typical case. They object that Congress has 'crossed the line distinguishing encouragement from coercion,' . . . in the way it has structured the funding: Instead of simply refusing to grant the new funds to States that will not accept the new conditions, Congress has also threatened to withhold those States' existing Medicaid funds. The States claim that this threat serves no purpose other than to force unwilling States to sign up for the dramatic expansion in health care coverage effected by the Act.

"Given the nature of the threat and the programs at issue here, we must agree. We have upheld Congress's authority to condition the receipt of funds on the States' complying with restrictions on the use of those funds, because that is the means by which Congress ensures that the funds are spent according to its view of the 'general Welfare.' Conditions that do not here govern the use of the funds, however, cannot be justified on that basis. When, for example, such conditions take the form of threats to terminate other significant independent grants, the conditions are properly viewed as a means of pressuring the States to accept policy changes.

"In *South Dakota* v. *Dole*, we considered a challenge to a federal law that threatened to withhold five percent of a State's federal highway funds if the State did not raise its drinking age to 21. The Court found that the condition was 'directly related to one of the main purposes for which highway funds are expended—safe interstate travel.' . . . At the same time, the condition was not a restriction on how the highway funds—set aside for specific highway improvement and maintenance efforts— were to be used.

"We accordingly asked whether 'the financial inducement offered by Congress' was 'so coercive as to pass the point at which "pressure turns into compulsion." ' . . . By 'financial inducement' the Court meant the threat of losing five percent of highway funds; no new money was offered to the States to raise their drinking ages. We found that the inducement was not impermissibly coercive, because Congress was offering only 'relatively mild encouragement to the States.' . . . We observed that 'all South Dakota would lose if she adheres to her chosen course as to a suitable minimum drinking age is 5%' of her highway funds. . . . In fact, the federal funds at stake constituted less than half of one percent of South Dakota's budget at the time. . . . In consequence, 'we conclude[d] that [the] encouragement to state action [was] a valid use of the spending power.' . . . Whether to accept the drinking age change 'remain[ed] the prerogative of the States not merely in theory but in fact.' . . .

"In this case, the financial 'inducement' Congress has chosen is much more than 'relatively mild encouragement'—it is a gun to the head. Section 1396c of the Medicaid Act provides that if a State's Medicaid plan does not comply with the Act's requirements, the Secretary of Health and Human Services may declare that 'further payments will not be made to the State.' 42 U. S. C. § 1396c. A State that opts out of the Affordable Care Act's expansion in health care coverage thus stands to lose not merely 'a relatively small percentage' of its existing Medicaid funding, but *all* of it. . . . Medicaid spending accounts for over 20 percent of the average State's total budget, with federal funds covering 50 to 83 percent of those costs. . . . The Federal Government estimates that it will pay out approximately $3.3 trillion between 2010 and 2019 in order to cover the costs of *pre*-expansion Medicaid. . . . In addition, the States have developed intricate statutory and administrative regimes over the course of many decades to implement their objectives under existing Medicaid. It is easy to see how the *Dole* Court could conclude that the threatened loss of less than half of one percent of South Dakota's budget left that State with 'prerogative' to reject Congress's desired policy, 'not merely in theory but in fact.' . . . The threatened loss of over 10 percent of a State's overall budget, in contrast, is economic dragooning that leaves the States with no real option but to acquiesce in the Medicaid expansion.

"Justice Ginsburg [in dissent] claims that *Dole* is distinguishable because here 'Congress has not threatened to withhold funds earmarked for any other program.' . . . But that begs the question: The States contend that the expansion is in reality a new program and that Congress is forcing them to accept it by threatening the funds for the existing Medicaid program. We cannot agree that existing Medicaid and the expansion dictated by the Affordable Care Act are all one program simply because 'Congress styled' them as such. . . . If the expansion is not properly viewed as a modification of the existing Medicaid program, Congress's decision to so title it is irrelevant.

"Here, the Government claims that the Medicaid expansion is properly viewed merely as a modification of the existing program because the States agreed that Congress could change the terms of Medicaid when they signed on in the first place. The Government observes that the Social Security Act, which includes the original Medicaid provisions, contains a clause expressly reserving '[t]he right to alter, amend, or repeal any provision' of that statute. 42 U. S. C. § 1304. So it does. But 'if Congress intends to impose a condition on the grant of federal moneys, it must do so unambiguously.' . . . A State confronted with statutory language reserving the right to 'alter' or 'amend' the pertinent provisions of the Social Security Act might reasonably assume that Congress was entitled to make adjustments to the Medicaid program as it developed. Congress has in fact done so, sometimes conditioning only the new funding, other times both old and new. See, *e.g.,* Social Security Amendments of 1972, 86 Stat. 1381–1382, 1465 (extending Medicaid eligibility, but partly conditioning only the new funding); Omnibus Budget Reconciliation Act of 1990, § 4601, 104 Stat. 1388–166 (extending eligibility, and conditioning old and new funds).

"The Medicaid expansion, however, accomplishes a shift in kind, not merely degree. The original program was designed to cover medical services for four particular categories of the needy: the disabled, the blind, the elderly, and needy families with dependent children. . . . Previous amendments to Medicaid eligibility merely altered and expanded the boundaries of these categories. Under the Affordable Care Act, Medicaid is transformed into a program to meet the health care needs of the entire nonelderly population with income below 133 percent of the poverty level. It is no longer a program to care for the neediest among us, but rather an element of a comprehensive national plan to provide universal health insurance coverage.

" . . .

"As we have explained, '[t]hough Congress' power to legislate under the spending power is broad, it does not include surprising participating States with postacceptance or 'retroactive' conditions.' . . . A State could hardly anticipate that Congress's reservation of the right to 'alter' or 'amend' the Medicaid program included the power to transform it so dramatically.

" . . .

"Nothing in our opinion precludes Congress from offering funds under the Affordable Care Act to expand the availability of health care, and requiring that States accepting such funds comply with the conditions on their use. What Congress is not free to do is to penalize States that choose not to participate in that new program by taking away their existing Medicaid funding. Section 1396c gives the Secretary of Health and Human Services the authority to do just that. It allows her to withhold *all* 'further [Medicaid] payments . . . to the State' if she determines that the State is out of compliance with any Medicaid requirement, including those contained in the expansion. 42 U. S. C. § 1396c. In light of the Court's holding, the Secretary cannot apply § 1396c to withdraw existing Medicaid funds for failure to comply with the requirements set out in the expansion.

"That fully remedies the constitutional violation we have identified. . . ."

A joint opinion by Justices Scalia, Kennedy, Thomas and Alito agreed that the Medicaid expansion provisions of the Act exceeded Congress's conditional spending powers, but would have found that the remedy for such a violation was not simply to prevent the federal government from withholding existing Medicaid funding from States choosing not to undertake the expansion, but also to invalidate other parts of the Act.

Justices Ginsburg and Sotomayor dissented from the Court's invalidation of the Medicaid expansion conditions, arguing that since, "to expand coverage, Congress could have recalled the existing legislation, and replaced it with a new law making Medicaid as embracive of the poor as Congress chose," there ought be no constitutional prohibition on Congress reaching the same place by amending the existing law. Justices Ginsburg and Sotomayor pointed out that, "[p]rior to today's decision, . . . the Court has never ruled that the terms of any grant crossed the indistinct line between temptation and coercion," and questioned the Court's ability to fashion coherent doctrinal lines in this area in subsequent cases:

"When future Spending Clause challenges arrive, as they likely will in the wake of today's decision, how will litigants and judges assess whether 'a State has a legitimate choice whether to accept the federal conditions in exchange for federal funds'? . . . Are courts to measure the number of dollars the Federal Government might withhold for noncompliance? The portion of the State's budget at stake? And which State's—or States'—budget is determinative: the lead plaintiff, all challenging States (26 in this case, many with quite different fiscal situations), or some national median? Does it matter that Florida, unlike most States, imposes no state income tax, and therefore might be able to replace foregone federal funds with new state revenue? Or that the coercion state officials in fact fear is punishment at the ballot box for turning down a politically popular federal grant?

"The coercion inquiry, therefore, appears to involve political judgments that defy judicial calculation. See Baker v. Carr, 369 U.S. 186, 217 (1962). Even commentators sympathetic to robust enforcement of *Dole*'s limitations, . . . have concluded that conceptions of 'impermissible coercion' premised on States' perceived inability to decline federal funds 'are just too amorphous to be judicially administrable.' . . ."

Justices Ginsburg and Sotomayor did agree with the Chief Justice's opinion, however, in its determination that any violation of Congress's Spending Clause powers would be remedied in this case by simply allowing unconsenting states to continue to receive their existing Medicaid funding.

CHAPTER 5

STATE SOVEREIGNTY AND FEDERAL REGULATION

1. STATE IMMUNITY FROM FEDERAL REGULATION

State Regulatory Immunity, 1936–1985

United States v. California, 297 U.S. 175 (1936), sustained a penalty imposed on a state-owned railroad for violation of the Federal Safety Appliance Act. It was not necessary to address California's argument that the non-profit operation of the railroad was performance of "a public function in its sovereign capacity." It was irrelevant whether operation of the railroad was in a sovereign or private capacity. "The sovereign power of the states is necessarily diminished to the extent of the grants of power to the federal government in the Constitution." Chief Justice Stone's opinion for the Court also rejected any analogy to a state's constitutional immunity from federal taxation. "[W]e look to the activities in which the states have traditionally engaged as marking the boundary of the restriction upon the federal taxing power. But there is no such limitation upon the plenary power to regulate commerce. The state can no more deny the power if its exercise has been authorized by Congress than can an individual."

Until 1976, constitutional attacks on application of federal regulatory statutes to state activities were uniformly rejected. Case v. Bowles, 327 U.S. 92 (1946), upheld application of a maximum price under the Emergency Price Control Act as applied to a timber sale by the State of Washington. State of California v. Taylor, 353 U.S. 553 (1957), rejected a challenge to application of the Railway Labor Act to a state owned railroad. (The Act made wages and working conditions subject to a collective bargaining agreement rather than state civil service laws.) Parden v. Terminal Ry. of Alabama State Docks Dept., 377 U.S. 184 (1964), held that a state owned railroad was subject to liability to an injured employee under the Federal Employers' Liability Act. Maryland v. Wirtz, 392 U.S. 183 (1968), sustained application of the wage and hour provisions of the Fair Labor Standards Act to employees of public schools and hospitals. Fry v. United States, 421 U.S. 542 (1975) sustained application of the Economic Stabilization Act to limit wage increases of public employees.

Significantly, however, Justices Douglas and Stewart dissented in Maryland v. Wirtz, arguing that the commerce power could not be exercised in a way that unreasonably interfered with a state's sovereign power. Justice Rehnquist's dissent in Fry v. United States argued that Maryland v. Wirtz should be overruled. Finally, a footnote to Justice Marshall's opinion for the Court in *Fry* contained this statement: "While the Tenth Amendment has been characterized as 'a truism,' . . . United States v. Darby, 312 U.S. 100, 124 (1941), it is not without significance. The Amendment expressly declares the constitutional policy that Congress may not exercise power in a fashion that impairs the States' integrity or their ability to function effectively in a federal system. . . ." 427 U.S. at 547, n. 7.

Maryland v. Wirtz was overruled in the five to four decision of the Court in National League of Cities v. Usery, 426 U.S. 833 (1976). 1974 amendments to the Fair Labor Standards Act extended the Act's maximum hour and minimum wage provisions to employees of the states and their political subdivisions. The Court held that the Act could not constitutionally be applied to state employees performing traditional governmental functions. Justice Rehnquist's opinion for the Court relied on the statement in the footnote to the *Fry* opinion that Congress could not "exercise power in a fashion that impairs the States' integrity or their ability to function effectively in a federal system." Applying the Fair Labor Standards Act to state employees would impose costs and limit flexibility. The Court concluded that "insofar as the challenged amendments operate to directly displace the States' freedom to structure integral operations in areas of traditional government functions, they are not within the authority granted Congress by" the Commerce Clause. Justice Blackmun joined the Court's opinion, but admitted in a concurrence that he was "not untroubled by certain possible implications of the Court's opinion." He explained that he joined the Court's opinion because he read it to adopt "a balancing approach" that permitted federal regulation "where the federal interest is demonstrably greater and where state . . . compliance with imposed federal standards would be essential." Justice Brennan's dissent, joined by Justices White and Marshall, argued that "restraints upon exercise by Congress of its plenary commerce power lies in the political process and not in the judicial process. . . . [T]he political branches of our Government are structured to protect the interests of the States, as well as the Nation as a whole, and . . . the States are fully able to protect their own interests. . . ." Justice Stevens' dissent emphasized the absence of standards distinguishing invalid federal regulation and "federal regulation of state activities that I consider unquestionably permissible."

In Hodel v. Virginia Surface Mining and Reclamation Association, Inc., 452 U.S. 264 (1981), the Court summarized three requirements that *National League of Cities* challenges to federal legislation must meet in order to succeed. "First, there must be a showing that the challenged statute regulates the 'states as states.' . . . Second, the federal regulation must address matters that are indisputably 'attribute[s] of state sovereignty.' . . . And, third, it must be apparent that the States' compliance with the federal law would directly impair their ability 'to structure integral operations in areas of traditional governmental functions.'" (The Court also mentioned in a footnote the possibility that a challenged federal law would be valid, even if all three requirements were satisfied, under the balancing test suggested by Justice Blackmun's concurrence in *National League of Cities*.)

In United Transportation Union v. Long Island Railroad Co., 455 U.S. 678 (1982), the Court was unanimous, concluding that a state-owned railroad was not immune from application of the labor provisions of the Railway Labor Act, because operation of a railroad was not a "traditional" state function. In Equal Employment Opportunity Commission v. Wyoming, 460 U.S. 226 (1983), however, the Court divided five to four with Justice Blackmun joining the four *National League of Cities* dissenters to form the majority. The Court upheld a 1974 amendment to the Age Discrimination in Employment Act extending the Act to state employees. The case arose out of the involuntary retirement of a state game warden at age 55, which violated provisions of the Act forbidding involuntary retirement prior to age 70. Justice Brennan's opinion for the Court concluded that state compliance with the Act would be less costly than, and would not impair flexibility to the same degree as, the minimum wage and maximum hour provisions at issue in *National League of Cities*. The prohibitions of the Age Discrimination Act thus involved federal intrusion that was "sufficiently less serious" and did not impair states' ability to structure their integral operations—a question that "must depend . . . on considerations of degree."

Garcia v. San Antonio Metropolitan Transit Authority

469 U.S. 528, 105 S.Ct. 1005, 83 L.Ed.2d 1016 (1985).

■ JUSTICE BLACKMUN delivered the opinion of the Court.

We revisit in these cases an issue raised in National League of Cities v. Usery, 426 U.S. 833 (1976). In that litigation, this Court, by a sharply divided vote, ruled that the Commerce Clause does not empower Congress to enforce the minimum-wage and overtime provisions of the Fair Labor Standards Act (FLSA) against the States "in areas of traditional governmental functions." Id., at 852. Although *National League of Cities* supplied some examples of "traditional governmental functions," it did not offer a general explanation of how a "traditional" function is to be distinguished from a "nontraditional" one. Since then, federal and state courts have struggled with the task, thus imposed, of identifying a traditional function for purposes of state immunity under the Commerce Clause.

In the present cases, a Federal District Court concluded that municipal ownership and operation of a mass-transit system is a traditional governmental function and thus, under *National League of Cities,* is exempt from the obligations imposed by the FLSA. Faced with the identical question, three Federal Courts of Appeals and one state appellate court have reached the opposite conclusion.

Our examination of this "function" standard applied in these and other cases over the last eight years now persuades us that the attempt to draw the boundaries of state regulatory immunity in terms of "traditional governmental function" is not only unworkable but is inconsistent with established principles of federalism and, indeed, with those very federalism principles on which *National League of Cities* purported to rest. That case, accordingly, is overruled.

I

. . .

The FLSA obligations of public mass-transit systems like SATS [San Antonio Transit System] were expanded in 1974 when Congress provided for the progressive repeal of the surviving overtime exemption for mass-transit employees. Fair Labor Standards Amendments of 1974, § 21(b), 88 Stat. 68. Congress simultaneously brought the States and their subdivisions further within the ambit of the FLSA by extending FLSA coverage to virtually all state and local-government employees. §§ 6(a)(1) and (6), 88 Stat. 58, 60, 29 U.S.C. §§ 203(d) and (x). SATS complied with the FLSA's overtime requirements until 1976, when this Court, in *National League of Cities,* supra, overruled *Maryland v. Wirtz,* and held that the FLSA could not be applied constitutionally to the "traditional governmental functions" of state and local governments. Four months after *National League of Cities* was handed down, SATS informed its employees that the decision relieved SATS of its overtime obligations under the FLSA.

. . .

. . . After initial argument, the cases were restored to our calendar for reargument, and the parties were requested to brief and argue the following additional question:

"Whether or not the principles of the Tenth Amendment as set forth in National League of Cities v. Usery, 426 U.S. 833 (1976), should be reconsidered?" . . .

II

The controversy in the present cases has focused on the third *Hodel* requirement—that the challenged federal statute trench on "traditional governmental functions." . . .

Thus far, this Court itself has made little headway in defining the scope of the governmental functions deemed *protected* under *National League of Cities*. In that case the Court set forth examples of protected and unprotected functions, . . . but provided no explanation of how those examples were identified. The only other case in which the Court has had occasion to address the problem is *Long Island*. We there observed: "The determination of whether a federal law impairs a state's authority with respect to 'areas of traditional [state] functions' may at times be a difficult one." . . . The accuracy of that statement is demonstrated by this Court's own difficulties in *Long Island* in developing a workable standard for "traditional governmental functions." We relied in large part there on "the *historical reality* that the operation of railroads is not among the functions *traditionally* performed by state and local governments," but we simultaneously disavowed "a static historical view of state functions generally immune from federal regulation." . . . Finally, having disclaimed a rigid reliance on the historical pedigree of state involvement in a particular area, we nonetheless found it appropriate to emphasize the extended historical record of federal involvement in the field of rail transportation.

Many constitutional standards involve "undoubte[d] . . . gray areas," . . . and, despite the difficulties that this Court and other courts have encountered so far, it normally might be fair to venture the assumption that case-by-case development would lead to a workable standard for determining whether a particular governmental function should be immune from federal regulation under the Commerce Clause. . . .

. . .

The distinction the Court discarded as unworkable in the field of tax immunity has proved no more fruitful in the field of regulatory immunity under the Commerce Clause. Neither do any of the alternative standards that might be employed to distinguish between protected and unprotected governmental functions appear manageable. We rejected the possibility of making immunity turn on a purely historical standard of "tradition" in *Long Island,* and properly so. The most obvious defect of a historical approach to state immunity is that it prevents a court from accommodating changes in the historical functions of States, changes that have resulted in a number of once-private functions like education being assumed by the States and their subdivisions. At the same time, the only apparent virtue of a rigorous historical standard, namely, its promise of a reasonably objective measure for state immunity, is illusory. Reliance on history as an organizing principle results in linedrawing of the most arbitrary sort; the genesis of state governmental functions stretches over a historical continuum from before the Revolution to the present, and courts would have to decide by fiat precisely how longstanding a pattern of state involvement had to be for federal regulatory authority to be defeated.

A nonhistorical standard for selecting immune governmental functions is likely to be just as unworkable as is a historical standard. . . .

We believe, however, that there is a more fundamental problem at work here, a problem that explains why the Court was never able to provide a basis for the governmental-proprietary distinction in the inter-governmental tax immunity cases and why an attempt to draw similar distinctions with respect to federal regulatory authority under *National League of Cities* is unlikely to succeed regardless of how the distinctions are phrased. The problem is that neither the governmental-proprietary distinction nor any other that purports to separate out important governmental functions can be faithful to the role of federalism in a democratic society. The essence of our federal system is that within the realm of authority left open to them under the Constitution, the States must be equally free to engage in any activity that their citizens choose for the common weal, no matter how unorthodox or unnecessary anyone else—including the judiciary—deems state involvement to be. Any rule of state immunity that looks to the "traditional," "integral," or "necessary" nature of governmental functions inevitably invites an unelected federal judiciary to make decisions about which state policies it favors and which ones it dislikes. . . .

We therefore now reject, as unsound in principle and unworkable in practice, a rule of state immunity from federal regulation that turns on a judicial appraisal of whether a particular governmental function is "integral" or "traditional." Any such rule leads to inconsistent results at the same time that it disserves principles of democratic self-governance, and it breeds inconsistency precisely because it is divorced from those principles. If there are to be limits on the Federal Government's power to interfere with state functions—as undoubtedly there are—we must look elsewhere to find them. We accordingly return to the underlying issue that confronted this Court in *National League of Cities*—the manner in which the Constitution insulates States from the reach of Congress' power under the Commerce Clause.

III

. . .

We doubt that courts ultimately can identify principled constitutional limitations on the scope of Congress' Commerce Clause powers over the States merely by relying on *a priori* definitions of state sovereignty. In part, this is because of the elusiveness of objective criteria for "fundamental" elements of state sovereignty, a problem we have witnessed in the search for "traditional governmental functions." There is, however, a more fundamental reason: the sovereignty of the States is limited by the Constitution itself. A variety of sovereign powers, for example, are withdrawn from the States by Article I, § 10. Section 8 of the same Article works an equally sharp contraction of state sovereignty by authorizing Congress to exercise a wide range of legislative powers and (in conjunction with the Supremacy Clause of Article VI) to displace contrary state legislation. . . .

The States unquestionably do "retai[n] a significant measure of sovereign authority." . . . They do so, however, only to the extent that the Constitution has not divested them of their original powers and transferred those powers to the Federal Government. . . .

. . .

When we look for the States' "residuary and inviolable sovereignty," The Federalist No. 39, p. 285 (B. Wright ed. 1961) (J. Madison), in the shape of the constitutional scheme rather than in predetermined notions of sovereign power, a different measure of state sovereignty emerges. Apart from the limitation on federal authority inherent in the delegated nature of Congress' Article I powers, the principal means chosen by the Framers to ensure the role of the States in the federal system lies in the structure of the Federal Government itself. It is no novelty to observe that the composition of the Federal Government was designed in large part to protect the States from overreaching by Congress.[11] The Framers thus gave the States a role in the selection both of the Executive and the Legislative Branches of the Federal

---

[11] See, e.g., J. Choper, Judicial Review and the National Political Process 175–184 (1980); Wechsler, The Political Safeguards of Federalism: The Role of the States in the Composition and Selection of the National Government, 54 Colum.L.Rev. 543 (1954); La Pierre, The Political Safeguards of Federalism Redux: Intergovernmental Immunity and the States as Agents of the Nation, 60 Wash.U.L.Q. 779 (1982).

Government. The States were vested with indirect influence over the House of Representatives and the Presidency by their control of electoral qualifications and their role in presidential elections. U.S. Const., Art. I, § 2, and Art. II, § 1. They were given more direct influence in the Senate, where each State received equal representation and each Senator was to be selected by the legislature of his State. Art. I, § 3. The significance attached to the States' equal representation in the Senate is underscored by the prohibition of any constitutional amendment divesting a State of equal representation without the State's consent. Art. V.

The extent to which the structure of the Federal Government itself was relied on to insulate the interests of the States is evident in the views of the Framers. . . . In short, the Framers chose to rely on a federal system in which special restraints on federal power over the States inhered principally in the workings of the National Government itself, rather than in discrete limitations on the objects of federal authority. State sovereign interests, then, are more properly protected by procedural safeguards inherent in the structure of the federal system than by judicially created limitations on federal power.

The effectiveness of the federal political process in preserving the States' interests is apparent even today in the course of federal legislation. On the one hand, the States have been able to direct a substantial proportion of federal revenues into their own treasuries in the form of general and program-specific grants in aid. The federal role in assisting state and local governments is a longstanding one; Congress provided federal land grants to finance state governments from the beginning of the Republic, and direct cash grants were awarded as early as 1887 under the Hatch Act. In the past quarter-century alone, federal grants to States and localities have grown from $7 billion to $96 billion. As a result, federal grants now account for about one-fifth of state and local government expenditures. The States have obtained federal funding for such services as police and fire protection, education, public health and hospitals, parks and recreation, and sanitation. Moreover, at the same time that the States have exercised their influence to obtain federal support, they have been able to exempt themselves from a wide variety of obligations imposed by Congress under the Commerce Clause. For example, the Federal Power Act, the National Labor Relations Act, the Labor-Management Reporting and Disclosure Act, the Occupational Safety and Health Act, the Employee Retirement Insurance Security Act, and the Sherman Act all contain express or implied exemptions for States and their subdivisions. The fact that some federal statutes such as the FLSA extend general obligations to the States cannot obscure the extent to which the political position of the States in the federal system has served to minimize the burdens that the States bear under the Commerce Clause.

We realize that changes in the structure of the Federal Government have taken place since 1789, not the least of which has been the substitution of popular election of Senators by the adoption of the Seventeenth Amendment in 1913, and that these changes may work to alter the influence of the States in the federal political process. Nonetheless, against this background, we are convinced that the fundamental limitation that the constitutional scheme imposes on the Commerce Clause to protect the "States as States" is one of process rather than one of result. Any substantive restraint on the exercise of Commerce Clause powers must find its justification in the procedural nature of this basic limitation, and it must be tailored to compensate for possible failings in the national political process rather than to dictate a "sacred province of state autonomy." EEOC v. Wyoming, 460 U.S., at 236.

Insofar as the present cases are concerned, then, we need go no further than to state that we perceive nothing in the overtime and minimum-wage requirements of the FLSA, as applied to SAMTA, that is destructive of state sovereignty or violative of any constitutional provision. SAMTA faces nothing more than the same minimum-wage and overtime obligations that hundreds of thousands of other employers, public as well as private, have to meet.

. . .

IV

. . .

We do not lightly overrule recent precedent. We have not hesitated, however, when it has become apparent that a prior decision has departed from a proper understanding of congressional power under the Commerce Clause. . . . Due respect for the reach of congressional power within the federal system mandates that we do so now.

National League of Cities v. Usery, 426 U.S. 833 (1976), is overruled. The judgment of the District Court is reversed, and these cases are remanded to that court for further proceedings consistent with this opinion.

It is so ordered.

■ JUSTICE POWELL, with whom THE CHIEF JUSTICE, JUSTICE REHNQUIST, and JUSTICE O'CONNOR join, dissenting.

The Court today, in its 5–4 decision, overrules National League of Cities v. Usery, 426 U.S. 833 (1976), a case in which we held that Congress lacked authority to impose the requirements of the Fair Labor Standards Act on state and local governments. Because I believe this decision substantially alters the federal system embodied in the Constitution, I dissent.

I

There are, of course, numerous examples over the history of this Court in which prior decisions have been reconsidered and overruled. There have been few cases, however, in which the principle of *stare decisis* and the rationale of recent decisions were ignored as abruptly as we now witness. . . .

. . .

Whatever effect the Court's decision may have in weakening the application of *stare decisis,* it is likely to be less important than what the Court has done to the Constitution itself. A unique feature of the United States is the *federal* system of government guaranteed by the Constitution and implicit in the very name of our country. Despite some genuflecting in the Court's opinion to the concept of federalism, today's decision effectively reduces the Tenth Amendment to meaningless rhetoric when Congress acts pursuant to the Commerce Clause. . . .

II

. . .

B

Today's opinion does not explain how the States' role in the electoral process guarantees that particular exercises of the Commerce Clause power will not infringe on residual State sovereignty. Members of Congress are elected from the various States, but once in office they are members of the federal government. Although the States participate in the Electoral College, this is hardly a reason to view the President as a representative of the States' interest against federal encroachment. We noted recently "the hydraulic pressure inherent within each of the separate Branches to exceed the outer limits of its power. . . ." Immigration and Naturalization Service v. Chadha, 462 U.S. 919, 951 (1983). The Court offers no reason to think that this pressure will not operate when Congress seeks to invoke its powers under the Commerce Clause, notwithstanding the electoral role of the States.[9]

. . .

. . . At least since *Marbury v. Madison* it has been the settled province of the federal judiciary "to say what the law is" with respect to the constitutionality of acts of Congress. . . . In rejecting the role of the judiciary in protecting the States from federal overreaching, the Court's opinion offers no explanation for ignoring the teaching of the most famous case in our history.

. . .

■ JUSTICE REHNQUIST, dissenting.

I join both Justice Powell's and Justice O'Connor's thoughtful dissents. Justice Powell's reference to the "balancing test" approved in *National League of Cities* is not identical with the language in that case, which recognized that Congress could not act under its commerce power to infringe on certain fundamental aspects of state sovereignty that are essential to "the States' separate and independent existence." Nor is either test, or Justice O'Connor's suggested approach, precisely congruent with Justice Blackmun's views in 1976, when he spoke of a balancing approach which did not outlaw federal power in areas "where the federal interest is demonstrably greater." But under any one of these approaches the judgment in this case should be affirmed, and I do not think it incumbent on those of us in dissent to spell out further the fine points of a principle that will, I am confident, in time again command the support of a majority of this Court.

■ JUSTICE O'CONNOR, with whom JUSTICE POWELL and JUSTICE REHNQUIST join, dissenting.

. . .

The problems of federalism in an integrated national economy are capable of more responsible resolution than holding that the States as States retain no status apart from that which Congress chooses to let them retain. The proper resolution, I suggest, lies in weighing state autonomy as a factor in the balance when interpreting the means by which Congress can exercise its authority on the States as States. It is insufficient, in assessing the validity of congressional regulation of a State pursuant to the commerce power, to ask only whether the same regulation would be valid if

---

[9]   At one time in our history, the view that the structure of the federal government sufficed to protect the States might have had a somewhat more practical, although not a more logical, basis. Professor Wechsler, whose seminal article in 1954 proposed the view adopted by the Court today, predicated his argument on assumptions that simply do not accord with current reality. Professor Wechsler wrote: "National action has . . . always been regarded as exceptional in our polity, an intrusion to be justified by some necessity, the special rather than the ordinary case." Wechsler, The Political Safeguards of Federalism: The Role of the States in the Composition and Selection of the National Government, 54 Colum.L.Rev. 543, 544 (1954). Not only is the premise of this view clearly at odds with the proliferation of national legislation over the past 30 years, but "a variety of structural and political changes in this century have combined to make Congress particularly *insensitive* to state and local values." Advisory Comm'n on Intergovernmental Relations [ACIR], Regulatory Federalism: Policy, Process, Impact and Reform 50 (1984). The adoption of the Seventeenth Amendment (providing for direct election of senators), the weakening of political parties on the local level, and the rise of national media, among other things, have made Congress increasingly less representative of State and local interests, and more likely to be responsive to the demands of various national constituencies. Id., at 50–51. As one observer explained, "As Senators and members of the House develop independent constituencies among groups such as farmers, businessmen, laborers, environmentalists, and the poor, each of which generally supports certain national initiatives, their tendency to identify with state interests and the positions of state officials is reduced." Kaden, "Federalism in the Courts: Agenda for the 1980s," in ACIR, The Future of Federalism in the '80s, at 97 (1981).

enforced against a private party. That reasoning, embodied in the majority opinion, is inconsistent with the spirit of our Constitution. . . .

. . .

New York v. United States

505 U.S. 144, 112 S.Ct. 2408, 120 L.Ed.2d 120 (1992).

■ JUSTICE O'CONNOR delivered the opinion of the Court.

This case implicates one of our Nation's newest problems of public policy and perhaps our oldest question of constitutional law. The public policy issue involves the disposal of radioactive waste: In this case, we address the constitutionality of three provisions of the Low-Level Radioactive Waste Policy Amendments Act of 1985, Pub.L. 99–240, 99 Stat. 1842, 42 U.S.C. § 2021b et seq. The constitutional question is as old as the Constitution: It consists of discerning the proper division of authority between the Federal Government and the States. We conclude that while Congress has substantial power under the Constitution to encourage the States to provide for the disposal of the radioactive waste generated within their borders, the Constitution does not confer upon Congress the ability simply to compel the States to do so. We therefore find that only two of the Act's three provisions at issue are consistent with the Constitution's allocation of power to the Federal Government.

I

We live in a world full of low level radioactive waste. Radioactive material is present in luminous watch dials, smoke alarms, measurement devices, medical fluids, research materials, and the protective gear and construction materials used by workers at nuclear power plants. Low level radioactive waste is generated by the Government, by hospitals, by research institutions, and by various industries. The waste must be isolated from humans for long periods of time, often for hundreds of years. Millions of cubic feet of low level radioactive waste must be disposed of each year. . . .

. . . [S]ince 1979 only three disposal sites—those in Nevada, Washington, and South Carolina—have been in operation. Waste generated in the rest of the country must be shipped to one of these three sites for disposal. . . . In 1979, both the Washington and Nevada sites were forced to shut down temporarily, leaving South Carolina to shoulder the responsibility of storing low level radioactive waste produced in every part of the country. The Governor of South Carolina, understandably perturbed, ordered a 50% reduction in the quantity of waste accepted at the Barnwell site. The Governors of Washington and Nevada announced plans to shut their sites permanently.

Faced with the possibility that the Nation would be left with no disposal sites for low level radioactive waste, Congress responded by enacting the Low-Level Radioactive Waste Policy Act, . . . Relying largely on a report submitted by the National Governors' Association, Congress declared a federal policy of holding each State "responsible for providing for the availability of capacity either within or outside the State for the disposal of low-level radioactive waste generated within its borders," and found that such waste could be disposed of "most safely and efficiently . . . on a regional basis." § 4(a)(1) . . . The 1980 Act authorized States to enter into regional compacts that, once ratified by Congress, would have the authority beginning in 1986 to restrict the use of their disposal facilities to waste generated within member States. § 4(a)(2)(B) . . . The 1980 Act included no penalties for States that failed to participate in this plan.

By 1985, only three approved regional compacts had operational disposal facilities; not surprisingly, these were the compacts formed around South Carolina, Nevada, and Washington, the three sited States. The following year, the 1980 Act would have given these three compacts the ability to exclude waste from nonmembers, and the remaining 31 States would have had no assured outlet for their low level radioactive waste. With this prospect looming, Congress once again took up the issue of waste disposal. The result was the legislation challenged here, the Low-Level Radioactive Waste Policy Amendments Act of 1985.

The 1985 Act was again based largely on a proposal submitted by the National Governors' Association. In broad outline, the Act embodies a compromise among the sited and unsited States. The sited States agreed to extend for seven years the period in which they would accept low level radioactive waste from other States. In exchange, the unsited States agreed to end their reliance on the sited States by 1992.

The mechanics of this compromise are intricate. The Act directs: "Each State shall be responsible for providing, either by itself or in cooperation with other States, for the disposal of . . . low-level radioactive waste generated within the State," . . . , with the exception of certain waste generated by the Federal Government . . . The Act authorizes States to "enter into such [interstate] compacts as may be necessary to provide for the establishment and operation of regional disposal facilities for low-level radioactive waste." . . . For an additional seven years beyond the period contemplated by the 1980 Act, from the beginning of 1986 through the end of 1992, the three existing disposal sites "shall make disposal capacity available for low-level radioactive waste generated by any source," with certain exceptions not relevant here. . . . But the three States in which the disposal sites are located are permitted to exact a graduated surcharge for waste arriving from outside the regional compact. . . . After the seven-year transition period expires, approved regional compacts may exclude radioactive waste generated outside the region. . . . The Act provides three types of incentives to encourage the States to comply with their statutory obligation to provide for the disposal of waste generated within their borders.

1.   Monetary incentives. One quarter of the surcharges collected by the sited States must be transferred to an escrow account held by the Secretary of Energy. . . . The Secretary then makes payments from this account to each State that has complied with a series of deadlines. By July 1, 1986, each State was to have ratified legislation either joining a regional compact or indicating an intent to develop a disposal facility within the State. . . . By January 1, 1988, each unsited compact was to have identified the State in which its facility would be located, and each compact or stand-alone State was to have developed a siting plan and taken other identified steps. . . . By January 1, 1990, each State or compact was to have filed a complete application for a license to operate a disposal facility, or the Governor of any State that had not filed an application was to have certified that the State would be capable of disposing of all waste generated in the State after 1992. . . . The rest of the account is to be paid out to those States or compacts able to dispose of all low level radioactive waste generated within their borders by January 1, 1993. . . . Each State that has not met the 1993 deadline must either take title to the waste generated within its borders or forfeit to the waste generators the incentive payments it has received. . . .

2.   Access incentives. The second type of incentive involves the denial of access to disposal sites. States that fail to meet the July 1986 deadline may be charged twice the ordinary surcharge for the remainder of 1986 and may be denied access to disposal facilities thereafter. . . . States that fail to meet the 1988 deadline may be charged double surcharges for the first half of 1988 and quadruple surcharges for the second half of 1988, and may be denied access thereafter. . . . States that fail to meet the 1990 deadline may be denied access. . . . Finally, States that have not filed complete

applications by January 1, 1992, for a license to operate a disposal facility, or States belonging to compacts that have not filed such applications, may be charged triple surcharges. . . .

3. The take title provision. The third type of incentive is the most severe. The Act provides: "If a State (or, where applicable, a compact region) in which low-level radioactive waste is generated is unable to provide for the disposal of all such waste generated within such State or compact region by January 1, 1996, each State in which such waste is generated, upon the request of the generator or owner of the waste, shall take title to the waste, be obligated to take possession of the waste, and shall be liable for all damages directly or indirectly incurred by such generator or owner as a consequence of the failure of the State to take possession of the waste as soon after January 1, 1996, as the generator or owner notifies the State that the waste is available for shipment." . . . These three incentives are the focus of petitioners' constitutional challenge.

In the seven years since the Act took effect, Congress has approved nine regional compacts, encompassing 42 of the States. All six unsited compacts and four of the unaffiliated States have met the first three statutory milestones.

New York, a State whose residents generate a relatively large share of the Nation's low level radioactive waste, did not join a regional compact. Instead, the State complied with the Act's requirements by enacting legislation providing for the siting and financing of a disposal facility in New York. The State has identified five potential sites, three in Allegany County and two in Cortland County. Residents of the two counties oppose the State's choice of location.

Petitioners—the State of New York and the two counties—filed this suit against the United States in 1990. They sought a declaratory judgment that the Act is inconsistent with the Tenth . . . Amendment to the Constitution, . . . and with the Guarantee Clause of Article IV of the Constitution. The States of Washington, Nevada, and South Carolina intervened as defendants. The District Court dismissed the complaint. The Court of Appeals affirmed. . . .

II

. . .

B

Petitioners do not contend that Congress lacks the power to regulate the disposal of low level radioactive waste. . . . Petitioners likewise do not dispute that under the Supremacy Clause Congress could, if it wished, pre-empt state radioactive waste regulation. Petitioners contend only that the Tenth Amendment limits the power of Congress to regulate in the way it has chosen. Rather than addressing the problem of waste disposal by directly regulating the generators and disposers of waste, petitioners argue, Congress has impermissibly directed the States to regulate in this field.

Most of our recent cases interpreting the Tenth Amendment have concerned the authority of Congress to subject state governments to generally applicable laws. The Court's jurisprudence in this area has traveled an unsteady path. See . . . San Antonio Metropolitan Transit Authority . . . (overruling *National League of Cities*) . . . This case presents no occasion to apply or revisit the holdings of any of these cases, as this is not a case in which Congress has subjected a State to the same legislation applicable to private parties. . . .

This case instead concerns the circumstances under which Congress may use the States as implements of regulation; that is, whether Congress may direct or otherwise motivate the States to regulate in a particular field or a particular way. Our cases have established a few principles that guide our resolution of the issue.

1

As an initial matter, Congress may not simply "commandee[r] the legislative processes of the States by directly compelling them to enact and enforce a federal regulatory program." Hodel v. Virginia Surface Mining & Reclamation Assn., Inc., 452 U.S. 264, 288 (1981). In *Hodel,* the Court upheld the Surface Mining Control and Reclamation Act of 1977 precisely because it did not "commandeer" the States into regulating mining. The Court found that "the States are not compelled to enforce the steep-slope standards, to expend any state funds, or to participate in the federal regulatory program in any manner whatsoever. If a State does not wish to submit a proposed permanent program that complies with the Act and implementing regulations, the full regulatory burden will be borne by the Federal Government." . . .

. . .

. . . While Congress has substantial powers to govern the Nation directly, including in areas of intimate concern to the States, the Constitution has never been understood to confer upon Congress the ability to require the States to govern according to Congress' instructions. . . .

Indeed, the question whether the Constitution should permit Congress to employ state governments as regulatory agencies was a topic of lively debate among the Framers. Under the Articles of Confederation, Congress lacked the authority in most respects to govern the people directly. In practice, Congress "could not directly tax or legislate upon individuals; it had no explicit 'legislative' or 'governmental' power to make binding 'law' enforceable as such." Amar, Of Sovereignty and Federalism, 96 Yale L.J. 1425, 1447 (1987).

The inadequacy of this governmental structure was responsible in part for the Constitutional Convention. . . .

The Convention generated a great number of proposals for the structure of the new Government, but two quickly took center stage. Under the Virginia Plan, as first introduced by Edmund Randolph, Congress would exercise legislative authority directly upon individuals, without employing the States as intermediaries. . . . Under the New Jersey Plan, as first introduced by William Paterson, Congress would continue to require the approval of the States before legislating, as it had under the Articles of Confederation. . . .

. . .

In the end, the Convention opted for a Constitution in which Congress would exercise its legislative authority directly over individuals rather than over States; for a variety of reasons, it rejected the New Jersey Plan in favor of the Virginia Plan. . . .

In providing for a stronger central government, therefore, the Framers explicitly chose a Constitution that confers upon Congress the power to regulate individuals, not States. As we have seen, the Court has consistently respected this choice. We have always understood that even where Congress has the authority under the Constitution to pass laws requiring or prohibiting certain acts, it lacks the power directly to compel the States to require or prohibit those acts. . . . The allocation of power contained in the Commerce Clause, for example, authorizes Congress to regulate interstate commerce directly; it does not authorize Congress to regulate state governments' regulation of interstate commerce.

2

This is not to say that Congress lacks the ability to encourage a State to regulate in a particular way, or that Congress may not hold out incentives to the States as a method of influencing a State's policy choices. Our cases have identified a variety of methods, short of outright coercion, by which Congress may urge a State to adopt a legislative program consistent with federal interests. Two of these methods are of particular relevance here.

First, under Congress' spending power, "Congress may attach conditions on the receipt of federal funds." South Dakota v. Dole, 483 U.S., at 206. Such conditions must (among other requirements) bear some relationship to the purpose of the federal spending, . . . ; otherwise, of course, the spending power could render academic the Constitution's other grants and limits of federal authority. Where the recipient of federal funds is a State, as is not unusual today, the conditions attached to the funds by Congress may influence a State's legislative choices. . . . *Dole* was one such case: The Court found no constitutional flaw in a federal statute directing the Secretary of Transportation to withhold federal highway funds from States failing to adopt Congress' choice of a minimum drinking age. . . .

Second, where Congress has the authority to regulate private activity under the Commerce Clause, we have recognized Congress' power to offer States the choice of regulating that activity according to federal standards or having state law pre-empted by federal regulation. Hodel v. Virginia Surface Mining & Reclamation Assn., Inc., supra, at 288. See also FERC v. Mississippi, supra, at 764–765. This arrangement, which has been termed "a program of cooperative federalism," *Hodel,* supra, at 289, is replicated in numerous federal statutory schemes. These include the Clean Water Act, . . . ; the Occupational Safety and Health Act of 1970, . . . the Resource Conservation and Recovery Act of 1976, . . . ; and the Alaska National Interest Lands Conservation Act, . . .

By either of these two methods, as by any other permissible method of encouraging a State to conform to federal policy choices, the residents of the State retain the ultimate decision as to whether or not the State will comply. If a State's citizens view federal policy as sufficiently contrary to local interests, they may elect to decline a federal grant. If state residents would prefer their government to devote its attention and resources to problems other than those deemed important by Congress, they may choose to have the Federal Government rather than the State bear the expense of a federally mandated regulatory program, and they may continue to supplement that program to the extent state law is not pre-empted. Where Congress encourages state regulation rather than compelling it, state governments remain responsive to the local electorate's preferences; state officials remain accountable to the people.

By contrast, where the Federal Government compels States to regulate, the accountability of both state and federal officials is diminished. If the citizens of New York, for example, do not consider that making provision for the disposal of radioactive waste is in their best interest, they may elect state officials who share their view. That view can always be pre-empted under the Supremacy Clause if it is contrary to the national view, but in such a case it is the Federal Government that makes the decision in full view of the public, and it will be federal officials that suffer the consequences if the decision turns out to be detrimental or unpopular. But where the Federal Government directs the States to regulate, it may be state officials who will bear the brunt of public disapproval, while the federal officials who devised the regulatory program may remain insulated from the electoral ramifications of their decision. Accountability is thus diminished when, due to federal coercion, elected state officials cannot regulate in accordance with the views of the local electorate in matters not pre-empted by federal regulation. . . .

With these principles in mind, we turn to the three challenged provisions of the Low-Level Radioactive Waste Policy Amendments Act of 1985.

III

The parties in this case advance two quite different views of the Act. As petitioners see it, the Act imposes a requirement directly upon the States that they regulate in the field of radioactive waste disposal in order to meet Congress' mandate that "[e]ach State shall be responsible for providing . . . for the disposal of . . . low-level radioactive waste." . . . Petitioners understand this provision as a direct command from Congress, enforceable independent of the three sets of incentives provided by the Act. Respondents, on the other hand, read this provision together with the incentives, and see the Act as affording the States three sets of choices. According to respondents, the Act permits a State to choose first between regulating pursuant to federal standards and losing the right to a share of the Secretary of Energy's escrow account; to choose second between regulating pursuant to federal standards and progressively losing access to disposal sites in other States; and to choose third between regulating pursuant to federal standards and taking title to the waste generated within the State. . . .

The Act could plausibly be understood either as a mandate to regulate or as a series of incentives. Under petitioners' view, however, . . . the Act would clearly "commandee[r] the legislative processes of the States by directly compelling them to enact and enforce a federal regulatory program." . . . We must reject this interpretation of the provision for two reasons. First, such an outcome would, to say the least, "upset the usual constitutional balance of federal and state powers." . . . Second, "where an otherwise acceptable construction of a statute would raise serious constitutional problems, the Court will construe the statute to avoid such problems unless such construction is plainly contrary to the intent of Congress." . . .

We therefore decline petitioners' invitation to construe § 2021c(a)(1)(A), alone and in isolation, as a command to the States independent of the remainder of the Act. Construed as a whole, the Act comprises three sets of "incentives" for the States to provide for the disposal of low level radioactive waste generated within their borders. We consider each in turn.

A

The first set of incentives works in three steps. First, Congress has authorized States with disposal sites to impose a surcharge on radioactive waste received from other States. Second, the Secretary of Energy collects a portion of this surcharge and places the money in an escrow account. Third, States achieving a series of milestones receive portions of this fund.

The first of these steps is an unexceptionable exercise of Congress' power to authorize the States to burden interstate commerce. . . . Whether or not the States would be permitted to burden the interstate transport of low level radioactive waste in the absence of Congress' approval, the States can clearly do so with Congress' approval, which is what the Act gives them.

The second step, the Secretary's collection of a percentage of the surcharge, is no more than a federal tax on interstate commerce, which petitioners do not claim to be an invalid exercise of either Congress' commerce or taxing power. . . .

The third step is a conditional exercise of Congress' authority under the Spending Clause: Congress has placed conditions—the achievement of the milestones—on the receipt of federal funds. . . .

The Act's first set of incentives, in which Congress has conditioned grants to the States upon the States' attainment of a series of milestones, is thus well within the authority of Congress under the Commerce and Spending Clauses. Because the first set of incentives is supported by affirmative constitutional grants of power to Congress, it is not inconsistent with the Tenth Amendment.

B

In the second set of incentives, Congress has authorized States and regional compacts with disposal sites gradually to increase the cost of access to the sites, and then to deny access altogether, to radioactive waste generated in States that do not meet federal deadlines. As a simple regulation, this provision would be within the power of Congress to authorize the States to discriminate against interstate commerce. . . . Where federal regulation of private activity is within the scope of the Commerce Clause, we have recognized the ability of Congress to offer states the choice of regulating that activity according to federal standards or having state law preempted by federal regulation. . . .

This is the choice presented to nonsited States by the Act's second set of incentives: States may either regulate the disposal of radioactive waste according to federal standards by attaining local or regional self-sufficiency, or their residents who produce radioactive waste will be subject to federal regulation authorizing sited States and regions to deny access to their disposal sites. The affected States are not compelled by Congress to regulate, because any burden caused by a State's refusal to regulate will fall on those who generate waste and find no outlet for its disposal, rather than on the State as a sovereign. A State whose citizens do not wish it to attain the Act's milestones may devote its attention and its resources to issues its citizens deem more worthy; the choice remains at all times with the residents of the State, not with Congress. The State need not expend any funds, or participate in any federal program, if local residents do not view such expenditures or participation as worthwhile. . . . Nor must the State abandon the field if it does not accede to federal direction; the State may continue to regulate the generation and disposal of radioactive waste in any manner its citizens see fit.

The Act's second set of incentives thus represents a conditional exercise of Congress' commerce power, along the lines of those we have held to be within Congress' authority. As a result, the second set of incentives does not intrude on the sovereignty reserved to the States by the Tenth Amendment.

C

The take title provision is of a different character. This third so-called "incentive" offers States, as an alternative to regulating pursuant to Congress' direction, the option of taking title to and possession of the low level radioactive waste generated within their borders and becoming liable for all damages waste generators suffer as a result of the States' failure to do so promptly. In this provision, Congress has crossed the line distinguishing encouragement from coercion.

The take title provision offers state governments a "choice" of either accepting ownership of waste or regulating according to the instructions of Congress. Respondents do not claim that the Constitution would authorize Congress to impose either option as a freestanding requirement. On one hand, the Constitution would not permit Congress simply to transfer radioactive waste from generators to state governments. Such a forced transfer, standing alone, would in principle be no different than a congressionally compelled subsidy from state governments to radioactive waste producers. The same is true of the provision requiring the States to become liable for the generators' damages. Standing alone, this provision would be indistinguishable from an Act of Congress directing the States to assume the liabilities of certain state residents. Either type of federal action would "commandeer" state governments into the service of federal regulatory purposes, and would for this reason be inconsistent with the Constitution's division of authority between federal and state governments.

On the other hand, the second alternative held out to state governments—regulating pursuant to Congress' direction—would, standing alone, present a simple command to state governments to implement legislation enacted by Congress. As we have seen, the Constitution does not empower Congress to subject state governments to this type of instruction.

Because an instruction to state governments to take title to waste, standing alone, would be beyond the authority of Congress, and because a direct order to regulate, standing alone, would also be beyond the authority of Congress, it follows that Congress lacks the power to offer the States a choice between the two. Unlike the first two sets of incentives, the take title incentive does not represent the conditional exercise of any congressional power enumerated in the Constitution. In this provision, Congress has not held out the threat of exercising its spending power or its commerce power; it has instead held out the threat, should the States not regulate according to one federal instruction, of simply forcing the States to submit to another federal instruction. A choice between two unconstitutionally coercive regulatory techniques is no choice at all. . . .

The take title provision appears to be unique. No other federal statute has been cited which offers a state government no option other than that of implementing legislation enacted by Congress.

. . .

IV

Respondents raise a number of objections to this understanding of the limits of Congress' power.

A

The United States proposes three alternative views of the constitutional line separating state and federal authority. While each view concedes that Congress generally may not compel state governments to regulate pursuant to federal direction, each purports to find a limited domain in which such coercion is permitted by the Constitution.

First, the United States argues that the Constitution's prohibition of congressional directives to state governments can be overcome where the federal interest is sufficiently important to justify state submission. . . . But whether or not a particularly strong federal interest enables Congress to bring state governments within the orbit of generally applicable federal regulation, no Member of the Court has ever suggested that such a federal interest would enable Congress to command a state government to enact state regulation. No matter how powerful the federal interest involved, the Constitution simply does not give Congress the authority to require the States to regulate. The Constitution instead gives Congress the authority to regulate matters directly and to pre-empt contrary state regulation. Where a federal interest is sufficiently strong to cause Congress to legislate, it must do so directly; it may not conscript state governments as its agents.

Second, the United States argues that the Constitution does, in some circumstances, permit federal directives to state governments. Various cases are cited for this proposition, but none support it. Some of these cases discuss the well established power of Congress to pass laws enforceable in state courts. See Testa v. Katt, 330 U.S. 386 (1947). . . . Federal statutes enforceable in state courts do, in a sense, direct state judges to enforce them, but this sort of federal "direction" of state judges is mandated by the text of the Supremacy Clause. No comparable constitutional provision authorizes Congress to command state legislatures to legislate.

Additional cases cited by the United States discuss the power of federal courts to order state officials to comply with federal law. . . . Again, however, the text of the Constitution plainly confers this authority on the federal courts, the "judicial Power" of which "shall extend to all Cases, in Law and Equity, arising under this Constitution, [and] the Laws of the United States . . . ; [and] to Controversies between two or more States; [and] between a State and Citizens of another State." U.S. Const., Art. III, § 2. The Constitution contains no analogous grant of authority to Congress. Moreover, the Supremacy Clause makes federal law paramount over the contrary positions of state officials; the power of federal courts to enforce federal law thus presupposes some authority to order state officials to comply. . . .

In sum, the cases relied upon by the United States hold only that federal law is enforceable in state courts and that federal courts may in proper circumstances order state officials to comply with federal law, propositions that by no means imply any authority on the part of Congress to mandate state regulation.

. . .

B

The sited State respondents focus their attention on the process by which the Act was formulated. They correctly observe that public officials representing the State of New York lent their support to the Act's enactment. . . . Respondents then pose what appears at first to be a troubling question: How can a federal statute be found an unconstitutional infringement of State sovereignty when state officials consented to the statute's enactment?

. . .

Where Congress exceeds its authority relative to the States . . . the departure from the constitutional plan cannot be ratified by the "consent" of state officials. An analogy to the separation of powers among the Branches of the Federal Government clarifies this point. The Constitution's division of power among the three Branches is violated where one Branch invades the territory of another, whether or not the encroached-upon Branch approves the encroachment. . . . The constitutional authority of Congress cannot be expanded by the "consent" of the governmental unit whose domain is thereby narrowed, whether that unit is the Executive Branch or the States.

. . . [a]

VI

Having determined that the take title provision exceeds the powers of Congress, we must consider whether it is severable from the rest of the Act.

. . .

. . . [T]he take title provision may be severed without doing violence to the rest of the Act. The Act is still operative and it still serves Congress' objective of encouraging the States to attain local or regional self-sufficiency in the disposal of low level radioactive waste. . . .

VII

. . .

States are not mere political subdivisions of the United States. . . .

---

[a] The Court held open the question whether a claim that the federal statute would violate the Guarantee Clause of the Constitution might be judicially reviewable, and said that in any event that neither the monetary incentives in the law nor the possibility that a State's waste producers may find themselves exclude from disposal sites in another State would pose any realistic threat to the form or method of functioning of New York's government.

. . . The Federal Government may not compel the States to enact or administer a federal regulatory program. . . . The Constitution enables the Federal Government to pre-empt state regulation contrary to federal interests, and it permits the Federal Government to hold out incentives to the States as a means of encouraging them to adopt suggested regulatory schemes. It does not, however, authorize Congress simply to direct the States to provide for the disposal of the radioactive waste generated within their borders. While there may be many constitutional methods of achieving regional self-sufficiency in radioactive waste disposal, the method Congress has chosen is not one of them. The judgment of the Court of Appeals is accordingly

Affirmed in part and reversed in part.

■ JUSTICE WHITE, with whom JUSTICE BLACKMUN and JUSTICE STEVENS join, concurring in part and dissenting in part.

. . .

I

My disagreement with the Court's analysis begins at the basic descriptive level of how the legislation at issue in this case came to be enacted. . . . The Low-Level Radioactive Waste Policy Act of 1980 . . . , and its amendatory Act of 1985, resulted from the efforts of state leaders to achieve a state-based set of remedies to the waste problem. They sought not federal pre-emption or intervention, but rather congressional sanction of interstate compromises they had reached.

. . .

. . . Unlike legislation that directs action from the Federal Government to the States, the 1980 and 1985 Acts reflected hard-fought agreements among States as refereed by Congress. The distinction is key, and the Court's failure properly to characterize this legislation ultimately affects its analysis of the take title provision's constitutionality.

II

. . .

. . . I am unmoved by the Court's vehemence in taking away Congress' authority to sanction a recalcitrant unsited State now that New York has reaped the benefits of the sited States' concessions.

A

In my view, New York's actions subsequent to enactment of the 1980 and 1985 Acts fairly indicate its approval of the interstate agreement process embodied in those laws within the meaning of Art. I, § 10, cl. 3. . . .

. . .

The State should be estopped from asserting the unconstitutionality of a provision that seeks merely to ensure that, after deriving substantial advantages from the 1985 Act, New York in fact must live up to its bargain by establishing an in-state low-level radioactive waste facility or assuming liability for its failure to act. . . .

. . .

III

The Court announces that it has no occasion to revisit such decisions as . . . Garcia v. San Antonio Metropolitan Transit Authority, 469 U.S. 528 (1985). . . . Although this statement sends the welcome signal that the Court does not intend to cut a wide swath through our recent Tenth Amendment precedents, it nevertheless is unpersuasive. I have several difficulties with the Court's analysis in this respect: it builds its rule around an insupportable and illogical distinction in the types of alleged incursions on state sovereignty; it derives its rule from cases that do not support its analysis; it fails to apply the appropriate tests from the cases on which it purports to base its rule; and it omits any discussion of the most recent and pertinent test for determining the take title provision's constitutionality.

The Court's distinction between a federal statute's regulation of States and private parties for general purposes, as opposed to a regulation solely on the activities of States, is unsupported by our recent Tenth Amendment cases. In no case has the Court rested its holding on such a distinction. . . . An incursion on state sovereignty hardly seems more constitutionally acceptable if the federal statute that "commands" specific action also applies to private parties. The alleged diminution in state authority over its own affairs is not any less because the federal mandate restricts the activities of private parties.

. . .

. . . In *Garcia,* we stated the proper inquiry. . . . [T]he Court tacitly concedes that a failing of the political process cannot be shown in this case because it refuses to rebut the unassailable arguments that the States were well able to look after themselves in the legislative process that culminated in the 1985 Act's passage.

Ultimately, I suppose, the entire structure of our federal constitutional government can be traced to an interest in establishing checks and balances to prevent the exercise of tyranny against individuals. But these fears seem extremely far distant to me in a situation such as this. . . . Congress has acceded to the wishes of the States by permitting local decisionmaking rather than imposing a solution from Washington. New York itself participated and supported passage of this legislation at both the gubernatorial and federal representative levels, and then enacted state laws specifically to comply with the deadlines and timetables agreed upon by the States in the 1985 Act. For me, the Court's civics lecture has a decidedly hollow ring at a time when action, rather than rhetoric, is needed to solve a national problem.

IV

Though I disagree with the Court's conclusion that the take title provision is unconstitutional, I do not read its opinion to preclude Congress from adopting a similar measure through its powers under the Spending or Commerce Clauses. . . . Congress could . . . condition the payment of funds on the State's willingness to take title if it has not already provided a waste disposal facility. . . . Similarly, should a State fail to establish a waste disposal facility by the appointed deadline . . . , Congress has the power pursuant to the Commerce Clause to regulate directly the producers of the waste. Thus, . . . Congress could amend the statute to say that if a State fails to meet the January 1, 1996 deadline for achieving a means of waste disposal, and has not taken title to the waste, no low-level radioactive waste may be shipped out of the State of New York. . . . [T]he threat of federal pre-emption may suffice to induce States to accept responsibility for failing to meet critical time deadlines for solving their low-level radioactive waste disposal problems, especially if that federal intervention also would strip state and local authorities of any input in locating sites for low-level radioactive waste disposal facilities. And of course, should Congress amend the statute to meet the Court's objection and a State refuse to act, the National Legislature will have ensured at least a federal solution to the waste management problem.

Finally, our precedents leave open the possibility that Congress may create federal rights of action in the generators of low-level radioactive waste against persons acting under color of state law for their failure to meet certain functions designated in federal-state programs. . . . In addition to compensating injured parties for the State's failure to act, the exposure to liability established by such suits also potentially serves as an inducement to compliance with the program mandate.

V

The ultimate irony of the decision today is that in its formalistically rigid obeisance to "federalism," the Court gives Congress fewer incentives to defer to the wishes of state officials in achieving local solutions to local problems. This legislation was a classic example of Congress acting as arbiter among the States in their attempts to accept responsibility for managing a problem of grave import. . . . By invalidating the measure designed to ensure compliance for recalcitrant States, such as New York, the Court upsets the delicate compromise achieved among the States and forces Congress to erect several additional formalistic hurdles to clear before achieving exactly the same objective. Because the Court's justifications for undertaking this step are unpersuasive to me, I respectfully dissent.

■ JUSTICE STEVENS, concurring in part and dissenting in part.

Under the Articles of Confederation, the Federal Government had the power to issue commands to the States. . . . Because that indirect exercise of federal power proved ineffective, the Framers of the Constitution empowered the Federal Government to exercise legislative authority directly over individuals within the States, even though that direct authority constituted a greater intrusion on State sovereignty. Nothing in that history suggests that the Federal Government may not also impose its will upon the several States as it did under the Articles. The Constitution enhanced, rather than diminished, the power of the Federal Government.

The notion that Congress does not have the power to issue "a simple command to state governments to implement legislation enacted by Congress," is incorrect and unsound. There is no such limitation in the Constitution. The Tenth Amendment surely does not impose any limit on Congress' exercise of the powers delegated to it by Article I. Nor does the structure of the constitutional order or the values of federalism mandate such a formal rule. To the contrary, the Federal Government directs state governments in many realms. The Government regulates state-operated railroads, state school systems, state prisons, state elections, and a host of other state functions. Similarly, there can be no doubt that, in time of war, Congress could either draft soldiers itself or command the States to supply their quotas of troops. I see no reason why Congress may not also command the States to enforce federal water and air quality standards or federal standards for the disposition of low-level radioactive wastes.

. . .

Printz v. United States

521 U.S. 898 (1997).

In 1993, Congress amended the Gun Control Act of 1968 by enacting the Brady Act. The Brady Act directed the U.S. Attorney General to set up a national instant background check system for the purchase of certain handguns by November 30, 1998, but before that time required the local law enforcement officials, in particular each "chief law enforcement officer" (CLEO) of the place where a purchaser desired to buy a covered gun, to perform the background checks and determine whether the proposed purchases would be in violation of the law, prior to purchase.

CLEOs for Ravalli County Montana and Graham County Arizona sued to challenge the constitutionality of the requirements imposed upon them. The district court invalided the challenged provisions, a divided panel of the Court of Appeals for the Ninth Circuit reversed, and the Supreme Court reversed again, in a 5–4 ruling authored by Justice Scalia. The Court began its explanation: "The Brady Act purports to direct state law enforcement officers to participate, albeit only temporarily, in the administration of a federally enacted regulatory scheme. . . . The petitioners here object to being pressed into federal service, and contend that congressional action compelling state officers to execute federal laws is unconstitutional. Because there is no constitutional text speaking to this precise question, the answer to the CLEOs' challenge must be sought in historical understanding and practice, in the structure of the Constitution, and in the jurisprudence of this Court."

With regard to history, the Court said that early practice "[e]stablishes, at most, that the Constitution was originally understood to permit imposition of an obligation on state *judges* to enforce federal prescriptions, insofar as those prescriptions related to matters appropriate for the judicial power. That assumption was perhaps implicit in one of the provisions of the Constitution, and was explicit in another. In accord with the so-called Madisonian Compromise, Article III, § 1, established only a Supreme Court, and made the creation of lower federal courts optional with the Congress—even though it was obvious that the Supreme Court alone could not hear all federal cases throughout the United States. . . . And the Supremacy Clause, Art. VI, cl. 2, announced that 'the Laws of the United States . . . shall be the supreme Law of the Land; and the Judges in every State shall be bound thereby.' It is understandable why courts should have been viewed distinctively in this regard; unlike legislatures and executives, they applied the law of other sovereigns all the time. . . . The Constitution itself, in the Full Faith and Credit Clause, Art. IV, § 1, generally required such enforcement with respect to obligations arising in other States. . . . For these reasons, we do not think the early statutes imposing obligations on state courts imply a power of Congress to impress the state executive into its service."

Finding this history less than conclusive, the Court turned to constitutional structure, echoing New York v. United States in finding that: the "Framers rejected the concept of a central government that would act upon and through the States, and instead designed a system in which the state and federal governments would exercise concurrent authority over the people. . . ."

As for precedent, the Court relied primarily on *New York*, concluding that its teaching applied fully: "The Government . . . maintains that requiring state officers to perform discrete, ministerial tasks specified by Congress does not violate the principle of *New York* because it does not diminish the accountability of state or federal officials. This argument fails even on its own terms. By forcing state governments to absorb the financial burden of implementing a federal regulatory program, Members of Congress can take credit for "solving" problems without having to ask their constituents to pay for the solutions with higher federal taxes. And even when the States are not forced to absorb the costs of implementing a federal program, they are still put in the position of taking the blame for its burdensomeness and for its defects. . . ."

Justice O'Connor concurred, emphasizing the Court "appropriately refrain[ed] from deciding whether other purely ministerial reporting requirements imposed by Congress on state and local authorities pursuant to its Commerce Clause powers are similarly invalid. See, e.g., 42 U.S.C. § 5779(a) (requiring state and local law enforcement agencies to report cases of missing children to the Department of Justice).

Justice Thomas also concurred, calling for a more fundamental revisiting of Commerce Clause jurisprudence. And Justice Stevens, joined by Justices Souter, Ginsburg, and Breyer, dissented, finding the question presented to be "remarkably similar to the question, heavily debated by the Framers of the Constitution, whether the Congress could require state agents to collect federal taxes. Or the question whether Congress could impress state judges into federal service to entertain and decide cases that they would prefer to ignore." Justice Souter also wrote a separate dissent, as did Justice Breyer, joined by Justice Stevens.

Reno v. Condon

528 U.S. 141 (2000).

The Driver's Privacy Protection Act of 1994 (DPPA) restricts the ability of state motor vehicle departments to disclose drivers' personal information without consent. (The Act also regulates disclosure by private persons who have obtained drivers' personal information from a state DMV.) South Carolina claimed that the DPPA violated the federalism principles of New York v. United States. A unanimous Court rejected that argument. DPPA did not require states to enact any laws or regulations, as did the statute in New York, nor require State officials to assist in the enforcement of federal statutes regulating private individuals, as did the law in Printz. DPPA regulated State activities, rather than controlling State regulation of private parties. It was not necessary to address South Carolina's argument that Congress may only regulate States by "generally applicable" laws that apply to individuals as well as States. DPPA is "generally applicable". It "regulates the universe of entities that participate as suppliers to the market for motor vehicle information—the States as initial suppliers of the information in interstate commerce and private resellers or rediscloser of that information in commerce."

2. ENFORCEMENT OF FEDERAL RIGHTS IN SUITS AGAINST STATE OFFICERS: THE ELEVENTH AMENDMENT

Pennhurst State School & Hospital v. Halderman

465 U.S. 89, 104 S.Ct. 900, 79 L.Ed.2d 67 (1984).

■ JUSTICE POWELL delivered the opinion of the Court.

This case presents the question whether a federal court may award injunctive relief against state officials on the basis of state law.

I

This litigation, here for the second time, concerns the conditions of care at petitioner Pennhurst State School and Hospital, a Pennsylvania institution for the care of the mentally retarded. . . .

. . . Respondents' amended complaint charged that conditions at Pennhurst violated the class members' rights under the Eighth and Fourteenth Amendments; § 504 of the Rehabilitation Act of 1973, 87 Stat. 394, as amended, 29 U.S.C. § 794 (1976 ed. and Supp. V); the Developmentally Disabled Assistance and Bill of Rights Act, 42 U.S.C. §§ 6001–6081 (1976 ed. and Supp. V); and the Pennsylvania Mental Health and Mental Retardation Act of 1966 (the "MH-MR Act"), Pa.Stat.Ann., Tit. 50, §§ 4101–4704 (Purdon 1969 and Supp.1982). Both damages and injunctive relief were sought.

. . .

The Court of Appeals for the Third Circuit [decided] that respondents had a right to habilitation in the least restrictive environment, but it grounded this right solely on the "bill of rights" provision in the Developmentally Disabled Assistance and Bill of Rights Act. . . .

This Court reversed the judgment of the Court of Appeals, finding that 42 U.S.C. § 6010 did not create any substantive rights. . . . We remanded the case to the Court of Appeals to determine if the remedial order could be supported on the basis of state law, the Constitution, or § 504 of the Rehabilitation Act. . . .

On remand the Court of Appeals . . . concluded that [the] state statute fully supported its prior judgment, and therefore did not reach the remaining issues of federal law. It also rejected petitioners' argument that the Eleventh Amendment barred a federal court from considering this pendent state-law claim. . . .

We . . . reverse and remand.

II

Petitioners [contend that] the Eleventh Amendment prohibited the District Court from ordering state officials to conform their conduct to state law. . . . We . . . find the Eleventh Amendment challenge dispositive.

A

Article III, § 2 of the Constitution provides that the federal judicial power extends, *inter alia,* to controversies "between a State and Citizens of another State." Relying on this language, this Court in 1793 assumed original jurisdiction over a suit brought by a citizen of South Carolina against the State of Georgia. Chisholm v. Georgia, 2 Dall. 419 (1793). The decision "created such a shock of surprise that the Eleventh Amendment was at once proposed and adopted." Monaco v. Mississippi, 292 U.S. 313, 325 (1934). The Amendment provides:

"The Judicial power of the United States shall not be construed to extend to any suit in law or equity, commenced or prosecuted against one of the United States by Citizens of another State, or by Citizens or Subjects of any Foreign State."

The Amendment's language overruled the particular result in *Chisholm,* but this Court has recognized that its greater significance lies in its affirmation that the fundamental principle of sovereign immunity limits the grant of judicial authority in Art. III. Thus, in Hans v. Louisiana, 134 U.S. 1 (1890), the Court held that, despite the limited terms of the Eleventh Amendment, a federal court could not entertain a suit brought by a citizen against his own State. After reviewing the constitutional debates concerning the scope of Art. III, the Court determined that federal jurisdiction over suits against unconsenting States "was not contemplated by the Constitution when establishing the judicial power of the United States." Id., at 15. See Monaco v. Mississippi, supra, 292 U.S., at 322–323 (1934). In short, the principle of sovereign immunity is a constitutional limitation on the federal judicial power established in Art. III:

. . .

B

This Court's decisions thus establish that "an unconsenting State is immune from suits brought in federal courts by her own citizens as well as by citizens of another state." *Employees, supra,* 411 U.S., at 280. There may be a question, however, whether a particular suit in fact is a suit against a State. It is clear, of course, that in the absence of consent a suit in which the State or one of its agencies or departments is named as the defendant is proscribed by the Eleventh Amendment. . . . This jurisdictional bar applies regardless of the nature of the relief sought. . . .

When the suit is brought only against state officials, a question arises as to whether that suit is a suit against the State itself. Although prior decisions of this Court have not been entirely consistent on this issue, certain principles are well established. The Eleventh Amendment bars a suit against state officials when "the state is the real, substantial party in interest." . . . And, as when the State itself is named as the defendant, a suit against state officials that is in fact a suit against a State is barred regardless of whether it seeks damages or injunctive relief. . . .

The Court has recognized an important exception to this general rule: a suit challenging the constitutionality of a state official's action is not one against the State. This was the holding in Ex parte Young, 209 U.S. 123 (1908), in which a federal court enjoined the Attorney General of the State of Minnesota from bringing suit to enforce a state statute that allegedly violated the Fourteenth Amendment. This Court held that the Eleventh Amendment did not prohibit issuance of this injunction. The theory of the case was that an unconstitutional enactment is "void" and therefore does not "impart to [the officer] any immunity from responsibility to the supreme authority of the United States." . . . Since the State could not authorize the action, the officer was "stripped of his official or representative character and [was] subjected to the consequences of his official conduct." . . .

While the rule permitting suits alleging conduct contrary to "the supreme authority of the United States" has survived, the theory of *Young* has not been provided an expansive interpretation. Thus, in Edelman v. Jordan, 415 U.S. 651 (1974), the Court emphasized that the Eleventh Amendment bars some forms of injunctive relief against state officials for violation of federal law. . . . In particular, *Edelman* held that when a plaintiff sues a state official alleging a violation of federal law, the federal court may award an injunction that governs the official's future conduct, but not one that awards retroactive monetary relief. Under the theory of *Young,* such a suit would not be one against the State since the federal-law allegation would strip the state officer of his official authority. Nevertheless, retroactive relief was barred by the Eleventh Amendment.

III

With these principles in mind, we now turn to the question whether the claim that petitioners violated *state law* in carrying out their official duties at Pennhurst is one against the State and therefore barred by the Eleventh Amendment. Respondents advance two principal arguments in support of the judgment below. [T]hey contend that under the doctrine of Edelman v. Jordan, supra, the suit is not against the State because the courts below ordered only prospective injunctive relief. . . .

A

. . . The Court of Appeals held that if the judgment below rested on federal law, it could be entered against petitioner state officials under the doctrine established in *Edelman* and *Young* even though the prospective financial burden was substantial and ongoing. The court assumed, and respondents assert, that this reasoning applies as well when the official acts in violation of state law. This argument misconstrues the basis of the doctrine established in *Young* and *Edelman.*

As discussed above, the injunction in *Young* was justified, notwithstanding the obvious impact on the State itself, on the view that sovereign immunity does not apply because an official who acts unconstitutionally is "stripped of his official or representative character,". . . . This rationale, of course, created the "well-recognized irony" that an official's unconstitutional conduct constitutes state action under the Fourteenth Amendment but not the Eleventh Amendment. . . . Nonetheless, the *Young* doctrine has been accepted as necessary to permit the federal courts to vindicate federal rights. . . .

The Court also has recognized, however, that the need to promote the supremacy of federal law must be accommodated to the constitutional immunity of the States. This is the significance of Edelman v. Jordan . . . [W]e declined to extend the fiction of *Young* to encompass retroactive relief, for to do so would effectively eliminate the constitutional immunity of the States. Accordingly, we concluded that . . . an award of retroactive relief necessarily "fall[s] afoul of the Eleventh Amendment if that basic constitutional provision is to be conceived of as having any present force." . . . In sum

Edelman's distinction between prospective and retroactive relief fulfills the underlying purpose of Ex parte Young while at the same time preserving to an important degree the constitutional immunity of the States.

This need to reconcile competing interests is wholly absent, however, when a plaintiff alleges that a state official has violated *state* law. In such a case the entire basis for the doctrine of *Young* and *Edelman* disappears. A federal court's grant of relief against state officials on the basis of state law, whether prospective or retroactive, does not vindicate the supreme authority of federal law. On the contrary, it is difficult to think of a greater intrusion on state sovereignty than when a federal court instructs state officials on how to conform their conduct to state law. Such a result conflicts directly with the principles of federalism that underlie the Eleventh Amendment. We conclude that *Young* and *Edelman* are inapplicable in a suit against state officials on the basis of state law.

B

The contrary view of Justice Stevens' dissent rests on fiction, is wrong on the law, and, most important, would emasculate the Eleventh Amendment. . . .

. . . To the extent there was a violation of state law in this case, it is a case of the State itself not fulfilling its legislative promises.

. . .

. . . Under the dissent's view of the *ultra vires* doctrine, the Eleventh Amendment would have force only in the rare case in which a plaintiff foolishly attempts to sue the State in its own name, or where he cannot produce some state statute that has been violated to his asserted injury. Thus, the *ultra vires* doctrine, a narrow and questionable exception, would swallow the general rule that a suit is against the State if the relief will run against it. . . .

. . .

D

Respondents urge that application of the Eleventh Amendment to pendent state-law claims will have a disruptive effect on litigation against state officials. . . .

It may be that applying the Eleventh Amendment to pendent claims results in federal claims being brought in state court, or in bifurcation of claims. That is not uncommon in this area. Under Edelman v. Jordan, supra, a suit against state officials for retroactive monetary relief, whether based on federal or state law, must be brought in state court. Challenges to the validity of state tax systems under 42 U.S.C. § 1983 also must be brought in state court. . . . Under the abstention doctrine, unclear issues of state law commonly are split off and referred to the state courts.

In any case, the answer to respondents' assertions is that such considerations of policy cannot override the constitutional limitation on the authority of the federal judiciary to adjudicate suits against a State. . . .

. . .

V

. . . We hold that these federal courts lacked jurisdiction to enjoin petitioner state institutions and state officials on the basis of this state law. The District Court also rested its decision on the Eighth and Fourteenth Amendments and § 504 of the Rehabilitation Act of 1973. On remand the Court of Appeals may consider to what extent, if any, the judgment may be sustained on these bases. The court also may consider whether relief may be granted to respondents under the Developmentally Disabled Assistance and Bill of Rights Act, 42 U.S.C. §§ 6011, 6063. The judgment of the Court of Appeals is reversed, and the case remanded for further proceedings consistent with this opinion.

It is so ordered.

■ JUSTICE BRENNAN, dissenting.

I fully agree with Justice Stevens' dissent. Nevertheless, I write separately to explain that in view of my continued belief that the Eleventh Amendment "bars federal court suits against States only by citizens of other States," . . . I would hold that petitioners are not entitled to invoke the protections of that Amendment in this federal court suit by citizens of Pennsylvania. . . .[a]

Application of the Eleventh Amendment in Suits for "Retroactive Relief"

Given prior law that the Eleventh Amendment applied to suits by a state's own citizens, and that it applied although only state officers were named parties if the state was the real party in interest, the "stripping doctrine" of Ex parte Young was crucial in permitting private federal court litigation to compel state compliance with the Constitution and federal laws.[1]

The stripping doctrine is not broad enough, however, to permit actions for "retroactive relief" that must be paid from public funds. While a judgment for damages that must be paid only from the state official's personal assets presents no Eleventh Amendment problem, Scheuer v. Rhodes, 416 U.S. 232 (1974), the Eleventh Amendment is still a serious obstacle if a private plaintiff's suit seeks the payment of state funds for past violations of federal law. That was the situation in Edelman v. Jordan, 415 U.S. 651 (1974), where welfare recipients were seeking reimbursement for past welfare payments withheld by state officials in violation of federal law. The Court held that, while the principle of Ex Parte Young supported the lower federal courts' judgment ordering state welfare officials to pay future benefits, the Eleventh Amendment barred any retroactive relief for benefits withheld in the past.

A second fiction—of state "consent" or "waiver" of sovereign immunity—had been applied to permit federal court damage actions against states for violation of federal statutes. Edelman v. Jordan, however, considerably limited that theory—concluding that a state could not be sued in federal court for retroactive relief unless Congress, "by the most express language or by such overwhelming implications from the text," demonstrated its intent to abrogate the state's immunity under the Eleventh Amendment.

---

[a] Justice Stevens, with whom Justices Brennan, Marshall and Blackmun joined, also filed a dissent.

[1] The Eleventh Amendment is inapplicable to suits by the federal government against states. United States v. Texas, 143 U.S. 621 (1892). Local political subdivisions, such as cities and counties are not "states" within the meaning of the Eleventh Amendment, and are fully subject to private party suits in the federal courts. Mt. Healthy City Sch. Dist. v. Doyle, 429 U.S. 274 (1977).

While the Eleventh Amendment has no application to suits against the United States, Indian tribes, or foreign countries, independent conceptions of sovereign immunity do apply. In private actions against federal officials, the stripping doctrine has been applied to determine the extent of federal sovereign immunity. Larson v. Domestic & Foreign Commerce Corp., 337 U.S. 682 (1949); Dugan v. Rank, 372 U.S. 609 (1963); Note, *The Sovereign Immunity Doctrine and Judicial Review of Federal Administrative Action,* 2 U.C.L.A.L.Rev. 382 (1955). In 1976, Public Law 94–574, § 1, 90 Stat. 2721, amended the Administrative Procedure Act (5 U.S.C. §§ 702, 703) to eliminate the defense of sovereign immunity in private suits seeking relief other than money damages against the United States. (Congress had long before consented to suit for money damages for tort and contract claims against the United States.) On the immunity of Indian tribes, see Santa Clara Pueblo v. Martinez, 436 U.S. 49, 58 (1978).

Congressional Power to Abrogate Eleventh Amendment Immunity and Subject States to Suit in Federal Court

The Court has held in a series of cases that Congress can subject States to damage liability in federal court when States violate federal statutory provisions that were validly adopted under the powers conferred to Congress by Section Five of the Fourteenth Amendment, but that the threshold for Congressional authority under Section Five is significant. Many of the most recent of such cases appear infra beginning at pp. 850. In Seminole Tribe of Florida v. Florida, 517 U.S. 44 (1996), the Court held that Congress enjoys no powers to abrogate Eleventh Amendment immunity under the Commerce Clause provisions in Article I. Relying on *Seminole Tribe*, the Court in College Savings Bank v. Florida Prepaid Postsecondary Education Expense Board, 527 U.S. 666 (1999) and Florida Prepaid Postsecondary Education Expense Board v. College Savings Bank, 527 U.S. 627 (1999), held that Congress could not abrogate Eleventh Amendment immunity from private damage claims brought for infringement of trademarks and patents.

Central Virginia Community College v. Katz
546 U.S. 356 (2006).

The Court, 5–4 (with Justice O'Connor, soon to leave the bench, in the majority), held that although "statements in both the majority and the dissenting opinions" in Seminole Tribe of Florida v. Florida "reflected an assumption that the holding in that case would apply" to state amenability to suit under the Bankruptcy Clause, Art. I, § 8, cl. 4, which empowers Congress to establish "uniform Laws on the subject of Bankruptcies throughout the United States," that assumption "was erroneous." The majority reasoned that the Bankruptcy Clause's history and rationale, as well as the legislation proposed and enacted under it immediately after ratification, suggest the Clause was more than an ordinary grant of authority to Congress; it was also a subordination of state sovereign immunity. According to the Court, the "ineluctable conclusion . . . is that States agreed in the plan of the Convention not to assert any sovereign immunity defense they might have had in proceedings brought pursuant to 'laws on the subject of Bankruptcies.' "

State Sovereign Immunity in State Court Suits

In Alden v. Maine, 527 U.S. 706 (1999), the Court held that States could assert sovereign immunity when sued in State court, that Congress lacked power to abrogate that immunity, and that States do not waive immunity by permitting suit in similar cases involving state law claims. Affirming a State court decision dismissing an overtime pay claim under the Fair Labor Standards Act, the Court said:

"the sovereign immunity of the States neither derives from nor is limited by the terms of the Eleventh Amendment. Rather, as the Constitution's structure, and its history, and the authoritative interpretations by this Court make clear, the States' immunity from suit is a fundamental aspect of the sovereignty which the States enjoyed before the ratification of the Constitution, and which they retain today . . . except as altered by the plan of the Convention or certain constitutional Amendments."

State Sovereign Immunity from Federal Administrative Proceedings

In Federal Maritime Commission v. South Carolina State Ports Authority, 535 U.S. 743 (2002), the Court held that a federal administrative proceeding which bore a "remarkably strong resemblance to civil litigation in federal courts" implicated the Eleventh Amendment immunity enjoyed by states. The Court rejected the arguments by the United States that a federal administrative proceeding should be treated differently than a judicial proceeding because the administrative agency's orders are not self-executing in the way that a court's orders are. The Court also found unavailing the federal government's suggestion that private actions brought against states before federal administrative bodies do not present the same threat that judicial litigation does to the financial integrity of states. The Court observed that sovereign immunity is designed to protect states not only from monetary liability, but also from the affront to their dignity that arises from suit itself.

CHAPTER 6

THE SCOPE OF STATE POWER

Introduction. In Chapter 4 we explored the early Nineteenth Century dispute in the Supreme Court between those who read the commerce clause as granting to Congress exclusive power to regulate interstate commerce and those who contended that the grant was merely concurrent, leaving full power in the states to regulate in the absence of conflicting federal regulation. In Cooley v. Board of Wardens, 53 U.S. (12 How.) 299 (1851), the Court reached a compromise position under which the commerce clause would permit some state regulations of interstate commerce but forbid others even in the absence of federal regulation. Ever since *Cooley* the Court has been struggling to find a formula to determine when state regulations of commerce are permissible.

In *Cooley* the Court attempted to resolve the problem by looking at the subjects being regulated. "Whatever subjects of this power are in their nature national, or admit only of one uniform system, or plan of regulation may justly be said to be of such a nature as to require exclusive legislation by Congress." Other subjects (such as harbor pilots, in that case) are of such a nature "as to leave no doubt of the superior fitness and propriety, not to say the absolute necessity, of different systems of regulation, drawn from local knowledge and experience, and conformed to local wants."

Later cases were more likely to speak in terms of "direct" burdens on commerce being forbidden, "indirect" burdens permitted. Thus in Erb v. Morasch, 177 U.S. 584 (1900) the Court said that a city ordinance regulating the speed of trains was "even as to interstate trains, one only indirectly affecting interstate commerce, and is within the power of the state until at least Congress shall take action in the matter." On the other hand, in Shafer v. Farmers' Grain Co. of Embden, 268 U.S. 189 (1925), the Court held invalid a state regulation of the purchase of wheat for interstate shipment because it constituted a "direct burden" on interstate commerce.

More recently the Court has addressed the problem in substantive rather than formal terms. In Brown-Forman Distillers Corporation v. New York State Liquor Authority, 476 U.S. 573, 578 (1986), for example, the Court said:

"This Court has adopted what amounts to a two-tiered approach to analyzing state economic regulation under the Commerce Clause. When a state statute directly regulates or discriminates against interstate commerce, or when its effect is to favor in-state economic interests over out-of-state interests, we have generally struck down the statute without further inquiry. . . . When, however, a statute has only indirect effects on interstate commerce and regulates evenhandedly, we have examined whether the State's interest is legitimate and whether the burden on interstate commerce clearly exceeds the local benefits. Pike v. Bruce Church, Inc., 397 U.S. 137, 142 (1970). We have also recognized that there is no clear line separating the category of state regulation that is virtually *per se* invalid under the Commerce Clause, and the category subject to the Pike v. Bruce Church balancing approach. In either situation the critical consideration is the overall effect of the statute on both local and interstate activity."

1. DISCRIMINATION AGAINST INTERSTATE COMMERCE

New Energy Co. of Indiana v. Limbach
486 U.S. 269, 108 S.Ct. 1803, 100 L.Ed.2d 302 (1988).

■ JUSTICE SCALIA delivered the opinion of the Court.

Appellant New Energy Company of Indiana has challenged the constitutionality of Ohio Rev.Code Ann. § 5735.145(B) (1986), a provision that awards a tax credit against the Ohio motor vehicle fuel sales tax for each gallon of ethanol sold (as a component of gasohol) by fuel dealers, but only if the ethanol is produced in Ohio or in a State that grants similar tax advantages to ethanol produced in Ohio. The question presented is whether § 5735.145(B) discriminates against interstate commerce in violation of the Commerce Clause, U.S. Const., Art. I, § 8, cl. 3.

I

Ethanol, or ethyl alcohol, is usually made from corn. In the last decade it has come into widespread use as an automotive fuel, mixed with gasoline in a ratio of 1:9 to produce what is called gasohol. The interest in ethanol emerged in reaction to the petroleum market dislocations of the early 1970's. The product was originally promoted as a means of achieving energy independence while providing a market for surplus corn; more recently, emphasis has shifted to its environmental advantages as a replacement for lead in enhancing fuel octane. . . . Ethanol was, however (and continues to be), more expensive than gasoline, and the emergence of ethanol production on a commercial scale dates from enactment of the first federal subsidy, in the form of an exemption from federal motor fuel excise taxes, in 1978. . . . Since then, many States, particularly those in the grain-producing areas of the country, have enacted their own ethanol subsidies. . . . Ohio first passed such a measure in 1981, providing Ohio gasohol dealers a credit of so many cents per gallon of ethanol used in their product against the Ohio motor vehicle fuel sales tax payable on both ethanol and gasoline. This credit was originally available without regard to the source of the ethanol. . . . In 1984, however, Ohio enacted § 5735.145(B), which denies the credit to ethanol coming from States that do not grant a tax credit, exemption, or refund to ethanol from Ohio, or, if a State grants a smaller tax advantage than Ohio's, granting only an equivalent credit. . . .

Appellant . . . manufactures ethanol in South Bend, Indiana, for sale in several States, including Ohio. Indiana repealed its tax exemption for ethanol, effective July 1, 1985, . . . at which time it also passed legislation providing a direct subsidy to Indiana ethanol producers (the sole one of which was appellant) . . . Thus, by reason of Ohio's reciprocity provision, appellant's ethanol sold in Ohio became ineligible for the Ohio tax credit. Appellant sought declaratory and injunctive relief in [an Ohio state court,] alleging that § 5735.145(B) violated the Commerce Clause by discriminating against out-of-state ethanol producers to the advantage of in-state industry. The court denied relief, and the Ohio Court of Appeals affirmed. A divided Ohio Supreme Court initially reversed, finding that § 5735.145(B) discriminated without adequate justification against products of out-of-state origin, and shielded Ohio producers from out-of-state competition. [On] rehearing [it] reversed itself, a majority of the court finding that the provision was not protectionist or unreasonably burdensome. . . .

II

It has long been accepted that the Commerce Clause not only grants Congress the authority to regulate commerce among the States, but also directly limits the power of the States to discriminate against interstate commerce. See, e.g., Hughes v.

Oklahoma, 441 U.S. 322, 326 (1979); H.P. Hood & Sons, Inc. v. Du Mond, 336 U.S. 525, 534–535 (1949); Welton v. Missouri, 91 U.S. 275 (1876). This "negative" aspect of the Commerce Clause prohibits economic protectionism—that is, regulatory measures designed to benefit in-state economic interests by burdening out-of-state competitors. See, e.g., Bacchus Imports, Ltd. v. Dias, 468 U.S. 263, 270–273 (1984); *H.P. Hood & Sons,* supra, at 532–533; Guy v. Baltimore, 100 U.S. 434, 443 (1880). Thus, state statutes that clearly discriminate against interstate commerce are routinely struck down, see, e.g., Sporhase v. Nebraska ex rel. Douglas, 458 U.S. 941 (1982); Lewis v. BT Investment Managers, Inc., 447 U.S. 27 (1980); Dean Milk Co. v. Madison, 340 U.S. 349 (1951), unless the discrimination is demonstrably justified by a valid factor unrelated to economic protectionism, see, e.g., Maine v. Taylor, 477 U.S. 131 (1986).

The Ohio provision at issue here explicitly deprives certain products of generally available beneficial tax treatment because they are made in certain other States, and thus on its face appears to violate the cardinal requirement of nondiscrimination. Appellees argue, however, that the availability of the tax credit to some out-of-state manufacturers (those in States that give tax advantages to Ohio-produced ethanol) shows that the Ohio provision, far from discriminating against interstate commerce, is likely to promote it, by encouraging other States to enact similar tax advantages that will spur the interstate sale of ethanol. We rejected a similar contention in an earlier "reciprocity" case, Great Atlantic & Pacific Tea Co. v. Cottrell, 424 U.S. 366 (1976). The regulation at issue there permitted milk from out of State to be sold in Mississippi only if the State of origin accepted Mississippi milk on a reciprocal basis. Mississippi put forward, among other arguments, the assertion that "the reciprocity requirement is in effect a free-trade provision, advancing the identical national interest that is served by the Commerce Clause." Id., at 378. In response, we said that "Mississippi may not use the threat of economic isolation as a weapon to force sister States to enter into even a desirable reciprocity agreement." Id., at 379. More recently, we characterized a Nebraska reciprocity requirement for the export of ground water from the State as "facially discriminatory legislation" which merited " 'strictest scrutiny.' " Sporhase v. Nebraska ex rel. Douglas, supra, at 958, quoting Hughes v. Oklahoma, supra, at 337.

It is true that in *Cottrell* and *Sporhase* the effect of a State's refusal to accept the offered reciprocity was total elimination of all transport of the subject product into or out of the offering State; whereas in the present case the only effect of refusal is that the out-of-state product is placed at a substantial commercial disadvantage through discriminatory tax treatment. That makes no difference for purposes of Commerce Clause analysis. In the leading case of Baldwin v. G.A.F. Seelig, Inc., 294 U.S. 511 (1935), the New York law excluding out-of-state milk did not impose an absolute ban, but rather allowed importation and sale so long as the initial purchase from the dairy farmer was made at or above the New York State-mandated price. In other words, just as the appellant here, in order to sell its product in Ohio, only has to cut its profits by reducing its sales price below the market price sufficiently to compensate the Ohio purchaser-retailer for the forgone tax credit, so also the milk wholesaler-distributor in *Baldwin,* in order to sell its product in New York, only had to cut its profits by increasing its purchase price above the market price sufficiently to meet the New York-prescribed minimum. We viewed the New York law as "an economic barrier against competition" that was "equivalent to a rampart of customs duties." Id., at 527. Similarly, in Hunt v. Washington Apple Advertising Comm'n, 432 U.S. 333, 349–351 (1977), we found invalid under the Commerce Clause a North Carolina statute that did not exclude apples from other States, but merely imposed additional costs upon Washington sellers and deprived them of the commercial advantage of their distinctive grading system. The present law likewise imposes an economic disadvantage upon out-of-state sellers; and the promise to remove that if reciprocity is accepted no more justifies disparity of treatment than it would justify categorical exclusion. We have indicated that reciprocity requirements are not *per se* unlawful. See *Cottrell,* supra, at 378. But the case we cited for that proposition, Kane v. New Jersey, 242 U.S. 160, 167–168 (1916), discussed a context in which, if a State offered the reciprocity did not accept it, the consequence was, to be sure, *less favored* treatment for its citizens, but nonetheless treatment that complied with the minimum requirements of the Commerce Clause. Here, quite to the contrary, the threat used to induce Indiana's acceptance is, in effect, taxing a product made by its manufacturers at a rate higher than the same product made by Ohio manufacturers, without (as we shall see) justification for the disparity.

Appellees argue that § 5735.145(B) should not be considered discrimination against interstate commerce because its practical scope is so limited. Apparently only one Ohio ethanol manufacturer exists (appellee South Point Ethanol) and only one out-of-state manufacturer (appellant) is clearly disadvantaged by the provision. Our cases, however, indicate that where discrimination is patent, as it is here, neither a widespread advantage to in-state interests nor a widespread disadvantage to out-of-state competitors need be shown. For example, in *Bacchus Imports, Ltd. v. Dias,* supra, we held unconstitutional under the Commerce Clause a special exemption from Hawaii's liquor tax for certain locally produced alcoholic beverages (okolehao and fruit wine), even though other locally produced alcoholic beverages were subject to the tax. 468 U.S., at 265, 271. And in *Lewis v. BT Investment Managers, Inc.,* supra, we held unconstitutional a Florida statute that excluded from certain business activities in Florida not all out-of-state entities, but only out-of-state bank holding companies, banks, or trust companies. In neither of these cases did we consider the size or number of the in-state businesses favored or the out-of-state businesses disfavored relevant to our determination. Varying the strength of the bar against economic protectionism according to the size and number of in-state and out-of-state firms affected would serve no purpose except the creation of new uncertainties in an already complex field.

. . .

It has not escaped our notice that the appellant here, which is eligible to receive a cash subsidy under Indiana's program for in-state ethanol producers, is the potential beneficiary of a scheme no less discriminatory than the one that it attacks, and no less effective in conferring a commercial advantage over out-of-state competitors. To believe the Indiana scheme is valid, however, is not to believe that the Ohio scheme must be valid as well. The Commerce Clause does not prohibit all state action designed to give its residents an advantage in the marketplace, but only action of that description *in connection with the State's regulation of interstate commerce.* Direct subsidization of domestic industry does not ordinarily run afoul of that prohibition; discriminatory taxation of out-of-state manufactures does. Of course, even if the Indiana subsidy were invalid, retaliatory violation of the Commerce Clause by Ohio would not be acceptable. See *Cottrell,* 424 U.S., at 379–380.

III

Our cases leave open the possibility that a State may validate a statute that discriminates against interstate commerce by showing that it advances a legitimate local purpose that cannot be adequately served by reasonable nondiscriminatory alternatives. See, e.g., Maine v. Taylor, 477 U.S., at 138, 151; Sporhase v. Nebraska ex rel. Douglas, 458 U.S., at 958; Hughes v. Oklahoma, 441 U.S., at 336–337; Dean Milk Co. v. Madison, 340 U.S., at 354. This is perhaps just another way of saying that what may appear to be a "discriminatory" provision in the constitutionally prohibited sense—that is, a protectionist enactment—may on closer analysis not be so. However it be put, the standards for such justification are high. Cf. Philadelphia v. New Jersey, 437 U.S. 617, 624 (1978) ("[W]here simple economic protectionism is effected by state legislation, a virtually *per se* rule of invalidity has been erected"); Hughes v. Oklahoma, 441 U.S., at 337 ("[F]acial discrimination by itself may be a fatal defect" and "[a]t a minimum . . . invokes the strictest scrutiny").

Appellees advance two justifications for the clear discrimination in the present case: health and commerce. As to the first, they argue that the provision encourages use of ethanol (in replacement of lead as a gasoline octane-enhancer) to reduce harmful exhaust emissions, both in Ohio itself and in surrounding States whose polluted atmosphere may reach Ohio. Certainly the protection of health is a legitimate state goal, and we assume for purposes of this argument that use of ethanol generally furthers it. But § 5735.145(B) obviously does not, except perhaps by accident. As far as ethanol use in Ohio itself is concerned, there is no reason to suppose that ethanol produced in a State that does not offer tax advantages to ethanol produced in Ohio is less healthy, and thus should have its importation into Ohio suppressed by denial of the otherwise standard tax credit. And as far as ethanol use outside Ohio is concerned, surely that is just as effectively fostered by other States' subsidizing ethanol production or sale in some fashion other than giving a tax credit to Ohio-produced ethanol; but these helpful expedients do not qualify for the tax credit. It could not be clearer that health is not the purpose of the provision, but is merely an occasional and accidental effect of achieving what is its purpose, favorable tax treatment for Ohio-produced ethanol. Essentially the same reasoning also responds to appellees' second (and related) justification for the discrimination, that the reciprocity requirement is designed to increase commerce in ethanol by encouraging other States to enact ethanol subsidies. What is encouraged is not ethanol subsidies in general, but only favorable treatment for Ohio-produced ethanol. In sum, appellees' health and commerce justifications amount to no more than implausible speculation, which does not suffice to validate this plain discrimination against products of out-of-state manufacture.

. . .

Reversed.

NOTE

New Energy presents the one doctrine on which all justices appear to agree—state statutes discriminating against interstate commerce will normally be found unconstitutional. Beyond this proposition there are wide areas of disagreement. Some commentators have argued that courts generally should not invalidate non-discriminatory state regulations on the basis that the burden on interstate commerce outweighs local benefits. For one example, see Regan, *The Supreme Court and State Protectionism: Making Sense of the Dormant Commerce Clause,* 84 Mich.L.Rev. 1091 (1986). For an article citing the attacks on the Court's use of the commerce clause and largely defending the Court, see Collins, *Economic Union as a Constitutional Value,* 63 New York U.L.Rev. 43 (1988). Justice Scalia rejects the balancing approach to negative commerce clause cases and says: "In my view, a state statute is invalid under the Commerce Clause if, and only if, it accords discriminatory treatment to interstate commerce in a respect not required to achieve a lawful state purpose. When such a validating purpose exists, it is for Congress and not us to determine it is not significant enough to justify the burden on commerce." Bendix Autolite Corp. v. Midwesco Enterprises, Inc., 486 U.S. 888, 898 (1988)(opinion concurring in judgment).

2. IMPLIED RESTRICTIONS OF THE COMMERCE CLAUSE— TRANSPORTATION

Kassel v. Consolidated Freightways Corporation

450 U.S. 662, 101 S.Ct. 1309, 67 L.Ed.2d 580 (1981).

■ JUSTICE POWELL announced the judgment of the Court and delivered an opinion in which JUSTICE WHITE, JUSTICE BLACKMUN, and JUSTICE STEVENS joined.

The question is whether an Iowa statute that prohibits the use of certain large trucks within the State unconstitutionally burdens interstate commerce.

I

Respondent Consolidated Freightways Corporation of Delaware (Consolidated) is one of the largest common carriers in the country. It offers service in 48 States under a certificate of public convenience and necessity issued by the Interstate Commerce Commission. Among other routes, Consolidated carries commodities through Iowa on Interstate 80, the principal east-west route linking New York, Chicago, and the west coast, and on Interstate 35, a major north-south route.

Consolidated mainly uses two kinds of trucks. One consists of a three-axle tractor pulling a 40-foot two-axle trailer. This unit, commonly called a single, or "semi," is 55 feet in length overall. Such trucks have long been used on the Nation's highways. Consolidated also uses a two-axle tractor pulling a single-axle trailer which, in turn, pulls a single-axle dolly and a second single-axle trailer. This combination, known as a double, or twin, is 65 feet long overall. Many trucking companies, including Consolidated, increasingly prefer to use doubles to ship certain kinds of commodities. Doubles have larger capacities, and the trailers can be detached and routed separately if necessary. Consolidated would like to use 65-foot doubles on many of its trips through Iowa.

The State of Iowa, however, by statute restricts the length of vehicles that may use its highways. Unlike all other States in the West and Midwest, Iowa generally prohibits the use of 65-foot doubles within its borders. Instead, most truck combinations are restricted to 55 feet in length. Doubles, mobile homes, trucks carrying vehicles such as tractors and other farm equipment, and singles hauling livestock, are permitted to be as long as 60 feet. Notwithstanding these restrictions, Iowa's statute permits cities abutting the state line by local ordinance to adopt the length limitations of the adjoining State. Iowa Code § 321.457(7) (1979). Where a city has exercised this option, otherwise oversized trucks are permitted within the city limits and in nearby commercial zones. Ibid.

Iowa also provides for two other relevant exemptions. An Iowa truck manufacturer may obtain a permit to ship trucks that are as large as 70 feet. Iowa Code § 321E.10 (1979). Permits also are available to move oversized mobile homes, provided that the unit is to be moved from a point within Iowa or delivered for an Iowa resident. Id., § 321E.28(5).[7]

---

[7] The parochial restrictions in the mobile home provision were enacted after Governor Ray vetoed a bill that would have permitted the interstate shipment of all mobile homes through Iowa. Governor Ray commented, in his veto message:

"This bill . . . would make Iowa a bridge state as these oversized units are moved into Iowa after being manufactured in another state and sold in a third. None of this activity would be of particular economic benefit to Iowa."

Because of Iowa's statutory scheme, Consolidated cannot use its 65-foot doubles to move commodities through the State. Instead, the company must do one of four things: (i) use 55-foot singles; (ii) use 60-foot doubles; (iii) detach the trailers of a 65-foot double and shuttle each through the State separately; or (iv) divert 65-foot doubles around Iowa.

Dissatisfied with these options, Consolidated filed this suit in the District Court averring that Iowa's statutory scheme unconstitutionally burdens interstate commerce. Iowa defended the law as a reasonable safety measure enacted pursuant to its police power. The State asserted that 65-foot doubles are more dangerous than 55-foot singles and, in any event, that the law promotes safety and reduces road wear within the State by diverting much truck traffic to other States.

In a 14-day trial, both sides adduced evidence on safety, and on the burden on interstate commerce imposed by Iowa's law. [T]he District Court found that the "evidence clearly establishes that the twin is as safe as the semi." . . . For that reason,

"there is no valid safety reason for barring twins from Iowa's highways because of their configuration."

. . .

In light of [its] findings, the District Court applied the standard we enunciated in Raymond Motor Transportation, Inc. v. Rice, 434 U.S. 429 (1978), and concluded that the state law impermissibly burdened interstate commerce. . . .

The . . . Eighth Circuit affirmed. . . .

. . . We now affirm.

II

. . .

. . . [A] State's power to regulate commerce is never greater than in matters traditionally of local concern. . . . For example, regulations that touch upon safety—especially highway safety—are those that "the Court has been most reluctant to invalidate." *Raymond,* supra, at 443; . . . Indeed, "if safety justifications are not illusory, the court will not second-guess legislative judgment about their importance in comparison with related burdens on interstate commerce." *Raymond,* supra, at 449 (Blackmun, J., concurring). Those who would challenge such bona fide safety regulations must overcome a "strong presumption of validity." Bibb v. Navajo Freight Lines, Inc., 359 U.S. 520, 524 (1959).

But the incantation of a purpose to promote the public health or safety does not insulate a state law from Commerce Clause attack. Regulations designed for that salutary purpose nevertheless may further the purpose so marginally, and interfere with commerce so substantially, as to be invalid under the Commerce Clause. . . .

III

Applying these general principles, we conclude that the Iowa truck-length limitations unconstitutionally burden interstate commerce.

In Raymond Motor Transportation, Inc. v. Rice, [434 U.S. 429 (1978),] the Court held that a Wisconsin statute that precluded the use of 65-foot doubles violated the Commerce Clause. This case is *Raymond* revisited. Here, as in *Raymond,* the State failed to present any persuasive evidence that 65-foot doubles are less safe than 55-foot singles. Moreover, Iowa's law is now out of step with the laws of all other Midwestern and Western States. Iowa thus substantially burdens the interstate flow of goods by truck. In the absence of congressional action to set uniform standards, some burdens associated with state safety regulations must be tolerated. But where, as here, the State's safety interest has been found to be illusory, and its regulations impair significantly the federal interest in efficient and safe interstate transportation, the state law cannot be harmonized with the Commerce Clause.

A

. . . As noted above, the District Court found that the "evidence clearly establishes that the twin is as safe as the semi." The record supports this finding.

. . .

. . . [T]he State points to only three ways in which the 55-foot single is even arguably superior: singles take less time to be passed and to clear intersections; they may back up for longer distances; and they are somewhat less likely to jackknife.

The first two of these characteristics are of limited relevance on modern interstate highways. As the District Court found, the negligible difference in the time required to pass, and to cross intersections, is insignificant on 4-lane divided highways because passing does not require crossing into oncoming traffic lanes, *Raymond,* 434 U.S., at 444, and interstates have few, if any, intersections. The concern over backing capability also is insignificant because it seldom is necessary to back up on an interstate. In any event, no evidence suggested any difference in backing capability between the 60-foot doubles that Iowa permits and the 65-foot doubles that it bans. Similarly, although doubles tend to jackknife somewhat more than singles, 65-foot doubles actually are less likely to jackknife than 60-foot doubles.

Statistical studies supported the view that 65-foot doubles are at least as safe overall as 55-foot singles and 60-foot doubles. . . . Iowa concedes that it can produce no study that establishes a statistically significant difference in safety between the 65-foot double and the kinds of vehicles the State permits. Nor . . . did Iowa present a single witness who testified that 65-foot doubles were more dangerous overall than the vehicles permitted under Iowa law. . . .

B

Consolidated, meanwhile, demonstrated that Iowa's law substantially burdens interstate commerce. Trucking companies that wish to continue to use 65-foot doubles must route them around Iowa or detach the trailers of the doubles and ship them through separately. Alternatively, trucking companies must use the smaller 55-foot singles or 60-foot doubles permitted under Iowa law. Each of these options engenders inefficiency and added expense. The record shows that Iowa's law added about $12.6 million each year to the costs of trucking companies. Consolidated alone incurred about $2 million per year in increased costs.

In addition to increasing the costs of the trucking companies (and, indirectly, of the service to consumers), Iowa's law may aggravate, rather than ameliorate, the problem of highway accidents. . . .

IV

Perhaps recognizing the weakness of the evidence supporting its safety argument, and the substantial burden on commerce that its regulations create, Iowa urges the Court simply to "defer" to the safety judgment of the State. It argues that the length of trucks is generally, although perhaps imprecisely, related to safety. The task of drawing a line is one that Iowa contends should be left to its legislature.

The Court normally does accord "special deference" to state highway safety regulations. *Raymond,* 434 U.S., at 444, n. 18. This traditional deference "derives in part from the assumption that where such regulations do not discriminate on their face against interstate commerce, their burden usually falls on local economic interests as well as other States' economic interests, thus insuring that a State's own political processes will serve as a check against unduly burdensome regulations." Ibid. Less deference to the legislative judgment is due, however, where the local regulation bears disproportionately on out-of-state residents and businesses. Such a disproportionate burden is apparent here. Iowa's scheme, although generally banning large doubles from the State, nevertheless has several exemptions that secure to Iowans many of the benefits of large trucks while shunting to neighboring States many of the costs associated with their use.

At the time of trial there were two particularly significant exemptions. First, singles hauling livestock or farm vehicles were permitted to be as long as 60 feet. Iowa Code §§ 321.457(5), 321.457(3) (1979). As the Court of Appeals noted, this provision undoubtedly was helpful to local interests. Cf. *Raymond,* supra, at 434 (exemption in Wisconsin for milk shippers). Second, cities abutting other States were permitted to enact local ordinances adopting the larger length limitation of the neighboring State. Iowa Code § 321.457(7) (1979). This exemption offered the benefits of longer trucks to individuals and businesses in important border cities without burdening Iowa's highways with interstate through traffic. Cf. *Raymond,* supra, at 446–447, and n. 24 (exemption in Wisconsin for shipments from local plants).

The origin of the "border cities exemption" also suggests that Iowa's statute may not have been designed to ban dangerous trucks, but rather to discourage interstate truck traffic. In 1974, the legislature passed a bill that would have permitted 65-foot doubles in the State. Governor Ray vetoed the bill. He said:

"I find sympathy with those who are doing business in our state and whose enterprises could gain from increased cargo carrying ability by trucks. However, with this bill, the Legislature has pursued a course that would benefit only a few Iowa-based companies while providing a great advantage for out-of-state trucking firms and competitors at the expense of our Iowa citizens."

After the veto, the "border cities exemption" was immediately enacted and signed by the Governor.

. . .

V

. . .

Because Iowa has imposed this burden without any significant countervailing safety interest, its statute violates the Commerce Clause. The judgment of the Court of Appeals is affirmed.

It is so ordered.

■ JUSTICE BRENNAN, with whom JUSTICE MARSHALL joins, concurring in the judgment.

. . .

For me, analysis of Commerce Clause challenges to state regulations must take into account three principles: (1) The courts are not empowered to second-guess the empirical judgments of lawmakers concerning the utility of legislation. (2) The burdens imposed on commerce must be balanced against the local benefits actually sought to be achieved by the State's lawmakers, and not against those suggested after the fact by counsel. (3) Protectionist legislation is unconstitutional under the Commerce Clause, even if the burdens and benefits are related to safety rather than economics.

I

Both the opinion of my Brother Powell and the opinion of my Brother Rehnquist are predicated upon the supposition that the constitutionality of a state regulation is determined by the factual record created by the State's lawyers in trial court. But that supposition cannot be correct, for it would make the constitutionality of state laws and regulations depend on the vagaries of litigation rather than on the judgments made by the State's lawmakers.

In considering a Commerce Clause challenge to a state regulation, the judicial task is to balance the burden imposed on commerce against the local benefits sought to be achieved by the State's *lawmakers*. See Pike v. Bruce Church, Inc., 397 U.S. 137, 142 (1970). In determining those benefits, a court should focus ultimately on the regulatory purposes identified by the lawmakers and on the evidence before or available to them that might have supported their judgment. . . . Since the court must confine its analysis to the purposes the lawmakers had for maintaining the regulation, the only relevant evidence concerns whether the lawmakers could rationally have believed that the challenged regulation would foster those purposes. . . . It is not the function of the court to decide whether *in fact* the regulation promotes its intended purpose, so long as an examination of the evidence before or available to the lawmaker indicates that the regulation is not wholly irrational in light of its purposes.

II

My Brothers Powell and Rehnquist make the mistake of disregarding the intention of Iowa's lawmakers and assuming that resolution of the case must hinge upon the argument offered by Iowa's attorneys: that 65-foot doubles are more dangerous than shorter trucks. . . . Iowa sought to discourage interstate truck traffic on Iowa's highways. Thus, the safety advantages and disadvantages of the types and lengths of trucks involved in this case are irrelevant to the decision.[3]

. . .

My Brother Powell concedes that "[i]t is . . . far from clear that Iowa was motivated primarily by a judgment that 65-foot doubles are less safe than 55-foot singles. Rather, Iowa seems to have hoped to limit the use of its highways by deflecting some through traffic." This conclusion is more than amply supported by the record and the legislative history of the Iowa regulation. . . .

. . .

Although the Court has stated that "[i]n no field has . . . deference to state regulation been greater than that of highway safety," Raymond Motor Transportation, Inc. v. Rice, supra, 434 U.S., at 443, it has declined to go so far as to presume that size restrictions are inherently tied to public safety. The Court has emphasized that the "strong presumption of validity" of size restrictions "cannot justify a court in closing its eyes to uncontroverted evidence of record,"—here the obvious fact that the safety characteristics of 65-foot doubles did not provide the motivation for either legislators or Governor in maintaining the regulation.

III

Though my Brother Powell recognizes that the State's actual purpose in maintaining the truck-length regulation was "to limit the use of its highways by

---

[3] My Brother Rehnquist claims that the "argument" that a Court should defer to the actual purposes of the lawmakers rather than to the *post hoc* justifications of counsel "has been consistently rejected by the Court in other contexts." . . .

If, as here, the only purpose ever articulated by the State's lawmakers for maintaining a regulation is illegitimate, I consider it contrary to precedent as well as to sound principles of constitutional adjudication for the courts to base their analysis on purposes never conceived by the lawmakers. This is especially true where, as the dissent's strained analysis of the relative safety of 65-foot doubles to shorter trucks amply demonstrates, the *post hoc* justifications are implausible as well as imaginary. I would emphasize that, although my Brother Powell's plurality opinion does not give as much weight to the illegitimacy of Iowa's actual purpose as I do, see Part III, infra, both that opinion and this concurrence have found the actual motivation of the Iowa lawmakers in maintaining the truck-length regulation highly relevant to, if not dispositive of, the case.

deflecting some through traffic," he fails to recognize that this purpose, being *protectionist* in nature, is *impermissible* under the Commerce Clause. The Governor admitted that he blocked legislative efforts to raise the length of trucks because the change "would benefit only a few Iowa-based companies while providing a great advantage for out-of-state trucking firms and competitors at the expense of our Iowa citizens." Appellant Raymond Kassel, Director of the Iowa Department of Transportation, while admitting that the greater 65-foot length standard would be *safer* overall, defended the more restrictive regulations because of their benefits *within Iowa* . . .

Iowa may not shunt off its fair share of the burden of maintaining interstate truck routes, nor may it create increased hazards on the highways of neighboring States in order to decrease the hazards on Iowa highways. . . .

This Court's heightened deference to the judgments of state lawmakers in the field of safety is largely attributable to a judicial disinclination to weigh the interests of safety against other societal interests, such as the economic interest in the free flow of commerce. Thus, "if safety justifications are not illusory, the Court will not second-guess legislative judgment about their importance *in comparison with related burdens on interstate commerce.*" Raymond Motor Transportation, Inc. v. Rice, supra, at 449 (Blackmun, J., concurring) (emphasis added). Here, the decision of Iowa's lawmakers to promote *Iowa's* safety and other interests at the direct expense of the safety and other interests of neighboring States merits no such deference. . . .

I therefore concur in the judgment.

■ JUSTICE REHNQUIST, with whom THE CHIEF JUSTICE and JUSTICE STEWART join, dissenting.

. . . Although the plurality and concurring opinions strike down Iowa's law by different routes, I believe the analysis in both opinions oversteps our "limited authority to review state legislation under the commerce clause," Brotherhood of Locomotive Firemen v. Chicago, R.I. & P.R. Co., 393 U.S. 129, 136 (1968), and seriously intrudes upon the fundamental right of the States to pass laws to secure the safety of their citizens. . . .

. . .

II

. . .

A determination that a state law is a rational safety measure does not end the Commerce Clause inquiry. A "sensitive consideration" of the safety purpose in relation to the burden on commerce is required. *Raymond,* supra, at 441. When engaging in such a consideration the Court does not directly compare safety benefits to commerce costs and strike down the legislation if the latter can be said in some vague sense to "outweigh" the former. Such an approach would make an empty gesture of the strong presumption of validity accorded state safety measures, particularly those governing highways. It would also arrogate to this Court functions of forming public policy, functions which, in the absence of congressional action, were left by the Framers of the Constitution to state legislatures. . . .

The purpose of the "sensitive consideration" referred to above is rather to determine if the asserted safety justification, although rational, is merely a pretext for discrimination against interstate commerce. We will conclude that it is if the safety benefits from the regulation are demonstrably trivial while the burden on commerce is great. Thus the Court in *Bibb* stated that the "strong presumption of validity" accorded highway safety measures could be overcome only when the safety benefits were "slight or problematical," 359 U.S., at 524. . . .

III

. . . There can be no doubt that the challenged statute is a valid highway safety regulation and thus entitled to the strongest presumption of validity against Commerce Clause challenges. . . . There can also be no question that the particular limit chosen by Iowa—60 feet—is rationally related to Iowa's safety objective. Most truck limits are between 55 and 65 feet, and Iowa's choice is thus well within the widely accepted range.

Iowa adduced evidence supporting the relation between vehicle length and highway safety. . . .

. . . In sum, there was sufficient evidence presented at trial to support the legislative determination that length is related to safety, and nothing in Consolidated's evidence undermines this conclusion.

. . .

My Brother Brennan argues that the Court should consider only *the* purpose the Iowa legislators *actually* sought to achieve by the length limit, and not the purposes advanced by Iowa's lawyers in defense of the statute. . . . The argument has been consistently rejected by the Court in other contexts, compare, e.g., United States Railroad Retirement Board v. Fritz, 449 U.S. 166, 187–188 (1980) with id., at 187–188 (Brennan, J., dissenting) and Michael M. v. Superior Court of Sonoma County, [450 U.S.] at 469–470 (1981) (plurality opinion) with id., at 494–496 (Brennan, J., dissenting), and Justice Brennan can cite no authority for the proposition that possible legislative purposes suggested by a State's lawyers should not be considered in Commerce Clause cases. The problems with [such] a view . . . are apparent. To name just a few, it assumes that individual legislators are motivated by one discernible "actual" purpose, and ignores the fact that different legislators may vote for a single piece of legislation for widely different reasons. . . . How, for example, would a court . . . approach a statute, the legislative history of which indicated that 10 votes were based on safety considerations, 10 votes were based on protectionism, and the statute passed by a vote of 40–20? What would the *actual* purpose of the *legislature* have been in that case? This Court has wisely "never insisted that a legislative body articulate its reasons for enacting a statute." *Fritz,* supra, at 177.

Both the plurality and concurring opinions attach great significance to the Governor's veto of a bill passed by the Iowa Legislature permitting 65-foot doubles. Whatever views one may have about the significance of legislative motives, it must be emphasized that the law which the Court strikes down today was not passed to achieve the protectionist goals the plurality and the concurrence ascribe to the Governor. Iowa's 60-foot length limit was established in 1963, at a time when very few States permitted 65-foot doubles. Striking down legislation on the basis of asserted legislative motives is dubious enough, but the plurality and concurrence strike down the legislation involved in this case because of asserted impermissible motives for *not* enacting *other* legislation, motives which could not possibly have been present when the legislation under challenge here was considered and passed. Such action is, so far as I am aware, unprecedented in this Court's history.

Furthermore, the effort in both the plurality and concurring opinions to portray the legislation involved here as protectionist is in error. Whenever a State enacts more stringent safety measures than its neighbors, in an area which affects commerce, the safety law will have the incidental effect of deflecting interstate commerce to the neighboring States. . . .

. . . The true problem with today's decision is that it gives no guidance whatsoever to these States as to whether their laws are valid or how to defend them. For that matter, the decision gives no guidance to Consolidated or other trucking firms either.

Perhaps, after all is said and done, the Court today neither says nor does very much at all. We know only that Iowa's law is invalid and that the jurisprudence of the "negative side" of the Commerce Clause remains hopelessly confused.

3. PREEMPTION OF STATE LEGISLATION BY FEDERAL LEGISLATION—THE IMPACT OF THE SUPREMACY CLAUSE

Introduction. We first met the preemption problem in Gibbons v. Ogden, supra p. 98, where the Court held the New York grant of a monopoly on a steamboat route to be inconsistent with the grant of a federal license to another steamboat to operate on the route. Marshall stated the ultimate principle—should there be a "collision" between an Act of Congress passed pursuant to the Constitution and a state statute, the state law "must yield to the law of Congress."

While simple to state, the principle is difficult to apply. The Supreme Court has applied a variety of verbal formulas over the years in seeking to determine when there is such a "collision" that the state law must fall. In many early cases it took a broad view of the subject, suggesting that merely by regulating in an area Congress should be taken as having "occupied the field" and determined that the states should not regulate in that field. See, e.g., Napier v. Atlantic Coast Line R. Co., 272 U.S. 605 (1926), in which the Court held that by granting power to the Interstate Commerce Commission to prescribe rules governing the safety of locomotives, Congress "intended to occupy the field" and state statutes requiring cab curtains and particular types of firebox doors were invalid even though the Commission had not issued any rules relating to cab curtains and firebox doors.

Beginning in the latter half of the twentieth century, the Court has often seemed less inclined to infer Congressional intent to supersede state laws in the absence of fairly direct conflict. In Rice v. Santa Fe Elevator Corp., 331 U.S. 218, 230 (1947), e.g., the Court said that when Congress has legislated "in a field which the States have traditionally occupied," we "start with the assumption that the historic police powers of the States were not to be superseded by the Federal Act unless that was the clear and manifest purpose of Congress. . . . Such a purpose may be evidenced in several ways. The scheme of federal regulation may be so pervasive as to make reasonable the inference that Congress left no room for the States to supplement it. . . . Or the Act of Congress may touch a field in which the federal interest is so dominant that the federal system will be assumed to preclude enforcement of state laws on the same subject. Likewise, the object sought to be obtained by the federal law and the character of obligations imposed by it may reveal the same purpose. . . . Or the state policy may produce a result inconsistent with the objective of the federal statute. . . . It is often a perplexing question whether Congress has precluded state action or by the choice of selective regulatory measures has left the police power of the States undisturbed except as the state and federal regulations collide."

A useful law review note—*Pre-emption as a Preferential Ground: A New Canon of Construction,* 12 Stan.L.Rev. 308 (1959), Selected Essays on Constitutional Law, 1938–1962 (1963), 310—contains the following paragraph:

"[T]he Court has adopted the same weighing of interests approach in pre-emption cases that it uses to determine whether a state law unjustifiably burdens interstate commerce. In a number of situations the Court has invalidated statutes on the pre-emption ground when it appeared that the state laws sought to favor local economic interests at the expense of the interstate market. On the other hand, when the Court has been satisfied that valid local interests, such as those in safety or in the reputable operation of local business, outweigh the restrictive effect on interstate commerce, the

Court has rejected the pre-emption argument and allowed state regulation to stand. . . ."

The case that follows illustrates the Court's approach to pre-emption cases. It is relevant to note that federal regulation may present pre-emption problems whether or not state law regulates interstate commerce. See, e.g., DeCanas v. Bica, 424 U.S. 351 (1976), involving an alleged conflict between a California statute regulating employment of illegal aliens and the federal immigration laws.

Gade v. National Solid Wastes Management Association

505 U.S. 88, 112 S.Ct. 2374, 120 L.Ed.2d 73 (1992).

■ JUSTICE O'CONNOR announced the judgment of the Court and delivered an opinion, Parts I, III, and IV of which represent the views of the Court, and Part II of which is joined by THE CHIEF JUSTICE, JUSTICE WHITE, and JUSTICE SCALIA.

In 1988, the Illinois General Assembly enacted the Hazardous Waste Crane and Hoisting Equipment Operators Licensing Act . . . and the Hazardous Waste Laborers Licensing Act. . . . The stated purpose of the acts is both "to promote job safety" and "to protect life, limb and property." . . . [W]e consider whether these "dual impact" statutes, which protect both workers and the general public, are pre-empted by the federal Occupational Safety and Health Act of 1970 . . . (OSH Act), and the standards promulgated . . . by the Occupational Safety and Health Administration (OSHA).

I

. . .

. . . OSHA . . . promulgated regulations on "Hazardous Waste Operations and Emergency Response," including detailed regulations on worker training requirements. . . . The OSHA regulations require . . . that workers engaged in an activity that may expose them to hazardous wastes receive a minimum of 40 hours of instruction off the site, and a minimum of three days actual field experience under the supervision of a trained supervisor. . . . On-site managers and supervisors directly responsible for hazardous waste operations must receive the same initial training as general employees, plus at least eight additional hours of specialized training on various health and safety programs. . . . Employees and supervisors are required to receive eight hours of refresher training annually. . . .

. . . [The] Illinois . . . [laws] at issue here. . . are designated as acts "in relation to environmental protection," and their stated aim is to protect both employees and the general public by licensing hazardous waste equipment operators and laborers working at certain facilities. Both acts require a license applicant to provide a certified record of at least 40 hours of training under an approved program conducted within Illinois, to pass a written examination, and to complete an annual refresher course of at least eight hours of instruction. . . . In addition, applicants for a hazardous waste crane operator's license must submit "a certified record showing operation of equipment used in hazardous waste handling for a minimum of 4,000 hours." . . .

. . .

. . . [T]he Association [sued] . . . to enjoin . . . enforc[ement of] the Illinois licensing acts, claiming [they] were pre-empted by the OSH Act and OSHA regulations and that they violated the Commerce Clause of the United States Constitution. . . . [T]he District Court held [the state] acts . . . not pre-empted because each protected public safety in addition to promoting job safety. . . . [It] invalidated the requirement that applicants for a hazardous waste license be trained "within Illinois" on the ground that the provision did not contribute to Illinois's stated purpose of protecting public safety

[and] declined to consider the Association's Commerce Clause challenge for lack of ripeness. . . .

. . . [The] Court of Appeals . . . affirmed in part and reversed in part. . . .

II

Before addressing the scope of the OSH Act's pre-emption of dual impact state regulations, we consider petitioner's threshold argument . . . that the Act does not pre-empt nonconflicting state regulations at all. "[T]he question whether a certain state action is pre-empted by federal law is one of congressional intent. 'The purpose of Congress is the ultimate touchstone.' " . . . "To discern Congress' intent we examine the explicit statutory language and the structure and purpose of the statute." . . .

In the OSH Act, Congress endeavored "to assure so far as possible every working man and woman in the Nation safe and healthful working conditions." . . . To that end, Congress authorized . . . mandatory occupational safety and health standards applicable to all businesses affecting interstate commerce, . . . and thereby brought the Federal Government into a field that traditionally had been occupied by the States. Federal regulation of the workplace was not intended to be all-encompassing, however. First, Congress expressly saved two areas from federal pre-emption. [One is state worker compensation laws. In addition,] Section 18(a) provides that the Act does not "prevent any State agency or court from asserting jurisdiction under State law over any occupational safety or health issue with respect to which no [federal] standard is in effect." . . .

Congress . . . also, in § 18(b) of the Act, gave the States the option of pre-empting federal regulation entirely. That section provides: . . .

"Any State which, at any time, desires to assume responsibility for development and enforcement therein of occupational safety and health standards relating to any occupational safety or health issue with respect to which a Federal standard has been promulgated [by the Secretary under the OSH Act] shall submit a State plan for the development of such standards and their enforcement." . . .

About half the States have received the Secretary's approval for their own state plans as described in this provision. . . . Illinois is not among them.

[We agree with] the Court of Appeals . . . that § 18(b) "unquestionably" pre-empts any state law or regulation that establishes an occupational health and safety standard on an issue for which OSHA has already promulgated a standard, unless the State has obtained the Secretary's approval for its own plan. . . .

Pre-emption may be either expressed or implied, and "is compelled whether Congress' command is explicitly stated in the statute's language or implicitly contained in its structure and purpose." Jones v. Rath Packing Co., 430 U.S. 519, 525 . . . (1977); . . . Absent explicit pre-emptive language, we have recognized at least two types of implied pre-emption: field pre-emption, where the scheme of federal regulation is "so pervasive as to make reasonable the inference that Congress left no room for the States to supplement it," . . . (quoting Rice v. Santa Fe Elevator Corp., 331 U.S. 218, 230 . . . (1947)), and conflict pre-emption, where "compliance with both federal and state regulations is a physical impossibility," Florida Lime & Avocado Growers, Inc. v. Paul, 373 U.S. 132, 142–143 . . . (1963), or where state law "stands as an obstacle to the accomplishment and execution of the full purposes and objectives of Congress." Hines v. Davidowitz, 312 U.S. 52, 67 . . . (1941); . . . .

Our ultimate task in any pre-emption case is to determine whether state regulation is consistent with the structure and purpose of the statute as a whole. Looking to "the provisions of the whole law, and to its object and policy," . . . we hold that nonapproved state regulation of occupational safety and health issues for which a federal standard is in effect is impliedly pre-empted as in conflict with the full purposes and objectives of the OSH Act. *Hines v. Davidowitz,* supra. The design of the statute persuades us that Congress intended to subject employers and employees to only one set of regulations, be it federal or state, and that the only way a State may regulate an OSHA-regulated occupational safety and health issue is pursuant to an approved state plan that displaces the federal standards.

The principal indication that Congress intended to pre-empt state law is § 18(b)'s statement that a State "shall" submit a plan if it wishes to "assume responsibility" for "development and enforcement . . . of occupational safety and health standards relating to any occupational safety or health issue with respect to which a Federal standard has been promulgated." The unavoidable implication of this provision is that a State may not enforce its own occupational safety and health standards without obtaining the Secretary's approval, and petitioner concedes that § 18(b) would require an approved plan if Illinois wanted to "assume responsibility" for the regulation of occupational safety and health within the State. Petitioner contends, however, that an approved plan is necessary only if the State wishes completely to replace the federal regulations, not merely to supplement them. . . .

Petitioner's interpretation . . . is not tenable in light of the OSH Act's surrounding provisions. . . . The OSH Act as a whole evidences Congress' intent to avoid subjecting workers and employers to duplicative regulation; a State may develop an occupational safety and health program tailored to its own needs, but only if it is willing completely to displace the applicable federal regulations.

Cutting against petitioner's interpretation of § 18(b) is the language of § 18(a), which saves from pre-emption any state law regulating an occupational safety and health issue with respect to which no federal standard is in effect. . . . [P]reservation of state authority in the absence of a federal standard presupposes a background pre-emption of all state occupational safety and health standards whenever a federal standard governing the same issue is in effect.

Our understanding of the implications of § 18(b) is likewise bolstered by § 18(c) of the Act, . . . which sets forth the conditions that must be satisfied before the Secretary can approve a plan submitted by a State under subsection (b). State standards that affect interstate commerce will be approved only if they "are required by compelling local conditions" and "do not unduly burden interstate commerce." . . . If a State could supplement federal regulations without undergoing the § 18(b) approval process, then the protections that § 18(c) offers to interstate commerce would easily be undercut. It would make little sense to impose such a condition on state programs intended to supplant federal regulation and not those that merely supplement it: the burden on interstate commerce remains the same.

Section 18(f) also confirms our view. . . . That provision gives the Secretary the authority to withdraw her approval of a state plan. . . . Once approval is withdrawn, the plan "cease[s] to be in effect". . . . Under petitioner's reading of § 18(b), § 18(f) should permit the continued exercise of state jurisdiction over purely "supplemental" and nonconflicting standards. Instead, § 18(f) assumes that the State loses the power to enforce all of its occupational safety and health standards once approval is withdrawn.

The same assumption of exclusive federal jurisdiction in the absence of an approved state plan is apparent in the transitional provisions contained in § 18(h) of the Act. . . . Section 18(h) authorized the Secretary of Labor, during the first two years after passage of the Act, to enter into an agreement with a State by which the State would be permitted to continue to enforce its own occupational health and safety standards for two years or until final action was taken by the Secretary pursuant to

§ 18(b), whichever was earlier. Significantly, § 18(h) does not say that such an agreement is only necessary when the State wishes fully to supplant federal standards. Indeed, the original Senate version of the provision would have allowed a State to enter into such an agreement only when it wished to enforce standards "not in conflict with Federal occupational health and safety standards," a category which included "any State occupational health and safety standard which provides for more stringent health and safety regulations than do the Federal standards." . . . Although that provision was eliminated from the final draft of the bill, thereby allowing agreements for the temporary enforcement of less stringent state standards, it is indicative of the congressional understanding that a State was required to enter into a transitional agreement even when its standards were stricter than federal standards. The Secretary's contemporaneous interpretation of § 18(h) also expresses that understanding. . . .

. . . Our review of the Act persuades us that Congress sought to promote occupational safety and health while at the same time avoiding duplicative, and possibly counterproductive, regulation. It thus established a system of uniform federal occupational health and safety standards, but gave States the option of pre-empting federal regulations by developing their own occupational safety and health programs. In addition, Congress offered the States substantial federal grant monies to assist them in developing their own programs. . . . To allow a State selectively to "supplement" certain federal regulations with ostensibly nonconflicting standards would be inconsistent with this federal scheme of establishing uniform federal standards, on the one hand, and encouraging States to assume full responsibility for development and enforcement of their own OSH programs, on the other.

We cannot accept petitioner's argument that the OSH Act does not pre-empt nonconflicting state laws because those laws, like the Act, are designed to promote worker safety. In determining whether state law "stands as an obstacle" to the full implementation of a federal law, . . . "it is not enough to say that the ultimate goal of both federal and state law" is the same. . . ."A state law also is pre-empted if it interferes with the methods by which the federal statute was designed to reach th[at] goal." . . . The OSH Act does not foreclose a State from enacting its own laws to advance the goal of worker safety, but it does restrict the ways in which it can do so. If a State wishes to regulate an issue of worker safety for which a federal standard is in effect, its only option is to obtain the prior approval of the Secretary of Labor, as described in § 18 of the Act.[2]

III

. . . We now consider whether a dual impact law can be an "occupational safety and health standard" subject to pre-emption under the Act.

----

[2]   Justice Kennedy, while agreeing on the pre-emptive scope of the OSH Act, finds that its pre-emption is express rather than implied. . . . In the end, even Justice Kennedy finds express pre-emption by relying on the negative "inference" of § 18(b), which governs when *state* law will pre-empt *federal* law. We cannot agree that the negative implications of the text, although ultimately dispositive to our own analysis, *expressly* address the issue of federal pre-emption of state law. We therefore prefer to place this case in the category of implied pre-emption. Although we have chosen to use the term "conflict" pre-emption, we could as easily have stated that the promulgation of a federal safety and health standard "pre-empts the field" for any nonapproved state law regulating the same safety and health issue. . . . ("[F]ield pre-emption may be understood as a species of conflict pre-emption: A state law that falls within a pre-empted field conflicts with Congress' intent (either express or plainly implied) to exclude state regulation"). . . . Frequently, the pre-emptive "label" we choose will carry with it substantive implications for the scope of pre-emption. In this case, however, it does not. Our disagreement with Justice Kennedy as to whether the OSH Act's pre-emptive effect is labelled "express" or "implied" is less important than our agreement that the implications of the text of the statute evince a congressional intent to pre-empt nonapproved state regulations when a federal standard is in effect.

... [P]etitioner asserts that if the state legislature articulates a purpose other than (or in addition to) workplace health and safety, then the OSH Act loses its pre-emptive force. We disagree.

Although "part of the pre-empted field is defined by reference to the purpose of the state law in question, ... another part of the field is defined by the state law's actual effect." ... In assessing the impact of a state law on the federal scheme, we have refused to rely solely on the legislature's professed purpose and have looked as well to the effects of the law. As we explained over two decades ago:

"We can no longer adhere to the aberrational doctrine ... that state law may frustrate the operation of federal law as long as the state legislature in passing its law had some purpose in mind other than one of frustration. Apart from the fact that it is at odds with the approach taken in nearly all our Supremacy Clause cases, such a doctrine would enable state legislatures to nullify nearly all unwanted federal legislation by simply publishing a legislative committee report articulating some state interest or policy—other than frustration of the federal objective—that would be tangentially furthered by the proposed state law.... [A]ny state legislation which frustrates the full effectiveness of federal law is rendered invalid by the Supremacy Clause." Perez v. Campbell, 402 U.S., at 651–652. ...

[A] dual impact state regulation cannot avoid OSH Act pre-emption simply because the regulation serves several objectives rather than one.... The key question is thus at what point the state regulation sufficiently interferes with federal regulation that it should be deemed pre-empted under the Act.

... [T]he Court of Appeals ... [held] that, in the absence of the approval of the Secretary, the OSH Act pre-empts all state law that "constitutes, in a direct, clear and substantial way, regulation of worker health and safety." ... We agree that this is the appropriate standard.... On the other hand, state laws of general applicability (such as laws regarding traffic safety or fire safety) that do not conflict with OSHA standards and that regulate the conduct of workers and non-workers alike would generally not be pre-empted. Although some laws of general applicability may have a "direct and substantial" effect on worker safety, they cannot fairly be characterized as "occupational" standards, because they regulate workers simply as members of the general public.... [Here,] a law directed at workplace safety is not saved from pre-emption simply because the State can demonstrate some additional effect outside of the workplace.

In sum, a state law requirement that directly, substantially, and specifically regulates occupational safety and health is an occupational safety and health standard within the meaning of the Act. That such a law may also have a nonoccupational impact does not render it any less of an occupational standard for purposes of pre-emption analysis. ...

IV

We recognize that "the States have a compelling interest in the practice of professions within their boundaries, and that as part of their power to protect the public health, safety, and other valid interests they have broad power to establish standards for licensing practitioners and regulating the practice of professions." ... But under the Supremacy Clause ... "any state law, however clearly within a State's acknowledged power, which interferes with or is contrary to federal law, must yield." ... We therefore reject petitioner's argument that the State's interest in licensing various occupations can save from OSH Act pre-emption those provisions that directly and substantially affect workplace safety.

... Because neither of the OSH Act's saving provisions are implicated, and because Illinois does not have an approved state plan under § 18(b), the state licensing acts are pre-empted by the OSH Act to the extent they establish occupational safety and health standards for training those who work with hazardous wastes. . . .

■ JUSTICE KENNEDY, concurring in part and concurring in the judgment.

Though I concur in the Court's judgment and with the ultimate conclusion that the state law is pre-empted, I would find express pre-emption from the terms of the federal statute. I cannot agree that we should denominate this case as one of implied pre-emption. The contrary view of the plurality is based on an undue expansion of our implied pre-emption jurisprudence. . . .

. . .

Our decisions establish that a high threshold must be met if a state law is to be pre-empted for conflicting with the purposes of a federal Act. . . . In my view, this type of pre-emption should be limited to state laws which impose prohibitions or obligations which are in direct contradiction to Congress' primary objectives, as conveyed with clarity in the federal legislation.

. . . Any potential tension between a scheme of federal regulation of the workplace and a concurrent, supplementary state scheme would not . . . rise to the level of "actual conflict" described in our pre-emption cases. Absent the express provisions of § 18 . . . , I would not say that state supplementary regulation conflicts with the purposes of the OSH Act, or that it "interferes with the methods by which the federal statute was designed to reach [its] goal."

. . .

The necessary implication of finding express pre-emption in this case is that the pre-emptive scope of the OSH Act is defined by the language of § 18(b). Because this provision requires federal approval of state occupational safety and health standards alone, only state laws fitting within the description are pre-empted. For that reason I agree with the Court that state laws of general applicability are not pre-empted. I also agree that "a state law requirement that directly, substantially, and specifically regulates occupational safety and health is an occupational safety and health standard within the meaning of the Act," and therefore falls within the scope of pre-emption. So-called "dual impact" state regulations which meet this standard are pre-empted by the OSH Act, regardless of any additional purpose the law may serve, or effect the law may have, outside the workplace. As a final matter, I agree that the Illinois Acts are not saved because they operate through a licensing mechanism rather than through direct regulation of the workplace. I therefore join all but Part II of the Court's opinion, and concur in the judgment of the Court.

■ JUSTICE SOUTER, with whom JUSTICE BLACKMUN, JUSTICE STEVENS, and JUSTICE THOMAS join, dissenting.

. . . In light of our rule that federal pre-emption of state law is only to be found in a clear congressional purpose to supplant exercises of the States' traditional police powers, the text of the Act fails to support the Court's conclusion.

I

. . .

. . . [W]hether the pre-emption at issue is described as occupation of each narrow field in which a federal standard has been promulgated, as pre-emption of those regulations that conflict with the federal objective of single regulation, or, as Justice Kennedy describes it, as express pre-emption, the key is congressional intent, and I find the language of the statute insufficient to demonstrate an intent to pre-empt state law in this way.

. . .

III

At first blush, respondent's strongest argument might seem to rest on § 18(a) of the Act. . . .

. . . The plurality reasons that there must be pre-emption . . . when there is a federal standard in effect, else § 18(a) would be rendered superfluous because "there is no possibility of conflict where there is no federal regulation."

. . . The plurality ignores the possibility that the provision simply rules out field pre-emption and is otherwise entirely compatible with the possibility that pre-emption will occur only when actual conflict between a federal regulation and a state rule renders compliance with both impossible. . . .

Respondent also relies on § 18(b). . . .

. . . [I]n actually providing a mechanism for a State to "assume responsibility" for an issue with respect to which a federal standard has been promulgated (that is, to pre-empt federal law), § 18(b) is far from pre-emptive of anything adopted by the States. Its heading . . . speaks expressly of the "development and enforcement of State standards to preempt applicable Federal standards." The provision does not in any way provide that absent such state pre-emption of federal rules, the State may not even supplement the federal standards with consistent regulations of its own. . . . The provision . . . makes perfect sense on the assumption that a dual regulatory scheme is permissible but subject to state pre-emption if the State wishes to shoulder enough of the federal mandate to gain approval of a plan.

. . .

Arizona v. United States
567 U.S. 387, 132 S.Ct. 2492, 183 L.Ed.2d 351 (2012).

■ JUSTICE KENNEDY delivered the opinion of the Court.

Arizona in 2010 enacted a statute called the Support Our Law Enforcement and Safe Neighborhoods Act[,] S. B. 1070, [whose] stated purpose is to "discourage and deter the unlawful entry and presence of aliens and economic activity by persons unlawfully present in the United States." . . . The law's provisions establish an official state policy of "attrition through enforcement." . . . The question before the Court is whether federal law preempts and renders invalid four separate provisions of the state law.

. . . Two create new state offenses. Section 3 makes failure to comply with federal alien registration requirements a state misdemeanor. . . . Section 5[(c)] makes it a misdemeanor for an unauthorized alien to seek or engage in work in the State. . . . Two other provisions give specific arrest authority and investigative duties with respect to certain aliens to state and local law enforcement officers. Section 6 authorizes officers to arrest without a warrant a person "the officer has probable cause to believe . . . has committed any public offense that makes the person removable from the United States." . . . Section 2(B) provides that officers who conduct a stop, detention, or arrest must in some circumstances make efforts to verify the person's immigration status with the Federal Government. . . .

The . . . District Court . . . issued a preliminary injunction preventing the four provisions . . . from taking effect. . . . The . . . Ninth Circuit affirmed[,] agree[ing] that the United States had established a likelihood of success on its preemption claims. . . .

II

A

The Government of the United States has broad, undoubted power over the subject of immigration and the status of aliens. See Toll v. Moreno, 458 U. S. 1, 10 (1982). . . . This authority rests, in part, on the National Government's constitutional power to "establish an uniform Rule of Naturalization," U. S. Const., Art. I, § 8, cl. 4, and its inherent power as sovereign to control and conduct relations with foreign nations, see *Toll, supra,* at 10 (citing United States v. Curtiss-Wright Export Corp., 299 U. S. 304, 318 (1936)).

The federal power to determine immigration policy is well settled. Immigration policy can affect trade, investment, tourism, and diplomatic relations for the entire Nation, as well as the perceptions and expectations of aliens in this country who seek the full protection of its laws. . . . Perceived mistreatment of aliens in the United States may lead to harmful reciprocal treatment of American citizens abroad. . . .

It is fundamental that foreign countries concerned about the status, safety, and security of their nationals in the United States must be able to confer and communicate on this subject with one national sovereign, not the 50 separate States. . . .

Federal governance of immigration and alien status is extensive and complex. Congress has specified categories of aliens who may not be admitted to the United States. See 8 U. S. C. § 1182. Unlawful entry and unlawful reentry into the country are federal offenses. §§ 1325, 1326. Once here, aliens are required to register with the Federal Government and to carry proof of status on their person. See §§ 1301–1306. Failure to do so is a federal misdemeanor. §§ 1304(e), 1306(a). Federal law also authorizes States to deny noncitizens a range of public benefits, § 1622; and it imposes sanctions on employers who hire unauthorized workers, § 1324a.

Congress has specified which aliens may be removed from the United States and the procedures for doing so. . . . Removal is a civil, not criminal, matter. A principal feature of the removal system is the broad discretion exercised by immigration officials. . . . Federal officials . . . must decide whether it makes sense to pursue removal at all. If removal proceedings commence, aliens may seek asylum and other discretionary relief allowing them to remain in the country or at least to leave without formal removal. See § 1229a(c)(4); see also, *e.g.,* §§ 1158 (asylum), 1229b (cancellation of removal), 1229c (voluntary departure).

Discretion in the enforcement of immigration law embraces immediate human concerns. Unauthorized workers trying to support their families, for example, likely pose less danger than alien smugglers or aliens who commit a serious crime. The equities of an individual case may turn on many factors, including whether the alien has children born in the United States, long ties to the community, or a record of distinguished military service. Some discretionary decisions involve policy choices that bear on this Nation's international relations. Returning an alien to his own country may be deemed inappropriate even where he has committed a removable offense or fails to meet the criteria for admission. The foreign state maybe mired in civil war, complicit in political persecution, or enduring conditions that create a real risk that the alien or his family will be harmed upon return. The dynamic nature of relations with other countries requires the Executive Branch to ensure that enforcement policies are consistent with this Nation's foreign policy with respect to these and other realities.

Agencies in the Department of Homeland Security play a major role in enforcing the country's immigration laws. . . . Immigration and Customs Enforcement (ICE) . . . "conducts criminal investigations involving the enforcement of immigration-related statutes." ICE also operates the Law Enforcement Support Center [(LESC), which] provides immigration status information to federal, state, and local officials around the clock. . . . ICE officers are responsible "for the identification, apprehension, and removal of illegal aliens from the United States." . . . Hundreds of thousands of aliens are removed by the Federal Government every year. . . .

B

The pervasiveness of federal regulation does not diminish the importance of immigration policy to the States. Arizona bears many of the consequences of unlawful immigration. Hundreds of thousands of deportable aliens are apprehended in Arizona each year. . . . Unauthorized aliens who remain in the State comprise, by one estimate, almost six percent of the population. . . . And in the State's most populous county, these aliens are reported to be responsible for a disproportionate share of serious crime. . . .

Statistics alone do not capture the full extent of Arizona's concerns. Accounts in the record suggest there is an "epidemic of crime, safety risks, serious property damage, and environmental problems" associated with the influx of illegal migration across private land near the Mexican border. . . . The problems posed to the State by illegal immigration must not be underestimated.

. . .

III

. . . There is no doubt that Congress may withdraw specified powers from the States by enacting a statute containing an express preemption provision. . . .

State law must also give way to federal law in at least two other circumstances. First, the States are precluded from regulating conduct in a field that Congress, acting within its proper authority, has determined must be regulated by its exclusive governance. See Gade v. National Solid Wastes Management Assn., 505 U. S. 88, 115 (1992).The intent to displace state law altogether can be inferred from a framework of regulation "so pervasive . . . that Congress left no room for the States to supplement it" or where there is a "federal interest . . . so dominant that the federal system will be assumed to preclude enforcement of state laws on the same subject." Rice v. Santa Fe Elevator Corp., 331 U. S. 218, 230 (1947). . . .

Second, state laws are preempted when they conflict with federal law. . . . This includes cases where "compliance with both federal and state regulations is a physical impossibility," Florida Lime & Avocado Growers, Inc. v. Paul, 373 U. S. 132, 142–143 (1963), and those instances where the challenged state law "stands as an obstacle to the accomplishment and execution of the full purposes and objectives of Congress," *Hines*, 312 U. S. [52,] 67 [(1941)]; see also Crosby [v. National Foreign Trade Council, 530 U. S. 363,] 373 [(2000)] ("What is a sufficient obstacle is a matter of judgment, to be informed by examining the federal statute as a whole and identifying its purpose and intended effects"). In preemption analysis, courts should assume that "the historic police powers of the States" are not superseded "unless that was the clear and manifest purpose of Congress." *Rice, supra,* at 230; see Wyeth v. Levine, 555 U. S. 555, 565 (2009).

. . .

IV

A

Section 3

Section 3 of S. B. 1070 creates a new state misdemeanor. It forbids the "willful failure to complete or carry an alien registration document . . . in violation of 8 United

States Code section 1304(e) or 1306(a)." . . . In effect, § 3 adds a state-law penalty for conduct proscribed by federal law. The United States contends that this state enforcement mechanism intrudes on the field of alien registration, a field in which Congress has left no room for States to regulate. . . .

The Court discussed federal alien-registration requirements in Hines v. Davidowitz, 312 U. S. 52. In 1940, as international conflict spread, Congress added to federal immigration law a "complete system for alien registration." *Id.*, at 70. The new federal law struck a careful balance. It punished an alien's willful failure to register but did not require aliens to carry identification cards. There were also limits on the sharing of registration records and fingerprints. The Court found that Congress intended the federal plan for registration to be a "single integrated and all-embracing system." *Id.*, at 74. Because this "complete scheme . . . for the registration of aliens" touched on foreign relations, it did not allow the States to "curtail or complement" federal law or to "enforce additional or auxiliary regulations." *Id.*, at 66–67. As a consequence, the Court ruled that Pennsylvania could not enforce its own alien-registration program. See *id.*, at 59, 74.

The present regime of federal regulation is not identical to the statutory framework considered in *Hines*, but it remains comprehensive. Federal law now includes a requirement that aliens carry proof of registration. . . . Other aspects, however, have stayed the same. Aliens who remain in the country for more than 30 days must apply for registration and be fingerprinted. . . . Detailed information is required, and any change of address has to be reported to the Federal Government. . . . The statute continues to provide penalties for the willful failure to register. . . .

The framework enacted by Congress leads to the conclusion here, as it did in *Hines*, that the Federal Government has occupied the field of alien registration. . . . Where Congress occupies an entire field, as it has in the field of alien registration, even complementary state regulation is impermissible. Field preemption reflects a congressional decision to foreclose any state regulation in the area, even if it is parallel to federal standards. . . .

Federal law makes a single sovereign responsible for maintaining a comprehensive and unified system to keep track of aliens within the Nation's borders. If § 3 of the Arizona statute were valid, every State could give itself independent authority to prosecute federal registration violations, "diminish[ing] the [Federal Government]'s control over enforcement" and "detract[ing] from the 'integrated scheme of regulation' created by Congress." . . . Even if a State may make violation of federal law a crime in some instances, it cannot do so in a field (like the field of alien registration) that has been occupied by federal law. . . .

. . .

B

Section 5(C)

Unlike § 3, which replicates federal statutory requirements, § 5(C) enacts a state criminal prohibition where no federal counterpart exists. The provision makes it a state misdemeanor for "an unauthorized alien to knowingly apply for work, solicit work in a public place or perform work as an employee or independent contractor" in Arizona. . . . The United States contends that the provision upsets the balance struck by the Immigration Reform and Control Act of 1986 (IRCA) and must be preempted as an obstacle to the federal plan of regulation and control.

When there was no comprehensive federal program regulating the employment of unauthorized aliens, this Court found that a State had authority to pass its own laws on the subject. In 1971, for example, California passed a law imposing civil penalties on the employment of aliens who were "not entitled to lawful residence in the United States if such employment would have an adverse effect on lawful resident workers." . . . The law was upheld against a preemption challenge in De Canas v. Bica, 424 U. S. 351 (1976). *De Canas* recognized that "States possess broad authority under their police powers to regulate the employment relationship to protect workers within the State." . . . At that point, however, the Federal Government had expressed no more than "a peripheral concern with [the] employment of illegal entrants." . . .

Current federal law is substantially different. . . . Congress enacted IRCA as a comprehensive framework for "combating the employment of illegal aliens." . . . The law makes it illegal for employers to knowingly hire, recruit, refer, or continue to employ unauthorized workers. . . . It also requires every employer to verify the employment authorization status of prospective employees. . . . These requirements are enforced through criminal penalties and an escalating series of civil penalties tied to the number of times an employer has violated the provisions. . . .

This comprehensive framework does not impose federal criminal sanctions on the employee side (*i.e.*, penalties on aliens who seek or engage in unauthorized work). Under federal law some civil penalties are imposed instead. . . . In addition, federal law makes it a crime for unauthorized workers to obtain employment through fraudulent means. . . . Congress has made clear, however, that any information employees submit to indicate their work status "may not be used" for purposes other than prosecution under specified federal criminal statutes for fraud, perjury, and related conduct. . . .

The legislative background of IRCA underscores the fact that Congress made a deliberate choice not to impose criminal penalties on aliens who seek, or engage in, unauthorized employment. . . .

. . .

. . . Under § 5(C) of S. B. 1070, Arizona law would interfere with the careful balance struck by Congress with respect to unauthorized employment of aliens. Although § 5(C) attempts to achieve one of the same goals as federal law—the deterrence of unlawful employment—it involves a conflict in the method of enforcement. . . .

C

Section 6

Section 6 of S. B. 1070 provides that a state officer, "without a warrant, may arrest a person if the officer has probable cause to believe . . . [the person] has committed any public offense that makes [him] removable from the United States." . . . The United States argues that arrests authorized by this statute would be an obstacle to the removal system Congress created.

As a general rule, it is not a crime for a removable alien to remain present in the United States. . . . If the police stop someone based on nothing more than possible removability, the usual predicate for an arrest is absent. When an alien is suspected of being removable, a federal official issues an administrative document called a Notice to Appear. . . . The form does not authorize an arrest. Instead, it gives the alien information about the proceedings, including the time and date of the removal hearing. . . . If an alien fails to appear, an *in absentia* order may direct removal. . . .

The federal statutory structure instructs when it is appropriate to arrest an alien during the removal process. . . . [W]arrants are executed by federal officers who have received training in the enforcement of immigration law. . . . If no federal warrant has been issued, those officers have more limited authority. . . . They may arrest an alien for being "in the United States in violation of any [immigration] law or regulation," for example, but only where the alien "is likely to escape before a warrant can be obtained." . . .

Section 6 attempts to provide state officers even greater authority to arrest aliens on the basis of possible removability than Congress has given to trained federal immigration officers. Under state law, officers who believe an alien is removable by reason of some "public offense" would have the power to conduct an arrest on that basis regardless of whether a federal warrant has issued or the alien is likely to escape. . . .

This is not the system Congress created. Federal law specifies limited circumstances in which state officers may perform the functions of an immigration officer. . . .

By authorizing state officers to decide whether an alien should be detained for being removable, § 6 violates the principle that the removal process is entrusted to the discretion of the Federal Government. . . .

. . .

Congress has put in place a system in which state officers may not make warrantless arrests of aliens based on possible removability except in specific, limited circumstances. By nonetheless authorizing state and local officers to engage in these enforcement activities as a general matter, § 6 creates an obstacle to the full purposes and objectives of Congress. . . . Section 6 is preempted by federal law.

D

Section 2(B)

Section 2(B) of S. B. 1070 requires state officers to make a "reasonable attempt . . . to determine the immigration status" of any person they stop, detain, or arrest on some other legitimate basis if "reasonable suspicion exists that the person is an alien and is unlawfully present in the United States." . . . The law also provides that "[a]ny person who is arrested shall have the person's immigration status determined before the person is released." . . . The accepted way to perform these status checks is to contact ICE, which maintains a database of immigration records.

Three limits are built into the state provision. First, a detainee is presumed not to be an alien unlawfully present in the United States if he or she provides a valid Arizona driver's license or similar identification. Second, officers "may not consider race, color or national origin . . . except to the extent permitted by the United States [and] Arizona Constitution[s]." . . . Third, the provisions must be "implemented in a manner consistent with federal law regulating immigration, protecting the civil rights of all persons and respecting the privileges and immunities of United States citizens." . . .

The United States and its *amici* contend that, even with these limits, the State's verification requirements pose an obstacle to the framework Congress put in place. The first concern is the mandatory nature of the status checks. The second is the possibility of prolonged detention while the checks are being performed.

1

Consultation between federal and state officials is an important feature of the immigration system. Congress has made clear that no formal agreement or special training needs to be in place for state officers to "communicate with the [Federal Government] regarding the immigration status of any individual, including reporting knowledge that a particular alien is not lawfully present in the United States.". . . And Congress has obligated ICE to respond to any request made by state officials for verification of a person's citizenship or immigration status. . . . ICE's Law Enforcement

Support Center operates "24 hours a day, seven days a week, 365 days a year" and provides, among other things, "immigration status, identity information and real-time assistance to local, state and federal law enforcement agencies." . . . LESC responded to more than one million requests for information in 2009 alone. . . .

The United States argues that making status verification mandatory interferes with the federal immigration scheme. It is true that . . . the officers must make an inquiry even in cases where it seems unlikely that the Attorney General would have the alien removed. . . .

Congress has done nothing to suggest it is inappropriate to communicate with ICE in these situations, however. Indeed, it has encouraged the sharing of information about possible immigration violations. . . . A federal statute regulating the public benefits provided to qualified aliens in fact instructs that "no State or local government entity may be prohibited, or in any way restricted, from sending to or receiving from [ICE] information regarding the immigration status, lawful or unlawful, of an alien in the United States." . . . The federal scheme thus leaves room for a policy requiring state officials to contact ICE as a routine matter. . . .

2

. . . Detaining individuals solely to verify their immigration status would raise constitutional concerns. . . . And it would disrupt the federal framework to put state officers in the position of holding aliens in custody for possible unlawful presence without federal direction and supervision. . . . The program put in place by Congress does not allow state or local officers to adopt this enforcement mechanism.

But § 2(B) could be read to avoid these concerns. . . . The state courts may conclude that, unless the person continues to be suspected of some crime for which he may be detained by state officers, it would not be reasonable to prolong the stop for the immigration inquiry. . . .

. . . Even if the law is read as an instruction to complete a check while the person is in custody, moreover, it is not clear at this stage and on this record that the verification process would result in prolonged detention.

However the law is interpreted, if § 2(B) only requires state officers to conduct a status check during the course of an authorized, lawful detention or after a detainee has been released, the provision likely would survive pre-emption—at least absent some showing that it has other consequences that are adverse to federal law and its objectives. There is no need in this case to address whether reasonable suspicion of illegal entry or another immigration crime would be a legitimate basis for prolonging a detention, or whether this too would be preempted by federal law. . . .

The nature and timing of this case counsel caution in evaluating the validity of § 2(B). The Federal Government has brought suit against a sovereign State to challenge the provision even before the law has gone into effect. There is a basic uncertainty about what the law means and how it will be enforced. At this stage, without the benefit of a definitive interpretation from the state courts, it would be inappropriate to assume § 2(B) will be construed in a way that creates a conflict with federal law. . . . As a result, the United States cannot prevail in its current challenge. . . . This opinion does not foreclose other preemption and constitutional challenges to the law as interpreted and applied after it goes into effect.

. . .

* * *

The United States has established that §§ 3, 5(C), and 6 of S. B. 1070 are preempted. It was improper, however, to enjoin § 2(B) before the state courts had an opportunity to construe it and without some showing that enforcement of the provision in fact conflicts with federal immigration law and its objectives.

The judgment is affirmed in part and reversed in part. The case is remanded for further proceedings consistent with this opinion.[a]

■ JUSTICE SCALIA, concurring in part and dissenting in part.

The United States is an indivisible "Union of sovereign States." Hinderlider v. La Plata River & Cherry Creek Ditch Co., 304 U. S. 92, 104 (1938). Today's opinion . . . deprives States of what most would consider the defining characteristic of sovereignty: the power to exclude from the sovereign's territory people who have no right to be there. Neither the Constitution itself nor even any law passed by Congress supports this result. I dissent.

I

As a sovereign, Arizona has the inherent power to exclude persons from its territory, subject only to those limitations expressed in the Constitution or constitutionally imposed by Congress. . . .

There is no doubt that "before the adoption of the constitution of the United States" each State had the authority to "prevent [itself] from being burdened by an influx of persons." Mayor of New York v. Miln, 11 Pet. 102, 132–133 (1837). And the Constitution did not strip the States of that authority. . . .

. . .

Notwithstanding "[t]he myth of an era of unrestricted immigration" in the first 100 years of the Republic, the States enacted numerous laws restricting the immigration of certain classes of aliens, including convicted criminals, indigents, persons with contagious diseases, and (in Southern States) freed blacks. . . .

In fact, the controversy surrounding the Alien and Sedition Acts involved a debate over whether, under the Constitution, the States had *exclusive* authority to enact such immigration laws. . . . The Kentucky and Virginia Resolutions, written in denunciation of these Acts, insisted that the power to exclude unwanted aliens rested solely in the States. . . .

. . .

II

. . . [A]fter the adoption of the Constitution there was some doubt about the power of the Federal Government to control immigration, but no doubt about the power of the States to do so. Since the founding era (though not immediately), doubt about the Federal Government's power has disappeared. . . .

I accept that as a valid exercise of federal power . . . because it is an inherent attribute of sovereignty no less for the United States than for the States. . . . That is why there was no need to set forth control of immigration as one of the enumerated powers of Congress . . . .

In light of the predominance of federal immigration restrictions in modern times, it is easy to lose sight of the States' traditional role in regulating immigration—and to overlook their sovereign prerogative to do so. I accept as a given that State regulation is excluded by the Constitution when (1) it has been prohibited by a valid federal law, or (2) it conflicts with federal regulation. . . .

Possibility (1) need not be considered here: there is no federal law prohibiting the States' sovereign power to exclude (assuming federal authority to enact such a law).

---

[a] Justice Kagan took no part in the consideration or decision of this case.

The mere existence of federal action in the immigration area—and the so-called field preemption arising from that action, upon which the Court's opinion so heavily relies—cannot be regarded as such a prohibition. . . .

. . .

What this case comes down to, then, is whether the Arizona law conflicts with federal immigration law—whether it excludes those whom federal law would admit, or admits those whom federal law would exclude. It does not purport to do so. It applies only to aliens who neither possess a privilege to be present under federal law nor have been removed pursuant to the Federal Government's inherent authority. . . .

[Finding no federal law prohibition or direct contradiction of any of the challenged provisions of S.B. 1070, Justice Scalia would have found none of them preempted. With respect to § 6, he said in part:]

. . . The most important point is that . . . Arizona is *entitled* to have "its own immigration policy"—including a more rigorous enforcement policy—so long as that does not conflict with federal law. . . .

. . .

. . . The State's whole complaint—the reason this law was passed and this case has arisen—is that the citizens of Arizona believe federal priorities are too lax. The State has the sovereign power to protect its borders more rigorously if it wishes, absent any valid federal prohibition. The Executive's policy choice of lax federal enforcement does not constitute such a prohibition.

. . .

Arizona has moved to protect its sovereignty—not in contradiction of federal law, but in complete compliance with it. The laws under challenge here do not extend or revise federal immigration restrictions, but merely enforce those restrictions more effectively. If securing its territory in this fashion is not within the power of Arizona, we should cease referring to it as a sovereign State. I dissent.

■ JUSTICE THOMAS, concurring in part and dissenting in part.

I agree with Justice Scalia that federal immigration law does not pre-empt any of the challenged provisions of S. B. 1070. I reach that conclusion, however, for the simple reason that there is no conflict between the "ordinary meanin[g]" of the relevant federal laws and that of the four provisions of Arizona law at issue here. . . .

. . .

■ JUSTICE ALITO, concurring in part and dissenting in part.

. . .

I agree with the Court that § 2(B) is not pre-empted. That provision does not authorize or require Arizona law enforcement officers to do anything they are not already allowed to do under existing federal law. The United States' argument that § 2(B) is pre-empted, not by any federal statute or regulation, but simply by the Executive's current enforcement policy is an astounding assertion of federal executive power that the Court rightly rejects.

I also agree with the Court that § 3 is pre-empted by virtue of our decision in Hines v. Davidowitz, 312 U. S. 52 (1941). . . .

. . . I part ways on § 5(C) and § 6. The Court's holding on § 5(C) is inconsistent with De Canas v. Bica, 424 U. S. 351 (1976), which held that employment regulation, even of aliens unlawfully present in the country, is an area of traditional state concern. Because state police powers are implicated here, our precedents require us to presume that federal law does not displace state law unless Congress' intent to do so is clear and manifest. I do not believe Congress has spoken with the requisite clarity to justify invalidation of § 5(C). Nor do I believe that § 6 is invalid. Like § 2(B), § 6 adds virtually nothing to the authority that Arizona law enforcement officers already exercise. And whatever little authority they have gained is consistent with federal law.

. . .

CHAPTER 7

SEPARATION OF POWERS

This chapter focuses on issues of division of power between the President and Congress. The coverage is, of necessity, both introductory and very selective, since the topic could easily be the sole concern of many volumes. Section 1 raises the question of the extent to which the President has the power to determine national policies. Section 2 deals with the other side of the coin, examining some instances where it is claimed that Congress has interfered with recognized Presidential powers. Section 3 is concerned with Presidential immunity from Congressional and judicial process.

1. THE PRESIDENT'S POWER TO DETERMINE NATIONAL POLICY

A. IN GENERAL

Introduction. A simplistic description of the division of powers between the legislature and the executive is that a nation's policies are set by the legislature in the laws, and carried into force by the executive. Even the casual student of American history knows that the reality of the division of authority between the President and Congress has been much more complex.

Youngstown Sheet & Tube Co. v. Sawyer
(The Steel Seizure Case)
343 U.S. 579, 72 S.Ct. 863, 96 L.Ed. 1153 (1952).

[This important decision emerged from a tangled background of labor legislation, price and wage negotiation in the steel industry, unhappiness between Congress and President Truman and the frustrating inability of the government to find an end for the war in Korea, then in its third year.[a]

[Part of the setting was disagreement between Congress and President Truman over the means of resolving major labor disputes. In 1947 Congress, over President Truman's veto, had passed the Taft-Hartley Act subjecting union practices to national control; one part of the Act provided that if a strike would endanger national health and safety the President was authorized to seek an injunction against the strike during a cooling-off period of eighty days during which a secret ballot of the workers could be held. These various provisions were bitterly resisted by labor. While this law was under consideration in Congress an amendment was offered for government seizure of industries to avoid serious shut-downs; Congress rejected the proposal. In his hard-hitting and astonishingly successful 1948 campaign for reelection, Truman

---

[a] The fullest account of the case is Westin, The Anatomy of a Constitutional Law Case (1958). Other accounts on which this discussion draws are Kauper, The Steel Seizure Case, 51 Mich.L.Rev. 141 (1952), Selected Essays, 129 (1963); Freund, Foreword: The Year of the Steel Case, 66 Harv.L.Rev. 89 (1952); McConnell, The Steel Seizure of 1952 (1958); The Steel Seizure Case, 82d Cong., 2d Sess., H.Doc.No. 534.

slashed at the "do-nothing" record of this session of Congress, and called for repeal of the "oppressive" Taft-Hartley Act.

[Another dimension to the problem was the Administration's controversy with the steel industry. Wage negotiations between the United Steel Workers and the industry had been opened in November 1951, five months before the final crisis. The negotiations were deadlocked, and in December the President referred this controversy to the Wage Stabilization Board—which was part of the program of controls over wages and prices that had been established during the Korean War. The Board did not have authority to dictate a settlement; its chief sanction was to decide the extent to which labor cost increases could be taken into account by the Office of Price Stabilization in acting on requests for increases in ceiling prices. The Wage Stabilization Board recommended certain wage increases; the steel industry rejected this recommendation unless it received a $12 per ton increase in the ceiling price. The stabilization officials refused to approve this increase on the ground that high earnings of the steel industry permitted the absorption of at least a part of the increase in labor costs.

[On April 3, Philip Murray, President of the United Steelworkers, called a general steel strike for 12:01 a.m., April 9. On the night of April 8, following a radio address to the nation, President Truman issued Executive Order 10340 directing the Secretary of Commerce "to take possession" and "to operate or arrange for the operation" of the production facilities of the steel industry. The Order outlined the vital part of steel in the war effort, and concluded that "a work stoppage would immediately jeopardize and imperil our national defense." The Secretary of Commerce was instructed to leave control, insofar as possible, in the hands of the present management, but the Order included a pointed authorization to "determine and prescribe terms and conditions of employment." The next morning, President Truman sent Congress a message reporting on this action and stating that if Congress preferred a different course of action, "That is a matter for the Congress to determine."

[Just before midnight on April 8, within an hour after the President's Order, attorneys for the steel companies arrived at the home of a United States District Judge with a motion for immediate relief. A hearing was set for 11:30 the next morning. The relief initially requested by the companies was the prevention of a change in wage rates during government management—a move designed to block the government's plan to force a settlement by establishing a new wage level that, as a practical matter, would be irreversible; but the case quickly reached larger dimensions and on April 29 District Judge David Pine held the seizure illegal and enjoined government officials from remaining in control of the industry. The case was rapidly carried to the Supreme Court.]

■ MR. JUSTICE BLACK delivered the opinion of the Court.

We are asked to decide whether the President was acting within his constitutional power when he issued an order directing the Secretary of Commerce to take possession of and operate most of the Nation's steel mills. The mill owners argue that the President's order amounts to lawmaking, a legislative function which the Constitution has expressly confided to the Congress and not to the President. The Government's position is that the order was made on findings of the President that his action was necessary to avert a national catastrophe which would inevitably result from a stoppage of steel production, and that in meeting this grave emergency the President was acting within the aggregate of his constitutional powers as the Nation's Chief Executive and the Commander-in-Chief of the Armed Forces of the United States. . . .

. . .

The President's power, if any, to issue the order must stem either from an act of Congress or from the Constitution itself. There is no statute that expressly authorizes the President to take possession of property as he did here. Nor is there any act of Congress to which our attention has been directed from which such a power can fairly be implied. . . .'

Moreover, the use of the seizure technique to solve labor disputes in order to prevent work stoppages was not only unauthorized by any congressional enactment; prior to this controversy, Congress had refused to adopt that method of settling labor disputes. When the Taft-Hartley Act was under consideration in 1947, Congress rejected an amendment which would have authorized such governmental seizures in cases of emergency. . . . Instead, the plan sought to bring about settlements by use of the customary devices of mediation, conciliation, investigation by boards of inquiry, and public reports. In some instances temporary injunctions were authorized to provide cooling-off periods. All this failing, unions were left free to strike after a secret vote by employees as to whether they wished to accept their employers' final settlement offer.

It is clear that if the President had authority to issue the order he did, it must be found in some provision of the Constitution. And it is not claimed that express constitutional language grants this power to the President. The contention is that presidential power should be implied from the aggregate of his powers under the Constitution. Particular reliance is placed on provisions in Article II which say that "the executive Power shall be vested in a President . . . "; that "he shall take Care that the Laws be faithfully executed"; and that he "shall be Commander in Chief of the Army and Navy of the United States."

The order cannot properly be sustained as an exercise of the President's military power as Commander in Chief of the Armed Forces. The Government attempts to do so by citing a number of cases upholding broad powers in military commanders engaged in day-to-day fighting in a theater of war. Such cases need not concern us here. Even though "theater of war" be an expanding concept, we cannot with faithfulness to our constitutional system hold that the Commander in Chief of the Armed Forces has the ultimate power as such to take possession of private property in order to keep labor disputes from stopping production. This is a job for the Nation's lawmakers, not for its military authorities.

Nor can the seizure order be sustained because of the several constitutional provisions that grant executive power to the President. In the framework of our Constitution, the President's power to see that the laws are faithfully executed refutes the idea that he is to be a lawmaker. The Constitution limits his functions in the lawmaking process to the recommending of laws he thinks wise and the vetoing of laws he thinks bad. And the Constitution is neither silent nor equivocal about who shall make laws which the President is to execute. The first section of the first article says that "All legislative Powers herein granted shall be vested in a Congress of the United States. . . ." After granting many powers to the Congress, Article I goes on to provide that Congress may "make all Laws which shall be necessary and proper for carrying into Execution the foregoing Powers and all other Powers vested by this Constitution in the Government of the United States, or in any Department or Officer thereof."

The President's order does not direct that a congressional policy be executed in a manner prescribed by Congress—it directs that a presidential policy be executed in a manner prescribed by the President. The preamble of the order itself, like that of many statutes, sets out reasons why the President believes certain policies should be adopted, proclaims these policies as rules of conduct to be followed, and again, like a statute, authorizes a government official to promulgate additional rules and regulations consistent with the policy proclaimed and needed to carry that policy into execution. The power of Congress to adopt such public policies as those proclaimed by the order is beyond question. It can authorize the taking of private property for public use. It can make laws regulating the relationships between employers and employees, prescribing rules designed to settle labor disputes, and fixing wages and working conditions in certain fields of our economy. The Constitution does not subject this lawmaking power of Congress to presidential or military supervision or control.

It is said that other Presidents without congressional authority have taken possession of private business enterprises in order to settle labor disputes. But even if this be true, Congress has not thereby lost its exclusive constitutional authority to make laws necessary and proper to carry out the powers vested by the Constitution "in the Government of the United States, or in any Department or Officer thereof."

The Founders of this Nation entrusted the lawmaking power to the Congress alone in both good and bad times. It would do no good to recall the historical events, the fears of power and the hopes for freedom that lay behind their choice. Such a review would but confirm our holding that this seizure order cannot stand.

The judgment of the District Court is affirmed.

Affirmed.

[All of the Justices who joined Justice Black's opinion for the Court also wrote individual concurring opinions. Justice Frankfurter stated that questions concerning the extent of Presidential power in the absence of legislation were not before the Court. The Labor Management Relations Act of 1947 was equivalent to an explicit Congressional negation of the authority asserted by the seizure. For Justice Burton the "controlling fact" was that Congress had prescribed specific procedures, not including seizure, for the present type of emergency. Justice Douglas argued that Congress, as the only branch with power to appropriate money to compensate for seizures, was the only branch with power to authorize or ratify them. A few often-quoted passages from Justice Jackson's lengthy concurring opinion follow.]

■ MR. JUSTICE JACKSON, concurring in the judgment and opinion of the Court.

. . .

The actual art of governing under our Constitution does not and cannot conform to judicial definitions of the power of any of its branches based on isolated clauses or even single Articles torn from context. While the Constitution diffuses power the better to secure liberty, it also contemplates that practice will integrate the dispersed powers into a workable government. It enjoins upon its branches separateness but interdependence, autonomy but reciprocity. Presidential powers are not fixed but fluctuate, depending upon their disjunction or conjunction with those of Congress. We may well begin by a somewhat over-simplified grouping of practical situations in which a President may doubt, or others may challenge, his powers, and by distinguishing roughly the legal consequences of this factor of relativity.

1.   When the President acts pursuant to an express or implied authorization of Congress, his authority is at its maximum, for it includes all that he possesses in his own right plus all that Congress can delegate. In these circumstances, and in these only, may he be said (for what it may be worth), to personify the federal sovereignty. If his act is held unconstitutional under these circumstances, it usually means that the Federal Government as an undivided whole lacks power. A seizure executed by the President pursuant to an Act of Congress would be supported by the strongest of presumptions and the widest latitude of judicial interpretation, and the burden of persuasion would rest heavily upon any who might attack it.

2. When the President acts in absence of either a congressional grant or denial of authority, he can only rely upon his own independent powers, but there is a zone of twilight in which he and Congress may have concurrent authority, or in which its distribution is uncertain. Therefore, congressional inertia, indifference or quiescence may sometimes, at least as a practical matter, enable, if not invite, measures on independent presidential responsibility. In this area, any actual test of power is likely to depend on the imperatives of events and contemporary imponderables rather than on abstract theories of law.

3. When the President takes measures incompatible with the expressed or implied will of Congress, his power is at its lowest ebb, for then he can rely only upon his own constitutional powers minus any constitutional powers of Congress over the matter. Courts can sustain exclusive Presidential control in such a case only by disabling the Congress from acting upon the subject. Presidential claim to a power at once so conclusive and preclusive must be scrutinized with caution, for what is at stake is the equilibrium established by our constitutional system.

. . .

. . . [T]he current seizure [can] be justified only by the severe tests under the third grouping, where it can be supported only by any remainder of executive power after subtraction of such powers as Congress may have over the subject. In short, we can sustain the President only by holding that seizure of such strike-bound industries is within his domain and beyond control by Congress. Thus, this Court's first review of such seizures occurs under circumstances which leave Presidential power most vulnerable to attack and in the least favorable of possible constitutional postures.

. . .

But I have no illusion that any decision by this Court can keep power in the hands of Congress if it is not wise and timely in meeting its problems. A crisis that challenges the President equally, or perhaps primarily, challenges Congress. If not good law, there was worldly wisdom in the maxim attributed to Napoleon that "The tools belong to the man who can use them." We may say that power to legislate for emergencies belongs in the hands of Congress, but only Congress itself can prevent power from slipping through its fingers.

. . .

■ MR. JUSTICE CLARK, concurring in the judgment of the Court . . .

I conclude that where Congress has laid down specific procedures to deal with the type of crisis confronting the President, he must follow those procedures . . .

■ MR. CHIEF JUSTICE VINSON, with whom MR. JUSTICE REED and MR. JUSTICE MINTON join, dissenting. . . .

. . .

One is not here called upon even to consider the possibility of executive seizure of a farm, a corner grocery store or even a single industrial plant. Such considerations arise only when one ignores the central fact of this case—that the Nation's entire basic steel production would have shut down completely if there had been no Government seizure. . . .'

. . .

A review of executive action demonstrates that our Presidents have on many occasions exhibited the leadership contemplated by the Framers when they made the President Commander in Chief, and imposed upon him the trust to "take Care that the Laws be faithfully executed." With or without explicit statutory authorization,

Presidents have at such times dealt with national emergencies by acting promptly and resolutely to enforce legislative programs, at least to save those programs until Congress could act. Congress and the courts have responded to such executive initiative with consistent approval. . . .'

. . .

Focusing now on the situation confronting the President on the night of April 8, 1952, we cannot but conclude that the President was performing his duty under the Constitution to "take Care that the Laws be faithfully executed"—a duty described by President Benjamin Harrison as "the central idea of the office." . . .

. . .

Hamdan v. Rumsfeld

548 U.S. 557 (2006).

The Court held 5–4 that the President's planned structure and procedures for military tribunals to try alleged terrorists being held after September 11, 2001 in Guantanamo Bay, Cuba (in this case Osama Bin Laden's alleged bodyguard) violated the limitations on military tribunals Congress had imposed in the Uniform Code of Military Justice, as well as certain provisions of the Geneva Conventions. In the course of doing so, the Court observed: "Whether or not the President has independent power, absent congressional authorization, to convene military commissions, he may not disregard limitations that Congress has, in proper exercise of its own war powers, placed on his powers. See Youngstown Sheet & Tube Co. v. Sawyer, 343 U.S. 579, 637 (1952) (Jackson, J., concurring). The Government does not argue otherwise."

B. INTERNATIONAL RELATIONS

Introduction. Most of the constitutional grants of power to the federal government relating to foreign affairs appear in the enumeration of executive powers: the President is made "Commander-in-Chief" of the armed forces; he is given the power, with the approval of two-thirds of the Senate, "to make Treaties"; and, with the "advice and consent" of the Senate, he "shall appoint Ambassadors, other public Ministers and Consuls," i.e., our representatives abroad (Art. II, § 2). Also, "he shall receive Ambassadors and other public Ministers" (Art. II, § 3). Those spare provisions, however, hardly begin to capture the scope of "the executive power" to conduct the nation's foreign affairs.

United States v. Curtiss-Wright Export Corp.

299 U.S. 304, 320 (1936).

A dispute arose as to the validity of a delegation of power from Congress to the President. In the course of upholding the delegation the Court noted that the legislative power was combined with "the very delicate, plenary and exclusive power of the President as the sole organ of the Federal government in the field of international relations—a power which does not require as a basis for its exercise an act of Congress, but which, of course, like every other governmental power, must be exercised in subordination to the applicable provisions of the Constitution. It is quite apparent that if, in the maintenance of our international relations, embarrassment—perhaps serious embarrassment—is to be avoided and success for our aims achieved, congressional legislation which is to be made effective through negotiation and inquiry within the international field must often accord to the President a degree of discretion and freedom from statutory restriction which would not be admissible were domestic affairs alone involved. Moreover, he, not Congress, has the better opportunity of knowing the conditions which prevail in foreign countries, and especially is this true in time of war. He has his confidential sources of information. He has his agents in the form of diplomatic, consular and other officials. Secrecy in respect of information gathered by them may be highly necessary, and the premature disclosure of it productive of harmful results. Indeed, so clearly is this true that the first President refused to accede to a request to lay before the House of Representatives the instructions, correspondence and documents relating to the negotiation of the Jay Treaty—a refusal the wisdom of which was recognized by the House itself and has never since been doubted."

International Agreements

The scope of national power to override state law and policy through the use of international agreements was discussed in Chapter 4. In that connection, United States v. Belmont, 301 U.S. 324 (1937), and United States v. Pink, 315 U.S. 203 (1942), relate to the power of the President to consummate international agreements without going through the process of having formal treaties ratified by the Senate and the effect of such agreements on state law.

Belmont and *Pink* raised a separate issue that has proved highly controversial— whether executive agreements can be employed to circumvent the role of the Senate embodied in Article 2 of the Constitution. Some commentators were critical. Borchard, *Shall the Executive Agreement Replace the Treaty?*, 53 Yale L.J. 664 (1944), 54 Yale L.J. 616 (1945). Others supported the use of executive agreements (buttressed in some cases by joint action by the two houses of Congress) as a well-established means to provide flexibility in dealing with international relations. McDougal & Lans, *Treaties and Congressional-Executive or Presidential Agreements: Interchangeable Instruments of National Policy,* 54 Yale L.J. 181, 534 (1945). This dispute does not concern the propriety of the bulk of agreements made between the heads of governments in their day-to-day handling of routine arrangements (like an agreement for the exchange of visits by naval vessels) or military arrangements like the line in conquered territory where allied armies will meet. Some such arrangements may fall within the independent power of the President as "commander-in-chief", others within "the executive power" of the President to conduct the day-to-day business of foreign relations. But one of the questions stirred by the *Belmont* and *Pink* cases is whether the President might use executive agreements for basic long-range commitments of the nation when it might be impossible to obtain the two-thirds vote of the Senate for treaty ratification.

Dames & Moore v. Regan

453 U.S. 654 (1981).

On January 20, 1981, Iran released hostages captured in the seizure of the American Embassy, in Teheran, pursuant to an agreement with the United States. One provision of the agreement provided for termination of litigation in American courts against Iran, with the arbitration of those claims before an International Claims Tribunal. On January 19, 1981, President Carter issued executive orders providing for transfer of blocked Iranian funds in the United States, and nullifying attachments issued against those funds. On February 24, 1981, President Reagan ratified the Executive Orders, and suspended all claims filed in United States courts that could be presented to the claims tribunal.

Petitioner was a company that had procured a judgment against Iran in a federal trial court for breach of its contract to conduct studies for a proposed nuclear plant in Iran. It brought this action against the Secretary of the Treasury to prevent enforcement of the Executive Orders. Reserving questions whether the Executive Orders' suspension of claims constituted an uncompensated taking of property, the Court held that the Executive Orders did not exceed Presidential powers.

The provisions of the Executive Orders suspending attachments against persons holding blocked Iranian funds, and directing the transfer of those funds to Iran, were held to be authorized by provisions of the International Emergency Economic Powers Act (IEEPA). The Court concluded, however, that neither IEEPA, nor the Hostage Act of 1868, specifically authorized the President to suspend claims pending in United States Courts. In upholding the validity of this aspect of the Executive Orders, Justice Rehnquist's opinion for the Court said, in part:

"Concluding that neither the IEEPA nor the Hostage Act constitutes specific authorization of the President's action suspending claims, however, is not to say that these statutory provisions are entirely irrelevant to the question of the validity of the President's action. We think both statutes highly relevant in the looser sense of indicating congressional acceptance of a broad scope for executive action in circumstances such as those presented in this case. . . ."

"Although we have declined to conclude that the IEEPA or the Hostage Act directly authorizes the President's suspension of claims . . . , we cannot ignore the general tenor of Congress' legislation in this area in trying to determine whether the President is acting alone or at least with the acceptance of Congress. . . . Congress cannot anticipate and legislate with regard to every possible action the President may find it necessary to take or every possible situation in which he might act. Such failure of Congress specifically to delegate authority does not, 'especially . . . in the areas of foreign policy and national security,' imply 'congressional disapproval' of action taken by the Executive. . . . On the contrary, the enactment of legislation closely related to the question of the President's authority in a particular case which evinces legislative intent to accord the President broad discretion may be considered to 'invite' 'measures on independent presidential responsibility.' *Youngstown*, . . . (Jackson, J., concurring). At least this is so where there is no contrary indication of legislative intent and when, as here, there is a history of congressional acquiescence in conduct of the sort engaged in by the President. . . ."

Recognition of Foreign Sovereignty

Zivotofsky v. Kerry

576 U.S. ___, 135 S.Ct. 2076, 192 L.Ed.2d 83 (2015).

■ JUSTICE KENNEDY delivered the opinion of the Court.

A delicate subject lies in the background of this case. That subject is Jerusalem. Questions touching upon the history of the ancient city and its present legal and international status are . . . committed to the Legislature and the Executive, not the Judiciary. . . .

The Court addresses two questions to resolve the inter-branch dispute now before it. First, it must determine whether the President has the exclusive power to grant formal recognition to a foreign sovereign. Second, if he has that power, the Court must determine whether Congress can command the President and his Secretary of State to issue a formal statement that contradicts the earlier recognition. The statement in question here is a congressional mandate that allows a United States citizen born in

Jerusalem to direct the President and Secretary of State, when issuing his passport, to state that his place of birth is "Israel."

I

A

. . . In 1948, President Truman formally recognized Israel in a signed statement of "recognition." . . . That statement did not recognize Israeli sovereignty over Jerusalem. Over the last 60 years, various actors have sought to assert full or partial sovereignty over the city, including Israel, Jordan, and the Palestinians. Yet, in contrast to a consistent policy of formal recognition of Israel, neither President Truman nor any later United States President has issued an official statement or declaration acknowledging any country's sovereignty over Jerusalem. Instead, the Executive Branch has maintained that "'the status of Jerusalem . . . should be decided not unilaterally but in consultation with all concerned.'" . . .

The President's position on Jerusalem is reflected in State Department policy regarding passports and consular reports of birth abroad. Understanding that passports will be construed as reflections of American policy, the State Department's Foreign Affairs Manual instructs its employees, in general, to record the place of birth on a passport as the "country [having] present sovereignty over the actual area of birth." Dept. of State, 7 Foreign Affairs Manual (FAM) § 1383.4 (1987). If a citizen objects to the country listed as sovereign by the State Department, he or she may list the city or town of birth rather than the country. . . . The FAM, however, does not allow citizens to list a sovereign that conflicts with Executive Branch policy. . . . Because the United States does not recognize any country as having sovereignty over Jerusalem, the FAM instructs employees to record the place of birth for citizens born there as "Jerusalem."

In 2002, Congress passed the Act at issue here, the Foreign Relations Authorization Act . . . . Section 214 of the Act is titled "United States Policy with Respect to Jerusalem as the Capital of Israel." . . . The subsection that lies at the heart of this case, § 214(d), addresses passports. That subsection seeks to override the FAM by allowing citizens born in Jerusalem to list their place of birth as "Israel." Titled "Record of Place of Birth as Israel for Passport Purposes," § 214(d) states "[f]or purposes of the registration of birth, certification of nationality, or issuance of a passport of a United States citizen born in the city of Jerusalem, the Secretary shall, upon the request of the citizen or the citizen's legal guardian, record the place of birth as Israel." . . .

When he signed the Act into law, President George W. Bush issued a statement declaring his position that § 214 would, "if construed as mandatory rather than advisory, impermissibly interfere with the President's constitutional authority to formulate the position of the United States, speak for the Nation in international affairs, and determine the terms on which recognition is given to foreign states." Statement on Signing the Foreign Relations Authorization Act, Fiscal Year 2003, Public Papers of the Presidents, George W. Bush, Vol. 2, Sept. 30, 2002, p. 1698 (2005). The President concluded, "U. S. policy regarding Jerusalem has not changed." *Ibid.*

. . .

B

In 2002, petitioner Menachem Binyamin Zivotofsky was born to United States citizens living in Jerusalem. . . . In December 2002, Zivotofsky's mother visited the American Embassy in Tel Aviv to request both a passport and a consular report of birth abroad for her son. . . . She asked that his place of birth be listed as "'Jerusalem,

Israel.' " . . . The Embassy clerks explained that, pursuant to State Department policy, the passport would list only "Jerusalem." . . . Zivotofsky's parents objected and, as his guardians, brought suit on his behalf in the United States District Court for the District of Columbia, seeking to enforce § 214(d).

Pursuant to § 214(d), Zivotofsky claims the right to have "Israel" recorded as his place of birth in his passport. . . . The arguments in Zivotofsky's brief center on his passport claim, as opposed to the consular report of birth abroad. Indeed, in the court below, Zivotofsky waived any argument that his consular report of birth abroad should be treated differently than his passport. . . . He has also waived the issue here by failing to differentiate between the two documents. As a result, the Court addresses Zivotofsky's passport arguments and need not engage in a separate analysis of the validity of § 214(d) as applied to consular reports of birth abroad.

. . .

II

In considering claims of Presidential power this Court refers to Justice Jackson's familiar tripartite framework from *Youngstown Sheet & Tube Co.* v. *Sawyer*, 343 U. S. 579, 635–638 (1952) (concurring opinion). The framework divides exercises of Presidential power into three categories: First, when "the President acts pursuant to an express or implied authorization of Congress, his authority is at its maximum, for it includes all that he possesses in his own right plus all that Congress can delegate." . . . Second, "in absence of either a congressional grant or denial of authority" there is a "zone of twilight in which he and Congress may have concurrent authority," and where "congressional inertia, indifference or quiescence may" invite the exercise of executive power. . . . Finally, when "the President takes measures incompatible with the expressed or implied will of Congress . . . he can rely only upon his own constitutional powers minus any constitutional powers of Congress over the matter." . . . To succeed in this third category, the President's asserted power must be both "exclusive" and "conclusive" on the issue. . . .

In this case the Secretary contends that § 214(d) infringes on the President's exclusive recognition power by "requiring the President to contradict his recognition position regarding Jerusalem in official communications with foreign sovereigns." . . . In so doing the Secretary acknowledges the President's power is "at its lowest ebb." . . . Because the President's refusal to implement § 214(d) falls into Justice Jackson's third category, his claim must be "scrutinized with caution," and he may rely solely on powers the Constitution grants to him alone. . . .

To determine whether the President possesses the exclusive power of recognition the Court examines the Constitution's text and structure, as well as precedent and history bearing on the question.

A

Recognition is a "formal acknowledgement" that a particular "entity possesses the qualifications for statehood" or "that a particular regime is the effective government of a state." Restatement (Third) of Foreign Relations Law of the United States § 203, Comment *a*, p. 84 (1986). It may also involve the determination of a state's territorial bounds. See 2 M. Whiteman, Digest of International Law § 1, p. 1 (1963) (Whiteman) ("[S]tates may recognize or decline to recognize territory as belonging to, or under the sovereignty of, or having been acquired or lost by, other states"). Recognition is often effected by an express "written or oral declaration." 1 J. Moore, Digest of International Law § 27, p. 73 (1906) (Moore). It may also be implied—for example, by concluding a bilateral treaty or by sending or receiving diplomatic agents. *Ibid.*; I. Brownlie, Principles of Public International Law 93 (7th ed. 2008) (Brownlie).

Legal consequences follow formal recognition. Recognized sovereigns may sue in United States courts, . . . and may benefit from sovereign immunity when they are sued . . . . The actions of a recognized sovereign committed within its own territory also receive deference in domestic courts under the act of state doctrine. . . .

Recognition at international law, furthermore, is a precondition of regular diplomatic relations. 1 Moore § 27, at 72. Recognition is thus "useful, even necessary," to the existence of a state. . . .

Despite the importance of the recognition power in foreign relations, the Constitution does not use the term "recognition," either in Article II or elsewhere. The Secretary asserts that the President exercises the recognition power based on the Reception Clause, which directs that the President "shall receive Ambassadors and other public Ministers." Art. II, § 3. As Zivotofsky notes, the Reception Clause received little attention at the Constitutional Convention. See Reinstein, Recognition: A Case Study on the Original Understanding of Executive Power, 45 U.Rich. L. Rev. 801, 860– 862 (2011). In fact, during the ratification debates, Alexander Hamilton claimed that the power to receive ambassadors was "more a matter of dignity than of authority," a ministerial duty largely "without consequence." The Federalist No. 69, p. 420 (C. Rossiter ed. 1961).

At the time of the founding, however, prominent international scholars suggested that receiving an ambassador was tantamount to recognizing the sovereignty of the sending state. See E. de Vattel, The Law of Nations § 78, p. 461 (1758) (J. Chitty ed. 1853) ("[E]very state, truly possessed of sovereignty, has a right to send ambassadors" and "to contest their right in this instance" is equivalent to "contesting their sovereign dignity"); see also 2 C. van Bynkershoek, On Questions of Public Law 156–157 (1737) (T. Frank ed. 1930) ("Among writers on public law it is usually agreed that only a sovereign power has a right to send ambassadors"); 2 H. Grotius, On the Law of War and Peace 440–441 (1625) (F. Kelsey ed. 1925) (discussing the duty to admit ambassadors of sovereign powers). It is a logical and proper inference, then, that a Clause directing the President alone to receive ambassadors would be understood to acknowledge his power to recognize other nations.

This in fact occurred early in the Nation's history when President Washington recognized the French Revolutionary Government by receiving its ambassador. See A. Hamilton, Pacificus No. 1, in The Letters of Pacificus and Helvidius 5, 13–14 (1845) (reprint 1976) (President "acknowledged the republic of France, by the reception of its minister"). After this incident the import of the Reception Clause became clear— causing Hamilton to change his earlier view. He wrote that the Reception Clause "includes th[e power] of judging, in the case of a revolution of government in a foreign country, whether the new rulers are competent organs of the national will, and ought to be recognised, or not." See id., at 12; see also 3 J. Story, Commentaries on the Constitution of the United States § 1560, p. 416 (1833) ("If the executive receives an ambassador, or other minister, as the representative of a new nation . . . it is an acknowledgment of the sovereign authority *de facto* of such new nation, or party"). As a result, the Reception Clause provides support, although not the sole authority, for the President's power to recognize other nations.

The inference that the President exercises the recognition power is further supported by his additional Article II powers. It is for the President, "by and with the Advice and Consent of the Senate," to "make Treaties, provided two thirds of the Senators present concur." Art. II, § 2, cl.2. In addition, "he shall nominate, and by and with the Advice and Consent of the Senate, shall appoint Ambassadors" as well as "other public Ministers and Consuls." *Ibid.*

As a matter of constitutional structure, these additional powers give the President control over recognition decisions. At international law, recognition may be effected by different means, but each means is dependent upon Presidential power. In addition to receiving an ambassador, recognition may occur on "the conclusion of a bilateral treaty," or the "formal initiation of diplomatic relations," including the dispatch of an ambassador. Brownlie 93; see also 1 Moore § 27, at 73. The President has the sole power to negotiate treaties, see *United States* v. *Curtiss-Wright Export Corp.*, 299 U. S. 304, 319 (1936), and the Senate may not conclude or ratify a treaty without Presidential action. The President, too, nominates the Nation's ambassadors and dispatches other diplomatic agents. Congress may not send an ambassador without his involvement. Beyond that, the President himself has the power to open diplomatic channels simply by engaging in direct diplomacy with foreign heads of state and their ministers. The Constitution thus assigns the President means to effect recognition on his own initiative. Congress, by contrast, has no constitutional power that would enable it to initiate diplomatic relations with a foreign nation. Because these specific Clauses confer the recognition power on the President, the Court need not consider whether or to what extent the Vesting Clause, which provides that the "executive Power" shall be vested in the President, provides further support for the President's action here. Art. II, § 1, cl. 1.

The text and structure of the Constitution grant the President the power to recognize foreign nations and governments. The question then becomes whether that power is exclusive. The various ways in which the President may unilaterally effect recognition—and the lack of any similar power vested in Congress—suggest that it is. So, too, do functional considerations. Put simply, the Nation must have a single policy regarding which governments are legitimate in the eyes of the United States and which are not. Foreign countries need to know, before entering into diplomatic relations or commerce with the United States, whether their ambassadors will be received; whether their officials will be immune from suit in federal court; and whether they may initiate lawsuits here to vindicate their rights. These assurances cannot be equivocal.

. . .

It remains true, of course, that many decisions affecting foreign relations—including decisions that may determine the course of our relations with recognized countries—require congressional action. Congress may "regulate Commerce with foreign Nations," "establish an uniform Rule of Naturalization," "define and punish Piracies and Felonies committed on the high Seas, and Offences against the Law of Nations," "declare War," "grant Letters of Marque and Reprisal," and "make Rules for the Government and Regulation of the land and naval Forces." U. S. Const., Art. I, § 8. In addition, the President cannot make a treaty or appoint an ambassador without the approval of the Senate. Art. II, § 2, cl. 2. The President, furthermore, could not build an American Embassy abroad without congressional appropriation of the necessary funds. Art. I, § 8, cl. 1. Under basic separation-of-powers principles, it is for the Congress to enact the laws, including "all Laws which shall be necessary and proper for carrying into Execution" the powers of the Federal Government. § 8, cl. 18.

. . .

B

No single precedent resolves the question whether the President has exclusive recognition authority and, if so, how far that power extends. In part that is because, until today, the political branches have resolved their disputes over questions of recognition. The relevant cases, though providing important instruction, address the division of recognition power between the Federal Government and the States, see, *e.g., Pink*, 315 U. S. 203, or between the courts and the political branches, see, *e.g., Banco Nacional de Cuba*, 376 U. S., at 410—not between the President and Congress. As the parties acknowledge, some isolated statements in those cases lend support to the position that Congress has a role in the recognition process. In the end, however, a fair reading of the cases shows that the President's role in the recognition process is both central and exclusive. . . .

. . .

C

Having examined the Constitution's text and this Court's precedent, it is appropriate to turn to accepted understandings and practice. In separation-of-powers cases this Court has often "put significant weight upon historical practice." *NLRB* v. *Noel Canning*, 573 U. S. ___, ___ (2014) (slip op., at 6) (emphasis deleted). Here, history is not all on one side, but on balance it provides strong support for the conclusion that the recognition power is the President's alone. . . .

. . .

III

As the power to recognize foreign states resides in the President alone, the question becomes whether § 214(d) infringes on the Executive's consistent decision to withhold recognition with respect to Jerusalem. See *Nixon* v. *Administrator of General Services*, 433 U. S. 425, 443 (1977) (action unlawful when it "prevents the Executive Branch from accomplishing its constitutionally assigned functions"). Section 214(d) requires that, in a passport or consular report of birth abroad, "the Secretary shall, upon the request of the citizen or the citizen's legal guardian, record the place of birth as Israel" for a "United States citizen born in the city of Jerusalem." 116 Stat. 1366. That is, § 214(d) requires the President, through the Secretary, to identify citizens born in Jerusalem who so request as being born in Israel. But according to the President, those citizens were not born in Israel. As a matter of United States policy, neither Israel nor any other country is acknowledged as having sovereignty over Jerusalem. In this way, § 214(d) "directly contradicts" the "carefully calibrated and longstanding Executive branch policy of neutrality toward Jerusalem." . . . If the power over recognition is to mean anything, it must mean that the President not only makes the initial, formal recognition determination but also that he may maintain that determination in his and his agent's statements. This conclusion is a matter of both common sense and necessity. If Congress could command the President to state a recognition position inconsistent with his own, Congress could override the President's recognition determination. . . .

. . .

* * *

In holding § 214(d) invalid the Court does not question the substantial powers of Congress over foreign affairs in general or passports in particular. This case is confined solely to the exclusive power of the President to control recognition determinations, including formal statements by the Executive Branch acknowledging the legitimacy of a state or government and its territorial bounds. Congress cannot command the President to contradict an earlier recognition determination in the issuance of passports. The judgment of the Court of Appeals for the District of Columbia Circuit is

Affirmed.

■ JUSTICE BREYER, concurring.

I continue to believe that this case presents a political question inappropriate for judicial resolution. . . . But because precedent precludes resolving this case on political question grounds, . . . , I join the Court's opinion.

■ JUSTICE THOMAS, concurring in the judgment in part and dissenting in part.

Our Constitution allocates the powers of the Federal Government over foreign affairs in two ways. First, it expressly identifies certain foreign affairs powers and vests them in particular branches, either individually or jointly. Second, it vests the residual foreign affairs powers of the Federal Government—*i.e.,* those not specifically enumerated in the Constitution—in the President by way of Article II's Vesting Clause.

Section 214(d) of the Foreign Relations Authorization Act, Fiscal Year 2003, ignores that constitutional allocation of power insofar as it directs the President, contrary to his wishes, to list "Israel" as the place of birth of Jerusalem-born citizens on their passports. The President has long regulated passports under his residual foreign affairs power, and this portion of § 214(d) does not fall within any of Congress' enumerated powers.

By contrast, § 214(d) poses no such problem insofar as it regulates consular reports of birth abroad. Unlike passports, these reports were developed to effectuate the naturalization laws, and they continue to serve the role of identifying persons who need not be naturalized to obtain U. S. citizenship. The regulation of these reports does not fall within the President's foreign affairs powers, but within Congress' enumerated powers under the Naturalization and Necessary and Proper Clauses.

Rather than adhere to the Constitution's division of powers, the Court relies on a distortion of the President's recognition power to hold both of these parts of § 214(d) unconstitutional. Because I cannot join this faulty analysis, I concur only in the portion of the Court's judgment holding § 214(d) unconstitutional as applied to passports. I respectfully dissent from the remainder of the Court's judgment.

. . .

■ CHIEF JUSTICE ROBERTS, with whom JUSTICE ALITO joins, dissenting.

Today's decision is a first: Never before has this Court accepted a President's direct defiance of an Act of Congress in the field of foreign affairs. We have instead stressed that the President's power reaches "its lowest ebb" when he contravenes the express will of Congress, "for what is at stake is the equilibrium established by our constitutional system." *Youngstown Sheet & Tube Co.* v. *Sawyer*, 343 U. S. 579, 637–638 (1952) (Jackson, J., concurring).

. . .

■ JUSTICE SCALIA, with whom THE CHIEF JUSTICE and JUSTICE ALITO join, dissenting.

. . . This case arises out of a dispute between the Executive and Legislative Branches about whether the United States should treat Jerusalem as a part of Israel. The Constitution contemplates that the political branches will make policy about the territorial claims of foreign nations the same way they make policy about other international matters: The President will exercise his powers on the basis of his views, Congress its powers on the basis of its views. That is just what has happened here.

. . .

II

. . .

The Court holds that the Constitution makes the President alone responsible for recognition and that § 214(d) invades this exclusive power. I agree that the Constitution *empowers* the President to extend recognition on behalf of the United States, but I find it a much harder question whether it makes that power exclusive. The Court tells us that "the weight of historical evidence" supports exclusive executive authority over "the formal determination of recognition." . . . But even with its attention confined to formal recognition, the Court is forced to admit that "history is not all on one side." . . . To take a stark example, Congress legislated in 1934 to grant independence to the Philippines, which were then an American colony. . . . In the course of doing so, Congress directed the President to "recognize the independence of the Philippine Islands as a separate and self-governing nation" and to "acknowledge the authority and control over the same of the government instituted by the people thereof." . . . Constitutional? And if Congress may control recognition when exercising its power "to dispose of . . . the Territory or other Property belonging to the United States," Art. IV, § 3, cl. 2, why not when exercising other enumerated powers? Neither text nor history nor precedent yields a clear answer to these questions. Fortunately, I have no need to confront these matters today—nor does the Court—because § 214(d) plainly does not concern recognition.

Recognition is more than an announcement of a policy. Like the ratification of an international agreement or the termination of a treaty, it is a formal legal act with effects under international law. It signifies acceptance of an international status, and it makes a commitment to continued acceptance of that status and respect for any attendant rights. . . .

. . .

Section 214(d) performs a more prosaic function than extending recognition. Just as foreign countries care about what our Government has to say about their borders, so too American citizens often care about what our Government has to say about their identities. . . .

. . .

C. WAR AND NATIONAL DEFENSE

Introduction. The Constitution is not silent about Congressional participation in one aspect of foreign affairs. Article I, Section 8, Clause 11, of the Constitution specifies that it is a Congressional prerogative "to declare war."

The Prize Cases
67 U.S. (2 Black) 635, 17 L.Ed. 459 (1863).

[In April, 1861, President Lincoln declared a blockade of southern ports. Pursuant to this blockade, in May and July, 1861, Union ships seized merchant vessels and cargoes of foreign neutrals and residents of the southern states. The ships were condemned by federal court order. The owners of the ships and cargo appealed. The Supreme Court regarded the first question to be: "Had the President authority to institute a blockade of southern ports which neutrals were bound to respect?" The following excerpts are addressed to that question.]

■ MR. JUSTICE GRIER.

. . .

By the Constitution, Congress alone has the power to declare a national or foreign war. It cannot declare war against a State or any number of States, by virtue of any clause in the Constitution. The Constitution confers on the President the whole executive power. He is bound to take care that the laws be faithfully executed. He is Commander-in-Chief of the Army and Navy of the United States, and of the militia of the several States when called into the actual service of the United States. He has no power to initiate or declare a war either against a foreign nation or a domestic State. But by the Acts of Congress of Feb. 28th, 1795 and 3d of March, 1807, he is authorized to call out the militia and use the military and naval forces of the United States in case of invasion by foreign nations, and to suppress insurrection against the government of a State or of the United States.

If a war be made by invasion of a foreign nation, the President is not only authorized but bound to resist force, by force. He does not initiate the war, but is bound to accept the challenge without waiting for any special legislative authority. And whether the hostile party be a foreign invader, or States organized in rebellion, it is none the less a war, although the declaration of it be "*unilateral.*" . . .

. . .

This greatest of civil wars was not gradually developed by popular commotion, tumultuous assemblies, or local unorganized insurrections. However long may have been its previous conception, it nevertheless sprung forth suddenly from the parent brain, a Minerva in the full panoply of war. The President was bound to meet it in the shape it presented itself, without waiting for Congress to baptize it with a name; and no name given to it by him or them could change the fact. . . .

Whether the President in fulfilling his duties, as Commander-in-Chief, in suppressing an insurrection, has met with such armed hostile resistance, and a civil war of such alarming proportions as will compel him to accord to them the character of belligerents, is a question to be decided by him, and this court must be governed by the decisions and acts of the Political Department of the government to which this power was intrusted. "He must determine what degree of force the crisis demands." The proclamation of blockade is, itself, official and conclusive evidence to the court that a state of war existed which demanded and authorized a recourse to such a measure, under the circumstances peculiar to the case.

. . .

If it were necessary to the technical existence of a war, that it should have a legislative sanction, we find it in almost every Act passed at the extraordinary session of the Legislature of 1861, which was wholly employed in enacting laws to enable the government to prosecute the war with vigor and efficiency. And finally, in 1861, we find Congress "*ex majore cautela*" and in anticipation of such astute objections, passing an Act "approving, legalizing and making valid all the acts, proclamations, and orders of the President, & c., as if they had been issued and done under the previous express authority and direction of the Congress of the United States."

Without admitting that such an Act was necessary under the circumstances, it is plain that if the President had in any manner assumed powers which it was necessary should have the authority or sanction of Congress, that . . . this ratification has operated to perfectly cure the defect. . . .'

[The decrees of condemnation were affirmed except for certain cargoes which were bought and paid for in the South before the war broke out and which were being removed shortly thereafter.]

■ MR. JUSTICE NELSON [joined by CHIEF JUSTICE TANEY and JUSTICES CATRON and CLIFFORD, dissenting]. . . .

The Acts of 1795 and 1807 did not, and could not, under the Constitution, confer on the President the power of declaring war against a State of this Union, or of deciding that war existed, and upon that ground authorize the capture and confiscation of the property of every citizen of the State whenever it was found on the waters. The laws of war, whether the war be civil or *inter gentes,* as we have seen, convert every citizen of the hostile State into a public enemy, and treat him accordingly, whatever may have been his previous conduct. This great power over the business and property of the citizen is reserved to the Legislative Department by the express words of the Constitution. It cannot be delegated or surrendered to the Executive. Congress alone can determine whether war exists or should be declared, and until they have acted, no citizen of the State can be punished in his person or property, unless he has committed some offense against a law of Congress passed before the act was committed, which made it a crime, and defined the punishment. The penalty of confiscation for the acts of others with which he had no concern cannot lawfully be inflicted. . . .'

[This dissenting opinion also came to the conclusion that congressional ratification of the seizures was . . . invalid.]

Mora v. McNamara

389 U.S. 934, 88 S.Ct. 282, 19 L.Ed.2d 287 (1967).

Petition for writ of certiorari to the United States Court of Appeals for the District of Columbia Circuit.

Nov. 6, 1967. Denied.

■ MR. JUSTICE MARSHALL took no part in the consideration or decision of this petition.

■ MR. JUSTICE STEWART, with whom MR. JUSTICE DOUGLAS joins, dissenting.

The petitioners were drafted into the United States Army in late 1965, and six months later were ordered to a West Coast replacement station for shipment to Vietnam. They brought this suit to prevent the Secretary of Defense and the Secretary of the Army from carrying out those orders, and requested a declaratory judgment that the present United States military activity in Vietnam is "illegal." The District Court dismissed the suit, and the Court of Appeals affirmed.

There exist in this case questions of great magnitude. . . .

I.   Is the present United States military activity in Vietnam a "war" within the meaning of Article I, Section 8, Clause 11 of the Constitution?

II.   If so, may the Executive constitutionally order the petitioners to participate in that military activity, when no war has been declared by the Congress?

III.   Of what relevance to Question II are the present treaty obligations of the United States?

IV.   Of what relevance to Question II is the Joint Congressional ("Tonkin Gulf") Resolution of August 10, 1964?[a] . . .

---

[a]   The Tonkin Gulf Resolution was enacted at the request of President Johnson as a result of specific naval incidents in the Gulf of Tonkin. It stated that "Congress approves and supports the determination of the President, as Commander-in-Chief, to take all necessary measures to repel any armed attack against the forces of the United States and to prevent further aggression." H.R.J.Res.

These are large and deeply troubling questions. Whether the Court would ultimately reach them depends, of course, upon the resolution of serious preliminary issues of justiciability. We cannot make these problems go away simply by refusing to hear the case of three obscure Army privates. I intimate not even tentative views upon any of these matters, but I think the Court should squarely face them by granting certiorari and setting this case for oral argument.

■ MR. JUSTICE DOUGLAS, with whom MR. JUSTICE STEWART concurs, dissenting.

The questions posed by Mr. Justice Stewart cover the wide range of problems which the Senate Committee on Foreign Relations recently explored, in connection with the SEATO treaty of February 19, 1955, and the Tonkin Gulf Resolution.

Mr. Katzenbach, representing the Administration, testified that he did not regard the Tonkin Gulf Resolution to be "a declaration of war" . . . He added:

"The use of the phrase 'to declare war' as it was used in the Constitution of the United States had a particular meaning in terms of the events and the practices which existed at the time it was adopted. . . ."

"[I]t was recognized by the Founding Fathers that the President might have to take emergency action to protect the security of the United States, but that if there was going to be another use of the armed forces of the United States, that was a decision which Congress should check the Executive on, which Congress should support. It was for that reason that the phrase was inserted in the Constitution.

". . .

"A declaration of war would not, I think, correctly reflect the very limited objectives of the United States with respect to Vietnam. It would not correctly reflect our efforts there, what we are trying to do, the reasons why we are there, to use an outmoded phraseology, to declare war."

The view that Congress was intended to play a more active role in the initiation and conduct of war than the above statements might suggest has been espoused by Senator Fulbright . . . , quoting Thomas Jefferson who said:

"We have already given in example one effectual check to the Dog of war by transferring the power of letting him loose from the Executive to the Legislative body, from those who are to spend to those who are to pay."

These opposed views are reflected in the Prize Cases, . . .

The Court and the Vietnam Controversy

After the *Mora* decision, efforts to obtain a Supreme Court ruling on whether or not American military operations in Vietnam amounted to an "unconstitutional" war continued, but without success. The lower courts generally ruled that the issue was not justiciable.

Professor Henkin argues that the "courts, despite sometimes-misguided efforts to compel them to do so (as on Vietnam), are not likely to step into intense confrontations between President and Congress, or inhibit either when the other does not object. Whether from the sense that the boundary between Congress and President . . . , cannot be defined by law, whether from realization of the inherent limitations of judicial power or from prudence, whether under a doctrine of 'political questions' or by other judicial devices and formulae for abstention, courts will not make certain what

1145, 88th Cong., 2d Sess., 78 Stat. 384 (1964). It was repealed December 31, 1970. Did the repeal have any effect on the President's powers to continue operations in Vietnam?

was left uncertain, will not curtail the power of the political branches, will not arbitrate their differences. Then, in time, the issues will recede, stirring neither controversy nor case." *Foreign Affairs and the Constitution,* 274–275 (1972).

See, generally, John Hart Ely, *War and Responsibility* (1993).

Boumediene v. Bush

553 U.S. 723, 128 S.Ct. 2229, 171 L.Ed.2d 41 (2008).

■ JUSTICE KENNEDY delivered the opinion of the Court.

Petitioners are aliens designated as enemy combatants and detained at the United States Naval Station at Guantanamo Bay, Cuba. There are others detained there, also aliens, who are not parties to this suit.

Petitioners present a question not resolved by our earlier cases relating to the detention of aliens at Guantanamo: whether they have the constitutional privilege of habeas corpus, a privilege not to be withdrawn except in conformance with the Suspension Clause, Art. I, § 9, cl. 2. We hold these petitioners do have the habeas corpus privilege. Congress has enacted a statute, the Detainee Treatment Act of 2005 (DTA), 119 Stat. 2739, that provides certain procedures for review of the detainees' status. We hold that those procedures are not an adequate and effective substitute for habeas corpus. Therefore § 7 of the Military Commissions Act of 2006(MCA), 28 U.S.C.A. § 2241(e) (Supp.2007), operates as an unconstitutional suspension of the writ. We do not address whether the President has authority to detain these petitioners nor do we hold that the writ must issue. These and other questions regarding the legality of the detention are to be resolved in the first instance by the District Court.

I

Under the Authorization for Use of Military Force (AUMF), § 2(a), 115 Stat. 224, note following 50 U.S.C. § 1541 (2000 ed., Supp. V), the President is authorized "to use all necessary and appropriate force against those nations, organizations, or persons he determines planned, authorized, committed, or aided the terrorist attacks that occurred on September 11, 2001, or harbored such organizations or persons, in order to prevent any future acts of international terrorism against the United States by such nations, organizations or persons."

In Hamdi v. Rumsfeld, 542 U.S. 507 (2004), five Members of the Court recognized that detention of individuals who fought against the United States in Afghanistan "for the duration of the particular conflict in which they were captured, is so fundamental and accepted an incident to war as to be an exercise of the 'necessary and appropriate force' Congress has authorized the President to use." (plurality opinion of O'Connor, J.), id., at 588–589 (Thomas, J., dissenting). After *Hamdi,* the Deputy Secretary of Defense established Combatant Status Review Tribunals (CSRTs) to determine whether individuals detained at Guantanamo were "enemy combatants," as the Department defines that term. . . . A later memorandum established procedures to implement the CSRTs. . . . The Government maintains these procedures were designed to comply with the due process requirements identified by the plurality in *Hamdi.* . . .

Interpreting the AUMF, the Department of Defense ordered the detention of these petitioners, and they were transferred to Guantanamo. Some of these individuals were apprehended on the battlefield in Afghanistan, others in places as far away from there as Bosnia and Gambia. All are foreign nationals, but none is a citizen of a nation now at war with the United States. Each denies he is a member of the al Qaeda terrorist network that carried out the September 11 attacks or of the Taliban regime that provided sanctuary for al Qaeda. Each petitioner appeared before a separate CSRT; was determined to be an enemy combatant; and has sought a writ of habeas corpus in the United States District Court for the District of Columbia.

The first actions commenced in February 2002. The District Court ordered the cases dismissed for lack of jurisdiction because the naval station is outside the sovereign territory of the United States. . . . The Court of Appeals for the District of Columbia Circuit affirmed. . . . We granted certiorari and reversed, holding that 28 U.S.C. § 2241 extended statutory habeas corpus jurisdiction to Guantanamo. See Rasul v. Bush, 542 U.S. 466, 473 (2004). The constitutional issue presented in the instant cases was not reached in *Rasul*. . . .

After *Rasul*, petitioners' cases were consolidated and entertained in two separate proceedings . . . .

While appeals were pending from the[se] District Court decisions, Congress passed the DTA. Subsection (e) of § 1005 of the DTA amended 28 U.S.C. § 2241 to provide that "no court, justice, or judge shall have jurisdiction to hear or consider . . . an application for a writ of habeas corpus filed by or on behalf of an alien detained by the Department of Defense at Guantanamo Bay, Cuba." 119 Stat. 2742. Section 1005 further provides that the Court of Appeals for the District of Columbia Circuit shall have "exclusive" jurisdiction to review decisions of the CSRTs. Ibid.

In Hamdan v. Rumsfeld, 548 U.S. 557, 576–577 (2006), the Court held this provision did not apply to cases (like petitioners') pending when the DTA was enacted. Congress responded by passing the MCA, 10 U.S.C.A. § 948a et seq. (Supp.2007), which again amended § 2241. The text of the statutory amendment is discussed below. See Part II, infra. . . .

Petitioners' cases were consolidated on appeal, and the parties filed supplemental briefs in light of our decision in *Hamdan*. The Court of Appeals' ruling . . . is the subject of our present review and today's decision.

The Court of Appeals concluded that MCA § 7 must be read to strip from it, and all federal courts, jurisdiction to consider petitioners' habeas corpus applications, . . . that petitioners are not entitled to the privilege of the writ or the protections of the Suspension Clause, . . . and, as a result, that it was unnecessary to consider whether Congress provided an adequate and effective substitute for habeas corpus in the DTA.

We granted certiorari. . . .

II

As a threshold matter, we must decide whether MCA § 7 denies the federal courts jurisdiction to hear habeas corpus actions pending at the time of its enactment. We hold the statute does deny that jurisdiction, so that, if the statute is valid, petitioners' cases must be dismissed.

. . .

III

In deciding the constitutional questions now presented we must determine whether petitioners are barred from seeking the writ or invoking the protections of the Suspension Clause either because of their status, i.e., petitioners' designation by the Executive Branch as enemy combatants, or their physical location, i.e., their presence at Guantanamo Bay. The Government contends that noncitizens designated as enemy combatants and detained in territory located outside our Nation's borders have no constitutional rights and no privilege of habeas corpus. Petitioners contend they do have cognizable constitutional rights and that Congress, in seeking to eliminate recourse to habeas corpus as a means to assert those rights, acted in violation of the Suspension Clause.

. . . [The Court then provided an overview of the history behind habeas corpus and the Suspension Clause.]

B

The broad historical narrative of the writ and its function is central to our analysis, but we seek guidance as well from founding-era authorities addressing the specific question before us: whether foreign nationals, apprehended and detained in distant countries during a time of serious threats to our Nation's security, may assert the privilege of the writ and seek its protection. . . .

. . .

. . . Petitioners argue the site of their detention is analogous to two territories outside of England to which the writ did run: the so-called "exempt jurisdictions," like the Channel Islands; and (in former times) India. There are critical differences between these places and Guantanamo, however.

. . .

. . . And given the unique status of Guantanamo Bay and the particular dangers of terrorism in the modern age, the common-law courts simply may not have confronted cases with close parallels to this one. We decline, therefore, to infer too much, one way or the other, from the lack of historical evidence on point. . . .

IV

Drawing from its position that at common law the writ ran only to territories over which the Crown was sovereign, the Government says the Suspension Clause affords petitioners no rights because the United States does not claim sovereignty over the place of detention.

Guantanamo Bay is not formally part of the United States. See DTA § 1005(g), 119 Stat. 2743. And under the terms of the lease between the United States and Cuba, Cuba retains "ultimate sovereignty" over the territory while the United States exercises "complete jurisdiction and control." See Lease of Lands for Coaling and Naval Stations, Feb. 23, 1903, U.S.-Cuba, Art. III, T.S. No. 418 (hereinafter 1903 Lease Agreement) . . . Under the terms of the 1934 Treaty, however, Cuba effectively has no rights as a sovereign until the parties agree to modification of the 1903 Lease Agreement or the United States abandons the base . . . . .

The United States contends, nevertheless, that Guantanamo is not within its sovereign control. This was the Government's position well before the events of September 11, 2001. . . . And in other contexts the Court has held that questions of sovereignty are for the political branches to decide . . . . . Even if this were a treaty interpretation case that did not involve a political question, the President's construction of the lease agreement would be entitled to great respect. . . .

We therefore do not question the Government's position that Cuba, not the United States, maintains sovereignty, in the legal and technical sense of the term, over Guantanamo Bay. But this does not end the analysis. Our cases do not hold it is improper for us to inquire into the objective degree of control the Nation asserts over foreign territory. As commentators have noted, " '[s]overeignty' is a term used in many senses and is much abused." See 1 Restatement (Third) of Foreign Relations Law of the United States § 206, Comment b, p. 94 (1986). When we have stated that sovereignty is a political question, we have referred not to sovereignty in the general, colloquial sense, meaning the exercise of dominion or power, see Webster's New

International Dictionary 2406 (2d ed.1934) ("sovereignty," definition 3), but sovereignty in the narrow, legal sense of the term, meaning a claim of right, see 1 Restatement (Third) of Foreign Relations, supra, § 206, Comment b, at 94 (noting that sovereignty "implies a state's lawful control over its territory generally to the exclusion of other states, authority to govern in that territory, and authority to apply law there").... Accordingly, for purposes of our analysis, we accept the Government's position that Cuba, and not the United States, retains de jure sovereignty over Guantanamo Bay. As we did in *Rasul*, however, we take notice of the obvious and uncontested fact that the United States, by virtue of its complete jurisdiction and control over the base, maintains de facto sovereignty over this territory....

Were we to hold that the present cases turn on the political question doctrine, we would be required first to accept the Government's premise that de jure sovereignty is the touchstone of habeas corpus jurisdiction. This premise, however, is unfounded....

A

The Court has discussed the issue of the Constitution's extraterritorial application on many occasions. These decisions undermine the Government's argument that, at least as applied to noncitizens, the Constitution necessarily stops where de jure sovereignty ends.

[The Court then canvassed its decisions in the Insular cases, Reid v. Covert and Johnson v. Eisentrager to conclude that de jure sovereignty is not the touchstone of constitutional reach.]

. . .

C

As we recognized in *Rasul* . . . the outlines of a framework for determining the reach of the Suspension Clause are suggested by the factors the Court relied upon in *Eisentrager*. In addition to the practical concerns discussed above, the *Eisentrager* Court found relevant that each petitioner:

"(a) is an enemy alien; (b) has never been or resided in the United States; (c) was captured outside of our territory and there held in military custody as a prisoner of war; (d) was tried and convicted by a Military Commission sitting outside the United States; (e) for offenses against laws of war committed outside the United States; (f) and is at all times imprisoned outside the United States." 339 U.S., at 777.

Based on this language from *Eisentrager*, and the reasoning in our other extraterritoriality opinions, we conclude that at least three factors are relevant in determining the reach of the Suspension Clause: (1) the citizenship and status of the detainee and the adequacy of the process through which that status determination was made; (2) the nature of the sites where apprehension and then detention took place; and (3) the practical obstacles inherent in resolving the prisoner's entitlement to the writ.

. . .

[Applying these factors], [w]e hold that Art. I, § 9, cl. 2, of the Constitution has full effect at Guantanamo Bay. If the privilege of habeas corpus is to be denied to the detainees now before us, Congress must act in accordance with the requirements of the Suspension Clause.... This Court may not impose a de facto suspension by abstaining from these controversies.... The MCA does not purport to be a formal suspension of the writ; and the Government, in its submissions to us, has not argued that it is. Petitioners, therefore, are entitled to the privilege of habeas corpus to challenge the legality of their detention.

V

In light of this holding the question becomes whether the statute stripping jurisdiction to issue the writ avoids the Suspension Clause mandate because Congress has provided adequate substitute procedures for habeas corpus. The Government submits there has been compliance with the Suspension Clause because the DTA review process in the Court of Appeals, see DTA § 1005(e), provides an adequate substitute. Congress has granted that court jurisdiction to consider

"(i) whether the status determination of the [CSRT] . . . was consistent with the standards and procedures specified by the Secretary of Defense . . . and (ii) to the extent the Constitution and laws of the United States are applicable, whether the use of such standards and procedures to make the determination is consistent with the Constitution and laws of the United States." § 1005(e)(2)(C), 119 Stat. 2742.

. . .

A

Our case law does not contain extensive discussion of standards defining suspension of the writ or of circumstances under which suspension has occurred. This simply confirms the care Congress has taken throughout our Nation's history to preserve the writ and its function. Indeed, most of the major legislative enactments pertaining to habeas corpus have acted not to contract the writ's protection but to expand it or to hasten resolution of prisoners' claims. . . .

. . .

B

We do not endeavor to offer a comprehensive summary of the requisites for an adequate substitute for habeas corpus. We do consider it uncontroversial, however, that the privilege of habeas corpus entitles the prisoner to a meaningful opportunity to demonstrate that he is being held pursuant to "the erroneous application or interpretation" of relevant law. . . . And the habeas court must have the power to order the conditional release of an individual unlawfully detained-though release need not be the exclusive remedy and is not the appropriate one in every case in which the writ is granted. . . . These are the easily identified attributes of any constitutionally adequate habeas corpus proceeding. But, depending on the circumstances, more may be required.

. . .

The idea that the necessary scope of habeas review in part depends upon the rigor of any earlier proceedings accords with our test for procedural adequacy in the due process context. See Mathews v. Eldridge, 424 U.S. 319, 335 (1976) (noting that the Due Process Clause requires an assessment of, inter alia, "the risk of an erroneous deprivation of [a liberty interest;] and the probable value, if any, of additional or substitute procedural safeguards"). This principle has an established foundation in habeas corpus jurisprudence as well, as Chief Justice Marshall's opinion in Ex parte Watkins, 3 Pet. 193 (1830), demonstrates. . . .

. . .

Petitioners identify what they see as myriad deficiencies in the CSRTs. The most relevant for our purposes are the constraints upon the detainee's ability to rebut the factual basis for the Government's assertion that he is an enemy combatant. As already noted . . . at the CSRT stage the detainee has limited means to find or present evidence to challenge the Government's case against him. He does not have the assistance of counsel and may not be aware of the most critical allegations that the

Government relied upon to order his detention. . . . The detainee can confront witnesses that testify during the CSRT proceedings. . . . But given that there are in effect no limits on the admission of hearsay evidence—the only requirement is that the tribunal deem the evidence "relevant and helpful," . . . the detainee's opportunity to question witnesses is likely to be more theoretical than real.

. . .

Although we make no judgment as to whether the CSRTs, as currently constituted, satisfy due process standards, we agree with petitioners that, even when all the parties involved in this process act with diligence and in good faith, there is considerable risk of error in the tribunal's findings of fact. . . .

For the writ of habeas corpus, or its substitute, to function as an effective and proper remedy in this context, the court that conducts the habeas proceeding must have the means to correct errors that occurred during the CSRT proceedings. . . .

. . .

C

We now consider whether the DTA allows the Court of Appeals to conduct a proceeding meeting these standards. . . .

The DTA does not explicitly empower the Court of Appeals to order the applicant in a DTA review proceeding released should the court find that the standards and procedures used at his CSRT hearing were insufficient to justify detention. This is troubling. Yet, for present purposes, we can assume congressional silence permits a constitutionally required remedy. In that case it would be possible to hold that a remedy of release is impliedly provided for. The DTA might be read, furthermore, to allow the petitioners to assert most, if not all, of the legal claims they seek to advance, including their most basic claim: that the President has no authority under the AUMF to detain them indefinitely. (Whether the President has such authority turns on whether the AUMF authorizes-and the Constitution permits-the indefinite detention of "enemy combatants" as the Department of Defense defines that term. Thus a challenge to the President's authority to detain is, in essence, a challenge to the Department's definition of enemy combatant, a "standard" used by the CSRTs in petitioners' cases.) At oral argument, the Solicitor General urged us to adopt both these constructions, if doing so would allow MCA § 7 to remain intact. . . .

The absence of a release remedy and specific language allowing AUMF challenges are not the only constitutional infirmities from which the statute potentially suffers, however. The more difficult question is whether the DTA permits the Court of Appeals to make requisite findings of fact. The DTA enables petitioners to request "review" of their CSRT determination in the Court of Appeals, DTA § 1005(e)(2)(B)(i), . . . but the "Scope of Review" provision confines the Court of Appeals' role to reviewing whether the CSRT followed the "standards and procedures" issued by the Department of Defense and assessing whether those "standards and procedures" are lawful. § 1005(e)(C). . . . Among these standards is "the requirement that the conclusion of the Tribunal be supported by a preponderance of the evidence . . . allowing a rebuttable presumption in favor of the Government's evidence." § 1005(e)(C)(i). . . .

Assuming the DTA can be construed to allow the Court of Appeals to review or correct the CSRT's factual determinations, as opposed to merely certifying that the tribunal applied the correct standard of proof, we see no way to construe the statute to allow what is also constitutionally required in this context: an opportunity for the detainee to present relevant exculpatory evidence that was not made part of the record in the earlier proceedings.

On its face the statute allows the Court of Appeals to consider no evidence outside the CSRT record.... [T]he DTA review proceeding falls short of being a constitutionally adequate substitute, for the detainee still would have no opportunity to present evidence discovered after the CSRT proceedings concluded.

. . .

By foreclosing consideration of evidence not presented or reasonably available to the detainee at the CSRT proceedings, the DTA disadvantages the detainee by limiting the scope of collateral review to a record that may not be accurate or complete. In other contexts, e.g., in post-trial habeas cases where the prisoner already has had a full and fair opportunity to develop the factual predicate of his claims, similar limitations on the scope of habeas review may be appropriate. . . . In this context, however, where the underlying detention proceedings lack the necessary adversarial character, the detainee cannot be held responsible for all deficiencies in the record.

. . .

We do not imply DTA review would be a constitutionally sufficient replacement for habeas corpus but for these limitations on the detainee's ability to present exculpatory evidence. For even if it were possible, as a textual matter, to read into the statute each of the necessary procedures we have identified, we could not overlook the cumulative effect of our doing so. To hold that the detainees at Guantanamo may, under the DTA, challenge the President's legal authority to detain them, contest the CSRT's findings of fact, supplement the record on review with exculpatory evidence, and request an order of release would come close to reinstating the § 2241 habeas corpus process Congress sought to deny them. The language of the statute, read in light of Congress' reasons for enacting it, cannot bear this interpretation. Petitioners have met their burden of establishing that the DTA review process is, on its face, an inadequate substitute for habeas corpus.

Although we do not hold that an adequate substitute must duplicate § 2241 in all respects, it suffices that the Government has not established that the detainees' access to the statutory review provisions at issue is an adequate substitute for the writ of habeas corpus. MCA § 7 thus effects an unconstitutional suspension of the writ. In view of our holding we need not discuss the reach of the writ with respect to claims of unlawful conditions of treatment or confinement.

VI

A

In light of our conclusion that there is no jurisdictional bar to the District Court's entertaining petitioners' claims the question remains whether there are prudential barriers to habeas corpus review under these circumstances.

. . .

The real risks, the real threats, of terrorist attacks are constant and not likely soon to abate. The ways to disrupt our life and laws are so many and unforeseen that the Court should not attempt even some general catalogue of crises that might occur. Certain principles are apparent, however. Practical considerations and exigent circumstances inform the definition and reach of the law's writs, including habeas corpus. The cases and our tradition reflect this precept.

In cases involving foreign citizens detained abroad by the Executive, it likely would be both an impractical and unprecedented extension of judicial power to assume that habeas corpus would be available at the moment the prisoner is taken into custody. If and when habeas corpus jurisdiction applies, as it does in these cases, then proper deference can be accorded to reasonable procedures for screening and initial detention under lawful and proper conditions of confinement and treatment for a reasonable period of time. Domestic exigencies, furthermore, might also impose such onerous burdens on the Government that here, too, the Judicial Branch would be required to devise sensible rules for staying habeas corpus proceedings until the Government can comply with its requirements in a responsible way. Cf. Ex parte Milligan, 4 Wall., at 127 ("If, in foreign invasion or civil war, the courts are actually closed, and it is impossible to administer criminal justice according to law, then, on the theatre of active military operations, where war really prevails, there is a necessity to furnish a substitute for the civil authority, thus overthrown, to preserve the safety of the army and society; and as no power is left but the military, it is allowed to govern by martial rule until the laws can have their free course"). Here, as is true with detainees apprehended abroad, a relevant consideration in determining the courts' role is whether there are suitable alternative processes in place to protect against the arbitrary exercise of governmental power.

The cases before us, however, do not involve detainees who have been held for a short period of time while awaiting their CSRT determinations. . . .

Our decision today holds only that the petitioners before us are entitled to seek the writ; that the DTA review procedures are an inadequate substitute for habeas corpus; and that the petitioners in these cases need not exhaust the review procedures in the Court of Appeals before proceeding with their habeas actions in the District Court. The only law we identify as unconstitutional is MCA § 7, 28 U.S.C.A. § 2241(e) (Supp.2007). Accordingly, both the DTA and the CSRT process remain intact. Our holding with regard to exhaustion should not be read to imply that a habeas court should intervene the moment an enemy combatant steps foot in a territory where the writ runs. The Executive is entitled to a reasonable period of time to determine a detainee's status before a court entertains that detainee's habeas corpus petition. The CSRT process is the mechanism Congress and the President set up to deal with these issues. Except in cases of undue delay, federal courts should refrain from entertaining an enemy combatant's habeas corpus petition at least until after the Department, acting via the CSRT, has had a chance to review his status.

B

. . .

Our opinion does not undermine the Executive's powers as Commander in Chief. On the contrary, the exercise of those powers is vindicated, not eroded, when confirmed by the Judicial Branch. Within the Constitution's separation-of-powers structure, few exercises of judicial power are as legitimate or as necessary as the responsibility to hear challenges to the authority of the Executive to imprison a person. Some of these petitioners have been in custody for six years with no definitive judicial determination as to the legality of their detention. Their access to the writ is a necessity to determine the lawfulness of their status, even if, in the end, they do not obtain the relief they seek.

Because our Nation's past military conflicts have been of limited duration, it has been possible to leave the outer boundaries of war powers undefined. If, as some fear, terrorism continues to pose dangerous threats to us for years to come, the Court might not have this luxury. This result is not inevitable, however. The political branches, consistent with their independent obligations to interpret and uphold the Constitution, can engage in a genuine debate about how best to preserve constitutional values while protecting the Nation from terrorism. . . .

It bears repeating that our opinion does not address the content of the law that governs petitioners' detention. That is a matter yet to be determined. We hold that petitioners may invoke the fundamental procedural protections of habeas corpus. The laws and Constitution are designed to survive, and remain in force, in extraordinary times. Liberty and security can be reconciled; and in our system they are reconciled within the framework of the law. The Framers decided that habeas corpus, a right of first importance, must be a part of that framework, a part of that law.

. . . The judgment of the Court of Appeals is reversed. The cases are remanded . . . for proceedings consistent with this opinion.[a]

■ CHIEF JUSTICE ROBERTS, with whom JUSTICE SCALIA, JUSTICE THOMAS, and JUSTICE ALITO join, dissenting.

Today the Court strikes down as inadequate the most generous set of procedural protections ever afforded aliens detained by this country as enemy combatants. The political branches crafted these procedures amidst an ongoing military conflict, after much careful investigation and thorough debate. The Court rejects them today out of hand, without bothering to say what due process rights the detainees possess, without explaining how the statute fails to vindicate those rights, and before a single petitioner has even attempted to avail himself of the law's operation. And to what effect? The majority merely replaces a review system designed by the people's representatives with a set of shapeless procedures to be defined by federal courts at some future date. One cannot help but think, after surveying the modest practical results of the majority's ambitious opinion, that this decision is not really about the detainees at all, but about control of federal policy regarding enemy combatants.

. . .

■ JUSTICE SCALIA, with whom CHIEF JUSTICE ROBERTS, JUSTICE THOMAS, and JUSTICE ALITO join, dissenting.

. . .

. . . Contrary to my usual practice, however, I think it appropriate to begin with a description of the disastrous consequences of what the Court has done today.

I

America is at war with radical Islamists. The enemy began by killing Americans and American allies abroad: 241 at the Marine barracks in Lebanon, 19 at the Khobar Towers in Dhahran, 224 at our embassies in Dar es Salaam and Nairobi, and 17 on the USS Cole in Yemen. See National Commission on Terrorist Attacks upon the United States, The 9/11 Commission Report, pp. 60–61, 70, 190 (2004). On September 11, 2001, the enemy brought the battle to American soil, killing 2,749 at the Twin Towers in New York City, 184 at the Pentagon in Washington, D. C., and 40 in Pennsylvania. See id., at 552, n. 9. It has threatened further attacks against our homeland; one need only walk about buttressed and barricaded Washington, or board a plane anywhere in the country, to know that the threat is a serious one. Our Armed Forces are now in the field against the enemy, in Afghanistan and Iraq. Last week, 13 of our countrymen in arms were killed.

The game of bait-and-switch that today's opinion plays upon the Nation's Commander in Chief will make the war harder on us. It will almost certainly cause more Americans to be killed. That consequence would be tolerable if necessary to preserve a time-honored legal principle vital to our constitutional Republic. But it is this Court's blatant abandonment of such a principle that produces the decision today. The President relied on our settled precedent in Johnson v. Eisentrager, 339 U.S. 763 (1950), when he established the prison at Guantanamo Bay for enemy aliens. Citing that case, the President's Office of Legal Counsel advised him "that the great weight of

---

[a]   Justice Souter, joined by Justices Ginsburg and Breyer, concurred.

legal authority indicates that a federal district court could not properly exercise habeas jurisdiction over an alien detained at [Guantanamo Bay]." . . . Had the law been otherwise, the military surely would not have transported prisoners there, but would have kept them in Afghanistan, transferred them to another of our foreign military bases, or turned them over to allies for detention. Those other facilities might well have been worse for the detainees themselves.

In the long term, then, the Court's decision today accomplishes little, except perhaps to reduce the well-being of enemy combatants that the Court ostensibly seeks to protect. In the short term, however, the decision is devastating. At least 30 of those prisoners hitherto released from Guantanamo Bay have returned to the battlefield. . . . Some have been captured or killed. . . . But others have succeeded in carrying on their atrocities against innocent civilians. . . .

. . .

II

. . .

B

The Court purports to derive from our precedents a "functional" test for the extraterritorial reach of the writ, which shows that the Military Commissions Act unconstitutionally restricts the scope of habeas. That is remarkable because the most pertinent of those precedents, Johnson v. Eisentrager, 339 U.S. 763 (1950) conclusively establishes the opposite. . . .

. . .

Eisentrager thus held-held beyond any doubt-that the Constitution does not ensure habeas for aliens held by the United States in areas over which our Government is not sovereign. . . .

. . . [b]

---

[b]   Prior to *Boumediene* the Court had decided several other significant so-called "War on Terror" cases arising out of the 9–11 attacks. In *Hamdi v. Rumsfeld*, 542 U.S. 507 (2004), the Court, without a majority opinion, allowed—under the Congressional Authorization of the Use of Military Force following 9–11—the detention of a United States citizen who was captured in Afghanistan and then transferred to a naval brig in Virginia where he was held as an "enemy combatant," but also required under due process that the United States provide the detained individual "a meaningful opportunity to contest the factual bases for that detention before a neutral decisionmaker."

The same day that *Hamdi* was decided, the Court issued two other decisions involving challenges to prolonged Executive detention of persons also alleged to be "enemy combatants." One, Rumsfeld v. Padilla, 542 U.S. 426 (2004), involved a habeas petition filed in New York on behalf of a United States citizen first held in criminal custody in New York as a material witness in connection with a federal grand jury investigation of the September 11th terrorist attacks and then transferred to a Naval Brig in South Carolina for indefinite detention pursuant to Presidential directive. A 5–4 majority remanded, holding that the habeas petition had to be brought in South Carolina where Padilla was confined by the time the petition had been filed. Justice Stevens' dissent, joined by Justices Souter, Ginsburg and Breyer (who had joined the plurality opinion in *Hamdi*), said in a footnote: "I believe that the Non-Detention Act . . . prohibits—and the Authorization for Use of Military Force Joint Resolution . . . does not authorize—the protracted, incommunicado detention of American citizens arrested in the United States." The dissent concluded as follows:

"At stake in this case is nothing less than the essence of a free society. Even more important than the method of selecting the people's rulers and their successors is the character of the constraints imposed on the Executive by the rule of law. Unconstrained Executive detention for the purpose of investigating and preventing subversive activity is the hallmark of the Star Chamber. Access to counsel for the purpose of protecting the citizen from official mistakes and mistreatment is the hallmark of due process.

"Executive detention of subversive citizens, like detention of enemy soldiers to keep them off the battlefield, may sometimes be justified to prevent persons from launching or becoming missiles of

D. THE LINE ITEM VETO

Delegation of Legislative Power to the Executive

Many disputes about executive power implicate concerns that are sometimes collectively referred to as the non-delegation doctrine—the idea that Congress may not delegate its legislative powers to the executive. Although the Court has not invoked the doctrine as a formal basis for invalidating a Congressional law since the New Deal, for at least 150 years the Court's decisions have been sprinkled with categorical statements that Congress may not relinquish any of its powers to enact legislation through grants to federal administrators. The following excerpt from Justice O'Connor's opinion for the Court in Touby v. United States, 500 U.S. 160, 163–65 (1991), is illustrative:

"The Constitution provides that '[a]ll legislative Powers herein granted shall be vested in a Congress of the United States.' U.S. Const., Art. I, § 1. From this language the Court has derived the nondelegation doctrine: that Congress may not constitutionally delegate its legislative power to another Branch of government. . . ."

". . . [T]he nondelegation doctrine does not prevent Congress from seeking assistance, within proper limits, from its coordinate Branches. . . . Thus, Congress does not violate the Constitution merely because it legislates in broad terms, leaving a certain degree of discretion to executive or judicial actors. So long as Congress 'lay[s] down by legislative act an intelligible principle to which the person or body authorized to [act] is directed to conform, such legislative action is not a forbidden delegation of legislative power.'. . .

". . . [The Court has] upheld as providing sufficient guidance statutes authorizing the War Department to recover 'excessive profits' earned on military contracts, see Lichter v. United States, 334 U.S. 742, 778–786 (1948); authorizing the Price Administrator to fix 'fair and equitable' commodities prices, see Yakus v. United States, 321 U.S. 414, 426–427 (1944); and authorizing the Federal Communications Commission to regulate broadcast licensing in the 'public interest,' see National Broadcasting Co. v. United States, 319 U.S. 190, 225–226 (1943)."

The non-delegation idea is said to have both textual and theoretical underpinnings. As a matter of text, Article I, Section 1 of the Constitution provides that "All legislative Powers herein granted shall be vested in a Congress of the United States, which shall consist of a Senate and House of Representatives." As a matter of theory, the non-delegation doctrine reflects the basic idea that all decisions by government ought to be traceable to the governmental body to which the people have conferred permission to make those particular decisions.

---

destruction. It may not, however, be justified by the naked interest in using unlawful procedures to extract information. Incommunicado detention for months on end is such a procedure. Whether the information so procured is more or less reliable than that acquired by more extreme forms of torture is of no consequence. For if this Nation is to remain true to the ideals symbolized by its flag, it must not wield the tools of tyrants even to resist an assault by the forces of tyranny."

The other decision involved aliens captured in Afghanistan during the military campaign against al Qaeda and the Taliban. The Court held that the habeas corpus jurisdiction of United States courts extends to judicial review of the legality of Executive detention of foreign nationals at the United States Naval Base in Guantanamo Bay, Cuba, over which the United States—by virtue of a lease agreement with Cuba—exercises plenary and exclusive jurisdiction, but not "ultimate sovereignty." Rasul v. Bush, 542 U.S. 466 (2004).

Of course, things are not so simple. To begin with, it is not clear that "vested" means "nondelegable." After all, Article II "vests" executive power in a President alone, and yet he permissibly delegates what would have to be conceded to be executive authority to his underlings in the executive branch. And if their exercise of authority on his behalf is allowed because it can be traced back to him, why not the same for the President's exercise of power on behalf of Congress?

Some might respond that the President is free to reclaim power from his underlings, and that Congress might have difficulty retrieving power given to the President. This refinement of the non-delegation idea—that power ought not to be delegated in a way that it cannot be reclaimed—might explain some cases, but it might call into question the results of others. It might also suggest that Congressional delegation to the President might be different than delegation by Congress to other bodies, like states. In the following case, as well as the *Chadha* decision in the next section, consider whether and how non-delegation principles bear on the Court's analyses.

Clinton v. City of New York

524 U.S. 417, 118 S.Ct. 2091, 141 L.Ed.2d 393 (1998).

■ JUSTICE STEVENS delivered the opinion of the Court.

The Line Item Veto Act (Act) . . . was enacted in April 1996 and became effective on January 1, 1997. The following day, six Members of Congress who had voted against the Act brought suit in the District Court for the District of Columbia challenging its constitutionality. . . . We determined, however, that the Members of Congress did not have standing to sue because they had not "alleged a sufficiently concrete injury to have established Article III standing," Raines v. Byrd, 521 U.S. 811 (1997). . . .'

Less than two months after our decision in that case, the President exercised his authority to cancel one provision in the Balanced Budget Act of 1997, . . . and two provisions in the Taxpayer Relief Act of 1997 . . . Appellees, claiming that they had been injured by two of those cancellations, filed these cases in the District Court. That Court again held the statute invalid, . . . and we again expedited our review. . . . We now hold that these appellees have standing to challenge the constitutionality of the Act and, reaching the merits, we agree that the cancellation procedures set forth in the Act violate the Presentment Clause, Art. I, § 7, cl. 2, of the Constitution.

I

We begin by reviewing the canceled items that are at issue in these cases.

. . .

[The Court then provided some background on the two cancellations at issue, one a new direct spending item involving New York's health care programs and the other a limited tax benefit involving agriculture.]

II

Appellees filed two separate actions against the President and other federal officials challenging these two cancellations. The plaintiffs in the first case are the City of New York, two hospital associations, one hospital, and two unions representing health care employees. The plaintiffs in the second are a farmers' cooperative consisting of about 30 potato growers in Idaho and an individual farmer who is a member and officer of the cooperative. The District Court consolidated the two cases and determined that at least one of the plaintiffs in each had standing under Article III of the Constitution.

. . .

On the merits, the District Court held that the cancellations did not conform to the constitutionally mandated procedures for the enactment or repeal of laws . . .

IV

The Line Item Veto Act gives the President the power to "cancel in whole" three types of provisions that have been signed into law: "(1) any dollar amount of discretionary budget authority; (2) any item of new direct spending; or (3) any limited tax benefit." . . . It is undisputed that the New York case involves an "item of new direct spending" and that the Snake River case involves a "limited tax benefit" as those terms are defined in the Act. It is also undisputed that each of those provisions had been signed into law pursuant to Article I, § 7, of the Constitution before it was canceled.

The Act requires the President to adhere to precise procedures whenever he exercises his cancellation authority. . . . He must determine, with respect to each cancellation, that it will "(i) reduce the Federal budget deficit; (ii) not impair any essential Government functions; and (iii) not harm the national interest." . . . Moreover, he must transmit a special message to Congress notifying it of each cancellation within five calendar days . . . after the enactment of the canceled provision. . . . It is undisputed that the President meticulously followed these procedures in these cases.

A cancellation takes effect upon receipt by Congress of the special message from the President. . . . If, however, a "disapproval bill" pertaining to a special message is enacted into law, the cancellations set forth in that message become "null and void." . . . [N]o such bill was passed for either of the cancellations involved in these cases. A majority vote of both Houses is sufficient to enact a disapproval bill. The Act does not grant the President the authority to cancel a disapproval bill, . . . but he does, of course, retain his constitutional authority to veto such a bill.

. . . With respect to both an item of new direct spending and a limited tax benefit, the cancellation prevents the item "from having legal force or effect." . . . Thus, under the plain text of the statute, the two actions of the President that are challenged in these cases prevented one section of the Balanced Budget Act of 1997 and one section of the Taxpayer Relief Act of 1997 "from having legal force or effect." The remaining provisions of those statutes, with the exception of the second canceled item in the latter, continue to have the same force and effect as they had when signed into law.

In both legal and practical effect, the President has amended two Acts of Congress by repealing a portion of each. . . . There is no provision in the Constitution that authorizes the President to enact, to amend, or to repeal statutes. . . .

There are important differences between the President's "return" of a bill pursuant to Article I, § 7, and the exercise of the President's cancellation authority pursuant to the Line Item Veto Act. The constitutional return takes place before the bill becomes law; the statutory cancellation occurs after the bill becomes law. The constitutional return is of the entire bill; the statutory cancellation is of only a part. Although the Constitution expressly authorizes the President to play a role in the process of enacting statutes, it is silent on the subject of unilateral Presidential action that either repeals or amends parts of duly enacted statutes.

There are powerful reasons for construing constitutional silence on this profoundly important issue as equivalent to an express prohibition. The procedures governing the enactment of statutes set forth in the text of Article I were the product of the great debates and compromises that produced the Constitution itself. . . . Our first President understood the text of the Presentment Clause as requiring that he either "approve all the parts of a Bill, or reject it in toto." What has emerged in these cases from the President's exercise of his statutory cancellation powers, however, are truncated versions of two bills that passed both Houses of Congress. They are not the product of the "finely wrought" procedure that the Framers designed.

. . .

V

The Government advances two related arguments to support its position that despite the unambiguous provisions of the Act, cancellations do not amend or repeal properly enacted statutes in violation of the Presentment Clause. First, relying primarily on Field v. Clark, 143 U.S. 649 (1892), the Government contends that the cancellations were merely exercises of discretionary authority granted to the President by the Balanced Budget Act and the Taxpayer Relief Act read in light of the previously enacted Line Item Veto Act. Second, the Government submits that the substance of the authority to cancel tax and spending items "is, in practical effect, no more and no less than the power to 'decline to spend' specified sums of money, or to 'decline to implement' specified tax measures."

In Field v. Clark, the Court upheld the constitutionality of the Tariff Act of 1890. . . . That statute contained a "free list" of almost 300 specific articles that were exempted from import duties "unless otherwise specially provided for in this act." . . . Section 3 was a special provision that directed the President to suspend that exemption for sugar, molasses, coffee, tea, and hides "whenever, and so often" as he should be satisfied that any country producing and exporting those products imposed duties on the agricultural products of the United States that he deemed to be "reciprocally unequal and unreasonable. . . ." . . . The section then specified the duties to be imposed on those products during any such suspension. The Court [concluded that] § 3 had not delegated legislative power to the President . . .

[There are] three critical differences between the power to suspend the exemption from import duties and the power to cancel portions of a duly enacted statute. First, the exercise of the suspension power was contingent upon a condition that did not exist when the Tariff Act was passed: the imposition of "reciprocally unequal and unreasonable" import duties by other countries. In contrast, the exercise of the cancellation power within five days after the enactment of the Balanced Budget and Tax Reform Acts necessarily was based on the same conditions that Congress evaluated when it passed those statutes. Second, under the Tariff Act, when the President determined that the contingency had arisen, he had a duty to suspend; in contrast, while it is true that the President was required by the Act to make three determinations before he canceled a provision, . . . , those determinations did not qualify his discretion to cancel or not to cancel. Finally, whenever the President suspended an exemption under the Tariff Act, he was executing the policy that Congress had embodied in the statute. In contrast, whenever the President cancels an item of new direct spending or a limited tax benefit he is rejecting the policy judgment made by Congress and relying on his own policy judgment. Thus, the conclusion in Field v. Clark that the suspensions mandated by the Tariff Act were not exercises of legislative power does not undermine our opinion that cancellations pursuant to the Line Item Veto Act are the functional equivalent of partial repeals of Acts of Congress that fail to satisfy Article I, § 7.

The Government's reliance upon other tariff and import statutes . . . is unavailing for the same reasons. . . .

The cited statutes all relate to foreign trade, and this Court has recognized that in the foreign affairs arena, the President has "a degree of discretion and freedom from statutory restriction which would not be admissible were domestic affairs alone involved." United States v. Curtiss-Wright Export Corp., 299 U.S. 304, 320 (1936). . . . More important, when enacting the statutes discussed in *Field*, Congress itself made the decision to suspend or repeal the particular provisions at issue upon the occurrence of particular events subsequent to enactment, and it left only the determination of whether such events occurred up to the President. . . .

Neither are we persuaded by the Government's contention that the President's authority to cancel new direct spending and tax benefit items is no greater than his traditional authority to decline to spend appropriated funds. The Government has reviewed in some detail the series of statutes in which Congress has given the Executive broad discretion over the expenditure of appropriated funds. . . . It is argued that the Line Item Veto Act merely confers comparable discretionary authority over the expenditure of appropriated funds. The critical difference between this statute and all of its predecessors, however, is that unlike any of them, this Act gives the President the unilateral power to change the text of duly enacted statutes. None of the Act's predecessors could even arguably have been construed to authorize such a change.

VI

. . .

If there is to be a new procedure in which the President will play a different role in determining the final text of what may "become a law," such change must come not by legislation but through the amendment procedures set forth in Article V of the Constitution. . . .

The judgment of the District Court is affirmed.

It is so ordered.

■ JUSTICE KENNEDY, concurring.

. . .

I write to respond to my colleague Justice Breyer, who observes that the statute does not threaten the liberties of individual citizens, a point on which I disagree. . . . Liberty is always at stake when one or more of the branches seek to transgress the separation of powers.

Separation of powers was designed to implement a fundamental insight: concentration of power in the hands of a single branch is a threat to liberty. . . .'

In recent years, perhaps, we have come to think of liberty as defined by that word in the Fifth and Fourteenth Amendments and as illuminated by the other provisions of the Bill of Rights. The conception of liberty embraced by the Framers was not so confined. They used the principles of separation of powers and federalism to secure liberty in the fundamental political sense of the term, quite in addition to the idea of freedom from intrusive governmental acts. The idea and the promise were that when the people delegate some degree of control to a remote central authority, one branch of government ought not possess the power to shape their destiny without a sufficient check from the other two. In this vision, liberty demands limits on the ability of any one branch to influence basic political decisions. . . .

. . .

The principal object of the statute, it is true, was not to enhance the President's power to reward one group and punish another, to help one set of taxpayers and hurt another, to favor one State and ignore another. Yet these are its undeniable effects.

The law establishes a new mechanism which gives the President the sole ability to hurt a group that is a visible target, in order to disfavor the group or to extract further concessions from Congress. The law is the functional equivalent of a line item veto and enhances the President's powers beyond what the Framers would have endorsed.

. . .

. . . With these observations, I join the opinion of the Court.

■ JUSTICE BREYER, with whom JUSTICE O'CONNOR and JUSTICE SCALIA join as to Part III, dissenting.

I

. . . In my view the Line Item Veto Act does not violate any specific textual constitutional command, nor does it violate any implicit Separation of Powers principle. Consequently, I believe that the Act is constitutional.

II

I approach the constitutional question before us with three general considerations in mind. First, the Act represents a legislative effort to provide the President with the power to give effect to some, but not to all, of the expenditure and revenue-diminishing provisions contained in a single massive appropriations bill. And this objective is constitutionally proper.

When our Nation was founded, Congress could easily have provided the President with this kind of power. . . . At that time, a Congress, wishing to give a President the power to select among appropriations, could simply have embodied each appropriation in a separate bill, each bill subject to a separate Presidential veto.

Today, however, . . . Congress cannot divide such a bill into thousands, or tens of thousands, of separate appropriations bills, each one of which the President would have to sign, or to veto, separately. Thus, the question is whether the Constitution permits Congress to choose a particular novel means to achieve this same, constitutionally legitimate, end.

Second, the case in part requires us to focus upon the Constitution's generally phrased structural provisions, provisions that delegate all "legislative" power to Congress and vest all "executive" power in the President. The Court, when applying these provisions, has interpreted them generously in terms of the institutional arrangements that they permit. . . .

Indeed, Chief Justice Marshall, in a well-known passage, explained,

"To have prescribed the means by which government should, in all future time, execute its powers, would have been to change, entirely, the character of the instrument, and give it the properties of a legal code. It would have been an unwise attempt to provide, by immutable rules, for exigencies which, if foreseen at all, must have been seen dimly, and which can be best provided for as they occur." McCulloch v. Maryland. . . .'

This passage . . . calls attention to the genius of the Framers' pragmatic vision, which . . . find[s] constitutional room for necessary institutional innovation.

Third, we need not here referee a dispute among the other two branches. . . .

These three background circumstances mean that, when one measures the literal words of the Act against the Constitution's literal commands, the fact that the Act may closely resemble a different, literally unconstitutional, arrangement is beside the point. . . .

. . .

III

The Court believes that the Act violates the literal text of the Constitution. A simple syllogism captures its basic reasoning:

Major Premise: The Constitution sets forth an exclusive method for enacting, repealing, or amending laws.

Minor Premise: The Act authorizes the President to "repea[l] or amen[d]" laws in a different way, namely by announcing a cancellation of a portion of a previously enacted law.

Conclusion: The Act is inconsistent with the Constitution.

I find this syllogism unconvincing, however, because its Minor Premise is faulty. When the President "canceled" the two appropriation measures now before us, he did not repeal any law nor did he amend any law. He simply followed the law, leaving the statutes, as they are literally written, intact.

. . .

. . . Literally speaking, the President has not "repealed" or "amended" anything. He has simply executed a power conferred upon him by Congress, which power is contained in laws that were enacted in compliance with the exclusive method set forth in the Constitution. See Field v. Clark, . . .

. . .

IV

Because I disagree with the Court's holding of literal violation, I must consider whether the Act nonetheless violates Separation of Powers principles . . . There are three relevant Separation of Powers questions here: (1) Has Congress given the President the wrong kind of power, i.e., "non-Executive" power? (2) Has Congress given the President the power to "encroach" upon Congress' own constitutionally reserved territory? (3) Has Congress given the President too much power, violating the doctrine of "nondelegation?" . . . [W]ith respect to this Act, the answer to all these questions is "no."

A

Viewed conceptually, the power the Act conveys is the right kind of power. It is "executive." . . . Conceptually speaking, it closely resembles the kind of delegated authority—to spend or not to spend appropriations, to change or not to change tariff rates—that Congress has frequently granted the President, any differences being differences in degree, not kind.

. . . This Court has frequently found that the exercise of a particular power, such as the power to make rules of broad applicability, . . . can fall within the constitutional purview of more than one branch of Government. . . .

The Court has upheld congressional delegation of rulemaking power and adjudicatory power to federal agencies, . . . and prosecutor-appointment power to judges . . . It is far easier conceptually to reconcile the power at issue here with the relevant constitutional description ("executive") than in many of these cases. . . .'

If there is a Separation of Powers violation, then, it must rest, not upon purely conceptual grounds, but upon some important conflict between the Act and a significant Separation of Powers objective.

B

The Act does not undermine what this Court has often described as the principal function of the Separation of Powers, which is to maintain the tripartite structure of the Federal Government—and thereby protect individual liberty . . .

. . . [O]ne cannot say that the Act "encroaches" upon Congress' power, when Congress retained the power to insert, by simple majority, into any future appropriations bill, into any section of any such bill, or into any phrase of any section, a provision that says the Act will not apply. . . . Thus this Act is not the sort of delegation "without . . . sufficient check" that concerns Justice Kennedy . . .

Nor can one say that the Act's basic substantive objective is constitutionally improper, for the earliest Congresses could have, and often did, confer on the President this sort of discretionary authority over spending, . . . Where the burden of overcoming legislative inertia lies is within the power of Congress to determine by rule. Where is the encroachment?

Nor can one say the Act's grant of power "aggrandizes" the Presidential office. The grant is limited to the context of the budget. It is limited to the power to spend, or not to spend, particular appropriated items, and the power to permit, or not to permit, specific limited exemptions from generally applicable tax law from taking effect. . . . The delegation of those powers to the President may strengthen the Presidency, but any such change in Executive Branch authority seems minute when compared with the changes worked by delegations of other kinds of authority that the Court in the past has upheld. . . .

C

The "nondelegation" doctrine represents an added constitutional check upon Congress' authority to delegate power to the Executive Branch. . . .

. . .

. . . The President must determine that, to "prevent" the item or amount "from having legal force or effect" will "reduce the Federal budget deficit; . . . not impair any essential Government functions; and . . . not harm the national interest." . . .

The resulting standards are broad. But this Court has upheld standards that are equally broad, or broader. . . .

. . .

. . . I believe that the power the Act grants the President to prevent spending items from taking effect does not violate the "nondelegation" doctrine.

. . .

. . . [T]he "limited tax benefit" provisions do not differ enough from the "spending" provisions to warrant a different "nondelegation" result.

V

In sum, I recognize that the Act before us is novel. In a sense, it skirts a constitutional edge. But that edge has to do with means, not ends. The means chosen do not amount literally to the enactment, repeal, or amendment of a law. Nor, for that matter, do they amount literally to the "line item veto" that the Act's title announces. Those means do not violate any basic Separation of Powers principle. They do not improperly shift the constitutionally foreseen balance of power from Congress to the President. Nor, since they comply with Separation of Powers principles, do they threaten the liberties of individual citizens. They represent an experiment that may, or may not, help representative government work better. The Constitution, in my view, authorizes Congress and the President to try novel methods in this way. Consequently, with respect, I dissent.

■ JUSTICE SCALIA, with whom JUSTICE O'CONNOR joins, and with whom JUSTICE BREYER joins as to Part III, concurring in part and dissenting in part.

. . .

III

. . . [T]here is not a dime's worth of difference between Congress's authorizing the President to cancel a spending item, and Congress's authorizing money to be spent on a particular item at the President's discretion. And the latter has been done since the Founding of the Nation. . . .

. . .

The short of the matter is this: Had the Line Item Veto Act authorized the President to "decline to spend" any item of spending contained in the Balanced Budget Act of 1997, there is not the slightest doubt that authorization would have been constitutional. What the Line Item Veto Act does instead—authorizing the President to "cancel" an item of spending—is technically different. But the technical difference does not relate to the technicalities of the Presentment Clause, which have been fully complied with; and the doctrine of unconstitutional delegation, which is at issue here, is preeminently not a doctrine of technicalities. The title of the Line Item Veto Act, which was perhaps designed to simplify for public comprehension, or perhaps merely to comply with the terms of a campaign pledge, has succeeded in faking out the Supreme Court. The President's action it authorizes in fact is not a line-item veto and thus does not offend Art. I, § 7; and insofar as the substance of that action is concerned, it is no different from what Congress has permitted the President to do since the formation of the Union.

. . .

2. CONGRESSIONAL INTERFERENCE WITH PRESIDENTIAL PREROGATIVES

A. THE LEGISLATIVE VETO

Immigration and Naturalization Service v. Chadha
462 U.S. 919, 103 S.Ct. 2764, 77 L.Ed.2d 317 (1983).

■ CHIEF JUSTICE BURGER delivered the opinion of the Court.

. . . [These cases present] a challenge to the constitutionality of the provision in § 244(c)(2) of the Immigration and Nationality Act . . . authorizing one House of Congress, by resolution, to invalidate the decision of the Executive Branch, pursuant to authority delegated by Congress to the Attorney General of the United States, to allow a particular deportable alien to remain in the United States.

I

Chadha . . . was lawfully admitted to the United States in 1966 on a non-immigrant student visa. His visa expired on June 30, 1972. On October 11, 1973, the District Director of the Immigration and Naturalization Service ordered Chadha to show cause why he should not be deported for having "remained in the United States for a longer time than permitted." . . . [A] deportation hearing was held before an immigration judge on January 11, 1974. Chadha conceded that he was deportable for overstaying his visa and the hearing was adjourned to enable him to file an application for suspension of deportation under § 244(a)(1) of the Act, [which authorizes suspension in the case of] "a person whose deportation would, in the opinion of the Attorney General, result in extreme hardship to the alien or to his spouse, parent, or child, who is a citizen of the United States or an alien lawfully admitted for permanent residence."

. . . [T]he immigration judge . . . ordered that Chadha's deportation be suspended. The immigration judge found that Chadha met the requirements of § 244(a)(1): he had resided continuously in the United States for over seven years, was of good moral character, and would suffer "extreme hardship" if deported.

Pursuant to (§ 244(c)(1) of the Act), . . . the immigration judge suspended Chadha's deportation and a report of the suspension was transmitted to Congress. Section 244(c)(1) provides:

"Upon application by any alien who is found by the Attorney General to meet the requirements of subsection (a) of this section the Attorney General may in his discretion suspend deportation of such alien. If the deportation of any alien is suspended under the provisions of this subsection, a complete and detailed statement of the facts and pertinent provisions of law in the case shall be reported to the Congress with the reasons for such suspension. Such reports shall be submitted on the first day of each calendar month in which Congress is in session."

Once the Attorney General's recommendation for suspension of Chadha's deportation was conveyed to Congress, Congress had the power under § 244(c)(2) of the Act . . . to veto the Attorney General's determination that Chadha should not be deported. Section 244(c)(2) provides:

"(2) . . . if during the session of the Congress at which a case is reported, or prior to the close of the session of the Congress next following the session at which a case is reported, either the Senate or the House of Representatives passes a resolution stating in substance that it does not favor the suspension of such deportation, the Attorney General shall thereupon deport such alien or authorize the alien's voluntary departure at his own expense under the order of deportation in the manner provided by law. If, within the time above specified, neither the Senate nor the House of Representatives shall pass such a resolution, the Attorney General shall cancel deportation proceedings."

The June 25, 1974 order of the immigration judge suspending Chadha's deportation remained outstanding as a valid order for a year and a half. For reasons not disclosed by the record, Congress did not exercise the veto authority reserved to it under § 244(c)(2) until the first session of the 94th Congress. This was the final session in which Congress, pursuant to § 244(c)(2), could act to veto the Attorney General's determination that Chadha should not be deported. . . .'

On December 12, 1975, Representative Eilberg, Chairman of the Judiciary Subcommittee on Immigration, Citizenship, and International Law, introduced a resolution opposing "the granting of permanent residence in the United States to [six] aliens", including Chadha. . . . On December 16, 1975, the resolution was discharged from further consideration by the House Committee on the Judiciary and submitted to the House of Representatives for a vote. . . . The resolution had not been printed and was not made available to other Members of the House prior to or at the time it was voted on. Ibid. . . . House consideration of the resolution was based on Representative Eilberg's statement from the floor that "[i]t was the feeling of the committee, after reviewing 340 cases, that the aliens contained in the resolution [Chadha and five others] did not meet these statutory requirements, particularly as it relates to hardship; and it is the opinion of the committee that their deportation should not be suspended.". . . .'

The resolution was passed without debate or recorded vote. Since the House action was pursuant to § 244(c)(2), the resolution was not treated as an Article I legislative act; it was not submitted to the Senate or presented to the President for his action.

After the House veto . . . , the immigration judge reopened the deportation proceedings . . . Chadha was ordered deported pursuant to the House action.

. . .

Pursuant to § 106(a) of the Act, . . . Chadha filed a petition for review of the deportation order in the United States Court of Appeals for the Ninth Circuit. The Immigration and Naturalization Service agreed with Chadha's position before the Court of Appeals and joined him in arguing that § 244(c)(2) is unconstitutional. In light of the importance of the question, the Court of Appeals invited both the Senate and the House of Representatives to file briefs *amici curiae*.

. . . [T]he Court of Appeals held that the House was without constitutional authority to order Chadha's deportation . . .

. . . [W]e . . . affirm.

II

. . .

F

Case or Controversy

It is also contended that this is not a genuine controversy but "a friendly, non-adversary, proceeding," Ashwander v. Tennessee Valley Authority, supra, 297 U.S., at 346 (Brandeis, J., concurring), upon which the Court should not pass. This argument rests on the fact that Chadha and the INS take the same position on the constitutionality of the one-House veto. But it would be a curious result if, in the administration of justice, a person could be denied access to the courts because the Attorney General of the United States agreed with the legal arguments asserted by the individual.

. . .

III

A

We turn now to the question whether action of one House of Congress under § 244(c)(2) violates strictures of the Constitution. We begin, of course, with the presumption that the challenged statute is valid. . . .

By the same token, the fact that a given law or procedure is efficient, convenient, and useful in facilitating functions of government, standing alone, will not save it if it is contrary to the Constitution. Convenience and efficiency are not the primary objectives—or the hallmarks—of democratic government and our inquiry is sharpened rather than blunted by the fact that Congressional veto provisions are appearing with increasing frequency in statutes which delegate authority to executive and independent agencies:

"Since 1932, when the first veto provision was enacted into law, 295 congressional veto-type procedures have been inserted in 196 different statutes as follows: from 1932 to 1939, five statutes were affected; from 1940–49, nineteen statutes; between 1950–59, thirty-four statutes; and from 1960–69, forty-nine. From the year 1970 through 1975, at least one hundred sixty-three such provisions were included in eighty-nine laws." *Abourezk, The Congressional Veto: A Contemporary Response to Executive Encroachment on Legislative Prerogatives,* 52 Ind.L.Rev. 323, 324 (1977).

. . .

. . . Explicit and unambiguous provisions of the Constitution prescribe and define the respective functions of the Congress and of the Executive in the legislative process. . . .

. . . [T]he purposes underlying the Presentment Clauses, Art. I, § 7, cls. 2, 3, and the bicameral requirement of Art. I, § 1 and § 7, cl. 2, guide our resolution of the important question presented in this case. . . .

B

The Presentment Clauses

The records of the Constitutional Convention reveal that the requirement that all legislation be presented to the President before becoming law was uniformly accepted by the Framers. Presentment to the President and the Presidential veto were considered so imperative that the draftsmen took special pains to assure that these requirements could not be circumvented. . . .

The decision to provide the President with a limited and qualified power to nullify proposed legislation by veto was based on the profound conviction of the Framers that the powers conferred on Congress were the powers to be most carefully circumscribed. It is beyond doubt that lawmaking was a power to be shared by both Houses and the President. . . .

The President's role in the lawmaking process also reflects the Framers' careful efforts to check whatever propensity a particular Congress might have to enact oppressive, improvident, or ill-considered measures. . . . Presentment Clauses serve the important purpose of assuring that a "national" perspective is grafted on the legislative process. . . .

C

Bicameralism

The bicameral requirement of Art. I, §§ 1, 7 was of scarcely less concern to the Framers than was the Presidential veto and indeed the two concepts are interdependent. By providing that no law could take effect without the concurrence of the prescribed majority of the Members of both Houses, the Framers reemphasized their belief, already remarked upon in connection with the Presentment Clauses, that legislation should not be enacted unless it has been carefully and fully considered by the Nation's elected officials. . . .

. . .

We see therefore that the Framers were acutely conscious that the bicameral requirement and the Presentment Clauses would serve essential constitutional functions. The President's participation in the legislative process was to protect the Executive Branch from Congress and to protect the whole people from improvident laws. The division of the Congress into two distinctive bodies assures that the legislative power would be exercised only after opportunity for full study and debate in separate settings. The President's unilateral veto power, in turn, was limited by the power of two thirds of both Houses of Congress to overrule a veto thereby precluding final arbitrary action of one person. See 1 M. Farrand, supra, at 99–104. It emerges clearly that the prescription for legislative action in Art. I, §§ 1, 7 represents the

Framers' decision that the legislative power of the Federal government be exercised in accord with a single, finely wrought and exhaustively considered, procedure.

IV

. . . [W]e must . . . establish that the challenged action under § 244(c)(2) is of the kind to which the procedural requirements of Art. I, § 7 apply. Not every action taken by either House is subject to the bicameralism and presentment requirements of Art. I. Whether actions taken by either House are, in law and fact, an exercise of legislative power depends not on their form but upon "whether they contain matter which is properly to be regarded as legislative in its character and effect." . . .

Examination of the action taken here by one House pursuant to § 244(c)(2) reveals that it was essentially legislative in purpose and effect. In purporting to exercise power defined in Art. I, § 8, cl. 4 to "establish an uniform Rule of Naturalization," the House took action that had the purpose and effect of altering the legal rights, duties and relations of persons, including the Attorney General, Executive Branch officials and Chadha, all outside the legislative branch. . . .

. . .

Since it is clear that the action by the House under § 244(c)(2) was not within any of the express constitutional exceptions authorizing one House to act alone, and equally clear that it was an exercise of legislative power, that action was subject to the standards prescribed in Article I.[21] . . .

The veto authorized by § 244(c)(2) doubtless has been in many respects a convenient shortcut; the "sharing" with the Executive by Congress of its authority over aliens in this manner is, on its face, an appealing compromise. In purely practical terms, it is obviously easier for action to be taken by one House without submission to the President; but it is crystal clear from the records of the Convention, contemporaneous writings and debates, that the Framers ranked other values higher than efficiency. The records of the Convention and debates in the States preceding ratification underscore the common desire to define and limit the exercise of the newly created federal powers affecting the states and the people. There is unmistakable expression of a determination that legislation by the national Congress be a step-by-step, deliberate and deliberative process.

. . .

V

We hold that the Congressional veto provision in § 244(c)(2) is . . . unconstitutional. Accordingly, the judgment of the Court of Appeals is

Affirmed.

■ JUSTICE POWELL, concurring in the judgment.

. . . [O]ur holding should be no more extensive than necessary to decide this case. In my view, the case may be decided on a narrower ground. When Congress finds that a particular person does not satisfy the statutory criteria for permanent residence in

---

[21] Justice Powell's position is that the one-House veto in this case is a *judicial* act and therefore unconstitutional as beyond the authority vested in Congress by the Constitution. We agree that there is a sense in which one-House action pursuant to § 244(c)(2) has a judicial cast, since it purports to "review" Executive action. . . . But the attempted analogy between judicial action and the one-House veto is less than perfect. . . . [N]o justiciable case or controversy was presented by the Attorney General's decision to allow Chadha to remain in this country. [N]o party to such action has either the motivation or the right to appeal from it. . . .

this country it has assumed a judicial function in violation of the principle of separation of powers. Accordingly, I concur in the judgment.

. . .

II

. . .

On its face, the House's action appears clearly adjudicatory. The House did not enact a general rule; rather it made its own determination that six specific persons did not comply with certain statutory criteria. It thus undertook the type of decision that traditionally has been left to other branches. Even if the House did not make a *de novo* determination, but simply reviewed the Immigration and Naturalization Service's findings, it still assumed a function ordinarily entrusted to the federal courts. . . .

■ JUSTICE WHITE, dissenting.

Today the Court not only invalidates § 244(c)(2) of the Immigration and Nationality Act, but also sounds the death knell for nearly 200 other statutory provisions in which Congress has reserved a "legislative veto." . . .

The prominence of the legislative veto mechanism in our contemporary political system and its importance to Congress can hardly be overstated. It has become a central means by which Congress secures the accountability of executive and independent agencies. Without the legislative veto, Congress is faced with a Hobson's choice: either to refrain from delegating the necessary authority, leaving itself with a hopeless task of writing laws with the requisite specificity to cover endless special circumstances across the entire policy landscape, or in the alternative, to abdicate its lawmaking function to the executive branch and independent agencies. To choose the former leaves major national problems unresolved; to opt for the latter risks unaccountable policymaking by those not elected to fill that role. Accordingly, over the past five decades, the legislative veto has been placed in nearly 200 statutes. The device is known in every field of governmental concern: reorganization, budgets, foreign affairs, war powers, and regulation of trade, safety, energy, the environment and the economy.

I

. . .

The history of the legislative veto . . . makes clear that it has not been a sword with which Congress has struck out to aggrandize itself at the expense of the other branches—the concerns of Madison and Hamilton. Rather, the veto has been a means of defense, a reservation of ultimate authority necessary if Congress is to fulfill its designated role under Article I as the nation's lawmaker. While the President has often objected to particular legislative vetoes, generally those left in the hands of congressional committees, the Executive has more often agreed to legislative review as the price for a broad delegation of authority. To be sure, the President may have preferred unrestricted power, but that could be precisely why Congress thought it essential to retain a check on the exercise of delegated authority.

II

For all these reasons, the apparent sweep of the Court's decision today is regrettable. The Court's Article I analysis appears to invalidate all legislative vetoes irrespective of form or subject. Because the legislative veto is commonly found as a check upon rulemaking by administrative agencies and upon broad-based policy decisions of the Executive Branch, it is particularly unfortunate that the Court reaches its decision in a case involving the exercise of a veto over deportation decisions regarding particular individuals. . . . Unfortunately, today's holding is not so limited.

. . .

III

. . .

If Congress may delegate lawmaking power to independent and executive agencies, it is most difficult to understand Article I as forbidding Congress from also reserving a check on legislative power for itself. Absent the veto, the agencies receiving delegations of legislative or quasi-legislative power may issue regulations having the force of law without bicameral approval and without the President's signature. It is thus not apparent why the reservation of a veto over the exercise of that legislative power must be subject to a more exacting test. In both cases, it is enough that the initial statutory authorizations comply with the Article I requirements.

. . .

IV

. . .

I do not suggest that all legislative vetoes are necessarily consistent with separation of powers principles. A legislative check on an inherently executive function, for example that of initiating prosecutions, poses an entirely different question. . . .

. . .

■ JUSTICE REHNQUIST, with whom JUSTICE WHITE joins, dissenting.

. . .

By severing [the legislative veto in] § 244(c)(2) [and leaving, the rest of the statute in place,] the Court permits suspension of deportation in a class of cases where Congress never stated that suspension was appropriate. I do not believe we should expand the statute in this way without some clear indication that Congress intended such an expansion. . . .

. . .

Mistretta v. United States

488 U.S. 361 (1989).

The Sentencing Reform Act of 1984 created the United States Sentencing Commission, consisting of seven voting members appointed by the President with the advice and consent of the Senate. At least three of its members must be federal judges, selected after consideration of a list of six judges recommended by the Judicial Conference of the United States. The commission, established "as an independent commission in the judicial branch of the United States," promulgates binding sentencing guidelines for federal crimes. The Court upheld the commission's sentencing guidelines against a claim that the Act violated the principle of separation of powers. The Court stressed that a "concern of encroachment and aggrandizement . . . has animated our separation of powers jurisprudence."

"Accordingly, we have not hesitated to strike down provisions of law that either accrete to a single branch powers more appropriately diffused among separate branches or that undermine the authority and independence of one or another coordinate branch. . . . By the same token, we have upheld statutory provisions that to some degree commingle the functions of the Branches, but that pose no danger of either aggrandizement or encroachment."

Locating the Commission within the judicial branch did not violate the provisions of Article III, limiting the judicial power to resolution of "cases" and "controversies." Analogous to the provisions for judicial rulemaking, "Congress may delegate to the Judicial Branch nonadjudicatory functions that do not trench upon the prerogatives of another Branch and that are appropriate to the central mission of the Judiciary." Although the Commission wields rulemaking authority, it has not aggrandized the authority of the judicial branch, since judges had, as an aggregate, determined appropriate criminal sentences prior to passage of the Act.

Although the Commission does not wield "judicial power," Article III does not prohibit Article III judges from undertaking extrajudicial duties "in their individual capacities." In each case, the issue is "whether a particular extrajudicial assignment undermines the integrity of the Judicial Branch." Service on the Commission is voluntary, and participation in promulgation of the sentencing guidelines would not affect member-judges' ability to adjudicate sentencing issues.

"Judicial contribution to the enterprise of creating rules to limit the discretion of sentencing judges does not enlist the resources or reputation of the Judicial Branch in either the legislative business of determining what conduct should be criminalized or the executive business of enforcing the law. Rather, judicial participation on the Commission ensures that judicial experience and expertise will inform the promulgation of rules for the exercise of the Judicial Branch's own business—that of passing sentence on every criminal defendant."

Justice Scalia dissented, saying:

"Today's decision follows the regrettable tendency of our recent separation-of-powers jurisprudence . . . to treat the Constitution as though it were no more than a generalized prescription that the functions of the Branches should not be commingled too much—how much is too much to be determined, case-by-case, by this Court. The Constitution is not that. Rather, as its name suggests, it is a prescribed structure, a framework, for the conduct of government. . . . Consideration of the degree of commingling that a particular disposition produces may be appropriate at the margins, where the outline of the framework itself is not clear; but it seems to me far from a marginal question whether our constitutional structure allows for a body which is not the Congress, and yet exercises no governmental powers except the making of rules that have the effect of laws.

". . . [T]here are many desirable dispositions that do not accord with the constitutional structure we live under. And in the long run the improvisation of a constitutional structure on the basis of currently perceived utility will be disastrous."

B. APPOINTMENT, DISCHARGE, AND SUPERVISION OF "OFFICERS OF THE UNITED STATES"

Morrison v. Olson

487 U.S. 654, 108 S.Ct. 2597, 101 L.Ed.2d 569 (1988).

■ CHIEF JUSTICE REHNQUIST delivered the opinion of the Court.

This case presents us with a challenge to the independent counsel provisions of the Ethics in Government Act of 1978 . . . We hold today that these provisions of the Act do not violate the Appointments Clause of the Constitution, Art. II, § 2, cl. 2, or the limitations of Article III, nor do they impermissibly interfere with the President's authority under Article II in violation of the constitutional principle of separation of powers.

I

Briefly stated, Title VI of the Ethics in Government Act (Title VI or the Act) . . . allows for the appointment of an "independent counsel" to investigate and, if appropriate, prosecute certain high ranking government officials for violations of federal criminal laws. The Act requires the Attorney General, upon receipt of information that he determines is "sufficient to constitute grounds to investigate whether any person [covered by the Act] may have violated any Federal criminal law," to conduct a preliminary investigation of the matter. When the Attorney General has completed this investigation, or 90 days has elapsed, he is required to report to a special court (the Special Division) created by the Act "for the purpose of appointing independent counsels." . . . If . . . the Attorney General has determined that there are "reasonable grounds to believe that further investigation or prosecution is warranted," then he "shall apply to the division of the court for the appointment of an independent counsel." . . . Upon receiving this application, the Special Division "shall appoint an appropriate independent counsel and shall define that independent counsel's prosecutorial jurisdiction." . . .

With respect to all matters within the independent counsel's jurisdiction, the Act grants the counsel "full power and independent authority to exercise all investigative and prosecutorial functions and powers of the Department of Justice, the Attorney General, and any other officer or employee of the Department of Justice." . . . Two statutory provisions govern the length of an independent counsel's tenure in office. The first defines the procedure for removing an independent counsel. Section 596(a)(1) provides:

"An independent counsel appointed under this chapter may be removed from office, other than by impeachment and conviction, only by the personal action of the Attorney General and only for good cause, physical disability, mental incapacity, or any other condition that substantially impairs the performance of such independent counsel's duties."

. . . [A]n independent counsel can obtain judicial review of the Attorney General's action by filing a civil action in the United States District Court for the District of Columbia. . . . The reviewing court is authorized to grant reinstatement or "other appropriate relief."

The other provision governing the tenure of the independent counsel defines the procedures for "terminating" the counsel's office. . . . [T]he office of an independent counsel terminates when he notifies the Attorney General that he has completed or substantially completed any investigations or prosecutions undertaken pursuant to the Act. In addition, the Special Division, acting either on its own or on the suggestion of the Attorney General, may terminate the office of an independent counsel at any time if it finds that "the investigation of all matters within the prosecutorial jurisdiction of such independent counsel . . . have been completed or so substantially completed that it would be appropriate for the Department of Justice to complete such investigations and prosecutions." . . .

Finally, the Act provides for Congressional oversight of the activities of independent counsels. An independent counsel may from time to time send Congress statements or reports on his activities. § 595(a)(2). The "appropriate committees of the Congress" are given oversight jurisdiction in regard to the official conduct of an independent counsel, and the counsel is required by the Act to cooperate with Congress in the exercise of this jurisdiction. . . .

. . .

. . . In 1985, the majority members of the [House] Judiciary Committee published a lengthy report [which] suggested that appellee Olson had given false and misleading testimony to the subcommittee . . . The Chairman of the Judiciary Committee forwarded a copy of the report to the Attorney General with a request, pursuant to 28 U.S.C. § 592(c), that he seek the appointment of an independent counsel . . .

. . . The Attorney General accordingly requested appointment of an independent counsel to investigate whether Olson's March 10, 1983, testimony ". . . violated 18 U.S.C. § 1505, § 1001, or any other provision of federal criminal law." . . . The Attorney General also requested that the independent counsel have authority to investigate "any other matter related to that allegation."

On April 23, 1986, the Special Division appointed James C. McKay as independent counsel. . . .

McKay later resigned as independent counsel, and on May 29, 1986, the Division appointed appellant Morrison as his replacement. . . .

. . .

. . . [I]n May and June 1987, appellant caused a grand jury to issue and serve subpoenas ad testificandum and duces tecum on appellees. All three appellees moved to quash the subpoenas, claiming, among other things, that the independent counsel provisions of the Act were unconstitutional and that appellant accordingly had no authority to proceed. On July 20, 1987, the District Court upheld the constitutionality of the Act and denied the motions to quash. . . .'

A divided Court of Appeals reversed. . . . We now reverse.

II

. . .

III

. . .

The parties do not dispute that "[t]he Constitution for purposes of appointment . . . divides all its officers into two classes.". . . . As we stated in Buckley v. Valeo, 424 U.S. 1, 132 (1976), "[p]rincipal officers are selected by the President with the advice and consent of the Senate. Inferior officers Congress may allow to be appointed by the President alone, by the heads of departments, or by the Judiciary." The initial question is, accordingly, whether appellant is an "inferior" or a "principal" officer. If she is the latter, as the Court of Appeals concluded, then the Act is in violation of the Appointments Clause.

The line between "inferior" and "principal" officers is one that is far from clear, and the Framers provided little guidance into where it should be drawn. . . . We need not attempt here to decide exactly where the line falls between the two types of officers, because in our view appellant clearly falls on the "inferior officer" side of that line. Several factors lead to this conclusion.

First, appellant is subject to removal by a higher Executive Branch official. Although appellant may not be "subordinate" to the Attorney General (and the President) insofar as she possesses a degree of independent discretion to exercise the powers delegated to her under the Act, the fact that she can be removed by the Attorney General indicates that she is to some degree "inferior" in rank and authority. Second, appellant is empowered by the Act to perform only certain, limited duties. An independent counsel's role is restricted primarily to investigation and, if appropriate, prosecution for certain federal crimes. Admittedly, the Act delegates to appellant "full power and independent authority to exercise all investigative and prosecutorial functions and powers of the Department of Justice," . . . but this grant of authority does not include any authority to formulate policy for the Government or the Executive Branch, nor does it give appellant any administrative duties outside of those necessary to operate her office. The Act specifically provides that in policy matters appellant is to comply to the extent possible with the policies of the Department. . . .

Third, appellant's office is limited in jurisdiction. Not only is the Act itself restricted in applicability to certain federal officials suspected of certain serious federal crimes, but an independent counsel can only act within the scope of the jurisdiction that has been granted by the Special Division pursuant to a request by the Attorney General. Finally, appellant's office is limited in tenure. There is concededly no time limit on the appointment of a particular counsel. Nonetheless, the office of independent counsel is "temporary" in the sense that an independent counsel is appointed essentially to accomplish a single task, and when that task is over the office is terminated, either by the counsel herself or by action of the Special Division. Unlike other prosecutors, appellant has no ongoing responsibilities that extend beyond the accomplishment of the mission that she was appointed for and authorized by the Special Division to undertake. In our view, these factors relating to the "ideas of tenure, duration . . . and duties" of the independent counsel, . . . are sufficient to establish that appellant is an "inferior" officer in the constitutional sense.

. . .

This does not, however, end our inquiry under the Appointments Clause. Appellees argue that even if appellant is an "inferior" officer, the Clause does not empower Congress to place the power to appoint such an officer outside the Executive Branch. They contend that the Clause does not contemplate congressional authorization of "interbranch appointments," in which an officer of one branch is appointed by officers of another branch. The relevant language of the Appointments Clause is worth repeating. It reads: ". . . but the Congress may by Law vest the Appointment of such inferior Officers, as they think proper, in the President alone, in the courts of Law, or in the Heads of Departments." On its face, the language of this "excepting clause" admits of no limitation on interbranch appointments. Indeed, the inclusion of "as they think proper" seems clearly to give Congress significant discretion to determine whether it is "proper" to vest the appointment of, for example, executive officials in the "courts of Law." We recognized as much in one of our few decisions in this area, *Ex parte Siebold,* supra, where we stated:

"It is no doubt usual and proper to vest the appointment of inferior officers in that department of the government, executive or judicial, or in that particular executive department to which the duties of such officers appertain. But there is no absolute requirement to this effect in the Constitution; and, if there were, it would be difficult in many cases to determine to which department an office properly belonged . . . " . . .

. . .

We do not mean to say that Congress' power to provide for interbranch appointments of "inferior officers" is unlimited. In addition to separation of powers concerns, which would arise if such provisions for appointment had the potential to impair the constitutional functions assigned to one of the branches, *Siebold* itself suggested that Congress' decision to vest the appointment power in the courts would be improper if there was some "incongruity" between the functions normally performed by the courts and the performance of their duty to appoint. . . . In *Siebold,* as well, we indicated that judicial appointment of federal marshals, who are "executive officer[s]," would not be inappropriate. . . .

IV

Appellees next contend that the powers vested in the Special Division by the Act conflict with Article III of the Constitution. . . .

. . . Clearly, once it is accepted that the Appointments Clause gives Congress the power to vest the appointment of officials such as the independent counsel in the "courts of Law," there can be no Article III objection to the Special Division's exercise of that power, as the power itself derives from the Appointments Clause, a source of authority for judicial action that is independent of Article III. Appellees contend, however, that the Division's Appointments Clause powers do not encompass the power to define the independent counsel's jurisdiction. We disagree. In our view, Congress' power under the Clause to vest the "Appointment" of inferior officers in the courts may, in certain circumstances, allow Congress to give the courts some discretion in defining the nature and scope of the appointed official's authority. . . .

. . .

We are more doubtful about the Special Division's power to terminate the office of the independent counsel . . . As appellees suggest, the power to terminate, especially when exercised by the Division on its own motion, is "administrative" to the extent that it requires the Special Division to monitor the progress of proceedings of the independent counsel and come to a decision as to whether the counsel's job is "completed." . . . It also is not a power that could be considered typically "judicial," as it has few analogues among the court's more traditional powers. Nonetheless, we do not, as did the Court of Appeals, view this provision as a significant judicial encroachment upon executive power or upon the prosecutorial discretion of the independent counsel.

. . . [I]t is the duty of federal courts to construe a statute in order to save it from constitutional infirmities, . . . and to that end we think a narrow construction is appropriate here. The termination provisions of the Act do not give the Special Division anything approaching the power to remove the counsel while an investigation or court proceeding is still underway—this power is vested solely in the Attorney General. As we see it, "termination" may occur only when the duties of the counsel are truly "completed" or "so substantially completed" that there remains no need for any continuing action by the independent counsel. . . .

. . .

V

We now turn to consider whether the Act is invalid under the constitutional principle of separation of powers. Two related issues must be addressed: The first is whether the provision of the Act restricting the Attorney General's power to remove the independent counsel to only those instances in which he can show "good cause," taken by itself, impermissibly interferes with the President's exercise of his constitutionally appointed functions. The second is whether, taken as a whole, the Act violates the separation of powers by reducing the President's ability to control the prosecutorial powers wielded by the independent counsel.

A

Two Terms ago we had occasion to consider whether it was consistent with the separation of powers for Congress to pass a statute that authorized a government official who is removable only by Congress to participate in what we found to be "executive powers." Bowsher v. Synar, 478 U.S. 714, 730 (1986). We held in *Bowsher* that "Congress cannot reserve for itself the power of removal of an officer charged with the execution of the laws except by impeachment." . . . A primary antecedent for this ruling was our 1925 decision in Myers v. United States, 272 U.S. 52 (1926). *Myers* had considered the propriety of a federal statute by which certain postmasters of the

United States could be removed by the President only "by and with the advice and consent of the Senate." There too, Congress' attempt to involve itself in the removal of an executive official was found to be sufficient grounds to render the statute invalid. . . .'

Unlike both *Bowsher* and *Myers,* this case does not involve an attempt by Congress itself to gain a role in the removal of executive officials other than its established powers of impeachment and conviction. The Act instead puts the removal power squarely in the hands of the Executive Branch; an independent counsel may be removed from office, "only by the personal action of the Attorney General, and only for good cause." . . . There is no requirement of congressional approval of the Attorney General's removal decision, though the decision is subject to judicial review. . . . In our view, the removal provisions of the Act make this case more analogous to Humphrey's Executor v. United States, 295 U.S. 602 (1935), and Wiener v. United States, 357 U.S. 349 (1958), than to *Myers* or *Bowsher.*

In *Humphrey's Executor,* the issue was whether a statute restricting the President's power to remove the commissioners of the Federal Trade Commission only for "inefficiency, neglect of duty, or malfeasance in office" was consistent with the Constitution. 295 U.S., at 619. We stated that whether Congress can "condition the [President's power of removal] by fixing a definite term and precluding a removal except for cause, will depend upon the character of the office." . . . Contrary to the implication of some dicta in *Myers,2*[24] the President's power to remove government officials simply was not "all-inclusive in respect of civil officers with the exception of the judiciary provided for by the Constitution." . . . At least in regard to "quasi-legislative" and "quasi-judicial" agencies such as the FTC, "[t]he authority of Congress, in creating [such] agencies, to require them to act in discharge of their duties independently of executive control . . . includes, as an appropriate incident, power to fix the period during which they shall continue in office, and to forbid their removal except for cause in the meantime." . . . In *Humphrey's Executor,* we found it "plain" that the Constitution did not give the President "illimitable power of removal" over the officers of independent agencies. . . . Were the President to have the power to remove FTC commissioners at will, the "coercive influence" of the removal power would "threate[n] the independence of [the] commission." . . .

Similarly, in *Wiener* we considered whether the President had unfettered discretion to remove a member of the War Claims Commission, which had been established by Congress in the War Claims Act of 1948 . . . The Commission's function was to receive and adjudicate certain claims for compensation from those who had suffered personal injury or property damage at the hands of the enemy during World War II. Commissioners were appointed by the President, with the advice and consent of the Senate, but the statute made no provision for the removal of officers, perhaps because the Commission itself was to have a limited existence. As in *Humphrey's Executor,* however, the Commissioners were entrusted by Congress with adjudicatory powers that were to be exercised free from executive control. In this context, "Congress did not wish to have hang over the Commission the Damocles' sword of removal by the President for no reason other than that he preferred to have on that Commission men of his own choosing." . . . Accordingly, we rejected the President's attempt to remove a Commissioner "merely because he wanted his own appointees on [the] Commission,"

---

[24] The Court expressly disapproved of any statements in *Myers* that "are out of harmony" with the views expressed in *Humphrey's Executor.* 295 U.S., at 626. We recognized that the only issue actually decided in *Myers* was that "the President had power to remove a postmaster of the first class, without the advice and consent of the Senate as required by act of Congress." . . .

stating that "no such power is given to the President directly by the Constitution, and none is impliedly conferred upon him by statute." . . .

Appellees contend that *Humphrey's Executor* and *Wiener* are distinguishable from this case because they did not involve officials who performed a "core executive function." They argue that our decision in *Humphrey's Executor* rests on a distinction between "purely executive" officials and officials who exercise "quasi-legislative" and "quasi-judicial" powers. In their view, when a "purely executive" official is involved, the governing precedent is *Myers,* not *Humphrey's Executor.* . . . And, under *Myers,* the President must have absolute discretion to discharge "purely" executive officials at will. See *Myers,* 272 U.S., at 132–134.

We undoubtedly did rely on the terms "quasi-legislative" and "quasi-judicial" to distinguish the officials involved in *Humphrey's Executor* and *Wiener* from those in *Myers,* but our present considered view is that the determination of whether the Constitution allows Congress to impose a "good cause"-type restriction on the President's power to remove an official cannot be made to turn on whether or not that official is classified as "purely executive." The analysis contained in our removal cases is designed not to define rigid categories of those officials who may or may not be removed at will by the President, but to ensure that Congress does not interfere with the President's exercise of the "executive power" and his constitutionally appointed duty to "take care that the laws be faithfully executed" under Article II. *Myers* was undoubtedly correct in its holding, and in its broader suggestion that there are some "purely executive" officials who must be removable by the President at will if he is to be able to accomplish his constitutional role. . . . But as the Court noted in *Wiener,*

"The assumption was short-lived that the *Myers* case recognized the President's inherent constitutional power to remove officials no matter what the relation of the executive to the discharge of their duties and no matter what restrictions Congress may have imposed regarding the nature of their tenure." 357 U.S., at 352.

At the other end of the spectrum from *Myers,* the characterization of the agencies in *Humphrey's Executor* and *Wiener* as "quasi-legislative" or "quasi-judicial" in large part reflected our judgment that it was not essential to the President's proper execution of his Article II powers that these agencies be headed up by individuals who were removable at will. We do not mean to suggest that an analysis of the functions served by the officials at issue is irrelevant. But the real question is whether the removal restrictions are of such a nature that they impede the President's ability to perform his constitutional duty, and the functions of the officials in question must be analyzed in that light.

Considering for the moment the "good cause" removal provision in isolation from the other parts of the Act at issue in this case, we cannot say that the imposition of a "good cause" standard for removal by itself unduly trammels on executive authority. . . .

Nor do we think that the "good cause" removal provision at issue here impermissibly burdens the President's power to control or supervise the independent counsel, as an executive official, in the execution of her duties under the Act. . . .

B

The final question to be addressed is whether the Act, taken as a whole, violates the principle of separation of powers by unduly interfering with the role of the Executive Branch. . . .

We observe first that this case does not involve an attempt by Congress to increase its own powers at the expense of the Executive Branch. . . .

Similarly, we do not think that the Act works any *judicial* usurpation of properly executive functions. . . . Finally, we do not think that the Act "impermissibly undermine[s]" the powers of the Executive Branch, . . . or "disrupts the proper balance between the coordinate branches [by] prevent[ing] the Executive Branch from accomplishing its constitutionally assigned functions," . . . It is undeniable that the Act reduces the amount of control or supervision that the Attorney General and, through him, the President exercises over the investigation and prosecution of a certain class of alleged criminal activity. . . . Nonetheless, the Act does give the Attorney General several means of supervising or controlling the prosecutorial powers that may be wielded by an independent counsel. . . .

VI

In sum, we conclude today that it does not violate the Appointments Clause for Congress to vest the appointment of independent counsels in the Special Division; that the powers exercised by the Special Division under the Act do not violate Article III; and that the Act does not violate the separation of powers principle by impermissibly interfering with the functions of the Executive Branch. The decision of the Court of Appeals is therefore

Reversed.

■ JUSTICE KENNEDY took no part in the consideration or decision of this case.

■ JUSTICE SCALIA, dissenting.

II

. . .

. . . It seems to me . . . that the decision of the Court of Appeals invalidating the present statute must be upheld on fundamental separation-of-powers principles if the following two questions are answered affirmatively: (1) Is the conduct of a criminal prosecution (and of an investigation to decide whether to prosecute) the exercise of purely executive power? (2) Does the statute deprive the President of the United States of exclusive control over the exercise of that power? Surprising to say, the Court appears to concede an affirmative answer to both questions, but seeks to avoid the inevitable conclusion that since the statute vests some purely executive power in a person who is not the President of the United States it is void.

. . .

. . . [I]t is ultimately irrelevant *how much* the statute reduces presidential control. The case is over when the Court acknowledges, as it must, that "[i]t is undeniable that the Act reduces the amount of control or supervision that the Attorney General and, through him, the President exercises over the investigation and prosecution of a certain class of alleged criminal activity." . . .

. . .

Is it unthinkable that the President should have such exclusive power, even when alleged crimes by him or his close associates are at issue? No more so than that Congress should have the exclusive power of legislation, even when what is at issue is its own exemption from the burdens of certain laws. . . . No more so than that this Court should have the exclusive power to pronounce the final decision on justiciable cases and controversies, even those pertaining to the constitutionality of a statute reducing the salaries of the Justices. . . . The checks against any Branch's abuse of its exclusive powers are twofold: First, retaliation by one of the other Branch's use of *its* exclusive powers: Congress, for example, can impeach the Executive who willfully fails to enforce the laws; the Executive can decline to prosecute under unconstitutional statutes . . . ; and the courts can dismiss malicious prosecutions: Second, and ultimately, there is the political check that the people will replace those in the political branches . . . who are guilty of abuse. Political pressures produced special prosecutors—for Teapot Dome and for Watergate, for example—long before this statute created the independent counsel. . . .'

. . .

III

Because appellant (who all parties and the Court agree is an officer of the United States) was not appointed by the President with the advice and consent of the Senate, but rather by the Special Division of the United States Court of Appeals, her appointment is constitutional only if (1) she is an "inferior" officer within the meaning of the above clause, and (2) Congress may vest her appointment in a court of law.

. . .

. . . [I]t is not clear from the Court's opinion why the factors it discusses—[putting aside the question whether they are] applied correctly to the facts of this case—are determinative of the question of inferior status. . . . I think it [is] preferable to look to the text of the Constitution and the division of power that it establishes. These demonstrate, I think, that the independent counsel is not an inferior officer because she is not *subordinate* to any officer in the Executive Branch (indeed, not even to the President). Dictionaries in use at the time of the Constitutional Convention gave the word "inferiour" two meanings which it still bears today: (1) "lower in place" . . . and (2) "subordinate." . . . At the only other point in the Constitution at which the word "inferior" appears, it plainly connotes a relationship of subordination. Article III vests the judicial power of the United States in "one supreme Court, and in such inferior Courts as the Congress may from time to time ordain and establish." . . .

That "inferior" means "subordinate" is . . . consistent with what little we know about the evolution of the Appointments Clause. . . .'

. . .

Because appellant is not subordinate to another officer, she is not an "inferior" officer and her appointment other than by the President with the advice and consent of the Senate is unconstitutional.

IV

. . . [T]he restrictions upon the removal of the independent counsel also violate our established precedent dealing with that specific subject. . . .'

. . .

V

Under our system of government, the primary check against prosecutorial abuse is a political one. The prosecutors who exercise this awesome discretion are selected and can be removed by a President, whom the people have trusted enough to elect. Moreover, when crimes are not investigated and prosecuted fairly, nonselectively, with a reasonable sense of proportion, the President pays the cost in political damage to his administration. . . .'

. . .

. . . [The Court] extends into the very heart of our most significant constitutional function the "totality of the circumstances" mode of analysis that this Court has in recent years become fond of. Taking all things into account, we conclude that the power taken away from the President here is not really *too* much. . . .'

The ad hoc approach to constitutional adjudication has real attraction, even apart from its work-saving potential. It is guaranteed to produce a result, in every case, that will make a majority of the Court happy with the law. The law is, by definition, precisely what the majority thinks, taking all things into account, it *ought* to be. I prefer to rely upon the judgment of the wise men who constructed our system, and of the people who approved it, and of two centuries of history that have shown it to be sound. Like it or not, that judgment says, quite plainly, that "[t]he executive Power shall be vested in a President of the United States."

Free Enterprise Fund v. Public Company Accounting Oversight Board
561 U.S. 477 (2010).

The Court distinguished *Morrison* in a 5–4 decision invalidating restrictions Congress had placed on the removal of members of the Public Company Accounting Oversight Board (Board). In the wake of highly publicized accounting scandals around the turn of the twenty-first century, Congress enacted the Sarbanes-Oxley Act of 2002 (Act), which, among other things, created the Board to facilitate tighter regulation of the accounting industry. The Board is composed of five members, appointed to staggered 5-year terms by the Securities and Exchange Commission (SEC or Commission). It was modeled on private self-regulatory organizations in the securities industry—such as the New York Stock Exchange—that investigate and discipline their own members, but unlike the self-regulatory organizations, "the Board is a Government-created, Government-appointed entity, with expansive powers to govern an entire industry." Among other things, "[t]he Board promulgates auditing and ethics standards, performs routine inspections of all accounting firms, demands documents and testimony, and initiates formal investigations and disciplinary proceedings." The Act places the Board under the SEC's oversight, particularly with respect to the issuance of rules or the imposition of sanctions (both of which are subject to Commission approval). But the individual members of the Board—like the officers and directors of the self-regulatory organizations—enjoy power to do many things on their own, and are substantially insulated from the Commission's control; the Commission cannot remove Board members at will, but only "for good cause shown," "in accordance with" certain procedures. And the parties to the case agreed that the Commissioners cannot themselves be removed by the President except under the standard laid out in *Humphrey's Executor* of "inefficiency, neglect of duty, or malfeasance in office."

Ruling in favor of a challenge brought by a regulated entity against the constitutionality of the Act's limits on Board member removal, Chief Justice Roberts, writing for himself and Justices Scalia, Kennedy, Thomas and Alito, framed the issue this way: "Since 1789, the Constitution has been understood to empower the President to keep these officers accountable—by removing them from office, if necessary. See generally Myers v. United States, 272 U.S. 52 (1926). This Court has determined, however, that this authority is not without limit. In *Humphrey's Executor*, we held that Congress can, under certain circumstances, create independent agencies run by principal officers appointed by the President, whom the President may not remove at will but only for good cause. Likewise, in . . . Morrison v. Olson, 487 U.S. 654 (1988), the Court sustained similar restrictions on the power of principal executive officers— themselves responsible to the President—to remove their own inferiors. The parties do not ask us to reexamine any of these precedents, and we do not do so.

"We are asked, however, to consider a new situation not yet encountered by the Court. The question is whether these separate layers of protection may be combined. May the President be restricted in his ability to remove a principal officer, who is in turn restricted in his ability to remove an inferior officer, even though that inferior officer determines the policy and enforces the laws of the United States?

"We hold that such multilevel protection from removal is contrary to Article II's vesting of the executive power in the President. The President cannot 'take Care that the Laws be faithfully executed' if he cannot oversee the faithfulness of the officers who execute them. Here the President cannot remove an officer who enjoys more than one level of good-cause protection, even if the President determines that the officer is neglecting his duties or discharging them improperly. That judgment is instead committed to another officer, who may or may not agree with the President's determination, and whom the President cannot remove simply because that officer disagrees with him. This contravenes the President's 'constitutional obligation to ensure the faithful execution of the laws.' . . ."

The Court elaborated: "The Act before us does something quite different [from past cases.] It not only protects Board members from removal except for good cause, but withdraws from the President any decision on whether that good cause exists. That decision is vested instead in other tenured officers—the Commissioners—none of whom is subject to the President's direct control. The result is a Board that is not accountable to the President, and a President who is not responsible for the Board.

"The added layer of tenure protection makes a difference. Without a layer of insulation between the Commission and the Board, the Commission could remove a Board member at any time, and therefore would be fully responsible for what the Board does. The President could then hold the Commission to account for its supervision of the Board, to the same extent that he may hold the Commission to account for everything else it does.

"A second level of tenure protection changes the nature of the President's review. Now the Commission cannot remove a Board member at will. The President therefore cannot hold the Commission fully accountable for the Board's conduct, to the same extent that he may hold the Commission accountable for everything else that it does. The Commissioners are not responsible for the Board's actions. They are only responsible for their own determination of whether the Act's rigorous good-cause standard is met. And even if the President disagrees with their determination, he is powerless to intervene—unless that determination is so unreasonable as to constitute 'inefficiency, neglect of duty, or malfeasance in office.' *Humphrey's Executor*, . . .

"This novel structure does not merely add to the Board's independence, but transforms it. Neither the President, nor anyone directly responsible to him, nor even an officer whose conduct he may review only for good cause, has full control over the Board. The President is stripped of the power our precedents have preserved, and his ability to execute the laws—by holding his subordinates accountable for their conduct—is impaired."

Justices Stevens, Ginsburg, Breyer and Sotomayor dissented, and, relying more on "function and context and not . . . bright-line rules," would have found the protections from removal imposed by Congress reasonable and consistent with the separation of powers. The dissenters, believing that the majority's reasoning "threatens to disrupt severely the fair and efficient administration of the laws," listed in an Appendix to the dissent "at least 24 additional offices, boards, or bureaus" seemingly called into question by the majority.

After finding that the Act unconstitutionally interfered with the vesting of executive power in the President, the Court found the provisions limiting the Commission's power to remove Board members to be severable, and so left intact all other aspects of the Act. "Concluding that the removal restrictions are invalid leaves the Board removable by the Commission at will, and leaves the President separated from Board members by only a single level of good-cause tenure. The Commission is then fully responsible for the Board's actions, which are no less subject than the Commission's own functions to Presidential oversight."

In a separate part of the opinion, the Court rejected other challenges mounted against the Act, including the argument that Board members are principal officers requiring Presidential appointment with the Senate's advice and consent: "We held in Edmond v. United States, 520 U.S. 651, 662–663 (1997), that '[w]hether one is an "inferior" officer depends on whether he has a superior,' and that 'inferior officers' are officers whose work is directed and supervised at some level' by other officers appointed by the President with the Senate's consent. In particular, we noted that '[t]he power to remove officers' at will and without cause 'is a powerful tool for control' of an inferior. . . . As explained above, the statutory restrictions on the Commission's power to remove Board members are unconstitutional and void. Given that the Commission is properly viewed, under the Constitution, as possessing the power to remove Board members at will, and given the Commission's other oversight authority, we have no hesitation in concluding that under *Edmond* the Board members are inferior officers whose appointment Congress may permissibly vest in a 'Hea[d] of Departmen[t].' "

The Court went on to hold that the Commission is indeed a "Department" for purposes of the appointments clause, and that the full Commission, rather than the Chair of the Commission, is the "Head" of the "Department."

NOTE ON THE UNITARY EXECUTIVE CONCEPT IN PRINTZ V. UNITED STATES

In Printz v. United States, appearing at pp. 190 infra, Justice Scalia's majority opinion had the following to say about the Brady Act's assignment of federally mandated gun-purchase background checks to local law enforcement officials:

"We have thus far discussed the effect that federal control of state officers would have upon . . . the division of power between State and Federal Governments. It would also have an effect upon . . . the separation and equilibration of powers between the three branches of the Federal Government itself. The Constitution does not leave to speculation who is to administer the laws enacted by Congress; the President, it says, "shall take Care that the Laws be faithfully executed," Art. II, § 3, personally and through officers whom he appoints. . . . The Brady Act effectively transfers this responsibility to thousands of CLEOs in the 50 States, who are left to implement the program without meaningful Presidential control (if indeed meaningful Presidential control is possible without the power to appoint and remove). The insistence of the Framers upon unity in the Federal Executive—to insure both vigor and accountability—is well known. See The Federalist No. 70 (A.Hamilton). . . . That unity would be shattered, and the power of the President would be subject to reduction, if Congress could act as effectively without the President as with him, by simply requiring state officers to execute its laws."

The Court then observed, in a footnote, that: ". . . control by the unitary Federal Executive is also sacrificed when States voluntarily administer federal programs, but the condition of voluntary state participation significantly reduces the ability of Congress to use this device as a means of reducing the power of the Presidency."

National Labor Relations Board v. Noel Canning

573 U.S. ___, 134 S.Ct. 2550, 189 L.Ed.2d 538 (2014).

■ JUSTICE BREYER delivered the opinion of the Court.

Ordinarily the President must obtain "the Advice and Consent of the Senate" before appointing an "Office[r] of the United States." U.S. Const., Art. II, § 2, cl. 2. But the Recess Appointments Clause creates an exception. It gives the President alone the power "to fill up all Vacancies that may happen during the Recess of the Senate, by granting Commissions which shall expire at the End of their next Session." Art. II, § 2, cl. 3. We here consider three questions about the application of this Clause.

The first concerns the scope of the words "recess of the Senate." Does that phrase refer only to an inter-session recess (*i.e.,* a break between formal sessions of Congress), or does it also include an intra-session recess, such as a summer recess in the midst of a session? We conclude that the Clause applies to both kinds of recess.

The second question concerns the scope of the words "vacancies that may happen." Does that phrase refer only to vacancies that first come into existence during a recess, or does it also include vacancies that arise prior to a recess but continue to exist during the recess? We conclude that the Clause applies to both kinds of vacancy. The third question concerns calculation of the length of a "recess." The President made the appointments here at issue on January 4, 2012. At that time the Senate was in recess pursuant to a December 17, 2011, resolution providing for a series of brief recesses punctuated by "*pro forma* session[s]," with "no business . . . transacted," every Tuesday and Friday through January 20, 2012. S. J., 112th Cong., 1st Sess., 923 (2011) (hereinafter 2011 S. J.). In calculating the length of a recess are we to ignore the *pro forma* sessions, thereby treating the series of brief recesses as a single, month-long recess? We conclude that we cannot ignore these *pro forma* sessions. Our answer to the third question means that, when the appointments before us took place, the Senate was in the midst of a 3-day recess. Three days is too short a time to bring a recess within the scope of the Clause. Thus we conclude that the President lacked the power to make the recess appointments here at issue.

I

The case before us arises out of a labor dispute. The National Labor Relations Board (NLRB) found that a Pepsi-Cola distributor, Noel Canning, had unlawfully refused to reduce to writing and execute a collective-bargaining agreement with a labor union. The Board ordered the distributor to execute the agreement and to make employees whole for any losses. . . . The Pepsi-Cola distributor subsequently asked the Court of Appeals for the District of Columbia Circuit to set the Board's order aside. It claimed that three of the five Board members had been invalidly appointed, leaving the Board without the three lawfully appointed members necessary for it to act. . . .

The three members in question were Sharon Block, Richard Griffin, and Terence Flynn. In 2011 the President had nominated each of them to the Board. As of January 2012, Flynn's nomination had been pending in the Senate awaiting confirmation for approximately a year. The nominations of each of the other two had been pending for a few weeks. On January 4, 2012, the President, invoking the Recess Appointments Clause, appointed all three to the Board.

The distributor argued that the Recess Appointments Clause did not authorize those appointments. It pointed out that on December 17, 2011, the Senate, by unanimous consent, had adopted a resolution providing that it would take a series of brief recesses beginning the following day. See 2011 S. J. 923. Pursuant to that resolution, the Senate held *pro forma* sessions every Tuesday and Friday until it returned for ordinary business on January 23, 2012. . . . The President's January 4 appointments were made between the January 3 and January 6 *pro forma* sessions. In the distributor's view, each *pro forma* session terminated the immediately preceding recess. Accordingly, the appointments were made during a 3-day adjournment, which is not long enough to trigger the Recess Appointments Clause.

. . .

II

Before turning to the specific questions presented, we shall mention two background considerations that we find relevant to all three. First, *the Recess Appointments Clause sets forth a subsidiary, not a primary, method for appointing officers of the United States*. The immediately preceding Clause—Article II, Section 2, Clause 2—provides the primary method of appointment. It says that the President "shall nominate, *and by and with the Advice and Consent of the Senate*, shall appoint Ambassadors, other public Ministers and Consuls, Judges of the supreme Court, and all other Officers of the United States" (emphasis added).

. . .

Thus the Recess Appointments Clause reflects the tension between, on the one hand, the President's continuous need for "the assistance of subordinates," *Myers* v. *United States*, 272 U.S. 52, 117 (1926), and, on the other, the Senate's practice, particularly during the Republic's early years, of meeting for a single brief session each year. . . . We seek to interpret the Clause as granting the President the power to make appointments during a recess but not offering the President the authority routinely to avoid the need for Senate confirmation.

Second, *in interpreting the Clause, we put significant weight upon historical practice*. For one thing, the interpretive questions before us concern the allocation of power between two elected branches of Government. Long ago Chief Justice Marshall wrote that

"a doubtful question, one on which human reason may pause, and the human judgment be suspended, in the decision of which the great principles of liberty are not concerned, but the respective powers of those who are equally the representatives of the people, are to be adjusted; if not put at rest by the practice of the government, ought to receive a considerable impression from that practice." *McCulloch* v. *Maryland*, 4 Wheat. 316, 401 (1819).

And we later confirmed that "[l]ong settled and established practice is a consideration of great weight in a proper interpretation of constitutional provisions" regulating the relationship between Congress and the President. *The Pocket Veto Case*, 279 U.S. 655, 689 (1929). . . .

. . .

III

The first question concerns the scope of the phrase *"the recess* of the Senate." Art. II, § 2, cl. 3 (emphasis added). The Constitution provides for congressional elections every two years. And the 2-year life of each elected Congress typically consists of two formal 1-year sessions, each separated from the next by an "inter-session recess." . . . The Senate or the House of Representatives announces an inter-session recess by approving a resolution stating that it will "adjourn *sine die*," *i.e.*, without specifying a date to return (in which case Congress will reconvene when the next formal session is scheduled to begin).

The Senate and the House also take breaks in the midst of a session. The Senate or the House announces any such "intra-session recess" by adopting a resolution stating that it will "adjourn" to a fixed date, a few days or weeks or even months later. All agree that the phrase "the recess of the Senate" covers inter-session recesses. The question is whether it includes intra-session recesses as well.

In our view, the phrase "the recess" includes an intra-session recess of substantial length. Its words taken literally can refer to both types of recess. Founding-era dictionaries define the word "recess," much as we do today, simply as "a period of cessation from usual work." 13 The Oxford English Dictionary 322–323 (2d ed. 1989) (hereinafter OED) (citing 18th-and 19th-century sources for that definition of "recess"); 2 N. Webster, An American Dictionary of the English Language (1828) ("[r]emission or suspension of business or procedure"); 2 S. Johnson, A Dictionary of the English Language 1602–1603 (4th ed. 1773) (hereinafter Johnson) (same). The Founders themselves used the word to refer to intra-session, as well as to inter-session, breaks. See, *e.g.,* 3 Records of the Federal Convention of 1787, p. 76 (M. Farrand rev. 1966) . . . ; *id.,* at 191 . . . ; 1 T. Jefferson, A Manual of Parliamentary Practice § LI, p. 165 (2d ed. 1812) (describing a "recess by adjournment" which did *not* end a session).

We recognize that the word "the" in "*the* recess" might suggest that the phrase refers to the single break separating formal sessions of Congress. That is because the word "the" frequently (but not always) indicates "a particular thing." 2 Johnson 2003. But the word can also refer "to a term used generically or universally." 17 OED 879. The Constitution, for example, directs the Senate to choose a President *pro tempore* "in *the* Absence of the Vice- President." Art. I, § 3, cl. 5 (emphasis added). And the Federalist Papers refer to the chief magistrate of an ancient Achaean league who "administered the government in *the* recess of the Senate." The Federalist No. 18, at 113 (J. Madison) (emphasis added). Reading "the" generically in this way, there is no linguistic problem applying the Clause's phrase to both kinds of recess. And, in fact, the phrase "the recess" was used to refer to intra-session recesses at the time of the founding. . . .

The constitutional text is thus ambiguous. And we believe the Clause's purpose demands the broader interpretation. The Clause gives the President authority to make appointments during "the recess of the Senate" so that the President can ensure the continued functioning of the Federal Government when the Senate is away. The Senate is equally away during both an inter-session and an intra-session recess, and its capacity to participate in the appointments process has nothing to do with the words it uses to signal its departure.

History also offers strong support for the broad interpretation. . . .

President Franklin Roosevelt, for example, commissioned Dwight Eisenhower as a permanent Major General during an intra-session recess; President Truman made Dean Acheson Under Secretary of State; and President George H. W. Bush reappointed Alan Greenspan as Chairman of the Federal Reserve Board. . . . .

We must note one contrary opinion authored by President Theodore Roosevelt's Attorney General Philander Knox. Knox advised the President that the Clause did not cover a 19-day intra-session Christmas recess. 23 Op. Atty. Gen. 599 (1901). But in doing so he relied heavily upon the use of the word "the," a linguistic point that we do not find determinative. . . . And Knox all but confessed that his interpretation ran contrary to the basic purpose of the Clause. . . . Moreover, only three days before Knox gave his opinion, the Solicitor of the Treasury came to the opposite conclusion. . . . . We therefore do not think Knox's isolated opinion can disturb the consensus advice within the Executive Branch taking the opposite position.

. . . [Also] . . . we are not aware of any formal action [the Senate itself] has taken to call into question the broad and functional definition of "recess" first set out in the 1905 Senate Report and followed by the Executive Branch since at least 1921. Nor has

Justice Scalia identified any. All the while, the President has made countless recess appointments during intra-session recesses.

. . .

We are aware of, but we are not persuaded by, three important arguments to the contrary. First, some argue that the Founders would likely have intended the Clause to apply only to inter-session recesses, for they hardly knew any other. . . . The problem with this argument, however, is that it does not fully describe the relevant founding intent. The question is not: Did the Founders at the time think about intra-session recesses? Perhaps they did not. The question is: Did the Founders intend to restrict the scope of the Clause to the form of congressional recess then prevalent, or did they intend a broader scope permitting the Clause to apply, where appropriate, to somewhat changed circumstances? . . .

Second, some argue that the intra-session interpretation permits the President to make "illogic[ally]" long recess appointments. . . . A recess appointment made between Congress' annual sessions would permit the appointee to serve for about a year, *i.e.*, until the "end" of the "next" Senate "session." Art. II, § 2, cl. 3. But an intra-session appointment made at the beginning or in the middle of a formal session could permit the appointee to serve for 1½ or almost 2 years (until the end of the following formal session).

We agree that the intra-session interpretation permits somewhat longer recess appointments, but we do not agree that this consequence is "illogical." . . . A recess appointment that lasts somewhat longer than a year will ensure the President the continued assistance of subordinates that the Clause permits him to obtain while he and the Senate select a regular appointee. An appointment should last until the Senate has "an opportunity to act on the subject," Story, § 1551, at 410, and the Clause embodies a determination that a full session is needed to select and vet a replacement.

Third, the Court of Appeals [below] believed that application of the Clause to intra-session recesses would introduce "vagueness" into a Clause that was otherwise clear. . . . One can find problems of uncertainty, however, either way. . . .

. . .

The greater interpretive problem is determining how long a recess must be in order to fall within the Clause. Is a break of a week, or a day, or an hour too short to count as a "recess"? The Clause itself does not say. And Justice Scalia claims that this silence itself shows that the Framers intended the Clause to apply only to an inter-session recess. . . .

We disagree. For one thing, the most likely reason the Framers did not place a textual floor underneath the word "recess" is that they did not foresee the *need* for one. . . .

Moreover, the lack of a textual floor raises a problem that plagues *both* interpretations—Justice Scalia's and ours. Today a brief inter-session recess is just as possible as a brief intra-session recess.

. . .

We agree with the Solicitor General that a 3-day recess would be too short. . . . The Adjournments Clause reflects the fact that a 3-day break is not a significant interruption of legislative business. As the Solicitor General says, it is constitutionally *de minimis*. . . . A Senate recess that is so short that it does not require the consent of the House is not long enough to trigger the President's recess-appointment power. That is not to say that the President may make recess appointments during any recess that is "more than three days." Art. I, § 5, cl. 4. The Recess Appointments Clause seeks to permit the Executive Branch to function smoothly when Congress is unavailable. And though Congress has taken short breaks for almost 200 years, and there have been many thousands of recess appointments in that time, we have not found a single example of a recess appointment made during an intra-session recess that was shorter than 10 days. Nor has the Solicitor General. . . . There are a few historical examples of recess appointments made during inter-session recesses shorter than 10 days. . . . But when considered against 200 years of settled practice, we regard these few scattered examples as anomalies. We therefore conclude, in light of historical practice, that a recess of more than 3 days but less than 10 days is presumptively too short to fall within the Clause. We add the word "presumptively" to leave open the possibility that some very unusual circumstance—a national catastrophe, for instance, that renders the Senate unavailable but calls for an urgent response—could demand the exercise of the recess-appointment power during a shorter break. (It should go without saying—except that Justice Scalia compels us to say it—that political opposition in the Senate would not qualify as an unusual circumstance.)

In sum, we conclude that the phrase "the recess" applies to both intra-session and inter-session recesses. If a Senate recess is so short that it does not require the consent of the House, it is too short to trigger the Recess Appointments Clause. See Art. I, § 5, cl. 4. And a recess lasting less than 10 days is presumptively too short as well.

IV

The second question concerns the scope of the phrase "vacancies *that may happen* during the recess of the Senate." Art. II, § 2, cl. 3 (emphasis added). All agree that the phrase applies to vacancies that initially occur during a recess. But does it also apply to vacancies that initially occur before a recess and continue to exist during the recess? In our view the phrase applies to both kinds of vacancy. We believe that the Clause's language, read literally, permits, though it does not naturally favor, our broader interpretation. We concede that the most natural meaning of "happens" as applied to a "vacancy" (at least to a modern ear) is that the vacancy "happens" when it initially occurs. See 1 Johnson 913 (defining "happen" in relevant part as meaning "[t]o fall out; to chance; to come to pass"). But that is not the only possible way to use the word. Thomas Jefferson wrote that the Clause is "certainly susceptible of [two] constructions." . . . It "may mean 'vacancies that may happen to be' or 'may happen to fall'" during a recess. . . .

. . .

In any event, the linguistic question here is not whether the phrase can be, but whether it must be, read more narrowly. The question is whether the Clause is ambiguous. *The Pocket Veto Case*, 279 U.S., at 690. And the broader reading, we believe, is at least a permissible reading of a " 'doubtful' " phrase. *Ibid.* We consequently go on to consider the Clause's purpose and historical practice.

The Clause's purpose strongly supports the broader interpretation. That purpose is to permit the President to obtain the assistance of subordinate officers when the Senate, due to its recess, cannot confirm them. . . .

. . .

Common sense also suggests that many recess appointees filled vacancies that arose before the recess began. [W]ith research assistance from the Supreme Court Library, we have examined a random sample of the recess appointments made by our two most recent Presidents, and have found that almost all of those appointments filled pre-recess vacancies: Of a sample of 21 recess appointments, 18 filled pre-recess vacancies and only 1 filled a vacancy that arose during the recess in which he was appointed. The precise date on which 2 of the vacancies arose could not be determined. . . .Taken together, we think it is a fair inference that a large proportion of the recess appointments in the history of the Nation have filled pre-existing vacancies.

Did the Senate object? Early on, there was some sporadic disagreement with the broad interpretation. . . . In any event, by 1862 Attorney General Bates could still refer to "the unbroken acquiescence of the Senate" in support of the broad interpretation. . . .

   . . .

In light of some linguistic ambiguity, the basic purpose of the Clause, and the historical practice we have described, we conclude that the phrase "all vacancies" includes vacancies that come into existence while the Senate is in session.

V

The third question concerns the calculation of the length of the Senate's "recess." On December 17, 2011, the Senate by unanimous consent adopted a resolution to convene "*pro forma* session[s]" only, with "no business . . . transacted," on every Tuesday and Friday from December 20,2011, through January 20, 2012. 2011 S. J. 923. At the end of each *pro forma* session, the Senate would "adjourn until" the following *pro forma* session. *Ibid.* During that period, the Senate convened and adjourned as agreed. It held *pro forma* sessions on December 20, 23, 27, and 30, and on January 3, 6, 10, 13, 17, and 20; and at the end of each *pro forma* session, it adjourned until the time and date of the next. *Id.,* at 923–924; . . . . The President made the recess appointments before us on January 4, 2012, in between the January 3 and the January 6 *pro forma* sessions. We must determine the significance of these sessions— that is, whether, for purposes of the Clause, we should treat them as periods when the Senate was in session or as periods when it was in recess. If the former, the period between January 3 and January 6 was a 3-day recess, which is too short to trigger the President's recess-appointment power. . . . If the latter, however, then the 3-day period was part of a much longer recess during which the President did have the power to make recess appointments,. . . .

In our view, however, the *pro forma* sessions count as sessions, not as periods of recess. We hold that, for purposes of the Recess Appointments Clause, the Senate is in session when it says it is, provided that, under its own rules, it retains the capacity to transact Senate business. The Senate met that standard here.

The standard we apply is consistent with the Constitution's broad delegation of authority to the Senate to determine how and when to conduct its business. The Constitution explicitly empowers the Senate to "determine the Rules of its Proceedings." Art. I, § 5, cl. 2. And we have held that "all matters of method are open to the determination" of the Senate, as long as there is "a reasonable relation between the mode or method of proceeding established by the rule and the result which is sought to be attained" and the rule does not "ignore constitutional restraints or violate fundamental rights." *United States* v. *Ballin*, 144 U.S. 1, 5 (1892).

   . . .

■ JUSTICE SCALIA, with whom CHIEF JUSTICE ROBERTS, JUSTICE THOMAS and JUSTICE ALITO join, concurring in the judgment.

Except where the Constitution or a valid federal law provides otherwise, all "Officers of the United States" must be appointed by the President "by and with the Advice and Consent of the Senate." U.S. Const., Art. II, § 2, cl. 2. That general rule is subject to an exception: "The President shall have Power to fill up all Vacancies that may happen during the Recess of the Senate, by granting Commissions which shall expire at the End of their next Session." *Id.,* § 2, cl. 3. This case requires us to decide whether the Recess Appointments Clause authorized three appointments made by President Obama to the National Labor Relations Board in January 2012 without the Senate's consent.

To prevent the President's recess-appointment power from nullifying the Senate's role in the appointment process, the Constitution cabins that power in two significant ways. First, it may be exercised only in "the Recess of the Senate," that is, the intermission between two formal legislative sessions. Second, it may be used to fill only those vacancies that "happen during the Recess," that is, offices that become vacant during that intermission. Both conditions are clear from the Constitution's text and structure, and both were well understood at the founding. The Court of Appeals correctly held that the appointments here at issue are invalid because they did not meet either condition.

Today's Court agrees that the appointments were invalid, but for the far narrower reason that they were made during a 3-day break in the Senate's session. On its way to that result, the majority sweeps away the key textual limitations on the recess-appointment power. It holds, first, that the President can make appointments without the Senate's participation even during short breaks in the middle of the Senate's session, and second, that those appointments can fill offices that became vacant long before the break in which they were filled. The majority justifies those atextual results on an adverse-possession theory of executive authority: Presidents have long claimed the powers in question, and the Senate has not disputed those claims with sufficient vigor, so the Court should not "upset the compromises and working arrangements that the elected branches of Government themselves have reached." . . .

The Court's decision transforms the recess-appointment power from a tool carefully designed to fill a narrow and specific need into a weapon to be wielded by future Presidents against future Senates. To reach that result, the majority casts aside the plain, original meaning of the constitutional text in deference to late-arising historical practices that are ambiguous at best. The majority's insistence on deferring to the Executive's untenably broad interpretation of the power is in clear conflict with our precedent and forebodes a diminution of this Court's role in controversies involving the separation of powers and the structure of government. I concur in the judgment only.

I.   Our Responsibility

Today's majority disregards two overarching principles that ought to guide our consideration of the questions presented here. First, the Constitution's core, government-structuring provisions are no less critical to preserving liberty than are the later adopted provisions of the Bill of Rights. . . .

Second and relatedly, when questions involving the Constitution's government-structuring provisions are presented in a justiciable case, it is the solemn responsibility of the Judicial Branch " 'to say what the law is.' " . . . This Court does not defer to the other branches' resolution of such controversies; as Justice Kennedy has previously written, our role is in no way "lessened" because it might be said that "the two political branches are adjusting their own powers between themselves." . . .

Our decision in [INS v.] Chadha [462 U.S. 919 (1984)] illustrates that principle. There, we held that a statutory provision authorizing one House of Congress to cancel an executive action taken pursuant to statutory authority—a so-called "legislative veto"—exceeded the bounds of Congress's authority under the Constitution. . . . We did not hesitate to hold the legislative veto unconstitutional even though Congress had enacted, and the President had signed, nearly 300 similar provisions over the course of 50 years. . . . Just the opposite: We said the other branches' enthusiasm for the legislative veto "sharpened rather than blunted" our review.... Likewise, when the charge is made that a practice "enhances the President's powers beyond" what the Constitution permits, "[i]t is no answer ... to say that Congress surrendered its authority by its own hand." *Clinton*, 524 U.S., at 451 (Kennedy, J., concurring). "[O]ne Congress cannot yield up its own powers, much less those of other Congresses to follow. Abdication of responsibility is not part of the constitutional design." ...

Of course, where a governmental practice has been open, widespread, and unchallenged since the early days of the Republic, the practice should guide our interpretation of an ambiguous constitutional provision.... But " '[p]ast practice does not, by itself, create power.'" *Medellín* v. *Texas*, 552 U.S. 491, 532 (2008) (quoting *Dames & Moore* v. *Regan*, 453 U.S. 654, 686 (1981)). That is a necessary corollary of the principle that the political branches cannot by agreement alter the constitutional structure. Plainly, then, a self-aggrandizing practice adopted by one branch well after the founding, often challenged, and never before blessed by this Court—in other words, the sort of practice on which the majority relies in this case—does not relieve us of our duty to interpret the Constitution in light of its text, structure, and original understanding.

. . .

I concur in the judgment only.

3. PRESIDENTIAL IMMUNITIES

United States v. Nixon

418 U.S. 683, 94 S.Ct. 3090, 41 L.Ed.2d 1039 (1974).

■ MR. CHIEF JUSTICE Burger delivered the opinion of the Court.

This litigation presents for review the denial of a motion, filed on behalf of the President of the United States, in the case of United States v. Mitchell et al.... to quash a third-party subpoena *duces tecum* issued by the United States District Court for the District of Columbia ... The subpoena directed the President to produce certain tape recordings and documents relating to his conversations with aides and advisers. The court rejected the President's claims of absolute executive privilege ... The President appealed to the Court of Appeals. We granted the United States' petition for certiorari before judgment, ...

On March 1, 1974, a grand jury of the United States District Court for the District of Columbia returned an indictment charging seven named individuals[3] with various offenses, including conspiracy to defraud the United States and to obstruct justice. Although he was not designated as such in the indictment, the grand jury named the President, among others, as an unindicted coconspirator. On April 18, 1974, upon motion of the Special Prosecutor, a subpoena *duces tecum* was issued ... to the President by the United States District Court and made returnable on May 2, 1974. This subpoena required the production, in advance of the September 9 trial date, of certain tapes, memoranda, papers, transcripts, or other writings relating to certain precisely identified meetings between the President and others.... On May 1, 1974,

---

[3]   The seven defendants were John N. Mitchell, H.R. Haldeman, John D. Ehrlichman, Charles W. Colson, Robert C. Mardian, Kenneth W. Parkinson, and Gordon Strachan. Each had occupied either a position of responsibility on the White House staff or the Committee for the Re-election of the President. Colson entered a guilty plea on another charge and is no longer a defendant.

the President's counsel, filed a "special appearance" and a motion to quash the subpoena . . .

On May 20, 1974, the District Court denied the motion to quash . . .

. . .

II.   Justiciability

In the District Court the President's counsel argued that the court lacked jurisdiction to issue the subpoena because the matter was an intra-branch dispute between a subordinate and superior officer of the Executive Branch and hence not subject to judicial resolution. . . . The President's counsel . . . views the present dispute as essentially a "jurisdictional" dispute within the Executive Branch which he analogizes to a dispute between two congressional committees. Since the Executive Branch has exclusive authority and absolute discretion to decide whether to prosecute a case, . . . , it is contended that a President's decision is final in determining what evidence is to be used in a given criminal case. . . .

Our starting point is the nature of the proceeding for which the evidence is sought—here a pending criminal prosecution. . . . [The regulation under which the Special Prosecutor is acting] gives the Special Prosecutor explicit power to contest the invocation of executive privilege. . . .

So long as this regulation is extant it has the force of law. . . .

[Although] it is theoretically possible for the Attorney General to amend or revoke the regulation defining the Special Prosecutor's authority . . . he has not done so. So long as the regulation remains in force the Executive Branch is bound by it. . . .

. . .

IV.   The Claim of Privilege

A.

. . . [W]e turn to the claim that the subpoena should be quashed because it demands "confidential conversations between a President and his close advisors that it would be inconsistent with the public interest to produce." The first contention is a broad claim that the separation of powers doctrine precludes judicial review of a President's claim of privilege. The second contention is that if he does not prevail on the claim of absolute privilege, the court should hold as a matter of constitutional law that the privilege prevails over the subpoena *duces tecum*.

In the performance of assigned constitutional duties each branch of the Government must initially interpret the Constitution, and the interpretation of its powers by any branch is due great respect from the others. The President's counsel, as we have noted, reads the Constitution as providing an absolute privilege of confidentiality for all presidential communications. Many decisions of this Court, however, have unequivocally reaffirmed the holding of Marbury v. Madison, . . . that "it is emphatically the province and duty of the judicial department to say what the law is." . . .

. . .

B.

In support of his claim of absolute privilege the President's counsel urges two grounds one of which is common to all governments and one of which is peculiar to our system of separation of powers. The first ground is the valid need for protection of communications between high Government officials and those who advise and assist them in the performance of their manifold duties; the importance of this confidentiality is too plain to require further discussion. Human experience teaches that those who expect public dissemination of their remarks may well temper candor with a concern for appearances and for their own interests to the detriment of the decisionmaking process. Whatever the nature of the privilege of confidentiality of presidential communications in the exercise of Art. II powers, the privilege can be said to derive from the supremacy of each branch within its own assigned area of constitutional duties. Certain powers and privileges flow from the nature of enumerated powers; the protection of the confidentiality of Presidential communications has similar constitutional underpinnings.

The second ground asserted by the President's counsel in support of the claim of absolute privilege rests on the doctrine of separation of powers. Here it is argued that the independence of the Executive Branch within its own sphere insulates a president from a judicial subpoena in an ongoing criminal prosecution, and thereby protects confidential Presidential communications.

However, neither the doctrine of separation of powers, nor the need for confidentiality of high level communications without more, can sustain an absolute, unqualified Presidential privilege of immunity from judicial process under all circumstances. The President's need for complete candor and objectivity from advisers calls for great deference from the courts. However, when the privilege depends solely on the broad, undifferentiated claim of public interest in the confidentiality of such conversations, a confrontation with other values arises. Absent a claim of need to protect military, diplomatic or sensitive national security secrets, we find it difficult to accept the argument that even the very important interest in confidentiality of Presidential communications is significantly diminished by production of such material for *in camera* inspection with all the protection that a district court will be obliged to provide.

The impediment that an absolute, unqualified privilege would place in the way of the primary constitutional duty of the Judicial Branch to do justice in criminal prosecutions would plainly conflict with the function of the courts under Art. III. In designing the structure of our Government and dividing and allocating the sovereign power among three coequal branches, the Framers of the Constitution sought to provide a comprehensive system, but the separate powers were not intended to operate with absolute independence. . . . To read the Art. II powers of the President as providing an absolute privilege as against a subpoena essential to enforcement of criminal statutes on no more than a generalized claim of the public interest in confidentiality of nonmilitary and nondiplomatic discussions would upset the constitutional balance of "a workable government" and gravely impair the role of the courts under Art. III.

C.

Since we conclude that the legitimate needs of the judicial process may outweigh Presidential privilege, it is necessary to resolve those competing interests in a manner that preserves the essential functions of each branch. The right and indeed the duty to resolve that question does not free the Judiciary from according high respect to the representations made on behalf of the President. United States v. Burr, 25 F. Cas. 187, 190, 191–192 (No. 14,694) (CC Va. 1807).

. . . The privilege is fundamental to the operation of Government and inextricably rooted in the separation of powers under the Constitution. . . .

But this presumptive privilege must be considered in light of our historic commitment to the rule of law. . . . The very integrity of the judicial system and public confidence in the system depend on full disclosure of all the facts, within the framework of the rules of evidence. To ensure that justice is done, it is imperative to the function of courts that compulsory process be available for the production of evidence needed either by the prosecution or by the defense.

Only recently the Court restated the ancient proposition of law, albeit in the context of a grand jury inquiry rather than a trial, "that 'the public . . . has a right to every man's evidence,' except for those persons protected by a constitutional, common-law or statutory privilege." . . .

. . .

The right to the production of all evidence at a criminal trial . . . has constitutional dimensions. The Sixth Amendment explicitly confers upon every defendant in a criminal trial the right "to be confronted with the witnesses against him" and "to have compulsory process for obtaining witnesses in his favor." Moreover, the Fifth Amendment also guarantees that no person shall be deprived of liberty without due process of law. It is the manifest duty of the courts to vindicate those guarantees, and to accomplish that it is essential that all relevant and admissible evidence be produced.

In this case we must weigh the importance of the general privilege of confidentiality of Presidential communications in performance of the President's responsibilities against the inroads of such a privilege on the fair administration of criminal justice. The interest in preserving confidentiality is weighty indeed and entitled to great respect. However we cannot conclude that advisers will be moved to temper the candor of their remarks by the infrequent occasions of disclosure because of the possibility that such conversations will be called for in the context of a criminal prosecution.

On the other hand, the allowance of the privilege to withhold evidence that is demonstrably relevant in a criminal trial would cut deeply into the guarantee of due process of law and gravely impair the basic function of the courts. . . .

We conclude that [the] generalized assertion of privilege must yield to the demonstrated, specific need for evidence in a pending criminal trial.

. . .

Affirmed.

■ MR. JUSTICE REHNQUIST took no part in the consideration or decision of these cases.

Clinton v. Jones

520 U.S. 681, 117 S.Ct. 1636, 137 L.Ed.2d 945 (1997).

■ JUSTICE STEVENS delivered the opinion of the Court.

This case raises a constitutional and a prudential question concerning the Office of the President of the United States. Respondent, a private citizen, seeks to recover damages from the current occupant of that office based on actions allegedly taken before his term began. The President submits that in all but the most exceptional cases the Constitution requires federal courts to defer such litigation until his term ends and that, in any event, respect for the office warrants such a stay. Despite the force of the arguments supporting the President's submissions, we conclude that they must be rejected.

I

. . . In 1991 [President Clinton] was the Governor of the State of Arkansas. Respondent, Paula Corbin Jones . . . lived in Arkansas [in 1991], and was an employee of the Arkansas Industrial Development Commission.

On May 6, 1994, she commenced this action in the United States District Court . . .

Th[e] allegations [in the complaint] principally describe events that are said to have occurred on the afternoon of May 8, 1991, during an official conference held at the Excelsior Hotel in Little Rock, Arkansas. The Governor delivered a speech at the conference; respondent—working as a state employee—staffed the registration desk. She alleges that . . . the Governor . . . made "abhorrent" sexual advances that she vehemently rejected. She further claims that her superiors at work subsequently dealt with her in a hostile and rude manner, and changed her duties to punish her for rejecting those advances. . . .

. . . Her complaint contains four counts. The first charges that petitioner, acting under color of state law, deprived her of rights protected by the Constitution, in violation of . . . 42 U.S.C. § 1983. . . . [T]he alleged misconduct of petitioner was unrelated to any of his official duties as President of the United States and, indeed, occurred before he was elected to that office.

II

. . .

The District Judge denied the motion to dismiss on immunity grounds and ruled that discovery in the case could go forward, but ordered any trial stayed until the end of petitioner's Presidency. . . .'

Both parties appealed. A divided panel of the Court of Appeals affirmed the denial of the motion to dismiss, but because it regarded the order postponing the trial until the President leaves office as the "functional equivalent" of a grant of temporary immunity, it reversed that order. . . .'

. . .

III

. . .

. . . [There are] two important constitutional issues not encompassed within the questions presented by the petition for certiorari that we need not address today.

First, because the claim of immunity is asserted in a federal court and relies heavily on the doctrine of separation of powers . . . , it is not necessary to consider or decide whether a comparable claim might succeed in a state tribunal. If this case were being heard in a state forum, instead of advancing a separation of powers argument, petitioner would presumably rely on federalism and comity concerns1[13] as well as the interest in protecting federal officials from possible local prejudice that underlies the authority to remove certain cases brought against federal officers from a state to a federal court . . .

Second, our decision rejecting the immunity claim and allowing the case to proceed does not require us to confront the question whether a court may compel the

---

[13] Because the Supremacy Clause makes federal law "the supreme Law of the Land," Art. VI, cl. 2, any direct control by a state court over the President, who has principal responsibility to ensure that those laws are "faithfully executed," Art. II, § 3, may implicate concerns that are quite different from the interbranch separation of powers questions addressed here. . . .

attendance of the President at any specific time or place. We assume that the testimony of the President, both for discovery and for use at trial, may be taken at the White House at a time that will accommodate his busy schedule, and that, if a trial is held, there would be no necessity for the President to attend in person, though he could elect to do so.[14]

IV

Petitioner's principal submission—that "in all but the most exceptional cases," the Constitution affords the President temporary immunity from civil damages litigation arising out of events that occurred before he took office—cannot be sustained on the basis of precedent.

Only three sitting Presidents have been defendants in civil litigation involving their actions prior to taking office. Complaints against Theodore Roosevelt and Harry Truman had been dismissed before they took office; the dismissals were affirmed after their respective inaugurations. Two companion cases arising out of an automobile accident were filed against John F. Kennedy in 1960 during the Presidential campaign. After taking office, he unsuccessfully argued that his status as Commander in Chief gave him a right to a stay under the Soldiers' and Sailors' Civil Relief Act of 1940. . . . The motion for a stay was denied by the District Court, and the matter was settled out of court. Thus, none of those cases sheds any light on the constitutional issue before us.

The principal rationale for affording certain public servants immunity from suits for money damages arising out of their official acts is inapplicable to unofficial conduct. . . . That rationale provided the principal basis for our holding that a former President of the United States was "entitled to absolute immunity from damages liability predicated on his official acts," [Nixon v.] *Fitzgerald*, 457 U.S. [731 (1982)] . . . Our central concern was to avoid rendering the President "unduly cautious in the discharge of his official duties." . . .

This reasoning provides no support for an immunity for *unofficial* conduct. As we explained in *Fitzgerald*, "the sphere of protected action must be related closely to the immunity's justifying purposes." . . . Because of the President's broad responsibilities, we recognized in that case an immunity from damages claims arising out of official acts extending to the "outer perimeter of his authority." . . . But we have never suggested that the President, or any other official, has an immunity that extends beyond the scope of any action taken in an official capacity. . . .'

. . .

Petitioner's effort to construct an immunity from suit for unofficial acts grounded purely in the identity of his office is unsupported by precedent.

. . .

VI

Petitioner's strongest argument supporting his immunity claim is based on the text and structure of the Constitution. He does not contend that the occupant of the Office of the President is "above the law," in the sense that his conduct is entirely immune from judicial scrutiny. The President argues merely for a postponement of the judicial proceedings that will determine whether he violated any law. His argument is grounded in the character of the office that was created by Article II of the

---

[14] Although Presidents have responded to written interrogatories, given depositions, and provided videotaped trial testimony, no sitting President has ever testified, or been ordered to testify, in open court.

Constitution, and relies on separation of powers principles that have structured our constitutional arrangement since the founding.

As a starting premise, petitioner contends that he occupies a unique office with powers and responsibilities so vast and important that the public interest demands that he devote his undivided time and attention to his public duties. He submits that—given the nature of the office—the doctrine of separation of powers places limits on the authority of the Federal Judiciary to interfere with the Executive Branch that would be transgressed by allowing this action to proceed.

We have no dispute with the initial premise of the argument. Former presidents, from George Washington to George Bush, have consistently endorsed petitioner's characterization of the office. . . . Thus, while we suspect that even in our modern era there remains some truth to Chief Justice Marshall's suggestion that the duties of the Presidency are not entirely "unremitting," United States v. Burr, 25 F. Cas. 30, 34 (C.C.Va.1807), we accept the initial premise of the Executive's argument.

It does not follow, however, that separation of powers principles would be violated by allowing this action to proceed. . . .

. . . [I]n this case there is no suggestion that the Federal Judiciary is being asked to perform any function that might in some way be described as "executive." Respondent is merely asking the courts to exercise their core Article III jurisdiction to decide cases and controversies. Whatever the outcome of this case, there is no possibility that the decision will curtail the scope of the official powers of the Executive Branch. The litigation of questions that relate entirely to the unofficial conduct of the individual who happens to be the President poses no perceptible risk of misallocation of either judicial power or executive power.

. . . [P]etitioner contends that this particular case—as well as the potential additional litigation that an affirmance of the Court of Appeals judgment might spawn—may impose an unacceptable burden on the President's time and energy, and thereby impair the effective performance of his office.

Petitioner's predictive judgment finds little support in either history or the relatively narrow compass of the issues raised in this particular case. As we have already noted, in the more than 200-year history of the Republic, only three sitting Presidents have been subjected to suits for their private actions. If the past is any indicator, it seems unlikely that a deluge of such litigation will ever engulf the Presidency. As for the case at hand, if properly managed by the District Court, it appears to us highly unlikely to occupy any substantial amount of petitioner's time.

Of greater significance, petitioner errs by presuming that interactions between the Judicial Branch and the Executive, even quite burdensome interactions, necessarily rise to the level of constitutionally forbidden impairment of the Executive's ability to perform its constitutionally mandated functions. . . . The fact that a federal court's exercise of its traditional Article III jurisdiction may significantly burden the time and attention of the Chief Executive is not sufficient to establish a violation of the Constitution. Two long-settled propositions, first announced by Chief Justice Marshall, support that conclusion.

First, we have long held that when the President takes official action, the Court has the authority to determine whether he has acted within the law. . . .

Second, it is also settled that the President is subject to judicial process in appropriate circumstances. Although Thomas Jefferson apparently thought otherwise, Chief Justice Marshall, when presiding in the treason trial of Aaron Burr, ruled that a subpoena *duces tecum* could be directed to the President. United States v. Burr, 25 F.

Cas. 30 (No. 14692D) (CC Va. 1807). We unequivocally and emphatically endorsed Marshall's position when we held that President Nixon was obligated to comply with a subpoena commanding him to produce certain tape recordings of his conversations with his aides. . . .

. . .

VII

The Court of Appeals described the District Court's discretionary decision to stay the trial as the "functional equivalent" of a grant of temporary immunity. . . . Although we ultimately conclude that the stay should not have been granted, we think the issue is more difficult than the opinion of the Court of Appeals suggests.

Strictly speaking the stay was not the functional equivalent of the constitutional immunity that petitioner claimed, because the District Court ordered discovery to proceed. Moreover, a stay of either the trial or discovery might be justified by considerations that do not require the recognition of any constitutional immunity. The District Court has broad discretion to stay proceedings as an incident to its power to control its own docket. . . . The high respect that is owed to the office of the Chief Executive, though not justifying a rule of categorical immunity, is a matter that should inform the conduct of the entire proceeding, including the timing and scope of discovery.

Nevertheless, we are persuaded that it was an abuse of discretion for the District Court to defer the trial until after the President leaves office. Such a lengthy and categorical stay takes no account whatever of the respondent's interest in bringing the case to trial. . . .

The decision to postpone the trial was, furthermore, premature. The proponent of a stay bears the burden of establishing its need. . . . In this case, at the stage at which the District Court made its ruling, there was no way to assess whether a stay of trial after the completion of discovery would be warranted. Other than the fact that a trial may consume some of the President's time and attention, there is nothing in the record to enable a judge to assess the potential harm that may ensue from scheduling the trial promptly after discovery is concluded. . . .'

VIII

We add a final comment on two matters that are discussed at length in the briefs: the risk that our decision will generate a large volume of politically motivated harassing and frivolous litigation, and the danger that national security concerns might prevent the President from explaining a legitimate need for a continuance.

We are not persuaded that either of these risks is serious. Most frivolous and vexatious litigation is terminated at the pleading stage or on summary judgment, with little if any personal involvement by the defendant. . . . Moreover, the availability of sanctions provides a significant deterrent to litigation directed at the President in his unofficial capacity for purposes of political gain or harassment. History indicates that the likelihood that a significant number of such cases will be filed is remote. . . .

If Congress deems it appropriate to afford the President stronger protection, it may respond with appropriate legislation. . . . If the Constitution embodied the rule that the President advocates, Congress, of course, could not repeal it. But our holding today raises no barrier to a statutory response to these concerns.

The Federal District Court has jurisdiction to decide this case. Like every other citizen who properly invokes that jurisdiction, respondent has a right to an orderly disposition of her claims. Accordingly, the judgment of the Court of Appeals is affirmed.

It is so ordered.[a]

NOTE ON THE APPLICABILITY OF EXECUTIVE PRIVILEGE TO THE VICE PRESIDENCY

In Cheney v. United States District Court for the District of Columbia, 542 U.S. 367 (2004), the Supreme Court was asked to apply Executive Privilege considerations to a case seeking information from, among others, Vice President Richard Cheney. The *Cheney* litigation began when various public interest groups sued the Vice President and the National Energy Policy Development Group (NEPDG) that President Bush directed him to head. The plaintiffs, relying on the Federal Advisory Committee Act (FACA), sought to obtain records of the group's meetings. The defendants responded by arguing, among other things, that applying FACA to the Vice-President in a case like this would be problematic under separation-of-powers/executive privilege-type doctrines. After having its arguments largely rejected in the district court and the Court of Appeals, the Vice President sought relief in the Supreme Court.

Although the Court did not direct an outcome in the case, but rather remanded it for more consideration, the Court did send signals that the lower courts should be respectful of the Executive Branch's need to be free from outside interference: "All courts should be mindful of the burdens imposed on the Executive Branch in any future proceedings. Special considerations applicable to the President and the Vice-President suggest that the courts should be sensitive to requests by the Government for [immediate] appeals to reexamine, for example, whether the [FACA really does apply in these circumstances]."

The Court distinguished U.S. v. Nixon on the ground that it had involved a criminal proceeding in which the necessity for relevant evidence was stronger. By contrast, civil cases—like those under the FACA—do not implicate such a compelling need for "every man's evidence."

Consider the implications of the following additional language in *Cheney* for two of the other major separation of powers cases presented earlier in this chapter— Morrison v. Olson and Clinton v. Jones:

"The observation in *Nixon* that production of confidential information would not disrupt the functioning of the Executive Branch cannot be applied in a mechanistic fashion to civil litigation. In the criminal justice system, there are various constraints, albeit imperfect, to filter out insubstantial legal claims. The decision to prosecute a criminal case, for example, is made by a publicly accountable prosecutor subject to budgetary considerations. . . . In contrast, there are no analogous checks in the civil discovery process here. Although under Federal Rule of Civil Procedure 11, sanctions are available, and private attorneys owe an obligation of candor to the judicial tribunal, those safeguards have proved insufficient to discourage filing of meritless claims against the executive Branch. 'In view of the visibility of' the Offices of the President and the Vice-President and the 'effect of their actions on countless people,' they are 'easily identifiable target[s] for suits for civil damages.' "

The *Cheney* Court did not discuss whether, why and how Executive Privilege claims by Vice Presidents might be different than those by the President or Cabinet members, in light of the fact that the Vice President performs some legislative duties

---

[a]   Justice Breyer filed an opinion concurring in the judgment.

(e.g., presiding over and casting tie-breaking votes in the Senate), is not removable by the President the way cabinet members are, and is not required by the Constitution to be elected on a Presidential ticket. For discussion of these issues, and the *Cheney* case more generally, see Vikram Amar, *The Cheney Decision—A Missed Chance to Straighten Out Some Muddled Issues*, 2004 Cato Sup. Ct. Review 185 (2004).

NOTE ON THE IMPEACHMENT OF PRESIDENT WILLIAM CLINTON

The Congressional Act upheld in the *Morrison* case, combined with information unearthed in the *Clinton v. Jones* litigation, helped set the stage for the impeachment of President William Jefferson Clinton by the House of Representatives in December 1998. President Clinton was ultimately acquitted by the Senate in February 1999, and served out the remainder of his second term. The Clinton impeachment experience raised a host of constitutional questions, including the following: What precisely does the Article II's "high crimes and misdemeanors" standard mean?; Can this standard be satisfied by "private" misdeeds that do not implicate misuse of federal resources?; How do the impeachment standards for Presidents relate to those for other officials, like federal judges?; Is Congress under any constitutional duty to impeach where "high crimes and misdemeanors" may be present?; What role should the views of the public play in Congressional impeachment proceedings?; and What alternatives does Congress have to impeachment in dealing with alleged Presidential misdeeds? These and other profound constitutional questions never made their way into a court, but had to be dealt with by conscientious legislators as well as the rest of the country. For an introduction to some of the most vexing issues, see Klarman, *Constitutional Fetishism and the Clinton Impeachment Debate*, 85 Va. L.Rev. 631 (1999) and Vikram Amar, *The Truth, the Whole Truth and Nothing But the Truth About 'High Crimes and Misdemeanors' and the Constitution's Impeachment Process,"* 16 Const. Comm. 403 (1999).

PART 3

GOVERNMENT AND THE INDIVIDUAL: THE PROTECTION OF LIBERTY AND PROPERTY UNDER THE DUE PROCESS AND EQUAL PROTECTION CLAUSES

In this Part, the emphasis shifts from exploring the constitutional relationships among different parts of the governmental structure to the protection of individual rights from interference by all levels and branches of government. The central question is definition of the proper judicial role in giving content to the vague language of the due process clauses of the fifth and fourteenth amendments, and of the equal protection clause of the fourteenth amendment.

Chapter 8 concerns the interrelationship between the bill of rights and the Civil War amendments to the Constitution. Chapter 9 deals with the application of the due process clause. Chapter 10 discusses the equal protection clause. Chapter 11 completes the analysis with an examination of constitutional norms of fair procedure. (The discrete problems of constitutional protection of speech and conscience under the first amendment are reserved for Part IV.)

Chapter 12 returns to an issue of division of national and state power. After examining the application of the Civil War amendments to private conduct, the bulk of this chapter concerns the extent of Congressional power to enforce the amendments.

he's not a civil war slavery denier

CHAPTER 8

THE BILL OF RIGHTS, THE CIVIL WAR AMENDMENTS AND THEIR INTER-RELATIONSHIP

Introduction. In Chapter 1 it was noted that the original constitution included only a few limitations upon government power to regulate life, liberty and property. The principal restraints on state regulation were those forbidding the impairment of the obligation of contracts (Art. I, § 10), banning bills of attainder and ex post facto laws (Art. I, § 10), and guaranteeing citizens of one state the right to enjoy in another state "all the Privileges and Immunities" of its own citizens (Art. IV, § 2).

The Bill of Rights (Amendments 1–10) adopted in 1791 imposed a substantial series of protections for the individual against government. Almost 80 years later the Civil War Amendments (13, 14, and 15) specifically imposed restraints on the power of states to regulate the personal and property interests of their citizens.

The primary purpose of this Chapter is to give a brief historical introduction to the Court's application of these three sets of restraints on the power of government to regulate liberty and property. A major focus will be the dispute over the interrelationship between the Bill of Rights and the Civil War Amendments.

Early interpretations of the individual rights provisions contained in the text of the original Constitution, the Bill of Rights, and the Civil War Amendments should be augmented, however, by a preliminary reference to the possibility of nontextual constitutional restraints stemming from principles of natural justice invoked and elaborated by courts. This possibility was raised early in Calder v. Bull, 3 U.S. (3 Dall.) 386 (1798), where two Justices sharply disagreed, in an historically important exchange of *dicta*, over the propriety of basing a determination of unconstitutionality on principles not specified in the Constitution. Justice Chase upheld the challenged state law, but wrote:

"I cannot subscribe to the omnipotence of a state Legislature, or that it is absolute and without control; although its authority should not be expressly restrained by the constitution, or fundamental law, of the state. The people of the United States erected their constitutions or forms of government, to establish justice, to promote the general welfare, to secure the blessings of liberty, and to protect their persons and property from violence. The purposes for which men enter into society will determine the nature and terms of the social compact; and as they are the foundation of the legislative power, they will decide what are the proper objects of it: The nature, and ends of legislative power will limit the exercise of it. This fundamental principle flows from the very nature of our free Republican governments, that no man should be compelled to do what the laws do not require; nor to refrain from acts which the laws permit. There are acts which the federal, or state, Legislature cannot do, without exceeding their authority. There are certain vital principles in our free Republican governments, which will determine and overrule an apparent and flagrant abuse of legislative power; as to authorize manifest injustice by positive law; or to take away that security for personal liberty, or private property, for the protection whereof the government was established. An act of the Legislature (for I cannot call it a law) contrary to the great first principles of the social compact, cannot be considered a rightful exercise of legislative authority. . . . A few instances will suffice to explain what I mean. A law that punished a citizen for an innocent action, or, in other words, for an act, which, when done, was in violation of no existing law; a law that destroys, or impairs, the lawful private contracts of citizens; a law that makes a man a judge in his own cause; or a law that takes property from A. and gives it to B. It is against all reason and justice, for a people to entrust a Legislature with such powers; and, therefore, it cannot be presumed that they have done it. The genius, the nature, and the spirit, of our state governments, amount to a prohibition of such acts of legislation; and the general principles of law and reason forbid them. . . . To maintain that our federal, or state, Legislature possesses such powers, if they had not been expressly restrained, would, in my opinion, be a political heresy, altogether inadmissible in our free republican governments."

Justice Iredell responded:

"[S]ome speculative jurists have held, that a legislative act against natural justice must, in itself, be void; but I cannot think that, under such a government, any court of justice would possess a power to declare it so. . . .

"[I]t has been the policy of all the American States, which have, individually, framed their state constitutions since the revolution, and of the people of the United States, when they framed the federal constitution, to define with precision the objects of the legislative power, and to restrain its exercise within marked and settled boundaries. If any act of Congress, or of the legislature of a state, violates those constitutional provisions, it is unquestionably void. . . . If on the other hand, the legislature of the union, or the legislature of any member of the union, shall pass a law, within the general scope of their constitutional power, the court cannot pronounce it to be void, merely because it is, in their judgment, contrary to the principles of natural justice. The ideas of natural justice are regulated by no fixed standard; the ablest and the purest men have differed upon the subject; and all that the court could properly say, in such an event, would be, that the legislature (possessed of an equal right of opinion) had passed an act which, in the opinion of the judges, was inconsistent with the abstract principles of natural justice."

The substance of this debate has been a continuing theme in constitutional law, whether framed as a debate about an expansive interpretation of an open-ended text or about a "noninterpretive" principle of fundamental right. For discussion of the contemporary dimensions of the debate, compare Grey, *Do We Have an Unwritten Constitution?*, 27 Stan.L.Rev. 703 (1975); Perry, *The Constitution, The Courts, and Human Rights* (1982); and Sedler, *The Legitimacy Debate in Constitutional Adjudication*, 44 Ohio St.L.J. 10 (1983); with Ely, *Foreword: On Discovering Fundamental Values*, 92 Harv.L.Rev. 5 (1978); and Linde, *Judges, Critics, and the Realist Tradition*, 82 Yale L.J. 227 (1972).

1.   THE PRE–CIVIL WAR BACKGROUND

The Privileges and Immunities Clause of Article IV—Early Interpretations

Corfield v. Coryell

4 Wash.C.C. 371, 6 Fed.Cas. 546 (1823).

A New Jersey statute of 1820 made it unlawful for any person who was not "an actual inhabitant and resident" of the state to rake or gather clams, oysters, or shells in any of the rivers, bays, or waters of the state. The statute was challenged by a

Pennsylvania citizen gathering oysters in New Jersey waters. In disposing of the claim made under Article IV, section 2, Supreme Court Justice Washington, sitting on circuit, said:

"The next question is, whether this act infringes that section of the constitution which declares that 'the citizens of each state shall be entitled to all the privileges and immunities of citizens in the several states?' The inquiry is, what are the privileges and immunities of citizens in the several states? We feel no hesitation in confining these expressions to those privileges and immunities which are, in their nature, fundamental; which belong, of right, to the citizens of all free governments; and which have, at all times, been enjoyed by the citizens of the several states which compose this Union, from the time of their becoming free, independent, and sovereign. What these fundamental principles are, it would perhaps be more tedious than difficult to enumerate. They may, however, be all comprehended under the following general heads: Protection by the government; the enjoyment of life and liberty, with the right to acquire and possess property of every kind, and to pursue and obtain happiness and safety; subject nevertheless to such restraints as the government may justly prescribe for the general good of the whole. The right of a citizen of one state to pass through, or to reside in any other state, for purposes of trade, agriculture, professional pursuits, or otherwise; to claim the benefit of the writ of habeas corpus; to institute and maintain actions of any kind in the courts of the state; to take hold and dispose of property, either real or personal; and an exemption from higher taxes or impositions than are paid by the other citizens of the state; may be mentioned as some of the particular privileges and immunities of citizens, which are clearly embraced by the general description of privileges deemed to be fundamental: to which may be added, the elective franchise, as regulated and established by the laws or constitution of the state in which it is to be exercised. These, and many others which might be mentioned, are, strictly speaking, privileges and immunities, and the enjoyment of them by the citizens of each state, in every other state, was manifestly calculated (to use the expressions of the preamble of the corresponding provision in the old articles of confederation) 'the better to secure and perpetuate mutual friendship and intercourse among the people of the different states of the Union.' But we cannot accede to the proposition which was insisted on by the counsel, that, under this provision of the constitution, the citizens of the several states are permitted to participate in all the rights which belong exclusively to the citizens of any other particular state, merely upon the ground that they are enjoyed by those citizens; much less, that in regulating the use of the common property of the citizens of such state, the legislature is bound to extend to the citizens of all the other states the same advantages as are secured to their own citizens. A several fishery, either as the right to it respects running fish, or such as are stationary, such as oysters, clams, and the like, is as much the property of the individual to whom it belongs, as dry land, or land covered by water; and is equally protected by the laws of the state against the aggressions of others, whether citizens or strangers. Where those private rights do not exist to the exclusion of the common right, that of fishing belongs to all the citizens or subjects of the state. It is the property of all; to be enjoyed by them in subordination to the laws which regulate its use. They may be considered as tenants in common of this property; and they are so exclusively entitled to the use of it, that it cannot be enjoyed by others without the tacit consent, or the express permission of the sovereign who has the power to regulate its use."

Paul v. Virginia

75 U.S. (8 Wall.) 168, 180 (1868).

The Court upheld a state law imposing special burdens on insurance companies incorporated in other states as a condition of doing business on the ground that a corporation is not a citizen protected by the privileges and immunities clause of Article IV. In construing the clause the Court said:

"It was undoubtedly the object of the clause in question to place the citizens of each State upon the same footing with citizens of other States, so far as the advantages resulting from citizenship in those States are concerned. It relieves them from the disabilities of alienage in other States; it inhibits discriminating legislation against them by other States; it gives them the right of free ingress into other States, and egress from them; it insures to them in other States the same freedom possessed by the citizens of those States in the acquisition and enjoyment of property and in the pursuit of happiness; and it secures to them in other States the equal protection of their laws. It has been justly said that no provision in the Constitution has tended so strongly to constitute the citizens of the United States one people as this. Lemmon v. People, 20 N.Y. 607.

"Indeed, without some provision of the kind removing from the citizens of each State the disabilities of alienage in the other States, and giving them equality of privilege with citizens of those States, the Republic would have constituted little more than a league of States; it would not have constituted the Union which now exists.

"But the privileges and immunities secured to citizens of each State in the several States, by the provision in question, are those privileges and immunities which are common to the citizens in the latter States under their Constitution and laws by virtue of their being citizens. Special privileges enjoyed by citizens in their own States are not secured in other States by this provision. It was not intended by the provision to give to the laws of one State any operation in other States. They can have no such operation, except by the permission, express or implied, of those States. The special privileges which they confer must, therefore, be enjoyed at home, unless the assent of other States to their enjoyment therein be given."

2. APPLICATION OF THE BILL OF RIGHTS TO THE STATES

Introduction. In Barron v. Mayor and City Council of Baltimore, 32 U.S. (7 Pet.) 243 (1833), Chief Justice Marshall held for the Court that the freedoms set forth in the Bill of Rights were "intended solely as . . . limitation[s] on the exercise of power by the government of the United States, and [are] not applicable to the legislation of the states" whose own constitutions provided their respective inhabitants with "safeguards to liberty from the apprehended encroachments of their particular governments." Soon after the Civil War, moreover, in the Slaughter-House Cases, 83 U.S. (16 Wall.) 36 (1872), the Court held that the provision of the fourteenth amendment declaring that "No State shall make or enforce any law which shall abridge the privileges or immunities of citizens of the United States" did not authorize the Court to be "a perpetual censor upon all legislation of the States, on the civil rights of their own citizens" or the Congress to exercise power over "the entire domain of civil rights heretofore belonging exclusively to the States[.]" Only the "privileges and immunities belonging to a citizen of the United States as such," not "those belonging to the citizen of the State as such," were now to be protected by the fourteenth amendment. That conclusion led Justice Field, in dissent, to note that if the provision referred "only . . . to such privileges and immunities as were before its adoption specifically designated in the Constitution or necessarily implied as belonging to citizens of the United States, it was a vain and idle enactment, which accomplished nothing, and most unnecessarily excited Congress and the people on its passage."

Later, however, the Court responded differently to the question of the relationship between the Bill of Rights and the due process clause of the fourteenth amendment. An early example of the Court's approach was Twining v. New Jersey, 211 U.S. 78 (1908). The question posed was whether the provision in the fifth amendment that no person "shall be compelled in any criminal case to be a witness against himself" applied to restrain the states. Twining argued first that the "privileges and immunities of citizens of the United States" protected against state action by the fourteenth amendment included those fundamental personal rights which were protected against national action by the first eight Amendments; that this was the intention of the framers of the fourteenth amendment. The Court rejected this argument, relying on the interpretation of the privileges and immunities clause in the Slaughterhouse Cases. Second, Twining argued that a denial of the privilege against self-incrimination constituted a denial of due process of law. The Court rejected this argument, holding that the privilege against self-incrimination was not "an immutable principle of justice which is the inalienable possession of every citizen of a free government" and hence to deny it was not to deny due process.

Whether the first eight amendments could be utilized to make more specific the meaning of "due process of law" was not settled by *Twining*. The subsequent cases involved primarily criminal procedure, and detailed consideration of those cases is left to criminal procedure courses. Presented here are just a few of the principal cases illustrating the dispute over the incorporation problem and the nature of judicial review itself.

One aspect of the incorporation doctrine has become the foundation for most of the modern developments concerning freedom of speech, press, and religion. Almost casually, the Court in 1925 asserted in Gitlow v. New York, 268 U.S. 652, 666: "For present purposes we may and do assume that freedom of speech and of the press— which are protected by the 1st Amendment from abridgment by Congress—are among the fundamental personal rights and 'liberties' protected by the due process clause of the 14th Amendment from impairment by the states."

The Incorporation Doctrine

In Chapter 9 we will see how the Court gave an early expansive meaning to such fourteenth amendment terms as "liberty", "property", and "due process of law" in the context of judicial review of the substance of economic regulations. We will also see the Court's withdrawal from that expansive interpretation in recent decades.

In the field of procedure (primarily procedure in criminal cases), a similar development had a different twist. In the early years the Court found in the fourteenth amendment restrictions upon state procedures that denied "immutable principles of justice" that are "the inalienable possession of every citizen of a free government" or that deprived the accused of "sufficient notice of the accusation" and "an adequate opportunity to defend himself." These expansive terms, and others, tended to limit rather than to expand (as was the case with respect to the substance of economic regulations) the scope of Court review of state procedures. More recently, through the idea that the fourteenth amendment applies to the states the more specific procedural guaranties in the Bill of Rights, the Court has expanded the scope of review of state court procedures while making somewhat more specific the applicable standards.

More recently, the Court extended the incorporation doctrine beyond these procedural cases, to cover the substantive liberty found to be protected by the second amendment right "to keep and bear Arms." That decision, McDonald v. City of Chicago, is set forth infra, p. 315, after the following case.

Duncan v. Louisiana

391 U.S. 145, 88 S.Ct. 1444, 20 L.Ed.2d 491 (1968).

■ Mr. Justice White delivered the opinion of the Court.

Appellant, Gary Duncan, was convicted of simple battery[,] a misdemeanor, punishable by two years' imprisonment and a $300 fine. Appellant sought trial by jury, but because the Louisiana Constitution grants jury trials only in cases in which capital punishment or imprisonment at hard labor may be imposed, the trial judge denied the request. Appellant was convicted and sentenced to serve 60 days in the parish prison and pay a fine of $150. Appellant [unsuccessfully] sought review in the Supreme Court of Louisiana, asserting that the denial of jury trial violated rights guaranteed to him by the United States Constitution. . . . [A]ppellant . . . alleg[es here] that the Sixth and Fourteenth Amendments to the United States Constitution secure the right to jury trial in state criminal prosecutions where a sentence as long as two years may be imposed. . . .

I.

The Fourteenth Amendment denies the States the power to "deprive any person of life, liberty, or property, without due process of law." In resolving conflicting claims concerning the meaning of this spacious language, the Court has looked increasingly to the Bill of Rights for guidance; many of the rights guaranteed by the first eight Amendments to the Constitution have been held to be protected against state action by the Due Process Clause of the Fourteenth Amendment. That clause now protects the right to compensation for property taken by the State; the rights of speech, press, and religion covered by the First Amendment; the Fourth Amendment rights to be free from unreasonable searches and seizures and to have excluded from criminal trials any evidence illegally seized; the right guaranteed by the Fifth Amendment to be free of compelled self-incrimination; and the Sixth Amendment rights to counsel, to a speedy and public trial, to confrontation of opposing witnesses, and to compulsory process for obtaining witnesses.

The test for determining whether a right extended by the Fifth and Sixth Amendments with respect to federal criminal proceedings is also protected against state action by the Fourteenth Amendment has been phrased in a variety of ways in the opinions of this Court. The question has been asked whether a right is among those "fundamental principles of liberty and justice which lie at the base of all our civil and political institutions," Powell v. Alabama, 287 U.S. 45, 67 (1932); whether it is "basic in our system of jurisprudence," In re Oliver, 333 U.S. 257, 273 (1948); and whether it is "a fundamental right, essential to a fair trial," Gideon v. Wainwright, 372 U.S. 335, 343–344 (1963); Malloy v. Hogan, 378 U.S. 1, 6 (1964); Pointer v. Texas, 380 U.S. 400, 403 (1965). The claim before us is that the right to trial by jury guaranteed by the Sixth Amendment meets these tests. The position of Louisiana, on the other hand, is that the Constitution imposes upon the States no duty to give a jury trial in any criminal case, regardless of the seriousness of the crime or the size of the punishment which may be imposed. Because we believe that trial by jury in criminal cases is fundamental to the American scheme of justice, we hold that the Fourteenth Amendment guarantees a right of jury trial in all criminal cases which—were they to be tried in a federal court—would come within the Sixth Amendment's guarantee.[14]

---

[14] In one sense recent cases applying provisions of the first eight amendments to the States represent a new approach to the "incorporation" debate. Earlier the Court can be seen as having asked,

Since we consider the appeal before us to be such a case, we hold that the Constitution was violated when appellant's demand for jury trial was refused.

The history of trial by jury in criminal cases has been frequently told. . . .

. . .

Even such skeletal history is impressive support for considering the right to jury trial in criminal cases to be fundamental to our system of justice, an importance frequently recognized in the opinions of this Court. . . .

Jury trial continues to receive strong support. The laws of every State guarantee a right to jury trial in serious criminal cases; no State has dispensed with it; nor are there significant movements underway to do so. . . .

. . .

The guarantees of jury trial in the Federal and State Constitutions reflect a profound judgment about the way in which law should be enforced and justice administered. A right to jury trial is granted to criminal defendants in order to prevent oppression by the Government. . . . The deep commitment of the Nation to the right of jury trial in serious criminal cases as a defense against arbitrary law enforcement qualifies for protection under the Due Process Clause of the Fourteenth Amendment, and must therefore be respected by the States.

. . .   LA argument

well established

assisted in an overreaching govt

. . . Louisiana urges that holding that the Fourteenth Amendment assures a right to jury trial will cast doubt on the integrity of every trial conducted without a jury.

---

when inquiring into whether some particular procedural safeguard was required of a State, if a civilized system could be imagined that would not accord the particular protection. For example, Palko v. Connecticut, 302 U.S. 319, 325 (1937), stated: "The right to trial by jury and the immunity from prosecution except as the result of an indictment may have value and importance. Even so, they are not of the very essence of a scheme of ordered liberty. . . . Few would be so narrow or provincial as to maintain that a fair and enlightened system of justice would be impossible without them." The recent cases, on the other hand, have proceeded upon the valid assumption that state criminal processes are not imaginary and theoretical schemes but actual systems bearing virtually every characteristic of the common-law system that has been developing contemporaneously in England and in this country. The question thus is whether given this kind of system a particular procedure is fundamental—whether, that is, a procedure is necessary to an Anglo-American regime of ordered liberty. It is this sort of inquiry that can justify the conclusions that state courts must exclude evidence seized in violation of the Fourth Amendment, Mapp v. Ohio, 367 U.S. 643 (1961); that state prosecutors may not comment on a defendant's failure to testify, Griffin v. California, 380 U.S. 609 (1965); and that criminal punishment may not be imposed for the status of narcotics addiction, Robinson v. California, 370 U.S. 660 (1962). Of immediate relevance for this case are the Court's holdings that the States must comply with certain provisions of the Sixth Amendment, specifically that the States may not refuse a speedy trial, confrontation of witnesses, and the assistance, at state expense if necessary, of counsel. . . . Of each of these determinations that a constitutional provision originally written to bind the Federal Government should bind the States as well it might be said that the limitation in question is not necessarily fundamental to fairness in every criminal system that might be imagined but is fundamental in the context of the criminal processes maintained by the American States.

When the inquiry is approached in this way the question whether the States can impose criminal punishment without granting a jury trial appears quite different from the way it appeared in the older cases opining that States might abolish jury trial. See, e.g., Maxwell v. Dow, 176 U.S. 581 (1900). A criminal process which was fair and equitable but used no juries is easy to imagine. It would make use of alternative guarantees and protections which would serve the purposes that the jury serves in the English and American systems. Yet no American State has undertaken to construct such a system. Instead, every American State, including Louisiana, uses the jury extensively, and imposes very serious punishments only after a trial at which the defendant has a right to a jury's verdict. In every State, including Louisiana, the structure and style of the criminal process—the supporting framework and the subsidiary procedures—are of the sort that naturally complement jury trial, and have developed in connection with and in reliance upon jury trial.

Plainly, this is not the import of our holding. Our conclusion is that in the American States, as in the federal judicial system, a general grant of jury trial for serious offenses is a fundamental right, essential for preventing miscarriages of justice and for assuring that fair trials are provided for all defendants. We would not assert, however, that every criminal trial—or any particular trial—held before a judge alone is unfair or that a defendant may never be as fairly treated by a judge as he would be by a jury. Thus we hold no constitutional doubts about the practices, common in both federal and state courts, of accepting waivers of jury trial and prosecuting petty crimes without extending a right to jury trial. However, the fact is that in most places more trials for serious crimes are to juries than to a court alone; a great many defendants prefer the judgment of a jury to that of a court. Even where defendants are satisfied with bench trials, the right to a jury trial very likely serves its intended purpose of making judicial or prosecutorial unfairness less likely.[30]

II.

Louisiana's final contention is that even if it must grant jury trials in serious criminal cases, the conviction before us is valid and constitutional because here the petitioner was tried for simple battery and was sentenced to only 60 days .... We are not persuaded. It is doubtless true that there is a category of petty crimes or offenses which is not subject to the Sixth Amendment jury trial provision and should not be subject to the Fourteenth Amendment jury trial requirement here applied to the States.... But the penalty authorized for a particular crime is of major relevance in determining whether it is serious or not and may in itself, if severe enough, subject the trial to the mandates of the Sixth Amendment.... In the case before us the Legislature of Louisiana has made simple battery a criminal offense punishable by imprisonment for two years and a fine. The question, then is whether a crime carrying such a penalty is an offense which Louisiana may insist on trying without a jury.

We think not....

. . .

The judgment below is reversed and the case is remanded for proceedings not inconsistent with this opinion.

■ MR. JUSTICE BLACK, with whom MR. JUSTICE DOUGLAS joins, concurring.

... The dissent in this case ... makes a spirited and forceful defense of [the] now discredited [*Twining*] doctrine. I do not believe that it is necessary for me to repeat the historical and logical reasons for my challenge to the *Twining* holding contained in my *Adamson* dissent and Appendix to it. My Brother Harlan's objections to my *Adamson*

---

[30] Louisiana also asserts that if due process is deemed to include the right to jury trial, States will be obligated to comply with all past interpretations of the Sixth Amendment, an amendment which in its inception was designed to control only the federal courts and which throughout its history has operated in this limited environment where uniformity is a more obvious and immediate consideration. In particular, Louisiana objects to application of the decisions of this Court interpreting the Sixth Amendment as guaranteeing a 12-man jury in serious criminal cases, Thompson v. Utah, 170 U.S. 343 (1898); as requiring a unanimous verdict before guilt can be found, Maxwell v. Dow, 176 U.S. 581, 586 (1900); and as barring procedures by which crimes subject to the Sixth Amendment jury trial provision are tried in the first instance without a jury but at the first appellate stage by de novo trial with a jury, Callan v. Wilson, 127 U.S. 540, 557 (1888). It seems very unlikely to us that our decision today will require widespread changes in state criminal processes. First, our decisions interpreting the Sixth Amendment are always subject to reconsideration, a fact amply demonstrated by the instant decision. In addition, most of the States have provisions for jury trials equal in breadth to the Sixth Amendment, if that amendment is construed, as it has been, to permit the trial of petty crimes and offenses without a jury. Indeed, there appear to be only four States in which juries of fewer than 12 can be used without the defendant's consent for offenses carrying a maximum penalty of greater than one year. Only in Oregon and Louisiana can a less-than-unanimous jury convict for an offense with a maximum penalty greater than one year....

dissent history, like that of most of the objectors, relies most heavily on a criticism written by Professor Charles Fairman[,] . . . 2 Stan.L.Rev. 5 (1949) . . . [, which] in my view . . . has completely failed to refute the inferences and arguments that I suggested in my *Adamson* dissent. Professor Fairman's "history" relies very heavily on what was *not* said in the state legislatures that passed on the Fourteenth Amendment. Instead of relying on this kind of negative pregnant, my legislative experience has convinced me that it is far wiser to rely on what *was* said, and most importantly, said by the men who actually sponsored the Amendment in the Congress. . . . [B]oth its sponsors and those who opposed it believed the Fourteenth Amendment made the first eight Amendments of the Constitution (The Bill of Rights) applicable to the States.

. . . [Contrary to the dissent's view,] the words "No State shall make or enforce any law which shall abridge the privileges or immunities of citizens of the United States" seem to me an eminently reasonable way of expressing the idea that henceforth the Bill of Rights shall apply to the States.[1] What more precious "privilege" of American citizenship could there be than that privilege to claim the protections of our great Bill of Rights? I suggest that any reading of "privileges or immunities of citizens of the United States" which excludes the Bill of Rights' safeguards renders the words of this section of the Fourteenth Amendment meaningless. . . .

[handwritten margin note: Meat of difference in opinion]

. . . Brother Harlan's . . . view, as was indeed the view of *Twining,* is that "due process is an evolving concept" and therefore that it entails a "gradual process of judicial inclusion and exclusion" to ascertain those "immutable principles of free government which no member of the Union may disregard." Thus the Due Process Clause is treated as prescribing no specific and clearly ascertainable constitutional command that judges must obey in interpreting the Constitution, but rather as leaving judges free to decide at any particular time whether a particular rule or judicial formulation embodies an "immutable principl[e] of free government" or "is implicit in the concept of ordered liberty," or whether certain conduct "shocks the judge's conscience" or runs counter to some other similar, undefined and undefinable standard. Thus due process, according to my Brother Harlan, is to be a word with no permanent meaning, but one which is found to shift from time to time in accordance with judges' predilections and understandings of what is best for the country. If due process means this, the Fourteenth Amendment, in my opinion, might as well have been written that "no person shall be deprived of life, liberty or property except by laws that the judges of the United States Supreme Court shall find to be consistent with the immutable principles of free government." It is impossible for me to believe that such unconfined power is given to judges in our Constitution that is a written one in order to limit governmental power.

. . . [Moreover,] the "fundamental fairness" test is one on a par with that of shocking the conscience of the Court. Each . . . depends entirely on the particular judge's idea of ethics and morals instead of requiring him to depend on the boundaries fixed by the written words of the Constitution. Nothing in the history of the phrase "due process of law" suggests that constitutional controls are to depend on any particular judge's sense of values. . . .

Finally . . . I am not bothered by the argument that applying the Bill of Rights to the States, "according to the same standards that protect those rights against federal encroachment," interferes with our concept of federalism in that it may prevent States from trying novel social and economic experiments. I have never believed that under the guise of federalism the States should be able to experiment with the protections

---

[1]   My view has been and is that the Fourteenth Amendment, *as a whole,* makes the Bill of Rights applicable to the States. This would certainly include the language of the Privileges and Immunities Clause, as well as the Due Process Clause.

afforded our citizens through the Bill of Rights. . . . It seems to me totally inconsistent to advocate on the one hand, the power of this Court to strike down any state law or practice which it finds "unreasonable" or "unfair," and on the other hand urge that the States be given maximum power to develop their own laws and procedures. Yet the due process approach of my Brothers Harlan and Fortas . . . does just that since in effect it restricts the States to practices which a majority of this Court is willing to approve on a case-by-case basis. No one is more concerned than I that the States be allowed to use the full scope of their powers as their citizens see fit. And that is why I have continually fought against the expansion of this Court's authority over the States through the use of a broad, general interpretation of due process that permits judges to strike down state laws they do not like.

. . . I believe as strongly as ever that the Fourteenth Amendment was intended to make the Bill of Rights applicable to the States. I have been willing to support the selective incorporation doctrine, however, as an alternative, although perhaps less historically supportable than complete incorporation. The selective incorporation process, if used properly, does limit the Supreme Court in the Fourteenth Amendment field to specific Bill of Rights' protections only and keeps judges from roaming at will in their own notions of what policies outside the Bill of Rights are desirable and what are not. And, most importantly for me, the selective incorporation process has the virtue of having already worked to make most of the Bill of Rights' protections applicable to the States.

■ MR. JUSTICE FORTAS, concurring.

I join the judgments and opinions of the Court in these cases because I agree that the Due Process Clause of the Fourteenth Amendment requires that the States accord the right to jury trial in prosecutions for offenses that are not petty. . . .

. . .

■ MR. JUSTICE HARLAN, whom MR. JUSTICE STEWART joins, dissenting.

Every American jurisdiction provides for trial by jury in criminal cases. The question before us is not whether jury trial is an ancient institution, which it is; nor whether it plays a significant role in the administration of criminal justice, which it does; nor whether it will endure, which it shall. The question in this case is whether the State of Louisiana, which provides trial by jury for all felonies, is prohibited by the Constitution from trying charges of simple battery to the court alone. In my view, the answer to that question, mandated alike by our constitutional history and by the longer history of trial by jury, is clearly "no."

. . .

I.

I believe I am correct in saying that every member of the Court for at least the last 135 years has agreed that our Founders did not consider the requirements of the Bill of Rights so fundamental that they should operate directly against the States. They were wont to believe rather that the security of liberty in America rested primarily upon the dispersion of governmental power across a federal system. . . .

. . .

A few members of the Court have taken the position that the intention of those who drafted the first section of the Fourteenth Amendment was simply, and exclusively, to make the provisions of the first eight amendments applicable to state action. This view has never been accepted by this Court. In my view, . . . the first section of the Fourteenth Amendment was meant neither to incorporate, nor to be limited to, the specific guarantees of the first eight amendments. The overwhelming historical evidence marshalled by Professor Fairman demonstrates, to me conclusively, that the Congressmen and state legislators who wrote, debated, and ratified the Fourteenth Amendment did not think they were "incorporating" the Bill of Rights[9] and the very breadth and generality of the Amendment's provisions suggests that its authors did not suppose that the Nation would always be limited to mid-19th century conceptions of "liberty" and "due process of law" . . . [N]either history, nor sense, supports using the Fourteenth Amendment to put the States in a constitutional straitjacket with respect to their own development in the administration of criminal or civil law.

Although I therefore fundamentally disagree with the total incorporation view of the Fourteenth Amendment, it seems to me that such a position does at least have the virtue, lacking in the Court's selective incorporation approach, of internal consistency: we look to the Bill of Rights, word for word, clause for clause, precedent for precedent because, it is said, the men who wrote the Amendment wanted it that way. . . .

Apart from the . . . absolute incorporationists, I can see only one method of analysis that has any internal logic. That is to start with the words "liberty" and "due process of law" and attempt to define them in a way that accords with American traditions and our system of government. This approach, involving a much more discriminating process of adjudication than does "incorporation," is, albeit difficult, the one that was followed throughout the Nineteenth and most of the present century. It entails a "gradual process of judicial inclusion and exclusion," seeking, with due recognition of constitutional tolerance for state experimentation and disparity, to ascertain those "immutable principles of free government which no member of the Union may disregard." . . .

. . .

Today's Court still remains unwilling to accept the total incorporationists' view. . . . The Court is also, apparently, unwilling to face the task of determining whether denial of trial by jury in the situation before us, or in other situations, is fundamentally unfair. Consequently, the Court has compromised on the ease of the incorporationist position, without its internal logic. It has simply assumed that the question before us is whether the Jury Trial Clause of the Sixth Amendment should be incorporated into the Fourteenth, jot-for-jot and case-for-case, or ignored. Then the Court merely declares that the clause in question is "in" rather than "out."

---

[9] Fairman, Does the Fourteenth Amendment Incorporate the Bill of Rights? The Original Understanding, 2 Stan.L.Rev. 5 (1949). Professor Fairman was not content to rest upon the overwhelming fact that the great words of the four clauses of the first section of the Fourteenth Amendment would have been an exceedingly peculiar way to say that "The rights heretofore guaranteed against federal intrusion by the first eight Amendments are henceforth guaranteed against state intrusion as well." He therefore sifted the mountain of material comprising the debates and committee reports relating to the Amendment in both Houses of Congress and in the state legislatures that passed upon it. He found that in the immense corpus of comments on the purpose and effects of the proposed amendment, and on its virtues and defects, there is almost no evidence whatever for "incorporation." The first eight amendments are so much as mentioned by only two members of Congress, one of whom effectively demonstrated (a) that he did not understand Barron v. Baltimore, 7 Pet. 243, and therefore did not understand the question of incorporation, and (b) that he was not himself understood by his colleagues. One state legislative committee report, rejected by the legislature as a whole, found § I of the Fourteenth Amendment superfluous because it duplicated the Bill of Rights: the committee obviously did not understand Barron v. Baltimore either. That is all Professor Fairman could find, in hundreds of pages of legislative discussion prior to passage of the Amendment, that even suggests incorporation.

To this negative evidence the judicial history of the Amendment could be added. For example, it proved possible for a court whose members had lived through Reconstruction to reiterate the doctrine of *Barron v. Baltimore,* that the Bill of Rights did not apply to the States, without so much as questioning whether the Fourteenth Amendment had any effect on the continued validity of that principle. E.g., Walker v. Sauvinet, 92 U.S. 90; see generally Morrison, Does the Fourteenth Amendment Incorporate the Bill of Rights? The Judicial Interpretation, 2 Stan.L.Rev. 140 (1949).

. . .

The Court has justified neither its starting place nor its conclusion. . . .

II.

. . . When a criminal defendant contends that his state conviction lacked "due process of law," the question before this Court, in my view, is whether he was denied any element of fundamental procedural fairness. Believing, as I do, that due process is an evolving concept and that old principles are subject to reevaluation in light of later experience, I think it appropriate to deal on its merits with the question whether Louisiana denied appellant due process of law when it tried him for simple assault without a jury. . . .

In sum, there is a wide range of views on the desirability of trial by jury, and on the ways to make it most effective when it is used; there is also considerable variation from State to State in local conditions such as the size of the criminal caseload, the ease or difficulty of summoning jurors, and other trial conditions bearing on fairness. . . . [This situation should invoke] the celebrated dictum of Mr. Justice Brandeis [that it is]

"one of the happy incidents of the federal system that a single courageous State may, if its citizens choose, serve as a laboratory. . . ." New State Ice Co. v. Liebmann, 285 U.S. 262, 280, 311 (dissenting opinion).

This Court, other courts, and the political process are available to correct any experiments in criminal procedure that prove fundamentally unfair to defendants. . . . [I]nstead, and quite without reason, the Court has chosen to impose upon every State one means of trying criminal cases; it is a good means, but it is not the only fair means, and it is not demonstrably better than the alternatives States might devise.

I would affirm the judgment of the Supreme Court of Louisiana.

Incorporation and the Jury Trial Cases

Before *Duncan* it had been assumed that the jury trial guaranteed in the sixth and seventh amendments was the traditional unanimous jury of twelve. Footnote 30 in *Duncan* opened the door to reconsideration of that assumption. The results are worth reporting.

In Williams v. Florida, 399 U.S. 78 (1970), the Court upheld as consistent with the sixth amendment, as made applicable to the states through the fourteenth, a state law permitting conviction by a unanimous jury of six in all non-capital criminal cases. Justice Harlan, concurring, accused the Court of diluting "a federal guarantee in order to reconcile the logic of 'incorporation,' the 'jot-for-jot and case-for-case' application of the federal right to the States, with the reality of federalism. Can one doubt that had Congress tried to undermine the common law right to trial by jury before *Duncan* came on the books the history today recited would have barred such action? Can we expect repeat performances when this Court is called upon to give definition and meaning to other federal guarantees that have been 'incorporated'?" Justice Black, concurring, responded: "Today's decision is in no way attributable to any desire to dilute the Sixth Amendment in order more easily to apply it to the States, but follows solely as a necessary consequence of our duty to re-examine prior decisions to reach the correct constitutional meaning in each case." In Colgrove v. Battin, 413 U.S. 149 (1973), the Court applied the logic of *Williams* in holding that a jury of six persons in a civil case in the federal courts was not in violation of the seventh amendment. However, in Ballew v. Georgia, 435 U.S. 223 (1978), the Court held that the constitutional minimum size for a jury in non-petty criminal offenses was six, invalidating a state statute providing for conviction by unanimous vote of a jury of five.

In Apodaca v. Oregon, 406 U.S. 404 (1972), the Court upheld an Oregon statute providing for conviction in criminal cases by a vote of 10 persons out of a jury of twelve. Justice Powell repeated Justice Harlan's objection in *Williams* that the Court was diluting the scope of sixth amendment rights in the federal courts in order to avoid imposing "unnecessarily rigid" requirements on the states. Most recently in Burch v. Louisiana, 441 U.S. 130 (1979), the Court held invalid a statute providing for trial "before a jury of six persons, five of whom must concur to render a verdict." The Court recognized that "having already departed from the strictly historical requirements of jury trial, it is inevitable that lines must be drawn somewhere if the substance of jury trial right is to be preserved." The Court left open the question whether it would be consistent with the sixth amendment to provide for a nonunanimous vote by any jury of less than twelve but more than six.

McDonald v. City of Chicago

561 U.S. 742, 130 S.Ct. 3020, 177 L.Ed.2d 894 (2010).

■ JUSTICE ALITO announced the judgment of the Court and delivered the opinion of the Court with respect to Parts I, II-A, II-B, II-D, III-A, and III-B, in which the CHIEF JUSTICE, JUSTICE SCALIA, JUSTICE KENNEDY, and JUSTICE THOMAS join, and an opinion with respect to Parts II-C, IV, and V, in which the CHIEF JUSTICE, JUSTICE SCALIA, and JUSTICE KENNEDY join.

Two years ago, in District of Columbia v. Heller, 554 U.S. 570, 128 S.Ct. 2783, 171 L.Ed.2d 637 (2008), we held that the Second Amendment protects the right to keep and bear arms for the purpose of self-defense, and we struck down a District of Columbia law that banned the possession of handguns in the home. The city of Chicago (City) and the village of Oak Park, a Chicago suburb, have laws that are similar to the District of Columbia's, but Chicago and Oak Park argue that their laws are constitutional because the Second Amendment has no application to the States. We have previously held that most of the provisions of the Bill of Rights apply with full force to both the Federal Government and the States. Applying the standard that is well established in our case law, we hold that the Second Amendment right is fully applicable to the States.

I

[Chicago and Oak Park effectively ban the possession of handguns by private residents. Fearful of becoming targets of threats and violence, particularly from drug dealers in the neighborhood, McDonald and others sued post-*Heller* to have these laws declared unconstitutional under the Second and Fourteenth Amendments. The lower courts rejected their claims, "relying on three 19th-century cases—United States v. Cruikshank, 92 U.S. 542 (1876), Presser v. Illinois, 116 U.S. 252 (1886), and Miller v. Texas, 153 U.S. 535 (1894)—that were decided in the wake of this Court's interpretation of the Privileges or Immunities Clause of the Fourteenth Amendment in the Slaughter-House Cases, 16 Wall. 36 (1873)."]

II

A

Petitioners argue that the Chicago and Oak Park laws violate the right to keep and bear arms for two reasons. Petitioners' primary submission is that this right is among the "privileges or immunities of citizens of the United States" and that the narrow interpretation of the Privileges or Immunities Clause adopted in the

Slaughter-House Cases, supra, should now be rejected. As a secondary argument, petitioners contend that the Fourteenth Amendment's Due Process Clause "incorporates" the Second Amendment right.

Chicago and Oak Park (municipal respondents) maintain that a right set out in the Bill of Rights applies to the States only if that right is an indispensable attribute of *any* " 'civilized' " legal system.... If it is possible to imagine a civilized country that does not recognize the right, the municipal respondents tell us, then that right is not protected by due process.... And since there are civilized countries that ban or strictly regulate the private possession of handguns, the municipal respondents maintain that due process does not preclude such measures....

B

. . .

Three years after ... the *Slaughter-House Cases,* the Court decided *Cruikshank,* ... [where] the Court reviewed convictions stemming from the infamous Colfax Massacre in Louisiana on Easter Sunday 1873. Dozens of blacks, many unarmed, were slaughtered by a rival band of armed white men.... Ninety-seven men were indicted for participating in the massacre, but only nine went to trial. Six of the nine were acquitted of all charges; the remaining three were acquitted of murder but convicted under the Enforcement Act of 1870 ... for banding and conspiring together to deprive their victims of various constitutional rights, including the right to bear arms.

The Court reversed all of the convictions.... The Court wrote that the right of bearing arms for a lawful purpose "is not a right granted by the Constitution" and is not "in any manner dependent upon that instrument for its existence." ... "The second amendment," the Court continued, "declares that it shall not be infringed; but this ... means no more than that it shall not be infringed by Congress." ... "Our later decisions in *Presser v. Illinois* ... and *Miller v. Texas* ... reaffirmed that the Second Amendment applies only to the Federal Government." *Heller,*....

C

. . .

... For many decades, the question of the rights protected by the Fourteenth Amendment against state infringement has been analyzed under the Due Process Clause of that Amendment and not under the Privileges or Immunities Clause. We therefore decline to disturb the *Slaughter-House* holding.

At the same time, however, ... *Cruikshank, Presser,* and *Miller* do not preclude us from considering whether the Due Process Clause of the Fourteenth Amendment makes the Second Amendment right binding on the States. See *Heller,* .... None of those cases "engage[d] in the sort of Fourteenth Amendment inquiry required by our later cases." *Ibid.* ... *Cruikshank, Presser,* and *Miller* all preceded the era in which the Court began the process of "selective incorporation" under the Due Process Clause, and we have never previously addressed the question whether the right to keep and bear arms applies to the States under that theory.

Indeed, *Cruikshank* has not prevented us from holding that other rights that were at issue in that case are binding on the States through the Due Process Clause. In *Cruikshank,* the Court held that the general "right of the people peaceably to assemble for lawful purposes," which is protected by the First Amendment, applied only against the Federal Government and not against the States.... Nonetheless, over 60 years later the Court held that the right of peaceful assembly was a "fundamental righ[t] ... safeguarded by the due process clause of the Fourteenth Amendment." De Jonge v. Oregon, 299 U.S. 353, 364 (1937). We follow the same path here and thus consider whether the right to keep and bear arms applies to the States under the Due Process Clause.

D

[handwritten: ISSUE ↗]

In the late 19th century, the Court began to consider whether the Due Process Clause prohibits the States from infringing rights set out in the Bill of Rights. . . . Five features of the approach taken during the ensuing era should be noted.

First, the Court viewed the due process question as entirely separate from the question whether a right was a privilege or immunity of national citizenship. See Twining v. New Jersey, 211 U.S. 78, 99 (1908). *[handwritten: 1st]*

Second, the Court explained that the only rights protected against state infringement by the Due Process Clause were those rights "of such a nature that they are included in the conception of due process of law." . . . *[handwritten: 2nd]*

The Court used different formulations in describing the boundaries of due process. For example, in *Twining,* the Court referred to "immutable principles of justice which inhere in the very idea of free government which no member of the Union may disregard." . . . In Snyder v. Massachusetts . . . (1934), the Court spoke of rights that are "so rooted in the traditions and conscience of our people as to be ranked as fundamental." And in *Palko,* the Court famously said that due process protects those rights that are "the very essence of a scheme of ordered liberty" and essential to "a fair and enlightened system of justice." . . . *[handwritten: Boundaries of Due Process]*

Third, in some cases decided during this era the Court "can be seen as having asked, when inquiring into whether some particular procedural safeguard was required of a State, if a civilized system could be imagined that would not accord the particular protection." Duncan v. Louisiana, 391 U.S. 145, 149, n. 14 (1968). . . . *[handwritten: 3rd]*

Fourth, the Court during this era was not hesitant to hold that a right set out in the Bill of Rights failed to meet the test for inclusion within the protection of the Due Process Clause. . . . See, *e.g., Hurtado, supra* (grand jury indictment requirement); *Twining, supra* (privilege against self-incrimination). *[handwritten: 4th]*

Finally, even when a right set out in the Bill of Rights was held to fall within the conception of due process, the protection or remedies afforded against state infringement sometimes differed from the protection or remedies provided against abridgment by the Federal Government. . . . *[handwritten: 5th]*

. . .

While Justice Black's ["total incorporation"] theory was never adopted, the Court eventually moved in that direction by initiating what has been called a process of "selective incorporation," *i.e.,* the Court began to hold that the Due Process Clause fully incorporates particular rights contained in the first eight Amendments. . . . *[handwritten: selective incorporation definition]*

The decisions during this time abandoned three of the previously noted characteristics of the earlier period. The Court made it clear that the governing standard is not whether *any* "civilized system [can] be imagined that would not accord the particular protection." *Duncan,.* . . . Instead, the Court inquired whether a particular Bill of Rights guarantee is fundamental to *our* scheme of ordered liberty and system of justice. *Id.* . . . *[handwritten: our fundamental rights gage our Due Process not other countries]*

The Court also shed any reluctance to hold that rights guaranteed by the Bill of Rights met the requirements for protection under the Due Process Clause. The Court eventually incorporated almost all of the provisions of the Bill of Rights. Only a handful of the Bill of Rights protections remain unincorporated.[13]

Finally, the Court . . . decisively held that incorporated Bill of Rights protections "are all to be enforced against the States under the Fourteenth Amendment according to the same standards that protect those personal rights against federal encroachment." . . .

. . .

III

With this framework in mind, . . . we must decide whether the right to keep and bear arms is fundamental to *our* scheme of ordered liberty, *Duncan,* . . . or as we have said in a related context, whether this right is "deeply rooted in this Nation's history and tradition," Washington v. Glucksberg, 521 U.S. 702, 721 (1997). . . .

A

Our decision in *Heller* points unmistakably to the answer. Self-defense is a basic right, recognized by many legal systems from ancient times to the present day, and in *Heller,* we held that individual self-defense is "the *central component*" of the Second Amendment right. . . .

Heller makes it clear that this right is "deeply rooted in this Nation's history and tradition." . . . *Heller* explored the right's origins, noting that the 1689 English Bill of Rights explicitly protected a right to keep arms for self-defense . . . and that by 1765, Blackstone was able to assert that the right to keep and bear arms was "one of the fundamental rights of Englishmen,". . . .

Blackstone's assessment was shared by the American colonists. . . .

The right to keep and bear arms was considered no less fundamental by those who drafted and ratified the Bill of Rights. . . . Antifederalists and Federalists alike agreed that the right to bear arms was fundamental to the newly formed system of government. . . .

This understanding persisted in the years immediately following the ratification of the Bill of Rights. In addition to the four States that had adopted Second Amendment analogues before ratification, nine more States adopted state constitutional provisions protecting an individual right to keep and bear arms between 1789 and 1820. . . . Founding-era legal commentators confirmed the importance of the right to early Americans. . . .

B

1

By the 1850's, the perceived threat that had prompted the inclusion of the Second Amendment in the Bill of Rights—the fear that the National Government would disarm the universal militia—had largely faded as a popular concern, but the right to keep and bear arms was highly valued for purposes of self-defense. . . . Abolitionist authors wrote in support of the right. . . .

After the Civil War, many of the over 180,000 African Americans who served in the Union Army returned to the States of the old Confederacy, where systematic

---

[13] In addition to the right to keep and bear arms (and the Sixth Amendment right to a unanimous jury verdict . . .), the only rights not fully incorporated are (1) the Third Amendment's protection against quartering of soldiers; (2) the Fifth Amendment's grand jury indictment requirement; (3) the Seventh Amendment right to a jury trial in civil cases; and (4) the Eighth Amendment's prohibition on excessive fines.

efforts were made to disarm them and other blacks. . . . The laws of some States formally prohibited African Americans from possessing firearms. . . .

Throughout the South, armed parties, often consisting of ex-Confederate soldiers serving in the state militias, forcibly took firearms from newly freed slaves. . . .

Union Army commanders took steps to secure the right of all citizens to keep and bear arms, but the 39th Congress concluded that legislative action was necessary. Its efforts to safeguard the right to keep and bear arms demonstrate that the right was still recognized to be fundamental.

The most explicit evidence of Congress' aim appears in § 14 of the Freedmen's Bureau Act of 1866, which provided that "the right . . . to have full and equal benefit of all laws and proceedings concerning personal liberty, personal security, and the acquisition, enjoyment, and disposition of estate, real and personal, *including the constitutional right to bear arms,* shall be secured to and enjoyed by all the citizens . . . without respect to race or color, or previous condition of slavery." . . . Section 14 thus explicitly guaranteed that "all the citizens," black and white, would have "the constitutional right to bear arms."

The Civil Rights Act of 1866 . . . , which was considered at the same time as the Freedmen's Bureau Act, similarly sought to protect the right of all citizens to keep and bear arms. . . . [T]he Civil Rights Act, like the Freedmen's Bureau Act, aimed to protect "the constitutional right to bear arms" and not simply to prohibit discrimination. . . .

Congress, however, ultimately . . . [was] persuaded . . . that a constitutional amendment was necessary to provide full protection for the rights of blacks. Today, it is generally accepted that the Fourteenth Amendment was understood to provide a constitutional basis for protecting the rights set out in the Civil Rights Act of 1866. . . .

In debating the Fourteenth Amendment, the 39th Congress referred to the right to keep and bear arms as a fundamental right deserving of protection. . . .

Evidence from the period immediately following the ratification of the Fourteenth Amendment only confirms that the right to keep and bear arms was considered fundamental. . . . [D]ebating the Civil Rights Act of 1871, Congress routinely referred to the right to keep and bear arms and decried the continued disarmament of blacks in the South. . . . Finally, legal commentators from the period emphasized the fundamental nature of the right. . . .

The right to keep and bear arms was also widely protected by state constitutions at the time when the Fourteenth Amendment was ratified. . . .

In sum, it is clear that the Framers and ratifiers of the Fourteenth Amendment counted the right to keep and bear arms among those fundamental rights necessary to our system of ordered liberty.

2

Despite all this evidence, . . . respondents contend that Congress, in the years immediately following the Civil War, merely sought to outlaw "discriminatory measures taken against freedmen, which it addressed by adopting a non-discrimination principle" and that even an outright ban on the possession of firearms was regarded as acceptable, "so long as it was not done in a discriminatory manner." . . . This argument is implausible.

First, while § 1 of the Fourteenth Amendment contains "an antidiscrimination rule," namely, the Equal Protection Clause, municipal respondents can hardly mean that § 1 does no more than prohibit discrimination. If that were so, then the First Amendment, as applied to the States, would not prohibit nondiscriminatory abridgments of the rights to freedom of speech or freedom of religion; the Fourth Amendment, as applied to the States, would not prohibit all unreasonable searches and seizures but only discriminatory searches and seizures—and so on. We assume that this is not [their] view, so what they must mean is that the Second Amendment should be singled out for special—and specially unfavorable—treatment. We reject that suggestion.

Second, [the] argument ignores the clear terms of the Freedmen's Bureau Act of 1866, . . . § 14 [of which] protects "the constitutional right to bear arms," an unmistakable reference to the right protected by the Second Amendment. And it protects the "full and equal benefit" of this right in the States. . . . It would have been nonsensical for Congress to guarantee the full and equal benefit of a constitutional right that does not exist.

Third, if the 39th Congress had outlawed only those laws that discriminate on the basis of race or previous condition of servitude, African Americans in the South would likely have remained vulnerable to attack by many of their worst abusers: the state militia and state peace officers. In the years immediately following the Civil War, a law banning the possession of guns by all private citizens would have been nondiscriminatory only in the formal sense. Any such law—like the Chicago and Oak Park ordinances challenged here—presumably would have permitted the possession of guns by those acting under the authority of the State and would thus have left firearms in the hands of the militia and local peace officers. . . . [T]hose groups were widely involved in harassing blacks in the South.

Fourth, [the] purely antidiscrimination theory . . . disregards the plight of whites in the South who opposed the Black Codes. If the 39th Congress and the ratifying public had simply prohibited racial discrimination with respect to the bearing of arms, opponents of the Black Codes would have been left without the means of self-defense— as had abolitionists in Kansas in the 1850's.

Fifth, the 39th Congress' response to proposals to disband and disarm the Southern militias is instructive. Despite recognizing and deploring the abuses of these militias, the 39th Congress balked at a proposal to disarm them. . . . Disarmament, it was argued, would violate the members' right to bear arms, and it was ultimately decided to disband the militias but not to disarm their members. . . . It cannot be doubted that the right to bear arms was regarded as a substantive guarantee, not a prohibition that could be ignored so long as the States legislated in an evenhanded manner.

IV

. . .

. . . According to municipal respondents, if it is possible to imagine *any* civilized legal system that does not recognize a particular right, then the Due Process Clause does not make that right binding on the States. . . . Therefore, . . . because such countries as England, Canada, Australia, Japan, Denmark, Finland, Luxembourg, and New Zealand either ban or severely limit handgun ownership, it must follow that no right to possess such weapons is protected by the Fourteenth Amendment.

This line of argument is, of course, inconsistent with the long-established standard we apply in incorporation cases. . . . And the present-day implications . . . are stunning. For example, many of the rights that our Bill of Rights provides for persons accused of criminal offenses are virtually unique to this country. If *our* understanding of the right to a jury trial, the right against self-incrimination, and the right to counsel were necessary attributes of *any* civilized country, it would follow that the United States is the only civilized Nation in the world.

... [S]uggesting that their argument applies only to substantive as opposed to procedural rights [still] flies in the face of more than a half-century of precedent. For example, in Everson v. Board of Ed. . . . (1947), the Court held that the Fourteenth Amendment incorporates the Establishment Clause of the First Amendment. Yet several of the countries that municipal respondents recognize as civilized have established state churches. If we were to adopt [their] theory, all of this Court's Establishment Clause precedents involving actions taken by state and local governments would go by the boards.

Municipal respondents maintain that the Second Amendment differs from all of the other provisions of the Bill of Rights because it concerns the right to possess a deadly implement and thus has implications for public safety. . . .

The right to keep and bear arms, however, is not the only constitutional right that has controversial public safety implications. All of the constitutional provisions that impose restrictions on law enforcement and on the prosecution of crimes fall into the same category. . . .

We likewise reject [their] argument that we should depart from our established incorporation methodology on the ground that making the Second Amendment binding on the States and their subdivisions is inconsistent with principles of federalism and will stifle experimentation. . . .

. . .

... Under our precedents, if a Bill of Rights guarantee is fundamental from an American perspective, then, unless *stare decisis* counsels otherwise, that guarantee is fully binding on the States and thus *limits* (but by no means eliminates) their ability to devise solutions to social problems that suit local needs and values. . . .

. . .

As evidence that the Fourteenth Amendment has not historically been understood to restrict the authority of the States to regulate firearms, municipal respondents and supporting *amici* cite a variety of state and local firearms laws that courts have upheld. But what is most striking about their research is the paucity of precedent sustaining bans comparable to those at issue here and in *Heller*. . . . It is important to keep in mind that *Heller*, while striking down a law that prohibited the possession of handguns in the home, recognized that the right to keep and bear arms is not "a right to keep and carry any weapon whatsoever in any manner whatsoever and for whatever purpose." . . . We made it clear in *Heller* that our holding did not cast doubt on such longstanding regulatory measures as "prohibitions on the possession of firearms by felons and the mentally ill," "laws forbidding the carrying of firearms in sensitive places such as schools and government buildings, or laws imposing conditions and qualifications on the commercial sale of arms." . . . We repeat those assurances here. Despite municipal respondents' doomsday proclamations, incorporation does not imperil every law regulating firearms.

Municipal respondents argue, finally, that the right to keep and bear arms is unique among the rights set out in the first eight Amendments "because the reason for codifying the Second Amendment (to protect the militia) differs from the purpose (primarily, to use firearms to engage in self-defense) that is claimed to make the right implicit in the concept of ordered liberty." . . . Municipal respondents suggest that the Second Amendment right differs from the rights heretofore incorporated because the latter were "valued for [their] own sake." . . . But we have never previously suggested that incorporation of a right turns on whether it has intrinsic as opposed to instrumental value, and quite a few of the rights previously held to be incorporated— for example the right to counsel and the right to confront and subpoena witnesses—are clearly instrumental by any measure. Moreover, this contention repackages one of the chief arguments that we rejected in *Heller, i.e.,* that the scope of the Second Amendment right is defined by the immediate threat that led to the inclusion of that right in the Bill of Rights. In *Heller,* we recognized that the codification of this right was prompted by fear that the Federal Government would disarm and thus disable the militias, but we rejected the suggestion that the right was valued only as a means of preserving the militias. . . . On the contrary, we stressed that the right was also valued because the possession of firearms was thought to be essential for self-defense. As we put it, self-defense was "the *central component* of the right itself."

V

[The plurality rejected the methodology advocated in Justice Stevens' dissenting argument that the due process question is not a question of incorporation of the Second Amendment right recognized in *Heller* but of whether due process, standing alone, requires recognition of the particular right respondents asserted, saying in part:]

[T]he Court, for the past half century, has moved away from the two-track approach. If we were now to accept Justice Stevens' theory across the board, decades of decisions would be undermined. We assume that this is not what is proposed. What is urged instead, it appears, is that this theory be revived solely for the individual right that *Heller* recognized, over vigorous dissents.

The relationship between the Bill of Rights' guarantees and the States must be governed by a single, neutral principle. It is far too late to exhume what Justice Brennan . . . derided as "the notion that the Fourteenth Amendment applies to the States only a watered-down, subjective version of the individual guarantees of the Bill of Rights." . . .

B

. . .

Justice Breyer's conclusion that the Fourteenth Amendment does not incorporate the right to keep and bear arms appears to rest primarily on four factors: First, "there is no popular consensus" that the right is fundamental; second, the right does not protect minorities or persons neglected by those holding political power; third, incorporation of the Second Amendment right would "amount to a significant incursion on a traditional and important area of state concern, altering the constitutional relationship between the States and the Federal Government" and preventing local variations; and fourth, determining the scope of the Second Amendment right in cases involving state and local laws will force judges to answer difficult empirical questions regarding matters that are outside their area of expertise. Even if we believed that these factors were relevant to the incorporation inquiry, none of the[m] undermines the case for incorporation of the right to keep and bear arms for self-defense.

First, we have never held that a provision of the Bill of Rights applies to the States only if there is a "popular consensus" that the right is fundamental, and we see no basis for such a rule. But . . . there is evidence of such a consensus. An *amicus* brief submitted by 58 Members of the Senate and 251 Members of the House of Representatives urges us to hold that the right to keep and bear arms is fundamental. . . . Another brief submitted by 38 States takes the same position. . . .

Second, petitioners and many others who live in high-crime areas dispute the proposition that the Second Amendment right does not protect minorities and those lacking political clout. . . .

Third, . . . [i]ncorporation always restricts experimentation and local variations, but that has not stopped the Court from incorporating virtually every other provision of the Bill of Rights. . . .

Finally, Justice Breyer is incorrect that incorporation will require judges to assess the costs and benefits of firearms restrictions and thus to make difficult empirical judgments in an area in which they lack expertise. [W]hile his opinion in *Heller* recommended an interest-balancing test, the Court specifically rejected that suggestion. . . .

* * *

In *Heller,* we held that the Second Amendment protects the right to possess a handgun in the home for the purpose of self-defense. Unless considerations of *stare decisis* counsel otherwise, a provision of the Bill of Rights that protects a right that is fundamental from an American perspective applies equally to the Federal Government and the States. . . . We therefore hold that the Due Process Clause of the Fourteenth Amendment incorporates the Second Amendment right recognized in *Heller*. The judgment of the Court of Appeals is reversed, and the case is remanded for further proceedings.[a]

■ JUSTICE THOMAS, concurring in part and concurring in the judgment.

. . .

Applying what is now a well-settled test, the plurality opinion concludes that the right to keep and bear arms applies to the States through the Fourteenth Amendment's Due Process Clause because it is "fundamental" to the American "scheme of ordered liberty," . . . and " 'deeply rooted in this Nation's history and tradition,' " . . . I agree with that description of the right. But I cannot agree that it is enforceable against the States through a clause that speaks only to "process." Instead, the right to keep and bear arms is a privilege of American citizenship that applies to the States through the Fourteenth Amendment's Privileges or Immunities Clause.

I

Privilege > Process [handwritten]

. . .

. . . The one theme that links the Court's substantive due process precedents together is their lack of a guiding principle to distinguish "fundamental" rights that warrant protection from nonfundamental rights that do not. . . .

. . .

---

[a] Justice Scalia wrote a separate concurring opinion "only to respond to" Justice Stevens' "broad condemnation of the theory of interpretation which underlies the Court's opinion, a theory that makes the traditions of our people paramount." Among other critiques, Justice Scalia said the following:

". . . the question to be decided is not whether the historically focused method is a *perfect means* of restraining aristocratic judicial Constitution-writing; but whether it is the *best means available* in an imperfect world. Or indeed, even more narrowly than that: whether it is demonstrably much better than what Justice Stevens proposes. I think it beyond all serious dispute that it is much less subjective, and intrudes much less upon the democratic process. It is less subjective because it depends upon a body of evidence susceptible of reasoned analysis rather than a variety of vague ethico-political First Principles whose combined conclusion can be found to point in any direction the judges favor. In the most controversial matters brought before this Court—for example, the constitutionality of prohibiting abortion, assisted suicide, or homosexual sodomy, or the constitutionality of the death penalty—*any* historical methodology, under *any* plausible standard of proof, would lead to the same conclusion. Moreover, the methodological differences that divide historians, and the varying interpretive assumptions they bring to their work, are nothing compared to the differences among the American people (though perhaps not among graduates of prestigious law schools) with regard to the moral judgments Justice Stevens would have courts pronounce. And whether or not special expertise is needed to answer historical questions, judges most certainly have no 'comparative . . . advantage,' . . . in resolving moral disputes. What is more, his approach would not eliminate, but multiply, the hard questions courts must confront, since he would not *replace* history with moral philosophy, but would have courts consider *both*."

... I believe ... that a return to [the original meaning of the Fourteenth Amendment] would allow this Court to enforce the rights the Fourteenth Amendment is designed to protect with greater clarity and predictability than the substantive due process framework has so far managed.

. . .

II

. . .

... [T]he objective ... is to discern what "ordinary citizens" at the time of ratification would have understood the Privileges or Immunities Clause to mean. . . .

. . .

[Justice Thomas canvassed early legal documents that spoke of "privileges" and "immunities," which he viewed as indicators that those terms were synonymous with "rights"; evidence "from the political branches in the years leading to the Fourteenth Amendment's adoption"; and statements of its sponsors and opponents, including "well-circulated speeches." To Justice Thomas, "[t]his evidence plainly shows that the ratifying public understood the Privileges or Immunities Clause to protect constitutionally enumerated rights, including the right to keep and bear arms. As the Court demonstrates, there can be no doubt that § 1 was understood to enforce the Second Amendment against the States. In my view, this is because the right to keep and bear arms was understood to be a privilege of American citizenship guaranteed by the Privileges or Immunities Clause."]

III

. . .

... *Cruikshank* squarely held that the right to keep and bear arms was not a privilege of American citizenship, thereby overturning the convictions of militia members responsible for the brutal Colfax Massacre. *Cruikshank* is not a precedent entitled to any respect. The flaws in its interpretation of the Privileges or Immunities Clause are made evident by the . . . evidence of its original meaning, and I would reject the holding on that basis alone. But, the consequences of *Cruikshank* warrant mention as well.

Cruikshank's holding that blacks could look only to state governments for protection of their right to keep and bear arms enabled private forces, often with the assistance of local governments, to subjugate the newly freed slaves and their descendants through a wave of private violence designed to drive blacks from the voting booth and force them into peonage, an effective return to slavery. Without federal enforcement of the inalienable right to keep and bear arms, these militias and mobs were tragically successful in waging a campaign of terror against the very people the Fourteenth Amendment had just made citizens.

. . .

The use of firearms for self-defense was often the only way black citizens could protect themselves from mob violence. . . .

In my view, the record makes plain that the Framers of the Privileges or Immunities Clause and the ratifying-era public understood—just as the Framers of the Second Amendment did—that the right to keep and bear arms was essential to the preservation of liberty. The record makes equally plain that they deemed this right necessary to include in the minimum baseline of federal rights that the Privileges or Immunities Clause established in the wake of the War over slavery. There is nothing about *Cruikshank*'s contrary holding that warrants its retention.

* * *

I agree with the Court that the Second Amendment is fully applicable to the States. I do so because the right to keep and bear arms is guaranteed by the Fourteenth Amendment as a privilege of American citizenship.

■ JUSTICE STEVENS, dissenting.

In District of Columbia v. Heller, . . . (2008), the Court answered the question whether a federal enclave's "prohibition on the possession of usable handguns in the home violates the Second Amendment to the Constitution." The question we should be answering in this case is whether the Constitution "guarantees individuals a fundamental right," enforceable against the States, "to possess a functional, personal firearm, including a handgun, within the home." Complaint ¶ 34. . . . That is a different—and more difficult—inquiry than asking if the Fourteenth Amendment "incorporates" the Second Amendment. The so-called incorporation question was squarely and, in my view, correctly resolved in the late 19th century.

. . .

This is a substantive due process case.

I

. . .

. . . It has been "settled" for well over a century that the Due Process Clause "applies to matters of substantive law as well as to matters of procedure."

The second principle woven through our cases is that substantive due process is fundamentally a matter of personal liberty. . . .

. . . [T]he term "incorporation," like the term "unenumerated rights," is something of a misnomer. Whether an asserted substantive due process interest is explicitly named in one of the first eight Amendments to the Constitution or is not mentioned, the underlying inquiry is the same: We must ask whether the interest is "comprised within the term liberty." . . .

. . . Inclusion in the Bill of Rights is neither necessary nor sufficient for an interest to be judicially enforceable under the Fourteenth Amendment. . . .

The third precept to emerge from our case law flows from the second: The rights protected against state infringement by the Fourteenth Amendment's Due Process Clause need not be identical in shape or scope to the rights protected against Federal Government infringement by the various provisions of the Bill of Rights. . . .

It is true . . . that we have made numerous provisions of the Bill of Rights fully applicable to the States. . . . But we have never accepted a "total incorporation" theory of the Fourteenth Amendment, whereby the Amendment is deemed to subsume the provisions of the Bill of Rights en masse. And we have declined to apply several provisions to the States in any measure. . . .

It is true, as well, that during the 1960's the Court decided a number of cases involving procedural rights in which it treated the Due Process Clause as if it transplanted language from the Bill of Rights into the Fourteenth Amendment. . . . In my judgment, this line of cases is best understood as having concluded that, to ensure a criminal trial satisfies essential standards of fairness, some procedures should be the same in state and federal courts: The need for certainty and uniformity is more pressing, and the margin for error slimmer, when criminal justice is at issue. That principle has little relevance to the question whether a *non*procedural rule set forth in the Bill of Rights qualifies as an aspect of the liberty protected by the Fourteenth Amendment.

... [T]he Second Amendment differs in fundamental respects from its neighboring provisions in the Bill of Rights, ... and if some 1960's opinions purported to establish a general method of incorporation, that hardly binds us in this case. ...

. . .

II

... [T]he Court's narrative fails to capture the continuity and flexibility in our doctrine.

... When confronted with a substantive due process claim, we must ask whether the allegedly unlawful practice violates values "implicit in the concept of ordered liberty." Palko v. Connecticut ... (1937). If the practice in question lacks any "oppressive and arbitrary" character, if judicial enforcement of the asserted right would not materially contribute to "a fair and enlightened system of justice," then the claim is unsuitable for substantive due process protection. ...

Justice Cardozo's test undeniably requires judges to apply their own reasoned judgment, but that does not mean it involves an exercise in abstract philosophy. In addition to other constraints I will soon discuss, see Part III, *infra,* historical and empirical data of various kinds ground the analysis. Textual commitments laid down elsewhere in the Constitution, judicial precedents, English common law, legislative and social facts, scientific and professional developments, practices of other civilized societies, and, above all else, the " 'traditions and conscience of our people,' " *Palko* . . . , are critical variables. They can provide evidence about which rights really are vital to ordered liberty, as well as a spur to judicial action.

. . .

Nor . . . did *Duncan* mark an irreparable break from *Palko,* swapping out liberty for history. *Duncan* limited its discussion to "particular procedural safeguard[s]" in the Bill of Rights relating to "criminal processes," 391 U.S., at 149, n. 14; it did not purport to set a standard for other types of liberty interests. ...

... To the extent the Court's opinion could be read to imply that the historical pedigree of a right is the exclusive or dispositive determinant of its status under the Due Process Clause, the opinion is seriously mistaken.

. . .

... The right to free speech, for instance, has been safeguarded from state infringement not because the States have always honored it, but because it is "essential to free government" and "to the maintenance of democratic institutions"— that is, because the right to free speech is implicit in the concept of ordered liberty. ...

More fundamentally, a rigid historical methodology is unfaithful to the Constitution's command. For if it were really the case that the Fourteenth Amendment's guarantee of liberty embraces only those rights "so rooted in our history, tradition, and practice as to require special protection," *Glucksberg,* ... then the guarantee would serve little function, save to ratify those rights that state actors have *already* been according the most extensive protection. ... That approach ... promises an objectivity it cannot deliver and masks the value judgments that pervade any analysis of what customs, defined in what manner, are sufficiently " 'rooted' "; it countenances the most revolting injustices in the name of continuity, for we must never forget that not only slavery but also the subjugation of women and other rank forms of discrimination are part of our history; and it effaces this Court's distinctive role in saying what the law is, leaving the development and safekeeping of liberty to majoritarian political processes. It is judicial abdication in the guise of judicial modesty.

. . . The judge who would outsource the interpretation of "liberty" to historical sentiment has turned his back on a task the Constitution assigned to him and drained the document of its intended vitality.

III

. . .

. . . [O]nly certain types of especially significant personal interests may qualify for especially heightened protection. . . . Government action that shocks the conscience, pointlessly infringes settled expectations, trespasses into sensitive private realms or life choices without adequate justification, perpetrates gross injustice, or simply lacks a rational basis will always be vulnerable to judicial invalidation. Nor does the fact that an asserted right falls within one of these categories end the inquiry. More fundamental rights may receive more robust judicial protection, but the strength of the individual's liberty interests and the State's regulatory interests must always be assessed and compared. No right is absolute.

Rather than seek a categorical understanding of the liberty clause, our precedents have thus elucidated a conceptual core. . . . Self-determination, bodily integrity, freedom of conscience, intimate relationships, political equality, dignity and respect— these are the central values we have found implicit in the concept of ordered liberty.

Another key constraint on substantive due process analysis is respect for the democratic process. . . .

Recognizing a new liberty right is a momentous step. . . . But sensitivity to the interaction between the intrinsic aspects of liberty and the practical realities of contemporary society provides an important tool for guiding judicial discretion.

This sensitivity is an aspect of a deeper principle: the need to approach our work with humility and caution. . . .

Several rules of the judicial process help enforce such restraint. . . . [T]he Court has applied both the doctrine of *stare decisis* . . . and the common-law method—taking cases and controversies as they present themselves, proceeding slowly and incrementally, building on what came before. . . .

Relatedly, rather than evaluate liberty claims on an abstract plane, the Court has "required in substantive-due-process cases a 'careful description' of the asserted fundamental liberty interest." . . .

. . . Even if the most expansive formulation of a claim does not qualify for substantive due process recognition, particular components of the claim might. . . .

[T]o acknowledge that the task of construing the liberty clause requires judgment is not to say that it is a license for unbridled judicial lawmaking. To the contrary, only an honest reckoning with our discretion allows for honest argumentation and meaningful accountability.

IV

The question in this case, then, is not whether the Second Amendment right to keep and bear arms (whatever that right's precise contours) applies to the States because the Amendment has been incorporated into the Fourteenth Amendment. It has not been. The question, rather, is whether the particular right asserted by petitioners applies to the States because of the Fourteenth Amendment itself, standing on its own bottom. . . .

. . .

Understood as a plea to keep their preferred type of firearm in the home, petitioners' argument has real force. . . .

Bolstering petitioners' claim, our law has long recognized that the home provides a kind of special sanctuary in modern life. . . .

While the individual's interest in firearm possession is thus heightened in the home, the State's corresponding interest in regulation is somewhat weaker. . . . [F]irearms kept inside the home generally pose a lesser threat to public welfare as compared to firearms taken outside. The historical case for regulation is likewise stronger outside the home, as many States have for many years imposed stricter, and less controversial, restrictions on the carriage of arms than on their domestic possession. . . .

It is significant, as well, that a rule limiting the federal constitutional right to keep and bear arms to the home would be less intrusive on state prerogatives and easier to administer. . . .

. . .

V

While I agree with the Court that our substantive due process cases offer a principled basis for holding that petitioners have a constitutional right to possess a usable firearm in the home, I am ultimately persuaded that a better reading of our case law supports the city of Chicago. . . .

First, firearms have a fundamentally ambivalent relationship to liberty. Just as they can help homeowners defend their families and property from intruders, they can help thugs and insurrectionists murder innocent victims. . . .

Hence, in evaluating an asserted right to be free from particular gun-control regulations, liberty is on both sides of the equation. Guns may be useful for self-defense, as well as for hunting and sport, but they also have a unique potential to facilitate death and destruction and thereby to destabilize ordered liberty. . . .

. . . The idea that deadly weapons pose a distinctive threat to the social order—and that reasonable restrictions on their usage therefore impose an acceptable burden on one's personal liberty—is as old as the Republic. . . .

. . . And, of course, guns that start out in the home may not stay in the home. . . .

Second, the right to possess a firearm of one's choosing is different in kind from the liberty interests we have recognized under the Due Process Clause. . . . [I]t does not appear to be the case that the ability to own a handgun, or any particular type of firearm, is critical to leading a life of autonomy, dignity, or political equality. . . .

. . .

The liberty interest asserted by petitioners is also dissimilar from those we have recognized in its capacity to undermine the security of others. To be sure, some of the Bill of Rights' procedural guarantees may place "restrictions on law enforcement" that have "controversial public safety implications." But those implications are generally quite attenuated. . . . The link between handgun ownership and public safety is much tighter. . . .

. . .

Third, the experience of other advanced democracies, including those that share our British heritage, undercuts the notion that an expansive right to keep and bear arms is intrinsic to ordered liberty. . . .

. . .

Fourth, the Second Amendment differs in kind from the Amendments that surround it, with the consequence that its inclusion in the Bill of Rights is not merely unhelpful but positively harmful to petitioners' claim. Generally, the inclusion of a liberty interest in the Bill of Rights points toward the conclusion that it is of fundamental significance and ought to be enforceable against the States. But the Second Amendment plays a peculiar role within the Bill, as announced by its peculiar opening clause. . . . [I]t remains undeniable that "the purpose for which the right was codified" was "to prevent elimination of the militia." *Heller.* . . . Notwithstanding the *Heller* Court's efforts to write the Second Amendment's preamble out of the Constitution, the Amendment still serves the structural function of protecting the States from encroachment by an overreaching Federal Government.

The Second Amendment . . . is directed at preserving the autonomy of the sovereign States, and its logic therefore "resists" incorporation by a federal court *against* the States. . . .

. . .

I accept that the evolution in Americans' understanding of the Second Amendment may help shed light on the question whether a right to keep and bear arms is comprised within Fourteenth Amendment "liberty." But the reasons that motivated the Framers to protect the ability of militiamen to keep muskets available for military use when our Nation was in its infancy, or that motivated the Reconstruction Congress to extend full citizenship to the freedmen in the wake of the Civil War, have only a limited bearing on the question that confronts the homeowner in a crime-infested metropolis today. . . .

Fifth, although it may be true that Americans' interest in firearm possession and state-law recognition of that interest are "deeply rooted" in some important senses, it is equally true that the States have a long and unbroken history of regulating firearms. . . .

. . . And let us not forget that this Court did not recognize *any* non-militia-related interests under the Second Amendment until two Terms ago, in *Heller*. Petitioners do not dispute the city of Chicago's observation that "[n]o other substantive Bill of Rights protection has been regulated nearly as intrusively" as the right to keep and bear arms. . . .

. . .

Nor will the Court's intervention bring any clarity to this enormously complex area of law. . . .

Furthermore, and critically, the Court's imposition of a national standard is still more unwise because the elected branches have shown themselves to be perfectly capable of safeguarding the interest in keeping and bearing arms. . . .

. . . Neither petitioners nor those most zealously committed to their views represent a group or a claim that is liable to receive unfair treatment at the hands of the majority. . . . Having failed to show why their asserted interest is intrinsic to the concept of ordered liberty or vulnerable to maltreatment in the political arena, they have failed to show why "the word liberty in the Fourteenth Amendment" should be "held to prevent the natural outcome of a dominant opinion" about how to deal with the problem of handgun violence in the city of Chicago. *Lochner,* . . . (Holmes, J., dissenting).

VI

. . .

. . . Justice Scalia's defense of his method, which holds out objectivity and restraint as its cardinal—and, it seems, only—virtues, is unsatisfying on its own terms. For a limitless number of subjective judgments may be . . . *buried* in the analysis. At least with my approach, the judge's cards are laid on the table for all to see, and to critique. . . .

. . . My method seeks to synthesize dozens of cases on which the American people have relied for decades. Justice Scalia's method seeks to vaporize them. So I am left to wonder, which of us is more faithful to this Nation's constitutional history? And which of us is more faithful to the values and commitments of the American people, as they stand today? . . .

. . . What if the evidence had shown that, whereas at one time firearm possession contributed substantially to personal liberty and safety, nowadays it contributes nothing, or even tends to undermine them? Would it still have been reasonable to constitutionalize the right?

. . .

. . . Under our constitutional scheme, I would have thought that a judicial approach to liberty claims such as the one I have outlined—an approach that investigates both the intrinsic nature of the claimed interest and the practical significance of its judicial enforcement, that is transparent in its reasoning and sincere in its effort to incorporate constraints, that is guided by history but not beholden to it, and that is willing to protect some rights even if they have not already received uniform protection from the elected branches—has the capacity to improve, rather than "[im]peril," our democracy. It all depends on judges' exercising careful, reasoned judgment. As it always has, and as it always will.

VII

. . .

. . . Thankfully, the Second Amendment right identified in *Heller* and its newly minted Fourteenth Amendment analogue are limited, at least for now, to the home. But neither the "assurances" provided by the plurality, nor the many historical sources cited in its opinion should obscure the reality that today's ruling marks a dramatic change in our law—or that the Justices who have joined it have brought to bear an awesome amount of discretion in resolving the legal question presented by this case.

I would proceed more cautiously. For the reasons set out at length above, I cannot accept either the methodology the Court employs or the conclusions it draws. . . .

■ JUSTICE BREYER, with whom JUSTICE GINSBURG and JUSTICE SOTOMAYOR join, dissenting.

In my view, Justice Stevens has demonstrated that the Fourteenth Amendment's guarantee of "substantive due process" does not include a general right to keep and bear firearms for purposes of private self-defense. . . .

The Court, however, does not expressly rest its opinion upon "substantive due process" concerns. Rather, it directs its attention to this Court's "incorporation" precedents and asks whether the Second Amendment right to private self-defense is "fundamental" so that it applies to the States through the Fourteenth Amendment.

I shall therefore separately consider the question of "incorporation." I can find nothing in the Second Amendment's text, history, or underlying rationale that could warrant characterizing it as "fundamental" insofar as it seeks to protect the keeping and bearing of arms for private self-defense purposes. Nor can I find any justification for interpreting the Constitution as transferring ultimate regulatory authority over the private uses of firearms from democratically elected legislatures to courts or from the States to the Federal Government. I therefore conclude that the Fourteenth Amendment does not "incorporate" the Second Amendment's right "to keep and bear Arms." . . .

I

. . .

Since *Heller,* historians, scholars, and judges have continued to express the view that the Court's historical account was flawed. . . .

. . .

The historians now tell us . . . that the right to which Blackstone referred had, not *nothing,* but *everything,* to do with the militia. . . . [W]hen Blackstone referred to " 'the right of having and using arms for self-preservation and defence,' " he was referring to the right of the people *"to take part in the militia* to defend their political liberties," and *to the right of Parliament* (which represented the people) to *raise a militia* even when the King sought to deny it that power. . . .

If history, and history alone, is what matters, why would the Court not now reconsider *Heller* in light of these more recently published historical views? . . . At the least, where *Heller's* historical foundations are so uncertain, why extend its applicability?

. . . In my own view, the Court should not look to history alone but to other factors as well—above all, in cases where the history is so unclear that the experts themselves strongly disagree. It should, for example, consider the basic values that underlie a constitutional provision and their contemporary significance. And it should examine as well the relevant consequences and practical justifications that might, or might not, warrant removing an important question from the democratic decisionmaking process. . . .

II

A

. . .

[T]his Court, in considering an incorporation question, has never stated that the historical status of a right is the only relevant consideration. Rather, the Court has either explicitly or implicitly made clear in its opinions that the right in question has remained fundamental over time. . . .

I thus think it proper, above all where history provides no clear answer, to look to other factors in considering whether a right is sufficiently "fundamental" to remove it from the political process in every State. I would include among those factors the nature of the right; any contemporary disagreement about whether the right is fundamental; the extent to which incorporation will further other, perhaps more basic, constitutional aims; and the extent to which incorporation will advance or hinder the Constitution's structural aims, including its division of powers among different governmental institutions (and the people as well). . . .

. . . Finally, I would take account of the Framers' basic reason for believing the Court ought to have the power of judicial review. . . . [According to Alexander Hamilton in Federalist No. 78, j]udges . . . may find it easier to resist popular pressure to suppress the basic rights of an unpopular minority. See United States v. Carolene Products Co., 304 U.S. 144, 152, n. 4 (1938). That being so, it makes sense to ask whether that particular comparative judicial advantage is relevant to the case at hand. . . .

B

. . . [T]he incorporation of the Second Amendment cannot be based on the militia-related aspect of what *Heller* found to be more extensive Second Amendment rights.

[A]s *Heller* concedes, the private self-defense right that the Court would incorporate has nothing to do with "the *reason*" the Framers "codified" the right to keep and bear arms "in a written Constitution." . . . *Heller* immediately adds that the self-defense right was nonetheless "the *central component* of the right." . . . In my view, this is the historical equivalent of a claim that water runs uphill. . . . But, taking it as valid, the Framers' basic *reasons* for including language in the Constitution would nonetheless seem more pertinent (in deciding about the contemporary *importance* of a right) than the particular *scope* 17th- or 18th-century listeners would have then assigned to the words they used. And examination of the Framers' motivation tells us they did not think the private armed self-defense right was of paramount importance. . . .

Further, there is no popular consensus that the private self-defense right described in *Heller* is fundamental. . . . [E]very State regulates firearms extensively, and public opinion is sharply divided on the appropriate level of regulation. . . . And the appropriate level of firearm regulation has . . . long been, and continues to be, a hotly contested matter of political debate. . . .

Moreover, there is no reason here to believe that incorporation of the private self-defense right will further any other or broader constitutional objective. We are aware of no argument that gun-control regulations target or are passed with the purpose of targeting "discrete and insular minorities." . . . Nor will incorporation help to assure equal respect for individuals. Unlike the First Amendment's rights of free speech, free press, assembly, and petition, the private self-defense right does not comprise a necessary part of the democratic process that the Constitution seeks to establish. . . . Unlike the First Amendment's religious protections, the Fourth Amendment's protection against unreasonable searches and seizures, the Fifth and Sixth Amendments' insistence upon fair criminal procedure, and the Eighth Amendment's protection against cruel and unusual punishments, the private self-defense right does not significantly seek to protect individuals who might otherwise suffer unfair or inhumane treatment at the hands of a majority. Unlike the protections offered by many of these same Amendments, it does not involve matters as to which judges possess a comparative expertise, by virtue of their close familiarity with the justice system and its operation. And, unlike the Fifth Amendment's insistence on just compensation, it does not involve a matter where a majority might unfairly seize for itself property belonging to a minority.

Finally, incorporation of the right *will* work a significant disruption in the constitutional allocation of decisionmaking authority, thereby interfering with the Constitution's ability to further its objectives.

First, on any reasonable accounting, the incorporation of the right recognized in *Heller* would amount to a significant incursion on a traditional and important area of state concern. . . .

Second, determining the constitutionality of a particular state gun law requires finding answers to complex empirically based questions of a kind that legislatures are better able than courts to make. . . .

Government regulation of the right to bear arms normally embodies a judgment that the regulation will help save lives. The determination whether a gun regulation is constitutional would thus almost always require the weighing of the constitutional right to bear arms against the "primary concern of every government—a concern for the safety and indeed the lives of its citizens." . . .

        . . .

        . . . How can the Court assess the strength of the government's regulatory interests without addressing issues of empirical fact? How can the Court determine if a regulation is appropriately tailored without considering its impact? And how can the Court determine if there are less restrictive alternatives without considering what will happen if those alternatives are implemented?

. . .

. . . The fact is that judges do not know the answers to the kinds of empirically based questions that will often determine the need for particular forms of gun regulation. . . .

[T]here is no institutional need to send judges off on this "mission-almost-impossible." Legislators are . . . far better suited than judges to uncover facts and to understand their relevance. And legislators, unlike Article III judges, can be held democratically responsible for their empirically based and value-laden conclusions. . . .

. . .

Third, the ability of States to reflect local preferences and conditions—both key virtues of federalism—here has particular importance. The incidence of gun ownership varies substantially as between crowded cities and uncongested rural communities, as well as among the different geographic regions of the country. . . .

. . .

Fourth, although incorporation of any right removes decisions from the democratic process, the incorporation of this particular right does so without strong offsetting justification. . . .

. . .

In sum, the police power, the superiority of legislative decisionmaking, the need for local decisionmaking, the comparative desirability of democratic decisionmaking, the lack of a manageable judicial standard, and the life-threatening harm that may flow from striking down regulations all argue against incorporation. Where the incorporation of other rights has been at issue, *some* of these problems have arisen. But in this instance *all* these problems are present, *all* at the same time, and *all* are likely to be present in most, perhaps nearly all, of the cases in which the constitutionality of a gun regulation is at issue. At the same time, the important factors that favor incorporation in other instances—*e.g.,* the protection of broader constitutional objectives—are not present here. The upshot is that all factors militate against incorporation—with the possible exception of historical factors.

III

. . . The plurality . . . looks to selected portions of the Nation's history . . .

. . .

. . . [M]any States have constitutional provisions protecting gun possession. But, as far as I can tell, those provisions typically do no more than guarantee that a gun regulation will be a *reasonable* police power regulation. . . . It is thus altogether unclear whether such provisions would prohibit cities such as Chicago from enacting laws, such as the law before us, banning handguns. . . .

. . . States and localities have consistently enacted firearms regulations, including regulations similar to those at issue here, throughout our Nation's history. Courts have repeatedly upheld such regulations. And it is, at the very least, possible, and perhaps likely, that incorporation will impose on every, or nearly every, State a different right to bear arms than they currently recognize—a right that threatens to destabilize settled state legal principles. . . .

I thus cannot find a historical consensus with respect to whether the right described by *Heller* is "fundamental" as our incorporation cases use that term. Nor can

I find sufficient historical support for the majority's conclusion that that right is "deeply rooted in this Nation's history and tradition." Instead, I find no more than ambiguity and uncertainty that perhaps even expert historians would find difficult to penetrate. And a historical record that is so ambiguous cannot itself provide an adequate basis for incorporating a private right of self-defense and applying it against the States.

The Eighteenth Century

First, . . . the history discussed in *Heller* shows that the Second Amendment was enacted primarily for the purpose of protecting militia-related rights. . . .

Second, historians now tell us that the right to which Blackstone referred, an important link in the *Heller* majority's historical argument, concerned the right of Parliament (representing the people) to form a militia to oppose a tyrant (the King) threatening to deprive the people of their traditional liberties (which did not include an unregulated right to possess guns). . . .

Third, scholarly articles indicate that firearms were heavily regulated at the time of the framing—perhaps more heavily regulated than the Court in *Heller* believed. . . .

Fourth, after the Constitution was adopted, several States continued to regulate firearms possession by, for example, adopting rules that would have prevented the carrying of loaded firearms in the city. . . .

The Pre–Civil War Nineteenth Century

. . .

First, additional States began to regulate the discharge of firearms in public places. . . .

Second, States began to regulate the possession of concealed weapons, which were both popular and dangerous. . . .

. . .

The Post–Civil War Nineteenth Century

. . .

First, the Court today properly declines to revisit our interpretation of the Privileges or Immunities Clause. . . .

. . .

There is . . . every reason to believe that the *fundamental* concern of the Reconstruction Congress was the eradication of discrimination, not the provision of a new substantive right to bear arms free from reasonable state police power regulation. . . .

Second, firearms regulation in the later part of the 19th century was common. . . .

. . .

[F]our States largely banned the possession of all nonmilitary handguns during this period. . . . Fifteen States banned the concealed carry of pistols and other deadly weapons. . . . And individual municipalities enacted stringent gun controls, often in response to local conditions. . . .

Further, much as they had during the period before the Civil War, state courts routinely upheld such restrictions. . . .

The Twentieth and Twenty-First Centuries

. . .

First, by the end of the 20th century, in every State and many local communities, highly detailed and complicated regulatory schemes governed (and continue to govern) nearly every aspect of firearm ownership: Who may sell guns and how they must be sold; who may purchase guns and what type of guns may be purchased; how firearms must be stored and where they may be used; and so on. . . .

Of particular relevance here, some municipalities ban handguns, even in States that constitutionally protect the right to bear arms. . . .

. . .

Second, as I stated earlier, state courts in States with constitutions that provide gun rights have almost uniformly interpreted those rights as providing protection only against *unreasonable* regulation of guns. . . .

. . .

Indeed, state courts have specifically upheld as constitutional (under their state constitutions) firearms regulations that have included handgun bans. . . .

. . .

* * *

. . . Read in the majority's favor, the historical evidence is at most ambiguous. And, in the absence of any other support for its conclusion, ambiguous history cannot show that the Fourteenth Amendment incorporates a private right of self-defense against the States.

. . .

Due Process as a Limitation on Procedures Not Forbidden by the Bill of Rights

Justice Black substantially won his argument that the fourteenth amendment should be construed to make the Bill of Rights applicable to the states. As the following case indicates, however, he lost his battle to confine Court review of state procedures to the "specific" provisions of the Bill of Rights.

In re Winship

397 U.S. 358 (1970).

In a case addressing what process must be accorded in juvenile proceedings, the Court examined the requirement that proof of criminal charges be beyond a reasonable doubt, concluding that it "plays a vital role in the American scheme of criminal procedure" and that its use "is indispensable to command the respect and confidence of the community in applications of the criminal law." based on such judgments as to the importance of the standard, the Court said:

"Lest there remain any doubt about the constitutional stature of the reasonable-doubt standard, we explicitly hold that the Due Process Clause protects the accused against conviction except upon proof beyond a reasonable doubt of every fact necessary to constitute the crime with which he is charged."

Justice Harlan concurred in the opinion and judgment. Justice Black dissented at length, opening his opinion with the following:

". . . The Court has never clearly held . . . that proof beyond a reasonable doubt is either expressly or impliedly commanded by any provision of the Constitution. The Bill of Rights, which in my view is made fully applicable to the States by the Fourteenth Amendment, see Adamson v. California, 332 U.S. 46, 71–75 (1947) (dissenting opinion), does by express language provide for, among other things, a right to counsel in criminal trials, a right to indictment, and the right of a defendant to be informed of the nature of the charges against him. And in two places the Constitution provides for trial by jury, but nowhere in that document is there any statement that conviction of crime requires proof of guilt beyond a reasonable doubt. The Constitution thus goes into some detail to spell out what kind of trial a defendant charged with crime should have, and I believe the Court has no power to add to or subtract from the procedures set forth by the Founders. I realize that it is far easier to substitute individual judges' ideas of 'fairness' for the fairness prescribed by the Constitution, but I shall not at any time surrender my belief that that document itself should be our guide, not our own concept of what is fair, decent, and right. That this old 'shock-the-conscience' test is what the Court is relying on, rather than the words of the Constitution, is clearly enough revealed by the reference of the majority to 'fair treatment' and to the statement by the dissenting judges in the New York Court of Appeals that failure to require proof beyond a reasonable doubt amounts to a 'lack of fundamental fairness.' As I have said time and time again, I prefer to put my faith in the words of the written Constitution itself rather than to rely on the shifting, day-to-day standards of fairness of individual judges."[a]

More recently, Court holdings that fourteenth amendment due process limits state procedures not forbidden by the Bill of Rights have provoked disagreement within the Court about what methodology the Court should employ in defining the additional prohibitions. For example, having previously held in Browning-Ferris Industries v. Kelco Disposal, Inc., 492 U.S. 257 (1989), that the Eighth Amendment ban on excessive fines does not apply to punitive damage awards in cases between private parties, the Court decided that the Due Process Clause does circumscribe state procedures for awarding punitive damages. Pacific Mutual Life Insurance Co. v. Haslip, 499 U.S. 1 (1991).

Justice Blackmun's majority opinion upheld Alabama's traditional common-law method of assessing punitive damages, under which the decisions of court-instructed juries were subject to trial and appellate review, but only after inquiring whether that method was "inherently unfair." Furthermore, even though "well established before the Fourteenth Amendment was enacted" and with "[n]othing in that Amendment's text or history indicat[ing] an intention on the part of its drafters to overturn the prevailing method[,]" "general concerns of reasonableness and adequate guidance from the court when the case is tried to a jury properly enter into the constitutional calculus."

Justice Scalia's concurrence objected to the Court's "fairness" or "reasonableness" inquiry. In his view, "jury-assessed punitive damages" are "categorically" valid, because no Bill of Rights provision is implicated and the Due Process Clause itself is not violated so long as a particular procedure is "a traditional one." Asserting that "it is not for the Members of this Court to decide from time to time whether a process approved by the legal traditions of our people is 'due process' . . . ," he concluded that

---

[a] In Apprendi v. New Jersey, 530 U.S. 466 (2000), the Court, invoking *Winship*, held, 5–4, that the Due Process Clause of the Fourteenth Amendment requires that "[o]ther than the fact of a prior conviction, any fact that increases the penalty for a crime beyond the prescribed statutory maximum must be submitted to a jury, and proved beyond a reasonable doubt." Accordingly, a state statute that permitted a trial judge, at sentencing, to extend the prison term of a defendant convicted of a crime carrying a maximum 10-year sentence beyond 10 years on a finding, by only a preponderance of the evidence, that the defendant had acted with a purpose to intimidate because of bias, was unconstitutional for not allowing a jury determination of the finding and for not requiring proof of the hate crime purpose "beyond a reasonable doubt." See also Blakely v. Washington, 542 U.S. 296 (2004); United States v. Booker, 543 U.S. 220 (2005).

"traditional practice (unless contrary to the Bill of Rights) is conclusive of 'fundamental fairness.' "

Justice Kennedy concurred separately, agreeing "that the judgment of history should govern the outcome" in this case, but disagreeing with Justice Scalia "that widespread adherence to a historical practice always forecloses further inquiry when a party challenges an ancient institution or procedure as violative of due process." Justice O'Connor's even more emphatic dissent said that "[i]t does not matter that the system has been around for a long time, or that the result in this particular case may not seem glaringly unfair." She responded to Justice Scalia as follows:

"Circumstances are different than they were 200 years ago, and nothing in the Fourteenth Amendment requires us to blind ourselves to this fact. . . . Just the opposite is true. Due process demands that we possess some degree of confidence that the procedures employed to deprive persons of life, liberty, and property are capable of producing fair and reasonable results. When we lose that confidence, a change must be made."[b]

---

[b] Compare with *Haslip* the Court's subsequent decision in Honda Motor Co. v. Oberg, 512 U.S. 415 (1994), invalidating under due process Oregon's denial of judicial review of the size of punitive damage awards. Noting that "[o]ur recent cases have recognized a substantive limit on the size of punitive damage awards" and that judicial review as a safeguard against excessive verdicts was a well-established common law tradition from which Oregon alone had deviated (and had done so without providing a substitute procedure), Justice Stevens observed for the majority in pertinent part:

"Oregon's abrogation of a well-established common law protection against arbitrary deprivations of property raises a presumption that its procedures violate the Due Process Clause. . . . [T]raditional practice provides a touchstone for constitutional analysis. . . . Because the basic procedural protections of the common law have been regarded as so fundamental, very few cases have arisen in which a party has complained of their denial. In fact, most of our Due Process decisions involve arguments that traditional protections provide too little protection and that additional safeguards are necessary to ensure compliance with the Constitution. . . . Pacific Mut. Life Ins. v. Haslip. . . ."

For a discussion of the substantive due process limitations the Court has applied to the review of punitive damages awards, see Note, "Due Process Limitations on State Punitive Damages Awards," infra p. 355.

CHAPTER 9

THE DUE PROCESS CLAUSE AND THE REVIEW OF THE REASONABLENESS OF LEGISLATION

1. ECONOMIC REGULATORY LEGISLATION—THE RISE AND FALL OF DUE PROCESS

Due Process as a Restraint on the Substance of Legislation

The due process clauses of the Fifth and Fourteenth Amendments presented two major initial problems of interpretation: (1) Were the clauses, like Magna Carta, intended only as a restraint upon the executive? Did they operate only to provide that the executive branch of the government shall operate in accordance with the common or statutory law in force? Or were they intended in the context of the United States to function as limitations upon the powers of Congress and of the state legislatures? (2) If they were intended to limit the legislatures, did they serve to restrain only the enactment of procedures which are not "due" or "fair"? Or did they serve to impose restraints on the substance of legislation?

In two cases arising under the fifth amendment before the Civil War the Court almost casually gave answers to these questions. In Murray's Lessee v. Hoboken Land & Improvement Co., 59 U.S. (18 How.) 272, 276 (1856), the Court answered the first question: "It is manifest that it was not left to the legislative power to enact any process which might be devised. The article is a restraint on the legislative as well as on the executive and judicial powers of government, and cannot be so constructed as to leave congress free to make any process 'due process of law' by its mere will." In Dred Scott v. Sandford, 60 U.S. (19 How.) 393, 450 (1857), the Court with equal casualness gave a substantive content to the clause: "And an Act of Congress which deprives a citizen of the United States of his liberty or property, merely because he came himself or brought his property into a particular Territory of the United States, and who had committed no offense against the laws, could hardly be dignified with the name of due process of law."

In the Slaughter-House Cases, 83 U.S. (16 Wall.) 36 (1872), the Court summarily rejected a challenge to a law granting a monopoly based on due process, in the face of a dissent by Justice Bradley arguing that "a law which prohibits a large class of citizens from adopting a lawful employment, or from following a lawful employment previously adopted, does deprive them of liberty as well as property, without due process of law. Their right of choice is a portion of their liberty; their occupation is their property."

The Court addressed the issues again in 1878 in Davidson v. New Orleans, 96 U.S. 97. The Court upheld an application of a Louisiana statute providing for a special assessment against property for drainage purposes. In discussing the meaning of the due process clause the Court said: "It is easy to see that when the great Barons of England wrung from King John, at the point of the sword, the concession that neither their lives nor their property should be disposed of by the Crown, except as provided by the law of the land, they meant by 'law of the land' the ancient and customary laws of the English people, or laws enacted by the Parliament of which those Barons were a controlling element. It was not in their minds, therefore, to protect themselves against the enactment of laws by the Parliament of England. But when, in the year of grace 1866, there is placed in the Constitution of the United States a declaration that 'no State shall deprive any person of life, liberty, or property without due process of law,' can a State make anything due process of law which, by its own legislation, it chooses to declare such? To affirm this is to hold that the prohibition to the States is of no avail, or has no application where the invasion of private rights is affected under the forms of state legislation. It seems to us that a statute which declared in terms, and without more, that the full and exclusive title of a described piece of land, which is now in A, shall be and is hereby vested in B, would, if effectual, deprive A of his property without due process of law, within the meaning of the constitutional provision. . . ."

Between 1877 and 1900, the Court gradually broadened its interpretation of the meaning of the due process clause with reference to economic regulations. In Mugler v. Kansas, 123 U.S. 623 (1887), the Court upheld a state law prohibiting the manufacture and sale of alcoholic beverages but stated that not every regulatory statute "is to be accepted as a legitimate exertion of the police powers of the State. There are, of necessity, limits beyond which legislation cannot rightfully go. . . . The courts are not bound by mere forms, nor are they to be misled by mere pretenses. They are at liberty—indeed, are under a solemn duty—to look at the substance of things, whenever they enter upon the inquiry whether the Legislature has transcended the limits of its authority. If therefore, a statute purporting to have been enacted to protect the public health, the public morals, or the public safety, has no real or substantial relations to those objects, or is a palpable invasion of rights secured by the fundamental law, it is the duty of the courts to so adjudge, and thereby give effect to the Constitution."

The first major use of the due process clause to invalidate state economic regulations arose in the context of state regulation of railroad rates. In Chicago, M. & St. P.R. Co. v. Minnesota, 134 U.S. 418 (1890), the Court held unconstitutional a Minnesota statute authorizing a state commission to fix rates to be charged by railroads and forbidding any judicial review of the rates set. The Court said in part: "If the company is deprived of the power of charging reasonable rates for the use of its property, and such deprivation takes place in the absence of an investigation by judicial machinery, it is deprived of the lawful use of its property, and thus, in substance and effect, of the property itself, without due process of law and in violation of the Constitution of the United States. . . ."

Allgeyer v. Louisiana
165 U.S. 578 (1897).

The Court held that under the due process clause Louisiana could not make it a misdemeanor for a resident to use the mails to enter into a contract in New York with an insurance company not licensed to do business in Louisiana to insure goods shipped from Louisiana to Europe. The court said: "The Supreme Court of Louisiana says that the act of writing within that State the letter of notification, was an act therein done to effect an insurance on property then in the State, in a marine insurance company which had not complied with its laws, and such act was, therefore, prohibited by the statute. As so construed we think the statute is a violation of the Fourteenth Amendment of the Federal Constitution, in that it deprives the defendants of their liberty without due process of law. The statute which forbids such act does not become due process of law, because it is inconsistent with the provisions of the Constitution of the Union. The liberty mentioned in that amendment means not only the right of the citizen to be free from the mere physical restraint of his person, as by incarceration, but the term is deemed to embrace the right of the citizen to be free in the enjoyment of all his faculties; to be free to use them in all lawful ways; to live and work where he will; to earn his livelihood by any lawful calling; to pursue any livelihood or avocation, and for that purpose to enter into all contracts which may be proper, necessary and essential to his carrying out to a successful conclusion the purposes above mentioned."

Lochner v. New York

198 U.S. 45, 25 S.Ct. 539, 49 L.Ed. 937 (1905).

■ MR. JUSTICE PECKHAM . . . delivered the opinion of the Court:

The indictment, it will be seen, charges that the plaintiff in error violated the 110th section of article 8, chapter 415, of the Laws of 1897, known as the labor law of the state of New York, in that he wrongfully and unlawfully required and permitted an employee working for him to work more than sixty hours in one week. . . .

It is not an act merely fixing the number of hours which shall constitute a legal day's work, but an absolute prohibition upon the employer permitting, under any circumstances, more than ten hours' work to be done in his establishment. The employee may desire to earn the extra money which would arise from his working more than the prescribed time, but this statute forbids the employer from permitting the employee to earn it.

The statute necessarily interferes with the right of contract between the employer and employees, concerning the number of hours in which the latter may labor in the bakery of the employer. The general right to make a contract in relation to his business is part of the liberty of the individual protected by the 14th Amendment of the Federal Constitution. Allgeyer v. Louisiana, 165 U.S. 578. Under that provision no state can deprive any person of life, liberty, or property without due process of law. The right to purchase or to sell labor is part of the liberty protected by this amendment, unless there are circumstances which exclude the right. There are, however, certain powers, existing in the sovereignty of each state in the Union, somewhat vaguely termed police powers, the exact description and limitation of which have not been attempted by the courts. Those powers, broadly stated, and without, at present, any attempt at a more specific limitation, relate to the safety, health, morals, and general welfare of the public. Both property and liberty are held on such reasonable conditions as may be imposed by the governing power of the state in the exercise of those powers, and with such conditions the 14th Amendment was not designed to interfere. Mugler v. Kansas, 123 U.S. 623. . . .

Therefore, when the state, by its legislature, in the assumed exercise of its police powers, has passed an act which seriously limits the right to labor or the right of contract in regard to their means of livelihood between persons who are *sui juris* (both employer and employee), it becomes of great importance to determine which shall prevail,—the right of the individual to labor for such time as he may choose, or the right of the state to prevent the individual from laboring, or from entering into any contract to labor, beyond a certain time prescribed by the state.

This court has recognized the existence and upheld the exercise of the police powers of the states in many cases which might fairly be considered as border ones, and it has, in the course of its determination of questions regarding the asserted invalidity of such statutes, on the ground of their violation of the rights secured by the Federal Constitution, been guided by rules of a very liberal nature, the application of which has resulted, in numerous instances, in upholding the validity of state statutes thus assailed. Among the later cases where the state law has been upheld by this court is that of Holden v. Hardy, 169 U.S. 366. A provision in the act of the legislature of Utah was there under consideration, the act limiting the employment of workmen in all underground mines or workings, to eight hours per day, "except in cases of emergency, where life or property is in imminent danger." It also limited the hours of labor in smelting and other institutions for the reduction or refining of ores or metals to eight hours per day, except in like cases of emergency. The act was held to be a valid exercise of the police powers of the state. . . .

It must, of course, be conceded that there is a limit to the valid exercise of the police power by the state. . . . In every case that comes before this court, therefore, where legislation of this character is concerned, and where the protection of the Federal Constitution is sought, the question necessarily arises: Is this a fair, reasonable, and appropriate exercise of the police power of the state, or is it an unreasonable, unnecessary, and arbitrary interference with the right of the individual to his personal liberty, or to enter into those contracts in relation to labor which may seem to him appropriate or necessary for the support of himself and his family? Of course the liberty of contract relating to labor includes both parties to it. The one has as much right to purchase as the other to sell labor.

This is not a question of substituting the judgment of the court for that of the legislature. If the act be within the power of the state it is valid, although the judgment of the court might be totally opposed to the enactment of such a law. But the question would still remain: Is it within the police power of the state? and that question must be answered by the court.

The question whether this act is valid as a labor law, pure and simple, may be dismissed in a few words. There is no reasonable ground for interfering with the liberty of persons or the right of free contract, by determining the hours of labor, in the occupation of a baker. . . . Viewed in the light of a purely labor law with no reference whatever to the question of health, we think that a law like the one before us involves neither the safety, the morals, nor the welfare of the public, and that the interest of the public is not in the slightest degree affected by such an act. The law must be upheld, if at all, as a law pertaining to the health of the individual engaged in the occupation of a baker. . . .

We think the limit of the police power has been reached and passed in this case. There is, in our judgment, no reasonable foundation for holding this to be necessary or appropriate as a health law to safeguard the public health, or the health of the individuals who are following the trade of a baker. . . .

It is also urged, pursuing the same line of argument, that it is to the interest of the state that its population should be strong and robust, and therefore any legislation which may be said to tend to make people healthy must be valid as health laws, enacted under the police power. If this be a valid argument and a justification for this kind of legislation, it follows that the protection of the Federal Constitution from undue interference with liberty of person and freedom of contract is visionary, wherever the law is sought to be justified as a valid exercise of the police power. Scarcely any law but might find shelter under such assumptions, and conduct, properly so called, as well as contract, would come under the restrictive sway of the legislature. Not only the hours of employees, but the hours of employers, could be regulated, and doctors, lawyers, scientists, all professional men, as well as athletes and artisans, could be forbidden to fatigue their brains and bodies by prolonged hours of exercise, lest the fighting strength of the state be impaired. We mention these extreme cases because the contention is extreme. We do not believe in the soundness of the views which uphold this law. . . . Statutes of the nature of that under review, limiting the hours in which grown and intelligent men may labor to earn their living, are mere meddlesome interferences with the rights of the individual, and they are not saved from condemnation by the claim that they are passed in the exercise of the police power and upon the subject of the health of the individual whose rights are interfered with, unless there be some fair ground, reasonable in and of itself, to say that there is material danger to the public health, or to the health of the employees, if the hours of labor are not curtailed. . . .

It is impossible for us to shut our eyes to the fact that many of the laws of this character, while passed under what is claimed to be the police power for the purpose of protecting the public health or welfare, are, in reality, passed from other motives. We are justified in saying so when, from the character of the law and the subject upon which it legislates, it is apparent that the public health or welfare bears but the most remote relation to the law. The purpose of a statute must be determined from the natural and legal effect of the language employed; and whether it is or is not repugnant to the Constitution of the United States must be determined from the natural effect of such statutes when put into operation, and not from their proclaimed purpose. . . .

It is manifest to us that the limitation of the hours of labor as provided for in this section of the statute under which the indictment was found, and the plaintiff in error convicted, has no such direct relation to, and no such substantial effect upon, the health of the employee, as to justify us in regarding the section as really a health law. It seems to us that the real object and purpose were simply to regulate the hours of labor between the master and his employees (all being men, *sui juris*), in a private business, not dangerous in any degree to morals, or in any real and substantial degree to the health of the employees. Under such circumstances the freedom of master and employee to contract with each other in relation to their employment, and in defining the same, cannot be prohibited or interfered with, without violating the Federal Constitution.

The judgment of the Court of Appeals of New York, as well as that of the Supreme Court and of the County Court of Oneida County, must be reversed and the case remanded to the County Court for further proceedings not inconsistent with this opinion.

Reversed.

■ MR. JUSTICE HARLAN (with whom MR. JUSTICE WHITE and MR. JUSTICE DAY concurred) dissenting:

. . .

I take it to be firmly established that what is called the liberty of contract may, within certain limits, be subjected to regulations designed and calculated to promote the general welfare, or to guard the public health, the public morals, or the public safety. "The liberty secured by the Constitution of the United States to every person within its jurisdiction does not import," this court has recently said, "an absolute right in each person to be at all times and in all circumstances wholly freed from restraint. There are manifold restraints to which every person is necessarily subject for the common good." . . .

Granting, then, that there is a liberty of contract which cannot be violated even under the sanction of direct legislative enactment, but assuming, as according to settled law we may assume, that such liberty of contract is subject to such regulations as the state may reasonably prescribe for the common good and the well-being of society, what are the conditions under which the judiciary may declare such regulations to be in excess of legislative authority and void? Upon this point there is no room for dispute; for the rule is universal that a legislative enactment, Federal or state, is never to be disregarded or held invalid unless it be, beyond question, plainly and palpably in excess of legislative power. . . . If there be doubt as to the validity of the statute, that doubt must therefore be resolved in favor of its validity and the courts must keep their hands off leaving the legislature to meet the responsibility for unwise legislation. If the end which the legislature seeks to accomplish be one to which its power extends, and if the means employed to that end, although not the wisest or best, are yet not plainly and palpably unauthorized by law, then the court cannot interfere. In other words, when the validity of a statute is questioned, the burden of proof, so to speak, is upon those who assert it to be unconstitutional. McCulloch v. Maryland, 4 Wheat. 316, 421.

Let these principles be applied to the present case. By the statute in question it is provided that "no employee shall be required, or permitted, to work in a biscuit, bread, or cake bakery, or confectionery establishment, more than sixty hours in any one week, or more than ten hours in any one day, unless for the purpose of making a shorter work day on the last day of the week; nor more hours in any one week than will make an average of ten hours per day for the number of days during such week in which such employee shall work."

It is plain that this statute was enacted in order to protect the physical well-being of those who work in bakery and confectionery establishments. It may be that the statute had its origin, in part, in the belief that employers and employees in such establishments were not upon an equal footing, and that the necessities of the latter often compelled them to submit to such exactions as unduly taxed their strength. Be this as it may, the statute must be taken as expressing the belief of the people of New York that, as a general rule, and in the case of the average man, labor in excess of sixty hours during a week in such establishments may endanger the health of those who thus labor. Whether or not this be wise legislation it is not the province of the court to inquire. Under our systems of government the courts are not concerned with the wisdom or policy of legislation. So that, in determining the question of power to interfere with liberty of contract, the court may inquire whether the means devised by the state are germane to an end which may be lawfully accomplished and have a real or substantial relation to the protection of health, as involved in the daily work of the persons, male and female, engaged in bakery and confectionery establishments. But when this inquiry is entered upon I find it impossible, in view of common experience, to say that there is here no real or substantial relation between the means employed by the state and the end sought to be accomplished by its legislation. Mugler v. Kansas, 123 U.S. 623, 661. Nor can I say that the statute has no appropriate or direct connection with that protection to health which each state owes to her citizens . . . or that it is not promotive of the health of the employees in question . . . or that the regulation prescribed by the state is utterly unreasonable and extravagant or wholly arbitrary. . . . Still less can I say that the statute, is, beyond question, a plain, palpable invasion of rights, secured by the fundamental law. . . . Therefore I submit that this court will transcend its functions if it assumes to annul the statute of New York. It must be remembered that this statute does not apply to all kinds of business. It applies only to work in bakery and confectionery establishments, in which, as all know, the air constantly breathed by workmen is not as pure and healthful as that to be found in some other establishments or out of doors.

. . .

■ MR. JUSTICE HOLMES dissenting:

I regret sincerely that I am unable to agree with the judgment in this case, and that I think it my duty to express my dissent.

This case is decided upon an economic theory which a large part of the country does not entertain. If it were a question whether I agreed with that theory, I should desire to study it further and long before making up my mind. But I do not conceive that to be my duty, because I strongly believe that my agreement or disagreement has nothing to do with the right of a majority to embody their opinions in law. It is settled by various decisions of this court that state constitutions and state laws may regulate life in many ways which we as legislators might think as injudicious, or if you like as tyrannical, as this, and which, equally with this, interfere with the liberty to contract. Sunday laws and usury laws are ancient examples. A more modern one is the prohibition of lotteries. The liberty of the citizen to do as he likes so long as he does not interfere with the liberty of others to do the same, which has been a shibboleth for some well-known writers, is interfered with by school laws, by the Postoffice, by every state or municipal institution which takes his money for purposes thought desirable, whether he likes it or not. The 14th Amendment does not enact Mr. Herbert Spencer's Social Statics. The other day we sustained the Massachusetts vaccination law. Jacobson v. Massachusetts, 197 U.S. 11. United States and state statutes and decisions cutting down the liberty to contract by way of combination are familiar to this court. Northern Securities Co. v. United States, 193 U.S. 197. Two years ago we upheld the prohibition of sales of stock on margins, or for future delivery, in the Constitution of California. Otis v. Parker, 187 U.S. 606. The decision sustaining an eight-hour law for miners is still recent. Holden v. Hardy, 169 U.S. 366. Some of these laws embody convictions or prejudices which judges are likely to share. Some may not. But a Constitution is not intended to embody a particular economic theory, whether of paternalism and the organic relation of the citizen to the state or of *laissez faire*. It is made for people of fundamentally differing views, and the accident of our finding certain opinions natural and familiar, or novel, and even shocking, ought not to conclude our judgment upon the question whether statutes embodying them conflict with the Constitution of the United States.

General propositions do not decide concrete cases. The decision will depend on a judgment or intuition more subtle than any articulate major premise. But I think that the proposition just stated, if it is accepted, will carry us far toward the end. Every opinion tends to become a law. I think that the word "liberty," in the 14th Amendment, is perverted when it is held to prevent the natural outcome of a dominant opinion, unless it can be said that a rational and fair man necessarily would admit that the statute proposed would infringe fundamental principles as they have been understood by the traditions of our people and our law. It does not need research to show that no such sweeping condemnation can be passed upon the statute before us. A reasonable man might think it a proper measure on the score of health. Men whom I certainly could not pronounce unreasonable would uphold it as a first instalment of a general regulation of the hours of work. Whether in the latter aspect it would be open to the charge of inequality I think it unnecessary to discuss.

*The Post-*Lochner *Developments*

(1) **Liberty of contract and labor legislation.** *Maximum hours.* In Muller v. Oregon, 208 U.S. 412 (1908), the Court upheld the validity of a statute forbidding the employment of women in factories or laundries more than 10 hours per day as applied to a laundry. The Court distinguished *Lochner* on the ground that the state had a stronger interest in regulating the hours of work of women than of men. The physical differences between women and men were emphasized and the Court said that "history discloses the fact that woman has always been dependent upon man." The Court, in taking judicial notice of the general belief that "woman's physical structure, and the functions she performs in consequence thereof, justify special legislation

restricting or qualifying the conditions under which she should be permitted to toil," relied on a brief filed in the Court by Mr. Louis D. (later Justice) Brandeis that included a large collection of opinions from non-judicial sources.[a] It then said: "Constitutional questions . . . are not settled by even a consensus of present public opinion, for it is the peculiar value of a written constitution that it places in unchanging form limitations upon legislative action, and thus gives a permanence and stability to popular government which otherwise would be lacking. At the same time, when a question of fact is debated and debatable, and the extent to which a special constitutional limitation goes is affected by the truth in respect to that fact, a widespread and long continued belief concerning it is worthy of consideration." Several years later, without mentioning *Lochner,* the Court upheld a law providing a maximum 10-hour day for factory workers of both sexes that also permitted up to three hours a day overtime at time-and-a-half rate. Bunting v. Oregon, 243 U.S. 426 (1917).

"Yellow-Dog" Contracts. In Adair v. United States, 208 U.S. 161 (1908) and Coppage v. Kansas, 236 U.S. 1 (1915), the Court held invalid federal and state legislation forbidding employers to require employees to agree not to become or remain members of any labor organizations during the period of their employment. In *Coppage* the Court said: "An interference with this liberty [to make contracts] so serious as that now under consideration, and so disturbing of equality of right, must be deemed to be arbitrary, unless it be supportable as a reasonable exercise of the police power of the State." The Court went on to reject the argument of the state that such legislation was necessary to protect the interests of employees who were not financially as able to be independent in making contracts as employers, saying: "[S]ince it is self-evident that, unless all things are held in common, some persons must have more property than others, it is from the nature of things impossible to uphold freedom of contract and the right of private property without at the same time recognizing as legitimate those inequalities of fortune that are the necessary result of the exercise of those rights."

Minimum Wages. Adkins v. Children's Hosp., 261 U.S. 525 (1923), involved an Act of Congress prescribing minimum wages for women and children in the District of Columbia. The Court held the statute invalid when challenged by a hospital that employed women at lower than the minimum rate and by a woman elevator operator who was discharged by her employer to avoid the penalties of the act. The Court prefaced its discussion by saying: "There is, of course, no such thing as absolute freedom of contract. It is subject to a great variety of restraints. But freedom of contract is, nevertheless, the general rule and restraint the exception; and the exercise of legislative authority to abridge it can be justified only by the existence of exceptional circumstances." In distinguishing Muller v. Oregon, the Court said:

"But the ancient inequality of the sexes, otherwise than physical, as suggested in the *Muller* case, has continued 'with diminishing intensity.' In view of the great—not to say revolutionary—changes which have taken place since that utterance, in the contractual, political and civil status of women, culminating in the Nineteenth Amendment, it is not unreasonable to say that these differences have now come almost, if not quite, to the vanishing point. In this aspect of the matter, while the physical differences must be recognized in appropriate cases, and legislation fixing

---

[a]   The famous "Brandeis Brief" has been lauded as introducing the Court "to a new technique in the weighing of constitutional issues. This occurred when Mr. Louis D. Brandeis handed the Court . . . his famous brief, three pages of which were devoted to a statement of the constitutional principles involved and 113 pages of which were devoted to the presentation of facts and statistics, backed by scientific authorities, to show the evil effects of too long hours on women, 'the mothers of the race'." Johnson, *Social Planning Under the Constitution,* 2 Selected Essays (1938) 131, 145.

hours or conditions of work may properly take them into account, we cannot accept the doctrine that women of mature age, sui juris, require or may be subjected to restrictions upon their liberty of contract which could not lawfully be imposed in the case of men under similar circumstances."

It then went on to say that the statute could not be justified as safeguarding the morals of women because it "cannot be shown that well paid women safeguard their morals more carefully than those who are poorly paid." It concluded that the real flaw in the statute was that "it exacts from the employer an arbitrary payment for a purpose and upon a basis having no causal connection with his business or the contract or the work the employee engages to do." This, the Court said, "is so clearly the product of a naked, arbitrary exercise of power that it cannot be allowed to stand under the Constitution of the United States."

Justice Holmes in dissent said: "It will need more than the Nineteenth Amendment to convince me that there are no differences between men and women, or that legislation cannot take those differences into account. I should not hesitate to take them into account if I thought it necessary to sustain this act. . . . But after Bunting v. Oregon, 243 U.S. 426, I had supposed that it was not necessary, and that Lochner v. New York, 198 U.S. 45, would be allowed a deserved repose."

(2) Liberty of contract and business regulations relating to prices and other economic issues. *Price Fixing.* In Tyson & Bro.-United Theatre Ticket Offices v. Banton, 273 U.S. 418 (1927), the court held invalid a statute regulating the prices of theater tickets. The Court said "that the right of the owner to fix a price at which his property shall be sold or used is an inherent attribute of the property itself." Hence, the power to fix prices "does not exist in respect of merely private property or business . . . but exists only where the business or the property involved has become 'affected with a public interest.'" A long line of cases developed marking out the distinction between ordinary businesses and those "affected with a public interest" and so subject to price regulations. See, e.g., Williams v. Standard Oil Co., 278 U.S. 235 (1929), holding invalid a state statute regulating the price of gasoline. For later modifications of this doctrine, see Nebbia v. New York, 291 U.S. 502 (1934), set out below.

Restrictions on Business Entry. The Court applied an approach similar to that in the price fixing cases with regard to legislation restricting entry into particular businesses. In New State Ice Co. v. Liebmann, 285 U.S. 262 (1932), it held invalid a statute requiring any person desiring to engage in the ice business to obtain a certificate of public convenience and necessity. It said that the question was "whether the business is so charged with a public use as to justify" the restriction. It also said: "Plainly, a regulation which has the effect of denying or unreasonably curtailing the common right to engage in a lawful private business, such as that under review, cannot be upheld consistent with the 14th Amendment."

(3) Regulations of business designed to protect public health and safety. Most business regulations that came before the court were upheld where the legislative objective was to protect public health and safety rather than to interfere with the free market. However, in some cases the Court held regulations invalid because they were not sufficiently related to the legislative objectives. In Weaver v. Palmer Bros. Co., 270 U.S. 402 (1926), e.g., the Court held invalid a statute completely forbidding the use of shoddy (cut up fabrics) in the manufacture of bedding and providing for the use of other second-hand materials and feathers only if sterilized. The parties conceded that shoddy could be made harmless by disinfection or sterilization and there was no evidence to show that sickness or disease had been caused by the use of shoddy. The Court recognized that state regulations designed to protect public health and to protect the public from deception were generally valid but held that this statute did not sufficiently serve those ends. The measure could not be sustained as a measure to protect health because sterilization would eliminate the danger. Nor could it be sustained as a measure to protect against deception because the regulation provided for adequate notice to the public of the contents of the bedding. It then concluded: "The constitutional guarantees may not be made to yield to mere convenience. . . . The business here involved is legitimate and useful; and, while it is subject to all reasonable regulation, the absolute prohibition of the use of shoddy in the manufacture of comfortables is purely arbitrary and violates the due process clause of the Fourteenth Amendment."

Nebbia v. New York

291 U.S. 502, 54 S.Ct. 505, 78 L.Ed. 940 (1934).

■ MR. JUSTICE ROBERTS delivered the opinion of the Court.

. . .

[A New York statute provided for the fixing of maximum and minimum prices for the sale of milk. The legislature, after extensive hearings, had determined that economic conditions and destructive trade practices jeopardized an adequate milk supply at reasonable prices to consumers and producers and that price controls would help. Nebbia, owner of a grocery store, was convicted for selling milk at a price below the minimum fixed. He contended, inter alia, that the statute deprived him of due process of law. The Court upheld the law by a vote of 5 to 4. Excerpts from Justice Roberts' long opinion follow.]

The reports of our decisions abound with cases in which the citizen, individual or corporate, has vainly invoked the Fourteenth Amendment in resistance to necessary and appropriate exertion of the police power.

. . .

But we are told that because the law essays to control prices it denies due process. . . . The argument runs that the public control of rates or prices is per se unreasonable and unconstitutional save as applied to businesses affected with a public interest; that a business so affected is one in which property is devoted to an enterprise of a sort which the public itself might appropriately undertake, or one whose owner relies on a public grant or franchise for the right to conduct the business, or in which he is bound to serve all who apply; in short, such as is commonly called a public utility; or a business in its nature a monopoly. The milk industry, it is said, possesses none of these characteristics, and therefore, not being affected with a public interest, its charges may not be controlled by the state. . . .

We may as well say at once that the dairy industry is not, in the accepted sense of the phrase, a public utility. We think the appellant is also right in asserting that there is in this case no suggestion of any monopoly or monopolistic practice. It goes without saying that those engaged in the business are in no way dependent upon public grants or franchises for the privilege of conducting their activities. But if, as must be conceded, the industry is subject to regulation in the public interest, what constitutional principle bars the state from correcting existing maladjustments by legislation touching prices? We think there is no such principle. The due process clause makes no mention of sales or of prices any more than it speaks of business or contracts or buildings or other incidents of property. The thought seems nevertheless to have persisted that there is something peculiarly sacrosanct about the price one may charge for what he makes or sells, and that, however able to regulate other elements of manufacture or trade, with incidental effect upon price, the state is incapable of directly controlling the price itself. This view was negatived many years ago. Munn v. Illinois, 94 U.S. 113. . . .

It is clear that there is no closed class or category of businesses affected with a public interest, and the function of courts in the application of the Fifth and Fourteenth Amendments is to determine in each case whether circumstances vindicate the challenged regulation as a reasonable exertion of governmental authority or condemn it as arbitrary or discriminatory.... The phrase "affected with a public interest" can, in the nature of things, mean no more than that an industry, for adequate reason, is subject to control for the public good. In several of the decisions of this court wherein the expressions "affected with a public interest," and "clothed with a public use," have been brought forward as the criteria of the validity of price control, it has been admitted that they are not susceptible of definition and form an unsatisfactory test of the constitutionality of legislation directed at business practices or prices. These decisions must rest, finally, upon the basis that the requirements of due process were not met because the laws were found arbitrary, in their operation and effect. But there can be no doubt that upon proper occasion and by appropriate measures the state may regulate a business in any of its aspects, including the prices to be charged for the products or commodities it sells.

So far as the requirement of due process is concerned, and in the absence of other constitutional restriction, a state is free to adopt whatever economic policy may reasonably be deemed to promote public welfare, and to enforce that policy by legislation adapted to its purpose. The courts are without authority either to declare such policy, or, when it is declared by the legislature, to override it. If the laws passed are seen to have a reasonable relation to a proper legislative purpose, and are neither arbitrary nor discriminatory, the requirements of due process are satisfied, and judicial determination to that effect renders a court functus officio.... With the wisdom of the policy adopted, with the adequacy or practicability of the law enacted to forward it, the courts are both incompetent and unauthorized to deal. The course of decision in this court exhibits a firm adherence to these principles. Times without number we have said that the Legislature is primarily the judge of the necessity of such an enactment, that every possible presumption is in favor of its validity, and that though the court may hold views inconsistent with the wisdom of the law, it may not be annulled unless palpably in excess of legislative power.... Price control, like any other form of regulation, is unconstitutional only if arbitrary, discriminatory, or demonstrably irrelevant to the policy the Legislature is free to adopt, and hence an unnecessary and unwarranted interference with individual liberty.

The Overturning of Adkins v. Children's Hospital

In Morehead v. New York ex rel. Tipaldo, 298 U.S. 587 (1936), Justice Roberts, author of the opinion in *Nebbia,* joined with the *Nebbia* dissenters in applying *Adkins* to hold invalid a New York law providing for minimum wages for women workers. The Court noted that the petitioner had not asked the Court to reconsider the constitutional question decided in *Adkins.* Finding no sufficient basis for distinction, the Court held the statute invalid.

The next year, however, the Court, by a vote of 5 to 4 with Justice Roberts joining the majority, specifically overruled Adkins v. Children's Hospital. West Coast Hotel Co. v. Parrish, 300 U.S. 379 (1937). The Court responded to the argument based on freedom of contract by saying:

"What is freedom? The Constitution does not speak of freedom of contract. It speaks of liberty and prohibits the deprivation of liberty without due process of law.... But the liberty safeguarded is liberty in a social organization which requires the protection of law against the evils which menace the health, safety, morals and welfare of the people. Liberty under the constitution is thus necessarily subject to the restraints of due process, and regulation which is reasonable in relation to its subject and is adopted in the interests of the community is due process. This essential limitation of liberty in general governs freedom of contract in particular.

"What can be closer to the public interest than the health of women and their protection from unscrupulous and overreaching employers? And if the protection of women is a legitimate end of the exercise of state power, how can it be said that the requirement of the payment of a minimum wage fairly fixed in order to meet the very necessities of existence is not an admissible means to that end? The legislature of the State was clearly entitled to consider the situation of women in employment, the fact that they are in the class receiving the least pay, that their bargaining power is relatively weak, and that they are the ready victims of those who would take advantage of their necessitous circumstances. The legislature was entitled to adopt measures to reduce the evils of the 'sweating system,' the exploiting of workers at wages so low as to be insufficient to meet the bare cost of living, thus making their very helplessness the occasion of a most injurious competition. . . . The adoption of similar requirements by many States evidences a deep-seated conviction both as to the presence of the evil and as to the means adapted to check it. Legislative response to that conviction cannot be regarded as arbitrary or capricious, and that is all we have to decide. Even if the wisdom of the policy be regarded as debatable and its effects uncertain, still the legislature is entitled to its judgment."

It should be noted that the decision in *West Coast Hotel* was announced while President Roosevelt's "Court packing" proposal was pending in Congress. For a reference to the question whether this decision was intended to have an impact on that proposal, see n. a, supra p. 110.

The Demise of Liberty of Contract

During the 1940s the Supreme Court (which received seven new members between 1937 and 1941) overturned the old precedents and rejected all challenges to legislation based on assertions of a constitutional preference for a free economic market place.

In United States v. Darby, 312 U.S. 100 (1941), the Court upheld the provisions of the Fair Labor Standards Act fixing maximum hours and minimum wages for all covered employees. The Court said that "it is no longer open to question" that it is within the legislative power to fix wages and hours for men as well as women.

In Phelps Dodge Corp. v. National Labor Relations Bd., 313 U.S. 177 (1941), the Court upheld the provision of the N.L.R.A. making it an unfair labor practice for an employer to encourage or discourage membership in any labor union, saying that "[t]he course of decisions in this Court since *Adair v. United States* . . . and *Coppage v. Kansas* . . . have completely sapped those cases of their authority."

In Olsen v. Nebraska, 313 U.S. 236 (1941), the Court upheld a state statute fixing the fees chargeable by a private employment agency and in Lincoln Fed. Labor Union v. Northwestern Iron & Metal Co., 335 U.S. 525 (1949), upheld a state law providing that no person should be denied an opportunity to obtain employment because he was or was not a member of a labor union. In the latter case it rejected a claim by a labor union that the "open shop" law was invalid by saying: "Just as we have held that the due process clause erects no obstacle to block legislative protection of union members, we now hold that legislative protection can be afforded non-union members."

In Daniel v. Family Sec. Life Ins. Co., 336 U.S. 220 (1949), the Court upheld a statute which prohibited life insurance companies and their agents from engaging in the undertaking business and undertakers from acting as life insurance agents. The statute was challenged by an undertaker selling "funeral insurance." His claim that the statute resulted from the activities of the "insurance lobby" was rejected by the

Fourth, the District Court held unconstitutional, as violative of the Due Process Clause of the Fourteenth Amendment, the provision of § 4 of the Oklahoma Act which reads as follows:

"No person, firm, or corporation engaged in the business of retailing merchandise to the general public shall rent space, sublease departments, or otherwise permit any person purporting to do eye examination or visual care to occupy space in such retail store."

It seems to us that this regulation is on the same constitutional footing as the denial to corporations of the right to practice dentistry. Semler v. Oregon State Board of Dental Examiners, supra, 294 U.S. at 611. It is an attempt to free the profession, to as great an extent as possible, from all taints of commercialism. It certainly might be easy for an optometrist with space in a retail store to be merely a front for the retail establishment. In any case, the opportunity for that nexus may be too great for safety, if the eye doctor is allowed inside the retail store. Moreover, it may be deemed important to effective regulation that the eye doctor be restricted to geographical locations that reduce the temptations of commercialism. Geographical location may be an important consideration in a legislative program which aims to raise the treatment of the human eye to a strictly professional level. We cannot say that the regulation has no rational relation to that objective and therefore is beyond constitutional bounds.

What we have said is sufficient to dispose of the appeal in No. 185 from the conclusion of the District Court that that portion of § 3 which makes it unlawful to solicit the sale of spectacles, eyeglasses, lenses, and prisms by the use of advertising media is constitutional.

. . .

■ MR. JUSTICE HARLAN took no part in the consideration or decision of this case.

Ferguson v. Skrupa

372 U.S. 726, 83 S.Ct. 1028, 10 L.Ed.2d 93 (1963).

■ MR. JUSTICE BLACK delivered the opinion of the Court.

In this case, . . . we are asked to review the judgment of a three-judge District Court enjoining, as being in violation of the Due Process Clause of the Fourteenth Amendment, a Kansas statute making it a misdemeanor for any person to engage "in the business of debt adjusting" except as an incident to "the lawful practice of law in this state." The statute defines "debt adjusting" as "the making of a contract, express, or implied with a particular debtor whereby the debtor agrees to pay a certain amount of money periodically to the person engaged in the debt adjusting business who shall for a consideration distribute the same among certain specified creditors in accordance with a plan agreed upon."

The complaint, filed by appellee Skrupa doing business as "Credit Advisors," alleged that Skrupa was engaged in the business of "debt adjusting" as defined by the statute, that his business was a "useful and desirable" one, that his business activities were not "inherently immoral or dangerous" or in any way contrary to the public welfare, and that therefore the business could not be "absolutely prohibited" by Kansas. The three-judge court heard evidence by Skrupa tending to show the usefulness and desirability of his business and evidence by the state officials tending to show that "debt adjusting" lends itself to grave abuses against distressed debtors, particularly in the lower income brackets, and that these abuses are of such gravity that a number of States have strictly regulated "debt adjusting" or prohibited it altogether. The court found that Skrupa's business did fall within the Act's proscription and concluded, one judge dissenting, that the Act was prohibitory, not regulatory, but that even if construed in part as regulatory it was an unreasonable regulation of a "lawful business," which the court held amounted to a violation of the Due Process Clause of the Fourteenth Amendment. The court accordingly enjoined enforcement of the statute.

The only case discussed by the court below as support for its invalidation of the statute was Commonwealth v. Stone, 191 Pa.Super. 117, 155 A.2d 453 (1959), in which the Superior Court of Pennsylvania struck down a statute almost identical to the Kansas act involved here. . . . In doing so, the Pennsylvania court relied heavily on Adams v. Tanner, 244 U.S. 590 (1917), which held that the Due Process Clause forbids a State to prohibit a business which is "useful" and not "inherently immoral or dangerous to public welfare."

Both the District Court in the present case and the Pennsylvania court in Stone adopted the philosophy of *Adams v. Tanner,* and cases like it, that it is the province of courts to draw on their own views as to the morality, legitimacy, and usefulness of a particular business in order to decide whether a statute bears too heavily upon that business and by so doing violates due process. Under the system of government created by our Constitution, it is up to legislatures, not courts, to decide on the wisdom and utility of legislation. There was a time when the Due Process Clause was used by this Court to strike down laws which were thought unreasonable, that is, unwise or incompatible with some particular economic or social philosophy. In this manner the Due Process Clause was used, for example, to nullify laws prescribing maximum hours for work in bakeries, Lochner v. New York, 198 U.S. 45 (1905), outlawing "yellow dog" contracts, Coppage v. Kansas, 236 U.S. 1 (1915), setting minimum wages for women, Adkins v. Children's Hospital, 261 U.S. 525 (1923), and fixing the weight of loaves of bread, Jay Burns Baking Co. v. Bryan, 264 U.S. 504 (1924). This intrusion by the judiciary into the realm of legislative value judgments was strongly objected to at the time, particularly by Mr. Justice Holmes and Mr. Justice Brandeis. . . .

The doctrine that prevailed in *Lochner, Coppage, Adkins, Burns,* and like cases— that due process authorizes courts to hold laws unconstitutional when they believe the legislature has acted unwisely—has long since been discarded. We have returned to the original constitutional proposition that courts do not substitute their social and economic beliefs for the judgment of legislative bodies, who are elected to pass laws. . . .

In the face of our abandonment of the use of the "vague contours" of the Due Process Clause to nullify laws which a majority of the Court believed to be economically unwise, reliance on *Adams v. Tanner* is as mistaken as would be adherence to *Adkins v. Children's Hospital,* overruled by West Coast Hotel Co. v. Parrish, 300 U.S. 379 (1937). . . . We conclude that the Kansas Legislature was free to decide for itself that legislation was needed to deal with the business of debt adjusting. Unquestionably, there are arguments showing that the business of debt adjusting has social utility, but such arguments are properly addressed to the legislature, not to us. We refuse to sit as a "superlegislature to weigh the wisdom of legislation," and we emphatically refuse to go back to the time when courts used the Due Process Clause "to strike down state laws, regulatory of business and industrial conditions, because they may be unwise, improvident, or out of harmony with a particular school of thought." Nor are we able or willing to draw lines by calling a law "prohibitory" or "regulatory." Whether the legislature takes for its textbook Adam Smith, Herbert Spencer, Lord Keynes, or some other is no concern of ours. The Kansas debt adjusting statute may be wise or unwise. But relief, if any be needed, lies not with us but with the body constituted to pass laws for the State of Kansas.

. . .

Reversed.

■ MR. JUSTICE HARLAN concurs in the judgment on the ground that this state measure bears a rational relation to a constitutionally permissible objective. See Williamson v. Lee Optical Inc., 348 U.S. 483, 491.

Does the Due Process Clause Today Impose Any Limitations on the Substance of Economic Regulatory Legislation?

Does the decision in *Ferguson v. Skrupa* constitute a complete abandonment by the Court of the use of due process to impose a minimum standard of rationality on legislation? Does Justice Harlan's concurring opinion indicate that he thought the Court was no longer going to insist that legislation "bear a rational relationship to a constitutionally permissible objective"?

If one looks only at the outcome of cases challenging economic regulatory legislation under due process, the answer would appear to be that no effective review is undertaken by the Court. No economic regulatory statute has been held invalid under due process since 1937. Only in cases where the Court has been able to find a "taking" of property without just compensation in violation of the taking clause of the fifth amendment or an impairment of contract within the meaning of the contract clause has it invalidated legislation in the economic area.

However, the Court continues to write opinions in which it states that it is applying a due process standard that requires legislation to bear a rational relationship to a legitimate state objective. In Exxon Corp. v. Governor of Maryland, 437 U.S. 117, 125 (1978), the Court, in upholding a statute prohibiting producers or refiners of petroleum products from operating retail service stations in the state, rejected a due process objection, stating: "[W]e have no hesitancy in concluding that it bears a reasonable relation to the State's legitimate purpose in controlling the gasoline retail market." And in PruneYard Shopping Center v. Robins, 447 U.S. 74 (1980), the Court rejected a due process challenge to a state court judgment ordering a private property owner to permit use of a portion of that property by persons soliciting signatures on petitions. It quoted from Nebbia v. New York, set out supra p. 348: "The guaranty of due process . . . demands only that the law shall not be unreasonable, arbitrary or capricious, and that the means selected shall have a real and substantial relation to the objective sought to be [obtained]." The Court then added: "Appellants have failed to provide sufficient justification for concluding that this test is not satisfied by the State's asserted interest in promoting more expansive rights of free speech and petition than conferred by the Federal Constitution."

Due Process Limitations on State Punitive Damages Awards

In contrast to its highly deferential approach to due process review of the reasonableness of economic *legislation*, the Court in the 1990's began to define substantive due process limits to assure the reasonableness of punitive damages awards imposed in civil trials, based on the perception that "[p]unitive damages pose an acute danger of arbitrary deprivation of property[,]" Honda Motor Co. v. Oberg, 512 U.S. 415, 432 (1994). In State Farm Mutual Automobile Insurance Co. v. Campbell, 538 U.S. 408 (2003), the Court affirmed that the "Due Process Clause of the Fourteenth Amendment prohibits the imposition of grossly excessive or arbitrary punishments on a tortfeasor" and overturned as "neither reasonable nor proportionate to the wrong committed, and . . . an irrational deprivation of the property of the defendant" a punitive damages award of $145 million, where full compensatory damages were $1 million. Justice Kennedy's majority opinion applied "three guideposts" the Court had adopted in BMW of North America, Inc. v. Gore, 517 U.S.

559 (1996), as instructions for courts reviewing punitive damages to consider: "(1) the degree of reprehensibility of the defendant's misconduct; (2) the disparity between the actual or potential harm suffered by the plaintiff and the punitive damages award; and (3) the difference between the punitive damages awarded by the jury and the civil penalties authorized or imposed in comparable cases." The majority also declared more generally:

"We decline . . . to impose a bright-line ratio which a punitive damages award cannot exceed. Our jurisprudence and the principles it has now established demonstrate, however, that, in practice, few awards exceeding a single-digit ratio between punitive and compensatory damages, to a significant degree, will satisfy due process. In [Pacific Mutual Life Insurance Co. v. Haslip, 499 U.S. 1, 23–24 (1991)], in upholding a punitive damages award, we concluded that an award of more than four times the amount of compensatory damages might be close to the line of constitutional impropriety. . . . We cited that 4-to-1 ratio again in Gore. . . . The Court further referenced a long legislative history, dating back over 700 years and going forward to today, providing for sanctions of double, treble, or quadruple damages to deter and punish. . . . While these ratios are not binding, they are instructive. They demonstrate what should be obvious: Single-digit multipliers are more likely to comport with due process, while still achieving the State's goals of deterrence and retribution, than awards with ratios in range of 500 to 1, or, in this case, of 145 to 1.

"Nonetheless, because there are no rigid benchmarks that a punitive damages award may not surpass, ratios greater than those we have previously upheld may comport with due process where 'a particularly egregious act has resulted in only a small amount of economic damages.' . . . The converse is also true, however. When compensatory damages are substantial, then a lesser ratio, perhaps only equal to compensatory damages, can reach the outermost limit of the due process guarantee. The precise award in any case, of course, must be based upon the facts and circumstances of the defendant's conduct and the harm to the plaintiff.

"In sum, courts must ensure that the measure of punishment is both reasonable and proportionate to the amount of harm to the plaintiff and to the general damages recovered."

Three Justices dissented. Justice Scalia "adhere[d] to the view expressed in my dissenting opinion in . . . Gore . . . that the Due Process Clause provides no substantive protections against 'excessive' or 'unreasonable' awards of punitive damages." He added "that the punitive damages jurisprudence which has sprung forth from BMW v. Gore is insusceptible of principled application. . . ." Justice Thomas " 'continue[d] to believe that the Constitution does not constrain the size of punitive damages awards.' Cooper Industries, Inc. v. Leatherman Tool Group, Inc., 532 U.S. 424, 443 (2001)." Finally, Justice Ginsburg opined that although "[t]he large size of the award upheld by the Utah Supreme Court in this case indicates why damage-capping legislation may be altogether fitting and proper[, n]either the amount of the award nor the trial record . . . justifies this Court's substitution of its judgment for that of Utah's competent decisionmakers." She also wrote: "In a legislative scheme or a state high court's design to cap punitive damages, the handiwork in setting single-digit and 1-to-1 benchmarks could hardly be questioned; in a judicial decree imposed on the States by this Court under the banner of substantive due process, the numerical controls today's decision installs seem to me boldly out of order." She concluded her opinion as follows: "I remain of the view that this Court has no warrant to reform state law governing awards of punitive damages. Gore, 517 U.S., at 607 (Ginsburg, J., dissenting). Even if I were prepared to accept the flexible guides prescribed in Gore, I would not join the Court's swift conversion of those guides into instructions that begin to resemble marching orders."

2. PROTECTION OF PERSONAL LIBERTIES

A. INTRODUCTION

In Section 1 of this chapter we saw how the Court determined that the word "liberty" in the due process clause gave special protection to the liberty to contract so that restrictions on that liberty, especially as reflected in labor legislation, were invalid unless specially justified by the state.

The liberty of contract cases have long since been overruled. But more recently the Court has derived from the word liberty a special constitutional protection for privacy, personal autonomy, and some family relationships requiring special justification for state infringements on those interests. The process by which an interest is singled out by the Court for special constitutional protection is worthy of examination as a means of understanding how general constitutional phrases become limitations on the power of legislatures.

Some issues that relate to privacy are governed by special constitutional language. The fourth amendment (incorporated by the fourteenth amendment against the states) protects persons, places, and possessions against indiscriminate searches and seizures. The fifth amendment protects against self-incrimination. But no language in the Constitution talks about privacy, family life, or personal autonomy.

In reading these cases ask yourself whether the Court adduces a principled basis for singling out these particular interests from all the other aspects of liberty that similarly might be protected.

Try also to determine what is the scope of this special protection. What kinds of regulations can be brought within the privacy rubric so as to require special state justification?

For useful general discussion, see Dixon, *The "New" Substantive Due Process and the Democratic Ethic: A Prolegomenon,* 1976 B.Y.U.L.Rev. 43; Henkin, *Privacy and Autonomy,* 74 Colum.L.Rev. 1410 (1974).

Two early cases from the *Lochner* era are frequently cited in current opinions. In Meyer v. Nebraska, 262 U.S. 390 (1923), a parochial school language teacher had been convicted of violating a law prohibiting the teaching of any subject in a language other than English in the first eight grades of public and private schools. In reversing his conviction, the Court said that the liberty protected by due process "denotes not merely freedom from bodily restraint, but also the right of the individual to contract, to engage in any of the common occupations of life, to acquire useful knowledge, to marry, establish a home and bring up children, to worship God according to the dictates of his own conscience, and, generally, to enjoy those privileges long recognized at common law as essential to the orderly pursuit of happiness by free men." The right of Meyer to teach German and the right of parents to engage him were within that zone of constitutionally-protected liberty. The Court concluded that, because no justifications for the complete abolition of the right to teach foreign languages had been shown, "the statute as applied is arbitrary, and without reasonable relation to any end within the competency of the state."

In Pierce v. Society of Sisters, 268 U.S. 510 (1925), the Court upheld a trial court injunction against the enforcement of an Oregon statute requiring parents to send children between the ages of 8 and 16 to a public school. The suit was brought by a Catholic society operating a school and a private corporation operating a military academy. The Court noted that the effect of the act would be to force private schools out of business. It then said that under the doctrine of *Meyer* "we think it entirely plain that the [statute] unreasonably interferes with the liberty of parents and guardians to direct the upbringing and education of children under their control. . . . The fundamental theory of liberty upon which all governments in this Union repose excludes any general power of the state to standardize its children by forcing them to accept instruction from public teachers only. The child is not the mere creature of the state; those who nurture him and direct his destiny have the right, coupled with the high duty, to recognize and prepare him for additional obligations."

Another case prior to Griswold v. Connecticut that referred to special constitutional protection for interests relating to personal autonomy and family relationships was Skinner v. Oklahoma, 316 U.S. 535 (1942). The Court held invalid under equal protection a statute providing for compulsory sterilization of criminals convicted two or more times of crimes of moral turpitude. Since the statute made grand larceny a felony of moral turpitude, while embezzlement was not, it violated the equal protection clause. The Court, in an opinion by Justice Douglas, began its discussion of the equal protection issue by saying: "We are dealing here with legislation which involves one of the basic civil rights of man. Marriage and procreation are fundamental to the very existence and survival of the race. The power to sterilize, if exercised, may have subtle, far-reaching and devastating effects. . . . There is no redemption for the individual whom the law touches. Any experiment which the State conducts is to his irreparable injury. He is forever deprived of a basic liberty. We mention these matters not to reexamine the scope of the police power of the States. We advert to them merely in emphasis of our view that strict scrutiny of the classification which a State makes in a sterilization law is essential. . . ."

Griswold v. Connecticut

381 U.S. 479, 85 S.Ct. 1678, 14 L.Ed.2d 510 (1965).

■ MR. JUSTICE DOUGLAS delivered the opinion of the Court.

Appellant Griswold is Executive Director of the Planned Parenthood League of Connecticut. Appellant Buxton is a licensed physician and a professor at the Yale Medical School who served as Medical Director for the League at its Center in New Haven—a center open and operating from November 1 to November 10, 1961, when appellants were arrested.

They gave information, instruction, and medical advice to *married persons* as to the means of preventing conception. They examined the wife and prescribed the best contraceptive device or material for her use. Fees were usually charged, although some couples were serviced free.

The statutes whose constitutionality is involved in this appeal are §§ 53–32 and 54–196 of the General Statutes of Connecticut (1938). The former provides:

"Any person who uses any drug, medicinal article or instrument for the purpose of preventing conception shall be fined not less than fifty dollars or imprisoned not less than sixty days nor more than one year or be both fined and imprisoned."

Section 54–196 provides:

"Any person who assists, abets, counsels, causes, hires or commands another to commit any offense may be prosecuted and punished as if he were the principal offender."

The appellants were found guilty as accessories and fined $100 each, against the claim that the accessory statute as so applied violated the Fourteenth Amendment. The Appellate Division of the Circuit Court affirmed. The Court of Errors affirmed that judgment. . . .

. . .

Coming to the merits, we are met with a wide range of questions that implicate the Due Process Clause of the Fourteenth Amendment. Overtones of some arguments suggest that Lochner v. State. of New York, 198 U.S. 45, should be our guide. But we decline that invitation as we did in West Coast Hotel Co. v. Parrish, 300 U.S. 379; Olsen v. State of Nebraska, 313 U.S. 236; Lincoln Federal Labor Union v. Northwestern Co., 335 U.S. 525; Williamson v. Lee Optical Co., 348 U.S. 483; Giboney v. Empire Storage Co., 336 U.S. 490. We do not sit as a super-legislature to determine the wisdom, need, and propriety of laws that touch economic problems, business affairs, or social conditions. This law, however, operates directly on an intimate relation of husband and wife and their physician's role in one aspect of that relation.

The association of people is not mentioned in the Constitution nor in the Bill of Rights. The right to educate a child in a school of the parents' choice—whether public or private or parochial—is also not mentioned. Nor is the right to study any particular subject or any foreign language. Yet the First Amendment has been construed to include certain of those rights.

By *Pierce v. Society of Sisters,* supra, the right to educate one's children as one chooses is made applicable to the States by the force of the First and Fourteenth Amendments. By *Meyer v. State of Nebraska,* supra, the same dignity is given the right to study the German language in a private school. In other words, the State may not, consistently with the spirit of the First Amendment, contract the spectrum of available knowledge. The right of freedom of speech and press includes not only the right to utter or to print, but the right to distribute, the right to receive, the right to read (Martin v. City of Struthers, 319 U.S. 141, 143) and freedom of inquiry, freedom of thought, and freedom to teach (see Wieman v. Updegraff, 344 U.S. 183, 195)—indeed the freedom of the entire university community. Sweezy v. State of New Hampshire, 354 U.S. 234, 249–250, 261–263; Barenblatt v. United States, 360 U.S. 109, 112; Baggett v. Bullitt, 377 U.S. 360, 369. Without those peripheral rights the specific rights would be less secure. And so we reaffirm the principle of the *Pierce* and the *Meyer* cases.

. . .

The foregoing cases suggest that specific guarantees in the Bill of Rights have penumbras, formed by emanations from those guarantees that help give them life and substance. See Poe v. Ullman, 367 U.S. 497, 516–522 (dissenting opinion). Various guarantees create zones of privacy. The right of association contained in the penumbra of the First Amendment is one, as we have seen. The Third Amendment in its prohibition against the quartering of soldiers "in any house" in time of peace without the consent of the owner is another facet of that privacy. The Fourth Amendment explicitly affirms the "right of the people to be secure in their persons, houses, papers, and effects, against unreasonable searches and seizures." The Fifth Amendment in its Self-Incrimination Clause enables the citizen to create a zone of privacy which government may not force him to surrender to his detriment. The Ninth Amendment provides: "The enumeration in the Constitution, of certain rights, shall not be construed to deny or disparage others retained by the people."

The Fourth and Fifth Amendments were described in Boyd v. United States, 116 U.S. 616, 630, as protection against all governmental invasions "of the sanctity of a man's home and the privacies of life." We recently referred in Mapp v. Ohio, 367 U.S. 643, 656, to the Fourth Amendment as creating a "right to privacy, no less important than any other right carefully and particularly reserved to the people." See Beaney, The Constitutional Right to Privacy, 1962 Sup.Ct.Rev. 212; Griswold, The Right to be Let Alone, 55 N.W.U.L.Rev. 216 (1960).

We have had many controversies over these penumbral rights of "privacy and repose." . . . These cases bear witness that the right of privacy which presses for recognition here is a legitimate one.

The present case, then, concerns a relationship lying within the zone of privacy created by several fundamental constitutional guarantees. And it concerns a law which, in forbidding the *use* of contraceptives rather than regulating their manufacture or sale, seeks to achieve its goals by means having a maximum destructive impact upon that relationship. Such a law cannot stand in light of the familiar principle, so often applied by this Court, that a "governmental purpose to control or prevent activities constitutionally subject to state regulation may not be achieved by means which sweep unnecessarily broadly and thereby invade the area of protected freedoms." NAACP v. Alabama, 377 U.S. 288, 307. Would we allow the police to search the sacred precincts of marital bedrooms for telltale signs of the use of contraceptives? The very idea is repulsive to the notions of privacy surrounding the marriage relationship.

We deal with a right of privacy older than the Bill of Rights—older than our political parties, older than our school system. Marriage is a coming together for better or for worse, hopefully enduring, and intimate to the degree of being sacred. It is an association that promotes a way of life, not causes; a harmony in living, not political faiths; a bilateral loyalty, not commercial or social projects. Yet it is an association for as noble a purpose as any involved in our prior decisions.

Reversed.

■ MR. JUSTICE GOLDBERG, whom THE CHIEF JUSTICE and MR. JUSTICE BRENNAN join, concurring.

I agree with the Court that Connecticut's birth control law unconstitutionally intrudes upon the right of marital privacy, and I join in its opinion and judgment. Although I have not accepted the view that " 'due process' as used in the Fourteenth Amendment includes all of the first eight Amendments," id., 367 U.S. at 516 (see my concurring opinion in Pointer v. Texas, 380 U.S. 400, 410, and the dissenting opinion of Mr. Justice Brennan in Cohen v. Hurley, 366 U.S. 117), I do agree that the concept of liberty protects those personal rights that are fundamental, and is not confined to the specific terms of the Bill of Rights. My conclusion that the concept of liberty is not so restricted and that it embraces the right of marital privacy though that right is not mentioned explicitly in the Constitution is supported both by numerous decisions of this Court, referred to in the Court's opinion, and by the language and history of the Ninth Amendment. In reaching the conclusion that the right of marital privacy is protected, as being within the protected penumbra of specific guarantees of the Bill of Rights, the Court refers to the Ninth Amendment. I add these words to emphasize the relevance of that Amendment to the Court's holding.

. . .

The Ninth Amendment reads, "The enumeration in the Constitution, of certain rights, shall not be construed to deny or disparage others retained by the people." . . .

While this Court has had little occasion to interpret the Ninth Amendment,[6] "[i]t cannot be presumed that any clause in the constitution is intended to be without

---

[6] This Amendment has been referred to as "The Forgotten Ninth Amendment," in a book with that title by Bennet B. Patterson (1955). Other commentary on the Ninth Amendment includes Redlich, Are There "Certain Rights . . . Retained by the People"? 37 N.Y.U.L.Rev. 787 (1962), and Kelsey, The Ninth Amendment of the Federal Constitution, 11 Ind.L.J. 309 (1936). As far as I am aware, until today this Court has referred to the Ninth Amendment only in United Public Workers v. Mitchell, 330 U.S. 75, 94–95; Tennessee Electric Power Co. v. TVA, 306 U.S. 118, 143–144; and

effect." Marbury v. Madison, 1 Cranch 137, 174. In interpreting the Constitution, "real effect should be given to all the words it uses." Myers v. United States, 272 U.S. 52, 151. The Ninth Amendment to the Constitution may be regarded by some as a recent discovery but since 1791 it has been a basic part of the Constitution which we are sworn to uphold. To hold that a right so basic and fundamental and so deep-rooted in our society as the right of privacy in marriage may be infringed because that right is not guaranteed in so many words by the first eight amendments to the Constitution is to ignore the Ninth Amendment and to give it no effect whatsoever. Moreover, a judicial construction that this fundamental right is not protected by the Constitution because it is not mentioned in explicit terms by one of the first eight amendments or elsewhere in the Constitution would violate the Ninth Amendment, which specifically states that "[t]he enumeration in the Constitution, of certain rights shall not be *construed* to deny or disparage others retained by the people." (Emphasis added.)

. . .

The entire fabric of the Constitution and the purposes that clearly underlie its specific guarantees demonstrate that the rights to marital privacy and to marry and raise a family are of similar order and magnitude as the fundamental rights specifically protected.

Although the Constitution does not speak in so many words of the right of privacy in marriage, I cannot believe that it offers these fundamental rights no protection. The fact that no particular provision of the Constitution explicitly forbids the State from disrupting the traditional relation of the family—a relation as old and as fundamental as our entire civilization—surely does not show that the Government was meant to have the power to do so. Rather, as the Ninth Amendment expressly recognizes, there are fundamental personal rights such as this one, which are protected from abridgment by the Government though not specifically mentioned in the Constitution.

. . .

The logic of the dissents would sanction federal or state legislation that seems to me even more plainly unconstitutional than the statute before us. . . . [I]f upon a showing of a slender basis of rationality, a law outlawing voluntary birth control by married persons is valid, then, by the same reasoning, a law requiring compulsory birth control also would seem to be valid. In my view, however, both types of law would unjustifiably intrude upon rights of marital privacy which are constitutionally protected.

. . .

In sum, I believe that the right of privacy in the marital relation is fundamental and basic—a personal right "retained by the people" within the meaning of the Ninth Amendment. Connecticut cannot constitutionally abridge this fundamental right, which is protected by the Fourteenth Amendment from infringement by the States. I agree with the Court that petitioners' convictions must therefore be reversed.

■ MR. JUSTICE HARLAN, concurring in the judgment.

I fully agree with the judgment of reversal, but find myself unable to join the Court's opinion. The reason is that it seems to me to evince an approach to this case very much like that taken by my Brothers Black and Stewart in dissent, namely: the Due Process Clause of the Fourteenth Amendment does not touch this Connecticut

---

Ashwander v. TVA, 297 U.S. 288, 330–331. See also Calder v. Bull, 3 Dall. 386, 388; Loan Ass'n v. City of Topeka, 20 Wall. 655, 662–663. . . .

statute unless the enactment is found to violate some right assured by the letter or penumbra of the Bill of Rights.

In other words, what I find implicit in the Court's opinion is that the "incorporation" doctrine may be used to *restrict* the reach of Fourteenth Amendment Due Process. For me this is just as unacceptable constitutional doctrine as is the use of the "incorporation" approach to *impose* upon the States all the requirements of the Bill of Rights as found in the provisions of the first eight amendments and in the decisions of this Court interpreting them. . . .

■ MR. JUSTICE WHITE, concurring in the judgment.

In my view this Connecticut law as applied to married couples deprives them of "liberty" without due process of law, as that concept is used in the Fourteenth Amendment. I therefore concur in the judgment of the Court reversing these convictions under Connecticut's aiding and abetting statute.

. . .

■ MR. JUSTICE BLACK, with whom MR. JUSTICE STEWART joins, dissenting.

I agree with my Brother Stewart's dissenting opinion. And like him I do not to any extent whatever base my view that this Connecticut law is constitutional on a belief that the law is wise or that its policy is a good one. In order that there may be no room at all to doubt why I vote as I do, I feel constrained to add that the law is every bit as offensive to me as it is to my Brethren of the majority and my Brothers Harlan, White and Goldberg who, reciting reasons why it is offensive to them, hold it unconstitutional. There is no single one of the graphic and eloquent strictures and criticisms fired at the policy of this Connecticut law either by the Court's opinion or by those of my concurring Brethren to which I cannot subscribe—except their conclusion that the evil qualities they see in the law make it unconstitutional.

. . .

The Court talks about a constitutional "right of privacy" as though there is some constitutional provision or provisions forbidding any law ever to be passed which might abridge the "privacy" of individuals. But there is not. . . .

. . .

I realize that many good and able men have eloquently spoken and written, sometimes in rhapsodical strains, about the duty of this Court to keep the Constitution in tune with the times. The idea is that the Constitution must be changed from time to time and that this Court is charged with a duty to make those changes. For myself, I must with all deference reject that philosophy. The Constitution makers knew the need for change and provided for it. Amendments suggested by the people's elected representatives can be submitted to the people or their selected agents for ratification. That method of change was good for our Fathers, and being somewhat old-fashioned I must add it is good enough for me. And so, I cannot rely on the Due Process Clause or the Ninth Amendment or any mysterious and uncertain natural law concept as a reason for striking down this state law. The Due Process Clause with an "arbitrary and capricious" or "shocking to the conscience" formula was liberally used by this Court to strike down economic legislation in the early decades of this century, threatening, many people thought, the tranquility and stability of the nation. See, e.g., Lochner v. State of New York, 198 U.S. 45. That formula, based on subjective considerations of "natural justice," is no less dangerous when used to enforce this Court's views about personal rights than those about economic rights. I had thought that we had laid that formula, as a means for striking down state legislation, to rest once and for all in cases like West Coast Hotel Co. v. Parrish, 300 U.S. 379; Olsen v.

State of Nebraska ex rel. Western Reference & Bond Assn., 313 U.S. 236, and many other opinions. . . .

. . . The late Judge Learned Hand, after emphasizing his view that judges should not use the due process formula suggested in the concurring opinions today or any other formula like it to invalidate legislation offensive to their "personal preferences,"[22] made the statement, with which I fully agree, that:

"For myself it would be most irksome to be ruled by a bevy of Platonic Guardians, even if I knew how to choose them, which I assuredly do not."

So far as I am concerned, Connecticut's law as applied here is not forbidden by any provision of the Federal Constitution as that Constitution was written, and I would therefore affirm.

■ MR. JUSTICE STEWART, whom MR. JUSTICE BLACK joins, dissenting.

Since 1879 Connecticut has had on its books a law which forbids the use of contraceptives by anyone. I think this is an uncommonly silly law. As a practical matter, the law is obviously unenforceable, except in the oblique context of the present case. As a philosophical matter, I believe the use of contraceptives in the relationship of marriage should be left to personal and private choice, based upon each individual's moral, ethical, and religious beliefs. As a matter of social policy, I think professional counsel about methods of birth control should be available to all, so that each individual's choice can be meaningfully made. But we are not asked in this case to say whether we think this law is unwise, or even asinine. We are asked to hold that it violates the United States Constitution. And that I cannot do.

. . .

What provisions of the Constitution, then, does make this state law invalid? The Court says it is the right of privacy "created by several fundamental constitutional guarantees." With all deference, I can find no such general right of privacy in the Bill of Rights, in any other part of the Constitution, or in any case ever before decided by this Court.[a]

. . .

Privacy as Autonomy Versus Privacy as Freedom from Intrusion and Disclosure

In *Griswold* the Court appeared to use the term "privacy" in the sense of protecting private matters from disclosure. It emphasized intrusion into "the sacred precincts of marital bedrooms." But in Roe v. Wade, infra p. 400, the Court gave the term a broader meaning protecting personal autonomy. In fact, in Carey v. Population Services Int'l., 431 U.S. 678, 687 (1977), the Court said that later decisions had "put *Griswold* in proper perspective. *Griswold* may no longer be read as holding only that a State may not prohibit a married couple's use of contraceptives. Read in the light of its progeny, the teaching of *Griswold* is that the Constitution protects individual decisions in matters of childbearing from unjustified intrusion by the State."

---

[22] Hand, The Bill of Rights (1958) 70. . . .

[a] Helpful discussion of the Court's approach to the Griswold case may be found in: *Symposium on the Griswold Case and the Right of Privacy,* 64 Mich.L.Rev. 197 (1965); Beaney, *The Griswold Case and the Expanding Right to Privacy,* 1966 Wis.L.Rev. 979; Katin, *Griswold v. Connecticut: The Justices and Connecticut's "Uncommonly Silly Law,"* 42 Notre Dame L. 680 (1967); Franklin, *The Ninth Amendment as Civil Law Method and Its Implications for a Republican Form of Government,* 40 Tul.L.Rev. 487 (1966).

Since *Griswold* the Court has decided very few claims that the state had unconstitutionally invaded privacy in the sense of requiring disclosure of personal matters. Whalen v. Roe, 429 U.S. 589 (1977), presented the question whether a state could record, in a centralized computer file, the names and addresses of all persons who had obtained, pursuant to a doctor's prescription, certain drugs for which there was both a lawful and an unlawful market. In response to an argument that the state requirement invaded a constitutionally protected zone of privacy, the Court noted: "The cases sometimes characterized as protecting 'privacy' have in fact involved at least two different kinds of interests. One is the individual interest in avoiding disclosure of personal matters, and another is the interest in independence in making certain kinds of important decisions." The Court upheld the statute on the ground that the state protections against public disclosure of the data were sufficient to avoid a serious threat to either interest. It concluded its opinion with the following paragraph:

"A final word about issues we have not decided. We are not unaware of the threat to privacy implicit in the accumulation of vast amounts of personal information in computerized data banks or other massive government files. The collection of taxes, the distribution of welfare and social security benefits, the supervision of public health, the direction of our armed forces and the enforcement of the criminal laws, all require the orderly preservation of great quantities of information, much of which is personal in character and potentially embarrassing or harmful if disclosed. The right to collect and use such data for public purposes is typically accompanied by a concomitant statutory or regulatory duty to avoid unwarranted disclosures. Recognizing that in some circumstances that duty arguably has its roots in the Constitution, nevertheless New York's statutory scheme, and its implementing administrative procedures, evidence a proper concern with, and protection of, the individual's interest in privacy. We therefore need not, and do not, decide any question which might be presented by the unwarranted disclosure of accumulated private data—whether intentional or unintentional—or by a system that did not contain comparable security provisions. We simply hold that this record does not establish an invasion of any right or liberty protected by the Fourteenth Amendment."

More than three decades later, in the context of a claim involving the collection of personal background data from employees of government contractors, the Court noted that since 1977 "no . . . decision has squarely addressed a constitutional right to informational privacy." National Aeronautics and Space Administration v. Nelson, 562 U.S. 134, 146 (2011). Again rejecting the claim, however, the Court followed the approach in *Whalen*, "assum[ed] that the Government's challenged inquiries implicate a privacy interest of constitutional significance[,]" but "h[e]ld that, whatever the scope of this interest, it does not prevent the Government from asking reasonable questions of the sort included [on the challenged forms] in an employment background investigation that is subject to the Privacy Act's safeguards against public disclosure." Concurring in the judgment, Justice Scalia, joined by Justice Thomas, would have resolved the case, not by balancing interests in privacy against government interests, but categorically by "simply hold[ing] that there is no constitutional right to 'informational privacy'" at all.

B. FAMILY AND MARITAL RELATIONSHIPS

Moore v. City of East Cleveland, Ohio

431 U.S. 494, 97 S.Ct. 1932, 52 L.Ed.2d 531 (1977).

■ MR. JUSTICE POWELL announced the judgment of the Court, and delivered an opinion in which MR. JUSTICE BRENNAN, MR. JUSTICE MARSHALL, and MR. JUSTICE BLACKMUN joined.

East Cleveland's housing ordinance, like many throughout the country, limits occupancy of a dwelling unit to members of a single family. § 1351.02. But the ordinance contains an unusual and complicated definitional section that recognizes as a "family" only a few categories of related individuals, § 1341.08.[2] Because her family, living together in her home, fits none of those categories, appellant stands convicted of a criminal offense. The question in this case is whether the ordinance violates the Due Process Clause of the Fourteenth Amendment.

I.

Appellant, Mrs. Inez Moore, lives in her East Cleveland home together with her son, Dale Moore Sr., and her two grandsons, Dale, Jr., and John Moore, Jr. The two boys are first cousins rather than brothers; we are told that John came to live with his grandmother and with the elder and younger Dale Moores after his mother's death.

In early 1973, Mrs. Moore received a notice of violation from the city, stating that John was an "illegal occupant" and directing her to comply with the ordinance. When she failed to remove him from her home, the city filed a criminal charge. Mrs. Moore moved to dismiss, claiming that the ordinance was constitutionally invalid on its face. Her motion was overruled, and upon conviction she was sentenced to five days in jail and a $25 fine. The Ohio Court of Appeals affirmed after giving full consideration to her constitutional claims, and the Ohio Supreme Court denied review. . . .

II.

The city argues that our decision in Village of Belle Terre v. Boraas, 416 U.S. 1 (1974), requires us to sustain the ordinance attacked here. Belle Terre, like East Cleveland, imposed limits on the types of groups that could occupy a single dwelling unit. Applying the constitutional standard announced in this Court's leading land-use case, Euclid v. Ambler Realty Co., 272 U.S. 365 (1926), we sustained the Belle Terre

---

[2]   Section 1341.08 (1966) provides:

" 'Family' means a number of individuals related to the nominal head of the household or to the spouse of the nominal head of the household living as a single housekeeping unit in a single dwelling unit, but limited to the following:

"(a) Husband or wife of the nominal head of the household.

"(b) Unmarried children of the nominal head of the household or of the spouse of the nominal head of the household, provided, however, that such unmarried children have no children residing with them.

"(c) Father or mother of the nominal head of the household or of the spouse of the nominal head of the household.

"(d) Notwithstanding the provisions of subsection (b) hereof, a family may include not more than one dependent married or unmarried child of the nominal head of the household or of the spouse of the nominal head of the household and the spouse and dependent children of such dependent child. For the purpose of this subsection, a dependent person is one who has more than fifty percent of his total support furnished for him by the nominal head of the household and the spouse of the nominal head of the household.

"(e) A family may consist of one individual."

ordinance on the ground that it bore a rational relationship to permissible state objectives.

But one overriding factor sets this case apart from *Belle Terre*. The ordinance there affected only *unrelated* individuals. It expressly allowed all who were related by "blood, adoption, or marriage" to live together, and in sustaining the ordinance we were careful to note that it promoted "family needs" and "family values." East Cleveland, in contrast, has chosen to regulate the occupancy of its housing by slicing deeply into the family itself. This is no mere incidental result of the ordinance. On its face it selects certain categories of relatives who may live together and declares that others may not. In particular, it makes a crime of a grandmother's choice to live with her grandson in circumstances like those presented here.

When a city undertakes such intrusive regulation of the family, neither *Belle Terre* nor *Euclid* governs; the usual judicial deference to the legislature is inappropriate. "This Court has long recognized that freedom of personal choice in matters of marriage and family life is one of the liberties protected by the Due Process Clause of the Fourteenth Amendment." . . . A host of cases, tracing their lineage to Meyer v. Nebraska, 262 U.S. 390, 399–401 (1923), and Pierce v. Society of Sisters, 268 U.S. 510, 534–535 (1925), have consistently acknowledged a "private realm of family life which the state cannot enter." Prince v. Massachusetts, 321 U.S. 158, 166 (1944). . . . Of course, the family is not beyond regulation. See Prince v. Massachusetts. But when the government intrudes on choices concerning family living arrangements, this Court must examine carefully the importance of the governmental interests advanced and the extent to which they are served by the challenged regulation. See *Poe v. Ullman* (Harlan, J., dissenting).

When thus examined, this ordinance cannot survive. The city seeks to justify it as a means of preventing overcrowding, minimizing traffic and parking congestion, and avoiding an undue financial burden on East Cleveland's school system. Although these are legitimate goals, the ordinance before us serves them marginally, at best. For example, the ordinance permits any family consisting only of husband, wife, and unmarried children to live together, even if the family contains a half-dozen licensed drivers, each with his or her own car. At the same time it forbids an adult brother and sister to share a household, even if both faithfully use public transportation. The ordinance would permit a grandmother to live with a single dependent son and children, even if his school-age children number a dozen, yet it forces Mrs. Moore to find another dwelling for her grandson John, simply because of the presence of his uncle and cousin in the same household. We need not labor the point. Section 1341.08 has but a tenuous relation to alleviation of the conditions mentioned by the city.

III.

The city would distinguish the cases based on *Meyer* and *Pierce*. It points out that none of them "gives grandmothers any fundamental rights with respect to grandsons," and suggests that any constitutional right to live together as a family extends only to the nuclear family—essentially a couple and its dependent children.

To be sure, these cases did not expressly consider the family relationship presented here. They were immediately concerned with freedom of choice with respect to childbearing, e.g., *LaFleur, Roe v. Wade, Griswold,* supra, or with the rights of parents to the custody and companionship of their own children, Stanley v. Illinois, supra, or with traditional parental authority in matters of child rearing and education. *Yoder, Ginsberg, Pierce, Meyer,* supra. But unless we close our eyes to the basic reasons why certain rights associated with the family have been accorded shelter under the Fourteenth Amendment's Due Process Clause, we cannot avoid applying the force and rationale of these precedents to the family choice involved in this case.

. . .

Substantive due process has at times been a treacherous field for this Court. There *are* risks when the judicial branch gives enhanced protection to certain substantive liberties without the guidance of the more specific provisions of the Bill of Rights. As the history of the *Lochner* era demonstrates, there is reason for concern lest the only limits to such judicial intervention become the predilections of those who happen at the time to be Members of this Court. That history counsels caution and restraint. But it does not counsel abandonment, nor does it require what the city urges here: cutting off any protection of family rights at the first convenient, if arbitrary boundary—the boundary of the nuclear family.

Appropriate limits on substantive due process come not from drawing arbitrary lines but rather from careful "respect for the teachings of history [and] solid recognition of the basic values that underlie our society." Griswold v. Connecticut, 381 U.S., at 501 (Harlan, J., concurring). . . . Our decisions establish that the Constitution protects the sanctity of the family precisely because the institution of the family is deeply rooted in this Nation's history and tradition. It is through the family that we inculcate and pass down many of our most cherished values, moral and cultural.

Ours is by no means a tradition limited to respect for the bonds uniting the members of the nuclear family. The tradition of uncles, aunts, cousins, and especially grandparents sharing a household along with parents and children has roots equally venerable and equally deserving of constitutional recognition. Over the years millions of our citizens have grown up in just such an environment, and most, surely, have profited from it. Even if conditions of modern society have brought about a decline in extended family households, they have not erased the accumulated wisdom of civilization, gained over the centuries and honored throughout our history, that supports a larger conception of the family. Out of choice, necessity, or a sense of family responsibility, it has been common for close relatives to draw together and participate in the duties and the satisfactions of a common home. Decisions concerning child rearing, which *Yoder, Meyer, Pierce* and other cases have recognized as entitled to constitutional protection, long have been shared with grandparents or other relatives who occupy the same household—indeed who may take on major responsibility for the rearing of the children. Especially in times of adversity, such as the death of a spouse or economic need, the broader family has tended to come together for mutual sustenance and to maintain or rebuild a secure home life. This is apparently what happened here.

Whether or not such a household is established because of personal tragedy, the choice of relatives in this degree of kinship to live together may not lightly be denied by the State. *Pierce* struck down an Oregon law requiring all children to attend the State's public schools, holding that the Constitution "excludes any general power of the State to standardize its children by forcing them to accept instruction from public teachers only." 268 U.S., at 535. By the same token the Constitution prevents East Cleveland from standardizing its children—and its adults—by forcing all to live in certain narrowly defined family patterns.

Reversed.

■ MR. JUSTICE BRENNAN, with whom MR. JUSTICE MARSHALL joins, concurring.

I join the plurality's opinion. . . .

In today's America, the "nuclear family" is the pattern so often found in much of white suburbia. Sanden, Sociology: A Systematic Approach, p. 320 (1965). The Constitution cannot be interpreted, however, to tolerate the imposition by government upon the rest of us of white suburbia's preference in patterns of family living. The "extended family" that provided generations of early Americans with social services and economic and emotional support in times of hardship, and was the beachhead for successive waves of immigrants who populated our cities, remains not merely still a pervasive living pattern, but under the goad of brutal economic necessity, a prominent pattern—virtually a means of survival—for large numbers of the poor and deprived minorities of our society. For them compelled pooling of scant resources requires compelled sharing of a household.

The "extended" form is especially familiar among black families. . . .

I do not wish to be understood as implying that East Cleveland's enforcement of its ordinance is motivated by a racially discriminatory purpose: the record of this case would not support that implication. But the prominence of other than nuclear families among ethnic and racial minority groups, including our black citizens, surely demonstrates that the "extended family" pattern remains a vital tenet of our society. It suffices that in prohibiting this pattern of family living as a means of achieving its objectives, appellee city has chosen a device that deeply intrudes into family associational rights that historically have been central, and today remain central, to a large proportion of our population.

. . .

■ MR. JUSTICE STEVENS, concurring in the judgment.

In my judgment the critical question presented by this case is whether East Cleveland's housing ordinance is a permissible restriction on appellant's right to use her own property as she sees fit.

. . .

■ MR. JUSTICE STEWART, with whom MR. JUSTICE REHNQUIST joins, dissenting.

. . .

. . . The question presented, as I view it, is whether the decision in *Belle Terre* is controlling, or whether the Constitution compels a different result because East Cleveland's definition of "family" is more restrictive than that before us in the *Belle Terre* case.

. . . The *Belle Terre* decision disposes of the appellant's contentions to the extent they focus not on her blood relationships with her sons and grandsons but on more general notions about the "privacy of the home." Her suggestion that every person has a constitutional right permanently to share his residence with whomever he pleases, and that such choices are "beyond the province of legitimate governmental intrusion," amounts to the same argument that was made and found unpersuasive in *Belle Terre*.

To be sure, the ordinance involved in *Belle Terre* did not prevent blood relatives from occupying the same dwelling, and the Court's decision in that case does not, therefore, foreclose the appellant's arguments based specifically on the ties of kinship present in this case. Nonetheless, I would hold, for the reasons that follow, that the existence of those ties does not elevate either the appellant's claim of associational freedom or her claim of privacy to a level invoking constitutional protection.

. . .

The "association" in this case is not for any purpose relating to the promotion of speech, assembly, the press, or religion. And wherever the outer boundaries of constitutional protection of freedom of association may eventually turn out to be, they surely do not extend to those who assert no interest other than the gratification, convenience, and economy of sharing the same residence.

The appellant is considerably closer to the constitutional mark in asserting that the East Cleveland ordinance intrudes upon "the private realm of family life which the state cannot enter." . . .

Although the appellant's desire to share a single-dwelling unit also involves "private family life" in a sense, that desire can hardly be equated with any of the interests protected in [previous cases.] The ordinance . . . did not impede her choice to have or not to have children, and it did not dictate to her how her own children were to be nurtured and reared. The ordinance clearly does not prevent parents from living together or living with their unemancipated offspring.

. . .[7]

. . . When the Court has found that the Fourteenth Amendment placed a substantive limitation on a State's power to regulate, it has been in those rare cases in which the personal interests at issue have been deemed "implicit in the concept of ordered liberty." See Roe v. Wade, supra, at 152, quoting Palko v. Connecticut, 302 U.S. 319, 325. The interest that the appellant may have in permanently sharing a single kitchen and a suite of contiguous rooms with some of her relatives simply does not rise to that level. To equate this interest with the fundamental decisions to marry and to bear and raise children is to extend the limited substantive contours of the Due Process Clause beyond recognition.

The appellant also challenges the single-family occupancy ordinance on equal protection grounds. Her claim is that the city has drawn an arbitrary and irrational distinction between groups of people who may live together as a "family" and those who may not. . . .

Obviously, East Cleveland might have as easily and perhaps as effectively hit upon a different definition of "family." But a line could hardly be drawn that would not sooner or later become the target of a challenge like the appellant's. If "family" included all of the householder's grandchildren there would doubtless be the hard case of an orphaned niece or nephew. If, as the appellant suggests, a "family" must include all blood relatives, what of longtime friends? The point is that any definition would produce hardships in some cases without materially advancing the legislative purpose. . . .

   . . .

■ MR. JUSTICE WHITE, dissenting.

   . . .

. . . Realizing that the present construction of the Due Process Clause represents a major judicial gloss on its terms, as well as on the anticipation of the Framers, and that much of the underpinning for the broad, substantive application of the Clause disappeared in the conflict between the executive and the judiciary in the 1930's and 1940's, the Court should be extremely reluctant to breathe still further substantive content into the Due Process Clause so as to strike down legislation adopted by a State or city to promote its welfare. Whenever the judiciary does so, it unavoidably pre-empts for itself another part of the governance of the country without express constitutional authority.

Accepting the cases as they are and the Due Process Clause as construed by them, however, I think it evident that the threshold question in any due process attack on legislation, whether the challenge is procedural or substantive, is whether there is a deprivation of life, liberty or property. . . .

---

[7] The opinion of Mr. Justice Powell and Mr. Justice Brennan's concurring opinion both emphasize the traditional importance of the extended family in American life. But I fail to understand why it follows that the residents of East Cleveland are constitutionally prevented from following what Mr. Justice Brennan calls the "pattern" of "white suburbia," even though that choice may reflect "cultural myopia." In point of fact, East Cleveland is a predominantly Negro community, with a Negro City Manager and City Commission.

It seems to me that Mr. Justice Douglas was closest to the mark in Poe v. Ullman . . . when he said that the trouble with the holdings of the "old Court" was not in its definition of liberty but in its definition of the protections guaranteed to that liberty— "not in entertaining inquiries concerning the constitutionality of social legislation but in applying the standards that it did."

The term "liberty" is not, therefore, to be given a crabbed construction. I have no more difficulty than Mr. Justice Powell apparently does in concluding that petitioner in this case properly asserts a liberty interest within the meaning of the Due Process Clause. The question is not one of liberty, *vel non.* Rather, there being no procedural issue at stake, the issue is whether the precise interest involved—the interest in having more than one set of grandchildren live in her home—is entitled to such substantive protection under the Due Process Clause that this ordinance must be held invalid.

. . .

[T]he general principle [is] that "liberty may not be interfered with, under the guise of protecting the public interest, by legislative action which is arbitrary or without reasonable relation to some purpose within the competency of the state to effect." Meyer v. Nebraska, supra, at 399–400. This means-end test appears to require that any statute restrictive of liberty have an ascertainable purpose and represent a rational means to achieve that purpose, whatever the nature of the liberty interest involved. . . .

There are various "liberties," however, which require that infringing legislation be given closer judicial scrutiny, not only with respect to existence of a purpose and the means employed, but also with respect to the importance of the purpose itself relative to the invaded interest. Some interests would appear almost impregnable to invasion, such as the freedoms of speech, press, and religion, and the freedom from cruel and unusual punishments. Other interests, for example, the right of association, the right to vote, and various claims sometimes referred to under the general rubric of the right to privacy, also weigh very heavily against state claims of authority to regulate. It is this category of interests which, as I understand it, Mr. Justice Stewart refers to as "implicit in the concept of ordered liberty." Because he would confine the reach of substantive due process protection to interests such as these and because he would not classify in this category the asserted right to share a house with the relatives involved here, he rejects the due process claim.

Given his premise, he is surely correct. Under our cases, the Due Process Clause extends substantial protection to various phases of family life, but none requires that the claim made here be sustained. I cannot believe that the interest in residing with more than one set of grandchildren is one that calls for any kind of heightened protection under the Due Process Clause. . . .

Mr. Justice Powell would apparently construe the Due Process Clause to protect from all but quite important state regulatory interests any right or privilege that in his estimate is deeply rooted in the country's traditions. For me, this suggests a far too expansive charter for this Court and a far less meaningful and less confining guiding principle than Mr. Justice Stewart would use for serious substantive due process review. . . .

. . . Had it been our task to legislate, we might have approached the problem in a different manner than did the drafters of this ordinance; but I have no trouble in concluding that the normal goals of zoning regulation are present here and that the ordinance serves these goals by limiting, in identifiable circumstances, the number of people who can occupy a single household. The ordinance does not violate the Due Process Clause.

For very similar reasons, the equal protection claim must fail, since it is not to be judged by the strict scrutiny standard employed when a fundamental interest or suspect classification is involved. . . .

[A dissenting opinion by Chief Justice Burger is omitted.][a]

Obergefell v. Hodges

576 U.S. ___, 135 S.Ct. 2584, 192 L.Ed.2d 609 (2015).

■ JUSTICE KENNEDY delivered the opinion of the Court.

The Constitution promises liberty to all within its reach, a liberty that includes certain specific rights that allow persons, within a lawful realm, to define and express their identity. The petitioners in these cases seek to find that liberty by marrying someone of the same sex and having their marriages deemed lawful on the same terms and conditions as marriages between persons of the opposite sex.

I

These cases come from Michigan, Kentucky, Ohio, and Tennessee, States that define marriage as a union between one man and one woman. [Fourteen same-sex couples, and two men whose same-sex partners are deceased, claimed in different actions that denying them the right to marry or to have their marriages (which were lawfully performed in another State) given full recognition, violated the Fourteenth Amendment. Judgments in their favor in various district courts were reversed by the Sixth Circuit in consolidated cases.]

. . . This Court granted review, limited to two questions. . . . The first, presented by the cases from Michigan and Kentucky, is whether the Fourteenth Amendment requires a State to license a marriage between two people of the same sex. The second, presented by the cases from Ohio, Tennessee, and, again, Kentucky, is whether the Fourteenth Amendment requires a State to recognize a same-sex marriage licensed and performed in a State which does grant that right.

II

. . .

A

. . . [T]he annals of human history reveal the transcendent importance of marriage. The lifelong union of a man and a woman always has promised nobility and dignity to all persons, without regard to their station in life. Marriage is sacred to those who live by their religions and offers unique fulfillment to those who find meaning in the secular realm. Its dynamic allows two people to find a life that could not be found alone, for a marriage becomes greater than just the two persons. Rising from the most basic human needs, marriage is essential to our most profound hopes and aspirations.

The centrality of marriage to the human condition makes it unsurprising that the institution has existed for millennia and across civilizations. . . . It is fair and necessary to say these references were based on the understanding that marriage is a union between two persons of the opposite sex.

That history is the beginning of these cases. The respondents say it should be the end as well. To them, it would demean a timeless institution if the concept and lawful status of marriage were extended to two persons of the same sex. Marriage, in their

---

[a] For a full discussion, see *Developments in the Law—The Constitution and the Family,* 93 Harv.L.Rev. 1156 (1980).

view, is by its nature a gender-differentiated union of man and woman. This view long has been held—and continues to be held—in good faith by reasonable and sincere people here and throughout the world.

The petitioners acknowledge this history but contend that these cases cannot end there. Were their intent to demean the revered idea and reality of marriage, the petitioners' claims would be of a different order. But that is neither their purpose nor their submission. To the contrary, it is the enduring importance of marriage that underlies the[ir] contentions. . . . Far from seeking to devalue marriage, the petitioners seek it for themselves because of their respect—and need—for its privileges and responsibilities. And their immutable nature dictates that same-sex marriage is their only real path to this profound commitment.

Recounting the circumstances of three of these cases illustrates the urgency of the petitioners' cause from their perspective. [Obergefell and his partner of over two decades had a "lasting, committed relation" in Ohio and chose to marry in Maryland after the latter was diagnosed with the progressive, debilitating, and incurable disease of ALS. He died three months later, but] Ohio law does not permit Obergefell to be listed as the surviving spouse on [his] death certificate. By statute, they must remain strangers even in death, a state-imposed separation Obergefell deems "hurtful for the rest of time." . . . He brought suit to be shown as the surviving spouse on [his partner's] death certificate.

[Two female nurses from Michigan, also in a committed relationship, are raising three adopted children together, one of whom needed "around-the-clock care" and another with special needs.] Michigan, however, permits only opposite-sex married couples or single individuals to adopt, so each child can have only one woman as his or her legal parent. If an emergency were to arise, schools and hospitals may treat the three children as if they had only one parent. And, were tragedy to befall either [woman], the other would have no legal rights over the children she had not been permitted to adopt. This couple seeks relief from the continuing uncertainty their unmarried status creates in their lives.

[A soldier married his partner in New York before being deployed to Afghanistan, and they settled in Tennessee on his return to work for the Army there.] Their lawful marriage is stripped from them whenever they reside in Tennessee, returning and disappearing as they travel across state lines. . . .

The[se] cases . . . involve other petitioners as well . . . . Their stories reveal that they seek not to denigrate marriage but rather to live their lives, or honor their spouses' memory, joined by its bond.

B

. . . The history of marriage is one of both continuity and change. That institution—even as confined to opposite-sex relations—has evolved over time.

For example, marriage was once viewed as an arrangement by the couple's parents based on political, religious, and financial concerns; but by the time of the Nation's founding it was understood to be a voluntary contract between a man and a woman. . . . As the role and status of women changed, the institution further evolved. Under the centuries-old doctrine of coverture, a married man and woman were treated by the State as a single, male-dominated legal entity. . . . As women gained legal, political, and property rights, and as society began to understand that women have their own equal dignity, the law of coverture was abandoned. . . . These . . . developments in the institution of marriage . . . worked deep transformations in its structure, affecting aspects of marriage long viewed by many as essential. . . .

These new insights have strengthened, not weakened, the institution of marriage. Indeed, changed understandings of marriage are characteristic of a Nation where new dimensions of freedom become apparent to new generations, often through perspectives that begin in pleas or protests and then are considered in the political sphere and the judicial process.

This dynamic can be seen in the Nation's experiences with the rights of gays and lesbians. Until the mid-20th century, same-sex intimacy long had been condemned as immoral by the state itself in most Western nations, a belief often embodied in the criminal law. For this reason, among others, many persons did not deem homosexuals to have dignity in their own distinct identity. . . . Even when a greater awareness of the humanity and integrity of homosexual persons came in the period after World War II, the argument that gays and lesbians had a just claim to dignity was in conflict with both law and widespread social conventions. . . .

For much of the 20th century, moreover, homosexuality was treated as an illness. . . . Only in more recent years have psychiatrists and others recognized that sexual orientation is both a normal expression of human sexuality and immutable. . . .

In the late 20th century, following substantial cultural and political developments, same-sex couples began to lead more open and public lives and to establish families. This development was followed by a quite extensive discussion of the issue in both governmental and private sectors and by a shift in public attitudes toward greater tolerance. As a result, questions about the rights of gays and lesbians soon reached the courts, where the issue could be discussed in the formal discourse of the law.

[Justice Kennedy recounted legal developments, including Bowers v. Hardwick, 478 U. S. 186 (1986), Romer v. Evans, 517 U. S. 620 (1996), and Lawrence v. Texas, 539 U. S. 558 (2003), as well as state court decisions and laws on both sides of the question, and the 1996 Defense of Marriage Act (DOMA), defining marriage for all federal-law purposes as "only a legal union between one man and one woman as husband and wife." He then continued:]

. . . Two Terms ago, in United States v. Windsor, 570 U. S. ___ (2013), this Court invalidated DOMA to the extent it barred the Federal Government from treating same-sex marriages as valid even when they were lawful in the State where they were licensed. DOMA, the Court held, impermissibly disparaged those same-sex couples "who wanted to affirm their commitment to one another before their children, their family, their friends, and their community." . . .

. . .

After years of litigation, legislation, referenda, and the discussions that attended these public acts, the States are now divided on the issue of same-sex marriage. . . .

III

. . .

The identification and protection of fundamental rights is an enduring part of the judicial duty to interpret the Constitution. That responsibility, however, "has not been reduced to any formula." Poe v. Ullman, 367 U. S. 497, 542 (1961) (Harlan, J., dissenting). Rather, it requires courts to exercise reasoned judgment in identifying interests of the person so fundamental that the State must accord them its respect. . . . History and tradition guide and discipline this inquiry but do not set its outer boundaries. . . . That method respects our history and learns from it without allowing the past alone to rule the present.

The nature of injustice is that we may not always see it in our own times. The generations that wrote and ratified the Bill of Rights and the Fourteenth Amendment did not presume to know the extent of freedom in all of its dimensions, and so they entrusted to future generations a charter protecting the right of all persons to enjoy liberty as we learn its meaning. When new insight reveals discord between the Constitution's central protections and a received legal stricture, a claim to liberty must be addressed.

Applying these established tenets, the Court has long held the right to marry is protected by the Constitution. . . . Loving v. Virginia, 388 U. S. 1, 12 (1967), . . . Zablocki v. Redhail, 434 U. S. 374, 384 (1978), . . . [and] Turner v. Safley, 482 U. S. 78, 95 (1987), which held the right to marry was abridged by regulations limiting the privilege of prison inmates to marry. Over time and in other contexts, the Court has reiterated that the right to marry is fundamental under the Due Process Clause. . . .

It cannot be denied that this Court's cases describing the right to marry presumed a relationship involving opposite-sex partners. The Court, like many institutions, has made assumptions defined by the world and time of which it is a part. This was evident in Baker v. Nelson, 409 U. S. 810, a one-line summary decision issued in 1972, holding the exclusion of same-sex couples from marriage did not present a substantial federal question.

Still, . . . in assessing whether the force and rationale of its cases apply to same-sex couples, the Court must respect the basic reasons why the right to marry has been long protected. . . .

This analysis compels the conclusion that same-sex couples may exercise the right to marry. The four principles and traditions to be discussed demonstrate that the reasons marriage is fundamental under the Constitution apply with equal force to same-sex couples.

A first premise of the Court's relevant precedents is that the right to personal choice regarding marriage is inherent in the concept of individual autonomy. . . .

Choices about marriage shape an individual's destiny. . . .

The nature of marriage is that, through its enduring bond, two persons together can find other freedoms, such as expression, intimacy, and spirituality. This is true for all persons, whatever their sexual orientation. . . . There is dignity in the bond between two men or two women who seek to marry and in their autonomy to make such profound choices. . . .

A second principle in this Court's jurisprudence is that the right to marry is fundamental because it supports a two-person union unlike any other in its importance to the committed individuals. This point was central to Griswold v. Connecticut . . . . And in *Turner*, the Court again acknowledged the intimate association protected by this right, holding prisoners could not be denied the right to marry because their committed relationships satisfied the basic reasons why marriage is a fundamental right. . . . The right to marry thus dignifies couples who "wish to define themselves by their commitment to each other." *Windsor*, ... Marriage responds to the universal fear that a lonely person might call out only to find no one there. It offers the hope of companionship and understanding and assurance that while both still live there will be someone to care for the other.

As this Court held in *Lawrence*, same-sex couples have the same right as opposite-sex couples to enjoy intimate association. *Lawrence* invalidated laws that made same-sex intimacy a criminal act. . . . But while *Lawrence* confirmed a dimension of freedom that allows individuals to engage in intimate association without criminal liability, it does not follow that freedom stops there. Outlaw to outcast may be a step forward, but it does not achieve the full promise of liberty.

A third basis for protecting the right to marry is that it safeguards children and families and thus draws meaning from related rights of childrearing, procreation, and education. . . . By giving recognition and legal structure to their parents' relationship, marriage allows children "to understand the integrity and closeness of their own family and its concord with other families in their community and in their daily lives." *Windsor* . . . . Marriage also affords the permanency and stability important to children's best interests. . . .

As all parties agree, many same-sex couples provide loving and nurturing homes to their children, whether biological or adopted. And hundreds of thousands of children are presently being raised by such couples. . . . Most States have allowed gays and lesbians to adopt, either as individuals or as couples, and many adopted and foster children have same-sex parents . . . . This provides powerful confirmation from the law itself that gays and lesbians can create loving, supportive families.

Excluding same-sex couples from marriage thus conflicts with a central premise of the right to marry. Without the recognition, stability, and predictability marriage offers, their children suffer the stigma of knowing their families are somehow lesser. They also suffer the significant material costs of being raised by unmarried parents, relegated through no fault of their own to a more difficult and uncertain family life. The marriage laws at issue here thus harm and humiliate the children of same-sex couples. See *Windsor* . . . .

That is not to say the right to marry is less meaningful for those who do not or cannot have children. An ability, desire, or promise to procreate is not and has not been a prerequisite for a valid marriage in any State. . . . The constitutional marriage right has many aspects, of which childbearing is only one.

Fourth and finally, this Court's cases and the Nation's traditions make clear that marriage is a keystone of our social order. . . . Marriage remains a building block of our national community.

. . . [W]hile the States are in general free to vary the benefits they confer on all married couples, they have throughout our history made marriage the basis for an expanding list of governmental rights, benefits, and responsibilities. These aspects of marital status include: taxation; inheritance and property rights; rules of intestate succession; spousal privilege in the law of evidence; hospital access; medical decisionmaking authority; adoption rights; the rights and benefits of survivors; birth and death certificates; professional ethics rules; campaign finance restrictions; workers' compensation benefits; health insurance; and child custody, support, and visitation rules. See Brief for United States as Amicus Curiae 6–9; Brief for American Bar Association as Amicus Curiae 8–29. Valid marriage under state law is also a significant status for over a thousand provisions of federal law. See *Windsor* . . . . The States have contributed to the fundamental character of the marriage right by placing that institution at the center of so many facets of the legal and social order.

There is no difference between same- and opposite-sex couples with respect to this principle. Yet by virtue of their exclusion from that institution, same-sex couples are denied the constellation of benefits that the States have linked to marriage. This harm results in more than just material burdens. Same-sex couples are consigned to an instability many opposite-sex couples would deem intolerable in their own lives. As the State itself makes marriage all the more precious by the significance it attaches to it, exclusion from that status has the effect of teaching that gays and lesbians are unequal in important respects. It demeans gays and lesbians for the State to lock them out of a central institution of the Nation's society. Same-sex couples, too, may aspire to the transcendent purposes of marriage and seek fulfillment in its highest meaning.

The limitation of marriage to opposite-sex couples may long have seemed natural and just, but its inconsistency with the central meaning of the fundamental right to marry is now manifest. With that knowledge must come the recognition that laws excluding same-sex couples from the marriage right impose stigma and injury of the kind prohibited by our basic charter.

. . . [R]espondents refer to Washington v. Glucksberg, 521 U. S. 702, 721 (1997), which called for a "'careful description'" of fundamental rights[, and] assert the petitioners do not seek to exercise the right to marry but rather a new and nonexistent "right to same-sex marriage." . . . *Glucksberg* did insist that liberty under the Due Process Clause must be defined in a most circumscribed manner, with central reference to specific historical practices. Yet while that approach may have been appropriate for the asserted right there involved (physician-assisted suicide), it is inconsistent with the approach this Court has used in discussing other fundamental rights, including marriage and intimacy. *Loving* did not ask about a "right to interracial marriage"; *Turner* did not ask about a "right of inmates to marry"; and *Zablocki* did not ask about a "right of fathers with unpaid child support duties to marry." Rather, each case inquired about the right to marry in its comprehensive sense, asking if there was a sufficient justification for excluding the relevant class from the right. . . .

That principle applies here. If rights were defined by who exercised them in the past, then received practices could serve as their own continued justification and new groups could not invoke rights once denied. This Court has rejected that approach, both with respect to the right to marry and the rights of gays and lesbians. See *Loving*, 388 U. S., at 12; *Lawrence*, 539 U. S., at 566–567.

The right to marry is fundamental as a matter of history and tradition, but rights come not from ancient sources alone. They rise, too, from a better informed understanding of how constitutional imperatives define a liberty that remains urgent in our own era. Many who deem same-sex marriage to be wrong reach that conclusion based on decent and honorable religious or philosophical premises, and neither they nor their beliefs are disparaged here. But when that sincere, personal opposition becomes enacted law and public policy, the necessary consequence is to put the imprimatur of the State itself on an exclusion that soon demeans or stigmatizes those whose own liberty is then denied. Under the Constitution, same-sex couples seek in marriage the same legal treatment as opposite-sex couples, and it would disparage their choices and diminish their personhood to deny them this right.

The right of same-sex couples to marry that is part of the liberty promised by the Fourteenth Amendment is derived, too, from that Amendment's guarantee of the equal protection of the laws. The Due Process Clause and the Equal Protection Clause are connected in a profound way, though they set forth independent principles. Rights implicit in liberty and rights secured by equal protection may rest on different precepts and are not always coextensive, yet in some instances each may be instructive as to the meaning and reach of the other. In any particular case one Clause may be thought to capture the essence of the right in a more accurate and comprehensive way, even as the two Clauses may converge in the identification and definition of the right. . . .

The Court's cases touching upon the right to marry reflect this dynamic. In *Loving* the Court invalidated a prohibition on interracial marriage under both the Equal Protection Clause and the Due Process Clause. . . . The reasons why marriage is a fundamental right became more clear and compelling from a full awareness and understanding of the hurt that resulted from laws barring interracial unions.

The synergy between the two protections is illustrated further in *Zablocki*[, where] . . . the essential nature of the marriage right . . . made apparent the law's incompatibility with requirements of equality. Each concept—liberty and equal protection—leads to a stronger understanding of the other.

. . . [I]nvidious sex-based classifications in marriage remained common through the mid-20th century [and t]hese classifications denied the equal dignity of men and women. . . . Responding to a new awareness, the Court invoked equal protection principles to invalidate laws imposing sex-based inequality on marriage. . . . Like *Loving* and *Zablocki*, these precedents show the Equal Protection Clause can help to identify and correct inequalities in the institution of marriage, vindicating precepts of liberty and equality under the Constitution.

. . .

In *Lawrence* the Court acknowledged the interlocking nature of these constitutional safeguards . . . [, drawing] upon principles of liberty and equality to define and protect the rights of gays and lesbians, holding the State "cannot demean their existence or control their destiny by making their private sexual conduct a crime." . . .

This dynamic also applies to same-sex marriage. It is now clear that the challenged laws burden the liberty of same-sex couples, and it must be further acknowledged that they abridge central precepts of equality. Here the marriage laws enforced by the respondents are in essence unequal: same-sex couples are denied all the benefits afforded to opposite-sex couples and are barred from exercising a fundamental right. Especially against a long history of disapproval of their relationships, this denial to same-sex couples of the right to marry works a grave and continuing harm. The imposition of this disability on gays and lesbians serves to disrespect and subordinate them. And the Equal Protection Clause, like the Due Process Clause, prohibits this unjustified infringement of the fundamental right to marry. . . .

These considerations lead to the conclusion that the right to marry is a fundamental right inherent in the liberty of the person, and under the Due Process and Equal Protection Clauses of the Fourteenth Amendment couples of the same-sex may not be deprived of that right and that liberty. The Court now holds that same-sex couples may exercise the fundamental right to marry. . . .

Baker v. Nelson must be and now is overruled, and the State laws challenged by Petitioners in these cases are now held invalid to the extent they exclude same-sex couples from civil marriage on the same terms and conditions as opposite-sex couples.

IV

There may be an initial inclination in these cases to proceed with caution—to await further legislation, litigation, and debate. . . .

Yet there has been far more deliberation than this argument acknowledges. There have been referenda, legislative debates, and grassroots campaigns, as well as countless studies, papers, books, and other popular and scholarly writings. There has been extensive litigation in state and federal courts. . . .

. . .

The dynamic of our constitutional system is that individuals need not await legislative action before asserting a fundamental right. . . . It is of no moment whether advocates of same-sex marriage now enjoy or lack momentum in the democratic process. The issue before the Court here is the legal question whether the Constitution protects the right of same-sex couples to marry.

This is not the first time the Court has been asked to adopt a cautious approach to recognizing and protecting fundamental rights. In *Bowers*, a bare majority upheld a law criminalizing same-sex intimacy. . . . Although *Bowers* was eventually repudiated in *Lawrence*, men and women were harmed in the interim, and the substantial effects of these injuries no doubt lingered long after *Bowers* was overruled. Dignitary wounds cannot always be healed with the stroke of a pen.

A ruling against same-sex couples would have the same effect—and, like *Bowers*, would be unjustified under the Fourteenth Amendment. The petitioners' stories make clear the urgency of the issue they present to the Court. James Obergefell now asks whether Ohio can erase his marriage . . . for all time. April DeBoer and Jayne Rowse now ask whether Michigan may continue to deny them the certainty and stability all mothers desire to protect their children, and for them and their children the childhood years will pass all too soon. Ijpe DeKoe and Thomas Kostura now ask whether Tennessee can deny to one who has served this Nation the basic dignity of recognizing his New York marriage. Properly presented with the petitioners' cases, the Court has a duty to address these claims and answer these questions.

. . .

The respondents also argue allowing same-sex couples to wed will harm marriage as an institution by leading to fewer opposite-sex marriages. . . . Decisions about whether to marry and raise children are based on many personal, romantic, and practical considerations; and it is unrealistic to conclude that an opposite-sex couple would choose not to marry simply because same-sex couples may do so. . . . The respondents have not shown a foundation for the conclusion that allowing same-sex marriage will cause the harmful outcomes they describe. Indeed, with respect to this asserted basis for excluding same-sex couples from the right to marry, it is appropriate to observe these cases involve only the rights of two consenting adults whose marriages would pose no risk of harm to themselves or third parties.

. . .

V

These cases also present the question whether the Constitution requires States to recognize same-sex marriages validly performed out of State. As made clear by the case of Obergefell and Arthur, and by that of DeKoe and Kostura, the recognition bans inflict substantial and continuing harm on same-sex couples.

. . . In light of the fact that many States already allow same-sex marriage—and hundreds of thousands of these marriages already have occurred—the disruption caused by the recognition bans is significant and ever-growing.

. . . The Court, in this decision, holds same-sex couples may exercise the fundamental right to marry in all States. It follows that the Court also must hold—and it now does hold—that there is no lawful basis for a State to refuse to recognize a lawful same-sex marriage performed in another State on the ground of its same-sex character.

* * *

. . . [Petitioners] ask for equal dignity in the eyes of the law. The Constitution grants them that right.

The judgment . . . is reversed.

■ CHIEF JUSTICE ROBERTS, with whom JUSTICE SCALIA and JUSTICE THOMAS join, dissenting.

Petitioners make strong arguments rooted in social policy and considerations of fairness. . . .

But this Court is not a legislature. Whether same-sex marriage is a good idea should be of no concern to us. Under the Constitution, judges have power to say what the law is, not what it should be. . . .

Although the policy arguments for extending marriage to same-sex couples may be compelling, the legal arguments for requiring such an extension are not. The fundamental right to marry does not include a right to make a State change its definition of marriage. And a State's decision to maintain the meaning of marriage that has persisted in every culture throughout human history can hardly be called irrational. In short, our Constitution does not enact any one theory of marriage. The people of a State are free to expand marriage to include same-sex couples, or to retain the historic definition.

. . . Many people will rejoice at this decision, and I begrudge none their celebration. But for those who believe in a government of laws, not of men, the majority's approach is deeply disheartening. Supporters of same-sex marriage have achieved considerable success persuading their fellow citizens—through the democratic process—to adopt their view. That ends today. Five lawyers have closed the debate and enacted their own vision of marriage as a matter of constitutional law. Stealing this issue from the people will for many cast a cloud over same-sex marriage, making a dramatic social change that much more difficult to accept.

The majority's decision is an act of will, not legal judgment. The right it announces has no basis in the Constitution or this Court's precedent. . . . [T]he Court invalidates the marriage laws of more than half the States and orders the transformation of a social institution that has formed the basis of human society for millennia, for the Kalahari Bushmen and the Han Chinese, the Carthaginians and the Aztecs. Just who do we think we are?

It can be tempting for judges to confuse our own preferences with the requirements of the law. But as this Court has been reminded throughout our history, the Constitution "is made for people of fundamentally differing views." Lochner v. New York, 198 U. S. 45, 76 (1905) (Holmes, J., dissenting). . . . The majority today[, however,] . . . seizes for itself a question the Constitution leaves to the people, at a time when the people are engaged in a vibrant debate on that question. And it answers that question based not on neutral principles of constitutional law, but on its own "understanding of what freedom is and must become." I have no choice but to dissent.

. . .

I

. . . There is no serious dispute that, under our precedents, the Constitution protects a right to marry and requires States to apply their marriage laws equally. The real question in these cases is what constitutes "marriage," or—more precisely—who decides what constitutes "marriage"?

. . .

A

As the majority acknowledges, marriage "has existed for millennia and across civilizations." For all those millennia, across all those civilizations, "marriage" referred to only one relationship: the union of a man and a woman. . . .

This universal definition of marriage . . . is no historical coincidence. . . . It arose in the nature of things to meet a vital need: ensuring that children are conceived by a mother and father committed to raising them in the stable conditions of a lifelong relationship. . . .

. . .

. . . [B]y bestowing a respected status and material benefits on married couples, society encourages men and women to conduct sexual relations within marriage rather than without. . . .

This singular understanding of marriage has prevailed in the United States throughout our history. . . .

The Constitution itself says nothing about marriage, and the Framers thereby entrusted the States with "[t]he whole subject of the domestic relations of husband and wife." *Windsor* . . . . There is no dispute that every State at the founding—and every State throughout our history until a dozen years ago—defined marriage in the traditional, biologically rooted way. . . .

. . .

This Court's precedents have repeatedly described marriage in ways that are consistent only with its traditional meaning. Early cases on the subject referred to marriage as "the union for life of one man and one woman," Murphy v. Ramsey, 114 U. S. 15, 45 (1885), which forms "the foundation of the family and of society, without which there would be neither civilization nor progress," Maynard v. Hill, 125 U. S. 190, 211 (1888). We later described marriage as "fundamental to our very existence and survival," an understanding that necessarily implies a procreative component. Loving v. Virginia, 388 U. S. 1, 12 (1967); see Skinner v. Oklahoma ex rel. Williamson, 316 U. S. 535, 541 (1942). More recent cases have directly connected the right to marry with the "right to procreate." Zablocki v. Redhail, 434 U. S. 374, 386 (1978).

As the majority notes, some aspects of marriage have changed over time. . . .

. . . [T]hese developments . . . did not, however, work any transformation in the core structure of marriage as the union between a man and a woman. . . .

. . .

II

. . . The majority . . . resolves these cases for petitioners based almost entirely on the Due Process Clause.

. . .

A

. . .

The need for restraint in administering the strong medicine of substantive due process is a lesson this Court has learned the hard way. . . .

. . .

[After recounting the history of *Lochner* and its progeny, and the Court's eventual recognition of "its error," Chief Justice Roberts continued:]

Rejecting *Lochner* does not require disavowing the doctrine of implied fundamental rights, and this Court has not done so. But to avoid repeating *Lochner*'s error of converting personal preferences into constitutional mandates, our modern substantive due process cases have stressed the need for "judicial self-restraint." . . . Our precedents have required that implied fundamental rights be "objectively, deeply rooted in this Nation's history and tradition," and "implicit in the concept of ordered liberty, such that neither liberty nor justice would exist if they were sacrificed." *Glucksberg* . . . .

. . .

. . . [G]iven the few "guideposts for responsible decisionmaking in this unchartered area," . . . "an approach grounded in history imposes limits on the judiciary that are more meaningful than any based on [an] abstract formula," . . . . Expanding a right suddenly and dramatically is likely to require tearing it up from its roots. . . . The only way to ensure restraint in this delicate enterprise is "continual insistence upon respect for the teachings of history, solid recognition of the basic values that underlie our society, and wise appreciation of the great roles [of] the doctrines of federalism and separation of powers." Griswold v. Connecticut, 381 U. S. 479, 501 (1965) (Harlan, J., concurring in judgment).

B

. . .

1

. . . As a matter of constitutional law, . . . the sincerity of petitioners' wishes is not relevant.

When the majority turns to the law, it relies primarily on precedents discussing the fundamental "right to marry." Turner v. Safley, 482 U. S. 78, 95 (1987); Zablocki, 434 U. S., at 383; see Loving, 388 U. S., at 12. . . .

None of the laws at issue in those cases purported to change the core definition of marriage as the union of a man and a woman. . . . As the majority admits, the institution of "marriage" discussed in every one of these cases "presumed a relationship involving opposite-sex partners."

In short, the "right to marry" cases stand for the important but limited proposition that particular restrictions on access to marriage *as traditionally defined* violate due process. These precedents say nothing at all about a right to make a State change its definition of marriage, which is the right petitioners actually seek here. . . .

2

. . .

Neither *Lawrence* nor any other precedent in the privacy line of cases supports the right that petitioners assert here [either]. Unlike criminal laws banning contraceptives and sodomy, the marriage laws at issue here involve no government intrusion. They create no crime and impose no punishment. Same-sex couples remain free to live together, to engage in intimate conduct, and to raise their families as they see fit. No one is "condemned to live in loneliness" by the laws challenged in these cases—no one. At the same time, the laws in no way interfere with the "right to be let alone."

. . .

In sum, the privacy cases provide no support for the majority's position, because petitioners do not seek privacy. Quite the opposite, they seek public recognition of their relationships, along with corresponding government benefits. . . .

3

. . .

Ultimately, only one precedent offers any support for the majority's methodology: Lochner v. New York . . . .

To be fair, the majority does not suggest that its individual autonomy right is entirely unconstrained. The constraints it sets are precisely those that accord with its own "reasoned judgment," informed by its "new insight" into the "nature of injustice," which was invisible to all who came before but has become clear "as we learn [the] meaning" of liberty. The truth is that today's decision rests on nothing more than the majority's own conviction that same-sex couples should be allowed to marry because they want to, and that "it would disparage their choices and diminish their personhood to deny them this right." Whatever force that belief may have as a matter of moral philosophy, it has no more basis in the Constitution than did the naked policy preferences adopted in *Lochner*. . . .

. . .

One immediate question invited by the majority's position is whether States may retain the definition of marriage as a union of two people. . . . Indeed, from the standpoint of history and tradition, a leap from opposite-sex marriage to same-sex marriage is much greater than one from a two-person union to plural unions, which have deep roots in some cultures around the world. If the majority is willing to take the big leap, it is hard to see how it can say no to the shorter one.

It is striking how much of the majority's reasoning would apply with equal force to the claim of a fundamental right to plural marriage. . . .

. . .

4

. . .

The majority's understanding of due process lays out a tantalizing vision of the future for Members of this Court: If an unvarying social institution enduring over all of recorded history cannot inhibit judicial policymaking, what can? But this approach is dangerous for the rule of law. . . .

III

. . . The majority does not seriously engage with [the Equal Protection Clause] claim. Its discussion is, quite frankly, difficult to follow. . . . Absent . . . is anything resembling our usual framework for deciding equal protection cases. . . .

. . . In any event, the marriage laws at issue here do not violate the Equal Protection Clause, because distinguishing between opposite-sex and same-sex couples is rationally related to the States' "legitimate state interest" in "preserving the traditional institution of marriage." Lawrence, 539 U. S., at 585 (O'Connor, J., concurring in judgment).

It is important to note with precision which laws petitioners have challenged. Although they discuss some of the ancillary legal benefits that accompany marriage, such as hospital visitation rights and recognition of spousal status on official documents, petitioners' lawsuits target the laws defining marriage generally rather than those allocating benefits specifically. The equal protection analysis might be different, in my view, if we were confronted with a more focused challenge to the denial of certain tangible benefits. Of course, those more selective claims will not arise now that the Court has taken the drastic step of requiring every State to license and recognize marriages between same-sex couples.

IV

. . .

. . . There will be consequences to shutting down the political process on an issue of such profound public significance. Closing debate tends to close minds. People denied a voice are less likely to accept the ruling of a court on an issue that does not seem to be the sort of thing courts usually decide. As a thoughtful commentator observed about another issue, "The political process was moving . . . , not swiftly enough for advocates of quick, complete change, but majoritarian institutions were listening and acting. Heavy-handed judicial intervention was difficult to justify and appears to have provoked, not resolved, conflict." Ginsburg, Some Thoughts on Autonomy and Equality in Relation to Roe v. Wade, 63 N. C. L. Rev. 375, 385–386 (1985) . . . . Indeed, however heartened the proponents of same-sex marriage might be on this day, it is worth acknowledging what they have lost, and lost forever: the opportunity to win the true acceptance that comes from persuading their fellow citizens of the justice of their cause. And they lose this just when the winds of change were freshening at their backs.

. . . Today's decision . . . creates serious questions about religious liberty. . . .

Respect for sincere religious conviction has led voters and legislators in every State that has adopted same-sex marriage democratically to include accommodations for religious practice. The majority's decision imposing same-sex marriage cannot, of course, create any such accommodations. . . .

Hard questions arise when people of faith exercise religion in ways that may be seen to conflict with the new right to same-sex marriage—when, for example, a religious college provides married student housing only to opposite-sex married couples, or a religious adoption agency declines to place children with same-sex married couples. Indeed, the Solicitor General candidly acknowledged that the tax exemptions of some religious institutions would be in question if they opposed same-sex marriage. . . . There is little doubt that these and similar questions will soon be before this Court. Unfortunately, people of faith can take no comfort in the treatment they receive from the majority today.

Perhaps the most discouraging aspect of today's decision is the extent to which the majority feels compelled to sully those on the other side of the debate. . . . By the majority's account, Americans who did nothing more than follow the understanding of marriage that has existed for our entire history—in particular, the tens of millions of people who voted to reaffirm their States' enduring definition of marriage—have acted to "lock . . . out," "disparage," "disrespect and subordinate," and inflict "[d]ignitary wounds" upon their gay and lesbian neighbors. These apparent assaults on the character of fairminded people . . . are entirely gratuitous. It is one thing for the majority to conclude that the Constitution protects a right to same-sex marriage; it is something else to portray everyone who does not share the majority's "better informed understanding" as bigoted.

. . .

If you are among the many Americans—of whatever sexual orientation—who favor expanding same-sex marriage, by all means celebrate today's decision. Celebrate the achievement of a desired goal. Celebrate the opportunity for a new expression of commitment to a partner. Celebrate the availability of new benefits. But do not celebrate the Constitution. It had nothing to do with it.

I respectfully dissent.

■ JUSTICE SCALIA, with whom JUSTICE THOMAS joins, dissenting.

I join the Chief Justice's opinion in full. I write separately to call attention to this Court's threat to American democracy.

. . . Today's decree says that . . . the Ruler of 320 million Americans . . . is a majority of the nine lawyers on the Supreme Court. The opinion in these cases is the furthest extension in fact—and the furthest extension one can even imagine—of the

Court's claimed power to create "liberties" that the Constitution and its Amendments neglect to mention. . . .

I

. . .

. . . When the Fourteenth Amendment was ratified in 1868, every State limited marriage to one man and one woman, and no one doubted the constitutionality of doing so. That resolves these cases. . . . We have no basis for striking down a practice that is not expressly prohibited by the Fourteenth Amendment's text, and that bears the endorsement of a long tradition of open, widespread, and unchallenged use dating back to the Amendment's ratification. Since there is no doubt whatever that the People never decided to prohibit the limitation of marriage to opposite-sex couples, the public debate over same-sex marriage must be allowed to continue.

. . .

. . . [T]o allow the policy question of same-sex marriage to be considered and resolved by a select, patrician, highly unrepresentative panel of nine is to violate a principle even more fundamental than no taxation without representation: no social transformation without representation.

II

But what really astounds is the hubris reflected in today's judicial Putsch. The five Justices who compose today's majority are entirely comfortable concluding that every State violated the Constitution for all of the 135 years between the Fourteenth Amendment's ratification and Massachusetts' permitting of same-sex marriages in 2003. They have discovered in the Fourteenth Amendment a "fundamental right" overlooked by every person alive at the time of ratification, and almost everyone else in the time since. . . . These Justices *know* that limiting marriage to one man and one woman is contrary to reason; they *know* that an institution as old as government itself, and accepted by every nation in history until 15 years ago, cannot possibly be supported by anything other than ignorance or bigotry. And they are willing to say that any citizen who does not agree with that, who adheres to what was, until 15 years ago, the unanimous judgment of all generations and all societies, stands against the Constitution.

. . .

. . . With each decision of ours that takes from the People a question properly left to them—with each decision that is unabashedly based not on law, but on the "reasoned judgment" of a bare majority of this Court—we move one step closer to being reminded of our impotence.

■ JUSTICE THOMAS, with whom JUSTICE SCALIA joins, dissenting.

The Court's decision today is at odds not only with the Constitution, but with the principles upon which our Nation was built. Since well before 1787, liberty has been understood as freedom from government action, not entitlement to government benefits. The Framers created our Constitution to preserve that understanding of liberty. Yet the majority invokes our Constitution in the name of a "liberty" that the Framers would not have recognized, to the detriment of the liberty they sought to protect. . . . [I]t rejects the idea—captured in our Declaration of Independence—that human dignity is innate and suggests instead that it comes from the Government. This distortion of our Constitution not only ignores the text, it inverts the relationship between the individual and the state in our Republic. I cannot agree with it.

. . .

II

Even if the doctrine of substantive due process were somehow defensible—it is not—petitioners still would not have a claim. To invoke the protection of the Due Process Clause at all—whether under a theory of "substantive" or "procedural" due process—a party must first identify a deprivation of "life, liberty, or property." The majority claims these state laws deprive petitioners of "liberty," but the concept of "liberty" it conjures up bears no resemblance to any plausible meaning of that word as it is used in the Due Process Clauses.

. . .

Both of the Constitution's Due Process Clauses reach back to Magna Carta. . . .

. . .

The Framers . . . adopt[ed] provisions in early State Constitutions that replicated Magna Carta's language, but were modified to refer specifically to "life, liberty, or property." State decisions interpreting these provisions between the founding and the ratification of the Fourteenth Amendment almost uniformly construed the word "liberty" to refer only to freedom from physical restraint. . . .

In enacting the Fifth Amendment's Due Process Clause, the Framers similarly chose to employ the "life, liberty, or property" formulation . . . . When read in light of the history of that formulation, it is hard to see how the "liberty" protected by the Clause could be interpreted to include anything broader than freedom from physical restraint. . . .

If the Fifth Amendment uses "liberty" in this narrow sense, then the Fourteenth Amendment likely does as well. . . . That the Court appears to have lost its way in more recent years does not justify deviating from the original meaning of the Clauses.

. . .

Even assuming that the "liberty" in those Clauses encompasses something more than freedom from physical restraint, it would not include the types of rights claimed by the majority. In the American legal tradition, liberty has long been understood as individual freedom from governmental action, not as a right to a particular governmental entitlement.

. . .

Whether we define "liberty" as locomotion or freedom from governmental action more broadly, petitioners have in no way been deprived of it. Petitioners cannot claim, under the most plausible definition of "liberty," that they have been imprisoned or physically restrained by the States for participating in same-sex relationships. To the contrary, they have been able to cohabitate and raise their children in peace. They have been able to hold civil marriage ceremonies in States that recognize same-sex marriages and private religious ceremonies in all States. They have been able to travel freely around the country, making their homes where they please. Far from being incarcerated or physically restrained, petitioners have been left alone to order their lives as they see fit.

Nor, under the broader definition, can they claim that the States have restricted their ability to go about their daily lives as they would be able to absent governmental restrictions. Petitioners do not ask this Court to order the States to stop restricting their ability to enter same-sex relationships, to engage in intimate behavior, to make vows to their partners in public ceremonies, to engage in religious wedding ceremonies, to hold themselves out as married, or to raise children. The States have imposed no such restrictions. Nor have the States prevented petitioners from approximating a number of incidents of marriage through private legal means, such as wills, trusts, and powers of attorney.

Instead, the States have refused to grant them governmental entitlements. Petitioners claim that as a matter of "liberty," they are entitled to access privileges and benefits that exist solely because of the government. They want, for example, to receive the State's imprimatur on their marriages—on state issued marriage licenses, death certificates, or other official forms. And they want to receive various monetary benefits, including reduced inheritance taxes upon the death of a spouse, compensation if a spouse dies as a result of a work-related injury, or loss of consortium damages in tort suits. But receiving governmental recognition and benefits has nothing to do with any understanding of "liberty" that the Framers would have recognized.

To the extent that the Framers would have recognized a natural right to marriage that fell within the broader definition of liberty, it would not have included a right to governmental recognition and benefits. . . . Petitioners misunderstand the institution of marriage when they say that it would "mean little" absent governmental recognition. . . .

. . . [Our] precedents all involved absolute prohibitions on private actions associated with marriage. Loving v. Virginia, . . . for example, involved a couple who was criminally prosecuted for marrying in the District of Columbia and cohabiting in Virginia, . . . In a similar vein, Zablocki v. Redhail . . . involved a man who was prohibited, on pain of criminal penalty, from "marry[ing] in Wisconsin or elsewhere" because of his outstanding child-support obligations . . . . And Turner v. Safley . . . involved state inmates who were prohibited from entering marriages without the permission of the superintendent of the prison, permission that could not be granted absent compelling reasons . . . . In *none* of those cases were individuals denied solely governmental recognition and benefits associated with marriage.

. . .

III

. . .

A

The majority apparently disregards the political process as a protection for liberty. . . . As a general matter, when the States act through their representative governments or by popular vote, the liberty of their residents is fully vindicated. . . .

. . .

B

. . .

. . . Had the majority allowed the definition of marriage to be left to the political process—as the Constitution requires—the People could have considered the religious liberty implications of deviating from the traditional definition as part of their deliberative process. Instead, the majority's decision short-circuits that process, with potentially ruinous consequences for religious liberty.

IV

. . . [T]he majority goes to great lengths to assert that its decision will advance the "dignity" of same-sex couples. The flaw in that reasoning, of course, is that the Constitution contains no "dignity" Clause, and even if it did, the government would be incapable of bestowing dignity.

Human dignity has long been understood in this country to be innate. . . .

The corollary . . . is that human dignity cannot be taken away by the government. Slaves did not lose their dignity (any more than they lost their humanity) because the government allowed them to be enslaved. Those held in internment camps did not lose their dignity because the government confined them. And those denied governmental benefits certainly do not lose their dignity because the government denies them those benefits. The government cannot bestow dignity, and it cannot take it away.

The majority's . . . rejection of laws preserving the traditional definition of marriage can have no effect on the dignity of the people who voted for them [either]. Its invalidation of those laws can have no effect on the dignity of the people who continue to adhere to the traditional definition of marriage. And its disdain for the understandings of liberty and dignity upon which this Nation was founded can have no effect on the dignity of Americans who continue to believe in them.

. . .

■ JUSTICE ALITO, with whom JUSTICE SCALIA and JUSTICE THOMAS join, dissenting.

. . .

I

. . .

To prevent five unelected Justices from imposing their personal vision of liberty upon the American people, the Court has held that "liberty" under the Due Process Clause should be understood to protect only those rights that are " 'deeply rooted in this Nation's history and tradition.' " Washington v. Glucksberg . . . . And it is beyond dispute that the right to same-sex marriage is not among those rights. See United States v. Windsor, . . . (Alito, J., dissenting) . . . .

For today's majority, it does not matter that the right to same-sex marriage lacks deep roots or even that it is contrary to long-established tradition. The Justices in the majority claim the authority to confer constitutional protection upon that right simply because they believe that it is fundamental.

II

Attempting to circumvent the problem presented by the newness of the right found in these cases, the majority claims that the issue is the right to equal treatment. Noting that marriage is a fundamental right, the majority argues that a State has no valid reason for denying that right to same-sex couples. This reasoning is dependent upon a particular understanding of the purpose of civil marriage. . . . [T]he Court['s] . . . argument is that the fundamental purpose of marriage is to promote the well-being of those who choose to marry. . . . This understanding of the States' reasons for recognizing marriage enables the majority to argue that same-sex marriage serves the States' objectives in the same way as opposite-sex marriage.

This understanding of marriage . . . is shared by many people today, but it is not the traditional one. For millennia, marriage was inextricably linked to the one thing that only an opposite-sex couple can do: procreate.

. . . [Respondents'] basic argument is that States formalize and promote marriage, unlike other fulfilling human relationships, in order to encourage potentially procreative conduct to take place within a lasting unit that has long been thought to provide the best atmosphere for raising children. They thus argue that there are reasonable secular grounds for restricting marriage to opposite-sex couples.

. . .

. . . States that do not want to recognize same-sex marriage have not yet given up on the traditional understanding. They worry that by officially abandoning the older understanding, they may contribute to marriage's further decay. It is far beyond the outer reaches of this Court's authority to say that a State may not adhere to the understanding of marriage that has long prevailed, not just in this country and others with similar cultural roots, but also in a great variety of countries and cultures all around the globe.

. . .

III

. . .

. . . If the issue of same-sex marriage had been left to the people of the States, it is likely that some States would recognize same-sex marriage and others would not. It is also possible that some States would tie recognition to protection for conscience rights. The majority today makes that impossible. By imposing its own views on the entire country, the majority facilitates the marginalization of the many Americans who have traditional ideas. . . .

. . .

Today's decision shows that decades of attempts to restrain this Court's abuse of its authority have failed. A lesson that some will take from today's decision is that preaching about the proper method of interpreting the Constitution or the virtues of judicial self-restraint and humility cannot compete with the temptation to achieve what is viewed as a noble end by any practicable means. I do not doubt that my colleagues in the majority sincerely see in the Constitution a vision of liberty that happens to coincide with their own. But this sincerity is cause for concern, not comfort. What it evidences is the deep and perhaps irremediable corruption of our legal culture's conception of constitutional interpretation.

. . .

Michael H. v. Gerald D.

491 U.S. 110, 109 S.Ct. 2333, 105 L.Ed.2d 91 (1989).

■ JUSTICE SCALIA announced the judgment of the Court and delivered an opinion, in which THE CHIEF JUSTICE joins, and in all but note 6 of which JUSTICE O'CONNOR and JUSTICE KENNEDY join.

Under California law, a child born to a married woman living with her husband is presumed to be a child of the marriage. Cal.Evid.Code Ann. § 621 (West Supp.1989). The presumption of legitimacy may be rebutted only by the husband or wife, and then only in limited circumstances. Ibid. The instant appeal presents the claim that this presumption infringes upon the due process rights of a man who wishes to establish his paternity of a child born to the wife of another man, and the claim that it infringes upon the constitutional right of the child to maintain a relationship with her natural father.

I

[In 1978, two years after Carole and Gerald D. married and began living in California, Carole began "an adulterous affair with her neighbor, Michael H." Three years later she gave birth to Victoria. Blood tests "showed a 98.07% probability that Michael was Victoria's father." Victoria always lived with Carole, but during her first three years they lived intermittently with Gerald in New York, with Michael in St. Thomas or Los Angeles, and with another man in California. Whenever they were with Michael, he "held Victoria out as his daughter."]

In November 1982, [when first] rebuffed in his attempts to visit Victoria, Michael filed a filiation action in California Superior Court to establish his paternity and right to visitation. . . . [Victoria's court-appointed attorney later] filed a cross-complaint asserting that if she had more than one psychological or de facto father, she was entitled to maintain her filial relationship . . . with both. . . .

[After Carole again became involved with Michael for a time, she eventually] reconciled with Gerald and joined him in New York, where they now live with Victoria and two other children since born into the marriage.

In May 1984, Michael and Victoria . . . [successfully] sought visitation rights for Michael pendente lite. . . .

[In October], Gerald, who had intervened in the action, [successfully] moved for summary judgment on the ground that under Cal.Evid.Code § 621 there were no triable issues of fact as to Victoria's paternity. This law provides that "the issue of a wife cohabiting with her husband, who is not impotent or sterile, is conclusively presumed to be a child of the marriage." . . . The presumption may be rebutted by blood tests, but only if a motion for such tests is made, within two years from the date of the child's birth, either by the husband or, if the natural father has filed an affidavit acknowledging paternity, by the wife. . . .

On January 28, 1985, having found that affidavits submitted by Carole and Gerald sufficed to demonstrate that the two were cohabiting at conception and birth and that Gerald was neither sterile nor impotent, the Superior Court granted Gerald's motion for summary judgment, rejecting Michael's and Victoria's challenges to the constitutionality of § 621. The court also denied . . . motions for continued visitation pending the appeal under Cal.Civ.Code § 4601, which provides that a court may, in its discretion, grant "reasonable visitation rights . . . to any . . . person having an interest in the welfare of the child." . . .

. . . [T]he California Court of Appeal affirmed the judgment . . . and upheld the constitutionality of the statute. . . . It interpreted that judgment, moreover, as having denied permanent visitation rights under § 4601. . . .

. . . [T]he California Supreme Court denied discretionary review. . . .

. . .

III

. . . All parental rights, including visitation, were automatically denied by denying Michael status as the father. While . . . § 4601 places it within the discretionary power of a court to award visitation rights to a nonparent, the [California courts] held that California law denies visitation, against the wishes of the mother, to a putative father who has been prevented by § 621 from establishing his paternity.

Michael raises two related challenges to the constitutionality of § 621. First, he asserts that requirements of procedural due process prevent the State from terminating his liberty interest in his relationship with his child without affording him an opportunity to demonstrate his paternity in an evidentiary hearing. We believe this claim derives from a fundamental misconception of the nature of the California statute. While § 621 is phrased in terms of a presumption, that rule of evidence is the implementation of a substantive rule of law [that it is] *irrelevant* for paternity purposes whether a child conceived during and born into an existing marriage was begotten by someone other than the husband and had a prior relationship with him. . . . [T]he conclusive presumption . . . exclud[es] inquiries into the child's paternity that would be destructive of family integrity and privacy.

. . . [T]here is no difference between a rule which says that the marital husband shall be irrebuttably presumed to be the father, and a rule which says that the adulterous natural father shall not be recognized as the legal father. *Both* rules deny someone in Michael's situation a hearing on whether, in the particular circumstances of his case, California's policies would best be served by giving him parental rights. . . . We therefore reject Michael's procedural due process challenge and proceed to his substantive claim.

Michael contends as a matter of substantive due process that because he has established a parental relationship with Victoria, protection of Gerald's and Carole's marital union is an insufficient state interest to support termination of that relationship. This argument is, of course, predicated on the assertion that Michael has a constitutionally protected liberty interest in his relationship with Victoria.

. . .

. . . [W]e have insisted . . . that the interest denominated as a "liberty" be "fundamental" (a concept that, in isolation, is hard to objectify) [and] that it be an interest traditionally protected by our society. As we have put it, the Due Process Clause affords only those protections "so rooted in the traditions and conscience of our people as to be ranked as fundamental." Snyder v. Massachusetts, 291 U.S. 97, 105 (1934) (Cardozo, J.). Our cases reflect "continual insistence upon respect for the teachings of history [and] solid recognition of the basic values that underlie our society. . . ." Griswold v. Connecticut, 381 U.S. 479, 501 (1965) (Harlan, J., concurring in judgment).

This insistence that the asserted liberty interest be rooted in history and tradition is evident . . . in our cases according constitutional protection to certain parental rights. Michael reads the landmark case of Stanley v. Illinois, 405 U.S. 645 (1972), and the subsequent cases of Quilloin v. Walcott, 434 U.S. 246 (1978), Caban v. Mohammed, 441 U.S. 380 (1979) and Lehr v. Robertson, 463 U.S. 248 (1983), as establishing that a liberty interest is created by biological fatherhood plus an established parental relationship—factors that exist in the present case as well. We think that distorts the rationale of those cases. As we view them, they rest not upon such isolated factors but upon the historic respect—indeed, sanctity would not be too strong a term—traditionally accorded to the relationships that develop within the unitary family. . . . In *Stanley,* for example, we forbade the destruction of such a family when, upon the death of the mother, the state had sought to remove children from the custody of a father who had lived with and supported them and their mother for 18 years. . . .

Thus, the legal issue in the present case reduces to whether the relationship between persons in the situation of Michael and Victoria has been treated as a protected family unit under the historic practices of our society, or whether on any other basis it has been accorded special protection. . . . [Q]uite to the contrary, our traditions have protected the marital family (Gerald, Carole, and the child they acknowledge to be theirs) against the sort of claim Michael asserts.

The presumption of legitimacy was a fundamental principle of the common law . . . rebutt[able] only by proof that a husband was incapable of procreation or had had no access to his wife during the relevant period. . . .

We have found nothing in the older sources, nor in the older cases, addressing specifically the power of the natural father to assert parental rights over a child born into a woman's existing marriage with another man. Since it is Michael's burden to establish that such a power (at least where the natural father has established a relationship with the child) is so deeply embedded within our traditions as to be a fundamental right, the lack of evidence alone might defeat his case. But the evidence shows that even in modern times . . . the ability of a person in Michael's position to claim paternity has not been generally acknowledged. . . .

Moreover, even if it were clear that one in Michael's position generally possesses, and has generally always possessed, standing to challenge the marital child's legitimacy, that would still not establish Michael's case.... What he must establish . . . is not that our society has traditionally allowed a natural father in his circumstances to establish paternity, but that it has traditionally accorded such a father parental rights, or at least has not traditionally denied them. . . . What counts is whether the States in fact award substantive parental rights to the natural father of a child conceived within and born into an extant marital union that wishes to embrace the child. We are not aware of a single case, old or new, that has done so. This is not the stuff of which fundamental rights qualifying as liberty interests are made.[6]

In Lehr v. Robertson, a case involving a natural father's attempt to block his child's adoption by the unwed mother's new husband, we observed that "[t]he significance of the biological connection is that it offers the natural father an opportunity that no other male possesses to develop a relationship with his offspring," . . . and we assumed that the Constitution might require some protection of that opportunity. . . . Where, however, the child is born into an extant marital family, the natural father's unique opportunity conflicts with the similarly unique opportunity of the husband of the marriage; and it is not unconstitutional for the State to give categorical preference to the latter. . . . In accord with our traditions, a limit is also imposed by the circumstance that the mother is, at the time of the child's conception and birth, married to and cohabiting with another man, both of whom wish to raise the child as the offspring of their union. It is a question of legislative policy and not constitutional law whether California will allow the presumed parenthood of a couple desiring to retain a child conceived within and born into their marriage to be rebutted.

---

[6]   Justice Brennan criticizes our methodology in using historical traditions specifically relating to the rights of an adulterous natural father, rather than inquiring more generally "whether parenthood is an interest that historically has received our attention and protection." There seems to us no basis for the contention that this methodology is "nove[l]." For example, in Bowers v. Hardwick, 478 U.S. 186 (1986), we noted that at the time the Fourteenth Amendment was ratified all but 5 of the 37 States had criminal sodomy laws, that all 50 of the States had such laws prior to 1961, and that 24 States and the District of Columbia continued to have them; and we concluded from that record, regarding that very specific aspect of sexual conduct, that "to claim that a right to engage in such conduct is 'deeply rooted in this Nation's history and tradition' or 'implicit in the concept of ordered liberty' is, at best, facetious." . . . In Roe v. Wade, 410 U.S. 113 (1973), we spent about a fifth of our opinion negating the proposition that there was a longstanding tradition of laws proscribing abortion. . . . We do not understand why, having rejected our focus upon the societal tradition regarding the natural father's rights vis-a-vis a child whose mother is married to another man, Justice Brennan would choose to focus instead upon "parenthood." Why should the relevant category not be even more general—perhaps "family relationships"; or "personal relationships"; or even "emotional attachments in general"? Though the dissent has no basis for the level of generality it would select, we do: We refer to the most specific level at which a relevant tradition protecting, or denying protection to, the asserted right can be identified. If, for example, there were no societal tradition, either way, regarding the rights of the natural father of a child adulterously conceived, we would have to consult, and (if possible) reason from, the traditions regarding natural fathers in general. But there is such a more specific tradition, and it unqualifiedly denies protection to such a parent. . . . Because . . . general traditions provide such imprecise guidance, they permit judges to dictate rather than discern the society's views. The need, if arbitrary decision-making is to be avoided, to adopt the most specific tradition as the point of reference—or at least to announce, as Justice Brennan declines to do, some other criterion for selecting among the innumerable relevant traditions that could be consulted—is well enough exemplified by the fact that in the present case Justice Brennan's opinion and Justice O'Connor's opinion, which disapproves this footnote, *both* appeal to tradition, but on the basis of the tradition they select reach opposite results. . . . [A] rule of law that binds neither by text nor by any particular, identifiable tradition, is no rule of law at all. Finally, we may note that this analysis is not inconsistent with the result in cases such as Griswold v. Connecticut, 381 U.S. 479 (1965), or Eisenstadt v. Baird, 405 U.S. 438 (1972). None of those cases acknowledged a longstanding and still extant societal tradition withholding the very right pronounced to be the subject of a liberty interest and then rejected it. . . . [T]he existence of such a tradition, continuing to the present day, refutes any possible contention that the alleged right is "so rooted in the traditions and conscience of our people as to be ranked as fundamental," Snyder v. Massachusetts, 291 U.S. 97, 105 (1934), or "implicit in the concept of ordered liberty," Palko v. Connecticut, 302 U.S. 319, 325 (1937).

. . .

IV

We have never had occasion to decide whether a child has a liberty interest, symmetrical with that of her parent, in maintaining her filial relationship. We need not do so here because, even assuming that such a right exists, Victoria's claim must fail. . . . [T]he claim that a State must recognize multiple fatherhood has no support in the history or traditions of this country. Moreover, even if [her claim is only that] she has a liberty interest in maintaining a filial relationship with her natural father, Michael, we find that, at best, her claim is the obverse of Michael's and fails for the same reasons.

. . .

The judgment of the California Court of Appeal is Affirmed.

■ JUSTICE O'CONNOR, with whom JUSTICE KENNEDY joins, concurring in part.

I concur in all but footnote 6 of Justice Scalia's opinion. This footnote sketches a mode of historical analysis to be used when identifying liberty interests protected by the Due Process Clause of the Fourteenth Amendment that may be somewhat inconsistent with our past decisions in this area. See Griswold v. Connecticut, 381 U.S. 479 (1965); Eisenstadt v. Baird, 405 U.S. 438 (1972). On occasion the Court has characterized relevant traditions protecting asserted rights at levels of generality that might not be "the most specific level" available. See Loving v. Virginia, 388 U.S. 1, 12 (1967); Turner v. Safley, 482 U.S. 78, 94 (1987). . . . I would not foreclose the unanticipated by the prior imposition of a single mode of historical analysis. Poe v. Ullman, 367 U.S. 497, 542, 544 (1961) (Harlan, J., dissenting).

■ JUSTICE STEVENS, concurring in the judgment.

. . .

. . . I . . . would not foreclose the possibility that a constitutionally protected relationship between a natural father and his child might exist in a case like this. Indeed, I am willing to assume for the purpose of deciding this case that Michael's relationship with Victoria is strong enough to give him a constitutional right to try to convince a trial judge that Victoria's best interest would be served by granting him visitation rights. I am satisfied, however, that the California statute, as applied in this case, gave him that opportunity.

Section 4601 . . . plainly gave the trial judge the authority to grant Michael "reasonable visitation rights."

. . .

. . . [T]he trial judge . . . considered the effect of § 4601 and expressly found "that, at the present time, it is not in the best interests of the child that the Plaintiff have visitation. The Court believes that the existence of two (2) 'fathers' as male authority figures will confuse the child and be counter-productive to her best interests." . . .

. . . Because I am convinced that the trial judge had the authority under state law both to hear Michael's plea for visitation rights and to grant him such rights if Victoria's best interests so warranted, I am satisfied that the California statutory scheme is consistent with the Due Process Clause of the Fourteenth Amendment.

. . .

■ JUSTICE BRENNAN, with whom JUSTICE MARSHALL and JUSTICE BLACKMUN join, dissenting.

In a case that has yielded so many opinions [I] begin by emphasizing the common ground shared by a majority of this Court. Five Members of the Court refuse to foreclose "the possibility that a natural father might ever have a constitutionally protected interest in his relationship with a child whose mother was married to and cohabiting with another man at the time of the child's conception and birth." (Stevens, J., concurring in judgment). Five Justices agree that the flaw inhering in a conclusive presumption that terminates a constitutionally protected interest without any hearing whatsoever is a *procedural* one. See infra; (White, J., dissenting); (Stevens, J., concurring in judgment). Four Members of the Court agree that Michael H. has a liberty interest in his relationship with Victoria, see infra; (White, J., dissenting), and one assumes for purposes of this case that he does, (Stevens, J., concurring in judgment).

In contrast, only two Members of the Court fully endorse Justice Scalia's view of the proper method of analyzing questions arising under the Due Process Clause. See O'Connor, J., concurring in part. . . .

I

. . .

. . . Because reasonable people can disagree about the content of particular traditions, and because they can disagree even about which traditions are relevant to the definition of "liberty," the plurality has not found the objective boundary that it seeks.

Even if we could agree . . . on the content and significance of particular traditions, we still would be forced to identify the point at which a tradition becomes firm enough to be relevant to our definition of liberty and the moment at which it becomes too obsolete to be relevant any longer. The plurality supplies no objective means by which we might make these determinations. . . .

. . .

It is not that tradition has been irrelevant to our prior decisions. Throughout our decisionmaking in this important area runs the theme that certain interests and practices—freedom from physical restraint, marriage, childbearing, childrearing, and others—form the core of our definition of "liberty." Our solicitude for these interests is partly the result of the fact that the Due Process Clause would seem an empty promise if it did not protect them, and partly the result of the historical and traditional importance of these interests in our society. In deciding cases arising under the Due Process Clause, therefore, we have considered whether the concrete limitation under consideration impermissibly impinges upon one of these more generalized interests.

Today's plurality, however, does not ask whether parenthood is an interest that historically has received our attention and protection; the answer to that question is too clear for dispute. Instead, the plurality asks whether the specific variety of parenthood under consideration—a natural father's relationship with a child whose mother is married to another man—has enjoyed such protection.

If we had looked to tradition with such specificity in past cases, many a decision would have reached a different result. Surely the use of contraceptives by unmarried couples, Eisenstadt v. Baird, 405 U.S. 438 (1972), or even by married couples, Griswold v. Connecticut, 381 U.S. 479 (1965); the freedom from corporal punishment in schools, Ingraham v. Wright, 430 U.S. 651 (1977); the freedom from an arbitrary transfer from a prison to a psychiatric institution, Vitek v. Jones, 445 U.S. 480 (1980); and even the right to raise one's natural but illegitimate children, Stanley v. Illinois, 405 U.S. 645 (1972), were not "interest[s] traditionally protected by our society," at the time of their consideration by this Court. If we had asked, therefore, in *Eisenstadt, Griswold, Ingraham, Vitek,* or *Stanley* itself whether the specific interest under consideration had been traditionally protected, the answer would have been a resounding "no." That we did not ask this question in those cases highlights the novelty of the interpretive method that the plurality opinion employs today.

. . .

II

. . .

. . . The better approach . . . is to ask whether the specific parent-child relationship under consideration is close enough to the interests that we already have protected to be deemed an aspect of "liberty" as well. [T]he question is . . . whether the relationship under consideration is sufficiently substantial to qualify as a liberty interest under our prior cases.

. . . [Those] cases have produced a unifying theme: although an unwed father's biological link to his child does not, in and of itself, guarantee him a constitutional stake in his relationship with that child, such a link combined with a substantial parent-child relationship will do so. . . .

. . .

The plurality's . . . language suggests that if Carole or Gerald alone wished to raise Victoria, or if both were dead and the State wished to raise her, Michael and Victoria might be found to have a liberty interest in their relationship with each other. But that would be to say that whether Michael and Victoria have a liberty interest varies with the State's interest in recognizing that interest, for it is the State's interest in protecting the marital family—and not Michael and Victoria's interest in their relationship with each other—that varies with the status of Carole and Gerald's relationship. It is a bad day for due process when the State's interest in terminating a parent-child relationship is reason to conclude that that relationship is not part of the "liberty" protected by the Fourteenth Amendment.

. . .

. . . [Also,] Michael's challenge in this Court does not depend on his ability ultimately to obtain visitation rights; it would be strange indeed if, before one could be granted a hearing, one were required to prove that one would prevail on the merits. The point of procedural due process is to give the litigant a fair chance at prevailing, not to ensure a particular substantive outcome. . . .

III

. . . [California's] refusal to hold a hearing is properly analyzed under our procedural due process cases, which instruct us to consider the State's interest in curtailing the procedures accompanying the termination of a constitutionally protected interest. California's interest, minute in comparison with a father's interest in his relationship with his child, cannot justify its refusal to hear Michael out on his claim that he is Victoria's father.

A

. . . What Michael wants is a chance to show that he is Victoria's father. By depriving him of this opportunity, California prevents Michael from taking advantage of the best-interest standard embodied in § 4601 of California's Civil Code, which directs that *parents* be given visitation rights unless "the visitation would be detrimental to the best interests of the child." . . .

As interpreted by the California courts, . . . § 621 . . . also deprives him of any chance of maintaining his relationship with the child he claims to be his own. When, as a result of § 621, a putative father may not establish his paternity, neither may he obtain discretionary visitation rights as a "nonparent" under § 4601. . . . Justice Stevens' assertion to the contrary is mere wishful thinking. . . .

. . .

. . . Gerald D. claims—and the plurality agrees—that whether a man is the biological father of a child whose family situation places the putative father within § 621 is simply irrelevant to the State. . . . Yet the claim that California does not care about factual paternity is patently false. California cares very much about factual paternity when the husband is impotent or sterile . . . ; it cares very much about it when the wife and husband do not share the same home . . . ; and it cares very much about it when the husband himself declares that he is not the father. . . . The State, though selective in its concern for factual paternity, certainly is not *indifferent* to it.[9] More fundamentally, . . . [t]o say that California does not care about factual paternity in the limited circumstances of this case—where the husband is neither impotent nor sterile nor living apart from his wife—is simply another way of describing its conclusive presumption.

. . .

B

. . .

[T]o say that the State must provide Michael with a hearing to prove his paternity is not to express any opinion of the ultimate state of affairs between Michael and Victoria and Carole and Gerald. . . . Michael first must convince a court that he is Victoria's father, and even if he is able to do this, he will be denied visitation rights if that would be in Victoria's best interests. See Cal.Civ.Code Ann. § 4601 (West Supp.1989). It is elementary that a determination that a State must afford procedures before it terminates a given right is not a prediction about the end result of those procedures.

. . .

■ JUSTICE WHITE, with whom JUSTICE BRENNAN joins, dissenting.

. . . [T]he fact that Michael H. is the biological father of Victoria is to me highly relevant to whether he has rights, as a father or otherwise, with respect to the child. Because I believe that Michael H. has a liberty interest that cannot be denied without due process of the law, I must dissent.

I

Like Justices Brennan, Marshall, Blackmun and Stevens, I do not agree with the plurality opinion's conclusion that a natural father can never "have a constitutionally protected interest in his relationship with a child whose mother was married to and cohabiting with another man at the time of the child's conception and birth." (Stevens, J., concurring in judgment). . . . The basic principle enunciated in the Court's unwed father cases is that an unwed father who has demonstrated a sufficient commitment to his paternity by way of personal, financial, or custodial responsibilities has a protected liberty interest in a relationship with his child.

. . .

. . . Michael H. is . . . a father who has asserted his interests in raising and providing for his child since the very time of the child's birth. . . . Michael and Victoria lived together (albeit intermittently, given Carole's itinerant life style.) There is a personal and emotional relationship between Michael and Victoria, who grew up

---

[9]   In this respect, the plurality is mistaken in suggesting that "there is no difference between a rule which says that the marital husband shall be irrebuttably presumed to be the father, and a rule which says that the adulterous natural father shall not be recognized as the legal father." In the latter case, the State has not made paternity the predominant concern in child-custody disputes and then told some putative fathers that they may not prove their paternity.

calling him "Daddy." Michael H. held Victoria out as his daughter and contributed to the child's financial support. The mother has never denied, and indeed has admitted that Michael H. is Victoria's father. . . ."When an unwed father demonstrates a full commitment to the responsibilities of parenthood by 'com[ing] forward to participate in the rearing of his child,' Caban, 441 U.S., at 392, his interest in personal contact with his child acquires substantial protection under the Due Process Clause." *Lehr,* supra, at 261. The facts in this case satisfy the *Lehr* criteria, which focused on the relationship between father and child, not on the relationship between father and mother. . . . It is clear enough that Michael H. . . . has a liberty interest entitled to protection under the Due Process Clause of the Fourteenth Amendment.

II

California plainly denies Michael this protection. . . . California law . . . even denies him the opportunity to introduce blood-test evidence to rebut the demonstrable fiction that Gerald is Victoria's father.[3] . . . The Court gives its blessing to § 621 by relying on the State's asserted interests in the integrity of the family (defined as Carole and Gerald) and in protecting Victoria from the stigma of illegitimacy and by balancing away Michael's interest in establishing that he is the father of the child.

The interest in protecting a child from the social stigma of illegitimacy lacks any real connection to the facts of a case where a father is seeking to establish, rather than repudiate, paternity. The "stigma of illegitimacy" argument harks back to ancient common law when there were no blood tests to ascertain that the husband could not "by the laws of nature" be the child's father. . . . It is hardly rare in this world of divorce and remarriage for a child to live with the "father" to whom her mother is married, and still have a relationship with her biological father.

The State's professed interest in the preservation of the existing marital unit is a more significant concern. To be sure, the intrusion of an outsider asserting that he is the father of a child whom the husband believes to be his own would be disruptive to say the least. On the facts of this case, however, Gerald was well aware of the liaison between Carole and Michael. . . .

. . .

. . . Michael H. eagerly grasped the opportunity to have a relationship with his daughter (he lived with her; he declared her to be his child; he provided financial support for her) and still, with today's opinion, his opportunity has vanished. He has been rendered a stranger to his child.

. . .

Troxel v. Granville
530 U.S. 57 (2000).

A Washington statute permitted "[a]ny person" to petition a superior court for visitation rights "at any time" and authorized the court to grant visitation whenever "visitation may serve the best interest of the child." The unwed father of two daughters separated from their mother in 1991, moved in with his parents, and regularly brought the girls for weekend visitation at their home until he committed suicide in 1993. After the girls' mother, Granville, informed the paternal grandparents, the Troxels, that she wanted to limit them to one short visit per month,

---

3   While the ultimate resolution of Michael's case, were he permitted to introduce such evidence, might well be visitation rights or even custody of the child, it is important to keep in mind that the question at issue here is not whether he should be granted visitation or custody but simply whether he can take the first step in any such proceeding. . . .

". . . If we embrace this unenumerated right, . . . we will be ushering in a new regime of judicially prescribed, and federally prescribed, family law. I have no reason to believe that federal judges will be better at this than state legislatures. . . ."

Finally, Justice Kennedy's dissent found the Washington Supreme Court's "sweeping ruling requiring the harm to the child standard" in error, and "so central" to its decision that he would have vacated and remanded on that "sole ground"—without addressing any application of the visitation statute or "whether, under the correct constitutional standards, the Washington statute can be invalidated on its face." His criticism of the lower court ruling "that a parent has a constitutional right to prevent visitation in all cases not involving harm" included the following:

"My principal concern is that the holding seems to proceed from the assumption that the parent or parents who resist visitation have always been the child's primary caregivers and that the third parties who seek visitation have no legitimate and established relationship with the child. . . .

"Cases are sure to arise—perhaps a substantial number of cases—in which a third party, by acting in a caregiving role over a significant period of time, has developed a relationship with a child which is not necessarily subject to absolute parental veto. . . .

" . . .

"In light of the inconclusive historical record and case law, as well as the almost universal adoption of the best interests standard for visitation disputes, I would be hard pressed to conclude the right to be free of such review in all cases is itself ' "implicit in the concept of ordered liberty.' " . . . [I]t would be more appropriate to conclude that the constitutionality of the application of the best interests standard depends on more specific factors. In short, a fit parent's right vis-a-vis a complete stranger is one thing; her right vis-a-vis another parent or a de facto parent may be another. The protection the Constitution requires, then, must be elaborated with care, using the discipline and instruction of the case law system. . . ."

C. PERSONAL AUTONOMY

Eisenstadt v. Baird
405 U.S. 438 (1972).

In a prosecution of a defendant for giving a contraceptive to an unmarried person the Court had before it, among others, the question whether it was a denial of equal protection of the laws to permit the distribution of contraceptives to married persons but not to unmarried. One argument made to sustain the classification was that contraceptives were considered immoral. The counter argument was that under Griswold v. Connecticut it would be a denial of due process to prohibit the distribution of contraceptives. The Court said it did not need to decide the issue, but did make the following observation: "if the right of privacy means anything, it is the right of the individual, married or single, to be free from unwarranted governmental intrusion into matters so fundamentally affecting a person as the decision whether to bear or beget a child."

Roe v. Wade

410 U.S. 113, 93 S.Ct. 705, 35 L.Ed.2d 147 (1973).

■ MR. JUSTICE BLACKMUN delivered the opinion of the Court.

This Texas federal appeal and its Georgia companion, Doe v. Bolton, post, 410 U.S. 179, present constitutional challenges to state criminal abortion legislation. The Texas statutes under attack here are typical of those that have been in effect in many States for approximately a century. The Georgia statutes, in contrast, have a modern cast and are a legislative product that, to an extent at least, obviously reflects the influences of recent attitudinal change, of advancing medical knowledge and techniques, and of new thinking about an old issue.

We forthwith acknowledge our awareness of the sensitive and emotional nature of the abortion controversy, of the vigorous opposing views, even among physicians, and of the deep and seemingly absolute convictions that the subject inspires. One's philosophy, one's experiences, one's exposure to the raw edges of human existence, one's religious training, one's attitudes toward life and family and their values, and the moral standards one establishes and seeks to observe, are all likely to influence and to color one's thinking and conclusions about abortion.

In addition, population growth, pollution, poverty, and racial overtones tend to complicate and not to simplify the problem.

Our task, of course, is to resolve the issue by constitutional measurement free of emotion and of predilection. We seek earnestly to do this, and, because we do, we have inquired into, and in this opinion place some emphasis upon, medical and medical-legal history and what that history reveals about man's attitudes toward the abortive procedure over the centuries. We bear in mind, too, Mr. Justice Holmes' admonition in his now vindicated dissent in Lochner v. New York, 198 U.S. 45, 76 (1905):

"It [the Constitution] is made for people of fundamentally differing views, and the accident of our finding certain opinions natural and familiar, or novel, and even shocking, ought not to conclude our judgment upon the question whether statutes embodying them conflict with the Constitution of the United States."

I.

The Texas statutes that concern us here are Arts. 1191–1194 and 1196 of the State's Penal Code, Vernon's Ann.P.C. These make it a crime to "procure an abortion," as therein defined, or to attempt one, except with respect to "an abortion procured or attempted by medical advice for the purpose of saving the life of the mother." Similar statutes are in existence in a majority of the States.

. . .

V.

The principal thrust of appellant's attack on the Texas statutes is that they improperly invade a right, said to be possessed by the pregnant woman, to choose to terminate her pregnancy. Appellant would discover this right in the concept of personal "liberty" embodied in the Fourteenth Amendment's Due Process Clause; or in personal, marital, familial, and sexual privacy said to be protected by the Bill of Rights or its penumbras, see Griswold v. Connecticut, 381 U.S. 479 (1965); Eisenstadt v. Baird, 405 U.S. 438 (1972); id., at 460 (White, J., concurring); or among those rights reserved to the people by the Ninth Amendment, Griswold v. Connecticut, 381 U.S., at 486 (Goldberg, J., concurring). Before addressing this claim, we feel it desirable briefly to survey, in several aspects, the history of abortion, for such insight as that history may afford us, and then to examine the state purposes and interests behind the criminal abortion laws.

. . .

[The Court's long historical discussion is omitted.]

VII.

Three reasons have been advanced to explain historically the enactment of criminal abortion laws in the 19th century and to justify their continued existence.

It has been argued occasionally that these laws were the product of a Victorian social concern to discourage illicit sexual conduct. Texas, however, does not advance this justification in the present case, and it appears that no court or commentator has taken the argument seriously. . . .

A second reason is concerned with abortion as a medical procedure. When most criminal abortion laws were first enacted, the procedure was a hazardous one for the woman. . . .

Modern medical techniques have altered this situation. Appellants and various *amici* refer to medical data indicating that abortion in early pregnancy, that is, prior to the end of first trimester, although not without its risk, is now relatively safe. Mortality rates for women undergoing early abortions, where the procedure is legal, appear to be as low as or lower than the rates for normal childbirth. Consequently, any interest of the State in protecting the woman from an inherently hazardous procedure, except when it would be equally dangerous for her to forgo it, has largely disappeared. Of course, important state interests in the area of health and medical standards do remain. The State has a legitimate interest in seeing to it that abortion, like any other medical procedure, is performed under circumstances that insure maximum safety for the patient. This interest obviously extends at least to the performing physician and his staff, to the facilities involved, to the availability of aftercare, and to adequate provision for any complication or emergency that might arise. The prevalence of high mortality rates at illegal "abortion mills" strengthens, rather than weakens, the State's interest in regulating the conditions under which abortions are performed. Moreover, the risk to the woman increases as her pregnancy continues. Thus the State retains a definite interest in protecting the woman's own health and safety when an abortion is proposed at a late stage of pregnancy.

The third reason is the State's interest—some phrase it in terms of duty—in protecting prenatal life. Some of the argument for this justification rests on the theory that a new human life is present from the moment of conception. The State's interest and general obligation to protect life then extends, it is argued, to prenatal life. Only when the life of the pregnant mother herself is at stake, balanced against the life she carries within her, should the interest of the embryo or fetus not prevail. Logically, of course, a legitimate state interest in this area need not stand or fall on acceptance of the belief that life begins at conception or at some other point prior to live birth. In assessing the State's interest, recognition may be given to the less rigid claim that as long as at least *potential* life is involved, the State may assert interests beyond the protection of the pregnant woman alone.

Parties challenging state abortion laws have sharply disputed in some courts the contention that a purpose of these laws, when enacted, was to protect prenatal life. Pointing to the absence of legislative history to support the contention, they claim that most state laws were designed solely to protect the woman. Because medical advances have lessened this concern, at least with respect to abortion in early pregnancy, they argue that with respect to such abortions the laws can no longer be justified by any state interest. There is some scholarly support for this view of original purpose. The few state courts called upon to interpret their laws in the late 19th and early 20th centuries did focus on the State's interest in protecting the woman's health rather than in preserving the embryo and fetus. Proponents of this view point out that in many States, including Texas, by statute or judicial interpretation, the pregnant woman herself could not be prosecuted for self-abortion or for cooperating in an abortion performed upon her by another. They claim that adoption of the "quickening" distinction through received common law and state statutes tacitly recognizes the greater health hazards inherent in late abortion and impliedly repudiates the theory that life begins at conception.

It is with these interests, and the weight to be attached to them, that this case is concerned.

VIII.

The Constitution does not explicitly mention any right of privacy. In a line of decisions, however, going back perhaps as far as Union Pacific R. Co. v. Botsford, 141 U.S. 250, 251 (1891), the Court has recognized that a right of personal privacy, or a guarantee of certain areas or zones of privacy, does exist under the Constitution. In varying contexts the Court or individual Justices have indeed found at least the roots of that right in the First Amendment, Stanley v. Georgia, 394 U.S. 557, 564 (1969); in the Fourth and Fifth Amendments, Terry v. Ohio, 392 U.S. 1, 8–9 (1968), Katz v. United States, 389 U.S. 347, 350 (1967); Boyd v. United States, 116 U.S. 616 (1886), see Olmstead v. United States, 277 U.S. 438, 478 (1928) (Brandeis, J., dissenting); in the penumbras of the Bill of Rights, Griswold v. Connecticut, 381 U.S. 479, 484–485 (1965); in the Ninth Amendment, id., at 486 (Goldberg, J., concurring); or in the concept of liberty guaranteed by the first section of the Fourteenth Amendment, see Meyer v. Nebraska, 262 U.S. 390, 399 (1923). These decisions make it clear that only personal rights that can be deemed "fundamental" or "implicit in the concept of ordered liberty," Palko v. Connecticut, 302 U.S. 319, 325 (1937), are included in this guarantee of personal privacy. They also make it clear that the right has some extension to activities relating to marriage, Loving v. Virginia, 388 U.S. 1, 12 (1967), procreation, Skinner v. Oklahoma, 316 U.S. 535 (1942), contraception, Eisenstadt v. Baird, 405 U.S. 438, 453–454 (1972); id., at 460, 463–465 (White, J., concurring), family relationships, Prince v. Massachusetts, 321 U.S. 158, 166 (1944), and child rearing and education, Pierce v. Society of Sisters, 268 U.S. 510, 535 (1925), Meyer v. Nebraska, supra.

This right of privacy, whether it be founded in the Fourteenth Amendment's concept of personal liberty and restrictions upon state action, as we feel it is, or, as the District Court determined, in the Ninth Amendment's reservation of rights to the people, is broad enough to encompass a woman's decision whether or not to terminate her pregnancy. The detriment that the State would impose upon the pregnant woman by denying this choice altogether is apparent. Specific and direct harm medically diagnosable even in early pregnancy may be involved. Maternity, or additional offspring, may force upon the woman a distressful life and future. Psychological harm may be imminent. Mental and physical health may be taxed by child care. There is also the distress, for all concerned, associated with the unwanted child, and there is the problem of bringing a child into a family already unable, psychologically and otherwise, to care for it. In other cases, as in this one, the additional difficulties and continuing stigma of unwed motherhood may be involved. All these are factors the woman and her responsible physician necessarily will consider in consultation.

On the basis of elements such as these, appellants and some *amici* argue that the woman's right is absolute and that she is entitled to terminate her pregnancy at whatever time, in whatever way, and for whatever reason she alone chooses. With this we do not agree. Appellants' arguments that Texas either has no valid interest at all in regulating the abortion decision, or no interest strong enough to support any limitation upon the woman's sole determination, is unpersuasive. The Court's decisions recognizing a right of privacy also acknowledge that some state regulation in areas protected by that right is appropriate. As noted above, a state may properly assert important interests in safeguarding health, in maintaining medical standards, and in protecting potential life. At some point in pregnancy, these respective interests become sufficiently compelling to sustain regulation of the factors that govern the abortion decision. The privacy right involved, therefore, cannot be said to be absolute. In fact, it is not clear to us that the claim asserted by some *amici* that one has an unlimited right to do with one's body as one pleases bears a close relationship to the right of privacy previously articulated in the Court's decisions. The Court has refused to recognize an unlimited right of this kind in the past. Jacobson v. Massachusetts, 197 U.S. 11 (1905) (vaccination); Buck v. Bell, 274 U.S. 200 (1927) (sterilization).

We therefore conclude that the right of personal privacy includes the abortion decision, but that this right is not unqualified and must be considered against important state interests in regulation.

We note that those federal and state courts that have recently considered abortion law challenges have reached the same conclusion. A majority, in addition to the District Court in the present case, have held state laws unconstitutional, at least in part, because of vagueness or because of overbreadth and abridgment of rights. . . .

Although the results are divided, most of these courts have agreed that the right of privacy, however based, is broad enough to cover the abortion decision; that the right, nonetheless, is not absolute and is subject to some limitations; and that at some point the state interests as to protection of health, medical standards, and prenatal life, become dominant. We agree with this approach.

Where certain "fundamental rights" are involved, the Court has held that regulation limiting these rights may be justified only by a "compelling state interest," Kramer v. Union Free School District, 395 U.S. 621, 627 (1969); Shapiro v. Thompson, 394 U.S. 618, 634 (1969); Sherbert v. Verner, 374 U.S. 398, 406 (1963), and that legislative enactments must be narrowly drawn to express only the legitimate state interests at stake. Griswold v. Connecticut, 381 U.S. 479, 485 (1965); Aptheker v. Secretary of State, 378 U.S. 500, 508 (1964); Cantwell v. Connecticut, 310 U.S. 296, 307–308 (1940); see Eisenstadt v. Baird, 405 U.S. 438, 460, 463–464 (1972) (White, J., concurring).

In the recent abortion cases . . . courts have recognized these principles. Those striking down state laws have generally scrutinized the State's interest in protecting health and potential life and have concluded that neither interest justified broad limitations on the reasons for which a physician and his pregnant patient might decide that she should have an abortion in the early stages of pregnancy. Courts sustaining state laws have held that the State's determinations to protect health or prenatal life are dominant and constitutionally justifiable.

IX.

The District Court held that the appellee failed to meet his burden of demonstrating that the Texas statute's infringement upon Roe's rights was necessary to support a compelling state interest, and that, although the defendant presented "several compelling justifications for state presence in the area of abortions," the statutes outstripped these justifications and swept "far beyond any areas of compelling state interest." 314 F.Supp., at 1222–1223. Appellant and appellee both contest that holding. Appellant . . . claims an absolute right that bars any state imposition of criminal penalties in the area. Appellee argues that the State's determination to recognize and protect prenatal life from and after conception constitutes a compelling state interest. As noted above, we do not agree fully with either formulation.

A.   The appellee and certain *amici* argue that the fetus is a "person" within the language and meaning of the Fourteenth Amendment. In support of this they outline at length and in detail the well-known facts of fetal development. If this suggestion of personhood is established, the appellant's case, of course, collapses, for the fetus' right to life is then guaranteed specifically by the Amendment. The appellant conceded as much on reargument. On the other hand, the appellee conceded on reargument that no case could be cited that holds that a fetus is a person within the meaning of the Fourteenth Amendment.

The Constitution does not define "person" in so many words. Section 1 of the Fourteenth Amendment contains three references to "person." The first, in defining "citizens," speaks of "persons born or naturalized in the United States." The word also appears both in the Due Process Clause and in the Equal Protection Clause. "Person" is used in other places in the Constitution: in the listing of qualifications for representatives and senators, Art. I, § 2, cl. 2, and § 3, cl. 3; in the Apportionment Clause, Art. I, § 2, cl. 3; in the Migration and Importation provision, Art. I, § 9, cl. 1; in the Emolument Clause, Art. I, § 9, cl. 8; in the Electors provisions, Art. II, § 1, cl. 2, and the superseded cl. 3; in the provision outlining qualifications for the office of President, Art. II, § 1, cl. 5; in the Extradition provisions, Art. IV, § 2, cl. 2, and the superseded Fugitive Slave cl. 3; and in the Fifth, Twelfth, and Twenty-second Amendments as well as in §§ 2 and 3 of the Fourteenth Amendment. But in nearly all these instances, the use of the word is such that it has application only postnatally. None indicates, with any assurance, that it has any possible prenatal application.[54]

All this, together with our observation, supra, that throughout the major portion of the 19th century prevailing legal abortion practices were far freer than they are today, persuades us that the word "person," as used in the Fourteenth Amendment, does not include the unborn. . . .

This conclusion, however, does not of itself fully answer the contentions raised by Texas, and we pass on to other considerations.

B.   The pregnant woman cannot be isolated in her privacy. She carries an embryo and, later, a fetus, if one accepts the medical definitions of the developing young in the human uterus. See Dorland's Illustrated Medical Dictionary, 478–479, 547 (24th ed. 1965). The situation therefore is inherently different from marital intimacy, or bedroom possession of obscene material, or marriage, or procreation, or education, with which *Eisenstadt, Griswold, Stanley, Loving, Skinner, Pierce,* and *Meyer* were respectively concerned. As we have intimated above, it is reasonable and appropriate for a State to decide that at some point in time another interest, that of health of the mother or that of potential human life, becomes significantly involved. The woman's privacy is no longer sole and any right of privacy she possesses must be measured accordingly.

Texas urges that, apart from the Fourteenth Amendment, life begins at conception and is present throughout pregnancy, and that, therefore, the State has a compelling interest in protecting that life from and after conception. We need not

---

[54] When Texas urges that a fetus is entitled to Fourteenth Amendment protection as a person, it faces a dilemma. Neither in Texas nor in any other State are all abortions prohibited. Despite broad proscription, an exception always exists. The exception contained in Art. 1196, for an abortion procured or attempted by medical advice for the purpose of saving the life of the mother, is typical. But if the fetus is a person who is not to be deprived of life without due process of law, and if the mother's condition is the sole determinant, does not the Texas exception appear to be out of line with the Amendment's command?

There are other inconsistencies between Fourteenth Amendment status and the typical abortion statute. [I]n Texas the woman is not a principal or an accomplice with respect to an abortion upon her. If the fetus is a person, why is the woman not a principal or an accomplice? Further, the penalty for criminal abortion specified by Art. 1195 is significantly less than the maximum penalty for murder prescribed by Art. 1257 of the Texas Penal Code. If the fetus is a person, may the penalties be different?

resolve the difficult question of when life begins. When those trained in the respective disciplines of medicine, philosophy, and theology are unable to arrive at any consensus, the judiciary, at this point in the development of man's knowledge, is not in a position to speculate as to the answer.

It should be sufficient to note briefly the wide divergence of thinking on this most sensitive and difficult question. There has always been strong support for the view that life does not begin until live birth. This was the belief of the Stoics. It appears to be the predominant, though not the unanimous, attitude of the Jewish faith. It may be taken to represent also the position of a large segment of the Protestant community, insofar as that can be ascertained; organized groups that have taken a formal position on the abortion issue have generally regarded abortion as a matter for the conscience of the individual and her family. [T]he common law found greater significance in quickening. Physicians and their scientific colleagues have regarded that event with less interest and have tended to focus either upon conception or upon live birth or upon the interim point at which the fetus becomes "viable," that is, potentially able to live outside the mother's womb, albeit with artificial aid.[59] Viability is usually placed at about seven months (28 weeks) but may occur earlier, even at 24 weeks.[60] The Aristotelian theory of "mediate animation," that held sway throughout the Middle Ages and the Renaissance in Europe, continued to be official Roman Catholic dogma until the 19th century, despite opposition to this "ensoulment" theory from those in the Church who would recognize the existence of life from the moment of conception. The latter is now, of course, the official belief of the Catholic Church. As one of the briefs *amicus* discloses, this is a view strongly held by many non-Catholics as well, and by many physicians. Substantial problems for precise definition of this view are posed, however, by new embryological data that purport to indicate that conception is a "process" over time, rather than an event, and by new medical techniques such as menstrual extraction, the "morning-after" pill, implantation of embryos, artificial insemination, and even artificial wombs.

In areas other than criminal abortion the law has been reluctant to endorse any theory that life, as we recognize it, begins before live birth or to accord legal rights to the unborn except in narrowly defined situations and except when the rights are contingent upon live birth. For example, the traditional rule of tort law had denied recovery for prenatal injuries even though the child was born alive. That rule has been changed in almost every jurisdiction. In most States recovery is said to be permitted only if the fetus was viable, or at least quick, when the injuries were sustained, though few courts have squarely so held. In a recent development, generally opposed by the commentators, some States permit the parents of a stillborn child to maintain an action for wrongful death because of prenatal injuries. Such an action, however, would appear to be one to vindicate the parents' interest and is thus consistent with the view that the fetus, at most, represents only the potentiality of life. Similarly, unborn children have been recognized as acquiring rights or interests by way of inheritance or other devolution of property, and have been represented by guardians *ad litem*. Perfection of the interests involved, again, has generally been contingent upon live birth. In short, the unborn have never been recognized in the law as persons in the whole sense.

X.

In view of all this, we do not agree that, by adopting one theory of life, Texas may override the rights of the pregnant woman that are at stake. We repeat, however, that

---

[59] L. Hellman & J. Pritchard, Williams Obstetrics 493 (14th ed. 1971); Dorland's Illustrated Medical Dictionary 1689 (24th ed. 1965).

[60] Hellman & Pritchard, supra, n. 59, at 493.

the State does have an important and legitimate interest in preserving and protecting the health of the pregnant woman, whether she be a resident of the State or a non-resident who seeks medical consultation and treatment there, and that it has still *another* important and legitimate interest in protecting the potentiality of human life. These interests are separate and distinct. Each grows in substantiality as the woman approaches term and, at a point during pregnancy, each becomes "compelling."

With respect to the State's important and legitimate interest in the health of the mother, the "compelling" point, in the light of present medical knowledge, is at approximately the end of the first trimester. This is so because of the now established medical fact, referred to above . . . that until the end of the first trimester mortality in abortion is less than mortality in normal childbirth. It follows that, from and after this point, a State may regulate the abortion procedure to the extent that the regulation reasonably relates to the preservation and protection of maternal health. Examples of permissible state regulation in this area are requirements as to the qualifications of the person who is to perform the abortion; as to the licensure of that person; as to the facility in which the procedure is to be performed, that is, whether it must be a hospital or may be a clinic or some other place of less-than-hospital status; as to the licensing of the facility; and the like.

This means, on the other hand, that, for the period of pregnancy prior to this "compelling" point, the attending physician, in consultation with his patient, is free to determine, without regulation by the State, that in his medical judgment the patient's pregnancy should be terminated. If that decision is reached, the judgment may be effectuated by an abortion free of interference by the State.

With respect to the State's important and legitimate interest in potential life, the "compelling" point is at viability. This is so because the fetus then presumably has the capability of meaningful life outside the mother's womb. State regulation protective of fetal life after viability thus has both logical and biological justifications. If the State is interested in protecting fetal life after viability, it may go so far as to proscribe abortion during that period except when it is necessary to preserve the life or health of the mother.

Measured against these standards, Art. 1196 of the Texas Penal Code, in restricting legal abortions to those "procured or attempted by medical advice for the purpose of saving the life of the mother," sweeps too broadly. The statute makes no distinction between abortions performed early in pregnancy and those performed later, and it limits to a single reason, "saving" the mother's life, the legal justification for the procedure. The statute, therefore, cannot survive the constitutional attack made upon it here.

This conclusion makes it unnecessary for us to consider the additional challenge to the Texas statute asserted on grounds of vagueness. See United States v. Vuitch, 402 U.S. 62, 67–72 (1971).

XI.

To summarize and to repeat:

1.   A state criminal abortion statute of the current Texas type, that excepts from criminality only a *life saving* procedure on behalf of the mother, without regard to pregnancy stage and without recognition of the other interests involved, is violative of the Due Process Clause of the Fourteenth Amendment.

(a)   For the stage prior to approximately the end of the first trimester, the abortion decision and its effectuation must be left to the medical judgment of the pregnant woman's attending physician.

(b)   For the stage subsequent to approximately the end of the first trimester, the State, in promoting its interest in the health of the mother, may, if it chooses, regulate the abortion procedure in ways that are reasonably related to maternal health.

(c)   For the stage subsequent to viability the State, in promoting its interest in the potentiality of human life, may, if it chooses, regulate, and even proscribe, abortion except where it is necessary, in appropriate medical judgment, for the preservation of the life or health of the mother.

2.   The State may define the term "physician," as it has been employed in the preceding numbered paragraphs of this Part XI of this opinion, to mean only a physician currently licensed by the State, and may proscribe any abortion by a person who is not a physician as so defined.

In Doe v. Bolton, 410 U.S. 179, procedural requirements contained in one of the modern abortion statutes are considered. That opinion and this one, of course, are to be read together.

This holding, we feel, is consistent with the relative weights of the respective interests involved, with the lessons and example of medical and legal history, with the lenity of the common law, and with the demands of the profound problems of the present day. The decision leaves the State free to place increasing restrictions on abortion as the period of pregnancy lengthens, so long as those restrictions are tailored to the recognized state interests. The decision vindicates the right of the physician to administer medical treatment according to his professional judgment up to the points where important state interests provide compelling justifications for intervention. Up to those points the abortion decision in all its aspects is inherently, and primarily, a medical decision, and basic responsibility for it must rest with the physician. If an individual practitioner abuses the privilege of exercising proper medical judgment, the usual remedies, judicial and intra-professional, are available.

. . .

■ MR. JUSTICE STEWART, concurring.

. . .

■ MR. JUSTICE REHNQUIST, dissenting.

The Court's opinion brings to the decision of this troubling question both extensive historical fact and a wealth of legal scholarship. While its opinion thus commands my respect, I find myself nonetheless in fundamental disagreement with those parts of it which invalidate the Texas statute in question, and therefore dissent.

. . .

I have difficulty in concluding, as the Court does, that the right of "privacy" is involved in this case. Texas by the statute here challenged bars the performance of a medical abortion by a licensed physician on a plaintiff such as Roe. A transaction resulting in an operation such as this is not "private" in the ordinary usage of that word. Nor is the "privacy" which the Court finds here even a distant relative of the freedom from searches and seizures protected by the Fourth Amendment to the Constitution which the Court has referred to as embodying a right to privacy. Katz v. United States, 389 U.S. 347 (1967).

. . .

The Court eschews the history of the Fourteenth Amendment in its reliance on the "compelling state interest" test. See Weber v. Aetna Cas. & Sur. Co., 406 U.S. 164, 179 (1972) (dissenting opinion). But the Court adds a new wrinkle to this test by transposing it from the legal considerations associated with the Equal Protection Clause of the Fourteenth Amendment to this case arising under the Due Process

Clause of the Fourteenth Amendment. Unless I misapprehend the consequences of this transplanting of the "compelling state interest test," the Court's opinion will accomplish the seemingly impossible feat of leaving this area of the law more confused than it found it.

While the Court's opinion quotes from the dissent of Mr. Justice Holmes in Lochner v. New York, 198 U.S. 45 (1905), the result it reaches is more closely attuned to the majority opinion of Mr. Justice Peckham in that case. As in *Lochner* and similar cases, applying substantive due process standards to economic and social welfare legislation, the adoption of the compelling state interest standard will inevitably require this Court to examine the legislative policies and pass on the wisdom of these policies in the very process of deciding whether a particular state interest put forward may or may not be "compelling." The decision here to break the term of pregnancy into three distinct terms and to outline the permissible restrictions the State may impose in each one, for example, partakes more of judicial legislation than it does of a determination of the intent of the drafters of the Fourteenth Amendment.

The fact that a majority of the States, reflecting after all the majority sentiment in those States, have had restrictions on abortions for at least a century is a strong indication, it seems to me, that the asserted right to an abortion is not "so rooted in the traditions and conscience of our people as to be ranked as fundamental," Snyder v. Massachusetts, 291 U.S. 97, 105 (1934). Even today, when society's views on abortion are changing, the very existence of the debate is evidence that the "right" to an abortion is not so universally accepted as the appellants would have us believe.[a]

[In the companion case of Doe v. Bolton, 410 U.S. 179 (1973), the Court held invalid a number of provisions of the Georgia statute regulating medical practice in abortion cases. The concurring and dissenting opinions which follow were addressed to both cases.]

■ MR. CHIEF JUSTICE BURGER, concurring [in *Wade* and *Bolton*].

I agree that, under the Fourteenth Amendment to the Constitution, the abortion statutes of Georgia and Texas impermissibly limit the performance of abortions necessary to protect the health of pregnant women, using the term health in its broadest medical context. See United States v. Vuitch, 402 U.S. 62, 71–72 (1971). I am somewhat troubled that the Court has taken notice of various scientific and medical data in reaching its conclusion; however, I do not believe that the Court has exceeded the scope of judicial notice accepted in other contexts.

. . .

I do not read the Court's holding today as having the sweeping consequences attributed to it by the dissenting Justices; the dissenting views discount the reality that the vast majority of physicians observe the standards of their profession, and act only on the basis of carefully deliberated medical judgments relating to life and health. Plainly, the Court today rejects any claim that the Constitution requires abortion on demand.

■ MR. JUSTICE DOUGLAS, concurring [in *Wade* and *Bolton*].

While I join the opinion of the Court, I add a few words.

The questions presented in the present cases go far beyond the issues of vagueness, which we considered in United States v. Vuitch, 402 U.S. 62. They involve

---

[a]   For an early view criticizing the method by which the Court reached its result in the original abortion decisions, see Ely, *The Wages of Crying Wolf: A Comment on Roe v. Wade,* 82 Yale L.J. 920 (1973). For other useful commentary at the time see Epstein, *Substantive Due Process by Any Other Name: The Abortion Cases,* 1973 Sup.Ct.Rev. 159; Tribe, *Foreword: Toward a Model of Roles in the Due Process of Life and Law,* 87 Harv.L.Rev. 1 (1973).

the right of privacy, one aspect of which we considered in Griswold v. Connecticut, 381 U.S. 479, 484, when we held that various guarantees in the Bill of Rights create zones of privacy. . . .

The Ninth Amendment obviously does not create federally enforceable rights. It merely says, "The enumeration in the Constitution of certain rights, shall not be construed to deny or disparage others retained by the people." But a catalogue of these rights includes customary, traditional, and time-honored rights, amenities, privileges, and immunities that come within the sweep of "the Blessings of Liberty" mentioned in the preamble to the Constitution. Many of them in my view come within the meaning of the term "liberty" as used in the Fourteenth Amendment.

First is the autonomous control over the development and expression of one's intellect, interests, tastes, and personality.

These are rights protected by the First Amendment and in my view they are absolute, permitting of no exceptions. . . .

Second is freedom of choice in the basic decisions of one's life respecting marriage, divorce, procreation, contraception, and the education and upbringing of children.

These rights, unlike those protected by the First Amendment, are subject to some control by the police power. Thus the Fourth Amendment speaks only of "unreasonable searches and seizures" and of "probable cause." These rights are "fundamental" and we have held that in order to support legislative action the statute must be narrowly and precisely drawn and that a "compelling state interest" must be shown in support of the limitation. . . .

The liberty to marry a person of one's own choosing, Loving v. Virginia, 388 U.S. 1; the right of procreation, Skinner v. Oklahoma, 316 U.S. 535; the liberty to direct the education of one's children, Pierce v. Soc'y of Sisters, 268 U.S. 510, and the privacy of the marital relation, Griswold v. Connecticut, supra, are in this category. . . .

This right of privacy was called by Mr. Justice Brandeis the right "to be let alone." Olmstead v. United States, 277 U.S. 438, 478. That right includes the privilege of an individual to plan his own affairs, for, "outside areas of plainly harmful conduct, every American is left to shape his own life as he thinks best, do what he pleases, go where he pleases." Kent v. Dulles, 357 U.S. 116, 126.

Third is the freedom to care for one's health and person, freedom from bodily restraint or compulsion, freedom to walk, stroll, or loaf.

These rights, though fundamental, are likewise subject to regulation on a showing of "compelling state interest." . . .

The present statute has struck the balance between the woman and the State's interests wholly in favor of the latter. I am not prepared to hold that a State may equate, as Georgia has done, all phases of maturation preceding birth. . . .

In summary, the enactment is overbroad. It is not closely correlated to the aim of preserving pre-natal life. In fact, it permits its destruction in several cases, including pregnancies resulting from sex acts in which unmarried females are below the statutory age of consent. At the same time, however, the measure broadly proscribes aborting other pregnancies which may cause severe mental disorders. Additionally, the statute is overbroad because it equates the value of embryonic life immediately after conception with the worth of life immediately before birth. . . .

I also agree that the superstructure of medical supervision which Georgia has erected violates the patient's right of privacy inherent in her choice of her own physician.

■ MR. JUSTICE WHITE, with whom MR. JUSTICE REHNQUIST joins, dissenting [in *Wade* and *Bolton*]. . . .

With all due respect, I dissent. I find nothing in the language or history of the Constitution to support the Court's judgment. The Court simply fashions and announces a new constitutional right for pregnant mothers and, with scarcely any reason or authority for its action, invests that right with sufficient substance to override most existing state abortion statutes. The upshot is that the people and the legislatures of the 50 States are constitutionally disentitled to weigh the relative importance of the continued existence and development of the fetus on the one hand against a spectrum of possible impacts on the mother on the other hand. As an exercise of raw judicial power, the Court perhaps has authority to do what it does today; but in my view its judgment is an improvident and extravagant exercise of the power of judicial review which the Constitution extends to this Court.

The Court apparently values the convenience of the pregnant mother more than the continued existence and development of the life or potential life which she carries. Whether or not I might agree with that marshalling of values, I can in no event join the Court's judgment because I find no constitutional warrant for imposing such an order of priorities on the people and legislatures of the States. In a sensitive area such as this, involving as it does issues over which reasonable men may easily and heatedly differ, I cannot accept the Court's exercise of its clear power of choice by interposing a constitutional barrier to state efforts to protect human life and by investing mothers and doctors with the constitutionally protected right to exterminate it. This issue, for the most part, should be left with the people and to the political processes the people have devised to govern their affairs.

It is my view, therefore, that the Texas statute is not constitutionally infirm because it denies abortions to those who seek to serve only their convenience rather than to protect their life or health. . . .

Planned Parenthood of Southeastern
Pennsylvania v. Casey

505 U.S. 833, 112 S.Ct. 2791, 120 L.Ed.2d 674 (1992).

■ JUSTICE O'CONNOR, JUSTICE KENNEDY, and JUSTICE SOUTER announced the judgment of the Court and delivered the opinion of the Court with respect to Parts I, II, III, V-A, V-C, and VI, an opinion with respect to Part V-E, in which JUSTICE STEVENS joins, and an opinion with respect to Parts IV, V-B, and V-D.

I

Liberty finds no refuge in a jurisprudence of doubt. Yet 19 years after our holding that the Constitution protects a woman's right to terminate her pregnancy in its early stages, Roe v. Wade, 410 U.S. 113 (1973), that definition of liberty is still questioned. [T]he United States, as it has done in five other cases in the last decade, again asks us to overrule *Roe.* . . .

[Five abortion clinics, and physicians providing abortion services, challenged on their face] five provisions of the Pennsylvania Abortion Control Act . . . . The Act requires that a woman seeking an abortion give her informed consent prior to the abortion procedure, and specifies that she be provided with certain information at least 24 hours before the abortion is performed. § 3205. For a minor to obtain an abortion, the Act requires the informed consent of one of her parents, but provides for a judicial bypass option if the minor does not wish to or cannot obtain a parent's consent. § 3206. [T]he Act requires that, unless certain exceptions apply, a married woman seeking an abortion must sign a statement indicating that she has notified her husband of her intended abortion. § 3209. The Act exempts compliance with these three requirements in the event of a "medical emergency," which is defined in § 3203 of the Act. . . . [It also] imposes certain reporting requirements on facilities that provide abortion services. . . .

. . . The District Court . . . held all [the provisions] unconstitutional. . . . The Court of Appeals . . . [upheld all but] the husband notification requirement. . . .

. . .

After considering the fundamental constitutional questions resolved by *Roe,* principles of institutional integrity, and the rule of *stare decisis*, we are led to conclude this: the essential holding of *Roe v. Wade* should be retained and once again reaffirmed.

. . . *Roe*'s essential holding, the holding we reaffirm, has three parts. First is a recognition of the right of the woman to choose to have an abortion before viability and to obtain it without undue interference from the State. Before viability, the State's interests are not strong enough to support a prohibition of abortion or the imposition of a substantial obstacle to the woman's effective right to elect the procedure. Second is a confirmation of the State's power to restrict abortions after fetal viability, if the law contains exceptions for pregnancies which endanger a woman's life or health. And third is the principle that the State has legitimate interests from the outset of the pregnancy in protecting the health of the woman and the life of the fetus that may become a child. These principles do not contradict one another; and we adhere to each.

II

. . .

Neither the Bill of Rights nor the specific practices of States at the time of the adoption of the Fourteenth Amendment marks the outer limits of the substantive sphere of liberty which the Fourteenth Amendment protects. See U.S. Const., Amend. 9. . . .

The inescapable fact is that adjudication of substantive due process claims may call upon the Court in interpreting the Constitution to exercise that same capacity which by tradition courts always have exercised: reasoned judgment. . . .

. . .

Our law affords constitutional protection to personal decisions relating to marriage, procreation, contraception, family relationships, child rearing, and education. . . . These matters, involving the most intimate and personal choices a person may make in a lifetime, choices central to personal dignity and autonomy, are central to the liberty protected by the Fourteenth Amendment. At the heart of liberty is the right to define one's own concept of existence, of meaning, of the universe, and of the mystery of human life. Beliefs about these matters could not define the attributes of personhood were they formed under compulsion of the State.

. . . Abortion is a unique act . . . fraught with consequences for others: for the woman who must live with the implications of her decision; for the persons who perform and assist in the procedure; for the spouse, family, and society which must confront the knowledge that these procedures exist, procedures some deem nothing short of an act of violence against innocent human life; and, depending on one's beliefs, for the life or potential life that is aborted. Though abortion is conduct, it does not follow that the State is entitled to proscribe it in all instances[,] because the liberty of the woman is at stake in a sense unique to the human condition and so unique to the law. The mother who carries a child to full term is subject to anxieties, to physical constraints, to pain that only she must bear. That these sacrifices have from the beginning of the human race been endured by woman with a pride that ennobles her in the eyes of others and gives to the infant a bond of love cannot alone be grounds for the State to insist she make the sacrifice. Her suffering is too intimate and personal for the State to insist, without more, upon its own vision of the woman's role, however dominant that vision has been in the course of our history and our culture. The destiny of the woman must be shaped to a large extent on her own conception of her spiritual imperatives and her place in society.

[I]n some critical respects the abortion decision is of the same character as the decision to use contraception, to which *Griswold v. Connecticut, Eisenstadt v. Baird,* and *Carey v. Population Services International,* afford constitutional protection. We have no doubt as to the correctness of those decisions. They support the reasoning in *Roe* relating to the woman's liberty because they involve personal decisions concerning not only the meaning of procreation but also human responsibility and respect for it. . . .

. . .

III

[Because "*Roe* . . . has in no sense proven 'unworkable,' "; because "people have organized intimate relationships and made choices that define their views of themselves and their places in society, in reliance on the availability of abortion in the event that contraception should fail[,]" and women's "ability . . . to participate equally in the economic and social life of the Nation has been facilitated by their ability to control their reproductive lives"; because "[n]o evolution of legal principle has left *Roe*'s doctrinal footings weaker than they were in 1973"; and because any "divergences from the factual premises of 1973 have no bearing on the validity of *Roe*'s central holding, that viability marks the earliest point at which the State's interest in fetal life is constitutionally adequate to justify a legislative ban on nontherapeutic abortions[,]" it follows that "[w]ithin the bounds of normal *stare decisis* analysis, . . . the stronger argument is for affirming *Roe*'s central holding, with whatever degree of personal reluctance any of us may have, not for overruling it." *Roe* having provoked "sustained and widespread debate[,]" however, the Court went on to compare the request to overrule it with the repudiations of the "line of cases identified with Lochner v. New York" by West Coast Hotel Co. v. Parrish, and of Plessy v. Ferguson by Brown v. Board of Education. As to the former, "the Depression [brought] the lesson that seemed unmistakable to most people by 1937, that the interpretation of contractual freedom protected in *Adkins* rested on fundamentally false factual assumptions about the capacity of a relatively unregulated market to satisfy minimal levels of human welfare." As to the latter, "whatever may have been the understanding in *Plessy*'s time of the power of segregation to stigmatize those who were segregated with a 'badge of inferiority,' it was clear by 1954 that legally sanctioned segregation had just such an effect. . . . Society's understanding of the facts . . . in 1954 was thus fundamentally different from the basis claimed for the decision in 1896. While we think *Plessy* was wrong the day it was decided, . . . the *Plessy* Court's explanation for its decision was so clearly at odds with the facts apparent to the Court in 1954 that the decision to reexamine *Plessy* was on this ground alone not only justified but required." By contrast, "because neither the factual underpinnings of *Roe*'s central holding nor our understanding of it has changed (and because no other indication of weakened precedent has been shown) the Court could not pretend to be reexamining the prior law with any justification beyond a present doctrinal disposition to come out differently from the Court of 1973."]

. . . [W]henever the Court's interpretation of the Constitution calls the contending sides of a national controversy to end their national division by accepting a common mandate rooted in the Constitution[,] . . . only the most convincing justification . . .

could suffice to demonstrate that a later decision overruling the first was anything but a surrender to political pressure, and an unjustified repudiation of the principle on which the Court staked its authority in the first instance. So to overrule under fire in the absence of the most compelling reason to reexamine a watershed decision would subvert the Court's legitimacy beyond any serious question. . . .

. . .

IV

. . . [Although] much criticism has been directed at *Roe*['s line-drawing], . . . [l]iberty must not be extinguished for want of a line that is clear. . . .

We conclude the line should be drawn at viability . . . for two reasons. First, . . . *stare decisis*. . . .

[S]econd[,] the concept of viability . . . is the time at which there is a realistic possibility of maintaining and nourishing a life outside the womb, so that the independent existence of the second life can in reason and all fairness be the object of state protection that now overrides the rights of the woman. . . . The viability line also has, as a practical matter, an element of fairness. In some broad sense it might be said that a woman who fails to act before viability has consented to the State's intervention on behalf of the developing child.

The woman's right to terminate her pregnancy before viability is the most central principle of *Roe v. Wade*. . . .

On the other side of the equation is the interest of the State in the protection of potential life. . . . The weight to be given this state interest, not the strength of the woman's interest, was the difficult question faced in *Roe*. . . .

[I]t must be remembered that *Roe v. Wade* speaks with clarity in establishing not only the woman's liberty but also the State's "important and legitimate interest in potential life." . . . That portion of the decision in *Roe* has been given too little acknowledgement and implementation by the Court in its subsequent cases[, which] decided that any regulation touching upon the abortion decision must survive strict scrutiny, to be sustained only if drawn in narrow terms to further a compelling state interest. . . .

. . .

The trimester framework no doubt was erected to ensure that the woman's right to choose not become so subordinate to the State's interest in promoting fetal life that her choice exists in theory but not in fact. We do not agree, however, that the trimester approach is necessary to accomplish this objective. A framework of this rigidity was unnecessary and in its later interpretation sometimes contradicted the State's permissible exercise of its powers.

Though the woman has a right to choose to terminate or continue her pregnancy before viability, it does not at all follow that the State is prohibited from taking steps to ensure that this choice is thoughtful and informed. Even in the earliest stages of pregnancy, the State may enact rules and regulations designed to encourage her to know that there are philosophic and social arguments of great weight that can be brought to bear in favor of continuing the pregnancy to full term and that there are procedures and institutions to allow adoption of unwanted children as well as a certain degree of state assistance if the mother chooses to raise the child herself. . . .

We reject the trimester framework, which we do not consider to be part of the essential holding of *Roe*. . . . Measures aimed at ensuring that a woman's choice contemplates the consequences for the fetus do not necessarily interfere with the right recognized in *Roe,* although those measures have been found to be inconsistent with the rigid trimester framework announced in that case.... The trimester framework ... misconceives the nature of the pregnant woman's interest[,] and in practice it undervalues the State's interest in potential life, as recognized in *Roe*.

. . .

... The fact that a law which serves a valid purpose, one not designed to strike at the right itself, has the incidental effect of making it more difficult or more expensive to procure an abortion cannot be enough to invalidate it. Only where state regulation imposes an undue burden on a woman's ability to make this decision does the power of the State reach into the heart of the liberty protected by the Due Process Clause....

. . .

The very notion that the State has a substantial interest in potential life leads to the conclusion that not all regulations must be deemed unwarranted. Not all burdens on the right to decide whether to terminate a pregnancy will be undue. In our view, the undue burden standard is the appropriate means of reconciling the State's interest with the woman's constitutionally protected liberty.

. . .

A finding of an undue burden is a shorthand for the conclusion that a state regulation has the purpose or effect of placing a substantial obstacle in the path of a woman seeking an abortion of a nonviable fetus. A statute with this purpose is invalid because the means chosen by the State to further the interest in potential life must be calculated to inform the woman's free choice, not hinder it. And a statute which, while furthering the interest in potential life or some other valid state interest, has the effect of placing a substantial obstacle in the path of a woman's choice cannot be considered a permissible means of serving its legitimate ends.... [A] law designed to further the State's interest in fetal life which imposes an undue burden on the woman's decision before fetal viability [is un]constitutional....

... Regulations which do no more than create a structural mechanism by which the State, or the parent or guardian of a minor, may express profound respect for the life of the unborn are permitted, if they are not a substantial obstacle to the woman's exercise of the right to choose.... Unless it has that effect on her right of choice, a state measure designed to persuade her to choose childbirth over abortion will be upheld if reasonably related to that goal. Regulations designed to foster the health of a woman seeking an abortion are valid if they do not constitute an undue burden.

... [W]ith respect to the undue burden standard[, w]e give this summary:

(a) ... An undue burden exists, and therefore a provision of law is invalid, if its purpose or effect is to place a substantial obstacle in the path of a woman seeking an abortion before the fetus attains viability.

(b) We reject the rigid trimester framework of *Roe v. Wade*. To promote the State's profound interest in potential life, throughout pregnancy the State may take measures to ensure that the woman's choice is informed, and measures designed to advance this interest will not be invalidated as long as their purpose is to persuade the woman to choose childbirth over abortion. These measures must not be an undue burden on the right.

(c) As with any medical procedure, the State may enact regulations to further the health or safety of a woman seeking an abortion. Unnecessary health regulations that have the purpose or effect of presenting a substantial obstacle to a woman seeking an abortion impose an undue burden on the right.

(d) Our adoption of the undue burden analysis does not disturb the central holding of *Roe v. Wade,* and we reaffirm that holding. Regardless of whether exceptions are made for particular circumstances, a State may not prohibit any woman from making the ultimate decision to terminate her pregnancy before viability.

(e)   We also reaffirm *Roe*'s holding that "subsequent to viability, the State in promoting its interest in the potentiality of human life may, if it chooses, regulate, and even proscribe, abortion except where it is necessary, in appropriate medical judgment, for the preservation of the life or health of the mother." . . .

These principles control our assessment of the . . . challenged provisions.

V

. . .

A

. . .

Petitioners argue that the [statute's] definition [of medical emergency] is too narrow, contending that it forecloses the possibility of an immediate abortion despite some significant health risks. If . . . correct, we would be required to invalidate . . . , for the essential holding of *Roe* forbids a State from interfering with a woman's choice . . . if continuing her pregnancy would constitute a threat to her health. . . .

. . . [A]s construed by the Court of Appeals, [however,] the medical emergency definition imposes no undue burden on a woman's abortion right.

B

We next consider the informed consent requirement. . . .

Our prior decisions establish that as with any medical procedure, the State may require a woman to give her written informed consent to an abortion. . . . Petitioners challenge the statute's definition of informed consent because it includes the provision of specific information by the doctor and the mandatory 24-hour waiting period. The conclusions reached by a majority of the Justices in the separate opinions filed today and the undue burden standard adopted in this opinion require us to overrule in part some of the Court's past decisions. . . .

In *Akron I,* . . . we invalidated an ordinance which required that a woman seeking an abortion be provided by her physician with specific information "designed to influence the woman's informed choice between abortion or childbirth." . . .

To the extent *Akron I* and *Thornburgh* find a constitutional violation when the government requires, as it does here, the giving of truthful, nonmisleading information about the nature of the procedure, the attendant health risks and those of childbirth, and the "probable gestational age" of the fetus, those cases go too far, are inconsistent with *Roe*'s acknowledgment of an important interest in potential life, and are overruled. . . . In attempting to ensure that a woman apprehend the full consequences of her decision, the State furthers the legitimate purpose of reducing the risk that a woman may elect an abortion, only to discover later, with devastating psychological consequences, that her decision was not fully informed. . . .

We also see no reason why the State may not require doctors to inform a woman seeking an abortion of the availability of materials relating to the consequences to the fetus, even when those consequences have no direct relation to her health. . . . We conclude [that] . . . requiring that the woman be informed of the availability of information relating to fetal development and the assistance available should she decide to carry the pregnancy to full term is a reasonable measure to insure an informed choice, one which might cause the woman to choose childbirth over abortion. This requirement cannot be considered a substantial obstacle to obtaining an abortion, and, it follows, there is no undue burden.

Our prior cases also suggest that the "straitjacket," *Thornburgh* . . . , of particular information which must be given in each case interferes with a constitutional right of privacy between a pregnant woman and her physician. [T]he statute now before us does not require a physician to comply with the informed consent provisions "if he or she can demonstrate by a preponderance of the evidence, that he or she reasonably believed that furnishing the information would have resulted in a severely adverse effect on the physical or mental health of the patient." . . . In this respect, the statute does not prevent the physician from exercising his or her medical judgment.

Whatever constitutional status the doctor-patient relation may have as a general matter, in the present context it is derivative of the woman's position. . . . Thus, a requirement that a doctor give a woman certain information as part of obtaining her consent to an abortion is, for constitutional purposes, no different from a requirement that a doctor give certain specific information about any medical procedure.

. . .

The Pennsylvania statute also requires us to reconsider the holding in *Akron I* that the State may not require that a physician, as opposed to a qualified assistant, provide information relevant to a woman's informed consent. . . . Since there is no evidence on this record that requiring a doctor to give the information as provided by the statute would amount in practical terms to a substantial obstacle to a woman seeking an abortion, we conclude that it is not an undue burden. . . .

Our analysis of Pennsylvania's 24-hour waiting period between the provision of the information deemed necessary to informed consent and the performance of an abortion under the undue burden standard requires us to reconsider the premise behind the decision in *Akron I* invalidating a parallel requirement. In *Akron I* we said: "Nor are we convinced that the State's legitimate concern that the woman's decision be informed is reasonably served by requiring a 24-hour delay as a matter of course." . . . We consider that conclusion to be wrong. The idea that important decisions will be more informed and deliberate if they follow some period of reflection does not strike us as unreasonable, particularly where the statute directs that important information become part of the background of the decision. The statute, as construed by the Court of Appeals, permits avoidance of the waiting period in the event of a medical emergency and the record evidence shows that in the vast majority of cases, a 24-hour delay does not create any appreciable health risk. In theory, at least, the waiting period is a reasonable measure to implement the State's interest in protecting the life of the unborn, a measure that does not amount to an undue burden.

Whether the mandatory 24-hour waiting period is nonetheless invalid because in practice it is a substantial obstacle to a woman's choice to terminate her pregnancy is a closer question. The findings of fact by the District Court indicate that because of the distances many women must travel to reach an abortion provider, the practical effect will often be a delay of much more than a day because the waiting period requires that a woman seeking an abortion make at least two visits to the doctor. The District Court also found that in many instances this will increase the exposure of women seeking abortions to "the harassment and hostility of anti-abortion protestors demonstrating outside a clinic." . . . As a result, the District Court found that for those women who have the fewest financial resources, those who must travel long distances, and those who have difficulty explaining their whereabouts to husbands, employers, or others, the 24-hour waiting period will be "particularly burdensome." . . .

These findings are troubling in some respects, but they do not demonstrate that the waiting period constitutes an undue burden. We do not doubt that . . . the waiting period has the effect of "increasing the cost and risk of delay of abortions," . . . but the District Court did not conclude that the increased costs and potential delays amount to substantial obstacles. . . . [U]nder the undue burden standard a State is permitted to enact persuasive measures which favor childbirth over abortion, even if those measures do not further a health interest. . . .

We also disagree with the District Court's conclusion that the "particularly burdensome" effects of the waiting period on some women require its invalidation. . . . [O]n the record before us, and in the context of this facial challenge, we are not convinced that the 24-hour waiting period constitutes an undue burden.

. . .

C

Section 3209 of Pennsylvania's abortion law provides, except in cases of medical emergency, that no physician shall perform an abortion on a married woman without receiving a signed statement from the woman that she has notified her spouse that she is about to undergo an abortion. The woman has the option of providing an alternative signed statement certifying that her husband is not the man who impregnated her; that her husband could not be located; that the pregnancy is the result of spousal sexual assault which she has reported; or that the woman believes that notifying her husband will cause him or someone else to inflict bodily injury upon her. A physician who performs an abortion on a married woman without receiving the appropriate signed statement will have his or her license revoked, and is liable to the husband for damages.

[The opinion here recounted at length the district court's findings with respect to the widespread incidence and dynamics of wife-battering, marital rape, and other coerced sexual activity, as well as studies of the frequency of psychological and physical abuse of women, including homicides, by their husbands or male partners.]

. . . In well-functioning marriages, spouses discuss important intimate decisions such as whether to bear a child. But there are millions of women in this country who are the victims of regular physical and psychological abuse at the hands of their husbands. Should these women become pregnant, they may have very good reasons for not wishing to inform their husbands of their decision to obtain an abortion. Many may have justifiable fears of physical abuse, but may be no less fearful of the consequences of reporting prior abuse. . . . Many may have a reasonable fear that notifying their husbands will provoke further instances of child abuse; these women are not exempt from § 3209's notification requirement. Many may fear devastating forms of psychological abuse from their husbands . . . [that] may act as even more of a deterrent to notification than the possibility of physical violence, but [they] are not exempt from § 3209's notification requirement. And many women who are pregnant as a result of sexual assaults by their husbands will be unable to avail themselves of the exception for spousal sexual assault, § 3209(b)(3), because the exception requires that the woman have notified law enforcement authorities within 90 days of the assault, and her husband will be notified of her report once an investigation begins. § 3128(c). . . . [V]ictims of spousal sexual assault are extremely reluctant to report the abuse to the government; hence, a great many . . . will not be exempt from the notification requirement . . . .

The spousal notification requirement is thus likely to prevent a significant number of women from obtaining an abortion. . . . We must not blind ourselves to the fact that the significant number of women who fear for their safety and the safety of their children are likely to be deterred from procuring an abortion as surely as if the Commonwealth had outlawed abortion in all cases.

. . . Respondents argue that . . . the statute affects fewer than one percent of women seeking abortions [and thus] the statute cannot be invalid on its face. . . . We disagree. . . .

... The proper focus of constitutional inquiry is the group for whom the law is a restriction, not the group for whom the law is irrelevant.

... [I]n a large fraction of the cases in which § 3209 is relevant, it will operate as a substantial obstacle to a woman's choice to undergo an abortion. It is an undue burden, and therefore invalid.

This conclusion is in no way inconsistent with our decisions upholding parental notification or consent requirements. ... Those enactments, and our judgment that they are constitutional, are based on the quite reasonable assumption that minors will benefit from consultation with their parents and that children will often not realize that their parents have their best interests at heart. We cannot adopt a parallel assumption about adult women.

... If this case concerned a State's ability to require the mother to notify the father before taking some action with respect to a living child raised by both, ... it would be reasonable to conclude ... that the father's interest in the welfare of the child and the mother's interest are equal.

Before birth, however, [i]t is an inescapable biological fact that state regulation with respect to the child a woman is carrying will have a far greater impact on the mother's liberty than on the father's. ...

[N]ot so long ago ... a different understanding of the family and of the Constitution prevailed. In Bradwell v. Illinois, 16 Wall. 130 (1873), three Members of this Court reaffirmed the common-law principle that "a woman had no legal existence separate from her husband. ..." ... Only one generation has passed since this Court observed that "woman is still regarded as the center of home and family life," with attendant "special responsibilities" that precluded full and independent legal status under the Constitution. ... These views, of course, are no longer consistent with our understanding of the family, the individual, or the Constitution.

... For the great many women who are victims of abuse inflicted by their husbands, or whose children are the victims of such abuse, a spousal notice requirement enables the husband to wield an effective veto over his wife's decision[... —a] veto found unconstitutional in *Danforth*. ...

The husband's interest in the life of the child his wife is carrying does not permit the State to empower him with this troubling degree of authority over his wife. ... A State may not give to a man the kind of dominion over his wife that parents exercise over their children.

... Women do not lose their constitutionally protected liberty when they marry. ...

D

... Except in a medical emergency, an unemancipated young woman under 18 may not obtain an abortion unless she and one of her parents (or guardian) provides consent. ... If neither ... consent[s], a court may authorize the performance of an abortion upon a determination that the young woman is mature and capable of giving informed consent and has in fact given her informed consent, or that an abortion would be in her best interests.

... Our cases establish, and we reaffirm today, that a State may require a minor seeking an abortion to obtain the consent of a parent or guardian, provided that there is an adequate judicial bypass procedure. ...

E

. . .

. . . *Danforth* . . . held that recordkeeping and reporting provisions "that are reasonably directed to the preservation of maternal health and that properly respect a patient's confidentiality and privacy are permissible." [U]nder this standard, all the [recordkeeping and reporting] provisions at issue here except that relating to spousal notice are constitutional. . . . The collection of information [about] actual patients is a vital element of medical research, and so it cannot be said that the requirements serve no purpose other than to make abortions more difficult. Nor do [they] impose a substantial obstacle to a woman's choice. At most they might increase the cost of some abortions by a slight amount. While at some point increased cost could become a substantial obstacle, there is no such showing on the record before us.

Subsection (12) . . . requires the reporting of . . . a married woman's "reason for failure to provide notice" to her husband. . . . Like the spousal notice requirement itself, this provision places an undue burden on a woman's choice, and must be invalidated for that reason.

VI

Our Constitution is a covenant running from the first generation of Americans to us and then to future generations. . . . We accept our responsibility not to retreat from interpreting the full meaning of the covenant in light of all our precedents. We invoke it once again to define the freedom guaranteed by the Constitution's own promise, the promise of liberty.

. . .

■ JUSTICE STEVENS, concurring in part and dissenting in part.

. . .

I

. . .

[I]mplicit in the Court's analysis [is] a reaffirmation of *Roe*'s explanation of why the State's obligation to protect the life or health of the mother must take precedence over any duty to the unborn. . . . [A]s a matter of federal constitutional law, a developing organism that is not yet a "person" does not have what is sometimes described as a "right to life." This has been and, by the Court's holding today, remains a fundamental premise of our constitutional law governing reproductive autonomy.

II

. . .

. . . [T]he interest in protecting potential life is not grounded in the Constitution. It is, instead, an indirect interest supported by both humanitarian and pragmatic concerns. . . .

In counterpoise is the woman's constitutional interest in liberty. One aspect of this liberty is a right to bodily integrity, a right to control one's person. . . . This right is neutral on the question of abortion: The Constitution would be equally offended by an absolute requirement that all women undergo abortions as by an absolute prohibition on abortions. . . .

The woman's constitutional liberty interest also involves her freedom to decide matters of the highest privacy and the most personal nature. . . . The authority to make such traumatic and yet empowering decisions is an element of basic human dignity. As the joint opinion so eloquently demonstrates, a woman's decision to terminate her pregnancy is nothing less than a matter of conscience.

Weighing the State's interest in potential life and the woman's liberty interest, I agree with the joint opinion that the State may " 'expres[s] a preference for normal childbirth,' " that the State may take steps to ensure that a woman's choice "is thoughtful and informed," and that "States are free to enact laws to provide a reasonable framework for a woman to make a decision that has such profound and lasting meaning." Serious questions arise, however, when a State attempts to "persuade the woman to choose childbirth over abortion." Decisional autonomy must limit the State's power to inject into a woman's most personal deliberations its own views of what is best. The State may promote its preferences by funding childbirth, by creating and maintaining alternatives to abortion, and by espousing the virtues of family; but it must respect the individual's freedom to make such judgments.

. . .

. . . [T]he Pennsylvania statute . . . require[s] a physician or counselor to provide the woman with a range of materials clearly designed to persuade her to choose not to undergo the abortion. While the State is free . . . to produce and disseminate such material, the State may not inject such information into the woman's deliberations just as she is weighing such an important choice.

. . . [By contrast, r]equir[ing] the physician to inform a woman of the nature and risks of the abortion procedure and the medical risks of carrying to term, are neutral requirements comparable to those imposed in other medical procedures. . . .

III

The 24-hour waiting period . . . raises even more serious concerns. . . .

. . . [T]here is no evidence that the mandated delay benefits women or that it is necessary to enable the physician to convey any relevant information to the patient. The mandatory delay thus appears to rest on outmoded and unacceptable assumptions about the decisionmaking capacity of women. . . .

. . .

Part of the constitutional liberty to choose is the equal dignity to which each of us is entitled. A woman who decides to terminate her pregnancy is entitled to the same respect as a woman who decides to carry the fetus to term. The mandatory waiting period denies women that equal respect.

IV

In my opinion, a correct application of the "undue burden" standard leads to the same conclusion. . . .

[With respect to t]he 24-hour delay requirement, . . . [t]he findings of the District Court establish the severity of the burden. . . . [E]ven [when] the delay is not especially onerous, it is . . . "undue" because there is no evidence [it] serves a useful and legitimate purpose. [T]here is no legitimate reason to require a woman who has agonized over her decision to leave the clinic or hospital and return again another day. . . . [A] rigid requirement that all patients wait 24 hours or (what is true in practice) much longer to evaluate the significance of information that is either common knowledge or irrelevant is an irrational and, therefore, "undue" burden.

The counseling provisions are similarly infirm. . . . [The mandated information] requirements . . . do not serve a useful purpose and thus constitute an unnecessary— and therefore undue—burden on the woman's constitutional liberty to decide to terminate her pregnancy.

Accordingly, while I disagree with Parts IV, V-B, and V-D of the joint opinion, I join the remainder of the Court's opinion.

■ JUSTICE BLACKMUN, concurring in part, concurring in the judgment in part, and dissenting in part.

I join parts I, II, III, V-A, V-C, and VI of the joint opinion of Justices O'Connor, Kennedy, and Souter.

. . .

I

Make no mistake, the joint opinion of Justices O'Connor, Kennedy, and Souter is an act of personal courage and constitutional principle. . . .

. . .

[W]hile . . . the joint opinion errs in failing to invalidate the other regulations, I am pleased that [it] has not ruled out the possibility that these regulations may be shown to impose an unconstitutional burden. The joint opinion makes clear that its specific holdings are based on the insufficiency of the record before it. . . .

II

. . .

. . . *Roe*'s requirement of strict scrutiny as implemented through a trimester framework should not be disturbed. No other approach has gained a majority, and no other is more protective of the woman's fundamental right. Lastly, no other approach properly accommodates the woman's constitutional right with the State's legitimate interests.

. . .

Application of the strict scrutiny standard results in the invalidation of all the challenged provisions. Indeed, as this Court has invalidated virtually identical provisions in prior cases, *stare decisis* requires that we again strike them down.

. . .

III

. . .

The Chief Justice's criticism of *Roe* follows from his stunted conception of individual liberty. . . . [He] construe[s] this Court's personal-liberty cases as establishing only a laundry list of particular rights, rather than a principled account of how these particular rights are grounded in a more general right of privacy. This constricted view is reinforced by The Chief Justice's exclusive reliance on tradition as a source of fundamental rights. . . .

Even more shocking than The Chief Justice's cramped notion of individual liberty is his complete omission of any discussion of the effects that compelled childbirth and motherhood have on women's lives. . . . [His] view of the State's compelling interest in maternal health has less to do with health than it does with compelling women to be maternal.

. . .

■ CHIEF JUSTICE REHNQUIST, with whom JUSTICE WHITE, JUSTICE SCALIA, and JUSTICE THOMAS join, concurring in the judgment in part and dissenting in part.

The joint opinion, following its newly-minted variation on *stare decisis*, retains the outer shell of *Roe v. Wade,* . . . but beats a wholesale retreat from the substance of that case. We believe that *Roe* . . . should be overruled consistently with our traditional approach to *stare decisis* in constitutional cases. We would . . . uphold the challenged provisions of the Pennsylvania statute in their entirety.

I

. . .

. . . Although they reject the trimester framework . . . , Justices O'Connor, Kennedy, and Souter adopt a revised undue burden standard . . . that . . . is an unjustified constitutional compromise. . . .

. . .

. . . [Our] opinions . . . do not endorse any all-encompassing "right of privacy."

. . . Unlike marriage, procreation and contraception, abortion "involves the purposeful termination of potential life." Harris v. McRae . . . (1980). The abortion decision must therefore "be recognized as *sui generis*, different in kind from the others that the Court has protected under the rubric of personal or family privacy and autonomy." . . .

Nor do the historical traditions of the American people support the view that the right to terminate one's pregnancy is "fundamental." . . . At the time of the adoption of the Fourteenth Amendment, statutory prohibitions or restrictions on abortion were commonplace; in 1868, at least 28 of the then 37 States and 8 Territories had statutes banning or limiting abortion. . . . By the turn of the century virtually every State had a law prohibiting or restricting abortion on its books. By the middle of the present century, a liberalization trend had set in. But 21 of the restrictive abortion laws in effect in 1868 were still in effect in 1973 when *Roe* was decided, and an overwhelming majority of the States prohibited abortion unless necessary to preserve the life or health of the mother. . . . On this record, it can scarcely be said that any deeply rooted tradition of relatively unrestricted abortion in our history supported the classification of the right to abortion as "fundamental" under the Due Process Clause of the Fourteenth Amendment.

. . .

II

The joint opinion['s] . . . discussion of the principle of *stare decisis* appears to be almost entirely dicta, because [it] does not apply that principle in dealing with *Roe*. *Roe* decided that a woman had a fundamental right to an abortion. The joint opinion rejects that view. *Roe* decided that abortion regulations were to be subjected to "strict scrutiny" and could be justified only in the light of "compelling state interests." The joint opinion rejects that view. . . . *Roe* analyzed abortion regulation under a rigid trimester framework, a framework which has guided this Court's decisionmaking for 19 years. The joint opinion rejects that framework.

. . . Decisions following *Roe*, such as *Akron* . . . (1983), and *Thornburgh* . . . (1986), are frankly overruled in part under the "undue burden" standard expounded in the joint opinion.

In our view, authentic principles of *stare decisis* do not require that any portion of the reasoning in *Roe* be kept intact. . . .

. . .

. . . [O]ne might inquire how the joint opinion can view the "central holding" of *Roe* as so deeply rooted in our constitutional culture, when it so casually uproots and disposes of that same decision's trimester framework. . . .

. . .

Taking the joint opinion on its own terms, we doubt that its distinction between *Roe,* on the one hand, and *Plessy* and *Lochner,* on the other, withstands analysis. . . .

. . .

When the Court finally recognized its error in *West Coast Hotel,* it did not ... state that *Lochner* had been based on an economic view that had fallen into disfavor.... [T]he theme of the opinion is that the Court had been mistaken as a matter of constitutional law when it embraced "freedom of contract" 32 years previously.

... [T]he same arguments made before the Court in *Brown* were made in *Plessy* as well. The Court in *Brown* simply recognized, as Justice Harlan had recognized beforehand, that the Fourteenth Amendment does not permit racial segregation. The rule of *Brown* is not tied to popular opinion about the evils of segregation; it is a judgment that the Equal Protection Clause does not permit racial segregation, no matter whether the public might come to believe that it is beneficial. On that ground it stands, and on that ground alone the Court was justified in properly concluding that the *Plessy* Court had erred.

. . .

... *Roe*['s "fundamental right"-"strict scrutiny"] standard ... at least had a recognized basis in constitutional law.... The same cannot be said for the "undue burden" standard, ... which even today does not command the support of a majority of this Court....

... [T]his standard is based even more on a judge's subjective determinations than was the trimester framework....

... [T]he undue burden standard presents nothing more workable than the trimester framework which it discards today. Under the guise of the Constitution, this Court will still impart its own preferences on the States in the form of a complex abortion code.

. . .

... A woman's interest in having an abortion is a form of liberty protected by the Due Process Clause, but States may regulate abortion procedures in ways rationally related to a legitimate state interest....

III

[Applying that standard, the dissent concluded that each of the challenged provisions was rationally related to one or more legitimate state interests. Notably, the dissent concluded that "the spousal notice requirement is a rational attempt by the State to improve truthful communication between spouses and encourage collaborative decision-making, and thereby fosters marital integrity."]

IV

... [O]ur conclusion ... does not carry with it any necessary approval of these regulations. Our task is, as always, to decide only whether the challenged provisions of a law comport with the United States Constitution. If, as we believe, these do, their wisdom as a matter of public policy is for the people of Pennsylvania to decide.

■ JUSTICE SCALIA, with whom THE CHIEF JUSTICE, JUSTICE WHITE, and JUSTICE THOMAS join, concurring in the judgment in part and dissenting in part.

. . .

[T]he issue in this case [is] whether the power of a woman to abort her unborn child ... is a liberty protected by the Constitution of the United States. I am sure it is not. I reach that conclusion ... because of two simple facts: (1) the Constitution says absolutely nothing about it, and (2) the longstanding traditions of American society have permitted it to be legally proscribed....

. . .

. . . [A]pplying the rational basis test, I would uphold the Pennsylvania statute in its entirety. I must, however, respond to a few of the more outrageous arguments in today's opinion, which it is beyond human nature to leave unanswered. . . .

. . .

. . . [T]he best the Court can do to explain how it is that the word "liberty" must be thought to include the right to destroy human fetuses is to rattle off a collection of adjectives that simply decorate a value judgment and conceal a political choice. . . . But it is obvious to anyone applying "reasoned judgment" that the same adjectives can be applied to many forms of conduct that this Court . . . has held are not entitled to constitutional protection—because, like abortion, they are forms of conduct that have long been criminalized in American society. Those adjectives might be applied, for example, to homosexual sodomy, polygamy, adult incest, and suicide, all of which are equally "intimate" and "deep[ly] personal" decisions involving "personal autonomy and bodily integrity," and all of which can constitutionally be proscribed because it is our unquestionable constitutional tradition that they are proscribable. . . .

. . .

. . . The shortcomings of *Roe* did not include lack of clarity; virtually all regulation of abortion before the third trimester was invalid. But . . . the joint opinion . . . calls upon federal district judges to apply an "undue burden" standard as doubtful in application as it is unprincipled in origin. . . .

. . .

The Court's reliance upon *stare decisis* can best be described as contrived. . . . I confess never to have heard of this new, keep-what-you-want-and-throw-away-the-rest version. . . .

. . . [T]he arbitrary trimester framework, which the Court today discards, was quite as central to *Roe* as the arbitrary viability test, which the Court today retains. . . .

. . .

The Court's description of the place of *Roe* in the social history of the United States is unrecognizable. . . .

Roe's mandate for abortion-on-demand destroyed the compromises of the past, rendered compromise impossible for the future, and required the entire issue to be resolved uniformly, at the national level. . . . [T]o portray *Roe* as the statesmanlike "settlement" of a divisive issue . . . is nothing less than Orwellian. *Roe* fanned into life an issue that has inflamed our national politics in general, and has obscured with its smoke the selection of Justices to this Court in particular, ever since. And by keeping us in the abortion-umpiring business, it is the perpetuation of that disruption, rather than of any *pax Roeana*, that the Court's new majority decrees.

. . .

. . . Among the five Justices who purportedly adhere to *Roe*, at most three agree upon the principle that constitutes adherence (the joint opinion's "undue burden" standard)—and that principle is inconsistent with *Roe*. . . . To make matters worse, two of the three, in order thus to remain steadfast, had to abandon previously stated positions. . . .

. . .

[T]he notion that we would decide a case differently from the way we otherwise would have in order to show that we can stand firm against public disapproval is frightening. . . .

. . .

. . . I am as distressed as the Court is . . . about the "political pressure" directed to the Court. . . . The Court would profit . . . from giving . . . more attention to the cause of it . . . : a new mode of constitutional adjudication that relies not upon text and traditional practice to determine the law, but upon what the Court calls "reasoned judgment," which turns out to be nothing but philosophical predilection and moral intuition. . . .

. . .

Gonzales v. Carhart

550 U.S. 124, 127 S.Ct. 1610, 167 L.Ed.2d 480 (2007).

■ JUSTICE KENNEDY delivered the opinion of the Court.

[Doctors who perform second-trimester abortions, and some Planned Parenthood groups and the City and County of San Francisco, brought separate successful facial challenges in the lower federal courts to the federal Partial-Birth Abortion Ban Act of 2003, 18 U.S.C. § 1531.]

I

A

. . .

. . . Between 85 and 90 percent of the approximately 1.3 million abortions performed each year in the United States take place in the first three months of pregnancy, . . . most common[ly by] the physician vacuum[ing] out the embryonic tissue. [A]n alternative is to use medication, such as . . . RU-486. . . . The Act does not regulate these procedures.

Of the remaining abortions . . . most occur in the second trimester. The surgical procedure referred to as "dilation and evacuation" or "D & E" is the usual abortion method in this trimester. . . .

After sufficient dilation the . . . doctor . . . inserts grasping forceps through the woman's cervix and into the uterus to grab the fetus. The doctor grips a fetal part with the forceps and pulls it back through the cervix and vagina, continuing to pull even after meeting resistance from the cervix. The friction causes the fetus to tear apart. . . . A doctor may make 10 to 15 passes with the forceps to evacuate the fetus in its entirety. . . .

Some doctors, especially later in the second trimester, may kill the fetus a day or two before performing the surgical evacuation[, making] . . . its removal . . . easier. . . .

The abortion procedure that was the impetus for the numerous bans on "partial-birth abortion," including the Act, is a variation of this standard D & E [sometimes called] . . . intact D & E. The main difference between the two procedures is that in intact D & E a doctor extracts the fetus intact or largely intact with only a few passes. There are no comprehensive statistics indicating what percentage of all D & Es are performed in this manner.

. . .

In an intact D & E procedure the doctor extracts the fetus in a way conducive to pulling out its entire body, instead of ripping it apart. . . .

Intact D & E [usually involves piercing the fetal skull and evacuating its contents, however, because cervical dilation is insufficient to allow the fetus's head to pass once it becomes lodged in the cervix.]

. . .

D & E and intact D & E are not the only second-trimester abortion methods. . . .

B

. . . By the time of . . . *Stenberg* [*v. Carhart*, 530 U.S.914 (2000),] about 30 States had enacted bans designed to prohibit the [intact D & E] procedure. . . . In 2003, . . . Congress passed the Act at issue here. . . .

The Act responded to *Stenberg* in two ways. First, Congress made factual findings. Congress determined that this Court in *Stenberg* "was required to accept the very questionable findings issued by the district court judge," . . . but that Congress was "not bound to accept the same factual findings,". . . . Congress found, among other things, that "[a] moral, medical, and ethical consensus exists that the practice of performing a partial-birth abortion . . . is a gruesome and inhumane procedure that is never medically necessary and should be prohibited." . . .

Second, and more relevant here, the Act's language differs from that of the Nebraska statute struck down in *Stenberg*. . . .

. . .

II

The principles set forth in the joint opinion in Planned Parenthood of Southeastern Pa. v. Casey, 505 U.S. 833 (1992), did not find support from all those who join the instant opinion. See id., . . . (Scalia, J., joined by Thomas, J., inter alios, concurring in judgment in part and dissenting in part). Whatever one's views concerning the *Casey* joint opinion, it is evident a premise central to its conclusion— that the government has a legitimate and substantial interest in preserving and promoting fetal life—would be repudiated were the Court now to affirm the judgments of the Courts of Appeals.

. . .

. . . [W]e must determine whether the Act furthers the legitimate interest of the Government in protecting the life of the fetus that may become a child.

To implement its holding, *Casey* rejected both *Roe*'s rigid trimester framework and the interpretation of *Roe* that considered all previability regulations of abortion unwarranted. . . . On this point *Casey* overruled the holdings in two cases because they undervalued the State's interest in potential life. . . . (. . . Thornburgh v. American College of Obstetricians and Gynecologists, 476 U.S. 747 (1986) and Akron v. Akron Center for Reproductive Health, Inc., 462 U.S. 416 (1983)).

We assume the following principles for the purposes of this opinion. Before viability, a State "may not prohibit any woman from making the ultimate decision to terminate her pregnancy." . . . (plurality opinion). It also may not impose upon this right an undue burden, which exists if a regulation's "purpose or effect is to place a substantial obstacle in the path of a woman seeking an abortion before the fetus attains viability." Id., ... On the other hand, "[r]egulations which do no more than create a structural mechanism by which the State, or the parent or guardian of a minor, may express profound respect for the life of the unborn are permitted, if they are not a substantial obstacle to the woman's exercise of the right to choose." Id. . . . *Casey* . . . struck a balance . . . central to its holding. . . .

III

. . .

. . . Respondents assert that . . . the Act is void for vagueness because its scope is indefinite. In the alternative, respondents argue the Act's text proscribes all D & Es.

Because D & E is the most common second-trimester abortion method, respondents suggest the Act imposes an undue burden. In this litigation the Attorney General does not dispute that the Act would impose an undue burden if it covered standard D & E.

We conclude that the Act is not void for vagueness, does not impose an undue burden from any overbreadth, and is not invalid on its face.

[Interpreting the Act to punish only those who vaginally deliver a living fetus, past the point at which "either the fetal head or the fetal trunk past the navel is outside the body of the mother," and who thereafter perform an overt act causing the fetus' death that is separate from the act of delivery—all done "deliberately and intentionally"—the Court rejected the vagueness challenge.]

C

... The Act prohibits intact D & E; and ... it does not prohibit the D & E procedure in which the fetus is removed in parts.

. . .

... If the doctor intends to remove the fetus in parts from the outset, the doctor will not have the requisite intent to incur criminal liability. . . .

. . .

... [T]he Act departs in material ways from the statute in *Stenberg*. It [covers only] ... extraction of an entire fetus rather than removal of fetal pieces. . . .

The identification of specific anatomical landmarks to which the fetus must be partially delivered also differentiates the Act from the statute at issue in *Stenberg*. . . . [T]he fetus [must] be delivered so that it is partially "outside the body of the mother." . . . [Under] the Nebraska statute, . . . no part of the fetus had to be outside the body of the mother before a doctor could face criminal sanctions. . . .

By adding an overt-act requirement Congress sought further to meet the Court's objections to the state statute considered in *Stenberg*. . . . The Act makes the distinction ... between the overall partial-birth abortion and the distinct overt act that kills the fetus. . . . The fatal overt act must occur after delivery to an anatomical landmark, and it must be something "other than [the] completion of delivery." . . . This distinction matters because, unlike intact D & E, standard D & E does not involve a delivery followed by a fatal act.

... [I]nterpreting the Act so that it does not prohibit standard D & E is the most reasonable reading and understanding of its terms.

. . .

The ... Act's intent requirements ... preclude liability from attaching to an accidental intact D & E. . . .

The evidence also supports a legislative determination that an intact delivery is almost always a conscious choice rather than a happenstance. . . .

... Respondents have not shown that requiring doctors to intend dismemberment before delivery to an anatomical landmark will prohibit the vast majority of D & E abortions. The Act, then, cannot be held invalid on its face on these grounds.

IV

Under the principles accepted as controlling here, the Act, as we have interpreted it, would be unconstitutional "if its purpose or effect is to place a substantial obstacle in the path of a woman seeking an abortion before the fetus attains viability." *Casey*, ... (plurality opinion). The abortions affected by the Act's regulations take place both previability and postviability; so the quoted language and the undue burden analysis it relies upon are applicable. The question is whether the Act, measured by its text in this facial attack, imposes a substantial obstacle to late-term, but previability, abortions. The Act does not on its face impose a substantial obstacle, and we reject this further facial challenge to its validity.

A

. . . The Act proscribes a method of abortion in which a fetus is killed just inches before completion of the birth process. Congress stated as follows: "Implicitly approving such a brutal and inhumane procedure by choosing not to prohibit it will further coarsen society to the humanity of not only newborns, but all vulnerable and innocent human life, making it increasingly difficult to protect such life." Congressional Findings (14)(N),. . . . The Act expresses respect for the dignity of human life.

Congress was concerned, furthermore, with the effects on the medical community and on its reputation caused by the practice of partial-birth abortion. The findings in the Act explain:

"Partial-birth abortion . . . confuses the medical, legal, and ethical duties of physicians to preserve and promote life, as the physician acts directly against the physical life of a child, whom he or she had just delivered, all but the head, out of the womb, in order to end that life." Congressional Findings (14)(J). . . .

There can be no doubt the government "has an interest in protecting the integrity and ethics of the medical profession." Washington v. Glucksberg, 521 U.S. 702, 731 (1997). . . .

Casey reaffirmed these governmental objectives. The government may use its voice and its regulatory authority to show its profound respect for the life within the woman. . . . The . . . premise . . . that the State, from the inception of the pregnancy, maintains its own regulatory interest in protecting the life of the fetus that may become a child, cannot be set at naught by interpreting *Casey*'s requirement of a health exception so it becomes tantamount to allowing a doctor to choose the abortion method he or she might prefer. Where it has a rational basis to act, and it does not impose an undue burden, the State may use its regulatory power to bar certain procedures and substitute others, all in furtherance of its legitimate interests in regulating the medical profession in order to promote respect for life, including life of the unborn.

The Act's ban on abortions that involve partial delivery of a living fetus furthers the Government's objectives. . . . Congress could . . . conclude that the type of abortion proscribed by the Act requires specific regulation because it implicates additional ethical and moral concerns that justify a special prohibition. Congress determined that the abortion methods it proscribed had a "disturbing similarity to the killing of a newborn infant," Congressional Findings (14)(L), . . . and thus it was concerned with "draw[ing] a bright line that clearly distinguishes abortion and infanticide." Congressional Findings (14)(G), . . .

. . . Whether to have an abortion requires a difficult and painful moral decision. . . . While we find no reliable data to measure the phenomenon, it seems unexceptionable to conclude some women come to regret their choice to abort the infant life they once created and sustained. . . . Severe depression and loss of esteem can follow. . . .

In a decision so fraught with emotional consequence some doctors may prefer not to disclose precise details of the means that will be used, confining themselves to the required statement of risks the procedure entails. . . .

It is, however, precisely this lack of information concerning the way in which the fetus will be killed that is of legitimate concern to the State. *Casey*. . . . The State has an interest in ensuring so grave a choice is well informed. It is self-evident that a mother who comes to regret her choice to abort must struggle with grief more anguished and sorrow more profound when she learns, only after the event, what she once did not know: that she allowed a doctor to pierce the skull and vacuum the fast-developing brain of her unborn child, a child assuming the human form.

It is a reasonable inference that a necessary effect of the regulation and the knowledge it conveys will be to encourage some women to carry the infant to full term, thus reducing the absolute number of late-term abortions. The medical profession, furthermore, may find different and less shocking methods to abort the fetus in the second trimester, thereby accommodating legislative demand. The State's interest in respect for life is advanced by the dialogue that better informs the political and legal systems, the medical profession, expectant mothers, and society as a whole of the consequences that follow from a decision to elect a late-term abortion.

. . . It was reasonable for Congress to think that partial-birth abortion, more than standard D & E, "undermines the public's perception of the appropriate role of a physician during the delivery process, and perverts a process during which life is brought into the world." Congressional Findings (14)(K). . . . In sum, we reject the contention that the congressional purpose of the Act was "to place a substantial obstacle in the path of a woman seeking an abortion." . . .

B

. . . The prohibition in the Act would be unconstitutional, under precedents we here assume to be controlling, if it "subject[ed] [women] to significant health risks." . . . In *Ayotte* the parties agreed a health exception to the challenged parental-involvement statute was necessary "to avert serious and often irreversible damage to [a pregnant minor's] health." . . . Here, by contrast, whether the Act creates significant health risks for women has been a contested factual question. The evidence presented in the trial courts and before Congress demonstrates both sides have medical support for their position.

. . .

. . . The medical uncertainty over whether the Act's prohibition creates significant health risks provides a sufficient basis to conclude in this facial attack that the Act does not impose an undue burden.

. . . Alternatives are available to the prohibited procedure. [T]he Act does not proscribe D & E. . . . If the intact D & E procedure is truly necessary in some circumstances, it appears likely an injection that kills the fetus is an alternative . . . that allows the doctor to perform the procedure.

The instant cases, then, are different from Planned Parenthood of Central Mo. v. Danforth, 428 U.S. 52, 77–79 (1976), in which the Court invalidated a ban on saline amniocentesis, the then-dominant second-trimester abortion method. . . . Here the Act allows, among other means, a commonly used and generally accepted method, so it does not construct a substantial obstacle to the abortion right.

In reaching the conclusion the Act does not require a health exception we reject certain arguments made by the parties on both sides of these cases. [T]he Attorney General urges us to uphold the Act on the basis of the congressional findings alone. . . . Although we review congressional factfinding under a deferential standard, we do not in the circumstances here place dispositive weight on Congress' findings. The Court retains an independent constitutional duty to review factual findings where constitutional rights are at stake. . . .

As respondents have noted, and the District Courts recognized, some recitations in the Act are factually incorrect. . . . Congress determined no medical schools provide instruction on the prohibited procedure.... The testimony in the District Courts, however, demonstrated intact D & E is taught at medical schools.... Congress also found there existed a medical consensus that the prohibited procedure is never medically necessary.... The evidence presented in the District Courts contradicts that conclusion.... Uncritical deference to Congress' factual findings in these cases is inappropriate.

On the other hand, relying on ... *Stenberg*, respondents contend that an abortion regulation must contain a health exception "if 'substantial medical authority supports the proposition that banning a particular procedure could endanger women's health.'"...

A zero tolerance policy would strike down legitimate abortion regulations, like the present one, if some part of the medical community were disinclined to follow the proscription. This is too exacting a standard.... Considerations of marginal safety, including the balance of risks, are within the legislative competence when the regulation is rational and in pursuit of legitimate ends.... The Act is not invalid on its face where there is uncertainty over whether the barred procedure is ever necessary to preserve a woman's health, given the availability of other abortion procedures that are considered to be safe alternatives.

V

[An] as-applied challenge ... is the proper manner to protect the health of the woman if it can be shown that in discrete and well-defined instances a particular condition has or is likely to occur in which the procedure prohibited by the Act must be used. In an as-applied challenge the nature of the medical risk can be better quantified and balanced than in a facial attack.

. . .

... [R]espondents have not demonstrated that the Act would be unconstitutional in a large fraction of relevant cases. *Casey*,....

. . .

■ JUSTICE THOMAS, with whom JUSTICE SCALIA joins, concurring.

I join the Court's opinion because it accurately applies current jurisprudence, including [*Casey*]. I write separately to reiterate my view that the Court's abortion jurisprudence, including *Casey* and Roe v. Wade, ... has no basis in the Constitution.... I also note that whether the Act constitutes a permissible exercise of Congress' power under the Commerce Clause is not before the Court....

■ JUSTICE GINSBURG, with whom JUSTICE STEVENS, JUSTICE SOUTER, and JUSTICE BREYER join, dissenting.

. . .

Today's decision is alarming. It refuses to take *Casey* and *Stenberg* seriously. It tolerates, indeed applauds, federal intervention to ban nationwide a procedure found necessary and proper in certain cases by the American College of Obstetricians and Gynecologists (ACOG). It blurs the line, firmly drawn in *Casey*, between previability and postviability abortions. And, for the first time since *Roe*, the Court blesses a prohibition with no exception safeguarding a woman's health.

. . .

I

A

. . .

. . . [T]he Court has consistently required that laws regulating abortion, at any stage of pregnancy and in all cases, safeguard a woman's health. . . .

. . .

In *Stenberg*, we expressly held that a statute banning intact D & E was unconstitutional in part because it lacked a health exception. . . . We noted that there existed a "division of medical opinion" about the relative safety of intact D & E, . . . but we made clear that as long as "substantial medical authority supports the proposition that banning a particular abortion procedure could endanger women's health," a health exception is required. . . .

B

. . . Congress passed the Partial-Birth Abortion Ban Act . . . without an exception for women's health. . . .[4] . . .

Many of the Act's recitations are incorrect. . . .

More important, Congress claimed there was a medical consensus that the banned procedure is never necessary. . . . But the evidence "very clearly demonstrate[d] the opposite." . . .

Similarly, Congress found that "[t]here is no credible medical evidence that partial-birth abortions are safe or are safer than other abortion procedures." Congressional Findings (14)(B). . . . But the congressional record includes letters from numerous individual physicians stating that pregnant women's health would be jeopardized under the Act, as well as statements from nine professional associations, including ACOG, the American Public Health Association, and the California Medical Association, attesting that intact D & E carries meaningful safety advantages over other methods. . . .

C

. . .

According to the expert testimony plaintiffs introduced, the safety advantages of intact D & E are marked for women with certain medical conditions, . . . for women with certain pregnancy-related conditions, . . . and for women carrying fetuses with certain abnormalities. . . .

Intact D & E, plaintiffs' experts explained, provides safety benefits over D & E by dismemberment for several reasons[, including] minimiz[ing] the number of times a physician must insert instruments through the cervix and into the uterus[;] . . . decreas[ing] the likelihood that fetal tissue will be retained in the uterus, a condition that can cause infection, hemorrhage, and infertility[;] diminish[ing] the chances of exposing the patient's tissues to sharp bony fragments sometimes resulting from dismemberment of the fetus[; and, because it] takes less operating time than D & E by dismemberment, [it] may reduce bleeding, the risk of infection, and complications relating to anesthesia. . . .

. . . [E]ach of the District Courts . . . rejected Congress' findings as unreasonable and not supported by the evidence. . . .

. . .

---

[4] The Act's sponsors left no doubt that their intention was to nullify our ruling in *Stenberg*. . . .

The Court . . . insists that, because some witnesses disagreed with the ACOG and other experts' assessment of risk, the Act can stand. [T]he Court brushes under the rug the District Courts' well-supported findings that the physicians who testified that intact D & E is never necessary to preserve the health of a woman had slim authority for their opinions. They had no training for, or personal experience with, the intact D & E procedure, and many performed abortions only on rare occasions. . . . Even indulging the assumption that the Government witnesses were equally qualified to evaluate the relative risks of abortion procedures, their testimony could not erase the "significant medical authority support[ing] the proposition that in some circumstances, [intact D & E] would be the safest procedure." *Stenberg*,. . . .

II

A

. . . The law saves not a single fetus from destruction, for it targets only a *method* of performing abortion. . . . And surely the statute was not designed to protect the lives or health of pregnant women. . . .

. . .

Delivery of an intact, albeit nonviable, fetus warrants special condemnation, the Court maintains, because a fetus that is not dismembered resembles an infant. But so, too, does a fetus delivered intact after it is terminated by injection a day or two before the surgical evacuation, or a fetus delivered through medical induction or cesarean. Yet, the availability of those procedures—along with D & E by dismemberment—the Court says, saves the ban on intact D & E from a declaration of unconstitutionality. Never mind that the procedures deemed acceptable might put a woman's health at greater risk. . . .

Ultimately, the Court admits that "moral concerns" are at work, concerns that could yield prohibitions on any abortion. . . .

Revealing in this regard, the Court invokes an antiabortion shibboleth for which it concededly has no reliable evidence: Women who have abortions come to regret their choices, and consequently suffer from "[s]evere depression and loss of esteem."[7] . . . The solution the Court approves . . . is not to require doctors to inform women, accurately and adequately, of the different procedures and their attendant risks. . . . Instead, the Court deprives women of the right to make an autonomous choice, even at the expense of their safety.

This way of thinking reflects ancient notions about women's place in the family and under the Constitution—ideas that have long since been discredited. . . .

. . .

B

. . .

. . . Instead of drawing the line at viability, the Court refers to Congress' purpose to differentiate "abortion and infanticide" based not on whether a fetus can survive outside the womb, but on where a fetus is anatomically located when a particular medical procedure is performed. . . .

One wonders how long a line that saves no fetus from destruction will hold in face of the Court's "moral concerns." . . . The Court's hostility to the right *Roe* and *Casey*

---

[7]   The Court is surely correct that, for most women, abortion is a painfully difficult decision. But "neither the weight of the scientific evidence to date nor the observable reality of 33 years of legal abortion in the United States comports with the idea that having an abortion is any more dangerous to a woman's long-term mental health than delivering and parenting a child that she did not intend to have. . . ." [Citing studies.]

secured is not concealed. . . . [M]ost troubling, *Casey*'s principles, confirming the continuing vitality of "the essential holding of *Roe*," are merely "assume[d]" for the moment, rather than "retained" or "reaffirmed," *Casey*. . . .

III

A

. . .

. . . [T]he absence of a health exception burdens all women for whom it is relevant—women who, in the judgment of their doctors, require an intact D & E because other procedures would place their health at risk. . . . It makes no sense to conclude that this facial challenge fails because respondents have not shown that a health exception is necessary for a large fraction of second-trimester abortions, including those for which a health exception is unnecessary: The very purpose of a health *exception* is to protect women in *exceptional* cases.

B

If there is anything at all redemptive [about] today's opinion, it is that the Court is not willing to foreclose entirely a constitutional challenge to the Act. . . .

. . .

. . . But it should not escape notice that the record already includes hundreds and hundreds of pages of testimony identifying "discrete and well-defined instances" in which recourse to an intact D & E would better protect the health of women with particular conditions. Record evidence also documents that medical exigencies, unpredictable in advance, may indicate to a well-trained doctor that intact D & E is the safest procedure. . . .

The Court's allowance only of an "as-applied challenge in a discrete case" jeopardizes women's health and places doctors in an untenable position. Even if courts were able to carve-out exceptions through piecemeal litigation for "discrete and well-defined instances," women whose circumstances have not been anticipated by prior litigation could well be left unprotected. In treating those women, physicians would risk criminal prosecution, conviction, and imprisonment if they exercise their best judgment as to the safest medical procedure for their patients. The Court is thus gravely mistaken to conclude that narrow as-applied challenges are "the proper manner to protect the health of the woman."

IV

. . .

In sum, the notion that the Partial-Birth Abortion Ban Act furthers any legitimate governmental interest is, quite simply, irrational. . . . In candor, the Act, and the Court's defense of it, cannot be understood as anything other than an effort to chip away at a right declared again and again by this Court—and with increasing comprehension of its centrality to women's lives. . . .

. . .

Whole Woman's Health v. Hellerstedt

579 U.S. ___, 136 S.Ct. 2292, 195 L.Ed.2d 665 (2016).

■ JUSTICE BREYER delivered the opinion of the Court.

In Planned Parenthood of Southeastern Pa. v. Casey, 505 U. S. 833, 878 (1992), a plurality of the Court concluded that there "exists" an "undue burden" on a woman's right to decide to have an abortion, and consequently a provision of law is constitutionally invalid, if the *"purpose or effect"* of the provision *"is to place a substantial obstacle* in the path of a woman seeking an abortion before the fetus attains viability." (Emphasis added.) The plurality added that "[u]nnecessary health regulations that have the purpose or effect of presenting a substantial obstacle to a woman seeking an abortion impose an undue burden on the right." *Ibid.*

We must here decide whether two provisions of Texas' House Bill 2 violate the Federal Constitution as interpreted in *Casey.* The first provision, which we shall call the *"admitting-privileges requirement,"* says that

"[a] physician performing or inducing an abortion . . . must, on the date the abortion is performed or induced, have active admitting privileges at a hospital that . . . is located not further than 30 miles from the location at which the abortion is performed or induced." Tex. Health & Safety Code Ann. § 171.0031(a) (West Cum. Supp. 2015).

This provision amended Texas law that had previously required an abortion facility to maintain a written protocol "for managing medical emergencies and the transfer of patients requiring further emergency care to a hospital." 38 Tex. Reg. 6546 (2013).

The second provision, which we shall call the *"surgical center requirement,"* says that

"the minimum standards for an abortion facility must be equivalent to the minimum standards adopted under [the Texas Health and Safety Code section] for ambulatory surgical centers." Tex. Health & Safety Code Ann. § 245.010(a).

We conclude that neither of these provisions offers medical benefits sufficient to justify the burdens upon access that each imposes. Each places a substantial obstacle in the path of women seeking a previability abortion, each constitutes an undue burden on abortion access, *Casey, supra,* at 878 (plurality opinion), and each violates the Federal Constitution. Amdt. 14, § 1.

I

[In a second suit, petitioners, a group of abortion providers, "sought an injunction preventing enforcement of the admitting-privileges provision as applied to physicians at two abortion facilities, one operated by Whole Woman's Health in McAllen and the other operated by Nova Health Systems in El Paso. They also sought an injunction prohibiting enforcement of the surgical-center provision anywhere in Texas."

[After trial, the District Court made extensive findings concluding that, before H.B. 2 was enacted, there were more than 40 licensed abortion facilities in Texas; that almost half of those disappeared in the period leading up to and in the wake of enforcement of the admitting-privileges requirement; that if the surgical-center provision were allowed to take effect, the number would be reduced to 7 or 8, which would not be able to meet the demand of the entire state; that the geographical distribution of the remaining facilities would leave 2 million women of reproductive age more than 50 miles from an abortion provider, 1.3 million more than 100 miles away, 900,000 more than 150 miles distant, and 750,000 more than 200 miles from an abortion provider. Other findings included that the "two requirements erect a particularly high barrier for poor, rural, or disadvantaged women"; that before the Act "abortion in Texas was extremely safe with particularly low rates of serious complications and virtually no deaths occurring on account of the procedure"; that abortion was shown to be "much safer . . . than many common medical procedures not subject to such intense regulation and scrutiny[,]" such as colonoscopies, vasectomies, endometrial biopsies, and plastic surgery; that "risks are not appreciably lowered for patients who undergo abortions at ambulatory surgical centers as compared to nonsurgical-center facilities"; and that the "cost of coming into compliance" with the surgical-center requirement "for existing clinics is significant," "undisputedly approach[ing] 1 million dollars," and "most likely exceed[ing] 1.5 million dollars," with "[s]ome . . . clinics" unable to "comply due to physical size limitations of their sites."]

On the basis of these and other related findings, the District Court determined that the surgical-center requirement "imposes an undue burden on the right of women throughout Texas to seek a previability abortion," and that the "admitting-privileges requirement, . . . in conjunction with the ambulatory-surgical-center requirement, imposes an undue burden on the right of women in the Rio Grande Valley, El Paso, and West Texas to seek a previability abortion.". . . [T]he court enjoined the enforcement of the two provisions. . . .

[The Fifth Circuit reversed, based partially on the conclusion that the two requirements were rationally related to the legitimate state interest in protecting the health and welfare of women seeking abortions, and the conclusion that the plaintiffs had failed to show that either of the provisions "imposes an undue burden on a large fraction of women." The Court of Appeals also concluded that "[t]he District Court erred in finding that, if the surgical-center requirement takes effect, there will be too few abortion providers in Texas to meet the demand." In particular, the " 'record lacks any actual evidence regarding the current or future capacity of the eight clinics' "; and there is no "evidence in the record that" the providers that currently meet the surgical-center requirement "are operating at full capacity or that they cannot increase capacity."]

. . . The Court of Appeals upheld in part the District Court's more specific holding that the requirements are unconstitutional as applied to the McAllen facility and . . . a doctor at that facility . . . , but it reversed the District Court's holding that the surgical-center requirement is unconstitutional as applied to the facility in El Paso[, suggesting] that women in El Paso wishing to have an abortion could use abortion providers in nearby New Mexico.

II

[The Court first held that because H.B. 2's effect on women seeking abortions had changed dramatically since petitioners' first challenge, "res judicata neither bars petitioners' challenges to the admitting-privileges requirement nor prevents us from awarding facial relief" Furthermore, the Court held that claim preclusion principles did not prevent the challenge to the surgical-center provision either, as it was a "separate, distinct provision[ ] of H.B. 2" from the admitting-privileges provision.]

III

Undue Burden—Legal Standard

. . .

The Court of Appeals' articulation of the relevant standard is incorrect. [It] may be read to imply that a district court should not consider the existence or nonexistence of medical benefits when considering whether a regulation of abortion constitutes an undue burden. The rule announced in *Casey*, however, requires that courts consider the burdens a law imposes on abortion access together with the benefits those laws confer. . . . And [it] is wrong to equate the judicial review applicable to the regulation of a constitutionally protected personal liberty with the less strict review applicable where, for example, economic legislation is at issue. . . . *Casey* . . . asks courts to consider whether any burden imposed on abortion access is "undue."

The statement that legislatures, and not courts, must resolve questions of medical uncertainty is also inconsistent with this Court's case law. Instead, the Court, when determining the constitutionality of laws regulating abortion procedures, has placed considerable weight upon evidence and argument presented in judicial proceedings. . . .

Unlike in Gonzales [v. Carhart, 550 U. S. 124 (2007)], the relevant statute here does not set forth any legislative findings. . . . For a district court to give significant weight to evidence in the judicial record in these circumstances is consistent with this Court's case law. As we shall describe, the District Court did so here. It did not simply substitute its own judgment for that of the legislature. It considered the evidence in the record—including expert evidence, presented in stipulations, depositions, and testimony. It then weighed the asserted benefits against the burdens. We hold that, in so doing, the District Court applied the correct legal standard.

IV

Undue Burden—Admitting-Privileges Requirement

. . . We conclude that there is adequate legal and factual support for the District Court's conclusion [that the admitting-privileges requirement imposed an "undue burden" on a woman's right to have an abortion.]

The purpose of the admitting-privileges requirement is to help ensure that women have easy access to a hospital should complications arise during an abortion procedure. . . . But the District Court found that it brought about no such health-related benefit. . . .

The evidence upon which the court based this conclusion included [peer-reviewed studies and expert testimony]. . . .

We have found nothing in Texas' record evidence that shows that, compared to prior law (which required a "working arrangement" with a doctor with admitting privileges), the new law advanced Texas' legitimate interest in protecting women's health.

We add that, when directly asked at oral argument whether Texas knew of a single instance in which the new requirement would have helped even one woman obtain better treatment, Texas admitted that there was no evidence in the record of such a case. See Tr. of Oral Arg. 47. . . .

At the same time, the record evidence indicates that the admitting-privileges requirement places a "substantial obstacle in the path of a woman's choice." *Casey*, 505 U. S., at 877 (plurality opinion). The District Court found, as of the time the admitting-privileges requirement began to be enforced, the number of facilities providing abortions dropped in half, from about 40 to about 20. . . . Eight abortion clinics closed in the months leading up to the requirement's effective date. . . . Eleven more closed on the day the admitting-privileges requirement took effect. . . .

Other evidence helps to explain why the new requirement led to the closure of clinics. We read that other evidence in light of a brief filed in this Court by the Society of Hospital Medicine[, which] describes the undisputed general fact that "hospitals often condition admitting privileges on reaching a certain number of admissions per year.". . . In a word, doctors would be unable to maintain admitting privileges or obtain those privileges for the future, because the fact that abortions are so safe meant that providers were unlikely to have any patients to admit.

. . . [And t]he admitting-privileges requirement does not serve any relevant credentialing function.

In our view, the record contains sufficient evidence that the admitting-privileges requirement led to the closure of half of Texas' clinics, or thereabouts. Those closures meant fewer doctors, longer waiting times, and increased crowding. Record evidence also supports the finding that after the admitting-privileges provision went into effect, the "number of women of reproductive age living in a county . . . more than 150 miles from a provider increased from approximately 86,000 to 400,000 . . . and the number of women living in a county more than 200 miles from a provider from approximately 10,000 to 290,000.". . . We recognize that increased driving distances do not always constitute an "undue burden.". . . But here, those increases are but one additional burden, which, when taken together with others that the closings brought about, and when viewed in light of the virtual absence of any health benefit, lead us to conclude that the record adequately supports the District Court's "undue burden" conclusion. . . .

The dissent's only argument why these clinic closures, as well as the ones discussed in Part V, *infra*, may not have imposed an undue burden is this: Although "H. B. 2 caused the closure of *some* clinics" (emphasis added), other clinics may have closed for other reasons (so we should not "actually count" the burdens resulting from those closures against H. B. 2). But petitioners satisfied their burden to present evidence of causation by presenting direct testimony as well as plausible inferences to be drawn from the timing of the clinic closures. . . . The dissent's speculation that perhaps other evidence, not presented at trial or credited by the District Court, might have shown that some clinics closed for unrelated reasons does not provide sufficient ground to disturb the District Court's factual finding on that issue.

. . .

V

Undue Burden—Surgical-Center Requirement

[Justice Breyer first reviewed the "host of health and safety requirements" Texas had in place before the surgical-center requirement, as well as the many additional standards that would have to be met for abortion providers to comply with ambulatory surgical center requirements.]

There is considerable evidence in the record supporting the District Court's findings indicating that the statutory provision requiring all abortion facilities to meet all surgical-center standards does not benefit patients and is not necessary. The District Court found that "risks are not appreciably lowered for patients who undergo abortions at ambulatory surgical centers as compared to nonsurgical-center facilities.". . . The court added that women "will not obtain better care or experience more frequent positive outcomes at an ambulatory surgical center as compared to a previously licensed facility.". . . And these findings are well supported.

The record makes clear that the surgical-center requirement provides no benefit when complications arise in the context of an abortion produced through medication. That is because, in such a case, complications would almost always arise only after the patient has left the facility. . . . The record also contains evidence indicating that abortions taking place in an abortion facility are safe—indeed, safer than numerous procedures that take place outside hospitals and to which Texas does not apply its surgical-center requirements. . . . Nationwide, childbirth is 14 times more likely than abortion to result in death, . . . but Texas law allows a midwife to oversee childbirth in the patient's own home. Colonoscopy, a procedure that typically takes place outside a hospital (or surgical center) setting, has a mortality rate 10 times higher than an abortion. . . . And Texas partly or wholly grandfathers (or waives in whole or in part the surgical-center requirement for) about two-thirds of the facilities to which the surgical-center standards apply. But it neither grandfathers nor provides waivers for any of the facilities that perform abortions. . . . These facts indicate that the surgical-center provision imposes "a requirement that simply is not based on differences" between abortion and other surgical procedures "that are reasonably related to" preserving women's health, the asserted "purpos[e] of the Act in which it is found.". . .

Moreover, many surgical-center requirements are inappropriate as applied to surgical abortions. . . . Further, since the few instances in which serious complications do arise following an abortion almost always require hospitalization, not treatment at a surgical center, . . . surgical-center standards will not help in those instances either.

The upshot is that this record evidence, along with the absence of any evidence to the contrary, provides ample support for the District Court's conclusion that "[m]any of the building standards mandated by the act and its implementing rules have such a tangential relationship to patient safety in the context of abortion as to be nearly arbitrary.". . . That conclusion, along with the supporting evidence, provides sufficient support for the more general conclusion that the surgical-center requirement "will not [provide] better care or . . . more frequent positive outcomes.". . . The record evidence thus supports the ultimate legal conclusion that the surgical-center requirement is not necessary.

At the same time, the record provides adequate evidentiary support for the District Court's conclusion that the surgical-center requirement places a substantial obstacle in the path of women seeking an abortion. . . .

. . .

For one thing, the record contains charts and oral testimony . . . that, as a result of the surgical-center requirement, the number of abortions that the clinics would have to provide would rise from " '14,000 abortions annually' " to " '60,000 to 70,000' "—an increase by a factor of about five. . . .

For another thing, common sense suggests that, more often than not, a physical facility that satisfies a certain physical demand will not be able to meet five times that demand without expanding or otherwise incurring significant costs. . . . The dissent takes issue with this general, intuitive point by arguing that many places operate below capacity and that in any event, facilities could simply hire additional providers. We disagree that, according to common sense, medical facilities, well known for their wait times, operate below capacity as a general matter. And the fact that so many facilities were forced to close by the admitting-privileges requirement means that hiring more physicians would not be quite as simple as the dissent suggests. Courts are free to base their findings on commonsense inferences drawn from the evidence. And that is what the District Court did here.

. . .

Texas suggests that the seven or eight remaining clinics could expand sufficiently to provide abortions for the 60,000 to 72,000 Texas women who sought them each year. Because petitioners had satisfied their burden, the obligation was on Texas, if it could, to present evidence rebutting that issue to the District Court. Texas admitted that it presented no such evidence. . . .

. . .

More fundamentally, in the face of no threat to women's health, Texas seeks to force women to travel long distances to get abortions in crammed-to-capacity superfacilities. Patients seeking these services are less likely to get the kind of individualized attention, serious conversation, and emotional support that doctors at less taxed facilities may have offered. Healthcare facilities and medical professionals are not fungible commodities. Surgical centers attempting to accommodate sudden, vastly increased demand, . . . may find that quality of care declines. Another commonsense inference that the District Court made is that these effects would be harmful to, not supportive of, women's health.

Finally, the District Court found that the costs that a currently licensed abortion facility would have to incur to meet the surgical-center requirements were considerable, ranging from $1 million per facility (for facilities with adequate space) to $3 million per facility (where additional land must be purchased). . . . This evidence supports the conclusion that more surgical centers will not soon fill the gap when licensed facilities are forced to close.

We agree with the District Court that the surgical-center requirement, like the admitting-privileges requirement, provides few, if any, health benefits for women, poses a substantial obstacle to women seeking abortions, and constitutes an "undue burden" on their constitutional right to do so.

VI

We consider three additional arguments that Texas makes and deem none persuasive.

First, Texas argues that facial invalidation of both challenged provisions is precluded by H. B. 2's severability clause. . . . But the challenged provisions of H. B. 2 close most of the abortion facilities in Texas and place added stress on those facilities able to remain open. They vastly increase the obstacles confronting women seeking abortions in Texas without providing any benefit to women's health capable of withstanding any meaningful scrutiny. . . .

. . .

Texas similarly argues that . . . we should invalidate (as applied to abortion clinics) only those specific surgical-center regulations that unduly burden the provision of abortions, while leaving in place other surgical-center regulations. . . . As we have explained, Texas' attempt to broadly draft a requirement to sever "applications" does not require us to proceed in piecemeal fashion when we have found the statutory provisions at issue facially unconstitutional.

Nor is that approach to the regulations even required by H. B. 2 itself. The statute was meant to require abortion facilities to meet the integrated surgical-center standards—not some subset thereof. . . .

Second, Texas claims that the provisions at issue here do not impose a substantial obstacle because the women affected by those laws are not a "large fraction" of Texan women "of reproductive age," which Texas reads *Casey* to have required. . . . But *Casey* used the language "large fraction" to refer to "a large fraction of cases in which [the provision at issue] is *relevant*," a class narrower than "all women," "pregnant women," or even "the class of *women seeking abortions* identified by the State." 505 U. S., at 894–895 (opinion of the Court) (emphasis added). Here, as in *Casey*, the relevant denominator is "those [women] for whom [the provision] is an actual rather than an irrelevant restriction."

Third, Texas looks for support to Simopoulos v. Virginia, 462 U. S. 506 (1983), a case in which this Court upheld a surgical-center requirement as applied to second-trimester abortions. This case, however, . . . involves restrictions applicable to all abortions, not simply to those that take place during the second trimester. Most abortions in Texas occur in the first trimester, not the second. . . . More importantly, in *Casey* we discarded the trimester framework, and we now use "viability" as the relevant point at which a State may begin limiting women's access to abortion for reasons unrelated to maternal health. . . . Because the second trimester includes time that is both previability and postviability, *Simopoulos* cannot provide clear guidance. Further, the Court in *Simopoulos* found that the petitioner in that case, unlike petitioners here, had waived any argument that the regulation did not significantly help protect women's health. . . .

* * *

For these reasons the judgment of the Court of Appeals is reversed, and the case is remanded for further proceedings consistent with this opinion.

■ JUSTICE GINSBURG, concurring.

. . . H. B. 2 inevitably will reduce the number of clinics and doctors allowed to provide abortion services. Texas argues that H. B. 2's restrictions are constitutional because they protect the health of women who experience complications from abortions. In truth, "complications from an abortion are both rare and rarely dangerous.". . . See Brief for American College of Obstetricians and Gynecologists et al. as *Amici Curiae* 6–10 (collecting studies and concluding "[a]bortion is one of the safest medical procedures performed in the United States"); Brief for Social Science Researchers as *Amici Curiae* 5–9 (compiling studies that show "[c]omplication rates from abortion are very low"). Many medical procedures, including childbirth, are far more dangerous to patients, yet are not subject to ambulatory-surgical-center or hospital admitting-privileges requirements. . . . Given those realities, it is beyond rational belief that H. B. 2 could genuinely protect the health of women, and certain that the law "would simply make it more difficult for them to obtain abortions.". . . When a State severely limits access to safe and legal procedures, women in desperate circumstances may resort to unlicensed rogue practitioners, *faute de mieux*, at great risk to their health and safety. . . . So long as this Court adheres to Roe v. Wade, 410 U. S. 113 (1973), and Planned Parenthood of Southeastern Pa. v. Casey, 505 U. S. 833 (1992), Targeted Regulation of Abortion Providers laws like H. B. 2 that "do little or nothing for health, but rather strew impediments to abortion,". . . cannot survive judicial inspection.

■ JUSTICE THOMAS, dissenting.

. . .

I remain fundamentally opposed to the Court's abortion jurisprudence. . . . Even taking *Casey* as the baseline, however, the majority radically rewrites the undue-burden test in three ways. First, today's decision requires courts to "consider the burdens a law imposes on abortion access together with the benefits those laws confer." Second, today's opinion tells the courts that, when the law's justifications are medically uncertain, they need not defer to the legislature, and must instead assess medical justifications for abortion restrictions by scrutinizing the record themselves. Finally, even if a law imposes no "substantial obstacle" to women's access to abortions, the law now must have more than a "reasonabl[e] relat[ion] to . . . a legitimate state interest." These precepts are nowhere to be found in *Casey* or its successors, and transform the undue-burden test to something much more akin to strict scrutiny.

. . .

. . . [T]he label the Court affixes to its level of scrutiny in assessing whether the government can restrict a given right—be it "rational basis," intermediate, strict, or something else—is increasingly a meaningless formalism. As the Court applies whatever standard it likes to any given case, nothing but empty words separates our constitutional decisions from judicial fiat.

. . .

. . . The Court should abandon the pretense that anything other than policy preferences underlies its balancing of constitutional rights and interests in any given case.

. . .

■ JUSTICE ALITO, with whom THE CHIEF JUSTICE and JUSTICE THOMAS join, dissenting.

. . .

. . . The Court . . . , determined to strike down two provisions of a new Texas abortion statute in all of their applications, . . . simply disregards basic rules that apply in all other cases.

. . .

In this abortion case, . . . [t]he Court awards a victory to petitioners on the very claim that they unsuccessfully pressed in the earlier case. . . .

. . . [Also, despite] what must surely be the most emphatic severability clause ever written . . . , the Court holds that no part of the challenged provisions and no application of any part of them can be saved. . . .

The Court's patent refusal to apply well-established law in a neutral way is indefensible and will undermine public confidence in the Court as a fair and neutral arbiter.

[Justice Alito's lengthy analysis of the res judicata issue concluded that "petitioners' facial attack on the ASC requirements, like their facial attack on the admitting privileges rule, is precluded."]

III

Even if res judicata did not bar either facial claim, a sweeping, statewide injunction against the enforcement of the admitting privileges and ASC requirements would still be unjustified. . . .

[W]hat matters for present purposes is not the effect of the H. B. 2 provisions on petitioners but the effect on their patients.... [I]n order to obtain . . . facial invalidation of those provisions[,] they must show, at a minimum, that these provisions have an unconstitutional impact on at least a "large fraction" of Texas women of reproductive age. . . . Such a situation could result if the clinics able to comply with the new requirements either lacked the requisite overall capacity or were located too far away to serve a "large fraction" of the women in question.

Petitioners did not make that showing. Instead of offering direct evidence, they relied on two crude inferences. First, they pointed to the number of abortion clinics that closed after the enactment of H. B. 2, and asked that it be inferred that all these closures resulted from the two challenged provisions. . . . They made little effort to show why particular clinics closed. Second, they pointed to the number of abortions performed annually at ASCs before H. B. 2 took effect and, because this figure is well below the total number of abortions performed each year in the State, they asked that it be inferred that ASC-compliant clinics could not meet the demands of women in the State. . . . Petitioners failed to provide any evidence of the actual capacity of the facilities that would be available to perform abortions in compliance with the new law—even though they provided this type of evidence in their first case to the District Court at trial and then to this Court in their application for interim injunctive relief.

A

. . .

While there can be no doubt that H. B. 2 caused some clinics to cease operation, the absence of proof regarding the reasons for particular closures is a problem because some clinics have or may have closed for at least four reasons other than the two H. B. 2 requirements at issue here. These are [(1) the provision of H. B. 2 that regulates medication abortion, which was previously upheld and not relitigated in this case, which was followed by a decrease of nearly 7,000 such abortions in the first six months after it took effect; (2) a Texas law preventing family planning grants to providers that perform abortions, which may have caused some clinics to close for lack of funding; (3)

a nationwide decline in abortion demand; and (4) physician retirements or other localized factors.]

At least nine Texas clinics may have ceased performing abortions (or reduced capacity) for one or more of the reasons having nothing to do with the provisions challenged here. . . .

Neither petitioners nor the District Court properly addressed these complexities in assessing causation—and for no good reason. . . .

Precise findings are important because the key issue here is not the number or percentage of clinics affected, but the effect of the closures on women seeking abortions, *i.e.*, on the capacity and geographic distribution of clinics used by those women. To the extent that clinics closed (or experienced a reduction in capacity) for any reason unrelated to the challenged provisions of H. B. 2, the corresponding burden on abortion access may not be factored into the access analysis. . . . Petitioners—who, as plaintiffs, bore the burden of proof—cannot simply point to temporal correlation and call it causation.

B

Even if the District Court had properly filtered out immaterial closures, its analysis would have been incomplete for a second reason. Petitioners offered scant evidence on the capacity of the clinics that are able to comply with the admitting privileges and ASC requirements, or on those clinics' geographic distribution. Reviewing the evidence in the record, it is far from clear that there has been a material impact on access to abortion.

. . .

. . . First, it is not unassailable "common sense" to hold that current utilization equals capacity. . . . Faced with increased demand, ASCs could potentially increase the number of abortions performed without prohibitively expensive changes. Among other things, they might hire more physicians who perform abortions, utilize their facilities more intensively or efficiently, or shift the mix of services provided. Second, what matters for present purposes is not the capacity of just those ASCs that performed abortions prior to the enactment of H. B. 2 but the capacity of those that would be available to perform abortions after the statute took effect. And since the enactment of H. B. 2, the number of ASCs performing abortions has increased by 50%—from six in 2012 to nine today.

The most serious problem with the Court's reasoning is that its conclusion is belied by petitioners' own submissions to this Court. . . .

. . .

. . . The important point is that petitioners put on evidence of actual clinic capacity in their earlier case, and there is no apparent reason why they could not have done the same here. Indeed, the Court asserts that, after the admitting privileges requirement took effect, clinics "were not able to accommodate increased demand," but petitioners' own evidence suggested that the requirement had *no* effect on capacity. . . . On this point, like the question of the reason for clinic closures, petitioners did not discharge their burden, and the District Court did not engage in the type of analysis that should have been conducted before enjoining an important state law.

So much for capacity. The other potential obstacle to abortion access is the distribution of facilities throughout the State. This might occur if the two challenged H. B. 2 requirements, by causing the closure of clinics in some rural areas, led to a situation in which a "large fraction" of women of reproductive age live too far away from any open clinic. Based on the Court's holding in . . . *Casey*, . . . it appears that the need to travel up to 150 miles is not an undue burden, and the evidence in this case shows that if the only clinics in the State were those that would have remained open if the judgment of the Fifth Circuit had not been enjoined, roughly 95% of the women of reproductive age in the State would live within 150 miles of an open facility (or lived outside that range before H. B. 2). Because the record does not show why particular facilities closed, the real figure may be even higher than 95%.

We should decline to hold that these statistics justify the facial invalidation of the H. B. 2 requirements. The possibility that the admitting privileges requirement *might* have caused a closure in Lubbock is no reason to issue a facial injunction exempting Houston clinics from that requirement. I do not dismiss the situation of those women who would no longer live within 150 miles of a clinic as a result of H. B. 2. But under current doctrine such localized problems can be addressed by narrow as-applied challenges.

IV

Even if the Court were right to hold that res judicata does not bar this suit and that H. B. 2 imposes an undue burden on abortion access—it is, in fact, wrong on both counts—it is still wrong to conclude that the admitting privileges and surgical center provisions must be enjoined in their entirety[, because of H. B. 2's] extraordinarily broad severability clause. . . .

A

Applying H. B. 2's severability clause to the admitting privileges requirement is easy. Simply put, the requirement must be upheld in every city in which its application does not pose an undue burden. It surely does not pose that burden anywhere in the eastern half of the State, where most Texans live and where virtually no woman of reproductive age lives more than 150 miles from an open clinic. . . . And petitioners would need to show that the requirement caused specific West Texas clinics to close . . . before they could be entitled to an injunction tailored to address those closures.

B

Applying severability to the surgical center requirement calls for the identification of the particular provisions of the ASC regulations that result in the imposition of an undue burden. These regulations are lengthy and detailed, and while compliance with some might be expensive, compliance with many others would not. And many serve important health and safety purposes. Thus, the surgical center requirements cannot be judged as a package. . . .

. . .

[H. B. 2's severability provision] indisputably requires that all surgical center regulations that are not themselves unconstitutional be left standing. . . .

. . .

By forgoing severability, the Court strikes down numerous provisions that could not plausibly impose an undue burden. . . .

Any responsible application of the H. B. 2 severability provision would leave much of the law intact. At a minimum, both of the requirements challenged here should be held constitutional as applied to clinics in any Texas city that will have a surgical center providing abortions (*i.e.*, those areas in which there cannot possibly have been an undue burden on abortion access). Moreover, as even the District Court found, the surgical center requirement is clearly constitutional as to new abortion facilities and facilities already licensed as surgical centers. . . . And we should uphold every application of every surgical center regulation that does not pose an undue burden—at the very least, all of the regulations as to which petitioners have never made a specific complaint supported by specific evidence. . . .

. . .

When we decide cases on particularly controversial issues, we should take special care to apply settled procedural rules in a neutral manner. The Court has not done that here.

I therefore respectfully dissent.

Lawrence v. Texas

539 U.S. 558, 123 S.Ct. 2472, 156 L.Ed.2d 508 (2003).

■ JUSTICE KENNEDY delivered the opinion of the Court.

Liberty protects the person from unwarranted government intrusions into a dwelling or other private places. . . . And there are other spheres of our lives and existence, outside the home, where the State should not be a dominant presence. Freedom extends beyond spatial bounds. Liberty presumes an autonomy of self that includes freedom of thought, belief, expression, and certain intimate conduct. The instant case involves liberty of the person both in its spatial and more transcendent dimensions.

I

The question before the Court is the validity of a Texas statute making it a crime for two persons of the same sex to engage in certain intimate sexual conduct.

In Houston, Texas, officers . . . respon[ding] to a reported weapons disturbance . . . entered an apartment where . . . Lawrence . . . resided [and] observed Lawrence and another man, Tyron Garner, engaging in a sexual act. The two petitioners were . . . convicted. . . .

The complaints described their crime as "deviate sexual intercourse, namely anal sex, with a member of the same sex (man)." . . . Tex. Penal Code Ann. § 21.06(a) (2003) . . . provides: "A person commits an offense if he engages in deviate sexual intercourse with another individual of the same sex." The statute defines "[d]eviate sexual intercourse" as follows:

"(A) any contact between any part of the genitals of one person and the mouth or anus of another person; or

"(B) the penetration of the genitals or the anus of another person with an object." § 21.01(1).

. . . The petitioners . . . were each fined $200 . . . .

The Court of Appeals for the Texas Fourteenth District . . . en banc . . . , in a divided opinion, . . . affirmed the convictions[,] consider[ing] our decision in Bowers v. Hardwick, 478 U.S. 186 (1986), to be controlling on the federal due process aspect of the case. . . .

. . .

II

We conclude the case should be resolved by determining whether the petitioners were free as adults to engage in the private conduct in the exercise of their liberty under the Due Process Clause . . . . For this inquiry we deem it necessary to reconsider the Court's holding in *Bowers*.

. . .

. . . One difference [from *Bowers*] is that the Georgia statute prohibited the conduct whether or not the participants were of the same sex, while the Texas statute . . . applies only to participants of the same sex. . . . [In *Bowers*, t]he Court, in an opinion by Justice White, sustained the Georgia law. Four Justices dissented. . . .

The Court began its substantive discussion in *Bowers* as follows: "The issue presented is whether the Federal Constitution confers a fundamental right upon homosexuals to engage in sodomy and hence invalidates the laws of the many States that still make such conduct illegal and have done so for a very long time." That statement, we now conclude, discloses the Court's own failure to appreciate the extent of the liberty at stake. To say that the issue in *Bowers* was simply the right to engage in certain sexual conduct demeans the claim the individual put forward, just as it would demean a married couple were it to be said marriage is simply about the right to have sexual intercourse. The laws involved in *Bowers* and here are, to be sure, statutes that purport to do no more than prohibit a particular sexual act. Their penalties and purposes, though, have more far-reaching consequences, touching upon the most private human conduct, sexual behavior, and in the most private of places, the home. The statutes do seek to control a personal relationship that, whether or not entitled to formal recognition in the law, is within the liberty of persons to choose without being punished as criminals.

This, as a general rule, should counsel against attempts by the State, or a court, to define the meaning of the relationship or to set its boundaries absent injury to a person or abuse of an institution the law protects. It suffices for us to acknowledge that adults may choose to enter upon this relationship in the confines of their homes and their own private lives and still retain their dignity as free persons. When sexuality finds overt expression in intimate conduct with another person, the conduct can be but one element in a personal bond that is more enduring. The liberty protected by the Constitution allows homosexual persons the right to make this choice.

Having misapprehended the claim [as one of] a fundamental right to engage in consensual sodomy, the *Bowers* Court said: "Proscriptions against that conduct have ancient roots." . . . In academic writings, and in many of the scholarly *amicus* briefs . . . in this case, there are fundamental criticisms of the historical premises relied upon by the majority and concurring opinions in *Bowers*. . . . We need not enter this debate in the attempt to reach a definitive historical judgment, but the following considerations counsel against adopting the definitive conclusions upon which *Bowers* placed such reliance.

[T]here is no longstanding history in this country of laws directed at homosexual conduct as a distinct matter. . . . The English [sodomy] prohibition was understood to include relations between men and women as well as relations between men and men. . . . Nineteenth-century commentators similarly read American sodomy, buggery, and crime-against-nature statutes as criminalizing certain relations between men and women and between men and men. . . . [E]arly American sodomy laws were not directed at homosexuals as such but instead sought to prohibit nonprocreative sexual activity more generally[, suggesting] that this particular form of conduct was not thought of as a separate category from like conduct between heterosexual persons.

Laws prohibiting sodomy do not seem to have been enforced against consenting adults acting in private. . . .

. . .

. . . [F]ar from possessing "ancient roots," *Bowers*. . . . , American laws targeting same-sex couples did not develop until the last third of the 20th century. The reported decisions concerning the prosecution of consensual, homosexual sodomy between adults for the years 1880–1995 are not always clear in the details, but a significant number involved conduct in a public place. . . .

It was not until the 1970's that any State singled out same-sex relations for criminal prosecution, and only nine States have done so. . . . Post-*Bowers* even some of these States did not adhere to the policy of suppressing homosexual conduct. Over the course of the last decades, States with same-sex prohibitions have moved toward abolishing them. . . .

In summary, the historical grounds relied upon in *Bowers* are more complex than the majority opinion and the concurring opinion by Chief Justice Burger indicate. . . .

[O]f course, . . . the Court in *Bowers* was making the broader point that for centuries there have been powerful voices to condemn homosexual conduct as immoral. The condemnation has been shaped by religious beliefs, conceptions of right and acceptable behavior, and respect for the traditional family. For many persons these are not trivial concerns but profound and deep convictions accepted as ethical and moral principles to which they aspire and which thus determine the course of their lives. These considerations do not answer the question before us, however. The issue is whether the majority may use the power of the State to enforce these views on the whole society through operation of the criminal law. "Our obligation is to define the liberty of all, not to mandate our own moral code." Planned Parenthood of Southeastern Pa. v. Casey, 505 U.S. 833, 850 (1992).

. . . [W]e think that our laws and traditions in the past half century are of most relevance here. These references show an emerging awareness that liberty gives substantial protection to adult persons in deciding how to conduct their private lives in matters pertaining to sex. "[H]istory and tradition are the starting point but not in all cases the ending point of the substantive due process inquiry." County of Sacramento v. Lewis, 523 U.S. 833, 857 (1998) (Kennedy, J., concurring).

This emerging recognition should have been apparent when *Bowers* was decided. In 1955 the American Law Institute promulgated the Model Penal Code and made clear that it did not recommend or provide for "criminal penalties for consensual sexual relations conducted in private." ALI, Model Penal Code § 213.2, Comment 2, p. 372 (1980). It justified its decision on three grounds: (1) The prohibitions undermined respect for the law by penalizing conduct many people engaged in; (2) the statutes regulated private conduct not harmful to others; and (3) the laws were arbitrarily enforced and thus invited the danger of blackmail. . . . In 1961 Illinois changed its laws to conform to the Model Penal Code. Other States soon followed. . . .

In *Bowers* the Court referred to the fact that before 1961 all 50 States had outlawed sodomy, and that at the time of the Court's decision 24 States and the District of Columbia had sodomy laws. . . . Justice Powell pointed out that these prohibitions often were being ignored, however. Georgia, for instance, had not sought to enforce its law for decades. . . .

. . . A committee advising the British Parliament recommended in 1957 repeal of laws punishing homosexual conduct. . . . Parliament enacted the substance of those recommendations 10 years later. . . .

Of even more importance, almost five years before *Bowers* was decided the European Court of Human Rights . . . held that [Northern Ireland] laws proscribing [consensual homosexual] conduct were invalid under the European Convention on Human Rights. Dudgeon v. United Kingdom, 45 Eur. Ct. H. R. (1981). . . . Authoritative in all countries that are members of the Council of Europe (21 nations then, 45 nations now), the decision is at odds with the premise in *Bowers* that the claim put forward was insubstantial in our Western civilization.

In our own constitutional system the deficiencies in *Bowers* became even more apparent in the years following its announcement. The 25 States with laws prohibiting the relevant conduct referenced in the *Bowers* decision are reduced now to 13, of which 4 enforce their laws only against homosexual conduct. In those States where sodomy is still proscribed, whether for same-sex or heterosexual conduct, there is a pattern of nonenforcement with respect to consenting adults acting in private. The State of Texas admitted in 1994 that as of that date it had not prosecuted anyone under those circumstances. . . .

Two principal cases decided after *Bowers* cast its holding into even more doubt. In Planned Parenthood of Southeastern Pa. v. Casey, 505 U.S. 833 (1992), the Court reaffirmed . . . that our laws and tradition afford constitutional protection to personal decisions relating to marriage, procreation, contraception, family relationships, child rearing, and education. . . . [W]e stated as follows:

"These matters, involving the most intimate and personal choices a person may make in a lifetime, choices central to personal dignity and autonomy, are central to the liberty protected by the Fourteenth Amendment. At the heart of liberty is the right to define one's own concept of existence, of meaning, of the universe, and of the mystery of human life. Beliefs about these matters could not define the attributes of personhood were they formed under compulsion of the State."

Persons in a homosexual relationship may seek autonomy for these purposes, just as heterosexual persons do. The decision in *Bowers* would deny them this right.

[S]econd[, in] Romer v. Evans, 517 U.S. 620 (1996)[,] the Court struck down class-based legislation directed at homosexuals as a violation of the Equal Protection Clause. *Romer* invalidated an amendment to Colorado's constitution which named as a solitary class persons who were homosexuals, lesbians, or bisexual either by "orientation, conduct, practices or relationships," . . . , and deprived them of protection under state antidiscrimination laws. We concluded that the provision was "born of animosity toward the class of persons affected" and further that it had no rational relation to a legitimate governmental purpose. . . .

[A]n alternative argument . . . contend[s] that *Romer* provides the basis for declaring the Texas statute invalid under the Equal Protection Clause. That is a tenable argument, but we conclude the instant case requires us to address whether *Bowers* itself has continuing validity. Were we to hold the statute invalid under the Equal Protection Clause some might question whether a prohibition would be valid if drawn differently, say, to prohibit the conduct both between same-sex and different-sex participants.

Equality of treatment and the due process right to demand respect for conduct protected by the substantive guarantee of liberty are linked in important respects, and a decision on the latter point advances both interests. If protected conduct is made criminal and the law which does so remains unexamined for its substantive validity, its stigma might remain even if it were not enforceable as drawn for equal protection reasons. When homosexual conduct is made criminal by the law of the State, that declaration in and of itself is an invitation to subject homosexual persons to discrimination both in the public and in the private spheres. The central holding of *Bowers* has been brought in question by this case, and it should be addressed. Its continuance as precedent demeans the lives of homosexual persons.

The stigma this criminal statute imposes, moreover, is not trivial. [Though] a minor offense in the Texas legal system . . . , it remains a criminal offense with all that imports for the dignity of the persons charged[—a] record[, . . . possible] registration [as] sex offenders . . . [in] at least four States [and] the other collateral consequences always following a conviction, such as notations on job application forms. . . .

The foundations of *Bowers* have sustained serious erosion from our recent decisions in *Casey* and *Romer*. When our precedent has been thus weakened, criticism from other sources is of greater significance. In the United States criticism of *Bowers* has been substantial and continuing, disapproving of its reasoning in all respects, not just as to its historical assumptions. See, *e.g.,* C. Fried, Order and Law: Arguing the Reagan Revolution—A Firsthand Account 81–84 (1991); R. Posner, Sex and Reason 341–350 (1992). The courts of five different States have declined to follow it in interpreting provisions in their own state constitutions parallel to the Due Process Clause of the Fourteenth Amendment. . . .

To the extent *Bowers* relied on values we share with a wider civilization, it should be noted that the reasoning and holding in *Bowers* have been rejected elsewhere. . . . The right the petitioners seek . . . has been accepted as an integral part of human freedom in many other countries. . . .

. . . [T]here has been no individual or societal reliance on *Bowers* of the sort that could counsel against overturning its holding once there are compelling reasons to do so. . . .

The rationale of *Bowers* does not withstand careful analysis. . . .

Bowers was not correct when it was decided, and it is not correct today. It . . . should be and now is overruled.

The present case does not involve minors. It does not involve persons who might be injured or coerced or who are situated in relationships where consent might not easily be refused. It does not involve public conduct or prostitution. It does not involve whether the government must give formal recognition to any relationship that homosexual persons seek to enter. The case does involve two adults who, with full and mutual consent from each other, engaged in sexual practices common to a homosexual lifestyle. The petitioners are entitled to respect for their private lives. The State cannot demean their existence or control their destiny by making their private sexual conduct a crime. Their right to liberty under the Due Process Clause gives them the full right to engage in their conduct without intervention of the government. . . . The Texas statute furthers no legitimate state interest which can justify its intrusion into the personal and private life of the individual.

Had those who drew and ratified the Due Process Clauses of the Fifth Amendment or the Fourteenth Amendment known the components of liberty in its manifold possibilities, they might have been more specific. They did not presume to have this insight. They knew times can blind us to certain truths and later generations can see that laws once thought necessary and proper in fact serve only to oppress. As the Constitution endures, persons in every generation can invoke its principles in their own search for greater freedom.

[R]eversed . . . and . . . remanded for further proceedings not inconsistent with this opinion.

■ JUSTICE O'CONNOR, concurring in the judgment.

. . . I joined *Bowers*, and do not join the Court in overruling it. Nevertheless, I agree . . . that Texas' statute banning same-sex sodomy is unconstitutional . . . base[d] on the Fourteenth Amendment's Equal Protection Clause.

. . .

. . . We have consistently held . . . that some objectives, such as "a bare . . . desire to harm a politically unpopular group," are not legitimate state interests. . . . When a law exhibits such a desire to harm a politically unpopular group, we have applied a more searching form of rational basis review to strike down such laws under the Equal Protection Clause.

We have been most likely to [do so] where, as here, the challenged legislation inhibits personal relationships. In *Department of Agriculture v. Moreno*, for example, we held that a law preventing those households containing an individual unrelated to any other member of the household from receiving food stamps violated equal protection because the purpose of the law was to " 'discriminate against hippies.' " . . . The asserted governmental interest in preventing food stamp fraud was not deemed sufficient to satisfy rational basis review. . . . In Eisenstadt v. Baird, 405 U.S. 438, 447–455 (1972), we refused to sanction a law that discriminated between married and unmarried persons by prohibiting the distribution of contraceptives to single persons. Likewise, in *Cleburne v. Cleburne Living Center*, . . . we held that it was irrational for a State to require a home for the mentally disabled to obtain a special use permit when other residences—like fraternity houses and apartment buildings—did not have to obtain such a permit. And in *Romer v. Evans*, we disallowed a state statute that "impos[ed] a broad and undifferentiated disability on a single named group"— specifically, homosexuals. . . .

. . . Sodomy between opposite-sex partners . . . is not a crime in Texas. . . .

. . .

. . . Texas' sodomy law brands all homosexuals as criminals, thereby making it more difficult for homosexuals to be treated in the same manner as everyone else. . . .

Texas attempts to justify its law, and the effects of the law, by arguing that the statute satisfies rational basis review because it furthers the legitimate governmental interest of the promotion of morality. In *Bowers*[—a substantive due process case only—]we . . . rejected the argument that no rational basis existed to justify the law, pointing to the government's interest in promoting morality. . . .

This case raises a different issue . . .: whether, under the Equal Protection Clause, moral disapproval is a legitimate state interest to justify by itself a statute that bans homosexual sodomy, but not heterosexual sodomy. It is not. . . .

Moral disapproval of a group cannot be a legitimate governmental interest under the Equal Protection Clause because legal classifications must not be "drawn for the purpose of disadvantaging the group burdened by the law." . . . And because Texas so rarely enforces its sodomy law as applied to private, consensual acts, the law serves more as a statement of dislike and disapproval against homosexuals than as a tool to stop criminal behavior. The . . . law "raise[s] the inevitable inference that the disadvantage imposed is born of animosity toward the class of persons affected." . . .

Texas argues, however, that the sodomy law does not discriminate against homosexual persons . . . [—]only against homosexual conduct. [But] the conduct targeted by this law is conduct that is closely correlated with being homosexual. Under such circumstances, Texas' sodomy law is targeted at more than conduct. It is instead directed toward gay persons as a class. . . . When a State makes homosexual conduct criminal, and not "deviate sexual intercourse" committed by persons of different sexes, "that declaration in and of itself is an invitation to subject homosexual persons to discrimination both in the public and in the private spheres."

Indeed, Texas law confirms that the sodomy statute is directed toward homosexuals as a class. In Texas, calling a person a homosexual is slander *per se* because the word "homosexual" "impute[s] the commission of a crime." . . . The State has admitted that because of the sodomy law, *being* homosexual carries the presumption of being a criminal. See State v. Morales, 826 S. W. 2d, at 202–203 ("[T]he statute brands lesbians and gay men as criminals and thereby legally sanctions discrimination against them in a variety of ways unrelated to the criminal law"). Texas' sodomy law therefore results in discrimination against homosexuals as a class in an array of areas outside the criminal law. . . . In *Romer v. Evans*, we refused to sanction a law that singled out homosexuals "for disfavored legal status." . . . The same is true here. The Equal Protection Clause " 'neither knows nor tolerates classes among citizens.' " . . . (quoting Plessy v. Ferguson, 163 U.S. 537, 559 (1896) (Harlan, J. dissenting)).

. . .

Whether a sodomy law . . . neutral both in effect and application, see Yick Wo v. Hopkins, 118 U.S. 356 (1886), would violate the substantive component of the Due Process Clause is an issue that need not be decided today. I am confident, however, that so long as the Equal Protection Clause requires a sodomy law to apply equally to the private consensual conduct of homosexuals and heterosexuals alike, such a law would not long stand in our democratic society. . . .

[This] does not mean that other laws distinguishing between heterosexuals and homosexuals would similarly fail under rational basis review. Texas cannot assert any legitimate state interest here, such as national security or preserving the traditional institution of marriage. Unlike the moral disapproval of same-sex relations—the asserted state interest in this case—other reasons exist to promote the institution of marriage beyond mere moral disapproval of an excluded group.

. . .

■ JUSTICE SCALIA, with whom THE CHIEF JUSTICE and JUSTICE THOMAS join, dissenting.

. . .

. . . [N]owhere does the Court's opinion declare that homosexual sodomy is a "fundamental right" under the Due Process Clause; nor does it subject the Texas law to the standard of review that would be appropriate (strict scrutiny) if homosexual sodomy *were* a "fundamental right." Thus, while overruling the *outcome* of *Bowers*, the Court leaves strangely untouched its central legal conclusion: "[R]espondent would have us announce . . . a fundamental right to engage in homosexual sodomy. This we are quite unwilling to do." . . . Instead the Court simply describes petitioners' conduct as "an exercise of their liberty"—which it undoubtedly is—and proceeds to apply an unheard-of form of rational-basis review that will have far-reaching implications beyond this case. . . .

I

. . .

. . . Countless judicial decisions and legislative enactments have relied on the ancient proposition that a governing majority's belief that certain sexual behavior is "immoral and unacceptable" constitutes a rational basis for regulation. . . . State laws against bigamy, same-sex marriage, adult incest, prostitution, masturbation, adultery, fornication, bestiality, and obscenity are likewise sustainable only in light of *Bowers'* validation of laws based on moral choices. Every single one of these laws is called into question by today's decision; the Court makes no effort to cabin the scope of its decision to exclude them from its holding. . . . The impossibility of distinguishing homosexuality from other traditional "morals" offenses is precisely why *Bowers* rejected the rational-basis challenge. . . .

. . .

III

. . .

. . . [T]he "definitive [historical] conclusion," . . . on which *Bowers* relied [is] that our Nation has a longstanding history of laws prohibiting *sodomy in general—* regardless of whether it was performed by same-sex or opposite-sex couples:

"It is obvious to us that neither of these formulations would extend a fundamental right to homosexuals to engage in acts of consensual sodomy. Proscriptions against that conduct have ancient roots. *Sodomy* was a criminal offense at common law and was forbidden by the laws of the original 13 States when they ratified the Bill of Rights. In 1868, when the Fourteenth Amendment was ratified, all but 5 of the 37 States in the Union had *criminal sodomy laws*. In fact, until 1961, all 50 States outlawed *sodomy*, and today, 24 States and the District of Columbia continue to provide criminal penalties for *sodomy* performed in private and between consenting adults. Against this background, to claim that a right to engage in such conduct is 'deeply rooted in this Nation's history and tradition' or 'implicit in the concept of ordered liberty' is, at best, facetious." . . . (. . . emphasis added).

It is (as *Bowers* recognized) entirely irrelevant whether the laws in our long national tradition criminalizing homosexual sodomy were "directed at homosexual conduct as a distinct matter." . . . [T]he only relevant point is that [homosexual sodomy] *was* criminalized—which suffices to establish that homosexual sodomy is not a right "deeply rooted in our Nation's history and tradition." . . .

. . .

[T]he Court . . . says: "[O]ur laws and traditions in the past half century are of most relevance here [and] show *an emerging awareness* that liberty gives substantial protection to adult persons in deciding how to conduct their private lives *in matters pertaining to sex*." (emphasis added). Apart from the fact that such an "emerging awareness" does not establish a "fundamental right," the statement is factually false. States continue to prosecute all sorts of crimes by adults "in matters pertaining to sex": prostitution, adult incest, adultery, obscenity, and child pornography. Sodomy laws, too, have been enforced "in the past half century," in which there have been 134 reported cases involving prosecutions for consensual, adult, homosexual sodomy. . . . In relying . . . upon the American Law Institute's 1955 recommendation not to criminalize " 'consensual sexual relations conducted in private,' " the Court ignores the fact that this recommendation was "a point of resistance in most of the states that considered adopting the Model Penal Code." Gaylaw 159.

In any event, an "emerging awareness" is by definition not "deeply rooted in this Nation's history and tradition[s]," as we have said "fundamental right" status requires. Constitutional entitlements do not spring into existence because some States choose to lessen or eliminate criminal sanctions on certain behavior. Much less do they spring into existence, as the Court seems to believe, because *foreign nations* decriminalize conduct. . . .

IV

[T]he contention that there is no rational basis for the law here under attack . . . is so out of accord with our jurisprudence—indeed, with the jurisprudence of *any* society we know—that it requires little discussion.

The Texas statute undeniably seeks to further the belief of its citizens that certain forms of sexual behavior are "immoral and unacceptable," *Bowers* . . . —the same interest furthered by criminal laws against fornication, bigamy, adultery, adult incest, bestiality, and obscenity. . . . The Court . . . effectively decrees the end of all morals legislation. If, as the Court asserts, the promotion of majoritarian sexual morality is not even a *legitimate* state interest, none of the above-mentioned laws can survive rational-basis review.

V

Finally, I turn to petitioners' equal-protection challenge, which no Member of the Court save Justice O'Connor . . . embraces. . . .

. . .

Justice O'Connor simply decrees application of "a more searching form of rational basis review" to the Texas statute. The cases she cites do not recognize such a standard, and reach their conclusions only after finding, as required by conventional rational-basis analysis, that no conceivable legitimate state interest supports the classification at issue. . . . [She] must at least mean, however, that laws exhibiting " 'a . . . desire to harm a politically unpopular group' " are invalid *even though* there may be a conceivable rational basis to support them.

This reasoning leaves on pretty shaky grounds state laws limiting marriage to opposite-sex couples. Justice O'Connor seeks to preserve them by the conclusory statement that "preserving the traditional institution of marriage" is a legitimate state interest. But "preserving the traditional institution of marriage" is just a kinder way of describing the State's *moral disapproval* of same-sex couples. Texas's interest in § 21.06 could be recast in similarly euphemistic terms: "preserving the traditional sexual mores of our society." In the jurisprudence Justice O'Connor has seemingly created, judges can validate laws by characterizing them as "preserving the traditions of society" (good); or invalidate them by characterizing them as "expressing moral disapproval" (bad).

. . .

. . . Today's opinion dismantles the structure of constitutional law that has permitted a distinction to be made between heterosexual and homosexual unions, insofar as formal recognition in marriage is concerned. If moral disapprobation of homosexual conduct is "no legitimate state interest" for purposes of proscribing that conduct; and if, . . . "[w]hen sexuality finds overt expression in intimate conduct with another person, the conduct can be but one element in a personal bond that is more enduring"; what justification could there possibly be for denying the benefits of marriage to homosexual couples exercising "[t]he liberty protected by the Constitution"? . . .

. . .

■ JUSTICE THOMAS, dissenting.

. . . I write separately to note that the law before the Court today "is . . . uncommonly silly." Griswold v. Connecticut, 381 U.S. 479, 527 (1965) (Stewart, J., dissenting). If I were a member of the Texas Legislature, I would vote to repeal it. Punishing someone for expressing his sexual preference through noncommercial consensual conduct with another adult does not appear to be a worthy way to expend valuable law enforcement resources.

Notwithstanding this, . . . just like Justice Stewart, I "can find [neither in the Bill of Rights nor any other part of the Constitution a] general right of privacy," . . . , or as the Court terms it today, the "liberty of the person both in its spatial and more transcendent dimensions."

Obergefell v. Hodges

576 U.S. ___, 135 S.Ct. 2584, 192 L.Ed.2d 609 (2015).

[The report of this case appears *supra*, at p. 371.]

Washington v. Glucksberg

521 U.S. 702, 117 S.Ct. 2258, 138 L.Ed.2d 772 (1997).

■ CHIEF JUSTICE REHNQUIST delivered the opinion of the Court.

The question presented ... is whether Washington's prohibition against "caus[ing]" or "aid[ing]" a suicide offends the Fourteenth Amendment. . . . We hold that it does not.

. . . Washington law provides: "A person is guilty of promoting a suicide attempt when he knowingly causes or aids another person to attempt suicide." Wash. Rev. Code 9A.36.060(1) (1994). . . . Washington's Natural Death Act, enacted in 1979, states that the "withholding or withdrawal of life-sustaining treatment" at a patient's direction "shall not, for any purpose, constitute a suicide." Wash. Rev. Code § 70.122.070(1). . . .

. . . [Washington p]hysicians who ... occasionally treat terminally ill, suffering patients, and declare that they would assist these patients in ending their lives if not for Washington's assisted-suicide ban . . . , along with three gravely ill, pseudonymous plaintiffs who have since died and Compassion in Dying, a nonprofit organization that counsels people considering physician-assisted suicide, sued ... seeking a declaration that Wash Rev. Code 9A.36.060(1) (1994) is, on its face, unconstitutional. . . .

The plaintiffs asserted "the existence of a liberty interest protected by the Fourteenth Amendment which extends to a personal choice by a mentally competent, terminally ill adult to commit physician-assisted suicide." . . . Relying primarily on Planned Parenthood v. Casey, 505 U.S. 833 (1992), and Cruzan v. Director, Missouri Dept. of Health, 497 U.S. 261 (1990), the District Court agreed . . . and concluded that Washington's assisted-suicide ban is unconstitutional because it "places an undue burden on the exercise of [that] constitutionally protected liberty interest." . . .

. . . The Ninth Circuit ... en banc ... affirmed ... [,] conclud[ing] that "the Constitution encompasses a due process liberty interest in controlling the time and manner of one's death—that there is, in short, a constitutionally-recognized 'right to die.'" . . . After "[w]eighing and then balancing" this interest against Washington's various interests, the court held that the State's assisted-suicide ban was unconstitutional "as applied to terminally ill competent adults who wish to hasten their deaths with medication prescribed by their physicians."[6] We . . . reverse.

I

We begin, as we do in all due-process cases, by examining our Nation's history, legal traditions, and practices. . . . In almost every State—indeed, in almost every western democracy—it is a crime to assist a suicide. . . .

[F]or over 700 years, the Anglo-American common-law tradition has punished or otherwise disapproved of both suicide and assisting suicide. . . .

. . .

. . . And the prohibitions against assisting suicide never contained exceptions for those who were near death. . . .

. . . By the time the Fourteenth Amendment was ratified, it was a crime in most States to assist a suicide. . . . In this century, the Model Penal Code also prohibited "aiding" suicide, prompting many States to enact or revise their assisted-suicide bans. The Code's drafters observed that "the interests in the sanctity of life that are

---

[6] It is ... the court's holding that Washington's physician-assisted suicide statute is unconstitutional as applied to the "class of terminally ill, mentally competent patients" that is before us today.

represented by the criminal homicide laws are threatened by one who expresses a willingness to participate in taking the life of another, even though the act may be accomplished with the consent, or at the request, of the suicide victim." . . .

Though deeply rooted, the States' assisted-suicide bans have in recent years been reexamined and, generally, reaffirmed. Because of advances in medicine and technology, Americans today are increasingly likely to die in institutions, from chronic illnesses. . . . Public concern and democratic action are therefore sharply focused on how best to protect dignity and independence at the end of life, with the result that there have been many significant changes in state laws and in the attitudes these laws reflect. Many States, for example, now permit "living wills," surrogate health-care decisionmaking, and the withdrawal or refusal of life-sustaining medical treatment. . . . At the same time, however, voters and legislators continue for the most part to reaffirm their States' prohibitions on assisting suicide.

The Washington statute . . . was enacted in 1975 . . . . Four years later, Washington passed its Natural Death Act, which specifically stated that the "withholding or withdrawal of life-sustaining treatment . . . shall not, for any purpose, constitute a suicide" and that "[n]othing in this chapter shall be construed to condone, authorize, or approve mercy killing. . . ." . . . In 1991, Washington voters rejected a ballot initiative which . . . would have permitted a form of physician-assisted suicide. Washington then added a provision to the Natural Death Act expressly excluding physician-assisted suicide. . . .

California voters rejected an assisted-suicide initiative similar to Washington's in 1993. On the other hand, in 1994, voters in Oregon enacted [the] "Death With Dignity Act," which legalized physician-assisted suicide for competent, terminally ill adults. Since the Oregon vote, many proposals to legalize assisted-suicide have been and continue to be introduced in the States' legislatures, but none has been enacted. And just last year, Iowa and Rhode Island joined the overwhelming majority of States explicitly prohibiting assisted suicide. . . . Also, on April 30, 1997, President Clinton signed the Federal Assisted Suicide Funding Restriction Act of 1997, which prohibits the use of federal funds in support of physician-assisted suicide. . . . [16]

Thus, the States are currently engaged in serious, thoughtful examinations of physician-assisted suicide and other similar issues. For example, New York State's Task Force on Life and the Law . . . [a]fter studying physician-assisted suicide . . . unanimously concluded that "[l]egalizing assisted suicide and euthanasia would pose profound risks to many individuals who are ill and vulnerable. . . . [T]he potential dangers of this dramatic change in public policy would outweigh any benefit that might be achieved." . . .

Attitudes toward suicide itself have changed since Bracton, but our laws have consistently condemned, and continue to prohibit, assisting suicide. Despite changes in medical technology and notwithstanding an increased emphasis on the importance of end-of-life decisionmaking, we have not retreated from this prohibition. Against this backdrop of history, tradition, and practice, we now turn to respondents' constitutional claim.

II

The Due Process Clause . . . provides heightened protection against government interference with certain fundamental rights and liberty interests. . . . We have . . . assumed, and strongly suggested, that the Due Process Clause protects the traditional right to refuse unwanted lifesaving medical treatment. *Cruzan*, 497 U.S., at 278–279.

---

[16] Other countries are embroiled in similar debates. . . .

But we . . . "exercise the utmost care whenever we are asked to break new ground in this field," . . . lest the liberty protected by the Due Process Clause be subtly transformed into the policy preferences of the members of this Court. . . .

Our established method of substantive-due-process analysis has two primary features: First, we have regularly observed that the Due Process Clause specially protects those fundamental rights and liberties which are, objectively, "deeply rooted in this Nation's history and tradition," . . . and "implicit in the concept of ordered liberty," such that "neither liberty nor justice would exist if they were sacrificed," Palko v. Connecticut, 302 U.S. 319, 325, 326 (1937). Second, we have required in substantive-due-process cases a "careful description" of the asserted fundamental liberty interest. . . . Our Nation's history, legal traditions, and practices thus provide the crucial "guideposts for responsible decisionmaking,". . . .

Justice Souter . . . would largely abandon this restrained methodology, and instead ask "whether [Washington's] statute sets up one of those 'arbitrary impositions' or 'purposeless restraints' at odds with the Due Process Clause of the Fourteenth Amendment". . . . In our view, however, the development of this Court's substantive-due-process jurisprudence . . . has been a process whereby the outlines of the "liberty" specially protected by the Fourteenth Amendment—never fully clarified, to be sure, and perhaps not capable of being fully clarified—have at least been carefully refined by concrete examples involving fundamental rights found to be deeply rooted in our legal tradition. This approach tends to rein in the subjective elements that are necessarily present in due-process judicial review. In addition, by establishing a threshold requirement—that a challenged state action implicate a fundamental right—before requiring more than a reasonable relation to a legitimate state interest to justify the action, it avoids the need for complex balancing of competing interests in every case.

. . . [W]e have a tradition of carefully formulating the interest at stake in substantive-due-process cases. For example, although *Cruzan* is often described as a "right to die" case, . . . we were, in fact, more precise: we assumed that the Constitution granted competent persons a "constitutionally protected right to refuse lifesaving hydration and nutrition." . . . The Washington statute at issue in this case prohibits "aid[ing] another person to attempt suicide," . . . and, thus, the question before us is whether the "liberty" specially protected by the Due Process Clause includes a right to commit suicide which itself includes a right to assistance in doing so.

. . . [A] consistent and almost universal tradition . . . has long rejected the asserted right, and continues explicitly to reject it today, even for terminally ill, mentally competent adults. . . .

Respondents contend, however, . . . [p]ointing to *Casey* and *Cruzan*, . . . that the "liberty" protected by the Due Process Clause includes "basic and intimate exercises of personal autonomy," . . . [and] protects the "liberty of competent, terminally ill adults to make end-of-life decisions free of undue government interference." . . . The question presented in this case, however, is whether the protections of the Due Process Clause include a right to commit suicide with another's assistance. With this "careful description" of respondents' claim in mind, we turn to *Casey* and *Cruzan*.

In *Cruzan*, we considered whether Nancy Beth Cruzan, who had been severely injured in an automobile accident and was in a persistive vegetative state, "ha[d] a right under the United States Constitution which would require the hospital to withdraw life-sustaining treatment" at her parents' request. . . . We began with the observation that "[a]t common law, even the touching of one person by another without consent and without legal justification was a battery." . . . We then discussed the related rule that "informed consent is generally required for medical treatment." . . . After reviewing a long line of relevant state cases, we concluded that "the common-law doctrine of informed consent is viewed as generally encompassing the right of a competent individual to refuse medical treatment." . . . Next, we reviewed our own cases on the subject, and stated that "[t]he principle that a competent person has a constitutionally protected liberty interest in refusing unwanted medical treatment may be inferred from our prior decisions." . . . Therefore, "for purposes of [that] case, we assume[d] that the United States Constitution would grant a competent person a constitutionally protected right to refuse lifesaving hydration and nutrition." . . . We concluded that, notwithstanding this right, the Constitution permitted Missouri to require clear and convincing evidence of an incompetent patient's wishes concerning the withdrawal of life-sustaining treatment. . . .

> . . .

The right assumed in *Cruzan* . . . was not simply deduced from abstract concepts of personal autonomy. Given the common-law rule that forced medication was a battery, and the long legal tradition protecting the decision to refuse unwanted medical treatment, our assumption was entirely consistent with this Nation's history and constitutional traditions. The decision to commit suicide with the assistance of another may be just as personal and profound as the decision to refuse unwanted medical treatment, but it has never enjoyed similar legal protection. Indeed, the two acts are widely and reasonably regarded as quite distinct. See Vacco v. Quill, [521 U.S. 793 (1997)].[a] In *Cruzan* itself, we recognized that most States outlawed assisted

---

[a] In *Quill*, decided with *Glucksberg*, the Court reversed a decision of the Second Circuit Court of Appeals holding that New York's prohibition on assisted suicide violated the Equal Protection Clause insofar as it prevented prescribing lethal medication for mentally competent, terminally ill patients, because New York law allowed such patients to refuse life-sustaining medical treatment, and the distinction was "not rationally related to any legitimate state interest." Chief Justice Rehnquist's majority opinion concluded that "the distinction between assisting suicide and withdrawing life-sustaining treatment, a distinction widely recognized and endorsed in the medical profession and in our legal traditions, is both important and logical; it is certainly rational." The Chief Justice continued:

"The distinction comports with fundamental legal principles of causation and intent. First, when a patient refuses life-sustaining medical treatment, he dies from an underlying fatal disease or pathology; but if a patient ingests lethal medication prescribed by a physician, he is killed by that medication. . . .

"Furthermore, a physician who withdraws, or honors a patient's refusal to begin, life-sustaining medical treatment purposefully intends, or may so intend, only to respect his patient's wishes and 'to cease doing useless and futile or degrading things to the patient when [the patient] no longer stands to benefit from them.' . . . The same is true when a doctor provides aggressive palliative care; in some cases, painkilling drugs may hasten a patient's death, but the physician's purpose and intent is, or may be, only to ease his patient's pain. A doctor who assists a suicide, however, 'must, necessarily and indubitably, intend primarily that the patient be made dead.' . . . Similarly, a patient who commits suicide with a doctor's aid necessarily has the specific intent to end his or her own life, while a patient who refuses or discontinues treatment might not. . . .

"The law has long . . . distinguishe[d] actions taken "because of" a given end from actions taken "in spite of" their unintended but foreseen consequences. . . .

". . . [M]any courts, including New York courts, have carefully distinguished refusing life-sustaining treatment from suicide. . . .

"Similarly, the overwhelming majority of state legislatures have drawn a clear line between assisting suicide and withdrawing or permitting the refusal of unwanted lifesaving medical treatment by prohibiting the former and permitting the latter. . . .

> ". . .

"This Court has also recognized, at least implicitly, the distinction between letting a patient die and making that patient die. In [*Cruzan*], . . . our assumption of a right to refuse treatment was grounded not . . . on the proposition that patients have a general and abstract 'right to hasten death,' but on well established, traditional rights to bodily integrity and freedom from unwanted touching. . . .

". . . Logic and contemporary practice support New York's judgment that the two acts are different, and New York may therefore, consistent with the Constitution, treat them differently. . . .

suicide—and even more do today—and we certainly gave no intimation that the right to refuse unwanted medical treatment could be somehow transmuted into a right to assistance in committing suicide. . . .

Respondents also . . . emphasize the statement in *Casey* that:

"At the heart of liberty is the right to define one's own concept of existence, of meaning, of the universe, and of the mystery of human life. Beliefs about these matters could not define the attributes of personhood were they formed under compulsion of the State." . . .

By choosing this language, the Court's opinion in *Casey* described, in a general way and in light of our prior cases, those personal activities and decisions that this Court has identified as so deeply rooted in our history and traditions, or so fundamental to our concept of constitutionally ordered liberty, that they are protected by the Fourteenth Amendment. . . . That many of the rights and liberties protected by the Due Process Clause sound in personal autonomy does not warrant the sweeping conclusion that any and all important, intimate, and personal decisions are so protected, . . . and *Casey* did not suggest otherwise.

The history of the law's treatment of assisted suicide in this country has been and continues to be one of the rejection of nearly all efforts to permit it. That being the case, our decisions lead us to conclude that the asserted "right" to assistance in committing suicide is not a fundamental liberty interest protected by the Due Process Clause. The Constitution also requires, however, that Washington's assisted-suicide ban be rationally related to legitimate government interests. . . . This requirement is unquestionably met here. . . .

First, Washington has an "unqualified interest in the preservation of human life." *Cruzan*. . . . The State's prohibition on assisted suicide, like all homicide laws, both reflects and advances its commitment to this interest. . . .

. . . Washington . . . insists that all persons' lives, from beginning to end, regardless of physical or mental condition, are under the full protection of the law. . . . As we have previously affirmed, the States "may properly decline to make judgments about the 'quality' of life that a particular individual may enjoy," *Cruzan*. . . . This remains true, as *Cruzan* makes clear, even for those who are near death.

Relatedly, all admit that suicide is a serious public-health problem, especially among persons in otherwise vulnerable groups. . . .

Those who attempt suicide—terminally ill or not—often suffer from depression or other mental disorders. . . . Research indicates, however, that many people who request physician-assisted suicide withdraw that request if their depression and pain are treated. H. Hendin, Seduced by Death: Doctors, Patients and the Dutch Cure 24–25 (1997) (suicidal, terminally ill patients "usually respond well to treatment for

---

"New York's reasons for recognizing and acting on this distinction . . . are discussed in greater detail in our opinion in *Glucksberg* [and] easily satisfy the constitutional requirement that a legislative classification bear a rational relation to some legitimate end."

Each of the concurring opinions in *Glucksberg* also applied to this case, except that Justice Souter here said this:

"Even though I do not conclude that assisted suicide is a fundamental right entitled to recognition at this time, I accord the claims raised by the patients and physicians in this case and Washington v. Glucksberg a high degree of importance, requiring a commensurate justification. . . . The reasons that lead me to conclude in *Glucksberg* that the prohibition on assisted suicide is not arbitrary under the due process standard also support the distinction between assistance to suicide, which is banned, and practices such as termination of artificial life support and death-hastening pain medication, which are permitted. I accordingly concur in the judgment of the Court."

depressive illness and pain medication and are then grateful to be alive"); New York Task Force 177–178. The New York Task Force, however, expressed its concern that, because depression is difficult to diagnose, physicians and medical professionals often fail to respond adequately to seriously ill patients' needs. Id., at 175. Thus, legal physician-assisted suicide could make it more difficult for the State to protect depressed or mentally ill persons, or those who are suffering from untreated pain, from suicidal impulses.

The State also has an interest in protecting the integrity and ethics of the medical profession.... [T]he American Medical Association, like many other medical and physicians' groups, has concluded that "[p]hysician-assisted suicide is fundamentally incompatible with the physician's role as healer." ... And physician-assisted suicide could, it is argued, undermine the trust that is essential to the doctor-patient relationship by blurring the time-honored line between healing and harming. ...

Next, the State has an interest in protecting vulnerable groups—including the poor, the elderly, and disabled persons—from abuse, neglect, and mistakes.... We have recognized ... the real risk of subtle coercion and undue influence in end-of-life situations. *Cruzan.* ... If physician-assisted suicide were permitted, many might resort to it to spare their families the substantial financial burden of end-of-life health-care costs.

The State's interest here goes beyond protecting the vulnerable from coercion; it extends to protecting disabled and terminally ill people from prejudice, negative and inaccurate stereotypes, and "societal indifference." ... The State's assisted-suicide ban reflects and reinforces its policy that the lives of terminally ill, disabled, and elderly people must be no less valued than the lives of the young and healthy, and that a seriously disabled person's suicidal impulses should be interpreted and treated the same way as anyone else's. ...

Finally, the State may fear that permitting assisted suicide will start it down the path to voluntary and perhaps even involuntary euthanasia.... [W]hat is couched as a limited right to "physician-assisted suicide" is likely, in effect, a much broader license, which could prove extremely difficult to police and contain. Washington's ban on assisting suicide prevents such erosion.

This concern is further supported by evidence about the practice of euthanasia in the Netherlands ... suggest[ing] that, despite the existence of various reporting procedures, euthanasia in the Netherlands has not been limited to competent, terminally ill adults who are enduring physical suffering, and that regulation of the practice may not have prevented abuses in cases involving vulnerable persons, including severely disabled neonates and elderly persons suffering from dementia.... Washington, like most other States, reasonably ensures against this risk by banning, rather than regulating, assisting suicide. ...

We need not weigh exactly the relative strengths of these various interests. They are unquestionably important and legitimate, and Washington's ban on assisted suicide is at least reasonably related to their promotion and protection. We therefore hold that Wash. Rev. Code § 9A.36.060(1) (1994) does not violate the Fourteenth Amendment, either on its face or "as applied to competent, terminally ill adults who wish to hasten their deaths by obtaining medication prescribed by their doctors." ... [24]

---

[24] ... We emphasize that we today reject the Court of Appeals' specific holding that the statute is unconstitutional "as applied" to a particular class. See n. 6, supra. Justice Stevens agrees with this holding, but would not "foreclose the possibility that an individual plaintiff seeking to hasten her death, or a doctor whose assistance was sought, could prevail in a more particularized challenge." Our opinion does not absolutely foreclose such a claim. However, given our holding that the Due Process Clause ... does not provide heightened protection to the asserted liberty interest in ending one's life

* * *

Throughout the Nation, Americans are engaged in an earnest and profound debate about the morality, legality, and practicality of physician-assisted suicide. Our holding permits this debate to continue, as it should in a democratic society. . . .

■ JUSTICE O'CONNOR, concurring.[*]

     . . .

     . . . I join the Court's opinions because I agree that there is no generalized right to "commit suicide." But respondents urge us to address the narrower question whether a mentally competent person who is experiencing great suffering has a constitutionally cognizable interest in controlling the circumstances of his or her imminent death. I see no need to reach that question in the context of the facial challenges to the New York and Washington laws at issue here. . . . The parties and *amici* agree that in these States a patient who is suffering from a terminal illness and who is experiencing great pain has no legal barriers to obtaining medication, from qualified physicians, to alleviate that suffering, even to the point of causing unconsciousness and hastening death. . . . In this light, even assuming that we would recognize such an interest, I agree that the State's interests in protecting those who are not truly competent or facing imminent death, or those whose decisions to hasten death would not truly be voluntary, are sufficiently weighty to justify a prohibition against physician-assisted suicide.

     Every one of us at some point may be affected by our own or a family member's terminal illness. There is no reason to think the democratic process will not strike the proper balance between the interests of terminally ill, mentally competent individuals who would seek to end their suffering and the State's interests in protecting those who might seek to end life mistakenly or under pressure. . . .

     . . .

■ JUSTICE STEVENS, concurring in the judgments.

     . . .

     . . . The value to others of a person's life is far too precious to allow the individual to claim a constitutional entitlement to complete autonomy in making a decision to end that life. Thus, I fully agree with the Court that the "liberty" protected by the Due Process Clause does not include a categorical "right to commit suicide which itself includes a right to assistance in doing so."

     But . . . upholding a general statutory prohibition of assisted suicide does not mean that every possible application of the statute would be valid. . . .

II

     . . . In most cases, the individual's constitutionally protected interest in his or her own physical autonomy, including the right to refuse unwanted medical treatment, will give way to the State's interest in preserving human life.

     Cruzan, however, was not the normal case. . . . I insist that the source of Nancy Cruzan's right to refuse treatment was not just a common-law rule [but] an aspect of a far broader and more basic concept of freedom . . . older than the common law. This

---

with a physician's assistance, such a claim would have to be quite different from the ones advanced . . . here.

     [*]   Justice Ginsburg concurs in the Court's judgments substantially for the reasons stated in this opinion. Justice Breyer joins this opinion except insofar as it joins the opinions of the Court.

freedom embraces, not merely a person's right to refuse a particular kind of unwanted treatment, but also her interest in dignity, and in determining the character of the memories that will survive long after her death. . . .

. . .

. . . The now-deceased plaintiffs in this action may in fact have had a liberty interest even stronger than Nancy Cruzan's because, not only were they terminally ill, they were suffering constant and severe pain. Avoiding intolerable pain and the indignity of living one's final days incapacitated and in agony is certainly "[a]t the heart of [the] liberty . . . to define one's own concept of existence, of meaning, of the universe, and of the mystery of human life." *Casey.* . . .

. . . *Cruzan* [gave] recognition, not just to vague, unbridled notions of autonomy, but to the more specific interest in making decisions about how to confront an imminent death. . . . The liberty interest at stake in a case like this differs from, and is stronger than, both the common-law right to refuse medical treatment and the unbridled interest in deciding whether to live or die. It is an interest in deciding how, rather than whether, a critical threshold shall be crossed.

III

. . .

. . . Allowing the individual, rather than the State, to make judgments " 'about the "quality" of life that a particular individual may enjoy,' " does not mean that the lives of terminally-ill, disabled people have less value than the lives of those who are healthy. Rather, it gives proper recognition to the individual's interest in choosing a final chapter that accords with her life story, rather than one that demeans her values and poisons memories of her. . . .

. . . I agree that the State has a compelling interest in preventing persons from committing suicide because of depression, or coercion by third parties. But the State's legitimate interest in preventing abuse does not apply to an individual who is not victimized by abuse, who is not suffering from depression, and who makes a rational and voluntary decision to seek assistance in dying. . . .

. . . [P]alliative care . . . cannot alleviate all pain and suffering. . . . An individual adequately informed of the care alternatives thus might make a rational choice for assisted suicide. For such an individual, the State's interest in preventing potential abuse and mistake is only minimally implicated.

The final major interest asserted by the State is . . . preserving the traditional integrity of the medical profession. . . . But for some patients, it would be a physician's refusal to dispense medication to ease their suffering and make their death tolerable and dignified that would be inconsistent with the healing role. . . . Furthermore, because physicians are already involved in making decisions that hasten the death of terminally ill patients—through termination of life support, withholding of medical treatment, and terminal sedation—there is in fact significant tension between the traditional view of the physician's role and the actual practice in a growing number of cases.[12]

. . . I do not . . . foreclose the possibility that an individual plaintiff seeking to hasten her death, or a doctor whose assistance was sought, could prevail in a more particularized challenge. . . .

---

[12] [T]here is evidence that a significant number of physicians support the practice of hastening death in particular situations. . . .

IV

In New York, a doctor must respect a competent person's decision to refuse or to discontinue medical treatment even though death will thereby ensue, but the same doctor would be guilty of a felony if she provided her patient assistance in committing suicide. Today we hold that the Equal Protection Clause is not violated by the resulting disparate treatment of two classes of terminally ill people who may have the same interest in hastening death. I agree that the distinction between permitting death to ensue from an underlying fatal disease and causing it to occur by the administration of medication or other means provides a constitutionally sufficient basis for the State's classification. Unlike the Court, however, I am not persuaded that in all cases there will in fact be a significant difference between the intent of the physicians, the patients or the families in the two situations.

. . . The illusory character of any differences in intent or causation is confirmed by the fact that the American Medical Association unequivocally endorses the practice of terminal sedation—the administration of sufficient dosages of pain-killing medication to terminally ill patients to protect them from excruciating pain even when it is clear that the time of death will be advanced. The purpose of terminal sedation is to ease the suffering of the patient and comply with her wishes, and the actual cause of death is the administration of heavy doses of lethal sedatives. This same intent and causation may exist when a doctor complies with a patient's request for lethal medication to hasten her death.

. . . Our holding today in Vacco v. Quill that the Equal Protection Clause is not violated by New York's classification, just like our holding in Washington v. Glucksberg that the Washington statute is not invalid on its face, does not foreclose the possibility that some applications of the New York statute may impose an intolerable intrusion on the patient's freedom.

. . .

■ JUSTICE SOUTER, concurring in the judgment.

. . . The question is whether the statute sets up one of those "arbitrary impositions" or "purposeless restraints" at odds with the Due Process Clause of the Fourteenth Amendment. Poe v. Ullman, 367 U.S. 497, 543 (1961) (Harlan, J., dissenting). . . .

. . .

III

. . .

This approach calls for a court to assess the relative "weights" or dignities of the contending interests, . . . subject . . . to two important constraints. . . . First, . . . a court is bound to confine the values that it recognizes to those truly deserving constitutional stature, either to those expressed in constitutional text, or those exemplified by "the traditions from which [the Nation] developed," or revealed by contrast with "the traditions from which it broke." . . .

[S]econd[,] . . . [i]t is only when the legislation's justifying principle, critically valued, is so far from being commensurate with the individual interest as to be arbitrarily or pointlessly applied that the statute must give way. . . .

The *Poe* dissent . . . reminds us that the process of substantive review by reasoned judgment . . . is one of close criticism going to the details of the opposing interests and to their relationships with the historically recognized principles that lend them weight or value.

. . . Exact analysis and characterization of any due process claim is critical to the method and to the result.

. . .

. . . [H]ere we are faced with an individual claim not to a right on the part of just anyone to help anyone else commit suicide under any circumstances, but to the right of a narrow class to help others also in a narrow class under a set of limited circumstances. And the claimants are met with the State's assertion, among others, that rights of such narrow scope cannot be recognized without jeopardy to individuals whom the State may concededly protect through its regulations.

IV

A

Respondents claim that a patient facing imminent death, who anticipates physical suffering and indignity, and is capable of responsible and voluntary choice, should have a right to a physician's assistance in providing counsel and drugs to be administered by the patient to end life promptly. . . .

. . .

It is . . . in the abortion cases that the most telling recognitions of the importance of bodily integrity and the concomitant tradition of medical assistance have occurred. In Roe v. Wade, . . . we stressed the importance of the relationship between patient and physician. . . .

The analogies between the abortion cases and this one are several. Even though the State has a legitimate interest in discouraging abortion, . . . the Court recognized a woman's right to a physician's counsel and care. Like the decision to commit suicide, the decision to abort potential life can be made irresponsibly and under the influence of others, and yet the Court has held in the abortion cases that physicians are fit assistants. Without physician assistance in abortion, the woman's right would have too often amounted to nothing more than a right to self-mutilation, and without a physician to assist in the suicide of the dying, the patient's right will often be confined to crude methods of causing death, most shocking and painful to the decedent's survivors.

[F]inally,. . . . the good physician . . . ministers to the patient. This idea of the physician as serving the whole person is a source of the high value traditionally placed on the medical relationship. Its value is surely as apparent here as in the abortion cases, for just as the decision about abortion is not directed to correcting some pathology, so the decision in which a dying patient seeks help is not so limited. The patients here sought not only an end to pain . . . but an end to their short remaining lives with a dignity that they believed would be denied them by powerful pain medication, as well as by their consciousness of dependency and helplessness as they approached death. In that period when the end is imminent, they said, the decision to end life is closest to decisions that are generally accepted as proper instances of exercising autonomy over one's own body, instances recognized under the Constitution and the State's own law, instances in which the help of physicians is accepted as falling within the traditional norm.

. . .

In my judgment, the importance of the individual interest here, as within that class of "certain interests" demanding careful scrutiny of the State's contrary claim, see Poe, . . . cannot be gainsaid. Whether that interest might in some circumstances, or at some time, be seen as "fundamental" to the degree entitled to prevail is not, however, a conclusion that I need draw here, for . . . the State's interests described in the following section are sufficiently serious to defeat the present claim that its law is arbitrary or purposeless.

B

The State ... interests [include] ... protecting life generally, ... discouraging suicide even if knowing and voluntary, ... and protecting terminally ill patients from involuntary suicide and euthanasia, both voluntary and nonvoluntary. ...

[T]he third is dispositive for me. That third justification is different from the first two, for it addresses specific features of respondents' claim, and it opposes that claim not with a moral judgment contrary to respondents', but with a recognized state interest in the protection of nonresponsible individuals and those who do not stand in relation either to death or to their physicians as do the patients whom respondents describe. ... [M]istaken decisions may result from inadequate palliative care or a terminal prognosis that turns out to be error; coercion and abuse may stem from the large medical bills that family members cannot bear or unreimbursed hospitals decline to shoulder. Voluntary and involuntary euthanasia may result once doctors are authorized to prescribe lethal medication in the first instance, for they might find it pointless to distinguish between patients who administer their own fatal drugs and those who wish not to, and their compassion for those who suffer may obscure the distinction between those who ask for death and those who may be unable to request it. The argument is that a progression would occur, obscuring the line between the ill and the dying, and between the responsible and the unduly influenced, until ultimately doctors and perhaps others would abuse a limited freedom to aid suicides by yielding to the impulse to end another's suffering under conditions going beyond the narrow limits the respondents propose. The State thus argues, essentially, that respondents' claim is not as narrow as it sounds, simply because no recognition of the interest they assert could be limited to vindicating those interests and affecting no others. ...

. . .

... Whether acting from compassion or under some other influence, a physician who would provide a drug for a patient to administer might well go the further step of administering the drug himself; so, the barrier between assisted suicide and euthanasia could become porous, and the line between voluntary and involuntary euthanasia as well. The case for the slippery slope is fairly made out here, not because recognizing one due process right would leave a court with no principled basis to avoid recognizing another, but because there is a plausible case that the right claimed would not be readily containable by reference to facts about the mind that are matters of difficult judgment, or by gatekeepers who are subject to temptation, noble or not.

Respondents propose ... the answer of state regulation with teeth. ...

But at least at this moment there are reasons for caution in predicting the effectiveness of the teeth proposed. Respondents' proposals ... sound much like the guidelines now in place in the Netherlands, the only place where experience with physician-assisted suicide and euthanasia has yielded empirical evidence about how such regulations might affect actual practice. ... Some commentators marshal evidence that the Dutch guidelines have in practice failed to protect patients from involuntary euthanasia and have been violated with impunity. ... This evidence is contested. ... The day may come when we can say with some assurance which side is right, but for now it is the substantiality of the factual disagreement, and the alternatives for resolving it, that matter. They are, for me, dispositive of the due process claim at this time.

. . .

Legislatures . . . have superior opportunities to obtain the facts necessary for a judgment about the present controversy. . . .

. . .

. . . While I do not decide for all time that respondents' claim should not be recognized, I acknowledge the legislative institutional competence as the better one to deal with that claim at this time.

. . .

■ JUSTICE BREYER, concurring in the judgments.

I believe that Justice O'Connor's views, which I share, have greater legal significance than the Court's opinion suggests. I join her separate opinion, except insofar as it joins the majority. . . .

I agree with the Court in Vacco v. Quill that the articulated state interests justify the distinction drawn between physician assisted suicide and withdrawal of life-support. I also agree with the Court that the critical question in both of the cases before us is whether "the 'liberty' specially protected by the Due Process Clause includes a right" of the sort that the respondents assert. . . . I do not agree, however, with the Court's formulation of that claimed "liberty" interest. The Court describes it as a "right to commit suicide with another's assistance." But I would not reject the respondents' claim without considering a different formulation, for which our legal tradition may provide greater support. That formulation would use words roughly like a "right to die with dignity." But irrespective of the exact words used, at its core would lie personal control over the manner of death, professional medical assistance, and the avoidance of unnecessary and severe physical suffering—combined.

As Justice Souter points out, Justice Harlan's dissenting opinion in Poe v. Ullman, 367 U.S. 497 (1961), offers some support for such a claim. . . .

. . . [R]espondents . . . argue that one can find a "right to die with dignity" by examining the protection the law has provided for related, but not identical, interests relating to personal dignity, medical treatment, and freedom from state-inflicted pain. . . .

I do not believe, however, that this Court need or now should decide whether or a not such a right is "fundamental." That is because, in my view, the avoidance of severe physical pain (connected with death) would have to comprise an essential part of any successful claim and because, as Justice O'Connor points out, the laws before us do not force a dying person to undergo that kind of pain. Rather, the laws of New York and of Washington do not prohibit doctors from providing patients with drugs sufficient to control pain despite the risk that those drugs themselves will kill. . . . And under these circumstances the laws of New York and Washington would overcome any remaining significant interests and would be justified, regardless.

. . .

Were the legal circumstances different—for example, were state law to prevent the provision of palliative care, including the administration of drugs as needed to avoid pain at the end of life—then the law's impact upon serious and otherwise unavoidable physical pain (accompanying death) would be more directly at issue. And as Justice O'Connor suggests, the Court might have to revisit its conclusions in these cases.

3. THE SECOND AMENDMENT AND PERSONAL LIBERTY

By itself the following case is an important development in the constitutional law of personal liberty. Although at first glance it may seem a sharp digression from the

Court's approach to assessing the reasonableness of legislation under the due process clauses, consider whether, how, and to what extent, its methodological approach to constitutional interpretation of the enumerated Second Amendment right to keep and bear arms in the end differs from, or is similar to, the Court's approach to defining the scope of enumerated liberties under the due process clauses. Note the emphasis on parsing text and original (and post-ratification) understanding.

District of Columbia v. Heller

554 U.S.570, 128 S.Ct. 2783, 171 L.Ed.2d 637 (2008).

■ JUSTICE SCALIA delivered the opinion of the Court.

We consider whether a District of Columbia prohibition on the possession of usable handguns in the home violates the Second Amendment. . . .

I

The District of Columbia generally prohibits the possession of handguns. . . . [It] also requires residents to keep their lawfully owned firearms, such as registered long guns, "unloaded and disassembled or bound by a trigger lock or similar device" unless they are located in a place of business or are being used for lawful recreational activities. . . .

. . . Heller . . . applied for a registration certificate for a handgun . . . to keep at home, but the District refused. [The District Court dismissed Heller's Second Amendment challenge, but the Court of Appeals for the District of Columbia Circuit reversed.]

II

. . .

The Second Amendment provides: "A well regulated Militia, being necessary to the security of a free State, the right of the people to keep and bear Arms, shall not be infringed." . . .

. . . Petitioners and today's dissenting Justices believe that it protects only the right to possess and carry a firearm in connection with militia service. . . . Respondent argues that it protects an individual right to possess a firearm unconnected with service in a militia, and to use that arm for traditionally lawful purposes, such as self-defense within the home. . . .

The Second Amendment is naturally divided into two parts: its prefatory clause and its operative clause. The former does not limit the latter grammatically, but rather announces a purpose. . . .

. . .

1. Operative Clause.

a. "Right of the People." The first salient feature of the operative clause is that it codifies a "right of the people." The unamended Constitution and the Bill of Rights use the phrase "right of the people" two other times, in the First Amendment's Assembly-and-Petition Clause and in the Fourth Amendment's Search-and-Seizure Clause. The Ninth Amendment uses very similar terminology. . . . All three of these instances unambiguously refer to individual rights, not "collective" rights, or rights that may be exercised only through participation in some corporate body.

. . .

. . . Reading the Second Amendment as protecting only the right to "keep and bear Arms" in an organized militia . . . fits poorly with the operative clause's description of the holder of that right as "the people."

We start therefore with a strong presumption that the Second Amendment right is exercised individually and belongs to all Americans.

b.   "Keep and bear Arms." . . .

. . .

The term ["Arms"] was applied, then as now, to weapons . . . not specifically designed for military use and . . . not employed in a military capacity. . . .

. . . [T]he Second Amendment extends, prima facie, to all instruments that constitute bearable arms, even those that were not in existence at the time of the founding.

. . .

. . . "Keep arms" was simply a common way of referring to possessing arms, for militiamen and everyone else.

At the time of the founding, as now, to "bear" meant to "carry." . . . When used with "arms," however, the term has a meaning that refers to carrying for a particular purpose—confrontation. . . . Although the phrase implies that the carrying of the weapon is for the purpose of "offensive or defensive action," it in no way connotes participation in a structured military organization.

From our review of founding-era sources, we conclude that this natural meaning was also the meaning that "bear arms" had in the 18th century. In numerous instances, "bear arms" was unambiguously used to refer to the carrying of weapons outside of an organized militia. The most prominent examples are those most relevant to the Second Amendment: Nine state constitutional provisions written in the 18th century or the first two decades of the 19th, which enshrined a right of citizens to "bear arms in defense of themselves and the state" or "bear arms in defense of himself and the state." It is clear from those formulations that "bear arms" did not refer only to carrying a weapon in an organized military unit. . . .

. . .

c.   Meaning of the Operative Clause. Putting all of these textual elements together, we find that they guarantee the individual right to possess and carry weapons in case of confrontation. This meaning is strongly confirmed by the historical background of the Second Amendment[, which] codified a *pre-existing* right . . . that . . . "shall not be infringed." . . .

. . . [T]he Stuart Kings . . . succeeded in using select militias loyal to them to suppress political dissidents, in part by disarming their opponents. . . . [T]he Catholic James II had ordered general disarmaments of regions home to his Protestant enemies. . . . These experiences caused Englishmen to be extremely wary of concentrated military forces run by the state and to be jealous of their arms. They accordingly obtained an assurance from William and Mary, in the Declaration of Right (. . . codified as the English Bill of Rights), that Protestants would never be disarmed: "That the subjects which are Protestants may have arms for their defense suitable to their conditions and as allowed by law." . . . (1689). This right has long been understood to be the predecessor to our Second Amendment. . . . It was clearly an individual right, having nothing whatever to do with service in a militia. . . . [I]t was secured to . . . individuals, according to "libertarian political principles," not as members of a fighting force. . . .

By the time of the founding, . . . Blackstone . . . cited th[is] arms provision . . . as one of the fundamental rights of Englishmen. . . . His description of it cannot possibly be thought to tie it to militia or military service. It was, he said, "the natural right of resistance and self-preservation," . . . and "the right of having and using arms for self-preservation and defence," . . . (1768). Other contemporary authorities concurred. . . . Thus, the right secured in 1689 . . . was by the time of the founding understood to be an individual right protecting against both public and private violence.

. . .

There seems to us no doubt, on the basis of both text and history, that the Second Amendment conferred an individual right to keep and bear arms. Of course the right was not unlimited, just as the First Amendment's right of free speech was not. . . .

2.   Prefatory Clause.

. . .

. . . Does the preface fit with an operative clause that creates an individual right to keep and bear arms? It fits perfectly, once one knows the history that the founding generation knew and that we have described above. That history showed that the way tyrants had eliminated a militia consisting of all the able-bodied men was not by banning the militia but simply by taking away the people's arms, enabling a select militia or standing army to suppress political opponents. This is what had occurred in England that prompted codification of the right to have arms in the English Bill of Rights.

The debate with respect to the right to keep and bear arms, as with other guarantees in the Bill of Rights, was not over whether it was desirable (all agreed that it was) but over whether it needed to be codified in the Constitution. During the 1788 ratification debates, the fear that the federal government would disarm the people in order to impose rule through a standing army or select militia was pervasive in Antifederalist rhetoric. . . . Federalists responded that because Congress was given no power to abridge the ancient right of individuals to keep and bear arms, such a force could never oppress the people. . . . It was understood across the political spectrum that the right helped to secure the ideal of a citizen militia, which might be necessary to oppose an oppressive military force if the constitutional order broke down.

It is therefore entirely sensible that the Second Amendment's prefatory clause announces the purpose for which the right was codified: to prevent elimination of the militia. The prefatory clause does not suggest that preserving the militia was the only reason Americans valued the ancient right; most undoubtedly thought it even more important for self-defense and hunting. But the threat that the new Federal Government would destroy the citizens' militia by taking away their arms was the reason that right—unlike some other English rights—was codified in a written Constitution. Justice Breyer's assertion that individual self-defense is merely a "subsidiary interest" of the right to keep and bear arms is profoundly mistaken. He bases that assertion solely upon the prologue—but that can only show that self-defense had little to do with the right's *codification;* it was the *central component* of the right itself.

. . . If . . . the Second Amendment right is no more than the right to keep and use weapons as a member of an organized militia . . . —if, that is, the *organized* militia is the sole institutional beneficiary of the Second Amendment's guarantee—it does not assure the existence of a "citizens' militia" as a safeguard against tyranny. For Congress retains plenary authority to organize the militia, which must include the authority to say who will belong to the organized force. . . .

B

Our interpretation is confirmed by analogous arms-bearing rights in state constitutions that preceded and immediately followed adoption of the Second Amendment. . . .

. . .

. . . That of the nine state constitutional protections for the right to bear arms enacted immediately after 1789 at least seven unequivocally protected an individual citizen's right to self-defense is strong evidence that that is how the founding generation conceived of the right. . . .

The historical narrative that petitioners must endorse would thus treat the Federal Second Amendment as an odd outlier, protecting a right unknown in state constitutions or at English common law, based on little more than an overreading of the prefatory clause.

. . .

D

. . . [V]irtually all interpreters of the Second Amendment in the century after its enactment interpreted the amendment as we do.

[Justice Scalia cited post-ratification commentary from St. George Tucker, William Rawle, Joseph Story, and antislavery advocates as support for the individual-rights view; concluded that the "19th-century [federal and state] cases that interpreted the Second Amendment universally support an individual right unconnected to militia service"; contended that after the Civil War—when freed blacks "were routinely disarmed by Southern States"—congressional efforts to protect them were based on the understanding that the Second Amendment secured an individual right to use arms for self-defense; and asserted that "[e]very late-19th-century legal scholar that we have read interpreted the Second Amendment to secure an individual right unconnected with militia service"—including "Thomas Cooley, who wrote a massively popular 1868 Treatise on Constitutional Limitations."]

E

We now ask whether any of our precedents forecloses the conclusions we have reached about the meaning of the Second Amendment.

United States v. Cruikshank . . . held that the Second Amendment does not by its own force apply to anyone other than the Federal Government. . . .

Presser v. Illinois, 116 U.S. 252 (1886), . . . said nothing about the Second Amendment's meaning or scope, beyond the fact that it does not prevent the prohibition of private paramilitary organizations.

. . . United States v. Miller, 307 U.S. 174 (1939)[,] . . . according to Justice Stevens . . . [held] that the Second Amendment "protects the right to keep and bear arms for certain military purposes, but . . . does not curtail the legislature's power to regulate the nonmilitary use and ownership of weapons."

. . . *Miller* did not hold that and cannot possibly be read to have held that. The judgment . . . upheld against a Second Amendment challenge two men's federal convictions for transporting an unregistered short-barreled shotgun in interstate commerce. . . . It is entirely clear that the Court's basis for saying that the Second Amendment did not apply was . . . that the *type of weapon at issue* was not eligible for Second Amendment protection. . . .

. . .

. . . We . . . read *Miller* to say only that the Second Amendment does not protect those weapons not typically possessed by law-abiding citizens for lawful purposes, such as short-barreled shotguns. That accords with the historical understanding of the scope of the right, see Part III, infra.

We conclude that nothing in our precedents forecloses our adoption of the original understanding of the Second Amendment. . . .

III

Like most rights, the right secured by the Second Amendment is not unlimited. From Blackstone through the 19th-century cases, commentators and courts routinely explained that the right was not a right to keep and carry any weapon whatsoever in any manner whatsoever and for whatever purpose. . . . For example, the majority of the 19th-century courts to consider the question held that prohibitions on carrying concealed weapons were lawful under the Second Amendment or state analogues. . . . Although we do not undertake an exhaustive historical analysis today of the full scope of the Second Amendment, nothing in our opinion should be taken to cast doubt on longstanding prohibitions on the possession of firearms by felons and the mentally ill, or laws forbidding the carrying of firearms in sensitive places such as schools and government buildings, or laws imposing conditions and qualifications on the commercial sale of arms.

We also recognize another important limitation on the right to keep and carry arms. *Miller* said . . . that the sorts of weapons protected were those "in common use at the time." . . . We think that limitation is fairly supported by the historical tradition of prohibiting the carrying of "dangerous and unusual weapons." See 4 Blackstone 148–149 (1769); 3 B. Wilson, Works of the Honourable James Wilson 79 (1804);. . . .

. . . It may well be true today that a militia, to be as effective as militias in the 18th century, would require sophisticated arms that are highly unusual in society at large. Indeed, it may be true that no amount of small arms could be useful against modern-day bombers and tanks. But the fact that modern developments have limited the degree of fit between the prefatory clause and the protected right cannot change our interpretation of the right.

IV

We turn finally to the law at issue [, which] totally bans handgun possession in the home [and] requires that any lawful firearm in the home be disassembled or bound by a trigger lock at all times, rendering it inoperable.

. . . [T]he inherent right of self-defense has been central to the Second Amendment right. The handgun ban amounts to a prohibition of an entire class of "arms" that is overwhelmingly chosen by American society for that lawful purpose. The prohibition extends, moreover, to the home, where the need for defense of self, family, and property is most acute. Under any of the standards of scrutiny that we have applied to enumerated constitutional rights,[27] banning from the home "the most preferred firearm in the nation to 'keep' and use for protection of one's home and family," . . . would fail constitutional muster.

---

[27] Justice Breyer correctly notes that this law, like almost all laws, would pass rational-basis scrutiny. But rational-basis scrutiny is a mode of analysis we have used when evaluating laws under constitutional commands that are themselves prohibitions on irrational laws. . . . In those cases, "rational basis" is not just the standard of scrutiny, but the very substance of the constitutional guarantee. Obviously, the same test could not be used to evaluate the extent to which a legislature may regulate a specific, enumerated right, be it the freedom of speech, the guarantee against double jeopardy, the right to counsel, or the right to keep and bear arms. . . . If all that was required to overcome the right to keep and bear arms was a rational basis, the Second Amendment would be redundant with the separate constitutional prohibitions on irrational laws, and would have no effect.

. . .

It is no answer to say . . . that it is permissible to ban the possession of handguns so long as the possession of other firearms (*i.e.*, long guns) is allowed. It is enough to note . . . that the American people have considered the handgun to be the quintessential self-defense weapon. . . . It is easier to store in a location that is readily accessible in an emergency; it cannot easily be redirected or wrestled away by an attacker; it is easier to use for those without the upper-body strength to lift and aim a long gun; it can be pointed at a burglar with one hand while the other hand dials the police. Whatever the reason, handguns are the most popular weapon chosen by Americans for self-defense in the home, and a complete prohibition of their use is invalid.

We must also address the District's requirement (as applied to respondent's handgun) that firearms in the home be rendered and kept inoperable at all times. This makes it impossible for citizens to use them for the core lawful purpose of self-defense and is hence unconstitutional. . . .

. . .

Justice Breyer[,] . . . pointing to various restrictive laws in the colonial period[, would uphold the law here even assuming the Second Amendment is a personal guarantee.] Of the laws he cites, only one offers even marginal support for his assertion[, and there is] reason to doubt that colonial Boston authorities would have enforced [it] against someone who temporarily loaded a firearm to confront an intruder. . . . The other laws Justice Breyer cites are gunpowder-storage laws that he concedes did not clearly prohibit loaded weapons, but required only that excess gunpowder be kept in a special container or on the top floor of the home. Nothing about those fire-safety laws undermines our analysis; they do not remotely burden the right of self-defense as much as an absolute ban on handguns. Nor, correspondingly, does our analysis suggest the invalidity of laws regulating the storage of firearms to prevent accidents.

Justice Breyer points to other founding-era laws that he says "restricted the firing of guns within the city limits to at least some degree" in Boston, Philadelphia and New York. . . . It is . . . implausible that [any of them] would have been enforced against a citizen acting in self-defense. . . .

. . . [None imposed] significant criminal penalties. . . . [W]e do not think that a law imposing a 5-shilling fine and forfeiture of the gun would have prevented a person in the founding era from using a gun to protect himself or his family from violence, or that if he did so the law would be enforced against him. The District law, by contrast, . . . threatens citizens with a year in prison (five years for a second violation) for even obtaining a gun. . . .

Justice Breyer . . . criticizes us for declining to establish a level of scrutiny for evaluating Second Amendment restrictions. He proposes, explicitly at least, none of the traditionally expressed levels (strict scrutiny, intermediate scrutiny, rational basis), but rather a judge-empowering "interest-balancing inquiry" that "asks whether the statute burdens a protected interest in a way or to an extent that is out of proportion to the statute's salutary effects upon other important governmental interests." . . . Justice Breyer['s] interest-balanced answer: because handgun violence is a problem, because the law is limited to an urban area, and because there were somewhat similar restrictions in the founding period (a false proposition . . .), the interest-balancing inquiry results in the constitutionality of the handgun ban. QED.

We know of no other enumerated constitutional right whose core protection has been subjected to a freestanding "interest-balancing" approach. The very enumeration of the right takes out of the hands of government—even the Third Branch of

Government—the power to decide on a case-by-case basis whether the right is *really worth* insisting upon. A constitutional guarantee subject to future judges' assessments of its usefulness is no constitutional guarantee at all. Constitutional rights are enshrined with the scope they were understood to have when the people adopted them, whether or not future legislatures or (yes) even future judges think that scope too broad. . . . The Second Amendment . . . [, l]ike the First, . . . is the very *product* of an interest-balancing by the people—which Justice Breyer would now conduct for them anew. And whatever else it leaves to future evaluation, it surely elevates above all other interests the right of law-abiding, responsible citizens to use arms in defense of hearth and home.

    . . .

We are aware of the problem of handgun violence in this country, and we take seriously the concerns raised by the many *amici* who believe that prohibition of handgun ownership is a solution. The Constitution leaves the District of Columbia a variety of tools for combating that problem, including some measures regulating handguns. . . . But the enshrinement of constitutional rights necessarily takes certain policy choices off the table. These include the absolute prohibition of handguns held and used for self-defense in the home. . . . [I]t is not the role of this Court to pronounce the Second Amendment extinct.

We affirm the judgment of the Court of Appeals.

■ JUSTICE STEVENS, with whom JUSTICE SOUTER, JUSTICE GINSBURG, and JUSTICE BREYER join, dissenting.

The question presented . . . is not whether the Second Amendment protects a "collective right" or an "individual right." Surely it protects a right that can be enforced by individuals. But . . . that . . . does not tell us anything about the scope of that right.

    . . .

The Second Amendment was adopted to protect the right of the people of each of the several States to maintain a well-regulated militia. It was a response to concerns raised during the ratification of the Constitution that the power of Congress to disarm the state militias and create a national standing army posed an intolerable threat to the sovereignty of the several States. . . . [T]here is no indication that the Framers of the Amendment intended to enshrine the common-law right of self-defense in the Constitution.

In 1934, Congress enacted the National Firearms Act, the first major federal firearms law. Upholding a conviction under that Act, this Court held that, "[i]n the absence of any evidence tending to show that possession or use of a 'shotgun having a barrel of less than eighteen inches in length' at this time has some reasonable relationship to the preservation or efficiency of a well regulated militia, we cannot say that the Second Amendment guarantees the right to keep and bear such an instrument." *Miller*. . . . The view of the Amendment we took in *Miller*—that it protects the right to keep and bear arms for certain military purposes, but that it does not curtail the Legislature's power to regulate the nonmilitary use and ownership of weapons—is both the most natural reading of the Amendment's text and the interpretation most faithful to the history of its adoption.

Since . . . *Miller,* hundreds of judges have relied on the view of the Amendment we endorsed there; we ourselves affirmed it in 1980. See Lewis v. United States, 445 U.S. 55, n. 8 (1980).[3] . . .

---

[3]   . . . Upholding a conviction for receipt of a firearm by a felon, we wrote: "These legislative restrictions on the use of firearms are neither based upon constitutionally suspect criteria, nor do they

The ... Court ... [s]takes its holding on a strained and unpersuasive reading of the Amendment's text; significantly different provisions in the 1689 English Bill of Rights, and in various 19th-century State Constitutions; postenactment commentary that was available to the Court when it decided *Miller;* and, ultimately, a feeble attempt to distinguish *Miller* that places more emphasis on the Court's decisional process than on the reasoning in the opinion itself.

. . .

I

. . .

The preamble to the Second Amendment ... identifies the preservation of the militia as the Amendment's purpose.... [P]rovisions in several State Declarations of Rights ... adopted roughly contemporaneously with the Declaration of Independence ... underscore the profound fear shared by many in that era of the dangers posed by standing armies....

... [T]he Framers' single-minded focus in crafting the constitutional guarantee "to keep and bear arms" was on military uses of firearms, which they viewed in the context of service in state militias.

. . .

[Justice Stevens disputed the majority's contention "that the words 'the people' as used in the Second Amendment must have the same meaning, and protect the same class of individuals, as when they are used in the First and Fourth Amendments." He also noted that the First Amendment rights of the people peaceably to assemble, and to petition the Government for a redress of grievances, "contemplate collective action".]

Similarly, the words "the people" in the Second Amendment refer back to the object announced in the Amendment's preamble. They remind us that it is the collective action of individuals having a duty to serve in the militia that the text directly protects and, perhaps more importantly, that the ultimate purpose of the Amendment was to protect the States' share of the divided sovereignty created by the Constitution.

. . .

[The words "to keep and bear arms"] describe a unitary right: to possess arms if needed for military purposes and to use them in conjunction with military activities.

. . .

... The absence of any reference to civilian uses of weapons tailors the text of the Amendment to the purpose identified in its preamble....

... The stand-alone phrase "bear arms" most naturally conveys a military meaning....

The ... term "keep" ... describe[s] the requirement that militia members store their arms at their homes, ready to be used for service when necessary...."[K]eep and bear arms" thus perfectly describes the responsibilities of a framing-era militia member.

... [T]he clause protects ... the single ... duty and ... right to have arms available and ready for military service, and to use them for military purposes when

---

entrench upon any constitutionally protected liberties. See United States v. Miller, 307 U.S. 174, 178 (1939) (the Second Amendment guarantees no right to keep and bear a firearm that does not have 'some reasonable relationship to the preservation or efficiency of a well regulated militia'). 445 U. S., at 65, n. 8.

necessary. Different language surely would have been used to protect nonmilitary use and possession of weapons from regulation if such an intent had played any role in the drafting of the Amendment.

* * *

When each word in the text is given full effect, the Amendment is most naturally read to secure to the people a right to use and possess arms in conjunction with service in a well-regulated militia. . . . And the Court's emphatic reliance on the claim "that the Second Amendment . . . codified a *pre-existing* right," is of course beside the point because the right to keep and bear arms for service in a state militia was also a pre-existing right.

. . .

II

. . .

Madison's decision to model the Second Amendment on the distinctly military Virginia proposal is . . . revealing, since it is clear that he considered and rejected formulations that would have unambiguously protected civilian uses of firearms. . . .

. . .

The history of the adoption of the Amendment . . . describes an overriding concern about the potential threat to state sovereignty that a federal standing army would pose, and a desire to protect the States' militias as the means by which to guard against that danger. But state militias could not effectively check the prospect of a federal standing army so long as Congress retained the power to disarm them, and so a guarantee against such disarmament was needed. As we explained in *Miller:* "With obvious purpose to assure the continuation and render possible the effectiveness of such forces the declaration and guarantee of the Second Amendment were made. It must be interpreted and applied with that end in view." . . . The evidence plainly refutes the claim that the Amendment was motivated by the Framers' fears that Congress might act to regulate any civilian uses of weapons. . . .

III

. . .

The English Bill of Rights . . . Article VII . . . was a response to . . . selective disarmament. . . . [It] did not establish a general right of all persons, or even of all Protestants, to possess weapons. . . .

The Court may well be correct that [it] protected the right of *some* English subjects to use *some* arms for personal self-defense free from restrictions by the Crown (but not Parliament). But that right—adopted in a different historical and political context and framed in markedly different language—tells us little about the meaning of the Second Amendment.

. . .

. . . Blackstone's invocation of " 'the natural right of resistance and self-preservation,' " and " 'the right of having and using arms for self-preservation and defence' " referred specifically to Article VII in the English Bill of Rights. The excerpt . . . , therefore, is, like Article VII itself, of limited use in interpreting the very differently worded, and differently historically situated, Second Amendment.

. . .

Story [tied] the significance of the Amendment directly to the paramount importance of the militia. . . . There is not so much as a whisper . . . that Story believed that the right secured by the Amendment bore any relation to private use or possession of weapons for activities like hunting or personal self-defense.

. . .

. . . Story's exclusive focus on the militia in his discussion of the Second Amendment confirms his understanding of the right protected by the Second Amendment as limited to military uses of arms.

. . .

IV

. . .

[F]or most of our history, the invalidity of Second-Amendment-based objections to firearms regulations has been well settled and uncontroversial. . . . After reviewing many of the same sources . . . discussed at greater length by the Court today, the *Miller* Court unanimously concluded that the Second Amendment did not apply to the possession of a firearm that did not have "some reasonable relationship to the preservation or efficiency of a well regulated militia." . . .

The key to that decision did not . . . turn on the difference between muskets and sawed-off shotguns; it turned, rather, on the basic difference between the military and nonmilitary use and possession of guns. Indeed, if the Second Amendment were not limited in its coverage to military uses of weapons, why should the Court in *Miller* have suggested that some weapons but not others were eligible for Second Amendment protection? If use for self-defense were the relevant standard, why did the Court not inquire into the suitability of a particular weapon for self-defense purposes?

. . .

V

. . .

Until today, it has been understood that legislatures may regulate the civilian use and misuse of firearms so long as they do not interfere with the preservation of a well-regulated militia. The Court's announcement of a new constitutional right to own and use firearms for private purposes upsets that settled understanding, but leaves for future cases the formidable task of defining the scope of permissible regulations. . . .

. . .

. . . The Court would have us believe that . . . the Framers made a choice to limit the tools available to elected officials wishing to regulate civilian uses of weapons, and to authorize this Court to use the common-law process of case-by-case judicial lawmaking to define the contours of acceptable gun control policy. Absent compelling evidence that is nowhere to be found in the Court's opinion, I could not possibly conclude that the Framers made such a choice.

. . .

■ JUSTICE BREYER, with whom JUSTICE STEVENS, JUSTICE SOUTER, and JUSTICE GINSBURG join, dissenting.

. . .

. . . [E]ven if . . . interpreted as protecting a wholly separate interest in individual self-defense[,] . . . the District's regulation, which focuses upon the presence of handguns in high-crime urban areas, represents a permissible legislative response to a serious, indeed life-threatening, problem.

. . . [A] legislature could reasonably conclude that the law will advance goals of great public importance, namely, saving lives, preventing injury, and reducing crime.

The law is tailored to the urban crime problem in that it is local in scope and thus affects only a geographic area both limited in size and entirely urban; the law concerns handguns, which are specially linked to urban gun deaths and injuries, and which are the overwhelmingly favorite weapon of armed criminals; and at the same time, the law imposes a burden upon gun owners that seems proportionately no greater than restrictions in existence at the time the Second Amendment was adopted. In these circumstances, the District's law falls within the zone that the Second Amendment leaves open to regulation by legislatures.

II

. . .

[C]olonial history itself offers important examples of the kinds of gun regulation that citizens would then have thought compatible with the "right to keep and bear arms," whether embodied in Federal or State Constitutions, or the background common law[—]includ[ing] substantial regulation of firearms in urban areas, [some of which] imposed obstacles to the use of firearms for the protection of the home.

Boston, Philadelphia, and New York City . . . all restricted the firing of guns within city limits to at least some degree. . . .

Furthermore, several towns and cities (including Philadelphia, New York, and Boston) regulated, for fire-safety reasons, the storage of gunpowder, a necessary component of an operational firearm. . . . Even assuming, as the majority does, that [Boston's] law included an implicit self-defense exception, it would nevertheless have prevented a homeowner from keeping in his home a gun that he could immediately pick up and use against an intruder. Rather, the homeowner would have had to get the gunpowder and load it into the gun, an operation that would have taken a fair amount of time to perform. . . .

. . .

[H]istorical evidence demonstrates that a self-defense assumption is the *beginning*, rather than the *end*, of any constitutional inquiry. . . .

III

. . .

Respondent proposes that the Court adopt a "strict scrutiny" test. . . . But the majority implicitly, and appropriately, rejects that suggestion by broadly approving a set of laws—prohibitions on concealed weapons, forfeiture by criminals of the Second Amendment right, prohibitions on firearms in certain locales, and governmental regulation of commercial firearm sales—whose constitutionality under a strict scrutiny standard would be far from clear.

. . .

I would simply adopt . . . an interest-balancing inquiry explicitly . . . [and] ask[ ] whether the statute burdens a protected interest in a way or to an extent that is out of proportion to the statute's salutary effects upon other important governmental interests. . . . Any answer would take account both of the statute's effects upon the competing interests and the existence of any clearly superior less restrictive alternative. . . . Contrary to the majority's unsupported suggestion that this sort of "proportionality" approach is unprecedented, the Court has applied it in various constitutional contexts, including election-law cases, speech cases, and due process cases. . . .

. . .

IV

. . .

No one doubts the constitutional importance of the statute's basic objective, saving lives. . . . But there is considerable debate about whether the District's statute helps to achieve that objective. . . .

[After considering the District's legislative hearings and reports, a wide array of statistics from both sides, and arguments about the relevance of these various sources, Justice Breyer summarized his conclusion as follows:]

The upshot is a set of studies and counterstudies that, at most, could leave a judge uncertain about the proper policy conclusion. But . . . legislators, not judges, have primary responsibility for drawing policy conclusions from empirical fact. . . .

. . .

. . . I conclude that the District's statute properly seeks to further the sort of life-preserving and public-safety interests that the Court has called "compelling." . . .

[With respect to "the extent to which the District's law burdens the interests that the Second Amendment seeks to protect," Justice Breyer concluded that (1) "the District's law burdens the Second Amendment's primary objective" of preserving a well regulated Militia "little, or not at all;" (2) for similar reasons—principally "that the District's law does not prohibit possession of rifles or shotguns, and [allows] opportunities for sporting activities in nearby States"—"the District's law burdens any sports-related or hunting-related objectives that the Amendment may protect little, or not at all"; but (3) because handguns are popular and easier to use, the prohibition "burdens to some degree an interest in self-defense that for present purposes I have assumed the Amendment seeks to further."]

In weighing needs and burdens, we must take account of the possibility that there are reasonable, but less restrictive alternatives. . . . Here I see none.

. . .

. . . [T]he very attributes that make handguns particularly useful for self-defense are also what make them particularly dangerous. That they are easy to hold and control means that they are easier for children to use. . . . That they are maneuverable and permit a free hand likely contributes to the fact that they are by far the firearm of choice for crimes such as rape and robbery. . . .

This symmetry suggests that any measure less restrictive in respect to the use of handguns for self-defense will, to that same extent, prove less effective in preventing the use of handguns for illicit purposes. . . . If it is indeed the case, as the District believes, that the number of guns contributes to the number of gun-related crimes, accidents, and deaths, then, although there may be less restrictive, *less effective* substitutes for an outright ban, there is no less restrictive *equivalent* of an outright ban.

. . .

The upshot is that the District's objectives are compelling; its predictive judgments as to its law's tendency to achieve those objectives are adequately supported; the law does impose a burden upon any self-defense interest that the Amendment seeks to secure; and there is no clear less restrictive alternative. I turn now to the final portion of the "permissible regulation" question: Does the District's law *disproportionately* burden Amendment-protected interests? Several considerations, taken together, convince me that it does not.

First, the District law is tailored to the life-threatening problems it attempts to address. The law concerns one class of weapons, handguns, leaving residents free to possess shotguns and rifles, along with ammunition. The area that falls within its scope is totally urban. . . . That urban area suffers from a serious handgun-fatality problem. The District's law directly aims at that compelling problem. And there is no less restrictive way to achieve the problem-related benefits that it seeks.

Second, the self-defense interest in maintaining loaded handguns in the home to shoot intruders is not the *primary* interest, but at most a subsidiary interest, that the Second Amendment seeks to serve. . . .

Further, . . . the Framers . . . are unlikely . . . to have thought of a right to keep loaded handguns in homes to confront intruders in urban settings as *central*. . . .

Nor, for that matter, am I aware of any evidence that *handguns* in particular were central to the Framers' conception of the Second Amendment. . . .

. . .

. . . [L]itigation over the course of many years, or the mere specter of such litigation, threatens to leave cities without effective protection against gun violence and accidents during that time.

. . . The majority . . . fails to list even one seemingly adequate replacement for the law it strikes down. I can understand how reasonable individuals can disagree about the merits of strict gun control as a crime-control measure, even in a totally urbanized area. But I cannot understand how one can take from the elected branches of government the right to decide whether to insist upon a handgun-free urban populace in a city now facing a serious crime problem. . . .

V

. . . [M]y . . . approach—requiring careful identification of the relevant interests and evaluating the law's effect upon them—limits the judge's choices; and the method's necessary transparency lays bare the judge's reasoning for all to see and to criticize.

The majority's methodology is . . . substantially less transparent . . . .

. . .

. . . The majority says that th[e] Amendment protects those weapons "typically possessed by law-abiding citizens for lawful purposes." This definition conveniently excludes machineguns, but permits handguns. . . . In essence, the majority determines what regulations are permissible by looking to see what existing regulations permit. There is no basis for believing that the Framers intended such circular reasoning.

I am similarly puzzled by the majority's list . . . of provisions that in its view would survive Second Amendment scrutiny. . . . Why these? . . .

[T]he majority ignores a more important question: Given the purposes for which the Framers enacted the Second Amendment, how should it be applied to modern-day circumstances that they could not have anticipated? Assume, for argument's sake, that the Framers did intend the Amendment to offer a degree of self-defense protection. Does that mean that the Framers also intended to guarantee a right to possess a loaded gun near swimming pools, parks, and playgrounds? That they would not have cared about the children who might pick up a loaded gun on their parents' bedside table? That they (who certainly showed concern for the risk of fire) would have lacked concern for the risk of accidental deaths or suicides that readily accessible loaded handguns in urban areas might bring? Unless we believe that they intended future generations to ignore such matters, answering questions such as the questions in this case requires judgment—judicial judgment exercised within a framework for constitutional analysis that guides that judgment and which makes its exercise transparent. One cannot answer those questions by combining inconclusive historical research with judicial *ipse dixit*.

. . .

McDonald v. City of Chicago

561 U.S. 742, 130 S.Ct. 3020, 177 L.Ed.2d 894 (2010).

[The report of this case appears *supra*, at p. 315.]

CHAPTER 10

THE EQUAL PROTECTION CLAUSE AND THE REVIEW OF THE REASONABLENESS OF LEGISLATION

1. INTRODUCTION—THE SCOPE OF EQUAL PROTECTION

The fourteenth amendment provision that no state shall "deny to any person within its jurisdiction the equal protection of the laws," raises a host of difficult analytical problems. It can hardly be taken to be a guarantee that every law shall treat every person the same, for almost all legislation involves classifications placing special burdens on or granting special benefits to individuals or groups. But if laws may classify, what content can be given to a guarantee of "equal protection of the laws"?

The Original Understanding

The Supreme Court originally took a narrow view of the scope of the equal protection clause. In the Slaughter-House Cases, 83 U.S. (16 Wall.) 36, 81 (1872), the Court said: "We doubt very much whether any action of a State not directed by way of discrimination against the negroes as a class, or on account of their race, will ever be held to come within the purview of this provision. It is so clearly a provision for that race and that emergency, that a strong case would be necessary for its application to any other." In Strauder v. West Virginia, 100 U.S. 303, 306, 307 (1880), which invalidated a statute limiting jury service to whites, the Court said: "[The fourteenth amendment] was designed to assure to the colored race the enjoyment of all the civil rights that under the law are enjoyed by white persons, and to give to that race the protection of the General Government, in that enjoyment, whenever it should be denied by the States." In referring to the equal protection clause the Court said: "What is this but declaring that the law in the States shall be the same for the black as for the white; that all persons whether colored or white, shall stand equal before the laws of the States and, in regard to the colored race, for whose protection the Amendment was primarily designed, that no discrimination shall be made against them by law because of their color."

The Court shortly expanded its view, however, and brought the full range of legislative classification within the restrictions of the clause. In Barbier v. Connolly, 113 U.S. 27 (1884), the Court upheld a statute prohibiting the operation of laundries from 10 p.m. to 6 a.m., but assumed that the equal protection clause applied. The Court said that the equal protection clause guaranteed, inter alia, that "all persons should be equally entitled to pursue their happiness and acquire and enjoy property;" that "no impediment should be interposed to the pursuits of any one except as applied to the same pursuits by others under like circumstances;" and that "no greater burdens should be laid upon one than are laid upon others in the same calling or condition." The promise of *Barbier* that the equal protection clause would be applied to economic regulations was fulfilled in the following case.

Gulf, Colorado & Santa Fe Railroad Co. v. Ellis

165 U.S. 150 (1897).

The Court invalidated a statute providing that successful plaintiffs in certain kinds of suits against railroad companies should receive in addition to costs reasonable attorney's fees "not to exceed $10." The following passages suggest its reasoning:

". . . The act singles out a certain class of debtors and punishes them when for like delinquencies it punishes no others. They are not treated as other debtors, or equally with other debtors. They cannot appeal to the courts as other litigants under like conditions and with like protection. If litigation terminates adversely to them, they are mulcted in the attorney's fees of the successful plaintiff; if it terminates in their favor, they recover no attorney's fees. It is no sufficient answer to say that they are punished only when adjudged to be in the wrong. They do not enter the courts upon equal terms. They must pay attorney's fees if wrong; they do not recover any if right; while their adversaries recover if right and pay nothing if wrong. In the suits, therefore, to which they are parties they are discriminated against, and are not treated as others. They do not stand equal before the law. They do not receive its equal protection. All this is obvious from a mere inspection of the statute.

. . .

"While good faith and a knowledge of existing conditions on the part of a legislature is to be presumed, yet to carry that presumption to the extent of always holding that there must be some undisclosed and unknown reason for subjecting certain individuals or corporations to hostile and discriminating legislation is to make the protecting clauses of the Fourteenth Amendment a mere rope of sand, in no manner restraining state action.

. . .

"But it is said that it is not within the scope of the Fourteenth Amendment to withhold from States the power of classification, and that if the law deals alike with all of a certain class it is not obnoxious to the charge of a denial of equal protection. While, as a general proposition, this is undeniably true, . . . yet it is equally true that such classification cannot be made arbitrarily. The State may not say that all white men shall be subjected to the payment of the attorney's fees of parties successfully suing them and all black men not. It may not say that all men beyond a certain age shall be alone thus subjected, or all men possessed of a certain wealth. These are distinctions which do not furnish any proper basis for the attempted classification. That must always rest upon some difference which bears a reasonable and just relation to the act in respect to which the classification is proposed, and can never be made arbitrarily and without any such basis."

. . .

The Doctrine of Reasonable Classification

In *Ellis* the Court articulated a doctrine of reasonable classification. To be valid a classification must be reasonably related to the object of the legislation and cannot be arbitrary. But what determines whether a classification is reasonable?

The following classic discussion of equal protection theory provides a framework of analysis. Tussman and tenBroek, *The Equal Protection of the Laws,* 37 Calif.L.Rev. 341 (1949):

"Here, then, is a paradox: The equal protection of the laws is a 'pledge of the protection of equal laws.' But laws may classify. And 'the very idea of classification is that of inequality.' In tackling this paradox the Court has neither abandoned the demand for equality nor denied the legislative right to classify. It has taken a middle course. It has resolved the contradictory demands of legislative specialization and constitutional generality by a doctrine of reasonable classification.

"The essence of that doctrine can be stated with deceptive simplicity. The Constitution does not require that things different in fact be treated in law as though they were the same. But it does require, in its concern for equality, that those who are similarly situated be similarly treated. The measure of the reasonableness of a classification is the degree of its success in treating similarly those similarly situated. . . .

. . .

". . . [W]here are we to look for the test of similarity of situation which determines the reasonableness of a classification? The inescapable answer is that we must look beyond the classification to the purpose of the law. A reasonable classification is one which includes all persons who are similarly situated with respect to the purpose of the law.

"The purpose of a law may be either the elimination of a public 'mischief' or the achievement of some positive public good. To simplify the discussion we shall refer to the purpose of a law in terms of the elimination of mischief, since the same argument holds in either case. We shall speak of the defining character or characteristics of the legislative classification as the trait. We can thus speak of the relation of the classification to the purpose of the law as the relation of the Trait to the Mischief.

. . .

"In other words, we are really dealing with the relation of two classes to each other. The first class consists of all individuals possessing the defining Trait; the second class consists of all individuals possessing, or rather, tainted by, the Mischief at which the law aims. The former is the legislative classification; the latter is the class of those similarly situated with respect to the purpose of the law. We shall refer to these two classes as T and M respectively.

"Now, since the reasonableness of any class T depends entirely upon its relation to a class M, it is obvious that it is impossible to pass judgment on the reasonableness of a classification without taking into consideration, or identifying, the purpose of the law. . . .

"There are five possible relationships between the class defined by the Trait and the class defined by the Mischief. These relationships can be indicated by the following diagrams:

(1)   (MT)   : All *T*'s are *M*'s and all *M*'s are *T*'s

(2)   (T)(M)   : No *T*'s are *M*'s

(3)   (M⟨T⟩)   : All *T*'s are *M*'s but some *M*'s are not *T*'s

(4)   (T⟨M⟩)   : All *M*'s are *T*'s but some *T*'s are not *M*'s

(5)   (T)(M)   : Some *T*'s are *M*'s; some *T*'s are not *M*'s; and some *M*'s are not *T*'s

One of these five relationships holds in fact in any case of legislative classification, and we will consider each from the point of view of its "reasonableness."

"The first two situations represent respectively the ideal limits of reasonableness and unreasonableness. . . .

"Classification of the third type may be called 'under-inclusive.' All who are included in the class are tainted with the mischief, but there are others also tainted whom the classification does not include. Since the classification does not include all who are similarly situated with respect to the purpose of the law, there is a prima facie violation of the equal protection requirement of reasonable classification.

"But the Court has recognized the very real difficulties under which legislatures operate—difficulties arising out of both the nature of the legislative process and of the society which legislation attempts perennially to reshape—and it has refused to strike down indiscriminately all legislation embodying the classificatory inequality here under consideration.

"In justifying this refusal, the Court has defended under-inclusive classifications on such grounds as: the legislature may attack a general problem in a piecemeal fashion; 'some play must be allowed for the joints of the machine'; 'a statute aimed at what is deemed an evil, and hitting it presumably where experience shows it to be most felt, is not to be upset . . . '; 'the law does all that is needed when it does all that it can . . . '; and—perhaps with some impatience—the equal protection clause is not 'a pedagogic requirement of the impracticable.'

"These generalities, while expressive of judicial tolerance, are not, however, very helpful. They do not constitute a clear statement of the circumstances and conditions which justify such tolerance—which justify a departure from the strict requirements of the principle of equality. . . .

"The fourth type of classification imposes a burden upon a wider range of individuals than are included in the class of those tainted with the mischief at which the law aims. It can thus be called 'over-inclusive.' Herod, ordering the death of all male children born on a particular day because one of them would some day bring about his downfall, employed such a classification. It is exemplified by the quarantine and the dragnet. The wartime treatment of American citizens of Japanese ancestry is a striking recent instance of the imposition of burdens upon a large class of individuals because some of them were believed to be disloyal.

"The prima facie case against such departures from the ideal standards of reasonable classification is stronger than the case against under-inclusiveness. For in the latter case, all who are included in the class are at least tainted by the mischief at which the law aims; while over-inclusive classifications reach out to the innocent bystander, the hapless victim of circumstance or association."[a]

2. Social and Economic Regulatory Legislation

Williamson v. Lee Optical of Oklahoma, Inc.
348 U.S. 483 (1955).

The due process portions of this case are set out supra, p. 351. The Court disposed of an equal protection challenge to the portion of the law exempting sellers of ready-to-wear glasses from regulations imposed on opticians as follows:

"The problem of legislative classification is a perennial one, admitting of no doctrinaire definition. Evils in the same field may be of different dimensions and propositions, requiring different remedies. Or so the legislature may think. . . . Or the reform may take one step at a time, addressing itself to the phase of the problem which seems most acute to the legislative mind. . . . The legislature may select one

---

[a]   Copyright ©, 1949, California Law Review, Inc. Reprinted by Permission.

Also see generally Note, *Developments in the Law—Equal Protection,* 82 Harv.L.Rev. 1065 (1969).

phase of one field, and apply a remedy there, neglecting the others. . . . The prohibition of the Equal Protection Clause goes no further than the invidious discrimination. We cannot say that that point has been reached here. For all this record shows, the ready-to-wear branch of this business may not loom large in Oklahoma or may present problems of regulation distinct from the other branch."

Scope and Legitimacy of Judicial Review of the Rationality of Legislation Under Equal Protection

Constitutional law scholars are sharply divided on the question whether the courts should examine ordinary economic legislation under the equal protection clause to insure that such legislation is at least minimally related to some general good. Three general views are identifiable.

Some scholars assert the view that courts should examine both the means and the ends of legislation. They argue that courts cannot escape the burden of examining the outcomes of the legislative process to determine whether the regulations are reasonably related to legitimate public purposes. See, e.g. Tribe, *American Constitutional Law* 582–5, 1440, 1451 (2d ed. 1988); Tussman and tenBroek, *Equal Protection of the Laws,* 37 Calif.L.Rev. 341, 350 (1949). One such scholar, building on a Madisonian republican vision that legitimate policy must be formulated by representatives deliberating to further the public good rather than simply reflecting interest-group pressures, suggests that "[j]udicial scrutiny of the legislative process might take the form of a more serious inquiry into both process and outcome, designed to ensure that what emerges is genuinely public rather than a reflection of existing relations of private power." Sunstein, *Interest Groups in American Public Law,* 38 Stan.L.Rev. 29, 86 (1985).

Others assert that courts should not reexamine legislative choices as to the ends to be served by legislation but should engage in a real inquiry to determine whether the means selected have a real and substantial relation to the object sought to be attained. See, e.g., Gunther, *Forward: In Search of Evolving Doctrine on a Changing Court: A Model for a Newer Equal Protection,* 86 Harv.L.Rev. 1 (1972).

A third view is that the proper role of the courts is to police the structural and procedural limitations the Constitution imposes on the legislative process but not to scrutinize the outcomes for reasonableness. The proponents of this view state that, except for those constitutional provisions which place substantive limits on legislative outcomes by extending special protection to interests against the legislative process, the reach and limits of otherwise valid laws are assumed to be adequately explained by the conflicting forces within the legislative process which shaped them. See, e.g., Linde, *Due Process of Lawmaking,* 55 Neb.L.Rev. 197 (1975); Barrett, *The Rational Basis Standard for Equal Protection Review of Ordinary Legislative Classifications,* 68 Ky.L.Rev. 845 (1980).

To what extent are these views reflected in the following cases?

Federal Communications Commission v. Beach Communications, Inc.

508 U.S. 307, 113 S.Ct. 2096, 124 L.Ed.2d 211 (1993).

■ JUSTICE THOMAS delivered the opinion of the Court.

In providing for the regulation of cable television facilities, Congress has drawn a distinction between facilities that serve separately owned and managed buildings and those that serve one or more buildings under common ownership or management.

Cable facilities in the latter category are exempt from regulation as long as they provide services without using public rights-of-way. The question . . . is whether there is any conceivable rational basis justifying this distinction for purposes of the Due Process Clause of the Fifth Amendment.

I

The Cable Communications Policy Act of 1984 (Cable Act) . . . provided for the franchising of cable systems by local governmental authorities. . . . Section 602(7) . . . determines the reach of the franchise requirement by defining the operative term "cable system[ ]" [as] any facility designed to provide video programming to multiple subscribers through "closed transmission paths," but . . . not . . .

"a facility that serves only subscribers in 1 or more multiple unit dwellings under common ownership, control, or management, unless such facility or facilities us[e] any public right-of-way." § 602(7)(B). . . .

In part, this provision tracks a regulatory "private cable" exemption previously promulgated by the Federal Communications Commission (FCC or Commission) pursuant to pre-existing authority under the Communications Act. . . .

[The] FCC . . . clarif[ied] the agency's interpretation of the term "cable system" . . . [i]n [a] proceeding [that] addressed the application of the exemption codified in § 602(7)(B) to satellite master antenna television (SMATV) facilities. Unlike a traditional cable television system, which delivers video programming to a large community of subscribers through coaxial cables laid under city streets or along utility lines, an SMATV system typically receives a signal from a satellite through a small satellite dish located on a rooftop and then retransmits the signal by wire to units within a building or complex of buildings. . . . The Commission ruled that an SMATV system that serves multiple buildings via a network of interconnected physical transmission lines is a cable system, unless it falls within the § 602(7)(B) exemption. . . . Consistent with the plain terms of the statutory exemption, the Commission concluded that such an SMATV system is subject to the franchise requirement if its transmission lines interconnect separately owned and managed buildings or if its lines use or cross any public right-of-way. . . .

Respondents . . . —SMATV operators that would be subject to franchising under the Cable Act as construed by the Commission—petitioned the Court of Appeals for review. . . . [A] majority . . . found merit in the claim that § 602(7) violates the implied equal protection guarantee of the Due Process Clause. . . . [A]bsen[t] what it termed "the predominant rationale for local franchising" (use of public rights-of-way), the court saw no rational basis "[o]n the record," and was "unable to imagine" any conceivable basis, for distinguishing between those facilities exempted by the statute and those SMATV cable systems that link separately owned and managed buildings. . . .

. . . We now reverse.

II

Whether embodied in the Fourteenth Amendment or inferred from the Fifth, equal protection is not a license for courts to judge the wisdom, fairness, or logic of legislative choices. In areas of social and economic policy, a statutory classification that neither proceeds along suspect lines nor infringes fundamental constitutional rights must be upheld against equal protection challenge if there is any reasonably conceivable state of facts that could provide a rational basis for the classification. See Sullivan v. Stroop, 496 U.S. 478, 485 (1990); Bowen v. Gilliard, 483 U.S. 587, 600–603 (1987); United States Railroad Retirement Bd. v. Fritz, 449 U.S. 166, 174–179 (1980); Dandridge v. Williams, 397 U.S. 471, 484–485 (1970). Where there are "plausible reasons" for Congress' action, "our inquiry is at an end." United States Railroad Retirement Bd. v. Fritz. . . . This standard of review is a paradigm of judicial restraint. "The Constitution presumes that, absent some reason to infer antipathy, even improvident decisions will eventually be rectified by the democratic process and that judicial intervention is generally unwarranted no matter how unwisely we may think a political branch has acted." Vance v. Bradley, 440 U.S. 93, 97 (1979) (footnote omitted).

On rational-basis review, a classification in a statute such as the Cable Act comes to us bearing a strong presumption of validity, see Lyng v. Automobile Workers, 485 U.S. 360, 370 (1988), and those attacking the rationality of the legislative classification have the burden "to negative every conceivable basis which might support it," Lehnhausen v. Lake Shore Auto Parts Co., 410 U.S. 356, 364 (1973). . . . Moreover, because we never require a legislature to articulate its reasons for enacting a statute, it is entirely irrelevant for constitutional purposes whether the conceived reason for the challenged distinction actually motivated the legislature. United States Railroad Retirement Bd. v. Fritz. . . . Thus, the absence of "legislative facts" explaining the distinction "[o]n the record," . . . has no significance in rational-basis analysis. . . . [A] legislative choice is not subject to courtroom fact-finding and may be based on rational speculation unsupported by evidence or empirical data. . . .

These restraints on judicial review have added force "where the legislature must necessarily engage in a process of line-drawing." . . . Defining the class of persons subject to a regulatory requirement—much like classifying governmental beneficiaries—"inevitably requires that some persons who have an almost equally strong claim to favored treatment be placed on different sides of the line, and the fact [that] the line might have been drawn differently at some points is a matter for legislative, rather than judicial, consideration." . . . The distinction . . . here represents such a line: By excluding from the definition of "cable system" those facilities that serve commonly owned or managed buildings without using public rights-of-way, § 602(7)(B) delineates the bounds of the regulatory field. Such scope-of-coverage provisions are unavoidable components of most economic or social legislation. In establishing the franchise requirement, Congress had to draw the line somewhere [and] choose which facilities to franchise. This necessity renders the precise coordinates of the resulting legislative judgment virtually unreviewable, since the legislature must be allowed leeway to approach a perceived problem incrementally. See, e.g., Williamson v. Lee Optical of Okla., Inc., 348 U.S. 483 (1955). . . .

Applying these principles, we conclude that the common-ownership distinction is constitutional. There are at least two possible bases for the distinction; either one suffices. First, . . . it is plausible that Congress . . . adopted the FCC's earlier rationale[, under which] common ownership was thought to be indicative of those systems for which the costs of regulation would outweigh the benefits to consumers. Because the number of subscribers was a similar indicator, the Commission also exempted cable facilities that served fewer than 50 subscribers. . . .

This regulatory-efficiency model . . . provides a conceivable basis for the common-ownership exemption. A legislator might rationally assume that systems serving only commonly owned or managed buildings without crossing public rights-of-way would typically be limited in size or would share some other attribute affecting their impact on the welfare of cable viewers such that regulators could "safely ignor[e]" these systems.

Respondents argue that Congress did not intend common ownership to be a surrogate for small size, since Congress simultaneously rejected the FCC's 50-subscriber exemption by omitting it from the Cable Act. . . . Whether the posited reason . . . actually motivated Congress is "constitutionally irrelevant," . . . and, in any event, the FCC's explanation indicates that both common ownership and number of subscribers were considered indicia of "very small" cable systems. Respondents also contend that an SMATV operator could increase his subscription base and still qualify for the exemption simply by installing a separate satellite dish on each building served. . . . The additional cost of multiple dishes and associated transmission equipment, however, would impose an independent constraint on system size.

Furthermore, small size is only one plausible ownership-related factor contributing to consumer welfare. Subscriber influence is another. Where an SMATV system serves a complex of buildings under common ownership or management, individual subscribers could conceivably have greater bargaining power vis-a-vis the cable operator (even if the number of dwelling units were large), since all the subscribers could negotiate with one voice through the common owner or manager. Such an owner might have substantial leverage, because he could withhold permission to operate the SMATV system on his property. He would also have an incentive to guard the interests of his tenants. Thus, there could be less need to establish regulatory safeguards for subscribers in commonly owned complexes. Respondents acknowledge such possibilities, . . . and we certainly cannot say that these assumptions would be irrational.

There is a second conceivable basis for the statutory distinction. Suppose competing SMATV operators wish to sell video programming to subscribers in a group of contiguous buildings, such as a single city block, which can be interconnected by wire without crossing a public right-of-way. If all the buildings belong to one owner or are commonly managed, that owner or manager could freely negotiate a deal for all subscribers on a competitive basis. But if the buildings are separately owned and managed, the first SMATV operator who gains a foothold by signing a contract and installing a satellite dish and associated transmission equipment on one of the buildings would enjoy a powerful cost advantage in competing for the remaining subscribers: he could connect additional buildings for the cost of a few feet of cable, whereas any competitor would have to recover the cost of his own satellite headend facility. Thus, the first operator could charge rates well above his cost and still undercut the competition. This potential for effective monopoly power might theoretically justify regulating the latter class of SMATV systems and not the former.

III

. . . [T]here are plausible rationales unrelated to the use of public rights-of-way for regulating cable facilities serving separately owned and managed buildings. The assumptions underlying these rationales may be erroneous, but the very fact that they are "arguable" is sufficient, on rational-basis review, to "immuniz[e]" the congressional choice from constitutional challenge. Vance v. Bradley, 440 U.S., at 112.

The judgment of the Court of Appeals is reversed. . . .

■ JUSTICE STEVENS, concurring in the judgment.

. . .

. . . In my opinion the interest in the free use of one's own property provides adequate support for an exception from burdensome regulation and franchising requirements even when the property is occupied not only by family members and guests, but by lessees and co-owners as well, and even when the property complex encompasses multiple buildings.

The master antenna serving multiple units in an apartment building is less unsightly than a forest of individual antennas, each serving a separate apartment. It was surely sensible to allow owners to make use of such an improvement without incurring the costs of franchising and economic regulation. . . .

That brings us to the "private cable" exemption. . . . A justification for [it] that rests on the presumption that an owner of property should be allowed to use an improvement on his own property as he sees fit unless there is a sufficient public interest in denying him that right simply does not apply [where] the improvement—here, the satellite antenna—is being used to distribute signals to subscribers on other people's property. In that situation, the property owner, or the SMATV operator, has reached out beyond the property line and is seeking to employ the satellite antenna in the broader market for television programming. While the crossing of that line need not trigger regulatory intervention, and the absence of such a crossing may not prevent such intervention, it certainly cannot be said that government is disabled, by the Constitution, from regulating in the case of the former and abstaining in the case of the latter. . . .

Thus, while I am not fully persuaded that the "private cable" exemption is justified by the size of the market which it encompasses,[1] or by the Court's "monopoly" rationale,[2] . . . it is reasonable to presume[3] that Congress was motivated by an interest in allowing property owners to exercise freedom in the use of their own property. Legislation so motivated surely does not violate the sovereign's duty to govern impartially. See Hampton v. Mow Sun Wong, 426 U.S. 88, 100 (1976). . . .

Ascertaining Legislative Purpose for Rational Basis Review

The Court's consistent refusal to require that legislative bodies articulate the purpose of a statutory classification, or be held to an identifiable "actual" or even "reasonably presumable" purpose, in order to have the classification survive judicial review for reasonableness, has in some circumstances provoked vigorous methodological dissent. Two decisions rejecting attacks on distinctions in benefits legislation are noteworthy in this regard.

In United States Railroad Retirement Board v. Fritz, 449 U.S. 166 (1980), Congress discontinued dual railroad retirement and social security benefits for some but not all former rail employees, in part drawing a line on the basis of how recent rather than how long an employee's railroad service had been. Justice Rehnquist's majority opinion, applying the rational basis standard, stated that "the plain language of [the provision drawing the distinction] marks the beginning and end of our inquiry" into purpose. Nor was that purpose "achieved . . . in a patently arbitrary or irrational way[,]" because "Congress could assume that those who had a current connection with the railroad industry when the Act was passed in 1974, or who returned to the industry before their retirement, were more likely than those who had left the industry prior to 1974, and who never returned, to be among the class of persons who pursue careers in the railroad industry, the class for whom the Railroad Retirement Act was designed." Having found "plausible reasons for Congress' action, our inquiry is at an end." Finally, the majority:

---

[1]   Approximately 25% of all multiple dwellings units are in complexes large enough to support an SMATV system. . . . Furthermore, whereas the FCC had, prior to [the Cable Act], exempted from regulation cable systems of less than 50 subscribers as well as those serving commonly owned multiple unit dwellings, Congress exempted only the latter when it passed the Cable Act, leaving out the exemption based on system size. Respondent thus makes a strong argument that Congress may have rejected the very rationale upon which the FCC, and the Court, rely.

[2]   . . . [T]he Court's analysis overlooks the competitive presence of traditional cable as a potential constraint on an SMATV operator's capacity to extract monopoly rents from landlords.

[3]   The Court['s] . . . formulation sweeps too broadly. . . . Judicial review under the "conceivable set of facts" test is tantamount to no review at all. . . . [W]hen the actual rationale for the legislative classification is unclear, we should inquire whether the classification is rationally related to "a legitimate purpose that we may reasonably presume to have motivated an impartial legislature.". . .

"disagree[d] with the District Court's conclusion that Congress was unaware of what it accomplished or that it was misled by the groups that appeared before it. If this test were applied literally to every member of any legislature that ever voted on a law, there would be very few laws which would survive it. The language of the statute is clear, and we have historically assumed that Congress intended what it enacted."

In dissent, Justice Brennan, joined by Justice Marshall, objected to the majority's "tautological approach to statutory purpose[,]" arguing that "the 'plain language' of the statute can tell us only what the classification is; it can tell us nothing about the purpose of the classification, let alone the relationship between the classification and that purpose." He continued:

". . . It may always be said that Congress intended to do what it in fact did. If that were the extent of our analysis, we would find every statute, no matter how arbitrary or irrational, perfectly tailored to achieve its purpose. But equal protection scrutiny under the rational basis test requires the courts first to deduce the independent objectives of the statute, usually from statements of purpose and other evidence in the statute and legislative history, and second to analyze whether the challenged classification rationally furthers achievement of those objectives. . . ."

Justice Brennan found in the legislative history "a 'principal purpose' . . . explicitly stated by Congress . . . to preserve the vested earned benefits of retirees who had already qualified for them." In his view, the classification, "which deprives some retirees of vested dual benefits that they had earned prior to 1974, directly conflicts with Congress' stated purpose" and, hence, is "not only rationally unrelated to the congressional purpose [but] inimical to it." In general, "[w]here Congress has expressly stated the purpose of a piece of legislation, but where the challenged classification is either irrelevant to or counter to that purpose, we must view any *post hoc* justifications proffered by Government attorneys with skepticism. A challenged classification may be sustained only if it is rationally related to achievement of an *actual* legitimate governmental purpose." Here, moreover, Congress had "asked railroad management and labor representatives to negotiate and submit a bill to restructure the Railroad Retirement system" and testimony "at congressional hearings perpetuated the inaccurate impression that all retirees with earned vested dual benefits under prior law would retain their benefits unchanged." While "a misstatement or several misstatements by witnesses before Congress would not ordinarily lead us to conclude that Congress misapprehended what it was doing . . . , where complex legislation was drafted by outside parties and Congress relied on them to explain it, where the misstatements are frequent and unrebutted, and where no Member of Congress can be found to have stated the effect of the classification correctly, we are entitled to suspect that Congress may have been misled." Accordingly, "I do not think that this classification was rationally related to an *actual* governmental purpose."

Justice Stevens, concurring in the judgment, shared Justice Brennan's concern that "judicial review [not] constitute a mere tautological recognition of the fact that Congress did what it intended to do" and urged that "[w]hen Congress deprives a small class of persons of vested rights that are protected . . . for others who are in a similar though not identical position, I believe the Constitution requires something more than merely a 'conceivable' or a 'plausible' explanation for the unequal treatment." But he did not

"share Justice Brennan's conclusion that every statutory classification must further an objective that can be confidently identified as the 'actual purpose' of the legislature. Actual purpose is sometimes unknown. Moreover, undue emphasis on actual motivation may result in identically worded statutes being held valid in one State and invalid in a neighboring State. I therefore believe that we must discover a correlation between the classification and either the actual purpose of the statute or a legitimate purpose that we may reasonably presume to have motivated an impartial legislature. If the adverse impact on the disfavored class is an apparent aim of the legislature, its impartiality would be suspect. If, however, the adverse impact may reasonably be viewed as an acceptable cost of achieving a larger goal, an impartial lawmaker could rationally decide that that cost should be incurred."

Here, though "Congress originally intended to protect *all* vested benefits, ... it ultimately sacrificed some benefits in the interest of achieving other objectives"— ending dual benefits and "protecting the solvency of the entire railroad retirement program." As "any distinction ... within the class of vested beneficiaries would involve a difference of degree rather than a difference in entitlement[,]" Justice Stevens was "satisfied that a distinction based upon currency of railroad employment represents an impartial method of identifying that sort of difference."

The following year the Court divided 5–4 over an equal protection challenge by residents of mental institutions denied a small welfare allowance Congress had authorized for inmates of only those public institutions receiving Medicaid payments on their behalf. Schweiker v. Wilson, 450 U.S. 221 (1981). The majority concluded that adopting the Medicaid eligibility criterion "must be considered Congress' deliberate, considered choice" and reasoned that Congress "may rationally limit the grant to Medicaid recipients, for whose care the Federal Government already has assumed the major portion of the expense" and leave it to the States, who "Congress believed ... have a 'traditional' responsibility to care for those institutionalized in public mental institutions[,] to provide an equivalent."

Justice Powell's dissent, joined by Justices Brennan, Marshall, and Stevens, said in part:

"The deference to which legislative accommodation of conflicting interests is entitled rests in part upon the principle that the political process of our majoritarian democracy responds to the wishes of the people. Accordingly, an important touchstone for equal protection review of statutes is how readily a policy can be discerned which the legislature intended to serve.... [W]hether a statutory classification discriminates arbitrarily cannot be divorced from whether it was enacted to serve an identifiable purpose. When a legislative purpose can be suggested only by the ingenuity of a government lawyer litigating the constitutionality of a statute, a reviewing court may be presented not so much with a legislative policy choice as its absence.

"In my view, the Court should receive with some skepticism *post hoc* hypotheses about legislative purpose, unsupported by the legislative history.[6] When no indication of legislative purpose appears other than the current position of the Secretary, the Court should require that the classification bear a 'fair and substantial relation' to the asserted purpose. See F.S. Royster Guano Co. v. Virginia, 253 U.S. 412, 415 (1920). This marginally more demanding scrutiny indirectly would test the plausibility of the tendered purpose....

"I conclude that Congress had no rational reason for refusing to pay a comfort allowance to appellees, while paying it to numerous otherwise identically situated

---

[6] Some of our cases suggest that the actual purpose of a statute is irrelevant, Flemming v. Nestor, 363 U.S. 603, 612 (1960), and that the statute must be upheld "if any state of facts reasonably may be conceived to justify" its discrimination, McGowan v. Maryland, 366 U.S. 420, 426 (1961). Although these cases preserve an important caution, they do not describe the importance of actual legislative purpose in our analysis. We recognize that a legislative body rarely acts with a single mind and that compromises blur purpose.... Ascertainment of actual purpose to the extent feasible, however, remains an essential step in equal protection.

disabled indigents. This unexplained difference in treatment must have been a legislative oversight. . . ."

Modern Rational Basis Review

Despite occasional dissenting expressions of discomfort with the "toothlessness" of rational basis review as applied in the realms of purely economic regulation and the provision of government benefits, the Court consistently has refused to invalidate any such measure, with one notable exception, for more than 50 years. In Morey v. Doud, 354 U.S. 457 (1957), the Court, with three dissenters, held that an Illinois statute imposing licensing and financial requirements on sellers and issuers of all money orders, except those of the "American Express Company[,]" violated equal protection. In reaching this conclusion, the Court took "all of these factors in conjunction—the remote relationship of the statutory classification to the Act's purpose or to business characteristics, and the creation of a closed class by the singling out of the money orders of a named company, with accompanying economic advantages."

Nearly twenty years later in a brief per curiam opinion, however, the Court concluded without dissent that *Morey* "was a needlessly intrusive judicial infringement on the State's legislative powers" and "so far departs from proper equal protection analysis in cases of exclusively economic regulation that it should be, and is, overruled." New Orleans v. Dukes, 427 U.S. 297 (1976). *Dukes,* which the Court found "essentially indistinguishable" from *Morey,* upheld an ordinance that exempted from a general prohibition against the selling of foodstuffs from pushcarts in New Orleans' French Quarter "vendors who have continually operated the same business [there] for eight years prior to January 1, 1972." The Court concluded that "[t]he city's classification rationally furthers the purpose . . . the city had identified as its objective . . . [;] that is, as a means 'to preserve the appearance and custom valued by the Quarter's residents and attractive to tourists.' " As for the "grandfather provision," the Court decided that "the city could rationally choose initially to eliminate vendors of more recent vintage" and gave the following rationale: "The city could reasonably decide that newer businesses were less likely to have built up substantial reliance interests in continued operations . . . and that the two vendors which qualified under the 'grandfather clause'—both of which had operated in the area for over 20 years . . . —had themselves become part of the distinctive character and charm that distinguishes the Vieux Carre."

The Court, purporting to apply the rational basis standard, has invalidated a number of legislative classifications in the modern era, but none involved solely economic regulation or distribution of government benefits.[a] For example, the Court

---

[a] Addressing allegations that a municipality unconstitutionally demanded a 33-foot easement as a condition of connecting a particular owner's property to the municipal water supply when only a 15-foot easement was demanded from other similarly situated property owners, the Court held the complaint "sufficient to state a claim for relief under traditional equal protection analysis," even if "brought by a 'class of one,' where the plaintiff alleges that she has been intentionally treated differently from others similarly situated and that there is no rational basis for the difference in treatment." Village of Willowbrook v. Olech, 528 U.S. 562 (2000). The Court so ruled, "quite apart from the Village's subjective motivation," which the plaintiff claimed was "ill will resulting from the . . . previous filing of an unrelated, successful lawsuit against the Village. . . ." For Justice Breyer, concurring in the result, only that "added factor" of vindictiveness ameliorated the concern that the Court not interpret the Equal Protection Clause "in a way that would transform many ordinary violations of city or state law[, such as common instances of faulty zoning decisions,] into violations of the Constitution."

In Engquist v. Oregon Dept. of Agriculture, 553 U.S. 591 (2008), however, the Court categorically rejected a public employee's " 'class-of-one' equal protection claim" that she was "fired . . . for 'arbitrary, vindictive, and malicious reasons.' " Chief Justice Roberts's majority opinion said that "[o]ur traditional view of the core concern of the Equal Protection Clause as a shield against arbitrary classifications,

invoked rational basis review in striking down a gender distinction in Reed v. Reed, 404 U.S. 71 (1971), infra, page 511. Similarly, in City of Cleburne v. Cleburne Living Center, 473 U.S. 432 (1985), infra, page 643, despite Justice Marshall's dissenting criticism that it was engaging in " 'second order' rational basis review," the Court held that a city ordinance, as applied to deny a special use permit for the operation of a group home for the mentally retarded, failed rational basis scrutiny and revealed "an irrational prejudice" against that group. Of like import but without reference to *Cleburne*, the Court later invalidated an amendment to the Colorado Constitution precluding any level of state government from protecting the status of persons on the basis of their "homosexual, lesbian or bisexual orientation, conduct, practices or relationships," because "its sheer breadth is so discontinuous with the reasons offered for it that the amendment seems inexplicable by anything but animus toward the class that it affects; it lacks a rational relationship to legitimate state interests." Romer v. Evans, 517 U.S. 620, 632 (1996), infra page 649. A further example includes the Court's professed use of rational basis review when invalidating legislative distinctions between newly-arrived and long-term state residents, as in Zobel v. Williams, 457 U.S. 55 (1982), infra, page 695. In these and similar cases one might ask whether and in what ways the Court may be applying a different form of rational basis review than in the opinions presented in this section, and why the Court might invoke the rational basis standard but apply it differently rather than invoke a different standard.

---

combined with unique considerations applicable when the government acts as employer as opposed to sovereign, lead us to conclude that the class-of-one theory of equal protection does not apply in the public employment context." He emphasized that "[w]hat seems to have been significant in *Olech* and the cases on which it relied was the existence of a clear standard against which departures, even for a single plaintiff, could be readily assessed." By contrast, "some forms of state action . . . by their nature involve discretionary decisionmaking based on a vast array of subjective, individualized assessments. In such cases the rule that people should be 'treated alike, under like circumstances and conditions' is not violated when one person is treated differently from others, because treating like individuals differently is an accepted consequence of the discretion granted. In such situations, allowing a challenge based on the arbitrary singling out of a particular person would undermine the very discretion that such state officials are entrusted to exercise." The principle that "[i]t is no proper challenge to what in its nature is a subjective, individualized decision that it was subjective and individualized[,] . . . applies most clearly in the employment context, for employment decisions are quite often subjective and individualized, resting on a wide array of factors that are difficult to articulate and quantify. . . . Unlike the context of arm's-length regulation, such as in *Olech,* treating seemingly similarly situated individuals differently in the employment context is par for the course."

The Chief Justice noted two additional points. First, "recognition of a class-of-one theory of equal protection in the public employment context—that is, a claim that the State treated an employee differently from others for a bad reason, or for no reason at all—is simply contrary to the concept of at-will employment." Second, "an allegation of arbitrary differential treatment could be made in nearly every instance of an assertedly wrongful employment action . . . on the theory that other employees were not treated wrongfully[,]" and the "practical problem . . . is not that it will be too easy for plaintiffs to prevail, but that governments will be forced to defend a multitude of such claims in the first place. . . ."

Justice Stevens, joined by Justices Souter and Ginsburg, dissented, finding "a clear distinction between an exercise of discretion and an arbitrary decision[,]" the former "represent[ing] a choice of one among two or more rational alternatives." Thus, he found "no need to create an exception for the public-employment context in order to prevent . . . discretionary decisions from giving rise to equal protection claims." Because "a random choice among rational alternatives does not violate the Equal Protection Clause[,]" and "[e]xperience . . . demonstrates that there are in fact rare cases in which a petty tyrant has misused governmental power . . . there is no compelling reason to carve arbitrary public-employment decisions out of the well-established category of equal protection violations when the familiar rational review standard can sufficiently limit these claims to only wholly unjustified employment actions."

3. SUSPECT CLASSIFICATIONS

Introduction. This section presents the cases where the classifying factor rather than the burden on a fundamental interest gives rise to a heightened standard of review. Subsection A deals with the most clearly suspect classifications—those disadvantaging racial minorities. Subsection B involves a special application of the racial classification doctrine to official racial segregation of schools and other public facilities. Subsection C addresses classifications dealing with gender, where the Court uses the classifying factor to justify a heightened standard of review but one not as rigorous as that applied to racial classifications.

The cases in Subsection D typically involve legislation lacking facially suspect classifications but having a differential impact on particular groups. The question addressed is whether "suspectness" turns on the "impact" of laws or the "intent" with which they are enacted.

Subsection E discusses the most controversial and divisive issue before the Court under the equal protection clause—the validity of the use of gender and racial classifications for the purpose of aiding women or minority groups.

Subsection F deals with classifications involving aliens, and Subsection G with other classifying factors that may trigger heightened scrutiny, such as illegitimacy, mental retardation, sexual orientation, age, and poverty.

A. CLASSIFICATIONS DISADVANTAGING RACIAL MINORITIES

Loving v. Virginia

388 U.S. 1, 87 S.Ct. 1817, 18 L.Ed.2d 1010 (1967).

■ MR. CHIEF JUSTICE WARREN delivered the opinion of the Court.

This case presents a constitutional question never addressed by this Court: whether a statutory scheme adopted by the State of Virginia to prevent marriages between persons solely on the basis of racial classifications violates the Equal Protection and Due Process Clauses of the Fourteenth Amendment. For reasons which seem to us to reflect the central meaning of those constitutional commands, we conclude that these statutes cannot stand consistently with the Fourteenth Amendment.

In June 1958, two residents of Virginia, Mildred Jeter, a Negro woman, and Richard Loving, a white man, were married in the District of Columbia pursuant to its laws. Shortly after their marriage, the Lovings returned to Virginia and established their marital abode in Caroline County.... [A County] grand jury issued an indictment charging the Lovings with violating Virginia's ban on interracial marriages. On January 6, 1959, the Lovings pleaded guilty to the charge and were sentenced to one year in jail; however, the trial judge suspended the sentence for a period of 25 years on the condition that the Lovings leave the State and not return to Virginia together for 25 years, stating that:

"Almighty God created the races white, black, yellow, malay, and red, and he placed them on separate continents. And but for the interference with his arrangement there would be no cause for such marriages. The fact that he separated the races shows that he did not intend for the races to mix."

After their convictions the Lovings took up residence in the District of Columbia. On November 6, 1963, they filed a motion in the state trial court to vacate the judgment and set aside the sentence on the ground that the statutes which they had violated were repugnant to the Fourteenth Amendment. The motion not having been decided by October 28, 1964, the Lovings instituted a class action in the United States District Court for the Eastern District of Virginia requesting that a three-judge court be convened to declare the Virginia antimiscegenation statutes unconstitutional and to enjoin state officials from enforcing their convictions. On January 22, 1965, the state trial judge denied the motion to vacate the sentences, and the Lovings perfected an appeal to the Supreme Court of Appeals of Virginia. On February 11, 1965, the three-judge District Court continued the case to allow the Lovings to present their constitutional claims to the highest state court.

The Supreme Court of Appeals upheld the constitutionality of the antimiscegenation statutes and, after modifying the sentence, affirmed the convictions. The Lovings appealed this decision, and we noted probable jurisdiction on December 12, 1966.

The two statutes under which appellants were convicted and sentenced are part of a comprehensive statutory scheme aimed at prohibiting and punishing interracial marriages. The Lovings were convicted of violating § 20–58 of the Virginia Code:

"Leaving State to Evade Law. If any white person and colored person shall go out of this State, for the purpose of being married, and with the intention of returning, and be married out of it, and afterwards return to and reside in it, cohabiting as man and wife, they shall be punished as provided in § 20–59, and the marriage shall be governed by the same law as if it had been solemnized in this State. The fact of their cohabitation here as man and wife shall be evidence of their marriage."

Section 20–59, which defines the penalty for miscegenation, provides:

"Punishment for Marriage. If any white person intermarry with a colored person, or any colored person intermarry with a white person, he shall be guilty of a felony and shall be punished by confinement in the penitentiary for not less than one nor more than five years."

Other central provisions in the Virginia statutory scheme are § 20–57, which automatically voids all marriages between "a white person and a colored person" without any judicial proceeding, and §§ 20–54 and 1–14 which, respectively, define "white persons" and "colored persons and Indians" for purposes of the statutory prohibitions. The Lovings have never disputed in the course of this litigation that Mrs. Loving is a "colored person" or that Mr. Loving is a "white person" within the meanings given those terms by the Virginia statutes.

Virginia is now one of 16 States which prohibit and punish marriages on the basis of racial classifications.[5] Penalties for miscegenation arose as an incident to slavery and have been common in Virginia since the colonial period. The present statutory scheme dates from the adoption of the Racial Integrity Act of 1924, passed during the period of extreme nativism which followed the end of the First World War. The central features of this Act, and current Virginia law, are the absolute prohibition of a "white person" marrying other than another "white person," a prohibition against issuing marriage licenses until the issuing official is satisfied that the applicants' statements as to their race are correct, certificates of "racial composition" to be kept by both local and state registrars, and the carrying forward of earlier prohibitions against racial intermarriage.

I.

In upholding the constitutionality of these provisions in the decision below, the Supreme Court of Appeals of Virginia referred to its 1955 decision in Naim v. Naim,

---

[5]   . . . Over the past 15 years, 14 States have repealed laws outlawing interracial marriage. . . .

197 Va. 80, 87 S.E.2d 749, as stating the reasons supporting the validity of these laws. In *Naim,* the state court concluded that the State's legitimate purposes were "to preserve the racial integrity of its citizens," and to prevent "the corruption of blood," "a mongrel breed of citizens," and "the obliteration of racial pride," obviously an endorsement of the doctrine of White Supremacy.... The court also reasoned that marriage has traditionally been subject to state regulation without federal intervention, and, consequently, the regulation of marriage should be left to exclusive state control by the Tenth Amendment.

While the state court is no doubt correct in asserting that marriage is a social relation subject to the State's police power, ... the State does not contend ... that its powers to regulate marriage are unlimited notwithstanding the commands of the Fourteenth Amendment. Nor could it do so in light of Meyer v. State of Nebraska, 262 U.S. 390 (1923), and Skinner v. State of Oklahoma, 316 U.S. 535 (1942). Instead, the State argues that the meaning of the Equal Protection Clause, as illuminated by the statements of the Framers, is only that state penal laws containing an interracial element as part of the definition of the offense must apply equally to whites and Negroes in the sense that members of each race are punished to the same degree. Thus, the State contends that, because its miscegenation statutes punish equally both the white and the Negro participants in an interracial marriage, these statutes, despite their reliance on racial classifications, do not constitute an invidious discrimination based upon race. The second argument advanced by the State assumes the validity of its equal application theory. The argument is that, if the Equal Protection Clause does not outlaw miscegenation statutes because of their reliance on racial classifications, the question of constitutionality would thus become whether there was any rational basis for a State to treat interracial marriages differently from other marriages. On this question, the State argues, the scientific evidence is substantially in doubt and, consequently, this Court should defer to the wisdom of the state legislature in adopting its policy of discouraging interracial marriages.

Because we reject the notion that the mere "equal application" of a statute containing racial classifications is enough to remove the classifications from the Fourteenth Amendment's proscription of all invidious racial discriminations, we do not accept the State's contention that these statutes should be upheld if there is any possible basis for concluding that they serve a rational purpose. The mere fact of equal application does not mean that our analysis of this statute should follow the approach we have taken in cases involving no racial discrimination where the Equal Protection Clause has been arrayed against a statute discriminating between the kinds of advertising which may be displayed on trucks in New York City, Railway Express Agency, Inc. v. People of State of New York, 336 U.S. 106 (1949), or an exemption in Ohio's ad valorem tax for merchandise owned by a non-resident in a storage warehouse, Allied Stores of Ohio, Inc. v. Bowers, 358 U.S. 522 (1959). In these cases, involving distinctions not drawn according to race, the Court has merely asked whether there is any rational foundation for the discriminations, and has deferred to the wisdom of the state legislatures. In the case at bar, however, we deal with statutes containing racial classifications, and the fact of equal application does not immunize the statute from the very heavy burden of justification which the Fourteenth Amendment has traditionally required of state statutes drawn according to race.

The State argues that statements in the Thirty-ninth Congress about the time of the passage of the Fourteenth Amendment indicate that the Framers did not intend the Amendment to make unconstitutional state miscegenation laws. Many of the statements alluded to by the State concern the debates over the Freedmen's Bureau Bill, which President Johnson vetoed, and the Civil Rights Act of 1866, enacted over his veto. While these statements have some relevance to the intention of Congress in submitting the Fourteenth Amendment, it must be understood that they pertained to the passage of specific statutes and not to the broader, organic purpose of a constitutional amendment. As for the various statements directly concerning the Fourteenth Amendment, we have said in connection with a related problem, that although these historical sources "cast some light" they are not sufficient to resolve the problem; "[a]t best, they are inconclusive. The most avid proponents of the post–War Amendments undoubtedly intended them to remove all legal distinctions among 'all persons born or naturalized in the United States.' Their opponents, just as certainly, were antagonistic to both the letter and the spirit of the Amendments and wished them to have the most limited effect." Brown et al. v. Board of Education of Topeka, et al., 347 U.S. 483 (1954). See also Strauder v. West Virginia, 100 U.S. 303, 310 (1880). We have rejected the proposition that the debates in the Thirty-ninth Congress or in the state legislatures which ratified the Fourteenth Amendment supported the theory advanced by the State, that the requirement of equal protection of the laws is satisfied by penal laws defining offenses based on racial classifications so long as white and Negro participants in the offense were similarly punished. McLaughlin et al. v. State of Florida, 379 U.S. 184 (1964).

The State finds support for its "equal application" theory in the decision of the Court in Pace v. Alabama, 106 U.S. 583 (1882). In that case, the Court upheld a conviction under an Alabama statute forbidding adultery or fornication between a white person and a Negro which imposed a greater penalty than that of a statute proscribing similar conduct by members of the same race. The Court reasoned that the statute could not be said to discriminate against Negroes because the punishment for each participant in the offense was the same. However, as recently as the 1964 Term, in rejecting the reasoning of that case, we stated "*Pace* represents a limited view of the Equal Protection Clause which has not withstood analysis in the subsequent decisions of this Court." *McLaughlin et al. v. Florida,* . . . As we there demonstrated, the Equal Protection Clause requires the consideration of whether the classifications drawn by any statute constitute an arbitrary and invidious discrimination. The clear and central purpose of the Fourteenth Amendment was to eliminate all official state sources of invidious racial discrimination in the States. Slaughter-House Cases, 16 Wall. 36, 71 (1873); Strauder v. State of West Virginia, 100 U.S. 303, 307–308 (1880); Ex parte Virginia, 100 U.S. 339, 344–345 (1880); Shelley v. Kraemer, 334 U.S. 1 (1948); Burton v. Wilmington Parking Authority, 365 U.S. 715 (1961).

There can be no question but that Virginia's miscegenation statutes rest solely upon distinctions drawn according to race. The statutes proscribe generally accepted conduct if engaged in by members of different races. Over the years, this Court has consistently repudiated "[d]istinctions between citizens solely because of their ancestry" as being "odious to a free people whose institutions are founded upon the doctrine of equality." Hirabayashi v. United States, 320 U.S. 81, 100 (1943). At the very least, the Equal Protection Clause demands that racial classifications, especially suspect in criminal statutes, be subjected to the "most rigid scrutiny," Korematsu v. United States, 323 U.S. 214, 216 (1944), and, if they are ever to be upheld, they must be shown to be necessary to the accomplishment of some permissible state objective, independent of the racial discrimination which it was the object of the Fourteenth Amendment to eliminate. Indeed, two members of this Court have already stated that they "cannot conceive of a valid legislative purpose . . . which makes the color of a person's skin the test of whether his conduct is a criminal offense." McLaughlin v. Florida, supra, 379 U.S. at 198 (Stewart, J., joined by Douglas, J., concurring).

There is patently no legitimate overriding purpose independent of invidious racial discrimination which justifies this classification. The fact that Virginia only prohibits interracial marriages involving white persons demonstrates that the racial classifications must stand on their own justification, as measures designed to maintain White Supremacy.[11] We have consistently denied the constitutionality of measures which restrict the rights of citizens on account of race. There can be no doubt that restricting the freedom to marry solely because of racial classifications violates the central meaning of the Equal Protection Clause.

. . .

These convictions must be reversed. It is so ordered.

■ MR. JUSTICE STEWART, concurring.

I have previously expressed the belief that "it is simply not possible for a state law to be valid under our Constitution which makes the criminality of an act depend upon the race of the actor." McLaughlin v. State of Florida, 379 U.S. 184, 198 (concurring opinion). Because I adhere to that belief, I concur in the judgment of the Court.

Palmore v. Sidoti

466 U.S. 429, 104 S.Ct. 1879, 80 L.Ed.2d 421 (1984).

■ CHIEF JUSTICE BURGER delivered the opinion of the Court.

We granted certiorari to review a judgment of a state court divesting a natural mother of the custody of her infant child because of her remarriage to a person of a different race.

I

When petitioner Linda Sidoti Palmore and respondent Anthony J. Sidoti, both Caucasians, were divorced in May 1980 in Florida, the mother was awarded custody of their three-year-old daughter.

In September 1981 the father sought custody of the child by filing a petition to modify the prior judgment because of changed conditions. The change was that the child's mother was then cohabiting with a Negro, Clarence Palmore, Jr., whom she married two months later. Additionally, the father made several allegations of instances in which the mother had not properly cared for the child.

After hearing testimony from both parties and considering a court counselor's investigative report, the court noted that the father had made allegations about the child's care, but the court made no findings with respect to these allegations. On the contrary, the court made a finding that "there is no issue as to either party's devotion to the child, adequacy of housing facilities, or respect[a]bility of the new spouse of either parent."

The court then addressed the recommendations of the court counselor, who had made an earlier report "in [another] case coming out of this circuit also involving the social consequences of an interracial marriage. Niles v. Niles, 299 So.2d 162." From this vague reference to that earlier case, the court turned to the present case and noted the counselor's recommendation for a change in custody because "[t]he wife

---

[11] Appellants point out that the State's concern in these statutes, as expressed in the words of the 1924 Act's title, "An Act to Preserve Racial Integrity," extends only to the integrity of the white race. While Virginia prohibits whites from marrying any nonwhite (subject to the exception for the descendants of Pocahontas), Negroes, Orientals, and any other racial class may intermarry without statutory interference. Appellants contend that this distinction renders Virginia's miscegenation statutes arbitrary and unreasonable even assuming the constitutional validity of an official purpose to preserve "racial integrity." We need not reach this contention because we find the racial classifications in these statutes repugnant to the Fourteenth Amendment, even assuming an even-handed state purpose to protect the "integrity" of all races.

[petitioner] has chosen for herself and for her child, a life-style unacceptable to her father *and to society*. . . . The child . . . is, or at school age will be, subject to environmental pressures not of choice."

The court then concluded that the best interests of the child would be served by awarding custody to the father. The court's rationale is contained in the following:

"The father's evident resentment of the mother's choice of a black partner is not sufficient to wrest custody from the mother. It is of some significance, however, that the mother did see fit to bring a man into her home and carry on a sexual relationship with him without being married to him. Such action tended to place gratification of her own desires ahead of her concern for the child's future welfare. *This Court feels that despite the strides that have been made in bettering relations between the races in this country, it is inevitable that Melanie will, if allowed to remain in her present situation and attains school age and thus more vulnerable to peer pressures, suffer from the social stigmatization that is sure to come.*"

The Second District Court of Appeal affirmed without opinion, thus denying the Florida Supreme Court jurisdiction to review the case. . . . We . . . reverse.

II

The judgment of a state court determining or reviewing a child custody decision is not ordinarily a likely candidate for review by this Court. However, the court's opinion, after stating that the "father's evident resentment of the mother's choice of a black partner is not sufficient" to deprive her of custody, then turns to what it regarded as the damaging impact on the child from remaining in a racially-mixed household. This raises important federal concerns arising from the Constitution's commitment to eradicating discrimination based on race.

The Florida court did not focus directly on the parental qualifications of the natural mother or her present husband, or indeed on the father's qualifications to have custody of the child. The court found that "there is no issue as to either party's devotion to the child, adequacy of housing facilities, or respect[a]bility of the new spouse of either parent." This, taken with the absence of any negative finding as to the quality of the care provided by the mother, constitutes a rejection of any claim of petitioner's unfitness to continue the custody of her child.

The court correctly stated that the child's welfare was the controlling factor. But that court was entirely candid and made no effort to place its holding on any ground other than race. Taking the court's findings and rationale at face value, it is clear that the outcome would have been different had petitioner married a Caucasian male of similar respectability.

A core purpose of the Fourteenth Amendment was to do away with all governmentally-imposed discrimination based on race. See Strauder v. West Virginia, 100 U.S. 303, 307–308, 310 (1880). Classifying persons according to their race is more likely to reflect racial prejudice than legitimate public concerns; the race, not the person, dictates the category. See Personnel Administrator v. Feeney, 442 U.S. 256, 272 (1979). Such classifications are subject to the most exacting scrutiny; to pass constitutional muster, they must be justified by a compelling governmental interest and must be "necessary . . . to the accomplishment" of its legitimate purpose, McLaughlin v. Florida, 379 U.S. 184, 196 (1964). See Loving v. Virginia, 388 U.S. 1, 11 (1967).

The State, of course, has a duty of the highest order to protect the interests of minor children, particularly those of tender years. In common with most states, Florida law mandates that custody determinations be made in the best interests of the children involved. Fla.Stat. § 61.13(2)(b)(1) (1983). The goal of granting custody based on the best interests of the child is indisputably a substantial governmental interest for purposes of the Equal Protection Clause.

It would ignore reality to suggest that racial and ethnic prejudices do not exist or that all manifestations of those prejudices have been eliminated. There is a risk that a child living with a step-parent of a different race may be subject to a variety of pressures and stresses not present if the child were living with parents of the same racial or ethnic origin.

The question, however, is whether the reality of private biases and the possible injury they might inflict are permissible considerations for removal of an infant child from the custody of its natural mother. We have little difficulty concluding that they are not. The Constitution cannot control such prejudices but neither can it tolerate them. Private biases may be outside the reach of the law, but the law cannot, directly or indirectly, give them effect. "Public officials sworn to uphold the Constitution may not avoid a constitutional duty by bowing to the hypothetical effects of private racial prejudice that they assume to be both widely and deeply held." Palmer v. Thompson, 403 U.S. 217, 260–261 (1971) (White, J., dissenting).

This is by no means the first time that acknowledged racial prejudice has been invoked to justify racial classifications. In Buchanan v. Warley, 245 U.S. 60 (1917), for example, this Court invalidated a Kentucky law forbidding Negroes from buying homes in white neighborhoods.

"It is urged that this proposed segregation will promote the public peace by preventing race conflicts. Desirable as this is, and important as is the preservation of the public peace, this aim cannot be accomplished by laws or ordinances which deny rights created or protected by the Federal Constitution."

Whatever problems racially-mixed households may pose for children in 1984 can no more support a denial of constitutional rights than could the stresses that residential integration was thought to entail in 1917. The effects of racial prejudice, however real, cannot justify a racial classification removing an infant child from the custody of its natural mother found to be an appropriate person to have such custody.

The judgment of the District Court of Appeal is reversed.

It is so ordered.

The Japanese Curfew and Evacuation Cases

At the outset of World War II, some military authorities asserted that citizens as well as aliens of Japanese ancestry on the West Coast posed a security threat; that there was among them an actual or incipient fifth column. On February 19, 1942, President Roosevelt, acting as President and Commander-in-Chief, issued Executive Order No. 9066 authorizing such military commanders as he might designate to prescribe military areas from which any or all persons might be excluded as a security measure. Pursuant to this order he designated General DeWitt as Military Commander of the Western Defense Command. Acting under the Executive Order, the General, on March 2, 1942, established Military Area No. 1 which included the Pacific Coast states. Not willing to have these security measures entirely a matter of executive and military power, Congress, by the Act of March 21, 1942, made criminal the violation of enforcement orders issued under Executive Order 9066. Beginning on March 24, 1942, General DeWitt issued a series of orders applying to persons of Japanese ancestry residing in Military Area No. 1. One of these established a curfew for such persons between the hours of 8:00 p.m. and 6:00 a.m.; others were "exclusion orders" requiring persons of Japanese ancestry to remove from designated districts in the Military Area to "relocation centers" established further inland.

Hirabayashi v. United States

320 U.S. 81 (1943).

Appellant, an American citizen of Japanese ancestry, was convicted in a federal district court of violating the curfew order and therefore the Act of March 21, 1942, by failing to remain in his residence between the hours of 8:00 p.m. and 6:00 a.m. The Court affirmed in an opinion by Chief Justice Stone, saying: "distinctions between citizens solely because of their ancestry are by their very nature odious to a free people whose institutions are founded upon the doctrine of equality." However, the Court held that while racial discriminations are in most cases irrelevant, there was an adequate showing in this case that persons of Japanese descent presented a special danger to the community in the context of the war with Japan and that it was not feasible to determine loyalty on an individual basis.

Korematsu v. United States

323 U.S. 214 (1944).

Petitioner, an American citizen of Japanese descent, was convicted in a federal district court for remaining in San Leandro, California, contrary to General Dewitt's Civilian Exclusion Order no. 34. No question was raised as to petitioner's loyalty to the United States. The Court upheld the conviction. It refused to rule on the validity of other orders which required the detention of excluded persons in relocation centers. Justice Black, speaking for the Court, said: "[a]ll legal restrictions which curtail the civil rights of a single racial group are immediately suspect. That is not to say that all such restrictions are unconstitutional. It is to say that courts must subject them to the most rigid scrutiny. Pressing public necessity may sometimes justify the existence of such restrictions; racial antagonism never can." He concluded his opinion by saying:

"To cast this case into outlines of racial prejudice, without reference to the real military dangers which were presented, merely confuses the issue. Korematsu was not excluded from the Military Area because of hostility to him or his race. He *was* excluded because we are at war with the Japanese Empire, because the properly constituted military authorities feared an invasion of our West Coast and felt constrained to take proper security measures, because they decided that the military urgency of the situation demanded that all citizens of Japanese ancestry be segregated from the West Coast temporarily, and finally, because Congress, reposing its confidence in this time of war in our military leaders—as inevitably it must— determined they should have the power to do just this. There was evidence of disloyalty on the part of some, the military authorities considered that the need for action was great, and time was short. We cannot—by availing ourselves of the calm perspective of hindsight—now say that at that time these actions were unjustified."

Justices Roberts, Murphy, and Jackson all dissented on the ground that the order constituted unjustified discrimination against loyal Japanese citizens on the basis of race. Justice Jackson noted the practical inability of the courts to interfere with military actions of this kind taken during times of war but said: "[O]nce a judicial opinion . . . rationalizes the Constitution to show that the Constitution sanctions such an order, the Court for all time has validated the principle of racial discrimination in criminal procedure and of transplanting American citizens. The principle then lies about like a loaded weapon ready for the hand of any authority that can bring forward a plausible claim of an urgent need."

Ex parte Mitsuye Endo

323 U.S. 283 (1944).

This case was decided the same day as Korematsu and involved a later phase of the Japanese relocation program, i.e., the continued detention of concededly loyal persons of Japanese ancestry in the relocation centers. This raised a question which had been expressly left open in Korematsu. Appellant, an American citizen of Japanese ancestry and unquestioned loyalty, was evacuated from Sacramento, California in 1942 and placed in an evacuation center, first in Modoc County, California, and then in Utah. In July, 1942, she filed a petition for writ of habeas corpus in the district court, which denied it in July, 1943. An appeal was taken to the circuit court of appeals which certified certain questions to the Supreme Court. Justice Douglas, for the Court, said that whatever power the war relocation authority had to detain persons of Japanese ancestry initially, or to detain those whose loyalty was questioned, it had no authority to subject concededly loyal citizens to its "leave" procedure. The detainee seeking "indefinite leave" had to meet a number of conditions, including a showing that "public sentiment" at the detainee's "proposed destination" had been investigated and approved. The Court rested on the conclusion that the detention of a loyal citizen under these circumstances exceeded what was authorized by the Act of March 21, 1942, and the President's executive orders, but there were constitutional overtones in the opinion: ". . . We must assume that the Chief Executive and members of Congress, as well as the courts, are sensitive to and respectful of the liberties of the citizen. In interpreting a wartime measure we must assume that their purpose was to allow for the greatest possible accommodation between those liberties and the exigencies of war. . . . The purpose and objective of the act and of these orders are plain. Their single aim was the protection of the war effort against espionage and sabotage. It is in light of that one objective that the powers conferred by the orders must be construed. . . . A citizen who is concededly loyal presents no problem of espionage or sabotage. . . . When the power to detain is derived from the power to protect the war effort against espionage and sabotage, detention which has no relationship to that objective is unauthorized. . . . If we assume (as we do) that the original evacuation was justified, its lawful character was derived from the fact that it was an espionage and sabotage measure, not that there was community hostility to this group of American citizens. The evacuation program rested explicitly on the former ground not on the latter as the underlying legislation shows. The authority to detain a citizen or to grant him a conditional release as protection against espionage or sabotage is exhausted at least when his loyalty is conceded. . . ."

The district court was reversed; Roberts and Murphy, JJ., concurred but stressed their view that the entire evacuation program was unconstitutional.[a]

---

[a] The Japanese evacuation cases have been subject to great criticism: Girdner & Loftis, *The Great Betrayal* (1969); Rostow, *The Japanese-American Cases—A Disaster,* in *The Sovereign Prerogative* 193 (1962); Dembitz, *Racial Discrimination and the Military Judgment,* 45 Colum.L.Rev. 175 (1945).

Cf. Chief Justice Warren, *The Bill of Rights and the Military,* in *Great Rights* 89 (Cahn ed. 1963).

For a comprehensive study of Japanese-American evacuation, see tenBroek, Barnhart & Matson, *Prejudice, War and the Constitution* (1954).

The 1980's witnessed a legal reconsideration of this historical chapter. In 1980 Congress established a Commission on Wartime Relocation and Internment of Civilians to review the evacuation episode and recommend appropriate remedies. Its report, *Personal Justice Denied* (1982), concluded that military necessity did not justify exclusion and internment and that a grave injustice had occurred. Further research published in Irons, *Justice at War* (1983), an account of the original trials and how they were prosecuted and defended, revealed internal memoranda indicating that when the government presented its arguments in these cases it deliberately misled the Court about the military judgments that actually had been made. Using these sources, Fred Korematsu and Gordon

What Groups Are Specially Protected Against Discrimination?

In the Slaughter-House Cases, 83 U.S. (16 Wall.) 36 (1872), the Court said: "We doubt very much whether any action of a State not directed by way of discrimination against the negroes as a class, or on account of their race, will ever be held to come within the purview of this provision. It is so clearly a provision for that race and that emergency, that a strong case would be necessary for its application to any other." A decade and a half later, however, the Court in Yick Wo v. Hopkins, 118 U.S. 356 (1886), invalidated a classification found to discriminate against aliens of Chinese ancestry, saying: "[The provisions of the fourteenth amendment] are universal in their application, to all persons within the territorial jurisdiction, without regard to any differences of race, or color, or of nationality." In Hernandez v. Texas, 347 U.S. 475 (1954), it was held a violation of the equal protection clause to subject a person of Mexican descent to trial before a jury from which persons of similar ancestry had been systematically excluded. In response to an argument by the state that the equal protection clause contemplated only two classes—white and Negro—the Court said:

"Throughout our history differences in race and color have defined easily identifiable groups which have at times required the aid of the courts in securing equal treatment under the laws. But community prejudices are not static, and from time to time other differences from the community norm may define other groups which need the same protection. Whether such a group exists within a community is a question of fact. When the existence of a distinct class is demonstrated, and it is further shown that the laws, as written or as applied, single out that class for different treatment not based on some reasonable classification, the guarantees of the Constitution have been violated. The Fourteenth Amendment is not directed solely against discrimination due to a 'two-class theory'—that is, based upon differences between 'white' and Negro."

Ascertaining the Existence of a Racial Classification

When a statute on its face classifies by race, as in *Loving,* no problem arises. But under what circumstances may racial discrimination be found even though a statute on its face makes no racial classification? Two distinct situations are involved.

First, a statute fair on its face may be administered in a way that results in racial discrimination. In Yick Wo v. Hopkins, supra, for example, the Court had before it an ordinance making it unlawful to operate a laundry in a wooden building without a permit from the board of supervisors. A laundryman of Chinese descent who had been

---

Hirabayashi successfully challenged their original convictions. Korematsu's conviction was vacated in 1984 based on a correction of "errors of fact." Korematsu v. United States, 584 F.Supp. 1406, 1420 (N.D.Cal.1984). Hirabayashi's convictions for violating the curfew and exclusion orders were later vacated "to make the judgments of the courts conform to the judgments of history." Hirabayashi v. United States, 828 F.2d 591, 593 (9th Cir.1987). The Court of Appeals concluded that the subsequent research "demonstrate[s] that there could have been no reasonable military assessment of an emergency at the time, that the orders were based upon racial stereotypes, and that the orders caused needless suffering and shame for thousands of American citizens." Congress subsequently enacted the Civil Liberties Act of 1988, 50 U.S.C.App. §§ 1989–1989d, which declared an official apology, urged the President to pardon those convicted who had refused to accept the discriminatory treatment, and appropriated funds for restitution of $20,000. to each individual of Japanese ancestry who, during the evacuation, relocation, and internment period, was a citizen or permanent resident alien, and was confined, held in custody, relocated, or otherwise deprived of liberty or property. An equal protection challenge to the Act by a citizen of German ancestry, interned with his father during the War after his father had received an individualized hearing, was rejected in Jacobs v. Barr, 959 F.2d 313 (D.C.Cir.1992), because "Congress's finding that Japanese Americans were the victims of prejudice, while German Americans were not" was "amply supported by historical evidence" and justified compensating "interns of Japanese but not German descent."

denied a permit to operate his laundry in a wooden building showed that the board had denied permits to the 200 Chinese who had petitioned but granted them to 80 non-Chinese. In holding that this constituted a violation of equal protection the Court said: "Though the law itself be fair on its face, and impartial in appearance, yet, if it is applied and administered by public authority with an evil eye and an unequal hand, so as practically to make unjust and illegal discriminations between persons in similar circumstances, material to their rights, the denial of equal justice is still within the prohibition of the constitution."

Second, the contention may be that a statute which does not on its face make a racial classification in fact was designed to discriminate against a racial group. At one extreme are cases where it is apparent from the face of the statute that an ostensibly nondiscriminatory classification in fact is based on race. See, e.g., Guinn v. United States, 238 U.S. 347 (1915). The Oklahoma Constitution was amended in 1910 to provide that no person shall be registered to vote unless able to read and write a section of that Constitution, but that no person who on Jan. 1, 1866, or any time prior thereto was entitled to vote under any form of government, and no lineal descendant of such person, shall be denied the right to vote because of inability to read and write a section of the Constitution. In holding the provision invalid as a forbidden racial discrimination in voting, the Court said that the discrimination appears from the mere statement of the text. "It is true it contains no express words of an exclusion from the standard which is established of any person on account of race, color, or previous condition of servitude, prohibited by the 15th Amendment, but the standard itself inherently brings that result into existence since it is based purely upon a period of time before the enactment of the 15th Amendment, and makes that period the controlling and dominant test of the right of suffrage." Similarly, saying in part that "[a]ncestry can be a proxy for race" and "[i]t is that proxy here[,]" a majority of the Court examined in context, and then invalidated as an impermissible racial discrimination, a voting qualification favoring the descendants of those who lived in Hawaii in 1778. Rice v. Cayetano, 528 U.S. 495 (2000), set forth infra at p. 680.

At the other extreme are cases where a statute which does not make a racial classification is shown to have a disproportionate impact on a particular racial group. See, e.g., Jefferson v. Hackney, 406 U.S. 535 (1972), in which the Court upheld a state welfare statute which funded old age assistance at 100% of recognized need but aid to dependent children at 75% of such need. The Court held that a showing that 40% of the recipients of old age assistance were African-Americans and Mexican-Americans while 87% of the recipients of aid to dependent children were from such groups was not sufficient to establish that the classification was based on race.

Because the problem of establishing the existence of the discrimination also arises in cases involving classifications based on gender, the cases dealing with proof of discriminatory purpose are postponed for consideration to page 547, infra.

B. RACIAL SEGREGATION IN SCHOOLS AND OTHER PUBLIC FACILITIES

Plessy v. Ferguson

163 U.S. 537, 16 S.Ct. 1138, 41 L.Ed. 256 (1896).

■ MR. JUSTICE BROWN delivered the opinion of the court.

This case turns upon the constitutionality of an act of the general assembly of the state of Louisiana, passed in 1890, providing for separate railway carriages for the white and colored races. . . .

. . .

The petition for the writ of prohibition averred that petitioner was seven-eighths Caucasian and one-eighth African blood; that the mixture of colored blood was not discernible in him; and that he was entitled to every right, privilege, and immunity secured to citizens of the United States of the white race; and that, upon such theory, he took possession of a vacant seat in a coach where passengers of the white race were accommodated, and was ordered by the conductor to vacate said coach, and take a seat in another, assigned to persons of the colored race, and, having refused to comply with such demand, he was forcibly ejected, with the aid of a police officer, and imprisoned in the parish jail to answer a charge of having violated the above act.

The constitutionality of this act is attacked upon the ground that it conflicts . . . with . . . the fourteenth amendment. . . .

. . .

The object of the amendment was undoubtedly to enforce the absolute equality of the two races before the law, but, in the nature of things, it could not have been intended to abolish distinctions based upon color, or to enforce social, as distinguished from political, equality, or a commingling of the two races upon terms unsatisfactory to either. Laws permitting, and even requiring, their separation, in places where they are liable to be brought into contact, do not necessarily imply the inferiority of either race to the other, and have been generally, if not universally, recognized as within the competency of the state legislatures in the exercise of their police power. The most common instance of this is connected with the establishment of separate schools for white and colored children, which have been held to be a valid exercise of the legislative power even by courts of states where the political rights of the colored race have been longest and most earnestly enforced.

. . .

Laws forbidding the intermarriage of the two races may be said in a technical sense to interfere with the freedom of contract, and yet have been universally recognized as within the police power of the state. . . .

. . .

In this connection, it is also suggested by the learned counsel for the plaintiff in error that the same argument that will justify the state legislature in requiring railways to provide separate accommodations for the two races will also authorize them to require separate cars to be provided for people whose hair is of a certain color, or who are aliens, or who belong to certain nationalities, or to enact laws requiring colored people to walk upon one side of the street, and white people upon the other, or requiring white men's houses to be painted white, and colored men's black, or their vehicles or business signs to be of different colors, upon the theory that one side of the street is as good as the other, or that a house or vehicle of one color is as good as one of another color. The reply to all this is that every exercise of the police power must be reasonable, and extend only to such laws as are enacted in good faith for the promotion of the public good, and not for the annoyance or oppression of a particular class. . . .

So far, then, as a conflict with the fourteenth amendment is concerned, the case reduces itself to the question whether the statute of Louisiana is a reasonable regulation, and with respect to this there must necessarily be a large discretion on the part of the legislature. In determining the question of reasonableness, it is at liberty to act with reference to the established usages, customs, and traditions of the people, and with a view to the promotion of their comfort, and the preservation of the public peace and good order. Gauged by this standard, we cannot say that a law which authorizes or even requires the separation of the two races in public conveyances is unreasonable, or more obnoxious to the fourteenth amendment than the acts of congress requiring separate schools for colored children in the District of Columbia, the constitutionality of which does not seem to have been questioned or the corresponding acts of state legislatures.

We consider the underlying fallacy of the plaintiff's argument to consist in the assumption that the enforced separation of the two races stamps the colored race with a badge of inferiority. If this be so, it is not by reason of anything found in the act, but solely because the colored race chooses to put that construction upon it. The argument necessarily assumes that if, as has been more than once the case, and is not unlikely to be so again, the colored race should become the dominant power in the state legislature, and should enact a law in precisely similar terms, it would thereby relegate the white race to an inferior position. We imagine that the white race, at least, would not acquiesce in this assumption. The argument also assumes that social prejudices may be overcome by legislation, and that equal rights cannot be secured to the negro except by an enforced commingling of the two races. We cannot accept this proposition. If the two races are to meet upon terms of social equality, it must be the result of natural affinities, a mutual appreciation of each other's merits, and a voluntary consent of individuals. . . . Legislation is powerless to eradicate racial instincts, or to abolish distinctions based upon physical differences, and the attempt to do so can only result in accentuating the difficulties of the present situation. If the civil and political rights of both races be equal, one cannot be inferior to the other civilly or politically. If one race be inferior to the other socially, the constitution of the United States cannot put them upon the same plane. . . .

The judgment of the court below is therefore affirmed.

■ MR. JUSTICE BREWER did not hear the argument or participate in the decision of this case.

■ MR. JUSTICE HARLAN dissenting. . . .

In respect of civil rights, common to all citizens, the constitution of the United States does not, I think, permit any public authority to know the race of those entitled to be protected in the enjoyment of such rights. Every true man has pride of race, and under appropriate circumstances, when the rights of others, his equals before the law, are not to be affected, it is his privilege to express such pride and to take such action based upon it as to him seems proper. But I deny that any legislative body or judicial tribunal may have regard to the race of citizens when the civil rights of those citizens are involved. Indeed, such legislation as that here in question is inconsistent not only with that equality of rights which pertains to citizenship, national and state, but with the personal liberty enjoyed by every one within the United States. . . .

[The thirteenth, fourteenth, and fifteenth amendments] were welcomed by the friends of liberty throughout the world. They removed the race line from our governmental systems. . . .

It was said in argument that the statute of Louisiana does not discriminate against either race, but prescribes a rule applicable alike to white and colored citizens. But this argument does not meet the difficulty. Everyone knows that the statute in question had its origin in the purpose, not so much to exclude white persons from railroad cars occupied by blacks; as to exclude colored people from coaches occupied by or assigned to white persons. Railroad corporations of Louisiana did not make discrimination among whites in the matter of accommodation for travelers. The thing to accomplish was, under the guise of giving equal accommodation for whites and blacks, to compel the latter to keep to themselves while traveling in railroad passenger coaches. No one would be so wanting in candor as to assert the contrary. The fundamental objection, therefore, to the statute, is that it interferes with the personal freedom of citizens. . . . If a white man and a black man choose to occupy the same public conveyance on a public highway, it is their right to do so; and no government, proceeding alone on grounds of race, can prevent it without infringing the personal liberty of each. . . .

The white race deems itself to be the dominant race in this country. And so it is, in prestige, in achievements, in education, in wealth, and in power. So, I doubt not, it will continue to be for all time, if it remains true to its great heritage, and holds fast to the principles of constitutional liberty. But in view of the constitution, in the eye of the law, there is in this country no superior, dominant, ruling class of citizens. There is no caste here. Our constitution is color-blind, and neither knows nor tolerates classes among citizens. In respect of civil rights, all citizens are equal before the law. The humblest is the peer of the most powerful. The law regards man as man, and takes no account of his surroundings or of his color when his civil rights as guaranteed by the supreme law of the land are involved. It is therefore to be regretted that this high tribunal, the final expositor of the fundamental law of the land, has reached the conclusion that it is competent for a state to regulate the enjoyment by citizens of their civil rights solely upon the basis of race.

. . .

If evils will result from the commingling of the two races upon public highways established for the benefit of all, they will be infinitely less than those that will surely come from state legislation regulating the enjoyment of civil rights upon the basis of race. We boast of the freedom enjoyed by our people above all other peoples. But it is difficult to reconcile that boast with a state of the law which, practically, puts the brand of servitude and degradation upon a large class of our fellow citizens,—our equals before the law. The thin disguise of "equal" accommodations for passengers in railroad coaches will not mislead any one, nor atone for the wrong this day done. . . .

Brown v. Board of Education of Topeka

347 U.S. 483, 74 S.Ct. 686, 98 L.Ed. 873 (1954).

■ MR. CHIEF JUSTICE WARREN delivered the opinion of the Court.

These cases come to us from the States of Kansas, South Carolina, Virginia, and Delaware. They are premised on different facts and different local conditions, but a common legal question justifies their consideration together in this consolidated opinion.

In each of the cases, minors of the Negro race, through their legal representatives, seek the aid of the courts in obtaining admission to the public schools of their community on a nonsegregated basis. In each instance, they have been denied admission to schools attended by white children under laws requiring or permitting segregation according to race. This segregation was alleged to deprive the plaintiffs of the equal protection of the laws under the Fourteenth Amendment. In each of the cases other than the Delaware case, a three-judge federal district court denied relief to the plaintiffs on the so-called "separate but equal" doctrine announced by this Court in Plessy v. Ferguson, 163 U.S. 537. Under that doctrine, equality of treatment is accorded when the races are provided substantially equal facilities, even though these facilities be separate. In the Delaware case, the Supreme Court of Delaware adhered to that doctrine, but ordered that the plaintiffs be admitted to the white schools because of their superiority to the Negro schools.

The plaintiffs contend that segregated public schools are not "equal" and cannot be made "equal," and that hence they are deprived of the equal protection of the laws. Because of the obvious importance of the question presented, the Court took jurisdiction. Argument was heard in the 1952 Term, and reargument was heard this Term on certain questions propounded by the Court.

Reargument was largely devoted to the circumstances surrounding the adoption of the Fourteenth Amendment in 1868. It covered exhaustively consideration of the Amendment in Congress, ratification by the states, then existing practices in racial segregation, and the views of proponents and opponents of the Amendment. This discussion and our own investigation convince us that, although these sources cast some light, it is not enough to resolve the problem with which we are faced. At best, they are inconclusive. The most avid proponents of the post–War Amendments undoubtedly intended them to remove all legal distinctions among "all persons born or naturalized in the United States." Their opponents, just as certainly were antagonistic to both the letter and the spirit of the Amendments and wished them to have the most limited effect. What others in Congress and the state legislatures had in mind cannot be determined with any degree of certainty.

An additional reason for the inconclusive nature of the Amendment's history, with respect to segregated schools, is the status of public education at that time. In the South, the movement toward free common schools, supported by general taxation, had not yet taken hold. Education of white children was largely in the hands of private groups. Education of Negroes was almost nonexistent, and practically all of the race were illiterate. In fact, any education of Negroes was forbidden by law in some states. Today, in contrast, many Negroes have achieved outstanding success in the arts and sciences as well as in the business and professional world. It is true that public school education at the time of the Amendment had advanced further in the North, but the effect of the Amendment on Northern States was generally ignored in the congressional debates. Even in the North, the conditions of public education did not approximate those existing today. The curriculum was usually rudimentary; ungraded schools were common in rural areas; the school term was but three months a year in many states; and compulsory school attendance was virtually unknown. As a consequence, it is not surprising that there should be so little in the history of the Fourteenth Amendment relating to its intended effect on public education.

In the first cases in this Court construing the Fourteenth Amendment, decided shortly after its adoption, the Court interpreted it as proscribing all state-imposed discriminations against the Negro race. The doctrine of "separate but equal" did not make its appearance in this Court until 1896 in the case of *Plessy v. Ferguson,* supra, involving not education but transportation. American courts have since labored with the doctrine for over half a century. In this Court, there have been six cases involving the "separate but equal" doctrine in the field of public education. In Cumming v. Board of Education of Richmond County, 175 U.S. 528, and Gong Lum v. Rice, 275 U.S. 78, the validity of the doctrine itself was not challenged. In more recent cases, all on the graduate school level, inequality was found in that specific benefits enjoyed by white students were denied to Negro students of the same educational qualifications. State of Missouri ex rel. Gaines v. Canada, 305 U.S. 337; Sipuel v. Board of Regents of University of Oklahoma, 332 U.S. 631; Sweatt v. Painter, 339 U.S. 629; McLaurin v. Oklahoma State Regents, 339 U.S. 637. In none of these cases was it necessary to reexamine the doctrine to grant relief to the Negro plaintiff. And in *Sweatt v. Painter,* supra, the Court expressly reserved decision on the question whether *Plessy v. Ferguson* should be held inapplicable to public education.

In the instant cases, that question is directly presented. Here, unlike *Sweatt v. Painter,* there are findings below that the Negro and white schools involved have been equalized, or are being equalized, with respect to buildings, curricula, qualifications and salaries of teachers, and other "tangible" factors. Our decision, therefore, cannot turn on merely a comparison of these tangible factors in the Negro and white schools involved in each of the cases. We must look instead to the effect of segregation itself on public education.

In approaching this problem, we cannot turn the clock back to 1868 when the Amendment was adopted, or even to 1896 when *Plessy v. Ferguson* was written. We must consider public education in the light of its full development and its present place in American life throughout the Nation. Only in this way can it be determined if segregation in public schools deprives these plaintiffs of the equal protection of the laws.

Today, education is perhaps the most important function of state and local governments. Compulsory school attendance laws and the great expenditures for education both demonstrate our recognition of the importance of education to our democratic society. It is required in the performance of our most basic public responsibilities, even service in the armed forces. It is the very foundation of good citizenship. Today it is a principal instrument in awakening the child to cultural values, in preparing him for later professional training, and in helping him to adjust normally to his environment. In these days, it is doubtful that any child may reasonably be expected to succeed in life if he is denied the opportunity of an education. Such an opportunity, where the state has undertaken to provide it, is a right which must be made available to all on equal terms.

We come then to the question presented: Does segregation of children in public schools solely on the basis of race, even though the physical facilities and other "tangible" factors may be equal, deprive the children of the minority group of equal educational opportunities? We believe that it does.

In *Sweatt v. Painter,* supra, in finding that a segregated law school for Negroes could not provide them equal educational opportunities, this Court relied in large part on "those qualities which are incapable of objective measurement but which make for greatness in a law school." In *McLaurin v. Oklahoma State Regents,* supra, the Court, in requiring that a Negro admitted to a white graduate school be treated like all other students, again resorted to intangible considerations: ". . . his ability to study, to engage in discussions and exchange views with other students, and, in general, to learn his profession." Such considerations apply with added force to children in grade and high schools. To separate them from others of similar age and qualifications solely because of their race generates a feeling of inferiority as to their status in the community that may affect their hearts and minds in a way unlikely ever to be undone. The effect of this separation on their educational opportunities was well stated by a finding in the Kansas case by a court which nevertheless felt compelled to rule against the Negro plaintiffs:

"Segregation of white and colored children in public schools has a detrimental effect upon the colored children. The impact is greater when it has the sanction of the law; for the policy of separating the races is usually interpreted as denoting the inferiority of the negro group. A sense of inferiority affects the motivation of a child to learn. Segregation with the sanction of law, therefore, has a tendency to [retard] the educational and mental development of negro children and to deprive them of some of the benefits they would receive in a racial[ly] integrated school system."

Whatever may have been the extent of psychological knowledge at the time of *Plessy v. Ferguson,* this finding is amply supported by modern authority.[11] Any language in *Plessy v. Ferguson* contrary to this finding is rejected.

---

[11] K.B. Clark, Effect of Prejudice and Discrimination on Personality Development (Midcentury White House Conference on Children and Youth, 1950); Wittmer and Kotinsky, Personality in the Making (1952), c. VI; Deutscher and Chein, The Psychological Effects of Enforced Segregation: A Survey of Social Science Opinion, 26 J.Psychol. 259 (1948); Chein, What are the Psychological Effects

We conclude that in the field of public education the doctrine of "separate but equal" has no place. Separate educational facilities are inherently unequal. Therefore, we hold that the plaintiffs and others similarly situated for whom the actions have been brought are, by reason of the segregation complained of, deprived of the equal protection of the laws guaranteed by the Fourteenth Amendment. This disposition makes unnecessary any discussion whether such segregation also violates the Due Process Clause of the Fourteenth Amendment.

Because these are class actions, because of the wide applicability of this decision, and because of the great variety of local conditions, the formulation of decrees in these cases presents problems of considerable complexity. On reargument, the consideration of appropriate relief was necessarily subordinated to the primary question—the constitutionality of segregation in public education. We have now announced that such segregation is a denial of the equal protection of the laws. In order that we may have the full assistance of the parties in formulating decrees, the cases will be restored to the docket, and the parties are requested to present further argument on Questions 4 and 5 previously propounded by the Court for the reargument this Term. The Attorney General of the United States is again invited to participate. The Attorneys General of the states requiring or permitting segregation in public education will also be permitted to appear as *amici curiae* upon request to do so by September 15, 1954, and submission of briefs by October 1, 1954.

It is so ordered.

Bolling v. Sharpe

347 U.S. 497, 74 S.Ct. 693, 98 L.Ed. 884 (1954).

■ MR. CHIEF JUSTICE WARREN delivered the opinion of the Court.

This case challenges the validity of segregation in the public schools of the District of Columbia. The petitioners, minors of the Negro race, allege that such segregation deprives them of due process of law under the Fifth Amendment. They were refused admission to a public school attended by white children solely because of their race. They sought the aid of the District Court for the District of Columbia in obtaining admission. That court dismissed their complaint. The Court granted a writ of certiorari before judgment in the Court of Appeals because of the importance of the constitutional question presented. 344 U.S. 873.

We have this day held that the Equal Protection Clause of the Fourteenth Amendment prohibits the states from maintaining racially segregated public schools. The legal problem in the District of Columbia is somewhat different, however. The Fifth Amendment, which is applicable in the District of Columbia, does not contain an equal protection clause as does the Fourteenth Amendment which applies only to the states. But the concepts of equal protection and due process, both stemming from our American ideal of fairness, are not mutually exclusive. The "equal protection of the laws" is a more explicit safeguard of prohibited unfairness than "due process of law," and, therefore, we do not imply that the two are always interchangeable phrases. But, as this Court has recognized, discrimination may be so unjustifiable as to be violative of due process.

---

of Segregation Under Conditions of Equal Facilities?, 3 Int.J.Opinion and Attitude Res. 229 (1949); Brameld, Educational Costs, in Discrimination and National Welfare (MacIver, ed., 1949), 44–48; Frazier, The Negro in the United States (1949), 674–681. And see generally Myrdal, An American Dilemma (1944).

Classifications based solely upon race must be scrutinized with particular care, since they are contrary to our traditions and hence constitutionally suspect. As long ago as 1896, this Court declared the principle "that the constitution of the United States, in its present form, forbids, so far as civil and political rights are concerned, discrimination by the general government, or by the states, against any citizen because of his race." And in Buchanan v. Warley, 245 U.S. 60, the Court held that a statute which limited the right of a property owner to convey his property to a person of another race was, as an unreasonable discrimination, a denial of due process of law.

Although the Court has not assumed to define "liberty" with any great precision, that term is not confined to mere freedom from bodily restraint. Liberty under law extends to the full range of conduct which the individual is free to pursue, and it cannot be restricted except for a proper governmental objective. Segregation in public education is not reasonably related to any proper governmental objective, and thus it imposes on Negro children of the District of Columbia a burden that constitutes an arbitrary deprivation of their liberty in violation of the Due Process Clause.

In view of our decision that the Constitution prohibits the states from maintaining racially segregated public schools, it would be unthinkable that the same Constitution would impose a lesser duty on the Federal Government. We hold that racial segregation in the public schools of the District of Columbia is a denial of the due process of law guaranteed by the Fifth Amendment to the Constitution.

For the reasons set out in *Brown v. Board of Education,* this case will be restored to the docket for reargument on Questions 4 and 5 previously propounded by the Court. 345 U.S. 972.

It is so ordered.

Brown *and the Relevance of Social Science and Historical Materials*

The Court in *Brown* relied to some extent on studies by psychologists and social scientists to support the conclusion that placing Negro children in separate schools generates feelings of inferiority unlikely to be undone. The Court's reference to this data generated immediate controversy among lawyers as to its propriety and relevance. Compare Cahn, *Science or Common Sense? A Dangerous Myth, in 1954 Annual Survey of American Law: Jurisprudence,* 30 N.Y.U.L.Rev. 150 (1955) with Honnold, *Book Review,* 33 Ind.L.J. 612, 614 (1958). More recent and elaborate consideration will be found in two symposia: *The Courts, Social Science, and School Desegregation,* 39 Law & Contemp.Prob. (No. 1, Winter, 1975, and No. 2, Spring, 1975); *School Desegregation: Lessons of the First Twenty-Five Years,* 42 Law & Contemp.Prob. (Summer 1978 and Autumn 1978).

The Court in *Brown* also directed attention to the historical background of the fourteenth amendment. For a discussion of the historical record, see Bickel, *The Original Understanding and the Segregation Decision,* 69 Harv.L.Rev. 1 (1955), *Selected Essays on Constitutional Law,* 1938–1962 (1963) 853.

For some of the voluminous literature which followed the desegregation cases and probed their implications, see Wechsler, *Toward Neutral Principles of Constitutional Law,* 73 Harv.L.Rev. 1 (1959); Black, *The Lawfulness of the Segregation Decisions,* 69 Yale L.J. 421 (1960); Pollak, *Racial Discrimination and Judicial Integrity,* 108 U.Pa.L.Rev. 1 (1959). These articles are reprinted in *Selected Essays on Constitutional Law,* 1938–1962 (1963) at 463, 844, and 819.

Segregation in Public Facilities Other than Schools

In *Brown* the Court emphasized the importance of education and gave reasons why segregation in schools was inherently unequal. When presented with the question whether the same reasoning would serve to invalidate segregation in other public facilities, the Court held such segregation invalid in a series of per curiam orders without explanatory opinions. In Mayor and City Council of Baltimore City v. Dawson, 350 U.S. 877 (1955), it summarily affirmed an order enjoining racial segregation in public beaches and bathhouses. In Holmes v. Atlanta, 350 U.S. 879 (1955) the Court summarily reversed a lower court order which appeared to permit the city to allocate a municipal golf course to different races on alternate days. In Gayle v. Browder, 352 U.S. 903 (1956) it summarily affirmed a judgment enjoining enforcement of racial segregation on city buses. Similar dispositions were made in cases involving other public facilities in New Orleans City Park Improvement Ass'n v. Detiege, 358 U.S. 54 (1958) (golf course and parks); State Athletic Comm'n v. Dorsey, 359 U.S. 533 (1959) (participation in athletic contests); Schiro v. Bynum, 375 U.S. 395 (1964) (municipal auditorium).

In Johnson v. Virginia, 373 U.S. 61 (1963), the Court wrote a brief per curiam opinion reversing a conviction of a defendant for sitting in a section of a segregated courtroom reserved for whites. The Court said, without further elaboration: "Such a conviction cannot stand for it is no longer open to question that a State may not constitutionally require segregation of public facilities."[a]

More than four decades later, in Johnson v. California, 543 U.S. 499 (2005), a divided Court insisted that strict scrutiny be applied to an unwritten California policy segregating prisoners in double cells (but not the prison generally) for up to 60 days after they arrive at a new prison, despite the claims of corrections officials that the temporary segregation was necessary during a period of inmate evaluation to prevent violence associated with racial gangs. With Chief Justice Rehnquist not participating, Justice O'Connor's majority opinion reasoned in part that "by insisting that inmates be housed only with other inmates of the same race, it is possible that prison officials will breed further hostility among prisoners and reinforce racial and ethnic divisions. By perpetuating the notion that race matters most, racial segregation of inmates 'may exacerbate the very patterns of [violence that it is] said to counteract.'" She "decline[d] the invitation" to make an exception for the prison context, where for certain fundamental constitutional rights the Court in Turner v. Safley, 482 U.S. 78, 89 (1987), has required only that a burdensome regulation be "reasonably related" to "legitimate penological interests." Unlike the constitutional rights to which the deferential standard of *Turner* properly applied, "[t]he right not to be discriminated against based on one's race is ... not a right that need necessarily be compromised for the sake of proper prison administration. On the contrary, compliance with the Fourteenth Amendment's ban on racial discrimination ... bolsters the legitimacy of the entire criminal justice system." The majority was convinced that "[i]n the prison context, when the government's power is at its apex, ... searching judicial review of racial classifications is necessary to guard against invidious discrimination"; that "[t]he 'necessities of prison security and discipline' ... are a compelling government interest justifying only those uses of race that are narrowly tailored to address those necessities"; and that on remand, although "[s]trict scrutiny does not preclude the ability of prison officials to address the compelling interest in prison safety[, p]rison administrators ... will have to demonstrate that any race-based policies are narrowly tailored to that end."

---

[a] For observations on the extent to which the Court uses per curiam decisions, see Brown, *Process of Law,* 72 Harv.L.Rev. 77 (1958).

A dissent by Justice Stevens concluded that the record as it stood showed the policy was unconstitutional, for it was "based on a conclusive presumption that housing inmates of different races together creates an unacceptable risk of racial violence"; "scant empirical evidence" supported that presumption; and a "very real risk that prejudice (whether conscious or not) partly underlies the . . . policy" undermined it. A polar opposite dissent by Justice Thomas, joined by Justice Scalia, emphasized "how limited the policy . . . is" of racial segregation of "a portion of [California's] inmates, in a part of its prisons, for brief periods . . . until the State can arrange permanent housing" and argued that the Court should apply *Turner* and defer to the expert judgment of prison officials. Those officials had asserted that "housing inmates in double cells without regard to race threatens not only prison discipline, but also the physical safety of inmates and staff . . . because double cells are especially dangerous. The risk of racial violence in public areas of prisons is high, and the tightly confined, private conditions of cells hazard even more violence." Furthermore, "Johnson has never argued that California's policy is motivated by anything other than a desire to protect inmates and staff." In any event, "the Constitution's usual demands . . . have always been lessened inside . . . prison walls" and the majority's "second-guessing" fell "far short of the compelling showing needed to overcome the deference we owe to prison administrators."

C. CLASSIFICATIONS BASED ON GENDER

Reed v. Reed

404 U.S. 71, 92 S.Ct. 251, 30 L.Ed.2d 225 (1971).

[Section 15–314C of the Idaho Code provided that in the choice of persons to administer an intestate estate "[o]f several persons claiming and equally entitled to administer, males must be preferred to females." Solely because of this statute an Idaho court appointed the father rather than the mother of a deceased child as administrator. The mother appealed the decision.]

■ MR. CHIEF JUSTICE BURGER delivered the opinion of the Court.

. . .

Section 15–314 is restricted in its operation to those situations where competing applications for letters of administration have been filed by both male and female members of the same entitlement class established by § 15–312. In such situations, § 15–314 provides that different treatment be accorded to the applicants on the basis of their sex; it thus establishes a classification subject to scrutiny under the Equal Protection Clause.

In applying that clause, this Court has consistently recognized that the Fourteenth Amendment does not deny to States the power to treat different classes of persons in different ways. Barbier v. Connolly, 113 U.S. 27; Lindsley v. Natural Carbonic Gas Co., 220 U.S. 61 (1911); Railway Express Agency, Inc. v. New York, 336 U.S. 106 (1949); McDonald v. Board of Election Commissioners, 394 U.S. 802 (1969). The Equal Protection Clause of that Amendment does, however, deny to States the power to legislate that different treatment be accorded to persons placed by a statute into different classes on the basis of criteria wholly unrelated to the objective of that statute. A classification "must be reasonable, not arbitrary, and must rest upon some ground of difference having a fair and substantial relation to the object of the legislation, so that all persons similarly circumstanced shall be treated alike." Royster Guano Co. v. Virginia, 253 U.S. 412, 415 (1920). The question presented by this case, then, is whether a difference in the sex of competing applicants for letters of administration bears a rational relationship to a state objective that is sought to be advanced by the operation of §§ 15–312 and 15–314.

In upholding the latter section, the Idaho Supreme Court concluded that its objective was to eliminate one area of controversy when two or more persons, equally entitled under § 15–312, seek letters of administration and thereby present the probate court "with the issue of which one should be named." The court also concluded that where such persons are not of the same sex, the elimination of females from consideration "is neither an illogical nor arbitrary method devised by the legislature to resolve an issue that would otherwise require a hearing as to the relative merits . . . of the two or more petitioning relatives. . . ." . . .

Clearly the objective of reducing the workload on probate courts by eliminating one class of contests is not without some legitimacy. The crucial question, however, is whether § 15–314 advances that objective in a manner consistent with the command of the Equal Protection Clause. We hold that it does not. To give a mandatory preference to members of either sex over members of the other, merely to accomplish the elimination of hearings on the merits, is to make the very kind of arbitrary legislative choice forbidden by the Equal Protection Clause of the Fourteenth Amendment; and whatever may be said as to the positive values of avoiding intrafamily controversy, the choice in this context may not lawfully be mandated solely on the basis of sex.

. . .

The judgment of the Idaho Supreme Court is reversed and the case remanded for further proceedings not inconsistent with this opinion.

Frontiero v. Richardson

411 U.S. 677, 93 S.Ct. 1764, 36 L.Ed.2d 583 (1973).

■ MR. JUSTICE BRENNAN announced the judgment of the Court in an opinion in which MR. JUSTICE DOUGLAS, MR. JUSTICE WHITE, and MR. JUSTICE MARSHALL join.

The question before us concerns the right of a female member of the uniformed services to claim her spouse as a "dependent" for the purposes of obtaining increased quarters allowances and medical and dental benefits under 37 U.S.C. §§ 401, 403, and 10 U.S.C. §§ 1072, 1076, on an equal footing with male members. Under these statutes, a serviceman may claim his wife as a "dependent" without regard to whether she is in fact dependent upon him for any part of her support. . . . A servicewoman, on the other hand, may not claim her husband as a "dependent" under these programs unless he is in fact dependent upon her for over one-half of his support. . . . Thus, the question for decision is whether this difference in treatment constitutes an unconstitutional discrimination against servicewomen in violation of the Due Process Clause of the Fifth Amendment. A three-judge District Court for the Middle District of Alabama, one judge dissenting, rejected this contention. . . . We reverse.

I.

In an effort to attract career personnel through reenlistment, Congress established . . . fringe benefits [for] members of the uniformed services on a competitive basis with business and industry. Thus, under 37 U.S.C. § 403, a member of the uniformed services with dependents is entitled to an increased "basic allowance for quarters" and, under 10 U.S.C. § 1076, a member's dependents are provided comprehensive medical and dental care.

Appellant Sharron Frontiero, a lieutenant in the United States Air Force, sought increased quarters allowances, and housing and medical benefits for her husband . . . on the ground that he was her "dependent." Although such benefits would automatically have been granted with respect to the wife of a male member of the uniformed services, appellant's application was denied because she failed to demonstrate that her husband was dependent on her for more than one-half of his support. Appellants then commenced this suit, contending that, by making this distinction, the statutes unreasonably discriminate on the basis of sex in violation of the Due Process Clause of the Fifth Amendment. In essence, appellants asserted that the discriminatory impact of the statutes is two-fold: first, as a procedural matter, a female member is required to demonstrate her spouse's dependency, while no such burden is imposed upon male members; and second, as a substantive matter, a male member who does not provide more than one-half of his wife's support receives benefits, while a similarly situated female member is denied such benefits. . . .

Although the legislative history of these statutes sheds virtually no light on the purposes underlying the differential treatment accorded male and female members, a majority of the three-judge District Court surmised that Congress might reasonably have concluded that, since the husband in our society is generally the "breadwinner" in the family—and the wife typically the "dependent" partner—"it would be more economical to require married female members claiming husbands to prove actual dependency than to extend the presumption of dependency to such members." 341 F.Supp., at 207. Indeed, given the fact that approximately 99% of all members of the uniformed services are male, the District Court speculated that such differential treatment might conceivably lead to a "considerable saving of administrative expense and manpower." Ibid.

II.

At the outset, appellants contend that classifications based upon sex, like classifications based upon race, alienage, and national origin, are inherently suspect and must therefore be subjected to close judicial scrutiny. We agree and, indeed, find at least implicit support for such an approach in our unanimous decision only last Term in Reed v. Reed, 404 U.S. 71 (1971). . . .

There can be no doubt that our Nation has had a long and unfortunate history of sex discrimination. Traditionally, such discrimination was rationalized by an attitude of "romantic paternalism" which, in practical effect, put women not on a pedestal, but in a cage. Indeed, this paternalistic attitude became so firmly rooted in our national consciousness that, exactly 100 years ago, a distinguished member of this Court was able to proclaim:

"Man is, or should be, woman's protector and defender. The natural and proper timidity and delicacy which belongs to the female sex evidently unfits it for many of the occupations of civil life. The constitution of the family organization, which is founded in the divine ordinance, as well as in the nature of things, indicates the domestic sphere as that which properly belongs to the domain and functions of womanhood. The harmony, not to say identity, of interests and views which belong, or should belong, to the family institution is repugnant to the ideas of a woman adopting a distinct and independent career from that of her husband. . . .

". . . The paramount destiny and mission of women are to fulfil the noble and benign offices of wife and mother. This is the law of the Creator." Bradwell v. Illinois, 83 U.S. [16 Wall.] 130, 141 (1873) (Bradley, J., concurring).

As a result of notions such as these, our statute books gradually became laden with gross, stereotypical distinctions between the sexes and, indeed, throughout much of the 19th century the position of women in our society was, in many respects, comparable to that of blacks under the pre–Civil War slave codes. Neither slaves nor women could hold office, serve on juries, or bring suit in their own names, and married women traditionally were denied the legal capacity to hold or convey property or to serve as legal guardians of their own children. See generally, L. Kanowitz, Women and the Law: The Unfinished Revolution 5–6 (1969); G. Mydral, An American Dilemma 1073 (2d ed. 1962). And although blacks were guaranteed the right to vote in 1870, women were denied even that right—which is itself "preservative of other basic civil and political rights"—until adoption of the Nineteenth Amendment half a century later.

It is true, of course, that the position of women in America has improved markedly in recent decades. Nevertheless, it can hardly be doubted that, in part because of the high visibility of the sex characteristic, women still face pervasive, although at times more subtle, discrimination in our educational institutions, on the job market and, perhaps most conspicuously, in the political arena.[17] See generally, K. Amundsen, The Silenced Majority: Women and American Democracy (1971); The President's Task Force on Women's Rights and Responsibilities, A Matter of Simple Justice (1970).

Moreover, since sex, like race and national origin, is an immutable characteristic determined solely by the accident of birth, the imposition of special disabilities upon the members of a particular sex because of their sex would seem to violate "the basic concept of our system that legal burdens should bear some relationship to individual responsibility. . . ." Weber v. Aetna Casualty & Surety Co., 406 U.S. 164, 175 (1972). And what differentiates sex from such nonsuspect statuses as intelligence or physical disability, and aligns it with the recognized suspect criteria, is that the sex characteristic frequently bears no relation to ability to perform or contribute to society. As a result, statutory distinctions between the sexes often have the effect of invidiously relegating the entire class of females to inferior legal status without regard to the actual capabilities of its individual members.

We might also note that, over the past decade, Congress has itself manifested an increasing sensitivity to sex-based classifications. In Tit. VII of the Civil Rights Act of 1964, for example, Congress expressly declared that no employer, labor union, or other organization subject to the provisions of the Act shall discriminate against any individual on the basis of "race, color, religion, *sex,* or national origin." Similarly, the Equal Pay Act of 1963 provides that no employer covered by the Act "shall discriminate . . . between employees on the basis of sex." And § 1 of the Equal Rights Amendment, passed by Congress on March 22, 1972, and submitted to the legislatures of the States for ratification, declares that "[e]quality of rights under the law shall not be denied or abridged by the United States or by any State on account of sex." Thus, Congress has itself concluded that classifications based upon sex are inherently invidious, and this conclusion of a coequal branch of Government is not without significance to the question presently under consideration. . . .

With these considerations in mind, we can only conclude that classifications based upon sex, like classifications based upon race, alienage, or national origin, are inherently suspect, and must therefore be subjected to strict judicial scrutiny. Applying the analysis mandated by that stricter standard of review, it is clear that the statutory scheme now before us is constitutionally invalid.

---

[17] It is true, of course, that when viewed in the abstract, women do not constitute a small and powerless minority. Nevertheless, in part because of past discrimination, women are vastly underrepresented in this Nation's decisionmaking councils. There has never been a female President, nor a female member of this Court. Not a single woman presently sits in the United States Senate, and only 14 women hold seats in the House of Representatives. And, as appellants point out, this underrepresentation is present throughout all levels of our State and Federal Government.

III.

The sole basis of the classification established in the challenged statutes is the sex of the individuals involved. . . .

Moreover, the Government concedes that the differential treatment accorded men and women under these statutes serves no purpose other than mere "administrative convenience." In essence, the Government maintains that, as an empirical matter, wives in our society frequently are dependent upon their husbands, while husbands rarely are dependent upon their wives. Thus, the Government argues that Congress might reasonably have concluded that it would be both cheaper and easier simply conclusively to presume that wives of male members are financially dependent upon their husbands, while burdening female members with the task of establishing dependency in fact.[22]

The Government offers no concrete evidence, however, tending to support its view that such differential treatment in fact saves the Government any money. In order to satisfy the demands of strict judicial scrutiny, the Government must demonstrate, for example, that it is actually cheaper to grant increased benefits with respect to *all* male members, than it is to determine which male members are in fact entitled to such benefits and to grant increased benefits only to those members whose wives actually meet the dependency requirement. Here, however, there is substantial evidence that, if put to the test, many of the wives of male members would fail to qualify for benefits. And in light of the fact that the dependency determination with respect to the husbands of female members is presently made solely on the basis of affidavits rather than through the more costly hearing process, the Government's explanation of the statutory scheme is, to say the least, questionable.

In any case, our prior decisions make clear that, although efficacious administration of governmental programs is not without some importance, "the Constitution recognizes higher values than speed and efficiency." Stanley v. Illinois, 405 U.S. 645, 656 (1972). And when we enter the realm of "strict judicial scrutiny," there can be no doubt that "administrative convenience" is not a shibboleth, the mere recitation of which dictates constitutionality. See Shapiro v. Thompson, 394 U.S. 618 (1969); Carrington v. Rash, 380 U.S. 89 (1965). On the contrary, any statutory scheme which draws a sharp line between the sexes, *solely* for the purpose of achieving administrative convenience, necessarily commands "dissimilar treatment for men and women who are . . . similarly situated," and therefore involves the "very kind of arbitrary legislative choice forbidden by the [Constitution]. . . ." Reed v. Reed. . . . We therefore conclude that, by according differential treatment to male and female members of the uniformed services for the sole purpose of achieving administrative convenience, the challenged statutes violate the Due Process Clause of the Fifth Amendment insofar as they require a female member to prove the dependency of her husband.

Reversed.

■ MR. JUSTICE STEWART concurs in the judgment, agreeing that the statutes before us work an invidious discrimination in violation of the Constitution. Reed v. Reed, 404 U.S. 71.

■ MR. JUSTICE REHNQUIST dissents for the reasons stated by Judge Rives in his opinion for the District Court, Frontiero v. Laird, 341 F.Supp. 201 (1972).

---

[22] It should be noted that these statutes are not in any sense designed to rectify the effects of past discrimination against women. . . . On the contrary, these statutes seize upon a group—women—who have historically suffered discrimination in employment, and rely on the effects of this past discrimination as a justification for heaping on additional economic disadvantages. . . .

■ MR. JUSTICE POWELL, with whom THE CHIEF JUSTICE and MR. JUSTICE BLACKMUN join, concurring in the judgment.

I agree that the challenged statutes constitute an unconstitutional discrimination against service women in violation of the Due Process Clause of the Fifth Amendment, but I cannot join the opinion of Mr. Justice Brennan, which would hold that all classifications based upon sex, "like classifications based upon race, alienage, and national origin," are "inherently suspect and must therefore be subjected to close judicial scrutiny." . . . It is unnecessary for the Court in this case to characterize sex as a suspect classification, with all of the far-reaching implications of such a holding. Reed v. Reed, 404 U.S. 71 (1971), which abundantly supports our decision today, did not add sex to the narrowly limited group of classifications which are inherently suspect. In my view, we can and should decide this case on the authority of *Reed* and reserve for the future any expansion of its rationale.

There is another, and I find compelling, reason for deferring a general categorizing of sex classifications as invoking the strictest test of judicial scrutiny. The Equal Rights Amendment, which if adopted will resolve the substance of this precise question, has been approved by the Congress and submitted for ratification by the States. If this Amendment is duly adopted, it will represent the will of the people accomplished in the manner prescribed by the Constitution. By acting prematurely and unnecessarily, as I view it, the Court has assumed a decisional responsibility at the very time when state legislatures, functioning within the traditional democratic process, are debating the proposed Amendment. It seems to me that this reaching out to preempt by judicial action a major political decision which is currently in process of resolution does not reflect appropriate respect for duly prescribed legislative processes.

There are times when this Court, under our system, cannot avoid a constitutional decision on issues which normally should be resolved by the elected representatives of the people. But democratic institutions are weakened, and confidence in the restraint of the Court is impaired, when we appear unnecessarily to decide sensitive issues of broad social and political importance at the very time they are under consideration within the prescribed constitutional processes.

Craig v. Boren

429 U.S. 190, 97 S.Ct. 451, 50 L.Ed.2d 397 (1976).

■ MR. JUSTICE BRENNAN delivered the opinion of the Court.

The interaction of two sections of an Oklahoma statute . . . prohibits the sale of "nonintoxicating" 3.2% beer to males under the age of 21 and to females under the age of 18. The question to be decided is whether such a gender-based differential constitutes a denial to males 18–20 years of age of the Equal Protection of the Laws in violation of the Fourteenth Amendment.

This action . . . by appellant Craig, a male then between 18 and 21 years of age, and by appellant Whitener, a licensed vendor of 3.2% beer . . . sought declaratory and injunctive relief against enforcement of the gender-based differential on the ground that it constituted invidious discrimination against males 18–20 years of age. A three-judge court . . . sustained [its] constitutionality and dismissed the action. . . . We reverse.

. . .

II.

A.

... To withstand constitutional challenge, previous cases establish that classifications by gender must serve important governmental objectives and must be substantially related to achievement of those objectives. Thus, in *Reed,* the objectives of "reducing the workload on probate courts," ... and "avoiding intra-family controversy," ... were deemed of insufficient importance to sustain use of an overt gender criterion in the appointment of intestate administrators. Decisions following *Reed* similarly have rejected administrative ease and convenience as sufficiently important objectives to justify gender-based classifications. See, e.g., Stanley v. Illinois, 405 U.S. 645, 656 (1972); Frontiero v. Richardson, 411 U.S. 677, 690 (1973); cf. Schlesinger v. Ballard, 419 U.S. 498, 506–507 (1975). And only two Terms ago Stanton v. Stanton, 421 U.S. 7 (1975), expressly stating that *Reed v. Reed* was "controlling," id., at 13, held that *Reed* required invalidation of a Utah differential age-of-majority statute, notwithstanding the statute's coincidence with and furtherance of the State's purpose of fostering "old notions" of role-typing and preparing boys for their expected performance in the economic and political worlds. Id., at 14–15.[6]

Reed v. Reed has also provided the underpinning for decisions that have invalidated statutes employing gender as an inaccurate proxy for other, more germane bases of classification. Hence, "archaic and overbroad" generalizations, *Schlesinger v. Ballard,* ... concerning the financial position of servicewomen, *Frontiero v. Richardson,* ... and working women, Weinberger v. Wiesenfeld, 420 U.S. 636, 643 (1975), could not justify use of a gender line in determining eligibility for certain governmental entitlements. Similarly, increasingly outdated misconceptions concerning the role of females in the home rather than in the "marketplace and world of ideas" were rejected as loose-fitting characterizations incapable of supporting state statutory schemes that were premised upon their accuracy. ... In light of the weak congruence between gender and the characteristic or trait that gender purported to represent, it was necessary that the legislatures choose either to realign their substantive laws in a gender-neutral fashion, or to adopt procedures for identifying those instances where the sex-centered generalization actually comported to fact. See, e.g., Stanley v. Illinois, ... ; cf. Cleveland Board of Educ. v. LaFleur, 414 U.S. 632, 650 (1974).

In this case, too, *"Reed* we feel, is controlling ... ," *Stanton v. Stanton.* ... We turn then to the question whether, under *Reed,* the difference between males and females with respect to the purchase of 3.2% beer warrants the differential in age drawn by the Oklahoma statute. We conclude that it does not.

. . .

C.

We accept for purposes of discussion the District Court's identification of the objective underlying §§ 241 and 245 as the enhancement of traffic safety.[7] Clearly, the

---

[6]   Kahn v. Shevin, 416 U.S. 351 (1974) and Schlesinger v. Ballard, 419 U.S. 498 (1975), upholding the use of gender-based classifications, rested upon the Court's perception of the laudatory purposes of those laws as remedying disadvantageous conditions suffered by women in economic and military life. See 416 U.S., at 353–354; 419 U.S., at 508. Needless to say, in this case Oklahoma does not suggest that the age-sex differential was enacted to ensure the availability of 3.2% beer for women as compensation for previous deprivations.

[7]   That this was the true purpose is not at all self-evident. The purpose is not apparent from the face of the statute and the Oklahoma Legislature does not preserve statutory history materials capable of clarifying the objectives served by its legislative enactments. ... [We] leav[e] for another day consideration of whether the statement of the State's Assistant Attorney General should suffice to

protection of public health and safety represents an important function of state and local governments. However, appellees' statistics in our view cannot support the conclusion that the gender-based distinction closely serves to achieve that objective and therefore the distinction cannot under *Reed* withstand equal protection challenge.

The appellees introduced a variety of statistical surveys. First, an analysis of arrest statistics for 1973 demonstrated that 18–20-year-old male arrests for "driving under the influence" and "drunkenness" substantially exceeded female arrests for that same age period.[8] Similarly, youths aged 17–21 were found to be overrepresented among those killed or injured in traffic accidents, with males again numerically exceeding females in this regard.[9] Third, a random roadside survey in Oklahoma City revealed that young males were more inclined to drive and drink beer than were their female counterparts.[10] Fourth, Federal Bureau of Investigation nationwide statistics exhibited a notable increase in arrests for "driving under the influence."[11] Finally, statistical evidence gathered in other jurisdictions, particularly Minnesota and Michigan, was offered to corroborate Oklahoma's experience by indicating the pervasiveness of youthful participation in motor vehicle accidents following the imbibing of alcohol. Conceding that "the case is not free from doubt," ... the District Court nonetheless concluded that this statistical showing substantiated "a rational basis for the legislative judgment underlying the challenged classification." ...

Even were this statistical evidence accepted as accurate, it nevertheless offers only a weak answer to the equal protection question presented here. The most focused and relevant of the statistical surveys, arrests of 18–20-year-olds for alcohol-related driving offenses, exemplifies the ultimate unpersuasiveness of this evidentiary record. Viewed in terms of the correlation between sex and the actual activity that Oklahoma seeks to regulate—driving while under the influence of alcohol—the statistics broadly establish that .18% of females and 2% of males in that age group were arrested for that offense. While such a disparity is not trivial in a statistical sense, it hardly can form the basis for employment of a gender line as a classifying device. Certainly if maleness is to serve as a proxy for drinking and driving a correlation of 2% must be considered an unduly tenuous "fit." Indeed, prior cases have consistently rejected the use of sex as a decisionmaking factor even though the statutes in question certainly rested on far more predictive empirical relationships than this.[13]

---

inform this Court of the legislature's objectives, or whether the Court must determine if the litigant simply is selecting a convenient, but false, *post-hoc* rationalization.

[8] The disparities in 18–20-year-old male-female arrests were substantial for both categories of offenses: 427 versus 24 for driving under the influence of alcohol and 966 versus 102 for drunkenness. Even if we assume that a legislature may rely on such arrest data in some situations, these figures do not offer support for a differential age line, for the disproportionate arrests of males persisted at older ages; indeed, in the case of arrests for drunkenness, the figures for all ages indicated "even more male involvement in such arrests at later ages." 399 F.Supp., at 1309. See also n. 14, *infra.*

[9] This survey drew no correlation between the accident figures for any age group and levels of intoxication found in those killed or injured.

[10] For an analysis of the results of this exhibit, see n. 16, *infra.*

[11] The FBI made no attempt to relate these arrest figures either to beer drinking or to an 18–21 age differential, but rather found that male arrests for all ages exceeded 90% of the total.

[13] For example, we can conjecture that in *Reed,* Idaho's apparent premise that women lacked experience in formal business matters (particularly compared to men) would have proved to be accurate in substantially more than 2% of all cases. And in both *Frontiero* and *Wiesenfeld,* we expressly found the government's empirical defense of mandatory dependency tests for men but not women to be unsatisfactory, even though we recognized that husbands still are far less likely to be dependent on their wives than vice versa. ...

Moreover, the statistics exhibit a variety of other shortcomings. . . . Setting aside the obvious methodological problems,[14] the surveys do not adequately justify the salient features of Oklahoma's gender-based traffic-safety law. None purports to measure the use and dangerousness of 3.2% beer as opposed to alcohol generally, a detail that is of particular importance since, in light of its low alcohol level, Oklahoma apparently considers the 3.2% beverage to be "non-intoxicating." 37 Okla.Stat. § 163.1 (1971); see State ex rel. Springer v. Bliss, 199 Okla. 198, 185 P.2d 220 (1947). Moreover, many of the studies, while graphically documenting the unfortunate increase in driving while under the influence of alcohol, make no effort to relate their findings to age-sex differentials as involved here. Indeed, the only survey that explicitly centered its attention upon young drivers and their use of beer—albeit apparently not of the diluted 3.2% variety—reached results that hardly can be viewed as impressive in justifying either a gender or age classification.[16]

There is no reason to belabor this line of analysis. It is unrealistic to expect either members of the judiciary or state officials to be well versed in the rigors of experimental or statistical technique. But this merely illustrates that proving broad sociological propositions by statistics is a dubious business, and one that inevitably is in tension with the normative philosophy that underlies the Equal Protection Clause. Suffice to say that the showing offered by the appellees does not satisfy us that sex represents a legitimate, accurate proxy for the regulation of drinking and driving. In fact, when it is further recognized that Oklahoma's statute prohibits only the selling of 3.2% beer to young males and not their drinking the beverage once acquired (even after purchase by their 18–20-year-old female companions), the relationship between gender and traffic safety becomes far too tenuous to satisfy *Reed's* requirement that the gender-based difference be substantially related to achievement of the statutory objective.

We hold, therefore, that under *Reed,* Oklahoma's 3.2% beer statute invidiously discriminates against males 18–20 years of age.

---

[14] The very social stereotypes that find reflection in age differential laws, see Stanton v. Stanton, . . . are likely substantially to distort the accuracy of these comparative statistics. Hence "reckless" young men who drink and drive are transformed into arrest statistics, whereas their female counterparts are chivalrously escorted home. See, e.g., W. Reckless & B. Kay, The Female Offender 4, 7, 13, 16–17 (Report to Pres. Comm'n on Law Enforcement & Admin. of Justice, 1967). Moreover, the Oklahoma surveys, gathered under a regime where the age-differential law in question has been in effect, are lacking in controls necessary for appraisal of the actual effectiveness of the male 3.2% beer prohibition. In this regard, the disproportionately high arrest statistics for young males—and, indeed, the growing alcohol-related arrest figures for all ages and sexes—simply may be taken to document the relative futility of controlling driving behavior by the 3.2 beer statute and like legislation, although we obviously have no means of estimating how many individuals, if any, actually were prevented from drinking by these laws.

[16] The random roadside survey of drivers conducted in Oklahoma City during August of 1972 found that 78% of drivers under 20 were male. Turning to an evaluation of their drinking habits and factoring out nondrinkers, 84% of the males versus 77% of the females expressed a preference for beer. Further 16.5% of the men and 11.4% of the women had consumed some alcoholic beverage within two hours of the interview. Finally, a blood alcohol concentration greater than .1% was discovered in 14.6% of the males compared to 11.5% of the females. "The 1973 figures, although they contain some variations, reflect essentiall y the same pattern." 399 F.Supp., at 1309. Plainly these statistical disparities between the sexes are not substantial. Moreover, when the 18–20 age boundaries are lifted and all drivers analyzed, the 1972 roadside survey indicates that male drinking rose slightly whereas female exposure to alcohol remained relatively constant. Again, in 1973, the survey established that "compared to all drivers interviewed, . . . the under-20 age group generally showed a lower involvement with alcohol in terms of having drunk within the past two hours or having a significant BAC (blood alcohol content)." Id., at 1309. In sum, this survey provides little support for a gender line among teenagers and actually runs counter to the imposition of drinking restrictions based upon age.

D.

Appellees argue, however, that §§ 241 and 245 enforce state policies concerning the sale and distribution of alcohol and by force of the Twenty-first Amendment should therefore be held to withstand the equal protection challenge. . . . The Twenty-first Amendment . . . primarily created an exception to the normal operation of the Commerce Clause. See, e.g., Hostetter v. Idlewild Bon Voyage Liquor Corp., 377 U.S. 324, 330 (1964);. . . .

[Its] relevance . . . to other constitutional provisions becomes increasingly doubtful. . . .

[B]oth federal and state courts uniformly have declared the unconstitutionality of gender lines that restrain the activities of customers of state-regulated liquor establishments irrespective of the operation of the Twenty-first Amendment. . . . Even when state officials have posited sociological or empirical justifications for these gender-based differentiations, the courts have struck down discriminations aimed at an entire class under the guise of alcohol regulation. In fact, social science studies that have uncovered quantifiable differences in drinking tendencies dividing along both racial and ethnic lines strongly suggest the need for application of the Equal Protection Clause in preventing discriminatory treatment that almost certainly would be perceived as invidious.[22] In sum, the principles embodied in the Equal Protection Clause are not to be rendered inapplicable by statistically measured but loose-fitting generalities concerning the drinking tendencies of aggregate groups. We thus hold that the operation of the Twenty-first Amendment does not alter the application of equal protection standards that otherwise govern this case.

We conclude that the gender-based differential contained in 37 Okla.Stat. § 245 constitutes a denial of the Equal Protection of the Laws to males aged 18–20[23] and reverse the judgment of the District Court.[24]

■ MR. JUSTICE POWELL, concurring.

I join the opinion of the Court [but] have reservations as to some of the discussion concerning the appropriate standard for equal protection analysis and the relevance of the statistical evidence. . . .

. . . I agree that Reed v. Reed, 404 U.S. 71 (1971), is the most relevant precedent. But I find it unnecessary . . . to read that decision as broadly as some of the Court's language may imply. *Reed* and subsequent cases involving gender-based classifications make clear that the Court subjects such classifications to a more critical examination than is normally applied when "fundamental" constitutional rights and "suspect classes" are not present.[*]

---

[22] Thus, if statistics were to govern the permissibility of state alcohol regulation without regard to the Equal Protection Clause as a limiting principle, it might follow that States could freely favor Jews and Italian Catholics at the expense of all other Americans, since available studies regularly demonstrate that the former two groups exhibit the lowest rates of problem drinking. . . .

In the past, . . . several States established criminal sanctions for the sale of alcohol to an Indian or "half or quarter breed Indian." . . . [S]tate alcohol beverage prohibitions also have been directed at other groups, notably German, Italian, and Catholic immigrants. . . . The repeal of most of these laws signals society's perception of the unfairness and questionable constitutionality of singling out groups to bear the brunt of alcohol regulation.

[23] Insofar as Goesaert v. Cleary, 335 U.S. 464 (1948), may be inconsistent, that decision is disapproved. . . .

[24] As noted in Stanton v. Stanton, . . . the Oklahoma Legislature is free to redefine any cutoff age for the purchase and sale of 3.2 beer that it may choose, provided that the redefinition operates in a gender-neutral fashion.

[*] As is evident from our opinions, the Court has had difficulty in agreeing upon a standard of equal protection analysis that can be applied consistently to the wide variety of legislative

. . .

■ MR. JUSTICE STEVENS, concurring.

There is only one Equal Protection Clause. It requires every State to govern impartially. It does not direct the courts to apply one standard of review in some cases and a different standard in other cases. Whatever criticism may be levelled at a judicial opinion implying that there are at least three such standards applies with the same force to a double standard.

I am inclined to believe that what has become known as the two-tiered analysis of equal protection claims does not describe a completely logical method of deciding cases, but rather is a method the Court has employed to explain decisions that actually apply a single standard in a reasonably consistent fashion. I also suspect that a careful explanation of the reasons motivating particular decisions may contribute more to an identification of that standard than an attempt to articulate it in all-encompassing terms. . . .

In this case, the classification is not as obnoxious as some the Court has condemned, nor as inoffensive as some the Court has accepted. It is objectionable because it is based on an accident of birth, because it is a mere remnant of the now almost universally rejected tradition of discriminating against males in this age bracket, and because, to the extent it reflects any physical difference between males and females, it is actually perverse. The question then is whether the traffic safety justification put forward by the State is sufficient to make an otherwise offensive classification acceptable.

The classification is not totally irrational. For the evidence does indicate that there are more males than females in this age bracket who drive and also more who drink. Nevertheless, . . . [i]t is difficult to believe that the statute was actually intended to cope with the problem of traffic safety, since it has only a minimal effect on access to a not-very-intoxicating beverage and does not prohibit its consumption. Moreover, the empirical data submitted by the State accentuates the unfairness of treating all 18–21-year-old males as inferior to their female counterparts. The legislation imposes a restraint on one hundred percent of the males in the class allegedly because about 2% of them have probably violated one or more laws relating to the consumption of alcoholic beverages. It is unlikely that this law will have a significant deterrent effect either on that 2% or on the law-abiding 98%. But even assuming some such slight benefit, it does not seem to me that an insult to all of the young men of the State can be justified by visiting the sins of the 2% on the 98%.

■ MR. JUSTICE BLACKMUN, concurring in part.

I join the Court's opinion except Part II-D thereof. I agree, however, that the Twenty-first Amendment does not save the challenged Oklahoma statute.

---

classifications. There are valid reasons for dissatisfaction with the "two-tier" approach that has been prominent in the Court's decisions in the past decade. Although viewed by many as a result-oriented substitute for more critical analysis, that approach—with its narrowly limited "upper-tier"—now has substantial precedential support. As has been true of *Reed* and its progeny, our decision today will be viewed by some as a "middle-tier" approach. While I would not endorse that characterization and would not welcome a further subdividing of equal protection analysis, candor compels the recognition that the relatively deferential "rational basis" standard of review normally applied takes on a sharper focus when we address a gender-based classification. So much is clear from our recent cases. For thoughtful discussions of equal protection analysis, see, e.g., Gunther, The Supreme Court, 1971 Term—Foreword: In Search of Evolving Doctrine on a Changing Court: A Model for Newer Equal Protection, 86 Harv.L.Rev. 1 (1972); Wilkinson, The Supreme Court, the Equal Protection Clause, and the Three Faces of Constitutional Equality, 61 Va.L.Rev. 945 (1975).

■ MR. JUSTICE STEWART, concurring in the judgment.

. . .

■ MR. CHIEF JUSTICE BURGER, dissenting.

I am in general agreement with Mr. Justice Rehnquist's dissent. . . .

. . .

Though today's decision does not go so far as to make gender-based classifications "suspect," it makes gender a disfavored classification. Without an independent constitutional basis supporting the right asserted or disfavoring the classification adopted, I can justify no substantive constitutional protection other than the normal McGowan v. Maryland, 366 U.S., at 425–426, protection afforded by the Equal Protection Clause.

. . .

■ MR. JUSTICE REHNQUIST, dissenting.

The Court's disposition of this case is objectionable on two grounds. First is its conclusion that *men* challenging a gender-based statute which treats them less favorably than women may invoke a more stringent standard of judicial review than pertains to most other types of classifications. Second is the Court's enunciation of this standard, without citation to any source, as being that "classifications by gender must serve *important* governmental objectives and must be *substantially* related to achievement of those objectives." (emphasis added). The only redeeming feature of the Court's opinion, to my mind, is that it apparently signals a retreat by those who joined the plurality opinion in Frontiero v. Richardson, 411 U.S. 677 (1973), from their view that sex is a "suspect" classification for purposes of equal protection analysis. I think the Oklahoma statute challenged here need pass only the "rational basis" equal protection analysis expounded in cases such as McGowan v. Maryland, 366 U.S. 420 (1961), and Williamson v. Lee Optical Co., 348 U.S. 483 (1955), and I believe that it is constitutional under that analysis.

. . .

Michael M. v. Superior Court

450 U.S. 464, 101 S.Ct. 1200, 67 L.Ed.2d 437 (1981).

■ JUSTICE REHNQUIST announced the judgment of the Court and delivered an opinion in which THE CHIEF JUSTICE, JUSTICE STEWART, and JUSTICE POWELL joined.

The question presented . . . is whether California's "statutory rape" law, § 261.5 of the Cal. Penal Code Ann. . . . violates the Equal Protection Clause of the Fourteenth Amendment. Section 261.5 defines unlawful sexual intercourse as "an act of sexual intercourse accomplished with a female not the wife of the perpetrator, where the female is under the age of 18 years." The statute thus makes men alone criminally liable for the act of sexual intercourse.

In July 1978, a complaint was filed . . . alleging that petitioner, then a 17½-year-old male, had had unlawful sexual intercourse with a female under the age of 18, in violation of § 261.5. . . . Prior to trial, petitioner sought to set aside the information on both state and federal constitutional grounds, asserting that § 261.5 unlawfully discriminated on the basis of gender. The trial court and the California Court of Appeal denied petitioner's request for relief and petitioner sought review in the Supreme Court of California.

The Supreme Court held that "section 261.5 discriminates on the basis of sex because only females may be victims, and only males may violate the section." The court then subjected the classification to "strict scrutiny," stating that it must be justified by a compelling state interest. It found that the classification was "supported not by mere social convention but by the immutable physiological fact that it is the female exclusively who can become pregnant." Canvassing "the tragic human cost of illegitimate teenage pregnancies," including the large number of teenage abortions, the increased medical risk associated with teenage pregnancies, and the social consequences of teenage childbearing, the court concluded that the State has a compelling interest in preventing such pregnancies. Because males alone can "physiologically cause the result which the law properly seeks to avoid," the court further held that the gender classification was readily justified as a means of identifying offender and victim. For the reasons stated below, we affirm the judgment. . . .

. . . Unlike the California Supreme Court, we have not held that gender-based classifications are "inherently suspect" and thus we do not apply so-called "strict scrutiny" to those classifications. . . . Our cases have held, however, that the traditional minimum rationality test takes on a somewhat "sharper focus" when gender-based classifications are challenged. See Craig v. Boren, 429 U.S. 190, 210 n. * (1976) (Powell, J., concurring). In Reed v. Reed, 404 U.S. 71 (1971), for example, the Court stated that a gender-based classification will be upheld if it bears a "fair and substantial relationship" to legitimate state ends, while in *Craig v. Boren, . . .* the Court restated the test to require the classification to bear a "substantial relationship" to "important governmental objectives."

Underlying these decisions is the principle that a legislature may not "make overbroad generalizations based on sex which are entirely unrelated to any differences between men and women or which demean the ability or social status of the affected class." Parham v. Hughes, 441 U.S. 347, 354 (1979) (plurality opinion of Stewart, J.). But because the Equal Protection Clause does not "demand that a statute necessarily apply equally to all persons" or require " 'things which are different in fact . . . to be treated in law as though they were the same,' " Rinaldi v. Yeager, 384 U.S. 305, 309 (1966), . . . this Court has consistently upheld statutes where the gender classification is not invidious, but rather realistically reflects the fact that the sexes are not similarly situated in certain circumstances. Parham v. Hughes, supra; Califano v. Webster, 430 U.S. 313 (1977); Schlesinger v. Ballard, 419 U.S. 498 (1975); Kahn v. Shevin, 416 U.S. 351 (1974). As the Court has stated, a legislature may "provide for the special problems of women." Weinberger v. Wiesenfeld, 420 U.S. 636, 653 (1975).

. . . [T]hat the California Legislature criminalized the act of illicit sexual intercourse with a minor female is a sure indication of its intent or purpose to discourage that conduct. Precisely why the legislature desired that result is of course somewhat less clear. This Court has long recognized that "[i]nquiries into congressional motives or purposes are a hazardous matter," United States v. O'Brien, 391 U.S. 367, 383–384 (1968); Palmer v. Thompson, 403 U.S. 217, 224 (1971), and the search for the "actual" or "primary" purpose of a statute is likely to be elusive. Arlington Heights v. Metropolitan Housing Dev. Corp., 429 U.S. 252, 265 (1977). . . . Here, for example, the individual legislators may have voted for the statute for a variety of reasons. Some legislators may have been concerned about preventing teenage pregnancies, others about protecting young females from physical injury or from the loss of "chastity," and still others about promoting various religious and moral attitudes towards premarital sex.

The justification for the statute offered by the State, and accepted by the Supreme Court of California, is that the legislature sought to prevent illegitimate teenage pregnancies. That finding, of course, is entitled to great deference. Reitman v. Mulkey, 387 U.S. 369, 373–374 (1967). And although our cases establish that the

State's asserted reason for the enactment of a statute may be rejected, if it "could not have been a goal of the legislation," *Weinberger v. Wiesenfeld, . . .* this is not such a case.

We are satisfied not only that the prevention of illegitimate pregnancy is at least one of the "purposes" of the statute, but that the State has a strong interest in preventing such pregnancy. At the risk of stating the obvious, teenage pregnancies, which have increased dramatically over the last two decades, have significant social, medical and economic consequences for both the mother and her child, and the State. Of particular concern to the State is that approximately half of all teenage pregnancies end in abortion. And of those children who are born, their illegitimacy makes them likely candidates to become wards of the State.[6]

We need not be medical doctors to discern that young men and young women are not similarly situated with respect to the problems and the risks of sexual intercourse. Only women may become pregnant, and they suffer disproportionately the profound physical, emotional, and psychological consequences of sexual activity. The statute at issue here protects women from sexual intercourse at an age when those consequences are particularly severe.[7]

The question thus boils down to whether a State may attack the problem of sexual intercourse and teenage pregnancy directly by prohibiting a male from having sexual intercourse with a minor female. We hold that such a statute is sufficiently related to the State's objectives to pass constitutional muster.

Because virtually all of the significant harmful and inescapably identifiable consequences of teenage pregnancy fall on the young female, a legislature acts well within its authority when it elects to punish only the participant who, by nature, suffers few of the consequences of his conduct. It is hardly unreasonable for a legislature acting to protect minor females to exclude them from punishment. Moreover, the risk of pregnancy itself constitutes a substantial deterrence to young females. No similar natural sanctions deter males. A criminal sanction imposed solely on males thus serves to roughly "equalize" the deterrents on the sexes.

We are unable to accept petitioner's contention that the statute is impermissibly underinclusive and must, in order to pass judicial scrutiny, be *broadened* so as to hold the female as criminally liable as the male. It is argued that this statute is not

---

[6]   . . .

Subsequent to the decision below, the California Legislature considered and rejected proposals to render § 261.5 gender neutral, thereby ratifying the judgment of the California Supreme Court. That is enough to answer petitioner's contention that the statute was the "accidental byproduct of a traditional way of thinking about women." Califano v. Webster, 430 U.S. 313 (1977) (quoting Califano v. Goldfarb, 430 U.S. 199 (1977) (Stevens, J., concurring)). Certainly this decision of the California Legislature is as good a source as is this Court in deciding what is "current" and what is "outmoded" in the perception of women.

[7]   Although petitioner concedes that the State has a "compelling" interest in preventing teenage pregnancy, he contends that the "true" purpose of § 261.5 is to protect the virtue and chastity of young women. As such, the statute is unjustifiable because it rests on archaic stereotypes. . . . Even if the preservation of female chastity were one of the motives of the statute, and even if that motive be impermissible, petitioner's argument must fail because "[i]t is a familiar practice of constitutional law that this court will not strike down an otherwise constitutional statute on the basis of an alleged illicit legislative motive." United States v. O'Brien, 391 U.S. 367, 383 (1968). In Orr v. Orr, 440 U.S. 268 (1979), for example, the Court rejected one asserted purpose as impermissible, but then considered other purposes to determine if they could justify the statute. Similarly, in Washington v. Davis, 426 U.S. 229, 243 (1976) the Court distinguished Palmer v. Thompson, 403 U.S. 217 (1971), on the grounds that the purposes of the ordinance there were not open to impeachment by evidence that the legislature was actually motivated by an impermissible purpose. See also Arlington Heights v. Metropolitan Housing Dev. Corp., 429 U.S. 252, 270, n. 21 (1977); Mobile v. Bolden, 446 U.S. 55, 91 (1980) (Stevens, J., concurring in judgment).

necessary to deter teenage pregnancy because a gender-neutral statute, where both male and female would be subject to prosecution, would serve that goal equally well. The relevant inquiry, however, is not whether the statute is drawn as precisely as it might have been, but whether the line chosen by the California Legislature is within constitutional limitations. . . .

In any event, we cannot say that a gender-neutral statute would be as effective as the statute California has chosen to enact. The State persuasively contends that a gender-neutral statute would frustrate its interest in effective enforcement. Its view is that a female is surely less likely to report violations of the statute if she herself would be subject to criminal prosecution. In an area already fraught with prosecutorial difficulties, we decline to hold that the Equal Protection Clause requires a legislature to enact a statute so broad that it may well be incapable of enforcement.[10]

We similarly reject petitioner's argument that § 261.5 is impermissibly overbroad because it makes unlawful sexual intercourse with prepubescent females, who are, by definition, incapable of becoming pregnant. Quite apart from the fact that the statute could well be justified on the grounds that very young females are particularly susceptible to physical injury from sexual intercourse, . . . it is ludicrous to suggest that the Constitution requires the California Legislature to limit the scope of its rape statute to older teenagers and exclude young girls.

There remains only petitioner's contention that the statute is unconstitutional as it is applied to him because he, like Sharon, was under 18 at the time of sexual intercourse. Petitioner argues that the statute is flawed because it presumes that as between two persons under 18, the male is the culpable aggressor. We find petitioner's contentions unpersuasive. Contrary to his assertions, the statute does not rest on the assumption that males are generally the aggressors. It is instead an attempt by a legislature to prevent illegitimate teenage pregnancy by providing an additional deterrent for men. The age of the man is irrelevant since young men are as capable as older men of inflicting the harm sought to be prevented.

In upholding the California statute we also recognize that this is not a case where a statute is being challenged on the grounds that it "invidiously discriminates" against females. To the contrary, the statute places a burden on males which is not shared by females. But we find nothing to suggest that men, because of past discrimination or peculiar disadvantages, are in need of the special solicitude of the courts. Nor is this a case where the gender classification is made "solely for . . . administrative convenience," as in Frontiero v. Richardson, 411 U.S. 677, 690 (1973) (emphasis omitted), or rests on "the baggage of sexual stereotypes" as in Orr v. Orr, 440 U.S., at 283. As we have held, the statute instead reasonably reflects the fact that the consequences of sexual intercourse and pregnancy fall more heavily on the female than on the male.

---

[10] The question whether a statute is *substantially* related to its asserted goals is at best an opaque one. It can be plausibly argued that a gender-neutral statute would produce fewer prosecutions than the statute at issue here. The dissent argues, on the other hand, that "even assuming that a gender-neutral statute would be more difficult to enforce. . . . [c]ommon sense . . . suggests that a gender-neutral statutory rape law is potentially a greater deterrent of sexual activity than a gender-based law, for the simple reason that a gender-neutral law subjects both men and women to criminal sanctions and thus arguably has a deterrent effect on twice as many potential violators."

Where such differing speculations as to the effect of a statute are plausible, we think it appropriate to defer to the decision of the California Supreme Court, "armed as it was with the knowledge of the facts and circumstances concerning the passage and potential impact of [the statute], and familiar with the milieu in which that provision would operate." Reitman v. Mulkey, 387 U.S. 369, 378–379 (1967).

Accordingly the judgment of the California Supreme Court is

Affirmed.

■ JUSTICE STEWART, concurring.

. . .

The Constitution is violated when government, state or federal, invidiously classifies similarly situated people on the basis of the immutable characteristics with which they were born. Thus, detrimental racial classifications by government always violate the Constitution, for the simple reason that, so far as the Constitution is concerned, people of different races are always similarly situated. . . . By contrast, while detrimental gender classifications by government often violate the Constitution, they do not always do so, for the reason that there are differences between males and females that the Constitution necessarily recognizes. In this case we deal with the most basic of these differences: females can become pregnant as the result of sexual intercourse; males cannot.

. . .

. . . Experienced observation confirms the common sense notion that adolescent males disregard the possibility of pregnancy far more than do adolescent females. And to the extent that § 261.5 may punish males for intercourse with prepubescent females, that punishment is justifiable because of the substantial physical risks for prepubescent females that are not shared by their male counterparts.

. . .

In short, the Equal Protection Clause does not mean that the physiological differences between men and women must be disregarded. While those differences must never be permitted to become a pretext for invidious discrimination, no such discrimination is presented by this case. . . .

■ JUSTICE BLACKMUN, concurring in the judgment.

It is gratifying that the plurality recognizes that "[a]t the risk of stating the obvious, teenage pregnancies . . . have increased dramatically over the last two decades" and "have significant social, medical, and economic consequences for both the mother and her child, and the State." There have been times when I have wondered whether the Court was capable of this perception, particularly when it has struggled with the different but not unrelated problems that attend abortion issues. See, for example, . . . today's opinion in *H.L. v. Matheson.* . . .

Some might conclude that the two uses of the criminal sanction—here flatly to forbid intercourse in order to forestall teenage pregnancies, and in *Matheson* to prohibit a physician's abortion procedure except upon notice to the parents of the pregnant minor—are vastly different proscriptions. But the basic social and privacy problems are much the same. Both Utah's statute in *Matheson* and California's statute in this case are legislatively created tools intended to achieve similar ends and addressed to the same societal concerns: the control and direction of young people's sexual activities. . . .

I, however, cannot vote to strike down the California statutory rape law, for I think it is a sufficiently reasoned and constitutional effort to control the problem at its inception. . . . I am persuaded that, although a minor has substantial privacy rights in intimate affairs connected with procreation, California's efforts to prevent teenage pregnancy are to be viewed differently from Utah's efforts to inhibit a woman from dealing with pregnancy once it has become an inevitability.

Craig v. Boren, 429 U.S. 190 (1976), was an opinion which, in large part, I joined. The plurality opinion in the present case points out the Court's respective phrasings of the applicable test in Reed v. Reed . . . and in Craig v. Boren. . . . I vote to . . . uphold the State's gender-based classification on that test and as exemplified by those two cases and by Schlesinger v. Ballard, 419 U.S. 498 (1975); Weinberger v. Wiesenfeld, 420 U.S. 636 (1975); and Kahn v. Shevin, 416 U.S. 351 (1974).

. . .

■ JUSTICE BRENNAN, with whom JUSTICES WHITE and MARSHALL join, dissenting.

I

It is disturbing to find the Court so splintered on a case that presents such a straightforward issue: whether the admittedly gender-based classification in Cal.Penal Code Ann. § 261.5 . . . bears a sufficient relationship to the State's asserted goal of preventing teenage pregnancies to survive the "mid-level" constitutional scrutiny mandated by Craig v. Boren, 429 U.S. 190 (1976). Applying . . . our precedents, . . . the classification must be declared unconstitutional. I fear that the plurality and Justices Stewart and Blackmun reach the opposite result by placing too much emphasis on the desirability of achieving the State's asserted statutory goal—prevention of teenage pregnancy—and not enough emphasis on the fundamental question of whether the sex-based discrimination in the California statute is *substantially* related to the achievement of that goal.

. . .

. . . [E]ven assuming that prevention of teenage pregnancy is an important governmental objective and that it is in fact an objective of § 261.5, California still has the burden of proving that there are fewer teenage pregnancies under its gender-based statutory rape law than there would be if the law were gender neutral. . . . [It] must show that because its statutory rape law punishes only males, and not females, it more effectively deters minor females from having sexual intercourse.

. . .

. . . [T]here are at least two serious flaws in the State's assertion that law enforcement problems created by a gender-neutral statutory rape law would make such a statute less effective than a gender-based statute in deterring sexual activity.

First, the experience of other jurisdictions, and California itself, belies the plurality's conclusion that a gender-neutral statutory rape law "may well be incapable of enforcement." . . .

. . .

[S]econd[,] . . . even assuming that a gender-neutral statute would be more difficult to enforce, the State has still not shown that those enforcement problems would make such a statute less effective than a gender-based statute in deterring minor females from engaging in sexual intercourse. Common sense, however, suggests that a gender-neutral statutory rape law is potentially a *greater* deterrent of sexual activity than a gender-based law, for the simple reason that a gender-neutral law subjects both men and women to criminal sanctions and thus arguably has a deterrent effect on twice as many potential violators. . . .

III

Until very recently, no California court or commentator had suggested that the purpose of California's statutory rape law was to protect young women from the risk of pregnancy. Indeed, the historical development of § 261.5 demonstrates that the law was initially enacted on the premise that young women, in contrast to young men, were to be deemed legally incapable of consenting to an act of sexual intercourse. Because their chastity was considered particularly precious, those young women were felt to be uniquely in need of the State's protection. In contrast, young men were assumed to be capable of making such decisions for themselves; the law therefore did not offer them any special protection.

It is perhaps because the gender classification in California's statutory rape law was initially designed to further these outmoded sexual stereotypes, rather than to reduce the incidence of teenage pregnancies, that the State has been unable to demonstrate a substantial relationship between the classification and its newly asserted goal. . . . But whatever the reason, the State has not shown that Cal.Penal Code § 261.5 is any more effective than a gender-neutral law would be in deterring minor females from engaging in sexual intercourse. It has therefore not met its burden of proving that the statutory classification is substantially related to the achievement of its asserted goal.

I would hold that § 261.5 violates the Equal Protection Clause. . . .

■ JUSTICE STEVENS, dissenting.

Local custom and belief—rather than statutory laws of venerable but doubtful ancestry—will determine the volume of sexual activity among unmarried teenagers. The empirical evidence cited by the plurality demonstrates the futility of the notion that a statutory prohibition will significantly affect the volume of that activity or provide a meaningful solution to the problems created by it. Nevertheless, as a matter of constitutional power, unlike my Brother Brennan, I would have no doubt about the validity of a state law prohibiting all unmarried teenagers from engaging in sexual intercourse. The societal interests in reducing the incidence of venereal disease and teenage pregnancy are sufficient, in my judgment, to justify a prohibition of conduct that increases the risk of those harms.

My conclusion that a nondiscriminatory prohibition would be constitutional does not help me answer the question whether a prohibition applicable to only half of the joint participants in the risk-creating conduct is also valid. It cannot be true that the validity of a total ban is an adequate justification for a selective prohibition; otherwise, the constitutional objection to discriminatory rules would be meaningless. The question . . . is whether the difference between males and females justifies this statutory discrimination based entirely on sex.

. . . I think the plurality is quite correct in making the assumption that the joint act that this law seeks to prohibit creates a greater risk of harm for the female than for the male. . . .

. . .

[However,] that a female confronts a greater risk of harm than a male is a reason for applying the prohibition to her—not a reason for granting her a license to use her own judgment on whether or not to assume the risk. . . .

. . .

Finally, even if . . . there actually is some speculative basis for treating equally guilty males and females differently, . . . any such speculative justification would be outweighed by the paramount interest in evenhanded enforcement of the law. A rule that authorizes punishment of only one of two equally guilty wrongdoers violates the essence of the constitutional requirement that the sovereign must govern impartially.

I respectfully dissent.

Rostker v. Goldberg

453 U.S. 57 (1981).

In 1980 President Carter recommended that Congress reactivate the draft registration process and provide for the registration of women as well as men. When Congress provided funds only for the registration of males, men subject to the draft sued as a class, claiming a violation of the Fifth Amendment's Due Process Clause. A District Court judgment in their favor was reversed by the Supreme Court. For the Court, Justice Rehnquist emphasized "[t]he customary deference accorded the judgments of Congress . . . when, as here, Congress specifically considered the question of the Act's constitutionality"; an even greater "healthy deference to legislative and executive judgments in the area of military affairs"; and a judicial "lack of competence" in this area that was "marked." Finding the District Court's "efforts to divorce registration from the military and national defense context, with all the deference called for in that context, singularly unpersuasive[,]" the Court nonetheless declined to adopt the Solicitor General's argument that it should apply the "rational relation" standard "and should not examine the Act under the heightened scrutiny with which we have approached gender-based discrimination, see Michael M. v. Superior Court of Sonoma County, 450 U.S. 464 (1981); Craig v. Boren, 429 U.S. 190; Reed v. Reed, supra[,]" saying in part:

"We do not think that the substantive guarantee of due process or certainty in the law will be advanced by any further 'refinement' in the applicable tests as suggested by the Government. Announced degrees of 'deference' to legislative judgments, just as levels of 'scrutiny' which this Court announces that it applies to particular classifications made by a legislative body, may all too readily become facile abstractions used to justify a result. . . . Simply labelling the legislative decision 'military' on the one hand or 'gender-based' on the other does not automatically guide a court to the correct constitutional result."

The majority found this case to be

"quite different from several of the gender-based discrimination cases we have considered in that . . . Congress did not act 'unthinkingly' or 'reflexively and not for any considered reason.' the question of registering women for the draft not only received considerable national attention and was the subject of wide-ranging public debate, but also was extensively considered by Congress in hearings, floor debate, and in committee. . . .

"The foregoing clearly establishes that the decision to exempt women from registration was not the 'accidental by-product of a traditional way of thinking about women.' Califano v. Webster, 430 U.S. 313, 320 (1977) (quoting Califano v. Goldfarb, 430 U.S. 199, 233 (1977) (Stevens, J., concurring)). In Michael M., 450 U.S., at 471, n. 6 (plurality), we rejected a similar argument because of action by the California Legislature considering and rejecting proposals to make a statute challenged on discrimination grounds gender-neutral. The cause for rejecting the argument is considerably stronger here. The issue was considered at great length, and Congress clearly expressed its purpose and intent. Contrast Califano v. Westcott, 443 U.S. 76, 87 (1979) ('the gender qualification . . . escaped virtually unnoticed in the hearings and floor debates')."

After identifying the "purpose of registration [to be] to prepare for a draft *of combat troops*[,]" the Court noted that by statute or policy women "as a group . . . are not eligible for combat" and that "Congress specifically recognized and endorsed the exclusion of women from combat in exempting women from registration." Accordingly, "[m]en and women, because of the combat restrictions on women, are simply not similarly situated for purposes of a draft or registration for a draft[,]" and "[t]he exemption of women from registration is not only sufficiently but also closely related to Congress' purpose in authorizing registration."

Finally, the Court thought the District Court had erred in "rel[ying] heavily on the President's decision to seek authority to register women and the testimony of members of the Executive Branch and the military in support of that decision[,]" including "testimony that in the event of a draft of 650,000 the military could absorb some 80,000 female inductees . . . to fill noncombat positions, freeing men to go to the front." In doing so, "the District Court palpably exceeded its authority when it ignored Congress' considered response to this line of reasoning." First, "assuming that a small number of women could be drafted for noncombat roles, Congress simply did not consider it worth the added burdens of including women in draft and registration plans." Second, "Congress also concluded that whatever the need for women for noncombat roles during mobilization, . . . it could be met by volunteers." And, "[m]ost significantly, Congress determined that staffing noncombat positions with women during a mobilization would be positively detrimental to the important goal of military flexibility." Rather than "undertaking an independent evaluation of this evidence," the District Court should have adopted "an appropriately deferential examination of *Congress'* evaluation of that evidence."

A dissent by Justice White, joined by Justice Brennan, "assume[d] what has not been challenged in this case—that excluding women from combat positions does not offend the constitution." But "[a]s I understand the record, . . . the Government cannot rely on volunteers and must register and draft not only to fill combat positions and those noncombat positions that must be filled by combat-trained men, but also to secure the personnel needed for jobs that can be performed by persons ineligible for combat without diminishing military effectiveness." Justice White could "discern no adequate justification" for "discrimination between men and women" with respect to "the latter category of positions[.]"

In a separate dissent, also joined by Justice Brennan, Justice Marshall objected to the Court upholding a statute that "categorically excludes women from a fundamental civic obligation." He, too, emphasized that "this case does not involve a challenge to the statutes or policies that prohibit female members of the Armed Forces from serving in combat." His review of "the discussion and findings contained in the Senate Report" led him to conclude that at most the Report "demonstrates that drafting *very large numbers* of women would frustrate the achievement of a number of important [military] objectives[,] . . . [b]ut . . . do[es] not enable the Government to carry its burden of demonstrating that *completely* excluding women from the draft by excluding them from registration substantially furthers important governmental objectives."

Mississippi University for Women v. Hogan

458 U.S. 718 (1982).ᵃ

The Court held invalid a state statute that excluded males from enrolling in a state-supported professional nursing school. Justice O'Connor, writing for the Court, said that the "test for determining the validity of a gender-based classification is straightforward." Without citing either Michael M. or Rostker she said: "Our decisions . . . establish that the party seeking to uphold a statute that classifies individuals on the basis of their gender must carry the burden of showing an 'exceedingly persuasive justification' for the classification. . . . The burden is met only by showing at least that the classification serves 'important governmental objectives and that the discriminatory means employed' are 'substantially related to the achievement of those objectives.' " She also noted that the "policy of excluding males from admission to the school of nursing tends to perpetuate the stereotyped view of nursing as an exclusively women's job."

For a fuller treatment of this case, see infra p. 565. Compare with its formulation of the test for measuring the constitutionality of sex-based classifications the approach taken in each of the next two decisions.

J.E.B. v. Alabama ex rel. T.B.

511 U.S. 127 (1994).

Beginning with Batson v. Kentucky, 476 U.S. 79 (1986), the Court had restricted the exercise of race-based peremptory challenges so that "whether the trial is criminal or civil, potential jurors, as well as litigants, have an equal protection right to jury selection procedures that are free from state-sponsored group stereotypes rooted in, and reflective of, historical prejudice." In this paternity and child support action, in which the State "used 9 of its 10 peremptory strikes to remove male jurors" (and "petitioner used all but one of his strikes to remove female jurors")—leaving the jury all-female due to a predominantly female pool—the Court extended Batson to "hold that gender, like race, is an unconstitutional proxy for juror competence and impartiality." It "reaffirm[ed]" that "[i]ntentional discrimination on the basis of gender by state actors violates the Equal Protection Clause, particularly where, as here, the discrimination serves to ratify and perpetuate invidious, archaic, and overbroad stereotypes about the relative abilities of men and women."

Justice Blackmun's majority opinion rejected the argument that unlike racial discrimination, "gender discrimination in the selection of the petit jury should be permitted," because " 'gender discrimination in this country . . . has never reached the level of discrimination' against African-Americans":

"While the prejudicial attitudes toward women in this country have not been identical to those held toward racial minorities, the similarities between the

---

ᵃ On March 22, 1972, Congress passed and submitted to the legislatures of the states for ratification the following proposed Equal Rights Amendment to the Constitution:

"Section 1. Equality of rights under the law shall not be denied or abridged by the United States or by any State on account of sex.

"Section 2. The Congress shall have the power to enforce, by appropriate legislation, the provisions of this article.

"Section 3. This amendment shall take effect two years after the date of ratification."

The statute proposing the amendment provided that the ratifications must occur within seven years. By 1978, 35 states (3 less than the required three-fourths) had ratified, but three of them had rescinded their previous ratification. Congress then passed a statute extending the time for ratification to June 30, 1982. The necessary number of states did not ratify by that deadline. The Hogan opinion was handed down the following day.

experiences of racial minorities and women, in some contexts, 'overpower those differences.' Note, Beyond Batson: Eliminating Gender-Based Peremptory Challenges, 105 Harv. L. Rev. 1920, 1921 (1992). . . . Certainly, with respect to jury service, African-Americans and women share a history of total exclusion, a history which came to an end for women many years after the embarrassing chapter in our history came to an end for African-Americans."

In any event, it sufficed "to acknowledge" the history of sex discrimination,

"a history which warrants the heightened scrutiny we afford all gender-based classifications today. Under our equal protection jurisprudence, gender-based classifications require 'an exceedingly persuasive justification' in order to survive constitutional scrutiny. . . . Thus, the only question is whether discrimination on the basis of gender in jury selection substantially furthers the State's legitimate interest in achieving a fair and impartial trial.[6] . . .

"Far from proffering an exceptionally persuasive justification for its gender-based peremptory challenges, respondent maintains that its decision to strike virtually all the males from the jury in this case 'may reasonably have been based upon the perception, supported by history, that men otherwise totally qualified to serve upon a jury might be more sympathetic and receptive to the arguments of a man alleged in a paternity action to be the father of an out-of-wedlock child, while women equally qualified to serve upon a jury might be more sympathetic and receptive to the arguments of the complaining witness who bore the child.' . . .

". . . Respondent offers virtually no support for the conclusion that gender alone is an accurate predictor of juror's attitudes; yet it urges this Court to condone the same stereotypes that justified the wholesale exclusion of women from juries and the ballot box.[11] . . .

"Discrimination in jury selection, whether based on race or on gender, causes harm to the litigants, the community, and the individual jurors who are wrongfully excluded from participation in the judicial process. The litigants are harmed by the risk that the prejudice which motivated the discriminatory selection of the jury will infect the entire proceedings. . . . The community is harmed by the State's participation in the perpetuation of invidious group stereotypes and the inevitable loss of confidence in our judicial system that state-sanctioned discrimination in the courtroom engenders.

"   . . .

". . . Striking individual jurors on the assumption that they hold particular views simply because of their gender is 'practically a brand upon them, affixed by law, an assertion of their inferiority.' Strauder v. West Virginia, 100 U.S. 303, 308 (1880). It denigrates the dignity of the excluded juror, and, for a woman, reinvokes a history of exclusion from political participation.[14] The message it sends to all those in the

---

[6]   Because we conclude that gender-based peremptory challenges are not substantially related to an important government objective, we once again need not decide whether classifications based on gender are inherently suspect. . . .

[11]   . . . [G]ender classifications that rest on impermissible stereotypes violate the Equal Protection Clause, even when some statistical support can be conjured up for the generalization. . . . The Equal Protection Clause . . . requires that state actors look beyond the surface before making judgments about people that are likely to stigmatize as well as to perpetuate historical patterns of discrimination.

[14]   The popular refrain is that all peremptory challenges are based on stereotypes of some kind, expressing various intuitive and frequently erroneous biases. But where peremptory challenges are made on the basis of group characteristics other than race or gender (like occupation, for example), they do not reinforce the same stereotypes about the group's competence or predispositions that have been used to prevent them from voting, participating on juries, pursuing their chosen professions, or

courtroom, and all those who may later learn of the discriminatory act, is that certain individuals, for no reason other than gender, are presumed unqualified by state actors to decide important questions upon which reasonable persons could disagree."

Justice Blackmun observed that the Court's conclusion did "not imply the elimination of all peremptory challenges." Rather, "gender simply may not serve as a proxy for bias." In fact, "[p]arties may . . . exercise their peremptory challenges to remove from the venire any group or class of individuals normally subject to 'rational basis' review." He also emphasized, in conclusion, the importance of equal opportunity in this context, because jury service constitutes direct "participation in our democratic processes[.]"

In a concurring opinion, Justice O'Connor urged that "today's holding should be limited to the government's use of gender-based peremptory strikes." It gave her "pause" that the decision would "increase the possibility that biased jurors will be allowed onto the jury, because sometimes a lawyer will be unable to provide an acceptable gender-neutral explanation even though the lawyer is in fact correct that the juror is unsympathetic." She elaborated:

". . . We know that like race, gender matters. A plethora of studies make clear that in rape cases, for example, female jurors are somewhat more likely to vote to convict than male jurors. . . . Moreover, though there have been no similarly definitive studies regarding, for example, sexual harassment, child custody, or spousal or child abuse, one need not be a sexist to share the intuition that in certain cases a person's gender and resulting life experience will be relevant to his or her view of the case. . . .

"Today's decision severely limits a litigant's ability to act on this intuition. . . . But to say that gender makes no difference as a matter of law is not to say that gender makes no difference as a matter of fact. I previously have said with regard to *Batson*: 'That the Court will not tolerate prosecutors' racially discriminatory use of the peremptory challenge, in effect, is a special rule of relevance, a statement about what this Nation stands for, rather than a statement of fact.' Brown v. North Carolina, 479 U.S. 940, 941–942 (1986) (O'Connor, J., concurring in denial of certiorari). Today's decision is a statement that . . . gender is now governed by the special rule of relevance formerly reserved for race. . . . [Yet] we have added an additional burden to the state and federal trial process, taken a step closer to eliminating the peremptory challenge, and diminished the ability of litigants to act on sometimes accurate gender-based assumptions about juror attitudes."

These concerns led Justice O'Connor to the "position that the Equal Protection Clause does not limit the exercise of peremptory challenges by private civil litigants and criminal defendants." She asked whether the Court later might preclude "the battered wife—on trial for wounding her abusive husband— . . . from using her peremptory challenges to ensure that the jury of her peers contains as many women members as possible?" Her own reply was: "I assume we will, but I hope we will not."

Concurring in the judgment, Justice Kennedy said of a peremptory challenge based on sex that the excluded juror "is no less injured than the individual denied jury service because of a law banning members of her sex from serving as jurors" and that "[t]he injury is to personal dignity and to the individual's right to participate in the political process." He also wrote that "[n]othing would be more pernicious to the jury system than for society to presume that persons of different backgrounds go to the jury room to voice prejudice. . . . The jury pool must be representative of the community, but that is a structural mechanism for preventing bias, not enfranchising it. . . ."

---

otherwise contributing to civic life. See B. Babcock, A Place in the Palladium, Women's Rights and Jury Service, 61 U. Cinn. L. Rev. 1139, 1173 (1993).

Chief Justice Rehnquist dissented, finding "sufficient differences between race and gender discrimination such that the principle of *Batson* should not be extended to peremptory challenges to potential jurors based on sex." Those differences include a "less searching standard of review" for gender classifications; that, unlike women, "[r]acial groups comprise numerical minorities in our society"; that "racial equality has proved a more challenging goal to achieve on many fronts than gender equality"; and that "*Batson* is best understood as a recognition that race lies at the core of the commands of the Fourteenth Amendment." He also observed that "[i]t is not merely 'stereotyping' to say that these differences may produce a difference in outlook which is brought to the jury room. Accordingly, use of peremptory challenges on the basis of sex is generally not the sort of derogatory and invidious act which peremptory challenges directed at black jurors may be."

In a separate dissent, Justice Scalia, joined by the Chief Justice and Justice Thomas, faulted the Court for "focusing unrealistically upon individual exercises of the peremptory challenge, and ignoring the totality of the practice." That all sides can exercise peremptories

"explains why peremptory challenges coexisted with the Equal Protection Clause for 120 years. . . . The situation would be different if both sides systematically struck individuals of one group, so that the strikes evinced group-based animus and served as a proxy for segregated venire lists. . . . The pattern here, however, displays not a systemic sex-based animus but each side's desire to get a jury favorably disposed to its case. That is why the Court's characterization of respondent's argument as 'reminiscent of the arguments advanced to justify the total exclusion of women from juries,' is patently false. Women were categorically excluded from juries because of doubt that they were competent; women are stricken from juries by peremptory challenge because of doubt that they are well disposed to the striking party's case. . . . There is discrimination and dishonor in the former, and not in the latter. . . ."

United States v. Virginia
518 U.S. 515, 116 S.Ct. 2264, 135 L.Ed.2d 735 (1996).

■ JUSTICE GINSBURG delivered the opinion of the Court.

Virginia's public institutions of higher learning include an incomparable military college, Virginia Military Institute (VMI). The United States maintains that the Constitution's equal protection guarantee precludes Virginia from reserving exclusively to men the unique educational opportunities VMI affords. We agree.

I

Founded in 1839, VMI is today the sole single-sex school among Virginia's 15 public institutions of higher learning. VMI's distinctive mission is to produce "citizen-soldiers," men prepared for leadership in civilian life and in military service. VMI pursues this mission through pervasive training of a kind not available anywhere else in Virginia[—] . . . an "adversative method" [that] constantly endeavors to instill physical and mental discipline in its cadets and impart to them a strong moral code. . . .

. . .

Neither the goal of producing citizen-soldiers nor VMI's implementing methodology is inherently unsuitable to women. And the school's impressive record in producing leaders has made admission desirable to some women. . . .

II

. . .

VMI['s] . . . ". . . adversative, or doubting, model of education" . . . features "[p]hysical rigor, mental stress, absolute equality of treatment, absence of privacy, minute regulation of behavior, and indoctrination in desirable values." . . .

VMI cadets live in spartan barracks where surveillance is constant and privacy nonexistent; they wear uniforms, eat together in the mess hall, and regularly participate in drills. . . . Entering students are incessantly exposed to the rat line, "an extreme form of the adversative model," comparable in intensity to Marine Corps boot camp. . . .

. . .

[The United States, prompted by a female applicant's complaint, sued Virginia and VMI in 1990. The District Court ruled in favor of VMI but the Fourth Circuit reversed and remanded,] suggest[ing] these options for the State: Admit women to VMI; establish parallel institutions or programs; or abandon state support, leaving VMI free to pursue its policies as a private institution. . . .

. . . Virginia proposed a parallel program for women: Virginia Women's Institute for Leadership (VWIL). The 4-year, state-sponsored undergraduate program would be located at Mary Baldwin College, a private liberal arts school for women, and would be open, initially, to about 25 to 30 students. Although VWIL would share VMI's mission—to produce "citizen-soldiers"—the VWIL program would differ, as does Mary Baldwin College, from VMI in academic offerings, methods of education, and financial resources. . . .

. . .

[T]he District Court . . . decided the plan met the requirements of the Equal Protection Clause. . . .

A divided Court of Appeals affirmed. . . .

. . .

III

[T]his case present[s] two ultimate issues. First, does Virginia's exclusion of women from the educational opportunities provided by VMI—extraordinary opportunities for military training and civilian leadership development—deny to women "capable of all of the individual activities required of VMI cadets," . . . the equal protection of the laws guaranteed by the Fourteenth Amendment? Second, if VMI's "unique" situation . . . as Virginia's sole single-sex public institution of higher education . . . offends the Constitution's equal protection principle, what is the remedial requirement?

IV

. . .

. . . Since *Reed*, the Court has repeatedly recognized that neither federal nor state government acts compatibly with the equal protection principle when a law or official policy denies to women, simply because they are women, full citizenship stature—equal opportunity to aspire, achieve, participate in and contribute to society based on their individual talents and capacities. . . .

. . . To summarize the Court's current directions for cases of official classification based on gender: Focusing on the differential treatment or denial of opportunity for which relief is sought, the reviewing court must determine whether the proffered justification is "exceedingly persuasive." The burden of justification is demanding and it rests entirely on the State. . . . The State must show "at least that the [challenged] classification serves 'important governmental objectives and that the discriminatory means employed' are 'substantially related to the achievement of those objectives.'" . . . The justification must be genuine, not hypothesized or invented *post hoc* in response to litigation. And it must not rely on overbroad generalizations about the different talents, capacities, or preferences of males and females. . . .

. . .

"Inherent differences" between men and women . . . remain cause for celebration, but not for denigration of the members of either sex or for artificial constraints on an individual's opportunity. Sex classifications may be used to compensate women "for particular economic disabilities [they have] suffered," . . . to "promot[e] equal employment opportunity," . . . to advance full development of the talent and capacities of our Nation's people[,] . . . [b]ut . . . not . . . , as they once were, . . . to create or perpetuate the legal, social, and economic inferiority of women.

[W]e conclude that Virginia has shown no "exceedingly persuasive justification" for excluding all women from the citizen-soldier training afforded by VMI. . . . Because the remedy proffered by Virginia—the Mary Baldwin VWIL program—does not cure the constitutional violation, i.e., it does not provide equal opportunity, we reverse. . . .

V

. . . Virginia . . . asserts two justifications in defense of VMI's exclusion of women. First, . . . "single-sex education provides important educational benefits," . . . and the option of single-sex education contributes to "diversity in educational approaches,". . . . Second, . . . "the unique VMI method of character development and leadership training," the school's adversative approach, would have to be modified were VMI to admit women. . . .

A

Single-sex education affords pedagogical benefits to at least some students, . . . and that reality is uncontested in this litigation. Similarly, it is not disputed that diversity among public educational institutions can serve the public good. But Virginia has not shown that VMI was established, or has been maintained, with a view to diversifying, by its categorical exclusion of women, educational opportunities within the State. In cases of this genre, our precedent instructs that "benign" justifications proffered in defense of categorical exclusions will not be accepted automatically; a tenable justification must describe actual state purposes, not rationalizations for actions in fact differently grounded. . . .

. . .

Neither recent nor distant history bears out Virginia's alleged pursuit of diversity through single-sex educational options. . . .

. . .

Virginia describes the current absence of public single-sex higher education for women as "an historical anomaly." . . . But the historical record indicates action more deliberate than anomalous: First, protection of women against higher education; next, schools for women far from equal in resources and stature to schools for men; finally, conversion of the separate schools to coeducation. . . .

Our 1982 decision in *Mississippi Univ. for Women* prompted VMI to reexamine its male-only admission policy. . . . A Mission Study Committee . . . studied the problem from October 1983 until May 1986, and in that month counseled against "change of VMI status as a single-sex college." . . . [W]e can hardly extract from that effort any state policy evenhandedly to advance diverse educational options. As the District

Court observed, the Committee's analysis "primarily focuse[d] on anticipated difficulties in attracting females to VMI," and the report, overall, supplied "very little indication of how th[e] conclusion was reached."

In sum, we find no persuasive evidence in this record that VMI's male-only admission policy "is in furtherance of a state policy of 'diversity.' " . . . A purpose genuinely to advance an array of educational options . . . is not served by VMI's historic and constant plan—a plan to "affor[d] a unique educational benefit only to males." . . . However "liberally" this plan serves the State's sons, it makes no provision whatever for her daughters. That is not equal protection.

B

Virginia next argues that VMI's adversative method of training provides educational benefits that cannot be made available, unmodified, to women. Alterations to accommodate women would necessarily be . . . so "drastic," . . . as to transform, indeed "destroy," VMI's program. . . .

The District Court forecast from expert witness testimony, and the Court of Appeals accepted, that coeducation would materially affect "at least these three aspects of VMI's program—physical training, the absence of privacy, and the adversative approach." . . . And it is uncontested that women's admission would require accommodations, primarily in arranging housing assignments and physical training programs for female cadets. . . . It is also undisputed, however, that "the VMI methodology could be used to educate women." . . . The District Court even allowed that some women may prefer it to the methodology a women's college might pursue. . . . ["S]ome women," the expert testimony established, "are capable of all of the individual activities required of VMI cadets," [and t]he parties . . . agree that "some women can meet the physical standards [VMI] now impose[s] on men." . . . In sum, as the Court of Appeals stated, "neither the goal of producing citizen soldiers," VMI's *raison d'etre*, "nor VMI's implementing methodology is inherently unsuitable to women." . . .

. . . [T]he District Court made "findings" on "gender-based developmental differences[,]" [that] restate the opinions of Virginia's expert witnesses, opinions about typically male or typically female "tendencies." . . . For example, "[m]ales tend to need an atmosphere of adversativeness," while "[f]emales tend to thrive in a cooperative atmosphere." . . .

The United States does not challenge any expert witness estimation on average capacities or preferences of men and women. Instead, the United States emphasizes that . . . we have cautioned reviewing courts to take a "hard look" at generalizations or "tendencies" of the kind pressed by Virginia, and relied upon by the District Court. . . . State actors controlling gates to opportunity, we have instructed, may not exclude qualified individuals based on "fixed notions concerning the roles and abilities of males and females." . . .

It may be assumed . . . that most women would not choose VMI's adversative method. . . . [H]owever, . . . it is also probable that "many men would not want to be educated in such an environment." . . . The issue . . . is . . . whether the State can constitutionally deny to women who have the will and capacity, the training and attendant opportunities that VMI uniquely affords. . . .

The notion that admission of women would downgrade VMI's stature, destroy the adversative system and, with it, even the school, is a judgment hardly proved, a prediction hardly different from other "self-fulfilling prophec[ies]," . . . once routinely used to deny rights or opportunities. When women first sought admission to the bar and access to legal education, concerns of the same order were expressed. . . .

Medical faculties similarly resisted men and women as partners in the study of medicine. . . .

Women's successful entry into the federal military academies, and their participation in the Nation's military forces, indicate that Virginia's fears for the future of VMI may not be solidly grounded. . . . The State's justification for excluding all women from "citizen-soldier" training for which some are qualified, in any event, cannot rank as "exceedingly persuasive," as we have explained and applied that standard.

. . .

VI

In the second phase of the litigation, Virginia presented its remedial plan—maintain VMI as a male-only college and create VWIL as a separate program for women. . . . [T]he Court of Appeals concluded that Virginia had arranged for men and women opportunities "sufficiently comparable" to survive equal protection evaluation. . . .

A

. . .

. . . For women only, . . . Virginia proposed a separate program, different in kind from VMI and unequal in tangible and intangible facilities. . . .

VWIL affords women no opportunity to experience the rigorous military training for which VMI is famed[,] . . . [i]nstead. . . "deemphasiz[ing]" military education, . . . and us[ing] a "cooperative method" of education "which reinforces self-esteem,". . . .

VWIL students participate in ROTC and a "largely ceremonial" Virginia Corps of Cadets, . . . but Virginia deliberately did not make VWIL a military institute. The VWIL House is not a military-style residence and VWIL students need not live together throughout the 4-year program, eat meals together, or wear uniforms during the school day. . . . VWIL students thus do not experience the "barracks" life "crucial to the VMI experience," the spartan living arrangements designed to foster an "egalitarian ethic." . . . Virginia deemed that core experience nonessential, indeed inappropriate, for training its female citizen-soldiers.

VWIL students . . . [are k]ept away from the pressures, hazards, and psychological bonding characteristic of VMI's adversative training . . . .

Virginia maintains that these methodological differences are "justified pedagogically," based on "important differences between men and women in learning and developmental needs," "psychological and sociological differences" Virginia describes as "real" and "not stereotypes." . . .

. . . [G]eneralizations about "the way women are," estimates of what is appropriate for *most women*, no longer justify denying opportunity to women whose talent and capacity place them outside the average description. Notably, Virginia never asserted that VMI's method of education suits *most men*. It is also revealing that Virginia accounted for its failure to make the VWIL experience "the entirely militaristic experience of VMI" on the ground that VWIL "is planned for women who do not necessarily expect to pursue military careers." . . . By that reasoning, VMI's "entirely militaristic" program would be inappropriate for men in general or *as a group*, for "[o]nly about 15% of VMI cadets enter career military service." . . .

In contrast to the generalizations about women on which Virginia rests [are] these dispositive realities: VMI's "implementing methodology" is not "inherently unsuitable to women," . . .; "some women . . . do well under [the] adversative model," . . .; "some women, at least, would want to attend [VMI] if they had the opportunity,"

. . . ; "some women are capable of all of the individual activities required of VMI cadets," . . . and "can meet the physical standards [VMI] now impose[s] on men,". . . . It is on behalf of these women that the United States has instituted this suit, and it is for them that a remedy must be crafted,[19] a remedy that will end their exclusion from a state-supplied educational opportunity for which they are fit, a decree that will "bar like discrimination in the future." . . .

B

In myriad respects other than military training, VWIL does not qualify as VMI's equal. VWIL's student body, faculty, course offerings, and facilities hardly match VMI's. Nor can the VWIL graduate anticipate the benefits associated with VMI's 157-year history, the school's prestige, and its influential alumni network.

. . . [T]he . . . VWIL program [is] fairly appraised as a "pale shadow" of VMI in terms of the range of curricular choices and faculty stature, funding, prestige, alumni support and influence. . . .

Virginia's VWIL solution is reminiscent of . . . Sweatt v. Painter, 339 U.S. 629 (1950). Reluctant to admit African Americans to its flagship University of Texas Law School, the State set up a separate school for Herman Sweatt and other black law students. . . .

. . . This Court contrasted resources at the new school with those at the school from which Sweatt had been excluded. . . .

More important than the tangible features, the Court emphasized, are "those qualities which are incapable of objective measurement but which make for greatness" in a school, including "reputation of the faculty, experience of the administration, position and influence of the alumni, standing in the community, traditions and prestige." . . . [T]he Court unanimously ruled that Texas had not shown "substantial equality in the [separate] educational opportunities" the State offered. . . . In line with *Sweatt*, we rule here that Virginia has not shown substantial equality in the separate educational opportunities the State supports at VWIL and VMI.

. . .

■ JUSTICE THOMAS took no part in the consideration or decision of this case.

■ CHIEF JUSTICE REHNQUIST, concurring in the judgment.

. . .

I

. . .

. . . [Not until the 1982 *Mississippi University for Women* decision was] Virginia [placed] on notice that VMI's men-only admissions policy was open to serious question.

. . .

. . . I agree with the Court that there is scant evidence in the record that [diversity in education with room for single-sex institutions] was the real reason that Virginia decided to maintain VMI as men only. But, unlike the majority, I would consider only evidence that postdates . . . *Hogan*, and would draw no negative inferences from the State's actions before that time. [A]fter *Hogan*, the State was

---

[19] Admitting women to VMI would undoubtedly require alterations necessary to afford members of each sex privacy from the other sex in living arrangements, and to adjust aspects of the physical training programs. . . . Experience shows such adjustments are manageable. See U.S. Military Academy, . . . Report of Admission of Women . . . (1977–1980) (4-year longitudinal study of the admission of women to West Point). . . .

entitled to reconsider its policy with respect to VMI, and to not have earlier justifications, or lack thereof, held against it.

Even if diversity in educational opportunity were the State's actual objective, the State's position would still be problematic[, because] . . . the diversity benefited only one sex; there was single-sex public education available for men at VMI, but no corresponding single-sex public education available for women. . . .

I do not think, however, that the State's options were as limited as the majority may imply. . . . Had Virginia made a genuine effort to devote comparable public resources to a facility for women, and followed through on such a plan, it might well have avoided an equal protection violation. . . .

But . . . neither the governing board of VMI nor the State took any action after 1982. If diversity in the form of single-sex, as well as coeducational, institutions of higher learning were to be available to Virginians, that diversity had to be available to women as well as to men.

. . .

[As for] Virginia['s] second justification[—] maintenance of the adversative method[—]I agree with the Court that [it] does not serve an important governmental objective. A State does not have substantial interest in the adversative methodology unless it is pedagogically beneficial[, and] . . . there is no . . . evidence in the record that an adversative method is pedagogically beneficial or is any more likely to produce character traits than other methodologies.

II

. . . [I]t is not the "exclusion of women" that violates the Equal Protection Clause, but the maintenance of an all-men school without providing any—much less a comparable—institution for women.

Accordingly, the remedy should not necessarily require either the admission of women to VMI, or the creation of a VMI clone for women. An adequate remedy . . . might be a demonstration by Virginia that its interest in educating men in a single-sex environment is matched by its interest in educating women in a single-sex institution. . . . It would . . . suffic[e] if the two institutions offered the same quality of education and were of the same overall calibre.

. . .

In the end, . . . VWIL . . . fails as a remedy, because it is distinctly inferior to the existing men's institution and will continue to be for the foreseeable future. . . . In particular, VWIL is . . . appended to a private college, not a self-standing institution; and VWIL is substantially underfunded as compared to VMI. I therefore ultimately agree with the Court that Virginia has not provided an adequate remedy.

■ JUSTICE SCALIA, dissenting.

. . .

. . . [W]hatever abstract tests we . . . devise, they cannot supersede—and indeed ought to be crafted *so as to reflect*—those constant and unbroken national traditions that embody the people's understanding of ambiguous constitutional texts. . . .

. . . [T]he tradition of having government-funded military schools for men is as well rooted in the traditions of this country as the tradition of sending only men into military combat. The people may decide to change the[m] through democratic processes; but the assertion that either tradition has been unconstitutional through the centuries is not law, but politics-smuggled-into-law.

And the same applies, more broadly, to single-sex education in general, which . . . is threatened by today's decision with the cut-off of all state and federal support. . . .

    . . .

II

Only the amorphous "exceedingly persuasive justification" phrase, and not the standard elaboration of intermediate scrutiny, can be made to yield th[e] conclusion that VMI's single-sex composition is unconstitutional because there exist several women (or, one would have to conclude under the Court's reasoning, a single woman) willing and able to undertake VMI's program. . . . There is simply no support in our cases for the notion that a sex-based classification is invalid unless it relates to characteristics that hold true in every instance.

[I]f the . . . applicable standard of review for sex-based classifications were . . . reconsider[ed], the stronger argument would be not for elevating the standard to strict scrutiny, but for reducing it to rational-basis review[, which] . . . would be much more in accord with the genesis of heightened standards of judicial review, the famous footnote in United States v. Carolene Products Co., 304 U.S. 144 (1938). . . . It is hard to consider women a "discrete and insular minorit[y]" unable to employ the "political processes ordinarily to be relied upon," when they constitute a majority of the electorate. And the suggestion that they are incapable of exerting that political power smacks of the same paternalism that the Court so roundly condemns. Moreover, a long list of legislation proves the proposition false. See, e.g., Equal Pay Act of 1963 . . . ; Title VII of the Civil Rights Act of 1964 . . . ; Title IX of the Education Amendments of 1972. . . . ; Women's Business Ownership Act of 1988. . . . ; Violence Against Women Act of 1994. . . .

III

    . . . [T]he question . . . is whether the exclusion of women from VMI is "substantially related to an important governmental objective."

A

    . . . Virginia has an important state interest in providing effective college education for its citizens. That single-sex instruction is an approach substantially related to that interest should be evident enough from the long and continuing history in this country of men's and women's colleges. . . .

    . . .

    . . . [S]o too a State's decision to maintain within its system one school that provides the adversative method is "substantially related" to its goal of good education. Moreover, it was uncontested that "if the state were to establish a women's VMI-type [i.e., adversative] program, the program would attract an insufficient number of participants to make the program work," . . . ; and it was found by the District Court that if Virginia were to include women in VMI, the school "would eventually find it necessary to drop the adversative system altogether,". . . . Thus, Virginia's options were an adversative method that excludes women or no adversative method at all.

[S]ingle-sex education and a distinctive educational method "represent legitimate contributions to diversity in the Virginia higher education system." . . .

    . . . [T]he Commonwealth has long proceeded on the principle that " '[h]igher education resources should be viewed as a whole—public and private' "—because such an approach enhances diversity and because " 'it is academic and economic waste to permit unwarranted duplication.' " . . . In these circumstances, Virginia's election to fund one public all-male institution and one on the adversative model—and to concentrate its resources in a single entity that serves both these interests in diversity—is substantially related to the State's important educational interests.

B

. . .

. . . [T]hat VMI would not have to change very much if it were to admit women . . . is irrelevant. . . .

But if . . . relevant, the Court would certainly be on the losing side[, given] . . . findings by two courts below, amply supported by the evidence, . . . that VMI would be fundamentally altered if it admitted women. . . .[5]

. . . Finally, the absence of a precise "all-women's analogue" to VMI is irrelevant. In Mississippi Univ. for Women v. Hogan, 458 U.S. 718 (1982), we attached no constitutional significance to the absence of an all-male nursing school. . . .

. . . VWIL [also] is . . . irrelevant, so long as VMI's all-male character is "substantially related" to an important state goal. . . .

. . .

C

[T]he concurrence . . . finds VMI unconstitutional on a basis that is more moderate than the Court's but only at the expense of being even more implausible. . . .

[T]he . . . pedagogical benefits of VMI's adversative approach were not only proved, but were a given in this litigation. The reason the woman applicant who prompted this suit wanted to enter VMI was . . . [that s]he wanted the distinctive adversative education that VMI provided. . . .

. . .

In any event, "diversity in the form of single-sex, as well as coeducational, institutions of higher learning," *is* "available to women as well as to men" in Virginia. The concurrence is able to assert the contrary only by disregarding the four all-women's private colleges in Virginia (generously assisted by public funds) and the Commonwealth's longstanding policy of coordinating public with private educational offerings. . . .

. . .

Nguyen v. Immigration and Naturalization Service
533 U.S. 53 (2001).

Born in Vietnam in 1969 to an unwed American citizen father and a Vietnamese citizen mother, Nguyen came to the United States at age six, became a lawful permanent resident, and was raised in Texas by his father, who obtained a state court DNA-based paternity declaration when Nguyen was 28. Later threatened with deportation as an alien convict, he challenged as a denial of "the equal protection guarantee embedded in the Due Process Clause of the Fifth Amendment" the more difficult criteria for citizenship set forth in 8 U.S.C. § 1409 for children born abroad of unwed citizen fathers and noncitizen mothers than for children born abroad of unwed citizen mothers and noncitizen fathers. Under § 1409(a), to be citizens the former must establish a blood relationship with the father by "clear and convincing evidence"; that the father "agreed in writing to provide financial support" up to 18; and that before 18 the child was either "legitimated under the law of the person's residence or domicile,"

---

[5] . . . West Point found it necessary upon becoming coeducational to "move away" from its adversative system. . . .

the father had acknowledged paternity in writing under oath, or paternity was "established by adjudication of a competent court." By contrast, the latter are automatically citizens at birth "if the mother had previously been physically present in the United States or one of its outlying possessions for a continuous period of one year." § 1409(c). The Court of Appeals rejected the equal protection challenge, and the Supreme Court affirmed. Justice Kennedy's opinion for the Court said in part:

"For a gender-based classification to withstand equal protection scrutiny, it must be established ' "at least that the [challenged] classification serves 'important governmental objectives and that the discriminatory means employed' are 'substantially related to the achievement of those objectives.' " ' United States v. Virginia.... § 1409 satisfies this standard. Given that determination, we need not decide whether some lesser degree of scrutiny pertains because the statute implicates Congress' immigration and naturalization power....

"...

" ... [W]hile the conditions necessary for a citizen mother to transmit citizenship under § 1409(c) exist at birth, citizen fathers and/or their children have 18 years to satisfy the requirements of § 1409(a)(4)....

"... [T]he imposition of the requirement for a paternal relationship, but not a maternal one, is justified by two important governmental objectives....

"The first ... is the importance of assuring that a biological parent-child relationship exists. In the case of the mother, the relation is verifiable from the birth itself. The mother's status is documented in most instances by the birth certificate or hospital records and the witnesses who attest to her having given birth.

"In the case of the father, the uncontestable fact is that he need not be present at the birth.... If he is present, furthermore, that circumstance is not incontrovertible proof of fatherhood. Fathers and mothers are not similarly situated with regard to the proof of biological parenthood. The imposition of a different set of rules for making that legal determination with respect to fathers and mothers is neither surprising nor troublesome from a constitutional perspective.... Section 1409(a)(4)'s provision of three options for a father seeking to establish paternity—legitimation, paternity oath, and court order of paternity—is designed to ensure an acceptable documentation of paternity.

"...

"The second important governmental interest furthered in a substantial manner by § 1409(a)(4) is the determination to ensure that the child and the citizen parent have some demonstrated opportunity or potential to develop not just a relationship that is recognized, as a formal matter, by the law, but one that consists of the real, everyday ties that provide a connection between child and citizen parent and, in turn, the United States.... In the case of a citizen mother and a child born overseas, the opportunity for a meaningful relationship between citizen parent and child inheres in the very event of birth, an event so often critical to our constitutional and statutory understandings of citizenship....

"The same opportunity does not result from the event of birth, as a matter of biological inevitability, in the case of the unwed father. [I]t is not always certain that a father will know that a child was conceived, nor is it always clear that even the mother will be sure of the father's identity.... One concern in this context has always been with young people, men for the most part, who are on duty with the Armed Forces in foreign countries....

"...

". . . Without an initial point of contact with the child by a father who knows the child is his own, there is no opportunity for father and child to begin a relationship. Section 1409 takes the unremarkable step of ensuring that such an opportunity, inherent in the event of birth as to the mother-child relationship, exists between father and child before citizenship is conferred upon the latter.

". . . [S]cientific proof of biological paternity does nothing, by itself, to ensure contact between father and child during the child's minority.

". . . It should be unobjectionable for Congress to require some evidence of a minimal opportunity for the development of a relationship with the child in terms the male can fulfill.

"...

". . . [T]he difference does not result from some stereotype, defined as a frame of mind resulting from irrational or uncritical analysis. . . ."

With respect to the means inquiry, Justice Kennedy responded as follows to the argument "that, although a mother will know of her child's birth, 'knowledge that one is a parent, no matter how it is acquired, does not guarantee a relationship with one's child'" and thus to impose "the additional requirements of § 1409(a)(4) only on the children of citizen fathers must reflect a stereotype that women are more likely than men to actually establish a relationship with their children":

"This line of argument misconceives the nature of both the governmental interest at issue and the manner in which we examine statutes alleged to violate equal protection. As to the former, Congress would of course be entitled to advance the interest of ensuring an actual, meaningful relationship in every case before citizenship is conferred. Or Congress could excuse compliance with the formal requirements when an actual father-child relationship is proved. It did neither here, perhaps because of the subjectivity, intrusiveness, and difficulties of proof that might attend an inquiry into any particular bond or tie. Instead, Congress enacted an easily administered scheme to promote the different but still substantial interest of ensuring at least an opportunity for a parent-child relationship to develop. Petitioners' argument confuses the means and ends of the equal protection inquiry; § 1409(a)(4) should not be invalidated because Congress elected to advance an interest that is less demanding to satisfy than some other alternative.

"Even if one conceives of the interest Congress pursues as the establishment of a real, practical relationship of considerable substance between parent and child in every case, as opposed simply to ensuring the potential for the relationship to begin, . . . [i]t is almost axiomatic that a policy which seeks to foster the opportunity for meaningful parent-child bonds to develop has a close and substantial bearing on the governmental interest in the actual formation of that bond. None of our gender-based classification equal protection cases have required that the statute under consideration must be capable of achieving its ultimate objective in every instance."

Justice Kennedy concluded his opinion this way:

". . . The distinction . . . at issue is not marked by misconception and prejudice, nor does it show disrespect for either class. The difference between men and women in relation to the birth process is a real one, and the principle of equal protection does not forbid Congress to address the problem at hand in a manner specific to each gender."[a]

---

[a]   Justice Scalia's concurring opinion, joined by Justice Thomas, is omitted.

Justice O'Connor dissented, joined by Justices Souter, Ginsburg, and Breyer. They found no "exceedingly persuasive justification for the sex-based classification" and faulted the Court's analysis:

"[T]he majority hypothesizes about the interests served by the statute and fails adequately to inquire into [its] actual purposes. . . . The Court also does not always explain adequately the importance of the interests that it claims to be served by the provision. The majority also fails carefully to consider whether the sex-based classification is being used impermissibly 'as a "proxy for other, more germane bases of classification," ' Mississippi Univ. for Women, . . . and instead casually dismisses the relevance of available sex-neutral alternatives. And . . . the fit between the means and ends of § 1409(a)(4) is far too attenuated for the provision to survive heightened scrutiny. In all, the majority opinion represents far less than the rigorous application of heightened scrutiny that our precedents require."

In the dissenters' view, the majority failed both to "elaborate on the importance of th[e] interest [in assuring that a biological parent-child relationship exists], which presumably lies in preventing fraudulent conveyances of citizenship" and to "demonstrate that this is one of the actual purposes of § 1409(a)(4)." The "gravest defect in the Court's reliance on this interest, however, is the insufficiency of the fit between § 1409(a)(4)'s discriminatory means and the asserted end." Because § 1409(a)(1) requires that "a blood relationship between the person and the father [be] established by clear and convincing evidence[,]" and given the "virtual certainty of a biological link that modern DNA testing affords[,]" § 1409(a)(4) is not needed to further this interest. Nor does "§ 1409(a)(4)'s limitation of the time allowed for obtaining proof of paternity substantially further[ ] the assurance of a blood relationship[,]" for "[m]odern DNA testing . . . essentially negates the evidentiary significance of the passage of time." In short, "[b]ecause § 1409(a)(4) adds little to the work that § 1409(a)(1) does on its own, it is difficult to say that § 1409(a)(4) 'substantially furthers' an important governmental interest."

Since "a mother will not always have formal legal documentation of birth because a birth certificate may not issue or may subsequently be lost [and c]onversely, a father's name may well appear on a birth certificate[,] . . . the majority has not shown that a mother's birth relation is uniquely verifiable by the INS, much less that any greater verifiability warrants a sex-based, rather than a sex-neutral, statute." Thus, requiring both mothers and fathers to prove parenthood would be a superior, sex-neutral alternative: "Far from being 'hollow,' the avoidance of gratuitous sex-based distinctions is the hallmark of equal protection."

The majority's focus on the second interest—" 'some demonstrated opportunity or potential to develop . . . real, everyday ties,'[—]appears to be the type of hypothesized rationale that is insufficient under heightened scrutiny." In any event, "it is questionable whether such an opportunity qualifies as an 'important' governmental interest apart from the existence of an actual relationship." Although "focusing on 'opportunity' rather than reality . . . presumably improves the chances of a sufficient means-end fit[,] in doing so, it dilutes significantly the weight of the interest." The dissent questioned "how . . . anyone profits from a 'demonstrated opportunity' for a relationship in the absence of the fruition of an actual tie. Children who have an 'opportunity' for such a tie with a parent . . . may never develop an actual relationship with that parent. . . . Likewise, where there is an actual relationship, it . . . does all the work in rendering appropriate a grant of citizenship, regardless of when and how the opportunity for that relationship arose." The dissent continued:

". . . [Also,] it is difficult to see how the requirement that proof of such opportunity be obtained before the child turns 18 substantially furthers the asserted interest. As the facts of this case demonstrate, it is entirely possible that a father and child will have the opportunity to develop a relationship and in fact will develop a relationship without obtaining the proof of the opportunity during the child's minority. . . .

        " . . .

"Moreover, available sex-neutral alternatives would at least replicate, and could easily exceed, whatever fit there is. . . . Congress could simply substitute . . . a requirement that the parent be present at birth or have knowledge of birth. . . . Congress could at least allow proof of such presence or knowledge to be one way of demonstrating an opportunity for a relationship. Under the present law, the statute on its face accords different treatment to a mother who is by nature present at birth and a father who is by choice present at birth even though those two individuals are similarly situated with respect to the 'opportunity' for a relationship. . . .

"Indeed, the idea that a mother's presence at birth supplies adequate assurance of an opportunity to develop a relationship while a father's presence at birth does not would appear to rest only on an overbroad sex-based generalization. A mother may not have an opportunity for a relationship if the child is removed from his or her mother on account of alleged abuse or neglect, or if the child and mother are separated by tragedy, such as disaster or war, of the sort apparently present in this case. There is no reason, other than stereotype, to say that fathers who are present at birth lack an opportunity for a relationship on similar terms. The '[p]hysical differences between men and women,' *Virginia*, . . . therefore do not justify § 1409(a)(4)'s discrimination."

        " . . .

"The question that then remains is the sufficiency of the fit between § 1409(a)(4)'s discriminatory means and the goal of 'establish[ing] . . . a real, practical relationship of considerable substance.' If Congress wishes to advance this end, it could easily do so by employing a sex-neutral classification . . . . For example, Congress could require some degree of regular contact between the child and the citizen parent over a period of time. . . .

        " . . .

"The claim that § 1409(a)(4) substantially relates to the achievement of the goal of a 'real, practical relationship' thus finds support not in biological differences but instead in a stereotype—i.e., 'the generalization that mothers are significantly more likely than fathers . . . to develop caring relationships with their children.' . . . Such a claim relies on 'the very stereotype the law condemns,' *J.E.B.* . . . , 'lends credibility' to the generalization, *Mississippi Univ. for Women* . . . , and helps to convert that 'assumption' into 'a self-fulfilling prophecy,' ibid. . . . Indeed, contrary to this stereotype, [his father] has reared Nguyen, while Nguyen apparently has lacked a relationship with his mother.

        " . . .

" . . . [T]he majority articulates a misshapen notion of 'stereotype' and its significance in our equal protection jurisprudence. . . . [I]n numerous cases where a measure of truth has inhered in the generalization, 'the Court has rejected official actions that classify unnecessarily and overbroadly by gender when more accurate and impartial functional lines can be drawn.' . . .

"Nor do stereotypes consist only of those overbroad generalizations that . . . 'show disrespect' for a class. . . . The hallmark of a stereotypical sex-based classification under this Court's precedents is not whether the classification is insulting, but whether it 'relie[s] upon the simplistic, outdated assumption that gender could be used as a "proxy for other, more germane bases of classification." ' . . .

" . . .

"Section 1409(a)(4) is . . . paradigmatic of a historic regime that left women with responsibility, and freed men from responsibility, for nonmarital children. . . . The majority, however, rather than confronting the stereotypical notion that mothers must care for these children and fathers may ignore them, quietly condones the 'very stereotype the law condemns,' *J.E.B.* . . . "

D. THE REQUIREMENT OF A DISCRIMINATORY PURPOSE—THE RELEVANCE OF DISCRIMINATORY IMPACT

Washington v. Davis

426 U.S. 229, 96 S.Ct. 2040, 48 L.Ed.2d 597 (1976).

■ MR. JUSTICE WHITE delivered the opinion of the Court.

This case involves the validity of a qualifying test administered to applicants for positions as police officers in the District of Columbia Metropolitan Police Department. The test was sustained by the District Court but invalidated by the Court of Appeals. We . . . reverse. . . .

I.

[Rejected applicants complained in the District Court] that the Department's recruiting procedures discriminated on the basis of race against black applicants by a series of practices including, but not limited to, a written personnel test which excluded a disproportionately high number of Negro applicants. These practices were asserted to violate respondents' rights "under the due process clause of the Fifth Amendment to the United States Constitution, under 42 U.S.C. § 1981 and under D.C.Code § 1–320." . . . [On cross-motions for summary judgment, the] District Court granted petitioners' and denied respondents' motions. . . .

According to the findings and conclusions of the District Court, to be accepted by the Department and to enter an intensive 17-week training program, the police recruit was required to satisfy certain physical and character standards, to be a high school graduate or its equivalent and to receive a grade of at least 40 on "Test 21," which is "an examination that is used generally throughout the federal service," which "was developed by the [United States] Civil Service Commission not the Police Department" and which was "designed to test verbal ability, vocabulary, reading and comprehension."

The validity of Test 21 was the sole issue before the court on the motions for summary judgment. The District Court noted that there was no claim of "an intentional discrimination or purposeful discriminatory actions" but only a claim that Test 21 bore no relationship to job performance and "has a highly discriminatory impact in screening out black candidates." Petitioners' evidence, the District Court said, warranted three conclusions: "(a) The number of black police officers, while substantial, is not proportionate to the population mix of the city. (b) A higher percentage of blacks fail the Test than whites. (c) The Test has not been validated to establish its reliability for measuring subsequent job performance." Ibid. This showing was deemed sufficient to shift the burden of proof to the defendants in the action, petitioners here; but the court nevertheless concluded that on the undisputed facts respondents were not entitled to relief. The District Court relied on several factors. Since August 1969, 44% of new police force recruits had been black; that figure also represented the proportion of blacks on the total force and was roughly equivalent to 20–29-year-old blacks in the 50-mile radius in which the recruiting efforts of the Police

Department had been concentrated. It was undisputed that the Department had systematically and affirmatively sought to enroll black officers many of whom passed the test but failed to report for duty. The District Court rejected the assertion that Test 21 was culturally slanted to favor whites and was "satisfied that the undisputable facts prove the test to be reasonably and directly related to the requirements of the police recruit training program and that it is neither so designed nor operated to discriminate against otherwise qualified blacks." It was thus not necessary to show that Test 21 was not only a useful indicator of training school performance but had also been validated in terms of job performance—"the lack of job performance validation does not defeat the test, given its direct relationship to recruiting and the valid part it plays in this process." The District Court ultimately concluded that "the proof is wholly lacking that a police officer qualifies on the color of his skin rather than ability" and that the Department "should not be required on this showing to lower standards or to abandon efforts to achieve excellence."

Having lost on both constitutional and statutory issues in the District Court, respondents brought the case to the Court of Appeals claiming that their summary judgment motion, which rested on purely constitutional grounds, should have been granted. The tendered constitutional issue was whether the use of Test 21 invidiously discriminated against Negroes and hence denied them due process of law contrary to the commands of the Fifth Amendment. The Court of Appeals, addressing that issue, announced that it would be guided by Griggs v. Duke Power Co., 401 U.S. 424 (1971), a case involving the interpretation and application of Title VII of the Civil Rights Act of 1964, and held that the statutory standards elucidated in that case were to govern the due process question tendered in this one. . . . The court went on to declare that lack of discriminatory intent in designing and administering Test 21 was irrelevant; the critical fact was rather that a far greater proportion of blacks—four times as many—failed the test than did whites. This disproportionate impact, standing alone and without regard to whether it indicated a discriminatory purpose, was held sufficient to establish a constitutional violation, absent proof by petitioners that the test was an adequate measure of job performance in addition to being an indicator of probable success in the training program, a burden which the court ruled petitioners had failed to discharge.[a]

. . .

II.

Because the Court of Appeals erroneously applied the legal standards applicable to Title VII cases in resolving the constitutional issue before it, we reverse its judgment in respondents' favor. Although the petition for certiorari did not present this ground for reversal, our Rule 40(1)(d)(2) provides that we "may notice a plain error not presented"; and this is an appropriate occasion to invoke the rule.

As the Court of Appeals understood Title VII, employees or applicants proceeding under it need not concern themselves with the employer's possibly discriminatory

---

[a] In Wards Cove Packing Co. v. Atonio, 490 U.S. 642 (1989), the Court interpreted *Griggs* narrowly by holding that once a plaintiff demonstrates that a particular employment practice caused an adverse disproportionate impact on nonwhites, the burden imposed on the employer is only a burden to "produce" a "legitimate business justification" for the practice, not a burden of "proof" of that or any higher level of justification. A plaintiff unable to persuade a trier of fact that a business necessity defense is illegitimate could only prevail by showing that the employer refused to adopt an equally effective alternate employment practice with less disparate impact. In the Civil Rights Act of 1991, P.L. 102–166, 105 Stat. 1071, Congress overrode *Wards Cove,* at least partially, by making the employer, not the challenger, carry the burden of "persuasion" in disparate impact cases that "the challenged practice is job related . . . and consistent with business necessity." The Act also forbids using an employer's "demonstration that an employment practice is required by business necessity . . . as a defense against a claim of intentional discrimination. . . ."

purpose but instead may focus solely on the racially differential impact of the challenged hiring or promotion practices. This is not the constitutional rule. We have never held that the constitutional standard for adjudicating claims of invidious racial discrimination is identical to the standards applicable under Title VII, and we decline to do so today.

The central purpose of the Equal Protection Clause of the Fourteenth Amendment is the prevention of official conduct discriminating on the basis of race. It is also true that the Due Process Clause of the Fifth Amendment contains an equal protection component prohibiting the United States from invidiously discriminating between individuals or groups. Bolling v. Sharpe, 347 U.S. 497 (1954). But our cases have not embraced the proposition that a law or other official act, without regard to whether it reflects a racially discriminatory purpose, is unconstitutional *solely* because it has a racially disproportionate impact.

Almost 100 years ago, Strauder v. West Virginia, 100 U.S. 303 (1879), established that the exclusion of Negroes from grand and petit juries in criminal proceedings violated the Equal Protection Clause, but the fact that a particular jury or a series of juries does not statistically reflect the racial composition of the community does not in itself make out an invidious discrimination forbidden by the Clause. "A purpose to discriminate must be present which may be proven by systematic exclusion of eligible jurymen of the prescribed race or by an unequal application of the law to such an extent as to show intentional discrimination." Akins v. Texas, 325 U.S. 398, 403–404 (1945). A defendant in a criminal case is entitled "to require that the State not deliberately and systematically deny to the members of his race the right to participate as jurors in the administration of justice." See also Carter v. Jury Commission, 396 U.S. 320, 335–337, 339 (1970); Cassell v. Texas, 339 U.S. 282, 287–290 (1950); Patton v. Mississippi, 332 U.S. 463, 468–469 (1947).

The rule is the same in other contexts. Wright v. Rockefeller, 376 U.S. 52 (1964), upheld a New York congressional apportionment statute against claims that district lines had been racially gerrymandered. The challenged districts were made up predominantly of whites or of minority races, and their boundaries were irregularly drawn. The challengers did not prevail because they failed to prove that the New York legislature "was either motivated by racial considerations or in fact drew the districts on racial lines"; the plaintiffs had not shown that the statute "was the product of a state contrivance to segregate on the basis of race or place of origin." . . . The dissenters were in agreement that the issue was whether the "boundaries . . . were purposefully drawn on racial lines." . . .

The school desegregation cases have also adhered to the basic equal protection principle that the invidious quality of a law claimed to be racially discriminatory must ultimately be traced to a racially discriminatory purpose. That there are both predominantly black and predominantly white schools in a community is not alone violative of the Equal Protection Clause. The essential element of *de jure* segregation is "a current condition of segregation resulting from intentional state action . . . the differentiating factor between *de jure* segregation and so-called *de facto* segregation . . . is *purpose* or *intent* to segregate." Keyes v. School District No. 1, 413 U.S. 189, 205, 208 (1973). The Court has also recently rejected allegations of racial discrimination based solely on the statistically disproportionate racial impact of various provisions of the Social Security Act because "the acceptance of appellant's constitutional theory would render suspect each difference in treatment among the grant classes, however lacking the racial motivation and however rational the treatment might be." Jefferson v. Hackney, 406 U.S. 535, 548 (1972). And compare Hunter v. Erickson, 393 U.S. 385 (1969), with James v. Valtierra, 402 U.S. 137 (1971).

This is not to say that the necessary discriminatory racial purpose must be express or appear on the face of the statute, or that a law's disproportionate impact is irrelevant in cases involving Constitution-based claims of racial discrimination. A statute, otherwise neutral on its face, must not be applied so as invidiously to discriminate on the basis of race. Yick Wo v. Hopkins, 118 U.S. 356 (1886). It is also clear from the cases dealing with racial discrimination in the selection of juries that the systematic exclusion of Negroes is itself such an "unequal application of the law ... as to show intentional discrimination." Akins v. Texas, supra, at 404. Smith v. Texas, 311 U.S. 128 (1940); Pierre v. Louisiana, 306 U.S. 354 (1939); Neal v. Delaware, 103 U.S. 370 (1881). A prima facie case of discriminatory purpose may be proved as well by the absence of Negroes on a particular jury combined with the failure of the jury commissioners to be informed of eligible Negro jurors in a community, Hill v. Texas, 316 U.S. 400, 404 (1942), or with racially nonneutral selection procedures, Alexander v. Louisiana, 405 U.S. 625 (1972); Avery v. Georgia, 345 U.S. 559 (1953); Whitus v. Georgia, 385 U.S. 545 (1967). With a prima facie case made out, "the burden of proof shifts to the State to rebut the presumption of unconstitutional action by showing that permissible racially neutral selection criteria and procedures have produced the monochromatic result." Alexander, supra, at 632. See also Turner v. Fouche, 396 U.S. 346, 361 (1970); Eubanks v. Louisiana, 356 U.S. 584, 587 (1958).

Necessarily, an invidious discriminatory purpose may often be inferred from the totality of the relevant facts, including the fact, if it is true, that the law bears more heavily on one race than another. It is also not infrequently true that the discriminatory impact—in the jury cases for example, the total or seriously disproportionate exclusion of Negroes from jury venires—may for all practical purposes demonstrate unconstitutionality because in various circumstances the discrimination is very difficult to explain on nonracial grounds. Nevertheless, we have not held that a law, neutral on its face and serving ends otherwise within the power of government to pursue, is invalid under the Equal Protection Clause simply because it may affect a greater proportion of one race than of another. Disproportionate impact is not irrelevant, but it is not the sole touchstone of an invidious racial discrimination forbidden by the Constitution. Standing alone, it does not trigger the rule, McLaughlin v. Florida, 379 U.S. 184 (1964), that racial classifications are to be subjected to the strictest scrutiny and are justifiable only by the weightiest of considerations.

There are some indications to the contrary in our cases. In Palmer v. Thompson, 403 U.S. 217 (1971), the city of Jackson, Miss., following a court decree to this effect, desegregated all of its public facilities save five swimming pools which had been operated by the city and which, following the decree, were closed by ordinance pursuant to a determination by the city council that closure was necessary to preserve peace and order and that integrated pools could not be economically operated. Accepting the finding that the pools were closed to avoid violence and economic loss, this Court rejected the argument that the abandonment of this service was inconsistent with the outstanding desegregation decree and that the otherwise seemingly permissible ends served by the ordinance could be impeached by demonstrating that racially invidious motivations had prompted the city council's action. The holding was that the city was not overtly or covertly operating segregated pools and was extending identical treatment to both whites and Negroes. The opinion warned against grounding decision on legislative purpose or motivation, thereby lending support for the proposition that the operative effect of the law rather than its purpose is the paramount factor. But the holding of the case was that the legitimate purposes of the ordinance—to preserve peace and avoid deficits—were not open to impeachment by evidence that the councilmen were actually motivated by racial considerations. Whatever dicta the opinion may contain, the decision did not involve, much less invalidate, a statute or ordinance having neutral purposes but disproportionate racial consequences.

Wright v. Council of the City of Emporia, 407 U.S. 451 (1972), also indicates that in proper circumstances, the racial impact of a law, rather than its discriminatory purpose, is the critical factor. That case involved the division of a school district. The issue was whether the division was consistent with an outstanding order of a federal court to desegregate the dual school system found to have existed in the area. The constitutional predicate for the District Court's invalidation of the divided district was "the enforcement until 1969 of racial segregation in the public school system of which Emporia had always been a part." Id., at 459. There was thus no need to find "an independent constitutional violation." Ibid. Citing *Palmer v. Thompson,* we agreed with the District Court that the division of the district had the effect of interfering with the federal decree and should be set aside.

That neither *Palmer* nor *Wright* was understood to have changed the prevailing rule is apparent from *Keyes v. School District No. 1,* supra, where the principal issue in litigation was whether and to what extent there had been purposeful discrimination resulting in a partially or wholly segregated school system. Nor did other later cases, *Alexander v. Louisiana,* supra, and *Jefferson v. Hackney,* supra, indicate that either *Palmer* or *Wright* had worked a fundamental change in equal protection law.[11]

Both before and after *Palmer v. Thompson,* however, various Courts of Appeals have held in several contexts, including public employment, that the substantially disproportionate racial impact of a statute or official practice standing alone and without regard to discriminatory purpose, suffices to prove racial discrimination violating the Equal Protection Clause absent some justification going substantially beyond what would be necessary to validate most other legislative classifications. The cases impressively demonstrate that there is another side to the issue; but, with all due respect, to the extent that those cases rested on or expressed the view that proof of discriminatory racial purpose is unnecessary in making out an equal protection violation, we are in disagreement.

As an initial matter, we have difficulty understanding how a law establishing a racially neutral qualification for employment is nevertheless racially discriminatory and denies "any person equal protection of the laws" simply because a greater proportion of Negroes fail to qualify than members of other racial or ethnic groups. Had respondents, along with all others who had failed Test 21, whether white or black, brought an action claiming that the test denied each of them equal protection of the laws as compared with those who had passed with high enough scores to qualify them as police recruits, it is most unlikely that their challenge would have been sustained. Test 21, which is administered generally to prospective government employees, concededly seeks to ascertain whether those who take it have acquired a particular level of verbal skill; and it is untenable that the Constitution prevents the government from seeking modestly to upgrade the communicative abilities of its employees rather than to be satisfied with some lower level of competence, particularly where the job requires special ability to communicate orally and in writing. Respondents, as Negroes, could no more successfully claim that the test denied them equal protection than could white applicants who also failed. The conclusion would not be different in

---

[11] To the extent that *Palmer* suggests a generally applicable proposition that legislative purpose is irrelevant in constitutional adjudication, our prior cases—as indicated in the text—are to the contrary; and very shortly after *Palmer,* all Members of the Court majority in that case joined the Court's opinion in Lemon v. Kurtzman, 403 U.S. 602 (1971), which dealt with the issue of public financing for private schools and which announced, as the Court had several times before, that the validity of public aid to church-related schools includes close inquiry into the purpose of the challenged statute.

the face of proof that more Negroes than whites had been disqualified by Test 21. That other Negroes also failed to score well would, alone, not demonstrate that respondents individually were being denied equal protection of the laws by the application of an otherwise valid qualifying test being administered to prospective police recruits.

Nor on the facts of the case before us would the disproportionate impact of Test 21 warrant the conclusion that it is a purposeful device to discriminate against Negroes and hence an infringement of the constitutional rights of respondents as well as other black applicants. As we have said, the test is neutral on its face and rationally may be said to serve a purpose the government is constitutionally empowered to pursue. Even agreeing with the District Court that the differential racial effect of Test 21 called for further inquiry, we think the District Court correctly held that the affirmative efforts of the Metropolitan Police Department to recruit black officers, the changing racial composition of the recruit classes and of the force in general, and the relationship of the test to the training program negated any inference that the Department discriminated on the basis of race or that "a police officer qualifies on the color of his skin rather than ability." 348 F.Supp., at 18.

Under Title VII, Congress provided that when hiring and promotion practices disqualifying substantially disproportionate numbers of blacks are challenged, discriminatory purpose need not be proved, and that it is an insufficient response to demonstrate some rational basis for the challenged practices. It is necessary, in addition, that they be "validated" in terms of job performance in any one of several ways, perhaps by ascertaining the minimum skill, ability or potential necessary for the position at issue and determining whether the qualifying tests are appropriate for the selection of qualified applicants for the job in question. However this process proceeds, it involves a more probing judicial review of, and less deference to, the seemingly reasonable acts of administrators and executives than is appropriate under the Constitution where special racial impact, without discriminatory purpose, is claimed. We are not disposed to adopt this more rigorous standard for the purposes of applying the Fifth and the Fourteenth Amendments in cases such as this.

A rule that a statute designed to serve neutral ends is nevertheless invalid, absent compelling justification, if in practice it benefits or burdens one race more than another would be far reaching and would raise serious questions about, and perhaps invalidate, a whole range of tax, welfare, public service, regulatory, and licensing statutes that may be more burdensome to the poor and to the average black than to the more affluent white.[14]

Given that rule, such consequences would perhaps be likely to follow. However, in our view, extension of the rule beyond those areas where it is already applicable by reason of statute, such as in the field of public employment, should await legislative prescription.

As we have indicated, it was error to direct summary judgment for respondents based on the Fifth Amendment.

III.

[The Court also rejected the statutory claims.]

---

[14] Goodman, De Facto School Segregation: Constitutional and Empirical Analysis, 60 Cal.L.Rev. 275, 300 (1972), suggests that disproportionate impact analysis might invalidate "tests and qualifications for voting, draft deferment, public employment, jury service and other government-conferred benefits and opportunities . . . ; [s]ales taxes, bail schedules, utility rates, bridge tolls, license fees, and other state-imposed charges." It has also been argued that minimum wage and usury laws as well as professional licensing requirements would require major modifications in light of the unequal impact rule. Silverman, Equal Protection, Economic Legislation and Racial Discrimination, 25 Vand.L.Rev. 1183 (1972). See also Demsetz, Minorities in the Market Place, 43 N.C.L.Rev. 271.

. . . Based on the evidence before him, the District Judge concluded that Test 21 was directly related to the requirements of the police training program and that a positive relationship between the test and training course performance was sufficient to validate the former, wholly aside from its possible relationship to actual performance as a police officer. . . .

. . .

The judgment of the Court of Appeals accordingly is reversed.

So ordered.

■ MR. JUSTICE STEWART joins Parts I and II of the Court's opinion.

■ MR. JUSTICE STEVENS, concurring.

While I agree with the Court's disposition of this case, I add these comments on the constitutional issue discussed in Part II. . . .

Frequently the most probative evidence of intent will be objective evidence of what actually happened rather than evidence describing the subjective state of mind of the actor. . . .

My point in making this observation is to suggest that the line between discriminatory purpose and discriminatory impact is not nearly as bright, and perhaps not quite as critical, as the reader of the Court's opinion might assume. I agree, of course, that a constitutional issue does not arise every time some disproportionate impact is shown. On the other hand, when the disproportion is as dramatic as in *Gomillion* or *Yick Wo,* it really does not matter whether the standard is phrased in terms of purpose or effect. Therefore, although I accept the statement of the general rule in the Court's opinion, I am not yet prepared to indicate how that standard should be applied in the many cases which have formulated the governing standard in different language.

. . .

■ MR. JUSTICE BRENNAN, with whom MR. JUSTICE MARSHALL joins, dissenting.

[This opinion addressed only the statutory issues explored in Part III of the Court's opinion.]

Village of Arlington Heights v. Metropolitan Housing Development Corp.
429 U.S. 252 (1977).

Metropolitan Housing submitted a request for the rezoning of a 15-acre parcel from single-family to multiple-family classification for the purpose of building apartments for low and moderate income families. The apartments were to be constructed under a federal program requiring an affirmative marketing plan to assure that the development would be racially integrated. Public hearings were held. Some persons objected to the introduction of low income racially integrated housing in the area. Many focused on the fact that the surrounding land had always been zoned for and occupied by single-family housing and neighboring citizens built or purchased their homes relying on the classification. They also noted that the city's consistent policy had been to zone for multiple-family housing only in areas that would serve as a buffer between single-family and commercial developments, whereas the parcel involved here did not adjoin any commercial district. The zoning request was denied and a suit was brought in the federal district court seeking declaratory and injunctive relief. The trial judge ruled for the city but the Court of Appeals reversed, finding that the "ultimate effect" of the denial was racially discriminatory. The Supreme Court reversed the Court of Appeals.

Justice Powell, speaking for the Court, said, in part:

III.

"Our decision last Term in Washington v. Davis, 426 U.S. 229 (1976), made it clear that official action will not be held unconstitutional solely because it results in a racially disproportionate impact. . . .

"*Davis* does not require a plaintiff to prove that the challenged action rested solely on racially discriminatory purposes. Rarely can it be said that a legislature or administrative body operating under a broad mandate made a decision motivated solely by a single concern, or even that a particular purpose was the 'dominant' or 'primary' one. In fact, it is because legislators and administrators are properly concerned with balancing numerous competing considerations that courts refrain from reviewing the merits of their decisions, absent a showing of arbitrariness or irrationality. But racial discrimination is not just another competing consideration. When there is a proof that a discriminatory purpose has been a motivating factor in the decision, this judicial deference is no longer justified.[12]

"Determining whether invidious discriminatory purpose was a motivating factor demands a sensitive inquiry into such circumstantial and direct evidence of intent as may be available. The impact of the official action—whether it 'bears more heavily on one race than another,' Washington v. Davis, 426 U.S., at 242—may provide an important starting point. Sometimes a clear pattern, unexplainable on grounds other than race, emerges from the effect of the state action even when the governing legislation appears neutral on its face. Yick Wo v. Hopkins, 118 U.S. 356 (1886); Guinn v. United States, 238 U.S. 347 (1915); Lane v. Wilson, 307 U.S. 268 (1939); Gomillion v. Lightfoot, 364 U.S. 339 (1960). The evidentiary inquiry is then relatively easy.[13] But such cases are rare. Absent a pattern as stark as that in *Gomillion* or *Yick Wo,* impact alone is not determinative,[14] and the Court must look to other evidence.[15]

"The historical background of the decision is one evidentiary source, particularly if it reveals a series of official actions taken for invidious purposes. . . . The specific sequence of events leading up to the challenged decision also may shed some light on the decisionmaker's purposes. . . . For example, if the property involved here always had been zoned R-5 but suddenly was changed to R-3 when the town learned of MHDC's plans to erect integrated housing, we would have a far different case. Departures from the normal procedural sequence also might afford evidence that improper purposes are playing a role. Substantive departures too may be relevant, particularly if the factors usually considered important by the decisionmaker strongly favor a decision contrary to the one reached.

"The legislative or administrative history may be highly relevant, especially where there are contemporary statements by members of the decision-making body,

---

[12] For a scholarly discussion of legislative motivation, see Brest, Palmer v. Thompson: An Approach to the Problem of Unconstitutional Legislative Motive, 1971 Sup.Ct.Rev. 95, 116–118.

[13] Several of our jury selection cases fall into this category. Because of the nature of the jury selection task, however, we have permitted a finding of constitutional violation even when the statistical pattern does not approach the extremes of *Yick Wo* or *Gomillion.* See, e.g., Turner v. Fouche, 396 U.S. 346, 359 (1970); Sims v. Georgia, 389 U.S. 404, 407 (1967).

[14] This is not to say that a consistent pattern of official racial discrimination is a necessary predicate to a violation of the equal protection clause. A single invidiously discriminatory governmental act—in the exercise of the zoning power as elsewhere—would not necessarily be immunized by the absence of such discrimination in the making of other comparable decisions. See City of Richmond v. United States, 422 U.S. 358, 378 (1975).

[15] In many instances, to recognize the limited probative value of disproportionate impact is merely to acknowledge the "heterogeneity" of the nation's population. Jefferson v. Hackney, 406 U.S. 535, 548 (1972); see also Washington v. Davis, 426 U.S., at 248.

minutes of its meetings, or reports. In some extraordinary instances the members might be called to the stand at trial to testify concerning the purpose of the official action, although even then such testimony frequently will be barred by privilege. . . . [18]

"The foregoing summary identifies, without purporting to be exhaustive, subjects of proper inquiry in determining whether racially discriminatory intent existed. With these in mind, we now address the case before us.

IV.

. . .

"We also have reviewed the evidence. The impact of the Village's decision does arguably bear more heavily on racial minorities. Minorities comprise 18% of the Chicago area population, and 40% of the income groups said to be eligible for Lincoln Green. But there is little about the sequence of events leading up to the decision that would spark suspicion. The area around the Victorian property has been zoned R-3 since 1959, the year when Arlington Heights first adopted a zoning map. Single-family homes surround the 80-acre site, and the Village is undeniably committed to single-family homes as its dominant residential land use. The rezoning request progressed according to the usual procedures. The Plan Commission even scheduled two additional hearings, at least in part to accommodate MHDC and permit it to supplement its presentation with answers to questions generated at the first hearing.

"The statements by the Plan Commission and Village Board members, as reflected in the official minutes, focused almost exclusively on the zoning aspects of the MHDC petition, and the zoning factors on which they relied are not novel criteria in the Village's rezoning decisions. There is no reason to doubt that there has been reliance by some neighboring property owners on the maintenance of single-family zoning in the vicinity. The Village originally adopted its buffer policy long before MHDC entered the picture and has applied the policy too consistently for us to infer discriminatory purpose from its application in this case. Finally, MHDC called one member of the Village Board to the stand at trial. Nothing in her testimony supports an inference of invidious purpose.

"In sum, the evidence does not warrant overturning the concurrent findings of both courts below. Respondents simply failed to carry their burden of proving that discriminatory purpose was a motivating factor in the Village's decision.[21] This conclusion ends the constitutional inquiry. The Court of Appeals' further finding that the Village's decision carried a discriminatory 'ultimate effect' is without independent constitutional significance."

---

[18] This Court has recognized, ever since Fletcher v. Peck, 6 Cranch 87, 130–131 (1810), that judicial inquiries into legislative or executive motivation represent a substantial intrusion into the workings of other branches of government. Placing a decisionmaker on the stand is therefore "usually to be avoided." Citizens to Preserve Overton Park v. Volpe, 401 U.S. 402, 420 (1971). The problems involved have prompted a good deal of scholarly commentary. See Tussman & TenBroek, The Equal Protection of the Laws, 37 Calif.L.Rev. 341, 356–361 (1949); A. Bickel, The Least Dangerous Branch, 208–221 (1962); Ely, Legislative and Administrative Motivation in Constitutional Law, 79 Yale L.J. 1205 (1970); Brest supra, n. 8.

[21] Proof that the decision by the Village was motivated in part by a racially discriminatory purpose would not necessarily have required invalidation of the challenged decision. Such proof would, however, have shifted to the Village the burden of establishing that the same decision would have resulted even had the impermissible purpose not been considered. If this were established, the complaining party in a case of this kind no longer fairly could attribute the injury complained of to improper consideration of a discriminatory purpose. In such circumstances, there would be no justification for judicial interference with the challenged decision. But in this case respondents failed to make the required threshold showing. See Mt. Healthy City School Dist. Bd. of Education v. Doyle, 429 U.S. 274.

Justices Marshall and Brennan concurred in Part III of the opinion set out above but indicated that in their view the case should be remanded to the court of appeals for it to reassess the evidence on discriminatory purpose. Justice White also dissented, calling for a remand to the court of appeals. Justice Stevens took no part in the decision.

Personnel Administrator of Massachusetts v. Feeney

442 U.S. 256 (1979).

Massachusetts' veterans' preference for state civil service positions was challenged as unconstitutional gender discrimination. Under the law, all veterans had an "absolute lifetime preference"; veterans with passing scores for classified civil service jobs were ranked above all other candidates. Since 98% of veterans were male, and the preference for veterans with passing scores was absolute, the impact of the law was, obviously, to disqualify female eligibles from consideration in much greater proportion than male eligibles. The Court rejected the argument that Massachusetts had discriminated against women in violation of the Equal Protection Clause. Justice Stewart's opinion for the Court said, in part:

"The cases of *Washington v. Davis,* and *Village of Arlington Heights v. Metropolitan Housing Development Corp.,* recognize that when a neutral law has a disparate impact upon a group that has historically been the victim of discrimination, an unconstitutional purpose may still be at work. But those cases signalled no departure from the settled rule that the Fourteenth Amendment guarantees equal laws, not equal results. . . .

"When a statute gender-neutral on its face is challenged on the ground that its effects upon women are disproportionately adverse, a two-fold inquiry is thus appropriate. The first question is whether the statutory classification is indeed neutral in the sense that it is not gender-based. If the classification itself, covert or overt, is not based upon gender, the second question is whether the adverse effect reflects invidious gender-based discrimination. . . . In this second inquiry, impact provides an 'important starting point,' but purposeful discrimination is 'the condition that offends the Constitution.' . . .

   . . .

"The question whether ch. 31, § 23 establishes a classification that is overtly or covertly based upon gender must first be considered. The appellee has conceded that ch. 31, § 23 is neutral on its face. . . .

". . . Apart from the fact that the definition of 'veterans' in the statute has always been neutral as to gender and that Massachusetts has consistently defined veteran status in a way that has been inclusive of women who have served in the military, this is not a law that can plausibly be explained only as a gender-based classification. Indeed, it is not a law that can rationally be explained on that ground. Veteran status is not uniquely male. Although few women benefit from the preference, the nonveteran class is not substantially all-female. To the contrary, significant numbers of nonveterans are men, and all nonveterans—male as well as female—are placed at a disadvantage. Too many men are affected to permit the inference that the statute is but a pretext for preferring men over women.

"Moreover, as the District Court implicitly found, the purposes of the statute provide the surest explanation for its impact. Just as there are cases in which impact alone can unmask an invidious classification, cf. *Yick Wo v. Hopkins,* there are others, in which—notwithstanding impact—the legitimate noninvidious purposes of a law cannot be missed. This is one. The distinction . . . is, as it seems to be, quite simply between veterans and nonveterans, not between men and women.

"The dispositive question, then, is whether the appellee has shown that a gender-based discriminatory purpose has, at least in some measure, shaped the Massachusetts veterans' preference legislation. . . .

"The contention that this veterans' preference is 'inherently non-neutral' or 'gender-based' presumes that the State, by favoring veterans, intentionally incorporated into its public employment policies the panoply of sex-based and assertedly discriminatory federal laws that have prevented all but a handful of women from becoming veterans. There are two serious difficulties with this argument. First, it is wholly at odds with the District Court's central finding that Massachusetts has not offered a preference to veterans for the purpose of discriminating against women. Second, it cannot be reconciled with the assumption made by both the appellee and the District Court that a more limited hiring preference for veterans could be sustained. Taken together, these difficulties are fatal.

. . .

"To be sure, this case is unusual in that it involves a law that by design is not neutral. The law overtly prefers veterans as such. As opposed to the written test at issue in *Davis,* it does not purport to define a job related characteristic. To the contrary, it confers upon a specifically described group—perceived to be particularly deserving—a competitive head start. But the District Court found, and the appellee has not disputed, that this legislative choice was legitimate. The basic distinction between veterans and nonveterans, having been found not gender-based, and the goals of the preference having been found worthy, Ch. 31 must be analyzed as is any other neutral law that casts a greater burden upon women as a group than upon men as a group. The enlistment policies of the armed services may well have discriminated on the basis of sex. See Frontiero v. Richardson, 411 U.S. 677; cf. Schlesinger v. Ballard, 419 U.S. 498. But the history of discrimination against women in the military is not on trial in this case.

"The appellee's ultimate argument rests upon the presumption, common to the criminal and civil law, that a person intends the natural and foreseeable consequences of his voluntary actions. . . .

". . . [I]t cannot seriously be argued that the legislature of Massachusetts could have been unaware that most veterans are men. It would thus be disingenuous to say that the adverse consequences of this legislation for women were unintended, in the sense that they were not volitional or in the sense that they were not foreseeable.

" 'Discriminatory purpose,' however, implies more than intent as volition or intent as awareness of consequences. . . . It implies that the decisionmaker, in this case a state legislature, selected or reaffirmed a particular course of action at least in part 'because of,' not merely 'in spite of,' its adverse effects upon an identifiable group. Yet nothing in the record demonstrates that this preference for veterans was originally devised or subsequently re-enacted because it would accomplish the collateral goal of keeping women in a stereotypic and predefined place in the Massachusetts Civil Service."

Justice Stevens' concurring opinion, joined by Justice White, said:

"While I concur in the Court's opinion, I confess that I am not at all sure that there is any difference between the two questions posed. . . . If a classification is not overtly based on gender, I am inclined to believe the question whether it is covertly gender-based is the same as the question whether its adverse effects reflect invidious gender-based discrimination. However the question is phrased, for me the answer is largely provided by the fact that the number of males disadvantaged by Massachusetts' Veterans Preference (1,867,000) is sufficiently large—and sufficiently close to the number of disadvantaged females (2,954,000)—to refute the claim that the rule was intended to benefit males as a class over females as a class."

Justice Marshall's dissent, joined by Justice Brennan, concluded that Massachusetts' veterans' preference system constituted "intentional" gender-based discrimination. The foreseeable impact of the law was so disproportionate that the State should have the burden to establish that "sex-based considerations played no part in the choice of the particular legislative scheme."

"Clearly, that burden was not sustained here. The legislative history of the statute reflects the Commonwealth's patent appreciation of the impact the preference system would have on women, and an equally evident desire to mitigate that impact only with respect to certain traditionally female occupations. Until 1971, the statute and implementing civil service regulations exempted from operation of the preference any job requisitions 'especially calling for women.' . . . In practice, this exemption, coupled with the absolute preference for veterans, has created a gender-based civil service hierarchy, with women occupying low grade clerical and secretarial jobs and men holding more responsible and remunerative positions.

"Thus, for over 70 years, the Commonwealth has maintained, as an integral part of its veteran's preference system, an exemption relegating female civil service applicants to occupations traditionally filled by women. Such a statutory scheme both reflects and perpetuates precisely the kind of archaic assumptions about women's roles which we have previously held invalid. . . ."

Hunter v. Underwood

471 U.S. 222 (1985).

Section 182 of the Alabama Constitution, adopted at a convention in 1901, disenfranchised persons convicted of, among other offenses, "any crime . . . involving moral turpitude." Edwards, a black, and Underwood, a white, were blocked from the voter roles because they each had been convicted of presenting a worthless check. Their federal district court suit contended that § 182 had been adopted intentionally to disenfranchise blacks on account of their race. On this issue the district court treated Edwards as the representative of a class of black members and ruled for the defendants. The Court of Appeals reversed, holding that the evidence showed that § 182 had disenfranchised 10 times as many blacks as whites, and that it had been adopted for the purpose of preventing blacks from voting. The Supreme Court affirmed, all joining an opinion by Justice Rehnquist (Justice Powell not participating).

The Court said first that a neutral state law producing racially disproportionate effects will be invalidated only if it is shown that racially discriminatory intent or purpose was a substantial factor behind enacting the law.

"Proving the motivation behind official action is often a problematic undertaking. See Rogers v. Lodge, 458 U.S. 613 (1982). When we move from an examination of a board of county commissioners such as was involved in Rogers to a body the size of the Alabama Constitutional Convention of 1901, the difficulties in determining the actual motivations of the various legislators that produced a given decision increase." But no such difficulties were present here. Evidence from historians and from speeches at the Convention made it clear that zeal for white supremacy ran rampant at the convention. Indeed, the appellants did not seriously dispute that fact. What appellants did argue was that the real purpose behind § 182 was to disenfranchise both poor whites and blacks.

"Even were we to accept this explanation as correct, it hardly saves § 182 from invalidity. The explanation concedes both that discrimination against blacks, as well as against poor whites, was a motivating factor for the provision and that § 182 certainly would not have been adopted by the convention or ratified by the electorate in the absence of the racially discriminatory motivation.

"Citing Palmer v. Thompson, 403 U.S., at 224, and Michael M. v. Superior Court of Sonoma County, 450 U.S. 464, 472, n. 7 (1981) (plurality opinion), appellants make the further argument that the existence of a permissible motive for § 182, namely the disenfranchisement of poor whites, trumps any proof of a parallel impermissible motive. Whether or not intentional disenfranchisement of poor whites would qualify as a 'permissible motive' within the meaning of *Palmer* and *Michael M.*, it is clear that where both impermissible racial motivation and racially discriminatory impact are demonstrated, *Arlington Heights* and *Mt. Healthy* supply the proper analysis. Under the view that the Court of Appeals could properly take of the evidence, an additional purpose to discriminate against poor whites would not render nugatory the purpose to discriminate against all blacks, and it is beyond peradventure that the latter was a 'but-for' motivation for the enactment of § 182.

. . .

"At oral argument in this Court, the State suggested that, regardless of the original purpose of § 182, events occurring in the succeeding 80 years had legitimated the provision. . . . Without deciding whether § 182 would be valid if enacted today without any impermissible motivation, we simply observe that its original enactment was motivated by a desire to discriminate against blacks on account of race and the section continues to this day to have that effect. As such, it violates equal protection under *Arlington Heights*.

"Finally, appellants contend that the State is authorized by the Tenth Amendment and § 2 of the Fourteenth Amendment to deny the franchise to persons who commit misdemeanors involving moral turpitude. For the reasons we have stated, the enactment of § 182 violated the Fourteenth Amendment, and the Tenth Amendment cannot save legislation prohibited by the subsequently enacted Fourteenth Amendment. The single remaining question is whether § 182 is excepted from the operation of the Equal Protection Clause of § 1 of the Fourteenth Amendment by the 'other crime' provision of § 2 of that Amendment. Without again considering the implicit authorization of § 2 to deny the vote to citizens 'for participation in rebellion, or other crime,' see Richardson v. Ramirez, 418 U.S. 24 (1974), we are confident that § 2 was not designed to permit the purposeful racial discrimination attending the enactment and operation of § 182 which otherwise violates § 1 of the Fourteenth Amendment. Nothing in our opinion in *Richardson v. Ramirez* . . . suggests the contrary."

E. "BENIGN" DISCRIMINATION: AFFIRMATIVE ACTION, QUOTAS, PREFERENCES BASED ON GENDER OR RACE

1. CLASSIFICATIONS ADVANTAGING FEMALES

Kahn v. Shevin

416 U.S. 351, 94 S.Ct. 1734, 40 L.Ed.2d 189 (1974).

■ MR. JUSTICE DOUGLAS delivered the opinion of the Court.

Since at least 1885, Florida has provided for some form of property tax exemption for widows. The current law granting all widows an annual $500 exemption, Fla.Stat.

§ 196.191(7), F.S.A., has been essentially unchanged since 1941. Appellant Kahn is a widower who lives in Florida and applied for the exemption to the Dade County Tax Assessor's Office. It was denied because the statute offers no analogous benefit for widowers. Kahn then sought a declaratory judgment in the Circuit Court for Dade County, Florida, and that court held the statute violative of the Equal Protection Clause of the Fourteenth Amendment because the classification "widow" was based upon gender. The Florida Supreme Court reversed, finding the classification valid because it has a "fair and substantial relation to the object of the legislation," that object being the reduction of "the disparity between the economic capabilities of a man and a woman." Kahn appealed here. . . . We affirm.

There can be no dispute that the financial difficulties confronting the lone woman in Florida or in any other State exceed those facing the man. Whether from overt discrimination or from the socialization process of a male dominated culture, the job market is inhospitable to the woman seeking any but the lowest paid jobs. There are of course efforts underway to remedy this situation. On the federal level Title VII of the Civil Rights Act of 1964 prohibits covered employers and labor unions from discrimination on the basis of sex, 42 U.S.C. § 2000e–2(a), (b), (c), as does the Equal Pay Act of 1963, 29 U.S.C. § 206(d). But firmly entrenched practices are resistant to such pressures, and indeed, data compiled by the Women's Bureau of the United States Department of Labor shows that in 1972 women working full time had a median income which was only 57.9% of the male median—a figure actually six points lower than had been achieved in 1955. Other data points in the same direction. The disparity is likely to be exacerbated for the widow. While the widower can usually continue in the occupation which preceded his spouse's death in many cases the widow will find herself suddenly forced into a job market with which she is unfamiliar, and in which, because of her former economic dependency, she will have fewer skills to offer.

There can be no doubt therefore that Florida's differing treatment of widows and widowers "rest[s] upon some ground of difference having a fair and substantial relation to the object of the legislation." Reed v. Reed, 404 U.S. 71, 76. . . .

This is not a case like Frontiero v. Richardson, 411 U.S. 677, where the Government denied its female employees both substantive and procedural benefits granted males "*solely* for administrative convenience." Id., at 690 (emphasis in original).[8] We deal here with a state tax law reasonably designed to further the state policy of cushioning the financial impact of spousal loss upon the sex for whom that loss imposes a disproportionately heavy burden. We have long held that "[w]here taxation is concerned and no specific federal right, apart from equal protection, is imperilled, the States have large leeway in making classifications and drawing lines which in their judgment produce reasonable systems of taxation." Lehnhausen v. Lake Shore Auto Parts Co., 410 U.S. 356, 359. A state tax law is not arbitrary although it "discriminate[s] in favor of a certain class . . . if the discrimination is founded upon a reasonable distinction, or difference in state policy," not in conflict with the Federal Constitution. Allied Stores v. Bowers, 358 U.S. 522, 528. This principle has weathered nearly a century of Supreme Court adjudication, and it applies here as well. The statute before us is well within those limits.[10]

---

[8] And in *Frontiero* the plurality opinion also noted that the statutes there were "not in any sense designed to rectify the effects of past discrimination against women. On the contrary, these statutes seize upon a group—women—who have historically suffered discrimination in employment, and rely on the effects of this past discrimination as a justification for heaping on additional economic disadvantages." . . . 411 U.S. 677, 689 n. 22. . . .

[10] The dissents argue that the Florida Legislature could have drafted the statute differently, so that its purpose would have been accomplished more precisely. But the issue of course is not whether the statute could have been drafted more wisely, but whether the lines chosen by the Florida

Affirmed.

■ MR. JUSTICE BRENNAN, with whom MR. JUSTICE MARSHALL joins, dissenting.

... In my view ... a legislative classification that distinguishes potential beneficiaries solely by reference to their gender-based status as widows or widowers, like classifications based upon race, alienage, and national origin, must be subjected to close judicial scrutiny, because it focuses upon generally immutable characteristics over which individuals have little or no control, and also because gender-based classifications too often have been inexcusably utilized to stereotype and stigmatize politically powerless segments of society. See Frontiero v. Richardson, 411 U.S. 677 (1973). The Court is not therefore free to sustain the statute on the ground that it rationally promotes legitimate governmental interests; rather, such suspect classifications can be sustained only when the State bears the burden of demonstrating that the challenged legislation serves overriding or compelling interests that cannot be achieved either by a more carefully tailored legislative classification or by the use of feasible less drastic means. While ... the statute serves a compelling governmental interest by "cushioning the financial impact of spousal loss upon the sex for whom that loss imposes a disproportionately heavy burden," I think [it] is invalid because the State's interest can be served equally well by a more narrowly drafted statute.

Gender-based classifications cannot be sustained merely because they promote legitimate governmental interests, such as efficacious administration of government. *Frontiero v. Richardson,* supra; Reed v. Reed, 404 U.S. 71 (1971). ... On the contrary, any statutory scheme which draws a sharp line between the sexes, *solely* for the purpose of achieving administrative convenience, necessarily commands "dissimilar treatment for men and women who are ... similarly situated," and therefore involves the "very kind of arbitrary legislative choice forbidden by the [constitution]. ..." Reed v. Reed, 404 U.S., at 77, 76. "*Frontiero v. Richardson,*. ... But Florida's justification of § 196.191(7) is not that it serves administrative convenience or helps to preserve the public fisc. Rather, the asserted justification is that § 196.191(7) is an affirmative step toward alleviating the effects of past economic discrimination against women."

I agree that, in providing special benefits for a needy segment of society long the victim of purposeful discrimination and neglect, the statute serves the compelling state interest of achieving equality for such groups. No one familiar with this country's history of pervasive sex discrimination against women can doubt the need for remedial measures to correct the resulting economic imbalances. Indeed, the extent of the economic disparity between men and women is dramatized by the data cited by the Court. By providing a property tax exemption for widows, § 196.01(7) assists in reducing that economic disparity for a class of women particularly disadvantaged by the legacy of economic discrimination. In that circumstance, the purpose and effect of the suspect classification is ameliorative; the statute neither stigmatizes nor denigrates widowers not also benefited by the legislation. Moreover, inclusion of needy widowers within the class of beneficiaries would not further the State's overriding interest in remedying the economic effects of past sex discrimination for needy victims

---

Legislature are within constitutional limitations. The dissent would use the Equal Protection Clause as a vehicle for reinstating notions of substantive due process that have been repudiated. ...

Gender has never been rejected as an impermissible classification in all instances. Congress has not so far drafted women into the Armed Services. 50 App.U.S.C. § 454. The famous Brandeis Brief in Muller v. Oregon, 208 U.S. 412, on which the court specifically relied, id., at 419–420, emphasized that the special physical organization of women has a bearing on the "conditions under which she should be permitted to toil." Id., at 420. These instances are pertinent to the problem in the tax field. ...

of that discrimination. While doubtless some widowers are in financial need, no one suggests that such need results from sex discrimination as in the case of widows.

The statute nevertheless fails to satisfy the requirements of equal protection, since the State has not borne its burden of proving that its compelling interest could not be achieved by a more precisely tailored statute or by use of feasible less drastic means. Section 196.191(7) is plainly overinclusive, for the $500 property tax exemption may be obtained by a financially independent heiress as well as by an unemployed widow with dependent children. The State has offered nothing to explain why inclusion of widows of substantial economic means was necessary to advance the State's interest in ameliorating the effects of past economic discrimination against women.

Moreover, alternative means of classification, narrowing the class of widow beneficiaries, appear readily available. The exemption is granted only to widows who complete and file with the tax assessor a form application establishing their status as widows. By merely redrafting that form to exclude widows who earn annual incomes, or possess assets, in excess of specified amounts, the State could readily narrow the class of beneficiaries to those widows for whom the effects of past economic discrimination against women have been a practical reality.

■ MR. JUSTICE WHITE, dissenting.

The Florida tax exemption at issue here is available to all widows but not to widowers. The presumption is that all widows are financially more needy and less trained or less ready for the job market than men. It may be that most widows have been occupied as housewife, mother and homemaker and are not immediately prepared for employment. But there are many rich widows who need no largess from the State; many others are highly trained and have held lucrative positions long before the death of their husbands. At the same time, there are many widowers who are needy and who are in more desperate financial straits and have less access to the job market than many widows. Yet none of them qualifies for the exemption.

I find the discrimination invidious and violative of the Equal Protection Clause. There is merit in giving poor widows a tax break, but gender-based classifications are suspect and require more justification than the State has offered.

I perceive no purpose served by the exemption other than to alleviate current economic necessity, but the State extends the exemption to widows who do not need the help and denies it to widowers who do. It may be administratively inconvenient to make individual determinations of entitlement and to extend the exemption to needy men as well as needy women, but administrative efficiency is not an adequate justification for discriminations based purely on sex. Frontiero v. Richardson, 411 U.S. 677 (1973); Reed v. Reed, 404 U.S. 71 (1971).

It may be suggested that the State is entitled to prefer widows over widowers because their assumed need is rooted in past and present economic discrimination against women. But this is not a credible explanation of Florida's tax exemption; for if the State's purpose was to compensate for past discrimination against females, surely it would not have limited the exemption to women who are widows. Moreover, even if past discrimination is considered to be the criterion for current tax exemption, the State nevertheless ignores all those widowers who have felt the effects of economic discrimination, whether as a member of a racial group or as one of the many who cannot escape the cycle of poverty. It seems to me that the State in this case is merely conferring an economic benefit in the form of a tax exemption and has not adequately explained why women should be treated differently than men.

I dissent.

Califano v. Webster

430 U.S. 313 (1977).

A complex formula for computing retirement benefits under social security permitted a female wage earner to exclude from the computation of her "average monthly wage" three more lower earning years than a similarly situated male wage earner could exclude. This resulted in a higher level of monthly old-age benefits for the retired female wage earner. In a Per Curiam opinion the Court held the classification valid, saying, in part:

"To withstand scrutiny under the equal protection component of the Fifth Amendment's Due Process Clause, 'classifications by gender must serve important governmental objectives and must be substantially related to achievement of those objectives.' Craig v. Boren, 429 U.S. 190, 197 (1976). Reduction of the disparity in economic condition between men and women caused by the long history of discrimination against women has been recognized as such an important governmental objective. Schlesinger v. Ballard, 419 U.S. 498 (1975); Kahn v. Shevin, 416 U.S. 351 (1974). But 'the mere recitation of a benign, compensatory purpose is not an automatic shield which protects against any inquiry into the actual purposes underlying a statutory scheme.' Weinberger v. Wiesenfeld, 420 U.S. 636, 648 (1975). Accordingly, we have rejected attempts to justify gender classifications as compensation for past discrimination against women when the classifications in fact penalized women wage earners, Califano v. Goldfarb, 430 U.S. 199, Weinberger v. Wiesenfeld, supra, at 645, or when the statutory structure and its legislative history revealed that the classification was not enacted as compensation for past discrimination. . . .

"The statutory scheme involved here is more analogous to those upheld in *Kahn* and *Ballard* than to those struck down in *Wiesenfeld* and *Goldfarb*. The more favorable treatment of the female wage earner enacted here was not a result of 'archaic and overbroad generalizations' about women, *Schlesinger v. Ballard* . . . or of 'the role-typing society has long imposed' upon women, Stanton v. Stanton, 421 U.S. 7, 15 (1975), such as casual assumptions that women are 'the weaker sex' or are more likely to be child-rearers or dependents. Cf. Califano v. Goldfarb, supra; Weinberger v. Wiesenfeld, supra. Rather, 'the only discernible purpose of [§ 215's more favorable treatment is] the permissible one of redressing our society's longstanding disparate treatment of women.' Califano v. Goldfarb. . . .

"The challenged statute operated directly to compensate women for past economic discrimination. Retirement benefits under the Act are based on past earnings. But as we have recognized: 'Whether from overt discrimination or from the socialization process of a male-dominated culture, the job market is inhospitable to the woman seeking any but the lowest paid jobs.' Kahn v. Shevin, 416 U.S. at 353. . . . Thus, allowing women, who as such have been unfairly hindered from earning as much as men, to eliminate additional low-earning years from the calculation of their retirement benefits works directly to remedy some part of the effect of past discrimination. Cf. Schlesinger v. Ballard, supra, at 508.

"The legislative history of § 215(b)(3) also reveals that Congress directly addressed the justification for differing treatment of men and women in the former version of that section and purposely enacted the more favorable treatment for female wage earners to compensate for past employment discrimination against women. . . ."

Chief Justice Burger, joined by Justices Stewart, Blackmun, and Rehnquist concurred in the judgment.

Orr v. Orr

440 U.S. 268 (1979).

The Court held unconstitutional Alabama's statutory scheme imposing alimony obligations on husbands but not wives. It rejected the argument that the gender distinction was justified, because of the disparity between the economic condition of men and women, to provide support for needy wives of broken marriages. Justice Brennan's opinion for the Court said in part:

"Ordinarily, we would begin the analysis of the 'needy spouse' objective by considering whether sex is a sufficiently 'accurate proxy' for dependency to establish that the gender classification rests 'upon some ground of difference having a fair and substantial relation to the object of the legislation.' Similarly, we would initially approach the 'compensation' rationale by asking whether women had in fact been significantly discriminated against in the sphere to which the statute applied a sex-based classification, leaving the sexes 'not similarly situated with respect to opportunities' in that sphere.[11]

"But in this case, even if sex were a reliable proxy for need, and even if the institution of marriage did discriminate against women, these factors still would 'not adequately justify the salient features of' Alabama's statutory scheme. Under the statute, individualized hearings at which the parties' relative financial circumstances are considered *already* occur. There is no reason, therefore, to use sex as a proxy for need. Needy males could be helped along with needy females with little if any additional burden on the State. In such circumstances, not even an administrative convenience rationale exists to justify operating by generalization or proxy. Similarly, since individualized hearings can determine which women were in fact discriminated against vis-a-vis their husbands, as well as which family units defied the stereotype and left the husband dependent on the wife, Alabama's alleged compensatory purpose may be effectuated without placing burdens solely on husbands. Progress toward fulfilling such a purpose would not be hampered, and it would cost the State nothing more, if it were to treat men and women equally by making alimony burdens independent of sex. 'Thus, the gender-based distinction is gratuitous; without it the statutory scheme would only provide benefits to those men who are in fact similarly situated to the women the statute aids,' and the effort to help those women would not in any way be compromised.

"Moreover, use of a gender classification actually produces perverse results in this case. As compared to a gender-neutral law placing alimony obligations on the spouse able to pay, the present Alabama statutes give an advantage only to the financially secure wife whose husband is in need. Although such a wife might have to pay alimony under a gender-neutral statute, the present statutes exempt her from that obligation. Thus, '[t]he [wives] who benefit from the disparate treatment are those who were . . . nondependent on their husbands.' They are precisely those who are not 'needy spouses' and who are 'least likely to have been victims of . . . discrimination,' by the institution of marriage. A gender-based classification which, as compared to a gender-neutral one, generates additional benefits only for those it has no reason to prefer cannot survive equal protection scrutiny.

"Legislative classifications which distribute benefits and burdens on the basis of gender carry the inherent risk of reinforcing the stereotypes about the 'proper place' of women and their need for special protection. Thus, even statutes purportedly designed to compensate for and ameliorate the effects of past discrimination must be carefully

---

[11] We would also consider whether the purportedly compensatory "classifications in fact penalized women," and whether "the statutory structure and its legislative history revealed that the classification was not enacted as compensation for past discrimination."

tailored. Where, as here, the State's compensatory and ameliorative purposes are as well served by a gender-neutral classification as one that gender-classifies and therefore carries with it the baggage of sexual stereotypes, the State cannot be permitted to classify on the basis of sex. And this is doubly so where the choice made by the State appears to redound—if only indirectly—to the benefit of those without need for special solicitude.

"Having found Alabama's alimony statutes unconstitutional, we reverse the judgment below and remand the cause for further proceedings not inconsistent with this opinion. That disposition, of course, leaves the state courts free . . . on remand to consider whether Mr. Orr's stipulated agreement to pay alimony, or other grounds of gender-neutral state law, bind him to continue his alimony payments."

Chief Justice Burger, Justice Powell, and Justice Rehnquist, dissenting on other issues, did not reach the equal protection question.

Mississippi University for Women v. Hogan
458 U.S. 718, 102 S.Ct. 3331, 73 L.Ed.2d 1090 (1982).

■ JUSTICE O'CONNOR delivered the opinion of the Court.

This case presents the narrow issue of whether a state statute that excludes males from enrolling in a state-supported professional nursing school violates the Equal Protection Clause of the Fourteenth Amendment.

I

The facts are not in dispute. In 1884, the Mississippi legislature created the Mississippi Industrial Institute and College for the Education of White Girls of the State of Mississippi, now the oldest state-supported all-female college in the United States. . . . The school, known today as Mississippi University for Women (MUW), has from its inception limited its enrollment to women.

In 1971, MUW established a School of Nursing, initially offering a two-year associate degree. Three years later, the school instituted a four-year baccalaureate program in nursing and today also offers a graduate program. The School of Nursing has its own faculty and administrative officers and establishes its own criteria for admission.

Respondent, Joe Hogan, is a registered nurse but does not hold a baccalaureate degree in nursing. Since 1974, he has worked as a nursing supervisor in a medical center in Columbus, the city in which MUW is located. In 1979, Hogan applied for admission to the MUW School of Nursing's baccalaureate program. Although he was otherwise qualified, he was denied admission to the School of Nursing solely because of his sex. School officials informed him that he could audit the courses in which he was interested, but could not enroll for credit.

Hogan [sued in federal district], claiming the single-sex admissions policy of MUW's School of Nursing violated the Equal Protection Clause . . . .

[T]he District Court denied preliminary injunctive relief. . . .

The . . . Fifth Circuit reversed, holding that, because the admissions policy discriminates on the basis of gender, the District Court improperly used a "rational relationship" test to judge the constitutionality of the policy. . . .

We . . . affirm. . . .[7]

II

We begin our analysis aided by several firmly-established principles. Because the challenged policy expressly discriminates among applicants on the basis of gender, it is subject to scrutiny under the Equal Protection Clause of the Fourteenth Amendment. Reed v. Reed, 404 U.S. 71, 75 (1971). That this statute discriminates against males rather than against females does not exempt it from scrutiny or reduce the standard of review.[8] Caban v. Mohammed, 441 U.S. 380, 394 (1979); Orr v. Orr, 440 U.S. 268, 279 (1979). Our decisions also establish that the party seeking to uphold a statute that classifies individuals on the basis of their gender must carry the burden of showing an "exceedingly persuasive justification" for the classification. Kirchberg v. Feenstra, 450 U.S. 455, 461 (1981); Personnel Administrator of Massachusetts v. Feeney, 442 U.S. 256, 273 (1979). The burden is met only by showing at least that the classification serves "important governmental objectives and that the discriminatory means employed" are "substantially related to the achievement of those objectives." Wengler v. Druggists Mutual Insurance Co., 446 U.S. 142, 150 (1980).

Although the test . . . is straightforward, it must be applied free of fixed notions concerning the roles and abilities of males and females. Care must be taken in ascertaining whether the statutory objective itself reflects archaic and stereotypic notions. Thus, if the statutory objective is to exclude or "protect" members of one gender because they are presumed to suffer from an inherent handicap or to be innately inferior, the objective itself is illegitimate. See Frontiero v. Richardson . . . (1973) (plurality opinion).

If the State's objective is legitimate and important, we next determine whether the requisite direct, substantial relationship between objective and means is present. The purpose of requiring that close relationship is to assure that the validity of a classification is determined through reasoned analysis rather than through the mechanical application of traditional, often inaccurate, assumptions about the proper roles of men and women. The need for the requirement is amply revealed by reference to the broad range of statutes already invalidated by this Court, statutes that relied upon the simplistic, outdated assumption that gender could be used as a "proxy for other, more germane bases of classification," Craig v. Boren, 429 U.S. 190, 198 (1976), to establish a link between objective and classification.

. . .

III

A

The State's primary justification for maintaining the single-sex admissions policy of MUW's School of Nursing is that it compensates for discrimination against women

---

[7] . . . Hogan sought only admission to the School of Nursing. . . . [W]e decline to address . . . whether MUW's admissions policy, as applied to males seeking admission to schools other than the School of Nursing, violates the Fourteenth Amendment.

[8] Without question, MUW's admissions policy worked to Hogan's disadvantage. Although Hogan could have attended classes and received credit in one of Mississippi's state-supported coeducational nursing programs, none of which was located in Columbus, he could attend only by driving a considerable distance from his home. A similarly situated female would not have been required to choose between foregoing credit and bearing that inconvenience. Moreover, since many students enrolled in the School of Nursing hold full-time jobs, Hogan's female colleagues had available an opportunity, not open to Hogan, to obtain credit for additional training. The policy of denying males the right to obtain credit toward a baccalaureate degree thus imposed upon Hogan "a burden he would not bear were he female." Orr v. Orr, 440 U.S. 268, 273 (1979).

and, therefore, constitutes educational affirmative action. As applied to the School of Nursing, we find the State's argument unpersuasive.

In limited circumstances, a gender-based classification favoring one sex can be justified if it intentionally and directly assists members of the sex that is disproportionately burdened. See Schlesinger v. Ballard, 419 U.S. 498 (1975). However, we consistently have emphasized that "the mere recitation of a benign, compensatory purpose is not an automatic shield which protects against any inquiry into the actual purposes underlying a statutory scheme." Weinberger v. Wiesenfeld, 420 U.S. 636, 648 (1975). The same searching analysis must be made, regardless of whether the State's objective is to eliminate family controversy, Reed v. Reed, supra, to achieve administrative efficiency, Frontiero v. Richardson, supra, or to balance the burdens borne by males and females.

It is readily apparent that a State can evoke a compensatory purpose to justify an otherwise discriminatory classification only if members of the gender benefited by the classification actually suffer a disadvantage related to the classification. We considered such a situation in Califano v. Webster, 430 U.S. 313 (1977), which involved a challenge to a statutory classification that allowed women to eliminate more low-earning years than men for purposes of computing Social Security retirement benefits. Although the effect of the classification was to allow women higher monthly benefits than were available to men with the same earning history, we upheld the statutory scheme, noting that it took into account that women "as such have been unfairly hindered from earning as much as men" and "work[ed] directly to remedy" the resulting economic disparity.

A similar pattern of discrimination against women influenced our decision in Schlesinger v. Ballard, 419 U.S. 498 (1975). There, we considered a federal statute that granted female Naval officers a 13-year tenure of commissioned service before mandatory discharge, but accorded male officers only a nine-year tenure. We recognized that, because women were barred from combat duty, they had had fewer opportunities for promotion than had their male counterparts. By allowing women an additional four years to reach a particular rank before subjecting them to mandatory discharge, the statute directly compensated for other statutory barriers to advancement.

In sharp contrast, Mississippi has made no showing that women lacked opportunities to obtain training in the field of nursing or to attain positions of leadership in that field when the MUW School of Nursing opened its door or that women currently are deprived of such opportunities. In fact, in 1970, the year before the School of Nursing's first class enrolled, women earned 94 percent of the nursing baccalaureate degrees conferred in Mississippi and 98.6 percent of the degrees earned nationwide.... When MUW's School of Nursing began operation, nearly 98 percent of all employed registered nurses were female....

Rather than compensate for discriminatory barriers faced by women, MUW's policy of excluding males from admission to the School of Nursing tends to perpetuate the stereotyped view of nursing as an exclusively women's job.... MUW's admissions policy lends credibility to the old view that women, not men, should become nurses, and makes the assumption that nursing is a field for women a self-fulfilling prophecy. See Stanton v. Stanton, 421 U.S. 7 (1975). Thus, we conclude that, although the State recited a "benign, compensatory purpose," it failed to establish that the alleged objective is the actual purpose underlying the discriminatory classification.

The policy is invalid also because it fails the second part of the equal protection test, for the State has made no showing that the gender-based classification is substantially and directly related to its proposed compensatory objective. To the contrary, MUW's policy of permitting men to attend classes as auditors fatally undermines its claim that women, at least those in the School of Nursing, are adversely affected by the presence of men.

MUW permits men who audit to participate fully in classes. Additionally, both men and women take part in continuing education courses offered by the School of Nursing, in which regular nursing students also can enroll. The uncontroverted record reveals that admitting men to nursing classes does not affect teaching style, that the presence of men in the classroom would not affect the performance of the female nursing students, and that men in coeducational nursing schools do not dominate the classroom. In sum, the record . . . is flatly inconsistent with the claim that excluding men from the School of Nursing is necessary to reach any of MUW's educational goals.

Thus, considering both the asserted interest and the relationship between the interest and the methods used by the State, we conclude that the State has fallen far short of establishing the "exceedingly persuasive justification" needed to sustain the gender-based classification. Accordingly, we hold that MUW's policy denying males the right to enroll for credit in its School of Nursing violates the Equal Protection Clause of the Fourteenth Amendment.

. . .

■ CHIEF JUSTICE BURGER, dissenting.

I agree generally with Justice Powell's dissenting opinion. I write separately, however, to emphasize that the Court's holding today is limited to the context of a professional nursing school. Since the Court's opinion relies heavily on its finding that women have traditionally dominated the nursing profession, it suggests that a State might well be justified in maintaining, for example, the option of an all-women's business school or liberal arts program.

■ JUSTICE BLACKMUN, dissenting.

. . .

I have come to suspect that it is easy to go too far with rigid rules in this area of claimed sex discrimination, and to lose—indeed destroy—values that mean much to some people by forbidding the State from offering them a choice while not depriving others of an alternate choice. . . .

. . .

■ JUSTICE POWELL, with whom JUSTICE REHNQUIST joins, dissenting.

The Court's opinion bows deeply to conformity. Left without honor—indeed, held unconstitutional—is an element of diversity that has characterized much of American education and enriched much of American life. The Court in effect holds today that no State now may provide even a single institution of higher learning open only to women students. . . .

. . .

II

The issue in this case is whether a State transgresses the Constitution when—within the context of a public system that offers a diverse range of campuses, curricula, and educational alternatives—it seeks to accommodate the legitimate personal preferences of those desiring the advantages of an all-women's college. In my view, the Court errs seriously by assuming—without argument or discussion—that the equal protection standard generally applicable to sex discrimination is appropriate here. That standard was designed to free women from "archaic and overbroad generalizations. . . ." Schlesinger v. Ballard, 419 U.S. 498, 508 (1975). In no previous case have we applied it to invalidate state efforts to *expand* women's choices. Nor are there prior sex discrimination decisions by this Court in which a male plaintiff, as in this case, had the choice of an equal benefit. . . .

By applying heightened equal protection analysis to this case, the Court frustrates the liberating spirit of the Equal Protection Clause. It forbids the States from providing women with an opportunity to choose the type of university they prefer. And yet it is these women whom the Court regards as the *victims* of an illegal, stereotyped perception of the role of women in our society. The Court reasons this way in a case in which no woman has complained, and the only complainant is a man who advances no claims on behalf of anyone else. His claim . . . is not that he is being denied a substantive educational opportunity, or even the right to attend an all-male or a coeducational college. It is *only* that the colleges open to him are located at inconvenient distances.

. . .

IV

A distinctive feature of America's tradition has been respect for diversity. This has been characteristic of the peoples from numerous lands who have built our country. It is the essence of our democratic system. At stake in this case as I see it is the preservation of a small aspect of this diversity. But that aspect is by no means insignificant, given our heritage of available choice between single-sex and coeducational institutions of higher learning. The Court answers that there is . . . discrimination of constitutional dimension. But, having found "discrimination," the Court finds it difficult to identify the victims. It hardly can claim that women are discriminated against. . . . In essence [Hogan] insists that he has a right to attend a college in his home community. This simply is not a sex discrimination case. The Equal Protection Clause was never intended to be applied to this kind of case.

Johnson v. Transportation Agency, Santa Clara County
480 U.S. 616 (1987).

A white male passed over for promotion in favor of a female employee with lower test scores sued under Title VII of the 1964 Civil Rights Act. He raised no constitutional issues, and the court decided the case entirely under Title VII. After much discussion the Court held "that the agency appropriately took into account as one factor the sex of Diane Joyce in determining that she should be promoted to the road dispatcher position. The decision to do so was made pursuant to an affirmative action plan that represents a moderate, flexible, case-by-case approach to effecting a gradual improvement in the representation of minorities and women in the Agency's work force." Three justices dissented.

2.   CLASSIFICATIONS ADVANTAGING RACIAL MINORITIES

Race-Conscious Affirmative Action, 1974–1989

During the last quarter of the 20th century the Court began to address the constitutionality of voluntary use of racial criteria for the avowed purpose of benefiting, rather than disadvantaging, racial minorities in the competition for valuable but finite opportunities such as public university admissions; government contracts, jobs and licenses; and voter representation. Earlier, in Swann v. Charlotte-Mecklenburg Board of Education, 402 U.S. 1 (1971), in the course of contrasting the legitimate scope of judicially-imposed race-conscious remedies for proven *de jure* school segregation with the broader scope of voluntary school board efforts, the Court had noted that "[s]chool authorities . . . traditionally charged with broad power to formulate and implement educational policy . . . might well conclude . . . that in order to prepare students to live in a pluralistic society each school should have a prescribed ratio of Negro to white students reflecting the proportion for the district as a whole."[a]

The first case that came to the Court squarely involving the constitutionality of a voluntary affirmative action program, however, was DeFunis v. Odegaard, 416 U.S. 312 (1974), but a majority of the Court dismissed as moot the action brought by a rejected white applicant to the University of Washington Law School, because by the time of the Court's opinion he was about to graduate by virtue of lower court proceedings. Justice Douglas dissented, addressed the merits, and said in part that "a finding that the state school employed a racial classification in selecting its students subjects it to the strictest scrutiny under the Equal Protection Clause." What is "key," he argued, "is the consideration of each application *in a racially neutral way*." (Emphasis in original.) That meant first that because the Law School Admissions Test (LSAT) "reflects questions touching on cultural backgrounds, the Admissions Committee acted properly . . . in setting minority applications apart for separate processing . . . in order better to probe their capacities and potentials." That meant second, however, that the "reason for the separate treatment of minorities as a class is to make more certain that racial factors do not militate *against an applicant or on his behalf*" (emphasis in original) and, specifically, that "[w]hatever [DeFunis'] race, he had a constitutional right to have his application considered on its individual merits in a racially neutral manner." Justice Douglas was concerned that "[t]he reservation of a proportion of the law school class for members of selected minority groups is fraught with . . . dangers, for one must immediately determine which groups are to receive such favored treatment and which are to be excluded, the proportions of the class that are to be allocated to each, and even the criteria by which to determine whether an individual is a member of a favored group." He also objected that the "State . . . may not proceed by racial classification to force strict population equivalencies for every group in every occupation, overriding individual preferences"; that "a segregated admissions process creates suggestions of stigma and caste no less than a segregated classroom, and in the end it may produce that result despite its contrary intentions"; and that since "[a]ll races can compete fairly at all professional levels . . . , any state-sponsored preference to one race over another in that competition is . . . 'invidious' and violative of the Equal Protection Clause."

A majority of the Court addressed the constitutional merits of a voluntary race-conscious affirmative action program for the first time in Regents of the University of California v. Bakke, 438 U.S. 265 (1978), although the Court could not muster consensus on a majority opinion—a frequent occurrence in affirmative action cases. Without reaching the constitutional question, Justice Stevens, joined by Chief Justice Burger and Justices Stewart and Rehnquist, concluded that the special admissions program of the Medical School of the University of California at Davis—which reserved 16 out of 100 places in the first year class for applicants who were either Black, Chicano, Asian or American Indian and were selected by a separate special admissions committee—violated Title VI of the Civil Rights Act of 1964. Of the five Justices who relied on the Constitution, one (Justice Powell) applied the "most exacting scrutiny" to the racial classification and concluded that the Davis special admissions program denied Bakke his "individual" equal protection rights by making him ineligible for consideration for any of the 16 seats reserved for minority applicants. Five Justices thus agreed that the particular Davis program was unlawful. Justice Powell also concluded, however, that unlike the Davis set-aside program, "a

---

[a]   A deeply divided Court revisited the meaning and significance of this statement more than 35 years later in Parents Involved in Community Schools v. Seattle School District No. 1, reported in full, infra, p. 620.

properly devised admissions program involving the competitive consideration of race and ethnic origin" for all seats in the class could be used by an institution of higher education to assemble "a diverse student body"—a "goal that is of paramount importance in the fulfillment of its mission." The remaining four Justices (Brennan, White, Marshall, and Blackmun) concluded in a joint opinion that "a state government may adopt race-conscious programs if the purpose . . . is to remove the disparate racial impact its actions might otherwise have and if there is reason to believe that the disparate impact is itself the product of past discrimination, whether its own or that of society at large"—and that there was "no question that Davis' program [was] valid under this test." The "articulated purpose of remedying the effects of past societal discrimination" was "sufficiently important to justify the use of race-conscious admissions programs where there is a substantial basis for concluding that minority underrepresentation is substantial and chronic, and that the handicap of past discrimination is impeding access of minorities to the medical school." And the "second prong of our test—whether the Davis program stigmatizes any discrete group or individual and whether race is reasonably used in light of the program's objectives—is clearly satisfied by the Davis program." The "use of racial preferences for remedial purposes does not inflict a pervasive injury upon individual whites in the sense that wherever they go or whatever they do there is a significant likelihood that they will be treated as second-class citizens because of their color. . . . Nor can the program reasonably be regarded as stigmatizing the program's beneficiaries or their race as inferior." (Justice Powell thought the "pliable notion of 'stigma' " was a standardless "subjective judgment," noting that "*[a]ll* state-imposed classifications that rearrange burdens and benefits on the basis of race are likely to be viewed with deep resentment by the individuals burdened" and thus "may outrage" them and "be perceived as invidious.") Taking Justice Powell's opinion together with their joint opinion, the four adherents to the joint opinion identified the constitutional common ground of a Court majority as having the following "central meaning": "Government may take race into account when it acts not to demean or insult any racial group but to remedy disadvantages cast on minorities by past racial prejudice, at least when appropriate findings have been made by judicial, legislative, or administrative bodies with competence to act in this area." (Many of the features of Justice Powell's influential opinion in *Bakke*, which have been widely employed since that decision in the formulation and administration of race-conscious affirmative action programs throughout higher education, are recounted in Grutter v. Bollinger, infra p. 590, and Gratz v. Bollinger, infra p. 602.)

In the 1980's voluntary affirmative action plans beyond the sphere of higher education were challenged. In Fullilove v. Klutznick, 448 U.S. 448 (1980), the Court, again with no majority opinion, upheld the "Minority Business Enterprise" (MBE) provision of the Public Works Employment Act of 1977, which appropriated federal funds for state and local public works projects. The MBE provision required the Secretary of Commerce, absent administrative waiver, to deny grant applications that did not include assurances that at least 10% of the grant amount would be expended for businesses owned 50% or more by minority group members, defined as "citizens of the United States who are Negroes, Spanish-speaking, Orientals, Indians, Eskimos and Aleuts." Administrative exceptions were available to eliminate MBE's that were not "bonafide" or that attempted price exploitation, or if grantees demonstrated that their best efforts had not and would not achieve the 10% target. Chief Justice Burger's opinion, joined by Justices White and Powell, invoked "appropriate deference to the Congress" but also "recognize[d] the need for careful judicial evaluation to assure that any congressional program that employs racial or ethnic criteria to accomplish the objective of remedying the present effects of past discrimination is narrowly tailored to the achievement of that goal." Applying the "most searching examination," however, he was satisfied that Congress' "comprehensive remedial power . . . to enforce equal protection guarantees" supported the "clear objective" of ensuring that grantees "would not employ procurement practices that Congress had decided might result in perpetuation of the effects of prior discrimination which had impaired or foreclosed access by minority business to public contracting opportunities." He also was satisfied that this limited preference (affecting only 0.25% of annual construction work expenditures in the United States), and the flexibility provided by the waiver and exemption provisions, supported the conclusion that the MBE program was a constitutionally permissible means of achieving that objective. Hence, Congress had not violated "the equal protection component of the Due Process Clause of the Fifth Amendment." A concurring opinion by Justice Marshall, joined by Justices Brennan and Blackmun, reiterated their view in *Bakke* that the "proper inquiry is whether racial classifications designed to further remedial purposes serve important governmental objectives and are substantially related to achievement of those objectives"—a standard he found easily satisfied in this case. Justice Stewart, Justice Rehnquist, and Justice Stevens dissented, the latter urging that "[r]acial classifications are simply too pernicious to permit any but the most exact connection between justification and classification."

By contrast, the Court next invalidated a race-sensitive collective bargaining provision explicitly protecting recently hired minority school teachers from being laid off in the customary reverse order of seniority. Wygant v. Jackson Board of Education, 476 U.S. 267 (1986). The policy required that "at no time will there be a greater percentage of minority personnel laid off than the current percentage of minority personnel employed at the time of the layoff." Justice Powell's plurality opinion, joined by Chief Justice Burger and Justices Rehnquist and O'Connor, criticized the lower courts' holding "that the Board's interest in providing minority role models for its minority students, as an attempt to alleviate the effects of societal discrimination, was sufficiently important to justify the racial classification embodied in the layoff provision." Neither "societal discrimination alone," nor the role model theory used by the lower courts (which compared the percentage of minority teachers to the percentage of minority students), sufficed. Societal discrimination was "too amorphous"; remedial racial classifications had to be supported by "convincing evidence" of "prior discrimination by the governmental unit involved" and that was absent here. The role model rationale had "no logical stopping point" and did "not necessarily bear a relationship to the harm caused by prior discriminatory hiring practices," especially where there was "no apparent connection" between the percentage of minority students and the percentage of minority faculty. In any event, in a portion of his opinion that Justice O'Connor did not join, Justice Powell found the means chosen to serve these ends inadequately justified. With layoffs, the "burden to be borne by innocent individuals" is "too intrusive," for in contrast to hiring goals, which "impose a diffuse burden, often foreclosing only one of several opportunities, layoffs impose the entire burden of achieving racial equality on particular individuals, often resulting in serious disruption of their lives." Justice White concurred in the judgment, saying in part: "Whatever the legitimacy of hiring goals or quotas may be, the discharge of white teachers to make room for blacks, none of whom has been shown to be a victim of any racial discrimination, is quite a different matter. I cannot believe that in order to integrate a work force, it would be permissible to discharge whites and hire blacks until the latter comprise a suitable percentage of the work force." Justice Marshall, joined by Justices Brennan and Blackmun, dissented, "believ[ing] that a public employer, with the full agreement of its employees, should be permitted to preserve the benefits of a legitimate and constitutional affirmative-action hiring plan even while reducing its work force. . . ." Justice Stevens dissented separately, believing it "not necessary to find that the Board of Education has been guilty of racial discrimination in the past to support the conclusion that it has a legitimate interest in employing more black teachers in the future." Although the "Equal Protection Clause absolutely prohibits the use of race in many governmental contexts" (such as "who may serve on juries, who may use public services, who may marry, and who may be fit parents"), "race is not always irrelevant to sound governmental decisionmaking." For example, "in law enforcement, if an undercover agent is needed to infiltrate a group suspected of ongoing criminal behavior—and if the members of the group are all of the same race—it would seem perfectly rational to employ an agent of that race. . . ." Similarly, employing and retaining more minority teachers was "rational and unquestionably legitimate" to serve the "valid public purpose" of having "an integrated faculty . . . able to provide benefits to the student body that could not be provided by an all white, or nearly all white, faculty."

"Strict Scrutiny" Applied to Race-Conscious Affirmative Action Plans After 1989

Building on President Reagan's appointments of Justice Scalia in 1986 and Justice Kennedy in 1988 (adding to his appointment of Justice O'Connor in 1981), and President George H.W. Bush's appointment of Justice Thomas in 1991, a majority of the Court in the next two cases coalesced around "strict scrutiny" as the proper standard for evaluating the validity of race-conscious affirmative action plans adopted by state and federal authorities, respectively. Those steps were deeply contested by dissenters, as has been the question of whether the strict scrutiny standard for these plans should be as strictly applied as when that standard of review is applied to racial classifications disadvantaging racial minorities. Attention should be paid not only to those disagreements and nuances, but also to the multiple considerations the Justices have found relevant in affirmative action cases.

City of Richmond v. J.A. Croson Company

488 U.S. 469, 109 S.Ct. 706, 102 L.Ed.2d 854 (1989).

■ JUSTICE O'CONNOR announced the judgment of the Court and delivered the opinion of the Court with respect to Parts I, III-B, and IV, an opinion with respect to Part II, in which THE CHIEF JUSTICE and JUSTICE WHITE join, and an opinion with respect to Parts III-A and V, in which THE CHIEF JUSTICE, JUSTICE WHITE and JUSTICE KENNEDY join.

. . .

I

[In 1983, Richmond, Virginia's City Council adopted a 5-year Plan requiring prime contractors to whom the city awarded construction contracts to subcontract at least 30% of the dollar amount of the contract to one or more Minority Business Enterprises (MBEs) located anywhere in the United States—MBE's being defined as "business[es] at least fifty-one (51) percent of which [are] . . . owned and controlled . . . by minority group members." In turn, "minority group members" were defined as "[c]itizens of the United States who are Blacks, Spanish-speaking, Orientals, Indians, Eskimos, or Aleuts." The Plan declared itself "remedial" in nature, authorized "waivers" on proof that the set-aside "cannot be achieved," and allowed a bidder denied an award for failure to comply with the MBE requirements a general right of protest. The record contained "no direct evidence of race discrimination on the part of the city in letting contracts or any evidence that the city's prime contractors had discriminated against minority-owned subcontractors."

[Croson, a contractor, submitted the only bid to provide and install toilet fixtures at the city jail. Croson contacted 5 or 6 potential MBE suppliers to supply the fixtures, but the only interested one reported at the bid opening that "difficulty in obtaining credit approval had hindered his submission of a bid." Six days later, still having not received a bid, Croson asked for a waiver of the 30% set-aside, saying the interested MBE was "unqualified" and others contacted "had been unresponsive or unable to quote." The interested MBE later submitted a bid 7% over the market price and higher than the fixtures price Croson had included in its bid. The MBE also informed city procurement officials that it could supply the fixtures. The city denied Croson's waiver request, leading Croson to sue in federal district court, "arguing that the Richmond ordinance was unconstitutional on its face and as applied in this case."

[The District Court "upheld the Plan in all respects" and a divided panel of the Fourth Circuit Court of Appeals affirmed. The Supreme Court vacated and remanded for further consideration in light of its "intervening decision in Wygant v. Jackson Board of Education, 476 U.S. 267 (1986)." After the Fourth Circuit on remand held that the "set-aside program" violated "both prongs of strict scrutiny under the Equal Protection Clause[,]" the Supreme Court here affirmed.]

II

. . .

Appellant . . . rel[ies] heavily on *Fullilove* for the proposition that a city council, like Congress, need not make specific findings of discrimination to engage in race-conscious relief. Thus, appellant argues "[i]t would be a perversion of federalism to hold that the federal government has a compelling interest in remedying the effects of racial discrimination in its own public works program, but a city government does not." . . .

What appellant ignores is that Congress, unlike any State or political subdivision, has a specific constitutional mandate to enforce the dictates of the Fourteenth Amendment. The power to "enforce" may at times also include the power to define situations which *Congress* determines threaten principles of equality and to adopt prophylactic rules to deal with those situations. . . .

That Congress may identify and redress the effects of society-wide discrimination does not mean that, *a fortiori*, the States and their political subdivisions are free to decide that such remedies are appropriate. Section 1 of the Fourteenth Amendment is an explicit *constraint* on state power, and the States must undertake any remedial efforts in accordance with that provision. . . .

. . .

It would seem equally clear, however, that a state or local subdivision . . . has the authority to eradicate the effects of private discrimination within its own legislative jurisdiction. . . . Richmond . . . can use its spending powers to remedy private discrimination, if it identifies the discrimination with the particularity required by the Fourteenth Amendment. . . .

Thus, if the city could show that it had essentially become a "passive participant" in a system of racial exclusion practiced by elements of the local construction industry, we think it clear that the city could take affirmative steps to dismantle such a system. It is beyond dispute that any public entity, state or federal, has a compelling interest in assuring that public dollars, drawn from the tax contributions of all citizens, do not serve to finance the evil of private prejudice. . . .

III

A

. . . [T]he "rights created by the first section of the Fourteenth Amendment are, by its terms, guaranteed to the individual. The rights established are personal rights." Shelley v. Kraemer, 334 U.S. 1, 22 (1948). The Richmond Plan denies certain citizens the opportunity to compete for a fixed percentage of public contracts based solely upon their race. To whatever racial group these citizens belong, their "personal rights" to be treated with equal dignity and respect are implicated by a rigid rule erecting race as the sole criterion in an aspect of public decisionmaking.

Absent searching judicial inquiry into the justification for such race-based measures, there is simply no way of determining what classifications are "benign" or "remedial" and what classifications are in fact motivated by illegitimate notions of racial inferiority or simple racial politics. Indeed, the purpose of strict scrutiny is to "smoke out" illegitimate uses of race by assuring that the legislative body is pursuing a goal important enough to warrant use of a highly suspect tool. The test also ensures that the means chosen "fit" this compelling goal so closely that there is little or no possibility that the motive for the classification was illegitimate racial prejudice or stereotype.

Classifications based on race carry a danger of stigmatic harm. Unless . . . strictly reserved for remedial settings, they may in fact promote notions of racial inferiority and lead to a politics of racial hostility. . . . We thus reaffirm the view expressed by the plurality in *Wygant* that the standard of review under the Equal Protection Clause is not dependent on the race of those burdened or benefited by a particular classification. . . .

. . .

Even were we to accept [that] the level of scrutiny varies according to the ability of different groups to defend their interests in the representative process, heightened scrutiny would still be appropriate in the circumstances of this case. . . . If one aspect of the judiciary's role under the Equal Protection Clause is to protect "discrete and insular minorities" from majoritarian prejudice or indifference, see United States v. Carolene Products Co., 304 U.S. 144, 153 n. 4 (1938), some maintain that these concerns are not implicated when the "white majority" places burdens upon itself. See J. Ely, Democracy and Distrust 170 (1980).

In this case, blacks comprise approximately 50% of the population of the city of Richmond. Five of the nine seats on the City Council are held by blacks. The concern that a political majority will more easily act to the disadvantage of a minority based on unwarranted assumptions or incomplete facts would seem to militate for, not against, the application of heightened judicial scrutiny in this case. . . .

. . .

III

B

We think it clear that the factual predicate offered in support of the Richmond Plan suffers from the same two defects identified as fatal in *Wygant.* The District Court found the city council's "findings sufficient to ensure that, in adopting the Plan, it was remedying the present effects of past discrimination in the *construction industry*." . . . (emphasis added). Like the "role model" theory employed in *Wygant,* a generalized assertion that there has been past discrimination in an entire industry provides no guidance for a legislative body to determine the precise scope of the injury it seeks to remedy. It "has no logical stopping point." *Wygant,.* . . . Relief for such an ill-defined wrong could extend until the percentage of public contracts awarded to MBEs in Richmond mirrored the percentage of minorities in the population as a whole.

. . .

. . . Like the claim that discrimination in primary and secondary schooling justifies a rigid racial preference in medical school admissions, an amorphous claim that there has been past discrimination in a particular industry cannot justify the use of an unyielding racial quota.

It is sheer speculation how many minority firms there would be in Richmond absent past societal discrimination, just as it was sheer speculation how many minority medical students would have been admitted to the medical school at Davis absent past discrimination in educational opportunities. . . .

. . . The 30% quota cannot in any realistic sense be tied to any injury suffered by anyone. The District Court relied upon five predicate "facts" in reaching its conclusion that there was an adequate basis for the 30% quota: (1) the ordinance declares itself to be remedial; (2) several proponents of the measure stated their views that there had been past discrimination in the construction industry; (3) minority businesses received .67% of prime contracts from the city while minorities constituted 50% of the city's population; (4) there were very few minority contractors in local and state contractors' associations; and (5) in 1977, Congress made a determination that the effects of past discrimination had stifled minority participation in the construction industry nationally.

None of these "findings," singly or together, provide the city of Richmond with a "strong basis in evidence for its conclusion that remedial action was necessary." *Wygant,*. . . . There is nothing approaching a prima facie case of a constitutional or statutory violation by *anyone* in the Richmond construction industry. . . .

. . . [T]hat the city council designated the Plan as "remedial" . . . is entitled to little or no weight. . . . Racial classifications are suspect, [so] simple legislative assurances of good intention cannot suffice.

. . . [Statements from proponents] are of little probative value in establishing identified discrimination in the Richmond construction industry. . . .

Reliance on the disparity between the number of prime contracts awarded to minority firms and the minority population of the city of Richmond is similarly misplaced. . . .

. . . [W]here special qualifications are necessary, the relevant statistical pool for purposes of demonstrating discriminatory exclusion must be the number of minorities qualified to undertake the particular task. . . .

In this case, the city does not even know how many MBEs in the relevant market are qualified to undertake prime or subcontracting work in public construction projects. . . . Nor does the city know what percentage of total city construction dollars minority firms now receive as subcontractors on prime contracts let by the city.

To a large extent, the set-aside of subcontracting dollars seems to rest on the unsupported assumption that white prime contractors simply will not hire minority firms. . . . Indeed, there is evidence in this record that overall minority participation in city contracts in Richmond is seven to eight percent, and that minority contractor participation in Community Block Development Grant *construction* projects is 17% to 22%. Without any information on minority participation in subcontracting, it is quite simply impossible to evaluate overall minority representation in the city's construction expenditures.

[E]vidence that MBE membership in local contractors' associations was extremely low . . . , standing alone[,] is [also] not probative of any discrimination in the local construction industry. There are numerous explanations for this dearth of minority participation, including past societal discrimination in education and economic opportunities as well as both black and white career and entrepreneurial choices. Blacks may be disproportionately attracted to industries other than construction. . . .

. . . If the statistical disparity between eligible MBEs and MBE membership were great enough, an inference of discriminatory exclusion could arise. In such a case, the city would have a compelling interest in preventing its tax dollars from assisting these organizations in maintaining a racially segregated construction market. . . .

Finally, . . . [with respect to] Congress' finding in connection with the set-aside approved in *Fullilove* that there had been nationwide discrimination in the construction industry[, t]he probative value . . . for demonstrating the existence of discrimination in Richmond is extremely limited. By its inclusion of a waiver procedure in the national program addressed in *Fullilove,* Congress explicitly recognized that the scope of the problem would vary from market area to market area. . . .

. . .

In sum, none of the evidence presented by the city points to any identified discrimination in the Richmond construction industry. We, therefore, hold that the city has failed to demonstrate a compelling interest in apportioning public contracting opportunities on the basis of race. . . .

The foregoing analysis applies only to the inclusion of blacks within the Richmond set-aside program. There is *absolutely no evidence* of past discrimination against Spanish-speaking, Oriental, Indian, Eskimo, or Aleut persons in any aspect of the Richmond construction industry. . . . It may well be that Richmond has never had an Aleut or Eskimo citizen. The random inclusion of racial groups that, as a practical matter, may never have suffered from discrimination in the construction industry in Richmond, suggests that perhaps the city's purpose was not in fact to remedy past discrimination.

If a 30% set-aside was "narrowly tailored" to compensate black contractors for past discrimination, one may legitimately ask why they are forced to share this "remedial relief" with an Aleut citizen who moves to Richmond tomorrow? The gross overinclusiveness of Richmond's racial preference strongly impugns the city's claim of remedial motivation. . . .

IV

[Being] almost impossible to assess whether the . . . Plan is narrowly tailored to remedy prior discrimination since it is not linked to identified discrimination in any way[, w]e limit ourselves to two observations . . . .

First, there does not appear to have been any consideration of the use of race-neutral means to increase minority business participation in city contracting. . . . Many of the barriers . . . appear to be race neutral. If MBEs disproportionately lack capital or cannot meet bonding requirements, a race-neutral program of city financing for small firms would, a fortiori, lead to greater minority participation. . . .

Second, the 30% quota cannot be said to be narrowly tailored to any goal, except perhaps outright racial balancing. It rests upon the "completely unrealistic" assumption that minorities will choose a particular trade in lockstep proportion to their representation in the local population. . . .

Since the city must already consider bids and waivers on a case-by-case basis, it is difficult to see the need for a rigid numerical quota. . . . Unlike the program upheld in

Fullilove, the Richmond Plan's waiver system focuses solely on the availability of MBEs; there is no inquiry into whether or not the particular MBE seeking a racial preference has suffered from the effects of past discrimination by the city or prime contractors.

. . . Under Richmond's scheme, a successful black, Hispanic, or Oriental entrepreneur from anywhere in the country enjoys an absolute preference over other citizens based solely on their race. We think it obvious that such a program is not narrowly tailored to remedy the effects of prior discrimination.

V

Nothing we say today precludes a state or local entity from taking action to rectify the effects of identified discrimination within its jurisdiction. If the City . . . had evidence . . . that nonminority contractors were systematically excluding minority businesses from subcontracting opportunities it could take action to end the discriminatory exclusion. Where there is a significant statistical disparity between the number of qualified minority contractors willing and able to perform a particular service and the number of such contractors actually engaged by the locality or the locality's prime contractors, an inference of discriminatory exclusion could arise. . . . Under such circumstances, the city could act to dismantle the closed business system by taking appropriate measures against those who discriminate on the basis of race or other illegitimate criteria. . . . In the extreme case, some form of narrowly tailored racial preference might be necessary to break down patterns of deliberate exclusion.

. . .

. . . [T]he city [also] has at its disposal a whole array of race-neutral devices to increase the accessibility of city contracting opportunities to small entrepreneurs of all races. . . .

. . .

Affirmed.

■ JUSTICE STEVENS, concurring in part and concurring in the judgment.

. . . I . . . do not agree with the premise . . . that a governmental decision that rests on a racial classification is never permissible except as a remedy for a past wrong. I do, however, agree with the Court's explanation of why the Richmond ordinance cannot be justified as a remedy for past discrimination, and therefore join Parts I, III-B, and IV of its opinion. . . .

. . .

. . . [I]nstead of carefully identifying the characteristics of the two classes of contractors that are respectively favored and disfavored by its ordinance, the Richmond City Council has merely engaged in the type of stereotypical analysis that is a hallmark of violations of the Equal Protection Clause. Whether we look at the class of persons benefited by the ordinance or at the disadvantaged class, the same conclusion emerges.

. . .

There is a special irony in the stereotypical thinking that prompts legislation of this kind. Although it stigmatizes the disadvantaged class with the unproven charge of past racial discrimination, it actually imposes a greater stigma on its supposed beneficiaries. . . .

■ JUSTICE KENNEDY, concurring in part and concurring in the judgment.

. . .

The moral imperative of racial neutrality is the driving force of the Equal Protection Clause. . . .

Nevertheless, given that a rule of automatic invalidity for racial preferences in almost every case would be a significant break with our precedents that require a case-by-case test, I am not convinced we need adopt it at this point. On the assumption that it will vindicate the principle of race neutrality . . . , I accept the less absolute rule . . . that any racial preference must face the most rigorous scrutiny by the courts. . . .

The ordinance before us falls far short of the standard we adopt. The nature and scope of the injury that existed; its historical or antecedent causes; the extent to which the City contributed to it, either by intentional acts or by passive complicity in acts of discrimination by the private sector; the necessity for the response adopted, its duration in relation to the wrong, and the precision with which it otherwise bore on whatever injury in fact was addressed, were all matters unmeasured, unexplored, unexplained by the City Council. We are left with an ordinance and a legislative record open to the fair charge that it is not a remedy but is itself a preference which will cause the same corrosive animosities that the Constitution forbids . . . .

■ JUSTICE SCALIA, concurring in the judgment.

I agree with much of the Court's opinion, and, in particular, with its conclusion that strict scrutiny must be applied to all governmental classification by race, whether or not its asserted purpose is "remedial" or "benign." I do not agree, however, . . . that . . . state and local governments may in some circumstances discriminate on the basis of race in order (in a broad sense) "to ameliorate the effects of past discrimination." . . .

We have in some contexts approved the use of racial classifications by the Federal Government to remedy the effects of past discrimination. I do not believe that we must or should extend those holdings to the States. . . .

A sound distinction between federal and state (or local) action based on race rests not only upon the substance of the Civil War Amendments, but upon social reality and governmental theory. . . . [R]acial discrimination against any group finds a more ready expression at the state and local than at the federal level. . . . An acute awareness of the heightened danger of oppression from political factions in small, rather than large, political units dates to the very beginning of our national history. . . .

. . . In my view there is only one circumstance in which the States may act *by race* to "undo the effects of past discrimination": where that is necessary to eliminate their own maintenance of a system of unlawful racial classification. . . . This distinction explains our school desegregation cases, in which we have made plain that States and localities sometimes have an obligation to adopt race-conscious remedies. While there is no doubt that those cases have taken into account the continuing "effects" of previously mandated racial school assignment, we have held those effects to justify a race-conscious remedy only because we have concluded, in that context, that they perpetuate a "dual school system." . . .

. . .

. . . [F]ar from justifying racial classification, identification of actual victims of discrimination makes it less supportable than ever, because more obviously unneeded.

. . .

. . . Since blacks have been disproportionately disadvantaged by racial discrimination, any race-neutral remedial program aimed at the disadvantaged *as such* will have a disproportionately beneficial impact on blacks. Only such a program, and not one that operates on the basis of race, is in accord with the letter and the spirit of our Constitution.

. . .

■ JUSTICE MARSHALL, with whom JUSTICE BRENNAN and JUSTICE BLACKMUN join, dissenting.

It is a welcome symbol of racial progress when the former capital of the Confederacy acts forthrightly to confront the effects of racial discrimination in its midst. In my view, nothing in the Constitution can be construed to prevent Richmond, Virginia, from allocating a portion of its contracting dollars for businesses owned or controlled by members of minority groups. Indeed, Richmond's set-aside program is indistinguishable in all meaningful respects from—and in fact was patterned upon—the federal set-aside plan . . . upheld in Fullilove v. Klutznick, 448 U.S. 448 (1980).

. . .

I

. . .

. . . So long as one views Richmond's local evidence of discrimination against the backdrop of systematic nationwide racial discrimination which Congress had so painstakingly identified in this very industry, this case is readily resolved.

II

. . . My view has long been that race-conscious classifications designed to further remedial goals "must serve important governmental objectives and must be substantially related to achievement of those objectives" in order to withstand constitutional scrutiny. . . .

A

1

. . . Richmond has two powerful interests in setting aside a portion of public contracting funds for minority-owned enterprises. The first is the city's interest in eradicating the effects of past racial discrimination. . . .

Richmond['s] second compelling interest . . . is . . . preventing the city's own spending decisions from reinforcing and perpetuating the exclusionary effects of past discrimination. . . .

. . .

2

The remaining question with respect to the "governmental interest" prong of equal protection analysis is whether Richmond has proffered satisfactory proof of past racial discrimination to support its twin interests in remediation and in governmental nonperpetuation. . . .

. . .

The varied body of evidence on which Richmond relied provides a "strong," "firm," and "unquestionably legitimate" basis upon which the City Council could determine that the effects of past racial discrimination warranted a remedial and prophylactic governmental response. . . . [T]hat just .67% of public construction expenditures over the previous five years had gone to minority-owned prime contractors, despite the city's racially mixed population, strongly suggests that construction contracting in the area was rife with "present economic inequities." . . . [T]hat area trade associations had virtually no minority members dramatized the extent of present inequities and suggested the lasting power of past discriminatory systems. . . .

. . .

. . . If Richmond indeed has a monochromatic contracting community . . . this most likely reflects the lingering power of past exclusionary practices. Certainly this is the explanation Congress has found persuasive at the national level. See *Fullilove,*. . . . The city's requirement that prime public contractors set aside 30% of their subcontracting assignments for minority-owned enterprises, subject to the ordinance's provision for waivers where minority-owned enterprises are unavailable or unwilling to participate, is designed precisely to ease minority contractors into the industry.

. . .

When the legislatures and leaders of cities with histories of pervasive discrimination testify that past discrimination has infected one of their industries, armchair cynicism like that exercised by the majority has no place. . . .

Finally, I vehemently disagree with the majority's dismissal of the congressional and Executive Branch findings noted in *Fullilove* as having "extremely limited" probative value in this case. . . .

No principle of federalism or of federal power . . . forbids a state or local government from drawing upon a nationally relevant historical record prepared by the Federal Government. . . .

B

. . . Richmond's set-aside plan also . . . is substantially related to the interests it seeks to serve. . . . [M]ost striking . . . is the similarity . . . to the "appropriately limited" federal set-aside provision upheld in *Fullilove.* . . . Like the federal provision, Richmond's is limited to five years in duration . . . and was not renewed when it came up for reconsideration in 1988. Like the federal provision, Richmond's contains a waiver provision freeing from its subcontracting requirements those nonminority firms that demonstrate that they cannot comply with its provisions. . . . Like the federal provision, Richmond's has a minimal impact on innocent third parties. While the measure affects 30% of public contracting dollars, that translates to only 3% of overall Richmond area contracting. . . .

Finally, like the federal provision, Richmond's does not interfere with any vested right . . . . [It] affects only future economic arrangements and imposes only a diffuse burden on nonminority competitors . . . . The plurality in *Wygant* emphasized the importance of this not disrupting the settled and legitimate expectations of innocent parties. . . .

. . . The majority takes issue . . . with . . . the city's refusal to explore the use of race-neutral measures . . . and the selection of a 30% set-aside figure. [As to the former,] the majority overlooks the fact that since 1975, Richmond has barred both discrimination by the city in awarding public contracts and discrimination by public contractors[, but] this ban has not succeeded in redressing the impact of past discrimination or in preventing city contract procurement from reinforcing racial homogeneity. [And] race-neutral measures . . . , while theoretically appealing, have been discredited by Congress as ineffectual in eradicating the effects of past discrimination in this very industry. . . .

As for Richmond's 30% target, . . . [it] affects only 3% of overall city contracting. . . . [M]ore important, . . . [it] was patterned directly on the *Fullilove* precedent. Congress' 10% figure fell "roughly halfway between the present percentage of minority contractors and the percentage of minority group members in the Nation." *Fullilove,* . . . (Powell, J., concurring). The . . . 30% figure similarly falls roughly halfway between the present percentage of Richmond-based minority contractors (almost zero) and the percentage of minorities in Richmond (50%). . . .

III

. . .

A

Today, for the first time, a majority of this Court has adopted strict scrutiny as its standard of Equal Protection Clause review of race-conscious remedial measures. This is an unwelcome development. A profound difference separates governmental actions that themselves are racist, and governmental actions that seek to remedy the effects of prior racism or to prevent neutral governmental activity from perpetuating the effects of such racism . . .

. . .

B

. . .

It cannot seriously be suggested that nonminorities in Richmond have any "history of purposeful unequal treatment." . . . Indeed, the numerical and political dominance of nonminorities within the State of Virginia and the Nation as a whole provide an enormous political check against the "simple racial politics" at the municipal level which the majority fears. . . .

. . .

C

. . .

To the degree that this parsimonious standard is grounded on a view that either section 1 or section 5 of the Fourteenth Amendment substantially disempowered States and localities from remedying past racial discrimination, the majority is seriously mistaken. . . .

. . .

. . . To interpret any aspect of these Amendments as proscribing state remedial responses . . . turns the Amendments on their heads. . . .

. . . [a]

Adarand Constructors, Inc. v. Pena

515 U.S. 200, 115 S.Ct. 2097, 132 L.Ed.2d 158 (1995).

■ JUSTICE O'CONNOR announced the judgment of the Court and delivered an opinion with respect to Parts I, II, III-A, III-B, III-D, and IV, which is for the Court except insofar as it might be inconsistent with the views expressed in JUSTICE SCALIA's concurrence, and an opinion with respect to Part III-C in which JUSTICE KENNEDY joins.

Petitioner Adarand Constructors, Inc., claims that the Federal Government's practice of giving general contractors on government projects a financial incentive to hire subcontractors controlled by "socially and economically disadvantaged individuals," and in particular, the Government's use of race-based presumptions in identifying such individuals, violates the equal protection component of the Fifth Amendment's Due Process Clause. The Court of Appeals rejected Adarand's claim. We conclude, however, that courts should analyze cases of this kind under a different standard of review than the one the Court of Appeals applied. We therefore vacate . . . and remand . . . for further proceedings.

---

[a] A separate dissenting opinion by Justice Blackmun, joined by Justice Brennan, is omitted.

I

[In 1989 an agency of the United States Department of Transportation (DOT) awarded the prime contract for a highway construction project in Colorado to Mountain Gravel & Construction Company. Mountain Gravel subcontracted the guardrail portion of the contract to Gonzales Construction Company rather than to Adarand, the low bidder, because the prime contract authorized additional compensation for hiring subcontractors certified as small businesses controlled by "socially and economically disadvantaged individuals."] Federal law requires [such] a subcontracting clause . . . in most federal agency contracts, and it also requires the clause to state that "[t]he contractor shall presume that socially and economically disadvantaged individuals include Black Americans, Hispanic Americans, Native Americans, Asian Pacific Americans, and other minorities, or any other individual found to be disadvantaged by the [Small Business] Administration [SBA] pursuant to section 8(a) of the Small Business Act." 15 U.S.C. §§ 637(d)(2), (3). Adarand claims that the presumption . . . [impermissibly] discriminates on the basis of race . . . .

. . .

. . . The . . . Tenth Circuit . . . understood . . . Fullilove v. Klutznick, 448 U.S. 448 (1980), to have adopted "a lenient standard, resembling intermediate scrutiny, in assessing" the constitutionality of federal race-based action. . . . Applying that "lenient standard," as further developed in Metro Broadcasting, Inc. v. FCC, 497 U.S. 547 (1990), the Court of Appeals upheld the use of subcontractor compensation clauses. . . .

. . .

III

. . . The Government concedes . . . that "the race-based rebuttable presumption used in some certification determinations under the Subcontracting Compensation Clause" is subject to some heightened level of scrutiny. . . .

. . .

B

. . .

[In Richmond v. J.A. Croson Co., 488 U.S. 469 (1989),] the Court finally agreed that the Fourteenth Amendment requires strict scrutiny of all race-based action by state and local governments. But *Croson* of course had no occasion to declare what standard of review the Fifth Amendment requires for such action taken by the Federal Government. . . .

Despite lingering uncertainty in the details, however, the Court's cases through *Croson* had established three general propositions with respect to governmental racial classifications. First, skepticism: " '[a]ny preference based on racial or ethnic criteria must necessarily receive a most searching examination,' " . . . Second, consistency: "the standard of review under the Equal Protection Clause is not dependent on the race of those burdened or benefited by a particular classification," Croson . . . , i. e., all racial classifications reviewable under the Equal Protection Clause must be strictly scrutinized. And third, congruence: "[e]qual protection analysis in the Fifth Amendment area is the same as that under the Fourteenth Amendment,". . . . Taken together, these three propositions lead to the conclusion that any person, of whatever race, has the right to demand that any governmental actor subject to the Constitution justify any racial classification subjecting that person to unequal treatment under the strictest judicial scrutiny. . . .

A year later, however, the Court took a surprising turn. Metro Broadcasting, Inc. v. FCC, 497 U.S. 547 (1990), involved a Fifth Amendment challenge to two race-based policies of the Federal Communications Commission. In *Metro Broadcasting*, the Court repudiated the long-held notion that "it would be unthinkable that the same Constitution would impose a lesser duty on the Federal Government" than it does on a State to afford equal protection of the laws . . . by holding that "benign" federal racial classifications need only satisfy intermediate scrutiny, even though *Croson* had recently concluded that such classifications enacted by a State must satisfy strict scrutiny. "[B]enign" federal racial classifications, the Court said, "—even if those measures are not 'remedial' in the sense of being designed to compensate victims of past governmental or societal discrimination—are constitutionally permissible to the extent that they serve important governmental objectives within the power of Congress and are substantially related to achievement of those objectives." . . . The Court did not explain how to tell whether a racial classification should be deemed "benign," other than to express "confiden[ce] that an 'examination of the legislative scheme and its history' will separate benign measures from other types of racial classifications." . . .

Applying this test, the Court . . . concluded that [the FCC policies] served the "important governmental objective" of "enhancing broadcast diversity," . . . and that they were "substantially related" to that objective. . . .

. . . *Metro Broadcasting* departed from prior cases in two significant respects. First, it turned its back on *Croson*'s explanation [that] strict scrutiny of all governmental racial classifications is essential . . . [in order] to 'smoke out' illegitimate uses of race . . . .

Second, [it] squarely rejected one of the three propositions established by the Court's earlier equal protection cases, namely, congruence between the standards applicable to federal and state racial classifications, and in so doing also undermined the other two—skepticism of all racial classifications, and consistency of treatment irrespective of the race of the burdened or benefited group. . . .

The three propositions undermined by *Metro Broadcasting* all derive from the basic principle that the Fifth and Fourteenth Amendments . . . protect persons, not groups. It follows . . . that all governmental action based on race . . . should be subjected to detailed judicial inquiry to ensure that the personal right to equal protection of the laws has not been infringed. . . . Accordingly, we hold today that all racial classifications, imposed by whatever federal, state, or local governmental actor, must be analyzed by a reviewing court under strict scrutiny. In other words, such classifications are constitutional only if they are narrowly tailored measures that further compelling governmental interests. To the extent that *Metro Broadcasting* is inconsistent with that holding, it is overruled.

. . .

. . . Justice Stevens concedes that "some cases may be difficult to classify"; all the more reason, in our view, to examine all racial classifications carefully. Strict scrutiny does not "trea[t] dissimilar race-based decisions as though they were equally objectionable"; to the contrary, it evaluates carefully all governmental race-based decisions in order to decide which are constitutionally objectionable and which are not. . . .

. . .

Perhaps it is not the standard of strict scrutiny itself, but our use of the concepts of "consistency" and "congruence" in conjunction with it, that leads Justice Stevens to dissent. . . . The principle of consistency simply means that whenever the government treats any person unequally because of his or her race, that person has suffered an injury that falls squarely within the language and spirit of the Constitution's guarantee of equal protection. It says nothing about the ultimate validity of any particular law; that determination is the job of the court applying strict scrutiny. . . .

Consistency does recognize that any individual suffers an injury when he or she is disadvantaged by the government because of his or her race, whatever that race may be. . . . Justice Stevens does not explain how his views square with *Croson*, or with the long line of cases understanding equal protection as a personal right.

. . .

C

. . .

. . . *Metro Broadcasting* itself departed from our prior cases—and did so quite recently. By refusing to follow *Metro Broadcasting*, then, we do not depart from the fabric of the law; we restore it. . . .

. . .

D

. . . [T]o the extent (if any) that *Fullilove* held federal racial classifications to be subject to a less rigorous standard, it is no longer controlling. But we need not decide today whether the program upheld in *Fullilove* would survive strict scrutiny as our more recent cases have defined it.

. . . *Korematsu* [*v. United States*, 323 U.S. 214 (1944),] demonstrates vividly that even "the most rigid scrutiny" can sometimes fail to detect an illegitimate racial classification. . . . Any retreat from the most searching judicial inquiry can only increase the risk of another such error occurring in the future.

Finally, we wish to dispel the notion that strict scrutiny is "strict in theory, but fatal in fact." . . . The unhappy persistence of both the practice and the lingering effects of racial discrimination against minority groups in this country is an unfortunate reality, and government is not disqualified from acting in response to it. . . . When race-based action is necessary to further a compelling interest, such action is within constitutional constraints if it satisfies the "narrow tailoring" test this Court has set out in previous cases.

IV

Because our decision today alters the playing field in some important respects, we think it best to remand . . . for further consideration in light of the principles we have announced. . . .

. . . [W]hether any of the ways in which the Government uses subcontractor compensation clauses can survive strict scrutiny . . . should be addressed in the first instance by the lower courts.

. . .

■ JUSTICE SCALIA, concurring in part and concurring in the judgment.

. . . In my view, government can never have a "compelling interest" in discriminating on the basis of race in order to "make up" for past racial discrimination in the opposite direction. . . . Individuals who have been wronged by unlawful racial discrimination should be made whole; but under our Constitution there can be no such thing as either a creditor or a debtor race. That concept is alien to the Constitution's focus upon the individual . . . and its rejection of dispositions based on race . . . . To pursue the concept of racial entitlement—even for the most admirable and benign of purposes—is to reinforce and preserve for future mischief the way of thinking that produced race slavery, race privilege and race hatred. In the eyes of government, we are just one race here. It is American.

. . .

■ JUSTICE THOMAS, concurring in part and concurring in the judgment.

. . . I write separately . . . to express my disagreement with the premise underlying Justice Stevens' and Justice Ginsburg's dissents: that there is a racial paternalism exception to the principle of equal protection. I believe that there is a "moral [and] constitutional equivalence" (Stevens, J., dissenting) between laws designed to subjugate a race and those that distribute benefits on the basis of race in order to foster some current notion of equality. Government cannot make us equal; it can only recognize, respect, and protect us as equal before the law.

. . . As far as the Constitution is concerned, it is irrelevant whether a government's racial classifications are drawn by those who wish to oppress a race or by those who have a sincere desire to help those thought to be disadvantaged. . . .

These programs . . . also undermine the moral basis of the equal protection principle. Purchased at the price of immeasurable human suffering, the equal protection principle reflects our Nation's understanding that such classifications ultimately have a destructive impact on the individual and our society. . . . [T]here can be no doubt that racial paternalism and its unintended consequences can be as poisonous and pernicious as any other form of discrimination. So-called "benign" discrimination teaches many that because of chronic and apparently immutable handicaps, minorities cannot compete with them without their patronizing indulgence. Inevitably, such programs engender attitudes of superiority or, alternatively, provoke resentment among those who believe that they have been wronged by the government's use of race. These programs stamp minorities with a badge of inferiority and may cause them to develop dependencies or to adopt an attitude that they are "entitled" to preferences. . . .

In my mind, government-sponsored racial discrimination based on benign prejudice is just as noxious as discrimination inspired by malicious prejudice. In each instance, it is racial discrimination, plain and simple.

■ JUSTICE STEVENS, with whom JUSTICE GINSBURG joins, dissenting.

. . .

II

The Court's concept of "consistency" assumes that there is no significant difference between a decision by the majority to impose a special burden on the members of a minority race and a decision by the majority to provide a benefit to certain members of that minority notwithstanding its incidental burden on some members of the majority. [T]hat assumption is untenable. There is no moral or constitutional equivalence between a policy that is designed to perpetuate a caste system and one that seeks to eradicate racial subordination. Invidious discrimination is an engine of oppression, subjugating a disfavored group to enhance or maintain the power of the majority. Remedial race-based preferences reflect the opposite impulse: a desire to foster equality in society. No sensible conception of the Government's constitutional obligation to "govern impartially" . . . should ignore this distinction.[1]

. . .

The consistency that the Court espouses would disregard the difference between a "No Trespassing" sign and a welcome mat. . . .

---

[1] . . . The Court suggests today that "strict scrutiny" means something different—something less strict—when applied to benign racial classifications. Although I agree that benign programs deserve different treatment than invidious programs, there is a danger that the fatal language of "strict scrutiny" will skew the analysis and place well-crafted benign programs at unnecessary risk.

... [With respect to the] supposed inability to differentiate between "invidious" and "benign" discrimination[,] the term "affirmative action" is common and well understood [and i]ts presence in everyday parlance shows that people understand the difference between good intentions and bad. . . .

. . .

As a matter of constitutional and democratic principle, a decision by representatives of the majority to discriminate against the members of a minority race is fundamentally different from those same representatives' decision to impose incidental costs on the majority of their constituents in order to provide a benefit to a disadvantaged minority.[5] . . .

III

The Court's concept of "congruence" assumes . . . no significant difference between a decision by the Congress . . . to adopt an affirmative-action program and such a decision by a State or a municipality. [T]hat assumption . . . ignores important practical and legal differences between federal and state or local decisionmakers.

. . . Metro Broadcasting, Inc. v. FCC, 497 U.S. 547 (1990), . . . identified the special "institutional competence" of our National Legislature [and] recalled the several opinions in *Fullilove* that admonished this Court to "approach our task with appropriate deference to the Congress, a co-equal branch charged by the Constitution with the power to 'provide for the . . . general Welfare of the United States' and 'to enforce, by appropriate legislation,' the equal protection guarantees of the Fourteenth Amendment. . . ." . . .

. . . In his separate opinion in Richmond v. J.A. Croson Co., 488 U.S. 469, 520–524 (1989), Justice Scalia discussed the basis for this distinction. . . .

In her plurality opinion in *Croson*, Justice O'Connor also emphasized the importance of this distinction . . . .

An additional reason for giving greater deference to the National Legislature than to a local law-making body is that federal affirmative-action programs represent the will of our entire Nation's elected representatives, whereas a state or local program may have an impact on nonresident entities who played no part in the decision to enact it. Thus, in the state or local context, individuals who were unable to vote for the local representatives who enacted a race-conscious program may nonetheless feel the effects of that program. . . .

. . .

. . . The Fourteenth Amendment . . . represents our Nation's consensus, achieved after hard experience throughout our sorry history of race relations, that the Federal Government must be the primary defender of racial minorities against the States,

---

[5] . . . Justice Thomas argues that the most significant cost associated with an affirmative-action program is its adverse stigmatic effect on its intended beneficiaries. Although I agree that this cost may be more significant than many people realize, . . . I do not think it applies to the facts of this case. First, . . . [n]o beneficiaries of the specific program . . . have challenged its constitutionality—perhaps because they do not find the preferences stigmatizing, or perhaps because their ability to opt out of the program provides them all the relief they would need. Second, . . . Justice Thomas' extreme proposition—that there is a moral and constitutional equivalence between an attempt to subjugate and an attempt to redress the effects of a caste system—[is not] at all persuasive. It is one thing to question the wisdom of affirmative-action programs. . . . It is another thing altogether to equate the many well-meaning and intelligent lawmakers and their constituents—whether members of majority or minority races—who have supported affirmative action over the years, to segregationists and bigots. Finally,. . . I am not persuaded that the psychological damage brought on by affirmative action is as severe as that engendered by racial subordination. That, in any event, is a judgment the political branches can be trusted to make. . . .

some of which may be inclined to oppress such minorities. A rule of "congruence" that ignores a purposeful "incongruity" so fundamental to our system of government is unacceptable.

. . .

IV

. . .

This is the third time in the Court's entire history that it has considered the constitutionality of a federal affirmative-action program. On each of the two prior occasions, the first in 1980, Fullilove v. Klutznick, 448 U.S. 448, and the second in 1990, Metro Broadcasting, Inc. v. FCC, 497 U.S. 547, the Court upheld the program. . . .

. . . *Today's* decision is an unjustified departure from settled law.

. . .

V

The Court's holding in *Fullilove* surely governs the result in this case. . . . [E]ven if my dissenting views in *Fullilove* had prevailed, this program would be valid.

Unlike the [10% set-aside in public contracts under the] 1977 Act, the present statutory scheme does not make race the sole criterion of eligibility for participation in the program. . . . [A] small business may qualify as a DBE, by showing that it is both socially and economically disadvantaged, even if it receives [no race-based] presumption[ ]. . . . Th[is] preference is more inclusive . . . because it does not make race a necessary qualification.

More importantly, race is not a sufficient qualification. Whereas a millionaire with a long history of financial successes . . . would have qualified for a preference under the 1977 Act merely because he was an Asian American or an African American, . . . [t]he DBE program excludes members of minority races who are not, in fact, socially or economically disadvantaged. . . . Unlike the 1977 set-asides, the current preference is designed to overcome the social and economic disadvantages that are often associated with racial characteristics. [I]n a particular case, . . . the presumptions can be rebutted. . . . The program is thus designed to allow race to play a part in the decisional process only when there is a meaningful basis for assuming its relevance.

. . .

Significantly, the current program, unlike the 1977 set-aside, does not establish any requirement—numerical or otherwise—that a general contractor must hire DBE subcontractors. . . . [T]he current program contains no quota. Although it provides monetary incentives to general contractors to hire DBE subcontractors, it does not require them to hire DBE's, and they do not lose their contracts if they fail to do so. The . . . preference here is far less rigid, and thus more narrowly tailored, than the 1977 Act. . . .

Finally, the record shows a dramatic contrast between the sparse deliberations that preceded the 1977 Act . . . and the extensive hearings conducted in several Congresses before the current program was developed. . . . [T]he Court of Appeals' judgment upholding this more carefully crafted program should be affirmed.

. . .

■ JUSTICE SOUTER, with whom JUSTICE GINSBURG and JUSTICE BREYER join, dissenting.

. . .

. . . [T]he Court's . . . recognition today that strict scrutiny can be compatible with the survival of a classification so reviewed demonstrates that our concepts of equal protection enjoy a greater elasticity than the standard categories might suggest. . . .

. . .

■ JUSTICE GINSBURG, with whom JUSTICE BREYER joins, dissenting.

. . .

The divisions in this difficult case should not obscure the Court's recognition of the persistence of racial inequality and a majority's acknowledgement of Congress' authority to act affirmatively, not only to end discrimination, but also to counteract discrimination's lingering effects. . . . Those effects, reflective of a system of racial caste only recently ended, are evident in our workplaces, markets, and neighborhoods. . . .

Given this history and its practical consequences, Congress surely can conclude that a carefully designed affirmative action program may help to realize, finally, the "equal protection of the laws" the Fourteenth Amendment has promised since 1868.

II

The lead opinion . . . strongly suggests that the strict standard announced is indeed "fatal" for classifications burdening groups that have suffered discrimination in our society. That seems to me, and, I believe, to the Court, the enduring lesson one should draw from Korematsu v. United States, 323 U.S. 214 (1944). . . .

For a classification made to hasten the day when "we are just one race," (Scalia, J., concurring in part and concurring in judgment), however, the lead opinion has dispelled the notion that "strict scrutiny" is " 'fatal in fact.' " . . . Properly, a majority of the Court calls for review that is searching, in order to ferret out classifications in reality malign, but masquerading as benign. . . .

Close review also is in order for this further reason. . . . [S]ome members of the historically favored race can be hurt by catch-up mechanisms designed to cope with the lingering effects of entrenched racial subjugation. Court review can ensure that preferences are not so large as to trammel unduly upon the opportunities of others or interfere too harshly with legitimate expectations of persons in once-preferred groups. . . .

* * *

While I would not disturb the programs challenged in this case, and would leave their improvement to the political branches, I see today's decision as one that allows our precedent to evolve, still to be informed by and responsive to changing conditions.

Rice v. Cayetano
528 U.S. 495 (2000).

The report in this case appears, infra, at p. 680.

Grutter v. Bollinger

539 U.S. 306, 123 S.Ct. 2325, 156 L.Ed.2d 304 (2003).

■ JUSTICE O'CONNOR delivered the opinion of the Court.

This case requires us to decide whether the use of race as a factor in student admissions by the University of Michigan Law School . . . is unlawful.

I

A

The Law School['s admissions policy seeks an academically capable, diverse student body through efforts that sought to] compl[y] with this Court's most recent ruling on the use of race in university admissions. See Regents of Univ. of Cal. v. Bakke, 438 U.S. 265 (1978). . . .

The hallmark of that policy is its focus on academic ability coupled with a flexible assessment of applicants' talents, experiences, and potential "to contribute to the learning of those around them." . . .

The policy makes clear . . . that even the highest possible score does not guarantee admission. . . . Nor does a low score automatically disqualify an applicant. . . .

The policy aspires to "achieve that diversity which has the potential to enrich everyone's education and thus make a law school class stronger than the sum of its parts." . . . The policy does not restrict the types of diversity contributions eligible for "substantial weight" in the admissions process, but instead recognizes "many possible bases for diversity admissions." . . . The policy does, however, reaffirm the Law School's longstanding commitment to "one particular type of diversity," that is, "racial and ethnic diversity with special reference to the inclusion of students from groups which have been historically discriminated against, like African-Americans, Hispanics and Native Americans, who without this commitment might not be represented in our student body in meaningful numbers." . . . By enrolling a " 'critical mass' of [underrepresented] minority students," the Law School seeks to "ensur[e] their ability to make unique contributions to the character of the Law School." . . .

. . .

B

Petitioner Barbara Grutter is a white Michigan resident who applied to the Law School in 1996 with a 3.8 grade point average and 161 LSAT score. The Law School [eventually] rejected her application [and she sued,] . . . alleg[ing unlawful racial discrimination] . . .

[The District Court heard extensive testimony that included the law school's Director of Admissions reporting that he would frequently consult "daily reports" keeping track of the racial and ethnic composition of the class to ensure that a critical mass of underrepresented minority students would be reached so as to realize the educational benefits of a diverse student body; a successor Director of Admissions stating that there is no number, percentage, or range of numbers or percentages that constitute critical mass but that without considering race a critical mass of underrepresented minority students could not be enrolled; and the Dean of the Law School indicating that critical mass means numbers such that underrepresented minority students do not feel isolated or like spokespersons for their race. Petitioner's expert testified that membership in certain minority groups " 'is an extremely strong factor in the decision for acceptance,' " but "conceded that race is not the predominant factor in the Law School's admissions calculus." The Law School's expert testified that a race-blind admissions system would have a "'very dramatic,'" negative effect on underrepresented minority admissions. Specifically, he testified that "in 2000, 35 percent of underrepresented minority applicants were admitted[, whereas he] predicted that if race were not considered, only 10 percent . . . would have been admitted." Underrepresented minority students would then have comprised 4 percent of the entering class instead of 14.5 percent.

[The District Court found the Law School's use of race unlawful. Sitting en banc, the Court of Appeals reversed, with four judges dissenting.]

We granted certiorari . . . to resolve [w]hether diversity is a compelling interest that can justify the narrowly tailored use of race in selecting applicants for admission to public universities. . . .

II

A

We last addressed the use of race in public higher education over 25 years ago. In the landmark *Bakke* case, we reviewed a racial set-aside program that reserved 16 out of 100 seats in a medical school class for members of certain minority groups. . . .

Since this Court's splintered decision in *Bakke*, Justice Powell's opinion announcing the judgment of the Court has served as the touchstone for constitutional analysis of race-conscious admissions policies. Public and private universities across the Nation have modeled their own admissions programs on Justice Powell's views on permissible race-conscious policies. . . .

. . . In Justice Powell's view, when governmental decisions "touch upon an individual's race or ethnic background, he is entitled to a judicial determination that the burden he is asked to bear on that basis is precisely tailored to serve a compelling governmental interest." . . .

. . .

Justice Powell approved the university's use of race to further only one interest: "the attainment of a diverse student body." . . . Justice Powell grounded his analysis in the academic freedom that "long has been viewed as a special concern of the First Amendment." . . .

. . . For Justice Powell, . . . "[t]he diversity that furthers a compelling state interest encompasses a far broader array of qualifications and characteristics of which racial or ethnic origin is but a single though important element." . . .

. . .

. . . [T]oday we endorse Justice Powell's view that student body diversity is a compelling state interest that can justify the use of race in university admissions.

narrowly tailored interest

Holding

B

. . . Because the Fourteenth Amendment "protect[s] *persons*, not *groups*," all "governmental action based on race—a *group* classification long recognized as in most circumstances irrelevant and therefore prohibited—should be subjected to detailed judicial inquiry to ensure that the *personal* right to equal protection of the laws has not been infringed." Adarand Constructors, Inc. v. Penã, 515 U.S. 200, 227 (1995) (emphasis in original . . .). . . .

We have held that all racial classifications imposed by government "must be analyzed by a reviewing court under strict scrutiny." . . . This means that such classifications are constitutional only if they are narrowly tailored to further compelling governmental interests. . . .

Strict scrutiny is not "strict in theory, but fatal in fact." *Adarand* . . . Although all governmental uses of race are subject to strict scrutiny, not all are invalidated by it. . . .

Context matters when reviewing race-based governmental action under the Equal Protection Clause. . . . Not every decision influenced by race is equally objectionable and strict scrutiny is designed to provide a framework for carefully examining the importance and the sincerity of the reasons advanced by the governmental decisionmaker for the use of race in that particular context.

III

A

With these principles in mind, we turn to the question whether the Law School's use of race is justified by a compelling state interest. [R]espondents assert only one justification for their use of race in the admissions process: obtaining "the educational benefits that flow from a diverse student body." . . .

. . . [S]ome language in [our affirmative-action cases decided since *Bakke*] might be read to suggest that remedying past discrimination is the only permissible justification for race-based governmental action. . . . But we have never held that. . . . Today, we hold that the Law School has a compelling interest in attaining a diverse student body.

The Law School's educational judgment that such diversity is essential to its educational mission is one to which we defer. . . . Our scrutiny . . . is no less strict for taking into account complex educational judgments in an area that lies primarily within the expertise of the university. Our holding today is in keeping with our tradition of giving a degree of deference to a university's academic decisions, within constitutionally prescribed limits. . . .

We have long recognized that, given the important purpose of public education and the expansive freedoms of speech and thought associated with the university environment, universities occupy a special niche in our constitutional tradition. . . . Our conclusion that the Law School has a compelling interest in a diverse student body is informed by our view that attaining a diverse student body is at the heart of the Law School's proper institutional mission, and that 'good faith' on the part of a university is 'presumed' absent 'a showing to the contrary.' " . . .

As part of its goal of "assembling a class that is both exceptionally academically qualified and broadly diverse," the Law School seeks to "enroll a 'critical mass' of minority students." . . . The Law School's interest is not simply "to assure within its student body some specified percentage of a particular group merely because of its race or ethnic origin." *Bakke*, . . . (opinion of Powell, J.). That would amount to outright racial balancing, which is patently unconstitutional. . . . Rather, the Law School's concept of critical mass is defined by reference to the educational benefits that diversity is designed to produce.

These benefits are substantial. As the District Court emphasized, the Law School's admissions policy promotes "cross-racial understanding," helps to break down racial stereotypes, and "enables [students] to better understand persons of different races." . . . These benefits are "important and laudable," because "classroom discussion is livelier, more spirited, and simply more enlightening and interesting" when the students have "the greatest possible variety of backgrounds." . . .

. . . [N]umerous studies show that student body diversity promotes learning outcomes, and "better prepares students for an increasingly diverse workforce and society, and better prepares them as professionals." Brief for American Educational Research Association et al. as *Amici Curiae* 3; see, *e.g.*, W. Bowen & D. Bok, The Shape of the River (1998); Diversity Challenged: Evidence on the Impact of Affirmative Action (G. Orfield & M. Kurlaender eds. 2001); Compelling Interest: Examining the Evidence on Racial Dynamics in Colleges and Universities (M. Chang, D. Witt, J. Jones, & K. Hakuta eds. 2003).

These benefits are not theoretical but real, as major American businesses have made clear that the skills needed in today's increasingly global marketplace can only be developed through exposure to widely diverse people, cultures, ideas, and viewpoints. Brief for 3M et al. as *Amici Curiae* 5; Brief for General Motors Corp. as *Amicus Curiae* 3–4. What is more, high-ranking retired officers and civilian leaders of the United States military assert that, "[b]ased on [their] decades of experience," a "highly qualified, racially diverse officer corps . . . is essential to the military's ability to fulfill its principle mission to provide national security." . . . The primary sources for the Nation's officer corps are the service academies and the Reserve Officers Training Corps (ROTC), the latter comprising students already admitted to participating colleges and universities. . . . At present, "the military cannot achieve an officer corps that is *both* highly qualified *and* racially diverse unless the service academies and the ROTC used limited race-conscious recruiting and admissions policies." *Ibid.* (emphasis in original). To fulfill its mission, the military "must be selective in admissions for training and education for the officer corps, *and* it must train and educate a highly qualified, racially diverse officer corps in a racially diverse setting." . . . (emphasis in original). We agree that "[i]t requires only a small step from this analysis to conclude that our country's other most selective institutions must remain both diverse and selective." *Ibid.*

We have repeatedly acknowledged the overriding importance of preparing students for work and citizenship . . . . Effective participation by members of all racial and ethnic groups in the civic life of our Nation is essential if the dream of one Nation, indivisible, is to be realized.

Moreover, universities, and in particular, law schools, represent the training ground for a large number of our Nation's leaders. . . . Individuals with law degrees occupy roughly half the state governorships, more than half the seats in the United States Senate, and more than a third of the seats in the United States House of Representatives. . . . The pattern is even more striking when it comes to highly selective law schools. A handful of these schools accounts for 25 of the 100 United States Senators, 74 United States Courts of Appeals judges, and nearly 200 of the more than 600 United States District Court judges. . . .

In order to cultivate a set of leaders with legitimacy in the eyes of the citizenry, it is necessary that the path to leadership be visibly open to talented and qualified individuals of every race and ethnicity. . . . Access to legal education (and thus the legal profession) must be inclusive of talented and qualified individuals of every race and ethnicity, so that all members of our heterogeneous society may participate in the educational institutions that provide the training and education necessary to succeed in America.

The Law School does not premise its need for critical mass on "any belief that minority students always (or even consistently) express some characteristic minority viewpoint on any issue." . . . To the contrary, diminishing the force of such stereotypes is both a crucial part of the Law School's mission, and one that it cannot accomplish with only token numbers of minority students. Just as growing up in a particular region or having particular professional experiences is likely to affect an individual's views, so too is one's own, unique experience of being a racial minority in a society, like our own, in which race unfortunately still matters. . . .

B

Even . . . when drawing racial distinctions is permissible to further a compelling state interest, . . . ". . . the means chosen to accomplish the [government's] asserted purpose must be specifically and narrowly framed to accomplish that purpose." . . .

. . . [T]he narrow-tailoring inquiry . . . must be calibrated to fit the distinct issues raised by the use of race to achieve student body diversity in public higher education. Contrary to Justice Kennedy's assertions, we do not "abandon[] strict scrutiny." Rather, . . . we adhere to *Adarand*'s teaching that the very purpose of strict scrutiny is to take such "relevant differences into account." . . .

. . .

We find that the Law School's admissions program bears the hallmarks of a narrowly tailored plan. As Justice Powell made clear in *Bakke*, truly individualized consideration demands that race be used in a flexible, nonmechanical way. It follows . . . that universities cannot establish quotas for members of certain racial groups or put members of those groups on separate admissions tracks. . . . Nor can universities insulate applicants who belong to certain racial or ethnic groups from the competition for admission. . . . Universities can, however, consider race or ethnicity more flexibly as a "plus" factor in the context of individualized consideration of each and every applicant. . . .

We are satisfied that the Law School's admissions program . . . does not operate as a quota. Properly understood, a "quota" is a program in which a certain fixed number or proportion of opportunities are "reserved exclusively for certain minority groups." . . . Quotas . . ."insulate the individual from comparison with all other candidates for the available seats." . . .

. . .

The Law School's goal of attaining a critical mass of underrepresented minority students does not transform its program into a quota. . . ."[S]ome attention to numbers," without more, does not transform a flexible admissions system into a rigid quota. . . . Nor, as Justice Kennedy posits, does the Law School's consultation of the "daily reports,' "which keep track of the racial and ethnic composition of the class (as well as of residency and gender), "suggest [] there was no further attempt at individual review save for race itself" during the final stages of the admissions process. To the contrary, the Law School's admissions officers testified without contradiction that they never gave race any more or less weight based on the information contained in these reports. . . . Moreover, as Justice Kennedy concedes, between 1993 and 2000, the number of African-American, Latino, and Native-American students in each class at the Law School varied from 13.5 to 20.1 percent, a range inconsistent with a quota.

The Chief Justice believes that the Law School's policy conceals an attempt to achieve racial balancing, and cites admissions data to contend that the Law School discriminates among different groups within the critical mass. But, as the Chief Justice concedes, the number of underrepresented minority students who ultimately enroll in the Law School differs substantially from their representation in the applicant pool and varies considerably for each group from year to year. . . .

That a race-conscious admissions program does not operate as a quota does not, by itself, satisfy the requirement of individualized consideration. . . .

Here, the Law School engages in a highly individualized, holistic review of each applicant's file, giving serious consideration to all the ways an applicant might contribute to a diverse educational environment. . . . Unlike the program at issue in Gratz v. Bollinger, [539 U.S. 244 (2003),] the Law School awards no mechanical, predetermined diversity "bonuses" based on race or ethnicity. . . .

We also find that . . . all factors that may contribute to student body diversity are meaningfully considered . . . .

. . .

. . . The Law School frequently accepts nonminority applicants with grades and test scores lower than underrepresented minority applicants (and other nonminority applicants) who are rejected. . . . This shows that the Law School seriously weighs many other diversity factors besides race that can make a real and dispositive difference for nonminority applicants as well. By this flexible approach, the Law School sufficiently takes into account, in practice as well as in theory, a wide variety of characteristics besides race and ethnicity that contribute to a diverse student body. . . .

Petitioner and the United States argue that the Law School's plan is not narrowly tailored because race-neutral means exist to obtain the educational benefits of student body diversity that the Law School seeks. We disagree. Narrow tailoring does not require exhaustion of every conceivable race-neutral alternative. Nor does it require a university to choose between maintaining a reputation for excellence or fulfilling a commitment to provide educational opportunities to members of all racial groups. . . . Narrow tailoring does, however, require serious, good faith consideration of workable race-neutral alternatives that will achieve the diversity the university seeks. . . .

We agree with the Court of Appeals that the Law School sufficiently considered *Narrowly tailored answer* workable race-neutral alternatives. The District Court took the Law School to task for failing to consider race-neutral alternatives such as "using a lottery system" or "decreasing the emphasis for all applicants on undergraduate GPA and LSAT scores." . . . But these alternatives would require a dramatic sacrifice of diversity, the academic quality of all admitted students, or both.

. . . [A] lottery would . . . sacrifice all other educational values, not to mention every other kind of diversity. . . . [L]lower[ing] admissions standards for all students [would be] a drastic remedy that would require the Law School to become a much different institution and sacrifice a vital component of its educational mission. The United States advocates "percentage plans," recently adopted by public undergraduate institutions in Texas, Florida, and California to guarantee admission to all students above a certain class-rank threshold in every high school in the State. . . . The United States does not, however, explain how such plans could work for graduate and professional schools. Moreover, even assuming such plans are race-neutral, they may preclude the university from conducting the individualized assessments necessary to assemble a student body that is not just racially diverse, but diverse along all the qualities valued by the university. We are satisfied that the Law School adequately considered race-neutral alternatives currently capable of producing a critical mass without forcing the Law School to abandon the academic selectivity that is the cornerstone of its educational mission.

. . .

We are satisfied that the Law School's admissions program does not [unduly harm members of any racial group]. Because the Law School considers "all pertinent elements of diversity," it can (and does) select nonminority applicants who have greater potential to enhance student body diversity over underrepresented minority applicants. . . . As Justice Powell recognized in *Bakke*, so long as a race-conscious admissions program uses race as a "plus" factor in the context of individualized consideration, a rejected applicant "will not have been foreclosed from all consideration for that seat simply because he was not the right color or had the wrong surname. . . . His qualifications would have been weighed fairly and competitively, and he would have no basis to complain of unequal treatment under the Fourteenth Amendment."

. . .

. . .

. . . [R]ace-conscious admissions policies must be limited in time. This requirement reflects that racial classifications, however compelling their goals, are potentially so dangerous that they may be employed no more broadly than the interest demands. . . .

. . .

We take the Law School at its word that it would "like nothing better than to find a race-neutral admissions formula" and will terminate its race-conscious admissions program as soon as practicable. . . . It has been 25 years since Justice Powell first approved the use of race to further an interest in student body diversity in the context of public higher education. Since that time, the number of minority applicants with high grades and test scores has indeed increased. . . . We expect that 25 years from now, the use of racial preferences will no longer be necessary to further the interest approved today.

. . . The judgment . . . is affirmed.

■ JUSTICE GINSBURG, with whom JUSTICE BREYER joins, concurring.

. . .

The Court . . . observes that "[i]t has been 25 years since Justice Powell . . . first approved the use of race to further an interest in student body diversity in the context of public higher education." For at least part of that time, however, the law could not fairly be described as "settled," and in some regions of the Nation, overtly race-conscious admissions policies have been proscribed. . . . Moreover, it was only 25 years before *Bakke* that this Court declared public school segregation unconstitutional, a declaration that, after prolonged resistance, yielded an end to a law-enforced racial caste system, itself the legacy of centuries of slavery. . . .

It is well documented that conscious and unconscious race bias, even rank discrimination based on race, remain alive in our land, impeding realization of our highest values and ideals. . . . As to public education, data for the years 2000–2001 show that 71.6% of African-American children and 76.3% of Hispanic children attended a school in which minorities made up a majority of the student body. . . . And schools in predominantly minority communities lag far behind others measured by the educational resources available to them. . . .

. . . [I]t remains the current reality that many minority students encounter markedly inadequate and unequal educational opportunities. Despite these inequalities, some minority students are able to meet the high threshold requirements set for admission to the country's finest undergraduate and graduate educational institutions. As lower school education in minority communities improves, an increase in the number of such students may be anticipated. From today's vantage point, one may hope, but not firmly forecast, that over the next generation's span, progress toward nondiscrimination and genuinely equal opportunity will make it safe to sunset affirmative action.

■ CHIEF JUSTICE REHNQUIST, with whom JUSTICE SCALIA, JUSTICE KENNEDY, and JUSTICE THOMAS join, dissenting.

. . . I do not believe . . . that the University of Michigan Law School's . . . means are narrowly tailored to the interest it asserts. . . . Stripped of its "critical mass" veil, the Law School's program is revealed as a naked effort to achieve racial balancing.

. . .

From 1995 through 2000, the Law School admitted between 1,130 and 1,310 students. Of those, between 13 and 19 were Native American, between 91 and 108 were African-Americans, and between 47 and 56 were Hispanic. If the Law School is admitting between 91 and 108 African-Americans in order to achieve "critical mass," thereby preventing African-American students from feeling "isolated or like spokespersons for their race," one would think that a number of the same order of magnitude would be necessary to accomplish the same purpose for Hispanics and Native Americans. Similarly, even if all of the Native American applicants admitted in a given year matriculate, which the record demonstrates is not at all the case, how can this possibly constitute a "critical mass" of Native Americans in a class of over 350 students? In order for this pattern of admission to be consistent with the Law School's explanation of "critical mass," one would have to believe that the objectives of "critical mass" offered by respondents are achieved with only half the number of Hispanics and one-sixth the number of Native Americans as compared to African-Americans. But respondents offer no race-specific reasons for such disparities. Instead, they simply emphasize the importance of achieving "critical mass," without any explanation of why that concept is applied differently among the three underrepresented minority groups.

These different numbers, moreover, come only as a result of substantially different treatment among the three underrepresented minority groups . . . .

Review of the record reveals only 67 [rejected underrepresented minority applicants between 1995 and 2000 with at least a 3.5 GPA and a 159 or higher on the LSAT (levels at which some nonminority applicants were admitted). Of these,] *56* were Hispanic, while only 6 were African-American, and only 5 were Native American. This discrepancy reflects a consistent practice. . . .

. . . [T]he Law School's disparate admissions practices with respect to these minority groups demonstrate that its alleged goal of "critical mass" is simply a sham. . . . Surely strict scrutiny cannot permit these sort of disparities without at least some explanation.

Only when the "critical mass" label is discarded does a likely explanation for these numbers emerge. . . .

[T]he correlation between the percentage of the Law School's pool of applicants who are members of the three minority groups and the percentage of the admitted applicants who are members of these same groups is far too precise to be dismissed as merely the result of the school paying "some attention to [the] numbers." . . . [F]rom 1995 through 2000 the percentage of admitted applicants who were members of these minority groups closely tracked the percentage of individuals in the school's applicant pool who were from the same groups.

. . .

For example, in 1995, when 9.7% of the applicant pool was African-American, 9.4% of the admitted class was African-American. By 2000, only 7.5% of the applicant pool was African-American, and 7.3% of the admitted class was African-American. This correlation is striking. . . . The tight correlation between the percentage of applicants and admittees of a given race . . . must result from careful race-based planning by the Law School. It suggests a formula for admission based on the aspirational assumption that all applicants are equally qualified academically, and therefore that the proportion of each group admitted should be the same as the proportion of that group in the applicant pool. . . .

. . . [T]he ostensibly flexible nature of the Law School's admissions program that the Court finds appealing appears to be, in practice, a carefully managed program designed to ensure proportionate representation of applicants from selected minority groups.

. . . The Law School has offered no explanation for its actual admissions practices and, unexplained, we are bound to conclude that the Law School has managed its admissions program, not to achieve a "critical mass," but to extend offers of admission to members of selected minority groups in proportion to their statistical representation in the applicant pool[—]precisely the type of racial balancing that the Court itself calls "patently unconstitutional."

Finally, I believe that the Law School's program fails strict scrutiny because it is devoid of any reasonably precise time limit on the Law School's use of race in admissions. . . .

. . .

The Court, in an unprecedented display of deference under our strict scrutiny analysis, upholds the Law School's program despite its obvious flaws. . . . Here the means actually used are forbidden by the Equal Protection Clause. . . .

■ JUSTICE KENNEDY, dissenting.

. . . The Court . . . does not apply strict scrutiny. . . .

. . . Our precedents provide a basis for the Court's acceptance of a university's considered judgment that racial diversity among students can further its educational task, when supported by empirical evidence. . . .

. . . [B]ut deference is not to be given with respect to the methods by which it is pursued. . . .

. . .

. . . There was little deviation among admitted minority students during the years from 1995 to 1998. The percentage of enrolled minorities fluctuated only by 0.3%, from 13.5% to 13.8%. The number of minority students to whom offers were extended varied by just a slightly greater magnitude of 2.2%, from the high of 15.6% in 1995 to the low of 13.4% in 1998.

The District Court relied on this uncontested fact to draw an inference that the Law School's pursuit of critical mass mutated into the equivalent of a quota. . . .

The narrow fluctuation band raises an inference that the Law School subverted individual determination, and strict scrutiny requires the Law School to overcome the inference. . . .

. . .

The consultation of daily reports during the last stages in the admissions process suggests there was no further attempt at individual review save for race itself. The admissions officers could use the reports to recalibrate the plus factor given to race depending on how close they were to achieving the Law School's goal of critical mass. The bonus factor of race would then become divorced from individual review; it would be premised instead on the numerical objective set by the Law School.

The Law School made no effort to guard against this danger. . . .

. . .

If universities are given the latitude to administer programs that are tantamount to quotas, they will have few incentives to make the existing minority admissions schemes transparent and protective of individual review. The unhappy consequence will be to perpetuate the hostilities that proper consideration of race is designed to avoid. . . .

It is regrettable the Court's important holding allowing racial minorities to have their special circumstances considered in order to improve their educational opportunities is accompanied by a suspension of the strict scrutiny which was the predicate of allowing race to be considered in the first place. . . . [T]hough I reiterate my approval of giving appropriate consideration to race in this one context, I must dissent in the present case.

■ JUSTICE SCALIA, with whom JUSTICE THOMAS joins, concurring in part and dissenting in part.

I join the opinion of The Chief Justice. As he demonstrates, the University of Michigan Law School's mystical "critical mass" justification for its discrimination by race challenges even the most gullible mind. The admissions statistics show it to be a sham to cover a scheme of racially proportionate admissions.

I also join Parts I through VII of Justice Thomas's opinion. I find particularly unanswerable his central point: that the allegedly "compelling state interest" at issue here is not the incremental "educational benefit" that emanates from the fabled "critical mass" of minority students, but rather Michigan's interest in maintaining a "prestige" law school whose normal admissions standards disproportionately exclude blacks and other minorities. If that is a compelling state interest, everything is.

. . .

. . . The Constitution proscribes government discrimination on the basis of race, and state-provided education is no exception.

■ JUSTICE THOMAS, with whom JUSTICE SCALIA joins as to Parts I-VII, concurring in part and dissenting in part.

. . . I believe blacks can achieve in every avenue of American life without the meddling of university administrators. . . .

. . . The Law School, of its own choosing, and for its own purposes, maintains an exclusionary admissions system that it knows produces racially disproportionate results. Racial discrimination is not a permissible solution to the self-inflicted wounds of this elitist admissions policy.

. . .

I

. . .

Where the Court has accepted only national security, and rejected even the best interests of a child, as a justification for racial discrimination, I conclude that only those measures the State must take to provide a bulwark against anarchy, or to prevent violence, will constitute a "pressing public necessity." . . .

The Constitution abhors classifications based on race, not only because those classifications can harm favored races or are based on illegitimate motives, but also because every time the government places citizens on racial registers and makes race relevant to the provision of benefits, it demeans us all. . . .

II

. . .

. . . It is the *educational benefits* that are the end, or allegedly compelling state interest, not "diversity."

. . . [T]he Law School seeks to improve marginally the education it offers without sacrificing too much of its exclusivity and elite status.

. . .

III

. . .

[T]here is no pressing public necessity in maintaining a public law school at all and, it follows, certainly not an elite law school. Likewise, marginal improvements in legal education do not qualify as a compelling state interest.

. . .

. . . [E]ven assuming that a State may, under appropriate circumstances, demonstrate a cognizable interest in having an elite law school, Michigan has failed to do so here.

. . .

. . . [I]t is precisely the Law School's status as an elite institution that causes it to be a way-station for the rest of the country's lawyers, rather than a training ground for those who will remain in Michigan. The Law School's decision to be an elite institution does little to advance the welfare of the people of Michigan or any cognizable interest of the State of Michigan.

. . .

IV

The interest in remaining elite and exclusive that the majority thinks so obviously critical requires the use of admissions "standards" that, in turn, create the Law School's "need" to discriminate on the basis of race. . . .

[A]ccepting all students who meet minimum qualifications . . . could achieve its vision of the racially aesthetic student body without the use of racial discrimination. . . .

. . .

. . . The Court relies heavily on social science evidence to justify its deference. . . . The Court never acknowledges, however, the growing evidence that racial (and other sorts) of heterogeneity actually impairs learning among black students. See, *e.g.,* Flowers & Pascarella, Cognitive Effects of College Racial Composition on African American Students After 3 Years of College, 40 J. of College Student Development 669, 674 (1999) (concluding that black students experience superior cognitive development at Historically Black Colleges (HBCs) and that, even among blacks, "a substantial diversity moderates the cognitive effects of attending an HBC"); Allen, The Color of Success: African-American College Student Outcomes at Predominantly White and Historically Black Public Colleges and Universities, 62 Harv. Educ. Rev. 26, 35 (1992) (finding that black students attending HBCs report higher academic achievement than those attending predominantly white colleges).

. . .

The majority grants deference to the Law School's "assessment that diversity will, in fact, yield educational benefits." It follows, therefore, that an HBC's assessment that racial homogeneity will yield educational benefits would similarly be given deference. An HBC's rejection of white applicants in order to maintain racial homogeneity seems permissible, therefore, under the majority's view of the Equal Protection Clause. . . .

. . .

. . . [T]he majority ignores the "experience" of those institutions that have been forced to abandon explicit racial discrimination in admissions.

The sky has not fallen at Boalt Hall at the University of California, Berkeley, for example. Prior to Proposition 209's adoption of Cal. Const., Art. 1, § 31(a), which bars the State from "grant[ing] preferential treatment . . . on the basis of race . . . in the operation of . . . public education," Boalt Hall enrolled 20 blacks and 28 Hispanics in its first-year class for 1996. In 2002, without deploying express racial discrimination in admissions, Boalt's entering class enrolled 14 blacks and 36 Hispanics. . . . Total underrepresented minority student enrollment at Boalt Hall now exceeds 1996 levels. Apparently [Michigan] Law School cannot be counted on to be as resourceful. The Court is willfully blind to the very real experience in California and elsewhere, which raises the inference that institutions with "reputation[s] for excellence" rivaling the Law School's have satisfied their sense of mission without resorting to prohibited racial discrimination.

V

. . .

[T]here is nothing ancient, honorable, or constitutionally protected about "selective" admissions . . .

. . . Since its inception, selective admissions has been the vehicle for racial, ethnic, and religious tinkering and experimentation by university administrators. . . . Columbia, Harvard, and others infamously determined that they had "too many" Jews, just as today the Law School argues it would have "too many" whites if it could not discriminate in its admissions process. . . .

Columbia employed intelligence tests precisely because Jewish applicants, who were predominantly immigrants, scored worse on such tests. . . .

Similarly no modern law school can claim ignorance of the poor performance of blacks, relatively speaking, on the Law School Admissions Test (LSAT). Nevertheless, law schools continue to use the test and then attempt to "correct" for black underperformance by using racial discrimination in admissions so as to obtain their aesthetic student body. The Law School's continued adherence to measures it knows produce racially skewed results is not entitled to deference by this Court. . . .

. . . The Law School may freely continue to employ the LSAT and other allegedly merit-based standards in whatever fashion it likes. What the Equal Protection Clause forbids, but the Court today allows, is the use of these standards hand-in-hand with racial discrimination. . . .

. . .

VI

. . .

. . . I [also] must contest the notion that the Law School's discrimination benefits those admitted as a result of it. . . . [N]owhere in any of the filings in this Court is any evidence that the purported "beneficiaries" of this racial discrimination prove themselves by performing at (or even near) the same level as those students who receive no preferences. . . .

. . . The Law School is not looking for those students who, despite a lower LSAT score or undergraduate grade point average, will succeed in the study of law. The Law School seeks only a facade—it is sufficient that the class looks right, even if it does not perform right.

. . .

Beyond the harm the Law School's racial discrimination visits upon its test subjects, no social science has disproved the notion that this discrimination "engender[s] attitudes of superiority or, alternatively, provoke[s] resentment among those who believe that they have been wronged by the government's use of race." . . .

. . . The majority of blacks are admitted to the Law School because of discrimination, and because of this policy all are tarred as undeserving. This problem of stigma does not depend on determinacy as to whether those stigmatized are actually the "beneficiaries" of racial discrimination. When blacks take positions in the highest places of government, industry, or academia, it is an open question today whether their skin color played a part in their advancement. The question itself is the stigma—because either racial discrimination did play a role, in which case the person may be deemed "otherwise unqualified," or it did not, in which case asking the question itself unfairly marks those blacks who would succeed without discrimination. Is this what the Court means by "visibly open"?

. . .

VII

[Although] I believe the Court's opinion to be, in most respects, erroneous[,] I . . . find two points on which I agree.

A

First, I note that the issue of unconstitutional racial discrimination among the groups the Law School prefers is not presented in this case . . . . I join the Court's opinion insofar as it confirms that this type of racial discrimination remains unlawful. . . .

B

. . .

I . . . understand the imposition of a 25-year time limit only as a holding that the deference the Court pays to the Law School's educational judgments and refusal to change its admissions policies will itself expire. . . . The Court defines this time limit in terms of narrow tailoring, but I believe this arises from its refusal to define rigorously the broad state interest vindicated today. . . . With these observations, I join the last sentence of Part III of the opinion of the Court.

. . .

Gratz v. Bollinger
539 U.S. 244 (2003).

In this companion case to Grutter, two white residents of Michigan who had been denied admission to the University of Michigan's undergraduate College of Literature, Science, and the Arts (LSA) brought a class action challenging the University's use of race in its admissions system. That system considered a number of factors in making admissions decisions, including high school grades, standardized test scores, high school quality, curriculum strength, geography, alumni relationships, leadership, and race. It employed a selection index that assigned points for the various factors considered; provided that 100 points would virtually assure admission; and assigned 20 points for being an underrepresented minority applicant. It was "undisputed that the University admits 'virtually every qualified . . . applicant' from" the groups the University considered to be "underrepresented minorities," namely, "African-Americans, Hispanics, and Native Americans." Chief Justice Rehnquist, speaking for a Court majority that included the four dissenters in Grutter plus Justice O'Connor, concluded "that because the University's use of race in its current freshman admissions policy is not narrowly tailored to achieve [its] asserted compelling interest in diversity, the admissions policy violates the Equal Protection Clause of the Fourteenth Amendment" as well as "Title VI and 42 U.S.C. § 1981." Responding to the argument "that 'diversity as a basis for employing racial preferences is simply too open-ended, ill-defined, and indefinite to constitute a compelling interest capable of supporting narrowly-tailored means[,]'" the Chief Justice wrote that "for the reasons set forth today in Grutter v. Bollinger, the Court has rejected these arguments. . . ." But, applying strict scrutiny, the majority found "that the University's policy, which automatically distributes 20 points, or one-fifth of the points needed to guarantee admission, to every single 'underrepresented minority' applicant solely because of race, is not narrowly tailored to achieve the interest in educational diversity that respondents claim justifies their program." The opinion said in pertinent part:

"The current LSA policy does not provide . . . individualized consideration. . . . The only consideration that accompanies [its] distribution of points is a factual review of an application to determine whether an individual is a member of one of these minority groups. Moreover, unlike Justice Powell's example, where the race of a 'particular black applicant' could be considered without being decisive, . . . the LSA's automatic distribution of 20 points has the effect of making 'the factor of race . . . decisive' for virtually every minimally qualified underrepresented minority applicant. . . ."

The "fact that the LSA has created the possibility of an applicant's file being flagged for individualized consideration . . . only emphasizes the flaws of the University's system as a whole when compared to that described by Justice Powell[,]" because "automatically awarding 20 points" virtually guaranteed that "every qualified underrepresented minority applicant [was] admitted" without needing to resort to individualized review (which was available "only . . . *after* admissions counselors automatically distribute the University's version of a 'plus'"), and individualized consideration was "the exception and not the rule" in any event. Finally, that the volume of undergraduate applications might make it impractical "to use the admissions system . . . upheld by the Court today in *Grutter*" did not matter, because "the fact that the implementation of a program capable of providing individualized consideration might present administrative challenges does not render constitutional an otherwise problematic system."

Justice O'Connor wrote a separate concurring opinion, which Justice Breyer joined except insofar as it joined the Court's opinion, contrasting the law school admissions process upheld in *Grutter* with the undergraduate policy invalidated in *Gratz*:

". . . The law school considers the various diversity qualifications of each applicant, including race, on a case-by-case basis. . . . By contrast, [the College] relies on the selection index to assign *every* underrepresented minority applicant the same, *automatic* 20-point bonus without consideration of the particular background, experiences, or qualities of each individual applicant. And this mechanized selection index score, by and large, automatically determines the admissions decision for each applicant. The selection index thus precludes admissions counselors from conducting the type of individualized consideration the Court's opinion in *Grutter* . . . requires: consideration of each applicant's individualized qualifications, including the contribution each individual's race or ethnic identity will make to the diversity of the student body, taking into account diversity within and among all racial and ethnic groups. . . ."

Justice Thomas also wrote a separate concurrence, saying that he "join[ed] the Court's opinion because . . . it correctly applies our precedents, including today's decision in *Grutter v. Bollinger*[, though he] would hold that a State's use of racial discrimination in higher education admissions is categorically prohibited by the Equal Protection Clause." He noted that the "admissions policy that the Court today invalidates does not suffer from the additional constitutional defect of allowing racial 'discriminat[ion]' among [the] groups' included within its definition of underrepresented minorities, . . . because it awards all underrepresented minorities the same racial preference." But "[u]nder today's decisions," it did fail to "allow for

(handwritten margin note: law school - v. - This case)

consideration of . . . nonracial distinctions among applicants on both sides of the single permitted racial classification."

Justice Breyer concurred in the judgment, agreeing with Justice O'Connor except for joining the Court's opinion, and with part of Justice Ginsburg's dissenting opinion. He specifically "agree[d] with Justice Ginsburg that . . . government decisionmakers may properly distinguish between policies of inclusion and exclusion, for the former are more likely to prove consistent with the basic constitutional obligation that the law respect each individual equally. . . ."

Justice Souter dissented, joined on the merits by Justice Ginsburg.[a] He found "the freshman admissions system here . . . closer to what *Grutter* approves than to [the quota system] *Bakke* condemns," because it "lets all applicants compete for all places and values an applicant's offering for any place not only on grounds of race, but on . . . all of the characteristics that the college thinks relevant to student diversity . . . " He noted that "[n]onminority students may receive 20 points for athletic ability, socioeconomic disadvantage, attendance at a socioeconomically disadvantaged or predominantly minority high school, or at the Provost's discretion; they may also receive 10 points for being residents of Michigan, 6 for residence in an underrepresented Michigan county, 5 for leadership and service, and so on." He continued:

"The very nature of a college's permissible practice of awarding value to racial diversity means that race must be considered in a way that increases some applicants' chances for admission. Since college admission is not left entirely to inarticulate intuition, it is hard to see what is inappropriate in assigning some stated value to a relevant characteristic, whether it be reasoning ability, writing style, running speed, or minority race. Justice Powell's plus factors necessarily are assigned some values. The college simply does by a numbered scale what the law school accomplishes in its 'holistic review,' *Grutter* . . . ; the distinction does not imply that applicants to the undergraduate college are denied individualized consideration or a fair chance to compete on the basis of all the various merits their applications may disclose.

"Nor is it possible to say that the 20 points convert race into a decisive factor comparable to reserving minority places as in *Bakke*. . . . The present record obviously shows that nonminority applicants may achieve higher selection point totals than minority applicants owing to characteristics other than race, and the fact that the university admits 'virtually every qualified under-represented minority applicant,' . . . may reflect nothing more than the likelihood that very few qualified minority applicants apply, . . . as well as the possibility that self-selection results in a strong minority applicant pool. It suffices . . . that there are no *Bakke*-like set-asides and that consideration of an applicant's whole spectrum of ability is no more ruled out by giving 20 points for race than by giving the same points for athletic ability or socioeconomic disadvantage.

. . .

". . . Drawing on admissions systems used at public universities in California, Florida, and Texas, the United States contends that Michigan could get student diversity in satisfaction of its compelling interest by guaranteeing admission to a fixed percentage of the top students from each high school in Michigan. . . .

"While there is nothing unconstitutional about such a practice, . . . [4] [t]he 'percentage plans' are just as race conscious as the point scheme (and fairly so), but

---

[a]   Justice Souter also joined a separate dissenting opinion by Justice Stevens, who urged dismissal for lack of jurisdiction and did not reach the merits.

[4]   Of course it might be pointless in the State of Michigan, where minorities are a much smaller fraction of the population than in California, Florida, or Texas. . . .

they get their racially diverse results without saying directly what they are doing or why they are doing it. In contrast, Michigan states its purpose directly.... Equal protection cannot become an exercise in which the winners are the ones who hide the ball."

Another dissent, by Justice Ginsburg, joined by Justice Souter, first asserted that "government decisionmakers may properly distinguish between policies of exclusion and inclusion"; that "[a]ctions designed to burden groups long denied full citizenship stature are not sensibly ranked with measures taken to hasten the day when entrenched discrimination and its after effects have been extirpated"; and that "[c]ontemporary human rights documents draw just this line; they distinguish between policies of oppression and measures designed to accelerate *de facto* equality. See ... the United Nations-initiated Conventions on the Elimination of All Forms of Racial Discrimination and on the Elimination of All Forms of Discrimination against Women. . . ." (Justice Breyer joined this portion of the opinion.) Justice Ginsburg then argued as follows:

"... The racial and ethnic groups to which the College accords special consideration ... historically have been relegated to inferior status by law and social practice; their members continue to experience class-based discrimination to this day.... There is no suggestion that the College adopted its current policy in order to limit or decrease enrollment by any particular racial or ethnic group, and no seats are reserved on the basis of race.... Nor has there been any demonstration that the College's program unduly constricts admissions opportunities for students who do not receive special consideration based on race.... [10]

"... [C]olleges and universities will seek to maintain their minority enrollment—and the networks and opportunities thereby opened to minority graduates—whether or not they can do so in full candor through adoption of affirmative action plans of the kind here at issue. Without recourse to such plans, [they] may resort to camouflage.... If honesty is the best policy, surely Michigan's accurately described, fully disclosed College affirmative action program is preferable to achieving similar numbers through winks, nods, and disguises."[a]

---

[10] The United States points to the "percentage plans" used in California, Florida, and Texas as one example of a "race-neutral alternativ[e]" that would permit the College to enroll meaningful numbers of minority students.... Calling such 10 or 20% plans "race-neutral" seems to me disingenuous, for they "unquestionably were adopted with the specific purpose of increasing representation of African-Americans and Hispanics in the public higher education system." ... Percentage plans depend for their effectiveness on continued racial segregation at the secondary school level: They can ensure significant minority enrollment in universities only if the majority-minority high school population is large enough to guarantee that, in many schools, most of the students in the top 10 or 20% are minorities. Moreover, because such plans link college admission to a single criterion—high school class rank—they create perverse incentives. They encourage parents to keep their children in low-performing segregated schools, and discourage students from taking challenging classes that might lower their grade point averages.... And even if percentage plans could boost the sheer numbers of minority enrollees at the undergraduate level, they do not touch enrollment in graduate and professional schools.

[a] Chief Justice Rehnquist's majority opinion found Justice Ginsburg's "observations" in this paragraph "remarkable for two reasons. First, they suggest that universities—to whose academic judgment we are told in *Grutter v. Bollinger* we should defer—will pursue their affirmative-action programs whether or not they violate the United States Constitution. Second, they recommend that these violations should be dealt with, not by requiring the universities to obey the Constitution, but by changing the Constitution so that it conforms to the conduct of the universities."

Fisher v. University of Texas at Austin

570 U.S. ___, 133 S.Ct. 2411 (2013).

A rejected white applicant contended that the undergraduate admissions process of the University of Texas at Austin (UT), which aimed to achieve a "critical mass" of racial minorities in the undergraduate population, denied her equal protection by impermissibly considering race in a manner that allegedly conflicted with *Grutter*, among other decisions. Reversing a grant of summary judgment by the Court of Appeals that—purporting to apply *Grutter*—had upheld the admissions program, the Supreme Court, with only Justice Ginsburg dissenting (and Justice Kagan not participating), held that the Court of Appeals "did not apply the correct standard of strict scrutiny" insofar as it "confined the strict scrutiny inquiry in too narrow a way by deferring to the University's good faith in its use of racial classifications and affirming the grant of summary judgment on that basis." Accordingly, the Court remanded the case "so that the admissions process can be considered and judged under a correct analysis. . . . Unlike *Grutter*, which was decided after trial, this case arises from cross-motions for summary judgment. In . . . determining whether summary judgment in favor of the University would be appropriate, the Court of Appeals must assess whether the University has offered sufficient evidence that would prove that its admissions program is narrowly tailored to obtain the educational benefits of diversity. Whether this record—and not 'simple . . . assurances of good intention,' *Croson* . . . —is sufficient is a question for the Court of Appeals in the first instance."

The record as it stood showed that following a pre-*Grutter*, 1996 Court of Appeals decision that invalidated a former race-conscious admissions program, the "Texas State Legislature . . . enacted . . . the Top Ten Percent Law grant[ing] automatic admission to any public state college, including the University, to all students in the top 10% of their class at high schools in Texas that comply with certain standards." Together with a new race-neutral, but "holistic" UT admissions process, UT ended up in the year before *Grutter* with an "entering class [that] was 4.5% African-American and 16.9% Hispanic"—compared to an "entering freshman class [that] was 4.1% African-American and 14.5% Hispanic" in the pre-1996 era of race-conscious admissions. Disappointed, however, by a study of undergraduate classes of 5–24 students showing few with "significant enrollment by members of racial minorities[,]" and by " 'anecdotal' reports from students regarding their 'interaction in the classroom[,]' " UT decided in 2004—after *Grutter*—to again take race into account as "a meaningful factor" in admissions.

Justice Kennedy's majority opinion emphasized that although among the Justices there "is disagreement about whether *Grutter* was consistent with the principles of equal protection in approving th[e] compelling interest in diversity[,] . . . the parties here do not ask the Court to revisit that aspect of *Grutter*'s holding." He then continued:

"Once the University has established that its goal of diversity is consistent with strict scrutiny, however, there must still be a further judicial determination that the admissions process meets strict scrutiny in its implementation. The University must prove that the means chosen by the University to attain diversity are narrowly tailored to that goal. On this point, the University receives no deference. *Grutter* made clear that it is for the courts, not for university administrators, to ensure that '[t]he means chosen to accomplish the [government's] asserted purpose must be specifically and narrowly framed to accomplish that purpose.' . . . True, a court can take account of a university's experience and expertise in adopting or rejecting certain admissions processes. But, as the Court said in *Grutter*, it remains at all times the University's obligation to demonstrate, and the Judiciary's obligation to determine, that admissions processes 'ensure that each applicant is evaluated as an individual and not in a way that makes an applicant's race or ethnicity the defining feature of his or her application.' . . .

"Narrow tailoring also requires that the reviewing court verify that it is 'necessary' for a university to use race to achieve the educational benefits of diversity. *Bakke*,. . . . This involves a careful judicial inquiry into whether a university could achieve sufficient diversity without using racial classifications. Although '[n]arrow tailoring does not require exhaustion of every *conceivable* race-neutral alternative,' strict scrutiny does require a court to examine with care, and not defer to, a university's 'serious, good faith consideration of workable race-neutral alternatives.' See *Grutter*, . . . (emphasis added). Consideration by the university is of course *necessary*, but it is not sufficient to satisfy strict scrutiny: The reviewing court must ultimately be satisfied that no workable race-neutral alternatives would produce the educational benefits of diversity. . . . A plaintiff, of course, bears the burden of placing the validity of a university's adoption of an affirmative action plan in issue. But strict scrutiny imposes on the university the ultimate burden of demonstrating, before turning to racial classifications, that available, workable race-neutral alternatives do not suffice.

"Rather than perform this searching examination, however, the Court of Appeals held petitioner could challenge only 'whether [the University's] decision to reintroduce race as a factor in admissions was made in good faith.' . . . And in considering such a challenge, the court would 'presume the University acted in good faith' and place on petitioner the burden of rebutting that presumption. . . . The Court of Appeals held that to 'second-guess the merits' of this aspect of the University's decision was a task it was 'ill-equipped to perform' and that it would attempt only to 'ensure that [the University's] decision to adopt a race-conscious admissions policy followed from [a process of] good faith consideration.' . . . The Court of Appeals thus concluded that 'the narrow-tailoring inquiry—like the compelling-interest inquiry—is undertaken with a degree of deference to the Universit[y].' . . . Because 'the efforts of the University have been studied, serious, and of high purpose,' the Court of Appeals held that the use of race in the admissions program fell within 'a constitutionally protected zone of discretion.' . . .

"These expressions of the controlling standard are at odds with *Grutter*'s command that 'all racial classifications imposed by government "must be analyzed by a reviewing court under strict scrutiny."' . . .

"*Grutter* did not hol𝑑 that good faith would forgive an impermissible consideration of race. It must be remembered that 'the mere recitation of a "benign" or legitimate purpose for a racial classification is entitled to little or no weight.' *Croson*,. . . . Strict scrutiny does not permit a court to accept a school's assertion that its admissions process uses race in a permissible way without a court giving close analysis to the evidence of how the process works in practice.

"The higher education dynamic does not change the narrow tailoring analysis of strict scrutiny applicable in other contexts. . . ."

Justice Kennedy concluded the majority opinion with these remarks:

"Strict scrutiny must not be ' "strict in theory, but fatal in fact," ' *Adarand* . . . ; see also *Grutter* . . . . But the opposite is also true. Strict scrutiny must not be strict in theory but feeble in fact. In order for judicial review to be meaningful, a university must make a showing that its plan is narrowly tailored to achieve the only interest that this Court has approved in this context: the benefits of a student body diversity that 'encompasses a . . . broa[d] array of qualifications and characteristics of which racial or ethnic origin is but a single though important element.' *Bakke*, . . . (opinion of Powell, J.)."

Justice Scalia "join[ed] the Court's opinion in full[,]" but concurred as well to reiterate his view in *Grutter* that the Constitution forbids race discrimination in state-provided education, and to emphasize that "petitioner in this case did not ask us to overrule *Grutter*'s holding that a 'compelling interest' in the educational benefits of diversity can justify racial preferences in university admissions." Justice Thomas also concurred, but added that he "would overrule *Grutter* . . . and hold that a State's use of race in higher education admissions decisions is categorically prohibited by the Equal Protection Clause." He reiterated his dissenting position in *Grutter* "that the educational benefits flowing from student body diversity—assuming they exist—hardly qualify as a compelling state interest. . . . [J]ust as the alleged educational benefits of segregation were insufficient to justify racial discrimination [at the time of *Brown v. Board of Education*], the alleged educational benefits of diversity cannot justify racial discrimination today." He elaborated in part:

"[I]n our desegregation cases, we rejected arguments that are virtually identical to those advanced by the University today. The University asserts, for instance, that the diversity obtained through its discriminatory admissions program prepares its students to become leaders in a diverse society. . . . The segregationists likewise defended segregation on the ground that it provided more leadership opportunities for blacks. . . .

"The University also asserts that student body diversity improves interracial relations. . . . In this argument, too, the University repeats arguments once marshaled in support of segregation. . . . We flatly rejected this line of arguments in McLaurin v. Oklahoma State Regents for Higher Ed., 339 U.S. 637 (1950), where we held that segregation would be unconstitutional even if white students never tolerated blacks. . . . It is, thus, entirely irrelevant whether the University's racial discrimination increases or decreases tolerance.

"Finally, while the University admits that racial discrimination in admissions is not ideal, it asserts that it is a temporary necessity because of the enduring race consciousness of our society. . . . Yet again, the University echoes the hollow justifications advanced by the segregationists. . . . The Fourteenth Amendment views racial bigotry as an evil to be stamped out, not as an excuse for perpetual racial tinkering by the State. . . ."

Justice Thomas went on to argue that "the lesson of history is clear enough: Racial discrimination is never benign. . . . The University's professed good intentions cannot excuse its outright racial discrimination any more than such intentions justified the now denounced arguments of slaveholders and segregationists." In addition, he asserted "that racial engineering does in fact have insidious consequences" in the form of injury not only to "white and Asian applicants who are denied admission because of their race[,]" but to "Blacks and Hispanics admitted to the University as a result of racial discrimination[, who] are, on average, far less prepared than their white and Asian classmates." Concerning the latter injury, he observed that the "University admits minorities who otherwise would have attended less selective colleges where they would have been more evenly matched. But, as a result of the mismatching, many blacks and Hispanics who likely would have excelled at less elite schools are placed in a position where underperformance is all but inevitable because they are less academically prepared than the white and Asian students with whom they must compete." He found "some evidence that students admitted as a result of racial discrimination are more likely to abandon their initial aspirations to become scientists and engineers than are students with similar qualifications who attend less selective schools[,]" and he suggested that "[t]hese students may well drift towards less competitive majors because the mismatch caused by racial discrimination in admissions makes it difficult for them to compete in more rigorous majors." Finally, he reiterated his view that "the University's discrimination . . . taints the accomplishment of all those who are admitted as a result" and "all those who are the same race as those [so] admitted . . . ." Thus, "[a]lthough cloaked in good intentions, the University's racial tinkering harms the very people it claims to be helping."

Justice Ginsburg's solo dissent urged that *Grutter*'s requirements had been satisfied. For her, it sufficed that "the University's admissions policy flexibly considers race only as a 'factor of a factor of a factor of a factor' in the calculus . . . ; followed a yearlong review through which the University reached the reasonable, good-faith judgment that supposedly race-neutral initiatives were insufficient to achieve, in appropriate measure, the educational benefits of student body diversity . . . ; and is subject to periodic review to ensure that the consideration of race remains necessary and proper to achieve the University's educational objectives[.]"

Fisher v. University of Texas at Austin (II)

579 U.S. ___, 136 S.Ct. 2198 (2016).

Following the Court's remand in *Fisher I*, the Court of Appeals again entered summary judgment in the University's favor, and this time the Supreme Court affirmed. Justice Kennedy again authored the majority opinion—in a 4–3 vote, however, with Justice Scalia having died, and Justice Kagan again recused.

Justice Kennedy noted that "up to 75 percent of the places in the freshman class are filled through the [Top Ten Percent] Plan[, though a]s a practical matter, this 75 percent cap, . . . now . . . fixed by statute, means that . . . a student actually needs to finish in the top seven or eight percent of his or her class . . . to be admitted in this category." The rest of the incoming class is "admitted based on a combination of their AI [Academic Index, a combination of SAT and high school academic performance] and PAI [Personal Achievement Index] scores." The PAI is "a numerical score based on a holistic review of an application." That review scores two required essays from 1–6, and separately involves another 1–6 score from a full-file evaluation (the "Personal Achievement Score" or PAS). The PAS involves a rereading of the essays, supplemental information like letters of recommendation, and an evaluation of "the applicant's potential contributions to the University's student body based on the applicant's leadership experience, extracurricular activities, awards/honors, community service, and other 'special circumstances.'" The "special circumstances" category includes "the socioeconomic status of the applicant's family, the socioeconomic status of the applicant's school, the applicant's family responsibilities, whether the applicant lives in a single-parent home, the applicant's SAT score in relation to the average SAT score at the applicant's school, the language spoken at the applicant's home, and, finally, the applicant's race." Justice Kennedy offered this characterization:

". . . Race enters the admissions process, then, at one stage and one stage only— the calculation of the PAS.

"Therefore, although admissions officers can consider race as a positive feature of a minority student's application, there is no dispute that race is but a 'factor of a factor of a factor' in the holistic-review calculus. . . . Furthermore, consideration of race is contextual and does not operate as a mechanical plus factor for underrepresented minorities. . . . There is also no dispute, however, that race, when considered in conjunction with other aspects of an applicant's background, can alter an applicant's PAS score. Thus, race, in this indirect fashion, considered with all of the other factors that make up an applicant's AI and PAI scores, can make a difference to whether an application is accepted or rejected."

Reiterating the legal principles set forth in *Fisher I*, Justice Kennedy wrote that the Court had remanded the case "with instructions to evaluate the record under the correct standard and to determine whether the University had made 'a showing that its plan is narrowly tailored to achieve' the educational benefits that flow from diversity." The Court majority was now satisfied that the University in fact had "met its burden of showing that the admissions policy it used at the time it rejected petitioner's application was narrowly tailored." Justice Kennedy's reasoning included the following:

III

"The University's program is *sui generis* [in that] it combines holistic review with a percentage plan. This approach gave rise to an unusual consequence in this case: The component of the University's admissions policy that had the largest impact on petitioner's chances of admission was not the school's consideration of race under its holistic-review process but rather the Top Ten Percent Plan. Because petitioner did not graduate in the top 10 percent of her high school class, she was categorically ineligible for more than three-fourths of the slots in the incoming freshman class. It seems quite plausible, then, to think that petitioner would have had a better chance of being admitted to the University if the school used race-conscious holistic review to select its entire incoming class. . . .

"Despite the Top Ten Percent Plan's outsized effect on petitioner's chances of admission, she has not challenged it. For that reason, throughout this litigation, the Top Ten Percent Plan has been taken, somewhat artificially, as a given premise.

"[That] complicates this Court's review. In particular, it has led to a record that is almost devoid of information about the students who secured admission to the University through the Plan. The Court thus cannot know how students admitted solely based on their class rank differ in their contribution to diversity from students admitted through holistic review.

". . . When petitioner's application was rejected, . . . the University's combined percentage-plan/holisticreview approach to admission had been in effect for just three years. While studies undertaken over the eight years since then may be of significant value in determining the constitutionality of the University's current admissions policy, that evidence has little bearing on whether petitioner received equal treatment when her application was rejected in 2008. If the Court were to remand, therefore, further factfinding would be limited to a narrow 3 year sample, review of which might yield little insight.

"Furthermore, . . . the University lacks any authority to alter the role of the [legislatively mandated] Top Ten Percent Plan in its admissions process. . . . If the University had no reason to think that it could deviate from the Top Ten Percent Plan, it similarly had no reason to keep extensive data on the Plan or the students admitted under it—particularly in the years before *Fisher I* clarified the stringency of the strict-scrutiny burden for a school that employs race-conscious review.

"[A] remand would do nothing more than prolong a suit that has already persisted for eight years and cost the parties on both sides significant resources. Petitioner long since has graduated from another college, and the University's policy—and the data on which it first was based—may have evolved or changed in material ways.

" . . .

"[The University does have a] continuing obligation to satisfy the burden of strict scrutiny in light of changing circumstances. The University engages in periodic reassessment of the constitutionality, and efficacy, of its admissions program. . . .

Going forward, that assessment must be undertaken in light of the experience the school has accumulated and the data it has gathered since the adoption of its admissions plan.

"As the University examines this data, it should remain mindful that diversity takes many forms. Formalistic racial classifications may sometimes fail to capture diversity in all of its dimensions and, when used in a divisive manner, could undermine the educational benefits the University values. Through regular evaluation of data and consideration of student experience, the University must tailor its approach in light of changing circumstances, ensuring that race plays no greater role than is necessary to meet its compelling interest. The University's examination of the data it has acquired in the years since petitioner's application, for these reasons, must proceed with full respect for the constraints imposed by the EqualProtection Clause. The type of data collected, and the manner in which it is considered, will have a significant bearing on how the University must shape its admissions policy to satisfy strict scrutiny in the years to come. Here, however, the Court is necessarily limited to the narrow question before it: whether, drawing all reasonable inferences in her favor, petitioner has shown by a preponderance of the evidence that she was denied equal treatment at the time her application was rejected.

IV

". . . [P]etitioner makes four arguments. First, she argues that the University has not articulated its compelling interest with sufficient clarity. According to petitioner, the University must set forth more precisely the level of minority enrollment that would constitute a 'critical mass.' . . .

"[H]owever, the compelling interest that justifies consideration of race in college admissions is not an interest in enrolling a certain number of minority students. Rather, a university may institute a race-conscious admissions program as a means of obtaining 'the educational benefits that flow from student body diversity.' *Fisher I,* . . . ; see also *Grutter.* . . . As this Court has said, enrolling adiverse student body 'promotes cross-racial understanding, helps to break down racial stereotypes, and enables students to better understand persons of different races.' . . . Equally important, 'student body diversity promotes learning outcomes, and better prepares students for an increasingly diverse workforce and society.' . . .

"Increasing minority enrollment may be instrumental to these educational benefits, but it is not, as petitioner seems to suggest, a goal that can or should be reduced to pure numbers. Indeed, since the University is prohibited from seeking a particular number or quota of minority students, it cannot be faulted for failing to specify the particular level of minority enrollment at which it believes the educational benefits of diversity will be obtained.

"On the other hand, asserting an interest in the educational benefits of diversity writ large is insufficient. A university's goals cannot be elusory or amorphous—they must be sufficiently measurable to permit judicial scrutiny of the policies adopted to reach them.

"The record reveals that in first setting forth its current admissions policy, the University articulated concrete and precise goals[, . . .] identif[ying] the educational values it seeks to realize through its admissions process: the destruction of stereotypes, the ' "promot[ion of] cross-racial understanding," ' the preparation of a student body ' "for an increasingly diverse workforce and society, " ' and the ' "cultivat[ion of] a set of leaders with legitimacy in the eyes of the citizenry. " ' . . . [Also,] the University explains that it strives to provide an 'academic environment' that offers a 'robust exchange of ideas, exposure to differing cultures, preparation for the challenges of an increasingly diverse workforce, and acquisition of competencies required of futureleaders.' . . . All of these objectives, as a general matter, mirror the 'compelling interest' this Court has approved in its prior cases.

"The University has provided in addition a 'reasoned, principled explanation' for its decision to pursue these goals. *Fisher I*, ... The University's 39-page proposal was written following a year-long study, which concluded that '[t]he use of race-neutral policies and programs ha[d] not been successful' in 'provid[ing] an educational setting that fosters cross-racial understanding, provid[ing] enlightened discussion and learning, [or] prepar[ing] students to function in an increasingly diverse workforce and society.' . . . Further support . . . can be found in the depositions and affidavits from various admissions officers. . . . Petitioner's contention that the University's goal was insufficiently concrete is rebutted by the record.

"Second, petitioner argues that the University has no need to consider race because it had already 'achieved critical mass' by 2003 using the Top Ten Percent Plan and race-neutral holistic review. . . . Petitioner is correct that a university bears a heavy burden in showing that it had not obtained the educational benefits of diversity before it turned to a race-conscious plan. The record reveals, however, that, at the time of petitioner's application, the University could not be faulted on this score. Before changing its policy the University conducted 'months of study and deliberation, including retreats, interviews, [and] review of data,' . . . and concluded that '[t]he use of race-neutral policies and programs ha[d] not been successful in achieving' sufficient racial diversity at the University. . . . At no stage in this litigation has petitioner challenged the University's good faith in conducting its studies, and the Court properly declines to consider the extrarecord materials the dissent relies upon, many of which are tangential to this case at best and none of which the University has had a full opportunity to respond to. . . .

"The record itself contains significant evidence, both statistical and anecdotal, in support of the University's position. [D]emographic data . . . show consistent stagnation in terms of the percentage of minority students enrolling at the University from 1996 to 2002. . . . Although demographics alone are by no means dispositive, they do have some value as a gauge of the University's ability to enroll students who can offer underrepresented perspectives.

"In addition . . . , the University put forward evidence that minority students admitted under the *Hopwood* [no consideration of race] regime experienced feelings of loneliness and isolation. . . .

"This anecdotal evidence is, in turn, bolstered by further, more nuanced quantitative data. . . . [O]nly 21 percent of undergraduate classes with five or more students in them had more than one African-American student enrolled. Twelve percent of these classes had no Hispanic students, as compared to 10 percent in 1996. . . . Though a college must continually reassess its need for race-conscious review, here that assessment appears to have been done with care, and a reasonable determination was made that the University had not yet attained its goals.

"Third, petitioner argues that considering race was not necessary because such consideration has had only a ' "minimal impact" in advancing the [University's] compelling interest.' Again, the record does not support this assertion. In 2003, 11 percent of the Texas residents enrolled through holistic review were Hispanic and 3.5 percent were African-American. . . . In 2007, by contrast, 16.9 percent of the Texas holistic-review freshmen were Hispanic and 6.8 percent were African-American. . . . Those increases—of 54 percent and 94 percent, respectively—show that consideration of race has had a meaningful, if still limited, effect on the diversity of the University's freshman class.

"In any event, it is not a failure of narrow tailoring for the impact of racial consideration to be minor. The fact that race consciousness played a role in only a small portion of admissions decisions should be a hallmark of narrow tailoring, not evidence of unconstitutionality.

"Petitioner's final argument is that 'there are numerous other available race-neutral means of achieving' the University's compelling interest. . . . A review of the record reveals, however, that, at the time of petitioner's application, none of her proposed alternatives was a workable means for the University to attain the benefits of diversity it sought. . . . [T]he University spent seven years attempting to achieve its compelling interest using race-neutral holistic review. None of these efforts succeeded, and petitioner fails to offer any meaningful way in which the University could have improved upon them at the time of her application.

"Petitioner also suggests altering the weight given to academic and socioeconomic factors in the University's admissions calculus. This proposal ignores the fact that the University tried, and failed, to increase diversity through enhanced consideration of socioeconomic and other factors. And it further ignores this Court's precedent making clear that the Equal Protection Clause does not force universities to choose between a diverse student body and a reputation for academic excellence. *Grutter*. . . .

"Petitioner's final suggestion is to uncap the Top Ten Percent Plan, and admit more—if not all—the University's students through a percentage plan. As an initial matter, petitioner overlooks the fact that the Top Ten Percent Plan, though facially neutral, cannot be understood apart from its basic purpose, which is to boost minority enrollment. . . . Consequently, petitioner cannot assert simply that increasing the University'sreliance on a percentage plan would make its admissions policy more race neutral.

"Even if, as a matter of raw numbers, minority enrollment would increase under such a regime, petitioner would be hard-pressed to find convincing support for the proposition that college admissions would be improved if they were a function of class rank alone. . . .

". . . [P]rivileging one characteristic above all others does not lead to a diverse student body. Indeed, to compel universities to admit students based on class rank alone is in deep tension with the goal of educational diversity as this Court's cases have defined it. See *Grutter*,. . . . At its center, the Top Ten Percent Plan is a blunt instrument that may well compromise the University's own definition of the diversity it seeks.

"In addition to these fundamental problems, an admissions policy that relies exclusively on class rank creates perverse incentives for applicants. Percentage plans 'encourage parents to keep their children in low-performing segregated schools, and discourage students from taking challenging classes that might lower their grade point averages.' *Gratz*, . . . (Ginsburg, J., dissenting).

". . .

"In short, none of petitioner's suggested alternatives—nor other proposals considered or discussed in the course of this litigation—have been shown to be 'available' and 'workable' means through which the University could have met its educational goals, as it understood and defined them in 2008. . . . The University has thus met its burden of showing that the admissions policy it used at the time it rejected petitioner's application was narrowly tailored.

* * *

". . . Considerable deference is owed to a university in defining those intangible characteristics, like student body diversity, that are central to its identity and educational mission. But still, it remains an enduring challenge to our Nation's education system to reconcile the pursuit of diversity with the constitutional promise of equal treatment and dignity.

"The University now has at its disposal valuable data about the manner in which different approaches to admissions may foster diversity or instead dilute it. The University must continue to use this data to scrutinize the fairness of its admissions program; to assess whether changing demographics have undermined the need for a race-conscious policy; and to identify the effects, both positive and negative, of the affirmative-action measures it deems necessary.

"The Court's affirmance of the University's admissions policy today does not necessarily mean the University may rely on that same policy without refinement. It is the University's ongoing obligation to engage in constant deliberation and continued reflection regarding its admissions policies."

Justice Alito dissented at length, joined by Chief Justice Roberts and Justice Thomas (who reiterated in a brief separate dissent that he "would overrule *Grutter*"). Justice Alito faulted the University for having failed to satisfy *Fisher I*'s "obligat[ion] (1) to identify the interests justifying its plan with enough specificity to permit a reviewing court to determine whether the requirements of strict scrutiny were met, and (2) to show that those requirements were in fact satisfied." His opinion states in pertinent part:

"To the extent that UT has ever moved beyond a plea for deference and identified the relevant interests in more specific terms, its efforts have been shifting, unpersuasive, and, at times, less than candid. When it adopted its race-based plan, UT said that the plan was needed to promote classroom diversity. . . . It pointed to a study showing that African-American, Hispanic, and Asian-American students were underrepresented in many classes. . . . But UT has never shown that its race-conscious plan actually ameliorates this situation. The University presents no evidence that its admissions officers, in administering the 'holistic' component of its plan, make any effort to determine whether an African-American, Hispanic, or Asian-American student is likely to enroll in classes in which minority students are underrepresented. And although UT's records should permit it to determine without much difficulty whether holistic admittees are any more likely than students admitted through the Top Ten Percent Law . . . to enroll in the classes lacking racial or ethnic diversity, UT either has not crunched those numbers or has not revealed what they show. Nor has UT explained why the underrepresentation of Asian-American students in many classes justifies its plan, which discriminates *against* those students.

"At times, UT has claimed that its plan is needed to achieve a 'critical mass' of African-American and Hispanic students, but it has never explained what this term means. . . .

"UT has also claimed at times that the race-based component of its plan is needed because the Top Ten Percent Plan admits *the wrong kind* of African-American and Hispanic students, namely, students from poor families who attend schools in which the student body is predominantly African-American or Hispanic. . . .

" . . .

"Although UT now disowns th[at] argument . . . , the Fifth Circuit majority . . . [accepted that] the Top Ten African-American and Hispanic admittees cannot match the holistic African-American and Hispanic admittees when it comes to 'records of personal achievement,' a 'variety of perspectives' and 'life experiences,' and 'unique skills.' . . .

"The Fifth Circuit reached this conclusion with little direct evidence regarding the characteristics of the Top Ten Percent and holistic admittees. Instead, the assumption behind the Fifth Circuit's reasoning is that most of the African-American and Hispanic students admitted under the race-neutral component of UT's plan were able to rank in the top decile of their high school classes only because they did not have to compete against white and Asian-American students. This insulting stereotype is not supported by the record. African-American and Hispanic students admitted under the Top Ten Percent Plan receive higher college grades than the African-American and Hispanic students admitted under the race-conscious program. . . .

". . .

"[I]f the majority is determined to give UT yet another chance, we should reverse and send this case back to the District Court. What the majority has now done—awarding a victory to UT in an opinion that fails to address the important issues in the case—is simply wrong."

Justice Alito's recounting of the evolution of UT's admissions system emphasized that, post-*Grutter*, UT's reintroduction of a race-conscious component "did not analyze the backgrounds, life experiences, leadership qualities, awards, extracurricular activities, community service, personal attributes, or other characteristics of the minority students who were already being admitted to UT under the holistic, race-neutral process." He also emphasized that "[e]ven though UT's classroom study showed that more classes lacked Asian-American students than lacked Hispanic students, . . . UT deemed Asian-Americans '*overrepresented*' based on state demographics"; that "[a]lthough UT claims that race is but a 'factor of a factor of a factor of a factor,' . . . UT acknowledges that 'race is the only one of [its] holistic factors that appears on the cover of every application,' [and, in his view, c]onsideration of race therefore pervades every aspect of UT's admissions process"; and that "UT asserts that it has no idea which students were admitted as a result of its race-conscious system and which students would have been admitted under a race-neutral process[,] thus mak[ing] no effort to assess how the individual characteristics of students admitted as the result of racial preferences differ (or do not differ) from those of students who would have been admitted without them."

Elaborating his criticisms, Justice Alito wrote that "UT has failed to define its interest in using racial preferences with clarity[, with the] result [that] the narrow tailoring inquiry is impossible, and UT cannot satisfy strict scrutiny"; that UT's "intentionally imprecise interest" in obtaining a "critical mass" of underrepresented minority students needed to obtain the full educational benefits of diversity was "designed to insulate UT's program from meaningful judicial review"; and that "without knowing in reasonably specific terms what critical mass is or how it can be measured, a reviewing court cannot conduct the requisite 'careful judicial inquiry' into whether the use of race was ' "necessary." ' *Fisher I*,. . . ." He continued:

"To be sure, I agree with the majority that our precedents do not require UT to pinpoint 'an interest in enrolling a certain number of minority students.' But in order for us to assess whether UT's program is narrowly tailored, the University must identify *some sort of concrete interest*. . . .

"The majority acknowledges that 'asserting an interest in the educational benefits of diversity writ large is insufficient,' and that '[a] university's goals cannot be elusory or amorphous—they must be sufficiently measurable to permit judicial scrutiny of the policies adopted to reach them.' According to the majority, however, UT has articulated the following 'concrete and precise goals': 'the destruction of stereotypes, the promot[ion of] cross-racial understanding, the preparation of a student body for an increasingly diverse workforce and society, and the cultivat[ion of] a set of leaders with legitimacy in the eyes of the citizenry.'

"These are laudable goals, but they are not concrete or precise, and they offer no limiting principle for the use of racial preferences. For instance, how will a court ever be able to determine whether stereotypes have been adequately destroyed? Or whether cross-racial understanding has been adequately achieved? If a university can justify racial discrimination simply by having a few employees opine that racial preferences are necessary to accomplish these nebulous goals, . . . then the narrow tailoring inquiry is meaningless. Courts will be required to defer to the judgment of university administrators, and affirmative-action policies will be completely insulated from judicial review.

". . .

"A court cannot ensure that an admissions process is narrowly tailored if it cannot pin down the goals that the process is designed to achieve. . . .

"Although UT's primary argument is that it need not point to any interest more specific than 'the educational benefits of diversity,' . . . it has—at various points in this litigation—identified four more specific goals: demographic parity, classroom diversity, intraracial diversity, and avoiding racial isolation. Neither UT nor the majority has demonstrated that any of these four goals provides a sufficient basis for satisfying strict scrutiny. And UT's arguments to the contrary depend on a series of invidious assumptions.

". . .

"To the extent that UT is pursuing parity with Texas demographics, that is nothing more than 'outright racial balancing,' which this Court has time and again held 'patently unconstitutional.' *Fisher I*, . . .); see *Grutter*, ...

"The record here demonstrates the pitfalls inherent in racial balancing. Although UT claims an interest in the educational benefits of diversity, it appears to have paid little attention to anything other than the number of minority students on its campus and in its classrooms. . . .

"The majority, for its part, claims that '[a]lthough demographics alone are by no means dispositive, they do have some value as a gauge of the University's ability to enroll students who can offer underrepresented perspectives.' But even if UT merely 'view[s] the demographic disparity as cause for concern,' Brief for United States as *Amicus Curiae* 29, and is seeking only to reduce—rather than eliminate—the disparity, that undefined goal cannot be properly subjected to strict scrutiny. In that case, there is simply no way for a court to know what specific demographic interest UT is pursuing, why a race-neutral alternative could not achieve that interest, and when that demographic goal would be satisfied. If a demographic discrepancy can serve as 'a gauge' that justifies the use of racial discrimination, then racial discrimination can be justified on that basis until demographic parity is reached. There is no logical stopping point short of patently unconstitutional racial balancing. Demographic disparities thus cannot be used to satisfy strict scrutiny here. . . .

"The other major explanation UT offered . . . was its desire to promote classroom diversity. . . . UT relied on a study of select classes containing five or more students. [T]he study indicated that 52% of these classes had no African-Americans, 16% had no Asian-Americans, and 12% had no Hispanics. . . . The study further suggested that only 21% of these classes had two or more African-Americans, 67% had two or more Asian-Americans, and 70% had two or more Hispanics. . . . Based on this study, UT concluded that it had a 'compelling educational interest' in employing racial preferences to ensure that it did not 'have large numbers of classes in which there are no students—or only a single student—of a given underrepresented race or ethnicity.'

"UT now equivocates, disclaiming any discrete interest in classroom diversity. . . . But UT has failed to identify the level of classroom diversity it deems sufficient, again making it impossible to apply strict scrutiny. . . .

"Putting aside UT's effective abandonment of its interest in classroom diversity, the evidence cited in support of that interest is woefully insufficient to show that UT's race-conscious plan was necessary to achieve the educational benefits of a diverse student body. As far as the record shows, UT failed to even scratch the surface of the available data before reflexively resorting to racial preferences. For instance, because UT knows which students were admitted through the Top Ten Percent Plan and which were not, as well as which students enrolled in which classes, it would seem relatively easy to determine whether Top Ten Percent students were more or less likely than holistic admittees to enroll in the types of classes where diversity was lacking. But UT never bothered to figure this out. . . . [UT] has not demonstrated that its race-conscious policy would promote classroom diversity any better than race-neutral options, such as expanding the Top Ten Percent Plan or using race-neutral holistic admissions.

"Moreover, . . . UT's own study . . . demonstrated that classroom diversity was more lacking for students classified as Asian-American than for those classified as Hispanic. . . . But the UT plan discriminates *against* Asian-American students. UT is apparently unconcerned that Asian-Americans 'may be made to feel isolated or may be seen as . . . "spokesperson[s]" of their race or ethnicity.' . . . And unless the University is engaged in unconstitutional racial balancing based on Texas demographics (where Hispanics outnumber Asian-Americans), . . . it seemingly views the classroom contributions of Asian-American students as less valuable than those of Hispanic students. . . .

"While both the majority and the Fifth Circuit rely on UT's classroom study, . . . they completely ignore its finding that Hispanics are better represented than Asian-Americans in UT classrooms. In fact, they act almost as if Asian-American students do not exist. . . .

"'. . .

"Perhaps the majority finds discrimination against Asian-American students benign, since Asian-Americans are "*overrepresented*" at UT. . . . But . . . [b]y accepting the classroom study as proof that UT satisfied strict scrutiny, the majority 'move[s] us from "separate but equal" to "unequal but benign."' *Metro Broadcasting*, . . . (Kennedy, J., dissenting).

"In addition to demonstrating that UT discriminates against Asian-American students, the classroom study also exhibits UT's use of a few crude, overly simplistic racial and ethnic categories. . . .

"For example, students labeled 'Asian American,' . . . seemingly include 'individuals of Chinese, Japanese, Korean, Vietnamese, Cambodian, Hmong, Indian and other backgrounds comprising roughly 60% of the world's population,' . . . . It would be ludicrous to suggest that all of these students have similar backgrounds and similar ideas and experiences to share. So why has UT lumped them together and concluded that it is appropriate to discriminate against Asian-American students because they are 'overrepresented' in the UT student body? UT has no good answer. And UT makes no effort to ensure that it has a critical mass of, say, 'Filipino Americans' or 'Cambodian Americans.' . . . As long as there are a sufficient number of 'Asian Americans,' UT is apparently satisfied.

"UT's failure to provide any definition of the various racial and ethnic groups is also revealing. . . . UT evidently labels each student as falling into only a single racial or ethnic group, . . . without explaining how individuals with ancestors from different groups are to be characterized. As racial and ethnic prejudice recedes, more and more students will have parents (or grandparents) who fall into more than one of UT's five groups. . . . UT's crude classification system is ill suited for the more integrated country that we are rapidly becoming. . . .

"Finally, it seems clear that the lack of classroom diversity is attributable in good part to factors other than the representation of the favored groups in the UT student population. UT offers . . . courses in subjects that are likely to have special appeal to members of the minority groups given preferential treatment under its challenged plan, and this of course diminishes the number of other courses in which these students can enroll. . . . Having designed an undergraduate program that virtually ensures a lack of classroom diversity, UT is poorly positioned to argue that this very result provides a justification for racial and ethnic discrimination, which the Constitution rarely allows.

"UT's purported interest in intraracial diversity . . . also falls short. At bottom, this argument relies on the unsupported assumption that there is something deficient or at least radically different about the African-American and Hispanic students admitted through the Top Ten Percent Plan.

". . .

"Ultimately, UT's intraracial diversity rationale relies on the baseless assumption that there is something wrong with African-American and Hispanic students admitted through the Top Ten Percent Plan, because they are 'from the lower-performing, racially identifiable schools.' [Tr. of Oral Arg.] (explaining that 'the basis' for UT's conclusion that it was 'not getting a variety of perspectives among African-Americans or Hispanics' was the fact that the Top Ten Percent Plan admits underprivileged minorities from highly segregated schools). . . . UT's assumptions appear to be based on the pernicious stereotype that the African-Americans and Hispanics admitted through the Top Ten Percent Plan only got in because they did not have to compete against very many whites and Asian-Americans. . . .

"In addition to relying on stereotypes, UT's argument that it needs racial preferences to admit privileged minorities turns the concept of affirmative action on its head. When affirmative action programs were first adopted, it was for the purpose of helping the disadvantaged. . . . Now we are told that a program that tends to admit poor and disadvantaged minority students is inadequate because it does not work to the advantage of those who aremore fortunate. This is affirmative action gone wild.

"It is also far from clear that UT's assumptions about the socioeconomic status of minorities admitted through the Top Ten Percent Plan are even remotely accurate. . . . As . . . statistics make plain, the minorities that UT characterizes as 'coming from depressed socioeconomic backgrounds,' . . . generally come from households with education levels exceeding the norm in Texas.

"Or consider income levels. . . . The household income levels for Top Ten Percent African-American and Hispanic admittees were on par [with the median annual household income in Texas.] . . . UT is asserting that it needs affirmative action to ensure that its minority students disproportionally come from families that are wealthier and better educated than the average Texas family.

"In addition[,] . . . UT argues that it needs race-conscious admissions to enroll academically superior minority students with higher SAT scores. Regrettably, the majority seems to embrace this argument as well. . . .

"This argument fails for a number of reasons. First, it is simply not true that Top Ten Percent minority admittees are academically inferior to holistic admittees.... Indeed, the statistics in the record reveal that, for each year between 2003 and 2007, African-American in-state freshmen who were admitted under the Top Ten Percent Law earned a higher mean grade point average than those admitted outside of the Top Ten Percent Law.... The same is true for Hispanic students....

"...

"Finally, UT's shifting positions on intraracial diversity,and the fact that intraracial diversity was not emphasized in the [Admissions] Proposal, suggest that it was not 'the actual purpose underlying the discriminatory classification.' Mississippi Univ. for Women v. Hogan, 458 U. S. 718, 730 (1982). Instead, it appears to be a *post hoc* rationalization.

"UT also alleges—and the majority embraces—an interest in avoiding 'feelings of loneliness and isolation' among minority students. In support of this argument, they cite only demographic data and anecdotal statements by UT officials that some students (we are not told how many) feel 'isolated.' This vague interest cannot possibly satisfy strict scrutiny.

"...

"... UT never explains why the Hispanic students—but not the Asian-American students—are isolated and lonely enough to receive an admissions boost, notwithstanding the fact that there are more Hispanics than Asian-Americans in the student population....

"Ultimately, UT has failed to articulate its interest in preventing racial isolation with any clarity, and it has provided no clear indication of how it will know when such isolation no longer exists. Like UT's purported interests in demographic parity, classroom diversity, and intraracial diversity, its interest in avoiding racial isolation cannot justify the use of racial preferences.

"Even assuming UT is correct that, under *Grutter*, it need only cite a generic interest in the educational benefits of diversity, its plan still fails strict scrutiny because it is not narrowly tailored.... [T]here is no evidence that race-blind, holistic review would not achieve UT's goals at least 'about as well' as UT's race-based policy. In addition, UT could have adopted other approaches to further its goals, such as intensifying its outreach efforts, uncapping the Top Ten Percent Law, or placing greater weight on socioeconomic factors.

"... [T]he majority devotes only a single, conclusory sentence to the most obvious race-neutral alternative: race-blind, holistic review that considers the applicant's unique characteristics and personal circumstances.... Because UT has failed to provide any evidence whatsoever that race-conscious holistic review will achieve its diversity objectives more effectively than race-blind holistic review, it cannot satisfy the heavy burden imposed by the strict scrutiny standard.

"The fact that UT's racial preferences are unnecessary to achieve its stated goals is further demonstrated by their minimal effect on UT's diversity.... [R]ace [probably] was determinative for only 15 African-American students and 18 Hispanic students in 2008 (representing 0.2% and 0.3%, respectively, of the total enrolled first-time freshmen from Texas high schools)....

"... Where, as here, racial preferences have only a slight impact on minority enrollment, a race-neutral alternative likely could have reached the same result.... And in this case, a race-neutral alternative could accomplish UT's objectives without gratuitously branding the covers of tens of thousands of applications with a bare racial stamp and 'tell[ing] each student he or she is to be defined by race.'

"...

"[S]omehow, the majority concludes that *petitioner* must lose as a result of UT's failure to provide evidence justifying its decision to employ racial discrimination. Tellingly, the Court frames its analysis as if petitioner bears the burden of proof here. But . . . [t]o the extent the record is inadequate, the responsibility lies with UT. . . .

". . . [T]he majority cites three reasons for breaking from the normal strict scrutiny standard. None . . . is convincing.

"First, the Court states that, while 'th[e] evidentiary gap perhaps could be filled by a remand to the district court for further factfinding' in 'an ordinary case,' that will not work here because '[w]hen petitioner's application was rejected, . . . the University's combined percentage-plan/holistic-review approach to admission had been in effect for just three years,' so 'further factfinding' 'might yield little insight.' This reasoning is dangerously incorrect. The Equal Protection Clause does not provide a 3-year grace period for racial discrimination. Under strict scrutiny, UT was required to identify evidence that race-based admissions were necessary to achieve a compelling interest *before* it put them in place—not three or more years after. . . .

"Second, in an effort to excuse UT's lack of evidence, the Court argues that because 'the University lacks any authority to alter the role of the Top Ten Percent Plan,' 'it similarly had no reason to keep extensive data on the Plan or the students admitted under it—particularly in the years before *Fisher I* clarified the stringency of the strict-scrutiny burden for a school that employs race-conscious review.' But UT has long been aware that it bears the burden of justifying its racial discrimination under strict scrutiny. . . . In light of this burden, UT had *every* reason to keep data on the students admitted through the Top Ten Percent Plan. . . . Its failure to do so demonstrates that UT unthinkingly employed a race-based process without examining whether the use of race was actually necessary. . . .

"...

"Third, the majority notes that this litigation has persisted for many years, that petitioner has already graduated from another college, that UT's policy may have changed over time, and that this case may offer little prospective guidance. At most, these considerations counsel in favor of dismissing this case as improvidently granted. . . . None of these considerations has any bearing whatsoever on the merits of this suit. The majority cannot side with UT simply because it is tired of this case."

Parents Involved in Community Schools
v. Seattle School District No. 1
551 U.S. 701, 127 S.Ct. 2738, 168 L.Ed.2d 508 (2007).

■ CHIEF JUSTICE ROBERTS announced the judgment of the Court, and delivered the opinion of the Court with respect to Parts I, II, III-A, and III-C, and an opinion with respect to Parts III-B and IV, in which JUSTICES SCALIA, THOMAS, and ALITO join.

The school districts in these cases voluntarily adopted student assignment plans that rely upon race to determine which public schools certain children may attend. The Seattle school district classifies children as white or nonwhite; the Jefferson County school district as black or "other." In Seattle, this racial classification is used to allocate slots in oversubscribed high schools. In Jefferson County, it is used to make certain elementary school assignments and to rule on transfer requests. In each case, the school district relies upon an individual student's race in assigning that student to a particular school, so that the racial balance at the school falls within a predetermined range based on the racial composition of the school district as a whole.

Parents of students denied assignment to particular schools under these plans solely because of their race brought suit, contending that allocating children to different public schools on the basis of race violated the Fourteenth Amendment guarantee of equal protection. The Courts of Appeals below upheld the plans. We . . . reverse.

I

Both cases present the same underlying legal question—whether a public school that had not operated legally segregated schools or has been found to be unitary may choose to classify students by race and rely upon that classification in making school assignments. . . .

A

Seattle School District No. 1 operates 10 regular public high schools. In 1998, it adopted the plan at issue[, which] allows incoming ninth graders to choose from among any of the district's high schools. . . .

. . . If too many students list the same school as their first choice, the district employs a series of "tiebreakers" [for] the oversubscribed school. The first [is] a sibling currently enrolled. . . . The next tiebreaker depends upon the racial composition of the particular school and the race of the individual student. In the district's public schools approximately 41 percent of enrolled students are white; the remaining 59 percent, comprising all other racial groups, are classified by Seattle for assignment purposes as nonwhite. . . . If an oversubscribed school is not within 10 percentage points of the district's overall white/nonwhite racial balance, . . . the district . . . assign[s] students whose race "will serve to bring the school into balance." . . . If . . . necessary . . . , the next tiebreaker is the geographic proximity of the school to the student's residence. . . .

Seattle has never operated segregated schools—legally separate schools for students of different races—nor has it ever been subject to court-ordered desegregation. It nonetheless employs the racial tiebreaker in an attempt to address the effects of racially identifiable housing patterns on school assignments. . . .

. . .

B

Jefferson County Public Schools operates the public school system in metropolitan Louisville, Kentucky. In 1973 a federal court found that Jefferson County had maintained a segregated school system, . . . and in 1975 the District Court entered a desegregation decree. . . . Jefferson County operated under this decree until 2000, when the District Court dissolved the decree after finding that the district had achieved unitary status by eliminating "[t]o the greatest extent practicable" the vestiges of its prior policy of segregation. . . .

In 2001, . . . Jefferson County adopted the voluntary student assignment plan at issue. . . . Approximately 34 percent of the district's 97,000 students are black; most of the remaining 66 percent are white. . . . The plan requires all nonmagnet schools to maintain a minimum black enrollment of 15 percent, and a maximum . . . of 50 percent. . . .

. . .

[A new kindergarten student whose local school was full was assigned instead to another school 10 miles from home. A transfer request to a school in a different cluster only a mile away was denied] because . . . "[t]he transfer would have an adverse effect on desegregation compliance" of [his assigned school]. . . .

. . .

III

A

It is well established that when the government distributes burdens or benefits on the basis of individual racial classifications, that action is reviewed under strict scrutiny. Johnson v. California, 543 U.S. 499, 505–506 (2005); Grutter v. Bollinger, 539 U.S. 306, 326 (2003). . . . In order to satisfy this searching standard of review, the school districts must demonstrate that the use of individual racial classifications in the assignment plans here under review is "narrowly tailored" to achieve a "compelling" government interest. . . .

[O]ur prior cases, in evaluating the use of racial classifications in the school context, have recognized two interests that qualify as compelling. The first is . . . remedying the effects of past intentional discrimination. . . . Yet the Seattle public schools have not shown that they were ever segregated by law, and were not subject to court-ordered desegregation decrees. The Jefferson County public schools were previously segregated by law . . . [but in 2000] achieved "unitary" status. . . .

   . . . [10]

The second government interest we have recognized as compelling . . . is the interest in diversity in higher education upheld in *Grutter*. . . .

   . . .

The entire gist of the analysis in *Grutter* was that the admissions program at issue there focused on each applicant as an individual, and not simply as a member of a particular racial group. . . .

In the present cases, by contrast, race is not considered as part of a broader effort to achieve "exposure to widely diverse people, cultures, ideas, and viewpoints," . . . ; race, for some students, is determinative standing alone. The districts argue that other factors, such as student preferences, affect assignment decisions under their plans, but under each plan when race comes into play, it is decisive by itself. . . .

Even when it comes to race, the plans here employ only a limited notion of diversity, viewing race exclusively in white/nonwhite terms in Seattle and black/"other" terms in Jefferson County. . . .

   . . .

In upholding the admissions plan in *Grutter*, . . . this Court relied upon considerations unique to institutions of higher education. . . . The present cases are not governed by *Grutter*.

B

. . . Each school district argues that educational and broader socialization benefits flow from a racially diverse learning environment, and each contends that because the diversity they seek is racial diversity—not the broader diversity at issue in *Grutter*—it makes sense to promote that interest directly by relying on race alone.

The parties and their *amici* dispute whether racial diversity in schools in fact has a marked impact on test scores and other objective yardsticks or achieves intangible

---

[10] The districts point to dicta in a prior opinion in which the Court suggested that, while not constitutionally mandated, it would be constitutionally permissible for a school district to seek racially balanced schools as a matter of "educational policy." See *Swann* v. *Charlotte-Mecklenburg Bd. of Ed.*, 402 U.S. 1, 16 (1971). . . . *Swann*, evaluating a school district engaged in court-ordered desegregation, had no occasion to consider whether a district's voluntary adoption of race-based assignments in the absence of a finding of prior *de jure* segregation was constitutionally permissible, an issue that was again expressly reserved in Washington v. Seattle School Dist. No. 1, 458 U.S. 457, 472, n. 15 (1982). . . .

socialization benefits. The debate is not one we need to resolve, however, because it is clear that the racial classifications employed by the districts are not narrowly tailored to the goal of achieving the educational and social benefits asserted to flow from racial diversity. In design and operation, the plans are directed only to racial balance, pure and simple, an objective this Court has repeatedly condemned as illegitimate.

The plans are tied to each district's specific racial demographics, rather than to any pedagogic concept of the level of diversity needed to obtain the asserted educational benefits. . . .

The districts offer no evidence that the level of racial diversity necessary to achieve the asserted educational benefits happens to coincide with the racial demographics of the respective school districts—or rather the white/nonwhite or black/"other" balance of the districts, since that is the only diversity addressed by the plans. . . . The [Seattle] district did not . . . demonstrate in any way how the educational and social benefits of racial diversity or avoidance of racial isolation are more likely to be achieved at a school that is 50 percent white and 50 percent Asian-American, which would qualify as diverse under Seattle's plan, than at a school that is 30 percent Asian-American, 25 percent African-American, 25 percent Latino, and 20 percent white, which under Seattle's definition would be racially concentrated.

Similarly, . . . [t]he Jefferson County plan . . . is based on a goal of replicating at each school "an African-American enrollment equivalent to the average district-wide African-American enrollment[,]" . . . [which has] nothing to do with preventing either the black or "other" group from becoming "small" or "isolated[.]" . . .

In fact, in each case . . . , enrolling students without regard to their race yields a substantially diverse student body under any definition of diversity.

. . .

[W]orking backward to achieve a particular type of racial balance, rather than working forward from some demonstration of the level of diversity that provides the purported benefits, is a fatal flaw under our existing precedent. . . .

. . . Allowing racial balancing as a compelling end in itself would "effectively assur[e] that race will always be relevant in American life, and that the 'ultimate goal' of 'eliminating entirely from governmental decisionmaking such irrelevant factors as a human being's race' will never be achieved." . . .

. . .

. . . [I]n Seattle the plans are defended as necessary to address the consequences of racially identifiable housing patterns. The sweep of the mandate claimed by the district is contrary to our rulings that remedying past societal discrimination does not justify race-conscious government action. . . .

. . .

. . . Even in the context of mandatory desegregation, we have stressed that racial proportionality is not required. . . .

. . .

C

The districts assert . . . that the way in which they have employed individual racial classifications is necessary to achieve their stated ends. The minimal effect these classifications have on student assignments, however, suggests that other means would be effective. Seattle's racial tiebreaker results, in the end, only in shifting a small number of students between schools. . . .

. . .

Similarly, Jefferson County's use of racial classifications has only a minimal effect on the assignment of students. . . .

While we do not suggest that *greater* use of race would be preferable, the minimal impact of the districts' racial classifications on school enrollment casts doubt on the necessity of using racial classifications. In *Grutter*, the consideration of race was viewed as indispensable in more than tripling minority representation at the law school—from 4 to 14.5 percent. . . .

The districts have also failed to show that they considered methods other than explicit racial classifications to achieve their stated goals. . . .

IV

. . .

Justice Breyer's dissent . . . relies heavily on dicta from *Swann* v. *Charlotte-Mecklenburg Bd. of Ed.*,. . . . [W]hen *Swann* was decided, this Court had not yet confirmed that strict scrutiny applies to racial classifications like those before us. . . .

. . . *Swann* addresses only a possible state objective; it says nothing of the permissible *means*—race conscious or otherwise—that a school district might employ to achieve that objective. . . .

. . .

Justice Breyer's dissent also asserts that these cases are controlled by *Grutter*. . . . We simply do not understand how Justice Breyer can maintain that classifying every schoolchild as black or white, and using that classification as a determinative factor in assigning children to achieve pure racial balance, can be regarded as "less burdensome, and hence more narrowly tailored" than the consideration of race in *Grutter*, when the Court in *Grutter* stated that "[t]he importance of . . . individualized consideration" in the program was "paramount," and consideration of race was one factor in a "highly individualized, holistic review." . . .

. . .

Th[e] argument that different rules should govern racial classifications designed to include rather than exclude is not new; it has been repeatedly pressed in the past, . . . and has been repeatedly rejected. . . .

. . .

Justice Breyer also suggests that other means for achieving greater racial diversity in schools are necessarily unconstitutional if the racial classifications at issue in these cases cannot survive strict scrutiny. These other means—*e.g.*, where to construct new schools, how to allocate resources among schools, and which academic offerings to provide to attract students to certain schools—implicate different considerations than the explicit racial classifications at issue in these cases, and we express no opinion on their validity . . . . Rather, we employ . . . strict scrutiny to evaluate the plans at issue today, an approach that in no way warrants the dissent's cataclysmic concerns. . . .

* * *

If the need for the racial classifications . . . is unclear, even on the districts' own terms, the costs are undeniable. "[D]istinctions between citizens solely because of their ancestry are by their very nature odious to a free people whose institutions are founded upon the doctrine of equality." . . . Government action dividing us by race is inherently suspect because such classifications promote "notions of racial inferiority and lead to a politics of racial hostility," *Croson*, . . . "reinforce the belief, held by too many for too much of our history, that individuals should be judged by the color of their skin," *Shaw* v. *Reno*, . . . and "endorse race-based reasoning and the conception of a Nation divided into racial blocs, thus contributing to an escalation of racial hostility and conflict." *Metro Broadcasting*, . . . (O'Connor, J., dissenting). As the Court explained in Rice v. Cayetano, 528 U.S. 495, 517 (2000), "[o]ne of the principal reasons race is treated as a forbidden classification is that it demeans the dignity and worth of a person to be judged by ancestry instead of by his or her own merit and essential qualities."

All this is true enough in the contexts in which these statements were made—government contracting, voting districts, allocation of broadcast licenses, and electing state officers—but when it comes to using race to assign children to schools, history will be heard. In *Brown* v. *Board of Education*, . . . we held that segregation deprived black children of equal educational opportunities regardless of whether school facilities and other tangible factors were equal, because government classification and separation on grounds of race themselves denoted inferiority. . . .

The parties and their *amici* debate which side is more faithful to the heritage of *Brown*, but the position of the plaintiffs in *Brown* was spelled out in their brief and could not have been clearer: "[T]he Fourteenth Amendment prevents states from according differential treatment to American children on the basis of their color or race." . . . What do the racial classifications at issue here do, if not accord differential treatment on the basis of race? . . . What do the racial classifications do in these cases, if not determine admission to a public school on a racial basis? Before *Brown*, schoolchildren were told where they could and could not go to school based on the color of their skin. The school districts in these cases have not carried the heavy burden of demonstrating that we should allow this once again—even for very different reasons. For schools that never segregated on the basis of race, such as Seattle, or that have removed the vestiges of past segregation, such as Jefferson County, the way "to achieve a system of determining admission to the public schools on a nonracial basis," *Brown II*, . . . is to stop assigning students on a racial basis. The way to stop discrimination on the basis of race is to stop discriminating on the basis of race.

. . . [R]eversed, and . . . remanded for further proceedings.

■ JUSTICE THOMAS, concurring.

. . . [T]he dissent would give school boards a free hand to make decisions on the basis of race—an approach reminiscent of that advocated by the segregationists in *Brown* . . . .

. . .

. . . [I]t is wrong to place the remediation of segregation on the same plane as the remediation of racial imbalance. First, . . . the further we get from the era of state-sponsored racial separation, the less likely it is that racial imbalance has a traceable connection to any prior segregation. . . .

Second, a school cannot "remedy" racial imbalance in the same way that it can remedy segregation. Remediation of past *de jure* segregation is a one-time process involving the redress of a discrete legal injury inflicted by an identified entity. . . . Unlike *de jure* segregation, there is no ultimate remedy for racial imbalance. Individual schools will fall in and out of balance in the natural course, and the appropriate balance itself will shift with a school district's changing demographics. Thus, racial balancing will have to take place on an indefinite basis—a continuous process with no identifiable culpable party and no discernable end point. In part for those reasons, the Court has never permitted outright racial balancing solely for the purpose of achieving a particular racial balance.

II

. . .

Given th[e] tenuous relationship between forced racial mixing and improved educational results for black children, the dissent cannot plausibly maintain that an educational element supports the integration interest, let alone makes it compelling. . . .

. . .

. . . [E]ven supposing interracial contact leads directly to improvements in racial attitudes and race relations, a program that assigns students of different races to the same schools might not capture those benefits. Simply putting students together under the same roof does not necessarily mean that the students will learn together or even interact.

Furthermore, it is unclear whether increased interracial contact improves racial attitudes and relations. . . .

. . .

. . . [*Grutter*] was critically dependent upon features unique to higher education[,n]one of [which] is present in elementary and secondary schools. Those schools do not select their own students, and education in the elementary and secondary environment generally does not involve the free interchange of ideas thought to be an integral part of higher education. . . .

. . .

III

Most of the dissent's criticisms of today's result can be traced to its rejection of the color-blind Constitution. . . .

. . .

The segregationists in *Brown* embraced the arguments the Court endorsed in *Plessy*. Though *Brown* decisively rejected those arguments, today's dissent replicates them to a distressing extent. . . .

. . .

In place of the color-blind Constitution, the dissent would permit measures to keep the races together and proscribe measures to keep the races apart. . . . The Constitution is not that malleable. . . . [O]ur history has taught us . . . to beware of elites bearing racial theories. . . . Can we really be sure that the racial theories that motivated *Dred Scott* and *Plessy* are a relic of the past or that future theories will be nothing but beneficent and progressive? That is a gamble I am unwilling to take, and it is one the Constitution does not allow.

. . .

■ JUSTICE KENNEDY, concurring in part and concurring in the judgment.

. . .

I

. . . The plurality . . . does not acknowledge that the school districts have identified a compelling interest here. For this reason, among others, I do not join Parts III-B and IV. Diversity, depending on its meaning and definition, is a compelling educational goal a school district may pursue.

. . . [T]he inquiry into less restrictive alternatives demanded by the narrow tailoring analysis requires . . . [that] government bears the burden of . . .

establish[ing], in detail, how decisions based on an individual student's race are made in a challenged governmental program. The Jefferson County Board of Education fails to meet this threshold mandate.

. . .

. . . [I]t fails to make clear, for example, who makes the decisions; what if any oversight is employed; the precise circumstances in which an assignment decision will or will not be made on the basis of race; or how it is determined which of two similarly situated children will be subjected to a given race-based decision. . . .

. . .

As for the Seattle case, the school district . . . has failed to explain why, in a district composed of a diversity of races, with fewer than half of the students classified as "white," it has employed the crude racial categories of "white" and "non-white" as the basis for its assignment decisions. . . .

. . . As the district fails to account for the classification system it has chosen, despite what appears to be its ill fit, Seattle has not shown its plan to be narrowly tailored to achieve its own ends; and thus it fails to pass strict scrutiny.

II

. . .

. . . [P]arts of the opinion by The Chief Justice imply an all-too-unyielding insistence that race cannot be a factor in instances when, in my view, it may be taken into account. The plurality opinion is too dismissive of the legitimate interest government has in ensuring all people have equal opportunity regardless of their race. . . . The plurality opinion is at least open to the interpretation that the Constitution requires school districts to ignore the problem of *de facto* resegregation in schooling. I cannot endorse that conclusion. To the extent the plurality opinion suggests the Constitution mandates that state and local school authorities must accept the status quo of racial isolation in schools, it is, in my view, profoundly mistaken.

. . .

In the administration of public schools by the state and local authorities it is permissible to consider the racial makeup of schools and to adopt general policies to encourage a diverse student body, one aspect of which is its racial composition. Cf. *Grutter* v. *Bollinger*,. . . . If school authorities are concerned that the student-body compositions of certain schools interfere with the objective of offering an equal educational opportunity to all of their students, they are free to devise race-conscious measures to address the problem in a general way and without treating each student in different fashion solely on the basis of a systematic, individual typing by race.

School boards may pursue the goal of bringing together students of diverse backgrounds and races through other means, including strategic site selection of new schools; drawing attendance zones with general recognition of the demographics of neighborhoods; allocating resources for special programs; recruiting students and faculty in a targeted fashion; and tracking enrollments, performance, and other statistics by race. These mechanisms are race conscious but do not lead to different treatment based on a classification that tells each student he or she is to be defined by race, so it is unlikely any of them would demand strict scrutiny to be found permissible. . . . Executive and legislative branches, which for generations now have considered these types of policies and procedures, should be permitted to employ them with candor and with confidence that a constitutional violation does not occur whenever a decisionmaker considers the impact a given approach might have on students of different races. Assigning to each student a personal designation according to a crude system of individual racial classifications is quite a different matter; and the legal analysis changes accordingly.

. . .

. . . I join Part III-C of the Court's opinion because I agree that in the context of these plans, the small number of assignments affected suggests that the schools could have achieved their stated ends through different means. These include the facially race-neutral means set forth above or, if necessary, a more nuanced, individual evaluation of school needs and student characteristics that might include race as a component. The latter approach would be informed by *Grutter*, though of course the criteria relevant to student placement would differ based on the age of the students, the needs of the parents, and the role of the schools.

III

. . .

[T]he general conclusions upon which [the dissent] relies have no principled limit and would result in the broad acceptance of governmental racial classifications in areas far afield from schooling. The dissent's permissive strict scrutiny (which bears more than a passing resemblance to rational-basis review) could invite widespread governmental deployment of racial classifications. . . .

[T]he dissent's reliance on . . . Gratz v. Bollinger, 539 U.S. 244 (2003), and *Grutter*, . . . is, with all respect, simply baffling.

Gratz involved a system where race was not the entire classification. The procedures . . . placed much less reliance on race than do the plans at issue here. The issue in *Gratz* arose, moreover, in the context of college admissions where students had other choices and precedent supported the proposition that First Amendment interests give universities particular latitude in defining diversity. . . . Even so the race factor was found to be invalid. . . . If *Gratz* is to be the measure, the racial classification systems here are *a fortiori* invalid. . . .

. . . *Grutter* . . . sustained a system that, it found, was flexible enough to take into account "all pertinent elements of diversity," . . . and considered race as only one factor among many. . . . Seattle's plan, by contrast, relies upon a mechanical formula that has denied hundreds of students their preferred schools on the basis of three rigid criteria: placement of siblings, distance from schools, and race. . . .

B

. . .

. . . Reduction of an individual to an assigned racial identity for differential treatment is among the most pernicious actions our government can undertake. The allocation of governmental burdens and benefits, contentious under any circumstances, is even more divisive when . . . made on the basis of individual racial classifications . . . .

Notwithstanding these concerns, [such] allocation . . . was found sometimes permissible in the context of remedies for *de jure* wrong. . . . The limitation of this power to instances where there has been *de jure* segregation serves to confine the nature, extent, and duration of governmental reliance on individual racial classifications.

. . . [W]hen *de facto* discrimination is at issue[,] the remedial rules are different. The State must seek alternatives to the classification and differential treatment of individuals by race, at least absent some extraordinary showing not present here.

C

The dissent refers to [lower court opinions], one of [whose] main concerns . . . was this: If it is legitimate for school authorities to work to avoid racial isolation in their schools, must they do so only by indirection and general policies? Does the Constitution mandate this inefficient result? Why may the authorities not recognize the problem in candid fashion and solve it altogether through resort to direct assignments based on student racial classifications? So, the argument proceeds, if race is the problem, then perhaps race is the solution.

The argument ignores the dangers presented by individual classifications, dangers that are not as pressing when the same ends are achieved by more indirect means. When the government classifies an individual by race, it must first define what it means to be of a race. Who exactly is white and who is nonwhite? To be forced to live under a state-mandated racial label is inconsistent with the dignity of individuals in our society. And it is a label that an individual is powerless to change. Governmental classifications that command people to march in different directions based on racial typologies can cause a new divisiveness. The practice can lead to corrosive discourse, where race serves not as an element of our diverse heritage but instead as a bargaining chip in the political process. On the other hand race-conscious measures that do not rely on differential treatment based on individual classifications present these problems to a lesser degree.

. . .

■ JUSTICE STEVENS, dissenting.

. . .

There is a cruel irony in the Chief Justice's reliance on . . . *Brown*. . . . [T]he history books do not tell stories of white children struggling to attend black schools. In this and other ways, the Chief Justice rewrites the history of one of this Court's most important decisions. . . .

The Chief Justice rejects the conclusion that the racial classifications at issue here should be viewed differently than others, because they do not impose burdens on one race alone and do not stigmatize or exclude. The only justification for refusing to acknowledge the obvious importance of that difference is the citation of a few recent opinions—none of which even approached unanimity—grandly proclaiming that all racial classifications must be analyzed under "strict scrutiny." . . .

. . . It is my firm conviction that no Member of the Court that I joined in 1975 would have agreed with today's decision.

■ JUSTICE BREYER, with whom JUSTICE STEVENS, JUSTICE SOUTER, and JUSTICE GINSBURG join, dissenting.

. . .

The plurality . . . distorts precedent, . . . misapplies the relevant constitutional principles, . . . announces legal rules that will obstruct efforts by state and local governments to deal effectively with the growing resegregation of public schools, . . . threatens to substitute for present calm a disruptive round of race-related litigation, and . . . undermines *Brown*'s promise of integrated primary and secondary education that local communities have sought to make a reality. . . .

I

Facts

. . . *Brown* . . . set the Nation on a path toward public school integration.

. . .

. . . [I]n respect to race-conscious desegregation measures that the Constitution *permitted,* but did not *require . . .* , this Court unanimously stated:

"School authorities are traditionally charged with broad power to formulate and implement educational policy and might well conclude, for example, that in order to prepare students to live in a pluralistic society each school should have a prescribed ratio of Negro to white students reflecting the proportion for the district as a whole. *To do this as an educational policy is within the broad discretionary powers of school authorities.*" Swann v. Charlotte-Mecklenburg Bd. of Ed., 402 U.S. 1, 16 (1971) (emphasis added).

. . .

[M]yriad school districts operating in myriad circumstances have devised myriad plans, often with race-conscious elements, all for the sake of eradicating earlier school segregation, bringing about integration, or preventing retrogression. . . .

I describe th[e] histories [of Seattle's and Lousiville's present plans] at length . . . to highlight three important features of these cases. First, the school districts' plans serve "compelling interests" and are "narrowly tailored" on any reasonable definition of those terms. Second, the distinction between *de jure* segregation (caused by school systems) and *de facto* segregation (caused, *e.g.,* by housing patterns or generalized societal discrimination) is meaningless in the present context. . . . Third, real-world efforts to substitute racially diverse for racially segregated schools (however caused) are complex, to the point where the Constitution cannot plausibly be interpreted to rule out categorically all local efforts to use means that are "conscious" of the race of individuals.

In both Seattle and Louisville, . . . plaintiffs filed lawsuits claiming unconstitutional segregation. . . . In Louisville, a federal court entered a remedial decree. In Seattle, the parties settled after the school district pledged to undertake a desegregation plan. . . . In each city the school board modified its plan several times in light of, for example, hostility to busing, the threat of resegregation, and the desirability of introducing greater student choice. And in each city, the school boards' plans have evolved over time in ways that progressively *diminish* the plans' use of explicit race-conscious criteria.

[Justice Breyer's lengthy, detailed recitation is omitted.]

Both districts sought greater racial integration for educational and democratic, as well as for remedial, reasons. Both sought to achieve these objectives while preserving their commitment to other educational goals, *e.g.,* districtwide commitment to high quality public schools, increased pupil assignment to neighborhood schools, diminished use of busing, greater student choice, reduced risk of white flight, and so forth. Consequently, the present plans expand student choice; they limit the burdens (including busing) that earlier plans had imposed upon students and their families; and they use race-conscious criteria in limited and gradually diminishing ways. In particular, they use race-conscious criteria only to mark the outer bounds of broad population-related ranges.

. . .

No one here disputes that Louisville's segregation was *de jure.* But what about Seattle's? Was it *de facto? De jure?* A mixture? . . .

A court finding of *de jure* segregation cannot be the crucial variable. . . .

. . .

Are courts really to treat as merely *de facto* segregated those school districts that avoided a federal order by voluntarily complying with *Brown*'s requirements?. . . .

. . .

II

The Legal Standard

A longstanding and unbroken line of legal authority tells us that the Equal Protection Clause permits local school boards to use race-conscious criteria to achieve positive race-related goals, even when the Constitution does not compel it. . . . *Swann* . . . .

[Justice Breyer quoted other opinions with similar statements.]

These statements nowhere suggest that this freedom is limited to school districts where court-ordered desegregation measures are also in effect. . . .

. . .

Lower state and federal courts had considered the matter settled and uncontroversial even before this Court decided *Swann*. . . .

. . .

. . . Numerous state and federal courts explicitly relied upon *Swann*'s guidance for decades to follow. . . .

. . .

. . . And . . . hundreds of local school districts have adopted student assignment plans that use race-conscious criteria. . . .

That *Swann*'s legal statement should find such broad acceptance is not surprising. . . . [A] well-established legal view of the Fourteenth Amendment . . . understands the basic objective of those who wrote the Equal Protection Clause as forbidding practices that lead to racial exclusion. The Amendment sought to bring into American society as full members those whom the Nation had previously held in slavery. . . .

There is reason to believe that those who drafted an Amendment with this basic purpose in mind would have understood the legal and practical difference between the use of race-conscious criteria in defiance of that purpose, namely to keep the races apart, and the use of race-conscious criteria to further that purpose, namely to bring the races together. . . .

. . . [N]o case . . . has followed Justice Thomas' "colorblind" approach [or] otherwise repudiated th[e] constitutional asymmetry between that which seeks to *exclude* and that which seeks to *include* members of minority races.

. . .

. . . [As for "the plurality's claim that later cases—in particular *Johnson*, *Adarand*, and *Grutter*—supplanted *Swann*[,]" those] cases . . . , though all applying strict scrutiny, do not treat exclusive and inclusive uses the same. Rather, they apply the strict scrutiny test in a manner that is "fatal in fact" only to racial classifications that harmfully *exclude;* they apply the test in a manner that is *not* fatal in fact to racial classifications that seek to *include*.

. . .

Second, as *Grutter* specified, "[c]ontext matters when reviewing race-based governmental action under the Equal Protection Clause." . . .

. . .

This context is *not* a context that involves the use of race to decide who will receive goods or services that are normally distributed on the basis of merit and which are in short supply. It is not one in which race-conscious limits stigmatize or exclude; the limits at issue do not pit the races against each other or otherwise significantly exacerbate racial tensions. They do not impose burdens unfairly upon members of one race alone but instead seek benefits for members of all races alike. The context here is one of racial limits that seek, not to keep the races apart, but to bring them together.

. . .

. . . In a word, [the plans] do not involve the kind of race-based harm that has led this Court, in other contexts, to find the use of race-conscious criteria unconstitutional.

. . .

[A] more lenient standard than "strict scrutiny" . . . in the present context would not imply abandonment of judicial efforts carefully to determine the need for race-conscious criteria and the criteria's tailoring in light of the need. And the present context requires a court to examine carefully the race-conscious program at issue . . . fully aware of the potential dangers and pitfalls that Justice Thomas and Justice Kennedy mention. . . .

. . . I believe that the law requires application here of a standard of review that is not "strict" in the traditional sense of that word, although it does require the careful review I have just described. . . .

Nonetheless, in light of *Grutter* and other precedents, . . . I shall apply the version of strict scrutiny that those cases embody. . . .

III

Applying the Legal Standard

A

Compelling Interest

The principal interest advanced . . . [is] promoting or preserving greater racial "integration" of public schools. . . .

. . . [T]he interest at stake possesses three essential elements. First, . . . a historical and remedial . . . interest in setting right the consequences of prior conditions of segregation[,] . . . . in maintaining hard-won gains [and] in preventing what gradually may become the *de facto* resegregation of America's public schools. . . .

Second, . . . an educational . . . interest in overcoming the adverse educational effects produced by and associated with highly segregated schools. . . .

. . .

Third, . . . a democratic . . . interest in producing an educational environment that reflects the "pluralistic society" in which our children will live. . . .

. . .

The compelling interest . . . includes an effort to help create citizens better prepared to know, to understand, and to work with people of all races and backgrounds, thereby furthering the kind of democratic government our Constitution foresees. If an educational interest that combines these three elements is not "compelling," what is?

. . .

B

Narrow Tailoring

. . . Several factors, taken together, lead me to conclude that the boards' use of race-conscious criteria in these plans passes even the strictest "tailoring" test.

First, the race-conscious criteria at issue only help set the outer bounds of *broad* ranges. . . .

. . . *Choice* . . . is the "predominant factor" in these plans. *Race* is not. . . .

. . .

Second, broad-range limits on voluntary school choice plans are less burdensome, and hence more narrowly tailored, . . . than other race-conscious restrictions this Court has previously approved[,] . . . [including those] approved in *Grutter*. Here, race becomes a factor only in a fraction of students' non-merit-based assignments—not in large numbers of students' merit-based applications. Moreover, the effect of applying race-conscious criteria here affects potentially disadvantaged students *less severely* . . . than . . . in *Grutter*. Disappointed students are not rejected from a State's flagship graduate program; they simply attend a different one of the district's many public schools, which in aspiration and in fact are substantially equal. . . .

Third, the manner in which the school boards developed these plans itself reflects "narrow tailoring." . . . Each plan is the product of a process that has sought to enhance student choice, while diminishing the need for mandatory busing. And each plan's use of race-conscious elements is *diminished* compared to the use of race in preceding integration plans.

. . .

Nor could the school districts have accomplished their desired aims (*e.g.*, avoiding forced busing, countering white flight, maintaining racial diversity) by other means. . . .

[A]s to "strategic site selection," Seattle has built one new high school in the last 44 years . . . . As to "drawing" neighborhood "attendance zones" on a racial basis, Louisville tried it, and it worked only when forced busing was also part of the plan. As to "allocating resources for special programs," Seattle and Louisville have both experimented with this; indeed, these programs are often referred to as "magnet schools," but the limited desegregation effect of these efforts extends at most to those few schools to which additional resources are granted. In addition, there is no evidence from the experience of these school districts that it will make any meaningful impact. . . . As to "recruiting faculty" on the basis of race, both cities have tried, but only as one part of a broader program. As to "tracking enrollments, performance and other statistics by race," tracking *reveals* the problem; it does not cure it.

. . .

The upshot is that these plans' specific features—(1) their limited and historically-diminishing use of race, (2) their strong reliance upon other non-race-conscious elements, (3) their history and the manner in which the districts developed and modified their approach, (4) the comparison with prior plans, and (5) the lack of reasonably evident alternatives—together show that the districts' plans are "narrowly tailored" to achieve their "compelling" goals. . . .

. . .

. . . [F]ive Members of this Court agree that "avoiding racial isolation" and "achiev[ing] a diverse student population" remain today compelling interests. *Ante,* . . . (opinion of Kennedy, J.). . . . For the reasons discussed above, however, I disagree with Justice Kennedy that Seattle and Louisville have not done enough to demonstrate that their present plans are necessary to continue upon the path set by *Brown*. . . .

. . .

. . . The plurality cites . . . those who argued in *Brown* against segregation, and Justice Thomas likens the approach that I have taken to that of segregation's defenders. . . . But segregation policies . . . perpetuated a caste system rooted in the institutions of slavery and 80 years of legalized subordination. The lesson of history is not that efforts to continue racial segregation are constitutionally indistinguishable from efforts to achieve racial integration. Indeed, it is a cruel distortion of history to compare Topeka, Kansas, in the 1950's to Louisville and Seattle in the modern day. . . .

. . .

. . . This is a decision that the Court and the Nation will come to regret.

I must dissent.

F. CLASSIFICATIONS DISADVANTAGING ALIENS

Graham v. Richardson

403 U.S. 365, 91 S.Ct. 1848, 29 L.Ed.2d 534 (1971).

■ MR. JUSTICE BLACKMUN delivered the opinion of the Court.

These are welfare cases. They provide yet another aspect of the widening litigation in this area. The issue here is whether the Equal Protection Clause of the Fourteenth Amendment prevents a State from conditioning welfare benefits either (a) upon the beneficiary's possession of United States citizenship, or (b) if the beneficiary is an alien, upon his having resided in this country for a specified number of years. . . .

I.

. . .

[Aliens denied welfare benefits challenged an Arizona law that provided welfare to citizens but not to aliens unless they had resided in the United States for 15 years and a Pennsylvania law that excluded aliens from certain state funded welfare benefits. In each case a three-judge district court ruled that the statute violated equal protection.]

II.

The appellants argue initially that the States, consistent with the Equal Protection Clause, may favor United States citizens over aliens in the distribution of welfare benefits. It is said that this distinction involves no "invidious discrimination" . . . for the State is not discriminating with respect to race or nationality.

The Fourteenth Amendment provides, "[N]or shall any State deprive any person of life, liberty, or property, without due process of law; nor deny to any person within its jurisdiction the equal protection of the laws." It has long been settled, and it is not disputed here, that the term "person" in this context encompasses lawfully admitted resident aliens as well as citizens of the United States and entitles both citizens and aliens to the equal protection of the laws of the State in which they reside. Yick Wo v. Hopkins, 118 U.S. 356, 369 (1886); Truax v. Raich, 239 U.S. 33, 39 (1915); Takahashi v. Fish & Game Commission, 334 U.S., at 420. Nor is it disputed that the Arizona and Pennsylvania statutes in question create two classes of needy persons, indistinguishable except with respect to whether they are or are not citizens of this country. Otherwise qualified United States citizens living in Arizona are entitled to federally funded categorical assistance benefits without regard to length of national residency, but aliens must have lived in this country for 15 years in order to qualify for aid. United States citizens living in Pennsylvania, unable to meet the requirements for federally funded benefits, may be eligible for state supported general assistance, but resident aliens as a class are precluded from that assistance.

Under traditional equal protection principles, a State retains broad discretion to classify as long as its classification has a reasonable basis. . . . This is so in "the area of economics and social welfare." Dandridge v. Williams, 397 U.S. 471, 485 (1970). But the Court's decisions have established that classifications based on alienage, like those based on nationality or race, are inherently suspect and subject to close judicial scrutiny. Aliens as a class are a prime example of a "discrete and insular" minority (see United States v. Carolene Products Co., 304 U.S. 144, 152–153 n. 4 (1938)) for whom such heightened judicial solicitude is appropriate. Accordingly, it was said in Takahashi, 334 U.S., at 420, that ". . . the power of a state to apply its laws exclusively to its alien inhabitants as a class is confined within narrow limits."

Arizona and Pennsylvania seek to justify their restrictions on the eligibility of aliens for public assistance solely on the basis of a State's "special public interest" in favoring its own citizens over aliens in the distribution of limited resources such as welfare benefits. . . .

. . . [W]e conclude that a State's desire to preserve limited welfare benefits for its own citizens is inadequate to justify Pennsylvania's making noncitizens ineligible for public assistance, and Arizona's restricting benefits to citizens and longtime resident aliens. . . .

. . .

We agree with the three-judge court in the Pennsylvania case that the "justification of limiting expenses is particularly inappropriate and unreasonable when the discriminated class consists of aliens. . . ." There can be no "special public interest" in tax revenues to which aliens have contributed on an equal basis with the residents of the State.

Accordingly, we hold that a state statute that denies welfare benefits to resident aliens and one that denies them to aliens who have not resided in the United States for a specified number of years violates the Equal Protection Clause.

III.

An additional reason why the state statutes at issue in these cases do not withstand constitutional scrutiny emerges from the area of federal-state relations. The National Government has "broad constitutional powers in determining what aliens shall be admitted to the United States, the period they may remain, regulation of their conduct before naturalization, and the terms and conditions of their naturalization." Takahashi v. Fish & Game Commission, 334 U.S., at 419; Hines v. Davidowitz, 312 U.S. 52, 66 (1941); see also Chinese Exclusion Case, 130 U.S. 581 (1889); United States ex rel. Turner v. Williams, 194 U.S. 279 (1904); Fong Yue Ting v. United States, 149 U.S. 698 (1893); Harisiades v. Shaughnessy, 342 U.S. 580 (1952). Pursuant to that power, Congress has provided, as part of a comprehensive plan for the regulation of immigration and naturalization, that "[A]liens who are paupers, professional beggars, or vagrants" or aliens who "are likely at any time to become public charges" shall be excluded from admission into the United States, 8 U.S.C. §§ 1182(a)(8) and 1182(a)(15), and that any alien lawfully admitted shall be deported who "has within five years after entry become a public charge from causes not affirmatively shown to have arisen after entry. . . ." 8 U.S.C. § 1251(a)(8). Admission of aliens likely to become public charges may be conditioned upon the posting of a bond or cash deposit. 8 U.S.C. § 1138. But Congress has not seen fit to impose any burden or restriction on aliens who become indigent after their entry into the United States. Rather, it has broadly declared that "All persons within the jurisdiction of the United States shall have the same right in every State and Territory . . . to the full and equal benefit of all laws and proceedings for the security of persons and property as is enjoyed by white citizens. . . ." 42 U.S.C. § 1981. The protection of this statute has been held to extend to aliens as well as to citizens. *Takahashi*. . . . Moreover, this Court has made it clear that, whatever may be the scope of the constitutional right of interstate travel, aliens lawfully within this country have a right to enter and abide in any State in the Union "on an equality of legal privileges with all citizens under nondiscriminatory laws." *Takahashi*. . . .

State laws that restrict the eligibility of aliens for welfare benefits merely because of their alienage conflict with these overriding national policies in an area constitutionally entrusted to the Federal Government. . . . State alien residency requirements, that either deny welfare benefits to noncitizens or condition them on longtime residency, equate with the assertion of a right, inconsistent with federal policy, to deny entrance and abode. Since such laws encroach upon exclusive federal power, they are constitutionally impermissible.

. . .

The judgments appealed from are affirmed.

It is so ordered.

■ MR. JUSTICE HARLAN joins in Parts III and IV of the Court's opinion, and in the judgment of the Court.

Bernal v. Fainter

467 U.S. 216, 104 S.Ct. 2312, 81 L.Ed.2d 175 (1984).

■ JUSTICE MARSHALL delivered the opinion of the Court.

The question . . . is whether a statute of the State of Texas violates the Equal Protection Clause of the Fourteenth Amendment . . . by denying aliens the opportunity to become notaries public. The Court of Appeals for the Fifth Circuit held that the statute does not offend the Equal Protection Clause. We . . . reverse.

I

Petitioner, a native of Mexico, is a resident alien who has lived in the United States since 1961. He works as a paralegal for Texas Rural Legal Aid, Inc., helping migrant farm workers on employment and civil rights matters. In order to administer oaths to these workers and to notarize their statements for use in civil litigation, petitioner applied in 1978 to become a notary public. Under Texas law, notaries public authenticate written instruments, administer oaths, and take out-of-court depositions. The Texas Secretary of State denied petitioner's application because he failed to satisfy the statutory requirement that a notary public be a citizen of the United States. Tex.Civ.Stat.Ann., Art. 5949(2). . . . After an unsuccessful administrative appeal, petitioner brought suit in the federal district court, claiming that the citizenship requirement mandated by Article 5949(2) violated the federal Constitution.

The District Court ruled in favor of petitioner. . . . A divided panel of the Court of Appeals for the Fifth Circuit reversed, concluding that the proper standard for review was the rational relationship test and that Article 5949(2) satisfied that test because it "bears a rational relationship to the state's interest in the proper and orderly handling of a countless variety of legal documents of importance to the state." Vargas v. Strake, 710 F.2d 190, 195 (C.A.5 1983).

II

As a general matter, a State law that discriminates on the basis of alienage can be sustained only if it can withstand strict judicial scrutiny. In order to withstand strict scrutiny, the law must advance a compelling State interest by the least restrictive means available. Applying this principle, we have invalidated an array of

State statutes that denied aliens the right to pursue various occupations. In Sugarman v. Dougall, 413 U.S. 634 (1973), we struck down a State statute barring aliens from employment in permanent positions in the competitive class of the State civil service. In In re Griffiths, 413 U.S. 717 (1973), we nullified a State law excluding aliens from eligibility for membership in the State bar. And in Examining Board v. Flores de Otero, 426 U.S. 572 (1976), we voided a State law that excluded aliens from the practice of civil engineering.

We have, however, developed a narrow exception to the rule that discrimination based on alienage triggers strict scrutiny. This exception has been labelled the "political function" exception and applies to laws that exclude aliens from positions intimately related to the process of democratic self-government. The contours of the "political function" exception are outlined by our prior decisions. In Foley v. Connelie, 435 U.S. 291 (1978), we held that a State may require police to be citizens because, in performing a fundamental obligation of government, police "are clothed with authority to exercise an almost infinite variety of discretionary powers" often involving the most sensitive areas of daily life. In Ambach v. Norwick, 441 U.S. 68 (1979), we held that a State may bar aliens who have not declared their intent to become citizens from teaching in the public schools because teachers, like police, possess a high degree of responsibility and discretion in the fulfillment of a basic governmental obligation. They have direct, day-to-day contact with students, exercise unsupervised discretion over them, act as role models and influence their students about the government and the political process. Finally, in Cabell v. Chavez-Salido, 454 U.S. 432 (1982), we held that a State may bar aliens from positions as probation officers because they, like police and teachers, routinely exercise discretionary power, involving a basic governmental function, that places them in a position of direct authority over other individuals.

The rationale behind the political function exception is that within broad boundaries a State may establish its own form of government and limit the right to govern to those who are full-fledged members of the political community. Some public positions are so closely bound up with the formulation and implementation of self-government that the State is permitted to exclude from those positions persons outside the political community, hence persons who have not become part of the process of democratic self-determination.

"The exclusion of aliens from basic governmental processes is not a deficiency in the democratic system but a necessary consequence of the community's process of political self-definition. Self-government, whether direct or through representatives, begins by defining the scope of the community of the governed and thus of the governors as well: Aliens are by definition those outside of this community."

We have therefore lowered our standard of review when evaluating the validity of exclusions that entrust only to citizens important elective and nonelective positions whose operations "go to the heart of representative government." Sugarman v. Dougall, supra, 413 U.S., at 647. "While not retreating from the position that restrictions on lawfully resident aliens that primarily affect economic interests are subject to heightened judicial scrutiny . . . we have concluded that strict scrutiny is out of place when the restriction primarily serves a political function. . . ." Cabell v. Chavez-Salido, supra, 454 U.S., at 439.

To determine whether a restriction based on alienage fits within the narrow political function exception, we devised in *Cabell* a two-part test.

"First, the specificity of the classification will be examined: a classification that is substantially overinclusive or underinclusive tends to undercut the governmental claim that the classification serves legitimate political ends. . . . Second, even if the classification is sufficiently tailored, it may be applied in the particular case only to 'persons holding state elective or important nonelective executive, legislative, and judicial positions,' those officers who 'participate directly in the formulation, execution, or review of broad public policy' and hence 'perform functions that go right to the heart of representative government.' "[7]

III

We now turn to Article 5949(2) to determine whether it satisfies the *Cabell* test. The statute provides that "[t]o be eligible for appointment as a Notary Public, a person shall be a resident citizen of the United States and of this state. . . ." Unlike the statute invalidated in *Sugarman,* Article 5949(2) does not indiscriminately sweep within its ambit a wide range of offices and occupations but specifies only one particular post with respect to which the State asserts a right to exclude aliens. Clearly, then, the statute is not overinclusive; it applies narrowly to only one category of persons: those wishing to obtain appointments as notaries. Less clear is whether Article 5942(2) is fatally underinclusive. Texas does not require court reporters to be United States citizens even though they perform some of the same services as notaries. Nor does Texas require that its Secretary of State be a citizen, even though he holds the highest appointive position in the State and performs many important functions, including supervision of the licensing of all notaries public. We need not decide this issue, however, because of our decision with respect to the second prong of the *Cabell* test.

In support of the proposition that notaries public fall within that category of officials who perform functions that "go to the heart of representative government," the State emphasizes that notaries are designated as public officers by the Texas Constitution. Texas maintains that this designation indicates that the State views notaries as important officials occupying posts central to the State's definition of itself as a political community. This Court, however, has never deemed the *source* of a position—whether it derives from a State's statute or its Constitution—as the dispositive factor in determining whether a State may entrust the position only to citizens. Rather, this Court has always looked to the actual *function* of the position as the dispositive factor. The focus of our inquiry has been whether a position was such that the officeholder would necessarily exercise broad discretionary power over the formulation or execution of public policies importantly affecting the citizen population—power of the sort that a self-governing community could properly entrust only to full-fledged members of that community. As the Court noted in *Cabell,* in determining whether the function of a particular position brings the position within the narrow ambit of the exception, "the Court will look to the importance of the function as a factor giving substance to the concept of democratic self-government."

The State maintains that even if the actual function of a post is the touchstone of a proper analysis, Texas notaries public should still be classified among those positions from which aliens can properly be excluded because the duties of Texas notaries entail the performance of functions sufficiently consequential to be deemed "political." . . .

We recognize the critical need for a notary's duties to be carried out correctly and with integrity. But a notary's duties, important as they are, hardly implicate responsibilities that go to the heart of representative government. Rather, these duties are essentially clerical and ministerial. In contrast to state troopers, *Foley v. Connelie,* notaries do not routinely exercise the State's monopoly of legitimate coercive force. Nor

---

[7]   We emphasize, as we have in the past, that the political-function exception must be narrowly construed; otherwise the exception will swallow the rule and depreciate the significance that should attach to the designation of a group as a "discrete and insular" minority for whom heightened judicial solicitude is appropriate. See Nyquist v. Mauclet, 432 U.S. 1, 11 (1977).

do notaries routinely exercise the wide discretion typically enjoyed by public school teachers when they present materials that educate youth respecting the information and values necessary for the maintenance of a democratic political system. See Ambach v. Norwick, 441 U.S., at 77. To be sure, considerable damage could result from the negligent or dishonest performance of a notary's duties. But the same could be said for the duties performed by cashiers, building inspectors, the janitors who clean up the offices of public officials, and numerous other categories of personnel upon whom we depend for careful, honest service. What distinguishes such personnel from those to which the political function exception is properly applied is that the latter are either invested with policy-making responsibility or broad discretion in the execution of public policy that requires the routine exercise of authority over individuals. Neither of these characteristics pertain to the functions performed by Texas notaries.

The inappropriateness of applying the political function exception to Texas notaries is further underlined by our decision in *In re Griffiths* ... in which we subjected to strict scrutiny a Connecticut statute that prohibited non-citizens from becoming members of the State bar. Along with the usual powers and privileges accorded to members of the bar, Connecticut gave to members of its bar additional authority that encompasses the very duties performed by Texas notaries—authority to "sign writs and subpoenas, take recognizances, administer oaths and take depositions and acknowledgement of deeds." In striking down Connecticut's citizenship requirement, we concluded that "[i]t in no way denigrates a lawyer's high responsibility to observe that [these duties] hardly involve matters of state policy or acts of such unique responsibility as to entrust them only to citizens." If it is improper to apply the political function exception to a citizenship requirement governing eligibility for membership in a State bar, it would be anomalous to apply the exception to the citizenship requirement that governs eligibility to become a Texas notary. We conclude, then, that the "political function" exception is inapplicable to Article 5949(2) and that the statute is therefore subject to strict judicial scrutiny.

IV

To satisfy strict scrutiny, the State must show that Article 5949(2) furthers a compelling State interest by the least restrictive means practically available. Respondent maintains that Article 5949(2) serves its "legitimate concern that notaries be reasonably familiar with state law and institutions" and "that notaries may be called upon years later to testify to acts they have performed." However both of these asserted justifications utterly fail to meet the stringent requirements of strict scrutiny. There is nothing in the record that indicates that resident aliens, as a class, are so incapable of familiarizing themselves with Texas law as to justify the State's absolute and class-wide exclusion. The possibility that some resident aliens are unsuitable for the position cannot justify a wholesale ban against all resident aliens. Furthermore, if the State's concern with ensuring a notary's familiarity with state law were truly "compelling," one would expect the State to give some sort of test actually measuring a person's familiarity with the law. The State, however, administers no such test. To become a notary public in Texas, one is merely required to fill out an application that lists one's name and address and that answers four questions pertaining to one's age, citizenship, residency and criminal record—nothing that reflects the State's asserted interest in insuring that notaries are familiar with Texas law. Similarly inadequate is the State's purported interest in insuring the later availability of notaries' testimony. This justification fails because the State fails to advance a factual showing that the unavailability of notaries' testimony presents a real, as opposed to a merely speculative, problem to the State. Without a factual underpinning, the State's asserted interest lacks the weight we have required of interests properly denominated as compelling.

V

We conclude that Article 5949(2) violates the Fourteenth Amendment.... Accordingly the judgment ... is reversed, and the case is remanded for further proceedings consistent with this opinion.

■ JUSTICE REHNQUIST, dissenting.

I dissent for the reasons stated in my dissenting opinion in Sugarman v. Dougall, 413 U.S. 634, 649 (1973).

Mathews v. Diaz

426 U.S. 67, 96 S.Ct. 1883, 48 L.Ed.2d 478 (1976).

■ MR. JUSTICE STEVENS delivered the opinion of the Court.

The question presented by the Secretary's appeal is whether Congress may condition an alien's eligibility for participation in a federal medical insurance program on continuous residence in the United States for a five-year period and admission for permanent residence. The District Court held that the first condition was unconstitutional and that it could not be severed from the second. Since we conclude that both conditions are constitutional, we reverse.

Each of the appellees is a resident alien who was lawfully admitted to the United States less than five years ago. Appellees Diaz and Clara are Cuban refugees who remain in this country at the discretion of the Attorney General; appellee Espinosa has been admitted for permanent residence. All three are over 65 years old and have been denied enrollment in the Medicare Part B supplemental medical insurance program established by ... the Social Security Act.... They brought this action to challenge the statutory basis for that denial. Specifically, they attack 42 U.S.C. § 1395o(2), which grants eligibility to resident citizens who are 65 or older but denies eligibility to such aliens unless they have been admitted for permanent residence and also have resided in the United States for at least five years....

   . . .

II.

There are literally millions of aliens within the jurisdiction of the United States. The Fifth Amendment, as well as the Fourteenth Amendment, protects every one of these persons from deprivation of life, liberty or property without due process of law. Wong Yang Sung v. McGrath, 339 U.S. 33, 48–51; Wong Wing v. United States, 163 U.S. 228, 238; see Russian Volunteer Fleet v. United States, 282 U.S. 481, 489. Even one whose presence in this country is unlawful, involuntary, or transitory, is entitled to that constitutional protection. *Wong Yang Sung,* supra; *Wong Wing,* supra.

The fact that all persons, aliens and citizens alike, are protected by the Due Process Clause does not lead to the further conclusion that all aliens are entitled to enjoy all the advantages of citizenship or, indeed, to the conclusion that all aliens must be placed in a single homogenous legal classification. For a host of constitutional and statutory provisions rest on the premise that a legitimate distinction between citizens and aliens may justify attributes and benefits for one class not accorded to the other;[12]

---

[12] The Constitution protects the privileges and immunities only of citizens, Amend. XIV, § 1; see Art. IV, § 2, cl. 1, and the right to vote only of citizens. Amends. XV, XIX, XXIV, XXVI. It requires that Representatives have been citizens for seven years, Art. I, § 2, cl. 2, and Senators citizens for nine, Art. I, § 3, cl. 3, and that the President be a "natural born Citizen." Art. II, § 1, cl. 5.

A multitude of federal statutes distinguish between citizens and aliens. The whole of Title 8 of the United States Code, regulating aliens and nationality, is founded on the legitimacy of distinguishing and the class of aliens is itself a heterogenous multitude of persons with a wide-ranging variety of ties to this country.

In the exercise of its broad power over naturalization and immigration, Congress regularly makes rules that would be unacceptable if applied to citizens. The exclusion of aliens and the reservation of the power to deport have no permissible counterpart in the Federal Government's power to regulate the conduct of its own citizenry. The fact that an act of Congress treats aliens differently from citizens does not in itself imply that such disparate treatment is "invidious."

In particular, the fact that Congress has provided some welfare benefits for citizens does not require it to provide like benefits for *all aliens*. Neither the overnight visitor, the unfriendly agent of a hostile foreign power, the resident diplomat, nor the illegal entrant, can advance even a colorable constitutional claim to a share in the bounty that a conscientious sovereign makes available to its own citizens and *some* of its guests. The decision to share that bounty with our guests may take into account the character of the relationship between the alien and this country: Congress may decide that as the alien's tie grows stronger, so does the strength of his claim to an equal share of that munificence.

The real question presented by this case is not whether discrimination between citizens and aliens is permissible; rather, it is whether the statutory discrimination *within* the class of aliens—allowing benefits to some aliens but not to others—is permissible. We turn to that question.

III.

For reasons long recognized as valid, the responsibility for regulating the relationship between the United States and our alien visitors has been committed to the political branches of the Federal Government. Since decisions in these matters may implicate our relations with foreign powers, and since a wide variety of classifications must be defined in the light of changing political and economic circumstances, such decisions are frequently of a character more appropriate to either the legislature or the executive than to the judiciary. This very case illustrates the need for flexibility in policy choices rather than the rigidity often characteristic of constitutional adjudication. Appellees Diaz and Clara are but two of over 440,000 Cuban refugees who arrived in the United States between 1961 and 1972. And the Cuban paroleees are but one of several categories of aliens who have been admitted in order to make a humane response to a natural catastrophe or an international political situation. Any rule of constitutional law that would inhibit the flexibility of the political branches of government to respond to changing world conditions should be adopted only with the greatest caution. The reasons that preclude judicial review of political questions also dictate a narrow standard of review of decisions made by the Congress or the President in the area of immigration and naturalization.

Since it is obvious that Congress has no constitutional duty to provide *all aliens* with the welfare benefits provided to citizens, the party challenging the constitutionality of the particular line Congress has drawn has the burden of advancing principled reasoning that will at once invalidate that line and yet tolerate a different line separating some aliens from others. In this case the appellees have challenged two requirements, first that the alien be admitted as a permanent resident, and second that his residence be of a duration of at least five years. But if these requirements were eliminated, surely Congress would at least require that the alien's entry be lawful; even then, unless mere transients are to be held constitutionally

---

citizens and aliens. A variety of other federal statutes provide for disparate treatment of aliens and citizens. . . .

entitled to benefits, *some* durational requirement would certainly be appropriate. In short, it is unquestionably reasonable for Congress to make an alien's eligibility depend on both the character and the duration of his residence. Since neither requirement is wholly irrational, this case essentially involves nothing more than a claim that it would have been more reasonable for Congress to select somewhat different requirements of the same kind.

We may assume that the five-year line drawn by Congress is longer than necessary to protect the fiscal integrity of the program. We may also assume that unnecessary hardship is incurred by persons just short of qualifying. But it remains true that some line is essential, that any line must produce some harsh and apparently arbitrary consequences, and, of greatest importance, that those who qualify under the test Congress has chosen may reasonably be presumed to have a greater affinity to the United States than those who do not. In short, citizens and those who are most like citizens qualify. Those who are less like citizens do not.

The task of classifying persons for medical benefits, like the task of drawing lines for federal tax purposes, inevitably requires that some persons who have an almost equally strong claim to favored treatment be placed on different sides of the line; the differences between the eligible and the ineligible are differences in degree rather than differences in the character of their respective claims. When this kind of policy choice must be made, we are especially reluctant to question the exercise of congressional judgment. In this case, since appellees have not identified a principled basis for prescribing a different standard than the one selected by Congress, they have, in effect, merely invited us to substitute our judgment for that of Congress in deciding which aliens shall be eligible to participate in the supplementary insurance program on the same conditions as citizens. We decline the invitation.

IV.

The cases on which appellees rely are consistent with our conclusion that this statutory classification does not deprive them of liberty or property without due process of law.

Graham v. Richardson, 403 U.S. 365, provides the strongest support for appellees' position. That case holds that state statutes that deny welfare benefits to resident aliens, or to aliens not meeting a requirement of durational residence within the United States, violate the Equal Protection Clause of the Fourteenth Amendment and encroach upon the exclusive federal power over the entrance and residence of aliens. Of course, the latter ground of decision actually supports our holding today that it is the business of the political branches of the Federal Government, rather than that of either the States or the federal judiciary, to regulate the conditions of entry and residence of aliens. The equal protection analysis also involves significantly different considerations because it concerns the relationship between aliens and the States rather than between aliens and the Federal Government.

Insofar as state welfare policy is concerned, there is little, if any, basis for treating persons who are citizens of another State differently from persons who are citizens of another country. Both groups are noncitizens as far as the State's interests in administering its welfare programs are concerned. Thus, a division by a State of the category of persons who are not citizens of that State into subcategories of United States citizens and aliens has no apparent justification, whereas, a comparable classification by the Federal Government is a routine and normally legitimate part of its business. Furthermore, whereas the Constitution inhibits every State's power to restrict travel across its own borders, Congress is explicitly empowered to exercise that type of control over travel across the borders of the United States.

We hold that § 1395*o*(2)(B) has not deprived appellees of liberty or property without due process of law.

The judgment of the District Court is reversed.

Nguyen v. Immigration and Naturalization Service
533 U.S. 53 (2001).

The report in this case appears, supra at p. 542.

G. WHAT OTHER CLASSIFICATIONS WILL PROVOKE HEIGHTENED SCRUTINY?

City of Cleburne v. Cleburne Living Center
473 U.S. 432, 105 S.Ct. 3249, 87 L.Ed.2d 313 (1985).

■ JUSTICE WHITE delivered the opinion of the Court.

A Texas city denied a special use permit for the operation of a group home for the mentally retarded, acting pursuant to a municipal zoning ordinance requiring permits for such homes. The Court of Appeals for the Fifth Circuit held that mental retardation is a "quasi-suspect" classification and that the ordinance violated the Equal Protection Clause because it did not substantially further an important governmental purpose. We hold that a lesser standard of scrutiny is appropriate, but conclude that under that standard the ordinance is invalid as applied in this case.

I

. . . [The] anticipated [group] home would house 13 retarded men and women . . . under the constant supervision of CLC staff members. . . .

. . . [A] special use permit, renewable annually, was required for the construction of "[h]ospitals for the insane or feeble-minded, or alcoholic [sic] or drug addicts, or penal or correctional institutions." The city had determined that the proposed group home should be classified as a "hospital for the feeble-minded." After holding a public hearing on CLC's application, the city council voted three to one to deny a special use permit.

CLC [sued] . . . alleging, *inter alia*, that the zoning ordinance was invalid on its face and as applied because it discriminated against the mentally retarded. . . . The [district] court deemed the ordinance, as written and applied, to be rationally related to the City's legitimate interests in "the legal responsibility of CLC and its residents, . . . the safety and fears of residents in the adjoining neighborhood," and the number of people to be housed. . . .

The . . . Fifth Circuit reversed, . . . [applying] intermediate-level scrutiny. . . . [It] held that the ordinance was invalid on its face because it did not substantially further any important governmental interests [and] that the ordinance was also invalid as applied. . . .

II

. . .

We have declined . . . to extend heightened review to differential treatment based on age:

"While the treatment of the aged in this Nation has not been wholly free of discrimination, such persons, unlike, say, those who have been discriminated against on the basis of race or national origin, have not experienced a 'history of purposeful unequal treatment' or been subjected to unique disabilities on the basis of stereotyped characteristics not truly indicative of their abilities." Massachusetts Board of Retirement v. Murgia, 427 U.S. 307, 313 (1976).[a]

The lesson of *Murgia* is that where individuals in the group affected by a law have distinguishing characteristics relevant to interests the state has the authority to implement, the courts have been very reluctant, as they should be in our federal system and with our respect for the separation of powers, to closely scrutinize legislative choices as to whether, how and to what extent those interests should be pursued. In such cases, the Equal Protection Clause requires only a rational means to serve a legitimate end.

III

[W]e conclude for several reasons that the Court of Appeals erred in holding mental retardation a quasi-suspect classification calling for a more exacting standard of judicial review than is normally accorded economic and social legislation. First, . . . th[e] mentally retarded have a reduced ability to cope with and function in the everyday world. . . . They are thus different, immutably so, in relevant respects, and the states' interest in dealing with and providing for them is plainly a legitimate one.[10] How this large and diversified group is to be treated under the law is a difficult and often a technical matter, very much a task for legislators guided by qualified professionals and not by the perhaps ill-informed opinions of the judiciary. Heightened scrutiny inevitably involves substantive judgments about legislative decisions, and we doubt that the predicate for such judicial oversight is present where the classification deals with mental retardation.

---

[a]   *Murgia* applied a rational basis standard and upheld a Massachusetts compulsory retirement law for state police officers who attained age fifty, rejecting the challenge of an officer who had passed an annual physical examination administered four months before he was retired involuntarily. The Court concluded that the objective of assuring physical fitness was rationally furthered by a maximum age limitation and that it was not necessary for the state to use individualized testing after age 50 even if that might determine fitness more precisely. The state did not have to choose the "best means" to accomplish its purpose, only a rational one.

The Court similarly has upheld a mandatory retirement age of 60 for Foreign Service officers, Vance v. Bradley, 440 U.S. 93 (1979), and a provision of the Missouri Constitution requiring nearly all state judges to retire at age 70. Gregory v. Ashcroft, 501 U.S. 452 (1991). In *Gregory* the Court rejected arguments "that the mandatory retirement provision makes two irrational distinctions: between judges who have reached age 70 and younger judges, and between judges 70 and over and other state employees of the same age who are not subject to mandatory retirement." The age distinction was rationally related to Missouri's "legitimate, indeed compelling, interest in maintaining a judiciary fully capable of performing the demanding tasks that judges must perform." The alternatives of voluntary retirement, impeachment, and retention elections rationally could be perceived as inadequate checks on judges whose performance has declined with advancing age. That judges serve longer terms, often run unopposed, and are less scrutinized by the public rationally explained "the distinction between judges and other state employees, in whom a deterioration in performance is more readily discernible and who are more easily removed." Although it is "probably not true that most" judges "suffer significant deterioration in performance at age 70" and "may not be true at all[,]" the "people of Missouri rationally could conclude that the threat of deterioration at age 70 is sufficiently great, and the alternatives for removal sufficiently inadequate, that they will require all judges to step aside at age 70."

[10]   As Dean Ely has observed:

"Surely one has to feel sorry for a person disabled by something he or she can't do anything about, but I'm not aware of any reason to suppose that elected officials are unusually unlikely to share that feeling. Moreover, classifications based on physical disability and intelligence are typically accepted as legitimate, even by judges and commentators who assert that immutability is relevant. The explanation, when one is given, is that *those* characteristics (unlike the one the commentator is trying to render suspect) are often relevant to legitimate purposes. At that point there's not much left of the immutability theory, is there?" J. Ely, Democracy and Distrust 150 (1980) (footnote omitted). See also id., at 154–155.

Second, . . . lawmakers have been addressing their difficulties in a manner that belies a continuing antipathy or prejudice and a corresponding need for more intrusive oversight by the judiciary. Thus, the federal government has not only outlawed discrimination against the mentally retarded in federally funded programs, see § 504 of the Rehabilitation Act of 1973, 29 U.S.C. § 794, but it has also provided the retarded with the right to receive "appropriate treatment, services, and habilitation" in a setting that is "least restrictive of [their] personal liberty." Developmental Disabilities Assistance and Bill of Rights Act, 42 U.S.C. §§ 6010(1), (2). In addition, the government has conditioned federal education funds on a State's assurance that retarded children will enjoy an education that, "to the maximum extent appropriate," is integrated with that of non-mentally retarded children. Education of the Handicapped Act, 20 U.S.C. § 1412(5)(B). The government has also facilitated the hiring of the mentally retarded into the federal civil service by exempting them from the requirement of competitive examination. . . . Texas has similarly enacted legislation that acknowledges the special status of the mentally retarded by conferring certain rights upon them, such as "the right to live in the least restrictive setting appropriate to [their] individual needs and abilities," including "the right to live . . . in a group home." Mentally Retarded Persons Act of 1977. . . .

. . . That a civilized and decent society expects and approves such legislation indicates that governmental consideration of those differences in the vast majority of situations is not only legitimate but desirable. It may be, as CLC contends, that legislation designed to benefit, rather than disadvantage, the retarded would generally withstand examination under a test of heightened scrutiny. The relevant inquiry, however, is whether heightened scrutiny is constitutionally mandated in the first instance. [M]erely requiring the legislature to justify its efforts in these terms may lead it to refrain from acting at all. Much recent legislation intended to benefit the retarded also assumes the need for measures that might be perceived to disadvantage them. The Education of the Handicapped Act, for example, requires an "appropriate" education, not one that is equal in all respects to the education of non-retarded children; clearly, admission to a class that exceeded the abilities of a retarded child would not be appropriate. Similarly, the Developmental Disabilities Assistance Act and the Texas act give the retarded the right to live only in the "least restrictive setting" appropriate to their abilities, implicitly assuming the need for at least some restrictions that would not be imposed on others. Especially given the wide variation in the abilities and needs of the retarded themselves, governmental bodies must have a certain amount of flexibility and freedom from judicial oversight in shaping and limiting their remedial efforts.

Third, the legislative response . . . negates any claim that the mentally retarded are politically powerless in the sense that they have no ability to attract the attention of the lawmakers. . . .

Fourth, if the large and amorphous class of the mentally retarded were deemed quasi-suspect . . . , it would be difficult to find a principled way to distinguish a variety of other groups who have perhaps immutable disabilities setting them off from others, who cannot themselves mandate the desired legislative responses, and who can claim some degree of prejudice from at least part of the public at large. One need mention . . . only the aging, the disabled, the mentally ill, and the infirm. We are reluctant to set out on that course. . . .

. . . Because mental retardation is a characteristic that the government may legitimately take into account in a wide range of decisions, and because both state and federal governments have recently committed themselves to assisting the retarded, we will not presume that any given legislative action, even one that disadvantages retarded individuals, is rooted in considerations that the Constitution will not tolerate.

Our refusal to recognize the retarded as a quasi-suspect class does not leave them entirely unprotected from invidious discrimination[;] legislation that distinguishes between the mentally retarded and others must be rationally related to a legitimate governmental purpose. . . .

IV

. . . We inquire first whether requiring a special use permit . . . in the circumstances here deprives respondents of the equal protection of the laws. If it does, there will be no occasion to decide whether the special use permit provision is facially invalid where the mentally retarded are involved. . . . This is the preferred course of adjudication since it enables courts to avoid making unnecessarily broad constitutional judgments. . . .

. . . The City does not require a special use permit in an R-3 zone for apartment houses, multiple dwellings, boarding and lodging houses, fraternity or sorority houses, dormitories, apartment hotels, hospitals, sanitariums, nursing homes for convalescents or the aged (other than for the insane or feeble-minded or alcoholics or drug addicts), private clubs or fraternal orders, and other specified uses. . . . May the city require the permit for this facility when other care and multiple dwelling facilities are freely permitted?

. . . Because in our view the record does not reveal any rational basis for believing that the . . . home would pose any special threat to the city's legitimate interests, we affirm the judgment below insofar as it holds the ordinance invalid as applied. . . .

The District Court found that the City Council's insistence on the permit rested on several factors. First, the Council was concerned with the negative attitude of the majority of property owners located within 200 feet of the Featherston facility, as well as with the fears of elderly residents of the neighborhood. But mere negative attitudes, or fear, unsubstantiated by factors which are properly cognizable in a zoning proceeding, are not permissible bases for treating a home for the mentally retarded differently from apartment houses, multiple dwellings, and the like. . . . [T]he City may not . . . defer[ ] to the wishes or objections of some fraction of the body politic. "Private biases may be outside the reach of the law, but the law cannot, directly or indirectly, give them effect." Palmore v. Sidoti, 466 U.S. 429, 433 (1984).

Second, the Council had two objections to the location of the facility. [It] was across the street from a junior high school, and [the Council] feared that the students might harass the occupants. . . . But the school itself is attended by about 30 mentally retarded students, and denying a permit based on such vague, undifferentiated fears is again permitting some portion of the community to validate what would otherwise be an equal protection violation. The other objection [was its location] on "a five hundred year flood plain." This concern . . . , however, can hardly be based on a distinction between the Featherston home and, for example, nursing homes, homes for convalescents or the aged, or sanitariums or hospitals. . . . The same may be said of another concern of the Council—doubts about the legal responsibility for actions which the mentally retarded might take. If there is no concern about legal responsibility with respect to other uses . . . such as boarding and fraternity houses, it is difficult to believe that . . . mildly or moderately mentally retarded individuals . . . would present any different or special hazard.

Fourth, . . . [given that] there would be no restrictions on the number of people who could occupy this home as a boarding house, nursing home, family dwelling, fraternity house, or dormitory[,] . . . this record does not clarify how . . . the characteristics of the intended occupants . . . rationally justify denying [them] what would be permitted to groups occupying the same site for different purposes. Th[ey] are the type of individuals who, with supporting staff, satisfy federal and state standards for group housing in the community; and there is no dispute that the home would meet the federal square-footage-per-resident requirement for facilities of this type. . . . In the words of the Court of Appeals, "The City never justifies its apparent view that other people can live under such 'crowded' conditions when mentally retarded persons cannot."

In the courts below the city also urged that the ordinance is aimed at avoiding concentration of population and at lessening congestion of the streets. These concerns obviously fail to explain why apartment houses, fraternity and sorority houses, hospitals and the like, may freely locate in the area without a permit. So, too, the expressed worry about fire hazards, the serenity of the neighborhood, and the avoidance of danger to other residents fail rationally to justify singling out [this] home . . . for the special use permit. . . .

The short of it is that requiring the permit in this case appears to us to rest on an irrational prejudice against the mentally retarded. . . .

   . . .

■ JUSTICE STEVENS, with whom THE CHIEF JUSTICE joins, concurring.

   . . . [O]ur cases reflect a continuum of judgmental responses to differing classifications . . . ranging from "strict scrutiny" at one extreme to "rational basis" at the other. I have never been persuaded that these so called "standards" adequately explain the decisional process. Cases involving classifications based on alienage, illegal residency, illegitimacy, gender, age, or—as in this case—mental retardation, do not fit well into sharply defined classifications.

   . . .

Every law that places the mentally retarded in a special class is not presumptively irrational. The differences between mentally retarded persons and those with greater mental capacity are obviously relevant to certain legislative decisions. An impartial lawmaker—indeed, even a member of a class of persons defined as mentally retarded—could rationally vote in favor of a law providing funds for special education and special treatment for the mentally retarded. A mentally retarded person could also recognize that he is a member of a class that might need special supervision in some situations, both to protect himself and to protect others. Restrictions on his right to drive cars or to operate hazardous equipment might well seem rational even though they deprived him of employment opportunities and the kind of freedom of travel enjoyed by other citizens. . . .

Even so, the Court of Appeals correctly observed that through ignorance and prejudice the mentally retarded "have been subjected to a history of unfair and often grotesque mistreatment." . . . The record convinces me that this permit was required because of the irrational fears of neighboring property owners, rather than for the protection of the mentally retarded persons who would reside in respondent's home.

   . . .

■ JUSTICE MARSHALL, with whom JUSTICE BRENNAN and JUSTICE BLACKMUN join, concurring in the judgment in part and dissenting in part.

   . . .

   . . . Cleburne's ordinance surely would be valid under the traditional rational basis test applicable to economic and commercial regulation. In my view, it is important to articulate, as the Court does not, the facts and principles that justify subjecting this zoning ordinance to the searching review—the heightened scrutiny— that actually leads to its invalidation. Moreover, in invalidating Cleburne's exclusion of the "feebleminded" only as applied . . . , rather than on its face, the Court radically departs from our equal protection precedents. . . .

I

. . .

. . . [B]y failing to articulate the factors that justify today's "second order" rational basis review, the Court provides no principled foundation for determining when more searching inquiry is to be invoked. . . .

II

I have long believed the level of scrutiny employed in an equal protection case should vary with "the constitutional and societal importance of the interest adversely affected and the recognized invidiousness of the basis upon which the particular classification is drawn." San Antonio Independent School District v. Rodriguez, 411 U.S. 1, 99 (1973) (Marshall, J., dissenting). . . . When a zoning ordinance works to exclude the retarded from all residential districts in a community, these two considerations require that the ordinance be convincingly justified as substantially furthering legitimate and important purposes. . . .

First, the interest of the retarded in establishing group homes is substantial. . . . [A]s deinstitutionalization has progressed, group homes have become the primary means by which retarded adults can enter life in the community. . . .

Second, the mentally retarded have been subject to a "lengthy and tragic history," . . . of segregation and discrimination that can only be called grotesque. . . .

. . . Marriages of the retarded were made, and in some states continue to be, not only voidable but also often a criminal offense. The purpose of such limitations . . . was unabashedly eugenic: to prevent the retarded from propagating. . . .

. . . [M]ost important, lengthy and continuing isolation of the retarded has perpetuated the ignorance, irrational fears, and stereotyping that long have plagued them.

In light of the importance of the interest at stake and the history of discrimination the retarded have suffered, the Equal Protection Clause requires us to do more than review the distinctions drawn by Cleburne's zoning ordinance as if they appeared in a taxing statute or in economic or commercial legislation. The searching scrutiny I would give to restrictions on the ability of the retarded to establish community group homes leads me to conclude that Cleburne's vague generalizations for classifying the "feeble minded" with drug addicts, alcoholics, and the insane, and excluding them where the elderly, the ill, the boarder, and the transient are allowed, are not substantial or important enough to overcome the suspicion that the ordinance rests on impermissible assumptions or outmoded and perhaps invidious stereotypes. . . .

III

. . .

The Court downplays the lengthy "history of purposeful unequal treatment" of the retarded, . . . by pointing to recent legislative action that is said to "beli[e] a continuing antipathy or prejudice." . . .

. . .

[L]egislative change . . . certainly does not eviscerate the underlying constitutional principle. The Court, for example, has never suggested that race-based classifications became any less suspect once extensive legislation had been enacted on the subject. . . .

For the retarded, just as for Negroes and women, much has changed in recent years, but much remains the same; out-dated statutes are still on the books, and irrational fears or ignorance, traceable to the prolonged social and cultural isolation of the retarded, continue to stymie recognition of the dignity and individuality of retarded people. Heightened judicial scrutiny of action appearing to impose unnecessary barriers to the retarded is required in light of increasing recognition that such barriers are inconsistent with evolving principles of equality embedded in the Fourteenth Amendment.

. . .

IV

In light of the scrutiny that should be applied here, Cleburne's ordinance sweeps too broadly to dispel the suspicion that it rests on a bare desire to treat the retarded as outsiders, pariahs who do not belong in the community. . . . [H]owever, the Court invalidates it merely as applied. . . . I must dissent from the novel proposition that "the preferred course of adjudication" is to leave standing a legislative act resting on "irrational prejudice" thereby forcing individuals in the group discriminated against to continue to run the act's gauntlet.

. . .

Invalidating on its face the ordinance's special treatment of the "feebleminded", in contrast, would place the responsibility for tailoring and updating Cleburne's unconstitutional ordinance where it belongs: with the legislative arm of the City of Cleburne. . . . [T]he city should not be allowed to keep its ordinance on the books intact and thereby shift to the courts the responsibility to confront the complex empirical and policy questions involved in updating statutes affecting the mentally retarded. A legislative solution would yield standards and provide the sort of certainty to retarded applicants and administrative officials that case-by-case judicial rulings cannot provide. . . .

Romer v. Evans

517 U.S. 620, 116 S.Ct. 1620, 134 L.Ed.2d 855 (1996).

■ JUSTICE KENNEDY delivered the opinion of the Court.

One century ago, the first Justice Harlan admonished this Court that the Constitution "neither knows nor tolerates classes among citizens." Plessy v. Ferguson, 163 U.S. 537, 559 (1896) (dissenting opinion). Unheeded then, those words now are understood to state a commitment to the law's neutrality where the rights of persons are at stake. The Equal Protection Clause enforces this principle and today requires us to hold invalid a provision of Colorado's Constitution.

I

[A]n amendment to the Constitution of . . . Colorado, adopted in a 1992 statewide referendum . . . as "Amendment 2," . . . [stemmed] in large part from ordinances that had been passed in various Colorado municipalities[,] bann[ing] discrimination in many transactions and activities, including housing, employment, education, public accommodations, and health and welfare services. . . . What gave rise to the statewide controversy was the protection . . . afforded to persons discriminated against by reason of their sexual orientation. . . .

Yet Amendment 2, in explicit terms, does more than repeal or rescind these provisions. It prohibits all legislative, executive or judicial action at any level of state or local government designed to protect the named class, a class we shall refer to as homosexual persons or gays and lesbians. The amendment reads:

"No Protected Status Based on Homosexual, Lesbian, or Bisexual Orientation. Neither the State of Colorado, through any of its branches or departments, nor any of its agencies, political subdivisions, municipalities or school districts, shall enact, adopt or enforce any statute, regulation, ordinance or policy whereby homosexual, lesbian or bisexual orientation, conduct, practices or relationships shall constitute or otherwise be the basis of or entitle any person or class of persons to have or claim any minority status, quota preferences, protected status or claim of discrimination. This Section of the Constitution shall be in all respects self-executing." ...

[This suit to enjoin Amendment 2 was brought successfully in state court by] homosexual persons [and] governmental entities which had acted earlier to protect homosexuals from discrimination . . . .

. . . [T]he State Supreme Court held that Amendment 2 was subject to strict scrutiny under the Fourteenth Amendment because it infringed the fundamental right of gays and lesbians to participate in the political process. . . . We . . . affirm . . . , but on a rationale different from that adopted by the State Supreme Court.

II

The State's principal argument in defense of Amendment 2 is that it puts gays and lesbians in the same position as all other persons. So, the State says, the measure does no more than deny homosexuals special rights. This reading of the amendment's language is implausible. We rely . . . upon the authoritative construction of Colorado's Supreme Court[, which] . . . found it invalid even on a modest reading of its implications. . . .

"The immediate objective of Amendment 2 is, at a minimum, to repeal existing statutes, regulations, ordinances, and policies of state and local entities that barred discrimination based on sexual orientation. . . .

"The 'ultimate effect' of Amendment 2 is to prohibit any governmental entity from adopting similar, or more protective statutes, regulations, ordinances, or policies in the future unless the state constitution is first amended to permit such measures." . . .

Sweeping and comprehensive is the change in legal status effected by this law. . . . Homosexuals, by state decree, are put in a solitary class with respect to transactions and relations in both the private and governmental spheres. The amendment withdraws from homosexuals, but no others, specific legal protection from the injuries caused by discrimination, and it forbids reinstatement of these laws and policies.

The change that Amendment 2 works in the legal status of gays and lesbians in the private sphere is far-reaching, both on its own terms and when considered in light of the structure and operation of modern anti-discrimination laws. . . . [M]ost States have chosen to counter discrimination by enacting detailed statutory schemes. . . .

Colorado's state and municipal laws typify this emerging tradition of statutory protection. . . . The laws first enumerate the persons or entities subject to a duty not to discriminate. . . . The Boulder ordinance, for example, has a comprehensive definition of entities deemed places of "public accommodation." . . . The Denver ordinance is of similar breadth, applying, for example, to hotels, restaurants, hospitals, dental clinics, theaters, banks, common carriers, travel and insurance agencies, and "shops and stores dealing with goods or services of any kind,". . . .

These statutes and ordinances also depart from the common law by enumerating the groups or persons within their ambit of protection. . . . Colorado's state and local governments have not limited anti-discrimination laws to groups that have so far been given the protection of heightened equal protection scrutiny under our cases. . . . Rather, they set forth an extensive catalogue of traits which cannot be the basis for discrimination, including age, military status, marital status, pregnancy, parenthood, custody of a minor child, political affiliation, physical or mental disability of an individual or of his or her associates—and, in recent times, sexual orientation. . . .

Amendment 2 bars homosexuals from securing protection against the injuries that these public-accommodations laws address . . . [and] nullifies specific legal protections for this targeted class in all transactions in housing, sale of real estate, insurance, health and welfare services, private education, and employment. . . .

Not confined to the private sphere, Amendment 2 also operates to repeal and forbid all laws or policies providing specific protection for gays or lesbians from discrimination by every level of Colorado government. The State Supreme Court cited two examples[—] . . . Colorado Executive Order D0035 (1990), which forbids employment discrimination against " 'all state employees, classified and exempt' on the basis of sexual orientation[,]" [and] "various provisions prohibiting discrimination based on sexual orientation at state colleges." . . . The repeal of these measures and the prohibition against their future reenactment demonstrates that Amendment 2 has the same force and effect in Colorado's governmental sector as it does elsewhere and that it applies to policies as well as ordinary legislation.

Amendment 2's reach may not be limited to specific laws passed for the benefit of gays and lesbians. It is a fair, if not necessary, inference from the broad language of the amendment that it deprives gays and lesbians even of the protection of general laws and policies that prohibit arbitrary discrimination in governmental and private settings. . . . At some point in the systematic administration of these laws, an official must determine whether homosexuality is an arbitrary and thus forbidden basis for decision. Yet a decision to that effect would itself amount to a policy prohibiting discrimination on the basis of homosexuality, and so would appear to be no more valid under Amendment 2 than the specific prohibitions against discrimination the state court held invalid.

If this consequence follows from Amendment 2, as its broad language suggests, it would compound the constitutional difficulties the law creates. . . . In any event, even if, as we doubt, homosexuals could find some safe harbor in laws of general application, we cannot accept the view that Amendment 2's prohibition on specific legal protections does no more than deprive homosexuals of special rights. To the contrary, the amendment imposes a special disability upon those persons alone. Homosexuals are forbidden the safeguards that others enjoy or may seek without constraint. They can obtain specific protection against discrimination only by enlisting the citizenry of Colorado to amend the state constitution or perhaps, on the State's view, by trying to pass helpful laws of general applicability. This is so no matter how local or discrete the harm, no matter how public and widespread the injury. We find nothing special in the protections Amendment 2 withholds. These are protections taken for granted by most people either because they already have them or do not need them; these are protections against exclusion from an almost limitless number of transactions and endeavors that constitute ordinary civic life in a free society.

III

. . . [E]qual protection of the laws must co-exist with the practical necessity that most legislation classifies for one purpose or another, with resulting disadvantage to various groups or persons. . . . We have attempted to reconcile the principle with the reality by stating that, if a law neither burdens a fundamental right nor targets a suspect class, we will uphold the legislative classification so long as it bears a rational relation to some legitimate end. See, e.g., Heller v. Doe, 509 U.S. 312, 319–320 (1993).

Amendment 2 fails, indeed defies, even this conventional inquiry. First, the amendment has the peculiar property of imposing a broad and undifferentiated disability on a single named group, an exceptional and, as we shall explain, invalid form of legislation. Second, its sheer breadth is so discontinuous with the reasons offered for it that the amendment seems inexplicable by anything but animus toward the class that it affects; it lacks a rational relationship to legitimate state interests.

Taking the first point, even in the ordinary equal protection case calling for the most deferential of standards, we insist on knowing the relation between the classification adopted and the object to be attained. The search for the link between classification and objective gives substance to the Equal Protection Clause; it provides guidance and discipline for the legislature, which is entitled to know what sorts of laws it can pass; and it marks the limits of our own authority. In the ordinary case, a law will be sustained if it can be said to advance a legitimate government interest, even if the law seems unwise or works to the disadvantage of a particular group, or if the rationale for it seems tenuous. . . . By requiring that the classification bear a rational relationship to an independent and legitimate legislative end, [however,] we ensure that classifications are not drawn for the purpose of disadvantaging the group burdened by the law. . . .

Amendment 2 confounds this normal process of judicial review. It is at once too narrow and too broad. It identifies persons by a single trait and then denies them protection across the board. The resulting disqualification of a class of persons from the right to seek specific protection from the law is unprecedented in our jurisprudence. . . .

It is not within our constitutional tradition to enact laws of this sort. Central both to the idea of the rule of law and to our own Constitution's guarantee of equal protection is the principle that government and each of its parts remain open on impartial terms to all who seek its assistance. . . . Respect for this principle explains why laws singling out a certain class of citizens for disfavored legal status or general hardships are rare. A law declaring that in general it shall be more difficult for one group of citizens than for all others to seek aid from the government is itself a denial of equal protection of the laws in the most literal sense. . . .

Davis v. Beason, 133 U.S. 333 (1890), . . . relied upon by the dissent, is not evidence that Amendment 2 is within our constitutional tradition . . . . In *Davis*, the Court approved an Idaho territorial statute denying Mormons, polygamists, and advocates of polygamy the right to vote and to hold office because, as the Court construed the statute, it "simply excludes from the privilege of voting, or of holding any office of honor, trust or profit, those who have been convicted of certain offences, and those who advocate a practical resistance to the laws of the Territory and justify and approve the commission of crimes forbidden by it." . . . To the extent *Davis* held that persons advocating a certain practice may be denied the right to vote, it is no longer good law. Brandenburg v. Ohio, 395 U.S. 444 (1969) (per curiam). To the extent it held that the groups designated in the statute may be deprived of the right to vote because of their status, its ruling could not stand without surviving strict scrutiny, a most doubtful outcome. . . . To the extent *Davis* held that a convicted felon may be denied the right to vote, its holding is not implicated by our decision and is unexceptionable. See Richardson v. Ramirez, 418 U.S. 24 (1974).

A second and related point is that laws of the kind now before us raise the inevitable inference that the disadvantage imposed is born of animosity toward the class of persons affected. "[I]f the constitutional conception of 'equal protection of the laws' means anything, it must at the very least mean that a bare . . . desire to harm a politically unpopular group cannot constitute a legitimate governmental interest." Department of Agriculture v. Moreno, 413 U.S. 528, 534 (1973). Even laws enacted for broad and ambitious purposes often can be explained by reference to legitimate public policies which justify the incidental disadvantages they impose on certain persons.

Amendment 2, however, in making a general announcement that gays and lesbians shall not have any particular protections from the law, inflicts on them immediate, continuing, and real injuries that outrun and belie any legitimate justifications that may be claimed for it. We conclude that, in addition to the far-reaching deficiencies of Amendment 2 that we have noted, the principles it offends, in another sense, are conventional and venerable; a law must bear a rational relationship to a legitimate governmental purpose, . . . and Amendment 2 does not.

The primary rationale the State offers for Amendment 2 is respect for other citizens' freedom of association, and in particular the liberties of landlords or employers who have personal or religious objections to homosexuality. Colorado also cites its interest in conserving resources to fight discrimination against other groups. The breadth of the Amendment is so far removed from these particular justifications that we find it impossible to credit them. We cannot say that Amendment 2 is directed to any identifiable legitimate purpose or discrete objective. It is a status-based enactment divorced from any factual context from which we could discern a relationship to legitimate state interests; it is a classification of persons undertaken for its own sake, something the Equal Protection Clause does not permit. . . .

We must conclude that Amendment 2 classifies homosexuals not to further a proper legislative end but to make them unequal to everyone else. This Colorado cannot do. A State cannot so deem a class of persons a stranger to its laws. Amendment 2 violates the Equal Protection Clause, and the judgment of the Supreme Court of Colorado is affirmed.

. . .

■ JUSTICE SCALIA, with whom THE CHIEF JUSTICE and JUSTICE THOMAS join, dissenting.

The Court has mistaken a Kulturkampf for a fit of spite. The constitutional amendment before us here is not the manifestation of a " 'bare . . . desire to harm' " homosexuals, but is rather a modest attempt by seemingly tolerant Coloradans to preserve traditional sexual mores against the efforts of a politically powerful minority to revise those mores through use of the laws. That objective, and the means chosen to achieve it, are not only unimpeachable under any constitutional doctrine hitherto pronounced . . . ; they have been specifically approved by . . . Congress . . . and by this Court.

In holding that homosexuality cannot be singled out for disfavorable treatment, the Court contradicts a decision, unchallenged here, pronounced only 10 years ago, see Bowers v. Hardwick, 478 U.S. 186 (1986), and places the prestige of this institution behind the proposition that opposition to homosexuality is as reprehensible as racial or religious bias. . . . Since the Constitution of the United States says nothing about this subject, it is left to be resolved by normal democratic means, including the democratic adoption of provisions in state constitutions. This Court has no business imposing upon all Americans the resolution favored by the elite class from which the Members of this institution are selected, pronouncing that "animosity" toward homosexuality is evil. I vigorously dissent.

I

. . .

. . . The clear import of the Colorado court's [decision] is that "general laws and policies that prohibit arbitrary discrimination" would continue to prohibit discrimination on the basis of homosexual conduct as well. . . . The amendment prohibits *special treatment* of homosexuals, and nothing more. . . .

[T]he Court's opinion ultimately . . . assumes [that t]he only denial of equal treatment . . . homosexuals have suffered is this: They may not obtain *preferential treatment* without amending the state constitution. . . .

The [Court's] central thesis . . . is that any group is denied equal protection when, to obtain advantage (or, presumably, to avoid disadvantage), it must have recourse to a more general and hence more difficult level of political decisionmaking than others. The world has never heard of such a principle. . . .

. . . The Court's entire novel theory rests upon the proposition that there is something *special*—something that cannot be justified by normal "rational basis" analysis—in making a disadvantaged group (or a nonpreferred group) resort to a higher decisionmaking level. That proposition finds no support in law or logic.

II

I turn next to whether there was a legitimate rational basis . . . for the prohibition of special protection for homosexuals.[1] . . . The case most relevant . . . is not even mentioned in the Court's opinion: In Bowers v. Hardwick, 478 U.S. 186 (1986), we held that the Constitution does not prohibit . . . making homosexual conduct a crime. . . . If it is constitutionally permissible . . . to make homosexual conduct criminal, surely it is constitutionally permissible for a State to enact other laws merely *disfavoring* homosexual conduct. . . . And *a fortiori* it is constitutionally permissible for a State to adopt a provision *not even* disfavoring homosexual conduct, but merely prohibiting all levels of state government from bestowing *special protections* upon homosexual conduct. Respondents . . . counter [by arguing] that [*Bowers*] cannot justify Amendment 2's application to individuals who do not engage in homosexual acts, but are merely of homosexual "orientation." . . .

But assuming that, in Amendment 2, a person of homosexual "orientation" is someone who does not engage in homosexual conduct but merely has a tendency or desire to do so, *Bowers* still suffices to establish a rational basis . . . . If it is rational to criminalize the conduct, surely it is rational to deny special favor and protection to those with a self-avowed tendency or desire to engage in the conduct. . . . Just as a policy barring the hiring of methadone users as transit employees does not violate equal protection simply because some methadone users pose no threat to passenger safety, see New York City Transit Authority v. Beazer, 440 U.S. 568 (1979), . . . Amendment 2 is not constitutionally invalid simply because it could have been drawn more precisely so as to withdraw special antidiscrimination protections only from those of homosexual "orientation" who actually engage in homosexual conduct. . . .

Moreover, even if the provision regarding homosexual "orientation" *were* invalid, . . . since, under *Bowers*, Amendment 2 is unquestionably constitutional as applied to those who engage in homosexual conduct, the facial challenge cannot succeed. . . .

III

. . . What [Colorado] has done is not only unprohibited, but eminently reasonable, with close, congressionally approved precedent in earlier constitutional practice.

First, . . . the only sort of "animus" at issue here [is] moral disapproval of homosexual conduct, the same sort of moral disapproval that produced the centuries-old criminal laws . . . held constitutional in *Bowers*. The Colorado amendment . . . , to

---

[1] The Court evidently agrees that "rational basis" . . . is the governing standard. The trial court rejected respondents' argument that homosexuals constitute a "suspect" or "quasi-suspect" class, and respondents elected not to appeal that ruling to the Supreme Court of Colorado. . . . And the Court implicitly rejects the Supreme Court of Colorado's holding . . . that Amendment 2 infringes upon a "fundamental right" of "independently identifiable class[es]" to "participate equally in the political process."

speak entirely precisely, [only] prohibits giving [*homosexuals*] favored status *because of their homosexual conduct*—that is, it prohibits favored status *for homosexuality.*

. . . Colorado not only is one of the 25 States that have repealed their antisodomy laws, but was among the first to do so. . . . But the society that eliminates criminal punishment for homosexual acts does not necessarily abandon the view that homosexuality is morally wrong and socially harmful; often, abolition simply reflects the view that enforcement of such criminal laws involves unseemly intrusion into the intimate lives of citizens. . . .

   . . .

By the time Coloradans were asked to vote on Amendment 2, . . . Aspen, Boulder, and Denver . . . had enacted ordinances that listed "sexual orientation" as an impermissible ground for discrimination, equating the moral disapproval of homosexual conduct with racial and religious bigotry. . . .

. . . Amendment 2 . . . sought to counter both the geographic concentration and the disproportionate political power of homosexuals by (1) resolving the controversy at the statewide level, and (2) making the election a single-issue contest for both sides. . . . The Court today asserts that this most democratic of procedures . . . *must* be unconstitutional, because it has never happened before. . . . [T]his is proved false every time a state law prohibiting or disfavoring certain conduct is passed . . . .

But . . . a much closer analogy . . . involves precisely the effort by the majority of citizens to preserve its view of sexual morality statewide, against the efforts of a geographically concentrated and politically powerful minority to undermine it. The constitutions of . . . Arizona, Idaho, New Mexico, Oklahoma, and Utah *to this day* contain provisions stating that polygamy is "forever prohibited." . . . Polygamists, and those who have a polygamous "orientation," have been "singled out" by these provisions for much more severe treatment than merely denial of favored status; and that treatment can only be changed by achieving amendment of the state constitutions. The Court's disposition today suggests that these provisions are unconstitutional, and that polygamy must be permitted in these States on a state-legislated, or perhaps even local-option, basis—unless, of course, polygamists for some reason have fewer constitutional rights than homosexuals.

. . . Congress . . . *required* the inclusion of . . . antipolygamy provisions in the constitutions . . . as a condition of their admission to statehood. . . . Thus, this "singling out" of the sexual practices of a single group for statewide, democratic vote . . . has received the explicit approval of . . . Congress.

[T]his Court has . . . approved a territorial statutory provision that went even further, depriving polygamists of the ability even to achieve a constitutional amendment, by depriving them of the power to vote. In Davis v. Beason, 133 U.S. 333 (1890), Justice Field wrote for a unanimous Court[,] . . . reject[ing] the argument that "such discrimination is a denial of the equal protection of the laws." . . . [3]

This Court cited *Beason* with approval as recently as 1993 . . . . It remains to be explained how . . . the Idaho [provision] was not an "impermissible targeting" of polygamists, but (the much more mild) Amendment 2 is an "impermissible targeting" of homosexuals. . . .

---

[3] . . . The Court . . . claim[s] that "[t]o the extent [*Beason*] held that the groups designated in the statute may be deprived of the right to vote because of their status, its ruling could not stand without surviving strict scrutiny, a most doubtful outcome." But if that is so, it is only because we have declared the right to vote to be a "fundamental political right," see, e.g., Dunn v. Blumstein, 405 U.S. 330, 336 (1972), deprivation of which triggers strict scrutiny. Amendment 2, of course, does not deny the fundamental right to vote, and the Court rejects the Colorado court's view that there exists a fundamental right to participate in the political process. Strict scrutiny is thus not in play here. . . .

. . .

Lawrence v. Texas

539 U.S. 558, 123 S.Ct. 2472, 156 L.Ed.2d 508 (2003).

[The report of this case appears *supra*, at p. 444.]

United States v. Windsor

570 U.S. ___, 133 S.Ct. 2675, 186 L.Ed.2d 808 (2013).

■ Justice Kennedy delivered the opinion of the Court.

Two women then resident in New York were married in a lawful ceremony in Ontario, Canada, in 2007. Edith Windsor and Thea Spyer returned to their home in New York City. When Spyer died in 2009, she left her entire estate to Windsor. Windsor sought to claim the estate tax exemption for surviving spouses. She was barred from doing so, however, by a federal law, the Defense of Marriage Act, which excludes a same-sex partner from the definition of "spouse" as that term is used in federal statutes. Windsor paid the taxes but filed suit to challenge the constitutionality of this provision. The United States District Court and the Court of Appeals ruled that this portion of the statute is unconstitutional and ordered the United States to pay Windsor a refund. This Court . . . now affirms the judgment in Windsor's favor.

I

In 1996, as some States were beginning to consider the concept of same-sex marriage, . . . and before any State had acted to permit it, Congress enacted the Defense of Marriage Act (DOMA) . . . . DOMA contains two operative sections: Section 2, which has not been challenged here, allows States to refuse to recognize same-sex marriages performed under the laws of other States. See 28 U.S.C. § 1738C.

Section 3 is at issue here. It amends the Dictionary Act in Title 1, § 7, of the United States Code to provide a federal definition of "marriage" and "spouse." Section 3 of DOMA provides as follows:

"In determining the meaning of any Act of Congress, or of any ruling, regulation, or interpretation of the various administrative bureaus and agencies of the United States, the word 'marriage' means only a legal union between one man and one woman as husband and wife, and the word 'spouse' refers only to a person of the opposite sex who is a husband or a wife." 1 U.S.C. § 7.

The definitional provision does not by its terms forbid States from enacting laws permitting same-sex marriages or civil unions or providing state benefits to residents in that status. The enactment's comprehensive definition of marriage for purposes of all federal statutes and other regulations or directives covered by its terms, however, does control over 1,000 federal laws in which marital or spousal status is addressed as a matter of federal law. . . .

. . . Windsor and Spyer registered as domestic partners when New York City gave that right to same-sex couples in 1993. Concerned about Spyer's health, the couple made the 2007 trip to Canada for their marriage, but they continued to reside in New York City. The State of New York deems their Ontario marriage to be a valid one. . . .

. . . Because DOMA denies federal recognition to same-sex spouses, Windsor did not qualify for the marital exemption from the federal estate tax, which excludes from taxation "any interest in property which passes or has passed from the decedent to his surviving spouse." 26 U.S.C. § 2056(a). Windsor paid $363,053 in estate taxes and sought a refund. The Internal Revenue Service denied the refund, concluding that, under DOMA, Windsor was not a "surviving spouse." Windsor['s] . . . refund suit . . . contended that DOMA violates the guarantee of equal protection, as applied to the Federal Government through the Fifth Amendment.

While the tax refund suit was pending, the Attorney General of the United States notified the Speaker of the House of Representatives, pursuant to 28 U.S.C. § 530D, that the Department of Justice would no longer defend the constitutionality of DOMA's § 3. Noting that "the Department has previously defended DOMA against . . . challenges involving legally married same-sex couples," . . . the Attorney General informed Congress that "the President has concluded that given a number of factors, including a documented history of discrimination, classifications based on sexual orientation should be subject to a heightened standard of scrutiny." . . . The Department of Justice has submitted many § 530D letters over the years refusing to defend laws it deems unconstitutional, when, for instance, a federal court has rejected the Government's defense of a statute and has issued a judgment against it. This case is unusual, however, because the § 530D letter was not preceded by an adverse judgment. The letter instead reflected the Executive's own conclusion, relying on a definition still being debated and considered in the courts, that heightened equal protection scrutiny should apply to laws that classify on the basis of sexual orientation.

Although "the President . . . instructed the Department not to defend the statute in *Windsor*," he also decided "that Section 3 will continue to be enforced by the Executive Branch" and that the United States had an "interest in providing Congress a full and fair opportunity to participate in the litigation of those cases." . . . The stated rationale for this dual-track procedure (determination of unconstitutionality coupled with ongoing enforcement) was to "recogniz[e] the judiciary as the final arbiter of the constitutional claims raised." . . .

[The Bipartisan Legal Advisory Group (BLAG) of the House of Representatives was permitted to intervene as an interested party to defend § 3's constitutionality. The District Court invalidated § 3, and on appeals by "[b]oth the Justice Department and BLAG[,]" the Court of Appeals affirmed.] It applied heightened scrutiny to classifications based on sexual orientation, as both the Department and Windsor had urged. The United States has not complied with the judgment. Windsor has not received her refund, and the Executive Branch continues to enforce § 3 of DOMA.

. . .

II

[Although the Government agreed with Windsor that § 3 is unconstitutional, and despite the fact that the District Court had ordered a refund, the majority ruled that the appeal by the United States still presented a justiciable controversy under Article III of the Constitution, given "Windsor's ongoing claim for funds that the United States refuses to pay." (The Court did note that "[i]t would be a different case if the Executive had taken the further step of paying Windsor the refund to which she was entitled under the District Court's ruling"). The majority acknowledged the serious concern that the "Executive's agreement with Windsor's legal argument raises the risk" of a lack of adversarial presentation—a concern it considered "prudential" and not constitutional. It found more persuasive, however, at least two "countervailing" prudential factors. First, "BLAG's sharp adversarial presentation of the issues satisfies the prudential concerns that otherwise might counsel against hearing an appeal from a decision with which the principal parties agree." Second, were the appeals to be dismissed, the lack of "precedential guidance . . . in cases involving the whole of DOMA's sweep involving over 1,000 federal statutes and a myriad of federal regulations" would result in "immense" judicial resource costs and litigation expenses "for all persons adversely affected." These "unusual and urgent circumstances" rendered it proper for the Court to rule on the appeal by the United States, and "the Court need not decide whether BLAG would have standing to challenge the District Court's ruling and its affirmance in the Court of Appeals on BLAG's own authority."

[The majority did perceive difficulties were it to become a "common practice in ordinary cases" for the Executive—in agreement with the challenger—to ask the Court to rule against the constitutionality of an Act of Congress, but it also declared that "if the Executive's agreement with a plaintiff that a law is unconstitutional is enough to preclude judicial review, then the Supreme Court's primary role in determining the constitutionality of a law that has inflicted real injury on a plaintiff who has brought a justiciable legal claim would become only secondary to the President's." And "[s]imilarly, with respect to the legislative power, when Congress has passed a statute and a President has signed it, it poses grave challenges to the separation of powers for the Executive at a particular moment to be able to nullify Congress' enactment solely on its own initiative and without any determination from the Court." These considerations were thought to "support the Court's decision to proceed to the merits."]

III

. . .

. . . [Over time,] New York recognized same-sex marriages performed elsewhere; and then it later amended its own marriage laws to permit same sex marriage. New York, in common with, as of this writing, 11 other States and the District of Columbia, decided that same-sex couples should have the right to marry and so live with pride in themselves and their union and in a status of equality with all other married persons. . . .

Against this background of lawful same-sex marriage in some States, the design, purpose, and effect of DOMA should be considered as the beginning point in deciding whether it is valid under the Constitution. By history and tradition the definition and regulation of marriage . . . has been treated as being within the authority and realm of the separate States. Yet it is further established that Congress, in enacting discrete statutes, can make determinations that bear on marital rights and privileges. . . .

. . .

Though . . . discrete examples establish the constitutionality of limited federal laws that regulate the meaning of marriage in order to further federal policy, DOMA has a far greater reach; for it enacts a directive applicable to over 1,000 federal statutes and the whole realm of federal regulations. And its operation is directed to a class of persons that the laws of New York, and of 11 other States, have sought to protect. . . .

In order to assess the validity of that intervention it is necessary to discuss the extent of the state power and authority over marriage as a matter of history and tradition. State laws defining and regulating marriage, of course, must respect the constitutional rights of persons, see, e.g., Loving v. Virginia, 388 U.S. 1 (1967); but, subject to those guarantees, "regulation of domestic relations" is "an area that has long been regarded as a virtually exclusive province of the States." Sosna v. Iowa, 419 U.S. 393, 404 (1975).

The recognition of civil marriages is central to state domestic relations law applicable to its residents and citizens. . . .

Consistent with this allocation of authority, the Federal Government, through our history, has deferred to state law policy decisions with respect to domestic relations. . . .

. . . Marriage laws vary in some respects from State to State. . . . But these rules are in every event consistent within each State.

. . . DOMA rejects the long established precept that the incidents, benefits, and obligations of marriage are uniform for all married couples within each State, though they may vary, subject to constitutional guarantees, from one State to the next. Despite these considerations, it is unnecessary to decide whether this federal intrusion on state power is a violation of the Constitution because it disrupts the federal balance. The State's power in defining the marital relation is of central relevance in this case quite apart from principles of federalism. Here the State's decision to give this class of persons the right to marry conferred upon them a dignity and status of immense import. When the State used its historic and essential authority to define the marital relation in this way, its role and its power in making the decision enhanced the recognition, dignity, and protection of the class in their own community. DOMA, because of its reach and extent, departs from this history and tradition of reliance on state law to define marriage. " '[D]iscriminations of an unusual character especially suggest careful consideration to determine whether they are obnoxious to the constitutional provision.' " Romer v. Evans, 517 U.S. 620, 633 (1996) . . . .

The Federal Government uses this state-defined class for the opposite purpose—to impose restrictions and disabilities. That result requires this Court now to address whether the resulting injury and indignity is a deprivation of an essential part of the liberty protected by the Fifth Amendment. What the State of New York treats as alike the federal law deems unlike by a law designed to injure the same class the State seeks to protect.

The States' interest in defining and regulating the marital relation, subject to constitutional guarantees, stems from the understanding that marriage is more than a routine classification for purposes of certain statutory benefits. Private, consensual sexual intimacy between two adult persons of the same sex may not be punished by the State, and it can form "but one element in a personal bond that is more enduring." Lawrence v. Texas, 539 U.S. 558, 567 (2003). By its recognition of the validity of same-sex marriages performed in other jurisdictions and then by authorizing same-sex unions and same-sex marriages, New York sought to give further protection and dignity to that bond. For same-sex couples who wished to be married, the State acted to give their lawful conduct a lawful status. This status is a far-reaching legal acknowledgment of the intimate relationship between two people, a relationship deemed by the State worthy of dignity in the community equal with all other marriages. It reflects both the community's considered perspective on the historical roots of the institution of marriage and its evolving understanding of the meaning of equality.

IV

DOMA seeks to injure the very class New York seeks to protect. By doing so it violates basic due process and equal protection principles applicable to the Federal Government. . . . The Constitution's guarantee of equality "must at the very least mean that a bare congressional desire to harm a politically unpopular group cannot" justify disparate treatment of that group. Department of Agriculture v. Moreno, 413 U.S. 528, 534–535 (1973). . . . DOMA's unusual deviation from the usual tradition of recognizing and accepting state definitions of marriage here operates to deprive same-sex couples of the benefits and responsibilities that come with the federal recognition of their marriages. This is strong evidence of a law having the purpose and effect of disapproval of that class. The avowed purpose and practical effect of the law here in question are to impose a disadvantage, a separate status, and so a stigma upon all who enter into same-sex marriages made lawful by the unquestioned authority of the States.

The history of DOMA's enactment and its own text demonstrate that interference with the equal dignity of same-sex marriages, a dignity conferred by the States in the exercise of their sovereign power, was more than an incidental effect of the federal statute. It was its essence. The House Report announced its conclusion that "it is both appropriate and necessary for Congress to do what it can to defend the institution of traditional heterosexual marriage. . . . H. R. 3396 is appropriately entitled the 'Defense of Marriage Act.' The effort to redefine 'marriage' to extend to homosexual couples is a truly radical proposal that would fundamentally alter the institution of marriage." H. R. Rep. No. 104–664, pp. 12–13 (1996). The House concluded that DOMA expresses "both moral disapproval of homosexuality, and a moral conviction that heterosexuality better comports with traditional (especially Judeo-Christian) morality." . . . The stated purpose of the law was to promote an "interest in protecting the traditional moral teachings reflected in heterosexual-only marriage laws." *Ibid.* Were there any doubt of this far-reaching purpose, the title of the Act confirms it: The Defense of Marriage.

. . . The Act's demonstrated purpose is to ensure that if any State decides to recognize same-sex marriages, those unions will be treated as second-class marriages for purposes of federal law. This raises a most serious question under the Constitution's Fifth Amendment.

. . . DOMA writes inequality into the entire United States Code. . . . Among the over 1,000 statutes and numerous federal regulations that DOMA controls are laws pertaining to Social Security, housing, taxes, criminal sanctions, copyright, and veterans' benefits.

DOMA's principal effect is to identify a subset of state sanctioned marriages and make them unequal. The principal purpose is to impose inequality, not for other reasons like governmental efficiency. Responsibilities, as well as rights, enhance the dignity and integrity of the person. And DOMA contrives to deprive some couples married under the laws of their State, but not other couples, of both rights and responsibilities. By creating two contradictory marriage regimes within the same State, DOMA forces same-sex couples to live as married for the purpose of state law but unmarried for the purpose of federal law, thus diminishing the stability and predictability of basic personal relations the State has found it proper to acknowledge and protect. By this dynamic DOMA undermines both the public and private significance of state-sanctioned same-sex marriages; for it tells those couples, and all the world, that their otherwise valid marriages are unworthy of federal recognition. This places same-sex couples in an unstable position of being in a second-tier marriage. The differentiation demeans the couple, whose moral and sexual choices the Constitution protects, see *Lawrence*, 539 U.S. 558, and whose relationship the State has sought to dignify. And it humiliates tens of thousands of children now being raised by same-sex couples. The law in question makes it even more difficult for the children to understand the integrity and closeness of their own family and its concord with other families in their community and in their daily lives.

Under DOMA, same-sex married couples have their lives burdened, by reason of government decree, in visible and public ways. By its great reach, DOMA touches many aspects of married and family life, from the mundane to the profound. It prevents same-sex married couples from obtaining government healthcare benefits they would otherwise receive. . . . It deprives them of the Bankruptcy Code's special protections for domestic-support obligations. . . . It forces them to follow a complicated procedure to file their state and federal taxes jointly. . . . It prohibits them from being buried together in veterans' cemeteries. . . .

. . .

What has been explained to this point should more than suffice to establish that the principal purpose and the necessary effect of this law are to demean those persons who are in a lawful same-sex marriage. This requires the Court to hold, as it now does, that DOMA is unconstitutional as a deprivation of the liberty of the person protected by the Fifth Amendment of the Constitution.

. . . While the Fifth Amendment itself withdraws from Government the power to degrade or demean in the way this law does, the equal protection guarantee of the Fourteenth Amendment makes that Fifth Amendment right all the more specific and all the better understood and preserved.

. . . DOMA instructs all federal officials, and indeed all persons with whom same-sex couples interact, including their own children, that their marriage is less worthy than the marriages of others. The federal statute is invalid, for no legitimate purpose overcomes the purpose and effect to disparage and to injure those whom the State, by its marriage laws, sought to protect in personhood and dignity. By seeking to displace this protection and treating those persons as living in marriages less respected than others, the federal statute is in violation of the Fifth Amendment. This opinion and its holding are confined to those lawful marriages.

. . .

■ CHIEF JUSTICE ROBERTS, dissenting.

I agree with Justice Scalia that this Court lacks jurisdiction to review the decisions of the courts below. On the merits of the constitutional dispute the Court decides to decide, I also agree with Justice Scalia that Congress acted constitutionally in passing the Defense of Marriage Act. . . . Interests in uniformity and stability amply justified Congress's decision to retain the definition of marriage that, at that point, had been adopted by every State in our Nation, and every nation in the world.

The majority sees a more sinister motive. . . . At least without some more convincing evidence that the Act's principal purpose was to codify malice, and that it furthered *no* legitimate government interests, I would not tar the political branches with the brush of bigotry.

But while I disagree with the result to which the majority's analysis leads it in this case, I think it more important to point out that its analysis leads no further. The Court does not have before it, and the logic of its opinion does not decide, the distinct question whether the States, in the exercise of their "historic and essential authority to define the marital relation" may continue to utilize the traditional definition of marriage.

The majority goes out of its way to make this explicit in the penultimate sentence of its opinion. . . . The dominant theme of the majority opinion is that the Federal Government's intrusion into an area "central to state domestic relations law applicable to its residents and citizens" is sufficiently "unusual" to set off alarm bells. I think the majority goes off course, . . . but it is undeniable that its judgment is based on federalism.

. . . [W]hile "[t]he State's power in defining the marital relation is of central relevance" to the majority's decision to strike down DOMA here, that power will come into play on the other side of the board in future cases about the constitutionality of state marriage definitions. So too will the concerns for state diversity and sovereignty that weigh against DOMA's constitutionality in this case.

. . .

■ JUSTICE SCALIA, with whom JUSTICE THOMAS joins, and with whom the CHIEF JUSTICE joins as to Part I, dissenting.

. . . We have no power to decide this case. And even if we did, we have no power under the Constitution to invalidate this democratically adopted legislation. . . .

I

[Because "Windsor won below, and so *cured* her injury, and the President was glad to see it[,]" the Court lacked power to decide the merits of this case. Doing so "is an assertion of judicial supremacy over the people's Representatives in Congress and the Executive [that] envisions a Supreme Court . . . at the apex of government, empowered to decide all constitutional questions, always and everywhere 'primary' in its role." In fact, "[a]s Justice Brandeis put it, we cannot 'pass upon the constitutionality of legislation in a friendly, non-adversary, proceeding'; absent a ' "real, earnest and vital controversy between individuals," ' we have neither any work to do nor any power to do it. Ashwander v. TVA, 297 U.S. 288, 346 (1936) (concurring opinion) . . ." Justice Scalia insisted that "[i]n the more than two centuries that this Court has existed as an institution, we have never suggested that we have the power to decide a question when every party agrees with both its nominal opponent *and the court below* on that question's answer." The Article III (not prudential) "question is whether there is any controversy (which requires *contradiction*) between the United States and Ms. Windsor. There is not."

[Nor did Justice Alito's contention that the Court had power to decide the merits based on the standing of BLAG to pursue the appeals suffice. Accepting BLAG's standing "would create a system in which Congress can hale the Executive before the courts not only to vindicate its own institutional powers to act, but to correct a perceived inadequacy in the execution of its laws." Rather than resolve such disputes through the courts, "[i]f majorities in both Houses of Congress care enough about the matter, they have available innumerable ways to compel executive action without a lawsuit—from refusing to confirm Presidential appointees to the elimination of funding." Direct confrontation of the President by Congress is the preferable and designed mechanism under our constitutional system in these circumstances.]

II

. . . We should vacate the decision below and remand . . . with instructions to dismiss the appeal. Given that the majority has volunteered its view of the merits, however, I proceed to discuss that as well.

A

[After complaining about "how rootless and shifting" the majority's justifications are—first "fooling many readers . . . into thinking that this is a federalism opinion" only to "disclaim[ ] reliance upon principles of federalism" and then shifting to "perplexing" references to equal protection—Justice Scalia continued:]

[I]f this is meant to be an equal-protection opinion, it is a confusing one. The opinion does not resolve and indeed does not even mention what had been the central question in this litigation: whether, under the Equal Protection Clause, laws restricting marriage to a man and a woman are reviewed for more than mere rationality. . . . In accord with my previously expressed skepticism about the Court's "tiers of scrutiny" approach, I would review this classification only for its rationality. . . . As nearly as I can tell, the Court agrees with that; its opinion does not apply strict scrutiny, and its central propositions are taken from rational-basis cases like *Moreno.* But the Court certainly does not *apply* anything that resembles that deferential framework. . . .

. . . [T]he opinion does not argue that same-sex marriage is "deeply rooted in this Nation's history and tradition," Washington v. Glucksberg, 521 U.S. 702, 720–721 (1997), a claim that would of course be quite absurd. So would the further suggestion (also necessary, under our substantive-due-process precedents) that a world in which DOMA exists is one bereft of " 'ordered liberty.' " *Id.*, at 721 . . . .

. . . The sum of all the Court's nonspecific hand-waving is that this law is invalid (maybe on equal-protection grounds, maybe on substantive-due process grounds, and perhaps with some amorphous federalism component playing a role) because it is motivated by a " 'bare . . . desire to harm' " couples in same-sex marriages. It is this proposition with which I will therefore engage.

B

. . . [T]he Constitution neither requires nor forbids our society to approve of same-sex marriage, much as it neither requires nor forbids us to approve of no-fault divorce, polygamy, or the consumption of alcohol.

However, even setting aside traditional moral disapproval of same-sex marriage (or indeed same-sex sex), there are many perfectly valid—indeed, downright boring— justifying rationales for this legislation. Their existence ought to be the end of this case. For they give the lie to the Court's conclusion that only those with hateful hearts could have voted "aye" on this Act. And more importantly, they serve to make the contents of the legislators' hearts quite irrelevant: "It is a familiar principle of constitutional law that this Court will not strike down an otherwise constitutional statute on the basis of an alleged illicit legislative motive." United States v. O'Brien, 391 U.S. 367, 383 (1968). Or at least it *was* a familiar principle. By holding to the contrary, the majority has declared open season on any law that (in the opinion of the law's opponents and any panel of like-minded federal judges) can be characterized as mean-spirited.

The majority concludes that the only motive for this Act was the "bare . . . desire to harm a politically unpopular group." Bear in mind that the object of this condemnation is . . . our respected coordinate branches, the Congress and Presidency of the United States. Laying such a charge against them should require the most extraordinary evidence. . . . The majority [instead] . . . affirmatively conceal[s] . . . the arguments that exist in justification. . . .

. . . DOMA avoids difficult choice-of-law issues that will now arise absent a uniform federal definition of marriage. . . . Imagine a pair of women who marry in Albany and then move to Alabama, which does not "recognize as valid any marriage of parties of the same sex." Ala. Code § 30–1–19(e) (2011). When the couple files their next federal tax return, may it be a joint one? Which State's law controls, for federal-law purposes: their State of celebration (which recognizes the marriage) or their State of domicile (which does not)? . . . DOMA avoided . . . uncertainty by specifying which marriages would be recognized for federal purposes. That is a classic purpose for a definitional provision.

Further, DOMA preserves the intended effects of prior legislation against then-unforeseen changes in circumstance. . . . DOMA's definitional section was enacted to ensure that state-level experimentation did not automatically alter the basic operation of federal law, unless and until Congress made the further judgment to do so on its own. That is not animus—just stabilizing prudence. . . .

The Court mentions none of this. Instead, it accuses the Congress that enacted this law and the President who signed it of . . . act[ing] with *malice*—with *the "purpose"* "to disparage and to injure" same-sex couples. It says that the motivation for DOMA was to "demean"; to "impose inequality"; to "impose . . . a stigma"; to deny people "equal dignity"; to brand gay people as "unworthy"; and to "*humiliat[e]*" their children (emphasis added).

I am sure these accusations are quite untrue. . . . [T]o defend traditional marriage is not to condemn, demean, or humiliate those who would prefer other arrangements, any more than to defend the Constitution of the United States is to condemn, demean, or humiliate other constitutions. To hurl such accusations so casually demeans *this institution*. . . . [The] Act . . . did no more than codify an aspect of marriage that had been unquestioned in our society for most of its existence—indeed, had been unquestioned in virtually all societies for virtually all of human history. It is one thing for a society to elect change; it is another for a court of law to impose change by adjudging those who oppose it . . . enemies of the human race.

* * *

. . . It takes real cheek for today's majority to assure us, as it is going out the door, that a constitutional requirement to give formal recognition to same-sex marriage is not at issue here—when what has preceded that assurance is a lecture on how superior the majority's moral judgment in favor of same-sex marriage is to the Congress's hateful moral judgment against it. . . .

I do not mean to suggest disagreement with the Chief Justice's view that lower federal courts and state courts can distinguish today's case when the issue before them is state denial of marital status to same-sex couples—or even that this Court could *theoretically* do so. . . .

In my opinion, however, the view that *this* Court will take of state prohibition of same-sex marriage is indicated beyond mistaking by today's opinion. . . . In sum, that Court which finds it so horrific that Congress irrationally and hatefully robbed same-sex couples of the "personhood and dignity" which state legislatures conferred upon them, will of a certitude be similarly appalled by state legislatures' irrational and hateful failure to acknowledge that "personhood and dignity" in the first place. . . .

By formally declaring anyone opposed to same-sex marriage an enemy of human decency, the majority arms well every challenger to a state law restricting marriage to its traditional definition. . . .

. . . Since DOMA's passage, citizens on all sides of the question have seen victories and they have seen defeats. There have been plebiscites, legislation, persuasion, and loud voices—in other words, democracy. . . .

. . . We might have covered ourselves with honor today, by promising all sides of this debate that it was theirs to settle and that we would respect their resolution. We might have let the People decide.

But that the majority will not do. . . .

■ Justice Alito, with whom Justice Thomas joins as to Parts II and III, dissenting.

. . . I would . . . hold that Congress did not violate Windsor's constitutional rights by enacting § 3. . . .

I

. . . The United States does not ask us to overturn the judgment of the court below or to alter that judgment in any way. Quite to the contrary, the United States argues emphatically in favor of the correctness of that judgment. We have never before reviewed a decision at the sole behest of a party that took such a position, and to do so would be to render an advisory opinion, in violation of Article III's dictates. For the reasons given in Justice Scalia's dissent, I do not find the Court's arguments to the contrary to be persuasive.

[But BLAG has standing to petition for review, because "in the narrow category of cases in which a court strikes down an Act of Congress and the Executive declines to defend the Act, Congress both has standing to defend the undefended statute and is a proper party to do so."]

II

. . .

Same-sex marriage presents a highly emotional and important question of public policy—but not a difficult question of constitutional law. The Constitution does not guarantee the right to enter into a same-sex marriage. Indeed, no provision of the Constitution speaks to the issue.

. . .

It is beyond dispute that the right to same-sex marriage is not deeply rooted in this Nation's history and tradition. . . .

What Windsor and the United States seek, therefore, is not the protection of a deeply rooted right but the recognition of a very new right, and they seek this innovation not from a legislative body elected by the people, but from unelected judges. Faced with such a request, judges have cause for both caution and humility.

. . .

. . . [I]f same sex marriage becomes widely accepted[, t]he long-term consequences . . . are not now known and are unlikely to be ascertainable for some time to come There are those who think that allowing same-sex marriage will seriously undermine the institution of marriage. . . . Others think that recognition of same-sex marriage will fortify a now-shaky institution. . . .

. . . [I]f the Constitution contained a provision guaranteeing the right to marry a person of the same sex, it would be our duty to enforce that right. But the Constitution simply does not speak to the issue of same-sex marriage. In our system of government, ultimate sovereignty rests with the people, and the people have the right to control their own destiny. Any change on a question so fundamental should be made by the people through their elected officials.

III

Perhaps because they cannot show that same-sex marriage is a fundamental right under our Constitution, Windsor and the United States couch their arguments in equal protection terms. . . .

. . . But that framework is ill suited for use in evaluating the constitutionality of laws based on the traditional understanding of marriage, which fundamentally turn on what marriage is.

. . .

By asking the Court to strike down DOMA as not satisfying some form of heightened scrutiny, Windsor and the United States are really seeking to have the Court resolve a debate between two competing views of marriage.

The first and older view, which I will call the "traditional" or "conjugal" view, sees marriage as an intrinsically opposite-sex institution. . . . While modern cultural changes have weakened the link between marriage and procreation in the popular mind, there is no doubt that, throughout human history and across many cultures, marriage has been viewed as an exclusively opposite-sex institution and as one inextricably linked to procreation and biological kinship.

The other, newer view is what I will call the "consent based" vision of marriage, a vision that primarily defines marriage as the solemnization of mutual commitment—

marked by strong emotional attachment and sexual attraction—between two persons. . . . Proponents of same-sex marriage argue that because gender differentiation is not relevant to this vision, the exclusion of same-sex couples from the institution of marriage is rank discrimination.

The Constitution does not codify either of these views of marriage. . . . The silence of the Constitution on this question should be enough to end the matter as far as the judiciary is concerned. . . . Because our constitutional order assigns the resolution of questions of this nature to the people, I would not presume to enshrine either vision of marriage in our constitutional jurisprudence.

. . . [B]oth Congress and the States are entitled to enact laws recognizing either of the two understandings of marriage. . . .

> . . .

To the extent that the Court takes the position that the question of same-sex marriage should be resolved primarily at the state level, I wholeheartedly agree. I hope that the Court will ultimately permit the people of each State to decide this question for themselves. Unless the Court is willing to allow this to occur, the whiffs of federalism in the today's opinion of the Court will soon be scattered to the wind.

In any event, § 3 of DOMA, in my view, does not encroach on the prerogatives of the States. . . . Section 3 does not prevent any State from recognizing same-sex marriage or from extending to same-sex couples any right, privilege, benefit, or obligation stemming from state law. All that § 3 does is to define a class of persons to whom federal law extends certain special benefits and upon whom federal law imposes certain special burdens. . . .

Obergefell v. Hodges

576 U.S. ___, 135 S.Ct. 2584, 192 L.Ed.2d 609 (2015).

[The report of this case appears *supra*, at p. 371.]

Wealth Classifications

Legislative classifications disadvantaging the poor most frequently take the form of financial charges applied to the indigent as well as the relatively more affluent, or withholding of welfare or other assistance from some indigents but not others. As a result, the issues normally involve disproportionate impact on the poor rather than explicit disadvantaging of them. Implicitly, these issues may involve whether equal protection not only requires treating similarly situated people similarly, but differently situated people differently, and whether the Constitution imposes affirmative obligations to assist the poor. The due process and equal protection dimensions of issues of poverty and the provision of government benefits and services are more fully discussed infra in section 4. C. (p. 708).

The Court generally states, however, that wealth classifications are not suspect. In Harper v. Virginia State Board of Elections, 383 U.S. 663 (1966) (set out fully infra p. 668), the Court did hold it a denial of equal protection to condition the right to vote in state elections on payment of a poll tax. Justice Douglas' opinion for the Court said: "Lines drawn on the basis of wealth or property, like those of race . . . , are traditionally disfavored." But subsequently, in other contexts, the Court has not followed this approach. In Ortwein v. Schwab, 410 U.S. 656 (1973), for example, the Court upheld a $25 state appellate court filing fee as applied to an indigent challenging a welfare agency determination. The Court said: "No suspect classification, such as race, nationality, or alienage, is present. . . . The applicable standard is that of rational justification." Similarly, in Harris v. McRae, 448 U.S. 297 (1980) (set out fully infra p. 718), the Court rejected an equal protection challenge to a federal statute prohibiting the expenditure of federal funds for abortions, despite conceding that the principal impact "falls on the indigent." The Court said that "that fact does not itself render the funding restriction constitutionally invalid, for this Court has held repeatedly that poverty, standing alone, is not a suspect classification. See, e.g., James v. Valtierra, 402 U.S. 137." Most recently, in Kadrmas v. Dickinson Public Schools, 487 U.S. 450 (1988), the Court rejected an indigent's equal protection challenge to a fee for bus service from a student's home to school. The Court declined "to apply a form of strict or 'heightened' scrutiny" and said: "We have previously rejected the suggestion that statutes having different effects on the wealthy and the poor should on that account alone be subjected to strict equal protection scrutiny. See, e.g., *Harris v. McRae* . . . ; *Ortwein v. Schwab*. . . . "

4. PROTECTION OF PERSONAL LIBERTIES

A. VOTING AND ELECTIONS

1. INTRODUCTION

The Constitution and the Franchise

(1) The Constitution of 1789. As originally adopted the Constitution left it to the States to determine who should have the right to vote in national as well as state elections. Art. II, § 1 provided for the selection of the President by electors appointed in each state "in such Manner as the Legislature thereof may direct"—a provision that has remained unchanged. Art. 1, § 2, cl. 1 provided that the persons voting for members of the House of Representatives "shall have the Qualifications requisite for Electors of the most numerous Branch of the State Legislature." Art. 1, § 3, cl. 1 provided that the members of the Senate should be chosen by the legislature of each State. It was not until the adoption of the seventeenth amendment in 1913 that it was provided that members of the Senate should be elected "by the people" of the respective States. That amendment also provided that the persons voting for members of the Senate "shall have the qualifications requisite for electors of the most numerous branch of the State legislatures." Art. I, § 4, cl. 1 provided that the "Times, Places and Manner of holding Elections for Senators and Representatives shall be prescribed in each State by the Legislature thereof; but the Congress may at any time by Law make or alter such Regulations, except as to the Places of choosing Senators."

(2) The Civil War Amendments. Before the Civil War all but six States discriminated against Negroes in establishing qualifications to vote. Stephanson, *Race Distinctions in American Law* 285 (1910). The fourteenth amendment did not directly forbid discrimination in voting. Section 2 of the amendment did provide for a reduction in representation in the House of Representatives in proportion to the number of "male inhabitants" who were not permitted to vote. However, the fifteenth amendment was soon adopted providing that the "right of citizens of the United States to vote shall not be denied or abridged by the United States or by any State on account of race, color, or previous condition of servitude." (For a modern interpretation of the Fifteenth Amendment, see the report of Rice v. Cayetano, 528 U.S. 495 (2000), infra at p. 680.)

(3) The Nineteenth, Twenty-Fourth, and Twenty-Sixth Amendments. The Civil War amendments did not extend the franchise to all. Women were, of course, citizens but citizenship did not carry the right to vote. Minor v. Happersett, 88 U.S. (21 Wall.) 162 (1875). Only after a long campaign for women's suffrage was the Nineteenth

Amendment ratified in 1920 providing that the right of citizens to vote "shall not be denied or abridged by the United States or by any State on account of sex." In 1964 the Twenty-Fourth Amendment was adopted providing that the right of any citizen to vote for the President, Vice-President, or members of Congress "shall not be denied or abridged by the United States or any State by reason of failure to pay any poll tax or other tax." Finally the Twenty-Sixth Amendment was adopted in 1971 providing that the right of any citizen eighteen years or older to vote "shall not be denied or abridged by the United States or by any State on account of age."

The Equal Protection Clause as the Source of a Right to Vote and Run for Elective Office

In reading the cases in this section two general questions should be considered: (1) Does the court use the general language of the equal protection clause to establish a substantive right to vote and participate in elections that goes beyond the specific constitutional provisions summarized above? (2) Is there special constitutional justification for the Court to go beyond the express language of the Constitution to guarantee the broadest access to the political processes? Cf. Ely, *Democracy and Distrust* 117 (1980): "[u]nblocking stoppages in the democratic process is what judicial review ought preeminently to be about, and denial of the vote seems the quintessential stoppage."

2.   QUALIFICATIONS OF VOTERS

Harper v. Virginia State Board of Elections

383 U.S. 663, 86 S.Ct. 1079, 16 L.Ed.2d 169 (1966).

■ MR. JUSTICE DOUGLAS delivered the opinion of the Court.[a]

These are suits by Virginia residents to have declared unconstitutional Virginia's poll tax. The three-judge District Court, feeling bound by our decision in Breedlove v. Suttles, 302 U.S. 277, dismissed the complaint. . . .

While the right to vote in federal elections is conferred by Art. I, § 2, of the Constitution . . . the right to vote in state elections is nowhere expressly mentioned. It is argued that the right to vote in state elections is implicit, particularly by reason of the First Amendment and that it may not constitutionally be conditioned upon the payment of a tax or fee. . . . We do not stop to canvass the relation between voting and political expression. For it is enough to say that once the franchise is granted to the electorate, lines may not be drawn which are inconsistent with the Equal Protection Clause of the Fourteenth Amendment. That is to say, the right of suffrage "is subject to the imposition of state standards which are not discriminatory and which do not contravene any restriction that Congress, acting pursuant to its constitutional powers, has imposed." Lassiter v. Northampton County Board of Elections, 360 U.S. 45, 51. We were speaking there of a state literacy test which we sustained, warning that the result would be different if a literacy test, fair on its face, were used to discriminate

---

[a]   In the two decades 1934–1954, five states abolished the poll tax: Louisiana, Florida, Georgia, South Carolina and Tennessee. This voluntary action then stopped—probably because of feelings stirred by the 1954 *Brown* decision. As of 1963, payment of a poll tax was a prerequisite to voting in five states: Alabama, Mississippi, Texas, Varmont and Virginia. Vermont abolished its poll tax while the *Harper* decision was pending. Burke Marshall reported: "By now the tax is a negligible, bi-racial deterrent to voting." 27 Law & Contemp.Pr. 455, 464 (1962). In 1962 Congress proposed, and by 1964 the requisite number of States had ratified, the Twenty-fourth Amendment outlawing the "poll tax or other tax" as a condition for voting in federal elections.

against a class. . . . But the *Lassiter* case does not govern the result here, because, unlike a poll tax, the "ability to read and write . . . has some relation to standards designed to promote intelligent use of the ballot." . . .

We conclude that a State violates the Equal Protection Clause of the Fourteenth Amendment whenever it makes the affluence of the voter or payment of any fee an electoral standard. Voter qualifications have no relation to wealth nor to paying or not paying this or any other tax. Our cases demonstrate that the Equal Protection Clause of the Fourteenth Amendment restrains the States from fixing voter qualifications which invidiously discriminate. Thus without questioning the power of a State to impose reasonable residence restrictions on the availability of the ballot . . . , we held in Carrington v. Rash, 380 U.S. 89, that a State may not deny the opportunity to vote to a bona fide resident merely because he is a member of the armed services. "By forbidding a soldier ever to controvert the presumption of non-residence, the Texas Constitution imposes an invidious discrimination in violation of the Fourteenth Amendment." . . . Previously we had said that neither homesite nor occupation "affords a permissible basis for distinguishing between qualified voters within the State." . . . We think the same must be true of requirements of wealth or affluence or payment of a fee.

Long ago in Yick Wo v. Hopkins, 118 U.S. 356, 370, the Court referred to "the political franchise of voting" as a "fundamental political right, because preservative of all rights." Recently in Reynolds v. Sims, 377 U.S. 533, 561–562, we said: "Undoubtedly, the right of suffrage is a fundamental matter in a free and democratic society. Especially since the right to exercise the franchise in a free and unimpaired manner is preservative of other basic civil and political rights, any alleged infringement of the right of citizens to vote must be carefully and meticulously scrutinized." . . .

It is argued that a State may exact fees from citizens for many different kinds of licenses; that if it can demand from all an equal fee for a driver's license, it can demand from all an equal poll tax for voting. But we must remember that the interest of the State, when it comes to voting, is limited to the power to fix qualifications. Wealth, like race, creed, or color, is not germane to one's ability to participate intelligently in the electoral process. Lines drawn on the basis of wealth or property, like those of race . . . , are traditionally disfavored. . . . To introduce wealth or payment of a fee as a measure of a voter's qualifications is to introduce a capricious or irrelevant factor. The degree of the discrimination is irrelevant. In this context—that is, as a condition of obtaining a ballot—the requirement of fee paying causes an "invidious" discrimination . . . that runs afoul of the Equal Protection Clause. Levy "by the poll," as stated in Breedlove v. Suttles, . . . is an old familiar form of taxation; and we say nothing to impair its validity so long as it is not made a condition to the exercise of the franchise. *Breedlove v. Suttles* sanctioned its use as "a prerequisite of voting." . . . To that extent the *Breedlove* case is overruled.

We agree, of course, with Mr. Justice Holmes that the Due Process Clause of the Fourteenth Amendment "does not enact Mr. Herbert Spencer's Social Statics". . . . Likewise, the Equal Protection Clause is not shackled to the political theory of a particular era. In determining what lines are unconstitutionally discriminatory, we have never been confined to historic notions of equality, any more than we have restricted due process to a fixed catalogue of what was at a given time deemed to be the limits of fundamental rights. . . . Notions of what constitutes equal treatment for purposes of the Equal Protection Clause *do* change. This Court in 1896 held that laws providing for separate public facilities for white and Negro citizens did not deprive the latter of the equal protection and treatment that the Fourteenth Amendment commands. . . . Seven of the eight Justices then sitting subscribed to the Court's opinion, thus joining in expressions of what constituted unequal and discriminatory treatment that sound strange to a contemporary ear. When, in 1954—more than a half-century later—we repudiated the "separate-but-equal" doctrine of *Plessy* as respects public education we stated: "In approaching this problem, we cannot turn the clock back to 1868 when the Amendment was adopted, or even to 1896 when Plessy v. Ferguson was written." Brown v. Board of Education. . . .

In a recent searching re-examination of the Equal Protection Clause, we held . . . that "the opportunity for equal participation by all voters in the election of state legislators" is required. Reynolds v. Sims. . . . We decline to qualify that principle by sustaining this poll tax. Our conclusion, like that in *Reynolds v. Sims,* is founded not on what we think governmental policy should be, but on what the Equal Protection Clause requires.

We have long been mindful that where fundamental rights and liberties are asserted under the Equal Protection Clause, classifications which might invade or restrain them must be closely scrutinized and carefully confined. . . .

Those principles apply here. For to repeat, wealth or fee paying has, in our view, no relation to voting qualifications; the right to vote is too precious, too fundamental to be so burdened or conditioned.

Reversed.

■ MR. JUSTICE BLACK, dissenting.

. . . The Court . . . overrules *Breedlove* in part, but its opinion reveals that it does so not by using its limited power to interpret the original meaning of the Equal Protection Clause, but by giving that clause a new meaning which it believes represents a better governmental policy. From this action I dissent.

. . .

The Court's justification for consulting its own notions rather than following the original meaning of the Constitution, as I would, apparently is based on the belief of the majority of the Court that for this Court to be bound by the original meaning of the Constitution is an intolerable and debilitating evil; that our Constitution should not be "shackled to the political theory of a particular era," and that to save the country from the original Constitution the Court must have constant power to renew it and keep it abreast with this Court's more enlightening theories of what is best for our society. It seems to me that this is not only an attack on the great value of our Constitution itself but also on the concept of a written constitution which is to survive through the years as originally written unless changed through the amendment process which the Framers wisely provided. Moreover, when a "political theory" embodied in our Constitution becomes outdated, it seems to me that a majority of the nine members of this Court are not only without constitutional power but are far less qualified to choose a new constitutional political theory than the people of this country proceeding in the manner provided by Article V.

The people have not found it impossible to amend their Constitution to meet new conditions. The Equal Protection Clause itself is the product of the peoples' desire to use their constitutional power to amend the Constitution to meet new problems. . . .

■ MR. JUSTICE HARLAN, whom MR. JUSTICE STEWART joins, dissenting.

The final demise of state poll taxes, already totally proscribed by the Twenty-Fourth Amendment with respect to federal elections and abolished by the States themselves in all but four States with respect to state elections, is perhaps in itself not of great moment. But the fact that the *coup de grace* has been administered by this Court instead of being left to the affected States or to the federal political process should be a matter of continuing concern to all interested in maintaining the proper role of this tribunal under our scheme of government.

   . . .

Dunn v. Blumstein
405 U.S. 330 (1972).

In holding invalid a statute imposing as a condition of voting residence in the state for one year and the county for three months before the election, the Court said:

"Durational residence requirements completely bar from voting all residents not meeting the fixed durational standards. By denying some citizens the right to vote, such laws deprive them of 'a fundamental political right, . . . preservative of all rights.' Reynolds v. Sims, 377 U.S. 533, 562 (1964). There is no need to repeat now the labors undertaken in earlier cases to analyze this right to vote and to explain in detail the judicial role in reviewing state statutes which selectively distribute the franchise. In decision after decision, this Court has made clear that a citizen has a constitutionally protected right to participate in elections on an equal basis with other citizens in the jurisdiction. See, e.g., Evans v. Cornman, 398 U.S. 419, 421–422 (1970);[a] Kramer v. Union Free School District No. 15, 395 U.S. 621, 626–628 (1969);[b] Cipriano v. City of Houma, 395 U.S. 701, 706 (1969);[c] Harper v. Virginia State Board of Elections, 383 U.S. 663, 667 (1966); Carrington v. Rash, 380 U.S. 89, 93–94 (1965);[d] Reynolds v. Sims, supra. This 'equal right to vote,' Evans v. Cornman, . . . is not absolute; the States have the power to impose voter qualifications, and to regulate access to the franchise in other ways. . . . But, as a general matter, 'before that right [to vote] can be restricted, the purpose of the restriction and the assertedly overriding interests served by it must meet close constitutional scrutiny.' Evans v. Cornman . . . ; see Bullock v. Carter, 405 U.S. 134 (1972).[e]

"Tennessee urges that this case is controlled by Drueding v. Devlin, 380 U.S. 125 (1965). *Drueding* was a decision upholding Maryland's durational residence

---

   [a] Persons living on the grounds of the National Institutes of Health, a federal reservation or enclave located within the boundaries of Maryland, were denied the right to vote in Maryland elections on the ground that they were not residents of Maryland. The Court held the denial unconstitutional: "In nearly every election, federal, state, and local, for offices from the Presidency to the school board, and on the entire variety of ballot propositions, appellees have a stake equal to that of other Maryland residents. As the District Court concluded, they are entitled under the Fourteenth Amendment to protect that stake by exercising the equal right to vote."

   [b] A New York law provided that residents of school districts could vote in school district elections only if they (1) own or lease taxable real property in the district, or (2) are parents or have custody of children enrolled in the local public schools. The Court noted that the statute was to be given "a close and exacting examination" because "statutes distributing the franchise constitute the foundation of our representative society." The Court then held the statute unconstitutional because the state had not demonstrated a "compelling state interest" justifying the limitation on the franchise.

   [c] A state provision giving only "property taxpayers" the right to vote in elections called to approve the issuance of revenue bonds by a municipal utility was held unconstitutional. The Court found no basis for the limitation since "the benefits and burdens of the bond issue fall indiscriminately on the property owner and nonproperty owner alike."

   [d] The Court held invalid a Texas constitutional provision prohibiting a member of the armed forces who moves his home to Texas from voting in any election so long as he is a member of the armed forces.

   [e] A Texas law requiring candidates to pay large filing fees in order to have their names placed on the ballot in primary elections was held invalid. The Court said:

"Because the Texas filing fee scheme has a real and appreciable impact on the exercise of the franchise, and because this impact is related to the resources of the voters supporting a particular candidate, we conclude, as in *Harper*, that the laws must be 'closely scrutinized' and found reasonably necessary to the accomplishment of legitimate state objectives in order to pass constitutional muster."

requirements. The District Court tested those requirements by the equal protection standard applied to ordinary state regulations: whether the exclusions are reasonably related to a permissible state interest. . . . We summarily affirmed *per curiam* without the benefit of argument. But if it was not clear then, it is certainly clear now that a more exacting test is required for any statute which 'place[s] a condition on the exercise of the right to vote.' Bullock v. Carter. . . . This development in the law culminated in Kramer v. Union Free School District No. 15, supra, 395 U.S. 621 (1969). There we canvassed in detail the reasons for strict review of statutes distributing the franchise, . . . noting *inter alia* that such statutes 'constitute the foundation of our representative society.' We concluded that if a challenged statute grants the right to vote to some citizens and denies the franchise to others, 'the Court must determine whether the exclusions are *necessary* to promote a *compelling* state interest.' Id., at 627 (emphasis added); Cipriano v. City of Houma, 395 U.S. 701, 704 (1969); City of Phoenix v. Kolodziejski, 399 U.S. 204, 205, 209 (1970).[f] Cf. Harper v. Virginia State Board of Elections, supra, 383 U.S., at 670. This is the test we apply here."

Marston v. Lewis

410 U.S. 679 (1973).

Arizona required a voter to have resided in the State for 50 days before an election and also to register at least 50 days prior. The Court held this requirement valid in light of a state showing that it would be difficult to do the necessary paper work in any shorter period before the election, stating: "In the present case, we are confronted with a recent and amply justifiable legislative judgment that 50 days rather than 30 is necessary to promote the State's important interest in accurate voter lists. The Constitution is not so rigid that that determination and others like it may not stand." A dissent argued that the Court had fixed in Dunn the line of 30 days as that beyond which reliance on administrative convenience is extremely questionable and "we can avoid an unprincipled numbers game only if we insist that any deviations from the line we have drawn, after mature consideration, be justified by far more substantial evidence than that produced" in this case.

Hill v. Stone

421 U.S. 289 (1975).

Issuance of bonds to finance construction of a city library was defeated in a Fort Worth election. Residents brought this federal court action challenging the provision of Texas law limiting the right to vote in city bond issue elections to persons who have "rendered" or listed real, mixed, or personal property for taxation in the election district. Under the law mere listing of the property—not the payment of any tax—was the prerequisite to voting. The Court, by a vote of five to three, held the statute invalid under the Equal Protection Clause, stating, in part:

"The basic principle . . . is that as long as the election in question is not one of special interest, any classification restricting the franchise on grounds other than residence, age, and citizenship cannot stand unless the district or State can demonstrate that the classification serves a compelling state interest. See *Kramer* . . . ; *Cipriano*. . . .

---

f   The Court held that a State could not restrict to real property taxpayers the vote in elections to approve the issuance of general obligation bonds.

"The appellant's claim that the Ft. Worth election was one of special interest and thus outside the principles of the *Kramer* case runs afoul of our decision in *City of Phoenix v. Kolodziejski*, supra. In the *Phoenix* case, we expressly stated that a general obligation bond issue—even where the debt service will be paid entirely out of property taxes as in Ft. Worth—is a matter of general interest, and that the principles of *Kramer* apply to classifications limiting eligibility among registered voters.

"In making the alternative contentions that the 'rendering requirement' creates no real 'classification,' or that the classification created should be upheld as being reasonable, the appellant misconceives the rationale of *Kramer* and its successors. Appellant argues that since all property is required to be rendered for taxation, and since anyone can vote in a bond election if he renders any property, no matter how little, the Texas scheme does not discriminate on the basis of wealth or property. Our cases, however, have not held or intimated that only property-based classifications are suspect; in an election of general interest, restrictions on the franchise of any character must meet a stringent test of justification. The Texas scheme creates a classification based on rendering, and it in effect disfranchises those who have not rendered their property for taxation in the year of the bond election. Mere reasonableness will therefore not suffice to sustain the classification created in this case.

B.

"The appellant has sought to justify the State's rendering requirement solely on the ground that it extends some protection to property owners, who will bear the direct burden of retiring the city's bonded indebtedness. The *Phoenix* case, however, rejected this analysis of the 'direct' imposition of costs on property owners. Even under a system in which the responsibility of retiring the bonded indebtedness falls directly on property taxpayers, all members of the community share in the cost in various ways. Moreover, the construction of a library is not likely to be of special interest to a particular, well-defined portion of the electorate. . . .

"The appellee city officials argue that the rendering qualifications furthers another state interest: it encourages prospective voters to render their property and thereby helps enforce the State's tax laws. This argument is difficult to credit. The use of the franchise to compel compliance with other, independent state objectives is questionable in any context. . . .

"In sum, the Texas rendering requirement erects a classification that impermissibly disenfranchises persons otherwise qualified to vote, solely because they have not rendered some property for taxation. The *Phoenix* case establishes that Ft. Worth's election was not a 'special interest' election, and the state interests proffered by appellant and the city officials fall far short of meeting the 'compelling state interest' test consistently applied in *Kramer, Cipriano,* and *Phoenix*."

Crawford v. Marion County Election Board
553 U.S. 181 (2008).

Indiana mandated presentation of government-issued photo identification before its citizens could vote in person (but not absentee), although it allowed indigent voters or those with a religious objection to being photographed to cast a provisional ballot that would be counted only if an affidavit were executed before a circuit court clerk within 10 days after an election. Without a majority opinion, the Court rejected a facial challenge to this Voter ID law. The lead opinion by Justice Stevens, joined by Chief Justice Roberts and Justice Kennedy, noted that "under . . . *Harper*, even rational restrictions on the right to vote are invidious if they are unrelated to voter qualifications[, but] 'evenhanded restrictions that protect the integrity and reliability of the electoral process itself' are not invidious and satisfy ... *Harper*." Applying a "balancing approach" that measures the severity of the burden on voters and demands a "corresponding [state] interest sufficiently weighty to justify the limitation," Justice Stevens found the state's interests "in deterring and detecting voter fraud[,]" seeking "to improve and modernize election procedures[,]" preventing voter fraud resulting from "its own maladministration—namely, that Indiana's voter registration rolls include a large number of names of persons who are either deceased or no longer live in Indiana[,]" and "safeguarding voter confidence" adequate justification, given that the evidence provided in this litigation did not demonstrate a severe burden on voting. Although the "record contains no evidence of any [in-person voter impersonation at polling places] actually occurring in Indiana at any time in its history[,] ... flagrant examples of such fraud in other parts of the country have been documented throughout this Nation's history by respected historians and journalists, ... occasional examples have surfaced in recent years, ... and ... Indiana's own experience with fraudulent voting in the 2003 Democratic primary for East Chicago Mayor—though perpetrated using absentee ballots and not in-person fraud—demonstrate that not only is the risk of voter fraud real but that it could affect the outcome of a close election." Justice Stevens also noted, in part:

"... [T]hat most voters already possess a valid driver's license, or some other form of acceptable identification, would not save the statute under our reasoning in *Harper,* if the State required voters to pay a tax or a fee to obtain a new photo identification. But ... the photo identification cards issued by Indiana's BMV are ... free. For most voters who need them, the inconvenience of making a trip to the BMV, gathering the required documents, and posing for a photograph surely does not qualify as a substantial burden on the right to vote, or even represent a significant increase over the usual burdens of voting.

"Both evidence in the record and facts of which we may take judicial notice, however, indicate that a somewhat heavier burden may be placed on a limited number of persons[,] includ[ing] elderly persons born out-of-state, who may have difficulty obtaining a birth certificate; persons who because of economic or other personal limitations may find it difficult either to secure a copy of their birth certificate or to assemble the other required documentation to obtain a state-issued identification; homeless persons; and persons with a religious objection to being photographed. ...

"The severity of that burden is ... mitigated by the fact that, if eligible, voters without photo identification may cast provisional ballots that will ultimately be counted. To do so, however, they must travel to the circuit court clerk's office within 10 days to execute the required affidavit. It is unlikely that such a requirement would pose a constitutional problem unless it is wholly unjustified. And even assuming that the burden may not be justified as to a few voters, that conclusion is by no means sufficient to establish petitioners' right to ... relief that would invalidate the statute in all its applications."

Absent "evidence in the record ... [of] the number of registered voters without photo identification" or about "the difficulties faced by either indigent voters or voters with religious objections to being photographed[,]" there was insufficient basis for invalidating this "neutral, nondiscriminatory regulation of voting procedure[.]"

An opinion concurring in the judgment by Justice Scalia, joined by Justices Thomas and Alito, urged "application of a deferential 'important regulatory interests' standard for nonsevere, nondiscriminatory restrictions, reserving strict scrutiny for laws that severely restrict the right to vote." The Voter ID law imposes "[o]rdinary and widespread burdens, ... requiring 'nominal effort' of everyone," and such burdens are "not severe." Moreover, "*everyone* must have and present a photo identification that can be obtained for free. The State draws no classifications, let alone discriminatory ones, except to establish *optional* absentee and provisional balloting for certain poor, elderly, and institutionalized voters and for religious objectors." Justice Scalia particularly objected to the idea of "weighing the burden of a nondiscriminatory voting law upon each voter and concomitantly requiring exceptions for vulnerable voters":

"A voter complaining about such a law's effect on him has no valid equal-protection claim because, without proof of discriminatory intent, a generally applicable law with disparate impact is not unconstitutional. . . . The Fourteenth Amendment does not regard neutral laws as invidious ones, *even when their burdens purportedly fall disproportionately on a protected class. A fortiori* it does not do so when, as here, the classes complaining of disparate impact are not even protected.*"

Justice Scalia emphasized that "voter-by-voter examination of the burdens of voting regulations would prove especially disruptive." He concluded:

"That sort of detailed judicial supervision of the election process would flout the Constitution's express commitment of the task to the States. See Art. I, § 4. It is for state legislatures to weigh the costs and benefits of possible changes to their election codes, and their judgment must prevail unless it imposes a severe and unjustified overall burden upon the right to vote, or is intended to disadvantage a particular class. Judicial review of their handiwork must apply an objective, uniform standard that will enable them to determine, *ex ante*, whether the burden they impose is too severe.

"The lead opinion's record-based resolution of these cases . . . provides no certainty, and will embolden litigants. . . ."

Justice Souter, joined by Justice Ginsburg, dissented, finding the "Indiana Voter ID Law . . . unconstitutional: the state interests fail to justify the practical limitations placed on the right to vote, and the law imposes an unreasonable and irrelevant burden on voters who are poor and old." He summarized his detailed objections as follows:

"Without a shred of evidence that in-person voter impersonation is a problem in the State, much less a crisis, Indiana has adopted one of the most restrictive photo identification requirements in the country. The State recognizes that tens of thousands of qualified voters lack the necessary federally issued or state-issued identification, but it insists on implementing the requirement immediately, without allowing a transition period for targeted efforts to distribute the required identification to individuals who need it. The State hardly even tries to explain its decision to force indigents or religious objectors to travel all the way to their county seats every time they wish to vote, and if there is any waning of confidence in the administration of elections it probably owes more to the State's violation of federal election law than to any imposters at the polling places. It is impossible to say, on this record, that the State's interest in adopting its signally inhibiting photo identification requirement has been shown to outweigh the serious burdens it imposes on the right to vote.

". . . If the Court's decision in *Harper* . . . stands for anything, it is that being poor has nothing to do with being qualified to vote. . . . The State's requirements here, that people without cars travel to a motor vehicle registry and that the poor who fail to do that get to their county seats within 10 days of every election, . . . translate into unjustified economic burdens uncomfortably close to the outright $1.50 fee we struck down 42 years ago. Like that fee, the onus of the Indiana law is illegitimate just

---

*   A number of our early right-to-vote decisions, purporting to rely upon the Equal Protection Clause, strictly scrutinized nondiscriminatory voting laws requiring the payment of fees. See, e.g., *Harper v. Virginia Bd. of Elections.* . . . [W]e have never held that legislatures must calibrate all election laws, even those totally unrelated to money, for their impacts on poor voters or must otherwise accommodate wealth disparities.

because it correlates with no state interest so well as it does with the object of deterring poorer residents from exercising the franchise."

Justice Breyer also dissented, because "the statute . . . imposes a disproportionate burden upon those eligible voters who lack a driver's license or other statutorily valid form of photo ID." Although "I share the general view of the lead opinion insofar as it holds that the Constitution does not *automatically* forbid Indiana from enacting a photo ID requirement[,]" Indiana's failure to phase in the requirement over two federal election cycles; to accommodate "Indiana nondriver[s], most likely to be poor, elderly, or disabled, [who] will find it difficult and expensive to travel to the Bureau of Motor Vehicles, particularly if he or she resides in one of the many Indiana counties lacking a public transportation system"; and to provide for many individuals who "may be uncertain about how to obtain the underlying documentation, usually a passport or a birth certificate, upon which the statute insists" and who "may find the costs associated with these documents unduly burdensome" (particularly when "two other States—Florida and Georgia—have put into practice photo ID requirements significantly less restrictive than Indiana's" and have not "insist[ed], as Indiana does, that indigent voters travel each election cycle to potentially distant places for the purposes of signing an indigency affidavit") render the voting burden disproportionate and, hence, unconstitutional.

NOTE

In Richardson v. Ramirez, 418 U.S. 24 (1974), the Court held valid California constitutional provisions and implementing statutes disenfranchising persons convicted of an "infamous crime." The Court said, in part:

"As we have seen, however, the exclusion of felons from the vote has an affirmative sanction in § 2 of the Fourteenth Amendment, a sanction which was not present in the case of the other restrictions on the franchise which were invalidated in the cases on which respondents rely. We hold that the understanding of those who adopted the Fourteenth Amendment, as reflected in the express language of § 2 and in the historical and judicial interpretation of the Amendment's applicability to state laws disenfranchising felons, is of controlling significance in distinguishing such laws from those other state limitations on the franchise which have been held invalid under the Equal Protection Clause by this Court."

Equal Protection and Ballot Evaluation

The Court has interpreted the Equal Protection Clause to restrict not only the setting of qualifications for eligibility to vote, but, at least in some circumstances, the standards and processes employed for determining which among disputed ballots in contested elections shall be counted, and how. It did so in the immediate, politically charged aftermath of the extremely close 2000 Presidential election, which hinged on Florida's 25 electoral votes. Just several hundred of nearly 6 million Florida votes cast separated Governor George W. Bush—the winner of the initial machine count and the state-mandated machine recount—and Vice President Albert Gore, Jr., who, among other legal actions, sued and eventually secured from the Florida Supreme Court on December 8 a judgment mandating, *inter alia*, an immediate statewide manual recounting of ballots on which vote tabulation machines had failed to detect a vote for President ("undervotes"). A bare majority of the Court stayed that judgment on December 9 and, in Bush v. Gore, 531 U.S. 98 (2000), reversed it on December 12, holding that the judgment contemplated "standardless manual recounts" in "violation of the Equal Protection Clause." Moreover, because the Court majority understood the

Florida Supreme Court to have said that the Florida legislature intended to have Florida's electors selected by December 12 in accordance with the "safe harbor provision" of the federal Electoral Count Act of 1887, 3 U.S.C. § 5—which requires any controversy or contest designed to lead to a conclusive selection of electors to be completed by that date—the Court concluded that it was too late to devise a constitutionally proper hand count.

The per curiam majority of five Justices said in part:

"The individual citizen has no federal constitutional right to vote for electors for the President of the United States unless and until the state legislature chooses a statewide election as the means to implement its power to appoint members of the Electoral College. U.S. Const., Art. II, § 1. . . . [I]t may . . . select the electors itself, which . . . State legislatures in several States [did] for many years after the Framing of our Constitution. . . . [N]ow . . . in each of the several States the citizens themselves vote for Presidential electors. When the state legislature vests the right to vote for President in its people, the right to vote as the legislature has prescribed is fundamental; and one source of its fundamental nature lies in the equal weight accorded to each vote and the equal dignity owed to each voter. . . .

"The right to vote is protected in more than the initial allocation of the franchise. Equal protection applies as well to the manner of its exercise. Having once granted the right to vote on equal terms, the State may not, by later arbitrary and disparate treatment, value one person's vote over that of another. See, e.g., Harper v. Virginia State Bd. of Elections, 383 U.S. 663, 665 (1966). . . . It must be remembered that 'the right of suffrage can be denied by a debasement or dilution of the weight of a citizen's vote just as effectively as by wholly prohibiting the free exercise of the franchise.' Reynolds v. Sims, 377 U.S. 533, 555 (1964)."

Finding "[m]uch of the controversy" focused on incompletely punched ballot cards with the "chads" hanging or just indented and hence unreadable by machine, the majority found the Florida Supreme Court's direction

"that the intent of the voter be discerned from such ballots . . . unobjectionable as an abstract proposition and a starting principle. The problem inheres in the absence of specific standards to ensure its equal application. The formulation of uniform rules to determine intent based on these recurring circumstances is practicable and, we conclude, necessary.

". . . The search for intent can be confined by specific rules designed to ensure uniform treatment.

"The want of those rules here has led to unequal evaluation of ballots in various respects. . . . [T]he standards for accepting or rejecting contested ballots might vary not only from county to county but indeed within a single county from one recount team to another.

"The record provides some examples. A monitor . . . observed that three members of [a] county canvassing board applied different standards in defining a legal vote. . . . [A]t least one county changed its evaluative standards during the counting process. . . . This is not a process with sufficient guarantees of equal treatment.

". . . [I]n the context of the Presidential selection process in Moore v. Ogilvie, 394 U.S. 814 (1969), . . . we invalidated a county-based procedure that diluted the influence of citizens in larger counties in the nominating process[,] observing that '[t]he idea that one group can be granted greater voting strength than another is hostile to the one man, one vote basis of our representative government.'

"The State Supreme Court ratified this uneven treatment. . . . [E]ach of the counties used varying standards to determine what was a legal vote. Broward County used a more forgiving standard than Palm Beach County, and uncovered almost three times as many new votes, a result markedly disproportionate to the difference in population between the counties."

The Court also objected to the Florida Supreme Court's failure to require the hand count to assess overvotes (ballots containing more than one fully punched chad) as well as undervotes; its willingness "to include whatever partial counts are done by the time of final certification"; and its failure to "specify who would recount the ballots"—forcing "county canvassing boards . . . to pull together ad hoc teams comprised of judges from various Circuits who had no previous training in handling and interpreting ballots." The Court then said:

"The recount process, in its features here described, is inconsistent with the minimum procedures necessary to protect the fundamental right of each voter in the special instance of a statewide recount under the authority of a single state judicial officer. Our consideration is limited to the present circumstances, for the problem of equal protection in election processes generally presents many complexities.

"The question . . . is not whether local entities, in the exercise of their expertise, may develop different systems for implementing elections. Instead, . . . a state court with the power to assure uniformity has ordered a statewide recount with minimal procedural safeguards. When a court orders a statewide remedy, there must be at least some assurance that the rudimentary requirements of equal treatment and fundamental fairness are satisfied."[a]

There were four separate dissents. Justice Stevens, joined by Justices Ginsburg and Breyer, concluded that "the failure of the Florida Supreme Court to specify in detail the precise manner in which the 'intent of the voter,' . . . is to be determined" did not "rise[ ] to the level of a constitutional violation." The Court had "never before called into question the substantive standard by which a State determines that a vote has been legally cast" and there was "no reason to think that the guidance provided to the factfinders, specifically the various canvassing boards, by the 'intent of the voter' standard" was insufficient. Although "[a]dmittedly, the use of differing substandards for determining voter intent in different counties employing similar voting systems may raise serious concerns[, t]hose concerns are alleviated—if not eliminated—by the fact that a single impartial magistrate will ultimately adjudicate all objections arising from the recount process." In any event, under the majority's "own reasoning, the appropriate course of action would be to remand to allow more specific procedures for implementing the legislature's uniform general standard to be established" rather than to "disenfranchise[ ] . . . an unknown number of voters whose [uncounted] ballots reveal their intent[.]" December 12 was not a fixed deadline, because the "safe harbor provisions" only "provide rules of decision for Congress to follow when selecting among conflicting slates of electors" and "do not prohibit a State from counting what the majority concedes to be legal votes until a bona fide winner is determined."

Justice Souter's dissent was joined by Justices Breyer, Stevens and Ginsburg, insofar as it criticized the Court's intervention at all rather than "allow[ing] the State to follow the course indicated by the opinions of its own Supreme Court" (which might have obviated any need for Supreme Court review), and insofar as it rejected any claimed violations of The Electoral Count Act or Article II. Only Justice Breyer joined that portion of his dissent that said in part:

---

[a] A concurring opinion by Chief Justice Rehnquist, joined by Justices Scalia and Thomas, found "additional grounds to reverse the Florida Supreme Court's decision"—namely, that its post-election decisions interpreting Florida's election statutes had so departed from the Florida legislature's scheme for appointing presidential electors, including the "legislative desire to attain the 'safe harbor' provided by § 5[,]" as to violate Art. II, § 1, cl.2. The four dissenters strongly disagreed, finding the Article II challenge to the Florida Supreme Court's statutory interpretations "not substantial."

". . . It is true that the Equal Protection Clause does not forbid the use of a variety of voting mechanisms within a jurisdiction, even though different mechanisms will have different levels of effectiveness in recording voters' intentions; local variety can be justified by concerns about cost, the potential value of innovation, and so on. But evidence in the record here suggests that a different order of disparity obtains under rules for determining a voter's intent that have been applied (and could continue to be applied) to identical types of ballots used in identical brands of machines and exhibiting identical physical characteristics (such as 'hanging' or 'dimpled' chads). . . . I can conceive of no legitimate state interest served by these differing treatments of the expressions of voters' fundamental rights. The differences appear wholly arbitrary."

He would have "remand[ed] the case . . . with instructions to establish uniform standards for evaluating the several types of ballots that have prompted differing treatments, to be applied within and among counties when passing on such identical ballots in any further recounting[,]" however, and he found "no justification for denying the State the opportunity to try to count all disputed ballots now."

Justice Ginsburg's dissent, in the portion addressing equal protection that was joined only by Justice Stevens, could not "agree that the recount adopted by the Florida court, flawed as it may be, would yield a result any less fair or precise than the certification that preceded that recount." She felt that "the Court's conclusion that a constitutionally adequate recount is impractical is a prophecy the Court's own judgment will not allow to be tested" and that "[s]uch an untested prophecy should not decide the Presidency of the United States."

Finally, Justice Breyer's dissent argued primarily—joined by Justices Stevens, Souter and Ginsburg—that the "Court was wrong to take this case[,] wrong to grant a stay [and] should now vacate that stay and permit the Florida Supreme Court to decide whether the recount should resume." With respect to the equal protection issues, joined only by Justice Souter, he rejected the complaints of failure to include overvotes and of recounts of all ballots, not just undervotes, in some but not all counties, because petitioner Bush had "presented no evidence . . . that a manual recount of overvotes would identify additional legal votes." However, the "absence of a uniform, specific standard to guide the recounts" did "implicate principles of fundamental fairness" and "in these very special circumstances, . . . may well have counseled the adoption of a uniform standard to address the problem." Given "the majority's disposition," he declined to "decide whether, or the extent to which, as a remedial matter, the Constitution would place limits upon the content of the uniform standard[,]" but he found "no justification for the majority's remedy" of "halt[ing] the recount entirely" rather than remanding to permit a recount "in accordance with a single-uniform substandard."[a]

The Fifteenth Amendment as a Limitation on State (and Federal) Power to Fix Qualifications for Voters

By its terms, the fifteenth amendment prohibits the United States or any State from denying or abridging the right of United States citizens to vote "on account of race, color, or previous condition of servitude." In Guinn v. United States, 238 U.S. 347 (1915), the Court found impermissible racial discrimination in a 1910 amendment to

---

[a] The Court's decision in Bush v. Gore called forth a torrent of commentary addressing the nature and propriety of the Court's intervention. For one sample of a wide range of views on many of the facets of the decision, including its equal protection analysis, see the various contributions to Symposium, *The Law of Presidential Elections: Issues in the Wake of Florida 2000*, 29 Florida State University Law Review 325–1029 (2001). For a general treatment of election disputes using the 2000 election in general, and Bush v. Gore in particular, as the organizing theme, see Issacharoff, Karlan & Pildes, *When Elections Go Bad: The Law of Democracy and the Presidential Election of 2000* (2001).

the Oklahoma Constitution that imposed a literacy requirement for voting but exempted all who were entitled to vote on or before January 1, 1866, and their lineal descendants. The Court also addressed the fifteenth amendment in the following modern case.

Rice v. Cayetano

528 U.S. 495 (2000).

In 1978 Hawaii amended its Constitution to create a state agency, the Office of Hawaiian Affairs (OHA), to administer programs benefiting two groups: (1) "native Hawaiians" (defined by statute "as descendants of not less than one-half part of the races inhabiting the Hawaiian islands prior to 1778"—the date when England's Captain Cook first landed in Hawaii), and (2) "Hawaiians" (defined more broadly as those descended from "the aboriginal peoples" inhabiting Hawaii in 1778). OHA is governed by nine trustees who "shall be Hawaiians" and who shall be "elected by qualified voters who are Hawaiians" in a statewide election. In a suit by a Hawaiian citizen lacking the ancestry required to vote in the trustee election, the Court found "a clear violation of the Fifteenth Amendment." Justice Kennedy's opinion for the majority first rejected the argument that the voting classification was not based on race but on whether one had an ancestor in Hawaii at a particular time, thus excluding fully Polynesian Hawaiians with no ancestors who lived there in 1778 and including those who could trace as little as 1/64th of their ancestry to a Hawaiian inhabitant from 1778. He wrote in part:

"Ancestry can be a proxy for race. It is that proxy here. Even if the residents of Hawaii in 1778 had been of more diverse ethnic backgrounds and cultures, it is far from clear that a voting test favoring their descendants would not be a race-based qualification. But that is not this case. For centuries Hawaii was isolated from migration. . . . The inhabitants shared common physical characteristics, and by 1778 they had a common culture. . . . The provisions before us reflect the State's effort to preserve that commonality of people to the present day. . . . The very object of the statutory definition in question and of its earlier congressional counterpart in the Hawaiian Homes Commission Act is to treat the early Hawaiians as a distinct people, commanding their own recognition and respect. The State, in enacting the legislation before us, has used ancestry as a racial definition and for a racial purpose."

Justice Kennedy found confirmation of this conclusion in the "history of the State's definition[,]" and he went on to say:

". . . Simply because a class defined by ancestry does not include all members of the race does not suffice to make the classification race neutral. Here, the State's argument is undermined by its express racial purpose and by its actual effects.

"The ancestral inquiry mandated by the State implicates the same grave concerns as a classification specifying a particular race by name. One of the principal reasons race is treated as a forbidden classification is that it demeans the dignity and worth of a person to be judged by ancestry instead of by his or her own merit and essential qualities. An inquiry into ancestral lines is not consistent with respect based on the unique personality each of us possesses, a respect the Constitution itself secures in its concern for persons and citizens.

"The ancestral inquiry mandated by the State is forbidden by the Fifteenth Amendment for the further reason that the use of racial classifications is corruptive of the whole legal order democratic elections seek to preserve. The law itself may not become the instrument for generating the prejudice and hostility all too often directed against persons whose particular ancestry is disclosed by their ethnic characteristics and cultural traditions. . . ."

Justice Kennedy then rejected Hawaii's "three principal defenses of its voting law." First, based on the special mission of the OHA trustees to protect the interests of native Hawaiians and afford them a measure of self-governance, Hawaii invoked *Morton v. Mancari*, 417 U.S. 535 (1974), which upheld employment preferences at the federal Bureau of Indian Affairs for individuals who were "one-fourth or more degree Indian blood and . . . member[s] of a Federally-recognized tribe." The BIA preference could be "tied rationally to the fulfillment of Congress' unique obligation toward the Indians," and was "reasonably and rationally designed to further Indian self-government." Without addressing "whether Congress may treat the native Hawaiians as it does the Indian tribes[,]" however, Justice Kennedy said that *Mancari*, which treated the BIA preference as "political rather than racial in nature," did not permit Congress to "authorize a State to establish a voting scheme that limits the electorate for its public officials to a class of tribal Indians, to the exclusion of all non-Indian citizens."

". . . If a non-Indian lacks a right to vote in tribal elections, it is for the reason that such elections are the internal affair of a quasi-sovereign. The OHA elections, by contrast, are the affair of the State of Hawaii. OHA is a state agency, established by the State Constitution, responsible for the administration of state laws and obligations. . . .

" . . .

"The validity of the voting restriction is the only question before us. [W]e assume the validity of the underlying administrative structure and trusts, without intimating any opinion on that point. Nonetheless, the elections for OHA trustee are elections of the State, not of a separate quasi-sovereign, and they are elections to which the Fifteenth Amendment applies. . . ."

Second, the majority rejected Hawaii's defense based on "cases holding that the rule of one person, one vote does not pertain to certain special purpose districts such as water or irrigation districts. See *Ball v. James*, 451 U.S. 355 (1981); *Salyer Land Co. v. Tulare Lake Basin Water Storage Dist.*, 410 U.S. 719 (1973)." Finding it "far from clear that the *Salyer* line of cases would be at all applicable to statewide elections for an agency with the powers and responsibilities of OHA[,]" the Court "would not find those cases dispositive in any event[,]" because "compliance with the one-person, one-vote rule of the Fourteenth Amendment" would not "excuse[ ] compliance with the Fifteenth Amendment[,]" which "has independent meaning and force." Nor, third, did Hawaii's argument that the "restriction is based on beneficiary status rather than race" succeed. Not only was there a mismatch between the bulk of the funds being earmarked to benefit "native Hawaiians" and the eligible voting group extending to the broader group of "Hawaiians," but "more essential[ly, t]he State's position rests . . . on the demeaning premise that citizens of a particular race are somehow more qualified than others to vote on certain matters."

Concurring in the result, Justice Breyer, joined by Justice Souter, saw "no need . . . to decide this case on the basis of so vague a concept as 'quasi-sovereign,' " and he would "not subscribe to the Court's consequently sweeping prohibition." Instead, he thought the Court "should reject Hawaii's effort to justify its rules through analogy to a trust for an Indian tribe because the record makes clear that (1) there is no 'trust' for native Hawaiians here, and (2) OHA's electorate, as defined in the statute, does not sufficiently resemble an Indian tribe." As to (1), OHA administers revenues from public lands granted by the United States at statehood for the benefit of all the people of Hawaii, receives funding by ordinary legislation, and does not spend all its money to benefit native Hawaiians, so that "OHA is simply a special purpose department of Hawaii's state government." As to (2), the State, not a tribe or its equivalent, defined the electorate to include, not just native Hawaiians (who might be "analogous to tribes of other Native Americans"), but "Hawaiians" who might be "less than one five-hundredth original Hawaiian (assuming nine generations between 1778 and the present)"—a definition "well beyond any reasonable limit." Although these factors "destroy[ed] the analogy on which Hawaii's justification must depend[, t]his is not to say that Hawaii's definitions themselves independently violated the Constitution . . . ; it is only to say that the analogies they here offer are too distant to save a race-based voting definition that in their absence would clearly violate the Fifteenth Amendment."

Justice Stevens dissented, emphasizing the Federal Government's "wide latitude in carrying out its obligations arising from the special relationship it has with the aboriginal peoples, a category that includes the native Hawaiians, . . . the State's own fiduciary responsibility—arising from its establishment of a public trust—for administering assets granted it by the Federal Government in part for the benefit of native Hawaiians[,]" and the absence of "invidious discrimination present in this effort to see that indigenous peoples are compensated for past wrongs, and to preserve a distinct and vibrant culture. . . ." The "well-established federal trust relationship with the native Hawaiians" made *Mancari* relevant and allowed "special benefits designed to restore a measure of native self-governance. . . ." With respect to the majority's concern "that we are confronted here with a state constitution and legislative enactment—passed by a majority of the entire population of Hawaii—rather than a law passed by Congress or a tribe itself[,] . . . OHA and its trustee elections can hardly be characterized simply as an 'affair of the State' alone; they are the instruments for implementing the Federal Government's trust relationship with a once sovereign indigenous people. This Court has held more than once that the federal power to pass laws fulfilling its trust relationship with the Indians may be delegated to the States." From that perspective, "as with the BIA preferences in *Mancari*, the OHA voting requirement is certainly reasonably designed to promote 'self-government' by the descendants of the indigenous Hawaiians, and to make OHA 'more responsive to the needs of its constituent groups.'" These reasons were "more than sufficient to justify the OHA trust system and trustee election provision under the Fourteenth Amendment."

As for the Fifteenth Amendment, Justice Stevens noted that it does not prohibit the use of ancestry per se, and he argued that in this case ancestry was not "a proxy for race, or a pretext for invidious racial discrimination." *Guinn* and like cases involved voting systems "designed to exclude one racial class (at least) from voting" and "have no application to a system designed to empower politically the remaining members of a class of once sovereign, indigenous people." That all of the eligible voters "are beneficiaries of the public trust created by the State and administered by OHA, and . . . have at least one ancestor who was a resident of Hawaii in 1778" established an acceptable trust scheme "whose terms provide that the trustees shall be elected by a class including beneficiaries"—a "classification th[at] exists wholly apart from race." Justice Stevens also said:

"... [T]here is surely nothing racially invidious about a decision to enlarge the class of eligible voters to include 'any descendant' of a 1778 resident of the Islands. The broader category of eligible voters serves quite practically to ensure that, regardless how 'dilute' the race of native Hawaiians becomes[,] . . . there will remain a voting interest whose ancestors were a part of a political, cultural community, and who have inherited through participation and memory the set of traditions the trust seeks to protect. The putative mismatch only underscores the reality that it cannot be purely a racial interest that either the trust or the election provision seeks to secure; the political and cultural interests served are—unlike racial survival—shared by both native Hawaiians and Hawaiians.[14]

"... The OHA voting qualification—part of a statutory scheme put in place by democratic vote of a multiracial majority of all state citizens, including those non-'Hawaiians' who are not entitled to vote in OHA trustee elections—appropriately includes every resident of Hawaii having at least one ancestor who lived in the Islands in 1778.... Unlike a class including only full-blooded Polynesians—as one would imagine were the class strictly defined in terms of race—the OHA election provision excludes all full-blooded Polynesians currently residing in Hawaii who are not descended from a 1778 resident of Hawaii. Conversely, unlike many of the old southern voting schemes in which any potential voter with a 'taint' of non-Hawaiian blood would be excluded, the OHA scheme excludes no descendant of a 1778 resident because he or she is also part European, Asian, or African as a matter of race. The classification here is thus both too inclusive and not inclusive enough to fall strictly along racial lines.

" . . .

"... [T]he classification here is not 'demeaning' at all.... It is based on the permissible assumption in this context that families with 'any' ancestor who lived in Hawaii in 1778, and whose ancestors thereafter continued to live in Hawaii, have a claim to compensation and self-determination that others do not. For the multiracial majority of the citizens of the State of Hawaii to recognize that deep reality is not to demean their own interests but to honor those of others.

"... Our traditional understanding of democracy and voting preferences makes it difficult to conceive that the majority of the State's voting population would have enacted a measure that discriminates against, or in any way represents prejudice and hostility toward, that self-same majority...."

Justice Ginsburg dissented separately "for the reasons stated by Justice Stevens in [that part] of his dissenting opinion ... relying on established federal authority over Native Americans...."

B. TRAVEL AND INTERSTATE MIGRATION AND LENGTH OF STATE RESIDENCE

Introduction. This section addresses a set of cases, all analyzed in the equal protection framework, that involve constitutional claims of freedom to seek opportunity through interstate movement, migration, or trade, without being disadvantaged relative to those who already live where the opportunity is sought. Moreover, these cases not only implicate constitutional values of federalism in interstate relationships, but they combine, as do many other equal protection cases, concern about highly valued personal liberty with concern about the nature of the disadvantaging classification. Thus they may usefully be compared with cases like Harper v. Virginia State Board of Elections, supra p. 668, which focused on both voting as a specially protected interest and wealth as a classification; the cases in Section C. infra on poverty and welfare; and many others.

Although the cases do not divide neatly into those emphasizing the liberty of interstate opportunity and those emphasizing distinctions based on the fact or length

---

[14] ...

... It is ... culture, rather than the Polynesian race, that is uniquely Hawaiian and in need of protection.

of residency, they are divided here into two subsections. The first addresses interstate travel and migration, the second distinctions among state residents based on their length of residence.

1.   TRAVEL AND INTERSTATE MIGRATION

Shapiro v. Thompson

394 U.S. 618, 89 S.Ct. 1322, 22 L.Ed.2d 600 (1969).

■ MR. JUSTICE BRENNAN delivered the opinion of the Court.

These three appeals were restored to the calendar for reargument. . . . Each is an appeal from a decision of a three-judge District Court holding unconstitutional a State or District of Columbia statutory provision which denies welfare assistance to residents of the State or District who have not resided within their jurisdictions for at least one year immediately preceding their applications for such assistance. We affirm. . . .

II.

There is no dispute that the effect of the waiting-period requirement in each case is to create two classes of needy resident families indistinguishable from each other except that one is composed of residents who have resided a year or more, and the second of residents who have resided less than a year, in the jurisdiction. On the basis of this sole difference the first class is granted and the second class is denied welfare aid upon which may depend the ability of the families to obtain the very means to subsist—food, shelter, and other necessities of life. In each case, the District Court found that appellees met the test for residence in their jurisdictions, as well as all other eligibility requirements except the requirement of residence for a full year prior to their applications. On reargument, appellees' central contention is that the statutory prohibition of benefits to residents of less than a year creates a classification which constitutes an invidious discrimination denying them equal protection of the laws. We agree. The interests which appellants assert are promoted by the classification either may not constitutionally be promoted by government or are not compelling governmental interests.

III.

Primarily, appellants justify the waiting-period requirement as a protective device to preserve the fiscal integrity of state public assistance programs. It is asserted that people who require welfare assistance during their first year of residence in a State are likely to become continuing burdens on state welfare programs. Therefore, the argument runs, if such people can be deterred from entering the jurisdiction by denying them welfare benefits during the first year, state programs to assist long-time residents will not be impaired by a substantial influx of indigent newcomers.

There is weighty evidence that exclusion from the jurisdiction of the poor who need or may need relief was the specific objective of these provisions. . . .

We do not doubt that the one-year waiting period device is well suited to discourage the influx of poor families in need of assistance. An indigent who desires to migrate, resettle, find a new job, start a new life will doubtless hesitate if he knows that he must risk making the move without the possibility of falling back on state welfare assistance during his first year of residence, when his need may be most acute. But the purpose of inhibiting migration by needy persons into the State is constitutionally impermissible.

This Court long ago recognized that the nature of our Federal Union and our constitutional concepts of personal liberty unite to require that all citizens be free to travel throughout the length and breadth of our land uninhibited by statutes, rules or regulations which unreasonably burden or restrict this movement. . . .

We have no occasion to ascribe the source of this right to travel interstate to a particular constitutional provision. It suffices that, as Mr. Justice Stewart said for the Court in United States v. Guest, 383 U.S. 745, 757–758 (1966):

"The constitutional right to travel from one State to another . . . occupies a position fundamental to the concept of our Federal Union. It is a right that has been firmly established and repeatedly recognized.

"[The] right finds no explicit mention in the Constitution. The reason, it has been suggested, is that a right so elementary was conceived from the beginning to be a necessary concomitant of the stronger Union the Constitution created. In any event, freedom to travel throughout the United States has long been recognized as a basic right under the Constitution."

Thus, the purpose of deterring the in-migration of indigents cannot serve as justification for the classification created by the one-year waiting period, since that purpose is constitutionally impermissible. . . .

Alternatively, appellants argue that even if it is impermissible for a State to attempt to deter the entry of all indigents, the challenged classification may be justified as a permissible state attempt to discourage those indigents who would enter the State solely to obtain larger benefits. We observe first that none of the statutes before us is tailored to serve that objective. . . .

More fundamentally, a State may no more try to fence out those indigents who seek higher welfare benefits than it may try to fence out indigents generally. Implicit in any such distinction is the notion that indigents who enter a State with the hope of securing higher welfare benefits are somehow less deserving than indigents who do not take this consideration into account. But we do not perceive why a mother who is seeking to make a new life for herself and her children should be regarded as less deserving because she considers, among other factors, the level of a State's public assistance. Surely such a mother is no less deserving than a mother who moves into a particular State in order to take advantage of its better educational facilities.

Appellants argue further that the challenged classification may be sustained as an attempt to distinguish between new and old residents on the basis of the contribution they have made to the community through the payment of taxes. We have difficulty seeing how long-term residents who qualify for welfare are making a greater present contribution to the State in taxes than indigent residents who have recently arrived. If the argument is based on contributions made in the past by the long-term residents, there is some question, as a factual matter, whether this argument is applicable in Pennsylvania where the record suggests that some 40% of those denied public assistance because of the waiting period had lengthy prior residence in the State. But we need not rest on the particular facts of these cases. Appellants' reasoning would logically permit the State to bar new residents from schools, parks, and libraries or deprive them of police and fire protection. Indeed it would permit the State to apportion all benefits and services according to the past tax contributions of its citizens. The Equal Protection Clause prohibits such an apportionment of state services.[10]

---

[10] We are not dealing here with state insurance programs which may legitimately tie the amount of benefits to the individual's contributions.

We recognize that a State has a valid interest in preserving the fiscal integrity of its programs. It may legitimately attempt to limit its expenditures, whether for public assistance, public education, or any other program. But a State may not accomplish such a purpose by invidious distinctions between classes of its citizens. It could not, for example, reduce expenditures for education by barring indigent children from its schools. Similarly, in the cases before us, appellants must do more than show that denying welfare benefits to new residents saves money. The saving of welfare costs cannot be an independent ground for an invidious classification.

In sum, neither deterrence of indigents from migrating to the State nor limitation of welfare benefits to those regarded as contributing to the State is a constitutionally permissible state objective.

IV.

Appellants next advance as justification certain administrative and related governmental objectives allegedly served by the waiting-period requirement. They argue that the requirement (1) facilitates the planning of the welfare budget; (2) provides an objective test of residency; (3) minimizes the opportunity for recipients fraudulently to receive payments from more than one jurisdiction; and (4) encourages early entry of new residents into the labor force.

At the outset, we reject appellants' argument that a mere showing of a rational relationship between the waiting period and these four admittedly permissible state objectives will suffice to justify the classification.... The waiting-period provision denies welfare benefits to otherwise eligible applicants solely because they have recently moved into the jurisdiction. But in moving from State to State or to the District of Columbia appellees were exercising a constitutional right, and any classification which serves to penalize the exercise of that right, unless shown to be necessary to promote a *compelling* governmental interest, is unconstitutional....

The argument that the waiting-period requirement facilitates budget predictability is wholly unfounded. The records in all three cases are utterly devoid of evidence that either State or the District of Columbia in fact uses the one-year requirement as a means to predict the number of people who will require assistance in the budget year....

The argument that the waiting period serves as an administratively efficient rule of thumb for determining residency similarly will not withstand scrutiny. The residence requirement and the one-year waiting-period requirement are distinct and independent prerequisites for assistance under these three statutes, and the facts relevant to the determination of each are directly examined by the welfare authorities. Before granting an application, the welfare authorities investigate the applicant's employment, housing, and family situation and in the course of the inquiry necessarily learn the facts upon which to determine whether the applicant is a resident.

Similarly, there is no need for a State to use the one-year waiting period as a safeguard against fraudulent receipt of benefits; for less drastic means are available, and are employed, to minimize that hazard. Of course, a State has a valid interest in preventing fraud by any applicant, whether a newcomer or a long-time resident. It is not denied however that the investigations now conducted entail inquiries into facts relevant to that subject. In addition, cooperation among state welfare departments is common. The District of Columbia, for example, provides interim assistance to its former residents who have moved to a State which has a waiting period. As a matter of course, District officials send a letter to the welfare authorities in the recipient's new community "to request the information needed to continue assistance." A like procedure would be an effective safeguard against the hazard of double payments. Since double payments can be prevented by a letter or a telephone call, it is unreasonable to accomplish this objective by the blunderbuss method of denying assistance to all indigent newcomers for an entire year.

Pennsylvania suggests that the one-year waiting period is justified as a means of encouraging new residents to join the labor force promptly. But this logic would also require a similar waiting period for long-term residents of the State. A state purpose to encourage employment provides no rational basis for imposing a one-year waiting-period restriction on new residents only.

We conclude therefore that appellants in these cases do not use and have no need to use the one-year requirement for the governmental purposes suggested. Thus, even under traditional equal protection tests a classification of welfare applicants according to whether they have lived in the State for one year would seem irrational and unconstitutional. But, of course, the traditional criteria do not apply in these cases. Since the classification here touches on the fundamental right of interstate movement, its constitutionality must be judged by the stricter standard of whether it promotes a *compelling* state interest. Under this standard, the waiting period requirement clearly violates the Equal Protection Clause.

V.

Connecticut and Pennsylvania argue, however, that the constitutional challenge to the waiting period requirements must fail because Congress expressly approved the imposition of the requirement by the States as part of the jointly funded AFDC program. . . .

But even if we were to assume, *arguendo,* that Congress did approve the imposition of a one-year waiting period, it is the responsive *state* legislation which infringes constitutional rights. By itself § 402(b) has absolutely no restrictive effect. It is therefore not that statute but only the state requirements which pose the constitutional question.

Finally, even if it could be argued that the constitutionality of § 402(b) is somehow at issue here, it follows from what we have said that the provision, insofar as it permits the one-year waiting-period requirement, would be unconstitutional. Congress may not authorize the States to violate the Equal Protection Clause. Perhaps Congress could induce wider state participation in school construction if it authorized the use of joint funds for the building of segregated schools. But could it seriously be contended that Congress would be constitutionally justified in such authorization by the need to secure state cooperation? Congress is without power to enlist state cooperation in a joint federal-state program by legislation which authorizes the States to violate the Equal Protection Clause. Katzenbach v. Morgan, 384 U.S. 641, 651 (1966).

VI.

The waiting-period requirement in the District of Columbia Code . . . is also unconstitutional even though it was adopted by Congress as an exercise of federal power. In terms of federal power, the discrimination created by the one-year requirement violates the Due Process Clause of the Fifth Amendment. "[W]hile the Fifth Amendment contains no equal protection clause, it does forbid discrimination that is 'so unjustifiable as to be violative of due process.'" Schneider v. Rusk, 377 U.S. 163, 168 (1964); Bolling v. Sharpe, 347 U.S. 497 (1954). For the reasons we have stated in invalidating the Pennsylvania and Connecticut provisions, the District of Columbia provision is also invalid—the Due Process Clause of the Fifth Amendment forbids Congress from denying public assistance to poor persons otherwise eligible solely on the ground that they have not been residents of the District of Columbia for one year at the time their applications are filed.

. . .

Affirmed.

■ MR. JUSTICE STEWART, concurring.

In joining the opinion of the Court, I add a word in response to the dissent of my Brother Harlan, who, I think, has quite misapprehended what the Court's opinion says.

The Court today does *not* "pick out particular human activities, characterize them as 'fundamental,' and give them added protection. . . ." To the contrary, the Court simply recognizes, as it must, an established constitutional right, and gives to that right no less protection than the Constitution itself demands. . . .

■ MR. CHIEF JUSTICE WARREN, with whom MR. JUSTICE BLACK joins, dissenting.

In my opinion the issue before us can be simply stated: may Congress, acting under one of its enumerated powers, impose minimal nationwide residence requirements or authorize the States to do so? Since I believe that Congress does have this power and has constitutionally exercised it in these cases, I must dissent. . . .

■ MR. JUSTICE HARLAN, dissenting.

. . .

In upholding the equal protection argument, the Court has applied an equal protection doctrine of relatively recent vintage: the rule that statutory classifications which either are based upon certain "suspect" criteria or affect "fundamental rights" will be held to deny equal protection unless justified by a "compelling" governmental interest. . . .

The "compelling interest" doctrine, which today is articulated more explicitly than ever before, constitutes an increasingly significant exception to the long-established rule that a statute does not deny equal protection if it is rationally related to a legitimate governmental objective. The "compelling interest" doctrine has two branches. The branch which requires that classifications based upon "suspect" criteria be supported by a compelling interest apparently had its genesis in cases involving racial classifications, which have at least since Korematsu v. United States, 323 U.S. 214, 216 (1944), been regarded as inherently "suspect." The criterion of "wealth" apparently was added to the list of "suspects" as an alternative justification for the rationale in Harper v. Virginia Bd. of Elections, 383 U.S. 663, 668 (1966), in which Virginia's poll tax was struck down. The criterion of political allegiance may have been added in Williams v. Rhodes, 393 U.S. 23 (1968). Today the list apparently has been further enlarged to include classifications based upon recent interstate movement, and perhaps those based upon the exercise of *any* constitutional right, . . .

I think that this branch of the "compelling interest" doctrine is sound when applied to racial classifications, for historically the Equal Protection Clause was largely a product of the desire to eradicate legal distinctions founded upon race. However, I believe that the more recent extensions have been unwise. . . .

The second branch of the "compelling interest" principle is even more troublesome. For it has been held that a statutory classification is subject to the "compelling interest" test if the result of the classification may be to affect a "fundamental right," regardless of the basis of the classification. . . .

I think this branch of the "compelling interest" doctrine particularly unfortunate and unnecessary. It is unfortunate because it creates an exception which threatens to swallow the standard equal protection rule. Virtually every state statute affects important rights. This Court has repeatedly held, for example, that the traditional equal protection standard is applicable to statutory classifications affecting such fundamental matters as the right to pursue a particular occupation, the right to receive greater or smaller wages or to work more or less hours, and the right to inherit property. Rights such as these are in principle indistinguishable from those involved here, and to extend the "compelling interest" rule to all cases in which such rights are affected would go far toward making this Court a "super-legislature." This branch of the doctrine is also unnecessary. When the right affected is one assured by the federal Constitution, any infringement can be dealt with under the Due Process Clause. But when a statute affects only matters not mentioned in the federal Constitution and is not arbitrary or irrational, I must reiterate that I know of nothing which entitles this Court to pick out particular human activities, characterize them as "fundamental," and give them added protection under an unusually stringent equal protection test. . . .

Dunn v. Blumstein

405 U.S. 330 (1972).

In this case the Court upheld a challenge to a Tennessee law providing that in order to vote one must be a resident of the state for one year and of the county for three months before the election. The Court, in an opinion by Justice Marshall, held that the residence requirement had to meet the Shapiro compelling state interest test because (1) it burdened the right to vote, and (2) it burdened the right to travel. The aspects of the case dealing with voting were considered supra, p. 671. The Court responded to the state's argument that durational residence requirements do not abridge the right to travel because they neither seek to deter travel nor actually do deter travel as follows:

"This view represents a fundamental misunderstanding of the law. It is irrelevant whether disenfranchisement or denial of welfare is the more potent deterrent to travel. *Shapiro* did not rest upon a finding that denial of welfare actually deterred travel. Nor have other 'right to travel' cases in this Court always relied on the presence of actual deterrence. In *Shapiro* we explicitly stated that the compelling state interest test would be triggered by 'any classification which serves to *penalize* the exercise of that right [to travel]. . . .

"Of course it is true that the two individual interests affected by Tennessee's durational residence requirements are affected in different ways. Travel is permitted, but only at a price; voting is prohibited. The right to travel is merely penalized, while the right to vote is absolutely denied. But these differences are irrelevant for present purposes. . . .

"The right to travel is 'an *unconditional* personal right,' a right whose exercise may not be conditioned. . . . Durational residence laws impermissibly condition and penalize the right to travel by imposing their prohibitions on only those persons who have recently exercised that right. In the present case, such laws force a person who wishes to travel and change residences to choose between travel and the basic right to vote. . . . Absent a compelling state interest, a State may not burden the right to travel in this way."

The Court also restated what the State must show to justify a statute burdening the right to travel or the right to vote:

"It is not sufficient for the State to show that durational residence requirements further a very substantial state interest. In pursuing that important interest, the State cannot choose means which unnecessarily burden or restrict constitutionally protected activity. Statutes affecting constitutional rights must be drawn with 'precision,' . . . and must be 'tailored' to serve their legitimate objectives. *Shapiro v. Thompson.* . . . And if there are other, reasonable ways to achieve those goals with a lesser burden on constitutionally protected activity, a State may not choose the way of greater interference. If it acts at all, it must choose 'less drastic means.' "

It then went on to hold that while the State had identified important and presumably "compelling" state interests—prevention of fraudulent voting and assuring knowledgeable voters—the durational residence requirement was not closely enough related to either of those interests.

Chief Justice Burger dissented. Justice Blackmun concurred in the result. Justices Powell and Rehnquist took no part in the decision.

Memorial Hospital v. Maricopa County
415 U.S. 250 (1974).

Applying *Shapiro* and *Dunn*, the Court held invalid an Arizona statute requiring a year's residence in a county as a condition to receiving nonemergency hospitalization or medical care at the county's expense. The challenge was brought by an indigent suffering from a chronic asthmatic and bronchial illness who suffered a severe respiratory attack within a month after he moved from New Mexico to Phoenix, Arizona. Justice Marshall's majority opinion said in part:

"The right of interstate travel has repeatedly been recognized as a basic constitutional freedom. Whatever its ultimate scope, however, the right to travel was involved in only a limited sense in *Shapiro.* The Court was there concerned only with the right to '[migrate], with intent to settle and abide' or, as the Court put it, 'to migrate, resettle, find a new job and start a new life.' Even a bona fide residence requirement would burden the right to travel, if travel meant merely movement. But, in *Shapiro,* the Court explained that '[t]he residence requirement and the one-year waiting-period requirement are distinct and independent prerequisites' for assistance and only the latter was held to be unconstitutional.... Later, in invalidating a durational residency requirement for voter registration on the basis of *Shapiro,* we cautioned that our decision was not intended to 'cast doubt on the validity of appropriately defined and uniformly applied bona fide residence requirements.' *Dunn v. Blumstein.* ...

The opinion later said:

"Although any durational residence requirement impinges to some extent on the right to travel, the Court in *Shapiro* did not declare such requirements to be *per se* unconstitutional. ...

"...

"Thus, *Shapiro* and *Dunn* stand for the proposition that a classification which 'operates to *penalize* those persons ... who have exercised their constitutional right of interstate migration,' must be justified by a compelling state interest.... Although any durational residency requirement imposes a potential cost on migration, the Court, in *Shapiro,* cautioned that some 'waiting-periods ... may not be penalties.' ... In *Dunn v. Blumstein,* supra, the Court found that the denial of the franchise, 'a fundamental political right,' ... was a penalty requiring application of the compelling state interest test. In *Shapiro,* the Court found denial of the basic 'necessities of life' to be a penalty. Nonetheless, the Court has declined to strike down state statutes requiring one year of residence as a condition to lower tuition at state institutions of higher education. [Citing Vlandis v. Kline, 412 U.S. 441, 452–453 n.9 (1973).]

"Whatever the ultimate parameters of the *Shapiro* penalty analysis, it is at least clear that medical care is as much 'a basic necessity of life' to an indigent as welfare assistance. And, governmental privileges or benefits necessary to basic sustenance have often been viewed as being of greater constitutional significance than less essential forms of governmental entitlements. See, e.g., *Shapiro,* supra; Goldberg v. Kelly, 397 U.S. 254, 264 (1970). . . . It would be odd, indeed, to find that the State of Arizona was required to afford Evaro welfare assistance to keep him from discomfort of inadequate housing or the pangs of hunger but could deny him the medical care necessary to relieve him from the wheezing and gasping for breath that attend his illness.

"...

"Not unlike the admonition of the Bible that, 'Ye shall have one manner of law, as well for the stranger as for one of your country.' Leviticus, 24:22, the right of interstate travel must be seen as insuring new residents the same right to vital government benefits and privileges in the States to which they migrate as are enjoyed by other residents. The State of Arizona's durational residency requirement for free medical care penalizes indigents for exercising their right to migrate to and settle in that State. Accordingly, the classification created by the residency requirement, 'unless shown to be necessary to promote a *compelling* [state] interest, is unconstitutional.' *Shapiro,* . . . (Emphasis original.)"

Using an analysis like that in *Shapiro,* Justice Marshall concluded that "[a]ppellees have not met their heavy burden of justification, nor demonstrated that the State, in pursuing legitimate objectives, has chosen means which do not unnecessarily impinge on constitutionally protected interests." Chief Justice Burger and Justice Blackmun concurred in the result.

Justice Douglas wrote separately to say that "[s]o far as interstate travel *per se* is considered, I share the doubts of my Brother Rehnquist" but that "in the setting of this case the invidious discrimination against the poor, Harper v. Virginia State Board of Elections, 383 U.S. 663 (1966), not the right to travel interstate is . . . the critical issue."

Justice Rehnquist dissented, saying in part:

"The legal question in this case is simply whether the State of Arizona has acted arbitrarily in determining that access to local hospital facilities for nonemergency medical care should be denied to persons until they have established residency for one year. The impediment which this quite rational determination has placed on petitioner Evaro's 'right to travel' is so remote as to be negligible: so far as the record indicates Evaro moved from New Mexico to Arizona three years ago and has remained ever since. The eligibility requirement has not the slightest resemblance to the actual barriers to the right of free ingress and egress protected by the Constitution, and struck down in cases such as *Crandall* and *Edwards.* And unlike *Shapiro* it does not involve an urgent need for the necessities of life or a benefit funded from current revenues to which the claimant may well have contributed. It is a substantial broadening of, and departure from, all of these holdings, all the more remarkable for the lack of explanation which accompanies the result."

Sosna v. Iowa

419 U.S. 393, 95 S.Ct. 553, 42 L.Ed.2d 532 (1975).

■ MR. JUSTICE REHNQUIST delivered the opinion of the Court.

Appellant Carol Sosna married Michael Sosna on September 5, 1964, in Michigan. They lived together in New York between October 1967 and August 1971, after which date they separated but continued to live in New York. In August 1972, appellant moved to Iowa with her three children, and the following month she petitioned the District Court of Jackson County, Iowa, for a dissolution of her marriage. . . . The Iowa court dismissed the petition for lack of jurisdiction, finding that Michael Sosna was not a resident of Iowa and appellant had not been a resident of the State of Iowa for one year preceding the filing of her petition. In so doing the Iowa court applied the provisions of Iowa Code § 598.6 requiring that the petitioner in such an action be "for the last year a resident of the state."

Instead of appealing this ruling to the Iowa appellate courts, appellant filed a complaint in [federal court] asserting that Iowa's durational residency requirement for invoking its divorce jurisdiction violated the . . . Constitution. . . .

A three-judge court . . . held that the Iowa durational residency requirement was constitutional. . . . We . . . decide that this case is not moot, and [up]hold the Iowa durational residency requirement for divorce. . . .

The durational residency requirement . . . is a part of Iowa's comprehensive statutory regulation of domestic relations, an area that has long been regarded as a virtually exclusive province of the States. . . .

The imposition of a durational residency requirement for divorce is scarcely unique to Iowa, since 48 States impose such a requirement as a condition for maintaining an action for divorce. As might be expected, the periods vary among the States and range from six weeks to two years. The one-year period selected by Iowa is the most common length of time prescribed.

Appellant contends that the Iowa requirement of one year's residence is unconstitutional . . . because it establishes two classes of persons and discriminates against those who have recently exercised their right to travel to Iowa, thereby contravening the Court's holdings in Shapiro v. Thompson, 394 U.S. 618 (1969); Dunn v. Blumstein, 405 U.S. 330 (1972), and Memorial Hospital v. Maricopa County, 415 U.S. 250 (1974); . . .

State statutes imposing durational residency requirements were of course invalidated when imposed by States as a qualification for welfare payments, *Shapiro,* supra, for voting, *Dunn,* supra, and for medical care, *Maricopa County,* supra. But none of those cases intimated that the States might never impose durational residency requirements, and such a proposition was in fact expressly disclaimed. What those cases had in common was that the durational residency requirements they struck down were justified on the basis of budgetary or record-keeping considerations which were held insufficient to outweigh the constitutional claims of the individuals. But Iowa's divorce residency requirement is of a different stripe. Appellant was not irretrievably foreclosed from obtaining some part of what she sought, as was the case with the welfare recipients in *Shapiro,* the voters in *Dunn,* or the indigent patient in *Maricopa County*. She would eventually qualify for the same sort of adjudication which she demanded virtually upon her arrival in the State. Iowa's requirement delayed her access to the courts, but, by fulfilling it, a plaintiff could ultimately obtain the same opportunity for adjudication which she asserts ought to be hers at an earlier point in time.

Iowa's residency requirement may reasonably be justified on grounds other than purely budgetary considerations or administrative convenience. . . . A decree of divorce is not a matter in which the only interested parties are the State as a sort of "grantor," and a plaintiff such as appellant in the role of "grantee." Both spouses are obviously interested in the proceedings, since it will affect their marital status and very likely their property rights. Where a married couple has minor children, a decree of divorce would usually include provisions for their custody and support. With consequences of such moment riding on a divorce decree issued by its courts, Iowa may insist that one seeking to initiate such a proceeding have the modicum of attachment to the State required here.

Such a requirement additionally furthers the State's parallel interests in both avoiding officious intermeddling in matters in which another State has a paramount interest, and in minimizing the susceptibility of its own divorce decrees to collateral attack. A State such as Iowa may quite reasonably decide that it does not wish to become a divorce mill for unhappy spouses who have lived there as short a time as appellant had when she commenced her action in the state court after having long resided elsewhere. Until such time as Iowa is convinced that appellant intends to remain in the State, it lacks the "nexus between person and place of such permanence as to control the creation of legal relations and responsibilities of the utmost significance." Williams v. North Carolina, 325 U.S. 226, 229 (1945). Perhaps even more importantly, Iowa's interests extend beyond its borders and include the recognition of its divorce decrees by other States under the Full Faith and Credit Clause of the Constitution, Art. IV, § 1. For that purpose, this Court has often stated that "judicial power to grant a divorce—jurisdiction, strictly speaking—is founded on domicil." *Williams,*. . . . Where a divorce decree is entered after a finding of domicile in *ex parte* proceedings, this Court has held that the finding of domicile is not binding upon another State and may be disregarded in the face of "cogent evidence" to the contrary. . . . For that reason, the State asked to enter such a decree is entitled to insist that the putative divorce plaintiff satisfy something more than the bare minimum of constitutional requirements before a divorce may be granted. The State's decision to exact a one-year residency requirement as a matter of policy is therefore buttressed by a quite permissible inference that this requirement not only effectuates state substantive policy but likewise provides a greater safeguard against successful collateral attack than would a requirement of bona fide residence alone. This is precisely the sort of determination that a State in the exercise of its domestic relations jurisdiction is entitled to make.

We therefore hold that the state interest in requiring that those who seek a divorce from its courts be genuinely attached to the State, as well as a desire to insulate divorce decrees from the likelihood of collateral attack, requires a different resolution of the constitutional issue presented than was the case in *Shapiro,* supra, *Dunn,* supra, and *Maricopa County,* supra.

. . .

[The Court also held that the statute did not violate due process by invoking a permanent and irrebuttable presumption of non-residence.]

Affirmed.

■ MR. JUSTICE WHITE, dissenting.

. . .

Because I find that the case before the Court has become moot, I must respectfully dissent.

■ MR. JUSTICE MARSHALL, with whom MR. JUSTICE BRENNAN joins, dissenting.

The Court today departs sharply from the course we have followed in analyzing durational residency requirements since Shapiro v. Thompson, 394 U.S. 618 (1969). Because I think the principles set out in that case and its progeny compel reversal here, I respectfully dissent.

As we have made clear in *Shapiro* and subsequent cases, any classification that penalizes exercise of the constitutional right to travel is invalid unless it is justified by a compelling governmental interest. . . .

The Court's failure to address the instant case in these terms suggests a new distaste for the mode of analysis we have applied to this corner of equal protection law. In its stead, the Court has employed what appears to be an *ad hoc* balancing test, under which the State's putative interest in ensuring that its divorce plaintiffs establish some roots in Iowa is said to justify the one-year residency requirement. I am concerned not only about the disposition of this case, but also about the implications of the majority's analysis for other divorce statutes and for durational residency requirement cases in general.

Jones v. Helms

452 U.S. 412 (1981).

A Georgia statute provided that parental abandonment of a child is a misdemeanor, but is a felony if the parent thereafter leaves the State. The lower federal court held the statute invalid because it infringed upon the right to travel, and the State's interests could be protected by less drastic means. On appeal, the Supreme Court unanimously reversed. Justice Stevens' opinion for the Court concluded that defendant's criminal conduct "necessarily qualified his right" to travel interstate. He noted, moreover, that this case did not involve, as did earlier "right to travel" cases, disparate treatment of residents and non-residents, or old and new residents. The question was the narrower one whether a State could enhance criminal punishment if the offender left the State after committing the crime. "Thus, although a simple penalty for leaving a State is plainly impermissible, if departure aggravates the consequences of conduct that is otherwise punishable, the State may treat the entire sequence of events, from the initial offense to departure from the State, as more serious than its separate components."

Bona Fide Residence Requirements

In McCarthy v. Philadelphia Civil Service Commission, 424 U.S. 645 (1976), the Court summarily rejected a city fire department employee's challenge to a requirement that city employees be residents of the city. The per curiam opinion distinguished *Shapiro, Dunn,* and *Memorial Hospital:*

". . . Neither in those cases, nor in any others, have we questioned the validity of a condition placed upon municipal employment that a person be a resident *at the time* of his application. In this case appellant claims a constitutional right to be employed by the city of Philadelphia *while* he is living elsewhere. There is no support in our cases for such a claim.

"We have previously differentiated between a requirement of continuing residency and a requirement of prior residency of a given duration. Thus in *Shapiro,* . . . we stated '[t]he residence requirement and the one-year waiting-period requirement are distinct and independent prerequisites'. And in *Memorial Hospital,* . . . quoting *Dunn,* . . . the Court explained that *Shapiro* and *Dunn* did not question 'the validity of appropriately defined and uniformly applied bona fide residence requirements.'

"This case involves that kind of bona fide continuing residence requirement. The judgment of the Commonwealth Court of Pennsylvania is therefore affirmed."

In Martinez v. Bynum, 461 U.S. 321 (1983), the Supreme Court upheld on its face a Texas law that permits a school district to deny tuition-free admission to a minor who lives apart from a parent or guardian, if the minor's presence in the school district is for the primary purpose of attending public schools. The durational residence cases permit "bona fide residence requirements." In Vlandis v. Kline, 412 U.S. 441, 453–454

(1973), the Court had stated that a state's interest in preserving the right of residents to attend state universities on a preferential tuition basis permits a state to "establish such reasonable criteria for in-state status as to make virtually certain that students who are not, in fact, bona fide residents of the State, but who have come there solely for educational purposes, cannot take advantage of the in-state rates." A school district would thus be justified in denying admission to all minor children whose parents did not satisfy traditional criteria of residency. The Texas statute was not invalid because it went further and allowed enrollment by children whose parents were present in the district, without intent to remain indefinitely, or children who were present in the district for some purpose other than attending school. Justice Marshall dissented. (A fuller report in this case appears infra, p. 743.)

Saenz v. Roe

526 U.S. 489, 119 S.Ct. 1518, 143 L.Ed.2d 689 (1999).

[The report of this case appears infra, at p. 703.]

2. LENGTH OF STATE RESIDENCE DISTINCTIONS

Zobel v. Williams

457 U.S. 55, 102 S.Ct. 2309, 72 L.Ed.2d 672 (1982).

■ CHIEF JUSTICE BURGER, delivered the opinion of the Court.

The question . . . is whether a statutory scheme by which a State distributes income derived from its natural resources to the adult citizens of the State in varying amounts, based on the length of each citizen's residence, violates the equal protection rights of newer state citizens. The Alaska Supreme Court sustained the constitutionality of the statute. . . .

We reverse.

I

[Beginning with the 1967 discovery of large oil reserves on state-owned land, Alaska began to receive huge petroleum revenues, portions of which it put in a Permanent Fund. In 1980, the legislature enacted a dividend program to distribute annually a portion of the Fund's earnings directly to each citizen over 18, each of whom was entitled to one dividend unit for each year of residency subsequent to 1959, the first year of statehood.]

Appellants, residents of Alaska since 1978, brought this suit in 1980 challenging the dividend distribution plan as violative of their right to equal protection guarantees and their constitutional right to migrate to Alaska, to establish residency there and thereafter to enjoy the full rights of Alaska citizenship on the same terms as all other citizens of the State. . . .

II

The Alaska dividend distribution law is quite unlike the durational residency requirements we examined in Sosna v. Iowa, 419 U.S. 393 (1975); Memorial Hospital v. Maricopa County, 415 U.S. 250 (1974); Dunn v. Blumstein, 405 U.S. 330 (1972); and Shapiro v. Thompson, 394 U.S. 618 (1969). . . .

The Alaska statute does not impose any threshold waiting period . . . [or] purport to establish a test of the *bona fides* of state residence. Instead, the dividend statute creates fixed, permanent distinctions between an ever increasing number of perpetual classes of concededly *bona fide* residents, based on how long they have been in the State.

Appellants established residence in Alaska two years before the dividend law was passed. The distinction they complain of is not one which the State makes between those who arrived in Alaska after the enactment of the dividend distribution law and those who were residents prior to its enactment. Appellants instead challenge the distinctions made within the class of persons who were residents when the dividend scheme was enacted in 1980. The distinctions appellants attack include the preference given to persons who were residents when Alaska became a State in 1959 over all those who have arrived since then, as well as the distinctions made between all *bona fide* residents who settled in Alaska at different times during the 1959 to 1980 period.[5]

. . . Appellants claim that the distinctions made by the Alaska law should be subjected to the higher level of scrutiny applied to the durational residency requirements in Shapiro v. Thompson, supra and Memorial Hospital v. Maricopa County, supra. The State, on the other hand, asserts that the law need only meet the minimum rationality test. In any event, if the statutory scheme cannot pass even the minimal test proposed by the State, we need not decide whether any enhanced scrutiny is called for.

A

The State advanced and the Alaska Supreme Court accepted three purposes justifying the distinctions made by the dividend program: (a) creation of a financial incentive for individuals to establish and maintain residence in Alaska; (b) encouragement of prudent management of the Permanent Fund; and (c) apportionment of benefits in recognition of undefined "contributions of various kinds, both tangible and intangible, which residents have made during their years of residency."

As the Alaska Supreme Court apparently realized, the first two state objectives— creating a financial incentive for individuals to establish and maintain Alaska residence, and assuring prudent management of the Permanent Fund and the State's natural and mineral resources—are not rationally related to the distinctions Alaska seeks to make between newer residents and those who have been in the State since 1959. Assuming *arguendo* that granting increased dividend benefits for each year of continued Alaska residence might give some residents an incentive to stay in the state in order to reap increased dividend benefits in the future, the State's interest is not in any way served by granting greater dividends to persons for their residency during the 21 years prior to the enactment.

Nor does the State's purpose of furthering the prudent management of the Permanent Fund and the state's resources support retrospective application of its plan to the date of statehood. . . . Even if we assume that the state interest is served by increasing the dividend for each year of residency beginning with the date of enactment, is it rationally served by granting greater dividends in varying amounts to those who resided in Alaska during the 21 years prior to enactment? We think not.

The last of the State's objectives—to reward citizens for past contributions—alone was relied upon by the Alaska Supreme Court to support the retrospective application of the law to 1959. However, that objective is not a legitimate state purpose. A similar "past contributions" argument was made and rejected in *Shapiro v. Thompson* . . . .

---

[5] . . .

The statute does not involve the kind of discrimination which the Privileges and Immunities Clause of Art. IV was designed to prevent. That Clause "was designed to insure to a citizen of State A who ventures into State B the same privileges which the citizens of State B enjoy." Toomer v. Witsell, 334 U.S. 385, 395 (1948). The Clause is thus not applicable to this case.

Similarly, in Vlandis v. Kline, 412 U.S. 441 (1973), we noted that "apportion[ment] of tuition rates on the basis of old and new residency ... would give rise to grave problems under the Equal Protection Clause of the Fourteenth Amendment."

If the States can make the amount of a cash dividend depend on length of residence, what would preclude varying university tuition on a sliding scale based on years of residence—or even limiting access to finite public facilities, eligibility for student loans, for civil service jobs, or for government contracts by length of domicile? Could States impose different taxes based on length of residence? Alaska's reasoning could open the door to state apportionment of other rights, benefits and services according to length of residency. It would permit the states to divide citizens into expanding numbers of permanent classes. Such a result would be clearly impermissible.

B

We need not consider whether the State could enact the dividend program prospectively only. . . .

III

. . .

We hold that the Alaska dividend distribution plan violates the ... Equal Protection Clause. . . . [T]he judgment ... is reversed and the case is remanded for further proceedings not inconsistent with this opinion.

■ JUSTICE BRENNAN, with whom JUSTICE MARSHALL, JUSTICE BLACKMUN, and JUSTICE POWELL join, concurring.

I ... agree ... that the retrospective aspects of Alaska's dividend-distribution law are not rationally related to a legitimate state purpose. I write separately only to emphasize that the pervasive discrimination embodied in the Alaska distribution scheme ... might well preclude even the prospective operation of Alaska's scheme.

. . .

. . . In my view, it is difficult to escape from the recognition that underlying any scheme of classification on the basis of duration of residence, we shall almost invariably find the unstated premise that "some citizens are more equal than others." We rejected that premise and, I believe, implicitly rejected most forms of discrimination based upon length of residence, when we adopted the Equal Protection Clause.

■ JUSTICE O'CONNOR, concurring in the judgment.

. . . The Court's ... holding depends on the assumption that Alaska's desire "to reward citizens for past contributions ... is not a legitimate state purpose." Nothing in the Equal Protection Clause itself, however, declares this objective illegitimate. Instead, as a full reading of Shapiro v. Thompson, 394 U.S. 618 (1969) and Vlandis v. Kline, 412 U.S. 441 (1973), reveals, the Court has rejected this objective only when its implementation would abridge an interest in interstate travel or migration.

I respectfully suggest ... that ... [a] desire to compensate citizens for their prior contributions is neither inherently invidious nor irrational. . . .

. . . Stripped to its essentials, the plan denies non-Alaskans settling in the State the same privileges afforded longer-term residents. The Privileges and Immunities Clause of Article IV, which guarantees "[t]he Citizens of each State ... all Privileges and Immunities of Citizens in the several States," addresses just this type of discrimination. Accordingly, I would measure Alaska's scheme against the principles implementing the Privileges and Immunities Clause. In addition to resolving the particular problems raised by Alaska's scheme, this analysis supplies a needed foundation for many of the "right to travel" claims discussed in the Court's prior opinions.

I

. . .

It could be argued that Alaska's scheme does not trigger the Privileges and Immunities Clause because it discriminates among classes of residents, rather than between residents and nonresidents. This argument, however, misinterprets the force of Alaska's distribution system. . . . Each group of citizens who migrated to Alaska in the past, or chooses to move there in the future, lives in the State on less favorable terms than those who arrived earlier. The circumstance that some of the disfavored citizens already live in Alaska does not negate the fact that "the citizen of State A who ventures into [Alaska]" to establish a home labors under a continuous disability.

. . . [O]ur prior opinions describe the proper standard of review. . . .

Once the Court ascertains that discrimination burdens an "essential activity," it will [assess] . . . the discrimination under a two-part test. First, there must be "something to indicate that noncitizens constitute a peculiar source of the evil at which the statute is aimed." Hicklin v. Orbeck, 437 U.S. 518, 525–526 (1978) (quoting Toomer v. Witsell, 334 U.S. 385, 398 (1948)). Second, the Court must find a "substantial relationship" between the evil and the discrimination practiced against the noncitizens.

Certainly the right infringed in this case is "fundamental." Alaska's statute burdens those nonresidents who choose to settle in the State. It is difficult to imagine a right more essential to the Nation as a whole than the right to establish residence in a new State. . . .

Alaska has not shown that its new residents are the "peculiar source" of any evil addressed by its disbursement scheme. . . .

Even if new residents were the peculiar source of these evils, Alaska has not chosen a cure that bears a "substantial relationship" to the malady. . . .

For these reasons, I conclude that Alaska's disbursement scheme violates Article IV's Privileges and Immunities Clause. I thus reach the same destination as the Court, but along a course that more precisely identifies the evils of the challenged statute.

. . .

■ Justice Rehnquist, dissenting.

Alaska's dividend distribution scheme . . . being in the nature of economic regulation, I am at a loss to see the rationality behind the Court's invalidation of it as a denial of equal protection. This Court has long held that state economic regulations are presumptively valid, and violate the Fourteenth Amendment only in the rarest of circumstances. . . .

. . . [T]he illegitimacy of a State's recognizing the past contributions of its citizens has been established by the Court only in certain cases considering an infringement of the right to travel, and the majority itself rightly declines to apply the strict scrutiny analysis of those right-to-travel cases. The distribution scheme at issue in this case impedes no person's right to travel to and settle in Alaska; if anything, the prospect of receiving annual cash dividends would encourage immigration to Alaska. The State's third justification cannot, therefore, be dismissed simply by quoting language about its legitimacy from right-to-travel cases which have no relevance to the question before us.

. . .

Attorney General of New York v. Soto-Lopez

476 U.S. 898, 106 S.Ct. 2317, 90 L.Ed.2d 899 (1986).

■ JUSTICE BRENNAN announced the judgment of the Court and delivered an opinion in which JUSTICE MARSHALL, JUSTICE BLACKMUN, and JUSTICE POWELL joined.

The question ... is whether a preference in civil service employment opportunities offered by the State of New York solely to resident veterans who lived in the State at the time they entered military service violates the constitutional rights of resident veterans who lived outside the State when they entered military service.

I

[The preference—which added points to examination scores for New York residents who are honorably-discharged veterans, served during time of war, and were residents of New York when they entered military service—could be used only once, either for original hiring or for one promotion. Appellees claimed to have met all the eligibility criteria for the preference except New York residence when they entered the Army. They sued after being denied the preference,] alleging that the requirement of residence when they joined the military violated the Equal Protection Clause of the Fourteenth Amendment and the constitutionally protected right to travel. . . .

The District Court dismissed appellees' complaint. . . . The . . . Second Circuit reversed[, holding] that the prior residence requirement . . . offends both the Equal Protection Clause and the right to travel. . . . We affirm.

"[F]reedom to travel throughout the United States has long been recognized as a basic right under the Constitution." *Dunn v. Blumstein.* . . . And, it is clear that the freedom to travel includes the "freedom to enter and abide in any State in the Union." *Dunn* . . .

The textual source of the constitutional right to travel, or, more precisely, the right of free interstate migration . . . has been variously assigned to the Privileges and Immunities Clause of Art. IV, . . . to the Commerce Clause, . . . and to the Privileges and Immunities Clause of the Fourteenth Amendment . . . . The right has also been inferred from the federal structure of government adopted by our Constitution. . . . Whatever its origin, the right to migrate is firmly established and has been repeatedly recognized by our cases. See, e.g., Hooper v. Bernalillo County Assessor, 472 U.S. 612, 618, n. 6 (1985); *Zobel,* . . .

A state law implicates the right to travel when it actually deters such travel, . . . when impeding travel is its primary objective, . . . , or when it uses " 'any classification which serves to penalize the exercise of that right.' " . . . Our right to migrate cases have principally involved the latter, indirect manner of burdening the right. More particularly, our recent cases have dealt with state laws that, by classifying residents according to the time they established residence, resulted in the unequal distribution of rights and benefits among otherwise qualified bona fide residents.[3]

Because the creation of different classes of residents raises equal protection concerns, we have also relied upon the Equal Protection Clause in these cases. Whenever a state law infringes a constitutionally protected right, we undertake intensified equal protection scrutiny of that law. . . . Thus, in several cases, we asked expressly whether the distinction drawn by the State between older and newer residents burdens the right to migrate. Where we found such a burden, we required

---

[3] We have always carefully distinguished between bona fide residence requirements, which seek to differentiate between residents and nonresidents, and residence requirements, such as durational, fixed date, and fixed point residence requirements, which treat established residents differently based on the time they migrated into the State. . . .

the State to come forward with a compelling justification. . . . In other cases, where we concluded that the contested classifications did not survive even rational basis scrutiny, we had no occasion to inquire whether enhanced scrutiny was appropriate. *Hooper,* supra; *Zobel,* supra. The analysis in all of these cases, however, is informed by the same guiding principle—the right to migrate protects residents of a State from being disadvantaged, or from being treated differently, simply because of the timing of their migration, from other similarly situated residents.. . .

. . .

Our task . . . is first to determine whether New York's restriction of its civil service preference . . . operates to penalize those persons who have exercised their right to migrate. If we find that it does, appellees must prevail unless New York can demonstrate that its classification is necessary to accomplish a compelling state interest. . . .

III

A

In previous cases, we have held that even temporary deprivations of very important benefits and rights can operate to penalize migration. For example, in *Shapiro,* supra, and in *Memorial Hospital,* supra, we found that recently arrived indigent residents were deprived of life's necessities by durational residence requirements for welfare assistance and for free, nonemergency medical care, respectively, which were available to other poor residents. In *Dunn,* supra, we held that new residents were denied a basic right by a durational residence requirement for establishing eligibility to vote. The fact that these deprivations were temporary did not offset the Court's conclusions that they were so severe and worked such serious inequities among otherwise qualified residents that they effectively penalized new residents for the exercise of their rights to migrate.

More recently, in Hooper v. Bernalillo, 472 U.S. 612 (1985), and *Zobel v. Williams,* supra, we struck down state laws that created permanent distinctions among residents based on the length or timing of their residence in the State. At issue in *Hooper* was a New Mexico statute that granted a tax exemption to Vietnam veterans who resided in the State before May 8, 1976. *Zobel* concerned an Alaska statute granting residents one state mineral income dividend unit for each year of residence subsequent to 1959. Because we employed rational basis equal protection analysis in those cases, we did not face directly the question whether the contested laws operated to penalize interstate migration. Nonetheless, the conclusion that they did penalize migration may be inferred from our determination that "the Constitution will not tolerate a state benefit program that 'creates fixed, permanent distinctions . . . between . . . classes of concededly bona fide residents, based on how long they have been in the State.' " *Hooper* . . . (quoting *Zobel* . . .).

. . . While the benefit sought here may not rise to the same level of importance as the necessities of life and the right to vote, it is unquestionably substantial. The award of bonus points can mean the difference between winning or losing civil service employment, with its attendant job security, decent pay, and good benefits. . . . Furthermore, appellees have been permanently deprived of the veterans' credits that they seek. . . . Such a permanent deprivation of a significant benefit, based only on the fact of nonresidence at a past point in time, clearly operates to penalize appellees for exercising their rights to migrate.

B

New York offers four interests in justification of its fixed point residence requirement: (1) the encouragement of New York residents to join the armed services;

(2) the compensation of residents for service in time of war by helping these veterans reestablish themselves upon coming home; (3) the inducement of veterans to return to New York after wartime service; and (4) the employment of a "uniquely valuable class of public servants" who possess useful experience acquired through their military service. All four justifications fail to withstand heightened scrutiny on a common ground—each of the State's asserted interests could be promoted fully by granting bonus points to *all* otherwise qualified veterans. New York residents would still be encouraged to join the services. Veterans who served in time of war would be compensated. And, both former New Yorkers and prior residents of other States would be drawn to New York after serving the Nation, thus providing the State with an even larger pool of potentially valuable public servants.

. . .

IV

. . . The State has not met its heavy burden of proving that it has selected a means of pursuing a compelling state interest which does not impinge unnecessarily on constitutionally protected interests. Consequently, we conclude that New York's veterans' preference violates appellees' constitutionally protected rights to migrate and to equal protection of the law.

. . .

Affirmed.

■ CHIEF JUSTICE BURGER, concurring in the judgment.

. . . Both *Zobel* and *Hooper* held that the classifications used by the States to award preferences to certain citizens failed to pass a rational basis test *under the Equal Protection Clause.* As a result, we had no occasion to reach the issues whether the classifications would survive heightened scrutiny or whether the right to travel was violated. . . .

. . .

I would affirm . . . based on our reasoning and holdings in *Hooper* and *Zobel,* rather than adding dicta concerning the right to travel.

■ JUSTICE WHITE, concurring in the judgment.

I agree with Justice O'Connor that the right to travel is not sufficiently implicated in this case to require heightened scrutiny. . . . But I agree with The Chief Justice that the New York statute at issue denies equal protection of the laws because the classification it employs is irrational. . . .[a]

■ JUSTICE O'CONNOR, with whom JUSTICE REHNQUIST and JUSTICE STEVENS join, dissenting.

. . . Because I believe that New York's veterans' preference scheme is not constitutionally offensive under the Equal Protection Clause, does not penalize some free-floating "right to migrate," and does not violate the Privileges and Immunities Clause of Art. IV, § 2, of the Constitution, I dissent.

I

. . .

In pursuing [its] new dual analysis, the Court simply rejects the equal protection approach the Court has previously employed in similar cases, . . . without bothering to explain why its novel use of both "right to migrate" analysis and strict equal protection scrutiny is more appropriate, necessary or doctrinally coherent. . . .

---

[a]   A dissent by Justice Stevens is omitted.

. . .

. . . I adhere to my belief that the Privileges and Immunities Clause of Art. IV, § 2, of the Constitution supplies the relevant basis for analysis in evaluating claims like appellees', where the principal allegation is that the state scheme impermissibly distinguishes between state residents, allegedly imposing a relative burden on those who have more recently exercised their right to establish residence in the State. See Zobel v. Williams . . . (O'Connor, J., concurring in judgment). I also continue to believe that a State's desire to compensate its citizens for their prior contributions is "neither inherently invidious nor irrational," either under the Court's "right to migrate" or under some undefined, substantive component of the Equal Protection Clause. . . . This case presents one of those instances in which the recognition of state citizens' past sacrifices constitutes a valid state interest that does not infringe any constitutionally protected interest, including the fundamental right to settle in another State which is protected by the Privileges and Immunities Clause of Art. IV, § 2. . . .

II

. . .

The New York law certainly does not directly restrict or burden appellees' freedom to move to New York and to establish residence there by imposing discriminatory fees, taxes, or other direct restraints. . . .

[And] the New York scheme does not effectively penalize those who exercise their fundamental right to settle in the State of their choice by requiring newcomers to accept a status inferior to that of all oldtime residents of New York upon their arrival. . . . Those veterans who were not New York residents when they joined the [military], who subsequently move to New York, and who endeavor to secure civil service employment are treated exactly the same as the vast majority of New York citizens; they are in no sense regarded as "second-class citizens" when compared with the vast majority of New Yorkers or even the majority of the candidates against whom they must compete in obtaining civil employment. . . .

. . . Moreover, the preference only increases the possibility of securing a civil service appointment; it does not guarantee it. Those newly arrived veterans who achieve a sufficiently high score on the exam may not be disadvantaged at all by the preference program; conversely, the chances of those who receive a very low score may not be affected by the fact that their competitors received bonus points. Finally, the bonus program is a one-time benefit. . . . Thus, . . . appellees are not forced to labor under a "continuous disability" by comparison even to this discrete group of New York citizens. . . .

. . .

In sum, finding that this scheme in theory or practical effect constitutes a "penalty" on appellees' fundamental right to settle in New York or on their "right to migrate" seems to me ephemeral, and completely unnecessary to safeguard the constitutional purpose of "maintaining a Union rather than a mere 'league of States.'" . . . [H]eightened scrutiny, either under the "right to migrate" or the Equal Protection Clause is inappropriate.

Under rational basis review, New York's program plainly passes constitutional muster. . . .

. . .

Whether this issue is tested under the "right to migrate," the Equal Protection Clause, or the Privileges and Immunities Clause of Art. IV, § 2, something more than the minimal effect on the right to travel or migrate that exists in this case must be required to trigger heightened scrutiny or the Court's right to travel analysis will swallow all the traditional deference shown to state economic and social regulation. . . .[a]

Saenz v. Roe

526 U.S. 489, 119 S.Ct. 1518, 143 L.Ed.2d 689 (1999).

■ JUSTICE STEVENS delivered the opinion of the Court.

In 1992, California enacted a statute limiting the maximum welfare benefits . . . payable to a family that has resided in the State for less than 12 months to the amount payable by the State of the family's prior residence. The questions presented . . . are whether the 1992 statute was constitutional when . . . enacted and, if not, whether an amendment to the Social Security Act enacted by Congress in 1996 affects that determination.

I

. . .

. . . [I]n order to make a relatively modest reduction in its vast welfare budget, the California Legislature enacted § 11450.03 . . . [I]n order to qualify for federal reimbursement, § 11450.03 required [federal] approval[, which California purportedly secured in] October 1992 . . . .

. . . [T]hree California residents . . . challeng[ed] the constitutionality of the durational residency requirement[, each] alleg[ing] that she had recently moved to California to live with relatives in order to escape abusive family circumstances [and] that her monthly AFDC grant for the ensuing 12 months would be substantially lower under § 11450.03 than if the statute were not in effect. . . .

The District Court . . . preliminarily enjoined implementation of the statute. The Court of Appeals summarily affirmed. . . .

We . . . were . . . unable to reach the merits because the . . . approval of § 11450.03 had been invalidated in a separate proceeding . . . . § 11450.03 remained inoperative until after Congress enacted the Personal Responsibility and Work Opportunity Reconciliation Act of 1996 (PRWORA) . . . .

PRWORA replaced the AFDC program with TANF [Temporary Assistance to Needy Families]. The new statute expressly authorizes any State that receives a block grant under TANF to "apply to a family the rules (including benefit amounts) of the [TANF] program . . . of another State if the family has moved to the State from the other State and has resided in the State for less than 12 months." 42 U.S.C. § 604(c) . . . . With this federal statutory provision in effect, California no longer needed specific approval from the Secretary to implement § 11450.03. . . .

. . . [Under the California rules,] the lower level of benefits applies regardless of whether the family was on welfare in the State of prior residence and regardless of the family's motive for moving to California. The instructions also explain that the residency requirement is inapplicable to families that recently arrived from another country.

II

[T]his action . . . also challeng[es] the constitutionality of PRWORA's approval of the durational residency requirement. . . .

. . .

---

[a] See generally Cohen, *Equal Treatment for Newcomers: The Core Meaning of National and State Citizenship,* 1 Const.Commentary 9 (1984).

. . . [The District Court] again enjoined the implementation of the statute. [T]he Court of Appeals affirmed. . . . We now affirm.

. . .

IV

The "right to travel" discussed in our cases embraces at least three different components. It protects the right of a citizen of one State to enter and to leave another State, the right to be treated as a welcome visitor rather than an unfriendly alien when temporarily present in the second State, and, for those travelers who elect to become permanent residents, the right to be treated like other citizens of that State.

. . . Given that § 11450.03 imposed no obstacle to respondents' entry into California, we think the State is correct when it argues that the statute does not directly impair the exercise of the right to free interstate movement. For the purposes of this case, therefore, we need not identify the source of that particular right in the text of the Constitution. The right of "free ingress and regress to and from" neighboring States, which was expressly mentioned in the text of the Articles of Confederation, may simply have been "conceived from the beginning to be a necessary concomitant of the stronger Union the Constitution created." Id., at 758.

The second component of the right to travel is, however, expressly protected by the . . . first sentence of Article IV, § 2, [which] provides:

"The Citizens of each State shall be entitled to all Privileges and Immunities of Citizens in the several States."

Thus, by virtue of a person's state citizenship, a citizen of one State who travels in other States, intending to return home at the end of his journey, is entitled to enjoy the "Privileges and Immunities of Citizens in the several States" that he visits. . . . Permissible justifications for discrimination between residents and nonresidents[, however,] are simply inapplicable to a nonresident's exercise of the right to move into another State and become a resident of that State.

What is at issue in this case, then, is this third aspect of the right to travel—the right of the newly arrived citizen to the same privileges and immunities enjoyed by other citizens of the same State. That right is protected not only by the new arrival's status as a state citizen, but also by her status as a citizen of the United States. That additional source of protection is plainly identified in the opening words of the Fourteenth Amendment:

"All persons born or naturalized in the United States, and subject to the jurisdiction thereof, are citizens of the United States and of the State wherein they reside. No State shall make or enforce any law which shall abridge the privileges or immunities of citizens of the United States; . . . ."

Despite fundamentally differing views concerning the coverage of the Privileges or Immunities Clause of the Fourteenth Amendment, most notably expressed in the majority and dissenting opinions in the Slaughter-House Cases, 16 Wall. 36 (1872), it has always been common ground that this Clause protects the third component of the right to travel. Writing for the majority in the *Slaughter-House Cases*, Justice Miller explained that one of the privileges conferred by this Clause "is that a citizen of the United States can, of his own volition, become a citizen of any State of the Union by a *bona fide* residence therein, with the same rights as other citizens of that State." . . . That newly arrived citizens "have two political capacities, one state and one federal," adds special force to their claim that they have the same rights as others who share their citizenship. Neither mere rationality nor some intermediate standard of review should be used to judge the constitutionality of a state rule that discriminates against some of its citizens because they have been domiciled in the State for less than a year.

The appropriate standard may be more categorical than that articulated in *Shapiro*, . . . but it is surely no less strict.

V

Because this case involves discrimination against citizens who have completed their interstate travel, the State's argument that its welfare scheme affects the right to travel only "incidentally" is beside the point. . . . [S]ince the right to travel embraces the citizen's right to be treated equally in her new State of residence, the discriminatory classification is itself a penalty.

It is undisputed that respondents . . . are citizens of California and that their need for welfare benefits is unrelated to the length of time that they have resided in California. We thus have no occasion to consider what weight might be given to a citizen's length of residence if the bona fides of her claim to state citizenship were questioned. Moreover, because whatever benefits they receive will be consumed while they remain in California, there is no danger that recognition of their claim will encourage citizens of other States to establish residency for just long enough to acquire some readily portable benefit, such as a divorce or a college education, that will be enjoyed after they return to their original domicile. See, e.g., Sosna v. Iowa, 419 U.S. 393 (1975); Vlandis v. Kline, 412 U.S. 441 (1973).

The classifications challenged in this case—and there are many—are defined entirely by (a) the period of residency in California and (b) the location of the prior residences of the disfavored class members. The favored class of beneficiaries includes all eligible California citizens who have resided there for at least one year, plus those new arrivals who last resided in another country or in a State that provides benefits at least as generous as California's. Thus, within the broad category of citizens who resided in California for less than a year, there are many who are treated like lifetime residents. And within the broad sub-category of new arrivals who are treated less favorably, there are many smaller classes whose benefit levels are determined by the law of the States from whence they came. To justify § 11450.03, California must therefore explain not only why it is sound fiscal policy to discriminate against those who have been citizens for less than a year, but also why it is permissible to apply such a variety of rules within that class.

. . .

Disavowing any desire to fence out the indigent, California has instead advanced an entirely fiscal justification for its multitiered scheme. The enforcement of § 11450.03 will save the State approximately $10.9 million a year. The question is not whether such saving is a legitimate purpose but whether the State may accomplish that end by the discriminatory means it has chosen. An evenhanded, across-the-board reduction of about 72 cents per month for every beneficiary would produce the same result. But our negative answer to the question does not rest on the weakness of the State's purported fiscal justification. It rests on the fact that the Citizenship Clause of the Fourteenth Amendment expressly equates citizenship with residence: "That Clause does not provide for, and does not allow for, degrees of citizenship based on length of residence." *Zobel*, 457 U.S., at 69. It is equally clear that the Clause does not tolerate a hierarchy of 45 subclasses of similarly situated citizens based on the location of their prior residence.[20] Thus § 11450.03 is doubly vulnerable: Neither the duration of respondents' California residence, nor the identity of their prior States of residence, has any relevance to their need for benefits. Nor do those factors bear any relationship

---

[20] See Cohen, Discrimination Against New State Citizens: An Update, 11 Const. Comm. 73, 79 (1994) ("[J]ust as it would violate the Constitution to deny these new arrivals state citizenship, it would violate the Constitution to concede their citizenship in name only while treating them as if they were still citizens of other states").

to the State's interest in making an equitable allocation of the funds to be distributed among its needy citizens. . . . In short, the State's legitimate interest in saving money provides no justification for its decision to discriminate among equally eligible citizens.

VI

The question that remains is whether congressional approval of durational residency requirements in the 1996 amendment to the Social Security Act somehow resuscitates the constitutionality of § 11450.03. That question is readily answered, for we have consistently held that Congress may not authorize the States to violate the Fourteenth Amendment. Moreover, the protection afforded to the citizen by the Citizenship Clause of that Amendment is a limitation on the powers of the National Government as well as the States.

. . .

Citizens of the United States, whether rich or poor, have the right to choose to be citizens "of the State wherein they reside." U.S. Const., Amdt. 14, § 1. The States, however, do not have any right to select their citizens. The Fourteenth Amendment, like the Constitution itself, was, as Justice Cardozo put it, "framed upon the theory that the peoples of the several states must sink or swim together, and that in the long run prosperity and salvation are in union and not division." Baldwin v. G.A.F. Seelig, Inc., 294 U.S. 511, 523 (1935).

. . .

■ CHIEF JUSTICE REHNQUIST, with whom JUSTICE THOMAS joins, dissenting.

The Court today breathes new life into the previously dormant Privileges or Immunities Clause of the Fourteenth Amendment . . . to strike down what I believe is a reasonable measure falling under the head of a "good-faith residency requirement."
. . .

I

. . . The right to travel clearly . . . prohibits States from impeding the free interstate passage of citizens. . . . The Court wisely holds that because . . . § 11450.03 . . . imposes no obstacle to respondents' entry into California, the statute does not infringe upon the right to travel. . . .

I also have no difficulty with aligning the right to travel with the protections afforded by the Privileges and Immunities Clause of Article IV, § 2, to nonresidents who enter other States "intending to return home at the end of [their] journey." . . . [T]his Clause [also] has no application here, because respondents expressed a desire to stay in California and become citizens of that State. . . .

Finally, I agree . . . that a "citizen of the United States can, of his own volition, become a citizen of any State of the Union by a *bona fide* residence therein, with the same rights as other citizens of that State." Slaughter-House Cases, 16 Wall. 36, 80 (1872).

But I cannot see how the right to become a citizen of another State is a necessary "component" of the right to travel, or why the Court tries to marry these separate and distinct rights. A person is no longer "traveling" in any sense of the word when he finishes his journey to a State which he plans to make his home. . . . The right to travel and the right to become a citizen are distinct, their relationship is not reciprocal, and one is not a "component" of the other. . . .

. . .

II

In unearthing from its tomb the right to become a state citizen and to be treated equally in the new State of residence, . . . the Court ignores a State's need to assure that only persons who establish a bona fide residence receive the benefits provided to current residents of the State.

. . .

. . . States employ objective criteria such as durational residence requirements to test a new resident's resolve to remain before these new citizens can enjoy certain in-state benefits. Recognizing the practical appeal of such criteria, this Court has repeatedly sanctioned the State's use of durational residence requirements before new residents receive in-state tuition rates at state universities. . . . The Court has done the same in upholding a 1-year residence requirement for eligibility to obtain a divorce in state courts, see Sosna v. Iowa, 419 U.S. 393, 406–409 (1975), and in upholding political party registration restrictions that amounted to a durational residency requirement for voting in primary elections, see Rosario v. Rockefeller, 410 U.S. 752, 760–762 (1973).

If States can require individuals to reside in-state for a year before exercising the right to educational benefits, the right to terminate a marriage, or the right to vote in primary elections that all other state citizens enjoy, then States may surely do the same for welfare benefits. . . . The welfare payment here and in-state tuition rates are cash subsidies provided to a limited class of people, and California's standard of living and higher education system make both subsidies quite attractive. . . . [T]he same deference should be given in the case of welfare payments. . . .

. . . I do not understand how the absence of a link between need and length of residency bears on the State's ability to objectively test respondents' resolve to stay in California. There is no link between the need for an education or for a divorce and the length of residence, and yet States may use length of residence as an objective yardstick to channel their benefits to those whose intent to stay is legitimate.

. . . The impact of a large number of new residents who immediately seek welfare payments will have a far greater impact on a State's operating budget than the impact of new residents seeking to attend a state university. . . .

The Court tries to distinguish education and divorce benefits by contending that the welfare payment here will be consumed in California, while a college education or a divorce produces benefits that are "portable" and can be enjoyed after individuals return to their original domicile. But this "you can't take it with you" distinction is more apparent than real . . . . Welfare payments . . . will no doubt be spent in California, but the benefits from receiving this income and having the opportunity to become employed or employable will stick with the welfare recipient if they stay in California or go back to their true domicile. Similarly, tuition subsidies are "consumed" in-state but the recipient takes the benefits of a college education with him wherever he goes. A welfare subsidy is thus as much an investment in human capital as is a tuition subsidy, and their attendant benefits are just as "portable." . . .

. . .

Finally, Congress' express approval in 42 U.S.C. § 604(c) of durational residence requirements for welfare recipients . . . only goes to show the reasonableness of a law like § 11450.03. The National Legislature, where people from Mississippi as well as California are represented, has recognized the need to protect state resources in a time of experimentation and welfare reform. As States like California revamp their total welfare packages, . . . they should have the authority and flexibility to ensure that their new programs are not exploited. Congress has decided that it makes good welfare policy to give the States this power. California has reasonably exercised it through an objective, narrowly tailored residence requirement. I see nothing in the Constitution that should prevent the enforcement of that requirement.

■ JUSTICE THOMAS, with whom THE CHIEF JUSTICE joins, dissenting.

. . . In my view, the majority attributes a meaning to the Privileges or Immunities Clause that likely was unintended when the Fourteenth Amendment was enacted and ratified.

. . .

. . . [R]epeated references to [Corfield v. Coryell, 6 Fed. Cas. 546 (No. 3, 230) (CCED Pa. 1825), by Members of the 39th Congress], combined with what appears to be the historical understanding of the Clause's operative terms, supports the inference that, at the time the Fourteenth Amendment was adopted, people understood that "privileges or immunities of citizens" were fundamental rights, rather than every public benefit established by positive law. Accordingly, the majority's conclusion—that a State violates the Privileges or Immunities Clause when it "discriminates" against citizens who have been domiciled in the State for less than a year in the distribution of welfare benefits—appears contrary to the original understanding and is dubious at best.

. . . Because I believe that the demise of the Privileges or Immunities Clause has contributed in no small part to the current disarray of our Fourteenth Amendment jurisprudence, I would be open to reevaluating its meaning in an appropriate case. Before invoking the Clause, however, we should endeavor to understand what the framers of the Fourteenth Amendment thought that it meant. . . .

. . .

C. COURT ACCESS, WELFARE, AND THE POOR

Introduction. The Court has addressed arguments for heightened scrutiny based on both the nature of the liberty interest affected and the nature of the disadvantaged class in a number of contexts. Here the emphasis is on two sets of claims: that fees for representation in, and resolution of, legal disputes unconstitutionally have deprived the poor of access to appropriate judicial services; and that the poor unconstitutionally have been denied welfare benefits. As suggested in the Note on Wealth Classifications, supra p. 708, the issues generally arise in the context of differential impact on the poor, rather than in the context of explicit disadvantaging of them for being poor as such. Another common thread linking these two groups of cases is that the basis of the claims may be due process, equal protection, or both. The court access and welfare cases are presented together to allow for consideration of these complexities and connections.

The Rights of the Poor Defendant in the Criminal Justice System

During the past 40 years the Court has had before it a number of cases involving the criminal appellate process. It invalidated a series of state statutes that by requiring filing fees and transcripts barred access to appeal by a defendant who was indigent. See, e.g., Griffin v. Illinois, 351 U.S. 12 (1956); Draper v. Washington, 372 U.S. 487 (1963). In Douglas v. California, 372 U.S. 353 (1963), the Court also held that a state had a duty to furnish counsel to an indigent taking his first appeal as of right. In Ross v. Moffitt, 417 U.S. 600 (1974), however, the Court held that an indigent defendant was not entitled to have counsel provided in taking a discretionary appeal to the highest state court or in petitioning for certiorari in the United States Supreme Court.

The Court said:

"The precise rationale for the *Griffin* and *Douglas* line of cases has never been explicitly stated, some support being derived from the Equal Protection Clause of the Fourteenth Amendment, and some from the Due Process Clause of that Amendment. Neither clause by itself provides an entirely satisfactory basis for the result reached, each depending on a different inquiry which emphasizes different factors. 'Due process' emphasizes fairness between the State and the individual dealing with the State, regardless of how other individuals in the same situation may be treated. 'Equal protection,' on the other hand, emphasizes disparity in treatment by a State between classes of individuals whose situations are arguably indistinguishable."

The Court went on to hold that the denial of counsel in this case was constitutional under either clause. The Court concluded:

"[T]he fact that a particular service might be of benefit to an indigent defendant does not mean that the service is constitutionally required. The duty of the State under our cases is not to duplicate the legal arsenal that may be privately retained by a criminal defendant in a continuing effort to reverse his conviction, but only to assure the indigent defendant an adequate opportunity to present his claims fairly in the context of the State's appellate process."

Justices Douglas, Brennan, and Marshall dissented.

In Pennsylvania v. Finley, 481 U.S. 551 (1987) the Court reaffirmed *Ross v. Moffitt,* holding that the state has no constitutional duty under either the due process or equal protection clauses to provide counsel to a defendant in postconviction proceedings.

In Murray v. Giarratano, 492 U.S. 1 (1989), indigent prisoners sentenced to death argued that due process and the Eighth Amendment ban on cruel and unusual punishment required the state to provide them with counsel in postconviction proceedings. Four Justices (Rehnquist, White, O'Connor, and Scalia) rejected these claims outright, finding no greater obligation to provide counsel on collateral review in capital cases than in any others. Justice Kennedy concurred in the judgment, concluding that the due process requirement of "meaningful access" to court recognized in Bounds v. Smith, 430 U.S. 817 (1977), was satisfied in this case. He rejected a categorical requirement of appointed counsel in every case, because the meaningful court access obligation "can be satisfied in various ways[.]" He also asserted that "collateral relief proceedings are a central part of the review process for prisoners sentenced to death" and that the "complexity of our jurisprudence in this area . . . makes it unlikely that capital defendants will be able to file successful petitions for collateral relief without the assistance of persons learned in the law." In this case, however, he was not prepared to find a violation of the meaningful court access right, because "no prisoner on death row in Virginia has been unable to obtain counsel to represent him in postconviction proceedings, and Virginia's prison system is staffed with institutional lawyers to assist in preparing petitions for postconviction relief."

In dissent, Justice Stevens, joined by Justices Brennan, Marshall and Blackmun, would have required the "appointment of counsel for indigent death row inmates who wish to pursue state postconviction relief."

The Due Process and Equal Protection Clauses were held to require the appointment of counsel, however, in connection with preparing an application for discretionary leave to seek a first-tier appeal from a challenged conviction based on a guilty plea or a plea of nolo contendere. Halbert v. Michigan, 545 U.S. 605 (2005). Justice Ginsburg's majority opinion reasoned that a discretionary first appeal should be treated the same as a first appeal as of right under Douglas v. California, rather than as a discretionary subsequent appeal under Ross v. Moffitt, largely because of two features of Michigan's appellate process following plea-based convictions: "First, in determining how to dispose of an application for leave to appeal, Michigan's intermediate appellate court looks to the merits of the claims made in the application. Second, indigent defendants pursuing first-tier review in the Court of Appeals are generally ill equipped to represent themselves." Unlike discretionary review following a first appeal as of right, as in *Ross,* when the first appeal is discretionary a "first-tier review applicant, forced to act *pro se,* will face a record unreviewed by appellate counsel, and will be equipped with no attorney's brief prepared for, or reasoned opinion by, a court of review[,]" rendering "a *pro se* applicant's entitlement to seek leave to appeal . . . more formal than real." Justice Ginsburg also noted the low rates of inmate literacy and reasoned that "[n]avigating the appellate process without a lawyer's assistance is a perilous endeavor for a layperson, and well beyond the competence of individuals, like Halbert, who have little education, learning disabilities, and mental impairments."

Justice Thomas, joined by Justice Scalia and Chief Justice Rehnquist, dissented, finding the Court's decision "an unwarranted extension of" *Douglas.*

Access of the Poor to the Courts in Civil Cases

Boddie v. Connecticut
401 U.S. 371 (1971).

A welfare recipient challenged the state procedures under which a plaintiff in a divorce action was required to pay fees of about $60 in order to file the action. The Court discussed the case as one involving procedural due process, concluding "that the State's refusal to admit these appellants to its courts, the sole means in Connecticut for obtaining a divorce, must be regarded as the equivalent of denying them an opportunity to be heard upon their claimed right to a dissolution of their marriages, and, in the absence of a sufficient countervailing justification for the state's action, a denial of due process." Justices Douglas and Brennan in concurring opinions argued that the decision should have been rested on the equal protection clause because of discrimination against the poor. Justice Black dissented. For a discussion which preceded Boddie, see Goodpaster, The Integration of Equal Protection, Due Process Standards, and the Indigent's Right of Free Access to the Courts, 56 Iowa L.Rev. 223 (1970).

United States v. Kras
409 U.S. 434 (1973).

An indigent petitioner seeking voluntary bankruptcy sought to proceed without paying the fees (not more than $50 in this case) that were a condition of discharge. The district court found for the petitioner, relying on Boddie. The Supreme Court reversed. Justice Blackmun, speaking for the Court, said, in part:

"We agree with the Government that our decision in *Boddie* does not control the disposition of this case and that the District Court's reliance upon *Boddie* is misplaced.

"A. *Boddie* was based on the notion that a State cannot deny access, simply because of one's poverty, to a 'judicial proceeding [that is] the only effective means of resolving the dispute at hand.' 401 U.S., at 376. Throughout the opinion there is constant and recurring reference to Connecticut's exclusive control over the establishment, enforcement, and dissolution of the marital relationship. The Court emphasized that 'marriage involves interests of basic importance in our society' ibid., and spoke of 'state monopolization of the means for legally dissolving this relationship.' '[R]esort to the state courts [was] the only avenue to dissolution of . . . marriages,' which was 'not only the paramount dispute-settlement technique, but, in fact the only available one.' . . . In the light of all this, we concluded that resort to the judicial process was 'no more voluntary in a realistic sense than that of the defendant called upon to defend his interests in court' and we resolved the case 'in light of the principles enunciated in our due process decisions that delimit rights of defendants compelled to litigate their differences in the judicial forum.'

"B. The appellants in *Boddie,* on the one hand, and Robert Kras, on the other stand in materially different postures. The denial of access to the judicial forum in *Boddie* touched directly, as has been noted, on the marital relationship and on the associational interests that surround the establishment and dissolution of that relationship. On many occasions we have recognized the fundamental importance of these interests under our Constitution. See, for example, Loving v. Virginia, 388 U.S. 1 (1967). . . . The *Boddie* appellants' inability to dissolve their marriages seriously impaired their freedom to pursue other protected associational activities. Kras' alleged interest in the elimination of his debt burden, and in obtaining his desired new start in life, although important and so recognized by the enactment of the Bankruptcy Act, does not rise to the same constitutional level. See Dandridge v. Williams, 397 U.S. 471 (1970); Richardson v. Belcher, 404 U.S. 78 (1971). If Kras is not discharged in bankruptcy, his position will not be materially altered in any constitutional sense. Gaining or not gaining a discharge will effect no change with respect to basic necessities. We see no fundamental interest that is gained or lost depending on the availability of a discharge in bankruptcy.

"C. Nor is the government's control over the establishment, enforcement, or dissolution of debts nearly so exclusive as Connecticut's control over the marriage relationship in *Boddie.* In contrast with divorce, bankruptcy is not the only method available to a debtor for the adjustment of his legal relationship with his creditors. The utter exclusiveness of court access and court remedy, as has been noted, was a potent factor in *Boddie.* But '[w]ithout a prior judicial imprimatur, individuals may freely enter into and rescind commercial contracts. . . .' 401 U.S., at 376.

"However unrealistic the remedy may be in a particular situation, a debtor, in theory, and often in actuality, may adjust his debts by negotiated agreement with his creditors. At times the happy passage of the applicable limitation period, or other acceptable creditor arrangement, will provide the answer. Government's role with respect to the private commercial relationship is qualitatively and quantitatively different than its role in the establishment, enforcement, and dissolution of marriage.

"Resort to the Court, therefore, is not Kras' sole path to relief. *Boddie's* emphasis on exclusivity finds no counterpart in the bankrupt's situation. . . .

"D. We are also of the opinion that the filing fee requirement does not deny Kras the equal protection of the laws. Bankruptcy is hardly akin to free speech or marriage or to those other rights, so many of which are imbedded in the First Amendment, that the Court has come to regard as fundamental and that demand the lofty requirement of a compelling governmental interest before they may be significantly regulated. See Shapiro v. Thompson, 394 U.S. 618, 638 (1969). Neither does it touch upon what has been said to be the suspect criteria of race, nationality or alienage. Graham v. Richardson, 403 U.S. 365, 375 (1971). Instead, bankruptcy legislation is in the area of economics and social welfare. See Dandridge v. Williams, 397 U.S., at 484–485; Richardson v. Belcher, 404 U.S., at 81; Lindsey v. Normet, 405 U.S. 56, 74 (1972); Jefferson v. Hackney, 406 U.S. 535, 546 (1972). This being so, the applicable standard, in measuring the propriety of Congress' classification, is that of rational justification."

Justices Stewart, Douglas, and Marshall, dissented.

Ortwein v. Schwab

410 U.S. 656 (1973).

Ortwein, a recipient of old-age assistance, had his award reduced by the county welfare agency. As provided by state law he appealed to the state public welfare agency, which held a hearing and upheld the county agency's decision. Judicial review of the state agency decision was provided by law in the state appellate court. Ortwein sought to appeal without paying the $25 filing fee required in all civil cases filed in that court, alleging that he was indigent and unable to pay the fee. The state court denied this contention and refused to hear the appeal without the fee. The Supreme Court, in a per curiam opinion, affirmed, indicating that Kras rather than Boddie was the controlling precedent. The Court gave three principal reasons for its decision:

(1)   The interest in increased welfare benefits "has far less constitutional significance" than the inability to dissolve one's marriage except through the courts.

(2)   Ortwein did receive a pre-termination evidentiary hearing (the required due process minimum) not conditioned on the payment of a fee. "This Court has long recognized that, even in criminal cases, due process does not require a State to provide an appellate system."

(3)   The filing fee does not violate the Equal Protection Clause by discriminating against the poor. The litigation, which deals with welfare payments, is in the area of economics and social welfare. "No suspect classification, such as race, nationality, or alienage, is present. . . . The applicable standard is that of rational justification." The filing fee makes a contribution toward the cost of operating the court system, hence the "requirement of rationality is met."

Justices Stewart, Douglas, Brennan and Marshall dissented.

Little v. Streater

452 U.S. 1 (1981).

A unanimous Court concluded that refusal to furnish blood grouping tests to an indigent defendant in a civil paternity case denied that defendant "a meaningful opportunity to be heard" within the rationale of Boddie v. Connecticut. The Court relied on these factors: this action was not simply a civil proceeding between private parties since the child's mother was compelled to bring the action by state welfare officials and the State Attorney General was a party to the action; under State Law, the defendant's testimony in a paternity action, standing alone, was insufficient to overcome the mother's testimony.

Lassiter v. Department of Social Services

452 U.S. 18 (1981).

A majority of the Court concluded that due process required the appointment of counsel, for an indigent parent in a proceeding brought by the state to terminate parental status, only in appropriate circumstances. The majority held that in this case, those special factors requiring the appointment of counsel were not present in that: no allegations of neglect or abuse had been made; no expert witness testified; and the presence of counsel could not have made a determinative difference in the result. The four dissenting Justices (Blackmun, Brennan, Marshall and Stevens) argued that due process should require the appointment of counsel for indigents in all proceedings brought by the state to terminate parental rights.

M.L.B. v. S.L.J.

519 U.S. 102 (1996).

The Court held that Mississippi could not deny an indigent mother the right to appeal the sufficiency of the evidence supporting a trial court's decision terminating all her parental rights based on her inability to pay substantial costs for preparing the trial record necessary to enable effective appellate review. The majority observed "that the Court's decisions concerning access to judicial processes ... Reflect both equal protection and due process concerns[,]" but that most had relied on equal protection, "as M.L.B.'s plea heavily does, for ... Due process does not independently require that the state provide a right to appeal." Though not controlled by precedent because this was a civil case involving indigency related to appellate review rather than any court access at all, the majority emphasized that a State must have strong justification when a matter of family association so fundamental as that of mother and child is at stake in a way as irrevocable as complete termination of any parental right. It also stressed the "considerable" risk of error evidenced by the frequency of appellate reversal of Mississippi trial court determinations to terminate parental rights, and the relative insignificance of the State's countervailing financial interest "in the tightly circumscribed category of parental status termination cases [where] appeals are few, and not likely to impose an undue burden on the State."

Unlike precedents holding that the Constitution does not mandate affirmative subsidies to exercise fundamental rights, such as freedom to speak or to choose an abortion procedure, which involved requests for "state aid to subsidize their privately initiated action or to alleviate the consequences of differences in economic circumstances that existed apart from state action[,]" here the objective was "to defend against the State's destruction of ... family bonds, and to resist the brand associated with a parental unfitness adjudication." Unlike cases holding that otherwise neutral laws do not presumptively violate equal protection simply because of disproportionate adverse effects on a racial minority, much less on the poor, here the rules were "wholly contingent on one's ability to pay, and thus 'visit different consequences on two categories of persons,' ... ; they apply to all indigents and do not reach anyone outside that class." As for concern that the Court's ruling inevitably would implicate greater financial obligations on the State to pay for transcripts in aid of appellate review in other important civil cases, the Court emphasized that the unique deprivation associated with terminating parental status set this case apart "even from other domestic relations matters such as divorce, paternity, and child custody."

Justice Kennedy concurred in the judgment, asserting that "due process is quite a sufficient basis for our holding." Justice Thomas dissented, joined in full by Justice Scalia and in part by Chief Justice Rehnquist (except for the portion of the opinion declaring Justice Thomas' "inclin[ation] to vote to overrule *Griffin* and its progeny").

Provision of Essential Governmental Benefits and Services to the Poor

The general question raised here is whether the Constitution provides a basis for a higher level of judicial scrutiny of legislation that relates to the provision by government to the poor of basic human necessities—food, medical care, education, housing—than it does to economic regulations. Three separate constitutional arguments may be made to support an affirmative answer to that question.

(1) Does the constitution (through the due process clause or otherwise) guarantee some minimum entitlement by the poor to the basic necessities of life? Is the due process clause not only a shield against governmental deprivations of liberty and property but also a sword which imposes affirmative obligations on government? Professor Michelman, *On Protecting the Poor Through the Fourteenth Amendment,* 83

Harv.L.Rev. 7, 9 (1969), argues that the purposes of the Supreme Court decisions dealing with equal protection and wealth classifications "could be more soundly and satisfyingly understood as vindication of a state's duty to protect against certain hazards which are endemic in an unequal society, rather than vindication of a duty to avoid complicity in unequal treatment." He goes on to elaborate the proposition that the Court should be talking of "minimum protection against economic hazard" rather than "equal protection." Professor Tribe refers to "[e]merging notions that government has an affirmative obligation somehow to provide at least a minimally decent subsistence with respect to the most basic human needs, subject to all of the familiar difficulties with judicial enforcement of affirmative duties." *American Constitutional Law,* 1336 (2d ed. 1988). Professor Michelman restated his thesis in *Welfare Rights in a Constitutional Democracy,* 1979 Wash.U.L.Q. 659. In commentary on that restatement Professor Bork asserted "that the argument for welfare rights is unconnected with either the Constitution or its history" and therefore "offers inadequate guidelines and so requires political decision making by the judiciary." *The Impossibility of Finding Welfare Rights in the Constitution,* 1979 Wash.U.L.Q. 695. See also Appleton, *Professor Michelman's Quest for a Constitutional Welfare Right,* 1979 Wash.U.L.Q. 715.

(2) Should classifications in statutes providing governmental services to the poor be subject to a heightened standard of review under the equal protection clause because they involve the basic economic needs of impoverished human beings?

(3) Should classifications based on wealth be held to be constitutionally "suspect" and hence to require special justification in order to be valid? This argument was discussed supra p. 666.

Welfare as a Fundamental Right Calling for Strict Scrutiny

A conscious attempt was made by lawyers involved in legal services programs to deal with what they regarded as inadequate welfare grants by persuading the Court to read a "right to life" into the equal protection clause that would guarantee an adequate minimum payment for every needy individual in society. The story of this attempt is told in Krislov, *The OEO Lawyers Fail to Constitutionalize a Right to Welfare: A Study in the Uses and Limits of the Judicial Process,* 58 Minn.L.Rev. 211 (1973); Sparer, *The Right to Welfare* in *The Rights of Americans* 65 (N. Dorsen, ed. 1971).

Dandridge v. Williams

397 U.S. 471, 90 S.Ct. 1153, 25 L.Ed.2d 491 (1970).

[Maryland participated in the federal Aid to Families with Dependent Children program (AFDC), providing grants of a certain amount for each child but imposing an upper limit of $250 per month that any family could receive. Recipients with large families that received less aid per child than smaller families not affected by the maximum challenged the regulation in federal district court. They contended that the state limit contravened the federal statute and discriminated against them merely because of the size of their families in violation of the equal protection clause. The Court upheld the state limit, rejecting both the statutory and the constitutional claims. Portions of the opinions relating to the constitutional issues are printed below.]

■ MR. JUSTICE STEWART delivered the opinion of the Court.

. . .

II.

Although a State may adopt a maximum grant system in allocating its funds available for AFDC payments without violating the Act, it may not, of course, impose a regime of invidious discrimination in violation of the Equal Protection Clause of the Fourteenth Amendment. Maryland says that its maximum grant regulation is wholly free of any invidiously discriminatory purpose or effect, and that the regulation is rationally supportable on at least four entirely valid grounds. The regulation can be clearly justified, Maryland argues, in terms of legitimate state interests in encouraging gainful employment, in maintaining an equitable balance in economic status as between welfare families and those supported by a wage-earner, in providing incentives for family planning, and in allocating available public funds in such a way as fully to meet the needs of the largest possible number of families. The District Court, while apparently recognizing the validity of at least some of these state concerns, nonetheless held that the regulation "is invalid on its face for overreaching,"—that it violates the Equal Protection Clause "[b]ecause it cuts too broad a swath on an indiscriminate basis as applied to the entire group of AFDC eligibles to which it purports to apply,. . . ."

If this were a case involving government action claimed to violate the First Amendment guarantee of free speech, a finding of "overreaching" would be significant and might be crucial. For when otherwise valid governmental regulation sweeps so broadly as to impinge upon activity protected by the First Amendment, its very overbreadth may make it unconstitutional. . . . But the concept of "overreaching" has no place in this case. For here we deal with state regulation in the social and economic field, not affecting freedoms guaranteed by the Bill of Rights, and claimed to violate the Fourteenth Amendment only because the regulation results in some disparity in grants of welfare payments to the largest AFDC families.[16] For this Court to approve the invalidation of state economic or social regulation as "overreaching" would be far too reminiscent of an era when the Court thought the Fourteenth Amendment gave it power to strike down state laws "because they may be unwise, improvident, or out of harmony with a particular school of thought." Williamson v. Lee Optical of Oklahoma, Inc., 348 U.S. 483, 488. That era long ago passed into history. Ferguson v. Skrupa, 372 U.S. 726.

In the area of economics and social welfare, a State does not violate the Equal Protection Clause merely because the classifications made by its laws are imperfect. If the classification has some "reasonable basis," it does not offend the Constitution simply because the classification "is not made with mathematical nicety or because in practice it results in some inequality." Lindsley v. Natural Carbonic Gas Co., 220 U.S. 61, 78. . . ."A statutory discrimination will not be set aside if any state of facts reasonably may be conceived to justify it." McGowan v. Maryland, 366 U.S. 420, 426.

To be sure, the cases cited, and many others enunciating this fundamental standard under the Equal Protection Clause, have in the main involved state regulation of business or industry. The administration of public welfare assistance, by contrast, involves the most basic economic needs of impoverished human beings. We recognize the dramatically real factual difference between the cited cases and this one,

---

[16] Cf. Shapiro v. Thompson, 394 U.S. 618, where by contrast, the Court found state interference with the constitutionally protected freedom of interstate travel.

but we can find no basis for applying a different constitutional standard.[17] . . . It is a standard that has consistently been applied to state legislation restricting the availability of employment opportunities. Goesaert v. Cleary, 335 U.S. 464; Kotch v. Board of River Port Pilot Comm'rs, 330 U.S. 552. . . . And it is a standard that is true to the principle that the Fourteenth Amendment gives the federal courts no power to impose upon the States their views of what constitutes wise economic or social policy.

Under this long-established meaning of the Equal Protection Clause, it is clear that the Maryland maximum grant regulation is constitutionally valid. We need not explore all the reasons that the State advances in justification of the regulation. It is enough that a solid foundation for the regulation can be found in the State's legitimate interest in encouraging employment and in avoiding discrimination between welfare families and the families of the working poor. By combining a limit on the recipient's grant with permission to retain money earned, without reduction in the amount of the grant, Maryland provides an incentive to seek gainful employment. And by keying the maximum family AFDC grants to the minimum wage a steadily employed head of a household receives, the State maintains some semblance of an equitable balance between families on welfare and those supported by an employed breadwinner.

It is true that in some AFDC families there may be no person who is employable. It is also true that with respect to AFDC families whose determined standard of need is below the regulatory maximum, and who therefore receive grants equal to the determined standard, the employment incentive is absent. But the Equal Protection Clause does not require that a State must choose between attacking every aspect of a problem or not attacking the problem at all. . . . It is enough that the State's action be rationally based and free from invidious discrimination. The regulation before us meets that test.

We do not decide today that the Maryland regulation is wise, that it best fulfills the relevant social and economic objectives that Maryland might ideally espouse, or that a more just and humane system could not be devised. Conflicting claims of morality and intelligence are raised by opponents and proponents of almost every measure, certainly including the one before us. But the intractable economic, social, and even philosophical problems presented by public welfare assistance programs are not the business of this Court. The Constitution may impose certain procedural safeguards upon systems of welfare administration, Goldberg v. Kelly, 397 U.S. 254. But the Constitution does not empower this Court to second-guess state officials charged with the difficult responsibility of allocating limited public welfare funds among the myriad of potential recipients.

The judgment is reversed.

[Justice Black, joined by Chief Justice Burger, and Justice Harlan filed concurring opinions. Justice Douglas dissented on the statutory issue.]

■ MR. JUSTICE MARSHALL, whom MR. JUSTICE BRENNAN joins, dissenting.

. . .

This classification process effected by the maximum grant regulation produces a basic denial of equal treatment. Persons who are concededly similarly situated (dependent children and their families), are not afforded equal, or even approximately equal, treatment under the maximum grant regulation. Subsistence benefits are paid with respect to some needy dependent children; nothing is paid with respect to others.

---

[17] It is important to note that there is no contention that the Maryland regulation is infected with a racially discriminatory purpose or effect such as to make it inherently suspect. Cf. McLaughlin v. Florida, 379 U.S. 184.

Some needy families receive full subsistence assistance as calculated by the State; the assistance paid to other families is grossly below their similarly calculated needs.

Yet, as a general principle, individuals should not be afforded different treatment by the State unless there is a relevant distinction between them and "a statutory discrimination must be based on differences that are reasonably related to the purposes of the Act in which it is found." Morey v. Doud, 354 U.S. 457, 465 (1957). . . . Consequently, the State may not, in the provision of important services or the distribution of governmental payments, supply benefits to some individuals while denying them to others who are similarly situated. . . .

In the instant case, the only distinction between those children with respect to whom assistance is granted and those children who are denied such assistance is the size of the family into which the child permits himself to be born. The class of individuals with respect to whom payments are actually made (the first four or five eligible dependent children in a family), is grossly underinclusive in terms of the class that the AFDC program was designed to assist, namely, *all* needy dependent children. Such underinclusiveness manifests "a prima facie violation of the equal protection requirement of reasonable classification," compelling the State to come forward with a persuasive justification for the classification.

The Court never undertakes to inquire for such a justification; rather it avoids the task by focusing upon the abstract dichotomy between two different approaches to equal protection problems that have been utilized by this Court.

Under the so-called "traditional test," a classification is said to be permissible under the Equal Protection Clause unless it is "without any reasonable basis." Lindsley v. Natural Carbonic Gas Co., 220 U.S. 61, 78 (1911). On the other hand, if the classification affects a "fundamental right," then the state interest in perpetuating the classification must be "compelling" in order to be sustained. See, e.g., *Shapiro v. Thompson,* supra;. . . .

This case simply defies easy characterization in terms of one or the other of these "tests." The cases relied on by the Court, in which a "mere rationality" test was actually used, e.g., Williamson v. Lee Optical of Oklahoma, Inc., 348 U.S. 483 (1955), are most accurately described as involving the application of equal protection reasoning to the regulation of business interests. The extremes to which the Court has gone in dreaming up rational bases for state regulation in that area may in many instances be ascribed to a healthy revulsion from the Court's earlier excesses in using the Constitution to protect interests that have more than enough power to protect themselves in the legislative halls. This case, involving the literally vital interests of a powerless minority—poor families without breadwinners—is far removed from the area of business regulation, as the Court concedes. Why then is the standard used in those cases imposed here? We are told no more than that this case falls in "the area of economics and social welfare," with the implication that from there the answer is obvious.

In my view, equal protection analysis of this case is not appreciably advanced by the *a priori* definition of a "right," fundamental or otherwise. Rather, concentration must be placed upon the character of the classification in question, the relative importance to individuals in the class discriminated against of the governmental benefits that they do not receive, and the asserted state interests in support of the classification. . . .

It is the individual interests here at stake that, as the Court concedes, most clearly distinguish this case from the "business regulation" equal protection cases. AFDC support to needy dependent children provides the stuff that sustains those children's lives: food, clothing, shelter. And this Court has already recognized several times that when a benefit, even a "gratuitous" benefit, is necessary to sustain life, stricter constitutional standards, both procedural and substantive, are applied to the deprivation of that benefit.

. . .

In any event, it cannot suffice merely to invoke the spectre of the past and to recite from *Lindsley v. Natural Carbonic Gas Co.* and *Williamson v. Lee Optical of Oklahoma, Inc.* to decide the case. Appellees are not a gas company or an optical dispenser; they are needy dependent children and families who are discriminated against by the State. The basis of that discrimination—the classification of individuals into large and small families—is too arbitrary and too unconnected to the asserted rationale, the impact on those discriminated against—the denial of even a subsistence existence—too great, and the supposed interests served too contrived and attenuated to meet the requirements of the Constitution. . . .

I would affirm the judgment of the District Court.

Harris v. McRae

448 U.S. 297, 100 S.Ct. 2671, 65 L.Ed.2d 784 (1980).

■ MR. JUSTICE STEWART delivered the opinion of the Court.

This case presents statutory and constitutional questions concerning the public funding of abortions under Title XIX of the Social Security Act, commonly known as the "Medicaid" Act, and recent annual appropriations acts containing the so-called "Hyde Amendment." The statutory question is whether Title XIX requires a State that participates in the Medicaid program to fund the cost of medically necessary abortions for which federal reimbursement is unavailable under the Hyde Amendment. The constitutional question, which arises only if Title XIX imposes no such requirement, is whether the Hyde Amendment, by denying public funding for certain medically necessary abortions, contravenes the liberty or equal protection guarantees of the Due Process Clause of the Fifth Amendment, or either of the Religion Clauses of the First Amendment.

I.

. . .

Since September 1976, Congress has prohibited . . . the use of any federal funds to reimburse the cost of abortions under the Medicaid program except under certain specified circumstances. This funding restriction is commonly known as the "Hyde Amendment," after its original congressional sponsor, Representative Hyde. The current version of the Hyde Amendment, applicable for fiscal year 1980, provides:

"[N]one of the funds provided by this joint resolution shall be used to perform abortions except where the life of the mother would be endangered if the fetus were carried to term; or except for such medical procedures necessary for the victims of rape or incest when such rape or incest has been reported promptly to a law enforcement agency or public health service." Pub.L. No. 96–123, § 109, 93 Stat. 926. See also Pub.L. No. 96–86, § 118, 93 Stat. 662.

. . .

[T]he District Court . . . invalidat[ed] all versions of the Hyde Amendment on constitutional grounds. . . .

. . .

II.

. . .

. . . [W]e conclude that Title XIX does not require a participating State to pay for those medically necessary abortions for which federal reimbursement is unavailable under the Hyde Amendment.[16]

III.

[Hence,] we must consider the constitutional validity of the Hyde Amendment. The appellees assert that the funding restrictions of the Hyde Amendment violate several rights secured by the Constitution—(1) the right of a woman, implicit in the Due Process Clause of the Fifth Amendment, to decide whether to terminate a pregnancy, (2) the prohibition under the Establishment Clause of the First Amendment against any "law respecting an establishment of religion," and (3) the right to freedom of religion protected by the Free Exercise Clause of the First Amendment. The appellees also contend that, quite apart from substantive constitutional rights, the Hyde Amendment violates the equal protection component of the Fifth Amendment.

. . .

A.

We address first the appellees' argument that the Hyde Amendment, by restricting the availability of certain medically necessary abortions under Medicaid, impinges on the "liberty" protected by the Due Process Clause as recognized in Roe v. Wade, 410 U.S. 113, and its progeny.

In the *Wade* case, this Court held . . . that the "liberty" protected by the Due Process Clause of the Fourteenth Amendment . . . includes the freedom of a woman to decide whether to terminate a pregnancy.

But the Court . . . also recognized that a State has legitimate interests during a pregnancy in both ensuring the health of the mother and protecting potential human life. These state interests, which were found to be "separate and distinct" and to "grow[ ]in substantiality as the woman approaches term," pose a conflict with a woman's untrammeled freedom of choice. . . .

In Maher v. Roe, 432 U.S. 464, the Court was presented with the question whether the scope of personal constitutional freedom recognized in *Roe v. Wade* included an entitlement to Medicaid payments for abortions that are not medically necessary. At issue in *Maher* was a Connecticut welfare regulation under which Medicaid recipients received payments for medical services incident to childbirth, but not for medical services incident to nontherapeutic abortions. The District Court held that the regulation violated the Equal Protection Clause of the Fourteenth Amendment because the unequal subsidization of childbirth and abortion impinged on the "fundamental right to abortion" recognized in *Wade* and its progeny.

It was the view of this Court that "the District Court misconceived the nature and scope of the fundamental right recognized in *Roe*." 432 U.S., at 471. The doctrine of *Roe v. Wade,* the Court held in *Maher,* "protects the woman from unduly burdensome interference with her freedom to decide whether to terminate her pregnancy," such as the severe criminal sanctions at issue in *Roe v. Wade,* supra, or the absolute requirement of spousal consent for an abortion challenged in Planned Parenthood of Central Missouri v. Danforth, 428 U.S. 52.

---

[16] A participating State is free, if it so chooses, to include in its Medicaid plan those medically necessary abortions for which federal reimbursement is unavailable. . . . We hold only that a State *need* not include such abortions in its Medicaid plan.

But the constitutional freedom recognized in *Wade* and its progeny, the *Maher* Court explained, did not prevent Connecticut from making "a value judgment favoring childbirth over abortion, and . . . implement[ing] that judgment by the allocation of public funds." As the Court elaborated:

"The Connecticut regulation before us is different in kind from the laws invalidated in our previous abortion decisions. The Connecticut regulation places no obstacles—absolute or otherwise—in the pregnant woman's path to an abortion. An indigent woman who desires an abortion suffers no disadvantage as a consequence of Connecticut's decision to fund childbirth; she continues as before to be dependent on private sources for the service she desires. The State may have made childbirth a more attractive alternative, thereby influencing the woman's decision, but it has imposed no restriction on access to abortions that was not already there. The indigency that may make it difficult—and in some cases, perhaps, impossible—for some women to have abortions is neither created nor in any way affected by the Connecticut regulation."

. . . In explaining why the constitutional principle recognized in *Wade* and later cases . . . did not translate into a constitutional obligation of Connecticut to subsidize abortions, the Court cited the "basic difference between direct state interference with a protected activity and state encouragement of an alternative activity consonant with legislative policy. Constitutional concerns are greatest when the State attempts to impose its will by force of law; the State's power to encourage actions deemed to be in the public interest is necessarily far broader." Thus, even though the Connecticut regulation favored childbirth over abortion by means of subsidization of one and not the other, the Court in *Maher* concluded that the regulation did not impinge on the constitutional freedom recognized in *Wade* because it imposed no governmental restriction on access to abortions.

The Hyde Amendment, like the Connecticut welfare regulation at issue in *Maher,* places no governmental obstacle in the path of a woman who chooses to terminate her pregnancy, but rather, by means of unequal subsidization of abortion and other medical services, encourages alternative activity deemed in the public interest. The present case does differ factually from *Maher* insofar as that case involved a failure to fund nontherapeutic abortions, whereas the Hyde Amendment withholds funding of certain medically necessary abortions. Accordingly, the appellees argue that because the Hyde Amendment affects a significant interest not present or asserted in *Maher*—the interest of a woman in protecting her health during pregnancy—and because that interest lies at the core of the personal constitutional freedom recognized in *Wade;* the present case is constitutionally different from *Maher.* . . .

. . . [True,] *Wade* emphasized . . . that the woman's decision carries with it significant personal health implications—both physical and psychological. In fact, . . . the Court held that even after fetal viability a State may not prohibit abortions "necessary to preserve the life or health of the mother." Because even the compelling interest of the State in protecting potential life after fetal viability was held to be insufficient to outweigh a woman's decision to protect her life or health, it could be argued that the freedom of a woman to decide whether to terminate her pregnancy for health reasons does in fact lie at the core of the constitutional liberty identified in *Wade.*

But, . . . it simply does not follow that a woman's freedom of choice carries with it a constitutional entitlement to the financial resources to avail herself of the full range of protected choices. The reason why was explained in *Maher:* although government may not place obstacles in the path of a woman's exercise of her freedom of choice, it need not remove those not of its own creation. Indigency falls in the latter category. The financial constraints that restrict an indigent woman's ability to enjoy the full range of constitutionally protected freedom of choice are the product not of governmental restrictions on access to abortions, but rather of her indigency. Although Congress has opted to subsidize medically necessary services generally, but not certain medically necessary abortions, the fact remains that the Hyde Amendment leaves an indigent woman with at least the same range of choice in deciding whether to obtain a medically necessary abortion as she would have had if Congress had chosen to subsidize no health care costs at all. We are thus not persuaded that the Hyde Amendment impinges on the constitutionally protected freedom of choice recognized in *Wade*.[19]

Although the liberty protected by the Due Process Clause affords protection against unwarranted government interference with freedom of choice in the context of certain personal decisions, it does not confer an entitlement to such funds as may be necessary to realize all the advantages of that freedom. To hold otherwise would mark a drastic change in our understanding of the Constitution. It cannot be that because government may not prohibit the use of contraceptives, Griswold v. Connecticut, 381 U.S. 479, or prevent parents from sending their child to a private school, Pierce v. Society of Sisters, 268 U.S. 510, government, therefore, has an affirmative constitutional obligation to ensure that all persons have the financial resources to obtain contraceptives or send their children to private schools. To translate the limitation on governmental power implicit in the Due Process Clause into an affirmative funding obligation would require Congress to subsidize the medically necessary abortion of an indigent woman even if Congress had not enacted a Medicaid program to subsidize other medically necessary services. Nothing in the Due Process Clause supports such an extraordinary result. Whether freedom of choice that is constitutionally protected warrants federal subsidization is a question for Congress to answer, not a matter of constitutional entitlement. Accordingly, we conclude that the Hyde Amendment does not impinge on the due process liberty recognized in *Wade*.

B.

The appellees also argue that the Hyde Amendment contravenes rights secured by the Religion Clauses of the First Amendment. . . .

. . .

[The Court held that the Hyde Amendment did not contravene the establishment clause of the first amendment and that the parties lacked standing to raise a challenge under the free exercise clause.]

---

[19] The appellees argue that the Hyde Amendment is unconstitutional because it "penalizes" the exercise of a woman's choice to terminate a pregnancy by abortion. See Memorial Hospital v. Maricopa County, 415 U.S. 250; Shapiro v. Thompson, 394 U.S. 618. This argument falls short of the mark. In *Maher,* the Court found only a "semantic difference" between the argument that Connecticut's refusal to subsidize nontherapeutic abortions "unduly interfere[d]" with the exercise of the constitutional liberty recognized in *Wade* and the argument that it "penalized" the exercise of that liberty. And, regardless of how the claim was characterized, the *Maher* Court rejected the argument that Connecticut's refusal to subsidize protected conduct, without more, impinged on the constitutional freedom of choice. This reasoning is equally applicable in the present case. A substantial constitutional question would arise if Congress had attempted to withhold all Medicaid benefits from an otherwise eligible candidate simply because that candidate had exercised her constitutionally protected freedom to terminate her pregnancy by abortion. This would be analogous to Sherbert v. Verner, 374 U.S. 398, where this Court held that a State may not, consistent with the First and Fourteenth Amendments, withhold *all* unemployment compensation benefits from a claimant who would otherwise be eligible for such benefits but for the fact that she is unwilling to work one day per week on her Sabbath. But the Hyde Amendment, unlike the statute at issue in *Sherbert,* does not provide for such a broad disqualification from receipt of public benefits. Rather, the Hyde Amendment, like the Connecticut welfare provision at issue in *Maher,* represents simply a refusal to subsidize certain protected conduct. A refusal to fund protected activity, without more, cannot be equated with the imposition of a "penalty" on that activity.

C.

It remains to be determined whether the Hyde Amendment violates the equal protection component of the Fifth Amendment. This challenge is premised on the fact that, although federal reimbursement is available under Medicaid for medically necessary services generally, the Hyde Amendment does not permit federal reimbursement of all medically necessary abortions. The District Court held, and the appellees argue here, that this selective subsidization violates the constitutional guarantee of equal protection.

The guarantee of equal protection under the Fifth Amendment is not a source of substantive rights or liberties,[25] but rather a right to be free from invidious discrimination in statutory classifications and other governmental activity. It is well-settled that where a statutory classification does not itself impinge on a right or liberty protected by the Constitution, the validity of classification must be sustained unless "the classification rests on grounds wholly irrelevant to the achievement of [any legitimate governmental] objective." McGowan v. Maryland, supra, 366 U.S., at 425. This presumption of constitutional validity, however, disappears if a statutory classification is predicated on criteria that are, in a constitutional sense, "suspect," the principal example of which is a classification based on race, e.g., Brown v. Board of Education, 347 U.S. 483.

1.

For the reasons stated above, we have already concluded that the Hyde Amendment violates no constitutionally protected substantive rights. We now conclude as well that it is not predicated on a constitutionally suspect classification. In reaching this conclusion, we again draw guidance from the Court's decision in *Maher v. Roe*. As to whether the Connecticut welfare regulation providing funds for childbirth but not for nontherapeutic abortions discriminated against a suspect class, the Court in *Maher* observed:

"An indigent woman desiring an abortion does not come within the limited category of disadvantaged classes so recognized by our cases. Nor does the fact that the impact of the regulation falls upon those who cannot pay lead to a different conclusion. In a sense, every denial of welfare to an indigent creates a wealth classification as compared to nonindigents who are able to pay for the desired goods or services. But this Court has never held that financial need alone identifies a suspect class for purposes of equal protection analysis." . . .

Thus, the Court in *Maher* found no basis for concluding that the Connecticut regulation was predicated on a suspect classification.

[T]he present case is indistinguishable from *Maher* in this respect. Here, as in *Maher,* the principal impact of the Hyde Amendment falls on the indigent. But that fact does not itself render the funding restriction constitutionally invalid, for this Court has held repeatedly that poverty, standing alone, is not a suspect classification. See, e.g., James v. Valtierra, 402 U.S. 137. That *Maher* involved the refusal to fund nontherapeutic abortions, whereas the present case involves the refusal to fund medically necessary abortions, has no bearing on the factors that render a classification "suspect" within the meaning of the constitutional guarantee of equal protection.

---

[25] An exception to this statement is to be found in Reynolds v. Sims, 377 U.S. 533, and its progeny. Although the Constitution of the United States does not confer the right to vote in state elections, see Minor v. Happersett, 21 Wall. 162, 178, *Reynolds* held that if a State adopts an electoral system, the Equal Protection Clause of the Fourteenth Amendment confers upon a qualified voter a substantive right to participate in the electoral process equally with other qualified voters. See, e.g., Dunn v. Blumstein, 405 U.S. 330, 336.

2.

The remaining question then is whether the Hyde Amendment is rationally related to a legitimate governmental objective. It is the Government's position that the Hyde Amendment bears a rational relationship to its legitimate interest in protecting the potential life of the fetus. We agree.

. . .

. . . By subsidizing the medical expenses of indigent women who carry their pregnancies to term while not subsidizing the comparable expenses of women who undergo abortions (except those whose lives are threatened), Congress has established incentives that make childbirth a more attractive alternative than abortion for persons eligible for Medicaid. These incentives bear a direct relationship to the legitimate congressional interest in protecting potential life. Nor is it irrational that Congress has authorized federal reimbursement for medically necessary services generally, but not for certain medically necessary abortions. Abortion is inherently different from other medical procedures, because no other procedure involves the purposeful termination of a potential life.

. . .

. . . It is not the mission of this Court or any other to decide whether the balance of competing interests reflected in the Hyde Amendment is wise social policy. If that were our mission, not every Justice who has subscribed to the judgment of the Court today could have done so. But we cannot, in the name of the Constitution, overturn duly enacted statutes simply "because they may be unwise, improvident, or out of harmony with a particular school of thought." . . . Rather, "when an issue involves policy choices as sensitive as those implicated [here] . . . , the appropriate forum for their resolution in a democracy is the legislature." Maher v. Roe. . . .

. . .

. . . [T]he judgment . . . is reversed, and the case is remanded . . . for further proceedings consistent with this opinion.

It is so ordered.

■ MR. JUSTICE WHITE, concurring.

. . .

■ MR. JUSTICE BRENNAN, with whom MR. JUSTICE MARSHALL and MR. JUSTICE BLACKMUN join, dissenting.

I agree entirely with my Brother Stevens that the State's interest in protecting the potential life of the fetus cannot justify the exclusion of financially and medically needy women from the benefits to which they would otherwise be entitled solely because the treatment that a doctor has concluded is medically necessary involves an abortion. I write separately to express my continuing disagreement with the Court's mischaracterization of the nature of the fundamental right recognized in Roe v. Wade, 410 U.S. 113 (1973), and its misconception of the manner in which that right is infringed by federal and state legislation withdrawing all funding for medically necessary abortions.

. . . Roe and its progeny established that the pregnant woman has a right to be free from state interference with her choice to have an abortion . . . The proposition for which these cases stand thus is not that the State is under an affirmative obligation to ensure access to abortions for all who may desire them; it is that the State must refrain from wielding its enormous power and influence in a manner that might burden the pregnant woman's freedom to choose whether to have an abortion. The Hyde Amendment's denial of public funds for medically necessary abortions plainly intrudes upon this constitutionally protected decision, for both by design and in effect it serves to coerce indigent pregnant women to bear children that they would otherwise elect not to have.[4]

. . . [T]he Hyde Amendment is nothing less than an attempt by Congress to . . . achieve indirectly what *Roe v. Wade* said it could not do directly. Under Title XIX of the Social Security Act, the Federal Government reimburses participating States for virtually all medically necessary services it provides to the categorically needy. The sole limitation of any significance is the Hyde Amendment's prohibition against the use of any federal funds to pay for the costs of abortions (except where the life of the mother would be endangered if the fetus were carried to term). As my Brother Stevens persuasively demonstrates, exclusion of medically necessary abortions from Medicaid coverage cannot be justified as a cost-saving device. Rather, the Hyde Amendment is a transparent attempt by the Legislative Branch to impose the political majority's judgment of the morally acceptable and socially desirable preference on a sensitive and intimate decision that the Constitution entrusts to the individual. Worse yet, the Hyde Amendment does not foist that majoritarian viewpoint with equal measure upon everyone in our Nation, rich and poor alike; rather, it imposes that viewpoint only upon that segment of our society which, because of its position of political powerlessness, is least able to defend its privacy rights from the encroachments of state-mandated morality. The instant legislation thus calls for more exacting judicial review than in most other cases. . . .

Moreover, it is clear that the Hyde Amendment not only was designed to inhibit, but does in fact inhibit the woman's freedom to choose abortion over childbirth. . . . [U]nder the Hyde Amendment, the Government will fund only those procedures incidental to childbirth. By thus injecting coercive financial incentives favoring childbirth into a decision that is constitutionally guaranteed to be free from governmental intrusion, the Hyde Amendment deprives the indigent woman of her freedom to choose abortion over maternity, thereby impinging on the due process liberty right recognized in *Roe v. Wade*.

. . . [T]he Court fails to appreciate . . . that it is not simply the woman's indigency that interferes with her freedom of choice, but the combination of her own poverty and the government's unequal subsidization of abortion and childbirth.

. . . By funding all of the expenses associated with childbirth and none of the expenses incurred in terminating pregnancy, the government literally makes an offer that the indigent woman cannot afford to refuse. It matters not that in this instance the government has used the carrot rather than the stick. What is critical is the realization that as a practical matter, many poverty-stricken women will choose to carry their pregnancy to term simply because the government provides funds for the associated medical services, even though these same women would have chosen to have an abortion if the government had also paid for that option, or indeed if the government had stayed out of the picture altogether and had defrayed the costs of neither procedure.

The fundamental flaw in the Court's due process analysis, then, is its failure to acknowledge that the discriminatory distribution of the benefits of governmental largesse can discourage the exercise of fundamental liberties just as effectively as can an outright denial of those rights through criminal and regulatory sanctions. . . .

---

[4] My focus throughout this opinion is upon the coercive impact of the congressional decision to fund one outcome of pregnancy—childbirth—while not funding the other—abortion. Because I believe this alone renders the Hyde Amendment unconstitutional, I do not dwell upon the other disparities that the Amendment produces in the treatment of rich and poor, pregnant and nonpregnant. I concur completely, however, in my Brother Stevens' discussion of those disparities. . . .

. . .

The Medicaid program cannot be distinguished from . . . other statutory schemes that unconstitutionally burdened fundamental rights.[6] . . .

I respectfully dissent.

■ MR. JUSTICE MARSHALL, dissenting.

. . .

. . . The Court's decision today marks a retreat from *Roe v. Wade* and represents a cruel blow to the most powerless members of our society. I dissent.

. . .

I.

The record developed below reveals that the standards set forth in the Hyde Amendment exclude the majority of cases in which the medical profession would recommend abortion as medically necessary. Indeed, in States that have adopted a standard more restrictive than the "medically necessary" test of the Medicaid Act, the number of funded abortions has decreased by over 98%.

. . .

An optimistic estimate indicates that as many as 100 excess deaths may occur each year as a result of the Hyde Amendment. The record contains no estimate of the health damage that may occur to poor women, but it shows that it will be considerable.

II.

. . .

A.

This case is perhaps the most dramatic illustration to date of the deficiencies in the Court's obsolete "two-tiered" approach to the Equal Protection Clause. . . . With all deference, I am unable to understand how the Court can afford the same level of scrutiny to the legislation involved here—whose cruel impact falls exclusively on indigent pregnant women—that it has given to legislation distinguishing opticians from ophthalmologists, or to other legislation that makes distinctions between economic interests more than able to protect themselves in the political process. . . . Heightened scrutiny of legislative classifications has always been designed to protect groups "saddled with such disabilities or subjected to such a history of purposeful unequal treatment, or relegated to such a position of political powerlessness as to command extraordinary protection from the majoritarian political process." San Antonio School District v. Rodriguez, supra, at 28 (1973).[4] And while it is now clear that traditional "strict scrutiny" is unavailable to protect the poor against classifications that disfavor them, Dandridge v. Williams, 397 U.S. 471 (1970), I do not

---

[6] . . . [I]t is no answer to assert that no "penalty" is being imposed because the State is only refusing to pay for the specific costs of the protected activity rather than withholding other Medicaid benefits to which the recipient would be entitled or taking some other action more readily characterized as "punitive." Surely the government could not provide free transportation to the polling booths only for those citizens who vote for Democratic candidates, even though the failure to provide the same benefit to Republicans "represents simply a refusal to subsidize certain protected conduct," ibid., and does not involve the denial of any other governmental benefits. Whether the State withholds only the special costs of a disfavored option or penalizes the individual more broadly for the manner in which she exercises her choice, it cannot interfere with a constitutionally protected decision through the coercive use of governmental largesse.

[4] For this reason the Court has on occasion suggested that classifications discriminating against the poor are subject to special scrutiny under the Fifth and Fourteenth Amendments. See McDonald v. Board of Election, 394 U.S. 802, 807 (1969); Harper v. Virginia Bd. of Elections, 383 U.S. 663, 668 (1966).

believe that legislation that imposes a crushing burden on indigent women can be treated with the same deference given to legislation distinguishing among business interests.

B.

. . .

The class burdened by the Hyde Amendment consists of indigent women, a substantial proportion of whom are members of minority races. As I observed in *Maher,* nonwhite women obtain abortions at nearly double the rate of whites. . . . In my view, the fact that the burden of the Hyde Amendment falls exclusively on financially destitute women suggests "a special condition, which tends seriously to curtail the operation of those political processes ordinarily to be relied upon to protect minorities, and which may call for a correspondingly more searching judicial inquiry." United States v. Carolene Products, 304 U.S. 144, 152–153, n. 4 (1938). For this reason, I continue to believe that "a showing that state action has a devastating impact on the lives of minority racial groups must be relevant" for purposes of equal protection analysis. Jefferson v. Hackney, 406 U.S. 535, 575–576 (1972) (Marshall, J., dissenting).

As I explained in *Maher,* the asserted state interest in protecting potential life is insufficient to "outweigh the deprivation or serious discouragement of a vital constitutional right of especial importance to poor and minority women." . . .

C.

Although I would abandon the strict-scrutiny-rational-basis dichotomy in equal protection analysis, it is by no means necessary to [do so] to conclude . . . that the Hyde Amendment is a denial of equal protection. My Brother Brennan has demonstrated that the Amendment is unconstitutional because it impermissibly infringes upon the individual's constitutional right to decide whether to terminate a pregnancy. And as my Brother Stevens demonstrates the Government's interest in protecting fetal life is not a legitimate one when it is in conflict with "the preservation of the life or health of the mother," *Roe v. Wade,* . . . and when the Government's effort to make serious health damage to the mother "a more attractive alternative than abortion" does not rationally promote the governmental interest in encouraging normal childbirth.

. . . *Maher* turned on the fact that the legislation there under consideration discouraged only nontherapeutic, or medically unnecessary, abortions. In the Court's view, denial of Medicaid funding for nontherapeutic abortions was not a denial of equal protection because Medicaid funds were available only for medically necessary procedures. Thus the plaintiffs were seeking benefits which were not available to others similarly situated. I continue to believe that *Maher* was wrongly decided. But it is apparent that while the plaintiffs in *Maher* were seeking a benefit not available to others similarly situated, respondents are protesting their exclusion from a benefit that is available to all others similarly situated[—]a crucial difference for equal protection purposes.

. . .

III.

. . .

Ultimately, the result reached today may be traced to the Court's unwillingness to apply the constraints of the Constitution to decisions involving the expenditure of governmental funds. . . .

. . .

In this case, the Federal Government has taken upon itself the burden of financing practically all medically necessary expenditures. One category of medically necessary expenditure has been singled out for exclusion, and the sole basis for the exclusion is a premise repudiated for purposes of constitutional law in *Roe v. Wade.* The consequence is a devastating impact on the lives and health of poor women. I do not believe that a Constitution committed to the equal protection of the laws can tolerate this result. I dissent.

■ Mr. Justice Blackmun, dissenting.

. . . [W]hat I said in dissent in Beal v. Doe, 432 U.S. 438, 442 (1977), and its two companion cases, Maher v. Roe, 432 U.S. 464 (1977), and Poelker v. Doe, 432 U.S. 519 (1977), continues for me to be equally pertinent and equally applicable in these Hyde Amendment cases. There is "condescension" in the Court's holding "that she may go elsewhere for her abortion"; this is "disingenuous and alarming"; the Government "punitively impresses upon a needy minority its own concepts of the socially desirable, the publicly acceptable, and the morally sound"; the "financial argument, of course, is specious"; there truly is "another world 'out there,' the existence of which the Court, I suspect, either chooses to ignore or fears to recognize"; the "cancer of poverty will continue to grow"; and "the lot of the poorest among us," once again, and still, is not to be bettered.

■ Mr. Justice Stevens, dissenting.

. . .

This case involves a special exclusion of women who, by definition, are confronted with a choice between two serious harms: serious health damage to themselves on the one hand and abortion on the other. The competing interests are the interest in maternal health and the interest in protecting potential human life. It is now part of our law that the pregnant woman's decision as to which of these conflicting interests shall prevail is entitled to constitutional protection.

. . .

. . . The Hyde Amendments not only exclude financially and medically needy persons from the pool of benefits for a constitutionally insufficient reason; they also require the expenditure of millions and millions of dollars in order to thwart the exercise of a constitutional right, thereby effectively inflicting serious and long lasting harm on impoverished women who want and need abortions for valid medical reasons. In my judgment, these amendments constitute an unjustifiable, and indeed blatant, violation of the sovereign's duty to govern impartially.

I respectfully dissent.

D. Education

San Antonio Independent School Dist. v. Rodriguez

411 U.S. 1, 93 S.Ct. 1278, 36 L.Ed.2d 16 (1973).

■ Mr. Justice Powell delivered the opinion of the Court.

This suit attacking the Texas system of financing public education was initiated by Mexican-American parents whose children attend the elementary and secondary schools in the Edgewood Independent School District, an urban school district in San Antonio, Texas. They brought a class action on behalf of school children throughout the State who are members of minority groups or who are poor and reside in school districts having a low property tax base [against] the State Board of Education, the

Commissioner of Education, the State Attorney General, and the Bexar County (San Antonio) Board of Trustees. . . . [The three-judge district court held] the Texas school finance system unconstitutional under the Equal Protection Clause of the Fourteenth Amendment. . . . [W]e reverse. . . .

I.

. . .

[The Court described at length the Texas system of school financing. For present purposes it is enough to note that half of the total educational expenditures in Texas came from the Texas Minimum Foundation School Program. State revenues financed 80% of the Program, with the remaining 20% (known as the Local Fund Assignment) coming from the local districts under a formula designed to reflect each district's relative taxpaying ability. Each school district imposed a property tax to raise funds to satisfy its Local Fund Assignment and to provide the revenues needed above those received under the Foundation Program.]

The school district in which appellees reside, the Edgewood Independent School District, has been compared throughout this litigation with the Alamo Heights Independent School District. This comparison between the least and most affluent districts in the San Antonio area serves to illustrate the manner in which the dual system of finance operates and to indicate the extent to which substantial disparities exist despite the State's impressive progress in recent years. Edgewood is one of seven public school districts in the metropolitan area. Approximately 22,000 students are enrolled in its 25 elementary and secondary schools. The district is situated in the core-city sector of San Antonio in a residential neighborhood that has little commercial or industrial property. The residents are predominantly of Mexican-American descent: approximately 90% of the student population is Mexican-American and over 6% is Negro. The average assessed property value per pupil is $5,960—the lowest in the metropolitan area—and the median family income ($4,686) is also the lowest. At an equalized tax rate of $1.05 per $100 of assessed property—the highest in the metropolitan area—the district contributed $26 to the education of each child for the 1967–1968 school year above its Local Fund Assignment for the Minimum Foundation Program. The Foundation Program contributed $222 per pupil for a state-local total of $248. Federal funds added another $108 for a total of $356 per pupil.

Alamo Heights is the most affluent school district in San Antonio. Its six schools, housing approximately 5,000 students, are situated in a residential community quite unlike the Edgewood District. The school population is predominantly Anglo, having only 18% Mexican-Americans and less than 1% Negroes. The assessed property value per pupil exceeds $49,000 and the median family income is $8,001. In 1967–1968 the local tax rate of $.85 per $100 of valuation yielded $333 per pupil over and above its contribution to the Foundation Program. Coupled with the $225 provided from that Program, the district was able to supply $558 per student. Supplemented by a $36 per pupil grant from federal sources, Alamo Heights spent $594 per pupil.

. . . [1970–1971] figures also reveal the extent to which these two districts' allotments were funded from their own required contributions to the Local Fund Assignment. Alamo Heights, because of its relative wealth, was required to contribute out of its local property tax collections approximately $100 per pupil, or about 20% of its Foundation grant. Edgewood, on the other hand, paid only $8.46 per pupil, which is about 2.4% of its grant. It does appear then that, at least as to these two districts, the Local Fund Assignment does reflect a rough approximation of the relative taxpaying potential of each.

Despite . . . recent increases, substantial interdistrict disparities in school expenditures found by the District Court to prevail in San Antonio and in varying degrees throughout the State still exist. And it was these disparities, largely attributable to differences in the amounts of money collected through local property taxation, that led the District Court to conclude that Texas' dual system of public school finance violated the Equal Protection Clause. . . .

Texas virtually concedes that its historically rooted dual system of financing education could not withstand the strict judicial scrutiny that this Court has found appropriate in reviewing legislative judgments that interfere with fundamental constitutional rights or that involve suspect classifications. If, as previous decisions have indicated, strict scrutiny means that the State's system is not entitled to the usual presumption of validity, that the State rather than the complainants must carry a "heavy burden of justification," that the State must demonstrate that its educational system has been structured with "precision" and is "tailored" narrowly to serve legitimate objectives and that it has selected the "least drastic means" for effectuating its objectives, the Texas financing system and its counterpart in virtually every other State will not pass muster. The State candidly admits that "[n]o one familiar with the Texas system would contend that it has yet achieved perfection." Apart from its concession that educational finance in Texas has "defects" and "imperfections," the State defends the system's rationality with vigor and disputes the District Court's finding that it lacks a "reasonable basis."

This, then, establishes the framework for our analysis. We must decide, first, whether the Texas system of financing public education operates to the disadvantage of some suspect class or impinges upon a fundamental right explicitly or implicitly protected by the Constitution, thereby requiring strict judicial scrutiny. If so, the judgment of the District Court should be affirmed. If not, the Texas scheme must still be examined to determine whether it rationally furthers some legitimate, articulated state purpose and therefore does not constitute an invidious discrimination in violation of the Equal Protection Clause of the Fourteenth Amendment.

II.

. . .

A.

The wealth discrimination discovered by the District Court in this case, and by several other courts that have recently struck down school financing laws in other States,[48] is quite unlike any of the forms of wealth discrimination heretofore reviewed by this Court. Rather than focusing on the unique features of the alleged discrimination, the courts in these cases have virtually assumed their findings of a suspect classification through a simplistic process of analysis: since, under the traditional systems of financing public schools, some poorer people receive less expensive educations than other more affluent people, these systems discriminate on the basis of wealth. This approach largely ignores the hard threshold questions, including whether it makes a difference for purposes of consideration under the Constitution that the class of disadvantaged "poor" cannot be identified or defined in customary equal protection terms, and whether the relative—rather than absolute— nature of the asserted deprivation is of significant consequence. Before a State's laws and the justifications for the classifications they create are subjected to strict judicial scrutiny, we think these threshold considerations must be analyzed more closely than they were in the court below.

. . .

---

[48] Serrano v. Priest, 96 Cal.Rptr. 601, 487 P.2d 1241, 5 Cal.3d 584 (1971); Van Dusartz v. Hatfield, 334 F.Supp. 870 (D.Minn.1971); Robinson v. Cahill, 118 N.J.Super. 223, 287 A.2d 187 (1972); Milliken v. Green, No. 53, 809 (Mich. 1973).

However described, it is clear that appellees' suit asks this Court to extend its most exacting scrutiny to review a system that allegedly discriminates against a large, diverse, and amorphous class, unified only by the common factor of residence in districts that happen to have less taxable wealth than other districts. The system of alleged discrimination and the class it defines have none of the traditional indicia of suspectness: the class is not saddled with such disabilities, or subjected to such a history of purposeful unequal treatment, or relegated to such a position of political powerlessness as to command extraordinary protection from the majoritarian political process.

We thus conclude that the Texas system does not operate to the peculiar disadvantage of any suspect class. But in recognition of the fact that this Court has never heretofore held that wealth discrimination alone provides an adequate basis for invoking strict scrutiny, appellees have not relied solely on this contention. They also assert that the State's system impermissibly interferes with the exercise of a "fundamental" right and that accordingly the prior decisions of this Court require the application of the strict standard of judicial review. . . . It is this question—whether education is a fundamental right, in the sense that it is among the rights and liberties protected by the Constitution—which has so consumed the attention of courts and commentators in recent years.

B.

In Brown v. Board of Education, 347 U.S. 483 (1954), a unanimous Court recognized that "education is perhaps the most important function of state and local governments." . . .

Nothing this Court holds today in any way detracts from our historic dedication to public education. We are in complete agreement with the conclusion of the three-judge panel below that "the grave significance of education both to the individual and to our society" cannot be doubted. But the importance of a service performed by the State does not determine whether it must be regarded as fundamental for purposes of examination under the Equal Protection Clause. Mr. Justice Harlan, dissenting from the Court's application of strict scrutiny to a law impinging upon the right of interstate travel, admonished that "[v]irtually every state statute affects important rights." Shapiro v. Thompson, 394 U.S. 618, 655, 661 (1969). In his view, if the degree of judicial scrutiny of state legislation fluctuated depending on a majority's view of the importance of the interest affected, we would have gone "far toward making this Court a 'super-legislature.'" We would indeed then be assuming a legislative role and one for which the Court lacks both authority and competence. But Mr. Justice Stewart's response in *Shapiro* to Mr. Justice Harlan's concern correctly articulates the limits of the fundamental rights rationale employed in the Court's equal protection decisions:

"The Court today does *not* 'pick out particular human activities, characterize them as' fundamental, 'and give them added protection. . . .' To the contrary, the Court simply recognizes, as it must, an established constitutional right, and gives to that right no less protection than the Constitution itself demands." 394 U.S., at 642. (Emphasis from original.)

. . .

. . . The right to interstate travel had long been recognized as a right of constitutional significance, and the Court's decision therefore did not require an *ad hoc* determination as to the social or economic importance of that right.

. . .

The lesson of these cases . . . is plain. It is not the province of this Court to create substantive constitutional rights in the name of guaranteeing equal protection of the laws. Thus the key to discovering whether education is "fundamental" is not to be found in comparisons of the relative societal significance of education as opposed to subsistence or housing. Nor is it to be found by weighing whether education is as important as the right to travel. Rather, the answer lies in assessing whether there is a right to education explicitly or implicitly guaranteed by the Constitution. Eisenstadt v. Baird, 405 U.S. 438 (1972);[73] Dunn v. Blumstein, 405 U.S. 330 (1972);[74] Police Department of the City of Chicago v. Mosley, 408 U.S. 92 (1972);[75] Skinner v. Oklahoma, 316 U.S. 535 (1942).[76]

Education, of course, is not among the rights afforded explicit protection under our Federal Constitution. Nor do we find any basis for saying it is implicitly so protected. . . .

We have carefully considered each of the arguments supportive of the District Court's finding that education is a fundamental right or liberty and have found those arguments unpersuasive. In one further respect we find this a particularly inappropriate case in which to subject state action to strict judicial scrutiny. . . . Each of our prior cases involved legislation which "deprived," "infringed," or "interfered" with the free exercise of some such fundamental personal right or liberty. See Skinner v. Oklahoma . . . ; Shapiro v. Thompson . . . ; Dunn v. Blumstein. . . . A critical distinction between those cases and the one now before us lies in what Texas is endeavoring to do with respect to education. . . . The Texas system of school finance . . . was implemented in an effort to *extend* public education and to improve its quality. Of course, every reform that benefits some more than others may be criticized for what it fails to accomplish. But we think it plain that, in substance, the thrust of the Texas system is affirmative and reformatory and, therefore, should be scrutinized under judicial principles sensitive to the nature of the State's efforts and to the rights reserved to the States under the Constitution.

C.

. . .

We need not rest our decision, however, solely on the inappropriateness of the strict scrutiny test. A century of Supreme Court adjudication under the Equal Protection Clause affirmatively supports the application of the traditional standard of review, which requires only that the State's system be shown to bear some rational

---

[73] In *Eisenstadt,* the Court struck down a Massachusetts statute that prohibited the distribution of contraceptive devices, finding that the law failed "to satisfy even the more lenient equal protection standard." . . . Nevertheless, in *dictum,* the Court recited the correct form of equal protection analysis: "if we were to conclude that the Massachusetts statute impinges upon fundamental freedoms under Griswold [v. Connecticut, 381 U.S. 479 (1965)], the statutory classification would have to be not merely *rationally related* to a valid public purpose but *necessary* to the achievement of a *compelling* state interest." . . . (emphasis from original).

[74] *Dunn* fully canvasses this Court's voting rights cases and explains that "this Court has made clear that a citizen has a *constitutionally protected right* to participate in elections on an equal basis with other citizens in the jurisdiction." . . . (emphasis supplied). The constitutional underpinnings of the right to equal treatment in the voting process can no longer be doubted even though, as the Court noted in Harper v. Virginia Bd. of Elections, 383 U.S. 663, 665 (1966), "the right to vote in state elections is nowhere expressly mentioned.". . .

[75] In *Mosley,* the Court struck down a Chicago antipicketing ordinance that exempted labor picketing from its prohibitions. The ordinance was held invalid under the Equal Protection Clause after subjecting it to careful scrutiny and finding that the ordinance was not narrowly drawn. The stricter standard of review was appropriately applied since the ordinance was one "affecting First Amendment interests.". . .

[76] *Skinner* applied the standard of close scrutiny to a state law permitting forced sterilization of "habitual criminals." Implicit in the Court's opinion is the recognition that the right of procreation is among the rights of personal privacy protected under the Constitution. See Roe v. Wade, 410 U.S. 113 (1973).

relationship to legitimate state purposes. This case represents far more than a challenge to the manner in which Texas provides for the education of its children. We have here nothing less than a direct attack on the way in which Texas has chosen to raise and disburse state and local tax revenues. We are asked to condemn the State's judgment in conferring on political subdivisions the power to tax local property to supply revenues for local interests. In so doing, appellees would have the Court intrude in an area in which it has traditionally deferred to state legislatures. This Court has often admonished against such interferences with the State's fiscal policies under the Equal Protection Clause. . . .

Thus we stand on familiar ground when we continue to acknowledge that the Justices of this Court lack both the expertise and the familiarity with local problems so necessary to the making of wise decisions with respect to the raising and disposition of public revenues. . . .

In addition to matters of fiscal policy, this case also involves the most persistent and difficult questions of educational policy, another area in which this Court's lack of specialized knowledge and experience counsels against premature interference with the informed judgments made at the state and local levels. . . .

. . .

The foregoing considerations buttress our conclusion that Texas' system of public school finance is an inappropriate candidate for strict judicial scrutiny. These same considerations are relevant to the determination whether that system, with its conceded imperfections, nevertheless bears some rational relationship to a legitimate state purpose. It is to this question that we next turn our attention.

III.

. . .

In sum, to the extent that the Texas system of school finance results in unequal expenditures between children who happen to reside in different districts, we cannot say that such disparities are the product of a system that is so irrational as to be invidiously discriminatory. Texas has acknowledged its shortcomings and has persistently endeavored—not without some success—to ameliorate the differences in levels of expenditures without sacrificing the benefits of local participation. The Texas plan is not the result of hurried, ill-conceived legislation. It certainly is not the product of purposeful discrimination against any group or class. On the contrary, it is rooted in decades of experience in Texas and elsewhere, and in major part is the product of responsible studies by qualified people. In giving substance to the presumption of validity to which the Texas system is entitled, . . . it is important to remember that at every stage of its development it has constituted a "rough accommodation" of interests in an effort to arrive at practical and workable solutions. . . . One also must remember that the system here challenged is not peculiar to Texas or to any other State. In its essential characteristics the Texas plan for financing public education reflects what many educators for a half century have thought was an enlightened approach to a problem for which there is no perfect solution. We are unwilling to assume for ourselves a level of wisdom superior to that of legislators, scholars, and educational authorities in 49 States, especially where the alternatives proposed are only recently conceived and nowhere yet tested. . . .

. . .

Reversed.

■ MR. JUSTICE STEWART, concurring.

. . .

Unlike other provisions of the Constitution, the Equal Protection Clause confers no substantive rights and creates no substantive liberties.[2] The function of the Equal Protection Clause, rather, is simply to measure the validity of *classifications* created by state laws.

There is hardly a law on the books that does not affect some people differently from others. But the basic concern of the Equal Protection Clause is with state legislation whose purpose or effect is to create discrete and objectively identifiable classes. And with respect to such legislation, it has long been settled that the Equal Protection Clause is offended only by laws that are invidiously discriminatory—only by classifications that are wholly arbitrary or capricious. . . .

. . .

■ MR. JUSTICE BRENNAN, dissenting.

Although I agree with my Brother White that the Texas statutory scheme is devoid of any rational basis, and for that reason is violative of the Equal Protection Clause, I also record my disagreement with the Court's rather distressing assertion that a right may be deemed "fundamental" for the purposes of equal protection analysis only if it is "explicitly or implicitly guaranteed by the Constitution." . . . As my Brother Marshall convincingly demonstrates, our prior cases stand for the proposition that "fundamentality" is, in large measure, a function of the right's importance in terms of the effectuation of those rights which are in fact constitutionally guaranteed. Thus, "[a]s the nexus between the specific constitutional guarantee and the nonconstitutional interest draws closer, the nonconstitutional interest becomes more fundamental and the degree of judicial scrutiny applied when the interest is infringed on a discriminatory basis must be adjusted accordingly." . . .

Here, there can be no doubt that education is inextricably linked to the right to participate in the electoral process and to the rights of free speech and association guaranteed by the First Amendment. . . . This being so, any classification affecting education must be subjected to strict judicial scrutiny, and since even the State concedes that the statutory scheme now before us cannot pass constitutional muster under this stricter standard of review, I can only conclude that the Texas school financing scheme is constitutionally invalid.

■ MR. JUSTICE WHITE, with whom MR. JUSTICE DOUGLAS and MR. JUSTICE BRENNAN join, dissenting.

. . .

The Equal Protection Clause permits discriminations between classes but requires that the classification bear some rational relationship to a permissible object sought to be attained by the statute. It is not enough that the Texas system before us seeks to achieve the valid, rational purpose of maximizing local initiative; the means chosen by the State must also be rationally related to the end sought to be achieved. . . .

---

[2] There is one notable exception to the above statement: It has been established in recent years that the Equal Protection Clause confers the substantive right to participate on an equal basis with other qualified voters whenever the State has adopted an electoral process for determining who will represent any segment of the State's population. See, e.g., Reynolds v. Sims, 377 U.S. 533; Kramer v. Union School District, 395 U.S. 621; Dunn v. Blumstein, 405 U.S. 330, 336. But there is no constitutional right to vote, as such. Minor v. Happersett, 88 U.S. 162. If there were such a right, both the Fifteenth Amendment and the Nineteenth Amendment would have been wholly unnecessary.

Neither Texas nor the majority heeds this rule. If the State aims at maximizing local initiative and local choice, by permitting school districts to resort to the real property tax if they choose to do so, it utterly fails in achieving its purpose in districts with property tax bases so low that there is little if any opportunity for interested parents, rich or poor, to augment school district revenues. Requiring the State to establish only that unequal treatment is in furtherance of a permissible goal, without also requiring the State to show that the means chosen to effectuate that goal are rationally related to its achievement, makes equal protection analysis no more than an empty gesture. In my view, the parents and children in Edgewood, and in like districts, suffer from an invidious discrimination violative of the Equal Protection Clause.

. . .

■ MR. JUSTICE MARSHALL, with whom MR. JUSTICE DOUGLAS concurs, dissenting.

. . .

. . . I must once more voice my disagreement with the Court's rigidified approach to equal protection analysis. See Dandridge v. Williams, 397 U.S. 471, 519–521 (1970) (dissenting opinion). . . . The Court apparently seeks to establish today that equal protection cases fall into one of two neat categories which dictate the appropriate standard of review—strict scrutiny or mere rationality. But this Court's decisions in the field of equal protection defy such easy categorization. A principled reading of what this Court has done reveals that it has applied a spectrum of standards in reviewing discrimination allegedly violative of the Equal Protection Clause. This spectrum clearly comprehends variations in the degree of care with which the Court will scrutinize particular classifications, depending, I believe, on the constitutional and societal importance of the interest adversely affected and the recognized invidiousness of the basis upon which the particular classification is drawn. I find in fact that many of the Court's recent decisions embody the very sort of reasoned approach to equal protection analysis for which I previously argued—that is, an approach in which "concentration [is] placed upon the character of the classification in question, the relative importance to the individuals in the class discriminated against of the governmental benefits they do not receive, and the asserted state interests in support of the classification." Dandridge v. Williams. . . .

I therefore cannot accept the majority's labored efforts to demonstrate that fundamental interests, which call for strict scrutiny of the challenged classification, encompass only established rights which we are somehow bound to recognize from the text of the Constitution itself. To be sure, some interests which the Court has deemed to be fundamental for purposes of equal protection analysis are themselves constitutionally protected rights. . . . But it will not do to suggest that the "answer" to whether an interest is fundamental for purposes of equal protection analysis is *always* determined by whether that interest "is a right . . . explicitly or implicitly guaranteed by the Constitution." . . .

. . .

The majority is, of course, correct when it suggests that the process of determining which interests are fundamental is a difficult one. But I do not think the problem is insurmountable. And I certainly do not accept the view that the process need necessarily degenerate into an unprincipled, subjective "picking-and-choosing" between various interests or that it must involve this Court in creating "substantive constitutional rights in the name of guaranteeing equal protection of the laws." . . . Although not all fundamental interests are constitutionally guaranteed, the determination of which interests are fundamental should be firmly rooted in the text of the Constitution. The task in every case should be to determine the extent to which constitutionally guaranteed rights are dependent on interests not mentioned in the Constitution. As the nexus between the specific constitutional guarantee and the nonconstitutional interest draws closer, the nonconstitutional interest becomes more fundamental and the degree of judicial scrutiny applied when the interest is infringed on a discriminatory basis must be adjusted accordingly. Thus, it cannot be denied that interests such as procreation, the exercise of the state franchise, and access to criminal appellate processes are not fully guaranteed to the citizen by our Constitution. But these interests have nonetheless been afforded special judicial consideration in the face of discrimination because they are, to some extent, interrelated with constitutional guarantees. Procreation is now understood to be important because of its interaction with the established constitutional right of privacy. The exercise of the state franchise is closely tied to basic civil and political rights inherent in the First Amendment. And access to criminal appellate processes enhances the integrity of the range of rights implicit in the Fourteenth Amendment guarantee of due process of law. Only if we closely protect the related interests from state discrimination do we ultimately ensure the integrity of the constitutional guarantee itself. This is the real lesson that must be taken from our previous decisions involving interests deemed to be fundamental.

. . .

. . . The majority suggests . . . that a variable standard of review would give this Court the appearance of a "super-legislature." . . . I cannot agree. Such an approach seems to me a part of the guarantees of our Constitution and of the historic experiences with oppression of and discrimination against discrete, powerless minorities which underlie that document. In truth, the Court itself will be open to the criticism raised by the majority so long as it continues on its present course of effectively selecting in private which cases will be afforded special consideration without acknowledging the true basis of its action.[67] . . .

. . .

As the Court points out, . . . no previous decision has deemed the presence of just a wealth classification to be sufficient basis to call forth "rigorous judicial scrutiny" of allegedly discriminatory state action. Compare, e.g., *Harper v. Virginia Board of Elections,* supra, with e.g., James v. Valtierra, 402 U.S. 137 (1971). That wealth classifications alone have not necessarily been considered to bear the same high degree of suspectness as have classifications based on, for instance, race or alienage may be explainable on a number of grounds. The "poor" may not be seen as politically powerless as certain discrete and insular minority groups. Personal poverty may entail much the same social stigma as historically attached to certain racial or ethnic groups. But personal poverty is not a permanent disability; its shackles may be escaped. Perhaps, most importantly, though, personal wealth may not necessarily share the general irrelevance as basis for legislative action that race or nationality is recognized to have. While the "poor" have frequently been a legally disadvantaged group, it cannot be ignored that social legislation must frequently take cognizance of the economic status of our citizens. Thus, we have generally gauged the invidiousness of wealth classifications with an awareness of the importance of the interests being affected and the relevance of personal wealth to those interests. See *Harper v. Virginia Board of Elections,* supra.

When evaluated with these considerations in mind, it seems to me that discrimination on the basis of group wealth in this case likewise calls for careful judicial scrutiny. . . .

---

[67] See generally Gunther, The Supreme Court, 1971 Term: Foreword, In Search of Evolving Doctrine on a Changing Court: A Model for a Newer Equal Protection, 86 Harv.L.Rev. 1 (1972).

. . .

Plyler v. Doe

457 U.S. 202, 102 S.Ct. 2382, 72 L.Ed.2d 786 (1982).

■ JUSTICE BRENNAN delivered the opinion of the Court.

The question presented by these cases is whether, consistent with the Equal Protection Clause of the Fourteenth Amendment, Texas may deny to undocumented school-age children the free public education that it provides to children who are citizens of the United States or legally admitted aliens.

I

Since the late nineteenth century, the United States has restricted immigration into this country. Unsanctioned entry into the United States is a crime, 8 U.S.C. § 1325, and those who have entered unlawfully are subject to deportation, 8 U.S.C. §§ 1251–1252. But despite the existence of these legal restrictions, a substantial number of persons have succeeded in unlawfully entering the United States. . . .

In May 1975, the Texas legislature revised its education laws to withhold from local school districts any state funds for the education of children who were not "legally admitted" into the United States. The 1975 revision also authorized local school districts to deny enrollment in their public schools to children not "legally admitted" to the country. . . . These cases involve constitutional challenges to those provisions.

. . .

II

The Fourteenth Amendment provides that "No State shall . . . deprive any person of life, liberty, or property, without due process of law; nor deny to *any person within its jurisdiction* the equal protection of the laws." Appellants argue at the outset that undocumented aliens, because of their immigration status, are not "persons within the jurisdiction" of the State of Texas, and that they therefore have no right to the equal protection of Texas law. We reject this argument. Whatever his status under the immigration laws, an alien is surely a "person" in any ordinary sense of that term. Aliens, even aliens whose presence in this country is unlawful, have long been recognized as "persons" guaranteed due process of law by the Fifth and Fourteenth Amendments. Shaughnessy v. Mezei, 345 U.S. 206, 212 (1953); Wong Wing v. United States, 163 U.S. 228, 238 (1896); Yick Wo v. Hopkins, 118 U.S. 356, 369 (1886). Indeed, we have clearly held that the Fifth Amendment protects aliens whose presence in this country is unlawful from invidious discrimination by the Federal Government. Mathews v. Diaz, 426 U.S. 67, 77 (1976).

. . .

III

. . .

. . . [W]e have treated as presumptively invidious those classifications that disadvantage a "suspect class,"[14] or that impinge upon the exercise of a "fundamental

---

[14] Several formulations might explain our treatment of certain classifications as "suspect." Some classifications are more likely than others to reflect deep-seated prejudice rather than legislative rationality in pursuit of some legitimate objective. Legislation predicated on such prejudice is easily recognized as incompatible with the constitutional understanding that each person is to be judged individually and is entitled to equal justice under the law. Classifications treated as suspect tend to be irrelevant to any proper legislative goal. See McLaughlin v. Florida, 379 U.S. 184, 192 (1964); Hirabayashi v. United States, 320 U.S. 81, 100 (1943). Finally, certain groups, indeed largely the same

right."[15] With respect to such classifications, [we] requir[e] the State to demonstrate that its classification has been precisely tailored to serve a compelling governmental interest. In addition, we have recognized that certain forms of legislative classification, while not facially invidious, nonetheless give rise to recurring constitutional difficulties; in these limited circumstances we have sought the assurance that the classification reflects a reasoned judgment consistent with the ideal of equal protection by inquiring whether it may fairly be viewed as furthering a substantial interest of the State.[16] We turn to a consideration of the standard appropriate for the evaluation of § 21.031.

A

Sheer incapability or lax enforcement of the laws barring entry into this country, coupled with the failure to establish an effective bar to the employment of undocumented aliens, has resulted in the creation of a substantial "shadow population" of illegal migrants—numbering in the millions—within our borders. This situation raises the specter of a permanent caste of undocumented resident aliens, encouraged by some to remain here as a source of cheap labor, but nevertheless denied the benefits that our society makes available to citizens and lawful residents. The existence of such an underclass presents most difficult problems for a Nation that prides itself on adherence to principles of equality under law.[19]

The children who are plaintiffs in these cases are special members of this underclass. Persuasive arguments support the view that a State may withhold its beneficence from those whose very presence within the United States is the product of

---

groups, have historically been "relegated to such a position of political powerlessness as to command extraordinary protection from the majoritarian political process." San Antonio School District v. Rodriguez, 411 U.S. 1, 28 (1973); Graham v. Richardson, 403 U.S. 365, 372 (1971); see United States v. Carolene Products Co., 304 U.S. 144, 152–153, n. 4 (1938). The experience of our Nation has shown that prejudice may manifest itself in the treatment of some groups. Our response to that experience is reflected in the Equal Protection Clause of the Fourteenth Amendment. Legislation imposing special disabilities upon groups disfavored by virtue of circumstances beyond their control suggests the kind of "class or caste" treatment that the Fourteenth Amendment was designed to abolish.

[15] In determining whether a class-based denial of a particular right is deserving of strict scrutiny under the Equal Protection Clause, we look to the Constitution to see if the right infringed has its source, explicitly or implicitly, therein. But we have also recognized the fundamentality of participation in state "elections on an equal basis with other citizens in the jurisdiction," Dunn v. Blumstein . . . , even though "the right to both, *per se,* is not a constitutionally protected right." San Antonio School District, 411 U.S., at 35, n. 78. With respect to suffrage, we have explained the need for strict scrutiny as arising from the significance of the franchise as the guardian of all other rights. See Harper v. Virginia Bd. of Elections, 383 U.S. 663, 667 (1966); Reynolds v. Sims, 377 U.S. 533, 562 (1964). . . .

[16] See Craig v. Boren, 429 U.S. 190 (1976); Lalli v. Lalli, 439 U.S. 259 (1978). This technique of "intermediate" scrutiny permits us to evaluate the rationality of the legislative judgment with reference to well-settled constitutional principles. . . . Only when concerns sufficiently absolute and enduring can be clearly ascertained from the Constitution and our cases do we employ this standard to aid us in determining the rationality of the legislative choice.

[19] We reject the claim that "illegal aliens" are a "suspect class." No case in which we have attempted to define a suspect class, see e.g., n. 14 supra, has addressed the status of persons unlawfully in our country. Unlike most of the classifications that we have recognized as suspect, entry into this class, by virtue of entry into this country, is the product of voluntary action. Indeed, entry into the class is itself a crime. In addition, it could hardly be suggested that undocumented status is a "constitutional irrelevancy." With respect to the actions of the federal government, alienage classifications may be intimately related to the conduct of foreign policy, to the federal prerogative to control access to the United States, and to the plenary federal power to determine who has sufficiently manifested his allegiance to become a citizen of the Nation. No State may independently exercise a like power. But if the Federal Government has by uniform rule prescribed what it believes to be appropriate standards for the treatment of an alien subclass, the States may, of course, follow the federal direction. See De Canas v. Bica, 424 U.S. 351 (1976).

their own unlawful conduct. These arguments do not apply with the same force to classifications imposing disabilities on the minor *children* of such illegal entrants. At the least, those who elect to enter our territory by stealth and in violation of our law should be prepared to bear the consequences, including, but not limited to, deportation. But the children of those illegal entrants are not comparably situated. Their "parents have the ability to conform their conduct to societal norms," and presumably the ability to remove themselves from the State's jurisdiction; but the children who are plaintiffs in these cases "can affect neither their parents' conduct nor their own status." Trimble v. Gordon, 430 U.S. 762, 770 (1977). Even if the State found it expedient to control the conduct of adults by acting against their children, legislation directing the onus of a parent's misconduct against his children does not comport with fundamental conceptions of justice. . . .

Of course, undocumented status is not irrelevant to any proper legislative goal. Nor is undocumented status an absolutely immutable characteristic since it is the product of conscious, indeed unlawful, action. But § 21.031 is directed against children, and imposes its discriminatory burden on the basis of a legal characteristic over which children can have little control. It is thus difficult to conceive of a rational justification for penalizing these children for their presence within the United States. Yet that appears to be precisely the effect of § 21.031.

Public education is not a "right" granted to individuals by the Constitution. San Antonio School District. . . . But neither is it merely some governmental "benefit" indistinguishable from other forms of social welfare legislation. Both the importance of education in maintaining our basic institutions, and the lasting impact of its deprivation on the life of the child, mark the distinction. The "American people have always regarded education and the acquisition of knowledge as matters of supreme importance." Meyer v. Nebraska, 262 U.S. 390, 400 (1923). We have recognized "the public school as a most vital civic institution for the preservation of a democratic system of government," Abington School District v. Schempp, 374 U.S. 203, 230 (1963) (Brennan, J., concurring), and as the primary vehicle for transmitting "the values on which our society rests." Ambach v. Norwick, 441 U.S. 68, 76 (1979). . . . In addition, education provides the basic tools by which individuals might lead economically productive lives to the benefit of us all. In sum, education has a fundamental role in maintaining the fabric of our society. We cannot ignore the significant social costs borne by our Nation when select groups are denied the means to absorb the values and skills upon which our social order rests.

In addition to the pivotal role of education in sustaining our political and cultural heritage, denial of education to some isolated group of children poses an affront to one of the goals of the Equal Protection Clause: the abolition of governmental barriers presenting unreasonable obstacles to advancement on the basis of individual merit. Paradoxically, by depriving the children of any disfavored group of an education, we foreclose the means by which that group might raise the level of esteem in which it is held by the majority. But more directly, "education prepares individuals to be self-reliant and self-sufficient participants in society." Wisconsin v. Yoder. . . . Illiteracy is an enduring disability. The inability to read and write will handicap the individual deprived of a basic education each and every day of his life. The inestimable toll of that deprivation on the social, economic, intellectual and psychological well-being of the individual, and the obstacle it poses to individual achievement, makes it most difficult to reconcile the cost or the principle of a status-based denial of basic education with the framework of equality embodied in the Equal Protection Clause. What we said 28 years ago in Brown v. Board of Education, 347 U.S. 483 (1954), still holds true:

"... In these days, it is doubtful that any child may reasonably be expected to succeed in life if he is denied the opportunity of an education. Such an opportunity, where the state has undertaken to provide it, is a right which must be made available to all on equal terms."

B

These well-settled principles allow us to determine the proper level of deference to be afforded § 21.031. Undocumented aliens cannot be treated as a suspect class because their presence in this country in violation of federal law is not a "constitutional irrelevancy." Nor is education a fundamental right; a State need not justify by compelling necessity every variation in the manner in which education is provided to its population. See San Antonio School Dist. v. Rodriguez, 411 U.S. 1, 28–39 (1973). But more is involved in this case than the abstract question whether § 21.031 discriminates against a suspect class, or whether education is a fundamental right. Section 21.031 imposes a lifetime hardship on a discrete class of children not accountable for their disabling status. The stigma of illiteracy will mark them for the rest of their lives. By denying these children a basic education, we deny them the ability to live within the structure of our civic institutions, and foreclose any realistic possibility that they will contribute in even the smallest way to the progress of our Nation. In determining the rationality of § 21.031, we may appropriately take into account its costs to the Nation and to the innocent children who are its victims. In light of these countervailing costs, the discrimination contained in § 21.031 can hardly be considered rational unless it furthers some substantial goal of the State.

IV

It is the State's principal argument, and apparently the view of the dissenting Justices, that the undocumented status of these children *vel non* establishes a sufficient rational basis for denying them benefits that a State might choose to afford other residents. The State notes that while other aliens are admitted "on an equality of legal privileges with all citizens under non-discriminatory laws," Takahashi v. Fish & Game Comm'n, 334 U.S. 410, 420 (1948), the asserted right of these children to an education can claim no implicit congressional imprimatur. Indeed, on the State's view, Congress' apparent disapproval of the presence of these children within the United States, and the evasion of the federal regulatory program that is the mark of undocumented status, provides authority for its decision to impose upon them special disabilities. Faced with an equal protection challenge respecting the treatment of aliens, we agree that the courts must be attentive to congressional policy; the exercise of congressional power might well affect the State's prerogatives to afford differential treatment to a particular class of aliens. But we are unable to find in the congressional immigration scheme any statement of policy that might weigh significantly in arriving at an equal protection balance concerning the State's authority to deprive these children of an education.

. . .

To be sure, like all persons who have entered the United States unlawfully, these children are subject to deportation. 8 U.S.C. §§ 1251–1252. But there is no assurance that a child subject to deportation will ever be deported. An illegal entrant might be granted federal permission to continue to reside in this country, or even to become a citizen. See, e.g., 8 U.S.C. §§ 1252, 1253(h), 1254. In light of the discretionary federal power to grant relief from deportation, a State cannot realistically determine that any particular undocumented child will in fact be deported until after deportation proceedings have been completed. It would of course be most difficult for the State to justify a denial of education to a child enjoying an inchoate federal permission to remain.

We are reluctant to impute to Congress the intention to withhold from these children, for so long as they are present in this country through no fault of their own, access to a basic education. In other contexts, undocumented status, coupled with some articulable federal policy, might enhance State authority with respect to the treatment of undocumented aliens. But in the area of special constitutional sensitivity presented by this case, and in the absence of any contrary indication fairly discernible in the present legislative record, we perceive no national policy that supports the State in denying these children an elementary education. The State may borrow the federal classification. But to justify its use as a criterion for its own discriminatory policy, the State must demonstrate that the classification is reasonably adapted to *"the purposes for which the state desires to use it."* Oyama v. California, 332 U.S. 633, 664–665 (1948) (Murphy, J., concurring) (emphasis added). We therefore turn to the state objectives that are said to support § 21.031.

V

Appellants argue that the classification at issue furthers an interest in the "preservation of the state's limited resources for the education of its lawful residents." Of course, a concern for the preservation of resources standing alone can hardly justify the classification used in allocating those resources. . . . The State must do more than justify its classification with a concise expression of an intention to discriminate. . . . Apart from the asserted state prerogative to act against undocumented children solely on the basis of their undocumented status—an asserted prerogative that carries only minimal force in the circumstances of this case—we discern three colorable state interests that might support § 21.031.

First, appellants appear to suggest that the State may seek to protect the State from an influx of illegal immigrants. While a State might have an interest in mitigating the potentially harsh economic effects of sudden shifts in population, § 21.031 hardly offers an effective method of dealing with an urgent demographic or economic problem. There is no evidence in the record suggesting that illegal entrants impose any significant burden on the State's economy. To the contrary, the available evidence suggests that illegal aliens underutilize public services, while contributing their labor to the local economy and tax money to the State fisc. . . .

Second, . . . appellants suggest that undocumented children are appropriately singled out for exclusion because of the special burdens they impose on the State's ability to provide high quality public education. But the record in no way supports the claim that exclusion of undocumented children is likely to improve the overall quality of education in the State. . . .

Finally, appellants suggest that undocumented children are appropriately singled out because their unlawful presence within the United States renders them less likely than other children to remain within the boundaries of the State, and to put their education to productive social or political use within the State. Even assuming that such an interest is legitimate, it is an interest that is most difficult to quantify. The State has no assurance that any child, citizen or not, will employ the education provided by the State within the confines of the State's borders. In any event, the record is clear that many of the undocumented children disabled by this classification will remain in this country indefinitely, and that some will become lawful residents or citizens of the United States. It is difficult to understand precisely what the State hopes to achieve by promoting the creation and perpetuation of a subclass of illiterates within our boundaries, surely adding to the problems and costs of unemployment, welfare, and crime. It is thus clear that whatever savings might be achieved by denying these children an education, they are wholly insubstantial in light of the costs involved to these children, the State, and the Nation.

VI

If the State is to deny a discrete group of innocent children the free public education that it offers to other children residing within its borders, that denial must be justified by a showing that it furthers some substantial state interest. No such showing was made here. Accordingly, the judgment of the Court of Appeals in each of these cases is

Affirmed.

■ Justice Marshall, concurring.

While I join the Court opinion, ... I continue to believe that an individual's interest in education is fundamental.... Furthermore, I believe that the facts of these cases demonstrate the wisdom of rejecting a rigidified approach to equal protection analysis, and of employing an approach that allows for varying levels of scrutiny depending upon "the constitutional and societal importance of the interest adversely affected and the recognized invidiousness of the basis upon which the particular classification is drawn." ...

■ Justice Blackmun, concurring.

I join the opinion and judgment of the Court.

Like Justice Powell, I believe that the children involved in this litigation "should not be left on the streets uneducated." I write separately, however, because in my view the nature of the interest at stake is crucial to the proper resolution of this case.

The "fundamental rights" aspect of the Court's equal protection analysis—the now-familiar concept that governmental classifications bearing on certain interests must be closely scrutinized—has been the subject of some controversy....

    ...

I joined Justice Powell's opinion for the Court in *Rodriguez,* and I continue to believe that it provides the appropriate model for resolving most equal protection disputes. Classifications infringing substantive constitutional rights necessarily will be invalid, if not by force of the Equal Protection Clause, then through operation of other provisions of the Constitution. Conversely, classifications bearing on nonconstitutional interests—even those involving "the most basic economic needs of impoverished human beings," Dandridge v. Williams, 397 U.S. 471, 485 (1970)— generally are not subject to special treatment under the Equal Protection Clause, because they are not distinguishable in any relevant way from other regulations in "the area of economics and social welfare." Ibid.

With all this said, however, I believe the Court's experience has demonstrated that the *Rodriguez* formulation does not settle every issue of "fundamental rights" arising under the Equal Protection Clause. Only a pedant would insist that there are *no* meaningful distinctions among the multitude of social and political interests regulated by the States, and *Rodriguez* does not stand for quite so absolute a proposition....

    ...

In my view, when the State provides an education to some and denies it to others, it immediately and inevitably creates class distinctions of a type fundamentally inconsistent with ... the Equal Protection Clause. Children denied an education are placed at a permanent and insurmountable competitive disadvantage, for an uneducated child is denied even the opportunity to achieve. And when those children are members of an identifiable group, that group—through the State's action—will have been converted into a discrete underclass. Other benefits provided by the State, such as housing and public assistance, are of course important; to an individual in immediate need, they may be more desirable than the right to be educated. But classifications involving the complete denial of education are in a sense unique, for they strike at the heart of equal protection values by involving the State in the creation of permanent class distinctions. . . . In a sense, then, denial of an education is the analogue of denial of the right to vote: the former relegates the individual to second-class social status; the latter places him at a permanent political disadvantage.

This conclusion is fully consistent with *Rodriguez*[, which] reserved judgment on the constitutionality of a state system that "occasioned an absolute denial of educational opportunities to any of its children," noting that "no charge fairly could be made that the system [at issue in *Rodriguez*] fails to provide each child with an opportunity to acquire . . . basic minimal skills." . . .

. . . Whatever the State's power to classify deportable aliens, . . . and whatever the Federal Government's ability to draw more precise and more acceptable alienage classifications, the statute at issue here sweeps within it a substantial number of children who will in fact, and who may well be entitled to, remain in the United States. Given the extraordinary nature of the interest involved, this makes the classification here fatally imprecise. And, as the Court demonstrates, the Texas legislation is not otherwise supported by any substantial interests.

. . .

■ JUSTICE POWELL, concurring.

I join the opinion of the Court, and write separately to emphasize the unique character of the case before us.

. . .

Although the analogy is not perfect, our holding today does find support in decisions of this Court with respect to the status of illegitimates. In Weber v. Aetna Casualty & Surety Co., 406 U.S. 164, 175 (1972) we said: "visiting . . . condemnation on the head of an infant" for the misdeeds of the parents is illogical, unjust, and "contrary to the basic concept of our system that legal burdens should bear some relationship to individual responsibility or wrongdoing."

. . .

In my view, the State's denial of education to these children bears no substantial relation to any substantial state interest. Both of the district courts found that an uncertain but significant percentage of illegal alien children will remain in Texas as residents and many eventually will become citizens. . . .

. . . [I]t hardly can be argued rationally that anyone benefits from the creation within our borders of a subclass of illiterate persons many of whom will remain in the State, adding to the problems and costs of both State and National Governments attendant upon unemployment, welfare and crime.

■ CHIEF JUSTICE BURGER, with whom JUSTICE WHITE, JUSTICE REHNQUIST, and JUSTICE O'CONNOR join, dissenting.

Were it our business to set the Nation's social policy, I would agree without hesitation that it is senseless for an enlightened society to deprive any children—including illegal aliens—of an elementary education. I fully agree that it would be folly—and wrong—to tolerate creation of a segment of society made up of illiterate persons, many having a limited or no command of our language. However, the Constitution does not constitute us as "Platonic Guardians" nor does it vest in this Court the authority to strike down laws because they do not meet our standards of desirable social policy, "wisdom," or "common sense." . . . We trespass on the assigned function of the political branches under our structure of limited and separated powers when we assume a policy making role as the court does today.

The Court makes no attempt to disguise that it is acting to make up for Congress' lack of "effective leadership" in dealing with the serious national problems caused by the influx of uncountable millions of illegal aliens across our borders. . . . However, it is not the function of the judiciary to provide "effective leadership" simply because the political branches of government fail to do so.

. . .

Once it is conceded—as the Court does—that illegal aliens are not a suspect class, and that education is not a fundamental right, our inquiry should focus on and be limited to whether the legislative classification at issue bears a rational relationship to a legitimate state purpose. . . .

. . .

. . . [T]hat there are sound *policy* arguments against the Texas legislature's choice does not render that choice an unconstitutional one.

. . .

Congress, "vested by the Constitution with the responsibility of protecting our borders and legislating with respect to aliens," bears primary responsibility for addressing the problems occasioned by the millions of illegal aliens flooding across our southern border. . . . While the "specter of a permanent caste" of illegal Mexican residents of the United States is indeed a disturbing one, it is but one segment of a larger problem, which is for the political branches to solve. I find it difficult to believe that Congress would long tolerate such a self-destructive result—that it would fail to deport these illegal alien families or to provide for the education of their children. Yet instead of allowing the political processes to run their course—albeit with some delay—the Court seeks to do Congress' job for it, compensating for congressional inaction. It is not unreasonable to think that this encourages the political branches to pass their problems to the judiciary.

The solution to this seemingly intractable problem is to defer to the political processes, unpalatable as that may be to some.

Martinez v. Bynum

461 U.S. 321 (1983).

A child born in Texas (and thus a United States citizen) lived with his parents in Mexico, where they were citizens, until he returned to Texas at age 8 to live with his sister in order to attend public school there. He challenged the constitutionality on its face of a Texas law denying tuition-free admission to local public schools to minors who live apart from their parents or guardians, if the minor's presence in the school district is "for the primary purpose of attending the public free schools." The Court rejected the facial attack. Justice Powell's majority opinion said that a "bona fide residence requirement, appropriately defined and uniformly applied, furthers the substantial state interest in assuring that services provided for its residents are enjoyed only by residents." As discussed in the report of this case supra p. 694, the Court concluded that the law "does not burden or penalize the constitutional right of interstate travel[.]" By granting "the benefits of residency to everyone who satisfies the traditional residence definition [of physical presence and an intention to remain indefinitely] and to some who legitimately could be classified as nonresidents"—those who do not intend to remain indefinitely in the district but currently reside there other than for the sole purpose of attending school—the State adopted a legitimate bona fide residence requirement. Justice Powell also found an "independent justification for local residence requirements in the public-school context" in the maintenance of school quality: "Absent residence requirements, . . . the proper planning and operation of the schools would suffer significantly."

Justice Brennan concurred separately "to stress that this case involves only a facial challenge." Justice Marshall dissented, concluding that "the statutory classification, which deprives some children of an education because of their motive for residing in Texas, is not adequately justified by the asserted state interests."

CHAPTER 11

DEFINING THE SCOPE OF "LIBERTY" AND "PROPERTY" PROTECTED BY THE DUE PROCESS CLAUSE—THE PROCEDURAL DUE PROCESS CASES

Introduction. In Chapter 8 we examined the due process clause and its relationship to requirements of fair procedure. In Chapter 9 we examined at length the substantive interests that are protected under the due process clause. The purpose of this chapter is to return to the issue of procedure in order to pursue the general question whether the interests protected by a requirement of fair procedure are the same as those protected by commands of fairness in substance. No attempt is made in this chapter to present a complete picture of the constitutional requirements of fair procedure in criminal, civil, and administrative proceedings. Those requirements are discussed at length in separate courses.

The materials here deal with whether there is, or ought to be, a difference in the interests protected by "substantive" and "procedural" due process. The question arises in two contexts. First, is every interest that is given substantive protection also accorded procedural protection? Does a determination that a particular interest is "liberty" or "property" that is substantively protected (in the sense that the state must establish some reason for imposing a burden on it) carry with it a correlative right to some kind of a hearing in which it can be determined whether the particular burden is justified? Second, does the requirement of fair procedure extend beyond those interests given substantive protection by the Constitution? When government extends protection to an interest it is not constitutionally required to recognize, is there a constitutionally imposed right to a hearing in which it can be determined that the particular burden on the interest is justified? For example, if a state provides for the payment of welfare to persons meeting certain criteria, may it also provide for the removal of individual recipients from the welfare rolls without some form of a hearing in which it can be determined whether the recipients meet the statutory criteria?

Board of Regents of State Colleges v. Roth

408 U.S. 564, 92 S.Ct. 2701, 33 L.Ed.2d 548 (1972).

■ MR. JUSTICE STEWART delivered the opinion of the Court.

In 1968 the respondent, David Roth, was hired for his first teaching job as assistant professor of political science at Wisconsin State University-Oshkosh. He was hired for a fixed term of one academic year. The notice of his faculty appointment specified that his employment would begin on September 1, 1968, and would end on June 30, 1969. The respondent completed that term. But he was informed that he would not be rehired for the next academic year.

The respondent had no tenure rights to continued employment. Under Wisconsin statutory law a state university teacher can acquire tenure as a "permanent" employee only after four years of year-to-year employment. Having acquired tenure, a teacher is entitled to continued employment "during efficiency and good behavior." A relatively new teacher without tenure, however, is under Wisconsin law entitled to nothing beyond his one-year appointment. There are no statutory or administrative standards defining eligibility for re-employment. State law thus clearly leaves the decision whether to rehire a nontenured teacher for another year to the unfettered discretion of University officials.

The procedural protection afforded a Wisconsin State University teacher before he is separated from the University corresponds to his job security. As a matter of statutory law, a tenured teacher cannot be "discharged except for cause upon written charges" and pursuant to certain procedures. A nontenured teacher, similarly, is protected to some extent *during* his one-year term. Rules promulgated by the Board of Regents provide that a nontenured teacher "dismissed" before the end of the year may have some opportunity for review of the "dismissal." But the Rules provide no real protection for a nontenured teacher who simply is not re-employed for the next year. He must be informed by February first "concerning retention or non-retention for the ensuing year." But "no reason for non-retention need be given. No review or appeal is provided in such case."

In conformance with these Rules, the President of Wisconsin State University-Oshkosh informed the respondent before February 1, 1969, that he would not be rehired for the 1969–1970 academic year. He gave the respondent no reason for the decision and no opportunity to challenge it at any sort of hearing.

The respondent then brought this action in a federal district court alleging that the decision not to rehire him for the next year infringed his Fourteenth Amendment rights. He attacked the decision both in substance and procedure. First, he alleged that the true reason for the decision was to punish him for certain statements critical of the University administration, and that it therefore violated his right to freedom of speech. Second, he alleged that the failure of University officials to give him notice of any reason for nonretention and an opportunity for a hearing violated his right to procedural due process of law.

The District Court granted summary judgment for the respondent on the procedural issue, ordering the University officials to provide him with reasons and a hearing. The Court of Appeals, with one judge dissenting, affirmed this partial summary judgment. We granted certiorari. The only question presented to us at this stage in the case is whether the respondent had a constitutional right to a statement of reasons and a hearing on the University's decision not to rehire him for another year. We hold that he did not.

I.

The requirements of procedural due process apply only to the deprivation of interests encompassed within the Fourteenth Amendment's protection of liberty and property. When protected interests are implicated the right to some kind of prior hearing is paramount. But the range of interests protected by procedural due process is not infinite.

. . .

"Liberty" and "property" are broad and majestic terms. They are among the "[g]reat [constitutional] concepts . . . purposely left to gather meaning from experience. . . . [T]hey relate to the whole domain of social and economic fact, and the statesmen who founded this Nation knew too well that only a stagnant society remains unchanged." National Ins. Co. v. Tidewater Co., 337 U.S. 582, 646 (Frankfurter, J., dissenting). For that reason the Court has fully and finally rejected the wooden distinction between "rights" and "privileges" that once seemed to govern the applicability of procedural due process rights. The Court has also made clear that the property interests protected by procedural due process extend well beyond actual ownership of real estate, chattels, or money. By the same token, the Court has required due process protection for deprivations of liberty beyond the sort of formal constraints imposed by the criminal process.

. . .

Yet, while the Court has eschewed rigid or formalistic limitations on the protection of procedural due process, it has at the same time observed certain boundaries. For the words "liberty" and "property" in the Due Process Clause of the Fourteenth Amendment must be given some meaning.

II.

. . .

There might be cases in which a State refused to re-employ a person under such circumstances that interests in liberty would be implicated. But this is not such a case.

The State, in declining to rehire the respondent, did not make any charge against him that might seriously damage his standing and associations in his community. It did not base the nonrenewal of his contract on a charge, for example, that he had been guilty of dishonesty, or immorality. Had it done so, this would be a different case. . . . In such a case, due process would accord an opportunity to refute the charge before University officials.[12] In the present case, however, there is no suggestion whatever that the respondent's interest in his "good name, reputation, honor or integrity" is at stake.

Similarly, there is no suggestion that the State, in declining to reemploy the respondent, imposed on him a stigma or other disability that foreclosed his freedom to take advantage of other employment opportunities. The State, for example, did not invoke any regulations to bar the respondent from all other public employment in State universities. Had it done so, this, again, would be a different case. . . .

To be sure, the respondent has alleged that the non-renewal of his contract was based on his exercise of his right to freedom of speech. But this allegation is not now before us. The District Court stayed proceedings on this issue, and the respondent has yet to prove that the decision not to rehire him was, in fact, based on his free speech activities.[14]

---

[12] The purpose of such notice and hearing is to provide the person an opportunity to clear his name. Once a person has cleared his name at a hearing, his employer, of course, may remain free to deny him future employment for other reasons.

[14] . . .

When a State would directly impinge upon interests in free speech or free press, this Court has on occasion held that opportunity for a fair adversary hearing must precede the action, whether or not the speech or press interest is clearly protected under substantive First Amendment standards. Thus we have required fair notice and opportunity for an adversary hearing before an injunction is issued against the holding of rallies and public meetings. Carroll v. Princess Anne, 393 U.S. 175. Similarly, we have indicated the necessity of procedural safeguards before a State makes a large-scale seizure of a person's allegedly obscene books, magazines and so forth. A Quantity of Books v. Kansas, 378 U.S. 205; Marcus v. Search Warrant, 367 U.S. 717. See Freedman v. Maryland, 380 U.S. 51; Bantam Books v. Sullivan, 372 U.S. 58. See generally Monaghan, First Amendment "Due Process," 83 Harv.L.Rev. 518.

In the respondent's case, however, the State has not directly impinged upon interests in free speech or free press in any way comparable to a seizure of books or an injunction against meetings. Whatever may be a teacher's rights of free speech, the interest in holding a teaching job at a state university, *simpliciter,* is not itself a free speech interest.

Hence, on the record before us, all that clearly appears is that the respondent was not rehired for one year at one University. It stretches the concept too far to suggest that a person is deprived of "liberty" when he simply is not rehired in one job but remains as free as before to seek another. . . .

III.

The Fourteenth Amendment's procedural protection of property is a safeguard of the security of interests that a person has already acquired in specific benefits. These interests—property interests—may take many forms.

. . .

Certain attributes of "property" interests protected by procedural due process emerge from these decisions. To have a property interest in a benefit, a person clearly must have more than an abstract need or desire for it. He must have more than a unilateral expectation of it. He must, instead, have a legitimate claim of entitlement to it. It is a purpose of the ancient institution of property to protect those claims upon which people rely in their daily lives, reliance that must not be arbitrarily undermined. It is a purpose of the constitutional right to a hearing to provide an opportunity for a person to vindicate those claims.

Property interests, of course, are not created by the Constitution. Rather, they are created and their dimensions are defined by existing rules or understandings that stem from an independent source such as state law—rules or understandings that secure certain benefits and that support claims of entitlement to those benefits. Thus the welfare recipients in *Goldberg v. Kelly,* supra, had a claim of entitlement to welfare payments that was grounded in the statute defining eligibility for them. The recipients had not yet shown that they were, in fact, within the statutory terms of eligibility. But we held that they had a right to a hearing at which they might attempt to do so.

Just as the welfare recipients' "property" interest in welfare payments was created and defined by statutory terms, so the respondent's "property" interest in employment at the Wisconsin State University-Oshkosh was created and defined by the terms of his appointment. Those terms secured his interest in employment up to June 30, 1969. But the important fact in this case is that they specifically provided that the respondent's employment was to terminate on June 30. They did not provide for contract renewal absent "sufficient cause." Indeed, they made no provision for renewal whatsoever.

Thus the terms of the respondent's appointment secured absolutely no interest in re-employment for the next year. They supported absolutely no possible claim of entitlement to re-employment. Nor, significantly, was there any state statute or University rule or policy that secured his interest in re-employment or that created any legitimate claim to it.[16] In these circumstances, the respondent surely had an abstract concern in being rehired, but he did not have a *property* interest sufficient to require the University authorities to give him a hearing when they declined to renew his contract of employment.

IV.

. . .

. . . [T]he respondent has not shown that he was deprived of liberty or property protected by the Fourteenth Amendment. The judgment of the Court of Appeals,

---

[16] To be sure, the respondent does suggest that most teachers hired on a year-to-year basis by the Wisconsin State University-Oshkosh are, in fact, rehired. But the District Court has not found that there is anything approaching a "common law" of re-employment, see Perry v. Sindermann, post, at 602, so strong as to require University officials to give the respondent a statement of reasons and a hearing on their decision not to rehire him.

accordingly, is reversed and the case is remanded for further proceedings consistent with this opinion.

It is so ordered.

■ MR. JUSTICE MARSHALL, dissenting.

. . .

In my view, every citizen who applies for a government job is entitled to it unless the government can establish some reason for denying the employment. This is the "property" right that I believe is protected by the Fourteenth Amendment and that cannot be denied "without due process of law." And it is also liberty—liberty to work—which is the "very essence of the personal freedom and opportunity" secured by the Fourteenth Amendment.

. . .

It may be argued that to provide procedural due process to all public employees or prospective employees would place an intolerable burden on the machinery of government. Cf. Goldberg v. Kelly, supra. The short answer to that argument is that it is not burdensome to give reasons when reasons exist. Whenever an application for employment is denied, an employee is discharged, or a decision not to rehire an employee is made, there should be some reason for the decision. It can scarcely be argued that government would be crippled by a requirement that the reason be communicated to the person most directly affected by the government's action.

Where there are numerous applicants for jobs, it is likely that few will choose to demand reasons for not being hired. But, if the demand for reasons is exceptionally great, summary procedures can be devised that would provide fair and adequate information to all persons. As long as the government has a good reason for its actions it need not fear disclosure. It is only where the government acts improperly that procedural due process is truly burdensome. And that is precisely when it is most necessary. . . . [a]

Town of Castle Rock v. Gonzales

545 U.S. 748 (2005).

In violation of a restraining order issued in conjunction with divorce proceedings, and without notice, an estranged father took his three daughters from the front of the family home. Tragically, several hours later he murdered them and thereafter was killed in a shoot-out with police. The mother sued the Town, alleging that her

---

[a] Dissenting opinions by Justice Douglas and Brennan are omitted. Justice Powell took no part in the decision.

In Perry v. Sindermann, 408 U.S. 593 (1972) a teacher's employment was terminated without notice of reasons or hearing after being employed by the college for four successive years under a series of one-year contracts. In his suit he alleged that the decision not to rehire him was based on his public criticism of policies of the college administration and thus infringed his right to free speech and that the failure to give him notice and hearing violated procedural due process. The trial court granted summary judgment for the defendant college on the basis of affidavits denying that plaintiff's criticism was involved and asserting no need to provide a hearing. The Court held that this decision was in error for two reasons: (1) Plaintiff was entitled to a full hearing on his free speech claim because "a teacher's public criticism of his superiors on matters of public concern may be constitutionally protected and may, therefore, be an impermissible basis for termination of his employment." (2) Plaintiff was also entitled to a hearing on his allegation that he had in fact some form of tenure under the practices of the college. There "may be an unwritten 'common law' in a particular university that certain employees shall have the equivalent of tenure." Plaintiff was entitled to show whether that existed in this case and, if it did, he would be entitled to an order obligating college officials to give him a hearing.

See Simon, *Liberty and Property in the Supreme Court: A Defense of Roth and Perry,* 71 Calif.L.Rev. 146 (1983).

repeated, unsuccessful efforts throughout the night to have the police enforce the restraining order were thwarted by a police department policy or custom of failing to respond properly and tolerating non-enforcement of restraining orders, thereby depriving her, without due process, of a statutorily-based property interest in police enforcement of the restraining order.

The Court held that she "did not, for purposes of the Due Process Clause, have a property interest in police enforcement of the restraining order against her husband." Noting that "a benefit is not a protected entitlement if government officials may grant or deny it in their discretion[,]" Justice Scalia's majority opinion said that "the central state-law question is whether Colorado law gave respondent a right to police enforcement of the restraining order"—a question as to which the Court found deference to the Tenth Circuit Court of Appeals "inappropriate," primarily because its opinion "did not draw upon a deep well of state-specific expertise, but consisted primarily of quoting language from the restraining order, the statutory text, and a state-legislative-hearing transcript." The Court's own examination led it to conclude that Colorado statutory provisions apparently obligating police to use "every reasonable means to enforce a restraining order," and to "arrest, or if an arrest would be impractical under the circumstances, seek a warrant for the arrest of a restrained person" when there is probable cause that the person has violated the order, did not "truly ma[k]e enforcement of restraining orders *mandatory*. A well established tradition of police discretion has long coexisted with apparently mandatory arrest statutes." Accordingly, "a true mandate of police action would require some stronger indication from the Colorado Legislature. . . ."

Justice Scalia also wrote:

"Respondent does not specify the precise means of enforcement that the Colorado restraining-order statute assertedly mandated—whether her interest lay in having police arrest her husband, having them seek a warrant for his arrest, or having them 'use every reasonable means, up to and including arrest, to enforce the order's terms . . .' Such indeterminacy is not the hallmark of a duty that is mandatory. Nor can someone be safely deemed 'entitled' to something when the identity of the alleged entitlement is vague. . . . The dissent ultimately contends that the obligations under the statute were quite precise: either make an arrest or (if that is impractical) seek an arrest warrant. The problem with this is that the seeking of an arrest warrant would be an entitlement to nothing but procedure—which . . . can[not] be the basis for a property interest. . . . After the warrant is sought, it remains within the discretion of a judge whether to grant it, and after it is granted, it remains within the discretion of the police whether and when to execute it. Respondent would have been assured nothing but the seeking of a warrant. This is not the sort of 'entitlement' out of which a property interest is created.

"Even if the statute could be said to have made enforcement of restraining orders 'mandatory' because of the domestic-violence context of the underlying statute, that would not necessarily mean that state law gave *respondent* an entitlement to *enforcement* of the mandate. Making the actions of government employees obligatory can serve various legitimate ends other than the conferral of a benefit on a specific class of people. . . .

"Respondent's alleged interest stems only from a State's *statutory* scheme—from a restraining order that was authorized by and tracked precisely the statute on which the Court of Appeals relied. She does not assert that she has any common-law or contractual entitlement to enforcement. If she was given a statutory entitlement, we would expect to see some indication of that in the statute itself. Although Colorado's statute spoke of 'protected person[s]' such as respondent, it did so in connection with matters other than a right to enforcement. . . . Perhaps most importantly, the statute spoke directly to the protected person's power to 'initiate contempt proceedings against the restrained person if the order [was] issued in a civil action or request the prosecuting attorney to initiate contempt proceedings if the order [was] issued in a criminal action.' . . . The protected person's express power to 'initiate' civil contempt proceedings contrasts tellingly with the mere ability to 'request' initiation of criminal contempt proceedings—and even more dramatically with the complete silence about any power to 'request' (much less demand) that an arrest be made.

"...

"Even if we were to think otherwise concerning the creation of an entitlement by Colorado, it is by no means clear that an individual entitlement to enforcement of a restraining order could constitute a 'property' interest for purposes of the Due Process Clause. Such a right would not, of course, resemble any traditional conception of property. Although that alone does not disqualify it from due process protection, as *Roth* and its progeny show, the right to have a restraining order enforced does not 'have some ascertainable monetary value,' as even our '*Roth*-type property-as-entitlement' cases have implicitly required. . . . Perhaps most radically, the alleged property interest here arises *incidentally*, not out of some new species of government benefit or service, but out of a function that government actors have always performed—to wit, arresting people who they have probable cause to believe have committed a criminal offense.

". . . In this case . . . '[t]he simple distinction between government action that directly affects a citizen's legal rights . . . and action that is directed against a third party and affects the citizen only indirectly or incidentally, provides a sufficient answer to' respondent's reliance on cases that found government-provided services to be entitlements."

Justice Souter's concurring opinion, joined by Justice Breyer, said in part:

"[Gonzales'] argument is unconventional because the state-law benefit for which it claims federal procedural protection is itself a variety of procedural regulation, a set of rules to be followed by officers exercising the State's executive power: use all reasonable means to enforce, arrest upon demonstrable probable cause, get a warrant, and so on.

"When her argument is [so] understood . . . , a further reason appears for rejecting its call to apply *Roth,* a reason that would apply even if the statutory mandates to the police were absolute, leaving the police with no discretion when the beneficiary of a protective order insists upon its enforcement. . . . [The] argument is at odds with the rule that '[p]rocess is not an end in itself. Its constitutional purpose is to protect a substantive interest to which the individual has a legitimate claim of entitlement.' . . . Just as a State cannot diminish a property right, once conferred, by attaching less than generous procedure to its deprivation, . . . neither does a State create a property right merely by ordaining beneficial procedure unconnected to some articulable substantive guarantee. . . . [W]e have not identified property with procedure as such. State rules of executive procedure, however important, may be nothing more than rules of executive procedure.

"Thus, in every instance of property recognized by this Court as calling for federal procedural protection, the property has been distinguishable from the procedural obligations imposed on state officials to protect it. Whether welfare benefits, Goldberg v. Kelly, 397 U.S. 254 (1970), attendance at public schools, Goss v. Lopez, 419 U.S. 565 (1975), utility services, Memphis Light, Gas & Water Div. v. Craft, 436 U.S. 1 (1978), public employment, Perry v. Sindermann, 408 U.S. 593 (1972), professional licenses, Barry v. Barchi, 443 U.S. 55 (1979), and so on, the property interest recognized in our cases has always existed apart from state procedural protection before the Court has recognized a constitutional claim to protection by federal process.... There is no articulable distinction between the object of Gonzales's asserted entitlement and the process she desires in order to protect her entitlement; both amount to certain steps to be taken by the police to protect her family and herself. Gonzales's claim would thus take us beyond *Roth* or any other recognized theory of Fourteenth Amendment due process, by collapsing the distinction between property protected and the process that protects it, and would federalize every mandatory state-law direction to executive officers whose performance on the job can be vitally significant to individuals affected.

"The procedural directions involved here ... presuppose no enforceable substantive entitlement, and *Roth* does not raise them to federally enforceable status in the name of due process."

Justice Stevens dissented, joined by Justice Ginsburg. Among the points he emphasized were that the States had passed a wave of "mandatory arrest" statutes in the domestic violence context in the 1980s and 1990s "with the unmistakable goal of eliminating police discretion in this area"; that "the Colorado statute at issue in this case was enacted for the benefit of the narrow class of persons who are beneficiaries of domestic restraining orders, and ... the order at issue in this case was specifically intended to provide protection to respondent and her children"; and "that a citizen's interest in the government's commitment to provide police enforcement in certain defined circumstances ... is just as concrete and worthy of protection as her interest in any other important service the government or a private firm has undertaken to provide." In his view, "under the statute, the police were *required* to provide enforcement; *they lacked the discretion to do nothing*.... Under the statute, if the police have probable cause that a violation has occurred, enforcement consists of either making an immediate arrest or seeking a warrant and then executing an arrest— traditional, well-defined tasks that law enforcement officers perform every day." Moreover, "[b]ecause the statute's guarantee of police enforcement is triggered by, and operates only in reference to, a judge's granting of a restraining order in favor of an identified 'protected person,' "there is simply no room to suggest that such a person has received merely an ' "incidental' " or ' "indirect' " benefit." In the concluding section of his dissent, Justice Stevens wrote in part:

"Given that Colorado law has quite clearly eliminated the police's discretion to deny enforcement, respondent is correct that she had much more than a 'unilateral expectation' that the restraining order would be enforced; rather, she had a 'legitimate claim of entitlement' to enforcement. *Roth*....

"Police enforcement of a restraining order is a government service that is no less concrete and no less valuable than other government services, such as education. The relative novelty of recognizing this type of property interest is explained by the relative novelty of the domestic violence statutes creating a mandatory arrest duty; before this innovation, the unfettered discretion that characterized police enforcement defeated any citizen's 'legitimate claim of entitlement' to this service.... Colorado law *guaranteed* the provision of a certain service, in certain defined circumstances, to a certain class of beneficiaries, and respondent reasonably relied on that guarantee. As we observed in *Roth*, '[i]t is a purpose of the ancient institution of property to protect those claims upon which people rely in their daily lives, reliance that must not be arbitrarily undermined.' ... Surely, if respondent had contracted with a private security firm to provide her and her daughters with protection from her husband, it would be apparent that she possessed a property interest in such a contract. Here, Colorado undertook a comparable obligation, and respondent—with restraining order in hand—justifiably relied on that undertaking. Respondent's claim of entitlement to this promised service is no less legitimate than the other claims our cases have upheld, and no less concrete than a hypothetical agreement with a private firm. The fact that it is based on a statutory enactment and a judicial order entered for her special protection, rather than on a formal contract, does not provide a principled basis for refusing to consider it 'property' worthy of constitutional protection.[20]"

. . .

Law That Defines Substantive Entitlements Together with Procedural Qualifications

Not long after *Roth* and *Sindermann*, the Court divided over the proper treatment of statutes that simultaneously appeared to create legitimate expectations of continued employment absent some kind of cause for dismissal and limited procedures for determining the existence of such cause. Should the entitlement provisions be thought to stand alone as creating a "property" interest whose deprivation required procedural protections mandated by the Due Process clauses? Or should the procedural qualification provisions be understood to define a more circumscribed "property" interest whose deprivation only required compliance with the requirements of the entitlement granting law?

In Arnett v. Kennedy, 416 U.S. 134 (1974), six Justices writing in separate concurring and dissenting opinions, seemed to take the former approach. In Bishop v. Wood, 426 U.S. 341 (1976), four of those dissented from a majority's decision that a discharged policeman was not deprived "of a property interest protected by the Fourteenth Amendment." Justice Stevens' majority opinion concluded that a "tenable" interpretation of state law by the lower federal courts was that the local ordinance, which provided that a permanent employee could be discharged for failing to perform work up to the standard of his classification, or for negligence, inefficiency or unfitness, might "be construed as granting no right to continued employment but merely conditioning an employee's removal on compliance with certain specified procedures" and thus "that petitioner 'held his position at the will and pleasure of the city.'" On that construction *Arnett* was irrelevant, the Court said, for there "the Court concluded that because the employee could only be discharged for cause, he had a property interest . . . entitled to constitutional protection."

Justice White's dissent, joined by Justices Brennan, Marshall and Blackmun, thought *Arnett* indistinguishable, for he understood the ordinance to contain "unequivocal language . . . that [petitioner] may be dismissed only for certain kinds of cause[,]" so that the majority's holding "rests . . . on the fact that state law provides no *procedures* for assuring that the City Manager dismiss him only for cause. The right to his job apparently given by the first two sentences of the ordinance is thus redefined, according to the majority, by the procedures provided for in the third sentence and as redefined is infringed only if the procedures are not followed." In a footnote, Justice White said that he did "not disagree with the majority or the courts below on the meaning of the state law"—that "as a matter of state law petitioner has no remedy no matter how arbitrarily or erroneously the City Manager has acted." Rather, "I differ . . . only with respect to the constitutional significance of an unambiguous state law. A majority of the Justices in Arnett v. Kennedy . . . stood on the proposition that the

---

[20] . . . Justice Souter . . . misunderstands respondent's claim. . . . [R]espondent is in fact asserting a substantive interest in the "enforcement of the restraining order"[—]a tangible, substantive act. If an estranged husband violates a restraining order by abducting children, and the police succeed in enforcing the order, the person holding the restraining order has undeniably just received a substantive benefit. As in other procedural due process cases, respondent is arguing that the police officers failed to follow fair procedures in ascertaining whether the statutory criteria that trigger their obligation to provide enforcement—*i.e.*, an outstanding order plus probable cause that it is being violated—were satisfied in her case. . . . It is Justice Souter, not respondent, who makes the mistake of "collapsing the distinction between property protected and the process that protects it."

Constitution required procedures *not* required by state law when the state conditions dismissal on 'cause.' "

Over a decade later, the Court addressed this problem more definitively in the following case.

Cleveland Board of Education v. Loudermill

470 U.S. 532 (1985).

An Ohio statute provided that classified civil service employees were entitled to retain their positions "during good behavior and efficient service" and could not be dismissed except for "misfeasance, malfeasance, or nonfeasance in office." It also required that an employee dismissed for cause be provided with an order of removal giving the reasons therefor and allowed an appeal to a state administrative board whose judgment could be reviewed in the state trial court.

A state security guard stated on his job application that he had never been convicted of a felony. Several months after he was hired the Board of Education discovered that he had been convicted of grand larceny, discharged him, and gave him a letter stating this reason. He appealed to the Civil Service Commission, which upheld his dismissal. He then filed this case in the federal district court, arguing that the state statute was unconstitutional on its face because it did not give him a chance to respond to charges before dismissal. A bus mechanic fired by the Parma Board of Education after failing an eye examination filed a similar suit after the Civil Service Commission ordered his reinstatement but without back pay. The district court rejected both claims, but the court of appeals reversed and the Supreme Court affirmed.

Justice White's opinion for the Court said:

". . . The statute plainly supports the conclusion, reached by both lower courts, that respondents possessed property rights in continued employment. . . .

"The Parma Board argues, however, that the property right is defined by, and conditioned on, the legislature's choice of procedures for its deprivation. . . . The procedures were adhered to in these cases. According to petitioner, '[t]o require additional procedures would in effect expand the scope of the property interest itself'. . . .

"This argument . . . has its genesis in the plurality opinion in *Arnett v. Kennedy*. . . . *Arnett* involved a challenge by a former federal employee to the procedures by which he was dismissed. The plurality reasoned that where the legislation conferring the substantive right also sets out the procedural mechanism for enforcing that right, the two cannot be separated:

'The employee's statutorily defined right is not a guarantee against removal without cause in the abstract, but such a guarantee as enforced by the procedures which Congress has designated for the determination of cause.

. . .

'. . . [W]here the grant of a substantive right is inextricably intertwined with the limitations on the procedures which are to be employed in determining that right, a litigant in the position of appellee must take the bitter with the sweet.' . . . "

After pointing out that six Justices in *Arnett* had specifically rejected this view and discussing subsequent cases, Justice White wrote:

"In light of these holdings, it is settled that the 'bitter with the sweet' approach misconceives the constitutional guarantee. If a clearer holding is needed, we provide it today. The point is straightforward: the Due Process Clause provides that certain substantive rights—life, liberty, and property—cannot be deprived except pursuant to constitutionally adequate procedures. The categories of substance and procedure are distinct. Were the rule otherwise, the Clause would be reduced to a mere tautology. 'Property' cannot be defined by the procedures provided for its deprivation any more than can life or liberty. The right to due process 'is conferred, not be legislative grace, but by constitutional guarantee. While the legislature may elect not to confer a property interest in [public] employment, it may not constitutionally authorize the deprivation of such an interest, once conferred, without appropriate procedural safeguards.' Arnett v. Kennedy, supra, 416 U.S., at 167 (Powell, J., concurring in part and concurring in result in part); see id., at 185 (White, J., concurring in part and dissenting in part).

"In short, once it is determined that the Due Process Clause applies, 'the question remains what process is due.' Morrissey v. Brewer, 408 U.S. 471, 481 (1972). The answer to that question is not to be found in the Ohio statute."

The Court then held that an employee must have some kind of hearing before discharge when he has a constitutionally protected property interest in his employment. But when a full administrative hearing and judicial review is available after termination, the employee does not have a right to a full adversarial evidentiary hearing before discharge. "The tenured public employee is entitled to oral or written notice of the charges against him, an explanation of the employer's evidence, and an opportunity to present his side of the story. . . . To require more than this prior to termination would intrude to an unwarranted extent on the government's interest in quickly removing an unsatisfactory employee."

Justice Marshall argued that the employee should receive a full adversarial evidentiary pre-termination hearing.

Justice Rehnquist dissented alone on the issue raised in *Arnett:*

"We ought to recognize the totality of the State's definition of the property right in question, and not merely seize upon one of several paragraphs in a unitary statute to proclaim that in that paragraph the State has inexorably conferred upon a civil service employee something which it is powerless under the United States Constitution to qualify in the next paragraph of the statute. This practice ignores our duty under *Roth* to rely on state law as the source of property interests for purposes of applying the Due Process Clause of the Fourteenth Amendment. While it does not impose a federal definition of property, the Court departs from the full breadth of the holding in *Roth* by its selective choice from among the sentences the Ohio legislature chooses to use in establishing and qualifying a right."

The Interrelationships of Substantive and Procedural Due Process

What is the relationship between the constitutional requirements of "fair substance" and "fair procedure"? In theory, the procedural requirement is conceptually distinct from any constitutional limit on the substance of government policy.

Hearings reinforce the rule of law by insuring official regularity and minimizing the scope for arbitrary decision-making. The procedural requirement may also serve, however, as a means for forcing the state to take more seriously than it might otherwise the substantive issues at stake. In Fuentes v. Shevin, 407 U.S. 67 (1972), the Court held invalid a state law which permitted summary seizure of property under a writ of replevin without prior notice or hearing to the possessor of the property. As part of its justification for requiring a prior hearing the Court said:

"The constitutional right to be heard is a basic aspect of the duty of government to follow a fair process of decisionmaking when it acts to deprive a person of his possessions. The purpose of this requirement is not only to ensure abstract fair play to the individual. Its purpose, more particularly, is to protect his use and possession of property from arbitrary encroachment—to minimize substantively unfair or mistaken deprivations of property, a danger that is especially great when the State seizes goods simply upon the application of and for the benefit of a private party. So viewed, the prohibition against the deprivation of property without due process of law reflects the high value, embedded in our constitutional and political history, that we place on a person's right to enjoy what is his, free of governmental interference. See Lynch v. Household Finance Corp., 405 U.S. 538.

"The requirement of notice and an opportunity to be heard raises no impenetrable barrier to the taking of a person's possessions. But the fair process of decisionmaking that it guarantees works, by itself, to protect against arbitrary deprivation of property. For when a person has an opportunity to speak up in his own defense, and when the State must listen to what he has to say, substantively unfair and simply mistaken deprivations of property interests can be prevented."

The problem of distinguishing substance and procedure is most complex where the state provides benefits it is not constitutionally compelled to provide. What are the procedural requirements, if any, when the state discharges an employee or terminates welfare benefits? Three situations must be distinguished:

(1)   The state in creating the benefit also creates standards to govern its termination. For example, a state provides that certain government employees can be discharged only for "good cause". Even though the government is not obligated to provide the job, is it required by procedural due process to provide a fair hearing in applying its own standards to take a job away?

(2)   The state in creating the benefit provides that it may be taken away at will. For example, a state provides that particular government employees may be fired in their superiors' discretion. The question now is whether the state may terminate a job in the unconstrained discretion of an administrative official. Is that question one of substantive due process? Or of procedural due process? If it is decided that the state can use standardless discretion to terminate the benefit, can there be any requirement of fair procedure? Or is the necessity for a hearing obviated in these situations because, as Justice Stevens observed in Codd v. Velger, 429 U.S. 624 (1977), "a hearing would [be] pointless because nothing plaintiff [can] prove [will] entitle him to keep his job"?

(3)   The state creates the benefit, establishes standards to govern its termination, and provides the procedures to be used in determining whether the standards for termination have been met. If those procedures do not meet the minimum standards of fairness required by due process, will they be held invalid? *Loudermill* says yes. Can that be reconciled with the view that the state may avoid any hearing requirement when it authorizes standardless discretion for termination of employment?

Michael H. v. Gerald D.

491 U.S. 110, 109 S.Ct. 2333, 105 L.Ed.2d 91 (1989).

[The report of this case appears *supra*, at p. 388.]

Sandin v. Conner

515 U.S. 472, 115 S.Ct. 2293, 132 L.Ed.2d 418 (1995).

■ CHIEF JUSTICE REHNQUIST delivered the opinion of the Court.

We granted certiorari to reexamine the circumstances under which state prison regulations afford inmates a liberty interest protected by the Due Process Clause.

I

[While serving an indeterminate sentence of 30 years to life in a Hawaii prison, Conner reacted angrily to a strip-search and was charged with "high misconduct" for physical interference with a correctional function and "low moderate misconduct" for using abusive or obscene language and for harassing employees. An adjustment committee held a hearing at which Conner appeared but was not allowed to present witnesses. The committee found him guilty and sentenced him, inter alia, to 30 days disciplinary segregation for the physical obstruction charge. On appeal, months after serving this punishment, the deputy administrator found unsupported, and so expunged, the high misconduct charge. In the interim, Conner had sued in federal court, claiming that the refusal to allow him to present witnesses deprived him of procedural due process.] The District Court granted summary judgment in favor of the prison officials.

The Court of Appeals . . . reversed. . . . It concluded that Conner had a liberty interest in remaining free from disciplinary segregation . . . based . . . on a prison regulation that instructs the committee to find guilt when a charge of misconduct is supported by substantial evidence. . . . [It] reasoned from Kentucky Department of Corrections v. Thompson, 490 U.S. 454 (1989), that the committee's duty to find guilt was nondiscretionary. From the language of the regulation, it drew a negative inference that the committee may not impose segregation if it does not find substantial evidence of misconduct. . . . It viewed this as a state-created liberty interest. . . . We . . . reverse.

II

Our due process analysis begins with Wolff [v. McDonnell, 418 U.S. 539 (1974), where] Nebraska inmates challenged the decision of prison officials to revoke good time credits without adequate procedures. . . . Inmates earned good time credits under a state statute that bestowed mandatory sentence reductions for good behavior, . . . revocable only for "flagrant or serious misconduct[.]" . . . We held that the Due Process Clause itself does not create a liberty interest in credit for good behavior, but that the statutory provision created a liberty interest in a "shortened prison sentence" which resulted from good time credits, credits which were revocable only if the prisoner was guilty of serious misconduct. . . . The Court characterized this liberty interest as one of "real substance". . . .

Inmates in Meachum [v. Fano, 427 U.S. 215 (1976), challenged] transfers from a Massachusetts medium security prison to a maximum security facility with substantially less favorable conditions. . . . The Court began with the proposition that the Due Process Clause does not protect every change in the conditions of confinement having a substantial adverse impact on the prisoner. It then held that the Due Process Clause did not itself create a liberty interest in prisoners to be free from intrastate prison transfers. . . . It reasoned that transfer to a maximum security facility, albeit one with more burdensome conditions, was "within the normal limits or range of custody which the conviction has authorized the State to impose." . . . The Court distinguished Wolff by noting that there the protected liberty interest in good time credit had been created by state law; here no comparable Massachusetts law stripped officials of the discretion to transfer prisoners to alternate facilities "for whatever reason or for no reason at all." . . .

Shortly after *Meachum*, the Court embarked on a different approach to defining state-created liberty interests. Because dictum in *Meachum* distinguished *Wolff* by focusing on whether state action was mandatory or discretionary, the Court in later cases laid ever greater emphasis on this somewhat mechanical dichotomy. . . .

[In Hewitt v. Helms, 459 U.S. 460 (1983), the Court] evaluat[ed] the claims of inmates who had been confined to administrative segregation[. I]t first rejected the inmates' claim of a right to remain in the general population. . . . The Due Process Clause standing alone confers no liberty interest in freedom from state action taken " 'within the sentence imposed[.]' " It then concluded that the transfer to less amenable quarters for nonpunitive reasons was "ordinarily contemplated by a prison sentence." . . . Examination of the possibility that the State had created a liberty interest by virtue of its prison regulations followed. Instead of looking to whether the State created an interest of "real substance" comparable to the good time credit scheme of *Wolff*, the Court asked whether the State had gone beyond issuing mere procedural guidelines and had used "language of an unmistakably mandatory character" such that the incursion on liberty would not occur "absent specified substantive predicates." . . . Finding such mandatory directives in the regulations before it, the Court decided that the State had created a protected liberty interest. . . .

As this methodology took hold, no longer did inmates need to rely on a showing that they had suffered a " 'grievous loss' " of liberty retained even after sentenced to terms of imprisonment. Morrissey v. Brewer, 408 U.S. 471, 481 (1972). . . . For the Court had ceased to examine the "nature" of the interest with respect to interests allegedly created by the State. . . . In a series of cases since *Hewitt*, the Court has wrestled with the language of intricate, often rather routine prison guidelines to determine whether mandatory language and substantive predicates created an enforceable expectation that the state would produce a particular outcome with respect to the prisoner's conditions of confinement.

. . .

By shifting the focus of the liberty interest inquiry to one based on the language of a particular regulation, and not the nature of the deprivation, the Court encouraged prisoners to comb regulations in search of mandatory language on which to base entitlements to various state-conferred privileges. Courts have, in response, and not altogether illogically, drawn negative inferences from mandatory language in the text of prison regulations. The Court of Appeals' approach in this case is typical: it inferred from the mandatory directive that a finding of guilt "shall" be imposed under certain conditions the conclusion that the absence of such conditions prevents a finding of guilt.

Such a conclusion may be entirely sensible in the ordinary task of construing a statute defining rights and remedies available to the general public. It is a good deal less sensible in the case of a prison regulation primarily designed to guide correctional officials in the administration of a prison. . . .

Hewitt has produced at least two undesirable effects. First, it creates disincentives for States to codify prison management procedures in the interest of uniform treatment. . . . States may avoid creation of "liberty" interests by having scarcely any regulations, or by conferring standardless discretion on correctional personnel.

Second, the *Hewitt* approach has led to the involvement of federal courts in the day-to-day management of prisons, often squandering judicial resources with little offsetting benefit to anyone. . . .

[W]e believe that the search for a negative implication from mandatory language in prisoner regulations has strayed from the real concerns undergirding the liberty protected by the Due Process Clause. The time has come to return to the due process principles . . . in *Wolff* and *Meachum.* Following *Wolff*, we recognize that States may under certain circumstances create liberty interests which are protected by the Due Process Clause. . . . But these interests will be generally limited to freedom from restraint which, while not exceeding the sentence in such an unexpected manner as to give rise to protection by the Due Process Clause of its own force, see, e.g., Vitek, 445 U.S., at 493 (transfer to mental hospital), and Washington, 494 U.S., at 221–222 (involuntary administration of psychotropic drugs), nonetheless imposes atypical and significant hardship on the inmate in relation to the ordinary incidents of prison life.

Conner asserts, incorrectly, that any state action taken for a punitive reason encroaches upon a liberty interest under the Due Process Clause even in the absence of any state regulation. Neither Bell v. Wolfish, 441 U.S. 520 (1979), nor Ingraham v. Wright, 430 U.S. 651 (1977), requires such a rule. *Bell* dealt with the interests of pretrial detainees and not convicted prisoners. . . .

. . . *Ingraham* . . . addressed the rights of schoolchildren to remain free from arbitrary corporal punishment. The Court noted that the Due Process Clause historically encompassed the notion that the state could not "physically punish an individual except in accordance with due process of law" and so found schoolchildren sheltered. . . .

The punishment of incarcerated prisoners, on the other hand, serves different aims than those found invalid in *Bell* and *Ingraham*. The process does not impose retribution in lieu of a valid conviction, nor does it maintain physical control over free citizens forced by law to subject themselves to state control over the educational mission. It effectuates prison management and prisoner rehabilitative goals. . . . Admittedly, prisoners do not shed all constitutional rights at the prison gate, . . . but " '[l]awful incarceration brings about the necessary withdrawal or limitation of many privileges and rights, a retraction justified by the considerations underlying our penal system.' " . . . Discipline by prison officials in response to a wide range of misconduct falls within the expected parameters of the sentence imposed by a court of law.

This case, though concededly punitive, does not present a dramatic departure from the basic conditions of Conner's indeterminate sentence. Although Conner points to dicta in cases implying that solitary confinement automatically triggers due process protection, . . . this Court has not had the opportunity to address in an argued case the question whether disciplinary confinement of inmates itself implicates constitutional liberty interests. We hold that Conner's discipline in segregated confinement did not present the type of atypical, significant deprivation in which a state might conceivably create a liberty interest. The record shows that . . . disciplinary segregation . . . mirrored those conditions imposed upon inmates in administrative segregation and protective custody. We note also that the State expunged Conner's disciplinary record with respect to the "high misconduct" charge 9 months after Conner served time in segregation. Thus, Conner's confinement did not exceed similar, but totally discretionary confinement in either duration or degree of restriction. . . . Based on a comparison between inmates inside and outside disciplinary segregation, the State's actions in placing him there for 30 days did not work a major disruption in his environment.

Nor does Conner's situation present a case where the State's action will inevitably affect the duration of his sentence. . . .

We hold, therefore, that neither the Hawaii prison regulation in question, nor the Due Process Clause itself, afforded Conner a protected liberty interest that would entitle him to the procedural protections set forth in *Wolff*. The regime to which he was subjected as a result of the misconduct hearing was within the range of confinement to be normally expected for one serving an indeterminate term of 30 years to life.

The judgment of the Court of Appeals is accordingly

Reversed.

■ JUSTICE GINSBURG, with whom JUSTICE STEVENS joins, dissenting.

. . .

Unlike the Court, I conclude that Conner had a liberty interest, protected by the Fourteenth Amendment's Due Process Clause, in avoiding the disciplinary confinement he endured. As Justice Breyer details, Conner's prison punishment effected a severe alteration in the conditions of his incarceration. Disciplinary confinement as punishment for "high misconduct" not only deprives prisoners of privileges for protracted periods; unlike administrative segregation and protective custody, disciplinary confinement also stigmatizes them and diminishes parole prospects. Those immediate and lingering consequences should suffice to qualify such confinement as liberty-depriving for purposes of Due Process Clause protection. . . .[1]

I see the Due Process Clause itself, not Hawaii's prison code, as the wellspring of the protection due Conner. Deriving protected liberty interests from mandatory language in local prison codes would make of the fundamental right something more in certain States, something less in others. . . .[2]

Deriving the prisoner's due process right from the code for his prison, moreover, yields this practical anomaly: a State that scarcely attempts to control the behavior of its prison guards may, for that very laxity, escape constitutional accountability; a State that tightly cabins the discretion of its prison workers may, for that attentiveness, become vulnerable to constitutional claims. An incentive for ruleless prison management disserves the State's penological goals and jeopardizes the welfare of prisoners.

. . .

■ JUSTICE BREYER, with whom JUSTICE SOUTER joins, dissenting.

. . .

II

. . . In determining whether state officials have deprived an inmate . . . of a procedurally protected "liberty," this Court traditionally has looked either (1) to the nature of the deprivation (how severe, in degree or kind) or (2) to the State's rules governing the imposition of that deprivation (whether they, in effect, give the inmate a "right" to avoid it). See, e.g., Kentucky Department of Corrections v. Thompson, 490 U.S. 454, 460–461, 464–465 (1989). Thus, this Court has said that certain changes in conditions may be so severe or so different from ordinary conditions of confinement

---

[1]   . . . The Court notes . . . that the State eventually expunged Conner's disciplinary record as a result of his successful administrative appeal. But hindsight cannot tell us whether a liberty interest existed at the outset. One must . . . know at the start the character of the interest at stake in order to determine then what process, if any, is constitutionally due. . . .

[2]   The Court describes a category of liberty interest that is something less than the one the Due Process Clause itself shields, something more than anything a prison code provides. The State may create a liberty interest, the Court tells us, when "atypical and significant hardship [would be borne by] the inmate in relation to the ordinary incidents of prison life." What design lies beneath these key words? The Court ventures no examples, leaving consumers of the Court's work at sea, unable to fathom what would constitute an "atypical, significant deprivation" and yet not trigger protection under the Due Process Clause directly.

that, whether or not state law gives state authorities broad discretionary power to impose them, the state authorities may not do so "without complying with minimum requirements of due process." Vitek v. Jones, 445 U.S. 480, 491–494 (1980) ("involuntary commitment to a mental hospital"); Washington v. Harper, 494 U.S. 210, 221–222 (1990) ("unwanted administration of antipsychotic drugs"). The Court has also said that deprivations that are less severe or more closely related to the original terms of confinement nonetheless will amount to deprivations of procedurally protected liberty, provided that state law (including prison regulations) narrowly cabins the legal power of authorities to impose the deprivation (thereby giving the inmate a kind of right to avoid it). See Hewitt v. Helms. . . .

If we apply these general pre-existing principles to the relevant facts before us, it seems fairly clear . . . that the prison punishment . . . deprived Conner of constitutionally protected "liberty." For one thing, the punishment worked a fairly major change in Conner's conditions. . . .

Moreover, irrespective of whether this punishment amounts to a deprivation of liberty independent of state law, here the prison's own disciplinary rules severely cabin the authority of prison officials to impose this kind of punishment. They . . . (1) impose a punishment that is substantial, (2) restrict its imposition as a punishment to instances in which an inmate has committed a defined offense, and (3) prescribe nondiscretionary standards for determining whether or not an inmate committed that offense.

Accordingly, under this Court's liberty-defining standards, imposing the punishment would "deprive" Conner of "liberty" within the meaning of the Due Process Clause. . . .

III

The majority . . . seeks to change, or to clarify, [those] "liberty" defining standards in one important respect[: by] . . . impos[ing] a minimum standard, namely that a deprivation falls within the Fourteenth Amendment's definition of "liberty" only if it "imposes atypical and significant hardship on the inmate in relation to the ordinary incidents of prison life."

I am not certain whether or not the Court means this standard to change prior law radically. . . . There is no need, however, for . . . significant change . . . to read the . . . Due Process Clause to protect inmates against deprivations of freedom that are important, not comparatively insignificant. Rather, . . . this concern simply requires elaborating, and explaining, the Court's present standards (without radical revision) [so as] not [to] create procedurally protected "liberty" interests where only minor matters are at stake.

Three sets of considerations, taken together, support my conclusion. . . . First, . . . it is not easy to specify just when, or how much of, a loss triggers . . . protection. There is a broad middle category of imposed restraints or deprivations that, considered by themselves, are neither obviously so serious as to fall within, nor obviously so insignificant as to fall without, the Clause's protection.

Second, the difficult line-drawing task that this middle category implies helps to explain why this Court developed its additional liberty-defining standard, which looks to local law (examining whether that local law creates a "liberty" by significantly limiting the discretion of local authorities to impose a restraint). . . . Despite its similarity to the way in which the Court determines the existence, or nonexistence, of "property" for Due Process Clause purposes, the justification for looking at local law is not the same in the prisoner liberty context. In protecting property, the Due Process Clause often aims to protect reliance, say, reliance upon an "entitlement" that local (i.e., nonconstitutional) law itself has created or helped to define. . . . In protecting liberty, however, the Due Process Clause protects . . . an absence of government restraint, the very absence of restraint that we call freedom. . . .

Nevertheless, there are several other important reasons, in the prison context, to consider the provisions of state law. The fact that a further deprivation of an inmate's freedom takes place under local rules that cabin the authorities' discretionary power to impose the restraint suggests, other things being equal, that the matter is more likely to have played an important role in the life of the inmate. . . . It suggests, other things being equal, that the matter is more likely of a kind to which procedural protections historically have applied, and where they normally prove useful, for such rules often single out an inmate and condition a deprivation upon the existence, or nonexistence, of particular facts. . . . It suggests, other things being equal, that the matter will not involve highly judgmental administrative matters that call for the wise exercise of discretion—matters where courts reasonably should hesitate to second-guess prison administrators. . . . It suggests, other things being equal, that the inmate will have thought that he himself, through control of his own behavior, could have avoided the deprivation, and thereby have believed that (in the absence of his misbehavior) the restraint fell outside the "sentence imposed" upon him. . . . Finally, courts can identify the presence or absence of cabined discretion fairly easily and objectively, at least much of the time. . . . These characteristics of "cabined discretion" mean that courts can use it as a kind of touchstone that can help them, when they consider the broad middle category of prisoner restraints, to separate those kinds of restraints that, in general, are more likely to call for constitutionally guaranteed procedural protection, from those that more likely do not. . . . I believe courts will continue to find this touchstone helpful as they seek to apply the majority's middle category standard.

Third, there is, therefore, no need to apply the "discretion-cabining" approach . . . where a deprivation is unimportant enough (or so similar in nature to ordinary imprisonment) that it rather clearly falls outside that middle category. . . . [T]his Court has never held that comparatively unimportant prisoner "deprivations" fall within the scope of the Due Process Clause even if local law limits the authority of prison administrators to impose such minor deprivations. . . . And . . . it should now simply specify that they do not.

I recognize that, as a consequence, courts must separate the unimportant from the potentially significant, without the help of the more objective "discretion-cabining" test. Yet, making that judicial judgment seems no more difficult than many other judicial tasks. . . . It seems to me possible to separate less significant matters such as television privileges . . . from more significant matters, such as the solitary confinement at issue here. Indeed, prison regulations themselves may help in this respect, such as the regulations here which separate (from more serious matters) "low moderate" and "minor" misconduct. . . .

[T]he problems that the majority identifies suggest . . . mak[ing] explicit the lower definitional limit, in the prison context, of "liberty" under the Due Process Clause—a limit . . . already implicit in this Court's precedent. . . . Th[ey] do not require abandoning that precedent. . . .

IV

The Court today reaffirms that the "liberty" protected by the Fourteenth Amendment includes interests that state law may create. It excludes relatively minor matters from that protection. . . . And, it does not question the vast body of case law . . . recognizing that segregation can deprive an inmate of constitutionally-protected "liberty." . . . That being so, it is difficult to see why the Court reverses, rather than affirms, the Court of Appeals in this case.

. . .

I agree [that the] conditions in administrative and disciplinary segregation are relatively similar in Hawaii [and that] the rules governing administrative segregation do, indeed, provide prison officials with broad leeway. But, I disagree with the majority's assertion about the relevance of the expungement. How can a later decision of prison authorities transform Conner's segregation for a violation of a specific disciplinary rule into a term of segregation under the administrative rules? How can a later expungement restore to Conner the liberty that, in fact, he had already lost? . . .

In sum, expungement or no, Conner suffered a deprivation that was significant, not insignificant. And, that deprivation took place under disciplinary rules that . . . do cabin official discretion sufficiently. I would therefore hold that Conner was deprived of "liberty" within the meaning of the Due Process Clause.

. . .

Wilkinson v. Austin
545 U.S. 209 (2005).

Prisoners challenged the procedures Ohio adopted for assignment to the Ohio State Penitentiary (OSP)—its most restrictive, highest security prison, designed to segregate the most dangerous prisoners from the general prison population. The Court unanimously held that under Sandin the inmates possessed a liberty interest in avoiding assignment to OSP but that Ohio's informal, nonadversary procedures were adequate to satisfy due process under Mathews v. Eldridge, 424 U.S. 319 (1976). With respect to the existence of a cognizable liberty interest, the Court noted but did not resolve a divergence among the Courts of Appeals about the application of Sandin's criterion of whether a freedom from restraint "imposes atypical and significant hardship on the inmate in relation to the ordinary incidents of prison life" stemming from the difficulty of "identifying the baseline from which to measure what is atypical and significant in any prison system." Instead, the Court said:

". . . [W]e are satisfied that assignment to OSP imposes an atypical and significant hardship under any plausible baseline.

"For an inmate placed in OSP, almost all human contact is prohibited, even to the point that conversation is not permitted cell to cell; the light, though it may be dimmed, is on for 24 hours; exercise is for 1 hour per day, but only in a small indoor room. Save perhaps for the especially severe limitations on all human contact, these conditions likely would apply to most solitary confinement facilities, but here there are two added components. First is the duration. Unlike the 30-day placement in *Sandin*, placement at OSP is indefinite and, after an initial 30-day review, is reviewed just annually. Second is that placement disqualifies an otherwise eligible inmate for parole consideration. . . . While any of these conditions standing alone might not be sufficient to create a liberty interest, taken together they impose an atypical and significant hardship within the correctional context. It follows that respondents have a liberty interest in avoiding assignment to OSP. . . .

"OSP's harsh conditions may well be necessary and appropriate in light of the danger that high-risk inmates pose both to prison officials and to other prisoners. That necessity, however, does not diminish our conclusion that the conditions give rise to a liberty interest in their avoidance."

Washington v. Harper
494 U.S. 210 (1990).

A mentally ill but not incompetent prisoner challenged, inter alia, the state's failure to provide him with a judicial hearing before administering antipsychotic medication against his will. The Washington Supreme Court held that due process required this and other procedural safeguards. It also held that the substance of the state's policy violated due process, because it allowed forced medication of any inmate found to be mentally ill and "gravely disabled" or dangerous to himself, others or their property, without also requiring proof that the state has a compelling interest in administering the medication and that the administration of the drugs is necessary and effective to further that interest. The Supreme Court overturned both holdings. Justice Kennedy's majority opinion said, in part:

"The Washington Supreme Court's decision . . . has both substantive and procedural aspects. It is axiomatic that procedural protections must be examined in terms of the substantive rights at stake. But identifying the contours of the substantive right remains a task distinct from deciding what procedural protections are necessary to protect that right. '[T]he substantive issue involves a definition of th[e] protected constitutional interest, as well as identification of the conditions under which competing state interests might outweigh it. The procedural issue concerns the minimum procedures required by the Constitution for determining that the individual's liberty interest actually is outweighed in a particular instance.' . . .

"Restated in the terms of this case, the substantive issue is what factual circumstances must exist before the State may administer antipsychotic drugs to the prisoner against his will; the procedural issue is whether the State's nonjudicial mechanisms used to determine the facts in a particular case are sufficient. . . .

"As a matter of state law, the Policy itself undoubtedly confers . . . a right to be free from the arbitrary administration of antipsychotic drugs. . . . By permitting a psychiatrist to treat an inmate with antipsychotic drugs against his wishes only if he is found to be (1) mentally ill and (2) gravely disabled or dangerous, the Policy creates a justifiable expectation on the part of the inmate that the drugs will not be administered unless those conditions exist. . . .

"We have no doubt that, in addition to the liberty interest created by the State's Policy, respondent possesses a significant liberty interest in avoiding the unwanted administration of antipsychotic drugs under the Due Process Clause of the Fourteenth Amendment. . . . Upon full consideration of the administrative scheme, however, we find that the Due Process Clause confers upon respondent no greater right than that recognized under state law.

"Respondent contends that the State, under the mandate of the Due Process Clause, may not override his choice to refuse antipsychotic drugs unless he has been found to be incompetent, and then only if the factfinder makes a substituted judgment that he, if competent, would consent to drug treatment. We disagree. The extent of a prisoner's right . . . must be defined in the context of the inmate's confinement. The Policy . . . requires the State to establish, by a medical finding, that a mental disorder exists which is likely to cause harm if not treated. Moreover, the fact that the medication must first be prescribed by a psychiatrist, and then approved by a reviewing psychiatrist, ensures that the treatment in question will be ordered only if it is in the prisoner's medical interests, given the legitimate needs of his institutional confinement. These standards, which recognize both the prisoner's medical interests and the State's interests, meet the demands of the Due Process Clause.

". . . [T]he proper standard for determining the validity of a prison regulation claimed to infringe on an inmate's constitutional rights is to ask whether the regulation is 'reasonably related to legitimate penological interests.' . . . This is true even when the constitutional right claimed to have been infringed is fundamental, and the State under other circumstances would have been required to satisfy a more rigorous standard of review. . . . The [Washington Supreme Court] erred in refusing to apply the standard of reasonableness."

Applying the reasonableness standard, the Court held "that, given the requirements of the prison environment, the Due Process Clause permits the State to treat a prison inmate who has a serious mental illness with antipsychotic drugs against his will, if the inmate is dangerous to himself or others and the treatment is in the inmate's medical interest." Then, "[h]aving determined that state law recognizes a liberty interest, also protected by the Due Process Clause, which permits refusal of antipsychotic drugs unless certain preconditions are met," the Court addressed "what procedural protections are necessary to ensure the decision to medicate . . . is neither arbitrary nor erroneous under the standards we have discussed above." Despite concluding that "[t]he forcible injection of medication into a nonconsenting person's body represents a substantial interference with that person's liberty" and that "[w]hile the therapeutic benefits of antipsychotic drugs are well documented, it is also true that the drugs can have serious, even fatal, side effects[,]" the Court held that a judicial hearing was unnecessary and that the particular administrative hearing procedures provided by the State satisfied procedural due process.

Justice Stevens dissented in an opinion joined by Justices Brennan and Marshall. He thought the majority had undervalued the liberty interest it had acknowledged:

"[T]he several dimensions of the liberty . . . are both physical and intellectual. Every violation of a person's bodily integrity is an invasion of his or her liberty. The invasion is particularly intrusive if it creates a substantial risk of permanent injury and premature death. Moreover, any such action is degrading if it overrides a competent person's choice to reject a specific form of medical treatment. And when the purpose or effect of forced drugging is to alter the will and the mind of the subject, it constitutes a deprivation of liberty in the most literal and fundamental sense."

Justice Stevens had "no doubt . . . that a competent individual's right to refuse such medication is a fundamental liberty interest deserving the highest order of protection." He found the state's policy invalid, because it "sweepingly sacrifices the inmate's substantive liberty interest to refuse psychotropic drugs, regardless of his medical interests, to institutional and administrative concerns." He also criticized the Court's opinion for failing to separate sufficiently the state's interest in institutional convenience from its interest in helping the inmate's medical condition. Finally, in view of the strength of the liberty interest implicated, he found the state's procedures constitutionally deficient for failing "to have the treatment decision made or reviewed by an impartial person or tribunal."

Kerry v. Din

576 U.S. ___, 135 S.Ct. 2128 (2015).

Din is a citizen and resident of the United States, whose husband is a citizen and resident of Afghanistan and a former civil servant in the Taliban regime. Din successfully petitioned to have her husband classified as her "immediate relative," a status under the Immigration and Nationality Act (INA) that allowed her to sponsor him via a special visa-application process for aliens for entry into the United States. When he applied for the visa, however, he was interviewed, and his application was denied, by the U.S. Embassy in Islamabad, Pakistan, pursuant to INA § 1182(a)(3)(B), which makes an otherwise admissible person inadmissible if he or she has engaged in a "terrorist activity," defined broadly to include "providing material support to a terrorist organization and serving as a terrorist organization's representative. § 1182(a)(3)(B)(i), (iii)–(vi)." After her husband was informed by a consular officer that "he was inadmissible under § 1182(a)(3)(B) but [was] provided no further explanation[,]" Din sued on his behalf, claiming "that the Government denied her due process of law when, without adequate explanation of the reason for the visa denial, it deprived her of her constitutional right to live in the United States with her spouse." (As an "unadmitted and nonresident alien, he[r husband] has no right of entry into the United States, and no cause of action to press in furtherance of his claim for admission.")

With no majority opinion, the Court rejected Din's due process claim. The plurality opinion of Justice Scalia, joined by Chief Justice Roberts and Justice Thomas, concluded that no process was due, because "[t]here is no such constitutional right" to live in the United States with one's spouse. He argued that the historical understanding of "liberty" in the Fifth Amendment derived from Magna Carta and was limited to freedom from imprisonment, confinement, or forcible detention. He argued further that "*even if* one accepts the textually unsupportable doctrine of implied fundamental rights, Din's arguments would fail." He elaborated as follows:

". . . [B]efore conferring constitutional status upon a previously unrecognized 'liberty,' we have required 'a careful description of the asserted fundamental liberty interest,' as well as a demonstration that the interest is 'objectively, deeply rooted in this Nation's history and tradition, and implicit in the concept of ordered liberty, such that neither liberty nor justice would exist if [it was] sacrificed.' . . .

"Din describes the denial of [the] visa application as implicating, alternately, a 'liberty interest in her marriage,' . . . , a 'right of association with one's spouse,' . . . 'a liberty interest in being reunited with certain blood relatives,' . . . and 'the liberty interest of a U. S. citizen under the Due Process Clause to be free from arbitrary restrictions on his right to live with his spouse,' . . . . To be sure, this Court has at times indulged a propensity for grandiloquence when reviewing the sweep of implied rights, describing them so broadly that they would include not only the interests Din asserts but many others as well. . . . But this Court is not bound by dicta, especially dicta that have been repudiated by the holdings of our subsequent cases. And the actual holdings of the cases Din relies upon hardly establish the capacious right she now asserts.

"Unlike the States in Loving v. Virginia, 388 U.S. 1 (1967), Zablocki v. Redhail, 434 U.S. 374 (1978), and Turner v. Safley, 482 U.S. 78 (1987), the Federal Government here has not attempted to forbid a marriage. . . .

" . . .

"Nothing in the cases Din cites establishes a free-floating and categorical liberty interest in marriage (or any other formulation Din offers) sufficient to trigger constitutional protection whenever a regulation in any way touches upon an aspect of the marital relationship. . . . Even if we might 'imply' a liberty interest in marriage generally speaking, that must give way when there is a tradition denying the specific application of that general interest. . . .

"Here, a long practice of regulating spousal immigration precludes Din's claim that the denial of [the] visa application has deprived her of a fundamental liberty interest. Although immigration was effectively unregulated prior to 1875, as soon as Congress began legislating in this area it enacted a complicated web of regulations that erected serious impediments to a person's ability to bring a spouse into the United States. . . .

" . . .

". . . Only by diluting the meaning of a fundamental liberty interest and jettisoning our established jurisprudence could we conclude that the denial of [the] visa application implicates any of Din's fundamental liberty interests."

As for Justice Breyer's dissenting arguments, Justice Scalia wrote this:

"Justice Breyer suggests that procedural due process rights attach to liberty interests that either are (1) created by nonconstitutional law, such as a statute, or (2) 'sufficiently important' so as to 'flow "implicit[ly]"' from the design, object, and nature of the Due Process Clause.'

"The first point is unobjectionable, at least given this Court's case law. . . . But it is unhelpful to Din, who does not argue that a statute confers on her a liberty interest protected by the Due Process Clause. . . . The legal benefits afforded to marriages and the preferential treatment accorded to visa applicants with citizen relatives are insufficient to confer on Din a right that can be deprived only pursuant to procedural due process.

"Justice Breyer's second point—that procedural due process rights attach even to some nonfundamental liberty interests that have not been created by statute—is much more troubling. . . . [H]e argues that the term 'liberty' in the Due Process Clause includes implied rights that, although not so fundamental as to deserve substantive-due-process protection, are important enough to deserve procedural-due-process protection. In other words, there are two categories of implied rights protected by the Due Process Clause: really fundamental rights, which cannot be taken away at all absent a compelling state interest; and not-so-fundamental rights, which can be taken away so long as procedural due process is observed.

"The dissent fails to cite a single case supporting its novel theory of implied nonfundamental rights. . . .

". . .

". . . Justice Breyer proposes . . . a dangerous doctrine. . . . Even shallow-rooted liberties would, thanks to this new procedural-rights-only notion of quasi-fundamental rights, qualify for judicially imposed procedural requirements. Moreover, Justice Breyer gives no basis for distinguishing the fundamental rights recognized in the cases he depends on from the nonfundamental right he believes they give rise to in the present case.

"Neither Din's right to live with her spouse nor her right to live within this country is implicated here. . . . The Government has not refused to recognize Din's marriage . . . , and Din remains free to live with her husband anywhere in the world that both individuals are permitted to reside. And the Government has not expelled Din from the country."

Justice Kennedy, joined by Justice Alito, concurred in the judgment, "[b]ut rather than deciding, as the plurality does, whether Din has a protected liberty interest, my view is that, even assuming she does, the notice she received regarding her husband's visa denial satisfied due process." Indeed, "[t]oday's disposition should not be interpreted as deciding whether a citizen has a protected liberty interest in the visa application of her alien spouse." Given the national security context, he relied on the analysis in Kleindienst v. Mandel, 408 U.S. 753 (1972), and concluded "that the Government satisfied any obligation it might have had to provide Din with a facially legitimate and bona fide reason for its action when it provided notice that her husband was denied admission to the country under § 1182(a)(3)(B)."

Justice Breyer's dissent was joined by Justices Ginsburg, Sotomayor, and Kagan. He wrote in pertinent part:

"The liberty interest that Ms. Din seeks to protect consists of her freedom to live together with her husband in the United States. She seeks procedural, not substantive, protection for this freedom. . . .

"Our cases make clear that the Due Process Clause entitles her to such procedural rights as long as (1) she seeks protection for a liberty interest sufficiently important for procedural protection to flow 'implicit[ly]' from the design, object, and nature of the Due Process Clause, or (2) nonconstitutional law (a statute, for example) creates 'an expectation' that a person will not be deprived of that kind of liberty without fair procedures. . . .

"The liberty for which Ms. Din seeks protection easily satisfies both standards. As this Court has long recognized, the institution of marriage, which encompasses the right of spouses to live together and to raise a family, is central to human life, requires and enjoys community support, and plays a central role in most individuals' 'orderly pursuit of happiness,' . . . . Similarly, the Court has long recognized that a citizen's right to live within this country, being fundamental, enjoys basic procedural due process protection. See Ng Fung Ho v. White, 259 U.S. 276, 284–285 (1922) . . . .

"At the same time, the law, including visa law, surrounds marriage with a host of legal protections to the point that it creates a strong expectation that government will not deprive married individuals of their freedom to live together without strong reasons and (in individual cases) without fair procedure. . . . Justice Scalia's response—that nonconstitutional law creates an 'expectation' that merits procedural protection under the Due Process Clause only if there is an unequivocal statutory right—is sorely mistaken. . . .

"Justice Scalia's more general response—claiming that I have created a new category of constitutional rights—misses the mark. I break no new ground here. Rather, this Court has already recognized that the Due Process Clause guarantees that the government will not, without fair procedure, deprive individuals of a host of rights, freedoms, and liberties that are no more important, and for which the state has created no greater expectation of continued benefit, than the liberty interest at issue here. . . . See, e.g., Wolff v. McDonnell, 418 U. S. 539, 556–557 (1974) (prisoner's right to maintain 'goodtime' credits shortening term of imprisonment; procedurally protected liberty interest based on nonconstitutional law); Paul v. Davis, 424 U. S. 693, 701 (1976) (right to certain aspects of reputation; procedurally protected liberty interest arising under the Constitution); Goss v. Lopez, 419 U. S. 565, 574–575 (1975) (student's right not to be suspended from school class; procedurally protected liberty interest arising under the Constitution); Vitek v. Jones, 445 U. S. 480, 491–495 (1980) (prisoner's right against involuntary commitment; procedurally protected liberty interest arising under the Constitution); Washington v. Harper, 494 U. S. 210, 221–222 (1990) (mentally ill prisoner's right not to take psychotropic drugs; procedurally protected liberty interest arising under the Constitution); see generally Goldberg [v. Kelly, 397 U. S. 254, 262–3 (1970)] (right to welfare benefits; procedurally protected property interest based on nonconstitutional law). How could a Constitution that protects individuals against the arbitrary deprivation of so diverse a set of interests not also offer some form of procedural protection to a citizen threatened with governmental deprivation of her freedom to live together with her spouse in America? . . .

II

A

"The more difficult question is the nature of the procedural protection required by the Constitution. . . .

"[H]ere, the Government makes individualized visa determinations through the application of a legal rule to particular facts. Individualized adjudication normally calls for the ordinary application of Due Process Clause procedures. . . . And those procedures normally include notice of an adverse action, an opportunity to present relevant proofs and arguments, before a neutral decisionmaker, and reasoned decisionmaking. See Hamdi v. Rumsfeld, 542 U. S. 507, 533 (2004) (plurality opinion) . . . . These procedural protections help to guarantee that government will not make a decision directly affecting an individual arbitrarily but will do so through the reasoned application of a rule of law. It is that rule of law, stretching back at least 800 years to Magna Carta, which in major part the Due Process Clause seeks to protect. . . .

"Here, we need . . . consider only the minimum procedure that Ms. Din has requested—namely, a statement of reasons, some kind of explanation, as to why the State Department denied her husband a visa.

" . . .

" . . . [A] statement of reasons, even one provided after a visa denial, serves much the same function as a 'notice' of a proposed action. It allows Ms. Din, who suffered a 'serious loss,' a fair 'opportunity to meet' 'the case' that has produced separation from her husband. . . . Properly apprised of the grounds for the Government's action, Ms. Din can then take appropriate action—whether this amounts to an appeal, internal agency review, or (as is likely here) an opportunity to submit additional evidence and obtain reconsideration . . . .

" . . . [I]n the absence of some highly unusual circumstance (not shown to be present here . . .), the Constitution requires the Government to provide an adequate reason why it refused to grant Ms. Din's husband a visa. That reason, in my view, could be either the factual basis for the Government's decision or a sufficiently specific statutory subsection that conveys effectively the same information."

Justice Breyer found inadequate the State Department's statement that the denial was under "8 U. S. C. § 1182 (a)(3)(B)—the terrorism and national security bars to admissibility":

"For one thing, . . . § 1182(a)(3)(B), sets forth, not one reason, but dozens. It is a complex provision with 10 different subsections, many of which cross-reference other provisions of law. . . . Taken together the subsections, directly or through cross-reference, cover a vast waterfront of human activity potentially benefitting, sometimes in major ways, sometimes hardly at all, sometimes directly, sometimes indirectly, sometimes a few people, sometimes many, sometimes those with strong links, sometimes those with hardly a link, to a loosely or strongly connected group of individuals, which, through many different kinds of actions, might fall within the broad statutorily defined term 'terrorist.' . . .

"For another thing, the State Department's reason did not set forth any factual basis for the Government's decision. . . .

"The generality of the statutory provision cited and the lack of factual support mean that here, the reason given is analogous to telling a criminal defendant only that he is accused of 'breaking the law'; telling a property owner only that he cannot build because environmental rules forbid it; or telling a driver only that police pulled him over because he violated traffic laws. As such, the reason given cannot serve its procedural purpose. It does not permit Ms. Din to assess the correctness of the State Department's conclusion; it does not permit her to determine what kinds of facts she might provide in response; and it does not permit her to learn whether, or what kind of, defenses might be available. In short, any 'reason' that Ms. Din received is not constitutionally adequate."

Finally, in response to Justice Kennedy's opinion, Justice Breyer said in part:

". . . [T]he presence of [national] security considerations does not suspend the Constitution. Hamdi, 542 U.S., at 527–537 (plurality opinion). Rather, it requires us to take security needs into account when determining, for example, what 'process' is 'due.' Ibid.

"Yet how can we take proper account of security considerations without knowing what they are, without knowing how and why they require modification of traditional due process requirements, and without knowing whether other, less restrictive alternatives are available? How exactly would it harm important security interests to give Ms. Din a better explanation? Is there no way to give Ms. Din such an explanation while also maintaining appropriate secrecy? I believe we need answers to these questions before we can accept as constitutional a major departure from the procedural requirements that the Due Process Clause ordinarily demands."

CHAPTER 12

APPLICATION OF THE POST–CIVIL WAR AMENDMENTS TO PRIVATE CONDUCT: CONGRESSIONAL POWER TO ENFORCE THE AMENDMENTS

Introduction. This chapter presents a mixture of issues that can best be described as those involved in the Civil Rights Cases with which this chapter begins. That 1883 decision took a narrow view of the reach of section 1 of the thirteenth amendment and section 1 of the fourteenth amendment in their application to private racial discrimination. The decision also adopted a correspondingly narrow view of Congressional power to enforce the amendments. After setting out the decision in the Civil Rights Cases in section 1, the remainder of this chapter explores the question whether its basic conceptions are still valid. Section 2, dealing with the "state action" concept, includes those cases concerning the application of constitutional limits of governmental action to private conduct. The subject of the rest of the chapter is Congressional power to enforce the Civil War Amendments, focusing particularly on the extent of the power to prohibit both private and state action that would be lawful in the absence of federal legislation. Section 3 presents a brief review of the surviving fragments of Reconstruction era legislation, and contemporary federal legislation protecting civil rights. Section 4 addresses the issue of Congressional power to prohibit private racial discrimination in enforcing the thirteenth amendment's prohibition of slavery and involuntary servitude. Section 5 focuses on Congressional power under the fourteenth amendment to prohibit private racial, and non-racial, discrimination. Section 6 broadens the focus beyond issues of private discrimination, examining the extent of Congressional power to prohibit state laws and practices that violate neither section 1 of the fourteenth amendment nor section 1 of the fifteenth amendment. This last section considers both the scope of Congressional power to provide broad remedies for conceded constitutional violations and, most controversial, to modify the substantive content of constitutional rights.

1. EARLY INTERPRETATION

Civil Rights Cases
109 U.S. 3, 3 S.Ct. 18, 27 L.Ed. 835 (1883).

■ BRADLEY, J.

These cases are all founded on the first and second sections of the act of congress known as the "Civil Rights Act," passed March 1, 1875, entitled "An act to protect all citizens in their civil and legal rights." 18 Stat. 335. Two of the cases, those against Stanley and Nichols, are indictments for denying to persons of color the accommodations and privileges of an inn or hotel; two of them, those against Ryan and

Singleton, are, one an information, the other an indictment, for denying to individuals the privileges and accommodations of a theater, the information against Ryan being for refusing a colored person a seat in the dress circle of Maguire's theater in San Francisco; and the indictment against Singleton being for denying to another person, whose color is not stated, the full enjoyment of the accommodations of the theater known as the Grand Opera House in New York, "said denial not being made for any reasons by law applicable to citizens of every race and color, and regardless of any previous condition of servitude." The case of Robinson and wife against the Memphis & Charleston Railroad Company was an action brought in the circuit court of the United States for the western district of Tennessee, to recover the penalty of $500 given by the second section of the act; and the *gravamen* was the refusal by the conductor of the railroad company to allow the wife to ride in the ladies' car, for the reason, as stated in one of the counts, that she was a person of African descent. The jury rendered a verdict for the defendants in this case upon the merits under a charge of the court, to which a bill of exceptions was taken by the plaintiffs. . . .

It is obvious that the primary and important question in all the cases is the constitutionality of the law; for if the law is unconstitutional none of the prosecutions can stand.

The sections of the law referred to provide as follows:

"Section 1. That all persons within the jurisdiction of the United States shall be entitled to the full and equal enjoyment of the accommodations, advantages, facilities, and privileges of inns, public conveyances on land or water, theaters, and other places of public amusement; subject only to the conditions and limitations established by law, and applicable alike to citizens of every race and color, regardless of any previous condition of servitude.

"Section 2. That any person who shall violate the foregoing section by denying to any citizen, except for reasons by law applicable to citizens of every race and color, and regardless of any previous condition of servitude, the full enjoyment of any of the accommodations, advantages, facilities, or privileges in said section enumerated, or by aiding or inciting such denial, shall, for every such offense, forfeit and pay the sum of $500 to the person aggrieved thereby, to be recovered in an action of debt, with full costs; and shall, also, for every such offense, be deemed guilty of a misdemeanor, and upon conviction thereof shall be fined not less than $500 nor more than $1,000, or shall be imprisoned not less than 30 days nor more than one year. . . ."

Has congress constitutional power to make such a law? Of course, no one will contend that the power to pass it was contained in the constitution before the adoption of the last three amendments. The power is sought, first, in the fourteenth amendment, and the views and arguments of distinguished senators, advanced while the law was under consideration, claiming authority to pass it by virtue of that amendment, are the principal arguments adduced in favor of the power. . . .

The first section of the fourteenth amendment,—which is the one relied on,—after declaring who shall be citizens of the United States, and of the several states, is prohibitory in its character, and prohibitory upon the states. It declares that "no state shall make or enforce any law which shall abridge the privileges or immunities of citizens of the United States; nor shall any state deprive any person of life, liberty, or property without due process of law; nor deny to any person within its jurisdiction the equal protection of the laws." It is state action of a particular character that is prohibited. Individual invasion of individual rights is not the subject-matter of the amendment. It has a deeper and broader scope. It nullifies and makes void all state legislation, and state action of every kind, which impairs the privileges and immunities of citizens of the United States, or which injures them in life, liberty, or property without due process of law, or which denies to any of them the equal protection of the laws. It not only does this, but, in order that the national will, thus declared, may not be a mere *brutum fulmen,* the last section of the amendment invests congress with power to enforce it by appropriate legislation. To enforce what? To enforce the prohibition. To adopt appropriate legislation for correcting the effects of such prohibited state laws and state acts, and thus to render them effectually null, void, and innocuous. This is the legislative power conferred upon congress, and this is the whole of it. It does not invest congress with power to legislate upon subjects which are within the domain of state legislation; but to provide modes of relief against state legislation, or state action, of the kind referred to. It does not authorize congress to create a code of municipal law for the regulation of private rights; but to provide modes of redress against the operation of state laws, and the action of state officers, executive or judicial, when these are subversive of the fundamental rights specified in the amendment. . . .

In this connection it is proper to state that civil rights, such as are guaranteed by the constitution against state aggression, cannot be impaired by the wrongful acts of individuals, unsupported by state authority in the shape of laws, customs, or judicial or executive proceedings. The wrongful act of an individual, unsupported by any such authority, is simply a private wrong, or a crime of that individual; an invasion of the rights of the injured party, it is true, whether they affect his person, his property, or his reputation; but if not sanctioned in some way by the state, or not done under state authority, his rights remain in full force, and may presumably be vindicated by resort to the laws of the state for redress. An individual cannot deprive a man of his right to vote, to hold property, to buy and to sell, to sue in the courts, or to be a witness or a juror; he may, by force or fraud, interfere with the enjoyment of the right in a particular case; he may commit an assault against the person, or commit murder, or use ruffian violence at the polls, or slander the good name of a fellow-citizen; but unless protected in these wrongful acts by some shield of state law or state authority, he cannot destroy or injure the right; he will only render himself amenable to satisfaction or punishment; and amenable therefor to the laws of the state where the wrongful acts are committed. . . .

Of course, these remarks do not apply to those cases in which congress is clothed with direct and plenary powers of legislation over the whole subject, accompanied with an express or implied denial of such power to the states, as in the regulation of commerce with foreign nations, among the several states, and with the Indian tribes, the coining of money, the establishment of post-offices and post-roads, the declaring of war, etc. In these cases congress has power to pass laws for regulating the subjects specified, in every detail and the conduct and transactions of individuals in respect thereof.

. . .

. . . [T]he power of congress to adopt direct and primary, as distinguished from corrective, legislation on the subject in hand, is sought, in the second place, from the thirteenth amendment, which abolishes slavery. This amendment declares "that neither slavery, nor involuntary servitude, except as a punishment for crime, whereof the party shall have been duly convicted, shall exist within the United States, or any place subject to their jurisdiction;" and it gives congress power to enforce the amendment by appropriate legislation. . . .

It is true that slavery cannot exist without law any more than property in lands and goods can exist without law, and therefore the thirteenth amendment may be regarded as nullifying all state laws which establish or uphold slavery. But it has a reflex character also, establishing and decreeing universal civil and political freedom throughout the United States; and it is assumed that the power vested in congress to enforce the article by appropriate legislation, clothes congress with power to pass all laws necessary and proper for abolishing all badges and incidents of slavery in the United States; and upon this assumption it is claimed that this is sufficient authority for declaring by law that all persons shall have equal accommodations and privileges in all inns, public conveyances, and places of public amusement; the argument being that the denial of such equal accommodations and privileges is in itself a subjection to a species of servitude within the meaning of the amendment. . . .

It may be that by the black code, (as it was called), in the times when slavery prevailed, the proprietors of inns and public conveyances were forbidden to receive persons of the African race, because it might assist slaves to escape from the control of their masters. This was merely a means of preventing such escapes, and was no part of the servitude itself. A law of that kind could not have any such object now, however justly it might be deemed an invasion of the party's legal right as a citizen, and amenable to the prohibitions of the fourteenth amendment.

The long existence of African slavery in this country gave us very distinct notions of what it was, and what were its necessary incidents. Compulsory service of the slave for the benefit of the master, restraint of his movements except by the master's will, disability to hold property, to make contracts, to have a standing in court, to be a witness against a white person, and such like burdens and incapacities were the inseparable incidents of the institution. Severer punishments for crimes were imposed on the slave than on free persons guilty of the same offenses. Congress, as we have seen, by the civil rights bill of 1866, passed in view of the thirteenth amendment, before the fourteenth was adopted, undertook to wipe out these burdens and disabilities, the necessary incidents of slavery, constituting its substance and visible form; and to secure to all citizens of every race and color, and without regard to previous servitude, those fundamental rights which are the essence of civil freedom, namely, the same right to make and enforce contracts, to sue, be parties, give evidence, and to inherit, purchase, lease, sell, and convey property, as is enjoyed by white citizens. Whether this legislation was fully authorized by the thirteenth amendment alone, without the support which it afterwards received from the fourteenth amendment, after the adoption of which it was re-enacted with some additions, it is not necessary to inquire. It is referred to for the purpose of showing that at that time (in 1866) congress did not assume, under the authority given by the thirteenth amendment, to adjust what may be called the social rights of men and races in the community; but only to declare and vindicate those fundamental rights which appertain to the essence of citizenship, and the enjoyment or deprivation of which constitutes the essential distinction between freedom and slavery. . . .

The only question under the present head, therefore, is, whether the refusal to any persons of the accommodations of an inn, or a public conveyance, or a place of public amusement, by an individual, and without any sanction or support from any state law or regulation, does inflict upon such persons any manner of servitude, or form of slavery, as those terms are understood in this country? . . .

Now, conceding, for the sake of the argument, that the admission to an inn, a public conveyance, or a place of public amusement, on equal terms with all other citizens, is the right of every man and all classes of men, is it any more than one of those rights which the states by the Fourteenth Amendment are forbidden to deny to any person? And is the Constitution violated until the denial of the right has some State sanction or authority? Can the act of a mere individual, the owner of the inn, the public conveyance, or place of amusement, refusing the accommodation, be justly regarded as imposing any badge of slavery or servitude upon the applicant, or only as inflicting an ordinary civil injury, properly cognizable by the laws of the state, and presumably subject to redress by those laws until the contrary appears?

After giving to these questions all the consideration which their importance demands, we are forced to the conclusion that such an act of refusal has nothing to do with slavery or involuntary servitude, and that if it is violative of any right of the party, his redress is to be sought under the laws of the state; or, if those laws are adverse to his rights and do not protect him, his remedy will be found in the corrective legislation which congress has adopted, or may adopt, for counteracting the effect of state laws, or state action, prohibited by the fourteenth amendment. It would be running the slavery argument into the ground to make it apply to every act of discrimination which a person may see fit to make as to the guests he will entertain, or as to the people he will take into his coach or cab or car, or admit to his concert or theater, or deal with in other matters of intercourse or business. Innkeepers and public carriers, by the laws of all the states, so far as we are aware, are bound, to the extent of their facilities, to furnish proper accommodation to all unobjectionable persons who in good faith apply for them. If the laws themselves make any unjust discrimination, amenable to the prohibitions of the fourteenth amendment, congress has full power to afford a remedy under that amendment and in accordance with it.

When a man has emerged from slavery, and by the aid of beneficent legislation has shaken off the inseparable concomitants of that state, there must be some stage in the progress of his elevation when he takes the rank of a mere citizen, and ceases to be the special favorite of the laws, and when his rights as a citizen, or a man, are to be protected in the ordinary modes by which other men's rights are protected. There were thousands of free colored people in this country before the abolition of slavery, enjoying all the essential rights of life, liberty, and property the same as white citizens; yet no one, at that time, thought that it was any invasion of their personal *status* as freemen because they were not admitted to all the privileges enjoyed by white citizens, or because they were subjected to discriminations in the enjoyment of accommodations in inns, public conveyances, and places of amusement. Mere discriminations on account of race or color were not regarded as badges of slavery. If, since that time, the enjoyment of equal rights in all these respects has become established by constitutional enactment, it is not by force of the thirteenth amendment, (which merely abolishes slavery,) but by force of the fourteenth and fifteenth amendments.

On the whole, we are of opinion that no countenance of authority for the passage of the law in question can be found in either the thirteenth or fourteenth amendment of the constitution; and no other ground of authority for its passage being suggested, it must necessarily be declared void, at least so far as its operation in the several states is concerned. . . .

■ MR. JUSTICE HARLAN dissenting:

The opinion in these cases proceeds, it seems to me, upon grounds entirely too narrow and artificial. I cannot resist the conclusion that the substance and spirit of the recent Amendments of the Constitution have been sacrificed by a subtle and ingenious verbal criticism. "It is not the words of the law but the internal sense of it that makes the law; the letter of the law is the body; the sense and reason of the law is the soul." Constitutional provisions, adopted in the interest of liberty, and for the purpose of securing, through national legislation, if need be, rights inhering in a state of freedom, and belonging to American citizenship, have been so construed as to defeat the ends the people desired to accomplish, which they attempted to accomplish, and which they supposed they had accomplished by changes in their fundamental law. . . .

[In a long opinion Justice Harlan argued that both the 13th and 14th Amendments gave Congress power to legislate directly with reference to private individuals engaged in such quasi-public businesses as those involved in this case.]

My brethren say, that when a man has emerged from slavery, and by the aid of beneficient legislation has shaken off the inseparable concomitants of that state, there must be some stage in the progress of his elevation when he takes the rank of a mere citizen, and ceases to be the special favorite of the laws, and when his rights as a citizen, or a man, are to be protected in the ordinary modes by which other men's rights are protected. It is, I submit, scarcely just to say that the colored race has been the special favorite of the laws. The Statute of 1875, now adjudged to be unconstitutional, is for the benefit of citizens of every race and color. What the Nation, through Congress, has sought to accomplish in reference to that race, is—what had already been done in every State of the Union for the white race—to secure and protect rights belonging to them as freemen and citizens; nothing more. It was not deemed enough "to help the feeble up, but to support him after." The one underlying purpose of congressional legislation has been to enable the black race to take the rank of mere citizens. The difficulty has been to compel a recognition of the legal right of the black race to take the rank of citizens, and to secure the enjoyment of privileges belonging, under the law, to them as a component part of the people for whose welfare and happiness government is ordained. At every step, in this direction, the Nation has been confronted with class tyranny, which a contemporary English historian says is, of tyrannies, the most intolerable, "For it is ubiquitous in its operation, and weighs, perhaps, most heavily on those whose obscurity or distance would withdraw them from the notice of a single despot." Today, it is the colored race which is denied, by corporations and individuals wielding public authority, rights fundamental in their freedom and citizenship. At some future time, it may be that some other race will fall under the ban of race discrimination. If the constitutional Amendments be enforced, according to the intent with which, as I conceive, they were adopted, there cannot be in this Republic, any class of human beings in practical subjection to another class, with power in the latter to dole out to the former just such privileges as they may choose to grant. The supreme law of the land has decreed that no authority shall be exercised in this country upon the basis of discrimination, in respect of civil rights, against freemen and citizens because of their race, color or previous condition of servitude. To that decree—for the due enforcement of which, by appropriate legislation, Congress has been invested with express power—every one must bow, whatever may have been, or whatever now are, his individual views as to the wisdom or policy, either of the recent changes in the fundamental law, or of the legislation which has been enacted to give them effect.

For the reasons stated I feel constrained to withhold my assent to the opinion of the court.

The Relationship Between Congressional Power to Enforce the Constitution and Self-Enforcing Provisions of the Constitution

While the ultimate issue in the Civil Rights Cases concerned the constitutional validity of a federal statute prohibiting private discrimination, the bulk of the opinion discusses the question whether private racial discrimination would violate the Constitution had there been no federal legislation. The case was a major decision concerning the application of the Constitution to private conduct only because the Court's rationale was that Congressional power to enforce the thirteenth and fourteenth amendments necessarily tracked the self-executing provisions of those amendments. The next section of this chapter will explore the extent to which the fourteenth amendment applies of its own force to private conduct. Sections 4 through 6 will return to the issue of Congressional power. It is appropriate at this point to entertain a preliminary inquiry whether the interpretations of section one of the thirteenth amendment and section one of the fourteenth amendment should mark the outer limits of Congress' power to "enforce" those amendments.

Consider the facts of one of the cases grouped for decision in the Civil Rights Cases—the owner of a private theater enforcing a racially discriminatory policy in the selection of patrons. What are the consequences of a judicial decision that section one of the fourteenth amendment requires preferring the rights of the excluded patrons to those of the owner? What are the consequences of a judicial decision that Congress has the power under section five of the fourteenth amendment to require the theater owner to desist from racial discrimination in choice of patrons? Do those different consequences suggest that there should be differences in the reach of the self-enforcing provisions of section one and Congressional power under section five? Can major differences in the reach of section one and Congressional power under section five be recognized without giving Congress limitless power no longer tied to any limitation that it be directed to "enforcing" the fourteenth amendment?

2. APPLICATION OF THE CONSTITUTION TO PRIVATE CONDUCT

Introduction to the State Action Concept. With the exception of the thirteenth amendment the Constitution is a restraint on governmental action and does not provide one private citizen with rights against another. The Bill of Rights restrains the action of the federal government. The fourteenth amendment provides that "no state shall" deprive any person of due process or equal protection. The fifteenth amendment prohibits denial of voting rights "by the United States or by any State. . . ." The same verbal formula appears in the voting right protections of the nineteenth, twenty-fourth and twenty-sixth amendments.

A basic conception of the opinion in the Civil Rights Cases was that "civil rights, such as are guaranteed by the Constitution against state aggression, cannot be impaired by the wrongful acts of individuals, unsupported by state authority in the shape of laws, customs, or judicial or executive proceedings." In a general sense, however, all private action is "supported by state authority" if the state has not chosen to make that private action illegal. It has proved to be extremely difficult to determine when state involvement with private action, beyond mere failure to prohibit it, brings into play the constitutional limitations on governmental action.

It has also proved to be difficult to organize the cases that involve the problem. Subsection A deals with the argument that constitutional limits apply because a private party is performing a function normally performed by government. Subsection B collects the cases where it is claimed that government has enforced the racially discriminatory decisions of private parties. Subsection C includes, quite simply, the rest of the cases where the argument has been made that government has "supported" the conduct of private parties by approving it, regulating it, or providing financial support to it.

From the end of World War II through 1968, all Supreme Court decisions that reached the question whether unconstitutional state action was present decided that it was. Since 1970, most Supreme Court decisions considering the same issue have not found unconstitutional state action. Part of the explanation may be found in significant changes in the Court's membership. (Compare Evans v. Newton, 382 U.S. 296 (1966), infra p. 780, with Evans v. Abney, 396 U.S. 435 (1970); infra p. 793, Amalgamated Food Employees Union Local 590 v. Logan Valley Plaza, Inc., 391 U.S. 308 (1968), with Lloyd Corp., Ltd. v. Tanner, 407 U.S. 551 (1972), both discussed infra p. 780.) Other explanations may stem from the fact that nearly all of the cases prior to 1968 dealt with racial discrimination. Since 1970, issues such as first amendment rights of access to private property and due process rights of fair procedure have been prominent. Is the extent of governmental action required to invoke constitutional protection less where racial discrimination is claimed than when other forms of discrimination, or other constitutional rights, are involved?

A related question concerns the impact of the growing body of federal legislation prohibiting private racial discrimination. (See sections 3, 4, 5 and 6 of this chapter.) The Civil Rights Act of 1964 prohibits private racial discrimination in places of public accommodation, employment, and activities—including private education—receiving Federal financial assistance. The 1968 Civil Rights Act prohibits racial discrimination in the private housing market, and provides criminal penalties for many forms of private racial violence. And, in 1968, the Court discovered that remaining fragments of the Civil Rights Act of 1866 reached broad areas of private racial discrimination. (See section 4 of this chapter.) There are few cases now where the issue whether federal law prohibits private racial discrimination will turn on whether sufficient indicia of state action are present to invoke the provisions of the fourteenth amendment. Does this suggest legitimate reasons for limiting state action doctrines, even as applied to racial discrimination?

A. PRIVATE PERFORMANCE OF "GOVERNMENT" FUNCTIONS

The White Primary Cases

Despite the clear terms of the fifteenth amendment, for three-quarters of a century an effective means to block voting by Blacks was their exclusion from the Democratic Party in Southern States. Initially, it was argued that primary voting was beyond constitutional protection, even if state law mandated exclusion of Black voters from participation in the Democratic primaries. In Nixon v. Herndon, 273 U.S. 536 (1927), however, a Texas statute excluding Blacks from Democratic primaries was held to be unconstitutional as racial discrimination by the state. Texas' response was to repeal the offending statute, and to provide that a party's executive committee had the power to determine the party's membership. Exclusion of Blacks from the Democratic primary was again held unconstitutional on the ground that the new Texas statute had made the committee an agent of the state. Nixon v. Condon, 286 U.S. 73 (1932). When the Texas Democratic Party once again excluded Blacks from party membership, however, the exclusion survived constitutional attack on the ground that it was not state action, but the action of a private group. Grovey v. Townsend, 295 U.S. 45 (1935). Grovey v. Townsend was overruled in Smith v. Allwright, 321 U.S. 649 (1944), because "the place of the primary in the electoral scheme makes clear that state delegation to a party of the power to fix the qualifications of primary elections is delegation of a state function that may make the party's action the action of the state." That the Constitution prohibited exclusion of Blacks from participating in elections, whatever form the election took, was dramatized in Terry v. Adams, 345 U.S. 461 (1953), where Blacks were excluded from voting in a pre-primary straw vote of a Texas county political organization called the Jaybird Democratic Organization. Because winners in the Jaybird primary ran unopposed in the formal Democratic primaries, the Court decided that exclusion of Blacks from the Jaybird primary was a violation of the fifteenth amendment, despite the absence of formal state involvement in their exclusion.

Steele v. Louisville and Nashville Railroad Co.

323 U.S. 192 (1944).

The Brotherhood of Locomotive Firemen and Enginemen, under the terms of the Railway Labor Act, was exclusive bargaining representative for the railway firemen. Blacks who constituted a substantial minority of the labor force, were excluded from membership in the brotherhood. As a result of negotiations an agreement was made in 1941 between the railroad and the brotherhood providing for restrictions on the hiring and promotion of blacks with the ultimate aim of their exclusion from work as firemen. Steele, a black fireman, brought suit against the railroad and the brotherhood based on the foregoing facts. The Supreme Court of Alabama affirmed the dismissal of the complaint. the United States Supreme Court, speaking through Chief Justice Stone, said:

"If, as the state court has held, the Act confers this power on the bargaining representative of a craft or class of employees without any commensurate statutory duty toward its members, constitutional questions arise. For the representative is clothed with power not unlike that of a legislature which is subject to constitutional limitations on its power to deny, restrict, destroy or discriminate against the rights of those for whom it legislates and which is also under an affirmative constitutional duty equally to protect those rights. . . .

"We think that the Railway Labor Act imposes upon the statutory representatives of a craft at least as exacting a duty to protect equally the interests of the members of the craft as the Constitution imposes upon a legislature to give equal protection to the interests of those for whom it legislates. Congress has seen fit to clothe the bargaining representative with powers comparable to those possessed by a legislative body both to create and restrict the rights of those whom it represents, . . . but it has also imposed on the representative a corresponding duty. . . .

"Reversed."

Justice Murphy, concurring, stated that the case presented "a grave constitutional issue that should be squarely faced." The Railway Labor Act must be construed to bar this discrimination: "Otherwise the Act would bear the stigma of unconstitutionality under the Fifth Amendment in this respect."

Access to Company Towns and Shopping Centers

Marsh v. Alabama, 326 U.S. 501 (1946), was one of two pre-1970 Supreme Court decisions, that presented the state action issue in some context other than racial discrimination. A member of Jehovah's Witnesses was prosecuted for trespass when she distributed religious literature on the streets of a company-owned town and refused to leave when ordered to do so. The town involved was described by the Court as being accessible to and freely used by the public in general with nothing to distinguish it from any other town except the fact that the title to the property belonged to a private corporation. In reversing the conviction the Court talked primarily about first amendment issues. It stated that had the corporation owned the segment of the state highway that paralleled the business street of the company town and operated that segment it would "have been the performance of a public function." The opinion then continued:

"We do not think it makes any significant constitutional difference as to the relationship between the rights of the owner and those of the public that here the State, instead of permitting the corporation to operate a highway, permitted it to use its property as a town, operate a 'business block' in the town and a street and sidewalk on that business block. . . . Whether a corporation or a municipality owns or possesses the town the public in either case has an identical interest in the functioning of the community in such manner that the channels of communication remain free."

The other pre-1970 case not involving racial discrimination was Amalgamated Food Employees Union Local 590 v. Logan Valley Plaza, Inc., 391 U.S. 308 (1968), which extended *Marsh* to require that picketers be given access to a large privately-owned shopping center. Justice Marshall's opinion for the majority concluded that there was no reason to draw a distinction between a privately owned business district surrounded by residential property under the same ownership, and one surrounded by property under other ownership. Justice Black, the author of the *Marsh* opinion but one of three dissenters in *Logan Valley,* argued that the company town in *Marsh* had all the attributes of a conventional municipality, but that the shopping center had only one—ownership of the business block. *Logan Valley* was criticized, but distinguished, in Lloyd Corp., Ltd. v. Tanner, 407 U.S. 551 (1972), where anti-war leafletters were held not to have a constitutional right of access to a large privately-owned shopping center. The four Justices in the *Logan Valley* majority who were still on the Court dissented in *Lloyd.* In Hudgens v. NLRB, 424 U.S. 507 (1976), the Court concluded that *Lloyd* had overruled *Logan Valley* and that speakers had no constitutional right of access to large privately-owned shopping centers.

Evans v. Newton
382 U.S. 296 (1966).

In 1911, Senator Augustus O. Bacon executed a will devising land to the city of Macon, Georgia, for a park for whites only. The city kept the park segregated for decades, but in some years prior to this suit permitted blacks to use it on the ground that the city could not constitutionally maintain a segregated park. (See Pennsylvania v. Board of City Trusts, infra, p. 791) This suit sought to remove the city as trustee. Black citizens of Macon intervened, asking the state court to refuse to appoint new private trustees. State courts accepted the resignation of the city as trustee and appointed private trustees. The united states supreme court reversed, holding that the park could not be maintained on a segregated basis, despite the city's resignation as trustee. Justice Douglas' opinion for the court gave two reasons. First, his opinion read the record below as showing that the city remained "entwined in the management or control of the park." Second, the opinion stated:

"This conclusion [that the substitution of trustees did not transfer the park to the 'private sector'] is buttressed by the nature of the service rendered the community by a park. The service rendered even by a private park of this character is municipal in nature. It is open to every white person, there being no selective element other than race. Golf clubs, social centers, luncheon clubs, schools such as Tuskegee was at least in origin, and other like organizations in the private sector are often racially oriented. A park, on the other hand, is more like a fire department or police department that traditionally serves the community. Mass recreation through the use of parks is plainly in the public domain, Watson v. Memphis, 373 U.S. 526; and state courts that aid private parties to perform that public function on a segregated basis implicate the State in conduct proscribed by the Fourteenth Amendment. Like the streets of the company town in Marsh v. Alabama, supra, the elective process of Terry v. Adams, supra, and the transit system of Public Util. Comm'n v. Pollak, supra, the predominant character and purpose of this park are municipal."

Justice White concurred in the result. Justices Black, Harlan and Stewart dissented.

Flagg Brothers, Inc. v. Brooks

436 U.S. 149, 98 S.Ct. 1729, 56 L.Ed.2d 185 (1978).

■ MR. JUSTICE REHNQUIST delivered the opinion of the Court.

The question presented by this litigation is whether a warehouseman's proposed sale of goods entrusted to him for storage, as permitted by New York Uniform Commercial Code § 7–210, is an action properly attributable to the State of New York. . . .

I.

According to her complaint, the allegations of which we must accept as true, respondent Shirley Brooks and her family were evicted from their apartment in Mount Vernon, N.Y., on June 13, 1973. The City Marshal arranged for Brooks' possessions to be stored by petitioner Flagg Brothers, Inc., in its warehouse. Respondent was informed of the cost of moving and storage, and she instructed the workmen to proceed, although she found the price too high. On August 25, 1973, after a series of disputes over the validity of the charges being claimed by petitioner, Flagg Brothers, Brooks received a letter demanding that her account be brought up to date within 10 days "or your furniture will be sold." . . . A series of subsequent letters from respondent and her attorneys produced no satisfaction.

Brooks thereupon initiated this class action in the District Court under 42 U.S.C. § 1983, seeking damages, an injunction against the threatened sale of her belongings, and the declaration that such a sale pursuant to § 7–210 would violate the Due Process and Equal Protection Clauses of the Fourteenth Amendment. . . . [T]he District Court, dismissed the complaint for failure to state a claim for relief under § 1983.

A divided panel of the Court of Appeals reversed.

. . .

II.

A claim upon which relief may be granted to respondents against Flagg Brothers under § 1983 must embody at least two elements. Respondents are first bound to show that they have been deprived of a right "secured by the Constitution and the laws" of the United States. They must secondly show that Flagg Brothers deprived them of this right acting "under color of any statute" of the State of New York. It is clear that these two elements denote two separate areas of inquiry. . . .

It must be noted that respondents have named no public officials as defendants in this action. The city marshal, who supervised their evictions, was dismissed from the case by the consent of all the parties. This total absence of overt official involvement plainly distinguishes this case from earlier decisions imposing procedural restrictions on creditors' remedies. . . . While as a factual matter any person with sufficient physical power may deprive a person of his property, only a State or a private person whose action "may fairly be treated as that of the State itself," . . . may deprive him of "an interest encompassed within the Fourteenth Amendment's protection," . . . Thus, the only issue presented by this case is whether Flagg Brothers' action may fairly be attributed to the State of New York. We conclude that it may not.

III.

Respondents' primary contention is that New York has delegated to Flagg Brothers a power "traditionally exclusively reserved to the State." . . . They argue that the resolution of private disputes is a traditional function of civil government, and that the State in § 7–210 has delegated this function to Flagg Brothers. Respondents, however, have read too much into the language of our previous cases. While many functions have been traditionally performed by governments, very few have been "exclusively reserved to the State."

One such area has been elections. While the Constitution protects private rights of association and advocacy with regard to the election of public officials, our cases make it clear that the conduct of the elections themselves is an exclusively public function. . . .

A second line of cases under the public function doctrine originated with Marsh v. Alabama . . . Just as the Texas Democratic Party in *Smith* and the Jaybird Democratic Association in *Terry* effectively performed the entire public function of selecting public officials, so too the Gulf Shipbuilding Corp. performed all the necessary municipal functions in the town of Chickasaw, Ala., which it owned. . . .

These two branches of the public function doctrine have in common the feature of exclusivity.[8] Although the elections held by the Democratic Party and its affiliates were the only meaningful elections in Texas, and the streets owned by the Gulf Shipbuilding Corp. were the only streets in Chickasaw, the proposed sale by Flagg Brothers under § 7–210 is not the only means of resolving this purely private dispute. . . .

Whatever the particular remedies available under New York law, we do not consider a . . . detailed description of them necessary to our conclusion that the settlement of disputes between debtors and creditors is not traditionally an exclusive public function. . . .

Thus, even if we were inclined to extend the sovereign function doctrine outside of its present carefully confined bounds, the field of private commercial transactions would be a particularly inappropriate area into which to expand it. We conclude that our sovereign function cases do not support a finding of state action here.

. . . [T]here are a number of state and municipal functions not covered by our election cases nor governed by the reasoning of *Marsh* which have been administered with a greater degree of exclusivity by States and municipalities than has the function of so-called "dispute resolution." Among these are such functions as education, fire and police protection, and tax collection. We express no view as to the extent, if any, to which a city or State might be free to delegate to private parties the performance of such functions and thereby avoid the strictures of the Fourteenth Amendment. The mere recitation of these possible permutations and combinations of factual situations suffices to caution us that their resolution should abide the necessity of deciding them.

IV.

Respondents further urge that Flagg Brothers' proposed action is properly attributable to the State because the State has authorized and encouraged it in enacting § 7–210. Our cases state "that a State is responsible for the . . . act of a private party when the State, by its law, has compelled the act." . . . This Court, however, has never held that a State's mere acquiescence in a private action converts that action into that of the State. . . .

. . .

---

[8] Respondents also contend that Evans v. Newton, 382 U.S. 296 (1966), establishes that the operation of a park for recreational purposes is an exclusively public function. We doubt that *Newton* intended to establish any such broad doctrine in the teeth of the experience of several American entrepreneurs who amassed great fortunes by operating parks for recreational purposes. We think *Newton* rests on a finding of ordinary state action under extraordinary circumstances. The Court's opinion emphasizes that the record showed "no change in the municipal maintenance and concern over this facility," id., at 301, after the transfer of title to private trustees. That transfer had not been shown to have eliminated the actual involvement of the city in the daily maintenance and care of the park.

Here, the State of New York has not compelled the sale of a bailor's goods, but has merely announced the circumstances under which its courts will not interfere with a private sale. Indeed, the crux of respondents' complaint is not that the State *has* acted, but that it has *refused* to act. This statutory refusal to act is no different in principle from an ordinary statute of limitations whereby the State declines to provide a remedy for private deprivations of property after the passage of a given period of time.

. . .

Reversed.

■ MR. JUSTICE BRENNAN took no part in the consideration or decision of this case.

■ MR. JUSTICE STEVENS, with whom MR. JUSTICE WHITE and MR. JUSTICE MARSHALL join, dissenting.

. . . In my judgment the Court's holding is fundamentally inconsistent with, if not foreclosed by, our prior decisions which have imposed procedural restrictions on the State's authorization of certain creditors' remedies. . . .

There is no question in this case but that respondents have a property interest in the possessions that the warehouseman proposes to sell. It is also clear that, whatever power of sale the warehouseman has, it does not derive from the consent of the respondents. The claimed power derives solely from the State, and specifically from § 7–210 of the New York Uniform Commercial Code. The question is whether a state statute which authorizes a private party to deprive a person of his property without his consent must meet the requirements of the Due Process Clause of the Fourteenth Amendment. This question must be answered in the affirmative unless the State has virtually unlimited power to transfer interests in private property without any procedural protections.

In determining that New York's statute cannot be scrutinized under the Due Process Clause, the Court reasons that the warehouseman's proposed sale is solely private action because the state statute "*permits* but does not compel" the sale, . . . (emphasis added), and because the warehouseman has not been delegated a power "*exclusively* reserved to the State," . . . (emphasis added). Under this approach a State could enact laws authorizing private citizens to use self-help in countless situations without any possibility of federal challenge. . . . [T]he distinctions between "permission" and "compulsion" on the one hand, and "exclusive" and "non-exclusive," on the other, cannot be determinative factors in state-action, analysis. . . . In this case, the State of New York, by enacting § 7–210 of the Uniform Commercial Code, has acted in the most effective and unambiguous way a State can act. This section specifically authorizes petitioner to sell respondents' possessions; it details the procedures that petitioner must follow; and it grants petitioner the power to convey good title to goods that are now owned by respondents to a third party.

While Members of this Court have suggested that statutory authorization alone may be sufficient to establish state action, it is not necessary to rely on those suggestions in this case because New York has authorized the warehouseman to perform what is clearly a state function. The test of what is a state function for purposes of the Due Process Clause has been variously phrased. Most frequently the issue is presented in terms of whether the State has delegated a function traditionally and historically associated with sovereignty. . . . In this Court, petitioners have attempted to argue that the nonconsensual transfer of property rights is not a traditional function of the sovereign. The overwhelming historical evidence is to the contrary, however, and the Court wisely does not adopt this position. Instead, the Court reasons that state action cannot be found because the State has not delegated to the warehouseman an *exclusive* sovereign function. This distinction, however, is not consistent with our prior decisions on state action[9]. . . .

. . .

Whether termed "traditional," "exclusive," or "significant," the state power to order binding, nonconsensual resolution of a conflict between debtor and creditor is exactly the sort of power with which the Due Process Clause is concerned. And the State's delegation of that power to a private party is, accordingly, subject to due process scrutiny. . . .

It is important to emphasize that, contrary to the Court's apparent fears, this conclusion does not even remotely suggest that "all private deprivations of property [will] be converted into public acts whenever the State, for whatever reason, denies relief sought by the putative property owner." . . . The focus is not on the private deprivation but on the state authorization. "[W]hat is always vital to remember is that it is the *state's* conduct, whether action or inaction, not the *private* conduct, that gives rise to constitutional attack." H. Friendly, The Dartmouth College Case and The Public-Private Penumbra, p. 17 (emphasis in original). The State's conduct in this case takes the concrete form of a statutory enactment, and it is that statute that may be challenged.

My analysis in this case thus assumes that petitioner's proposed sale will conform to the procedure specified by the state legislature and that respondents' challenge therefore will be to the constitutionality of that process. It is only what the State itself has enacted that they may ask the federal court to review in a § 1983 case. If there should be a deviation from the state statute—such as a failure to give the notice required by the state law—the defect could be remedied by a state court and there would be no occasion for § 1983 relief. . . .

On the other hand, if there is compliance with the New York statute, the state legislative action which enabled the deprivation to take place must be subject to constitutional challenge in a federal court. Under this approach, the federal courts do not have jurisdiction to review every foreclosure proceeding in which the debtor claims that there has been a procedural defect constituting a denial of due process of law. Rather, the Federal District Court's jurisdiction under § 1983 is limited to challenges to the constitutionality of the state procedure itself. . . .

Finally, it is obviously true that the overwhelming majority of disputes in our society are resolved in the private sphere. But it is no longer possible, if it ever was, to believe that a sharp line can be drawn between private and public actions. The Court today holds that our examination of state delegations of power should be limited to those rare instances where the State has ceded one of its "exclusive" powers. As indicated, I believe that this limitation is neither logical nor practical. More troubling, this description of what is state action does not even attempt to reflect the concerns of the Due Process Clause, for the state action doctrine is, after all, merely one aspect of this broad constitutional protection.

In the broadest sense, we expect government "to provide a reasonable and fair framework of rules which facilitate commercial transactions. . . ." Mitchell v. W.T. Grant, . . . 416 U.S., at 624 (Powell, J., concurring). This "framework of rules" is premised on the assumption that the State will control nonconsensual deprivations of property and that the State's control will, in turn, be subject to the restrictions of the

---

[9] The Court, for instance, attempts to distinguish Evans v. Newton, . . . *Newton* concededly involved a function which is not exclusively sovereign—the operation of a park, but the Court claims that *Newton* actually rested on a determination that the City was still involved in the "daily maintenance and care of the park." This stark attempt to rewrite the rationale of the *Newton* opinion is fully answered by Mr. Justice White's opinion in that case. . . .

Due Process Clause. The power to order legally binding surrenders of property and the constitutional restrictions on that power are necessary correlatives in our system. In effect, today's decision allows the State to divorce these two elements by the simple expedient of transferring the implementation of its policy to private parties. Because the Fourteenth Amendment does not countenance such a division of power and responsibility, I respectfully dissent.[a]

San Francisco Arts & Athletics, Inc. v. United States Olympic Committee
483 U.S. 522 (1987).

Section 110 of the Amateur Sports Act of 1978 grants the committee the right to prohibit commercial and promotional uses of the word "olympic." The court rejected an argument that the committee violated the equal protection component of the Fifth Amendment by discriminatory enforcement of its exclusive right. The committee was not a governmental actor and did not perform functions that have been traditionally the exclusive prerogative of the federal government. There was no evidence of governmental involvement in the committee's choice of how it enforced its right. Four dissenters argued that the committee was a governmental actor because there was a "symbiotic relationship" between the committee and the federal government in coordinating amateur athletics in international competition. Two of the four dissenters argued, in addition, that the committee performed a public function in governing international amateur athletics.

B. GOVERNMENTAL ENFORCEMENT OF "PRIVATE" DECISIONS

Shelley v. Kraemer
334 U.S. 1, 68 S.Ct. 836, 92 L.Ed. 1161 (1948).

■ MR. CHIEF JUSTICE VINSON delivered the opinion of the Court.

These cases present for our consideration questions relating to the validity of court enforcement of private agreements, generally described as restrictive covenants, which have as their purpose the exclusion of persons of designated race or color from the ownership or occupancy of real property. Basic constitutional issues of obvious importance have been raised.

The first of these cases comes to this Court on certiorari to the Supreme Court of Missouri. On February 16, 1911, thirty out of a total of thirty-nine owners of property fronting both sides of Labadie Avenue between Taylor Avenue and Cora Avenue in the city of St. Louis, signed an agreement, which was subsequently recorded providing in part:

". . . the said property is hereby restricted to the use and occupancy for the term of Fifty (50) years from this date, so that it shall be a condition all the time and whether recited and referred to as [sic] not in subsequent conveyances and shall attach to the land, as a condition precedent to the sale of the same, that hereafter no part of said property or any portion thereof shall be, for said term of Fifty-years, occupied by any person not of the Caucasian race, it being intended hereby to restrict the use of said property for said period of time against the occupancy as owners or tenants of any portion of said property for resident or other purpose by people of the Negro or Mongolian Race."

---

[a] See Brest, *State Action and Liberal Theory: A Casenote on* Flagg Brothers v. Brooks, 130 U.Pa.L.Rev. 1296 (1982).

The entire district described in the agreement included fifty-seven parcels of land. The thirty owners who signed the agreement held title to forty-seven parcels, including the particular parcel involved in this case. . . .

On August 11, 1945, pursuant to a contract of sale, petitioners Shelley, who are Negroes, for valuable consideration received from one Fitzgerald a warranty deed to the parcel in question. The trial court found that petitioners had no actual knowledge of the restrictive agreement at the time of the purchase.

On October 9, 1945, respondents, as owners of other property subject to the terms of the restrictive covenant, brought suit in the Circuit Court of the city of St. Louis praying that petitioners Shelley be restrained from taking possession of the property and that judgment be entered divesting title out of petitioners Shelley and revesting title in the immediate grantor or in such other person as the court should direct. The trial court denied the requested relief on the ground that the restrictive agreement, upon which respondents based their action, had never become final and complete. . . .

The Supreme Court of Missouri sitting *en banc* reversed and directed the trial court to grant the relief for which respondents had prayed. That court held the agreement effective and concluded that enforcement of its provisions violated no rights guaranteed to petitioners by the Federal Constitution. At the time the court rendered its decision, petitioners were occupying the property in question.

The second of the cases under consideration comes to this Court from the Supreme Court of Michigan. The circumstances presented do not differ materially from the Missouri case. . . .

Petitioners have placed primary reliance on their contentions, first raised in the state courts, that judicial enforcement of the restrictive agreements in these cases has violated rights guaranteed to petitioners by the Fourteenth Amendment of the Federal Constitution and Acts of Congress passed pursuant to that Amendment. Specifically, petitioners urge that they have been denied the equal protection of the laws, deprived of property without due process of law, and have been denied privileges and immunities of citizens of the United States. We pass to a consideration of those issues.

I.

Whether the equal protection clause of the Fourteenth Amendment inhibits judicial enforcement by state courts of restrictive covenants based on race or color is a question which this Court has not heretofore been called upon to consider. . . .

. . .

It should be observed that these covenants do not seek to proscribe any particular use of the affected properties. Use of the properties for residential occupancy, as such, is not forbidden. The restrictions of these agreements, rather are directed toward a designated class of persons and seek to determine who may and who may not own or make use of the properties for residential purposes. The excluded class is defined wholly in terms of race or color; "simply that and nothing more."

It cannot be doubted that among the civil rights intended to be protected from discriminatory state action by the Fourteenth Amendment are the rights to acquire, enjoy, own and dispose of property. . . .

It is likewise clear that restrictions on the right of occupancy of the sort sought to be created by the private agreements in these cases could not be squared with the requirements of the Fourteenth Amendment if imposed by state statute or local ordinance. We do not understand respondents to urge the contrary. In the case of Buchanan v. Warley [245 U.S. 60] a unanimous Court declared unconstitutional the provisions of a city ordinance which denied to colored persons the right to occupy houses in blocks in which the greater number of houses were occupied by white persons, and imposed similar restrictions on white persons with respect to blocks in which the greater number of houses were occupied by colored persons. During the course of the opinion in that case, this Court stated: "The Fourteenth Amendment and these statutes enacted in furtherance of its purpose operate to qualify and entitle a colored man to acquire property without state legislation discriminating against him solely because of color."

In Harmon v. Tyler, 273 U.S. 668 (1927), a unanimous court, on the authority of *Buchanan v. Warley,* supra, declared invalid an ordinance which forbade any Negro to establish a home on any property in a white community or any white person to establish a home in a Negro community, "except on the written consent of a majority of the persons of the opposite race inhabiting such community or portion of the City to be affected."

But the present cases, unlike those just discussed, do not involve action by state legislatures or city councils. Here the particular patterns of discrimination and the areas in which the restrictions are to operate, are determined, in the first instance, by the terms of agreements among private individuals. Participation of the State consists in the enforcement of the restrictions so defined. The crucial issue with which we are here confronted is whether this distinction removes these cases from the operation of the prohibitory provisions of the Fourteenth Amendment.

Since the decision of this Court in the Civil Rights Cases, 109 U.S. 3 (1883), the principle has become firmly embedded in our constitutional law that the action inhibited by the first section of the Fourteenth Amendment is only such action as may fairly be said to be that of the States. That Amendment erects no shield against merely private conduct, however discriminatory or wrongful.

We conclude, therefore, that the restrictive agreements standing alone cannot be regarded as a violation of any rights guaranteed to petitioners by the Fourteenth Amendment. So long as the purposes of those agreements are effectuated by voluntary adherence to their terms, it would appear clear that there has been no action by the State and the provisions of the Amendment have not been violated. . . .

But here there was more. These are cases in which the purposes of the agreements were secured only by judicial enforcement by state courts of the restrictive terms of the agreements. The respondents urge that judicial enforcement of private agreements does not amount to state action; or, in any event, the participation of the State is so attenuated in character as not to amount to state action within the meaning of the Fourteenth Amendment. Finally, it is suggested, even if the States in these cases may be deemed to have acted in the constitutional sense, their action did not deprive petitioners of rights guaranteed by the Fourteenth Amendment. We move to a consideration of these matters.

II.

That the action of state courts and of judicial officers in their official capacities is to be regarded as action of the State within the meaning of the Fourteenth Amendment, is a proposition which has long been established by decisions of this Court. That principle was given expression in the earliest cases involving the construction of the terms of the Fourteenth Amendment. . . .

One of the earliest applications of the prohibitions contained in the Fourteenth Amendment to action of state judicial officials occurred in cases in which Negroes had been excluded from jury service in criminal prosecutions by reason of their race or color. These cases demonstrate, also, the early recognition by this Court that state action in violation of the Amendment's provisions is equally repugnant to the constitutional commands whether directed by state statute or taken by a judicial official in the absence of statute. . . .

The action of state courts in imposing penalties or depriving parties of other substantive rights without providing adequate notice and opportunity to defend, has, of course, long been regarded as a denial of the due process of law guaranteed by the Fourteenth Amendment. . . .

In numerous cases, this Court has reversed criminal convictions in state courts for failure of those courts to provide the essential ingredients of a fair hearing. . . .

But the examples of state judicial action which have been held by this Court to violate the Amendment's commands are not restricted to situations in which the judicial proceedings were found in some manner to be procedurally unfair. It has been recognized that the action of state courts in enforcing a substantive common-law rule formulated by those courts, may result in the denial of rights guaranteed by the Fourteenth Amendment, even though the judicial proceedings in such cases may have been in complete accord with the most rigorous conceptions of procedural due process. Thus in American Federation of Labor v. Swing, 1941, 312 U.S. 321, enforcement by state courts of the common-law policy of the State, which resulted in the restraining of peaceful picketing, was held to be state action of the sort prohibited by the Amendment's guaranties of freedom of discussion. . . .

The short of the matter is that from the time of the adoption of the Fourteenth Amendment until the present, it has been the consistent ruling of this Court that the action of the States to which the Amendment has reference, includes action of state courts and state judicial officials. Although, in construing the terms of the Fourteenth Amendment, differences have from time to time been expressed as to whether particular types of state action may be said to offend the Amendment's prohibitory provisions, it has never been suggested that state court action is immunized from the operation of those provisions simply because the act is that of the judicial branch of the state government.

III.

Against this background of judicial construction, extending over a period of some three-quarters of a century, we are called upon to consider whether enforcement by state courts of the restrictive agreements in these cases may be deemed to be the acts of those States; and, if so, whether that action has denied these petitioners the equal protection of the laws which the Amendment was intended to insure.

We have no doubt that there has been state action in these cases in the full and complete sense of the phrase. The undisputed facts disclose that petitioners were willing purchasers of properties upon which they desired to establish homes. The owners of the properties were willing sellers; and contracts of sale were accordingly consummated. It is clear that but for the active intervention of the state courts, supported by the full panoply of state power, petitioners would have been free to occupy the properties in question without restraint.

These are not cases, as has been suggested, in which the States have merely abstained from action, leaving private individuals free to impose such discriminations as they see fit. Rather, these are cases in which the States have made available to such individuals the full coercive power of government to deny to petitioners, on the grounds of race or color, the enjoyment of property rights in premises which petitioners are willing and financially able to acquire and which the grantors are willing to sell. The difference between judicial enforcement and nonenforcement of the restrictive covenants is the difference to petitioners between being denied rights of property available to other members of the community and being accorded full enjoyment of those rights on an equal footing.

The enforcement of the restrictive agreements by the state courts in these cases was directed pursuant to the common-law policy of the States as formulated by those courts in earlier decisions. In the Missouri case, enforcement of the covenant was directed in the first instance by the highest court of the State after the trial court had determined the agreement to be invalid for want of the requisite number of signatures. In the Michigan case, the order of enforcement by the trial court was affirmed by the highest state court. The judicial action in each case bears the clear and unmistakable imprimatur of the State. We have noted that previous decisions of this Court have established the proposition that judicial action is not immunized from the operation of the Fourteenth Amendment simply because it is taken pursuant to the state's common-law policy. Nor is the Amendment ineffective simply because the particular pattern of discrimination, which the State has enforced, was defined initially by the terms of a private agreement. State action, as that phrase is understood for the purposes of the Fourteenth Amendment, refers to exertions of state power in all forms. And when the effect of that action is to deny rights subject to the protection of the Fourteenth Amendment, it is the obligation of this Court to enforce the constitutional commands.

We hold that in granting judicial enforcement of the restrictive agreements in these cases, the States have denied petitioners the equal protection of the laws and that, therefore, the action of the state courts cannot stand. We have noted that freedom from discrimination by the States in the enjoyment of property rights was among the basic objectives sought to be effectuated by the framers of the Fourteenth Amendment. That such discrimination has occurred in these cases is clear. Because of the race or color of these petitioners they have been denied rights of ownership or occupancy enjoyed as a matter of course by other citizens of different race or color. . . .

Respondents urge, however, that since the state courts stand ready to enforce restrictive covenants excluding white persons from the ownership or occupancy of property covered by such agreements, enforcement of covenants excluding colored persons may not be deemed a denial of equal protection of the laws to the colored persons who are thereby affected. This contention does not bear scrutiny. The parties have directed our attention to no case in which a court, state or federal, has been called upon to enforce a covenant excluding members of the white majority from ownership or occupancy of real property on grounds of race or color. But there are more fundamental considerations. The rights created by the first section of the Fourteenth Amendment are, by its terms, guaranteed to the individual. The rights established are personal rights. It is, therefore, no answer to these petitioners to say that the courts may also be induced to deny white persons rights of ownership and occupancy on grounds of race or color. Equal protection of the laws is not achieved through indiscriminate imposition of inequalities. . . .

. . .

For the reasons stated, the judgment of the Supreme Court of Missouri and the judgment of the Supreme Court of Michigan must be reversed.

Reversed.

■ MR. JUSTICE REED, MR. JUSTICE JACKSON, and MR. JUSTICE RUTLEDGE took no part in the consideration or decision of these cases.

Restrictive Covenants

Restrictive covenants directed against minorities were used widely prior to the *Shelley* case, particularly in large cities in the North and West. These covenants were not only against Blacks but also Armenians, Jews, Mexicans, Syrians, Japanese, Chinese and American Indians. It has been estimated that 80% of the land in Chicago was restricted. *To Secure These Rights—The Report of the President's Committee on Civil Rights 67–70* (1947).

The use of these covenants prior to *Shelley* contributed to the isolation of Blacks in congested and substandard housing. Partly as a result of limitations of Blacks' access to housing, they often were forced to pay higher rentals than Whites. Helfeld & Groner, *Race Discrimination in Housing,* 57 Yale L.J. 426, 426–33 (1948). Would such evidence have been relevant to the *Shelley* decision? See Martin, *Segregation of Residences of Negroes,* 32 Mich.L.Rev. 721 (1934).[1]

Barrows v. Jackson

346 U.S. 249 (1953).

Plaintiff's predecessor and defendant, owners of real estate in the same neighborhood, entered into an agreement, recorded on the deeds and running against subsequent takers, that their property would be occupied only by Whites. Plaintiff sued defendant for damages alleging that, in violation of their agreement, defendant had sold his property without including the agreed restriction in the deed, and had permitted non-Whites to move in and occupy the premises. The California courts sustained a demurrer to the complaint on the authority of Shelley.

The United States Supreme Court affirmed California's denial of relief. Justice Minton, for the Court, wrote: "This Court will not permit or require California to coerce respondent to respond in damages for failure to observe a restrictive covenant that this Court would deny California the right to enforce in equity. . . ."

Prosecution of "Sit-In" Demonstrators in the 1960s

A significant phase of the civil rights struggle was the use of "sit-in" demonstrations at Southern restaurants or lunch counters where Blacks were segregated or refused service. Typically, Blacks would sit at a table or counter, be asked to leave, and be arrested and convicted of trespass when they refused. The Supreme Court reviewed the constitutionality of the convictions of literally hundreds of sit-in demonstrators in the early sixties. While the convictions were reversed, a majority of the Court never faced squarely the question whether enforcement of a private property owner's discrimination was unconstitutional state action under Shelley v. Kraemer. In some cases, convictions were reversed on the ground that the state trespass statute gave inadequate warning as to whether it prohibited remaining on private property after being asked to leave as well as unauthorized "entry." Bouie v. City of Columbia, 378 U.S. 347 (1964). Where convictions were reversed because of unconstitutional state action, the grounds were narrow. E.g., Robinson v. Florida, 378 U.S. 153 (1964) (city ordinance required segregation although restaurant manager stated that Blacks were excluded for business reasons); Griffin v. Maryland, 378 U.S. 130 (1964) (amusement park employee who asked Blacks to leave and arrested them was also deputized as a sheriff).

The *Griffin* case is particularly interesting. The state argued that the constitutional issues in the case were indistinguishable from those where the trespass arrest had been made by a police officer not employed by the park. The Court did not resolve the state's broad contention that no constitutional violation followed from a police arrest and state conviction for trespass of a person refusing to leave private property. The Court noted that Collins, the park employee who asked the defendants to leave, wore a sheriff's badge and "consistently identified himself as a deputy sheriff"

---

[1]   See also: Karst & Van Alstyne, *State Action,* 14 Stan.L.Rev. 3 (1961); Henkin, *Shelley v. Kraemer: Notes for a Revised Opinion,* 110 U.Pa.L.Rev. 473 (1962); *Effect of State Court Interpretation of a Contract,* 55 Mich.L.Rev. 871 (1957); *Police Enforcement of Private Discrimination,* 52 N.W.U.L.Rev. 774 (1958); *Criminal Penalties to Enforce Private Discrimination,* 57 Mich.L.Rev. 122 (1958); *Impact of Shelley v. Kraemer on the State Action Concept,* 44 Cal.L.Rev. 718 (1956).

when asking defendants to leave and placing them under arrest. Collins had a contractual obligation to enforce the park's policy. The case thus fell within the rule that a state (Collins) could not undertake an obligation to enforce a private policy of racial discrimination. The three dissenters conceded that Collins was exercising state authority, but argued that "the involvement of the State is no different from what it would have been had the arrests been made by a regular policeman dispatched from police headquarters." Suppose Collins had not worn his badge nor identified himself as a sheriff when he asked defendants to leave the amusement park. When they refused, he called a regular policeman who arrived and made the arrest. Can you think of a tenable theory that supports a conclusion that there was unconstitutional state action on the facts in *Griffin,* but that there would not be on the supposed facts?

The sit-in cases came to an end with the enactment of Title II of the Civil Rights Act of 1964 which prohibited discrimination in places of public accommodation. (The Court held that the statute abated sit-in prosecutions that had occurred prior to its enactment. Hamm v. City of Rock Hill, 379 U.S. 306 [1964].) In one of the last of the sit-in cases, five Justices did reach the broader issue of the application of Shelley v. Kraemer to the sit-in situation. Bell v. Maryland, 378 U.S. 226 (1964). Justice Douglas, joined by Justice Goldberg, argued that *Shelley* should govern when trespass convictions were used to enforce private discrimination that represented business preferences rather than personal prejudices. (Justice Goldberg, joined by Chief Justice Warren and Justice Douglas, also argued that access to public accommodations was a privilege of national citizenship). Justice Black's dissent, joined by Justices Harlan and White, argued that *Shelley* was inapplicable. A citizen who sought the law's protection of his property rights was not cast outside the law's protection because he called on law officers to enforce those rights. Shelley v. Kraemer was a case, according to Justice Black, where enforcement of a restrictive covenant operated to prohibit a willing seller from conveying to a Black purchaser and its principle did not apply to cases where the property owner was unwilling to permit occupation of his property by Blacks.

Pennsylvania v. Board of City Trusts

353 U.S. 230, 77 S.Ct. 806, 1 L.Ed.2d 792 (1957).

■ PER CURIAM.

The motion to dismiss the appeal for want of jurisdiction is granted, 28 U.S.C. § 1257(2). Treating the papers whereon the appeal was taken as a petition for writ of certiorari, 28 U.S.C. § 2103, the petition is granted. 28 U.S.C. § 1257(3).

Stephen Girard, by a will probated in 1831, left a fund in trust for the erection, maintenance, and operation of a "college." The will provided that the college was to admit "as many poor white male orphans, between the ages of six and ten years, as the said income shall be adequate to maintain." The will named as trustee the City of Philadelphia. The provisions of the will were carried out by the State and City and the college was opened in 1848. Since 1869, by virtue of an act of the Pennsylvania Legislature, the trust has been administered and the college operated by the "Board of Directors of City Trusts of the City of Philadelphia." . . . [a]

---

[a]   The Board is composed of 15 persons, including the mayor, the president of the City Council and twelve other citizens appointed by the judges of the Court of Common Pleas of the County of Philadelphia. The treasurer of the city serves as treasurer of the board. Pursuant to the terms of the will the funds of the trust were held and invested by the city treasurer and an annual accounting made to the legislature. The expenses of operating the school were defrayed wholly from the trust fund. It appears that the Board of City Trusts took an active role in directing the administration of the School.

In February 1954, the petitioners Foust and Felder applied for admission to the college. They met all qualifications except that they were Negroes. For this reason the Board refused to admit them. They petitioned the Orphans' Court of Philadelphia County for an order directing the Board to admit them, alleging that their exclusion because of race violated the Fourteenth Amendment to the Constitution. The State of Pennsylvania and the City of Philadelphia joined in the suit also contending the Board's action violated the Fourteenth Amendment. The Orphans' Court rejected the constitutional contention and refused to order the applicants' admission. . . . This was affirmed by the Pennsylvania Supreme Court. . . .

The Board which operates Girard College is an agency of the State of Pennsylvania. Therefore, even though the Board was acting as a trustee, its refusal to admit Foust and Felder to the college because they were Negroes was discrimination by the State. Such discrimination is forbidden by the Fourteenth Amendment. . . . Accordingly, the judgment of the Supreme Court of Pennsylvania is reversed and the cause is remanded for further proceedings not inconsistent with this opinion.

It is so ordered.

State Enforcement of Charitable Trusts

After the decision in Pennsylvania v. Board of City Trusts, Pennsylvania courts substituted private trustees to effectuate Stephen Girard's "dominant purpose" to limit the College to White orphans. In re Girard College Trusteeship, 391 Pa. 434, 138 A.2d 844 (1958). The Supreme Court never reached the merits of the questions whether Girard College could be administered by private trustees and continue to exclude Blacks or whether the state court's substitution of trustees to permit continued exclusion of Blacks was itself unconstitutional state action. (The appeal was dismissed for lack of jurisdiction and certiorari was denied. 357 U.S. 570 (1958).) The grounds of decision in Evans v. Newton, supra p. 780, made it unnecessary to decide whether state enforcement of discriminatory testamentary trusts was in all cases unconstitutional state action.

Charitable trusts do not have identifiable beneficiaries and are enforced, at least nominally, by state officials. States will not enforce such trusts unless they serve worthy purposes. Finally, charitable trusts are exempt from taxation, and are free from otherwise applicable restrictions on indefinite accumulation of trust property. (The Girard trust grew from 2 to 98 million dollars.) Do these elements of state contact impose a constitutional obligation on all private trusts to avoid racial discrimination? See Clark, *Charitable Trusts, the Fourteenth Amendment and the Will of Stephen Girard*, 66 Yale L.J. 979 (1957). An additional issue presented in both the Girard trust litigation and Evans v. Newton was whether, under the doctrine of Shelley v. Kraemer, the action of a state court in replacing a government trustee with a private trustee, for the purpose of effectuating a testator's desire to discriminate, was in itself unconstitutional state action.

Lower federal courts have dealt with some of these issues in the context of educational testamentary trusts. The Court of Appeals for the Third Circuit held the state courts' substitution of private trustees in the *Girard College* case was unconstitutional state action. Commonwealth of Pennsylvania v. Brown, 392 F.2d 120 (3d Cir.1968), cert. denied 391 U.S. 921 (1968). Earlier, a United States District Court decided that the terms of an 1833 bequest limiting Tulane University to the education of Whites were no longer binding. Guillory v. Administrators of Tulane University of

---

See In re Girard's Estate, 386 Pa. 548, 127 A.2d 287 (1956), certiorari granted, judgment reversed 353 U.S. 230 (1957).

La., 212 F.Supp. 674 (E.D.La.1962). Does the Supreme Court's decision in Evans v. Abney, which follows, cast doubt on the soundness of those lower court decisions?

Evans v. Abney

396 U.S. 435 (1970).

After the decision in Evans v. Newton, the Supreme Court of Georgia ruled that Senator Bacon's intention to provide a park for Whites only had become impossible to fulfill and that accordingly the trust had failed and the parkland and other trust property had reverted by operation of Georgia law to the heirs of the senator. The Supreme Court upheld this action. Justice Black, writing for the Court, said, in part:

"When a city park is destroyed because the Constitution required it to be integrated, there is reason for everyone to be disheartened. We agree with petitioners that in such a case it is not enough to find that the state court's result was reached through the application of established principles of state law. . . . Here, however, the action of the Georgia Supreme Court declaring the Baconsfield trust terminated presents no violation of constitutionally protected rights, and any harshness that may have resulted from the State court's decision can be attributed solely to its intention to effectuate as nearly as possible the explicit terms of Senator Bacon's will.

"Petitioners first argue that the action of the Georgia court violates the United States Constitution in that it imposes a drastic 'penalty,' the 'forfeiture' of the park, merely because of the city's compliance with the constitutional mandate expressed by this Court in Evans v. Newton. Of course, Evans v. Newton did not speak to the problem of whether Baconsfield should or could continue to operate as a park; it held only that its continued operation as a park had to be without racial discrimination. But petitioners now want to extend that holding to forbid the Georgia courts from closing Baconsfield on the ground that such a closing would penalize the city and its citizens for complying with the Constitution. We think, however, that the will of Senator Bacon and Georgia law provide all the justification necessary for imposing such a 'penalty.' The construction of wills is essentially a state-law question . . . and in this case the Georgia Supreme Court, as we read its opinion, interpreted Senator Bacon's will as embodying a preference for termination of the park rather than its integration. Given this, the Georgia court had no alternative under its relevant trust laws, which are long standing and neutral with regard to race, but to end the Baconsfield trust and return the property to the Senator's heirs."

Peremptory Challenges to Exclude Jurors on Account of Race

In Powers v. Ohio, 499 U.S. 400 (1991), the Court held that a prosecutor's exclusion of petit jurors through race-based peremptory challenges denied the excluded jurors equal protection, and that the criminal defendant had third-party standing to raise that issue. In two subsequent cases, the principal issue was whether there was state action in juror challenges by a private litigant and a criminal defendant.

Edmonson v. Leesville Concrete Co., Inc., 500 U.S. 614 (1991), held that the Constitution prohibited juror challenges by a private litigant. The Court applied a two part test to determine the state action question. First, did a private party's exercise of a right or privilege have its "source in state authority"? Peremptory challenges are permitted only when government allows them through statute or decisional law. Second, can the private party charged with constitutional violation "be described in all fairness as a state actor"? Private parties could not exercise juror challenges "absent the overt, significant assistance of the court," and juror challenges involved the performance of a traditional public function—selecting an entity (the jury) that is a "quintessential governmental body." The Court distinguished Polk County v. Dodson, 454 U.S. 312 (1981), which had held that a public defender, although employed by government, was not a state actor in a case claiming constitutionally inadequate representation. A defense lawyer in a criminal case is ethically committed to be an adversary to the government, while there is no adversarial relationship between the private litigant and government in the jury selection process.

Dodson was harder to distinguish in Georgia v. McCollum, 505 U.S. 42 (1992), where the Court held that it is unconstitutional for a criminal defense lawyer to use race-based peremptory challenges. Whether a public defender is a state actor "depends on the nature and context of the function he is performing." The public defender's function in exercising a peremptory challenge is different from other actions taken in the accused's defense, because it involves "the power to choose a quintessential governmental body."

Brentwood Academy v. Tennessee Secondary School Athletic Association

531 U.S. 288, 121 S.Ct. 924, 148 L.Ed.2d 807 (2001).

■ JUSTICE SOUTER delivered the opinion of the Court.

The issue is whether a statewide association incorporated to regulate interscholastic athletic competition among public and private secondary schools may be regarded as engaging in state action when it enforces a rule against a member school. . . . We hold that the association's regulatory activity may and should be treated as state action owing to the pervasive entwinement of state school officials in the structure of the association, there being no offsetting reason to see the association's acts in any other way.

I

Respondent Tennessee Secondary School Athletic Association (Association) is a not-for-profit membership corporation organized to regulate interscholastic sport among the public and private high schools in Tennessee that belong to it. No school is forced to join, but without any other authority actually regulating interscholastic athletics, it enjoys the memberships of almost all the State's public high schools (some 290 of them or 84% of the Association's voting membership), far outnumbering the 55 private schools that belong. A member school's team may play or scrimmage only against the team of another member, absent a dispensation.

The Association's rulemaking arm is its legislative council, while its board of control tends to administration. The voting membership of each of these nine-person committees is limited under the Association's bylaws to high school principals, assistant principals, and superintendents elected by the member schools, and the public school administrators who so serve typically attend meetings during regular school hours. Although the Association's staff members are not paid by the State, they are eligible to join the State's public retirement system for its employees. Member schools pay dues to the Association, though the bulk of its revenue is gate receipts at member teams' football and basketball tournaments, many of them held in public arenas rented by the Association.

The constitution, bylaws, and rules of the Association set standards of school membership and the eligibility of students to play in interscholastic games. . . .

Ever since the Association was incorporated in 1925, Tennessee's State Board of Education (State Board) has (to use its own words) acknowledged the corporation's functions "in providing standards, rules and regulations for interscholastic competition in the public schools of Tennessee," ... More recently, ... in 1972, it went so far as to adopt a rule expressly "designat[ing]" the Association as "the organization to supervise and regulate the athletic activities in which the public junior and senior high schools in Tennessee participate on an interscholastic basis." ... In 1996, however, the State Board dropped the original Rule ... expressly designating the Association as regulator; it substituted a statement "recogniz[ing] the value of participation in interscholastic athletics and the role of [the Association] in coordinating interscholastic athletic competition," while "authoriz[ing] the public schools of the state to voluntarily maintain membership in [the Association]." ...

The action before us responds to a 1997 regulatory enforcement proceeding brought against petitioner, Brentwood Academy, a private parochial high school member of the Association. The Association's board of control found that Brentwood violated a rule prohibiting "undue influence" in recruiting athletes, when it wrote to incoming students and their parents about spring football practice. The Association accordingly placed Brentwood's athletic program on probation for four years, declared its football and boys' basketball teams ineligible to compete in playoffs for two years, and imposed a $3,000 fine. When these penalties were imposed, all the voting members of the board of control and legislative council were public school administrators.

Brentwood sued the Association and its executive director in federal court under ... 42 U.S.C. § 1983, claiming that enforcement of the Rule was state action and a violation of the First and Fourteenth Amendments. The District Court entered summary judgment for Brentwood. . . .

The United States Court of Appeals for the Sixth Circuit reversed. . . . Rehearing en banc was later denied over the dissent of two judges. . . .

We granted certiorari, . . . and now reverse.

Our cases try to plot a line between state action subject to Fourteenth Amendment scrutiny and private conduct (however exceptionable) that is not. . . . If the Fourteenth Amendment is not to be displaced . . . its ambit cannot be a simple line between States and people operating outside formally governmental organizations, and the deed of an ostensibly private organization or individual is to be treated sometimes as if a State had caused it to be performed. . . .

What is fairly attributable is a matter of normative judgment, and the criteria lack rigid simplicity. From the range of circumstances that could point toward the State behind an individual face, no one fact can function as a necessary condition across the board for finding state action; nor is any set of circumstances absolutely sufficient, for there may be some countervailing reason against attributing activity to the government. . . .

Our cases have identified a host of facts that can bear on the fairness of such an attribution. . . .

Amidst such variety, examples may be the best teachers, and examples from our cases are unequivocal in showing that the character of a legal entity is determined neither by its expressly private characterization in statutory law, nor by the failure of the law to acknowledge the entity's inseparability from recognized government officials or agencies. . . . Pennsylvania v. Board of Directors of City Trusts of Philadelphia . . . held the privately endowed Gerard College to be a state actor and enforcement of its private founder's limitation of admission to whites attributable to the State, because, consistent with the terms of the settlor's gift, the college's board of directors was a state agency established by state law. Ostensibly the converse situation occurred in Evans v. Newton, . . . which held that private trustees to whom a city had transferred a park were nonetheless state actors barred from enforcing racial segregation, since the park served the public purpose of providing community recreation, and "the municipality remain[ed] entwined in [its] management [and] control," . . .

These examples of public entwinement in the management and control of ostensibly separate trusts or corporations foreshadow this case, as this Court itself anticipated in [National Collegiate Athletic Assn. v. Tarkanian, 488 U.S. 179 (1988)]. *Tarkanian* arose when an undoubtedly state actor, the University of Nevada, suspended its basketball coach, Tarkanian, in order to comply with rules and recommendations of the National Collegiate Athletic Association (NCAA). The coach charged the NCAA with state action, arguing that the state university had delegated its own functions to the NCAA, clothing the latter with authority to make and apply the university's rules, the result being joint action making the NCAA a state actor.

. . .

B

. . . The nominally private character of the Association is overborne by the pervasive entwinement of public institutions and public officials in its composition and workings, and there is no substantial reason to claim unfairness in applying constitutional standards to it.

The Association is not an organization of natural persons acting on their own, but of schools, and of public schools to the extent of 84% of the total. . . .

. . . Interscholastic athletics obviously play an integral part in the public education of Tennessee. . . . Since a pickup system of interscholastic games would not do, these public teams need some mechanism to produce rules and regulate competition. The mechanism is an organization overwhelmingly composed of public school officials who select representatives (all of them public officials at the time in question here), who in turn adopt and enforce the rules that make the system work. Thus, by giving these jobs to the Association, the 290 public schools of Tennessee belonging to it can sensibly be seen as exercising their own authority to meet their own responsibilities. Unsurprisingly, then, the record indicates that half the council or board meetings documented here were held during official school hours, and that public schools have largely provided for the Association's financial support. A small portion of the Association's revenue comes from membership dues paid by the schools, and the principal part from gate receipts at tournaments among the member schools. Unlike mere public buyers of contract services, whose payments for services rendered do not convert the service providers into public actors, . . . the schools here obtain membership in the service organization and give up sources of their own income to their collective association. The Association thus exercises the authority of the predominantly public schools to charge for admission to their games; the Association does not receive this money from the schools, but enjoys the schools' moneymaking capacity as its own.

In sum, to the extent of 84% of its membership, the Association is an organization of public schools represented by their officials acting in their official capacity to provide an integral element of secondary public schooling. There would be no recognizable Association, legal or tangible, without the public school officials, who do not merely control but overwhelmingly perform all but the purely ministerial acts by which the Association exists and functions in practical terms. Only the 16% minority of private school memberships prevents this entwinement of the Association and the public school system from being total and their identities totally indistinguishable.

To complement the entwinement of public school officials with the Association from the bottom up, the State of Tennessee has provided for entwinement from top down. State Board members are assigned ex officio to serve as members of the board of control and legislative council, and the Association's ministerial employees are treated as state employees to the extent of being eligible for membership in the state retirement system.

. . .

C

Entwinement is also the answer to the Association's several arguments offered to persuade us that the facts would not support a finding of state action under various criteria applied in other cases. These arguments are beside the point, simply because the facts justify a conclusion of state action under the criterion of entwinement, a conclusion in no sense unsettled merely because other criteria of state action may not be satisfied by the same facts.

The Association places great stress, for example, on the application of a public function test, as exemplified in Rendell-Baker v. Kohn, 457 U.S. 830 (1982). There, an apparently private school provided education for students whose special needs made it difficult for them to finish high school. . . . [W]e held that the performance of such a public function did not permit a finding of state action on the part of the school unless the function performed was exclusively and traditionally public, as it was not in that case. The Association argues that application of the public function criterion would produce the same result here, and we will assume, arguendo, that it would. But this case does not turn on a public function test, any more than Rendell-Baker had anything to do with entwinement of public officials in the special school.

For the same reason, it avails the Association nothing to stress that the State neither coerced nor encouraged the actions complained of. "Coercion" and "encouragement" are like "entwinement" in referring to kinds of facts that can justify characterizing an ostensibly private action as public instead. Facts that address any of these criteria are significant, but no one criterion must necessarily be applied. When, therefore, the relevant facts show pervasive entwinement to the point of largely overlapping identity, the implication of state action is not affected by pointing out that the facts might not loom large under a different test.

D

This is not to say that all of the Association's arguments are rendered beside the point by the public officials' involvement in the Association, for after application of the entwinement criterion, or any other, there is a further potential issue. . . . Even facts that suffice to show public action (or, standing alone, would require such a finding) may be outweighed in the name of some value at odds with finding public accountability in the circumstances. . . .

. . .

The judgment of the Court of Appeals for the Sixth Circuit is reversed, and the case is remanded for further proceedings consistent with this opinion.

It is so ordered.

■ JUSTICE THOMAS, with whom THE CHIEF JUSTICE, JUSTICE SCALIA, and JUSTICE KENNEDY join, dissenting.

We have never found state action based upon mere "entwinement." Until today, we have found a private organization's acts to constitute state action only when the organization performed a public function; was created, coerced, or encouraged by the government; or acted in a symbiotic relationship with the government. . . . I respectfully dissent.

. . . Although we have used many different tests to identify state action, they all have a common purpose. Our goal in every case is to determine whether an action "can fairly be attributed to the State." . . .

A

Regardless of these various tests for state action, common sense dictates that the TSSAA's actions cannot fairly be attributed to the State, and thus cannot constitute state action. . . . The TSSAA's rules are enforced not by a state agency but by its own board of control, which comprises high school principals, assistant principals, and superintendents, none of whom must work at a public school. Of course, at the time the recruiting rule was enforced in this case, all of the board members happened to be public school officials. However, each board member acts in a representative capacity on behalf of all the private and public schools in his region of Tennessee, and not simply his individual school.

The State of Tennessee did not create the TSSAA. The State does not fund the TSSAA and does not pay its employees. . . . The only state pronouncement acknowledging the TSSAA's existence is a rule providing that the State Board of Education permits public schools to maintain membership in the TSSAA if they so choose.

Moreover, the State of Tennessee has never had any involvement in the particular action taken by the TSSAA in this case: the enforcement of the TSSAA's recruiting rule prohibiting members from using "undue influence" on students or their parents or guardians "to secure or to retain a student for athletic purposes." There is no indication that the State has ever had any interest in how schools choose to regulate recruiting. . . .

B

. . .

The TSSAA has not performed a function that has been "traditionally exclusively reserved to the State." . . . The TSSAA no doubt serves the public, particularly the public schools, but the mere provision of a service to the public does not render such provision a traditional and exclusive public function. . . .

. . . It is also obvious that the TSSAA is not an entity created and controlled by the government for the purpose of fulfilling a government objective. . . . Indeed, no one claims that the State of Tennessee played any role in the creation of the TSSAA as a private corporation in 1925. . . .

In addition, the State of Tennessee has not "exercised coercive power or . . . provided such significant encouragement [to the TSSAA], either overt or covert," . . . To be sure, public schools do provide a small portion of the TSSAA's funding through their membership dues, but no one argues that these dues are somehow conditioned on the TSSAA's enactment and enforcement of recruiting rules. Likewise, even if the TSSAA were dependent on state funding to the extent of 90%, as was the case in Blum, instead of less than 4%, mere financial dependence on the State does not convert the TSSAA's actions into acts of the State. . . . Furthermore, there is no evidence of "joint participation," . . . between the State and the TSSAA in the TSSAA's enforcement of its recruiting rule. The TSSAA's board of control enforces its recruiting rule solely in accordance with the authority granted to it under the contract that each member signs.

. . .

Because I do not believe that the TSSAA's action of enforcing its recruiting rule is fairly attributable to the State of Tennessee, I would affirm.

II

Although the TSSAA's enforcement activities cannot be considered state action as a matter of common sense or under any of this Court's existing theories of state action, the majority presents a new theory. Under this theory, the majority holds that the combination of factors it identifies evidences "entwinement" of the State with the TSSAA, and that such entwinement converts private action into state action. . . .

. . .

* * *

Because the majority never defines "entwinement," the scope of its holding is unclear. If we are fortunate, the majority's fact-specific analysis will have little bearing beyond this case. But if the majority's new entwinement test develops in future years, it could affect many organizations that foster activities, enforce rules, and sponsor extracurricular competition among high schools—not just in athletics, but in such diverse areas as agriculture, mathematics, music, marching bands, forensics, and cheerleading. Indeed, this entwinement test may extend to other organizations that are composed of, or controlled by, public officials or public entities, such as firefighters, policemen, teachers, cities, or counties. I am not prepared to say that any private organization that permits public entities and public officials to participate acts as the State in anything or everything it does, and our state-action jurisprudence has never reached that far. The state-action doctrine was developed to reach only those actions that are truly attributable to the State, not to subject private citizens to the control of federal courts hearing § 1983 actions.

I respectfully dissent.

C. GOVERNMENT FINANCING, REGULATION AND AUTHORIZATION OF PRIVATE CONDUCT

1. PRIVATE ACTIVITY ON GOVERNMENT PROPERTY

Burton v. Wilmington Parking Authority
365 U.S. 715, 81 S.Ct. 856, 6 L.Ed.2d 45 (1961).

[The Eagle Coffee Shoppe is a restaurant located within an offstreet automobile parking building in Wilmington, Delaware. The parking building is owned and operated by the Wilmington Parking Authority, an agency of the State of Delaware, and the restaurant is the Authority's lessee. Before it began actual construction of the facility, the Authority was advised by its retained experts that the anticipated revenue from the parking of cars and proceeds from sale of its bonds would not be sufficient to finance the construction costs of the facility. Moreover, the bonds were not expected to be marketable if payable solely out of parking revenues. To secure additional capital needed for its "debt-service" requirements, and thereby to make bond financing practicable, the Authority decided it was necessary to enter long-term leases with responsible tenants for commercial use of some of the space available in the projected "garage building." The public was invited to bid for these leases.

[In April 1957 such a private lease, for 20 years and renewable for another 10 years, was made with Eagle Coffee Shoppe, Inc., for use as a "restaurant, dining room, banquet hall, cocktail lounge and bar and for no other use and purpose." Other portions of the structure were leased to other tenants, including a bookstore, a retail jeweler, and a food store. Upon completion of the building, the Authority located at appropriate places thereon official signs indicating the public character of the building, and flew from mastheads on the roof both the state and national flags.

[In August 1958 Burton parked his car in the building and walked around to enter the restaurant by its front door on Ninth Street. He was refused service. He then filed this action seeking a declaratory judgment, alleging that he was refused service solely because he was a Negro. On motions for summary judgment the trial court ruled for Burton. The Delaware Supreme Court reversed on the ground that Eagle Coffee Shoppe was under no duty to serve because of a state statute providing: "No keeper of an inn, tavern, hotel, or restaurant, or other place of public entertainment or refreshment of travelers, guests, or customers shall be obliged, by law, to furnish entertainment or refreshment to persons whose reception or entertainment by him would be offensive to the major part of his customers and would injure his business. . . ."]

■ MR. JUSTICE CLARK delivered the opinion of the Court.

. . .

It is clear, as it always has been since the Civil Rights Cases . . . that "Individual invasion of individual rights is not the subject-matter of the amendment," and that private conduct abridging individual rights does no violence to the Equal Protection Clause unless to some significant extent the State in any of its manifestations has been found to have become involved in it. Because the virtue of the right to equal protection of the laws could lie only in the breadth of its application, its constitutional assurance was reserved in terms whose imprecision was necessary if the right were to be enjoyed in the variety of individual-state relationships which the Amendment was designed to embrace. For the same reason, to fashion and apply a precise formula for recognition of state responsibility under the Equal Protection Clause is an "impossible task" . . . Only by sifting facts and weighing circumstances can the nonobvious involvement of the State in private conduct be attributed its true significance. . . .

Addition of all these activities, obligations and responsibilities of the Authority, the benefits mutually conferred, together with the obvious fact that the restaurant is operated as an integral part of a public building devoted to a public parking service, indicates that degree of state participation and involvement in discriminatory action which it was the design of the Fourteenth Amendment to condemn. It is irony amounting to grave injustice that in one part of a single building, erected and maintained with public funds by an agency of the State to serve a public purpose, all persons have equal rights, while in another portion, also serving the public, a Negro is a second-class citizen, offensive because of his race, without rights and unentitled to service, but at the same time fully enjoys equal access to nearby restaurants in wholly privately owned buildings. As the Chancellor pointed out, in its lease with Eagle the Authority could have affirmatively required Eagle to discharge the responsibilities under the Fourteenth Amendment imposed upon the private enterprise as a consequence of state participation. But no State may effectively abdicate its responsibilities by either ignoring them or by merely failing to discharge them whatever the motive may be. It is of no consolation to an individual denied the equal protection of the laws that it was done in good faith. Certainly the conclusions drawn in similar cases by the various Courts of Appeals do not depend upon such a distinction. By its inaction, the Authority, and through it the State, has not only made itself a party to the refusal of service, but has elected to place its power, property and prestige behind the admitted discrimination. The State has so far insinuated itself into a position of interdependence with Eagle that it must be recognized as a joint participant in the challenged activity, which, on that account, cannot be considered to have been so "purely private" as to fall without the scope of the Fourteenth Amendment.

Because readily applicable formulae may not be fashioned, the conclusions drawn from the facts and circumstances of this record are by no means declared as universal truths on the basis of which every state leasing agreement is to be tested. . . . Specifically defining the limits of our inquiry, what we hold today is that when a State leases public property in the manner and for the purpose shown to have been the case here, the proscriptions of the Fourteenth Amendment must be complied with by the lessee as certainly as though they were binding covenants written into the agreement itself.

The judgment of the Supreme Court of Delaware is reversed and the cause remanded for further proceedings consistent with this opinion.

[Justice Stewart concurred. Justices Frankfurter, Harlan, and Whittaker, dissented.]

Reality vs. Appearance of State Action

Consider the following hypothesis. In cases concerning racial discrimination, an important factor of decision is whether all of the circumstances create a public perception that the state approves the private discriminatory decision. Are appearances of state approval more important than an inquiry whether, appearances aside, racial discrimination can be traced to governmental decisions? The suggested hypothesis would support the results in the preceding cases of Pennsylvania v. Board of Trusts and Burton v. Wilmington Parking Authority. So long as the city ran the school, it appeared that the city and not the testator was making the choice to engage in a policy of racial discrimination. So long as the city operated the parking garage, it would appear that it approved racial discrimination by tenants in the parking structure. It can also be argued that the hypothesis explains the disparate results in the two cases concerning Senator Bacon's will—Evans v. Newton, supra p. 780, and Evans v. Abney, supra p. 793. The city had operated the park for so long as a segregated park that merely turning it over to a private trustee for continued segregated operation would not remove the appearance of a segregated city park. On the other hand, terminating the operation of the park because the city could no longer follow Senator Bacon's wish that it be segregated did not give the appearance that the city approved the testator's choice. (Consider the case of a private university refusing to accept a bequest because it *disapproves* conditions attached to it.)

Are you persuaded that *Abney* and *Newton* are both appropriately decided under the hypothesis suggested here? Do you think that the hypothesis is useful in marking the limits of state action doctrine? Is the hypothesis useful in explaining the disparate state-action and no-state-action conclusions in the cases that follow?

Gilmore v. Montgomery, Ala.

417 U.S. 556 (1974).

The case involved actions by a city in permitting the use of public park recreational facilities by private segregated school groups and any other non-school groups that allegedly discriminate in their membership on the basis of race. The Court held it invalid for the city to allocate use of park facilities to private segregated school groups where that action facilitated the avoidance of an outstanding school desegregation order. With respect to the use by other segregated groups the Court found the facts insufficiently developed to permit a ruling and sent the case back to the district court. In concluding its opinion the Court said:

"We close with this word of caution. It should be obvious that the exclusion of any person or group—all-Negro, all-oriental, or all-white—from public facilities infringes upon the freedom of the individual to associate as he chooses. Mr. Justice Douglas emphasized this in his dissent, joined by Mr. Justice Marshall, in *Moose Lodge*. He observed, 'The associational rights which our system honors permit all white, all black, all brown and all yellow clubs to be formed. They also permit all Catholic, all Jewish, or all agnostic clubs to be established. Government may not tell a man or woman who his or her associates must be. The individual can be as selective as he desires.' . . . The freedom to associate applies to the beliefs we share, and to those we consider reprehensible. It tends to produce the diversity of opinion that oils the machine of democratic government and insures peaceful, orderly change. Because its exercise is largely dependent on the right to own or use property, . . . any denial of access to public facilities must withstand close scrutiny and be carefully circumscribed. Certainly, a person's mere membership in an organization which possesses a discriminatory admissions policy would not alone be ground for his exclusion from public facilities. Having said this, however, we must also be aware that the very exercise of the freedom to associate by some may serve to infringe that freedom for others. Invidious discrimination takes its own toll on the freedom to associate, and it is not subject to affirmative constitutional protection when it involves state action. Norwood v. Harrison, 413 U.S., at 470."

2.   GOVERNMENT FINANCIAL ASSISTANCE TO PRIVATE ACTIVITIES

Norwood v. Harrison

413 U.S. 455 (1973).

Mississippi had a statutory program under which textbooks were purchased by the state and lent to students in both public and private schools. A suit was brought challenging the application of this statute in lending textbooks to students attending schools with racially discriminatory admission policies. The Court held the statute invalid as applied to such schools. The Court said:

"This Court has consistently affirmed decisions enjoining state tuition grants to students attending racially discriminatory private schools. A textbook lending program is not legally distinguishable from the forms of state assistance foreclosed by the prior cases. Free textbooks, like tuition grants directed to private school students, are a form of financial assistance inuring to the benefit of the private schools themselves. An inescapable educational cost for students in both public and private schools is the expense of providing all necessary learning materials. When, as here, that necessary expense is borne by the State, the economic consequence is to give aid to the enterprise; if the school engages in discriminatory practices the State by tangible aid in the form of textbooks thereby gives support to such discrimination. Racial discrimination in state-operated schools is barred by the Constitution and '[i]t is also axiomatic that a state may not induce, encourage or promote private persons to accomplish what it is constitutionally forbidden to accomplish.' . . .

"We do not suggest that a State violates its constitutional duty merely because it has provided *any* form of state service that benefits private schools said to be racially discriminatory. Textbooks are a basic educational tool and, like tuition grants, they are provided only in connection with schools; they are to be distinguished from generalized services government might provide to schools in common with others. Moreover, the textbooks provided to private school students by the State in this case are a form of assistance readily available from sources entirely independent of the State—unlike, for example, 'such necessities of life as electricity, water, and police and fire protection.' Moose Lodge No. 107 v. Irvis, 407 U.S. 163, 173 (1972). The State has neither an absolute nor operating monopoly on the procurement of school textbooks; anyone can purchase them on the open market.

"The District Court laid great stress on the absence of showing by appellants that 'any child enrolled in private school, if deprived of free textbooks, would withdraw from private school and subsequently enroll in the public schools.' We can accept this factual assertion; we cannot and do not know, on this record at least, whether state textbook assistance is the determinative factor in the enrollment of any students in any of the private schools in Mississippi. We do not agree with the District Court in its analysis of the legal consequences of this uncertainty, for the Constitution does not permit the State to aid discrimination even when there is no precise causal relationship between state financial aid to a private school and the continued well-being of that school. A State may not grant the type of tangible financial aid here involved if that aid has a significant tendency to facilitate, reinforce, and support private discrimination."

Blum v. Yaretsky

457 U.S. 991 (1982).

A class of medicaid patients brought suit claiming that private nursing homes violated their rights to procedural due process in transferring them to lower levels of care, or discharging them. The nursing homes receive reimbursement from the state for their services in caring for medicaid patients. Decisions by the nursing home result in lower medicaid benefits. The Court held that there was no state action that would trigger the fourteenth amendment's requirement of procedural due process. Justice Rehnquist's opinion for the court said, in part:

"Respondents . . . argue that the State 'affirmatively commands' the summary discharge or transfer of Medicaid patients who are thought to be inappropriately placed in their nursing facilities. Were this characterization accurate, we would have a different question before us. However, our review of the statutes and regulations identified by respondents does not support respondents' characterization of them.

. . .

". . . [R]espondents' complaint is about nursing home decisions to discharge or transfer, not to admit, Medicaid patients. But we are not satisfied that the State is responsible for those decisions. . . . The regulations cited by respondents require [nursing homes] 'to make all efforts possible to transfer patients to the appropriate level of care or home as indicated by the patient's medical condition or needs' . . . The nursing homes are required to complete patient care assessment forms designed by the State and 'provide the receiving facility or provider with a current copy of same at the time of discharge to an alternate level of care facility or home.' . . .

"These regulations do not require the nursing homes to rely on the forms in making discharge or transfer decisions, nor do they demonstrate that the State is responsible for the decision to discharge or transfer particular patients. Those decisions ultimately turn on medical judgments made by private parties according to professional standards that are not established by the State. This case, therefore, is not unlike Polk County v. Dodson, 454 U.S. 312 (1981), in which the question was whether a public defender acts 'under color of' state law within the meaning of 42 U.S.C. § 1983 when representing an indigent defendant in a state criminal proceeding. Although the public defender was employed by the State and appointed by the State to represent the respondent, we concluded that '[t]his assignment entailed functions and obligations in no way dependent on state authority.' . . . The decisions made by the public defender in the course of representing his client were framed in accordance with professional canons of ethics, rather than dictated by any rule of conduct imposed by the State. The same is true of nursing home decisions to discharge or transfer particular patients because the care they are receiving is medically inappropriate."

Justices Brennan and Marshall dissented.

Rendell-Baker v. Kohn

457 U.S. 830 (1982).

Plaintiffs were discharged teachers, previously employed by a private school for maladjusted high school students. Most of the school's students had been referred to it by city and state agencies. Public funds account for 90 to 99% of the school's operating budget. Plaintiffs brought suit under 42 U.S.C. § 1983, claiming that their discharges were for constitutionally protected speech, in violation of the First Amendment, and that they had been denied procedural due process. The Court held that the private school did not act under color of state law in dismissing the plaintiffs. Chief Justice Burger's opinion said, in part:

"The school . . . is not fundamentally different from many private corporations whose business depends primarily on contracts to build roads, bridges, dams, ships, or submarines for the government. Acts of such private contractors do not become acts of the government by reason of their significant or even total engagement in performing public contracts."

Justices Marshall and Brennan dissented.

3.   GOVERNMENT REGULATION OF PRIVATE ACTIVITY

Moose Lodge No. 107 v. Irvis

407 U.S. 163, 92 S.Ct. 1965, 32 L.Ed.2d 627 (1972).

■ MR. JUSTICE REHNQUIST delivered the opinion of the Court.

Appellee Irvis, a Negro . . . , was refused service by appellant Moose Lodge, a local branch of the national fraternal organization located in Harrisburg, Pennsylvania. Appellee then brought this action under 42 U.S.C. § 1983 for injunctive relief in the United States District Court for the Middle District of Pennsylvania. He claimed that because the Pennsylvania liquor board had issued appellant Moose Lodge a private club license that authorized the sale of alcoholic beverages on its premises, the refusal of service to him was "state action" for the purposes of the Equal Protection Clause of the Fourteenth Amendment. He named both Moose Lodge and the Pennsylvania Liquor Authority as defendants, seeking injunctive relief that would have required the defendant liquor board to revoke Moose Lodge's license so long as it continued its discriminatory practices. Appellee sought no damages.

A three-judge district court, convened at appellee's request, upheld his contention on the merits, and entered a decree declaring invalid the liquor license issued to Moose Lodge "as long as it follows a policy of racial discrimination in its membership or operating policies or practices." Moose Lodge alone appealed from the decree . . .

I.

The District Court in its opinion found that "a Caucasian member in good standing brought plaintiff, a Negro, to the Lodge's dining room and bar as his guest and requested service of food and beverages. The Lodge through its employees refused service to plaintiff solely because he is a Negro." It is undisputed that each local Moose Lodge is bound by the constitution and general by-laws of the Supreme Lodge, the latter of which contains a provision limiting membership in the lodges to white male Caucasians. The District Court in this connection found that "[t]he lodges accordingly maintain a policy and practice of restricting membership to the Caucasian race and permitting members to bring only Caucasian guests on lodge premises, particularly to the dining room and bar."

. . .

Any injury to appellee from the conduct of Moose Lodge stemmed not from the lodge's membership requirements, but from its policies with respect to the serving of guests of members. Appellee has standing to seek redress for injuries done to him, but may not seek redress for injuries done to others. . . . [A]ppellee was not injured by Moose Lodge's membership policy since he never sought to become a member. . . .

Because appellee had no standing to litigate a constitutional claim arising out of Moose Lodge's membership practices, the District Court erred in reaching that issue on the merits. But it did not err in reaching the constitutional claim of appellee that Moose Lodge's guest service practices under these circumstances violated the Fourteenth Amendment. . . .

II.

Moose Lodge is a private club in the ordinary meaning of that term. It is a local chapter of a national fraternal organization having well defined requirements for membership. It conducts all of its activities in a building that is owned by it. It is not publicly funded. Only members and guests are permitted in any lodge of the order; one may become a guest only by invitation of a member or upon invitation of the house committee.

Appellee, while conceding the right of private clubs to choose members upon a discriminatory basis, asserts that the licensing of Moose Lodge to serve liquor by the Pennsylvania Liquor Control Board amounts to such State involvement with the club's activities as to make its discriminatory practices forbidden by the Equal Protection Clause of the Fourteenth Amendment. The relief sought and obtained by appellee in the District Court was an injunction forbidding the licensing by the liquor authority of Moose Lodge until it ceased its discriminatory practices. We conclude that Moose Lodge's refusal to serve food and beverages to a guest by reason of the fact that he was a Negro does not, under the circumstances here presented, violate the Fourteenth Amendment.

. . .

While the principle is easily stated, the question of whether particular discriminatory conduct is private, on the one hand, or amounts to "state action," on the other hand, frequently admits of no easy answer. . . .

Our cases make clear that the impetus for the forbidden discrimination need not originate with the State if it is state action that enforces privately originated discrimination. Shelley v. Kraemer, supra. . . .

The Court has never held, of course, that discrimination by an otherwise private entity would be violative of the Equal Protection Clause if the private entity receives any sort of benefit or service at all from the State, or if it is subject to state regulation in any degree whatever. Since state-furnished services include such necessities of life as electricity, water, and police and fire protection, such a holding would utterly emasculate the distinction between private as distinguished from state conduct set forth in The Civil Rights Cases, supra, and adhered to in subsequent decisions. Our holdings indicate that where the impetus for the discrimination is private, the State must have "significantly involved itself with invidious discriminations," Reitman v.

Mulkey, 387 U.S. 369, 380 (1967), in order for the discriminatory action to fall within the ambit of the constitutional prohibition.

. . .

Here there is nothing approaching the symbiotic relationship between lessor and lessee that was present in *Burton,* where the private lessee obtained the benefit of locating in a building owned by the state created parking authority, and the parking authority was enabled to carry out its primary public purpose of furnishing parking space by advantageously leasing portions of the building constructed for that purpose to commercial lessees such as the owner of the Eagle Restaurant. Unlike *Burton,* the Moose Lodge building is located on land owned by it, not by any public authority. Far from apparently holding itself out as a place of public accommodation, Moose Lodge quite ostentatiously proclaims the fact that it is not open to the public at large. Nor is it located and operated in such surroundings that although private in name, it discharges a function or performs a service that would otherwise in all likelihood be performed by the State. In short, while Eagle was a public restaurant in a public building, Moose Lodge is a private social club in a private building.

With the exception hereafter noted, the Pennsylvania Liquor Control Board plays absolutely no part in establishing or enforcing the membership or guest policies of the club that it licenses to serve liquor. There is no suggestion in this record that the Pennsylvania law, either as written or as applied, discriminates against minority groups either in their right to apply for club licenses themselves or in their right to purchase and be served liquor in places of public accommodation. The only effect that the state licensing of Moose Lodge to serve liquor can be said to have on the right of any other Pennsylvanian to buy or be served liquor on premises other than those of Moose Lodge is that for some purposes club licenses are counted in the maximum number of licenses which may be issued in a given municipality. Basically each municipality has a quota of one retail license for each 1,500 inhabitants. Licenses issued to hotels, municipal golf courses and airport restaurants are not counted in this quota, nor are club licenses until the maximum number of retail licenses is reached. Beyond that point, neither additional retail licenses nor additional club licenses may be issued so long as the number of issued and outstanding retail licenses remains at or above the statutory maximum.

The District Court was at pains to point out in its opinion what it considered to be the "pervasive" nature of the regulation of private clubs by the Pennsylvania Liquor Control Board. . . .

However detailed this type of regulation may be in some particulars, it cannot be said to in any way foster or encourage racial discrimination. Nor can it be said to make the State in any realistic sense a partner or even a joint venturer in the club's enterprise. The limited effect of the prohibition against obtaining additional club licenses when the maximum number of retail licenses allotted to a municipality has been issued, when considered together with the availability of liquor from hotel, restaurant, and retail licensees falls far short of conferring upon club licensees a monopoly in the dispensing of liquor in any given municipality or in the State as a whole. We therefore hold that, with the exception hereafter noted, the operation of the regulatory scheme enforced by the Pennsylvania Liquor Control Board does not sufficiently implicate the State in the discriminatory guest policies of Moose Lodge so as to make the latter "state action" within the ambit of the Equal Protection Clause of the Fourteenth Amendment.

The District Court found that the regulations of the Liquor Control Board adopted pursuant to statute affirmatively require that "every club licensee shall adhere to all the provisions of its Constitution and By-Laws." Appellant argues that the purpose of this provision "is purely and simply and plainly the prevention of subterfuge," pointing out that the *bona fides* of a private club, as opposed to a place of public accommodation masquerading as a private club, is a matter with which the State Liquor Control Board may legitimately concern itself. Appellee concedes this to be the case, and expresses disagreement with the District Court on this point. There can be no doubt that the label "private club" can and has been used to evade both regulations of state and local liquor authorities, and statutes requiring places of public accommodation to serve all persons without regard to race, color, religion, or national origin. This Court in Daniel v. Paul, 395 U.S. 298 (1969), had occasion to address this issue in connection with the application of Title II of the Civil Rights Act of 1964, 78 Stat. 243, 42 U.S.C. § 2000a et seq.

. . .

Even though the Liquor Control Board regulation in question is neutral in its terms, the result of its application in a case where the constitution and by-laws of a club required racial discrimination would be to invoke the sanctions of the State to enforce a concededly discriminatory private rule. State action, for purposes of the Equal Protection Clause, may emanate from rulings of administrative and regulatory agencies as well as from legislative or judicial action. . . . Shelley v. Kraemer . . . makes it clear that the application of state sanctions to enforce such a rule would violate the Fourteenth Amendment. Although the record before us is not as clear as one would like, appellant has not persuaded us that the District Court should have denied any and all relief.

Appellee was entitled to a decree enjoining the enforcement of § 113.09 of the regulations promulgated by the Pennsylvania Liquor Control Board insofar as that regulation requires compliance by Moose Lodge with provisions of its constitution and by-laws containing racially discriminatory provisions. He was entitled to no more. The judgment of the District Court is reversed, and the cause remanded with instructions to enter a decree in conformity with this opinion.

■ MR. JUSTICE DOUGLAS, with whom MR. JUSTICE MARSHALL joins, dissenting.

. . .

Were this regulation [enforcing the discriminatory membership clause] the only infirmity in Pennsylvania's licensing scheme, I would perhaps agree with the majority that the appropriate relief would be a decree enjoining its enforcement. But there is another flaw in the scheme not so easily cured. Liquor licenses in Pennsylvania, unlike driver's licenses, or marriage licenses, are not freely available to those who meet racially neutral qualifications. There is a complex quota system, which the majority accurately describes. What the majority neglects to say is that the Harrisburg quota, where Moose Lodge No. 107 is located, has been full for many years. No more club licenses may be issued in that city.

This state-enforced scarcity of licenses restricts the ability of blacks to obtain liquor, for liquor is commercially available *only* at private clubs for a significant portion of each week. Access by blacks to places that serve liquor is further limited by the fact that the state quota is filled. A group desiring to form a nondiscriminatory club which would serve blacks must purchase a license held by an existing club, which can exact a monopoly price for the transfer. The availability of such a license is speculative at best, however, for, as Moose Lodge itself concedes, without a liquor license a fraternal organization would be hard-pressed to survive.

Thus, the State of Pennsylvania is putting the weight of its liquor license, concededly a valued and important adjunct to a private club, behind racial discrimination. . . .

I would affirm the judgment below.

■ MR. JUSTICE BRENNAN, with whom MR. JUSTICE MARSHALL joins, dissenting.

When Moose Lodge obtained its liquor license, the State of Pennsylvania became an active participant in the operation of the Lodge bar. Liquor licensing laws are only incidentally revenue measures; they are primarily pervasive regulatory schemes under which the State dictates and continually supervises virtually every detail of the operation of the licensee's business. Very few, if any, other licensed businesses experience such complete state involvement. Yet the Court holds that that involvement does not constitute "state action" making the Lodge's refusal to serve a guest liquor solely because of his race a violation of the Fourteenth Amendment. The vital flaw in the Court's reasoning is its complete disregard of the fundamental value underlying the "state action" concept. . . .

Plainly, the State of Pennsylvania's liquor regulations intertwine the State with the operation of the Lodge bar in a "significant way [and] lend [the State's] authority to the sordid business of racial discrimination." . . .

This is thus a case requiring application of the principle that until today has governed our determinations of the existence of "state action": "Our prior decisions leave no doubt that the mere existence of efforts by the State, through legislation or otherwise, to authorize, encourage, or otherwise support racial discrimination in a particular facet of life constitutes illegal state involvement in those pertinent private acts of discrimination that subsequently occur." . . .

I therefore dissent and would affirm the final decree entered by the District Court.

Jackson v. Metropolitan Edison Co.

419 U.S. 345, 95 S.Ct. 449, 42 L.Ed.2d 477 (1974).

[Plaintiff brought suit against defendant, a privately owned and operated utility corporation which holds a certificate of public convenience issued by the Pennsylvania Utilities Commission, seeking damages and injunctive relief under 42 U.S.C. § 1983 for termination of her electric service allegedly before she had been afforded notice, a hearing, and an opportunity to pay any amounts due. Plaintiff claimed that under state law she was entitled to reasonably continuous electric service and that respondent's termination for alleged nonpayment, permitted by a provision of its general tariff filed with the Commission, was state action depriving her of her property without due process of law. The Court of Appeals affirmed the District Court's dismissal of her complaint. The Supreme Court affirmed.]

■ MR. JUSTICE REHNQUIST delivered the opinion of the Court.

. . .

Here the action complained of was taken by a utility company which is privately owned and operated, but which in many particulars of its business is subject to extensive state regulation. The mere fact that a business is subject to state regulation does not by itself convert its action into that of the State for purposes of the Fourteenth Amendment. Moose Lodge No. 107 v. Irvis, supra, 407 U.S. at 176–177. Nor does the fact that the regulation is extensive and detailed, as in the case of most public utilities, do so. Public Utilities Comm'n v. Pollak, 343 U.S. 451, 462 (1952). It may well be that acts of a heavily regulated utility with at least something of a governmentally protected monopoly will more readily be found to be "state" acts than will the acts of an entity lacking these characteristics. But the inquiry must be whether there is a sufficiently close nexus between the State and the challenged action of the regulated entity so that the action of the latter may be fairly treated as that of the State itself. . . . The true nature of the State's involvement may not be immediately obvious, and detailed inquiry may be required in order to determine whether the test is met. . . .

Petitioner advances a series of contentions which, in her view, lead to the conclusion that this case should fall on the *Burton* side of the line drawn in the *Civil Rights Cases,* supra, rather than on the *Moose Lodge* side of that line. We find none of them persuasive.

Petitioner first argues that "state action" is present because of the monopoly status allegedly conferred upon Metropolitan by the State of Pennsylvania. As a factual matter, it may well be doubted that the State ever granted or guaranteed Metropolitan a monopoly. But assuming that it had, this fact is not determinative in considering whether Metropolitan's termination of service to petitioner was "state action" for purposes of the Fourteenth Amendment. In *Pollak,* supra, where the Court dealt with the activities of the District of Columbia Transit Company, a congressionally established monopoly, we expressly disclaimed reliance on the monopoly status of the transit authority. Id., . . . Similarly, although certain monopoly aspects were presented in *Moose Lodge No. 107,* supra, we found that the Lodge's action was not subject to the provisions of the Fourteenth Amendment. In each of those cases, there was insufficient relationship between the challenged actions of the entities involved and their monopoly status. There is no indication of any greater connection here.

Petitioner next urges that state action is present because respondent provides an essential public service required to be supplied on a reasonably continuous basis by 66 Pa.Stat. § 1171, and hence performs a "public function." We have of course found state action present in the exercise by a private entity of powers traditionally exclusively reserved to the State. See, e.g., Nixon v. Condon, 286 U.S. 73 (1932) (election); Terry v. Adams, 345 U.S. 461 (1953) (election); Marsh v. Alabama, 326 U.S. 501 (1946) (company town); Evans v. Newton, 382 U.S. 296 (1966) (municipal park). If we were dealing with the exercise by Metropolitan of some power delegated to it by the State which is traditionally associated with sovereignty, such as eminent domain, our case would be quite a different one. But while the Pennsylvania statute imposes an obligation to furnish service on regulated utilities, it imposes no such obligation on the State. The Pennsylvania courts have rejected the contention that the furnishing of utility services is either a state function or a municipal duty. . . .

Perhaps in recognition of the fact that the supplying of utility service is not traditionally the exclusive prerogative of the State, petitioner invites the expansion of the doctrine of this limited line of cases into a broad principle that all businesses "affected with the public interest" are state actors in all their actions.

We decline the invitation for reasons stated long ago in Nebbia v. New York, 291 U.S. 502 (1934), in the course of rejecting a substantive due process attack on state legislation: . . .

Doctors, optometrists, lawyers, Metropolitan, and Nebbia's upstate New York grocery selling a quart of milk are all in regulated businesses, providing arguably essential goods and services, "affected with a public interest." We do not believe that such a status converts their every action, absent more, into that of the State.

We also reject the notion that Metropolitan's termination is state action because the State "has specifically authorized and approved" the termination practice. In the instant case, Metropolitan filed with the Public Utilities Commission a general tariff— a provision of which states Metropolitan's right to terminate service for nonpayment.

This provision has appeared in Metropolitan's previously filed tariffs for many years and has never been the subject of a hearing or other scrutiny by the Commission. . . .

. . . [T]he sole connection of the Commission with this regulation was Metropolitan's simple notice filing with the Commission and the lack of any Commission action to prohibit it.

The case most heavily relied on by petitioner is Public Utilities Comm'n v. Pollak, supra. There the Court dealt with the contention that Capital Transit's installation of a piped music system on its buses violated the First Amendment rights of the bus riders. It is not entirely clear whether the Court alternatively held that Capital Transit's action was action of the "State" for First Amendment purposes, or whether it merely assumed *arguendo* that it was and went on to resolve the First Amendment question adversely to the bus riders. In either event, the nature of the state involvement there was quite different than it is here. The District of Columbia Public Utilities Commission, on its own motion, commenced an investigation of the effects of the piped music, and after a full hearing concluded not only that Capital Transit's practices were "not inconsistent with public convenience, comfort, and safety," . . . but also that the practice "in fact through the creation of better will among passengers, . . . tends to improve the conditions under which the public rides." . . . Here, on the other hand, there was no such imprimatur placed on the practice of Metropolitan about which petitioner complains. The nature of governmental regulation of private utilities is such that a utility may frequently be required by the state regulatory scheme to obtain approval for practices a business regulated in less detail would be free to institute without any approval from a regulatory body. Approval by a state utility commission of such a request from a regulated utility, where the commission has not put its own weight on the side of the proposed practice by ordering it, does not transmute a practice initiated by the utility and approved by the commission into "state action." At most, the Commission's failure to overturn this practice amounted to no more than a determination that a Pennsylvania utility was authorized to employ such a practice if it so desired. Respondent's exercise of the choice allowed by state law where the initiative comes from it and not from the State, does not make its action in doing so "state action" for purposes of the Fourteenth Amendment.

We also find absent in the instant case the symbiotic relationship presented in Burton v. Wilmington Parking Authority, 365 U.S. 715 (1961). . . .

Metropolitan is a privately owned corporation, and it does not lease its facilities from the State of Pennsylvania. It alone is responsible for the provision of power to its customers. In common with all corporations of the State it pays taxes to the State, and it is subject to a form of extensive regulation by the State in a way that most other business enterprises are not. But this was likewise true of the appellant club in Moose Lodge No. 107 v. Irvis, . . .

All of petitioner's arguments taken together show no more than that Metropolitan was a heavily regulated private utility, enjoying at least a partial monopoly in the providing of electrical service within its territory, and that it elected to terminate service to petitioner in a manner which the Pennsylvania Public Utilities Commission found permissible under state law. Under our decision this is not sufficient to connect the State of Pennsylvania with respondent's action so as to make the latter's conduct attributable to the State for purposes of the Fourteenth Amendment.

We conclude that the State of Pennsylvania is not sufficiently connected with respondent's action in terminating petitioner's service so as to make respondent's conduct in so doing attributable to the State for purposes of the Fourteenth Amendment. We therefore have no occasion to decide whether petitioner's claim to continued service was "property" for purposes of that Amendment, or whether "due process of law" would require a State taking similar action to accord petitioner the procedural rights for which she contends. The judgment of the Court of Appeals for the Third Circuit is therefore

Affirmed.

■ MR. JUSTICE DOUGLAS, dissenting.

I reach the opposite conclusion from that reached by the majority on the state action issue. . . .

■ MR. JUSTICE BRENNAN, dissenting.

I do not think that a controversy existed between petitioner and respondent entitling petitioner to be heard in this action. . . .

■ MR. JUSTICE MARSHALL, dissenting.

I agree with my Brother Brennan that this case is a very poor vehicle for resolving the difficult and important questions presented today. . . . Since the Court has disposed of the case by finding no state action, however, I think it appropriate to register my dissent on that point. . . .

. . .

The fact that the Metropolitan Edison Company supplies an essential public service that is in many communities supplied by the government weighs more heavily for me than for the majority. . . .

Private parties performing functions affecting the public interest can often make a persuasive claim to be free of the constitutional requirements applicable to governmental institutions because of the value of preserving a private sector in which the opportunity for individual choice is maximized. . . . Maintaining the private status of parochial schools, cited by the majority, advances just this value. . . . But it is hard to imagine any such interests that are furthered by protecting public utility companies from meeting the constitutional standards that would apply if the companies were state-owned. The values of pluralism and diversity are simply not relevant when the private company is the only electric company in town.

. . .

What is perhaps most troubling about the Court's opinion is that it would appear to apply to a broad range of claimed constitutional violations by the company. The Court has not adopted the notion, accepted elsewhere, that different standards should apply to state action analysis when different constitutional claims are presented. . . . Thus, the majority's analysis would seemingly apply as well to a company that refused to extend service to Negroes, welfare recipients, or any other group that the company preferred, for its own reasons, not to serve. I cannot believe that this Court would hold that the State's involvement with the utility company was not sufficient to impose upon the company an obligation to meet the constitutional mandate of nondiscrimination. Yet nothing in the analysis of the majority opinion suggests otherwise.

I dissent.

3. FEDERAL POWER TO REGULATE PRIVATE CONDUCT UNDER THE THIRTEENTH AMENDMENT

Introduction. It will be recalled that the decision in the Civil Rights Cases conceded that Congressional power to enforce the thirteenth amendment extended to private racial discrimination that could be described as a badge of slavery. Its narrow construction of that concept, however, led to a narrow definition of Congressional power under the thirteenth amendment to regulate private racial discrimination. The cases discussed in this section, all decided since 1968, raise two questions. First, under the modern decisions, are there any forms of private racial discrimination that are *not* within Congressional power to prohibit? Second, to the extent that the thirteenth amendment empowers Congress to prohibit private *racial* discrimination, would the thirteenth amendment power sustain prohibition of similar *non-racial* discrimination, such as discrimination based on national origin, religion, gender, age or physical handicap?

Jones v. Alfred H. Mayer Co.

392 U.S. 409, 88 S.Ct. 2186, 20 L.Ed.2d 1189 (1968).

■ MR. JUSTICE STEWART delivered the opinion of the Court.

In this case we are called upon to determine the scope and the constitutionality of an Act of Congress, 42 U.S.C. § 1982, which provides that:

"All citizens of the United States shall have the same right, in every State and Territory, as is enjoyed by white citizens thereof to inherit, purchase, lease, sell, hold, and convey real and personal property."

On September 2, 1965, the petitioners filed a complaint in the District Court for the Eastern District of Missouri, alleging that the respondents had refused to sell them a home in the Paddock Woods community of St. Louis County for the sole reason that petitioner Joseph Lee Jones is a Negro. Relying in part upon § 1982, the petitioners sought injunctive and other relief. The District Court sustained the respondents' motion to dismiss the complaint, and the Court of Appeals for the Eighth Circuit affirmed, concluding that § 1982 applies only to state action and does not reach private refusals to sell. We granted certiorari to consider the questions thus presented. For the reasons that follow, we reverse the judgment of the Court of Appeals. We hold that § 1982 bars *all* racial discrimination, private as well as public, in the sale or rental of property, and that the statute, thus construed, is a valid exercise of the power of Congress to enforce the Thirteenth Amendment.

I.

At the outset, it is important to make clear precisely what this case does *not* involve. Whatever else it may be, 42 U.S.C. § 1982 is not a comprehensive open housing law. In sharp contrast to the Fair Housing Title (Title VIII) of the Civil Rights Act of 1968 . . . the statute in this case deals only with racial discrimination and does not address itself to discrimination on grounds of religion or national origin. It does not deal specifically with discrimination in the provision of services or facilities in connection with the sale or rental of a dwelling. It does not prohibit advertising or other representations that indicate discriminatory preferences. It does not refer explicitly to discrimination in financing arrangements or in the provision of brokerage services. It does not empower a federal administrative agency to assist aggrieved parties. It makes no provision for intervention by the Attorney General. And, although it can be enforced by injunction, it contains no provision expressly authorizing a federal court to order the payment of damages.

Thus, although § 1982 contains none of the exemptions that Congress included in the Civil Rights Act of 1968, it would be a serious mistake to suppose that § 1982 in any way diminishes the significance of the law recently enacted by Congress. . . .

. . .

III.

We begin with the language of the statute itself. In plain and unambiguous terms, § 1982 grants to all citizens, without regard to race or color, "the same right" to purchase and lease property "as is enjoyed by white citizens." As the Court of Appeals in this case evidently recognized, that right can be impaired as effectively by "those who place property on the market" as by the State itself. For, even if the State and its agents lend no support to those who wish to exclude persons from their communities on racial grounds, the fact remains that, whenever property "is placed on the market for whites only, whites have a right denied to Negroes." So long as a Negro citizen who wants to buy or rent a home can be turned away simply because he is not white, he cannot be said to enjoy "the *same* right . . . as is enjoyed by white citizens . . . to . . . purchase [and] lease . . . real and personal property." 42 U.S.C. § 1982. (Emphasis added.)

On its face, therefore, § 1982 appears to prohibit *all* discrimination against Negroes in the sale or rental of property—discrimination by private owners as well as discrimination by public authorities. Indeed, even the respondents seem to concede that, if § 1982 "means what it says"—to use the words of the respondents' brief—then it must encompass every racially motivated refusal to sell or rent and cannot be confined to officially sanctioned segregation in housing. Stressing what they consider to be the revolutionary implications of so literal a reading of § 1982, the respondents argue that Congress cannot possibly have intended any such result. Our examination of the relevant history, however, persuades us that Congress meant exactly what it said.

. . .

V.

The remaining question is whether Congress has power under the Constitution to do what § 1982 purports to do: to prohibit all racial discrimination, private and public, in the sale and rental of property. Our starting point is the Thirteenth Amendment, for it was pursuant to that constitutional provision that Congress originally enacted what is now § 1982. . . .

As its text reveals, the Thirteenth Amendment "is not a mere prohibition of State laws establishing or upholding slavery, but an absolute declaration that slavery or involuntary servitude shall not exist in any part of the United States." Civil Rights Cases, 109 U.S. 3, 20. It has never been doubted, therefore, "that the power vested in Congress to enforce the article by appropriate legislation," ibid., includes the power to enact laws "direct and primary, operating upon the acts of individuals, whether sanctioned by State legislation or not." Id., at 23.

Thus, the fact that § 1982 operates upon the unofficial acts of private individuals, whether or not sanctioned by state law, presents no constitutional problem. If Congress has power under the Thirteenth Amendment to eradicate conditions that prevent Negroes from buying and renting property because of their race or color, then no federal statute calculated to achieve that objective can be thought to exceed the constitutional power of Congress simply because it reaches beyond state action to regulate the conduct of private individuals. The constitutional question in this case, therefore, comes to this: Does the authority of Congress to enforce the Thirteenth Amendment "by appropriate legislation" include the power to eliminate all racial barriers to the acquisition of real and personal property? We think the answer to that question is plainly yes.

"By its own unaided force and effect," the Thirteenth Amendment "abolished slavery, and established universal freedom." Civil Rights Cases, 109 U.S. 3, 20. Whether or not the Amendment *itself* did any more than that—a question not involved in this case—it is at least clear that the Enabling Clause of that Amendment empowered Congress to do much more. For that clause clothed "Congress with power to pass *all laws necessary and proper for abolishing all badges and incidents of slavery in the United States.*" Ibid. (Emphasis added.)

. . .

. . . Surely Congress has the power under the Thirteenth Amendment rationally to determine what are the badges and the incidents of slavery, and the authority to translate that determination into effective legislation. Nor can we say that the determination Congress has made is an irrational one. For this Court recognized long ago that, whatever else they may have encompassed, the badges and incidents of slavery—its "burdens and disabilities"—included restraints upon "those fundamental rights which are the essence of civil freedom, namely, the same right . . . to inherit, purchase, lease, sell and convey property, as is enjoyed by white citizens." Civil Rights Cases, 109 U.S. 3, 22. Just as the Black Codes, enacted after the Civil War to restrict the free exercise of those rights, were substitutes for the slave system, so the exclusion of Negroes from white communities became a substitute for the Black Codes. And when racial discrimination herds men into ghettos and makes their ability to buy property turn on the color of their skin, then it too is a relic of slavery.

Negro citizens North and South, who saw in the Thirteenth Amendment a promise of freedom—freedom to "go and come at pleasure" and to "buy and sell when they please"—would be left with "a mere paper guarantee" if Congress were powerless to assure that a dollar in the hands of a Negro will purchase the same thing as a dollar in the hands of a white man. At the very least, the freedom that Congress is empowered to secure under the Thirteenth Amendment includes the freedom to buy whatever a white man can buy, the right to live wherever a white man can live. If Congress cannot say that being a free man means at least this much, then the Thirteenth Amendment made a promise the Nation cannot keep.

Representative Wilson of Iowa was the floor manager in the House for the Civil Rights Act of 1866. In urging that Congress had ample authority to pass the pending bill, he recalled the celebrated words of Chief Justice Marshall in McCulloch v. Maryland, 4 Wheat. 316, 421:

"Let the end be legitimate, let it be within the scope of the constitution, and all means which are appropriate, which are plainly adapted to that end, which are not prohibited, but consist with the letter and spirit of the constitution, are constitutional."

"The end is legitimate," the Congressman said, "because it is defined by the Constitution itself. The end is the maintenance of freedom. . . . A man who enjoys the civil rights mentioned in this bill cannot be reduced to slavery. . . . This settles the appropriateness of this measure, and that settles its constitutionality."

We agree. The judgment is reversed.[a]

■ MR. JUSTICE HARLAN, whom MR. JUSTICE WHITE joins, dissenting.

The decision in this case appears to me to be most ill-considered and ill-advised.

. . .

For reasons which follow, I believe that the Court's construction of § 1982 as applying to purely private action is almost surely wrong, and at the least is open to serious doubt. The issue of the constitutionality of § 1982, as construed by the Court, and of liability under the Fourteenth Amendment alone, also present formidable difficulties. Moreover, the political processes of our own era have, since the date of oral argument in this case, given birth to a civil rights statute embodying "fair housing"

---

[a] A concurring opinion by Justice Douglas is omitted.

provisions which would at the end of this year make available to others, though apparently not to the petitioners themselves, the type of relief which the petitioners now seek. It seems to me that this latter factor so diminishes the public importance of this case that by far the wisest course would be for this Court to refrain from decision and to dismiss the writ as improvidently granted.

. . .

Like the Court, I began analysis of § 1982 by examining its language. . . . The Court finds it "plain and unambiguous" that this language forbids purely private as well as state-authorized discrimination. With all respect, I do not find it so. For me, there is an inherent ambiguity in the term "right," as used in § 1982. The "right" referred to may either be a right to equal status under the law, in which case the statute operates only against state-sanctioned discrimination, or it may be an "absolute" right enforceable against private individuals. To me, the words of the statute, taken alone, suggest the former interpretation, not the latter.[9]

. . .

In sum, the most which can be said with assurance about the intended impact of the 1866 Civil Rights Act upon purely private discrimination is that the Act probably was envisioned by most members of Congress as prohibiting official, community-sanctioned discrimination in the South, engaged in pursuant to local "customs" which in the recent time of slavery probably were embodied in laws or regulations. Acts done under the color of such "customs" were, of course, said by the Court in the Civil Rights Cases . . . to constitute "state action" prohibited by the Fourteenth Amendment. . . . Adoption of a "state action" construction of the Civil Rights Act would therefore have the additional merit of bringing its interpretation into line with that of the Fourteenth Amendment, which this Court has consistently held to reach only "state action." This seems especially desirable in light of the wide agreement that a major purpose of the Fourteenth Amendment, at least in the minds of its congressional proponents, was to assure that the rights conferred by the then recently enacted Civil Rights Act could not be taken away by a subsequent Congress.

. . .

Civil Rights Legislation and the Commerce and Spending Powers

Whatever the scope of Congressional power under the thirteenth amendment to prohibit private racial discrimination, current decisions have not addressed the question of the reach of that power to other forms of discrimination. While the equal protection component of the fourteenth amendment has been extended beyond issues of racial discrimination, there are still unanswered questions about the reach of the fourteenth amendment enforcement power as applied to private conduct. It may be asked, however, whether it will ever be necessary to resolve those questions to sustain Congressional legislation prohibiting private discrimination. Modern civil rights laws have often been based upon Congress' power to regulate the economy and to control

---

[9] . . . In the Civil Rights Cases, 109 U.S. 3, the Court said of identical language in the predecessor statute to § 1982:

"[C]ivil rights, such as are guaranteed by the constitution against state aggression, cannot be impaired by the wrongful acts of individuals, unsupported by state authority. . . . The wrongful act of an individual, unsupported by any such authority, is simply a private wrong, or a crime of that individual; an invasion of the rights of the injured party, it is true . . . ; but if not sanctioned in some way by the state, or not done under State authority, his rights remain in full force, and may presumably be vindicated by resort to the laws of the State for redress. An individual cannot deprive a man of his right . . . to hold property, to buy and sell . . . ; he may, by force or fraud, interfere with the enjoyment of the right in a particular case; . . . but, unless protected in these wrongful acts by some shield of state law or state authority, he cannot destroy or injure the right. . . ." 109 U.S., at 17.

the conduct of federal grantees, and not upon the enforcement powers under the Reconstruction Amendments. The public accommodation provisions of the 1964 Civil Rights Act were based squarely upon the commerce power, for example, and were sustained by the Court in Heart of Atlanta Motel v. United States, supra p. 113, and Katzenbach v. McClung, supra p. 115, on that basis. In United Brotherhood of Carpenters v. Scott, 463 U.S. 825 (1983), the Court held that a private conspiracy to infringe first amendment rights, not motivated by racial bias, was not a violation of 42 U.S.C. § 1985(3). The four dissenters (Justice Blackmun, joined by Justices Brennan, Marshall and O'Connor) interpreted § 1985(3) to provide a cause of action for private conspiracies to interfere with first amendment rights. Both the majority and the dissent stated that if § 1985(3) were interpreted to reach private interference with first amendment rights, Congress would have power to ban such conspiracies under the commerce clause. Under those decisions, can you think of any case where it would be necessary to determine the reach of Congress' power under section 5 of the fourteenth amendment in order to define Congress' power to regulate private conduct? Consider, particularly, those cases in Section 2 of this Chapter that have found insufficient state action to subject private conduct to the provisions of section one of the fourteenth amendment. Would any of those situations be beyond Congressional regulatory power under the commerce clause?

Privileges of National Citizenship

Curiously, one long established source of federal power to control private conduct stems from the concept of privileges of national citizenship recognized by the Slaughter-House Cases, 83 U.S. 36 (1872). The curiosity is that the only express constitutional recognition of privileges of national citizenship is contained in section one of the fourteenth amendment. Nevertheless, the rationale of the Civil Rights Cases—that since section one of the fourteenth amendment prohibited only state action the enforcement power under section five did not extend to private conduct—was never held applicable to Congressional legislation that protected privileges of national citizenship from private interference. That is because the Slaughter-House Cases defined privileges of national citizenship as those "which owe their existence to the Federal government, its National character, its Constitution, or its laws." Under that definition, privileges of national citizenship did not "owe their existence" to their inclusion in the fourteenth amendment, and Congressional power to protect them stemmed from implied federal power that was not limited to the enforcement power under the fourteenth amendment.

The decision in the Slaughter-House Cases doomed much of the Reconstruction legislation by its narrow interpretation of the privileges and immunities clause. But, within that narrow interpretation, portions of those laws that were directed at purely private conduct were upheld as applied, and those provisions have survived. In this connection, the provisions of 18 U.S.C. § 241, penalizing private conspiracies to injure "any citizen in the free exercise or enjoyment of any right or privilege secured to him by the Constitution or laws of the United States," and of 42 U.S.C. § 1985(3), providing a civil action for private conspiracies to deny any person "equal privileges or immunities under the law," continue to be relevant.

A list of the privileges of national citizenship is contained in Justice Moody's opinion in Twining v. New Jersey, 211 U.S. 78, 97 (1908). Dicta or holdings in prosecutions under § 241 have identified these privileges of national citizenship, with concomitant federal power to protect them from private conduct. In United States v. Cruikshank, 92 U.S. 542 (1876), the Court held that the general rights of speech and assembly were not within the privileges of national citizenship, but announced in dicta that there was a federal right to assemble to petition Congress for a redress of grievances. Ex parte Yarbrough (Ku Klux Cases), 110 U.S. 651 (1884), added the right to vote in federal elections. (A more modern case, United States v. Classic, 313 U.S. 299 [1941], extended the right to primary elections for federal officers.) Logan v. United States, 144 U.S. 263 (1892), sustained prosecution of members of a lynch mob conspiring to injure a prisoner in custody of a United States Marshal. (Compare the decision nine years earlier, United States v. Harris, 106 U.S. 629 [1883], which declared unconstitutional a provision of the 1875 Act as applied to a lynch mob killing a state prisoner.) In re Quarles, 158 U.S. 532 (1895) decided that one right of federal citizenship was the right to inform federal officials of a violation of federal law.

In more recent cases, the "right to pass freely from State to State," which appeared first in Justice Moody's list of national privileges in *Twining,* has been prominent. One aspect of the decision in United States v. Guest, 383 U.S. 745 (1966), sustained an indictment under § 241 that alleged that defendants conspired to intimidate "Negro citizens of the United States" in their right to "travel freely to and from the State of Georgia." (That case grew out of the murder of Lemuel Penn, a nationally prominent incident involving Southern violence by Whites against Blacks, in 1964. Other aspects of the *Guest* decision will be discussed in the two notes that follow this one.) The Court concluded that not only did Congress have power under the commerce clause to protect free interstate travel, but that the right was one of those privileges protected by § 241. The *Guest* holding was reaffirmed in Griffin v. Breckenridge, 403 U.S. 88 (1971), which held that a private conspiracy to prevent persons from traveling interstate was actionable under § 1985(3).

Whether § 241 is applicable to other yet undefined privileges beyond those discussed in the preceding paragraphs is doubtful. The Court's opinion in *Guest* noted that criminal prosecution under § 241 was permissible for a conspiracy to interfere with interstate travel only because the right had been specifically defined in previous cases, and a specific intent by defendants to interfere with that right must be proved. (See Screws v. United States, discussed supra, p. 817) Justice Brennan, in his separate opinion, noted that § 241 was not "model legislation," and that relying on courts to "determine on a case-by-case basis whether the right purportedly threatened is a federal right . . . brings § 241 close to the danger line of being void for vagueness." 18 U.S.C. § 245, enacted two years later as part of the 1968 Civil Rights Act, is more specific. Among the private violence and intimidation made criminal by that statute are intended interferences with participation in programs, facilities or activities provided or administered by the United States, with federal employment, with service as a federal juror, and with participation in programs receiving federal financial assistance. Section 245 also punishes private interference with voting or campaigning in *any* election. The concept of privileges of national citizenship would sustain that statute as applied to federal elections. What theory sustains its application to elections for state and local offices? (See the note on *Private Interference with Fourteenth Amendment Rights* below, p. 818.)

Denial of Fourteenth Amendment Rights Under Color of Law or Custom

Even under the narrowest interpretation of the Civil Rights Cases, federal legislation can reach private conduct interfering with fourteenth amendment rights when that conduct contains sufficient indicia of state action to be prohibited by section one of the fourteenth amendment. Two important fragments of Reconstruction legislation explicitly reach denial of constitutional rights under color of law or "custom." Criminal penalties are provided by 18 U.S.C. § 242, and a civil action by 42 U.S.C. § 1983.

The two leading cases construing these statutes both involved allegations of unlawful police conduct. In Screws v. United States, 325 U.S. 91 (1945), the indictment under § 242 alleged that Screws, who held a grudge against his Black victim and had threatened to "get" him, had beaten him to death after arresting him and bringing him to the courthouse square where the jail was located. Monroe v. Pape, 365 U.S. 167 (1961), was a civil action under § 1983, alleging that the defendant police illegally invaded the plaintiff's home and searched it. In both cases, the Court rejected arguments that the police did not act "under color of law" if their conduct violated state law.

United States v. Price, 383 U.S. 787 (1966), for example, grew out of the widely publicized murder of three civil rights workers, Chaney, Goodman and Schwerner, outside Philadelphia, Mississippi in 1964. The indictment alleged a conspiracy between three law enforcement officials and fifteen private individuals to deprive the victims of their fourteenth amendment rights not to be "punished" without due process of law. The lower court had dismissed the indictments against the private defendants on the ground that they had not acted under color of law. The Court reversed and reinstated the indictments, holding that private parties jointly engaged with state officials in prohibited action are acting under color of law within the meaning of § 242. More recently, in Lugar v. Edmondson Oil Co., Inc., 457 U.S. 922 (1982), the same rationale was applied to a creditor using unconstitutional judicial procedures to collect a private debt, because he "acted in joint participation with state officials in seizure of the disputed property."

In United States v. Guest, supra, the indictment charged that defendants conspired to deprive Blacks of fourteenth amendment rights by, among other things, causing their arrest by false reports that they had committed criminal acts. The indictment was held to be a sufficient allegation of state involvement which could be proved by showing active connivance of state agents in making of the false reports "or other conduct amounting to official discrimination." (The opinion, although ambiguous, can be read to conclude by implication that there would be no state action if the proof merely showed that private individuals had made the false reports, without any involvement by public officials, and public officials had acted on those reports in good faith. The Court did state, however, that the case did not require, in order to sustain the indictment, any "determination of the threshold level that state action must attain in order to create rights under the Equal Protection Clause.")

Adickes v. Kress & Co., 398 U.S. 144 (1970), was a civil action under 42 U.S.C. § 1983 by a white woman who had been refused service in a lunch counter that she entered in the company of Blacks. Plaintiff claimed that the defendant had refused her service pursuant to a "custom of the community to segregate the races in public eating places." The majority of the Court interpreted the statute as requiring a showing of "state involvement" and "not simply a practice that reflects longstanding social habits, generally observed by the people in a locality." Hence, the plaintiff was required to show that custom "have the force of law by virtue of persistent practices of state officials." Justice Douglas, dissenting, asserted that it should be sufficient for plaintiff to show a custom in the sense of "the unwritten commitment, stronger than ordinances, statutes and regulations, by which men live and arrange their lives." Justice Brennan's dissent said it "means custom of the people of a State, not custom of state officials."

Private Interference with Fourteenth Amendment Rights

It is time to return, once more, to a basic conception of the Civil Rights Cases. It will be recalled that the Court reasoned that, because section one of the fourteenth amendment prohibited only discrimination by the state, Congress lacked power under section five to prohibit private discrimination in public accommodations. Would that still be true? Could Congress have passed Title II of the 1964 Act (public accommodations), Title VII of the 1964 Act (employment), and Title VIII of the 1968 Act (housing), under its power to enforce the fourteenth amendment's guarantee of equal protection of the laws? (Note that all three statutes reach beyond racial discrimination, unlike the public accommodations law invalidated in the Civil Rights Cases.) While six Justices in *United States v. Guest,* supra, agreed to an important dictum that section five of the fourteenth amendment empowers Congress to enact laws punishing private interference with fourteenth amendment rights, the answers to the questions posed are still not clear.

To understand the ambiguity, it is necessary to analyze the *Guest* decision in some detail. The indictment alleged that the defendants, all private individuals, had conspired to deny Blacks the right to "equal utilization, without discrimination upon the basis of race" of state owned facilities. The district court had dismissed the indictment on the ground that the criminal provisions of § 241, which contain no requirement that defendants act under color of law, were limited to privileges of national citizenship and did not reach fourteenth amendment rights. In the *Price* case, supra, decided the same day, the Court had held that conspiracies under color of law to deprive victims of fourteenth amendment rights were punishable under § 241. In *Guest,* a majority of the Court concluded that a conspiracy to deny victims' fourteenth amendment rights could not be prosecuted under § 241 in the absence of proof of state action. (As indicated in the previous note, dismissal of the indictment was reversed on the ground that the indictment could be read to allege state action.)

Justice Brennan, Chief Justice Warren and Justice Douglas dissented from the Court's conclusion that all conspiracies to deprive persons of fourteenth amendment rights were beyond the reach of § 241 unless state involvement in the conspiracy was proved. Justice Brennan concluded that Congress had the power to enact § 241, if it were construed to reach private conspiracies to deny fourteenth amendment rights, and criticized the Court's opinion as casting doubt on that Congressional power. That, in turn, led three members of the majority (Justices Clark, Black and Fortas) to write separately, stressing that the majority had merely construed the statute, and had decided no questions concerning the scope of Congress' power to "punish private conspiracies that interfere with fourteenth amendment rights, such as the right to utilize public facilities." They concluded summarily that there was "no doubt" that Congress had that power. Justice Brennan then responded that a majority of the Court had expressed the view that Congress could control private conduct interfering with the exercise of fourteenth amendment rights.

It should be emphasized that the portion of the indictment at issue in *Guest* alleged that the private defendants had conspired to deny their victims equal access to state facilities. The focus of the constitutional discussion in Justice Brennan's dissent and Justice Clark's separate opinion was the power to reach that conduct. Justice Brennan's rationale was that, in order to protect the constitutional right to equal utilization of state facilities, it was appropriate for Congress to punish private individuals who made it impossible for their victims to exercise those rights. (Contrast that with the position of the Civil Rights Cases that individuals who made it impossible for others to exercise their rights had not deprived them of those rights, and that Congress could not reach that individual conduct.) Would the theory also authorize Congress to control private conduct unrelated to any relationship between the victim and the state?

United States v. Morrison

529 U.S. 598 (2000).

The Court held that 42 U.S.C. § 13981, which provided a federal civil remedy for victims of gender-motivated violence, could not be sustained under § 5 of the fourteenth amendment. (That portion of the opinion concluding that the statute could not be sustained under the commerce clause appears supra, page 116.) Plaintiff argued that, because of pervasive bias against victims of gender-motivated violence, state justice systems failed to protect those victims. Chief Justice Rehnquist's opinion, joined by Justices O'Connor, Scalia, Kennedy and Thomas, rejected the argument that Congress acted appropriately under § 5 of the Fourteenth Amendment to remedy state bias and deter discrimination in state courts.

"[T]he language and purpose of the Fourteenth Amendment place certain limitations on the manner in which Congress may attack discriminatory conduct. These limitations are necessary to prevent the Fourteenth Amendment from obliterating the Framers' carefully crafted balance of power between the States and the National Government.... Foremost among these limitations is the time-honored principle that the Fourteenth Amendment, by its very terms, prohibits only state action....

. . .

"[I]n the Civil Rights Cases ..., we held that the public accommodation provisions of the Civil Rights Act of 1875, which applied to purely private conduct, were beyond the scope of the § 5 enforcement power....

"Petitioners ... rely on United States v. Guest ... for the proposition that the rule laid down in the Civil Rights Cases is no longer good law. In *Guest*, the Court reversed the construction of an indictment under 18 U.S.C. § 241, saying in the course of its opinion that 'we deal here with issues of statutory construction, not with issues of constitutional power.' ... Three Members of the Court, in a separate opinion by Justice Brennan, expressed the view that the Civil Rights Cases were wrongly decided, and that Congress could under § 5 prohibit actions by private individuals.... Three other Members of the Court, who joined the opinion of the Court, joined a separate opinion by Justice Clark which in two or three sentences stated the conclusion that Congress could 'punis[h] all conspiracies—with or without state action—that interfere with Fourteenth Amendment rights.' ...

"Though these three Justices saw fit to opine on matters not before the Court in *Guest*, the Court had no occasion to revisit the Civil Rights Cases ..., having determined 'the indictment [charging private individuals with conspiring to deprive blacks of equal access to state facilities] in fact contain[ed] an express allegation of state involvement.'

. . .

"To accept petitioners' argument, moreover, one must add to the three Justices joining Justice Brennan's reasoned explanation for his belief that the Civil Rights Cases were wrongly decided, the three Justices joining Justice Clark's opinion who gave no explanation whatever for their similar view. This is simply not the way that reasoned constitutional adjudication proceeds. We accordingly have no hesitation in saying that it would take more than the naked dicta contained in Justice Clark's opinion, when added to Justice Brennan's opinion, to cast any doubt upon the enduring vitality of the Civil Rights Cases ...

. . .

"Petitioners alternatively argue that, unlike the situation in the Civil Rights Cases, here there has been gender-based disparate treatment by state authorities, whereas in those cases there was no indication of such state action. There is abundant evidence, however, to show that the Congresses that enacted the Civil Rights Acts of 1871 and 1875 had a purpose similar to that of Congress in enacting § 13981 . . .

"But even if that distinction were valid, we do not believe it would save § 13981's civil remedy. For the remedy is simply not 'corrective in its character, adapted to counteract and redress the operation of such prohibited [s]tate laws or proceedings of [s]tate officers.' Civil Rights Cases, 109 U.S., at 18. . . . Section 13981 is not aimed at proscribing discrimination by officials which the Fourteenth Amendment might not itself proscribe; it is directed not at any State or state actor, but at individuals who have committed criminal acts motivated by gender bias.

"In the present cases, for example, § 13981 visits no consequence whatever on any Virginia public official . . . "

Justice Breyer's dissent was joined by Justice Stevens:

"Given my conclusion on the Commerce Clause question, I need not consider Congress' authority under § 5 of the Fourteenth Amendment. Nonetheless, I doubt the Court's reasoning rejecting that source of authority. . . .

. . .

"[W]hy can Congress not provide a remedy against private actors? Those private actors, of course, did not themselves violate the Constitution. But this Court has held that Congress at least sometimes can enact remedial '[l]egislation . . . [that] prohibits conduct which is not itself unconstitutional.' . . . The statutory remedy . . . intrudes little upon either States or private parties. It may lead state actors to improve their own remedial systems, primarily through example. It restricts private actors only by imposing liability for private conduct that is, in the main, already forbidden by state law. Why is the remedy 'disproportionate'? And given the relation between remedy and violation—the creation of a federal remedy to substitute for constitutionally inadequate state remedies—where is the lack of 'congruence'?"

. . .

"Despite my doubts about the majority's § 5 reasoning, I need not, and do not, answer the § 5 question, which I would leave for more thorough analysis if necessary on another occasion. Rather, in my view, the Commerce Clause provides an adequate basis for the statute before us. . . ."

4. THE SCOPE OF CONGRESSIONAL POWER TO REDEFINE THE AMENDMENTS

Over the past few decades, the Court decided a number of important cases addressing what role, if any, Congress has in interpreting and defining the specific content of constitutional provisions. Many of them construed Congress' power under Section 5 of the Fourteenth Amendment. In reading them, consider how much of the Court's reasoning is grounded in separation of powers concerns, and how much is grounded in federalism considerations.

Shelby County v. Holder

570 U.S. ___, 133 S.Ct. 2612, 186 L.Ed.2d 651 (2013).

■ CHIEF JUSTICE ROBERTS delivered the opinion of the Court.

The Voting Rights Act of 1965 employed extraordinary measures to address an extraordinary problem. Section 5 of the Act required States to obtain federal permission before enacting any law related to voting—a drastic departure from basic principles of federalism. And § 4 of the Act applied that requirement only to some States—an equally dramatic departure from the principle that all States enjoy equal sovereignty. This was strong medicine, but Congress determined it was needed to address entrenched racial discrimination in voting, "an insidious and pervasive evil which had been perpetuated in certain parts of our country through unremitting and ingenious defiance of the Constitution." *South Carolina v. Katzenbach*, 383 U.S. 301, 309 (1966). As we explained in upholding the law, "exceptional conditions can justify legislative measures not otherwise appropriate." *Id.*, at 334. Reflecting the unprecedented nature of these measures, they were scheduled to expire after five years. See Voting Rights Act of 1965, § 4(a), 79 Stat. 438.

Nearly 50 years later, they are still in effect; indeed, they have been made more stringent, and are now scheduled to last until 2031. There is no denying, however, that the conditions that originally justified these measures no longer characterize voting in the covered jurisdictions. By 2009, "the racial gap in voter registration and turnout [was] lower in the States originally covered by § 5 than it [was] nationwide." *Northwest Austin Municipal Util. Dist. No. One v. Holder*, 557 U.S. 193, 203–204 (2009). Since that time, Census Bureau data indicate that African-American voter turnout has come to exceed white voter turnout in five of the six States originally covered by § 5, with a gap in the sixth State of less than one half of one percent. . . .

At the same time, voting discrimination still exists; no one doubts that. The question is whether the Act's extraordinary measures, including its disparate treatment of the States, continue to satisfy constitutional requirements. As we put it a short time ago, "the Act imposes current burdens and must be justified by current needs." *Northwest Austin*, 557 U.S., at 203.

I

A

The Fifteenth Amendment was ratified in 1870, in the wake of the Civil War. It provides that "[t]he right of citizens of the United States to vote shall not be denied or abridged by the United States or by any State on account of race, color, or previous condition of servitude," and it gives Congress the "power to enforce this article by appropriate legislation."

"The first century of congressional enforcement of the Amendment, however, can only be regarded as a failure." *Id.*, at 197. In the 1890s, Alabama, Georgia, Louisiana, Mississippi, North Carolina, South Carolina, and Virginia began to enact literacy tests for voter registration and to employ other methods designed to prevent African-Americans from voting. *Katzenbach*, 383 U.S., at 310. Congress passed statutes outlawing some of these practices and facilitating litigation against them, but litigation remained slow and expensive, and the States came up with new ways to discriminate as soon as existing ones were struck down. Voter registration of African-Americans barely improved. *Id.*, at 313–314.

Inspired to action by the civil rights movement, Congress responded in 1965 with the Voting Rights Act. Section 2 was enacted to forbid, in all 50 States, any "standard, practice, or procedure . . . imposed or applied . . . to deny or abridge the right of any citizen of the United States to vote on account of race or color." 79 Stat. 437. The current version forbids any "standard, practice, or procedure" that "results in a denial or abridgement of the right of any citizen of the United States to vote on account of race or color." 42 U.S.C. § 1973(a). Both the Federal Government and individuals have sued to enforce § 2, . . . and injunctive relief is available in appropriate cases to block voting laws from going into effect, see 42 U.S.C. § 1973j(d). Section 2 is permanent, applies nationwide, and is not at issue in this case.

Other sections targeted only some parts of the country. At the time of the Act's passage, these "covered" jurisdictions were those States or political subdivisions that had maintained a test or device as a prerequisite to voting as of November 1, 1964, and had less than 50 percent voter registration or turnout in the 1964 Presidential election. § 4(b), 79 Stat. 438. Such tests or devices included literacy and knowledge tests, good moral character requirements, the need for vouchers from registered voters, and the like. § 4(c), *id.*, at 438–439. A covered jurisdiction could "bail out" of coverage if it had not used a test or device in the preceding five years "for the purpose or with the effect of denying or abridging the right to vote on account of race or color." § 4(a), *id.*, at 438. In 1965, the covered States included Alabama, Georgia, Louisiana, Mississippi, South Carolina, and Virginia. The additional covered subdivisions included 39 counties in North Carolina and one in Arizona. . . .

In those jurisdictions, § 4 of the Act banned all such tests or devices. § 4(a), 79 Stat. 438. Section 5 provided that no change in voting procedures could take effect until it was approved by federal authorities in Washington, D.C.—either the Attorney General or a court of three judges. *Id.*, at 439. A jurisdiction could obtain such "preclearance" only by proving that the change had neither "the purpose [nor] the effect of denying or abridging the right to vote on account of race or color." *Ibid.*

Sections 4 and 5 were intended to be temporary; they were set to expire after five years. See § 4(a), *id.*, at 438; *Northwest Austin, supra,* at 199. In *South Carolina v. Katzenbach*, we upheld the 1965 Act against constitutional challenge, explaining that it was justified to address "voting discrimination where it persists on a pervasive scale." 383 U.S., at 308. In 1970, Congress reauthorized the Act for another five years, and extended the coverage formula in § 4(b) to jurisdictions that had a voting test and less than 50 percent voter registration or turnout as of 1968. Voting Rights Act Amendments of 1970, §§ 3–4, 84 Stat. 315. That swept in several counties in California, New Hampshire, and New York. . . . Congress also extended the ban in § 4(a) on tests and devices nationwide. § 6, 84 Stat. 315.

In 1975, Congress reauthorized the Act for seven more years, and extended its coverage to jurisdictions that had a voting test and less than 50 percent voter registration or turnout as of 1972. Voting Rights Act Amendments of 1975, §§ 101, 202, 89 Stat. 400, 401. Congress also amended the definition of "test or device" to include the practice of providing English-only voting materials in places where over five percent of voting-age citizens spoke a single language other than English. § 203, *id.*, at 401–402. As a result of these amendments, the States of Alaska, Arizona, and Texas, as well as several counties in California, Florida, Michigan, New York, North Carolina, and South Dakota, became covered jurisdictions. . . . Congress correspondingly amended sections 2 and 5 to forbid voting discrimination on the basis of membership in a language minority group, in addition to discrimination on the basis of race or color. §§ 203, 206, 89 Stat. 401, 402. Finally, Congress made the nationwide ban on tests and devices permanent. § 102, *id.*, at 400.

In 1982, Congress reauthorized the Act for 25 years, but did not alter its coverage formula. See Voting Rights Act Amendments, 96 Stat. 131. Congress did, however, amend the bailout provisions, allowing political subdivisions of covered jurisdictions to bail out. Among other prerequisites for bailout, jurisdictions and their subdivisions must not have used a forbidden test or device, failed to receive preclearance, or lost a § 2 suit, in the ten years prior to seeking bailout. § 2, *id.*, at 131–133.

We upheld each of these reauthorizations against constitutional challenge. See *Georgia v. United States*, 411 U.S. 526 (1973); *City of Rome v. United States*, 446 U.S. 156 (1980); *Lopez v. Monterey County*, 525 U.S. 266 (1999).

In 2006, Congress again reauthorized the Voting Rights Act for 25 years, again without change to its coverage formula. Fannie Lou Hamer, Rosa Parks, and Coretta Scott King Voting Rights Act Reauthorization and Amendments Act, 120 Stat. 577. Congress also amended § 5 to prohibit more conduct than before. § 5, *id.*, at 580–581. . . . Section 5 now forbids voting changes with "any discriminatory purpose" as well as voting changes that diminish the ability of citizens, on account of race, color, or language minority status, "to elect their preferred candidates of choice." 42 U.S.C. §§ 1973c(b)–(d).

Shortly after this reauthorization, a Texas utility district brought suit, seeking to bail out from the Act's coverage and, in the alternative, challenging the Act's constitutionality. See *Northwest Austin*, 557 U.S., at 200–201. A three-judge District Court explained that only a State or political subdivision was eligible to seek bailout under the statute, and concluded that the utility district was not a political subdivision, a term that encompassed only "counties, parishes, and voter-registering subunits." *Northwest Austin Municipal Util. Dist. No. One v. Mukasey*, 573 F.Supp.2d 221, 232 (D.D.C.2008). The District Court also rejected the constitutional challenge. *Id.*, at 283.

We reversed. We explained that " 'normally the Court will not decide a constitutional question if there is some other ground upon which to dispose of the case.' " *Northwest Austin, supra*, at 205 (quoting *Escambia County v. McMillan*, 466 U.S. 48, 51(1984) (per curiam)). Concluding that "underlying constitutional concerns," among other things, "compel[led] a broader reading of the bailout provision," we construed the statute to allow the utility district to seek bailout. *Northwest Austin*, 557 U.S., at 207. In doing so we expressed serious doubts about the Act's continued constitutionality.

We explained that § 5 "imposes substantial federalism costs" and "differentiates between the States, despite our historic tradition that all the States enjoy equal sovereignty." *Id.*, at 202, 203. We also noted that "[t]hings have changed in the South. Voter turnout and registration rates now approach parity. Blatantly discriminatory evasions of federal decrees are rare. And minority candidates hold office at unprecedented levels." *Id.*, at 202. Finally, we questioned whether the problems that § 5 meant to address were still "concentrated in the jurisdictions singled out for preclearance." *Id.*, at 203.

Eight Members of the Court subscribed to these views, and the remaining Member would have held the Act unconstitutional. Ultimately, however, the Court's construction of the bailout provision left the constitutional issues for another day.

B

Shelby County is located in Alabama, a covered jurisdiction. It has not sought bailout, as the Attorney General has recently objected to voting changes proposed from within the county. . . . Instead, in 2010, the county sued the Attorney General in Federal District Court in Washington, D.C., seeking a declaratory judgment that sections 4(b) and 5 of the Voting Rights Act are facially unconstitutional, as well as a permanent injunction against their enforcement. The District Court ruled against the county and upheld the Act. . . . The court found that the evidence before Congress in 2006 was sufficient to justify reauthorizing § 5 and continuing the § 4(b) coverage formula.

The Court of Appeals for the D.C. Circuit affirmed. In assessing § 5, the D.C. Circuit considered six primary categories of evidence: Attorney General objections to voting changes, Attorney General requests for more information regarding voting changes, successful § 2 suits in covered jurisdictions, the dispatching of federal observers to monitor elections in covered jurisdictions, § 5 preclearance suits involving covered jurisdictions, and the deterrent effect of § 5. See 679 F. 3d 848, 862–63 (2012). After extensive analysis of the record, the court accepted Congress's conclusion that § 2 litigation remained inadequate in the covered jurisdictions to protect the rights of minority voters, and that § 5 was therefore still necessary.

Turning to § 4, the D.C. Circuit noted that the evidence for singling out the covered jurisdictions was "less robust" and that the issue presented "a close question." *Id.* at 879. But the court looked to data comparing the number of successful § 2 suits in the different parts of the country. Coupling that evidence with the deterrent effect of § 5, the court concluded that the statute continued "to single out the jurisdictions in which discrimination is concentrated," and thus held that the coverage formula passed constitutional muster. *Id.*, at 883.

Judge Williams dissented. He found "no positive correlation between inclusion in § 4(b)'s coverage formula and low black registration or turnout." *Id.*, at 891. Rather, to the extent there was any correlation, it actually went the other way: "condemnation under § 4(b) is a marker of higher black registration and turnout." *Ibid.* (emphasis added). Judge Williams also found that "[c]overed jurisdictions have *far more* black officeholders as a proportion of the black population than do uncovered ones." *Id.*, at 892. As to the evidence of successful § 2 suits, Judge Williams disaggregated the reported cases by State, and concluded that "[t]he five worst uncovered jurisdictions . . . have worse records than eight of the covered jurisdictions." *Id.*, at 897. He also noted that two covered jurisdictions—Arizona and Alaska—had not had any successful reported § 2 suit brought against them during the entire 24 years covered by the data. *Ibid.* Judge Williams would have held the coverage formula of § 4(b) "irrational" and unconstitutional. *Id.*, at 885.

We granted certiorari. 568 U.S. ___ (2012).

II

In *Northwest Austin*, we stated that "the Act imposes current burdens and must be justified by current needs." 557 U.S., at 203. And we concluded that "a departure from the fundamental principle of equal sovereignty requires a showing that a statute's disparate geographic coverage is sufficiently related to the problem that it targets." *Ibid.* These basic principles guide our review of the question before us.

A

The Constitution and laws of the United States are "the supreme Law of the Land." U.S. Const., Art. VI, cl. 2. State legislation may not contravene federal law. The Federal Government does not, however, have a general right to review and veto state enactments before they go into effect. A proposal to grant such authority to "negative" state laws was considered at the Constitutional Convention, but rejected in favor of allowing state laws to take effect, subject to later challenge under the Supremacy Clause. See 1 Records of the Federal Convention of 1787, pp. 21, 164–168 (M. Farrand ed. 1911); 2 id., at 27–29, 390–392.

Outside the strictures of the Supremacy Clause, States retain broad autonomy in structuring their governments and pursuing legislative objectives. Indeed, the Constitution provides that all powers not specifically granted to the Federal Government are reserved to the States or citizens. Amdt. 10. This "allocation of powers in our federal system preserves the integrity, dignity, and residual sovereignty of the States." *Bond v. United States*, 564 U.S. ___, ___ (2011). But the federal balance "is not just an end in itself: Rather, federalism secures to citizens the liberties that derive from the diffusion of sovereign power." *Ibid.*

More specifically, " 'the Framers of the Constitution intended the States to keep for themselves, as provided in the Tenth Amendment, the power to regulate elections.'" *Gregory v. Ashcroft*, 501 U.S. 452, 461–462 (1991) (quoting *Sugarman v. Dougall*, 413 U.S. 634, 647 (1973). Of course, the Federal Government retains significant control over federal elections. For instance, the Constitution authorizes Congress to establish the time and manner for electing Senators and Representatives. Art. I, § 4, cl. 1. . . . But States have "broad powers to determine the conditions under which the right of suffrage may be exercised." *Carrington v. Rash*, 380 U.S. 89, 91(1965). . . . And "[e]ach State has the power to prescribe the qualifications of its officers and the manner in which they shall be chosen." *Boyd v. Nebraska ex rel. Thayer*, 143 U.S. 135 (1892). Drawing lines for congressional districts is likewise "primarily the duty and responsibility of the State." *Perry v. Perez*, 565 U.S. ___, ___ (2012) (per curiam).

Not only do States retain sovereignty under the Constitution, there is also a "fundamental principle of *equal* sovereignty" among the States. *Northwest Austin*, *supra*, at 203 (citing *United States v. Louisiana*, 363 U.S. 1, 16 (1960); *Lessee of Pollard v. Hagan*, 3 How. 212, 223(1845); and *Texas v. White*, 7 Wall. 700, 725–726 (1869); emphasis added). Over a hundred years ago, this Court explained that our Nation "was and is a union of States, equal in power, dignity and authority." *Coyle v. Smith*, 221 U.S. 559, 567 (1911). Indeed, "the constitutional equality of the States is essential to the harmonious operation of the scheme upon which the Republic was organized." *Id.*, at 580. *Coyle* concerned the admission of new States, and *Katzenbach* rejected the notion that the principle operated as a *bar* on differential treatment outside that context. 383 U.S., at 328–329. At the same time, as we made clear in *Northwest Austin*, the fundamental principle of equal sovereignty remains highly pertinent in assessing subsequent disparate treatment of States. 557 U.S., at 203.

The Voting Rights Act sharply departs from these basic principles. It suspends "all changes to state election law—however innocuous—until they have been precleared by federal authorities in Washington, D.C." *Id.*, at 202. States must beseech the Federal Government for permission to implement laws that they would otherwise have the right to enact and execute on their own, subject of course to any injunction in a § 2 action. The Attorney General has 60 days to object to a preclearance request, longer if he requests more information. If a State seeks preclearance from a three-judge court, the process can take years.

And despite the tradition of equal sovereignty, the Act applies to only nine States (and several additional counties). While one State waits months or years and expends funds to implement a validly enacted law, its neighbor can typically put the same law into effect immediately, through the normal legislative process. Even if a noncovered jurisdiction is sued, there are important differences between those proceedings and preclearance proceedings; the preclearance proceeding "not only switches the burden of proof to the supplicant jurisdiction, but also applies substantive standards quite different from those governing the rest of the nation." 679 F.3d, at 884 (Williams, J., dissenting) (case below).

All this explains why, when we first upheld the Act in 1966, we described it as "stringent" and "potent." *Katzenbach*, 383 U.S., at 308. We recognized that it "may have been an uncommon exercise of congressional power," but concluded that "legislative measures not otherwise appropriate" could be justified by "exceptional conditions." *Id.*, at 334. We have since noted that the Act "authorizes federal intrusion into sensitive areas of state and local policymaking," *Lopez*, 525 U.S., at 282, and represents an "extraordinary departure from the traditional course of relations between the States and the Federal Government," *Presley v. Etowah County Comm'n*, 502 U.S. 491, 500–501 (1992). As we reiterated in *Northwest Austin*, the Act constitutes "extraordinary legislation otherwise unfamiliar to our federal system." 557 U.S., at 211.

B

In 1966, we found these departures from the basic features of our system of government justified. The "blight of racial discrimination in voting" had "infected the electoral process in parts of our country for nearly a century." *Katzenbach*, 383 U.S., at 308. Several States had enacted a variety of requirements and tests "specifically designed to prevent" African-Americans from voting. *Id.*, at 310. Case-by-case litigation had proved inadequate to prevent such racial discrimination in voting, in part because States "merely switched to discriminatory devices not covered by the federal decrees," "enacted difficult new tests," or simply "defied and evaded court orders." *Id.*, at 314. Shortly before enactment of the Voting Rights Act, only 19.4 percent of African-Americans of voting age were registered to vote in Alabama, only 31.8 percent in Louisiana, and only 6.4 percent in Mississippi. *Id.*, at 313. Those figures were roughly 50 percentage points or more below the figures for whites. *Ibid.*

In short, we concluded that "[u]nder the compulsion of these unique circumstances, Congress responded in a permissibly decisive manner." *Id.*, at 334, 335. We also noted then and have emphasized since that this extraordinary legislation was intended to be temporary, set to expire after five years. *Id.*, at 333; *Northwest Austin*, *supra*, at 199.

At the time, the coverage formula—the means of linking the exercise of the unprecedented authority with the problem that warranted it—made sense. We found that "Congress chose to limit its attention to the geographic areas where immediate action seemed necessary." *Katzenbach*, 383 U.S., at 328. The areas where Congress found "evidence of actual voting discrimination" shared two characteristics: "the use of tests and devices for voter registration, and a voting rate in the 1964 presidential election at least 12 points below the national average." *Id.*, at 330. We explained that "[t]ests and devices are relevant to voting discrimination because of their long history as a tool for perpetrating the evil; a low voting rate is pertinent for the obvious reason that widespread disenfranchisement must inevitably affect the number of actual voters." *Ibid.* We therefore concluded that "the coverage formula [was] rational in both practice and theory." *Ibid.* It accurately reflected those jurisdictions uniquely characterized by voting discrimination "on a pervasive scale," linking coverage to the devices used to effectuate discrimination and to the resulting disenfranchisement. *Id.*, at 308. The formula ensured that the "stringent remedies [were] aimed at areas where voting discrimination ha[d] been most flagrant." *Id.*, at 315.

C

Nearly 50 years later, things have changed dramatically. Shelby County contends that the preclearance requirement, even without regard to its disparate coverage, is now unconstitutional. Its arguments have a good deal of force. In the covered jurisdictions, "[v]oter turnout and registration rates now approach parity. Blatantly discriminatory evasions of federal decrees are rare. And minority candidates hold office at unprecedented levels." *Northwest Austin*, 557 U.S., at 202. The tests and devices that blocked access to the ballot have been forbidden nationwide for over 40 years. See § 6, 84 Stat. 315; § 102, 89 Stat. 400.

Those conclusions are not ours alone. Congress said the same when it reauthorized the Act in 2006, writing that "[s]ignificant progress has been made in eliminating first generation barriers experienced by minority voters, including increased numbers of registered minority voters, minority voter turnout, and minority representation in Congress, State legislatures, and local elected offices." § 2(b)(1), 120 Stat. 577. The House Report elaborated that "the number of African-Americans who are registered and who turn out to cast ballots has increased significantly over the last 40 years, particularly since 1982," and noted that "[i]n some circumstances, minorities register to vote and cast ballots at levels that surpass those of white voters." H.R.Rep. 109–478, at 12 (2006), 2006 U.S.C.C.A.N. 618, 627. That Report also explained that there have been "significant increases in the number of African-Americans serving in elected offices"; more specifically, there has been approximately a 1,000 percent increase since 1965 in the number of African-American elected officials in the six States originally covered by the Voting Rights Act. *Id.*, at 18.

The following chart, compiled from the Senate and House Reports, compares voter registration numbers from 1965 to those from 2004 in the six originally covered States. These are the numbers that were before Congress when it reauthorized the Act in 2006:

	1965			2004		
	White	Black	Gap	White	Black	Gap
Alabama	69.2	19.3	49.9	73.8	72.9	0.9
Georgia	62.[6]	27.4	35.2	63.5	64.2	–0.7
Louisiana	80.5	31.6	48.9	75.1	71.1	4.0
Mississippi	69.9	6.7	63.2	72.3	76.1	–3.8
South Carolina	75.7	37.3	38.4	74.4	71.1	3.3
Virginia	61.1	38.3	22.8	68.2	57.4	10.8

See S.Rep. No. 109–295, p. 11 (2006); H.R.Rep. No. 109–478, at 12. The 2004 figures come from the Census Bureau. Census Bureau data from the most recent election indicate that African-American voter turnout exceeded white voter turnout in five of the six States originally covered by § 5, with a gap in the sixth State of less than one half of one percent. . . . The preclearance statistics are also illuminating. In the first decade after enactment of § 5, the Attorney General objected to 14.2 percent of proposed voting changes. H. R Rep. No. 109–478, at 22. In the last decade before reenactment, the Attorney General objected to a mere 0.16 percent. S.Rep. No. 109–295, at 13.

There is no doubt that these improvements are in large part *because of* the Voting Rights Act. The Act has proved immensely successful at redressing racial discrimination and integrating the voting process. See § 2(b)(1), 120 Stat. 577. During the "Freedom Summer" of 1964, in Philadelphia, Mississippi, three men were murdered while working in the area to register African-American voters. See *United States v. Price*, 383 U.S. 787, 790 (1966). On "Bloody Sunday" in 1965, in Selma, Alabama, police beat and used tear gas against hundreds marching in support of African-American enfranchisement. . . . Today both of those towns are governed by African-American mayors. Problems remain in these States and others, but there is no denying that, due to the Voting Rights Act, our Nation has made great strides.

Yet the Act has not eased the restrictions in § 5 or narrowed the scope of the coverage formula in § 4(b) along the way. Those extraordinary and unprecedented features were reauthorized—as if nothing had changed. In fact, the Act's unusual remedies have grown even stronger. . . .

We have also previously highlighted the concern that "the preclearance requirements in one State [might] be unconstitutional in another." *Northwest Austin,*

557 U.S., at 203; see *Georgia v. Ashcroft*, 539 U.S., at 491(Kennedy, J., concurring) ("considerations of race that would doom a redistricting plan under the Fourteenth Amendment or § 2 [of the Voting Rights Act] seem to be what save it under § 5"). Nothing has happened since to alleviate this troubling concern about the current application of § 5.

Respondents do not deny that there have been improvements on the ground, but argue that much of this can be attributed to the deterrent effect of § 5, which dissuades covered jurisdictions from engaging in discrimination that they would resume should § 5 be struck down. Under this theory, however, § 5 would be effectively immune from scrutiny; no matter how "clean" the record of covered jurisdictions, the argument could always be made that it was deterrence that accounted for the good behavior.

The provisions of § 5 apply only to those jurisdictions singled out by § 4. We now consider whether that coverage formula is constitutional in light of current conditions.

III

A

When upholding the constitutionality of the coverage formula in 1966, we concluded that it was "rational in both practice and theory." *Katzenbach*, 383 U.S., at 330. The formula looked to cause (discriminatory tests) and effect (low voter registration and turnout), and tailored the remedy (preclearance) to those jurisdictions exhibiting both.

By 2009, however, we concluded that the "coverage formula raise[d] serious constitutional questions." *Northwest Austin*, 557 U.S., at 204. As we explained, a statute's "current burdens" must be justified by "current needs," and any "disparate geographic coverage" must be "sufficiently related to the problem that it targets." *Id.*, at 203. The coverage formula met that test in 1965, but no longer does so.

Coverage today is based on decades-old data and eradicated practices. The formula captures States by reference to literacy tests and low voter registration and turnout in the 1960s and early 1970s. But such tests have been banned nationwide for over 40 years. § 6, 84 Stat. 315; § 102, 89 Stat. 400. And voter registration and turnout numbers in the covered States have risen dramatically in the years since. H.R.Rep. No. 109–478, at 12. Racial disparity in those numbers was compelling evidence justifying the preclearance remedy and the coverage formula. . . . There is no longer such a disparity.

In 1965, the States could be divided into two groups: those with a recent history of voting tests and low voter registration and turnout, and those without those characteristics. Congress based its coverage formula on that distinction. Today the Nation is no longer divided along those lines, yet the Voting Rights Act continues to treat it as if it were.

B

The Government's defense of the formula is limited. First, the Government contends that the formula is "reverse-engineered": Congress identified the jurisdictions to be covered and *then* came up with criteria to describe them. Brief for Federal Respondent 48–49. Under that reasoning, there need not be any logical relationship between the criteria in the formula and the reason for coverage; all that is necessary is that the formula happen to capture the jurisdictions Congress wanted to single out.

The Government suggests that *Katzenbach* sanctioned such an approach, but the analysis in *Katzenbach* was quite different. *Katzenbach* reasoned that the coverage formula was rational because the "formula . . . was relevant to the problem": "Tests and devices are relevant to voting discrimination because of their long history as a tool for perpetrating the evil; a low voting rate is pertinent for the obvious reason that widespread disenfranchisement must inevitably affect the number of actual voters." 383 U.S., at 329.

Here, by contrast, the Government's reverse-engineering argument does not even attempt to demonstrate the continued relevance of the formula to the problem it targets. And in the context of a decision as significant as this one—subjecting a disfavored subset of States to "extraordinary legislation otherwise unfamiliar to our federal system," *Northwest Austin, supra*, at 211—that failure to establish even relevance is fatal.

The Government falls back to the argument that because the formula was relevant in 1965, its continued use is permissible so long as any discrimination remains in the States Congress identified back then—regardless of how that discrimination compares to discrimination in States unburdened by coverage. Brief for Federal Respondent 49–50. This argument does not look to "current political conditions," *Northwest Austin, supra*, at 203, but instead relies on a comparison between the States in 1965. That comparison reflected the different histories of the North and South. It was in the South that slavery was upheld by law until uprooted by the Civil War, that the reign of Jim Crow denied African-Americans the most basic freedoms, and that state and local governments worked tirelessly to disenfranchise citizens on the basis of race. The Court invoked that history—rightly so—in sustaining the disparate coverage of the Voting Rights Act in 1966. See *Katzenbach, supra*, at 308 ("The constitutional propriety of the Voting Rights Act of 1965 must be judged with reference to the historical experience which it reflects.").

But history did not end in 1965. By the time the Act was reauthorized in 2006, there had been 40 more years of it. In assessing the "current need[ ]" for a preclearance system that treats States differently from one another today, that history cannot be ignored. During that time, largely because of the Voting Rights Act, voting tests were abolished, disparities in voter registration and turnout due to race were erased, and African-Americans attained political office in record numbers. And yet the coverage formula that Congress reauthorized in 2006 ignores these developments, keeping the focus on decades-old data relevant to decades-old problems, rather than current data reflecting current needs.

The Fifteenth Amendment commands that the right to vote shall not be denied or abridged on account of race or color, and it gives Congress the power to enforce that command. The Amendment is not designed to punish for the past; its purpose is to ensure a better future. See *Rice v. Cayetano*, 528 U.S. 495, 512 (2000) ("Consistent with the design of the Constitution, the [Fifteenth] Amendment is cast in fundamental terms, terms transcending the particular controversy which was the immediate impetus for its enactment."). To serve that purpose, Congress—if it is to divide the States—must identify those jurisdictions to be singled out on a basis that makes sense in light of current conditions. It cannot rely simply on the past. We made that clear in *Northwest Austin*, and we make it clear again today.

C

In defending the coverage formula, the Government, the intervenors, and the dissent also rely heavily on data from the record that they claim justify disparate coverage. Congress compiled thousands of pages of evidence before reauthorizing the Voting Rights Act. The court below and the parties have debated what that record shows—they have gone back and forth about whether to compare covered to noncovered jurisdictions as blocks, how to disaggregate the data State by State, how to weigh § 2 cases as evidence of ongoing discrimination, and whether to consider evidence not before Congress, among other issues. . . . Regardless of how to look at the record, however, no one can fairly say that it shows anything approaching the "pervasive," "flagrant," "widespread," and "rampant" discrimination that faced Congress in 1965, and that clearly distinguished the covered jurisdictions from the rest of the Nation at that time. *Katzenbach, supra*, at 308, 315, 331; *Northwest Austin*, 557 U.S., at 201.

But a more fundamental problem remains: Congress did not use the record it compiled to shape a coverage formula grounded in current conditions. It instead reenacted a formula based on 40-year-old facts having no logical relation to the present day. The dissent relies on "second-generation barriers," which are not impediments to the casting of ballots, but rather electoral arrangements that affect the weight of minority votes. That does not cure the problem. Viewing the preclearance requirements as targeting such efforts simply highlights the irrationality of continued reliance on the § 4 coverage formula, which is based on voting tests and access to the ballot, not vote dilution. We cannot pretend that we are reviewing an updated statute, or try our hand at updating the statute ourselves, based on the new record compiled by Congress. Contrary to the dissent's contention, . . . we are not ignoring the record; we are simply recognizing that it played no role in shaping the statutory formula before us today.

The dissent also turns to the record to argue that, in light of voting discrimination in Shelby County, the county cannot complain about the provisions that subject it to preclearance. . . . But that is like saying that a driver pulled over pursuant to a policy of stopping all redheads cannot complain about that policy, if it turns out his license has expired. Shelby County's claim is that the coverage formula here is unconstitutional in all its applications, because of how it selects the jurisdictions subjected to preclearance. The county was selected based on that formula, and may challenge it in court.

D

The dissent proceeds from a flawed premise. It quotes the famous sentence from McCulloch v. Maryland, 4 Wheat. 316 (1819), with the following emphasis: "Let the end be legitimate, let it be within the scope of the constitution, and *all means which are appropriate, which are plainly adapted to that end*, which are not prohibited, but consist with the letter and spirit of the constitution, are constitutional." . . . But this case is about a part of the sentence that the dissent does not emphasize—the part that asks whether a legislative means is "consist[ent] with the letter and spirit of the constitution." The dissent states that "[i]t cannot tenably be maintained" that this is an issue with regard to the Voting Rights Act, . . . but four years ago, in an opinion joined by two of today's dissenters, the Court expressly stated that "[t]he Act's preclearance requirement and its coverage formula raise serious constitutional questions." *Northwest Austin, supra*, at 204. The dissent does not explain how those "serious constitutional questions" became untenable in four short years.

The dissent treats the Act as if it were just like any other piece of legislation, but this Court has made clear from the beginning that the Voting Rights Act is far from ordinary. At the risk of repetition, *Katzenbach* indicated that the Act was "uncommon" and "not otherwise appropriate," but was justified by "exceptional" and "unique" conditions. 383 U.S., at 334, 335. Multiple decisions since have reaffirmed the Act's "extraordinary" nature. See, *e.g.*, *Northwest Austin, supra*, at 211. Yet the dissent goes so far as to suggest instead that the preclearance requirement and disparate treatment of the States should be upheld into the future "unless there [is] no or almost no evidence of unconstitutional action by States." . . .

In other ways as well, the dissent analyzes the question presented as if our decision in *Northwest Austin* never happened. For example, the dissent refuses to consider the principle of equal sovereignty, despite *Northwest Austin*'s emphasis on its significance. *Northwest Austin* also emphasized the "dramatic" progress since 1965, 557 U.S., at 201, but the dissent describes current levels of discrimination as "flagrant," "widespread," and "pervasive," . . . Despite the fact that *Northwest Austin* requires an Act's "disparate geographic coverage" to be "sufficiently related" to its targeted problems, 557 U.S., at 203, the dissent maintains that an Act's limited coverage actually eases Congress's burdens, and suggests that a fortuitous relationship should suffice. Although *Northwest Austin* stated definitively that "current burdens" must be justified by "current needs," *ibid.*, the dissent argues that the coverage formula can be justified by history, and that the required showing can be weaker on reenactment than when the law was first passed.

There is no valid reason to insulate the coverage formula from review merely because it was previously enacted 40 years ago. If Congress had started from scratch in 2006, it plainly could not have enacted the present coverage formula. It would have been irrational for Congress to distinguish between States in such a fundamental way based on 40-year-old data, when today's statistics tell an entirely different story. And it would have been irrational to base coverage on the use of voting tests 40 years ago, when such tests have been illegal since that time. But that is exactly what Congress has done.

* * *

Striking down an Act of Congress "is the gravest and most delicate duty that this Court is called on to perform." *Blodgett v. Holden*, 275 U.S. 142, 148 (Holmes, J., concurring). We do not do so lightly. That is why, in 2009, we took care to avoid ruling on the constitutionality of the Voting Rights Act when asked to do so, and instead resolved the case then before us on statutory grounds. But in issuing that decision, we expressed our broader concerns about the constitutionality of the Act. Congress could have updated the coverage formula at that time, but did not do so. Its failure to act leaves us today with no choice but to declare § 4(b) unconstitutional. The formula in that section can no longer be used as a basis for subjecting jurisdictions to preclearance.

Our decision in no way affects the permanent, nationwide ban on racial discrimination in voting found in § 2. We issue no holding on § 5 itself, only on the coverage formula. Congress may draft another formula based on current conditions. Such a formula is an initial prerequisite to a determination that exceptional conditions still exist justifying such an "extraordinary departure from the traditional course of relations between the States and the Federal Government." *Presley*, 502 U.S., at 500–501. Our country has changed, and while any racial discrimination in voting is too much, Congress must ensure that the legislation it passes to remedy that problem speaks to current conditions.

The judgment of the Court of Appeals is reversed.

It is so ordered.

■ JUSTICE THOMAS, concurring.

I join the Court's opinion in full but write separately to explain that I would find § 5 of the Voting Rights Act unconstitutional as well. The Court's opinion sets forth the reasons.

. . .

■ JUSTICE GINSBURG, with whom JUSTICE BREYER, JUSTICE SOTOMAYOR, and JUSTICE KAGAN join, dissenting.

In the Court's view, the very success of § 5 of the Voting Rights Act demands its dormancy. Congress was of another mind. Recognizing that large progress has been made, Congress determined, based on a voluminous record, that the scourge of discrimination was not yet extirpated. The question this case presents is who decides whether, as currently operative, § 5 remains justifiable, this Court, or a Congress charged with the obligation to enforce the post–Civil War Amendments "by appropriate legislation." With overwhelming support in both Houses, Congress concluded that, for two prime reasons, § 5 should continue in force, unabated. First, continuance would facilitate completion of the impressive gains thus far made; and second, continuance would guard against backsliding. Those assessments were well within Congress' province to make and should elicit this Court's unstinting approbation.

I

. . . [Although no one doubts that voting discrimination still exists,] the Court today terminates the remedy that proved to be best suited to block that discrimination. The Voting Rights Act of 1965 (VRA) has worked to combat voting discrimination where other remedies had been tried and failed. Particularly effective is the VRA's requirement of federal preclearance for all changes to voting laws in the regions of the country with the most aggravated records of rank discrimination against minority voting rights.

A century after the Fourteenth and Fifteenth Amendments guaranteed citizens the right to vote free of discrimination on the basis of race, the "blight of racial discrimination in voting" continued to "infec[t] the electoral process in parts of our country." *South Carolina v. Katzenbach*, 383 U.S. 301 (1966). Early attempts to cope with this vile infection resembled battling the Hydra. Whenever one form of voting discrimination was identified and prohibited, others sprang up in its place. This Court repeatedly encountered the remarkable "variety and persistence" of laws disenfranchising minority citizens. *Id.*, at 311. To take just one example, the Court, in 1927, held unconstitutional a Texas law barring black voters from participating in primary elections, *Nixon v. Herndon*, 273 U.S. 536, 541; in 1944, the Court struck down a "reenacted" and slightly altered version of the same law, *Smith v. Allwright*, 321 U.S. 649, 658; and in 1953, the Court once again confronted an attempt by Texas to "circumven[t]" the Fifteenth Amendment by adopting yet another variant of the all-white primary, *Terry v. Adams*, 345 U.S. 461, 469.

During this era, the Court recognized that discrimination against minority voters was a quintessentially political problem requiring a political solution. As Justice Holmes explained: If "the great mass of the white population intends to keep the blacks from voting," "relief from [that] great political wrong, if done, as alleged, by the people of a State and the State itself, must be given by them or by the legislative and political department of the government of the United States." *Giles v. Harris*, 189 U.S. 475, 488 (1903).

Congress learned from experience that laws targeting particular electoral practices or enabling case-by-case litigation were inadequate to the task. . . . Patently, a new approach was needed.

Answering that need, the Voting Rights Act became one of the most consequential, efficacious, and amply justified exercises of federal legislative power in our Nation's history. Requiring federal preclearance of changes in voting laws in the covered jurisdictions—those States and localities where opposition to the Constitution's commands were most virulent—the VRA provided a fit solution for minority voters as well as for States. Under the preclearance regime established by § 5 of the VRA, covered jurisdictions must submit proposed changes in voting laws or procedures to the Department of Justice (DOJ), which has 60 days to respond to the changes. 79 Stat. 439, codified at 42 U.S.C. § 1973c(a). A change will be approved unless DOJ finds it has "the purpose [or] . . . the effect of denying or abridging the right to vote on account of race or color." *Ibid.* In the alternative, the covered jurisdiction may seek approval by a three-judge District Court in the District of Columbia.

. . .

Although the VRA wrought dramatic changes in the realization of minority voting rights, the Act, to date, surely has not eliminated all vestiges of discrimination against the exercise of the franchise by minority citizens. Jurisdictions covered by the preclearance requirement continued to submit, in large numbers, proposed changes to voting laws that the Attorney General declined to approve, auguring that barriers to minority voting would quickly resurface were the preclearance remedy eliminated. *City of Rome v. United States*, 446 U.S. 156, 181 (1980). Congress also found that as "registration and voting of minority citizens increas[ed], other measures may be resorted to which would dilute increasing minority voting strength." *Ibid.* (quoting H.R.Rep. No. 94–196, p. 10 (1975)). See also *Shaw v. Reno*, 509 U.S. 630, 640 (1993) ("[I]t soon became apparent that guaranteeing equal access to the polls would not suffice to root out other racially discriminatory voting practices" such as voting dilution). Efforts to reduce the impact of minority votes, in contrast to direct attempts to block access to the ballot, are aptly described as "second-generation barriers" to minority voting.

Second-generation barriers come in various forms. One of the blockages is racial gerrymandering, the redrawing of legislative districts in an "effort to segregate the races for purposes of voting." *Id.*, at 642. Another is adoption of a system of at-large voting in lieu of district-by-district voting in a city with a sizable black minority. By switching to at-large voting, the overall majority could control the election of each city council member, effectively eliminating the potency of the minority's votes. . . . A similar effect could be achieved if the city engaged in discriminatory annexation by incorporating majority-white areas into city limits, thereby decreasing the effect of VRA-occasioned increases in black voting. Whatever the device employed, this Court has long recognized that vote dilution, when adopted with a discriminatory purpose, cuts down the right to vote as certainly as denial of access to the ballot. . . .

In response to evidence of these substituted barriers, Congress reauthorized the VRA for five years in 1970, for seven years in 1975, and for 25 years in 1982. . . . Each time, this Court upheld the reauthorization as a valid exercise of congressional power. . . . As the 1982 reauthorization approached its 2007 expiration date, Congress again considered whether the VRA's preclearance mechanism remained an appropriate response to the problem of voting discrimination in covered jurisdictions.

Congress did not take this task lightly. Quite the opposite. The 109th Congress that took responsibility for the renewal started early and conscientiously. In October 2005, the House began extensive hearings, which continued into November and resumed in March 2006. S.Rep. No. 109–295, p. 2 (2006). In April 2006, the Senate followed suit, with hearings of its own. *Ibid.* In May 2006, the bills that became the VRA's reauthorization were introduced in both Houses. *Ibid.* The House held further hearings of considerable length, as did the Senate, which continued to hold hearings into June and July. H.R. Rep. 109–478, at 5; S. Rep. 109–295, at 3–4. In mid-July, the House considered and rejected four amendments, then passed the reauthorization by a vote of 390 yeas to 33 nays. 152 Cong. Rec. H5207 (July 13, 2006). . . . The bill was read and debated in the Senate, where it passed by a vote of 98 to 0. 152 Cong. Rec.

S8012 (July 20, 2006). President Bush signed it a week later, on July 27, 2006, recognizing the need for "further work . . . in the fight against injustice," and calling the reauthorization "an example of our continued commitment to a united America where every person is valued and treated with dignity and respect." 152 Cong. Rec. S8781 (Aug. 3, 2006).

In the long course of the legislative process, Congress "amassed a sizable record." *Northwest Austin Municipal Util. Dist. No. One v. Holder*, 557 U.S. 193, 205 (2009). See also 679 F.3d 848, 865–873 (C.A.D.C.2012) (describing the "extensive record" supporting Congress' determination that "serious and widespread intentional discrimination persisted in covered jurisdictions"). The House and Senate Judiciary Committees held 21 hearings, heard from scores of witnesses, received a number of investigative reports and other written documentation of continuing discrimination in covered jurisdictions. In all, the legislative record Congress compiled filled more than 15,000 pages. H.R. Rep. 109–478, at 5, 11–12; S. Rep. 109–295, at 2–4, 15. The compilation presents countless "examples of flagrant racial discrimination" since the last reauthorization; Congress also brought to light systematic evidence that "intentional racial discrimination in voting remains so serious and widespread in covered jurisdictions that section 5 preclearance is still needed." 679 F.3d, at 866.

After considering the full legislative record, Congress made the following findings: The VRA has directly caused significant progress in eliminating first-generation barriers to ballot access, leading to a marked increase in minority voter registration and turnout and the number of minority elected officials. 2006 Reauthorization § 2(b)(1). But despite this progress, "second generation barriers constructed to prevent minority voters from fully participating in the electoral process" continued to exist, as well as racially polarized voting in the covered jurisdictions, which increased the political vulnerability of racial and language minorities in those jurisdictions. §§ 2(b)(2)–(3), 120 Stat. 577. Extensive "[e]vidence of continued discrimination," Congress concluded, "clearly show[ed] the continued need for Federal oversight" in covered jurisdictions. §§ 2(b)(4)–(5), *id.*, at 577–578. The overall record demonstrated to the federal lawmakers that, "without the continuation of the Voting Rights Act of 1965 protections, racial and language minority citizens will be deprived of the opportunity to exercise their right to vote, or will have their votes diluted, undermining the significant gains made by minorities in the last 40 years." § 2(b)(9), *id.*, at 578.

Based on these findings, Congress reauthorized preclearance for another 25 years, while also undertaking to reconsider the extension after 15 years to ensure that the provision was still necessary and effective. 42 U.S.C. § 1973b(a)(7), (8) (2006 ed., Supp. V). The question before the Court is whether Congress had the authority under the Constitution to act as it did.

II

In answering this question, the Court does not write on a clean slate. It is well established that Congress' judgment regarding exercise of its power to enforce the Fourteenth and Fifteenth Amendments warrants substantial deference. The VRA addresses the combination of race discrimination and the right to vote, which is "preservative of all rights." *Yick Wo v. Hopkins*, 118 U.S. 356, 370 (1886). When confronting the most constitutionally invidious form of discrimination, and the most fundamental right in our democratic system, Congress' power to act is at its height.

The basis for this deference is firmly rooted in both constitutional text and precedent. The Fifteenth Amendment, which targets precisely and only racial discrimination in voting rights, states that, in this domain, "Congress shall have power to enforce this article by appropriate legislation." In choosing this language, the

Amendment's framers invoked Chief Justice Marshall's formulation of the scope of Congress' powers under the Necessary and Proper Clause:

"Let the end be legitimate, let it be within the scope of the constitution, and *all means which are appropriate, which are plainly adapted to that end*, which are not prohibited, but consist with the letter and spirit of the constitution, are constitutional." *McCulloch v. Maryland*, 4 Wheat. 316, 421(1819) (emphasis added).

It cannot tenably be maintained that the VRA, an Act of Congress adopted to shield the right to vote from racial discrimination, is inconsistent with the letter or spirit of the Fifteenth Amendment, or any provision of the Constitution read in light of the Civil War Amendments. Nowhere in today's opinion, or in *Northwest Austin*, is there clear recognition of the transformative effect the Fifteenth Amendment aimed to achieve. Notably, "the Founders' first successful amendment told Congress that it could 'make no law' over a certain domain"; in contrast, the Civil War Amendments used "language [that] authorized transformative new federal statutes to uproot all vestiges of unfreedom and inequality" and provided "sweeping enforcement powers . . . to enact 'appropriate' legislation targeting state abuses." A. Amar, America's Constitution: A Biography 361, 363, 399 (2005). See also McConnell, Institutions and Interpretation: A Critique of City of Boerne v. Flores, 111 Harv. L.Rev. 153, 182 (1997) (quoting Civil War-era framer that "the remedy for the violation of the fourteenth and fifteenth amendments was expressly not left to the courts. The remedy was legislative.").

The stated purpose of the Civil War Amendments was to arm Congress with the power and authority to protect all persons within the Nation from violations of their rights by the States. In exercising that power, then, Congress may use "all means which are appropriate, which are plainly adapted" to the constitutional ends declared by these Amendments. *McCulloch*, 4 Wheat., at 421. So when Congress acts to enforce the right to vote free from racial discrimination, we ask not whether Congress has chosen the means most wise, but whether Congress has rationally selected means appropriate to a legitimate end. "It is not for us to review the congressional resolution of [the need for its chosen remedy]. It is enough that we be able to perceive a basis upon which the Congress might resolve the conflict as it did." *Katzenbach v. Morgan*, 384 U.S. 641, 653 (1966).

Until today, in considering the constitutionality of the VRA, the Court has accorded Congress the full measure of respect its judgments in this domain should garner. *South Carolina v. Katzenbach* supplies the standard of review: "As against the reserved powers of the States, Congress may use any rational means to effectuate the constitutional prohibition of racial discrimination in voting." 383 U.S., at 324. Faced with subsequent reauthorizations of the VRA, the Court has reaffirmed this standard. *E.g.*, *City of Rome*, 446 U.S., at 178. Today's Court does not purport to alter settled precedent establishing that the dispositive question is whether Congress has employed "rational means."

For three reasons, legislation *reauthorizing* an existing statute is especially likely to satisfy the minimal requirements of the rational-basis test. First, when reauthorization is at issue, Congress has already assembled a legislative record justifying the initial legislation. Congress is entitled to consider that preexisting record as well as the record before it at the time of the vote on reauthorization. This is especially true where, as here, the Court has repeatedly affirmed the statute's constitutionality and Congress has adhered to the very model the Court has upheld. See id., at 174 ("The appellants are asking us to do nothing less than overrule our decision in *South Carolina v. Katzenbach* . . . , in which we upheld the constitutionality of the Act."); *Lopez v. Monterey County*, 525 U.S. 266, 283 (1999) (similar).

Second, the very fact that reauthorization is necessary arises because Congress has built a temporal limitation into the Act. It has pledged to review, after a span of years (first 15, then 25) and in light of contemporary evidence, the continued need for the VRA. Cf. *Grutter v. Bollinger*, 539 U.S. 306, 343 (2003) (anticipating, but not guaranteeing, that, in 25 years, "the use of racial preferences [in higher education] will no longer be necessary").

Third, a reviewing court should expect the record supporting reauthorization to be less stark than the record originally made. Demand for a record of violations equivalent to the one earlier made would expose Congress to a catch-22. If the statute was working, there would be less evidence of discrimination, so opponents might argue that Congress should not be allowed to renew the statute. In contrast, if the statute was not working, there would be plenty of evidence of discrimination, but scant reason to renew a failed regulatory regime. . . .

This is not to suggest that congressional power in this area is limitless. It is this Court's responsibility to ensure that Congress has used appropriate means. The question meet for judicial review is whether the chosen means are "adapted to carry out the objects the amendments have in view." *Ex parte Virginia*, 100 U.S. 339, 346 (1880). The Court's role, then, is not to substitute its judgment for that of Congress, but to determine whether the legislative record sufficed to show that "Congress could rationally have determined that [its chosen] provisions were appropriate methods." *City of Rome*, 446 U.S., at 176–177.

In summary, the Constitution vests broad power in Congress to protect the right to vote, and in particular to combat racial discrimination in voting. This Court has repeatedly reaffirmed Congress' prerogative to use any rational means in exercise of its power in this area. And both precedent and logic dictate that the rational-means test should be easier to satisfy, and the burden on the statute's challenger should be higher, when what is at issue is the reauthorization of a remedy that the Court has previously affirmed, and that Congress found, from contemporary evidence, to be working to advance the legislature's legitimate objective.

III

The 2006 reauthorization of the Voting Rights Act fully satisfies the standard stated in *McCulloch* . . . : Congress may choose any means "appropriate" and "plainly adapted to" a legitimate constitutional end. . . .

A

. . .

True, conditions in the South have impressively improved since passage of the Voting Rights Act. Congress noted this improvement and found that the VRA was the driving force behind it. 2006 Reauthorization § 2(b)(1). But Congress also found that voting discrimination had evolved into subtler second-generation barriers, and that eliminating preclearance would risk loss of the gains that had been made. §§ 2(b)(2), (9). Concerns of this order, the Court previously found, gave Congress adequate cause to reauthorize the VRA. *City of Rome*, 446 U.S., at 180–182 (congressional reauthorization of the preclearance requirement was justified based on "the number and nature of objections interposed by the Attorney General" since the prior reauthorization; extension was "necessary to preserve the limited and fragile achievements of the Act and to promote further amelioration of voting discrimination"). Facing such evidence then, the Court expressly rejected the argument that disparities in voter turnout and number of elected officials were the only metrics capable of justifying reauthorization of the VRA. *Ibid.*

B

I turn next to the evidence on which Congress based its decision to reauthorize the coverage formula in § 4(b). Because Congress did not alter the coverage formula, the same jurisdictions previously subject to preclearance continue to be covered by this remedy. . . .

There is no question . . . that the covered jurisdictions have a unique history of problems with racial discrimination in voting. . . .

Of particular importance, even after 40 years and thousands of discriminatory changes blocked by preclearance, conditions in the covered jurisdictions demonstrated that the formula was still justified by "current needs." *Northwest Austin*, 557 U.S., at 203.

Congress learned of these conditions through a report, known as the Katz study, that looked at § 2 suits between 1982 and 2004. . . .

Although covered jurisdictions account for less than 25 percent of the country's population, the Katz study revealed that they accounted for 56 percent of successful § 2 litigation since 1982. . . . Controlling for population, there were nearly four times as many successful § 2 cases in covered jurisdictions as there were in noncovered jurisdictions. . . . The Katz study further found that § 2 lawsuits are more likely to succeed when they are filed in covered jurisdictions than in noncovered jurisdictions. . . . From these findings—ignored by the Court—Congress reasonably concluded that the coverage formula continues to identify the jurisdictions of greatest concern.

The evidence before Congress, furthermore, indicated that voting in the covered jurisdictions was more racially polarized than elsewhere in the country. H.R.Rep. No. 109–478, at 34–35. While racially polarized voting alone does not signal a constitutional violation, it is a factor that increases the vulnerability of racial minorities to discriminatory changes in voting law. The reason is twofold. First, racial polarization means that racial minorities are at risk of being systematically outvoted and having their interests underrepresented in legislatures. Second, "when political preferences fall along racial lines, the natural inclinations of incumbents and ruling parties to entrench themselves have predictable racial effects. Under circumstances of severe racial polarization, efforts to gain political advantage translate into race-specific disadvantages." Ansolabehere, Persily, & Stewart, Regional Differences in Racial Polarization in the 2012 Presidential Election: Implications for the Constitutionality of Section 5 of the Voting Rights Act, 126 Harv. L.Rev. Forum 205, 209 (2013).

In other words, a governing political coalition has an incentive to prevent changes in the existing balance of voting power. When voting is racially polarized, efforts by the ruling party to pursue that incentive "will inevitably discriminate against a racial group." *Ibid.* Just as buildings in California have a greater need to be earthquake-proofed, places where there is greater racial polarization in voting have a greater need for prophylactic measures to prevent purposeful race discrimination. This point was understood by Congress and is well recognized in the academic literature. See 2006 Reauthorization § 2(b)(3), 120 Stat. 577 ("The continued evidence of racially polarized voting in each of the jurisdictions covered by the [preclearance requirement] demonstrates that racial and language minorities remain politically vulnerable"); H.R.Rep. No. 109–478, at 35 (2006), 2006 U.S.C.C.A.N. 618. . . .

. . .

IV

Congress approached the 2006 reauthorization of the VRA with great care and seriousness. The same cannot be said of the Court's opinion today. The Court makes no genuine attempt to engage with the massive legislative record that Congress assembled. Instead, it relies on increases in voter registration and turnout as if that were the whole story. . . . Without even identifying a standard of review, the Court dismissively brushes off arguments based on "data from the record," and declines to enter the "debat[e about] what [the] record shows." . . . One would expect more from an opinion striking at the heart of the Nation's signal piece of civil-rights legislation.

I note the most disturbing lapses. First, by what right, given its usual restraint, does the Court even address Shelby County's facial challenge to the VRA? Second, the Court veers away from controlling precedent regarding the "equal sovereignty" doctrine without even acknowledging that it is doing so. Third, hardly showing the respect ordinarily paid when Congress acts to implement the Civil War Amendments, and as just stressed, the Court does not even deign to grapple with the legislative record.

A

Shelby County launched a purely facial challenge to the VRA's 2006 reauthorization. "A facial challenge to a legislative Act," the Court has other times said, "is, of course, the most difficult challenge to mount successfully, since the challenger must establish that no set of circumstances exists under which the Act would be valid." *United States v. Salerno*, 481 U.S. 739, 745 (1987).

. . . "Embedded in the traditional rules governing constitutional adjudication is the principle that a person to whom a statute may constitutionally be applied will not be heard to challenge that statute on the ground that it may conceivably be applied unconstitutionally to others, in other situations not before the Court." *Broadrick [v. Oklahoma]*, 413 U.S., at 610 [1973]. Yet the Court's opinion in this case contains not a word explaining why Congress lacks the power to subject to preclearance the particular plaintiff that initiated this lawsuit—Shelby County, Alabama. The reason for the Court's silence is apparent, for as applied to Shelby County, the VRA's preclearance requirement is hardly contestable.

Alabama is home to Selma, site of the "Bloody Sunday" beatings of civil-rights demonstrators that served as the catalyst for the VRA's enactment. Following those events, Martin Luther King, Jr., led a march from Selma to Montgomery, Alabama's capital, where he called for passage of the VRA. If the Act passed, he foresaw, progress could be made even in Alabama, but there had to be a steadfast national commitment to see the task through to completion. In King's words, "the arc of the moral universe is long, but it bends toward justice." G. May, Bending Toward Justice: The Voting Rights Act and the Transformation of American Democracy 144 (2013).

History has proved King right. Although circumstances in Alabama have changed, serious concerns remain. Between 1982 and 2005, Alabama had one of the highest rates of successful § 2 suits, second only to its VRA-covered neighbor Mississippi. 679 F.3d, at 897 (Williams, J., dissenting). In other words, even while subject to the restraining effect of § 5, Alabama was found to have "deni[ed] or abridge[d]" voting rights "on account of race or color" more frequently than nearly all other States in the Union. 42 U.S.C. § 1973(a). This fact prompted the dissenting judge below to concede that "a more narrowly tailored coverage formula" capturing Alabama and a handful of other jurisdictions with an established track record of racial discrimination in voting "might be defensible." 679 F.3d, at 897 (opinion of Williams, J.). That is an understatement. Alabama's sorry history of § 2 violations alone provides sufficient justification for Congress' determination in 2006 that the State should remain subject to § 5's preclearance requirement.

> . . .

[R]ecent episodes forcefully demonstrate that § 5's preclearance requirement is constitutional as applied to Alabama and its political subdivisions. And under our case law, that conclusion should suffice to resolve this case. See *United States v. Raines*, 362 U.S. 17, 24–25 (1960) ("[I]f the complaint here called for an application of the statute clearly constitutional under the Fifteenth Amendment, that should have been an end to the question of constitutionality."). See also *Nevada Dept. of Human Resources v. Hibbs*, 538 U.S. 721, 743 (2003) (Scalia, J., dissenting) (where, as here, a state or local government raises a facial challenge to a federal statute on the ground that it exceeds Congress' enforcement powers under the Civil War Amendments, the challenge fails if the opposing party is able to show that the statute "could constitutionally be applied to some jurisdictions").

> . . .

B

The Court stops any application of § 5 by holding that § 4(b)'s coverage formula is unconstitutional. It pins this result, in large measure, to "the fundamental principle of equal sovereignty." In *Katzenbach*, however, the Court held, in no uncertain terms, that the principle "*applies only to the terms upon which States are admitted to the Union*, and not to the remedies for local evils which have subsequently appeared." 383 U.S., at 328–329 (emphasis added).

. . . [T]he Court clouds [this] once clear understanding by citing dictum from *Northwest Austin* to convey that the principle of equal sovereignty "remains highly pertinent in assessing subsequent disparate treatment of States." . . . If the Court is suggesting that dictum in *Northwest Austin* silently overruled *Katzenbach*'s limitation of the equal sovereignty doctrine to "the admission of new States," the suggestion is untenable. *Northwest Austin* cited *Katzenbach*'s holding in the course of *declining to decide* whether the VRA was constitutional or even what standard of review applied to the question. 557 U.S., at 203–204. In today's decision, the Court ratchets up what was pure dictum in *Northwest Austin*, attributing breadth to the equal sovereignty principle in flat contradiction of *Katzenbach*. The Court does so with nary an explanation of why it finds *Katzenbach* wrong, let alone any discussion of whether *stare decisis* nonetheless counsels adherence to *Katzenbach*'s ruling on the limited "significance" of the equal sovereignty principle.

Today's unprecedented extension of the equal sovereignty principle outside its proper domain—the admission of new States—is capable of much mischief. Federal statutes that treat States disparately are hardly novelties. See, e.g., 28 U.S.C. § 3704 (no State may operate or permit a sports-related gambling scheme, unless that State conducted such a scheme "at any time during the period beginning January 1, 1976, and ending August 31, 1990"); 26 U.S.C. § 142(*l*) (EPA required to locate green building project in a State meeting specified population criteria); 42 U.S.C. § 3796bb (at least 50 percent of rural drug enforcement assistance funding must be allocated to States with "a population density of fifty-two or fewer persons per square mile or a State in which the largest county has fewer than one hundred and fifty thousand people, based on the decennial census of 1990 through fiscal year 1997"); §§ 13925, 13971 (similar population criteria for funding to combat rural domestic violence); § 10136 (specifying rules applicable to Nevada's Yucca Mountain nuclear waste site, and providing that "[n]o State, other than the State of Nevada, may receive financial assistance under this subsection after December 22, 1987"). Do such provisions remain safe given the Court's expansion of equal sovereignty's sway?

Of gravest concern, Congress relied on our pathmarking *Katzenbach* decision in each reauthorization of the VRA. It had every reason to believe that the Act's limited geographical scope would weigh in favor of, not against, the Act's constitutionality. See, *e.g.*, *United States v. Morrison*, 529 U.S. 598, 626–627 (2000) (confining preclearance regime to States with a record of discrimination bolstered the VRA's constitutionality). Congress could hardly have foreseen that the VRA's limited geographic reach would render the Act constitutionally suspect. . . .

In the Court's conception, it appears, defenders of the VRA could not prevail upon showing what the record overwhelmingly bears out, *i.e.*, that there is a need for continuing the preclearance regime in covered States. In addition, the defenders would have to disprove the existence of a comparable need elsewhere. See Tr. of Oral Arg. 61–62 (suggesting that proof of egregious episodes of racial discrimination in covered jurisdictions would not suffice to carry the day for the VRA, unless such episodes are shown to be absent elsewhere). I am aware of no precedent for imposing such a double burden on defenders of legislation.

C

The Court has time and again declined to upset legislation of this genre unless there was no or almost no evidence of unconstitutional action by States. See, *e.g.*, *City of Boerne v. Flores*, 521 U.S. 507, 530 (1997) (legislative record "mention[ed] no episodes [of the kind the legislation aimed to check] occurring in the past 40 years"). No such claim can be made about the congressional record for the 2006 VRA reauthorization. Given a record replete with examples of denial or abridgment of a paramount federal right, the Court should have left the matter where it belongs: in Congress' bailiwick.

Instead, the Court strikes § 4(b)'s coverage provision because, in its view, the provision is not based on "current conditions." . . . It discounts, however, that one such condition was the preclearance remedy in place in the covered jurisdictions, a remedy Congress designed both to catch discrimination before it causes harm, and to guard against return to old ways. 2006 Reauthorization § 2(b)(3), (9). Volumes of evidence supported Congress' determination that the prospect of retrogression was real. Throwing out preclearance when it has worked and is continuing to work to stop discriminatory changes is like throwing away your umbrella in a rainstorm because you are not getting wet.

. . .

* * *

For the reasons stated, I would affirm the judgment of the Court of Appeals.

City of Boerne v. Flores

521 U.S. 507, 117 S.Ct. 2157, 138 L.Ed.2d 624 (1997).

■ JUSTICE KENNEDY delivered the opinion of the Court.*

A decision by local zoning authorities to deny a church a building permit was challenged under the Religious Freedom Restoration Act of 1993 (RFRA) . . . The case calls into question the authority of Congress to enact RFRA. We conclude the statute exceeds Congress' power.

---

*   Justice Scalia joins all but Part III-A-1 of this opinion.

I

[A church in Texas was denied permission to alter and enlarge its building to accommodate more worshippers under a Boerne City Council ordinance designed to protect historic landmarks or buildings in a historic district. The church's Archbishop sued in federal court, invoking its rights under the RFRA. The district court found that RFRA was unconstitutional because Congress lacked power under Section 5 of the Fourteenth Amendment to enact it. The Fifth Circuit reversed, and the Supreme Court reversed the Court of Appeals.]

II

Congress enacted RFRA in direct response to the Court's decision in Employment Div., Dept. of Human Resources of Ore. v. Smith, 494 U.S. 872 (1990). There we considered a Free Exercise Clause claim brought by members of the Native American Church who were denied unemployment benefits when they lost their jobs because they had used peyote. Their practice was to ingest peyote for sacramental purposes, and they challenged an Oregon statute of general applicability which made use of the drug criminal. In evaluating the claim, we declined to apply the balancing test set forth in Sherbert v. Verner, 374 U.S. 398 (1963), under which we would have asked whether Oregon's prohibition substantially burdened a religious practice and, if it did, whether the burden was justified by a compelling government interest. We stated: "[G]overnment's ability to enforce generally applicable prohibitions of socially harmful conduct . . . cannot depend on measuring the effects of a governmental action on a religious objector's spiritual development. . . ." . . .

. . .

. . . *Smith* held that neutral, generally applicable laws may be applied to religious practices even when not supported by a compelling governmental interest.

Four Members of the Court disagreed. They argued the law placed a substantial burden on the Native American Church members so that it could be upheld only if the law served a compelling state interest and was narrowly tailored to achieve that end. . . .

These points of constitutional interpretation were debated by Members of Congress in hearings and floor debates. Many criticized the Court's reasoning, and this disagreement resulted in the passage of RFRA. Congress announced:

"(1) [T]he framers of the Constitution, recognizing free exercise of religion as an unalienable right, secured its protection in the First Amendment to the Constitution;

"(2) laws 'neutral' toward religion may burden religious exercise as surely as laws intended to interfere with religious exercise;

"(3) governments should not substantially burden religious exercise without compelling justification;

"(4) in Employment Division v. Smith, 494 U.S. 872 (1990), the Supreme Court virtually eliminated the requirement that the government justify burdens on religious exercise imposed by laws neutral toward religion; and

"(5) the compelling interest test as set forth in prior Federal court rulings is a workable test for striking sensible balances between religious liberty and competing prior governmental interests." 42 U.S.C. § 2000bb(a).

The Act's stated purposes are:

"(1) to restore the compelling interest test as set forth in Sherbert v. Verner, 374 U.S. 398 (1963) and Wisconsin v. Yoder, 406 U.S. 205 (1972) and to guarantee its application in all cases where free exercise of religion is substantially burdened; and

"(2) to provide a claim or defense to persons whose religious exercise is substantially burdened by government." § 2000bb(b).

RFRA prohibits "[g]overnment" from "substantially burden[ing]" a person's exercise of religion even if the burden results from a rule of general applicability unless the government can demonstrate the burden "(1) is in furtherance of a compelling governmental interest; and (2) is the least restrictive means of furthering that compelling governmental interest." . . . The Act's mandate applies to any "branch, department, agency, instrumentality, and official (or other person acting under color of law) of the United States," as well as to any "State, or . . . subdivision of a State." . . . The Act's universal coverage is confirmed in § 2000bb–3(a), under which RFRA "applies to all Federal and State law, and the implementation of that law, whether statutory or otherwise, and whether adopted before or after [RFRA's enactment]." In accordance with RFRA's usage of the term, we shall use "state law" to include local and municipal ordinances.

III

A

Under our Constitution, the Federal Government is one of enumerated powers. McCulloch v. Maryland . . . The judicial authority to determine the constitutionality of laws, in cases and controversies, is based on the premise that the "powers of the legislature are defined and limited; and that those limits may not be mistaken, or forgotten, the constitution is written." Marbury v. Madison . . .

Congress relied on its Fourteenth Amendment enforcement power in enacting the most far reaching and substantial of RFRA's provisions, those which impose its requirements on the States. . . .

In defense of the Act respondent contends, with support from the United States as *amicus*, that RFRA is permissible enforcement legislation. Congress, it is said, is only protecting by legislation one of the liberties guaranteed by the Fourteenth Amendment's Due Process Clause, the free exercise of religion, beyond what is necessary under *Smith*. It is said the congressional decision to dispense with proof of deliberate or overt discrimination and instead concentrate on a law's effects accords with the settled understanding that § 5 includes the power to enact legislation designed to prevent as well as remedy constitutional violations. It is further contended that Congress' § 5 power is not limited to remedial or preventive legislation.

. . . Legislation which deters or remedies constitutional violations can fall within the sweep of Congress' enforcement power even if in the process it prohibits conduct which is not itself unconstitutional and intrudes into "legislative spheres of autonomy previously reserved to the States." . . . For example, the Court upheld a suspension of literacy tests and similar voting requirements under Congress' parallel power to enforce the provisions of the Fifteenth Amendment . . . as a measure to combat racial discrimination in voting, South Carolina v. Katzenbach, 383 U.S. 301, 308 (1966), despite the facial constitutionality of the tests under Lassiter v. Northampton County Bd. of Elections, 360 U.S. 45 (1959). We have also concluded that other measures protecting voting rights are within Congress' power to enforce the Fourteenth and Fifteenth Amendments, despite the burdens those measures placed on the States. . . .

It is also true, however, that "[a]s broad as the congressional enforcement power is, it is not unlimited." . . . In assessing the breadth of § 5's enforcement power, we begin with its text. Congress has been given the power "to enforce" the "provisions of this article." We agree with respondent, of course, that Congress can enact legislation under § 5 enforcing the constitutional right to the free exercise of religion. . . .

Congress' power under § 5, however, extends only to "enforc[ing]" the provisions of the Fourteenth Amendment. The Court has described this power as "remedial," . . . The design of the Amendment and the text of § 5 are inconsistent with the suggestion that Congress has the power to decree the substance of the Fourteenth Amendment's restrictions on the States. Legislation which alters the meaning of the Free Exercise Clause cannot be said to be enforcing the Clause. Congress does not enforce a constitutional right by changing what the right is. It has been given the power "to enforce," not the power to determine what constitutes a constitutional violation. Were it not so, what Congress would be enforcing would no longer be, in any meaningful sense, the "provisions of [the Fourteenth Amendment]."

While the line between measures that remedy or prevent unconstitutional actions and measures that make a substantive change in the governing law is not easy to discern, and Congress must have wide latitude in determining where it lies, the distinction exists and must be observed. There must be a congruence and proportionality between the injury to be prevented or remedied and the means adopted to that end. Lacking such a connection, legislation may become substantive in operation and effect. History and our case law support drawing the distinction, one apparent from the text of the Amendment.

1

. . .

The design of the Fourteenth Amendment has proved significant . . . in maintaining the traditional separation of powers between Congress and the Judiciary. . . . As enacted, the Fourteenth Amendment confers substantive rights against the States which, like the provisions of the Bill of Rights, are self-executing. . . . The power to interpret the Constitution in a case or controversy remains in the Judiciary.

2

The remedial and preventive nature of Congress' enforcement power, and the limitation inherent in the power, were confirmed in our earliest cases on the Fourteenth Amendment. In the Civil Rights Cases, 109 U.S. 3 (1883), the Court invalidated sections of the Civil Rights Act of 1875 which prescribed criminal penalties for denying to any person "the full enjoyment of" public accommodations and conveyances, on the grounds that it exceeded Congress' power by seeking to regulate private conduct. The Enforcement Clause, the Court said, did not authorize Congress to pass "general legislation upon the rights of the citizen, but corrective legislation; that is, such as may be necessary and proper for counteracting such laws as the States may adopt or enforce, and which, by the amendment, they are prohibited from making or enforcing. . . ." . . . Although the specific holdings of these early cases might have been superseded or modified, see, e.g., Heart of Atlanta Motel, Inc. v. United States, 379 U.S. 241 (1964); United States v. Guest, 383 U.S. 745 (1966), their treatment of Congress' § 5 power as corrective or preventive, not definitional, has not been questioned.

Recent cases have continued to revolve around the question of whether § 5 legislation can be considered remedial. In South Carolina v. Katzenbach . . . we upheld various provisions of the Voting Rights Act of 1965, finding them to be "remedies aimed at areas where voting discrimination has been most flagrant," . . . and necessary to "banish the blight of racial discrimination in voting, which has infected the electoral process in parts of our country for nearly a century,". . . . We noted evidence in the record reflecting the subsisting and pervasive discriminatory—and therefore unconstitutional—use of literacy tests. . . . The Act's new remedies, which used the administrative resources of the Federal Government, included the suspension of both literacy tests and, pending federal review, all new voting regulations in covered jurisdictions, as well as the assignment of federal examiners to list qualified applicants enabling those listed to vote. The new, unprecedented remedies were deemed necessary given the ineffectiveness of the existing voting rights laws, ... and the slow costly character of case-by-case litigation. ...

After South Carolina v. Katzenbach, the Court continued to acknowledge the necessity of using strong remedial and preventive measures to respond to the widespread and persisting deprivation of constitutional rights resulting from this country's history of racial discrimination. ...

3

Any suggestion that Congress has a substantive, non-remedial power under the Fourteenth Amendment is not supported by our case law. In Oregon v. Mitchell, ... a majority of the Court concluded Congress had exceeded its enforcement powers by enacting legislation lowering the minimum age of voters from 21 to 18 in state and local elections. The five Members of the Court who reached this conclusion explained that the legislation intruded into an area reserved by the Constitution to the States. ...

There is language in our opinion in Katzenbach v. Morgan, 384 U.S. 641 (1966), which could be interpreted as acknowledging a power in Congress to enact legislation that expands the rights contained in § 1 of the Fourteenth Amendment. This is not a necessary interpretation, however, or even the best one. In *Morgan*, the Court considered the constitutionality of § 4(e) of the Voting Rights Act of 1965, which provided that no person who had successfully completed the sixth primary grade in a public school in, or a private school accredited by, the Commonwealth of Puerto Rico in which the language of instruction was other than English could be denied the right to vote because of an inability to read or write English. New York's Constitution, on the other hand, required voters to be able to read and write English. The Court provided two related rationales for its conclusion that § 4(e) could "be viewed as a measure to secure for the Puerto Rican community residing in New York nondiscriminatory treatment by government." ... Under the first rationale, Congress could prohibit New York from denying the right to vote to large segments of its Puerto Rican community, in order to give Puerto Ricans "enhanced political power" that would be "helpful in gaining nondiscriminatory treatment in public services for the entire Puerto Rican community." ... Section 4(e) thus could be justified as a remedial measure to deal with "discrimination in governmental services." ... The second rationale, an alternative holding, did not address discrimination in the provision of public services but "discrimination in establishing voter qualifications." ... The Court perceived a factual basis on which Congress could have concluded that New York's literacy requirement "constituted an invidious discrimination in violation of the Equal Protection Clause." ... Both rationales for upholding § 4(e) rested on unconstitutional discrimination by New York and Congress' reasonable attempt to combat it. As Justice Stewart explained in Oregon v. Mitchell, ... interpreting *Morgan* to give Congress the power to interpret the Constitution "would require an enormous extension of that decision's rationale."

If Congress could define its own powers by altering the Fourteenth Amendment's meaning, no longer would the Constitution be "superior paramount law, unchangeable by ordinary means." It would be "on a level with ordinary legislative acts, and, like other acts, ... alterable when the legislature shall please to alter it." Marbury v. Madison ... Under this approach, it is difficult to conceive of a principle that would limit congressional power. ... Shifting legislative majorities could change the Constitution and effectively circumvent the difficult and detailed amendment process contained in Article V.

We now turn to consider whether RFRA can be considered enforcement legislation under § 5 of the Fourteenth Amendment.

B

Respondent contends that RFRA is a proper exercise of Congress' remedial or preventive power. The Act, it is said, is a reasonable means of protecting the free exercise of religion as defined by *Smith*. It prevents and remedies laws which are enacted with the unconstitutional object of targeting religious beliefs and practices. . . . If Congress can prohibit laws with discriminatory effects in order to prevent racial discrimination in violation of the Equal Protection Clause, . . . then it can do the same, respondent argues, to promote religious liberty.

While preventive rules are sometimes appropriate remedial measures, there must be a congruence between the means used and the ends to be achieved. The appropriateness of remedial measures must be considered in light of the evil presented. . . . Strong measures appropriate to address one harm may be an unwarranted response to another, lesser one. . . .

A comparison between RFRA and the Voting Rights Act is instructive. In contrast to the record which confronted Congress and the judiciary in the voting rights cases, RFRA's legislative record lacks examples of modern instances of generally applicable laws passed because of religious bigotry. The history of persecution in this country detailed in the hearings mentions no episodes occurring in the past 40 years. . . . Rather, the emphasis of the hearings was on laws of general applicability which place incidental burdens on religion. . . . It is difficult to maintain that they are examples of legislation enacted or enforced due to animus or hostility to the burdened religious practices or that they indicate some widespread pattern of religious discrimination in this country. Congress' concern was with the incidental burdens imposed, not the object or purpose of the legislation. . . . This lack of support in the legislative record, however, is not RFRA's most serious shortcoming. Judicial deference, in most cases, is based not on the state of the legislative record Congress compiles but "on due regard for the decision of the body constitutionally appointed to decide." . . . As a general matter, it is for Congress to determine the method by which it will reach a decision.

Regardless of the state of the legislative record, RFRA cannot be considered remedial, preventive legislation, if those terms are to have any meaning. RFRA is so out of proportion to a supposed remedial or preventive object that it cannot be understood as responsive to, or designed to prevent, unconstitutional behavior. It appears, instead, to attempt a substantive change in constitutional protections. Preventive measures prohibiting certain types of laws may be appropriate when there is reason to believe that many of the laws affected by the congressional enactment have a significant likelihood of being unconstitutional. . . .

RFRA is not so confined. Sweeping coverage ensures its intrusion at every level of government, displacing laws and prohibiting official actions of almost every description and regardless of subject matter. RFRA's restrictions apply to every agency and official of the Federal, State, and local Governments. . . . RFRA applies to all federal and state law, statutory or otherwise, whether adopted before or after its enactment . . . RFRA has no termination date or termination mechanism. Any law is subject to challenge at any time by any individual who alleges a substantial burden on his or her free exercise of religion.

The reach and scope of RFRA distinguish it from other measures passed under Congress' enforcement power, even in the area of voting rights. In South Carolina v. Katzenbach, the challenged provisions were confined to those regions of the country where voting discrimination had been most flagrant, . . . and affected a discrete class of state laws, i.e., state voting laws. Furthermore, to ensure that the reach of the

Voting Rights Act was limited to those cases in which constitutional violations were most likely (in order to reduce the possibility of overbreadth), the coverage under the Act would terminate "at the behest of States and political subdivisions in which the danger of substantial voting discrimination has not materialized during the preceding five years." . . . The provisions restricting and banning literacy tests, upheld in Katzenbach v. Morgan, . . . and Oregon v. Mitchell, . . . attacked a particular type of voting qualification, one with a long history as a "notorious means to deny and abridge voting rights on racial grounds." . . . In *City of Rome*, . . . the Court rejected a challenge to the constitutionality of a Voting Rights Act provision which required certain jurisdictions to submit changes in electoral practices to the Department of Justice for preimplementation review. The requirement was placed only on jurisdictions with a history of intentional racial discrimination in voting. . . . Like the provisions at issue in South Carolina v. Katzenbach, this provision permitted a covered jurisdiction to avoid preclearance requirements under certain conditions and, moreover, lapsed in seven years. This is not to say, of course, that § 5 legislation requires termination dates, geographic restrictions or egregious predicates. Where, however, a congressional enactment pervasively prohibits constitutional state action in an effort to remedy or to prevent unconstitutional state action, limitations of this kind tend to ensure Congress' means are proportionate to ends legitimate under § 5.

The stringent test RFRA demands of state laws reflects a lack of proportionality or congruence between the means adopted and the legitimate end to be achieved. If an objector can show a substantial burden on his free exercise, the State must demonstrate a compelling governmental interest and show that the law is the least restrictive means of furthering its interest. Claims that a law substantially burdens someone's exercise of religion will often be difficult to contest. . . . Requiring a State to demonstrate a compelling interest and show that it has adopted the least restrictive means of achieving that interest is the most demanding test known to constitutional law. . . . Laws valid under *Smith* would fall under RFRA without regard to whether they had the object of stifling or punishing free exercise. We make these observations not to reargue the position of the majority in *Smith* but to illustrate the substantive alteration of its holding attempted by RFRA. Even assuming RFRA would be interpreted in effect to mandate some lesser test, say one equivalent to intermediate scrutiny, the statute nevertheless would require searching judicial scrutiny of state law with the attendant likelihood of invalidation. This is a considerable congressional intrusion into the States' traditional prerogatives and general authority to regulate for the health and welfare of their citizens.

The substantial costs RFRA exacts, both in practical terms of imposing a heavy litigation burden on the States and in terms of curtailing their traditional general regulatory power, far exceed any pattern or practice of unconstitutional conduct under the Free Exercise Clause as interpreted in *Smith*. Simply put, RFRA is not designed to identify and counteract state laws likely to be unconstitutional because of their treatment of religion. In most cases, the state laws to which RFRA applies are not ones which will have been motivated by religious bigotry. If a state law disproportionately burdened a particular class of religious observers, this circumstance might be evidence of an impermissible legislative motive. . . . RFRA's substantial burden test, however, is not even a discriminatory effects or disparate impact test. It is a reality of the modern regulatory state that numerous state laws, such as the zoning regulations at issue here, impose a substantial burden on a large class of individuals. When the exercise of religion has been burdened in an incidental way by a law of general application, it does not follow that the persons affected have been burdened any more than other citizens, let alone burdened because of their religious beliefs. In addition, the Act imposes in every case a least restrictive means requirement—a requirement that was not used in the pre-*Smith* jurisprudence RFRA purported to codify—which also indicates that the legislation is broader than is appropriate if the goal is to prevent and remedy constitutional violations.

When Congress acts within its sphere of power and responsibilities, it has not just the right but the duty to make its own informed judgment on the meaning and force of the Constitution. This has been clear from the early days of the Republic. In 1789, when a Member of the House of Representatives objected to a debate on the constitutionality of legislation based on the theory that "it would be officious" to consider the constitutionality of a measure that did not affect the House, James Madison explained that "it is incontrovertibly of as much importance to this branch of the Government as to any other, that the constitution should be preserved entire. It is our duty." Were it otherwise, we would not afford Congress the presumption of validity its enactments now enjoy.

Our national experience teaches that the Constitution is preserved best when each part of the government respects both the Constitution and the proper actions and determinations of the other branches. When the Court has interpreted the Constitution, it has acted within the province of the Judicial Branch, which embraces the duty to say what the law is. Marbury v. Madison. When the political branches of the Government act against the background of a judicial interpretation of the Constitution already issued, it must be understood that in later cases and controversies the Court will treat its precedents with the respect due them under settled principles, including stare decisis, and contrary expectations must be disappointed. RFRA was designed to control cases and controversies, such as the one before us; but as the provisions of the federal statute here invoked are beyond congressional authority, it is this Court's precedent, not RFRA, which must control.

It is for Congress in the first instance to "determin[e] whether and what legislation is needed to secure the guarantees of the Fourteenth Amendment," and its conclusions are entitled to much deference. Katzenbach v. Morgan, 384 U.S., at 651. Congress' discretion is not unlimited, however, and the courts retain the power, as they have since Marbury v. Madison, to determine if Congress has exceeded its authority under the Constitution. Broad as the power of Congress is under the Enforcement Clause of the Fourteenth Amendment, RFRA contradicts vital principles necessary to maintain separation of powers and the federal balance. The judgment of the Court of Appeals sustaining the Act's constitutionality is reversed.

It is so ordered.

■ JUSTICE STEVENS, concurring.

In my opinion, the Religious Freedom Restoration Act of 1993 (RFRA) is a "law respecting an establishment of religion" that violates the First Amendment to the Constitution.

If the historic landmark on the hill in Boerne happened to be a museum or an art gallery owned by an atheist, it would not be eligible for an exemption from the city ordinances that forbid an enlargement of the structure. Because the landmark is owned by the Catholic Church, it is claimed that RFRA gives its owner a federal statutory entitlement to an exemption from a generally applicable, neutral civil law. Whether the Church would actually prevail under the statute or not, the statute has provided the Church with a legal weapon that no atheist or agnostic can obtain. This governmental preference for religion, as opposed to irreligion, is forbidden by the First Amendment. . . .

■ JUSTICE SCALIA, with whom JUSTICE STEVENS joins, concurring in part.

I write to respond briefly to the claim of Justice O'Connor's dissent . . . that historical materials support a result contrary to the one reached in Employment Div., Dept. of Human Resources of Ore. v. Smith, 494 U.S. 872 (1990). . . .

■ JUSTICE O'CONNOR, with whom JUSTICE BREYER joins except as to a portion of Part I, dissenting.

I dissent from the Court's disposition of this case. I agree with the Court that the issue before us is whether the Religious Freedom Restoration Act (RFRA) is a proper exercise of Congress' power to enforce § 5 of the Fourteenth Amendment. But as a yardstick for measuring the constitutionality of RFRA, the Court uses its holding in Employment Div., Dept. of Human Resources of Ore. v. Smith, 494 U.S. 872 (1990), the decision that prompted Congress to enact RFRA as a means of more rigorously enforcing the Free Exercise Clause. I remain of the view that *Smith* was wrongly decided, and I would use this case to reexamine the Court's holding there. . . .

I

I agree with much of the reasoning set forth in Part III-A of the Court's opinion. Indeed, if I agreed with the Court's standard in *Smith*, I would join the opinion. . . .

The Court's analysis of whether RFRA is a constitutional exercise of Congress' § 5 power, set forth in Part III-B of its opinion, is premised on the assumption that *Smith* correctly interprets the Free Exercise Clause. This is an assumption that I do not accept. I continue to believe that *Smith* adopted an improper standard for deciding free exercise claims. . . .

. . .

■ JUSTICE SOUTER, dissenting.

To decide whether the Fourteenth Amendment gives Congress sufficient power to enact the Religious Freedom Restoration Act, the Court measures the legislation against the free-exercise standard of Employment Div., Dept. of Human Resources of Ore. v. Smith, 494 U.S. 872 (1990). For the reasons stated in my opinion in Church of Lukumi Babalu Aye, Inc. v. Hialeah, 508 U.S. 520, 564–577 (1993) . . . I have serious doubts about the precedential value of the *Smith* rule and its entitlement to adherence. . . . [W]ithout briefing and argument on the merits of that rule . . . , I am not now prepared to join Justice O'Connor in rejecting it or the majority in assuming it to be correct. In order to provide full adversarial consideration, this case should be set down for reargument permitting plenary reexamination of the issue. . . .

■ JUSTICE BREYER, dissenting.

I agree with Justice O'Connor that the Court should direct the parties to brief the question whether Employment Div., Dept. of Human Resources of Ore. v. Smith, 494 U.S. 872 (1990) was correctly decided, and set this case for reargument. I do not, however, find it necessary to consider the question whether, assuming *Smith* is correct, § 5 of the Fourteenth Amendment would authorize Congress to enact the legislation before us. . . . I therefore join Justice O'Connor's dissent, with the exception of the first paragraph of Part I.

Kimel v. Florida Board of Regents

528 U.S. 62 (2000).

The Age Discrimination in Employment Act (ADEA) prohibits employment discrimination because of age. The Court held that ADEA was not authorized by § 5 of the Fourteenth Amendment. Justice O'Connor wrote the opinion for the Court.

"Applying the . . . 'congruence and proportionality' test . . . , we conclude that the ADEA is not 'appropriate legislation' under § 5 of the Fourteenth Amendment. . . .

"States may discriminate on the basis of age without offending the Fourteenth Amendment if the age classification in question is rationally related to a legitimate state interest. The rationality commanded by the Equal Protection Clause does not require States to match age distinctions and the legitimate interests they serve with razorlike precision. . . .

. . .

"Judged against the backdrop of our equal protection jurisprudence, it is clear that the ADEA is 'so out of proportion to a supposed remedial or preventive object that it cannot be understood as responsive to, or designed to prevent, unconstitutional behavior.' City of Boerne, 521 U.S., at 532. The Act, through its broad restriction on the use of age as a discriminating factor, prohibits substantially more state employment decisions and practices than would likely be held unconstitutional under the applicable equal protection, rational basis standard. . . ."

Board of Trustees of the University
of Alabama v. Garrett

531 U.S. 356, 121 S.Ct. 955, 148 L.Ed.2d 866 (2001).

■ CHIEF JUSTICE REHNQUIST delivered the opinion of the Court.

We decide here whether employees of the State of Alabama may recover money damages by reason of the State's failure to comply with the provisions of Title I of the Americans with Disabilities Act of 1990 (ADA or Act). . . .[1] We hold that such suits are barred by the Eleventh Amendment.

The ADA prohibits certain employers, including the States, from "discriminat[ing] against a qualified individual with a disability because of the disability of such individual in regard to job application procedures, the hiring, advancement, or discharge of employees, employee compensation, job training, and other terms, conditions, and privileges of employment." . . . To this end, the Act requires employers to "mak[e] reasonable accommodations to the known physical or mental limitations of an otherwise qualified individual with a disability who is an applicant or employee, unless [the employer] can demonstrate that the accommodation would impose an undue hardship on the operation of the [employer's] business." . . .

Respondent Patricia Garrett, a registered nurse, was employed as the Director of Nursing, OB/Gyn/Neonatal Services, for the University of Alabama in Birmingham Hospital. In 1994, Garrett was diagnosed with breast cancer and subsequently underwent a lumpectomy, radiation treatment, and chemotherapy. Garrett's treatments required her to take substantial leave from work. Upon returning to work in July 1995, Garrett's supervisor informed Garrett that she would have to give up her Director position. Garrett then applied for and received a transfer to another, lower paying position as a nurse manager.

Respondent Milton Ash worked as a security officer for the Alabama Department of Youth Services (Department). Upon commencing this employment, Ash informed the Department that he suffered from chronic asthma and that his doctor recommended he avoid carbon monoxide and cigarette smoke, and Ash requested that

---

[1]   . . . Title II of the ADA, [deals] with the "services, programs, or activities of a public entity," . . . We are not disposed to decide the constitutional issue whether Title II, which has somewhat different remedial provisions from Title I, is appropriate legislation under § 5 of the Fourteenth Amendment. . . .

the Department modify his duties to minimize his exposure to these substances. Ash was later diagnosed with sleep apnea and requested, again pursuant to his doctor's recommendation, that he be reassigned to daytime shifts to accommodate his condition. Ultimately, the Department granted none of the requested relief. Shortly after Ash filed a discrimination claim with the Equal Employment Opportunity Commission, he noticed that his performance evaluations were lower than those he had received on previous occasions.

Garrett and Ash filed separate lawsuits in the District Court, both seeking money damages under the ADA. Petitioners moved for summary judgment, claiming that the ADA exceeds Congress' authority to abrogate the State's Eleventh Amendment immunity. . . . [T]he District Court agreed with petitioners' position and granted their motions for summary judgment. . . . The Court of Appeals reversed. . . .

. . .

I

. . .

We have recognized . . . that Congress may abrogate the States' Eleventh Amendment immunity when it both unequivocally intends to do so and "act[s] pursuant to a valid grant of constitutional authority." . . .

Congress may not . . . base its abrogation of the States' Eleventh Amendment immunity upon the powers enumerated in Article I. . . . Congress may subject nonconsenting States to suit in federal court when it does so pursuant to a valid exercise of its [Fourteenth Amendment] § 5 power. . . . Accordingly, the ADA can apply to the States only to the extent that the statute is appropriate § 5 legislation.[3]

. . .

City of Boerne . . . confirmed . . . the long-settled principle that it is the responsibility of this Court, not Congress, to define the substance of constitutional guarantees. . . . Accordingly, § 5 legislation reaching beyond the scope of § 1's actual guarantees must exhibit "congruence and proportionality between the injury to be prevented or remedied and the means adopted to that end." . . .

II

The first step in applying these now familiar principles is to identify with some precision the scope of the constitutional right at issue. Here, that inquiry requires us to examine the limitations § 1 of the Fourteenth Amendment places upon States' treatment of the disabled. As we did last Term in *Kimel*, . . . we look to our prior decisions under the Equal Protection Clause dealing with this issue.

In Cleburne v. Cleburne Living Center, Inc., 473 U.S. 432 (1985), we considered an equal protection challenge to a city ordinance requiring a special use permit for the operation of a group home for the mentally retarded. The specific question before us was whether . . . mental retardation qualified as a "quasi-suspect" classification under our equal protection jurisprudence. . . . We . . . [concluded] instead that such legislation incurs only the minimum "rational-basis" review applicable to general social and economic legislation.[4] . . . In a statement that today seems quite prescient, we explained that

"if the large and amorphous class of the mentally retarded were deemed quasi-suspect for the reasons given by the Court of Appeals, it would be difficult to find a principled

---

³   It is clear that Congress intended to invoke § 5 as one of its bases for enacting the ADA. . . .

⁴   Applying the basic principles of rationality review, *Cleburne* struck down the city ordinance in question. . . . The Court's reasoning was that the city's purported justifications for the ordinance made no sense in light of how the city treated other groups similarly situated . . .

way to distinguish a variety of other groups who have perhaps immutable disabilities setting them off from others, who cannot themselves mandate the desired legislative responses, and who can claim some degree of prejudice from at least part of the public at large. One need mention in this respect only the aging, the disabled, the mentally ill, and the infirm. We are reluctant to set out on that course, and we decline to do so." . . .

Under rational-basis review, where a group possesses "distinguishing characteristics relevant to interests the State has the authority to implement," a State's decision to act on the basis of those differences does not give rise to a constitutional violation. . . .

Justice Breyer suggests that *Cleburne* stands for the broad proposition that state decisionmaking reflecting "negative attitudes" or "fear" necessarily runs afoul of the Fourteenth Amendment. Although such biases may often accompany irrational (and therefore unconstitutional) discrimination, their presence alone does not a constitutional violation make. As we noted in *Cleburne*: "[M]ere negative attitudes, or fear, unsubstantiated by factors which are properly cognizable in a zoning proceeding, are not permissible bases for treating a home for the mentally retarded differently. . . ." . . . This language, read in context, simply states the unremarkable and widely acknowledged tenet of this Court's equal protection jurisprudence that state action subject to rational-basis scrutiny does not violate the Fourteenth Amendment when it "rationally furthers the purpose identified by the State." Massachusetts Bd. of Retirement v. Murgia, 427 U.S. 307 (1976) (per curiam).

Thus, the result of *Cleburne* is that States are not required by the Fourteenth Amendment to make special accommodations for the disabled, so long as their actions towards such individuals are rational. They could quite hard headedly—and perhaps hardheartedly—hold to job-qualification requirements which do not make allowance for the disabled. If special accommodations for the disabled are to be required, they have to come from positive law and not through the Equal Protection Clause.[5]

III

Once we have determined the metes and bounds of the constitutional right in question, we examine whether Congress identified a history and pattern of unconstitutional employment discrimination by the States against the disabled. Just as § 1 of the Fourteenth Amendment applies only to actions committed "under color of state law," Congress' § 5 authority is appropriately exercised only in response to state transgressions. . . . The legislative record of the ADA, however, simply fails to show that Congress did in fact identify a pattern of irrational state discrimination in employment against the disabled.

Respondents contend that the inquiry as to unconstitutional discrimination should extend not only to States themselves, but to units of local governments, such as cities and counties. All of these, they say, are "state actors" for purposes of the Fourteenth Amendment. This is quite true, but the Eleventh Amendment does not extend its immunity to units of local government. . . . These entities are subject to private claims for damages under the ADA without Congress' ever having to rely on § 5 of the Fourteenth Amendment to render them so. It would make no sense to consider constitutional violations on their part, as well as by the States themselves, when only the States are the beneficiaries of the Eleventh Amendment.

---

[5]   It is worth noting that by the time that Congress enacted the ADA in 1990, every State in the Union had enacted such measures. At least one Member of Congress remarked that "this is probably one of the few times where the States are so far out in front of the Federal Government, it's not funny." . . . A number of these provisions, however, did not go as far as the ADA did in requiring accommodation.

Congress made a general finding in the ADA that "historically, society has tended to isolate and segregate individuals with disabilities, and, despite some improvements, such forms of discrimination against individuals with disabilities continue to be a serious and pervasive social problem." . . . The record assembled by Congress includes many instances to support such a finding. But the great majority of these incidents do not deal with the activities of States.

Respondents in their brief cite half a dozen examples from the record that did involve States. A department head at the University of North Carolina refused to hire an applicant for the position of health administrator because he was blind; similarly, a student at a state university in South Dakota was denied an opportunity to practice teach because the dean at that time was convinced that blind people could not teach in public schools. A microfilmer at the Kansas Department of Transportation was fired because he had epilepsy; deaf workers at the University of Oklahoma were paid a lower salary than those who could hear. The Indiana State Personnel Office informed a woman with a concealed disability that she should not disclose it if she wished to obtain employment.

Several of these incidents undoubtedly evidence an unwillingness on the part of state officials to make the sort of accommodations for the disabled required by the ADA. Whether they were irrational under our decision in *Cleburne* is more debatable, particularly when the incident is described out of context. But even if it were to be determined that each incident upon fuller examination showed unconstitutional action on the part of the State, these incidents taken together fall far short of even suggesting the pattern of unconstitutional discrimination on which § 5 legislation must be based. . . . In 1990, the States alone employed more than 4.5 million people. . . . It is telling, we think, that given these large numbers, Congress assembled only such minimal evidence of unconstitutional state discrimination in employment against the disabled.

Justice Breyer maintains that Congress applied Title I of the ADA to the States in response to a host of incidents representing unconstitutional state discrimination in employment against persons with disabilities. A close review of the relevant materials, however, undercuts that conclusion. Justice Breyer's Appendix C consists not of legislative findings, but of unexamined, anecdotal accounts of "adverse, disparate treatment by state officials." Of course, as we have already explained, "adverse, disparate treatment" often does not amount to a constitutional violation where rational-basis scrutiny applies. These accounts, moreover, were submitted not directly to Congress but to the Task Force on the Rights and Empowerment of Americans with Disabilities, which made no findings on the subject of state discrimination in employment. . . . And, had Congress truly understood this information as reflecting a pattern of unconstitutional behavior by the States, one would expect some mention of that conclusion in the Act's legislative findings. There is none. . . .

Even were it possible to squeeze out of these examples a pattern of unconstitutional discrimination by the States, the rights and remedies created by the ADA against the States would raise the same sort of concerns as to congruence and proportionality as were found in *City of Boerne*, supra. For example, whereas it would be entirely rational (and therefore constitutional) for a state employer to conserve scarce financial resources by hiring employees who are able to use existing facilities, the ADA requires employers to "mak[e] existing facilities used by employees readily accessible to and usable by individuals with disabilities." . . . The ADA does except employers from the "reasonable accommodatio[n]" requirement where the employer "can demonstrate that the accommodation would impose an undue hardship on the operation of the business of such covered entity." . . . However, even with this exception, the accommodation duty far exceeds what is constitutionally required in that it makes unlawful a range of alternate responses that would be reasonable but would fall short of imposing an "undue burden" upon the employer. . . .

The ADA also forbids "utilizing standards, criteria, or methods of administration" that disparately impact the disabled, without regard to whether such conduct has a rational basis. . . . Although disparate impact may be relevant evidence of racial discrimination, . . . such evidence alone is insufficient even where the Fourteenth Amendment subjects state action to strict scrutiny. . . .

The ADA's constitutional shortcomings are apparent when the Act is compared to Congress' efforts in the Voting Rights Act of 1965 to respond to a serious pattern of constitutional violations. In South Carolina v. Katzenbach, 383 U.S. 301 (1966), . . . we noted that "[b]efore enacting the measure, Congress explored with great care the problem of racial discrimination in voting." . . .

In that Act, Congress documented a marked pattern of unconstitutional action by the States. State officials, Congress found, routinely applied voting tests in order to exclude African-American citizens from registering to vote. . . . Congress also determined that litigation had proved ineffective and that there persisted an otherwise inexplicable 50-percentage-point gap in the registration of white and African-American voters in some States. . . . Congress' response was to promulgate in the Voting Rights Act a detailed but limited remedial scheme designed to guarantee meaningful enforcement of the Fifteenth Amendment in those areas of the Nation where abundant evidence of States' systematic denial of those rights was identified.

. . . The contrast between this kind of evidence, and the evidence that Congress considered in the present case, is stark. Congressional enactment of the ADA represents its judgment that there should be a "comprehensive national mandate for the elimination of discrimination against individuals with disabilities." . . . Congress is the final authority as to desirable public policy, but in order to authorize private individuals to recover money damages against the States, there must be a pattern of discrimination by the States which violates the Fourteenth Amendment, and the remedy imposed by Congress must be congruent and proportional to the targeted violation. Those requirements are not met here, and to uphold the Act's application to the States would allow Congress to rewrite the Fourteenth Amendment law laid down by this Court in Cleburne. Section 5 does not so broadly enlarge congressional authority. The judgment of the Court of Appeals is therefore Reversed.

■ JUSTICE KENNEDY, with whom JUSTICE O'CONNOR joins, concurring.

Prejudice, we are beginning to understand, rises not from malice or hostile animus alone. . . . There can be little doubt . . . that persons with mental or physical impairments are confronted with prejudice which can stem from indifference or insecurity as well as from malicious ill will.

. . . I do not doubt that the Americans with Disabilities Act of 1990 will be a milestone on the path to a more decent, tolerant, progressive society.

It is a question of quite a different order, however, to say that the States in their official capacities, the States as governmental entities, must be held in violation of the Constitution on the assumption that they embody the misconceived or malicious perceptions of some of their citizens. . . . The failure of a State to revise policies now seen as incorrect under a new understanding of proper policy does not always constitute the purposeful and intentional action required to make out a violation of the Equal Protection Clause. . . .

. . .

It must be noted, moreover, that what is in question is not whether the Congress, acting pursuant to a power granted to it by the Constitution, can compel the States to act. What is involved is only the question whether the States can be subjected to liability in suits brought not by the Federal Government (to which the States have consented, . . . but by private persons seeking to collect moneys from the state treasury without the consent of the State). The predicate for money damages against an unconsenting State in suits brought by private persons must be a federal statute enacted upon the documentation of patterns of constitutional violations committed by the State in its official capacity. That predicate . . . has not been established. With these observations, I join the Court's opinion.

■ JUSTICE BREYER, with whom JUSTICE STEVENS, JUSTICE SOUTER and JUSTICE GINSBERG join, dissenting.

. . .

. . . In my view, Congress reasonably could have concluded that the remedy before us constitutes an "appropriate" way to enforce this basic equal protection requirement. And that is all the Constitution requires.

I

The Court says that its primary problem with this statutory provision is one of legislative evidence. It says that "Congress assembled only . . . minimal evidence of unconstitutional state discrimination in employment." In fact, Congress compiled a vast legislative record documenting " 'massive, society-wide discrimination' " against persons with disabilities. . . .

The powerful evidence of discriminatory treatment throughout society in general, including discrimination by private persons and local governments, implicates state governments as well, for state agencies form part of that same larger society. There is no particular reason to believe that they are immune from the "stereotypic assumptions" and pattern of "purposeful unequal treatment" that Congress found prevalent. The Court claims that it "make[s] no sense" to take into consideration constitutional violations committed by local governments. But the substantive obligation that the Equal Protection Clause creates applies to state and local governmental entities alike. . . . Local governments often work closely with, and under the supervision of, state officials, and in general, state and local government employers are similarly situated. . . .

. . .

The congressionally appointed task force collected numerous specific examples, provided by persons with disabilities themselves, of adverse, disparate treatment by state officials. They reveal, not what the Court describes as "half a dozen" instances of discrimination, but hundreds of instances of adverse treatment at the hands of state officials—instances in which a person with a disability found it impossible to obtain a state job, to retain state employment, to use the public transportation that was readily available to others in order to get to work, or to obtain a public education, which is often a prerequisite to obtaining employment. . . .

As the Court notes, those who presented instances of discrimination rarely provided additional, independent evidence sufficient to prove in court that, in each instance, the discrimination they suffered lacked justification from a judicial standpoint. Perhaps this explains the Court's view that there is "minimal evidence of unconstitutional state discrimination." But a legislature is not a court of law. And Congress, unlike courts, must, and does, routinely draw general conclusions . . .

Regardless, Congress expressly found substantial unjustified discrimination against persons with disabilities. . . . In making these findings, Congress followed our decision in *Cleburne*, which established that not only discrimination against persons with disabilities that rests upon "a bare . . . desire to harm a politically unpopular group," . . . violates the Fourteenth Amendment, but also discrimination that rests solely upon "negative attitude [s]," "fea[r]," . . . or "irrational prejudice,". . . .

The evidence in the legislative record bears out Congress' finding that the adverse treatment of persons with disabilities was often arbitrary or invidious in this sense, and thus unjustified. . . .

II

The Court's failure to find sufficient evidentiary support may well rest upon its decision to hold Congress to a strict, judicially created evidentiary standard, particularly in respect to lack of justification. . . .

The problem with the Court's approach is that neither the "burden of proof" that favors States nor any other rule of restraint applicable to judges applies to Congress when it exercises its § 5 power. "Limitations stemming from the nature of the judicial process . . . have no application to Congress." . . . Rational-basis review—with its presumptions favoring constitutionality—is "a paradigm of judicial restraint." . . . And the Congress of the United States is not a lower court.

Indeed, the Court in *Cleburne* drew this very institutional distinction. We emphasized that "courts have been very reluctant, as they should be in our federal system and with our respect for the separation of powers, to closely scrutinize legislative choices." . . .

There is simply no reason to require Congress, seeking to determine facts relevant to the exercise of its § 5 authority, to adopt rules or presumptions that reflect a court's institutional limitations. Unlike courts, Congress can readily gather facts from across the Nation, assess the magnitude of a problem, and more easily find an appropriate remedy. . . . Unlike courts, Congress directly reflects public attitudes and beliefs, enabling Congress better to understand where, and to what extent, refusals to accommodate a disability amount to behavior that is callous or unreasonable to the point of lacking constitutional justification. Unlike judges, Members of Congress can directly obtain information from constituents who have first-hand experience with discrimination and related issues.

Moreover, unlike judges, Members of Congress are elected. . . . To apply a rule designed to restrict courts as if it restricted Congress' legislative power is to stand the underlying principle—a principle of judicial restraint—on its head. But without the use of this burden of proof rule or some other unusually stringent standard of review, it is difficult to see how the Court can find the legislative record here inadequate. Read with a reasonably favorable eye, the record indicates that state governments subjected those with disabilities to seriously adverse, disparate treatment. And Congress could have found, in a significant number of instances, that this treatment violated the substantive principles of justification—shorn of their judicial-restraint-related presumptions—that this Court recognized in *Cleburne*.

III

The Court argues in the alternative that the statute's damage remedy is not "congruent" with and "proportional" to the equal protection problem that Congress found. . . .

[W]hat is wrong with a remedy that, in response to unreasonable employer behavior, requires an employer to make accommodations that are reasonable? Of course, what is "reasonable" in the statutory sense and what is "unreasonable" in the constitutional sense might differ. In other words, the requirement may exceed what is necessary to avoid a constitutional violation. But it is just that power—the power to require more than the minimum that § 5 grants to Congress, as this Court has repeatedly confirmed. . . .

. . .

. . . [E]ven today, the Court purports to apply, not to depart from, these standards. But the Court's analysis and ultimate conclusion deprive its declarations of practical significance. The Court "sounds the word of promise to the ear but breaks it to the hope."

IV

The Court's harsh review of Congress' use of its § 5 power is reminiscent of the similar (now-discredited) limitation that it once imposed upon Congress' Commerce Clause power. Compare Carter v. Carter Coal Co., 298 U.S. 238 (1936), with United States v. Darby, 312 U.S. 100 (1941) (rejecting *Carter Coal's* rationale). I could understand the legal basis for such review were we judging a statute that discriminated against those of a particular race or gender . . . , or a statute that threatened a basic constitutionally protected liberty such as free speech, . . . The legislation before us, however, does not discriminate against anyone, nor does it pose any threat to basic liberty. And it is difficult to understand why the Court, which applies "minimum 'rational-basis' review" to statutes that burden persons with disabilities, subjects to far stricter scrutiny a statute that seeks to help those same individuals.

. . . Rules for interpreting § 5 that would provide States with special protection . . . run counter to the very object of the Fourteenth Amendment. . . . I doubt that today's decision serves any constitutionally based federalism interest.

The Court, through its evidentiary demands, its non-deferential review, and its failure to distinguish between judicial and legislative constitutional competencies, improperly invades a power that the Constitution assigns to Congress. . . . Whether the Commerce Clause does or does not enable Congress to enact this provision, . . . in my view, § 5 gives Congress the necessary authority.

For the reasons stated, I respectfully dissent.

Nevada Department of Human Resources v. Hibbs

538 U.S. 721, 123 S.Ct. 1972, 155 L.Ed.2d 953 (2003).

■ CHIEF JUSTICE REHNQUIST delivered the opinion of the Court.

The Family and Medical Leave Act of 1993 (FMLA or Act) entitles eligible employees to take up to 12 work weeks of unpaid leave annually for any of several reasons, including the onset of a "serious health condition" in an employee's spouse, child, or parent. . . . The Act creates a private right of action to seek both equitable relief and money damages "against any employer (including a public agency) in any Federal or State court of competent jurisdiction," . . . should that employer "interfere with, restrain, or deny the exercise of" FMLA rights . . . We hold that employees of the State of Nevada may recover money damages in the event of the State's failure to comply with the family-care provision of the Act.

. . . Respondent . . . worked for the Department's Welfare Division. In April and May 1997, he sought leave under the FMLA to care for his ailing wife, who was recovering from a car accident and neck surgery. The Department granted his request for the full 12 weeks of FMLA leave. . . . In October 1997, the Department informed respondent that he had exhausted his FMLA leave, that no further leave would be granted, and that he must report to work by November 12, 1997. Respondent failed to do so and was terminated.

Respondent sued petitioners in the United States District Court seeking damages and injunctive and declaratory relief for . . . violations of [FMLA]. The District Court awarded petitioners summary judgment on the grounds that the FMLA claim was barred by the Eleventh Amendment and that respondent's Fourteenth Amendment rights had not been violated. . . . The Ninth Circuit reversed.

. . .

Congress may . . . abrogate . . . immunity in federal court if it makes its intention to abrogate unmistakably clear in the language of the statute and acts pursuant to a valid exercise of its power under § 5 of the Fourteenth Amendment. . . . This case turns, then, on whether Congress acted within its constitutional authority when it sought to abrogate the States' immunity for purposes of the FMLA's family-leave provision.

In enacting the FMLA, Congress relied on two of the powers vested in it by the Constitution: its Article I commerce power and its power under § 5 of the Fourteenth Amendment to enforce that Amendment's guarantees. Congress may not abrogate the States' sovereign immunity pursuant to its Article I power over commerce. . . . Congress may, however, abrogate States' sovereign immunity through a valid exercise of its § 5 power . . .

Two provisions of the Fourteenth Amendment are relevant here: Section 5 grants Congress the power "to enforce" the substantive guarantees of § 1—among them, equal protection of the laws—by enacting "appropriate legislation." Congress may, in the exercise of its § 5 power, do more than simply proscribe conduct that we have held unconstitutional. "Congress' power 'to enforce' the Amendment includes the authority both to remedy and to deter violation of rights guaranteed thereunder by prohibiting a somewhat broader swath of conduct, including that which is not itself forbidden by the Amendment's text." . . . In other words, Congress may enact so-called prophylactic legislation that proscribes facially constitutional conduct, in order to prevent and deter unconstitutional conduct.

City of Boerne also confirmed, however, that it falls to this Court, not Congress, to define the substance of constitutional guarantees. . . . We distinguish appropriate prophylactic legislation from "substantive redefinition of the Fourteenth Amendment right at issue," . . . by applying the test set forth in *City of Boerne:* Valid § 5 legislation must exhibit "congruence and proportionality between the injury to be prevented or remedied and the means adopted to that end." . . .

The FMLA aims to protect the right to be free from gender-based discrimination in the workplace. We have held that statutory classifications that distinguish between males and females are subject to heightened scrutiny. . . . For a gender-based classification to withstand such scrutiny, it must "serv[e] important governmental objectives," and "the discriminatory means employed [must be] substantially related to the achievement of those objectives." . . . The State's justification for such a classification "must not rely on overbroad generalizations about the different talents, capacities, or preferences of males and females." . . . We now inquire whether Congress had evidence of a pattern of constitutional violations on the part of the States in this area.

The history of the many state laws limiting women's employment opportunities is chronicled in—and, until relatively recently, was sanctioned by—this Court's own opinions.

. . .

Congress responded to this history of discrimination by abrogating States' sovereign immunity in Title VII of the Civil Rights Act of 1964 . . . But state gender discrimination did not cease. . . . According to evidence that was before Congress when it enacted the FMLA, States continue to rely on invalid gender stereotypes in the employment context, specifically in the administration of leave benefits. Reliance on such stereotypes cannot justify the States' gender discrimination in this area. . . . The long and extensive history of sex discrimination prompted us to hold that measures that differentiate on the basis of gender warrant heightened scrutiny; here . . . the persistence of such unconstitutional discrimination by the States justifies Congress' passage of prophylactic § 5 legislation.

As the FMLA's legislative record reflects, a 1990 Bureau of Labor Statistics (BLS) survey stated that 37 percent of surveyed private-sector employees were covered by maternity leave policies, while only 18 percent were covered by paternity leave policies. . . .

Congress also heard testimony that "[p]arental leave for fathers . . . is rare. Even . . . [w]here child-care leave policies do exist, men, *both in the public and private sectors*, receive notoriously discriminatory treatment in their requests for such leave." . . .

Finally, Congress had evidence that, even where state laws and policies were not facially discriminatory, they were applied in discriminatory ways. . . .

In spite of all of the above evidence, Justice Kennedy argues in dissent that Congress' passage of the FMLA was unnecessary because "the States appear to have been ahead of Congress in providing gender-neutral family leave benefits," and points to Nevada's leave policies in particular. However, it was only "[s]ince Federal family leave legislation was first introduced" that the States had even "begun to consider similar family leave initiatives." . . .

Furthermore, the dissent's statement that some States "had adopted some form of family-care leave" before the FMLA's enactment glosses over important shortcomings of some state policies. First, seven States had childcare leave provisions that applied to women only. . . . These laws reinforced the very stereotypes that Congress sought to remedy through the FMLA. Second, 12 States provided their employees no family leave, beyond an initial childbirth or adoption, to care for a seriously ill child or family member. Third, many States provided no statutorily guaranteed right to family leave, offering instead only voluntary or discretionary leave programs. Three States left the amount of leave time primarily in employers' hands. Congress could reasonably conclude that such discretionary family-leave programs would do little to combat the stereotypes about the roles of male and female employees that Congress sought to eliminate. Finally, four States provided leave only through administrative regulations or personnel policies, which Congress could reasonably conclude offered significantly less firm protection than a federal law. Against the above backdrop of limited state leave policies, no matter how generous petitioner's own may have been, Congress was justified in enacting the FMLA as remedial legislation.

In sum, the States' record of unconstitutional participation in, and fostering of, gender-based discrimination in the administration of leave benefits is weighty enough to justify the enactment of prophylactic § 5 legislation.

We reached the opposite conclusion in *Garrett* and *Kimel*. In those cases, the § 5 legislation under review responded to a purported tendency of state officials to make age-or disability-based distinctions. Under our equal protection case law, discrimination on the basis of such characteristics is not judged under a heightened review standard . . .

Here, however, Congress directed its attention to state gender discrimination, which triggers a heightened level of scrutiny. . . . Because the standard for demonstrating the constitutionality of a gender-based classification is more difficult to meet than our rational-basis test . . . it was easier for Congress to show a pattern of state constitutional violations. Congress was similarly successful in South Carolina v.

Katzenbach, 383 U.S. 301, 308–313 (1966), where we upheld the Voting Rights Act of 1965: Because racial classifications are presumptively invalid, most of the States' acts of race discrimination violated the Fourteenth Amendment.

. . .

Stereotypes about women's domestic roles are reinforced by parallel stereotypes presuming a lack of domestic responsibilities for men. Because employers continued to regard the family as the woman's domain, they often denied men similar accommodations or discouraged them from taking leave. These mutually reinforcing stereotypes created a self-fulfilling cycle of discrimination that forced women to continue to assume the role of primary family caregiver, and fostered employers' stereotypical views about women's commitment to work and their value as employees. Those perceptions, in turn, Congress reasoned, lead to subtle discrimination that may be difficult to detect on a case-by-case basis.

. . .

By creating an across-the-board, routine employment benefit for all eligible employees, Congress sought to ensure that family-care leave would no longer be stigmatized as an inordinate drain on the workplace caused by female employees, and that employers could not evade leave obligations simply by hiring men. By setting a minimum standard of family leave for *all* eligible employees, irrespective of gender, the FMLA attacks the formerly state-sanctioned stereotype that only women are responsible for family caregiving, thereby reducing employers' incentives to engage in discrimination by basing hiring and promotion decisions on stereotypes.

The dissent characterizes the FMLA as a "substantive entitlement program" rather than a remedial statute because it establishes a floor of 12 weeks' leave. In the dissent's view, in the face of evidence of gender-based discrimination by the States in the provision of leave benefits, Congress could do no more in exercising its § 5 power than simply proscribe such discrimination. But this position cannot be squared with our recognition that Congress "is not confined to the enactment of legislation that merely parrots the precise wording of the Fourteenth Amendment," but may prohibit "a somewhat broader swath of conduct, including that which is not itself forbidden by the Amendment's text." . . . For example, this Court has upheld certain prophylactic provisions of the Voting Rights Act as valid exercises of Congress' § 5 power, including the literacy test ban and preclearance requirements for changes in States' voting procedures. . . .

Indeed, in light of the evidence before Congress, a statute mirroring Title VII, that simply mandated gender equality in the administration of leave benefits, would not have achieved Congress' remedial object. Such a law would allow States to provide for no family leave at all. Where "[t]wo-thirds of the nonprofessional caregivers for older, chronically ill, or disabled persons are working women," . . . and state practices continue to reinforce the stereotype of women as caregivers, such a policy would exclude far more women than men from the workplace.

Unlike the statutes at issue in *City of Boerne*, *Kimel*, and *Garrett*, which applied broadly to every aspect of state employers' operations, the FMLA is narrowly targeted at the fault line between work and family—precisely where sex-based overgeneralization has been and remains strongest—and affects only one aspect of the employment relationship. . . .

. . .

For the above reasons, we conclude that [FMLA] is congruent and proportional to its remedial object, and can "be understood as responsive to, or designed to prevent, unconstitutional behavior." . . .

The judgment of the Court of Appeals is therefore

Affirmed.

■ JUSTICE SOUTER, with whom JUSTICE GINSBURG and JUSTICE BREYER join, concurring.

. . . I join the Court's opinion here without conceding the dissenting . . . views expressed in Seminole Tribe of Fla. v. Florida . . .

■ JUSTICE STEVENS, concurring in the judgment.

Because I have never been convinced that an Act of Congress can amend the Constitution and because I am uncertain whether the congressional enactment before us was truly " 'needed to secure the guarantees of the Fourteenth Amendment,' " I write separately to explain why I join the Court's judgment. . . .

. . . As long as it clearly expresses its intent, Congress may abrogate that common-law defense pursuant to its power to regulate commerce "among the several States." . . . The family-care provision of the Family and Medical Leave Act of 1993 is unquestionably a valid exercise of a power that is "broad enough to support federal legislation regulating the terms and conditions of state employment." . . .

■ JUSTICE SCALIA, dissenting.

I join Justice Kennedy's dissent, and add one further observation: The constitutional violation that is a prerequisite to "prophylactic" congressional action to "enforce" the Fourteenth Amendment is a violation *by the State against which the enforcement action is taken.* There is no guilt by association, enabling the sovereignty of one State to be abridged under § 5 of the Fourteenth Amendment because of violations by another State, or by most other States, or even by 49 other States. Congress has sometimes displayed awareness of this self-evident limitation. That is presumably why the most sweeping provisions of the Voting Rights Act of 1965— which we upheld in *City of Rome v. United States,* 446 U.S. 156 (1980), as a valid exercise of congressional power under § 2 of the Fifteenth Amendment—were restricted to States "with a demonstrable history of intentional racial discrimination in voting," . . .

Today's opinion for the Court does not even attempt to demonstrate that each one of the 50 States . . . was in violation of the Fourteenth Amendment. It treats "the States" as some sort of collective entity which is guilty or innocent as a body. . . .

. . . [T]he court may, if asked, proceed to analyze whether the statute . . . can be validly applied to the litigant. In the context of § 5 prophylactic legislation applied against a State, this would entail examining whether the State has itself engaged in discrimination sufficient to support the exercise of Congress's prophylactic power.

. . . I think Nevada will be entitled to assert that the mere facts that (1) it is a State, and (2) some States are bad actors, is not enough; it can demand that *it* be shown to have been acting in violation of the Fourteenth Amendment.

■ JUSTICE KENNEDY, with whom JUSTICE SCALIA and JUSTICE THOMAS join, dissenting.

. . . [T]he family leave provision of the Act . . . is invalid to the extent it allows for private suits against the unconsenting States.

Congress does not have authority to define the substantive content of the Equal Protection Clause; it may only shape the remedies warranted by the violations of that guarantee. *City of Boerne, supra* . . . This requirement has special force in the context of the Eleventh Amendment, which protects a State's fiscal integrity from federal intrusion by vesting the States with immunity from private actions for damages pursuant to federal laws. The Commerce Clause likely would permit the National Government to enact an entitlement program such as this one; but when Congress couples the entitlement with the authorization to sue the States for monetary damages, it blurs the line of accountability the State has to its own citizens. . . .

The Court is unable to show that States have engaged in a pattern of unlawful conduct which warrants the remedy of opening state treasuries to private suits. The inability to adduce evidence of alleged discrimination, coupled with the inescapable fact that the federal scheme is not a remedy but a benefit program, demonstrate the lack of the requisite link between any problem Congress has identified and the program it mandated.

. . . All would agree that women historically have been subjected to conditions in which their employment opportunities are more limited than those available to men. As the Court acknowledges, however, Congress responded to this problem by abrogating States' sovereign immunity in Title VII of the Civil Rights Act of 1964 . . . The provision now before us . . . has a different aim than Title VII. It seeks to ensure that eligible employees, irrespective of gender, can take a minimum amount of leave time to care for an ill relative.

The relevant question, as the Court seems to acknowledge, is whether, notwithstanding the passage of Title VII and similar state legislation, the States continued to engage in widespread discrimination on the basis of gender in the provision of family leave benefits. . . . The evidence to substantiate this charge must be far more specific, however, than a simple recitation of a general history of employment discrimination against women. . . .

Respondents fail to make the requisite showing. . . .

As the Court seems to recognize, the evidence considered by Congress concerned discriminatory practices of the private sector, not those of state employers. . . .

. . .

The Court's reliance on evidence suggesting States provided men and women with the parenting leave of different length . . . concerns the Act's grant of parenting leave, . . . and is too attenuated to justify the family leave provision. The Court of Appeals' conclusion to the contrary was based on an assertion that "if states discriminate along gender lines regarding the one kind of leave, then they are likely to do so regarding the other." The charge that a State has engaged in a pattern of unconstitutional discrimination against its citizens is a most serious one. It must be supported by more than conjecture.

The Court maintains the evidence pertaining to the parenting leave is relevant because both parenting and family leave provisions respond to "the same gender stereotype: that women's family duties trump those of the workplace." This sets the contours of the inquiry at too high a level of abstraction. The question is not whether the family leave provision is a congruent and proportional response to general gender-based stereotypes in employment . . . ; the question is whether it is a proper remedy to an alleged pattern of unconstitutional discrimination by States in the grant of family leave. The evidence of gender-based stereotypes is too remote to support the required showing.

The Court next argues that "even where state laws and policies were not facially discriminatory, they were applied in discriminatory ways."

Even if there were evidence that individual state employers, in the absence of clear statutory guidelines, discriminated in the administration of leave benefits, this circumstance alone would not support a finding of a state-sponsored pattern of discrimination. The evidence could perhaps support the charge of disparate impact, but not a charge that States have engaged in a pattern of intentional discrimination prohibited by the Fourteenth Amendment. . . .

The federal-state equivalence upon which the Court places such emphasis is a deficient rationale at an even more fundamental level, however; for the States appear to have been ahead of Congress in providing gender-neutral family leave benefits. Thirty States, the District of Columbia, and Puerto Rico had adopted some form of family-care leave in the years preceding the Act's adoption. . . . At the very least, the history of the Act suggests States were in the process of solving any existing gender-based discrimination in the provision of family leave.

The Court acknowledges that States have adopted family leave programs prior to federal intervention, but argues these policies suffered from serious imperfections. Even if correct, this observation proves, at most, that programs more generous and more effective than those operated by the States were feasible. That the States did not devise the optimal programs is not, however, evidence that the States were perpetuating unconstitutional discrimination. Given that the States assumed a pioneering role in the creation of family leave schemes, it is not surprising these early efforts may have been imperfect. This is altogether different, however, from purposeful discrimination.

. . .

Our concern with gender discrimination, which is subjected to heightened scrutiny, as opposed to age-or disability-based distinctions, which are reviewed under rational standard, . . . does not alter this conclusion. The application of heightened scrutiny is designed to ensure gender-based classifications are not based on the entrenched and pervasive stereotypes which inhibit women's progress in the workplace. . . . Given the insufficiency of the evidence that States discriminated in the provision of family leave, the unfortunate fact that stereotypes about women continue to be a serious and pervasive social problem would not alone support the charge that a State has engaged in a practice designed to deny its citizens the equal protection of the laws.

The paucity of evidence to support the case the Court tries to make demonstrates that Congress was not responding with a congruent and proportional remedy to a perceived course of unconstitutional conduct. Instead, it enacted a substantive entitlement program of its own. If Congress had been concerned about different treatment of men and women with respect to family leave, a congruent remedy would have sought to ensure the benefits of any leave program enacted by a State are available to men and women on an equal basis. Instead, the Act imposes, across the board, a requirement that States grant a minimum of 12 weeks of leave per year. . . .

. . .

To be sure, the Nevada scheme did not track that devised by the Act in all respects. The provision of unpaid leave was discretionary and subject to a possible reporting requirement. . . . A congruent remedy to any discriminatory exercise of discretion, however, is the requirement that the grant of leave be administered on a gender-equal basis, not the displacement of the State's scheme by a federal one. The scheme enacted by the Act does not respect the States' autonomous power to design their own social benefits regime.

Were more proof needed to show that this is an entitlement program, not a remedial statute, it should suffice to note that the Act does not even purport to bar discrimination in some leave programs the States do enact and administer. Under the Act, a State is allowed to provide women with, say, 24 weeks of family leave per year but provide only 12 weeks of leave to men. As the counsel for the United States conceded during the argument, a law of this kind might run afoul of the Equal Protection Clause or Title VII, but it would not constitute a violation of the Act. The

Act on its face is not drawn as a remedy to gender-based discrimination in family leave.

. . . The dual requirement that Congress identify a pervasive pattern of unconstitutional state conduct and that its remedy be proportional and congruent to the violation is designed to separate permissible exercises of congressional power from instances where Congress seeks to enact a substantive entitlement under the guise of its § 5 authority.

The Court's precedents upholding the Voting Rights Act of 1965 as a proper exercise of Congress' remedial power are instructive. In South Carolina v. Katzenbach, 383 U.S. 301 (1966), the Court concluded that the Voting Rights Act's prohibition on state literacy tests was an appropriate method of enforcing the constitutional protection against racial discrimination in voting. This measure was justified because "Congress documented a marked pattern of unconstitutional action by the States." This scheme was both congruent, because it "aimed at areas where voting discrimination has been most flagrant," . . . and proportional, because it was necessary to "banish the blight of racial discrimination in voting, which has infected the electoral process in parts of our country for nearly a century," . . .

. . .

. . . The family leave benefit conferred by the Act is, by contrast, a substantive benefit Congress chose to confer upon state employees. . . .

. . .

Tennessee v. Lane

541 U.S. 509 (2004).

A disabled state criminal defendant who had to crawl to the second floor of a state courthouse because it was not accessible to the disabled sued Tennessee for damages under Title II of the Americans with Disabilities Act of 1990 (ADA or Act), which provides that "no qualified individual with a disability shall, by reason of such disability, be excluded from participation in or be denied the benefits of the services, programs or activities of a public entity, or be subjected to discrimination by any such entity." The Court in a 5–4 ruling found the lawsuit not to be barred by the Eleventh Amendment because Title II was, as applied to this lawsuit, a valid enactment under Section Five. As it did in *Hibbs*, the Court afforded Congress greater latitude to legislate under Section Five when Congress is protecting rights that themselves trigger heightened scrutiny; because the right to vote, serve on a jury, get married, etc., are fundamental rights—the burdening of which triggers heightened scrutiny— and because these rights are covered by Title II's protection in the realm of public "services, programs or activities," Justice Stevens' opinion for the Court found the *Boerne* test to be satisfied: "Title II, like Title I, seeks to enforce this prohibition on irrational disability discrimination. But it also seeks to enforce a variety of other basic constitutional guarantees, infringements of which are subject to more searching judicial review. . . . These rights include some, like the right of access to the courts at issue in this case, that are protected by the Due Process Clause of the Fourteenth Amendment." In a footnote, the opinion for the Court also reinforced a point implicit in *Hibbs* (but perhaps inconsistent with *Garrett*)—that the evidence of illegality on which Congress may base Section Five legislation is not limited to constitutional violations committed by state-level actors, but can include actions of nonstate government actors and even private actors.

Justice Souter, joined by Justice Ginsburg, wrote a concurrance, expressing criticism of the way *Boerne* has been applied in cases like *Garrett*. Justice Ginsburg also wrote a concurrence, joined by Justices Souter and Breyer.

Chief Justice Rehnquist wrote a dissent, joined by Justice Kennedy and Justice Thomas, in which he criticized the majority for, among other things, essentially ignoring the broad sweep of the statute, Title II, at issue: "[The majority] recounts historical discrimination against the disabled through institutionalization laws, restrictions on marriage, voting, and public education, conditions in mental hospitals, and various other forms of unequal treatment in the administration of public programs and services. Some of this evidence would be relevant if the Court were considering the constitutionality of the statute as a whole; but the Court rejects that approach in favor of a narrower "as-applied" inquiry. . . . Title II is not tailored to provide prophylactic protection of these rights; instead, it applies to any service, program, or activity provided by any entity. Its provisions affect transportation, health, education, and recreation programs, among many others, all of which are accorded only rational-basis scrutiny under the Equal Protection Clause. A requirement of accommodation for the disabled at a state-owned amusement park or sports stadium, for example, bears no permissible prophylactic relationship to enabling disabled persons to exercise their fundamental constitutional rights. . . . Viewed as a whole, then, there is little doubt that Title II of the ADA does not validly abrogate state sovereign immunity.

Justice Scalia and Justice Thomas also each wrote separate dissents.

Coleman v. Court of Appeals of Maryland

566 U.S. 30 (2012).

An employee of the Maryland court system alleged that his employer had not given him the required time to tend to his own serious medical condition, and sued for damages, under the provision of the Family and Medical Leave Act (FMLA) that requires employers to provide unpaid leave for employee self-care for a serious medical condition. By a 5–4 vote, the Court held that this provision was not validly enacted pursuant to Section Five. Writing for himself and three others, Justice Anthony Kennedy, distinguishing the part of the FMLA held to be valid under Section Five in *Hibbs*, found no pattern of gender discrimination with respect to the self-care leave provision. In the self-care leave part of the statute, he wrote, Congress was responding to the economic burdens created by illness-related job loss. Congress was, in other words, concerned with employer discrimination based on illness, not employer discrimination based on sex. Justice Kennedy noted that, at the very worst, when public employers deny self-care leave, there might be a disparate impact that hurts women more than men (because single parents tend to be women, and the self-care leave provision helps single parents a great deal). But he quickly added that any such uneven impact, unaccompanied by demonstrable malicious gender-discriminatory intent, is not a constitutional problem that gives Congress much latitude under Section Five. Justice Scalia concurred in the result, and expressed the view that Congress should be limited under Section 5 of the Fourteenth Amendment even more tightly than current doctrine permits. More specifically, Scalia opined that in most settings even "congruent and proportional" remedies are impermissible if they extend beyond the precise constitutional violations themselves. Justice Ginsburg, joined by Justices Breyer, Sotomayor and Kagan, dissented, pointing out in that Congress did have some anecdotal evidence in FMLA hearings conducted between 1986 and 1993 that some women were fired for needing self-care leave after becoming pregnant or giving birth.

Dickerson v. United States

530 U.S. 428, 120 S.Ct. 2326, 147 L.Ed.2d 405 (2000).

■ CHIEF JUSTICE REHNQUIST delivered the opinion of the Court.

In Miranda v. Arizona, 384 U.S. 436 (1966), we held that certain warnings must be given before a suspect's statement made during custodial interrogation could be admitted in evidence. In the wake of that decision, Congress enacted 18 U.S.C. § 3501, which in essence laid down a rule that the admissibility of such statements should turn only on whether or not they were voluntarily made. We hold that Miranda, being a constitutional decision of this Court, may not be in effect overruled by an Act of Congress, and we decline to overrule Miranda ourselves. We therefore hold that Miranda and its progeny in this Court govern the admissibility of statements made during custodial interrogation in both state and federal courts.

Petitioner Dickerson was indicted for bank robbery, conspiracy to commit bank robbery, and using a firearm in the course of committing a crime of violence, all in violation of the applicable provisions of Title 18 of the United States Code. Before trial, Dickerson moved to suppress a statement he had made at a Federal Bureau of Investigation field office, on the grounds that he had not received "Miranda warnings" before being interrogated. The District Court granted his motion . . . [T]he United States Court of Appeals for the Fourth Circuit . . . reversed . . . It [held] that § 3501 . . . was satisfied in this case. It then concluded that our decision in Miranda was not a constitutional holding, and that therefore Congress could by statute have the final say on the question of admissibility.

. . . [W]e . . . reverse.

. . .

In Miranda, we . . . concluded that the coercion inherent in custodial interrogation blurs the line between voluntary and involuntary statements, and thus heightens the risk that an individual will not be "accorded his privilege under the Fifth Amendment . . . not to be compelled to incriminate himself." . . . Accordingly, we laid down "concrete constitutional guidelines for law enforcement agencies and courts to follow." . . . Those guidelines established that the admissibility in evidence of any statement given during custodial interrogation of a suspect would depend on whether the police provided the suspect with four warnings. . . .

Two years after Miranda was decided, Congress enacted § 3501. That section provides, in relevant part:

"(a) In any criminal prosecution brought by the United States or by the District of Columbia, a confession . . . shall be admissible in evidence if it is voluntarily given. Before such confession is received in evidence, the trial judge shall, out of the presence of the jury, determine any issue as to voluntariness. If the trial judge determines that the confession was voluntarily made it shall be admitted in evidence and the trial judge shall permit the jury to hear relevant evidence on the issue of voluntariness and shall instruct the jury to give such weight to the confession as the jury feels it deserves under all the circumstances.

"(b) The trial judge in determining the issue of voluntariness shall take into consideration all the circumstances surrounding the giving of the confession, including (1) the time elapsing between arrest and arraignment of the defendant making the confession, if it was made after arrest and before arraignment, (2) whether such defendant knew the nature of the offense with which he was charged or of which he was suspected at the time of making the confession, (3) whether or not such defendant was advised or knew that he was not required to make any statement and that any such statement could be used against him, (4) whether or not such defendant had been advised prior to questioning of his right to the assistance of counsel; and (5) whether or not such defendant was without the assistance of counsel when questioned and when giving such confession.

"The presence or absence of any of the above-mentioned factors to be taken into consideration by the judge need not be conclusive on the issue of voluntariness of the confession."

. . . Congress intended by its enactment to overrule *Miranda*. . . . [W]e must address whether Congress has constitutional authority to thus supersede *Miranda*. If Congress has such authority, § 3501's totality-of-the-circumstances approach must prevail over *Miranda*'s requirement of warnings; if not, that section must yield to *Miranda*'s more specific requirements.

. . . This Court has supervisory authority over the federal courts, and we may use that authority to prescribe rules of evidence and procedure that are binding in those tribunals. . . . Congress retains the ultimate authority to modify or set aside any judicially created rules of evidence and procedure that are not required by the Constitution.

But Congress may not legislatively supersede our decisions interpreting and applying the Constitution. See, e.g., City of Boerne v. Flores . . . This case therefore turns on whether the *Miranda* Court announced a constitutional rule or merely exercised its supervisory authority to regulate evidence in the absence of congressional direction. . . .

. . . [F]irst and foremost of the factors . . . [supporting the conclusion] that *Miranda* is a constitutional decision—is that both *Miranda* and two of its companion cases applied the rule to proceedings in state courts . . . [W]e do not hold a supervisory power over the courts of the several States. . . . With respect to proceedings in state courts, our "authority is limited to enforcing the commands of the United States Constitution." . . .

The *Miranda* opinion itself begins by stating that the Court granted certiorari "to explore some facets of the problems . . . of applying the privilege against self-incrimination to in-custody interrogation, and to give concrete constitutional guidelines for law enforcement agencies and courts to follow.". . . . In fact, the majority opinion is replete with statements indicating that the majority thought it was announcing a constitutional rule. Indeed, the Court's ultimate conclusion was that the unwarned confessions obtained in the four cases before the Court in *Miranda* "were obtained from the defendant under circumstances that did not meet constitutional standards for protection of the privilege." . . .

Additional support for our conclusion that *Miranda* is constitutionally based is found in the *Miranda* Court's invitation for legislative action to protect the constitutional right against coerced self-incrimination. . . . [T]he *Miranda* Court concluded that, "[i]n order to combat these pressures and to permit a full opportunity to exercise the privilege against self-incrimination, the accused must be adequately and effectively appraised of his rights and the exercise of those rights must be fully honored." . . . However, the Court . . . opined that the Constitution would not preclude legislative solutions that differed from the prescribed *Miranda* warnings but which were "at least as effective in apprising accused persons of their right of silence and in assuring a continuous opportunity to exercise it.". . . .

. . .

. . . [T]he court-invited amicus curiae contends that the section complies with the requirement that a legislative alternative to *Miranda* be equally as effective in preventing coerced confessions. See Brief for Paul G. Cassell as Amicus Curiae. We agree with the amicus' contention that there are more remedies available for abusive police conduct than there were at the time *Miranda* was decided. . . . But we do not agree that these additional measures supplement § 3501's protections sufficiently to meet the constitutional minimum. *Miranda* requires procedures that will warn a suspect in custody of his right to remain silent and which will assure the suspect that the exercise of that right will be honored. . . . As discussed above, § 3501 explicitly eschews a requirement of pre-interrogation warnings in favor of an approach that looks to the administration of such warnings as only one factor in determining the voluntariness of a suspect's confession. The additional remedies cited by amicus do not, in our view, render them, together with § 3501 an adequate substitute for the warnings required by *Miranda*.

The dissent argues that it is judicial overreaching for this Court to hold § 3501 unconstitutional unless we hold that the *Miranda* warnings are required by the Constitution, in the sense that nothing else will suffice to satisfy constitutional requirements. But we need not go farther than *Miranda* to decide this case. In *Miranda*, the Court noted that reliance on the traditional totality-of-the-circumstances test raised a risk of overlooking an involuntary custodial confession, . . . , a risk that the Court found unacceptably great when the confession is offered in the case in chief to prove guilt. The Court therefore concluded that something more than the totality test was necessary. . . .

Whether or not we would agree with *Miranda*'s reasoning and its resulting rule, were we addressing the issue in the first instance, the principles of *stare decisis* weigh heavily against overruling it now. . . .

We do not think there is such justification for overruling *Miranda*. *Miranda* has become embedded in routine police practice to the point where the warnings have become part of our national culture. . . . [O]ur subsequent cases have reduced the impact of the *Miranda* rule on legitimate law enforcement while reaffirming the decision's core ruling that unwarned statements may not be used as evidence in the prosecution's case in chief.

The disadvantage of the *Miranda* rule is that statements which may be by no means involuntary, made by a defendant who is aware of his "rights," may nonetheless be excluded and a guilty defendant go free as a result. But experience suggests that the totality-of-the-circumstances test which § 3501 seeks to revive is more difficult than *Miranda* for law enforcement officers to conform to, and for courts to apply in a consistent manner. . . .

In sum, we conclude that *Miranda* announced a constitutional rule that Congress may not supersede legislatively. . . . [W]e decline to overrule *Miranda* ourselves. The judgment of the Court of Appeals is therefore

Reversed.

■ JUSTICE SCALIA, with whom JUSTICE THOMAS joins, dissenting.

. . . [T]oday's decision is not a reaffirmation of *Miranda*, but a radical revision of the most significant element of *Miranda* (as of all cases): the rationale that gives it a permanent place in our jurisprudence.

Marbury v. Madison, 1 Cranch 137 (1803), held that an Act of Congress will not be enforced by the courts if what it prescribes violates the Constitution of the United States. . . . One will search today's opinion in vain, however, for a statement . . . that what 18 U.S.C. § 3501 prescribes . . . violates the Constitution. The reason the statement does not appear is . . . that Justices whose votes are needed to compose today's majority are on record as believing that a violation of Miranda is not a violation of the Constitution. . . . And so, to justify today's agreed-upon result, the Court must adopt a significant new, if not entirely comprehensible, principle of constitutional law. As the Court chooses to describe that principle, statutes of Congress can be disregarded, not only when what they prescribe violates the Constitution, but when what they prescribe contradicts a decision of this Court that "announced a constitutional rule." . . . [T]he only thing that can possibly mean in the context of this case is that this Court has the power, not merely to apply the Constitution but to expand it, imposing what it regards as useful "prophylactic" restrictions upon Congress and the States. That is an immense and frightening antidemocratic power, and it does not exist.

. . . [The Court cannot say that] custodial interrogation that is not preceded by *Miranda* warnings or their equivalent violates the Constitution of the United States . . . because a majority of the Court does not believe it. The Court therefore acts in plain violation of the Constitution when it denies effect to this Act of Congress.

I

. . .

It was once possible to characterize the so-called *Miranda* rule as resting (however implausibly) upon the proposition that what the statute here before us permits—the admission at trial of un-Mirandized confessions—violates the Constitution. That is the fairest reading of the *Miranda* case itself. . . .

. . .

. . . [T]he decision in *Miranda*, if read as an explication of what the Constitution requires, is preposterous. There is, for example, simply no basis in reason for concluding that a response to the very first question asked, by a suspect who already knows all of the rights described in the *Miranda* warning, is anything other than a volitional act. . . . And even if one assumes that the elimination of compulsion absolutely requires informing even the most knowledgeable suspect of his right to remain silent, it cannot conceivably require the right to have counsel present. . . .

. . .

II

[S]ince *Miranda* we have explicitly, and repeatedly, interpreted that decision as having announced, not the circumstances in which custodial interrogation runs afoul of the Fifth or Fourteenth Amendment, but rather only "prophylactic" rules that go beyond the right against compelled self-incrimination. . . . The Court has squarely concluded that it is possible—indeed not uncommon—for the police to violate *Miranda* without also violating the Constitution.

. . .

. . . In light of these cases, . . . it is simply no longer possible for the Court to conclude . . . that a violation of *Miranda*'s rules is a violation of the Constitution. . . . [T]hat is what is required before the Court may disregard a law of Congress governing the admissibility of evidence in federal court. . . .

. . .

Finally, the Court asserts that *Miranda* must be a "constitutional decision" announcing a "constitutional rule," and thus immune to congressional modification, because we have since its inception applied it to the States. . . . If . . . the argument is meant as an appeal to logic rather than stare decisis, it is a classic example of begging the question . . .

III

There was available to the Court a means of reconciling the established proposition that a violation of *Miranda* does not itself offend the Fifth Amendment with the Court's assertion of a right to ignore the present statute. . . .

Petitioner and the United States contend that there is nothing at all exceptional, much less unconstitutional, about the Court's adopting prophylactic rules to buttress constitutional rights, and enforcing them against Congress and the States. . . .

. . .

. . . [W]hat the Court did in *Miranda* . . . is in fact extraordinary. That the Court has, on rare and recent occasion, repeated the mistake does not transform error into truth . . . The power with which the Court would endow itself under a "prophylactic" justification for *Miranda* goes far beyond what it has permitted Congress to do under authority of that text. Whereas we have insisted that congressional action under § 5 of the Fourteenth Amendment must be "congruent" with, and "proportional" to, a constitutional violation, see City of Boerne v. Flores, . . . the *Miranda* nontextual power to embellish confers authority to prescribe preventive measures against not only constitutionally prohibited compelled confessions, but also . . . foolhardy ones.

I applaud, therefore, the refusal of the Justices in the majority to enunciate this boundless doctrine of judicial empowerment . . . Since there is in fact no other principle that can reconcile today's judgment with the post-*Miranda* cases that the Court refuses to abandon, what today's decision will stand for . . . is the power of the Supreme Court to write a prophylactic, extraconstitutional Constitution, binding on Congress and the States.

IV

Thus, while I agree with the Court that § 3501 cannot be upheld without also concluding that *Miranda* represents an illegitimate exercise of our authority to review state-court judgments, I do not share the Court's hesitation in reaching that conclusion. . . .

. . .

Federalism and Congressional Approval of "Unconstitutional" State Laws

A number of constitutional limitations—the contract clause of Article I, Section 10, and the privileges and immunities clause of Article IV, Section 2, for example— apply only as limitations on the states. Other constitutional limitations that restrict both the national government and the states do so in different ways. Despite the "incorporation" of equal protection standards into the fifth amendment, Congress can adopt policies for the treatment of aliens that would be unconstitutional if contained in state legislation.[1] Limits on state territorial jurisdiction, such as the rules under the due process clause of the fourteenth amendment concerning the scope of in personam jurisdiction of state courts,[2] will not apply to a national government with nationwide territorial jurisdiction.

---

[1] See Mathews v. Diaz, 426 U.S. 67 (1976), supra p. 640; Hampton v. Mow Sun Wong, 426 U.S. 88 (1976); Plyler v. Doe, 457 U.S. 202 (1982), supra p. 736.

[2] The Court described the inability of a state court to bind an absent defendant as stemming from the due process clause of the fourteenth amendment in Pennoyer v. Neff, 95 U.S. (5 Otto) 714, 733–734 (1878). Even before the adoption of the fourteenth amendment, however, the Court enforced limitations on state judicial jurisdiction without tying them to any particular clause of the constitution. Commerce clause limitations on state power have sometimes been concerned with the extraterritorial impact of state laws. See Baldwin v. G.A.F. Seelig, Inc., 294 U.S. 511 (1935). Most recent cases limiting state power to tax interstate business have relied more on limits of territorial power imposed by the

In one context, it is clear beyond dispute that Congress can "consent" to state laws that would otherwise violate a constitutional limit applicable to the states, but inapplicable to the national government. By ordinary legislation, Congress can validate state laws that would be unconstitutional unreasonable burdens on interstate commerce. The traditional explanation for the power to consent has been two-fold: the limitation on state power is not express, but an implication from Congressional power to regulate interstate commerce; the limitation stems from an assumption that, if Congress is silent, it is presumed that Congress desired an unburdened interstate market.[4] Notice that those explanations are inapplicable to other constitutional limitations on state power that are express, and not merely implied from the existence of federal power. Justice Rutledge's opinion for the Court in Prudential Ins. Co. v. Benjamin, 328 U.S. 408 (1946) stated, however, that the conventional explanations "did not go to the heart of the matter," and do not explain the power of Congress to consent to state laws unreasonably burdening commerce.

Benjamin involved the McCarran-Ferguson Act of 1945, which provided that "silence on the part of the Congress shall not be construed to impose any barrier" to state regulation or taxation of insurance.[5] The Court held that the Act validated discriminatory state taxes on out-of-state insurance companies that would otherwise violate the commerce clause. Justice Rutledge's opinion explained that:

"The power of Congress over commerce exercised without reference to coordinated action of the states is not restricted . . . by any limitation which forbids it to discriminate against interstate commerce and in favor of local trade. . . . This broad authority Congress may exercise alone [subject to constitutional limits on Congress' power], or in conjunction with coordinated action by the states, in which case limitations imposed for the preservation of their powers become inoperative and only those designed to forbid action altogether by any power or combination of powers in our governmental system remain effective. . . . Clear and gross must be the evil which would nullify such an exertion, one which could arise only by exceeding . . . limitation[s] imposed by a constitutional provision or provisions designed and intended to outlaw the action entirely from our constitutional framework."

Does this mean that Congress can validate any state law, so long as Congress would have had the power to enact an identical or analogous law? For an argument along those lines, see W. Cohen, *Congressional Power to Validate Unconstitutional State Laws: A Forgotten Solution to an Old Enigma,* 35 Stan.L.Rev. 387 (1983).

In Metropolitan Life Insurance Co. v. Ward, 470 U.S. 869 (1985), the Court held that a discriminatory tax identical to that in *Benjamin,* was unconstitutional as a violation of the equal protection clause. The Court concluded that Congress had not intended to validate laws that violated the due process or equal protection clause. If Congress had specifically provided that discriminatory taxes on out-of-state insurance companies were valid as against an equal protection challenge, would this have changed the outcome in *Ward*? For an argument that it would, see W. Cohen, *Federalism in Equality Clothing: A Comment on* Metropolitan Life Insurance Company v. Ward, 38 Stan.L.Rev. 1 (1985). Compare Northeast Bancorp, Inc. v. Board of Governors of the Federal Reserve System, 472 U.S. 159 (1985).

---

due process clause of the fourteenth amendment than on the limitations imposed by the commerce clause.

[4] See Dowling, *Interstate Commerce and State Power—Revised Version,* 47 Colum.L.Rev. 547 (1947).

[5] The Act was a response to the decision in United States v. South-Eastern Underwriters Ass'n, 322 U.S. 533 (1944).

Saenz v. Roe

526 U.S. 489, 119 S.Ct. 1518, 143 L.Ed.2d 689 (1999).

[The report of this case appears *supra*, at p. 703.]

PART 4

CONSTITUTIONAL PROTECTION OF EXPRESSION AND CONSCIENCE

CHAPTER **13**   Governmental Control of the Content of Expression

CHAPTER **14**   Religion and the Constitution

Chapter 13 is an introduction to issues of freedom of expression. It examines the definition of constitutionally protected speech, and focuses on doctrine dealing with laws punishing expression because of its content. It also deals with government restriction that purports to control the time, place, or manner of speaking rather than its content. The protection of religious conscience and conduct is reserved for Chapter 14, which introduces the sometimes conflicting demands of the Free Exercise and Establishment Clauses.

CHAPTER 13

GOVERNMENTAL CONTROL OF THE CONTENT OF EXPRESSION

Introduction. This chapter focuses on the core problem in defining the contours of freedom of expression—the extent to which speech can be punished by government because of its content. Section 1 deals at length with speech advocating the violent overthrow of government. Section 2 is a deliberate digression, examining judicial techniques for avoiding decision whether speech can be controlled because of its content. This section examines the doctrine of prior restraint, and the doctrines of vagueness and overbreadth. Section 3 returns to the problem of content control, examining the Court's efforts to draw the distinction between protected and unprotected speech in four different contexts—defamation and privacy, obscenity, fighting words and offensive speech, and commercial speech.

1. AN INTRODUCTION TO PROBLEMS OF CONTENT CONTROL OF SPEECH

A. HISTORICAL INTRODUCTION—THE STATUS OF FREE SPEECH UP TO THE 1920'S

1. THE ENGLISH BACKGROUND

Freedom of thought and expression is taken so much as a matter of course in most western societies today that we are apt to forget how recently it has come to be accepted. As the distinguished English historian, J.B. Bury, emphasized in *A History of Freedom of Thought* (1913), "human societies (there are some brilliant exceptions) have been generally opposed to freedom of thought" and "it has taken centuries to persuade the most enlightened peoples that liberty to publish one's opinions and to discuss all questions is a good and not a bad thing" (Home University Library Ed., 1952, p. 2). This is due in part to the persistent inclination of people to cling to familiar and accepted opinion, and to dislike what is new, but other reasons are not difficult to discover.

Both the society and outlook of the Middle Ages were authoritarian; truth was divinely revealed and error was sin. Consequently, to extirpate erroneous views was not only permissible but a high moral obligation, and the unifying structure of the medieval Church provided the central authority for determining what was true and what was false. Thus the churchmen who in 1633 condemned Galileo to live the rest of his life in seclusion because he insisted that the earth was not the stationary center of the universe were only performing their duty as determined by the standards under which they had lived.[1]

Even after the impact of the Renaissance and Reformation, the rebirth of learning, and the development of nation-states, the modern concept of freedom of thought was slow to develop. Diversity replaced the unity of the Middle Ages, and the

---

[1] This incident is told in detail in De Santillana, *The Crime of Galileo* (1955).

invention of the printing press brought a new and previously unequaled medium of communication. But on the whole the dissenters and reformers sought only to establish a new brand of truth (their own) and did not recognize the value of general freedom of thought and speech as the means of arriving at truth.

The three centuries that elapsed between the appearance of the first book printed in England, by Caxton in 1476, and the Declaration of Independence in 1776 provide the immediate background of the American constitutional system, and the struggles of this period are particularly relevant in the area of freedom of thought and expression. They concerned two issues above all others, the separation of the English Church from that of Rome and the limitation of the prerogative of the Crown. Neither of these developments assured the freedom of the individual, but supplanted one religious establishment with another and made parliament supreme in areas that theretofore had been the province of the King. Dispute and domestic turmoil fomented discussion, as they always do, but the very limited freedom permitted to thought and speech is shown by the position of the press.

The invention of printing was almost as frightening to the mind of the fifteenth century as the discovery of atomic fission to the mind of the twentieth. The printing press, unless rigidly controlled, gave to dissident groups a powerful medium for "dangerous doctrine." No friend of the established order could view this situation with complacency at a time when religious truth, then an all-consuming subject, was deemed a matter of prior revelation, and when political controversy was entering the crisis of the life-and-death struggle between King and Parliament. Three instruments for the legal control of discussion were used: (1) the concept of constructive treason; (2) the doctrine of seditious libel; and (3) the domination of the press through state monopoly and licensing.

The law of treason was based on the Statute 25 Edward III (1351), which defined the crime to include (1) compassing or imagining the King's death, (2) levying war against the King, or (3) adhering to his enemies. These three clauses, strictly construed, did not offer complete protection for the security of the monarch and of the state, or so it was believed. Hence there arose in the seventeenth century that judicial extension of the statute known as constructive treason. Compassing or imagining the King's death, like intending to wage war against him, being a mental state, could be proved only by overt acts. During the latter part of the seventeenth century the judges ruled that printed and sometimes spoken words could constitute overt acts. Thus John Twyn was convicted of treason and hanged, drawn, and quartered in 1664 for printing a book asserting that the King was accountable to the people, who were entitled to revolt and take the government into their own hands.[2]

Prosecutions for constructive treason were rare, however: only two printers were executed for the crime during the seventeenth century and one during the eighteenth.[3] A more effective method of suppression—the law of seditious libel—was used in hundreds of convictions. Conviction for this crime did not bring death, but the penalties were often severe, including indefinite imprisonment and heavy fines. The law of seditious libel was developed in prosecutions before the Court of Star Chamber in the late sixteenth century, and when that body was abolished in 1641, the rules were taken over by the common law courts. The original theory of the offense was that the King was the fountainhead of justice and law whose acts were beyond popular criticism and that consequently it was wrong to censure him openly.[4] This doctrine

---

[2]   This and similar cases are recounted in Siebert, *Freedom of the Press in England,* 1476–1776 (1952), p. 267.

[3]   Siebert, op. cit., p. 365.

[4]   Stephen, *History of Criminal Law in England* (1883) Vol. II, p. 299.

was carried to such lengths that any reflection on the government in written or printed form might be held seditious libel. In 1704 Chief Justice Holt declared: "If people should not be called to account for possessing the people with an ill opinion of the government, no government can subsist. For it is very necessary for all governments that the people should have a good opinion of it. And nothing can be worse to any government than to endeavour to procure animosities as to the management of it; this has always been looked upon as a crime, and no government can be safe without it."[5]

As the eighteenth century progressed, juries became less inclined to reach guilty verdicts in seditious libel cases. The judges then took the position that truth was no defense and that the only issue to be submitted to the jury was whether or not the defendant had published the allegedly seditious statements. Whether or not the statements constituted a libel was a matter of law to be determined by the judge. This trend was strenuously opposed by the distinguished English barrister Thomas Erskine, among others, who contended that the jury should be asked to bring in a general verdict of guilty or not guilty and to determine the defendant's criminal intent as in other criminal cases. The final result of this struggle was the passage in 1792 of Fox's Libel Act, which established Erskine's views and gave the jury the power to render a general verdict on the whole issue in a libel case rather than merely on the issue of publication.

The French revolution brought a flurry of seditious libel cases, including the prosecution of Thomas Paine in 1792 for the publication of his "Rights of Man," but these prosecutions and the enactment of Fox's Libel Act marked the end of seditious libel as an instrument for the suppression of free speech in England.[6]

The third method of controlling expression of opinion, and on the whole the most effective one, was the elaborate system of printing monopolies and licensing. The Crown claimed authority to regulate the printing press in England as one of its prerogative rights until the supremacy of Parliament was established by the revolution of 1688. Beginning with Henry VIII (1509–1547), the press was held in check through royal proclamations, licenses, patents of monopoly, orders in Council, and Star Chamber decrees. The first English index of prohibited "heretical and blasphemous" books was created by royal proclamation in 1529 and a licensing system for all books was established in 1538 by a proclamation designed to stamp out "seditious opinions," as well as heretical views. Licensors were appointed, and no book could lawfully be printed and distributed without their prior approval. The system was modified and extended by the charter granted the Stationers Company in 1557. Members of the Company were given extensive control over the press by the provision of the Charter prohibiting all printing within the realm except by members of the Company or by those having special license from the Crown. The Company enforced both its own licensing ordinances and those issued by the Crown; all member printers were required to obtain a license from the officers of the Company before printing any works, and all presses were required to be registered with the Company.

The seventeenth century brought great changes to England in the form of the Puritan Revolution, the Commonwealth, and the triumph of Parliament through the revolution of 1688, but it did not bring freedom of the press, although eloquent voices, such as John Milton's,[7] were raised in its behalf. The licensing and other controls

---

[5]   Rex v. Tutchin, 14 *State Trials,* p. 1095, quoted in Siebert, op. cit., p. 271.

[6]   The efforts of Thomas Erskine on behalf of liberalism in eighteenth century England, including his defense of Thomas Paine, are told in Lloyd Paul Stryker's biography of Erskine, *For the Defense* (1947).

[7]   Milton had difficulties with the Stationers Company and the authorities over the publication of his pamphlets on divorce. He made his reply in Areopagitica (1644), which was a plea for the abolition of the licensing system. See Siebert, op. cit., p. 195. Milton's argument for freedom of the press cannot

became less effective during this century, but the principal change was the shift in power from the Crown to Parliament. The objection of the Puritans to the control of the press was not so much to the control as to the fact that it was exercised by the King. With the fall of Charles I (1649), power passed to Parliament, and after the struggles of the Commonwealth (1649–1653), the Protectorate (1653–1659), and the Stuart restoration (1660–1689), the supremacy of Parliament was confirmed by the Revolution of 1688 and the Bill of Rights of 1689. However, that great document of English constitutional development did not contain any statement espousing general freedom of speech or the press. Its only provision on the subject merely stated: "That the freedom of speech and debates or proceedings in parliament ought not to be impeached or questioned in any court or place out of parliament". It was freedom of speech *in* Parliament, *not outside,* that was recognized.

The control of the press exercised by Parliament gradually relaxed during the century following the Bill of Rights. At the end of the seventeenth century the power of the Stationers Company was broken by the refusal of Parliament to continue its monopolies and special privileges. The methods of control then shifted from licensing to subsidization and taxation. The government resorted to subsidization in order to promote the opinion it desired; such literary figures as Defoe, Swift, Addison, Steele, and Fielding all engaged in political pamphleteering or journalism for which they were compensated in one form or another by the government or political leaders. In 1712, newspapers, pamphlets, advertisements, and paper were subjected to taxes that had the effect of suppressing many of the smaller ephemeral publications then sniping at the policies of the government. That this was the purpose of the taxes is suggested by the fact that books were exempted. These taxes were continued with varying degrees of effectiveness until the first half of the nineteenth century.

It was in the light of this background that Blackstone discussed freedom of thought and expression in his Commentaries, first published in 1765. It is important to note that he wrote at a time when licensing had been abandoned but the law of seditious libel was still in full vigor. His comments are as follows:

"The liberty of the press is indeed essential to the nature of a free state; but this consists in laying no *previous* restraints upon publications, and not in freedom from censure for criminal matter when published. Every freeman has an undoubted right to lay what sentiments he pleases before the public: to forbid this, is to destroy the freedom of the press; but if he publishes what is improper, mischievous, or illegal, he must take the consequence of his own temerity. To subject the press to the restrictive power of a licenser, as was formerly done, both before and since the revolution, is to subject all freedom of sentiment to the prejudices of one man, and make him the arbitrary and infallible judge of all controverted points in learning, religion, and government. But to punish (as the law does at present) any dangerous or offensive writings, which, when published, shall on a fair and impartial trial be adjudged of a pernicious tendency, is necessary for the preservation of peace and good order, of government and religion, the only solid foundations of civil liberty. Thus the will of

---

be given here, but the following sentences deserve quotation: "Where there is much desire to learn, there of necessity will be much arguing, much writing, many opinions; for opinion in good men is but knowledge in the making. . . . And though all the winds of doctrine were let loose to play upon the earth, so Truth be in the field we do injuriously, by licensing and prohibiting, to misdoubt her strength. Let her and Falsehood grapple; whoever knew Truth put to the worse, in a free and open encounter? Her confuting is the best and surest suppressing. . . ." Apparently Milton had reservations about complete freedom of expression, however, for he also said he would not tolerate "popery and open superstition."? Furthermore that "which is impious or evil absolutely either against faith or manners no law can possibly permit, that intends not to unlaw itself. . . ." *The Tradition of Freedom* (Mayer ed. 1957) pp. 26, 28, 29.

individuals is still left free; the abuse only of that free will is the object of legal punishment. Neither is any restraint hereby laid upon freedom of thought or inquiry: liberty of private sentiment is still left; the disseminating, or making public, of bad sentiments, destructive of the ends of society, is the crime which society corrects." (*Commentaries,* Book IV, pp. 151–152.)[8]

2.   THE ADOPTION OF THE FIRST AMENDMENT AND THE CONTROVERSY OVER THE ALIEN AND SEDITION LAWS

(1)   The original intent. Scholars have not been able to agree as to the purpose intended to be served by the first amendment. The basic question is whether it was intended as a charter of freedom or as no more than a determination that regulation of speech and press according to common law principles should be reserved to the states. The most recent scholarship supports the latter position. Leonard Levy concludes, for example, that the amendment was intended only as a restraint on Congress and not on the courts in enforcing the common law crime of seditious libel and "that the prohibition on Congress was motivated far less by a desire to give immunity to political expression than by a solicitude for states' rights and the federal principle. The primary purpose of the first amendment was to reserve to the states an exclusive authority, as far as legislation was concerned, in the field of speech and press." *Freedom of Press from Zenger v. Jefferson* lix (1966).[1] For a different view, see Brant, *The Bill of Rights* 223–236 (1965).

(2)   The Sedition Act. In 1798, the Sedition Act (part of a package known as the Alien and Sedition Laws) made it a crime carrying imprisonment up to two years to write, utter, or publish "any false, scandalous and malicious writing . . . against the government of the United States, or either house of the congress . . . or the President . . . with intent to defame [them] . . . or to bring them . . . into contempt or disrepute; or to excite against them . . . the hatred of the good people of the United States, or to stir up sedition within the United States, or to excite any unlawful combinations therein, for opposing or resisting any law of the United States, or any act of the President of the United States, done in pursuance of any such law, or of the powers vested in him by the constitution of the United States, or to resist, oppose, or defeat any such law or act. . . ." The Act also provided that truth could be offered in defense and that the jury "shall have a right to determine the law and the fact, under the direction of the court, as in other cases." 1 Stat. 596 (1798).

The Sedition Act became the center of an enormous political controversy. Much attention was paid to the question whether it violated the first amendment. Levy contends that in this controversy there was a sudden breakthrough in libertarian thought with the Jeffersonian Republicans abandoning common law notions, arguing that free government required freedom of discussion, and asserting that only injurious conduct as manifested by deeds rather than words should be subjected to criminal punishment. *Freedom of the Press from Zenger to Jefferson* lxx–lxxix (1966).[2]

---

[8]   For a general review of the English background of our Bill of Rights, see Brant, *The Bill of Rights,* 3–219 (1965). See also Chafee, *How Human Rights Got into the Constitution* (1952) and *Three Human Rights in the Constitution of 1787* (1956). For a convenient collection of the documentary sources, see Perry and Cooper, *Sources of our Liberties* (1959).

[1]   Professor Levy in *Legacy of Suppression* (1960) reviews freedom of expression in early American history and concludes that in colonial America the people did not understand that freedom of thought means equal freedom for others, especially those with hated ideas.

[2]   More recently another author contends that the opposition to the Sedition Act was founded primarily on notions of states' rights rather than civil liberties with a primary motivation being the preservation of slavery. Berns, *Freedom of the Press and the Alien and Sedition Laws: A Reappraisal,*

The Sedition Act by its own terms was to be in force only until March 3, 1801. One of Jefferson's first acts as President was to pardon all persons convicted under the act. Jefferson's own view of the first amendment, however, seemed to be one of federalism rather than freedom—at least in his role as President subject to scurrilous attacks in opposition newspapers. In 1803 he wrote a letter to Governor McKean of Pennsylvania referring to the licentiousness and lying of the press and then asserting: "This is a dangerous state of things, and the press ought to be restored to its credibility if possible. The restraints provided by the laws of the states are sufficient for this if applied. And I have therefore long thought that a few prosecutions of the most prominent offenders would have a wholesome effect in restoring the integrity of the presses. Not a general prosecution, for that would look like persecution: but a selected one. The paper I now inclose appears to me to offer as good an instance in every respect to make an example of, as can be selected."[3]

In 1806 a common law prosecution of Connecticut editors for libel of President Jefferson and the Congress was brought in the federal courts. That avenue for controlling the press was eliminated by the Supreme Court on appeal from the conviction in that case—not because the prosecution violated the first amendment, but rather on the general proposition that federal courts had no common law criminal jurisdiction. *United States v. Hudson* and *Goodwin*, 11 U.S. (7 Cranch) 32 (1812).[4]

3. FREEDOM OF SPEECH AND PRESS IN THE NINETEENTH CENTURY

(1) Introduction. The Supreme Court did not begin to elaborate the protection accorded by the first amendment until the time of World War I. One should not draw from that fact the conclusion that there were no intrusions on freedom of speech and the press during this period of time. Developments in the states were unaffected by the first amendment. It was not until 1925 that the Court indicated that the fourteenth amendment had made the first applicable to the states. But there were episodes involving federal control, particularly of the press, that were not subjected to testing by the Supreme Court.[1]

(2) Punishment for contempt of court. Under the Judiciary Act of 1789, which authorized federal courts to punish "all contempts of authority in any cause or hearing" before them, federal courts early asserted the authority to punish newspapers and others who criticized court decisions. In one early case a federal district judge, James H. Peck, had one Lawless imprisoned and disbarred for publishing a criticism of a decision by Peck that was on appeal. Lawless had powerful political friends and as a result impeachment proceedings were brought against Judge Peck. Peck was acquitted but immediately thereafter Congress amended the statute to limit the contempt power to "misbehaviour of any person or persons in the presence of the said courts, or so near thereto as to obstruct the administration of justice." The story of this episode is told in *Nye v. United States*, 313 U.S. 33, 45 (1941). As a result of the change in the statute the federal courts for a long time did not assert the power to punish critics. (State

---

1970 Sup.Ct.Rev. 109. For a general historical introduction to this episode, see Stone, *Perilous Times: Free Speech in Wartime From the Sedition Act of 1798 to the War on Terrorism* 33–73 (2004).

    3   The letter is set out in Levy, *Freedom of the Press from Zenger to Jefferson* 364 (1966). In a letter to Abigail Adams in 1804 he also said: "While we deny that Congress have a right to control the freedom of the press, we have ever asserted the right of the States, and their exclusive right, to do so." Id. at 366, 367.

    4   For the story of the case and Jefferson's somewhat belated disapproval of the prosecution, see Levy, *Jefferson and Civil Liberties—The Darker Side* 61 (1963).

    1   For an excellent brief general account of this period see Nelson, *Freedom of the Press from Hamilton to the Warren Court* xix–xxxvii (1967).

courts, however, began increasingly to use contempt to punish comments outside the court on the ground that they tended to interfere with the administration of justice.) In 1918 in Toledo Newspaper Co. v. United States, 247 U.S. 402 (1918), the Supreme Court interpreted the federal statute as not applying a geographical limitation on the contempt power of the federal courts and said that the test under the statute was "the character of the act done and its direct tendency to prevent and obstruct the discharge of judicial duty." The Court also rejected the claim that freedom of the press was violated when contempt was used to punish under this test. To state that proposition was to answer it, the Court said, "since it involves in its very statement the contention that the freedom of the press is the freedom to do wrong with impunity, and implies the right to frustrate and defeat the discharge of those governmental duties upon the performance of which the freedom of all, including that of the press, depends." By 1928 the judicial use of the contempt power to punish the press was widespread, with most of the cases involving comments impugning the fairness, independence, or integrity of the judge.[2]

(3) Control of public discussion of the slavery question. Antislavery speech was regarded in the South as presenting a very real danger to the institution of slavery. While local dissenters were easily dealt with, the South also sought to exclude from the South any antislavery publications. In 1835 President Jackson asked Congress to enact a law prohibiting the circulation in the South through the mails "of incendiary publications intended to instigate the slaves to insurrection." Calhoun opposed this as a violation of freedom of the press, as being similar to the Sedition Act, but then he proposed a statute making it unlawful for a postmaster to receive and put into the mail any paper "touching the subject of slavery" and addressed to any person in a state which forbade by law the circulation of such materials. Neither of these bills passed, but in practice postmasters in the South responded to local pressures and refused to deliver antislavery materials. By 1863 the Postmaster General was asserting the power—not challenged for a long time—to remove from the mails or prevent delivery of anti-Union writings or material considered to be obscene. This restraint on discussion of slavery carried over into Congress, in which the House by a series of gag rules refused from 1836 to 1845 to entertain or to discuss any petition relating to slavery.[3]

(4) The Civil War. During the war there existed both a substantial amount of press freedom and a substantial amount of suppression by the military and the President. In one case President Lincoln went so far as to suppress newspapers and order trials of the publishers before military tribunals. For the documents in that case see Nelson, supra note 1, at 232–247. For a fuller account of the relationships between Lincoln and the press, see Randall, *Constitutional Problems Under Lincoln* 477–510 (1951).

(5) Obscenity, and control of the mails. In 1873 Congress passed the "Comstock law" providing for punishment of those who used the mails to transport obscene materials. State and federal prosecutions for obscenity reached new highs after the turn of the century.[4]

---

[2] For an account of the times, see Nelles & King, *Contempt by Publication in the United States,* 28 Colum.L.Rev. 401, 524 (1928).

[3] For a fuller treatment of these episodes, see Berns, *Freedom of the Press and the Alien and Sedition Laws: A Reappraisal,* 1970, Sup.Ct.Rev. 109, 142, 150; Nelson, *Freedom of the Press from Hamilton to the Warren Court* xxii–xxvi (1967); Miller, *Arguing About Slavery: The Great Battle in the United States Congress* (1995).

[4] See generally on this period, Nelson, *Freedom of the Press from Hamilton to the Warren Court* xxviii–xxxii (1967). For an account of postal censorship see Deutsch, *The Freedom of the Press and of the Mails,* 36 Mich.L.Rev. 703 (1938).

(6) Civil and criminal libel under state law. Even if the Sedition Act controversy were viewed as excluding federal libel laws, states remained free of federal constitutional restraint. As late as 1922, the Supreme Court maintained that "neither the Fourteenth Amendment nor any other provision of the Constitution of the United States imposes upon the States any restrictions about 'freedom of speech'. . . ." Prudential Ins. Co. v. Cheek, 259 U.S. 530, 543 (1922). While decisional law established truth as a complete defense in civil libel cases, the press was subject to practically strict liability for statements that were innocently false. Criminal libel laws often provided only a qualified defense of truth. Prosecutions for criminal libel in the state courts increased sharply in the later 1800's and stayed high through World War I. In 1918, a law review author could still assert:

"There is no such thing as an unlimited right to print whatever one may choose to print, regardless of its character and effect. Without law there can be no liberty, and freedom of the press does not mean irresponsibility for what is printed. All right-thinking men will join with Alexander Hamilton in his reprobation of 'the pestilential doctrine of an unchecked press,' and agree with him that ill-fated would be our country were this doctrine to prevail.

"It is for the state to say what publications are harmful, what use of the press is permissible. It would be an act of tyranny under normal conditions to deprive a citizen of the right to own a gun, but it is essential to public safety to prevent him from using it to the injury of others. So it is with the printing press, an instrument not less dangerous than a shot gun. It is not tyrannous nor inconsistent with the freedom of the press that its owner should be held accountable for any improper use he may make of it."[5]

B. WORLD WAR I AND THE POST-WAR YEARS: PENALIZING THE ADVOCACY OF THE OVERTHROW OF GOVERNMENT BY FORCE OR VIOLENCE

The Concern for Radical Speech in the First Quarter of the Twentieth Century

In the early years, principal free speech and press disputes had involved the role of newspapers and periodicals—typically those of a different political persuasion than the party in power—in acting as critics of government. A rising concern with radicals began to surface at the turn of the century. Following President McKinley's assassination, the New York Criminal Anarchy law, which became a model for later state and federal legislation, made it a crime to belong to an organization that taught the doctrine that government should be overthrown by force of violence. The Immigration Act of 1903 provided that persons who believed in or advocated the overthrow of government by force and violence should be barred from entering the country, or deported if already here.

The fear of radicals was brought to a head, and fused with concern over enemy sympathizers, by the country's entry into the First World War.

In 1917 Congress passed the Espionage Act. This act made it a crime when the country was at war to "willfully make or convey false reports or false statements with intent to interfere" with the prosecution of the war or to promote the success of enemies, or willfully to "cause or attempt to cause" insubordination, disloyalty, mutiny, or refusal of duty, in the military or naval forces of the United States, or

---

[5] Long, *The Freedom of the Press,* 5 Va.L.Rev. 225, 228, 229 (1918).

willfully to "obstruct the recruiting or enlistment service of the United States." Another provision of the act forbade the mailing of any material in violation of the provisions of the act or "advocating or urging treason, insurrection, or forcible resistance to any law of the United States. . . ." In 1918 the statute was amended to make criminal the utterance of language "intended to bring the form of government of the United States into contempt, scorn, contumely, or disrepute." This 1918 version of the Sedition Act was repealed in 1921. There were nearly 2,000 prosecutions under the 1917 and 1918 Acts, many publications were excluded from the mails, and a series of challenges under the first amendment came quickly to the Supreme Court.[1]

The antiradical sentiment of the war years became more intense after the war ended. The country was plagued by rumors of radical takeover of government. There was labor unrest, and the news featured incidents of riots and bombings. Radical leaders were prosecuted under state laws modeled after the 1902 New York Criminal Anarchy Law. Some of these cases, too, reached the Supreme Court and renewed the judicial debate concerning the meaning of free speech in the context of attempts to punish the advocates of radical doctrines.[2]

Masses Publishing Co. v. Patten
244 Fed. 535 (S.D.N.Y.1917).

The publisher of a revolutionary journal called "The Masses" brought suit to enjoin the postmaster of New York from refusing to accept the magazine in the mails. The postmaster argued that the magazine was nonmailable under the provision of the espionage act making nonmailable any publication that violated the other provisions of the act. Part of the focus here was on the provisions of the act penalizing the willful causing of disaffection in the military services and the willful obstruction of recruitment. On these points Judge Learned Hand construed the statute[3] as follows:

"The next phrase relied upon is that which forbids any one from willfully causing insubordination, disloyalty, mutiny, or refusal of duty in the military or naval forces of the United States. The defendant's position is that to arouse discontent and disaffection among the people with the prosecution of the war and with the draft tends to promote a mutinous and insubordinate temper among the troops. This, too, is true; men who become satisfied that they are engaged in an enterprise dictated by the unconscionable selfishness of the rich, and effectuated by a tyrannous disregard for the will of those who must suffer and die, will be more prone to insubordination than those who have faith in the cause and acquiesce in the means. Yet to interpret the word 'cause' so broadly would, as before, involve necessarily as a consequence the suppression of all hostile criticism, and of all opinion except what encouraged and supported the existing policies, or which fell within the range of temperate argument. It would contradict the normal assumption of democratic government that the suppression of hostile criticism does not turn upon the justice of its substance or the decency and propriety of its temper. Assuming that the power to repress such opinion may rest in Congress in the throes of a struggle for the very existence of the state, its exercise is so contrary to the use and wont of our people that only the clearest expression of such a power justifies the conclusion that it was intended.

---

[1]   See generally Chafee, *Freedom of Speech* (1920) for an account of the period.

[2]   For a review of the cases from *Schenck* to *Whitney,* see Cover, *The Left, The Right and the First Amendment,* 40 Md.L.Rev. 349 (1981).

[3]   Hand's grant of an injunction, based on that construction, was reversed by the Court of Appeals. 246 Fed. 24 (2d Cir.1917).

"The defendant's position, therefore, in so far as it involves the suppression of the free utterance of abuse and criticism of the existing law, or of the policies of the war, is not, in my judgment, supported by the language of the statute. Yet there has always been a recognized limit to such expressions, incident indeed to the existence of any compulsive power of the state itself. One may not counsel or advise others to violate the law as it stands. Words are not only the keys of persuasion, but the triggers of action, and those which have no purport but to counsel the violation of law cannot by any latitude of interpretation be a part of that public opinion which is the final source of government in a democratic state. The defendant asserts not only that the magazine indirectly through its propaganda leads to a disintegration of loyalty and a disobedience of law, but that in addition it counsels and advises resistance to existing law, especially to the draft. The consideration of this aspect of the case more properly arises under the third phrase of section 3, which forbids any willful obstruction of the recruiting or enlistment service of the United States, but, as the defendant urges that the magazine falls within each phrase, it is as well to take it up now. To counsel or advise a man to an act is to urge upon him either that it is his interest or his duty to do it. While, of course, this may be accomplished as well by indirection as expressly, since words carry the meaning that they impart, the definition is exhaustive, I think, and I shall use it. Political agitation, by the passions it arouses or the convictions it engenders, may in fact stimulate men to the violation of law. Detestation of existing policies is easily transformed into forcible resistance of the authority which puts them in execution, and it would be folly to disregard the causal relation between the two. Yet to assimilate agitation, legitimate as such, with direct incitement to violent resistance, is to disregard the tolerance of all methods of political agitation which in normal times is a safeguard of free government. The distinction is not a scholastic subterfuge, but a hard-bought acquisition in the fight for freedom, and the purpose to disregard it must be evident when the power exists. If one stops short of urging upon others that it is their duty or their interest to resist the law, it seems to me one should not be held to have attempted to cause its violation. If that be not the test, I can see no escape from the conclusion that under this section every political agitation which can be shown to be apt to create a seditious temper is illegal. I am confident that by such language Congress had no such revolutionary purpose in view.

"It seems to me, however, quite plain that none of the language and none of the cartoons in this paper can be thought directly to counsel or advise insubordination or mutiny, without a violation of their meaning quite beyond any tolerable understanding. I come, therefore, to the third phrase of the section, which forbids any one from willfully obstructing the recruiting or enlistment service of the United States. I am not prepared to assent to the plaintiff's position that this only refers to acts other than words, nor that the act thus defined must be shown to have been successful. One may obstruct without preventing, and the mere obstruction is an injury to the service; for it throws impediments in its way. Here again, however, since the question is of the expression of opinion, I construe the sentence, so far as it restrains public utterance, as I have construed the other two, and as therefore limited to the direct advocacy of resistance to the recruiting and enlistment service. If so, the inquiry is narrowed to the question whether any of the challenged matter may be said to advocate resistance to the draft, taking the meaning of the words with the utmost latitude which they can bear."

Schenck v. United States

249 U.S. 47 (1919).

Section 3 of title I of the Espionage Act of 1917 established three offenses: "[1] whoever, when the United States is at war, shall willfully make or convey false reports or false statements with intent to interfere with the operation or success of the military or naval forces of the United States or to promote the success of its enemies and [2] whoever, when the United States is at war, shall willfully cause or attempt to cause insubordination, disloyalty, mutiny, or refusal of duty, in the military or naval forces of the United States, or [3] shall willfully obstruct the recruiting or enlistment service of the United States, to the injury of the service or of the United States, shall be punished by a fine of not more than $10,000 or imprisonment for not more than twenty years, or both."[a] Section 4 of the same title punished persons conspiring to violate section 3, if any one of them did any act to effect the object of the conspiracy. Schenck and the other defendants were indicted and convicted of a conspiracy to violate section 3, by sending to drafted men, circulars calculated to cause insubordination in the armed services and to obstruct the recruiting and enlistment service of the United States. The circulars asserted that conscription violated the idea of the thirteenth amendment and was despotism in the interest of Wall Street's chosen few. Although the message "in form at least confined itself to peaceful measures," it urged the conscript not to "submit to intimidation" and denied the power of the government to send citizens abroad to shoot persons of other lands. Defendant did not deny that the tendency of the circulars was to influence persons to obstruct the draft, but contended that any such tendency was protected by the first amendment.

Justice Holmes' unanimous opinion for the Supreme Court contains the following statement:

"We admit that in many places and in ordinary times the defendants in saying all that was said in the circular would have been within their constitutional rights. But the character of every act depends upon the circumstances in which it is done. . . . The most stringent protection of free speech would not protect a man in falsely shouting fire in a theatre and causing a panic. It does not even protect a man from an injunction against uttering words that may have all the effect of force. . . . The question in every case is whether the words used are used in such circumstances and are of such a nature as to create a clear and present danger that they will bring about the substantive evils that Congress has a right to prevent. It is a question of proximity and degree. When a nation is at war many things that might be said in time of peace are such a hindrance to its effort that their utterance will not be endured so long as men fight and that no Court could regard them as protected by any constitutional right. It seems to be admitted that if an actual obstruction of the recruiting service were proved, liability for words that produced that effect might be enforced. The statute of 1917 in § 4 punishes conspiracies to obstruct as well as actual obstruction. If the act, (speaking, or circulating a paper) its tendency and the intent with which it is done are the same, we perceive no ground for saying that success alone warrants making the act a crime."

The convictions were affirmed.[b]

---

[a]   40 Stat. 219, which became 50 U.S.C. § 33, repealed June 25, 1948 when the present United States Code was enacted. The numbers have been inserted to indicate the different clauses of the provision.

[b]   One week later, on the authority of the *Schenck* decision, the Court sustained the conviction of a prominent socialist, Eugene V. Debs, under the same statute. In the course of a general address on socialism and opposition to the war, Debs praised draft resisters and stated: "You need to know that you are fit for something better than slavery and cannon fodder." Debs' 10 year sentence was affirmed because the jury could find that his remarks had a tendency to obstruct recruiting, and Debs had that intent. Justice Holmes stated that, even if the tendency of the speech and Debs' intent were incidental to Debs' main point in his speech—opposition to the war—his speech was not "protected by reason of its being part of a general program and expressions of a general and conscientious belief." Debs v. United States, 249 U.S. 211, 215 (1919).

Abrams v. United States

250 U.S. 616 (1919).

The 1918 amendment to the Espionage Act made criminal uttering, printing, writing, or publishing any disloyal, profane, scurrilous or abusive language or language intended to cause contempt, scorn, contumely or disrepute as regards the form of government of the United States; any language intended to incite resistance to the United States or promote the cause of its enemies; or any language urging curtailment of production of any things necessary to the prosecution of war with intent to hinder such prosecution. Abrams and his fellow defendants were indicted and convicted of conspiring to violate these provisions of the 1918 amendment, in that they printed and distributed some 5000 circulars in New York City on about August 22, 1918, which circulars were intended to bring the form of government of the United States into contempt; to encourage resistance to the United States in World War I; and to incite curtailment of war production. In the circulars, President Wilson was denounced as a hypocrite and a coward for sending troops into Russia to support the Anti-Bolshevik forces; the workers of the world were urged to awake and put down the common enemy—capitalism; the general strike was advocated as the necessary reply to the "barbaric intervention" in Russia; and the toilers of America were to pledge themselves "to create so great a disturbance that the autocrats of America shall be compelled to keep their armies at home, and not be able to spare any for Russia."

The majority concluded that any question regarding the constitutionality of the Espionage Act as a whole had been disposed of by *Schenck* and related cases, leaving, as the major issue, the sufficiency of the evidence to sustain the guilty verdict. They held that it had been proved that the defendants published their circulars with intent to encourage resistance to the war with Germany and to incite curtailment of war production.[a]

Justice Holmes, joined by Justice Brandeis, wrote a dissenting opinion in which he concluded that the circulars did not show the requisite intent to provoke resistance to the war with Germany or to curtail production in order to cripple the war effort. The opinion concludes with the following paragraphs.

"In this case sentences of twenty years imprisonment have been imposed for the publishing of two leaflets that I believe the defendants had as much right to publish as the Government has to publish the Constitution of the United States now vainly invoked by them. Even if I am technically wrong and enough can be squeezed from these poor and puny anonymities to turn the color of legal litmus paper; I will add, even if what I think the necessary intent were shown; the most nominal punishment seems to me all that possibly could be inflicted, unless the defendants are to be made to suffer not for what the indictment alleges but for the creed that they avow—a creed that I believe to be the creed of ignorance and immaturity when honestly held, as I see no reason to doubt that it was held here, but which, although made the subject of examination at the trial, no one has a right even to consider in dealing with the charges before the Court.

"Persecution for the expression of opinions seems to me perfectly logical. If you have no doubt of your premises or your power and want a certain result with all your heart you naturally express your wishes in law and sweep away all opposition. To allow opposition by speech seems to indicate that you think the speech impotent, as when a man says that he has squared the circle, or that you do not care whole-heartedly for the result, or that you doubt either your power or your premises. But

---

[a]   The majority found it unnecessary to review defendants' conviction on the count charging that the circulars were intended to bring the form of government of the United States into contempt.

when men have realized that time has upset many fighting faiths, they may come to believe even more than they believe the very foundations of their own conduct that the ultimate good desired is better reached by free trade in ideas—that the best test of truth is the power of the thought to get itself accepted in the competition of the market, and that truth is the only ground upon which their wishes safely can be carried out. That at any rate is the theory of our Constitution. It is an experiment, as all life is an experiment. Every year if not every day we have to wager our salvation upon some prophecy based upon imperfect knowledge. While that experiment is part of our system I think that we should be eternally vigilant against attempts to check the expression of opinions that we loathe and believe to be fraught with death, unless they so imminently threaten immediate interference with the lawful and pressing purposes of the law that an immediate check is required to save the country. I wholly disagree with the argument of the Government that the First Amendment left the common law as to seditious libel in force. History seems to me against the notion. I had conceived that the United States through many years had shown its repentance for the Sedition Act of 1798, by repaying fines that it imposed. Only the emergency that makes it immediately dangerous to leave the correction of evil counsels to time warrants making any exception to the sweeping command, 'Congress shall make no law . . . abridging the freedom of speech.' Of course I am speaking only of expressions of opinion and exhortations, which were all that were uttered here, but I regret that I cannot put into more impressive words my belief that in their conviction upon this indictment the defendants were deprived of their rights under the Constitution of the United States."[b]

Hand's "Advocacy" Test vs. Holmes' "Clear and Present" Test

Professor Corwin summarized the holdings of the *Schenck* and *Abrams* cases as follows:

"To sum up, the following propositions seem to be established with respect to constitutional freedom of speech and press: first, Congress is not limited to forbidding words which are of a nature 'to create a clear and present danger' to national interest, but it may forbid words which are intended to endanger those interests if in the exercise of a fair legislative discretion it finds it 'necessary and proper' to do so; second, the intent of the accused in uttering the alleged forbidden words may be presumed from the reasonable consequences of such words, though the presumption is a rebuttable one; third, the court will not scrutinize on appeal the findings of juries in this class of cases more strictly than in other penal cases. In short, the cause of freedom of speech and press is largely in the custody of legislative majorities and of juries, which, so far as there is evidence to show, is just where the framers of the Constitution intended it to be." Corwin, *Freedom of Speech and Press Under the First Amendment: A Resume*, 30 Yale L.J. 48, 55 (1920), reprinted in 2 Selected Essays on Constitutional Law 1060, 1067 (1938).

---

[b]   The Abrams case was the only one under the 1918 Act to reach the Supreme Court. That Act was repealed in 1921 (41 Stat. 1359), leaving the original 1917 Act to become what is now 18 U.S.C. § 2388. There have been intermittent prosecutions under the legislation. See Hartzel v. United States, 322 U.S. 680 (1944); United States v. Powell, 156 F.Supp. 526 (N.D.Cal.1957). The 1917 Act (by its original terms and as carried into 18 U.S.C. § 2388) applies only "when the United States is at war."

Related to the above legislation is a provision of the Universal Military Training and Service Act of 1948 which provides that one "who knowingly counsels, aids, or abets another to refuse or evade registration or service in the armed forces or any of the requirements of this title" is guilty of a crime. 50 U.S.C.App. § 462(a). Under this section, a dean of a college was convicted for telling a student who was refusing to register, "Do not let them coerce you into registering." Gara v. United States, 178 F.2d 38 (6th Cir.1949), affirmed by an equally divided vote, 340 U.S. 857 (1950).

Gunther, *Learned Hand and the Origins of Modern First Amendment Doctrine: Some Fragments of History,* 27 Stan.L.Rev. 719 (1975), sets forth contemporary correspondence between Judge Hand and Justice Holmes, making it clear that they had quite different points of view as to the appropriate limits on the punishment of radical speech. Holmes, in fact, started with the observation that "free speech stands no differently than freedom from vaccination." In a letter to Professor Chafee in 1921 Hand summarized his objections to the Holmes approach as set forth in *Schenck* and *Abrams:*

"I am not wholly in love with Holmesy's test and the reason is this. Once you admit that the matter is one of degree, while you may put it where it genuinely belongs, you so obviously make it a matter of administration, i.e. you give to Tomdickandharry, D.J., so much latitude that the jig is at once up. Besides their ineffabilities, the Nine Elder Statesmen, have not shown themselves wholly immune from the 'herd instinct' and what seems 'immediate and direct' today may seem very remote next year even though the circumstances surrounding the utterance be unchanged. I own I should prefer a qualitative formula, hard, conventional, difficult to evade." Id. at 770.

The *Abrams* case suggested a somewhat different problem than *Schenck.* In *Schenck,* the statutory language prohibited conduct. *Abrams* involved a statute making criminal "language intended to incite resistance to the United States" and "language urging curtailment of production of any things necessary to the prosecution of war with intent to hinder such prosecution." In Gitlow v. New York, which is set out below, New York's statute penalized the advocacy of the "duty, necessity, or propriety" of overturning the government by force or violence.

Gitlow v. New York

268 U.S. 652, 45 S.Ct. 625, 69 L.Ed. 1138 (1925).

■ MR. JUSTICE SANFORD delivered the opinion of the Court.

Benjamin Gitlow was indicted in the Supreme Court of New York, with three others, for the statutory crime of criminal anarchy. New York Penal Law §§ 160, 161. He was separately tried, convicted, and sentenced to imprisonment. The judgment was affirmed by the Appellate Division and by the Court of Appeals. . . .

The contention here is that the statute, by its terms and as applied in this case, is repugnant to the due process clause of the Fourteenth Amendment. Its material provisions are:

"§ 160. *Criminal anarchy defined.* Criminal anarchy is the doctrine that organized government should be overthrown by force or violence, or by assassination of the executive head or of any of the executive officials of government, or by any unlawful means. The advocacy of such doctrine either by word of mouth or writing is a felony.

"§ 161. *Advocacy of criminal anarchy.* Any person who:

"1. By word of mouth or writing advocates, advises or teaches the duty, necessity or propriety of overthrowing or overturning organized government by force or violence, or by assassination of the executive head or of any of the executive officials of government, or by any unlawful means; or,

"2. Prints, publishes, edits, issues or knowingly circulates, sells, distributes or publicly displays any book, paper, document, or written or printed matter in any form, containing or advocating, advising or teaching the doctrine that organized government should be overthrown by force, violence or any unlawful means, . . .

"Is guilty of a felony and punishable" by imprisonment or fine, or both.

The indictment was in two counts. The first charged that the defendant had advocated, advised and taught the duty, necessity and propriety of overthrowing and overturning organized government by force, violence and unlawful means, by certain writings therein set forth entitled "The Left Wing Manifesto"; the second that he had printed, published and knowingly circulated and distributed a certain paper called "The Revolutionary Age," containing the writings set forth in the first count advocating, advising and teaching the doctrine that organized government should be overthrown by force, violence and unlawful means.

The following facts were established on the trial by undisputed evidence and admissions: . . . It was admitted that the defendant signed a card subscribing to the Manifesto and Program of the Left Wing, which all applicants were required to sign before being admitted to membership; that he went to different parts of the State to speak to branches of the Socialist Party about the principles of the Left Wing and advocated their adoption; and that he was responsible for the Manifesto as it appeared, that "he knew of the publication, in a general way and he knew of its publication afterwards, and is responsible for its circulation."

There was no evidence of any effect resulting from the publication and circulation of the Manifesto.

No witnesses were offered in behalf of the defendant.

. . .

The court, among other things, charged the jury, in substance, that they must determine what was the intent, purpose and fair meaning of the Manifesto; that its words must be taken in their ordinary meaning, as they would be understood by people whom it might reach; that a mere statement or analysis of social and economic facts and historical incidents, in the nature of an essay, accompanied by prophecy as to the future course of events, but with no teaching, advice or advocacy of action, would not constitute the advocacy, advice or teaching of a doctrine for the overthrow of government within the meaning of the statute; that a mere statement that unlawful acts might accomplish such a purpose would be insufficient, unless there was a teaching, advising and advocacy of employing such unlawful acts for the purpose of overthrowing government; and that if the jury had a reasonable doubt that the Manifesto did teach, advocate or advise the duty, necessity or propriety of using unlawful means for the overthrowing of organized government, the defendant was entitled to an acquittal.

The defendant's counsel submitted two requests to charge which embodied in substance the statement that to constitute criminal anarchy within the meaning of the statute it was necessary that the language used or published should advocate, teach or advise the duty, necessity or propriety of doing "some definite or immediate act or acts" of force, violence or unlawfulness directed toward the overthrowing of organized government. These were denied further than had been charged. Two other requests to charge embodied in substance the statement that to constitute guilt the language used or published must be "reasonably and ordinarily calculated to incite certain persons" to acts of force, violence or unlawfulness, with the object of overthrowing organized government. These were also denied.

. . .

. . . The sole contention here is, essentially, that as there was no evidence of any concrete result flowing from the publication of the Manifesto or of circumstances showing the likelihood of such result, the statute as construed and applied by the trial court penalizes the mere utterance, as such, of "doctrine" having no quality of incitement, without regard either to the circumstances of its utterance or to the likelihood of unlawful sequences; and that, as the exercise of the right of free expression with relation to government is only punishable "in circumstances involving likelihood of substantive evil," the statute contravenes the due process clause of the Fourteenth Amendment. . . .

. . .

The statute does not penalize the utterance or publication of abstract "doctrine" or academic discussion having no quality of incitement to any concrete action. It is not aimed against mere historical or philosophical essays. It does not restrain the advocacy of changes in the form of government by constitutional and lawful means. What it prohibits is language advocating, advising or teaching the overthrow of organized government by unlawful means. These words imply urging to action. . . .

The Manifesto, plainly, is neither the statement of abstract doctrine nor, as suggested by counsel, mere prediction that industrial disturbances and revolutionary mass strikes will result spontaneously in an inevitable process of evolution in the economic system. It advocates and urges in fervent language mass action which shall progressively foment industrial disturbances and through political mass strikes and revolutionary mass action overthrow and destroy organized parliamentary government. It concludes with a call to action in these words:

"The proletariat revolution and the Communist reconstruction of society—*the struggle for these*—is now indispensable. . . . The Communist International calls the proletariat of the world to the final struggle!"

This is not the expression of philosophical abstraction, the mere prediction of future events; it is the language of direct incitement.

The means advocated for bringing about the destruction of organized parliamentary government, namely, mass industrial revolts usurping the functions of municipal government, political mass strikes directed against the parliamentary state, and revolutionary mass action for its final destruction, necessarily imply the use of force and violence, and in their essential nature are inherently unlawful in a constitutional government of law and order. That the jury were warranted in finding that the Manifesto advocated not merely the abstract doctrine of overthrowing organized government by force, violence and unlawful means, but action to that end, is clear.

For present purposes we may and do assume that freedom of speech and of the press—which are protected by the First Amendment from abridgment by Congress— are among the fundamental personal rights and "liberties" protected by the due process clause of the Fourteenth Amendment from impairment by the States. . . .

. . .

By enacting the present statute the State has determined, through its legislative body, that utterances advocating the overthrow of organized government by force, violence and unlawful means, are so inimical to the general welfare and involve such danger of substantive evil that they may be penalized in the exercise of its police power. That determination must be given great weight. . . . That utterances inciting to the overthrow of organized government by unlawful means, present a sufficient danger of substantive evil to bring their punishment within the range of legislative discretion, is clear. Such utterances, by their very nature, involve danger to the public peace and to the security of the State. They threaten breaches of the peace and ultimate revolution. And the immediate danger is none the less real and substantial, because the effect of a given utterance cannot be accurately foreseen. The State cannot reasonably be required to measure the danger from every such utterance in the nice balance of a jeweler's scale. A single revolutionary spark may kindle a fire that, smouldering for a time, may burst into a sweeping and destructive conflagration. It cannot be said that the State is acting arbitrarily or unreasonably when in the exercise of its judgment as to the measures necessary to protect the public peace and safety, it seeks to extinguish the spark without waiting until it has enkindled the flame or blazed into the conflagration. It cannot reasonably be required to defer the adoption of measures for its own peace and safety until the revolutionary utterances lead to actual disturbances of the public peace or imminent and immediate danger of its own destruction; but it may, in the exercise of its judgment, suppress the threatened danger in its incipiency. . . .

We cannot hold that the present statute is an arbitrary or unreasonable exercise of the police power of the State unwarrantably infringing the freedom of speech or press; and we must and do sustain its constitutionality.

This being so it may be applied to every utterance—not too trivial to be beneath the notice of the law—which is of such a character and used with such intent and purpose as to bring it within the prohibition of the statute. . . . In other words, when the legislative body has determined generally, in the constitutional exercise of its discretion, that utterances of a certain kind involve such danger of substantive evil that they may be punished, the question whether any specific utterance coming within the prohibited class is likely, in and of itself, to bring about the substantive evil, is not open to consideration. It is sufficient that the statute itself be constitutional and that the use of the language comes within its prohibition.

It is clear that the question in such cases is entirely different from that involved in those cases where the statute merely prohibits certain acts involving the danger of substantive evil, without any reference to language itself, and it is sought to apply its provisions to language used by the defendant for the purpose of bringing about the prohibited results. There, if it be contended that the statute cannot be applied to the language used by the defendant because of its protection by the freedom of speech or press, it must necessarily be found, as an original question, without any previous determination by the legislative body, whether the specific language used involved such likelihood of bringing about the substantive evil as to deprive it of the constitutional protection. In such cases it has been held that the general provisions of the statute may be constitutionally applied to the specific utterance of the defendant if its natural tendency and probable effect was to bring about the substantive evil which the legislative body might prevent. Schenck v. United States . . . ; Debs v. United States . . . And the general statement in the *Schenck Case,* . . . that the "question in every case is whether the words used are used in such circumstances and are of such a nature as to create a clear and present danger that they will bring about the substantive evils,"—upon which great reliance is placed in the defendant's argument—was manifestly intended, as shown by the context, to apply only in cases of this class, and has no application to those like the present, where the legislative body itself has previously determined the danger of substantive evil arising from utterances of a specified character. . . .

And finding, for the reasons stated, that the statute is not in itself unconstitutional, and that it has not been applied in the present case in derogation of any constitutional right, the judgment of the Court of Appeals is

Affirmed.

■ MR. JUSTICE HOLMES, dissenting.

Mr. Justice Brandeis and I are of opinion that this judgment should be reversed. The general principle of free speech, it seems to me, must be taken to be included in the Fourteenth Amendment, in view of the scope that has been given to the word "liberty" as there used, although perhaps it may be accepted with a somewhat larger latitude of interpretation than is allowed to Congress by the sweeping language that governs or ought to govern the laws of the United States. If I am right then I think that the criterion sanctioned by the full Court in Schenck v. United States ... applies. . . . It is true that in my opinion this criterion was departed from in Abrams v. United States, 250 U.S. 616, but the convictions that I expressed in that case are too deep for it to be possible for me as yet to believe that it . . . settled the law. If what I think the correct test is applied, it is manifest that there was no present danger of an attempt to overthrow the government by force on the part of the admittedly small minority who shared the defendant's views. It is said that this manifesto was more than a theory, that it was an incitement. Every idea is an incitement. It offers itself for belief and if believed it is acted on unless some other belief outweighs it or some failure of energy stifles the movement at its birth. The only difference between the expression of an opinion and an incitement in the narrower sense is the speaker's enthusiasm for the result. Eloquence may set fire to reason. But whatever may be thought of the redundant discourse before us it had no chance of starting a present conflagration. If in the long run the beliefs expressed in proletarian dictatorship are destined to be accepted by the dominant forces of the community, the only meaning of free speech is that they should be given their chance and have their way.

If the publication of this document had been laid as an attempt to induce an uprising against government at once and not at some indefinite time in the future it would have presented a different question. The object would have been one with which the law might deal, subject to the doubt whether there was any danger that the publication could produce any result, or in other words whether it was not futile and too remote from possible consequences. But the indictment alleges the publication and nothing more.

Whitney v. California

274 U.S. 357 (1927).

This case arose under the California criminal syndicalism act that defined "criminal syndicalism" as any doctrine advocating, teaching or abetting sabotage or other unlawful acts of violence as a means of accomplishing industrial or political change. It was a crime for any person to organize, assist in organizing, or knowingly become a member of any organization or group of persons associated to advocate, teach or abet criminal syndicalism.

Ms. Whitney was a socialist who in 1919 became a temporary member of the new Communist Labor Party and went as a delegate to a convention for organizing a California branch. There she supported a resolution which would have committed the organization to the use of peaceful and lawful methods of change, but this resolution lost and the convention adopted a program resembling Gitlow's Left Wing Manifesto. Whitney was found guilty under the act in that she assisted in organizing and knowingly became a member of a group formed to advocate criminal syndicalism.

The United States Supreme Court sustained the conviction. The majority opinion made two principal points: (a) Whether or not Miss Whitney helped organize and became a member of the Communist Labor Party with knowledge of its program of criminal syndicalism was a question of fact upon which the verdict of the jury was conclusive. (b) The California act "may not be declared unconstitutional unless it is an arbitrary or unreasonable attempt to exercise the authority vested in the state in the public interest." Because of the danger to the public peace and security from an organization advocating violent and unlawful methods of change, the act could not be regarded as an unreasonable exercise of the police power, unwarrantably infringing any right of free speech and assembly.

Justice Brandeis, although concurring in affirmance for procedural reasons, wrote a major opinion, joined by Justice Holmes, disagreeing with the Court's analysis. He said in part:

"Those who won our independence believed that the final end of the State was to make men free to develop their faculties, and that in its government the deliberative forces should prevail over the arbitrary. They valued liberty both as an end and as a means. They believed liberty to be the secret of happiness and courage to be the secret of liberty. They believed that freedom to think as you will and to speak as you think are means indispensable to the discovery and spread of political truth; that without free speech and assembly discussion would be futile; that with them, discussion affords ordinarily adequate protection against the dissemination of noxious doctrine; that the greatest menace to freedom is an inert people; that public discussion is a political duty; and that this should be a fundamental principle of the American government. They recognized the risks to which all human institutions are subject. But they knew that order cannot be secured merely through fear of punishment for its infraction; that it is hazardous to discourage thought, hope and imagination; that fear breeds repression; that repression breeds hate; that hate menaces stable government; that the path of safety lies in the opportunity to discuss freely supposed grievances and proposed remedies; and that the fitting remedy for evil counsels is good ones. Believing in the power of reason as applied through public discussion, they eschewed silence coerced by law—the argument of force in its worst form. Recognizing the occasional tyrannies of governing majorities, they amended the Constitution so that free speech and assembly should be guaranteed.

"Fear of serious injury cannot alone justify suppression of free speech and assembly. Men feared witches and burnt women. It is the function of speech to free men from the bondage of irrational fears. To justify suppression of free speech there must be reasonable ground to fear that serious evil will result if free speech is practiced. There must be reasonable ground to believe that the danger apprehended is imminent. There must be reasonable ground to believe that the evil to be prevented is a serious one. Every denunciation of existing law tends in some measure to increase the probability that there will be a violation of it. Condonation of a breach enhances the probability. Expressions of approval add to the probability. Propagation of the criminal state of mind by teaching syndicalism increases it. Advocacy of law-breaking heightens it still further. But even advocacy of violation, however reprehensible morally, is not a justification for denying free speech where the advocacy falls short of incitement and there is nothing to indicate that the advocacy would be immediately acted on. The wide difference between advocacy and incitement, between preparation and attempt, between assembling and conspiracy, must be borne in mind. In order to support a finding of clear and present danger it must be shown either that immediate serious violence was to be expected or was advocated, or that the past conduct furnished reason to believe that such advocacy was then contemplated."

"Those who won our independence by revolution were not cowards. They did not fear political change. They did not exalt order at the cost of liberty. To courageous, self-reliant men, with confidence in the power of free and fearless reasoning applied through the processes of popular government, no danger flowing from speech can be deemed clear and present, unless the incidence of the evil apprehended is so imminent that it may befall before there is opportunity for full discussion. If there be time to expose through discussion the falsehood and fallacies, to avert the evil by the processes of education, the remedy to be applied is more speech, not enforced silence. Only an emergency can justify repression. Such must be the rule if authority is to be reconciled with freedom. Such, in my opinion, is the command of the Constitution. It is therefore always open to Americans to challenge a law abridging free speech and assembly by showing that there was no emergency justifying it.

"Moreover, even imminent danger cannot justify resort to prohibition of these functions essential to effective democracy, unless the evil apprehended is relatively serious. Prohibition of free speech and assembly is a measure so stringent that it would be inappropriate as the means for averting a relatively trivial harm to society. A police measure may be unconstitutional merely because the remedy, although effective as means of protection, is unduly harsh or oppressive. Thus, a State might, in the exercise of its police power, make any trespass upon the land of another a crime, regardless of the results or of the intent or purpose of the trespasser. It might, also, punish an attempt, a conspiracy, or an incitement to commit the trespass. But it is hardly conceivable that this Court would hold constitutional a statute which punished as a felony the mere voluntary assembly with a society formed to teach that pedestrians had the moral right to cross unenclosed, unposted, waste lands and to advocate their doing so, even if there was imminent danger that advocacy would lead to a trespass. The fact that speech is likely to result in some violence or in destruction of property is not enough to justify its suppression. There must be the probability of serious injury to the State. Among free men, the deterrents ordinarily to be applied to prevent crime are education and punishment for violations of the law, not abridgement of the rights of free speech and assembly. . . ."[a]

The Basis of the Brandeis Concurrence in the Whitney Case

Because Justice Brandeis' opinion in *Whitney* is both the most articulate and passionate defense of the clear and present danger test, it is often forgotten that he and Justice Holmes voted to affirm Anita Whitney's conviction. The reason for concurrence was explained as follows:

"Whether in 1919, when Miss Whitney did the things complained of, there was in California such clear and present danger of serious evil, might have been made the important issue in the case. She might have required that the issue be determined either by the court or the jury. She claimed below that the statute as applied to her violated the Federal Constitution; but she did not claim that it was void because there was no clear and present danger of serious evil, nor did she request that the existence of these conditions of a valid measure thus restricting the rights of free speech and assembly be passed upon by the court or a jury. On the other hand, there was evidence on which the court or jury might have found that such danger existed. I am unable to assent to the suggestion in the opinion of the Court that assembling with a political party, formed to advocate the desirability of a proletarian revolution by mass action at some date necessarily far in the future, is not a right within the protection of the Fourteenth Amendment. In the present case, however, there was other testimony which tended to establish the existence of a conspiracy, on the part of members of the International Workers of the World, to commit present serious crimes; and likewise to show that such a conspiracy would be furthered by the activity of the society of which Miss Whitney was a member. Under these circumstances the judgment of the state court cannot be disturbed."

Note that the defendant was not charged with illegal advocacy, but was convicted for organizing and being a member of a group engaged in unlawful advocacy. Moreover, there was no evidence that she engaged personally in the unlawful

---

[a]   The Whitney case and its background are discussed in Chafee, *Free Speech in the United States* (1941), pp. 343–354. Shortly after the Supreme Court's decision, she was pardoned by Governor Young of California, who in giving reasons for his action made reference to the opinion of Justice Brandeis.

advocacy. To the contrary, she had sponsored a competing resolution at the group's organizing meeting calling for peaceful and lawful change. Suppose the clear and present danger defense had been raised at the criminal trial, but it had been found, on sufficient evidence, that the party advocated present serious crimes, and that there was a clear and present danger that those crimes would be committed. Under the position of Justices Brandeis and Holmes, would the fact that defendant disagreed with the advocacy of criminal conduct and did not personally participate in that advocacy be the basis of a viable first amendment defense? Would it be sufficient for conviction that she remained as an active party member, knowing of its illegal advocacy?

De Jonge v. Oregon
299 U.S. 353 (1937).

De Jonge was convicted on an indictment charging violation of the Oregon criminal syndicalism law that defined "criminal syndicalism" as "the doctrine which advocates crime, physical violence, sabotage or any unlawful acts or methods as a means of accomplishing or effecting industrial or political change or revolution." Among the offenses created were the teaching of criminal syndicalism, the printing or distribution of material advocating the doctrine, the organization of a society or group which advocates it, and presiding at or assisting in conducting a meeting of such an organization, society or group.

The indictment charged that the defendant had unlawfully presided at, and assisted in conducting "an assemblage of persons", to wit, the Communist Party, "which said assemblage of persons" did then and there unlawfully teach and advocate the doctrine of criminal syndicalism.

The evidence showed that De Jonge was a member of the Communist Party; that he presided over and otherwise participated in the public meeting held in Portland, Oregon, under the auspices of the Communist Party; that the meeting was held to protest against illegal raids on workers' halls and homes, and against the shooting of striking longshoremen by the Portland police; and at the meeting there were no unlawful acts done, nor any advocacy of criminal syndicalism. The Supreme Court of Oregon affirmed the conviction on the ground that in addition to the above evidence, there was evidence to show, as the indictment had charged, that the Communist Party at other times and places in Oregon, had taught and advocated criminal syndicalism.

Chief Justice Hughes, speaking for a unanimous Court, delivered an opinion containing the following paragraphs:

"Conviction upon a charge not made would be sheer denial of due process. It thus appears that, while defendant was a member of the Communist Party, he was not indicted for participating in its organization, or for joining it, or for soliciting members or for distributing its literature. He was not charged with teaching or advocating criminal syndicalism or sabotage or any unlawful acts, either at the meeting or elsewhere. He was accordingly deprived of the benefit of evidence as to the orderly and lawful conduct of the meeting and that it was not called or used for the advocacy of criminal syndicalism or sabotage or any unlawful action. His sole offense as charged, and for which he was convicted and sentenced to imprisonment for seven years, was that he had assisted in the conduct of a public meeting, albeit otherwise lawful, which was held under the auspices of the Communist Party.

"...

"Freedom of speech and of the press are fundamental rights which are safeguarded by the due process clause of the Fourteenth Amendment of the Federal

Constitution. . . . The right of peaceable assembly is a right cognate to those of free speech and free press and is equally fundamental. As this Court said in United States v. Cruikshank, 92 U.S. 542, 552: 'The very idea of a government, republican in form, implies a right on the part of its citizens to meet peaceably for consultation in respect to public affairs and to petition for a redress of grievances.' The First Amendment of the Federal Constitution expressly guarantees that right against abridgment by Congress. But explicit mention there does not argue exclusion elsewhere. For the right is one that cannot be denied without violating those fundamental principles of liberty and justice which lie at the base of all civil and political institutions—principles which the Fourteenth Amendment embodies in the general terms of its due process clause. . . .

"...

"It follows from these considerations that, consistently with the Federal Constitution, peaceable assembly for lawful discussion cannot be made a crime. The holding of meetings for peaceable political action cannot be proscribed. Those who assist in the conduct of such meetings cannot be branded as criminals on that score. The question, if the rights of free speech and peaceable assembly are to be preserved, is not as to the auspices under which the meeting is held but as to its purpose; not as to the relations of the speakers, but whether their utterances transcend the bounds of the freedom of speech which the Constitution protects. If the persons assembling have committed crimes elsewhere, if they have formed or are engaged in a conspiracy against the public peace and order, they may be prosecuted for their conspiracy or other violation of valid laws. But it is a different matter when the State, instead of prosecuting them for such offenses, seizes upon mere participation in a peaceable assembly and a lawful public discussion as the basis for a criminal charge.

"We are not called upon to review the findings of the state court as to the objectives of the Communist Party. Notwithstanding those objectives, the defendant still enjoyed his personal right of free speech and to take part in a peaceable assembly having a lawful purpose, although called by that Party. The defendant was none the less entitled to discuss the public issues of the day and thus in a lawful manner, without incitement to violence or crime, to seek redress of alleged grievances. That was of the essence of his guaranteed personal liberty."

C. THE POST WORLD WAR II COLD WAR ERA: PROSECUTION OF COMMUNISTS UNDER THE SMITH ACT

The Smith Act

During the years that followed the Second World War, anti-radical hysteria surpassed that of the Great Red Scare of the 1920's. The focus this time was the Russian threat, and the specific concern was espionage and subversion by the Communist Party of the United States. The output of both the national and state legislatures, passing laws dealing with loyalty and security, was enormous during this period. So too, were the number of cases, many decided by the United States Supreme Court. The cases that follow are only a small part of the story of the Supreme Court's treatment of anti-Communist legislation during the years of the cold war and after. They are, however, an important part since they continue the debate begun in *Schenck, Abrams, Gitlow* and *Whitney*.

The *Dennis* case, which follows, resulted from federal prosecution of the Communist Party's top national leaders. The *Yates* and *Scales* cases involved prosecutions of lower level Communist Party officials, that followed in the wake of the Court's affirmance of the convictions in *Dennis*. Ironically, the legislation under which the prosecutions were initiated had been enacted before the war. The Smith Act was passed in 1940 as a rider to other legislation and received little attention in or out of Congress until it was employed, after the war, as the vehicle for prosecution of Communist Party officials. The Smith Act was patterned on the New York Criminal Anarchy Act that had been sustained in Gitlow v. New York.

Dennis v. United States

341 U.S. 494 (1951).

Petitioners, leaders of the Communist Party, were prosecuted and convicted in a federal district court in New York of violating the Smith Act. The Act provided:

"Sec. 2(a). It shall be unlawful for any person:

"(1) to knowingly or willfully advocate, abet, advise, or teach the duty, necessity, desirability, or propriety of overthrowing or destroying any government in the United States by force or violence, or by the assassination of any officer of any such government;

" . . .

"(3) to organize or help to organize any society, group, or assembly of persons who teach, advocate, or encourage the overthrow or destruction of any government in the United States by force or violence; or to be or become a member of, or affiliate with, any such society, group, or assembly of persons, knowing the purposes thereof. . . .

"Sec. 3. It shall be unlawful for any person to attempt to commit, or to conspire to commit, any of the acts prohibited by the provisions of this title."

The indictment charged petitioners with conspiring (1) to organize as the Communist Party of the United States a group of persons who teach and advocate the overthrow of the Government of the United States by force and violence, and (2) to advocate and teach the duty and necessity of overthrowing the government of the United States by force and violence. After a protracted trial, the judge gave the jury instructions which included the following:

"In further construction and interpretation of the statute I charge you that it is not the abstract doctrine of overthrowing or destroying organized government by unlawful means which is denounced by this law, but the teaching and advocacy of action for the accomplishment of that purpose, by language reasonably and ordinarily calculated to incite persons to such action. Accordingly, you cannot find the defendants or any of them guilty of the crime charged unless you are satisfied beyond a reasonable doubt that they conspired to organize a society, group and assembly of persons who teach and advocate the overthrow or destruction of the Government of the United States by force and violence and to advocate and teach the duty and necessity of overthrowing or destroying the Government of the United States by force and violence, with the intent that such teaching and advocacy be of a rule or principle of action and by language reasonably and ordinarily calculated to incite persons to such action, all with the intent to cause the overthrow or destruction of the Government of the United States by force and violence as speedily as circumstances would permit.

" . . .

"If you are satisfied that the evidence establishes beyond a reasonable doubt that the defendants, or any of them, are guilty of a violation of the statute, as I have interpreted it to you, I find as matter of law that there is sufficient danger of a substantive evil that the Congress has a right to prevent to justify the application of the statute under the First Amendment of the Constitution.

"This is [a] matter of law about which you have no concern. It is a finding on a matter of law which I deem essential to support my ruling that the case should be submitted to you to pass upon the guilt or innocence of the defendants."

The convictions were affirmed by the Court of Appeals and the Supreme Court granted certiorari limited to the question of the constitutionality of the Smith Act as construed and applied. Several opinions were written, none of which obtained the approval of sufficient Justices to make it the opinion of the Court.

The opinion receiving the greatest assent was by Chief Justice Vinson, joined by Justices Reed, Burton and Minton. "The obvious purpose of the statute," said the Chief Justice, "is to protect existing Government, not from change by peaceable, lawful and constitutional means, but from change by violence, revolution and terrorism." Although the statute was inapplicable to "peaceful studies and discussions or teaching and advocacy in the realm of ideas," it did limit speech. Therefore, the case "squarely presented" the Court with the application of the "clear and present danger" test and required a decision as to "what that phrase imports."[a]

"Obviously, the words cannot mean that before the Government may act, it must wait until the *putsch* is about to be executed, the plans have been laid and the signal is awaited. If Government is aware that a group aiming at its overthrow is attempting to indoctrinate its members and to commit them to a course whereby they will strike when the leaders feel the circumstances permit, action by the Government is required. The argument that there is no need for Government to concern itself, for Government is strong, it possesses ample powers to put down a rebellion, it may defeat the revolution with ease needs no answer. For that is not the question. Certainly an attempt to overthrow the Government by force, even though doomed from the outset because of inadequate numbers or power of the revolutionists, is a sufficient evil for Congress to prevent. . . .

"The situation with which Justices Holmes and Brandeis were concerned in *Gitlow* was a comparatively isolated event, bearing little relation in their minds to any substantial threat to the safety of the community. . . . They were not confronted with any situation comparable to the instant one—the development of an apparatus designed and dedicated to the overthrow of the Government, in the context of world crisis after crisis.

"Chief Judge Learned Hand, writing for the majority below, interpreted the phrase as follows: 'In each case [courts] must ask whether the gravity of the "evil," discounted by its improbability, justifies such invasion of free speech as is necessary to avoid the danger.' 183 F.2d at 212. We adopt this statement of the rule. As articulated by Chief Judge Hand, it is as succinct and inclusive as any other we might devise at this time. It takes into consideration those factors which we deem relevant, and relates their significances. More we cannot expect from words.

"Likewise, we are in accord with the court below, which affirmed the trial court's finding that the requisite danger existed. The mere fact that from the period 1945 to 1948 petitioners' activities did not result in an attempt to overthrow the Government by force and violence is of course no answer to the fact that there was a group that was ready to make the attempt. The formation by petitioners of such a highly organized conspiracy, with rigidly disciplined members subject to call when the leaders, these petitioners, felt that the time had come for action, coupled with the inflammable nature of world conditions, similar uprisings in other countries, and the touch-and-go

---

[a] The Chief Justice made it clear that he regarded the views of Holmes and Brandeis as having won the acceptance of the Court. "Although no case subsequent to *Whitney* and *Gitlow* has expressly overruled the majority opinions in those cases, there is little doubt that subsequent opinions have inclined toward the Holmes-Brandeis rationale."

nature of our relations with countries with whom petitioners were in the very least ideologically attuned, convince us that their convictions were justified on this score. And this analysis disposes of the contention that a conspiracy to advocate, as distinguished from the advocacy itself, cannot be constitutionally restrained, because it comprises only the preparation. It is the existence of the conspiracy which creates the danger. . . . If the ingredients of the reaction are present, we cannot bind the Government to wait until the catalyst is added."

The Chief Justice also approved of the ruling below that withheld the issue of clear and present danger from the jury. "Bearing, as it does, the marks of a 'question of law,' the issue is properly one for the judge to decide."

He concluded that the convictions should be affirmed.

Justice Frankfurter wrote an extensive concurring opinion in which he emphasized the importance of a careful examination of the conflicting interests of national security and free speech which the Court was required to assess in order to arrive at its decision. He believed that the prior decisions resolving conflicts between speech and competing interests, when viewed as a whole, expressed an attitude toward the judicial function and a standard of values which were decisive of the case. "Free-speech cases are not an exception to the principle that we are not legislators, that direct policy-making is not our province. How best to reconcile competing interests is the business of legislatures, and the balance they strike is a judgment not to be displaced by ours, but to be respected unless outside the pale of fair judgment."

Justice Jackson's concurring opinion contended that the clear and present danger test was inapplicable since the prosecution was for conspiracy and under circumstances greatly different from those in *Gitlow, Whitney,* and earlier cases. "I would save it, unmodified, for application as a 'rule of reason' in the kind of case for which it was devised. When the issue is criminality of a hot-headed speech on a street corner, or circulation of a few incendiary pamphlets, or parading by some zealots behind a red flag, or refusal of a handful of school children to salute our flag, it is not beyond the capacity of the judicial process to gather, comprehend, and weigh the necessary materials for decision whether it is a clear and present danger of substantive evil or a harmless letting off of steam."

Justice Black's dissenting opinion emphasized that petitioners were not charged with an attempt to overthrow the Government, or with overt acts designed to overthrow the Government, or even with saying anything or writing anything designed to overthrow the Government. He argued that section 3 of the Smith Act was unconstitutional as a "virulent form of prior censorship of speech and press" in violation of the First Amendment. Justice Douglas also dissented, warning against the dangers of basing a prosecution for seditious conspiracy on speech alone. To make the criminality of the teaching of doctrine turn solely on the intent with which it is taught, made the offense similar to the old English crime of constructive treason. As to the clear and present danger rule, he observed:

"There comes a time when even speech loses its constitutional immunity. Speech innocuous one year may at another time fan such destructive flames that it must be halted in the interests of the safety of the Republic. That is the meaning of the clear and present danger test. When conditions are so critical that there will be no time to avoid the evil that the speech threatens, it is time to call a halt. Otherwise, free speech which is the strength of the Nation will be the cause of its destruction.

"Yet free speech is the rule, not the exception. The restraint to be constitutional must be based on more than fear, on more than passionate opposition against the speech, on more than a revolted dislike for its contents. There must be some immediate injury to society that is likely if speech is allowed."

Justice Clark did not participate in the disposition of the case. The convictions were affirmed by a vote of six to two.

Clear and Present Danger as a Test for the Validity of Legislation

It will be recalled that the Court in Gitlow v. New York rejected the clear and present danger test, noting that it had been used in Schenck v. United States only for the purpose of deciding when a defendant's speech violated a law that punished conduct. The *Gitlow* majority held that clear and present danger was an irrelevant concept when a law criminally punished certain categories of speech. Chief Justice Vinson's plurality opinion in Dennis v. United States conceded that the *Gitlow* rationale would make the clear and present danger test inapplicable to the Smith Act convictions reviewed by the Court, but he concluded that intervening Court opinions "have inclined toward the Holmes-Brandeis rationale." Accordingly, he interpreted that rationale as requiring an inquiry as to whether a clear and present danger justified application of the Smith Act to the particular facts. (The Court did not, however, review the sufficiency of the evidence to sustain the convictions, since that question had been removed from the case by the Court's limited grant of certiorari.)

Hans Linde argues that, although the decision was wrong in its result, the *Gitlow* Court was right in rejecting clear and present danger as a test for determining the validity of laws that punish speech. Linde, *"Clear and Present Danger" Reexamined: Dissonance in the Brandenburg Concerto,* 22 Stan.L.Rev. 1163 (1970). He summarizes his position as follows: "The objective conditions under which the particular expression occurs . . . —whether stated as 'clear and present danger' or some other formula—can be a factor at the time when suppression of that particular occurrence is before a court. It cannot easily be an element in the constitutionality of the decision to make a law proscribing a kind of speech or publication for the future." (Linde would reserve the clear and present danger test for cases, like *Schenck,* where the statute punished conduct and the defendant's speech was claimed to be a violation. He would invalidate the Smith Act under his standard for reviewing legislation directed against the communicative content of speech or press, arguing that the first amendment invalidates a law punishing speech if the proscribed content falls *under any circumstances* within the protection of the first amendment.)

Yates v. United States
354 U.S. 298, 77 S.Ct. 1064, 1 L.Ed.2d 1356 (1957).

■ MR. JUSTICE HARLAN delivered the opinion of the Court.

We brought these cases here to consider certain questions arising under the Smith Act . . . and otherwise to review the convictions of these petitioners for conspiracy to violate that Act. Among other things, the convictions are claimed to rest upon an application of the Smith Act which is hostile to the principles upon which its constitutionality was upheld in Dennis v. United States, 341 U.S. 494.

These 14 petitioners stand convicted, after a jury trial in the United States District Court for the Southern District of California, upon a single count indictment charging them with conspiring (1) to advocate and teach the duty and necessity of overthrowing the Government of the United States by force and violence, and (2) to organize, as the Communist Party of the United States, a society of persons who so advocate and teach, all with the intent of causing the overthrow of the Government by force and violence as speedily as circumstances would permit. . . .

. . .

Petitioners contend that the instructions to the jury were fatally defective in that the trial court refused to charge that, in order to convict, the jury must find that the advocacy which the defendants conspired to promote was of a kind calculated to "incite" persons to action for the forcible overthrow of the Government. It is argued that advocacy of forcible overthrow as mere *abstract doctrine* is within the free speech protection of the First Amendment; that the Smith Act, consistently with that constitutional provision, must be taken as proscribing only the sort of advocacy which incites to illegal *action;* and that the trial court's charge, by permitting conviction for mere advocacy, unrelated to its tendency to produce forcible action, resulted in an unconstitutional application of the Smith Act. The Government, which at the trial also requested the court to charge in terms of "incitement," now takes the position, however, that the true constitutional dividing line is not between inciting and abstract advocacy of forcible overthrow, but rather between advocacy as such, irrespective of its inciting qualities, and the mere discussion or exposition of violent overthrow as an abstract theory. . . .

There can be no doubt from the record that in so instructing the jury the court regarded as immaterial, and intended to withdraw from the jury's consideration, any issue as to the character of the advocacy in terms of its capacity to stir listeners to forcible action. . . .

We are thus faced with the question whether the Smith Act prohibits advocacy and teaching of forcible overthrow as an abstract principle, divorced from any effort to instigate action to that end, so long as such advocacy or teaching is engaged in with evil intent. We hold that it does not.

The distinction between advocacy of abstract doctrine and advocacy directed at promoting unlawful action is one that has been consistently recognized in the opinions of this Court, beginning with Fox v. Washington, 236 U.S. 273; and Schenck v. United States, 249 U.S. 47. This distinction was heavily underscored in Gitlow v. New York, 268 U.S. 652. . . .

We need not, however, decide the issue before us in terms of constitutional compulsion, for our first duty is to construe this statute. In doing so we should not assume that Congress chose to disregard a constitutional danger zone so clearly marked, or that it used the words "advocate" and "teach" in their ordinary dictionary meanings when they had already been construed as terms of art carrying a special and limited connotation. . . .

. . .

In failing to distinguish between advocacy of forcible overthrow as an abstract doctrine and advocacy of action to that end, the District Court appears to have been led astray by the holding in *Dennis* that advocacy of violent action to be taken at some future time was enough. It seems to have considered that, since "inciting" speech is usually thought of as something calculated to induce immediate action, and since *Dennis* held advocacy of action for future overthrow sufficient, this meant that advocacy, irrespective of its tendency to generate action, is punishable, provided only that it is uttered with a specific intent to accomplish overthrow. In other words, the District Court apparently thought that *Dennis* obliterated the traditional dividing line between advocacy of abstract doctrine and advocacy of action.

This misconceives the situation confronting the Court in *Dennis* and what was held there. Although the jury's verdict, interpreted in light of the trial court's instructions, did not justify the conclusion that the defendants' advocacy was directed at, or created any danger of, immediate overthrow, it did establish that the advocacy was aimed at building up a seditious group and maintaining it in readiness for action at a propitious time. . . . The essence of the *Dennis* holding was that indoctrination of a group in preparation for future violent action, as well as exhortation to immediate action, by advocacy found to be directed to "action for the accomplishment" of forcible overthrow, to violence as "a rule or principle of action," and employing "language of incitement," . . . is not constitutionally protected when the group is of sufficient size and cohesiveness, is sufficiently oriented towards action, and other circumstances are such as reasonably to justify apprehension that action will occur. This is quite a different thing from the view of the District Court here that mere doctrinal justification of forcible overthrow, if engaged in with the intent to accomplish overthrow, is punishable *per se* under the Smith Act. That sort of advocacy, even though uttered with the hope that it may ultimately lead to violent revolution, is too remote from concrete action to be regarded as the kind of indoctrination preparatory to action which was condemned in *Dennis*. As one of the concurring opinions in *Dennis* put it: "Throughout our decisions there has recurred a distinction between the statement of an idea which may prompt its hearers to take unlawful action, and advocacy that such action be taken." . . . There is nothing in *Dennis* which makes that historic distinction obsolete.

. . .

In light of the foregoing we are unable to regard the District Court's charge upon this aspect of the case as adequate. The jury was never told that the Smith Act does not denounce advocacy in the sense of preaching abstractly the forcible overthrow of the Government. We think that the trial court's statement that the proscribed advocacy must include the "urging," "necessity," and "duty" of forcible overthrow, and not merely its "desirability" and "propriety," may not be regarded as a sufficient substitute for charging that the Smith Act reaches only advocacy of action for the overthrow of government by force and violence. The essential distinction is that those to whom the advocacy is addressed must be urged to *do* something, now or in the future, rather than merely to *believe* in something. . . .

. . .

[The Court ordered an acquittal of five of the 14 petitioners,[a] finding "no adequate evidence in the record" to sustain their convictions on retrial.][b]

■ MR. JUSTICE BRENNAN and MR. JUSTICE WHITTAKER took no part in the consideration or decision of this case.

■ MR. JUSTICE BLACK, with whom MR. JUSTICE DOUGLAS joins, concurring in part and dissenting in part.

I would reverse every one of these convictions and direct that all the defendants be acquitted. In my judgment the statutory provisions on which these prosecutions are based abridge freedom of speech, press and assembly in violation of the First Amendment to the United States Constitution. See my dissent and that of Mr. Justice Douglas in Dennis v. United States, 341 U.S. 494, 579, 581. . . .

. . .

■ MR. JUSTICE CLARK, dissenting.

The petitioners, principal organizers and leaders of the Communist Party in California, have been convicted for a conspiracy covering the period 1940 to 1951. They

---

[a] Upon remand of the *Yates* case, the lower court dismissed the indictments against the remaining defendants who had not been acquitted by the Supreme Court. This action was "reluctantly" requested by the Government because it could not "satisfy the evidentiary requirements laid down by the Supreme Court in its opinion reversing the conviction in this matter." New York Times, Dec. 3, 1957, p. 71.

[b] The types of evidence that led the Court to order the five acquitted, and not the remaining nine, are summarized in *Scales v. United States,* infra.

were engaged in this conspiracy with the defendants in Dennis v. United States, 341 U.S. 494 (1951). . . .

. . .

The conspiracy includes the same group of defendants as in the *Dennis* case though petitioners here occupied a lower echelon in the party hierarchy. . . . The convictions here were based upon evidence closely paralleling that adduced in *Dennis* . . .

I would affirm the convictions. . . .

. . .

Scales v. United States

367 U.S. 203, 81 S.Ct. 1469, 6 L.Ed.2d 782 (1961).

[Petitioner, Chairman of the North and South Carolina Districts of the Communist Party, was convicted of violating the membership clause of the Smith Act (18 U.S.C. § 2385), which made it a crime to become a member of an organization advocating the overthrow of the government by force or violence, knowing the purposes of such organization.[1] The trial court had instructed the jury that in order to convict it must find that (1) the Communist Party advocated the violent overthrow of the government, in the sense of present "advocacy of action" to accomplish that end as soon as circumstances were propitious; and (2) petitioner was an "active" member of the Party, and not merely "a nominal, passive, inactive, or purely technical" member, with knowledge of the Party's illegal advocacy and a specific intent to bring about overthrow "as speedily as circumstances would permit." The Supreme Court affirmed the conviction.]

■ MR. JUSTICE HARLAN delivered the opinion of the Court.

. . .

1.   *Constitutional Challenge to the Membership Clause on Its Face.* . . .

Any thought that due process puts beyond the reach of the criminal law all individual associational relationships, unless accompanied by the commission of specific acts of criminality, is dispelled by familiar concepts of the law of conspiracy and complicity. . . . In this instance it is an organization which engages in criminal activity, and we can perceive no reason why one who actively and knowingly works in the ranks of that organization, intending to contribute to the success of those specifically illegal activities, should be any more immune from prosecution than he to whom the organization has assigned the task of carrying out the substantive criminal act . . .

. . . It must indeed be recognized that a person who merely becomes a member of an illegal organization, by that "act" alone need be doing nothing more than signifying his assent to its purposes and activities on one hand, and providing, on the other, only

---

[1]   Section 2385 (whose membership clause we place in italics) reads: . . .

"Whoever organizes or helps or attempts to organize any society, group, or assembly of persons who teach, advocate, or encourage the overthrow or destruction of any such government by force or violence; *or becomes or is a member of,* or affiliates with, *any such society, group, or assembly of persons, knowing the purposes thereof*:

"Shall be fined not more than $20,000 or imprisoned not more than twenty years, or both, and shall be ineligible for employment by the United States or any department or agency thereof, for the five years next following his conviction." . . .

the sort of moral encouragement which comes from the knowledge that others believe in what the organization is doing. . . .

. . . [T]hese factors have weight and must be found to be overborne in a total constitutional assessment of the statute. We think, however, they are duly met when the statute is found to reach only "active" members having also a guilty knowledge and intent, and which therefore prevents a conviction on what otherwise might be regarded as merely an expression of sympathy with the alleged criminal enterprise, unaccompanied by any significant action in its support or any commitment to undertake such action.

. . .

. . . It was settled in *Dennis* that the advocacy with which we are here concerned is not constitutionally protected speech, and it was further established that a combination to promote such advocacy, albeit under the aegis of what purports to be a political party, is not such association as is protected by the First Amendment. We can discern no reason why membership, when it constitutes a purposeful form of complicity in a group engaging in this same forbidden advocacy, should receive any greater degree of protection from the guarantees of that Amendment. . . .

2.   Evidentiary Challenge

. . .

On this phase of the case petitioner's principal contention is that the evidence was insufficient to establish that the Communist Party was engaged in present advocacy of violent overthrow of the Government in the sense required by the Smith Act, that is, in "advocacy of action" for the accomplishment of such overthrow either immediately or as soon as circumstances proved propitious, and uttered in terms reasonably calculated to "incite" to such action. . . . This contention rests largely on the proposition that the evidence on this aspect of the case does not differ materially from that which the Court in *Yates* stated was inadequate to establish that sort of Party advocacy there.

. . .

We agree with petitioner that the evidentiary question here is controlled in large part by *Yates*. The decision in *Yates* rested on the view (not articulated in the opinion, though perhaps it should have been) that the Smith Act offenses, involving as they do subtler elements than are present in most other crimes, call for strict standards in assessing the adequacy of the proof needed to make out a case of illegal advocacy. This premise is as applicable to prosecutions under the membership clause of the Smith Act as it is to conspiracy prosecutions under that statute as we had in *Yates*.

The impact of *Yates* with respect to this petitioner's evidentiary challenge is not limited, however, to that decision's requirement of strict standards of proof. *Yates* also articulates general criteria for the evaluation of evidence in determining whether this requirement is met. The *Yates* opinion, through its characterizations of large portions of the evidence which were either described in detail or referred to by reference to the record, indicates what type of evidence is needed to permit a jury to find that (a) there was "advocacy of action" and (b) the Party was responsible for such advocacy.

First, *Yates* makes clear what type of evidence is not *in itself* sufficient to show illegal advocacy. This category includes evidence of the following: the teaching of Marxism-Leninism and the connected use of Marxist "classics" as textbooks; the official general resolutions and pronouncements of the Party at past conventions; dissemination of the Party's general literature, including the standard outlines on Marxism; the Party's history and organizational structure; the secrecy of meetings and the clandestine nature of the Party generally; statements by officials evidencing sympathy for and alliance with the U.S.S.R. It was the predominance of evidence of this type which led the Court to order the acquittal of several *Yates* defendants, with the comment that they had not themselves "made a single remark or been present when someone else made a remark which would tend to prove the charges against them." However, this kind of evidence, while insufficient in itself to sustain a conviction, is not irrelevant. Such evidence in the context of other evidence, may be of value in showing illegal advocacy.

Second, the *Yates* opinion also indicates what kind of evidence is sufficient. There the Court pointed to two series of events which justified the denial of directed acquittals as to nine of the *Yates* defendants. The Court noted that with respect to seven of the defendants, meetings in San Francisco . . . might be considered to be "the systematic teaching and advocacy of illegal action which is condemned by the statute." . . . In those meetings, a small group of members were not only taught that violent revolution was inevitable, but they were also taught techniques for achieving that end. For example, the *Yates* record reveals that members were directed to be prepared to convert a general strike into a revolution and to deal with Negroes so as to prepare them specifically for revolution. In addition to the San Francisco meetings, the Court referred to certain activities in the Los Angeles area "which might be considered to amount to 'advocacy of action' " and with which two *Yates* defendants were linked. . . . Thus, one member was "surreptitiously indoctrinated in methods . . . of moving 'masses of people in time of crisis' "; others were told to adopt such Russian prerevolutionary techniques as the development of a special communication system through a newspaper similar to Pravda. . . . Viewed together, these events described in *Yates* indicate at least two patterns of evidence sufficient to show illegal advocacy: (a) the teaching of forceful overthrow, accompanied by directions as to the type of illegal action which must be taken when the time for the revolution is reached; and (b) the teaching of forceful overthrow, accompanied by a contemporary, though legal, course of conduct clearly undertaken for the specific purpose of rendering effective the later illegal activity which is advocated. . . .

Finally, *Yates* is also relevant here in indicating, at least by implication, the type and quantum of evidence necessary to attach liability for illegal advocacy to the Party. In discussing the Government's "conspiratorial-nexus theory" the Court found that the evidence there was insufficient because the incidents of illegal advocacy were infrequent, sporadic, and not fairly related to the period covered by the indictment. In addition, the Court indicated that the illegal advocacy was not sufficiently tied to officials who spoke for the Party as such.

Thus, in short, *Yates* imposes a strict standard of proof, and indicates the kind of evidence that is insufficient to show illegal advocacy under that standard, the kind of evidence that is sufficient, and what pattern of evidence is necessary to hold the Party responsible for such advocacy. With these criteria in mind, we now proceed to an examination of the evidence in this case.

[The Court's summary of the evidence is omitted.]

We conclude that this evidence sufficed to make a case for the jury on the issue of illegal Party advocacy. *Dennis* and *Yates* have definitely laid at rest any doubt that present advocacy of *future* action for violent overthrow satisfies statutory and constitutional requirements equally with advocacy of *immediate* action to that end. . . . Hence this record cannot be considered deficient because it contains no evidence of advocacy for immediate overthrow.

Since the evidence amply showed that Party leaders were continuously preaching during the indictment period the inevitability of eventual forcible overthrow, the first and basic question is a narrow one: whether the jury could permissibly infer that such preaching, in whole or in part, "was aimed at building up a seditious group and maintaining it in readiness for action at a propitious time . . . the kind of indoctrination preparatory to action which was condemned in *Dennis*." . . . On this score, we think that the jury, under instructions which fully satisfied the requirements of *Yates,* was entitled to infer from this systematic preaching . . . that "advocacy of action" was engaged in.

. . .

Affirmed.

■ MR. JUSTICE BLACK, dissenting.

. . .

. . . I think it is important to point out the manner in which this case re-emphasizes the freedom-destroying nature of the "balancing test" presently in use by the Court to justify its refusal to apply specific constitutional protections of the Bill of Rights. . . . Petitioner is being sent to jail for the express reason that he has associated with people who have entertained unlawful ideas and said unlawful things, and that of course is a *direct* abridgment of his freedoms of speech and assembly—under any definition that has ever been used for that term. . . .

. . .

■ MR. JUSTICE DOUGLAS, dissenting.

. . .

The case is not saved by showing that petitioner was an active member. None of the activity constitutes a crime. . . .

Not one single illegal act is charged to petitioner. That is why the essence of the crime covered by the indictment is merely belief—belief in the proletarian revolution, belief in Communist creed.

. . .

■ MR. JUSTICE BRENNAN, with whom THE CHIEF JUSTICE and MR. JUSTICE DOUGLAS join, dissenting.

[These justices argued that in § 4(f) of the Internal Security Act Congress legislated immunity from prosecution under the membership clause of the Smith Act.][a]

Aftermath of the Yates, Scales *and* Noto *Cases*

Of 141 people indicted under the Smith Act, 29 served prison terms. These included the 11 defendants in *Dennis,* 17 defendants in two cases prior to *Yates* that the Court declined to review, and the single defendant in *Scales.* Emerson, *The System of Freedom of Expression* 124 (1970). The government had turned to membership clause prosecutions after *Yates,* because it concluded that it would be unable to satisfy the Court's requirement that each defendant be proved to have personally advocated specific illegal acts or have participated in such advocacy by others. While the Court

---

[a]   Decided the same day as *Scales,* Noto v. United States, 367 U.S. 290 (1961), involved another prosecution under the membership clause of the Smith Act. The conviction was reversed because there was insufficient evidence of illegal Communist Party advocacy. Dicta stated that there must also be proof of the defendant's personal criminal purpose. "This element of the membership crime, like its others, must be judged *strictissimi juris,* for otherwise there is a danger that one in sympathy with the legitimate aims of such an organization, but not specifically intending to accomplish them by resort to violence, might be punished for his adherence to lawful and constitutionally protected purposes, because of other and unprotected purposes which he does not necessarily share." See United States v. Spock, 416 F.2d 165 (1st Cir.1969), reversing the conviction of Dr. Spock and others for conspiracy to counsel, aid, and abet registrants to resist the draft.

SECTION 1 AN INTRODUCTION TO PROBLEMS OF CONTENT CONTROL OF SPEECH 907

sustained the constitutionality of the membership clause in *Scales,* and also sustained the conviction, the *Scales* case marked the end of Smith Act prosecutions. Under the *Scales* and *Noto* cases, was the government required, in a membership clause case, to satisfy the same proof requirements imposed by *Yates?*

Consider, also, whether proof meeting the criteria imposed by the *Yates, Scales* and *Noto* cases would also sustain conviction under two older statutes contained in the federal criminal code, United States Code, Title 18:

§ 2383.   Rebellion or Insurrection

Whoever incites, sets on foot, assists, or engages in any rebellion or insurrection against the authority of the United States or the laws thereof, or gives aid or comfort thereto, shall be fined not more than $10,000 or imprisoned not more than ten years, or both; and shall be incapable of holding any office under the United States.

§ 2384.   Seditious Conspiracy

If two or more persons in any State or Territory, or in any place subject to the jurisdiction of the United States, conspire to overthrow, put down, or to destroy by force the Government of the United States, or to levy war against them, or to oppose by force the authority thereof, or by force to prevent, hinder, or delay the execution of any law of the United States, or by force to seize, take, or possess any property of the United States contrary to the authority thereof, they shall each be fined not more than $20,000 or imprisoned not more than twenty years, or both.

D. THE CURRENT STATUS OF THE CLEAR AND PRESENT DANGER TEST—THE "BRANDENBURG CONCERTO"[a]

Brandenburg v. Ohio
395 U.S. 444, 89 S.Ct. 1827, 23 L.Ed.2d 430 (1969).

■ PER CURIAM.

The appellant, a leader of a Ku Klux Klan group, was convicted under the Ohio Criminal Syndicalism statute for "advocat[ing] . . . the duty, necessity, or propriety of crime, sabotage, violence, or unlawful methods of terrorism as a means of accomplishing industrial or political reform" and for "voluntarily assembl[ing] with any society, group, or assemblage of persons formed to teach or advocate the doctrines of criminal syndicalism." Ohio Rev. Code Ann. § 2923.13. He was fined $1,000 and sentenced to one to 10 years' imprisonment. The appellant challenged the constitutionality of the criminal syndicalism statute under the First and Fourteenth Amendments to the United States Constitution, but the intermediate appellate court of Ohio affirmed his conviction without opinion. The Supreme Court of Ohio dismissed his appeal, *sua sponte,* "for the reason that no substantial constitutional question exists herein." . . . Appeal was taken to this Court. . . . We reverse.

The record shows that a man, identified at trial as the appellant, telephoned an announcer-reporter on the staff of a Cincinnati television station and invited him to come to a Ku Klux Klan "rally" to be held at a farm in Hamilton County. With the cooperation of the organizers, the reporter and a cameraman attended the meeting and filmed the events. Portions of the films were later broadcast on the local station and on a national network.

---

a   Linde, supra, p. 900.

The prosecution's case rested on the films and on testimony identifying the appellant as the person who communicated with the reporter and who spoke at the rally. The State also introduced into evidence several articles appearing in the film, including a pistol, a rifle, a shotgun, ammunition, a Bible, and a red hood worn by the speaker in the films.

One film showed 12 hooded figures, some of whom carried firearms. They were gathered around a large wooden cross, which they burned. No one was present other than the participants and the newsmen who made the film. Most of the words uttered during the scene were incomprehensible when the film was projected, but scattered phrases could be understood that were derogatory of Negroes and, in one instance, of Jews.[1] Another scene on the same film showed the appellant, in Klan regalia, making a speech. The speech, in full, was as follows:

"This is an organizers' meeting. We have had quite a few members here today which are—we have hundreds, hundreds of members throughout the State of Ohio. I can quote from a newspaper clipping from the Columbus, Ohio Dispatch, five weeks ago Sunday morning. The Klan has more members in the State of Ohio than does any other organization. We're not a revengent organization, but if our President, our Congress, our Supreme court, continues to suppress the white, Caucasian race, it's possible that there might have to be some revengeance taken.

"We are marching on Congress July the Fourth, four hundred thousand strong. From there we are dividing into two groups, one group to march on St. Augustine, Florida, the other group to march into Mississippi. Thank you."

The second film showed six hooded figures one of whom, later identified as the appellant, repeated a speech very similar to that recorded on the first film. The reference to the possibility of "revengeance" was omitted, and one sentence was added: "Personally, I believe the nigger should be returned to Africa, the Jew returned to Israel." Though some of the figures in the films carried weapons, the speaker did not.

The Ohio Criminal Syndicalism Statute was enacted in 1919. From 1917 to 1920, identical or quite similar laws were adopted by 20 States and two territories. E. Dowell, A History of Criminal Syndicalism Legislation in the United States 21 (1939). In 1927, this Court sustained the constitutionality of California's Criminal Syndicalism Act, . . . the text of which is quite similar to that of the laws of Ohio. *Whitney v. California*, 274 U.S. 357 (1927). The Court upheld the statute on the ground that, without more, "advocating" violent means to effect political and economic change involves such danger to the security of the State that the State may outlaw it. Cf. *Fiske v. Kansas*, 274 U.S. 380 (1927). But *Whitney* has been thoroughly discredited by later decisions. See *Dennis v. United States*, 341 U.S. 494, at 507 (1951). These later decisions have fashioned the principle that the constitutional guarantees of free

---

[1]   The significant portions that could be understood were:

"How far is the nigger going to—yeah."

"This is what we are going to do to the niggers."

"A dirty nigger."

"Send the Jews back to Israel."

"Let's give them back to the dark garden."

"Save America."

"Let's go back to constitutional betterment."

"Bury the niggers."

"We intend to do our part."

"Give us our state rights."

"Freedom for the whites."

"Nigger will have to fight for every inch he gets from now on."

speech and free press do not permit a State to forbid or proscribe advocacy of the use of force or of law violation except where such advocacy is directed to inciting or producing imminent lawless action and is likely to incite or produce such action.[2] As we said in Noto v. United States, 367 U.S. 290, 297–298 (1961), "the mere abstract teaching . . . of the moral propriety or even moral necessity for a resort to force and violence, is not the same as preparing a group for violent action and steeling it to such action." See also Herndon v. Lowry, 301 U.S. 242, 259–261 (1937); Bond v. Floyd, 385 U.S. 116, 134 (1966). A statute which fails to draw this distinction impermissibly intrudes upon the freedoms guaranteed by the First and Fourteenth Amendments. It sweeps within its condemnation speech which our Constitution has immunized from governmental control. Cf. Yates v. United States, 354 U.S. 298 (1957); De Jonge v. Oregon, 299 U.S. 353 (1937); Stromberg v. California, 283 U.S. 359 (1931). . . .

Measured by this test, Ohio's Criminal Syndicalism Act cannot be sustained. The Act punishes persons who "advocate or teach the duty necessity, or propriety" of violence "as a means of accomplishing industrial or political reform"; or who publish or circulate or display any book or paper containing such advocacy; or who "justify" the commission of violent acts "with intent to exemplify, spread or advocate the propriety of the doctrines of criminal syndicalism"; or who "voluntarily assemble" with a group formed "to teach or advocate the doctrines of criminal syndicalism." Neither the indictment nor the trial judge's instructions to the jury in any way refined the statute's bald definition of the crime in terms of mere advocacy not distinguished from incitement to imminent lawless action.[3]

Accordingly, we are here confronted with a statute which, by its own words and as applied, purports to punish mere advocacy and to forbid, on pain of criminal punishment, assembly with others merely to advocate the described type of action.[4] Such a statute falls within the condemnation of the First and Fourteenth Amendments. The contrary teaching of Whitney v. California, supra, cannot be supported, and that decision is therefore overruled.

Reversed.

■ MR. JUSTICE BLACK, concurring.

I agree with the views expressed by Mr. Justice Douglas in his concurring opinion in this case that the "clear and present danger" doctrine should have no place in the interpretation of the First Amendment. I join the Court's opinion, which, as I understand it, simply cites Dennis v. United States, 341 U.S. 494 (1951), but does not

---

[2]   It was on the theory that the Smith Act, 54 Stat. 670, 18 U.S.C. § 2385, embodied such a principle and that it had been applied only in conformity with it that this Court sustained the Act's constitutionality. Dennis v. United States, 341 U.S. 494 (1951). That this was the basis for *Dennis* was emphasized in Yates v. United States, 354 U.S. 298, 320–324 (1957), in which the Court overturned convictions for advocacy of the forcible overthrow of the Government under the Smith Act, because the trial judge's instructions had allowed conviction for mere advocacy, unrelated to its tendency to produce forcible action.

[3]   The first count of the indictment charged that appellant "did unlawfully by word of mouth advocate the necessity, or propriety of crime, violence, or unlawful methods of terrorism as a means of accomplishing political reform. . . ." The second count charged that appellant "did unlawfully voluntarily assemble with a group or assemblage of persons formed to advocate the doctrines of criminal syndicalism. . . ." The trial judge's charge merely followed the language of the indictment. No construction of the statute by the Ohio courts has brought it within constitutionally permissible limits. The Ohio Supreme Court has considered the statute in only one previous case, State v. Kassay, 126 Ohio St. 177, 184 N.E. 521 (1932), where the constitutionality of the statute was sustained.

[4]   Statutes affecting the right of assembly, like those touching on freedom of speech, must observe the established distinctions between mere advocacy and incitement to imminent lawless action, for as Chief Justice Hughes wrote in De Jonge v. Oregon, supra at 364: "The right of peaceable assembly is a right cognate to those of free speech and free press and is equally fundamental." . . .

indicate any agreement on the Court's part with the "clear and present danger" doctrine on which *Dennis* purported to rely.

■ MR. JUSTICE DOUGLAS, concurring.

While I join the opinion of the Court, I desire to enter a *caveat*.

. . .

. . . I see no place in the regime of the First Amendment for any "clear and present danger" test, whether strict and tight as some would make it, or free-wheeling as the Court in *Dennis* rephrased it.

When one reads the opinions closely and sees when and how the "clear and present danger" test has been applied, great misgivings are aroused. First, the threats were often loud but always puny and made serious only by judges so wedded to the *status quo* that critical analysis made them nervous. Second, the test was so twisted and perverted in *Dennis* as to make the trial of those teachers of Marxism an all-out political trial which was part and parcel of the cold war that has eroded substantial parts of the First Amendment.

. . .

The line between what is permissible and not subject to control and what may be made impermissible and subject to regulation is the line between ideas and overt acts.

The example usually given by those who would punish speech is the case of one who falsely shouts fire in a crowded theatre.

This is, however, a classic case where speech is brigaded with action. They are indeed inseparable and a prosecution can be launched for the overt acts actually caused. Apart from rare instances of that kind, speech is, I think, immune from prosecution. Certainly there is no constitutional line between advocacy of abstract ideas as in *Yates* and advocacy of political action as in *Scales*. The quality of advocacy turns on the depth of the conviction; and government has no power to invade that sanctuary of belief and conscience.[a]

The Constitutional Law Implications of the Court's Smith Act Interpretation

Despite the fact that it is a *per curiam* decision[1] and despite possible arguments that much of the discussion of clear and present danger is dicta, *Brandenburg* has been read as an authoritative statement of the Court's position on the minimum protection afforded speech.[2] Subsequent cases have converted other aspects of the Court's construction of the Smith Act in the *Yates* and *Scales* cases into constitutional doctrine.

---

[a] For a review of the development of clear and present danger doctrine from prior to World War I through *Brandenburg,* see Rabban, *The Emergence of Modern First Amendment Doctrine,* 50 U.Chi.L.Rev. 1205 (1983).

[1] It is unusual that the Court's major expression of contemporary first amendment doctrine is contained in an unsigned opinion. The editors have been informed by a reliable source that the opinion had been written by Justice Fortas, who resigned prior to the Court's announcement of the decision. The same source states that the case was regarded as easy in its result, and very little attention was paid to what the opinion said.

[2] E.g., a state conviction for disorderly conduct based on an intemperate speech at a campus anti-war demonstration was reversed, on the authority of *Brandenburg,* in Hess v. Indiana, 414 U.S. 105 (1973). Specifically, the Court held that the *Brandenburg* criteria had not been met both because the defendant's speech did not advocate specific unlawful action, and there was insufficient evidence that his words were likely to produce imminent disorder.

Even under the position taken by Justices Brandeis and Holmes, people could be punished for knowing membership in an organization advocating the commission of serious crimes, if there was a clear and present danger that those crimes would be committed. Justice Brandeis' *Whitney* concurrence did not require proof that the defendant participated in the advocacy or shared the organization's illegal purposes. Dicta in the *Scales* and *Noto* cases, however, required that there be proof, beyond defendant's knowledge of illegal advocacy by the organization, of the defendant's "active membership" and specific intent to accomplish the organization's illegal aims. Application of those requirements would have required the acquittal of the defendant in the *Whitney* case, even upon proof that her organization advocated specific criminal conduct and that there was a clear and present danger. Those requirements have, however, been converted from interpretations of the Smith Act to first amendment doctrine. The development occurred in a series of cases dealing with government requests for information, qualification for government employment and loyalty oaths; none of the cases involved criminal punishment.[3]

Deference to Legislative Judgment Concerning the Presence and Extent of Danger

A major issue in the clear and present danger debate is whether courts should defer to legislative judgments concerning the danger posed by classes of speech or the defendant's speech. It will be recalled that, in *Gitlow,* the Court noted the New York legislature's implicit determination that *all* revolutionary speech was dangerous, and concluded "it must be given great weight." Justice Frankfurter's concurring opinion in *Dennis* argued that the case presented a clash of interests "[i]t is not for us to decide" since Congress had decided that the danger created by Communist Party speech justified its restriction. 341 U.S. at 550. Chief Justice Vinson's plurality opinion accepted clear and present danger as the appropriate standard, with the obligation of courts to examine whether there is a clear and present danger to justify application of the statute to the specific situation, and thus did not articulately refer to sustaining of legislative judgments. (The rejection of any requirement of imminence allowed the plurality to discover the requisite danger. The Court had, moreover, not granted certiorari to consider the sufficiency of the evidence, so the Court was not required to determine whether any particular Communist Party speech created danger.) Chief Justice Vinson's opinion can be read as implicitly deferring to contemporary legislative and executive judgments concerning the danger to internal security presented by the Communist Party.

The Court discussed the issue of deference to legislative judgment in Landmark Communications, Inc. v. Virginia, 435 U.S. 829 (1978). Chief Justice Burger's opinion for the Court said, in part:

". . . Properly applied, the test requires a court to make its own inquiry into the imminence and magnitude of the danger said to flow from the particular utterance and then to balance the character of the evil, as well as its likelihood, against the need for free and unfettered expression. The possibility that other measures will serve the State's interests should also be weighed.

. . .

"A legislature appropriately inquires into and may declare the reasons impelling legislative action but the judicial function commands analysis of whether the specific conduct charged falls within the reach of the statute and if so whether the legislation

---

[3]   Elfbrandt v. Russell, 384 U.S. 11, 15–16 (1966); Keyishian v. Board of Regents, 385 U.S. 589, 606 (1967); Law Students Civil Rights Research Council, Inc. v. Wadmond, 401 U.S. 154, 165 (1971).

is consonant with the Constitution. Were it otherwise, the scope of freedom of speech and of the press would be subject to legislative definition and the function of the First Amendment as a check on legislative power would be nullified."

The Clear and Present Danger Debate—Some General Considerations

The earlier debate, in an extensive literature, argued whether a tightly-drawn clear and present danger test was a *necessary* condition for protection of freedom of speech.[1] The Court's current adherence to it has muted that debate, and brought to the fore the question whether any version of the clear and present danger test is a *sufficient* condition for protection of freedom of speech.[2] Before turning to some of the arguments made in the debate, however, it is important to note that clear and present danger is not a doctrine for all first amendment seasons. In its focus on the danger of illegal conduct, at most its literal application is limited to those cases where the only societal interest asserted for restricting speech is that danger. As will be seen in Section 3 of this chapter, and in the following two chapters, whether or not clear and present danger is the appropriate test for speech urging violation of the law, it is not helpful in other problem areas.[3] Some general themes in the debate are, however, of broader application. Some of those themes are singled out for brief mention, below.

(1) Political speech contrasted with other forms of speech. While the clear and present danger test is by its terms directed at any speech advocating the commission of a crime, all of the Supreme Court's cases have, in fact, involved some form of political speech—whether the general platform of a radical organization or a hot-tempered street-corner protest speech. A major criticism of the clear and present danger approach is that it permits stifling of radical political speech based on problematic assessments of public danger, while it over-protects dangerous speech in a non-political context.

The application of first amendment principles to criminal defendants who incite or solicit others, or agree among themselves to commit specific, serious crimes in a non-political context has not been much explored.[4] Professor Chafee, the most ardent

---

[1] The most articulate defense of the clear and present danger test is contained in Chafee, *Free Speech in the United States* (1941). For a contemporary defense, see Redish, *Advocacy of Unlawful Conduct and The First Amendment: In Defense of Clear and Present Danger,* 70 Calif.L.Rev. 1159 (1982).

[2] The earliest critical scholarly attack on the test as insufficiently protective of speech is Meiklejohn, *Free Speech and Its Relation to Self-Government* (1948).

[3] Before the *Dennis* case, the Court had employed the clear and present danger test in the context of a state contempt of court conviction of a newspaper and a labor leader for allegedly prejudicial statements concerning pending cases. Justice Black's opinion for the Court in Bridges v. California, 314 U.S. 252 (1941), held that these publications could not constitutionally constitute contempt in the absence of a clear and present danger to the administration of justice. Later cases involving contempt prosecutions for media criticism of judicial decisions have continued to reverse the convictions using the idiom of clear and present danger. Pennekamp v. Florida, 328 U.S. 331 (1946); Craig v. Harney, 331 U.S. 367 (1947); Wood v. Georgia, 370 U.S. 375 (1962). Those cases, however, can be read as imposing an absolute ban on contempt prosecution for media statements concerning pending cases, or criticism of judicial action. See Baltimore Radio Show, Inc. v. State, 193 Md. 300, 67 A.2d 497 (1949), cert. denied 338 U.S. 912 (1950).

Bridges, Pennekamp and *Craig* were prominent among the cases cited by Chief Justice Vinson in his opinion in the *Dennis* case for the proposition that the Court had "inclined toward the Holmes-Brandeis rationale." 341 U.S. at 507.

[4] Compare, however, State v. Robertson, 293 Or. 402, 649 P.2d 569 (1982). The Oregon Supreme Court, in an opinion by Justice Linde, invalidated a statute making "criminal coercion" a crime. The challenged statute concerned compelling or inducing a person to do something he has a legal right not to do by making a threat to inflict specific harms, including exposing a secret. For extended comment on the decision, see Greenawalt, *Criminal Coercion and Freedom of Speech,* 78 Northwestern L.Rev. 1081 (1983).

defender of Holmes' clear and present danger approach, argued that its source could be found in the general criminal law of attempt, which required that the defendant had made "dangerous progress toward the consummation" of the crime.[5] It will be recalled, however, that Holmes' opinions in *Schenck* and *Abrams* focused at least as much on the speakers' "intent" as on their "dangerous progress." The requirement of progress toward consummation of the criminal conduct urged by speech seems not to be clearly reflected in criminal law doctrines of solicitation and conspiracy, which also focus primarily on issues of proof of the defendant's intent. The Model Penal Code, § 5.02, provides that a person is guilty of solicitation to commit a crime "if with the purpose of facilitating its commission he commands, encourages or requests another person to engage in specific conduct which would constitute such crime." No requirement that the person solicited is likely to commit the crime has been imposed. The crime of conspiracy, whether or not it requires the commission of an overt act as well as the agreement, has similarly not required a showing that the ultimate object of the conspiracy would occur.

The argument that clear and present danger affords too little protection in the arena of political speech was first put forward by Alexander Meiklejohn.[6] He argued that the principle of freedom of speech was rooted in principles of self-government, and that there should be absolute protection for the discussion of public issues, but considerably less protection for speech that did not discuss issues of public interest.[7] Critics of the Meiklejohn approach have questioned the ability to draw the distinction between political and other forms of speech, and have objected to the low level of protection afforded non-political speech under his theory.[8] Advocates of a political speech principle have disagreed with Meiklejohn's assessment of the level of protection to be afforded political speech[9] or with his conclusion that the first amendment was inapplicable to non-political speech.[10] It is, however, a useful inquiry to consider whether the pattern of the Court's decisions reflects a distinction between speech discussing public affairs and other kinds of communication.

(2) Absolutes and balances. Justice Black was a consistent opponent of balancing competing interests as a technique of judicial adjudication. While his early opinions spoke of clear and present danger, he indicated in his *Dennis* dissent that he believed clear and present danger did not mark the outer boundaries of protected expression. For him, clear and present danger had become simply another technique for balancing competing interests. (Justice Frankfurter's *Dennis* concurrence, by contrast, criticized clear and present danger as too wooden a standard to permit the sensitive balancing of competing interests.) The position adopted by Justices Black and Douglas was that the first amendment forbids any government restriction on "speech" but permits the government to regulate "conduct." In their opinions in a number of cases, Justices Black and Harlan debated the question whether freedom of speech was absolutely protected[11] with Justice Black consistently maintaining that

---

[5] Chafee, supra note 1, at 47.

[6] Meiklejohn, supra note 2.

[7] Specifically, Meiklejohn argued that "freedom of speech" protected by the first amendment was non-abridgable, but that "liberty of speech" was protected only by the concept of due process and could be regulated for sufficient reasons. Id. at 37–39.

[8] E.g., Emerson, *The System of Freedom of Expression* 541 (1970); Chafee, *Book Review of Meiklejohn's Free Speech and its Relation to Self-Government,* 62 Harv.L.Rev. 891 (1949).

[9] Bork, *Neutral Principles and Some First Amendment Problems,* 47 Ind.L.J. 1 (1971).

[10] Be Vier, The First Amendment and Political Speech: An Inquiry into the Substance and Limits of Principle, 30 Stan.L.Rev. 299 (1978).

[11] E.g., Barenblatt v. United States, 360 U.S. 109 (1959); Konigsberg v. State Bar, 366 U.S. 36 (1961); cf. Cohen v. California, 403 U.S. 15 (1971).

"the men who drafted our Bill of Rights did all the 'balancing' that was to be done in this field."[12]

Criticisms of both the balancers and the absolutists should be obvious. Given the intractable problem of assigning values to competing interests, it is claimed that balancing is not a process but simply a convenient method of rationalizing subjective conclusions. Moreover, it often has been employed with excessive deference to the interests that justify suppression of speech. Absolute protection, it is argued, over-protects intolerable speech, or requires sophistry in drawing speech-conduct distinctions, or both.[13] The clash of contentions about absolutism and balancing has abated in contemporary free speech cases, but some of the competing arguments may have re-appeared in a new form.

(3) Ad hoc and definitional balancing. A major dispute in the debate surrounding clear and present danger was whether it was appropriate to focus on the danger of all revolutionary speech, or the danger of the defendant's particular speech in its context.[14] An analogous argument concerns the method for reconciling free speech values with competing governmental interests. Ad hoc balancing requires weighing the value of particular speech against the strength of competing interests in the particular case. Definitional balancing suggests that the competing interests should result not in ad hoc decisions but the framing of rules of general application.[15] For a "definitional balancer," the proper rule in a particular context may be one of absolute protection for speech, which may trigger at least part of the controversy between absolutism and balancing. Moreover, the distinction between ad hoc and definitional balancing is itself slippery, since it turns on the level of generality at which a balance is struck or whether there is predictable content in a rule. The student should be alert, in the materials that follow, to the question whether particular free speech issues have been resolved by ad hoc or definitional balancing. A final question is whether the results reached, or the reasons given, represent a single, coherent theory of freedom of expression.

---

[12]   366 U.S. at 61.

[13]   A sampling of the law review discussion includes Griswold, *Absolute is in the Dark—A Discussion of the Approach of the Supreme Court to Constitutional Questions,* 8 Utah L.Rev. 167 (1963); Frantz, *The First Amendment in the Balance,* 71 Yale L.J. 1424 (1962); Mendelson, *On the Meaning of the First Amendment: Absolutes in the Balance,* 50 Calif.L.Rev. 821 (1962); Frantz, *Is the First Amendment Law—A Reply to Professor Mendelson,* 51 Calif.L.Rev. 729 (1963); Kalven, *Upon Re-reading Mr. Justice Black on the First Amendment,* 14 U.C.L.A.L.Rev. 428 (1967); Gunther, *In Search of Judicial Quality on a Changing Court: The Case of Justice Powell,* 24 Stanf.L.Rev. 1001 (1972); Powe, *Evolution to Absolutism: Justice Douglas and the First Amendment,* 74 Colum.L.Rev. 371 (1974).

It can be argued that Justice Black was forced to manipulate the boundaries separating expression and action. In Giboney v. Empire Storage and Ice Co., 336 U.S. 490 (1949), he wrote the opinion for a unanimous court sustaining a restraint of trade conviction of union picketers whose placards urged an ice distributor to stop selling ice to nonunion peddlers. His opinion stated that the placards were to effectuate an unlawful purpose, and the defendants had engaged in illegal conduct "carried out by means of language." In Cohen v. California, 403 U.S. 15 (1971), infra, p. 1012, the Court overturned a breach of the peace conviction of a person who wore a jacket in a courthouse bearing the words "Fuck the Draft." Justice Black joined Justice Blackmun's dissent, which stated that the defendant's "antic . . . was mainly conduct and little speech."

[14]   See Linde, supra p. 900.

[15]   The term "definitional balancing" first appears in Nimmer, *The Right to Speak from Times to Time: First Amendment Theory Applied to Libel and Misapplied to Privacy,* 56 Cal.L.Rev. 935 (1968), which still contains the most lucid description of the distinction between definitional and ad hoc balancing. Id. at 939–948. The most comprehensive treatment of freedom of expression issues which rejects both absolutism and ad hoc balancing is contained in Emerson, supra note 8. Another attempt to construct a general structure avoiding ad hoc balancing is contained in a series of articles by Professor C. Edwin Baker. They are cited in Shiffrin, *The First Amendment and Economic Regulation: Away from a General Theory of the First Amendment,* 78 Northwestern L.Rev. 1212, 1224 n. 83 (1983), and Baker's approach is both explained and criticized, id. at 1239–1251.

E. SPEECH PROVIDING "MATERIAL SUPPORT" TO DESIGNATED FOREIGN TERRORIST ORGANIZATIONS

Holder v. Humanitarian Law Project

561 U.S. 1, 130 S.Ct. 2705, 177 L.Ed.2d 355 (2010).

■ CHIEF JUSTICE ROBERTS delivered the opinion of the Court.

Congress has prohibited the provision of "material support or resources" to certain foreign organizations that engage in terrorist activity. 18 U. S. C. § 2339B(a)(1). That prohibition is based on a finding that the specified organizations "are so tainted by their criminal conduct that any contribution to such an organization facilitates that conduct." Antiterrorism and Effective Death Penalty Act of 1996 (AEDPA). . . . [P]laintiffs . . . seek to provide support to two such organizations. Plaintiffs claim that they seek to facilitate only the lawful, nonviolent purposes of those groups. . . . [T]hey claim that the statute is too vague, in violation of the Fifth Amendment, and that it infringes their rights to freedom of speech and association, in violation of the First Amendment. We conclude that the material-support statute is constitutional as applied to the particular activities plaintiffs have told us they wish to pursue. We do not, however, address the resolution of more difficult cases that may arise under the statute in the future.

I

. . . 18 U. S. C. § 2339B . . . makes it a federal crime to "knowingly provid[e] material support or resources to a foreign terrorist organization." . . .

The authority to designate an entity a "foreign terrorist organization" rests with the Secretary of State. . . . She may, in consultation with the Secretary of the Treasury and the Attorney General, so designate an organization upon finding that it is foreign, engages in "terrorist activity" or "terrorism," and thereby "threatens the security of United States nationals or the national security of the United States." . . . An entity designated a foreign terrorist organization may seek review of that designation before the D. C. Circuit within 30 days of that designation. . . .

In 1997, the Secretary of State designated . . . as foreign terrorist organizations . . . the Kurdistan Workers' Party (. . . PKK) and the Liberation Tigers of Tamil Eelam (LTTE). The PKK . . . aim[s to] establish[] an independent Kurdish state in southeastern Turkey. . . . The LTTE [seeks to] creat[e] an independent Tamil state in Sri Lanka. . . . The District Court . . . found that the PKK and the LTTE engage in political and humanitarian activities. . . . The Government has presented evidence that both groups have also committed numerous terrorist attacks, some of which have harmed American citizens. . . . The LTTE sought judicial review of its designation as a foreign terrorist organization; the D. C. Circuit upheld that designation. . . . The PKK did not challenge its designation. . . .

. . . In 1998, plaintiffs . . . [sued,] claim[ing] that they wished to provide support for the humanitarian and political activities of the PKK and the LTTE in the form of monetary contributions, other tangible aid, legal training, and political advocacy, but . . . could not do so for fear of prosecution. . . .

[P]laintiffs claimed that the material-support statute . . . violated their freedom of speech and freedom of association under the First Amendment, because it criminalized their provision of material support to the PKK and the LTTE, without requiring the Government to prove that plaintiffs had a specific intent to further the unlawful ends of those organizations. . . . Second, plaintiffs argued that the statute was unconstitutionally vague. . . .

. . .

[During the lower court proceedings,] in 2001, Congress amended the definition of "material support or resources" to add the term "expert advice or assistance." . . . Patriot Act. . . . In 2003, plaintiffs filed a second action challenging the constitutionality of that term as applied to them. . . .

. . .

[Before further lower court proceedings concluded,] . . . Congress again amended § 2339B and the definition of "material support or resources." Intelligence Reform and Terrorism Prevention Act of 2004 (IRTPA), . . .

In IRTPA, Congress clarified the mental state necessary to violate § 2339B, requiring knowledge of the foreign group's designation as a terrorist organization or the group's commission of terrorist acts. § 2339B(a)(1). Congress also added the term "service" to the definition of "material support or resources," § 2339A(b)(1), and defined "training" to mean "instruction or teaching designed to impart a specific skill, as opposed to general knowledge," § 2339A(b)(2). It also defined "expert advice or assistance" to mean "advice or assistance derived from scientific, technical or other specialized knowledge." § 2339A(b)(3). Finally, IRTPA clarified the scope of the term "personnel" by providing:

"No person may be prosecuted under [§ 2339B] in connection with the term 'personnel' unless that person has knowingly provided, attempted to provide, or conspired to provide a foreign terrorist organization with 1 or more individuals (who may be or include himself) to work under that terrorist organization's direction or control or to organize, manage, supervise, or otherwise direct the operation of that organization. Individuals who act entirely independently of the foreign terrorist organization to advance its goals or objectives shall not be considered to be working under the foreign terrorist organization's direction and control." § 2339B(h).

. . .

[Subsequent lower court proceedings culminated in a Ninth Circuit ruling rejecting plaintiffs' First Amendment claims and upholding some of their vagueness claims. Certiorari petitions from both sides were granted.]

II

Plaintiffs challenge § 2339B's prohibition on four types of material support—"training," "expert advice or assistance," "service," and "personnel." . . . First, plaintiffs claim that § 2339B violates the Due Process Clause of the Fifth Amendment because these four statutory terms are impermissibly vague. Second, plaintiffs claim that § 2339B violates their freedom of speech under the First Amendment. Third, plaintiffs claim that § 2339B violates their First Amendment freedom of association.

Plaintiffs do not challenge the above statutory terms in all their applications. Rather, plaintiffs claim that § 2339B is invalid to the extent it prohibits them from engaging in certain specified activities. . . . With respect to [one set of plaintiffs] those activities are: (1) "train[ing] members of [the] PKK on how to use humanitarian and international law to peacefully resolve disputes"; (2) "engag[ing] in political advocacy on behalf of Kurds who live in Turkey"; and (3) "teach[ing] PKK members how to petition various representative bodies such as the United Nations for relief." . . . With respect to the other plaintiffs, those activities are: (1) "train[ing] members of [the] LTTE to present claims for tsunami-related aid to mediators and international bodies"; (2) "offer[ing] their legal expertise in negotiating peace agreements between the LTTE and the Sri Lankan government"; and (3) "engag[ing] in political advocacy on behalf of Tamils who live in Sri Lanka." . . .

[Because] "the LTTE was recently defeated militarily in Sri Lanka," . . . "[m]uch of the support [plaintiffs] sought to provide is now moot." . . . Plaintiffs thus seek only to support the LTTE "as a political organization outside Sri Lanka advocating for the rights of Tamils." . . . [P]laintiffs no longer seek to teach the LTTE how to present claims for tsunami-related aid, because the LTTE now "has no role in Sri Lanka." . . . For that reason, helping the LTTE negotiate a peace agreement with Sri Lanka appears to be moot as well. Thus, we do not consider the application of § 2339B to those activities here.

. . .

III

Plaintiffs . . . contend that we should interpret the material-support statute, when applied to speech, to require proof that a defendant intended to further a foreign terrorist organization's illegal activities. . . .

We reject plaintiffs' interpretation of § 2339B because . . . [in] the text of the statute . . . Congress plainly . . . chose knowledge about the organization's connection to terrorism, not specific intent to further the organization's terrorist activities.

. . .

Scales is . . . readily distinguishable. . . . Section 2339B does not criminalize mere membership in a designated foreign terrorist organization. It instead prohibits providing "material support" to such a group. Nothing about *Scales* suggests the need for a specific intent requirement in such a case. . . .

. . .

IV

. . .

[P]laintiffs' claims of vagueness lack merit. Plaintiffs do not argue that the material-support statute grants too much enforcement discretion to the Government. We therefore address only whether the statute "provide[s] a person of ordinary intelligence fair notice of what is prohibited." . . .

. . .

Congress . . . took care to add narrowing definitions to the material-support statute over time[, which] increased the clarity of the statute's terms. . . . And the knowledge requirement of the statute further reduces any potential for vagueness . . . .

. . . [T]he dispositive point . . . is that the statutory terms are clear in their application to plaintiffs' proposed conduct . . . .

. . . A person of ordinary intelligence would understand that instruction on resolving disputes through international law falls within the statute's definition of "training" because it imparts a "specific skill," not "general knowledge." § 2339A(b)(2). Plaintiffs' activities also fall comfortably within the scope of "expert advice or assistance": A reasonable person would recognize that teaching the PKK how to petition for humanitarian relief before the United Nations involves advice derived from, as the statute puts it, "specialized knowledge." § 2339A(b)(3). . . .

. . .

Plaintiffs also contend that they want to engage in "political advocacy" on behalf of Kurds living in Turkey and Tamils living in Sri Lanka [, but] . . . that such advocacy might be regarded as "material support" in the form of providing "personnel" or "service[s]," [meaning] that the statute is unconstitutionally vague because they cannot tell.

. . . The statute makes clear that "personnel" does not cover *independent* advocacy . . . .

"[S]ervice" similarly refers to concerted activity, not independent advocacy. . . . We think a person of ordinary intelligence would understand that independently advocating for a cause is different from providing a service to a group that is advocating for that cause.

. . . [A]ny independent advocacy in which plaintiffs wish to engage is not prohibited by § 2339B. On the other hand, a person of ordinary intelligence would understand the term "service" to cover advocacy performed in coordination with, or at the direction of, a foreign terrorist organization.

. . .

V

A

We next consider whether the material-support statute, as applied to plaintiffs, violates the freedom of speech guaranteed by the First Amendment. Both plaintiffs and the Government take extreme positions on this question. Plaintiffs claim that Congress has banned their "pure political speech." . . . It has not. Under the material-support statute, plaintiffs may say anything they wish on any topic. They may speak and write freely about the PKK and LTTE, the governments of Turkey and Sri Lanka, human rights, and international law. They may advocate before the United Nations. As the Government states: "The statute does not prohibit independent advocacy or expression of any kind." . . . Section 2339B also "does not prevent [plaintiffs] from becoming members of the PKK and LTTE or impose any sanction on them for doing so." . . . Congress has not, therefore, sought to suppress ideas or opinions in the form of "pure political speech." Rather, Congress has prohibited "material support," which most often does not take the form of speech at all. And when it does, the statute is carefully drawn to cover only a narrow category of speech to, under the direction of, or in coordination with foreign groups that the speaker knows to be terrorist organizations.[4]

For its part, the Government takes the foregoing too far, claiming that the only thing truly at issue in this litigation is conduct, not speech[, where] . . . we appl[y] . . . "intermediate scrutiny," under which a "content-neutral regulation will be sustained under the First Amendment if it advances important governmental interests unrelated to the suppression of free speech and does not burden substantially more speech than necessary to further those interests." Turner Broadcasting System, Inc. v. FCC, 520 U. S. 180, 189 (1997). . . .

. . . § 2339B regulates speech on the basis of its content. Plaintiffs want to speak to the PKK and the LTTE, and whether they may do so under § 2339B depends on what they say. If plaintiffs' speech to those groups imparts a "specific skill" or communicates advice derived from "specialized knowledge"—for example, training on the use of international law or advice on petitioning the United Nations—then it is barred. . . . On the other hand, plaintiffs' speech is not barred if it imparts only general or unspecialized knowledge. . . .

---

[4]   The dissent also analyzes the statute as if it prohibited "[p]eaceful political advocacy" or "pure speech and association," without more. Section 2339B does not do that, and we do not address the constitutionality of any such prohibitions. The dissent's claim that our decision is inconsistent with this Court's cases analyzing those sorts of restrictions is accordingly unfounded.

The Government argues that § 2339B should nonetheless receive intermediate scrutiny because it *generally* functions as a regulation of conduct. That argument runs headlong into . . . our precedents, most prominently Cohen v. California, 403 U. S. 15 (1971). *Cohen* also involved a generally applicable regulation of conduct, barring breaches of the peace. . . . But when Cohen was convicted for wearing a jacket bearing an epithet, we . . . recognized that the generally applicable law was directed at Cohen because of what his speech communicated—he violated the breach of the peace statute because of the offensive content of his particular message. We accordingly applied more rigorous scrutiny and reversed his conviction. . . .

. . . The law here may be described as directed at conduct, [too . . .], but as applied to plaintiffs the conduct triggering coverage under the statute consists of communicating a message. . . .

B

The First Amendment issue . . . is instead whether the Government may prohibit what plaintiffs want to do—provide material support to the PKK and LTTE in the form of speech.

Everyone agrees that the Government's interest in combating terrorism is an urgent objective of the highest order. . . . Plaintiffs' complaint is that the ban on material support, applied to what they wish to do, is not "necessary to further that interest.". . . . [P]laintiffs argue [that] their support will advance only the legitimate activities of the designated terrorist organizations, not their terrorism. . . .

Whether foreign terrorist organizations meaningfully segregate support of their legitimate activities from support of terrorism is an empirical question. When it enacted § 2339B in 1996, Congress made specific findings regarding the serious threat posed by international terrorism. . . . One of those findings explicitly rejects plaintiffs' contention that their support would not further the terrorist activities of the PKK and LTTE: "[F]oreign organizations that engage in terrorist activity are so tainted by their criminal conduct that *any contribution to such an organization* facilitates that conduct." . . .

. . . Congress considered and rejected the view that ostensibly peaceful aid would have no harmful effects.

We are convinced that Congress was justified in rejecting that view. The PKK and the LTTE are deadly groups. "The PKK's insurgency has claimed more than 22,000 lives." Declaration of Kenneth R. McKune, . . . The LTTE has engaged in extensive suicide bombings and political assassinations, including killings of the Sri Lankan President, Security Minister, and Deputy Defense Minister. . . . It is not difficult to conclude as Congress did that the "tain[t]" of such violent activities is so great that working in coordination with or at the command of the PKK and LTTE serves to legitimize and further their terrorist means. AEDPA § 301(a)(7). . . .

Material support meant to "promot[e] peaceable, lawful conduct," Brief for Plaintiffs 51, can further terrorism by foreign groups in multiple ways. "Material support" is a valuable resource by definition. Such support frees up other resources within the organization that may be put to violent ends. It also importantly helps lend legitimacy to foreign terrorist groups—legitimacy that makes it easier for those groups to persist, to recruit members, and to raise funds—all of which facilitate more terrorist attacks. . . .

Money is fungible, and . . . "[f]unds raised ostensibly for charitable purposes have in the past been redirected by some terrorist groups to fund the purchase of arms and explosives." *Id.*, [McKune Affidavit] at 134, ¶ 10. . . . There is evidence that the PKK and the LTTE, in particular, have not "respected the line between humanitarian and violent activities." . . . *id.*, . . .

The dissent argues that there is "no natural stopping place" for the proposition that aiding a foreign terrorist organization's lawful activity promotes the terrorist organization as a whole. But Congress has settled on just such a natural stopping place: The statute reaches only material support coordinated with or under the direction of a designated foreign terrorist organization. Independent advocacy that might be viewed as promoting the group's legitimacy is not covered.

Providing foreign terrorist groups with material support in any form also furthers terrorism by straining the United States' relationships with its allies and undermining cooperative efforts between nations to prevent terrorist attacks. . . . The material-support statute furthers this international effort by prohibiting aid for foreign terrorist groups that harm the United States' partners abroad. . . .

For example, the Republic of Turkey—a fellow member of NATO—is defending itself against a violent insurgency waged by the PKK. . . . That nation and our other allies would react sharply to Americans furnishing material support to foreign groups like the PKK, and would hardly be mollified by the explanation that the support was meant only to further those groups' "legitimate" activities. . . .

C

. . . The State Department informs us that "[t]he experience and analysis of the U. S. government agencies charged with combating terrorism strongly suppor[t]" Congress's finding that all contributions to foreign terrorist organizations further their terrorism. . . .

That evaluation of the facts by the Executive, like Congress's assessment, is entitled to deference. This litigation implicates sensitive and weighty interests of national security and foreign affairs. . . .

Our precedents, old and new, make clear that concerns of national security and foreign relations do not warrant abdication of the judicial role. . . . But when it comes to collecting evidence and drawing factual inferences in this area, "the lack of competence on the part of the courts is marked," . . . and respect for the Government's conclusions is appropriate.

One reason for that respect is that national security and foreign policy concerns arise in connection with efforts to confront evolving threats in an area where information can be difficult to obtain and the impact of certain conduct difficult to assess. The dissent slights these real constraints in demanding hard proof—with "detail," "specific facts," and "specific evidence"—that plaintiffs' proposed activities will support terrorist attacks. That would be a dangerous requirement. In this context, conclusions must often be based on informed judgment rather than concrete evidence, and that reality affects what we may reasonably insist on from the Government. The material-support statute is . . . a preventive measure—it criminalizes not terrorist attacks themselves, but aid that makes the attacks more likely to occur. The Government, when seeking to prevent imminent harms in the context of international affairs and national security, is not required to conclusively link all the pieces in the puzzle before we grant weight to its empirical conclusions. . . .

. . .

We also find it significant that Congress has been conscious of its own responsibility to consider how its actions may implicate constitutional concerns. First, § 2339B only applies to designated foreign terrorist organizations. There is, and always has been, a limited number of those organizations designated by the Executive Branch, . . . and any groups so designated may seek judicial review of the designation.

Second, in response to the lower courts' holdings in this litigation, Congress added clarity to the statute by providing narrowing definitions of the terms "training," "personnel," and "expert advice or assistance," as well as an explanation of the knowledge required to violate § 2339B. Third, in effectuating its stated intent not to abridge First Amendment rights, see § 2339B(i), Congress has also displayed a careful balancing of interests in creating limited exceptions to the ban on material support[, . . .] for example, exclud[ing] medicine and religious materials. See § 2339A(b)(1). In this area perhaps more than any other, the Legislature's superior capacity for weighing competing interests means that "we must be particularly careful not to substitute our judgment of what is desirable for that of Congress." *Rostker* . . . . Finally, and most importantly, Congress has avoided any restriction on independent advocacy, or indeed any activities not directed to, coordinated with, or controlled by foreign terrorist groups.

. . . Given the sensitive interests in national security and foreign affairs at stake, the political branches have adequately substantiated their determination that, to serve the Government's interest in preventing terrorism, it was necessary to prohibit providing material support in the form of training, expert advice, personnel, and services to foreign terrorist groups, even if the supporters meant to promote only the groups' nonviolent ends.

We turn to the particular speech plaintiffs propose to undertake. First, plaintiffs propose to "train members of [the] PKK on how to use humanitarian and international law to peacefully resolve disputes." . . . Congress can, consistent with the First Amendment, prohibit this direct training. It is wholly foreseeable that the PKK could use the "specific skill[s]" that plaintiffs propose to impart, § 2339A(b)(2), as part of a broader strategy to promote terrorism. The PKK could . . . pursue peaceful negotiation as a means of buying time to recover from short-term setbacks, lulling opponents into complacency, and ultimately preparing for renewed attacks. . . . A foreign terrorist organization introduced to the structures of the international legal system might use the information to threaten, manipulate, and disrupt. This possibility is real, not remote.

Second, plaintiffs propose to "teach PKK members how to petition various representative bodies such as the United Nations for relief." . . . The Government acts within First Amendment strictures in banning this proposed speech because it teaches the organization how to acquire "relief," . . . which could readily include monetary aid. . . . Indeed, earlier in this litigation, plaintiffs sought to teach the LTTE "to present claims for tsunami-related aid to mediators and international bodies," . . . . Money is fungible, and Congress logically concluded that money a terrorist group such as the PKK obtains using the techniques plaintiffs propose to teach could be redirected to funding the group's violent activities.

Finally, plaintiffs propose to "engage in political advocacy . . ." . . . [without] specify[ing] their expected level of coordination with the PKK or LTTE or suggest[ing] what exactly their "advocacy" would consist of. Plaintiffs' proposals are phrased at such a high level of generality that they cannot prevail in this preenforcement challenge. . . .

In responding to the foregoing, the dissent fails to address the real dangers at stake. It instead considers only the possible benefits of plaintiffs' proposed activities in the abstract. . . .

. . .

All this is not to say that any future applications of the material-support statute to speech or advocacy will survive First Amendment scrutiny. It is also not to say that any other statute relating to speech and terrorism would satisfy the First Amendment.

In particular, we in no way suggest that a regulation of independent speech would pass constitutional muster, even if the Government were to show that such speech benefits foreign terrorist organizations. We also do not suggest that Congress could extend the same prohibition on material support at issue here to domestic organizations. We simply hold that, in prohibiting the particular forms of support that plaintiffs seek to provide to foreign terrorist groups, § 2339B does not violate the freedom of speech.

VI

Plaintiffs' final claim is that the material-support statute violates their freedom of association under the First Amendment [by] criminaliz[ing] the mere fact of their associating with the PKK and the LTTE. . . .

The Court of Appeals correctly rejected this claim because the statute does not penalize mere association with a foreign terrorist organization. As the Ninth Circuit put it: "The statute does not prohibit being a member of one of the designated groups or vigorously promoting and supporting the political goals of the group. . . . What [§ 2339B] prohibits is the act of giving material support . . .". . . . Our decisions scrutinizing penalties on simple association or assembly are therefore inapposite. . . .

. . . It would be strange if the Constitution permitted Congress to prohibit certain forms of speech that constitute material support, but did not permit Congress to prohibit that support only to particularly dangerous and lawless foreign organizations. Congress is not required to ban material support to every group or none at all.

* * *

The Preamble to the Constitution proclaims that the people of the United States ordained and established that charter of government in part to "provide for the common defence." . . . We hold that, in regulating the particular forms of support that plaintiffs seek to provide to foreign terrorist organizations, Congress has pursued that objective consistent with the limitations of the First and Fifth Amendments.

■ JUSTICE BREYER, with whom JUSTICES GINSBURG and SOTOMAYOR join, dissenting.

Like the Court, and substantially for the reasons it gives, I do not think this statute is unconstitutionally vague. But I cannot agree . . . that the Constitution permits the Government to prosecute the plaintiffs criminally for engaging in coordinated teaching and advocacy furthering the designated organizations' lawful political objectives. . . .

I

. . .

[T]he Government has not made the strong showing necessary . . . . All the activities involve the communication and advocacy of political ideas and lawful means of achieving political ends. Even the subjects the plaintiffs wish to teach—using international law to resolve disputes peacefully or petitioning the United Nations, for instance—concern political speech. We cannot avoid the constitutional significance of these facts on the basis that some of this speech takes place outside the United States and is directed at foreign governments, for the activities also involve advocacy in *this* country directed to *our* government and *its* policies. The plaintiffs, for example, wish to write and distribute publications and to speak before the United States Congress. . . .

That this speech and association for political purposes is the *kind* of activity to which the First Amendment ordinarily offers its strongest protection is elementary. . . .

. . .

... [W]here, as here, a statute applies criminal penalties and at least arguably does so on the basis of content-based distinctions, I should think we would scrutinize the statute and justifications "strictly"—to determine whether the prohibition is justified by a "compelling" need that cannot be "less restrictively" accommodated....

But, even if we assume for argument's sake that "strict scrutiny" does not apply, ... I doubt that the statute, as the Government would interpret it, can survive any reasonably applicable First Amendment standard. See, *e.g.,* Turner Broadcasting System, Inc. v. FCC, 520 U.S. 180, 189 (1997) (describing intermediate scrutiny)....

The Government does identify a compelling countervailing interest, namely, the interest in protecting the security of the United States and its nationals from the threats that foreign terrorist organizations pose by denying those organizations financial and other fungible resources. I do not dispute the importance of this interest. But I do dispute whether the interest can justify the statute's criminal prohibition. To put the matter more specifically, precisely how does application of the statute to the protected activities before us *help achieve* that important security-related end? ...

. . .

... There is no *obvious* way in which undertaking advocacy for political change through peaceful means or teaching the PKK and LTTE, say, how to petition the United Nations for political change is fungible with other resources that might be put to more sinister ends in the way that donations of money, food, or computer training are fungible. It is far from obvious that these advocacy activities can themselves be redirected, or will free other resources that can be directed, towards terrorist ends. Thus, we must determine whether the Government has come forward with evidence to support its claim.

The Government has provided us with no empirical information that might convincingly support this claim....

The most one can say in the Government's favor about the[ ] statements [from Congress and the State Department official's affidavit] is that they *might* be read as offering highly general support for its argument. The statements do not, however, explain in any detail how the plaintiffs' political-advocacy-related activities might actually be "fungible" and therefore capable of being diverted to terrorist use. Nor do they indicate that Congress itself was concerned with "support" of this kind. The affidavit refers to "funds," "financing," and "goods"—none of which encompasses the plaintiffs' activities.... The statutory statement and the House Report ... are more naturally understood as referring to contributions of goods, money, or training and other services (say, computer programming) that could be diverted to, or free funding for, terrorist ends....

. . .

[Nor can the] "legitimacy" justification ... by itself warrant suppression of political speech, advocacy, and association. Speech, association, and related activities on behalf of a group will often, perhaps always, help to legitimate that group. Thus, were the law to accept a "legitimating" effect, in and of itself and without qualification, as providing sufficient grounds for imposing such a ban, the First Amendment battle would be lost in untold instances where it should be won. Once one accepts this argument, there is no natural stopping place. The argument applies as strongly to "independent" as to "coordinated" advocacy....

... Even were we to find some ... line of distinction, its application would seem so inherently uncertain that it would often, perhaps always, "chill" protected speech beyond its boundary....

Regardless, the "legitimacy" justification itself is inconsistent with critically important First Amendment case law. Consider the cases involving the protection the First Amendment offered those who joined the Communist Party intending only to further its peaceful activities. In those cases, this Court took account of congressional findings that the Communist Party not only advocated theoretically but also sought to put into practice the overthrow of our Government through force and violence. The Court had previously accepted Congress' determinations that the American Communist Party was a "Communist action organization" which (1) acted under the "control, direction, and discipline" of the world Communist movement, a movement that sought to employ "espionage, sabotage, terrorism, and any other means deemed necessary, to establish a Communist totalitarian dictatorship," and (2) "endeavor[ed]" to bring about "the overthrow of existing governments by . . . force if necessary." Communist Party of United States v. Subversive Activities Control Bd., 367 U. S. 1, 5–6 (1961). . . .

Nonetheless, the Court held that the First Amendment protected an American's right to belong to that party—despite whatever "legitimating" effect membership might have had—as long as the person did not share the party's unlawful purposes. . . . [T]hose cases draw further support from other cases permitting pure advocacy of even the most unlawful activity—as long as that advocacy is not "directed to inciting or producing imminent lawless action and . . . likely to incite or produce such action." *Brandenburg*,. . . . The Government's "legitimating" theory would seem to apply to these cases with equal justifying force; and, if recognized, it would have led this Court to conclusions other than those it reached.

Nor can the Government overcome these considerations simply by narrowing the covered activities to those that involve *coordinated*, rather than *independent,* advocacy. Conversations, discussions, or logistical arrangements might well prove necessary to carry out the speech-related activities here at issue (just as conversations and discussions are a necessary part of *membership* in any organization). The Government does not distinguish this kind of "coordination" from any other. I am not aware of any form of words that might be used to describe "coordination" that would not, at a minimum, seriously chill not only the kind of activities the plaintiffs raise before us, but also the "independent advocacy" the Government purports to permit. And, as for the Government's willingness to distinguish *independent* advocacy from *coordinated* advocacy, the former is *more* likely, not *less* likely, to confer legitimacy than the latter. Thus, other things being equal, the distinction "coordination" makes is arbitrary in respect to furthering the statute's purposes. And a rule of law that finds the "legitimacy" argument adequate in respect to the latter would have a hard time distinguishing a statute that sought to attack the former.

. . .

[T]he majority's arguments stretch the concept of "fungibility" beyond constitutional limits. . . . I am not aware of any case in this Court—not Gitlow v. New York, 268 U.S. 652 (1925), not Schenck v. United States, 249 U.S. 47 (1919), not *Abrams*, 250 U.S. 616, not the later Communist Party cases decided during the heat of the Cold War—in which the Court accepted anything like a claim that speech or teaching might be criminalized lest it, *e.g.*, buy negotiating time for an opponent who would put that time to bad use.

Moreover, the risk that those who are taught will put otherwise innocent speech or knowledge to bad use is omnipresent, at least where that risk rests on little more than (even informed) speculation. Hence to accept this kind of argument without more and to apply it to the teaching of a subject such as international human rights law is to adopt a rule of law that, contrary to the Constitution's text and First Amendment precedent, would automatically forbid the teaching of any subject in a case where national security interests conflict with the First Amendment. The Constitution does not allow all such conflicts to be decided in the Government's favor.

. . .

I concede that the Government's expertise in foreign affairs may warrant deference in respect to many matters, *e.g.*, our relations with Turkey. But it remains for this Court to decide whether the Government has shown that such an interest justifies criminalizing speech activity otherwise protected by the First Amendment. And the fact that other nations may like us less for granting that protection cannot in and of itself carry the day.

. . .

II

. . .

. . . I would read the statute as criminalizing First-Amendment-protected pure speech and association only when the defendant knows or intends that those activities will assist the organization's unlawful terrorist actions. . . .

. . .

. . . [T]his reading does not require the Government to undertake the difficult task of proving which, as between peaceful and nonpeaceful purposes, a defendant specifically preferred; knowledge is enough.

. . .

[T]extually speaking, a statutory requirement that the defendant *knew* the support was material can be read to require the Government to show that the defendant knew that the consequences of his acts had a significant likelihood of furthering the organization's terrorist, not just its lawful, aims.

. . .

The statute's history strongly supports this reading. . . .

. . .

2. INTERMEZZO: AN INTRODUCTION TO THE CONCEPTS OF VAGUENESS, OVERBREADTH AND PRIOR RESTRAINT

Introduction. Section 3 of this chapter will continue the inquiry begun in Section 1—exploring the societal interests that justify government control of the content of expression. This section involves judicial techniques that permit courts to reverse a defendant's conviction, or invalidate a statute, without deciding whether or not the content of expression or publication is constitutionally protected. The question to be asked is whether these techniques, as they are employed, respond to legitimate constitutional concerns or whether they are devices to avoid or postpone harder decisions concerning the limits of constitutionally protected speech. This section will not exhaust the study of vagueness, overbreadth and prior restraint. Decisions included in the remainder of this chapter, and the succeeding three chapters, are often based on these concepts.

A. VAGUENESS AND OVERBREADTH

Herndon v. Lowry

301 U.S. 242 (1937).

Herndon, an African American, had gone to Alabama as a paid organizer for the Communist Party during the depression years of the 1930's. He enrolled at least five members and held some meetings. When he was arrested he had in his possession Communist literature, including a pamphlet urging self determination for blacks and advocating strikes, boycotts and a revolutionary struggle for power. It did not appear that he had distributed the literature found in his possession nor that he had advocated anything other than relief for the needy. Herndon received a heavy sentence under a Georgia statute that had been aimed at slave insurrections in its earlier form, before the Civil War. (The statute would have permitted imposition of the death penalty in Herndon's case.) The statute defined "attempt to incite insurrection" as "any attempt, by persuasion or otherwise, to induce others to join in any combined resistance to the lawful authority of the state." Herndon appealed his conviction to the Georgia Supreme Court, arguing that the evidence was insufficient to sustain his conviction, because there was no proof that immediate serious violence was expected or advocated. The Georgia Supreme Court affirmed the conviction, ruling that such proof was unnecessary. A defendant did not have to intend that an insurrection should follow "instantly or at any given time, but it would be sufficient that he intended it to happen at any time, as a result of his influence, by those whom he sought to incite."

Herndon's major argument in the Supreme Court was that the insurrection statute as construed was unconstitutional, since no clear and present danger was required for conviction. The Court, however, reversed the conviction without overruling the holding of Gitlow v. New York, 268 U.S. 652 (1925), that a legislature could make revolutionary speech a crime without requiring proof of clear and present danger. The Court first analyzed the evidence, and concluded that Herndon had been convicted for merely talking about unemployment relief, since there was no proof he had distributed the single copies of the more inflammatory literature in his possession. Relying in part on De Jonge v. Oregon, 299 U.S. 353 (1937) (Section 1, supra), the Court held on these facts that Herndon's conviction was an "unwarranted invasion of the right of freedom of speech." The Court's second ground of decision was that the insurrection statute was unconstitutional. Portions of Justice Roberts' discussion of that ground follow:

"The statute, as construed and applied in the appellant's trial, does not furnish a sufficiently ascertainable standard of guilt. . . .

". . . To be guilty under the law, as construed, a defendant need not advocate resort to force. He need not teach any particular doctrine to come within its purview. Indeed, he need not be active in the formation of a combination or group if he agitate for a change in the frame of government, however peaceful his own intent. If, by the exercise of prophesy, he can forecast that, as a result of a chain of causation, following his proposed action a group may arise at some future date which will resort to force, he is bound to make the prophesy and abstain, under pain of punishment, possibly of execution. Every person who attacks existing conditions, who agitates for a change in the form of government, must take the risk that if a jury should be of opinion he ought to have foreseen that his utterances might contribute in any measure to some future forcible resistance to the existing government he may be convicted of the offense of inciting insurrection. Proof that the accused in fact believed that his effort would cause a violent assault upon the state would not be necessary to conviction. It would be sufficient if the jury thought he reasonably might foretell that those he persuaded to join the party might, at some time in the indefinite future, resort to forcible resistance of government. The question thus proposed to a jury involves pure speculation as to future trends of thought and action. Within what time might one reasonably expect that an attempted organization of the Communist Party in the United States would result in violent action by that party? If a jury returned a special verdict saying twenty years or even fifty years the verdict could not be shown to be wrong. The law, as thus construed, licenses the jury to create its own standard in each case. . . .

". . .

"The statute as construed and applied, amounts merely to a dragnet which may enmesh any one who agitates for a change of government if a jury can be persuaded that he ought to have foreseen his words would have some effect in the future conduct of others. No reasonably ascertainable standard of guilt is prescribed. So vague and indeterminate are the boundaries thus set to the freedom of speech and assembly that the law necessarily violates the guarantees of liberty embodied in the Fourteenth Amendment."[a]

Coates v. Cincinnati

402 U.S. 611, 91 S.Ct. 1686, 29 L.Ed.2d 214 (1971).

■ MR. JUSTICE STEWART delivered the opinion of the Court.

A Cincinnati, Ohio, ordinance makes it a criminal offense for "three or more persons to assemble . . . on any of the sidewalks . . . and there conduct themselves in a manner annoying to persons passing by. . . ." The issue before us is whether this ordinance is unconstitutional on its face.

The appellants were convicted of violating the ordinance, and the convictions were ultimately affirmed by a closely divided vote in the Supreme Court of Ohio, upholding the constitutional validity of the ordinance. An appeal from that judgment was brought here. . . . The record brought before the reviewing courts tells us no more than that the appellant Coates was a student involved in a demonstration and the other appellants were pickets involved in a labor dispute. For throughout this litigation it has been the appellants' position that the ordinance on its face violates the First and Fourteenth Amendments of the Constitution. . . .

In rejecting this claim and affirming the convictions the Ohio Supreme Court did not give the ordinance any construction at variance with the apparent plain import of its language. . . .

. . .

We are thus relegated, at best, to the words of the ordinance itself. If three or more people meet together on a sidewalk or street corner, they must conduct themselves so as not to annoy any police officer or other person who should happen to pass by. In our opinion this ordinance is unconstitutionally vague because it subjects the exercise of the right of assembly to an unascertainable standard, and unconstitutionally broad because it authorizes the punishment of constitutionally protected conduct.

Conduct that annoys some people does not annoy others. Thus, the ordinance is vague not in the sense that it requires a person to conform his conduct to an imprecise but comprehensible normative standard, but rather in the sense that no standard of

---

[a] For an interesting discussion of Herndon v. Lowry, see Chafee, *Free Speech in the United States* 388–398 (1941).

conduct is specified at all. As a result, "men of common intelligence must necessarily guess at its meaning." . . .

It is said that the ordinance is broad enough to encompass many types of conduct clearly within the city's constitutional power to prohibit. And so, indeed, it is. The city is free to prevent people from blocking sidewalks, obstructing traffic, littering streets, committing assaults, or engaging in countless other forms of anti-social conduct. It can do so through the enactment and enforcement of ordinances directed with reasonable specificity toward the conduct to be prohibited. . . . It cannot constitutionally do so through the enactment and enforcement of an ordinance whose violation may entirely depend upon whether or not a policeman is annoyed.

But the vice of the ordinance lies not alone in its violation of the due process standard of vagueness. The ordinance also violates the constitutional right of free assembly and association. Our decisions establish that mere public intolerance or animosity cannot be the basis for abridgment of these constitutional freedoms. . . . The First and Fourteenth Amendments do not permit a State to make criminal the exercise of the right of assembly simply because its exercise may be "annoying" to some people. If this were not the rule, the right of the people to gather in public places for social or political purposes would be continually subject to summary suspension through the good-faith enforcement of a prohibition against annoying conduct. And such a prohibition, in addition, contains an obvious invitation to discriminatory enforcement against those whose association together is "annoying" because their ideas, their lifestyle or their physical appearance is resented by the majority of their fellow citizens.

The ordinance before us makes a crime out of what under the Constitution cannot be a crime. It is aimed directly at activity protected by the Constitution. We need not lament that we do not have before us the details of the conduct found to be annoying. It is the ordinance on its face that sets the standard of conduct and warns against transgression. The details of the offense could no more serve to validate this ordinance than could the details of an offense charged under an ordinance suspending unconditionally the right of assembly and free speech.

The judgment is reversed.

■ MR. JUSTICE WHITE, with whom THE CHIEF JUSTICE and MR. JUSTICE BLACKMUN join, dissenting.

The claim in this case, in part, is that the Cincinnati ordinance is so vague that it may not constitutionally be applied to any conduct. But the ordinance prohibits persons from assembling with others and "conduct[ing] themselves in a manner annoying to persons passing by. . . ." . . . Any man of average comprehension should know that some kinds of conduct, such as assault or blocking passage on the street, will annoy others and are clearly covered by the "annoying conduct" standard of the ordinance. It would be frivolous to say that these and many other kinds of conduct are not within the foreseeable reach of the law.

It is possible that a whole range of other acts, defined with unconstitutional imprecision, is forbidden by the ordinance. But as a general rule, when a criminal charge is based on conduct constitutionally subject to proscription and clearly forbidden by a statute, it is no defense that the law would be unconstitutionally vague if applied to other behavior. Such a statute is not vague on its face. It may be vague as applied in some circumstances, but ruling on such a challenge obviously requires knowledge of the conduct with which a defendant is charged.

. . .

So . . . in United States v. National Dairy Corp., 372 U.S. 29 (1963), where we considered a statute forbidding sales of goods at "unreasonably" low prices to injure or eliminate a competitor, 15 U.S.C. § 13a, we thought the statute gave a seller adequate notice that sales below costs were illegal. The statute was therefore not facially vague, although it might be difficult to tell whether certain other kinds of conduct fell within this language. . . . This approach is consistent with the host of cases holding that "one to whom application of a statute is constitutional will not be heard to attack the statute on the ground that impliedly it might also be taken as applying to other persons or other situations in which its application might be unconstitutional." United States v. Raines, 362 U.S. 17, 21 (1960), and cases there cited.

Our cases, however, including *National Dairy,* recognize a different approach where the statute at issue purports to regulate or proscribe rights of speech or press protected by the First Amendment. . . . Although a statute may be neither vague, overbroad, nor otherwise invalid as applied to the conduct charged against a particular defendant, he is permitted to raise its vagueness or unconstitutional overbreadth as applied to others. And if the law is found deficient in one of these respects, it may not be applied to him either, until and unless a satisfactory limiting construction is placed on the statute. . . . The statute, in effect, is stricken down on its face. This result is deemed justified since the otherwise continued existence of the statute in unnarrowed form would tend to suppress constitutionally protected rights. . . .

Even accepting the overbreadth doctrine with respect to statutes clearly reaching speech, the Cincinnati ordinance does not purport to bar or regulate speech as such. It prohibits persons from assembling and "conduct[ing]" themselves in a manner annoying to other persons. Even if the assembled defendants in this case were demonstrating and picketing, we have long recognized that picketing is not solely a communicative endeavor and has aspects which the State is entitled to regulate even though there is incidental impact on speech. In Cox v. Louisiana, 379 U.S. 559 (1965), the Court held valid on its face a statute forbidding picketing and parading near a courthouse. This was deemed a valid regulation of conduct rather than pure speech. . . .

In the case before us, I would deal with the Cincinnati ordinance as we would with the ordinary criminal statute. The ordinance clearly reaches certain conduct but may be illegally vague with respect to other conduct. The statute is not infirm on its face and since we have no information from this record as to what conduct was charged against these defendants, we are in no position to judge the statute as applied. That the ordinance may confer wide discretion in a wide range of circumstances is irrelevant when we may be dealing with conduct at its core.

I would therefore affirm the judgment of the Ohio Supreme Court.

■ MR. JUSTICE BLACK.

. . .

. . . [T]he First Amendment which forbids the State to abridge freedom of speech, would invalidate this city ordinance if it were used to punish the making of a political speech, even if that speech were to annoy other persons. In contrast, however, the ordinance could properly be applied to prohibit the gathering of persons in the mouths of alleys to annoy passersby by throwing rocks or by some other conduct not at all connected with speech. It is a matter of no little difficulty to determine when a law can be held void on its face and when such summary action is inappropriate. This difficulty has been aggravated in this case, because the record fails to show in what conduct these defendants had engaged to annoy other people. In my view, a record showing the facts surrounding the conviction is essential to adjudicate the important constitutional issues in this case. I would therefore, vacate the judgment and remand the case to the court below to give both parties an opportunity to supplement the record so that we may determine whether the conduct actually punished is the kind of conduct which it is within the power of the State to punish.

Broadrick v. Oklahoma

413 U.S. 601 (1973).

An Oklahoma statute proscribed partisan political activity by state civil servants. Plaintiffs, who had engaged in partisan political activities (including solicitation of money) among their co-workers, brought suit to enjoin enforcement of the statute. They conceded that the statute validly could prohibit the conduct in which they had engaged but sought to have it declared unconstitutional because it forbade the wearing of political buttons and displaying bumper stickers—activity in which they had not engaged. They argued that the statute was overbroad because buttons and stickers were protected expression.

Justice White, writing for the Court, rejected this contention:

"[T]he Court has altered its traditional rules of standing to permit—in the First Amendment area—'attacks on overly broad statutes with no requirement that the person making the attack demonstrate that his own conduct could not be regulated by a statute drawn with the requisite specificity.' Dombrowski v. Pfister, 380 U.S. 479, 486 (1965). Litigants, therefore, are permitted to challenge a statute not because their own rights of free expression are violated, but because of a judicial prediction or assumption that the statute's very existence may cause others not before the court to refrain from constitutionally protected speech or expression.

"Such claims of facial overbreadth have been entertained in cases involving statutes which, by their terms, seek to regulate 'only spoken words.' Gooding v. Wilson, 405 U.S. 518, 520 (1972). . . . In such cases, it has been the judgment of this Court that the possible harm to society in permitting some unprotected speech to go unpunished is outweighed by the possibility that protected speech of others may be muted and perceived grievances left to fester because of the possible inhibitory effects of overly broad statutes. Overbreadth attacks have also been allowed where the Court thought rights of association were ensnared in statutes which, by their broad sweep, might result in burdening innocent associations. . . . Facial overbreadth claims have also been entertained where statutes, by their terms, purport to regulate the time, place and manner of expressive or communicative conduct, . . . and where such conduct has required official approval under laws that delegated standardless discretionary power to local functionaries, resulting in virtually unreviewable prior restraints on First Amendment rights. . . .

"The consequence of our departure from traditional rules of standing in the First Amendment area is that any enforcement of a statute thus placed at issue is totally forbidden until and unless a limiting construction or partial invalidation so narrows it as to remove the seeming threat or deterrence to constitutionally protected expression. Application of the overbreadth doctrine in this manner is, manifestly, strong medicine. It has been employed by the Court sparingly and only as a last resort. . . .

"It remains a 'matter of no little difficulty' to determine when a law may properly be held void on its face and when 'such summary action' is inappropriate. . . . But the plain import of our cases is, at the very least, that facial overbreadth adjudication is an exception to our traditional rules of practice and that its function, a limited one at the outset, attenuates as the otherwise unprotected behavior that it forbids the State to sanction moves from 'pure speech' towards conduct and that conduct—even if expressive—falls within the scope of otherwise valid criminal laws that reflect legitimate state interests in maintaining comprehensive controls over harmful, constitutionally unprotected conduct. Although such laws, if too broadly worded, may deter protected speech to some unknown extent, there comes a point where that effect—at best a prediction—cannot, with confidence, justify invalidating a statute on its face and so prohibiting a State from enforcing the statute against conduct that is admittedly within its power to proscribe.... To put the matter another way, particularly where conduct and not merely speech is involved, we believe that the overbreadth of a statute must not only be real, but substantial as well, judged in relation to the statute's plainly legitimate sweep. It is our view that § 818 is not substantially overbroad and that whatever overbreadth may exist should be cured through case-by-case analysis of the fact situations to which its sanctions, assertedly, may not be applied.[14]"

Justice Douglas dissented on the ground that the whole statute violated the first amendment. Justice Brennan concluded a dissenting opinion joined by Justices Stewart and Marshall as follows:

"At this stage, it is obviously difficult to estimate the probable impact of today's decision. If the requirement of 'substantial' overbreadth is construed to mean only that facial review is inappropriate where the likelihood of an impermissible application of the statute is too small to generate a 'chilling effect' on protected speech or conduct, then the impact is likely to be small. On the other hand, if today's decision necessitates the drawing of artificial distinctions between protected speech and protected conduct, and if the 'chill' on protected conduct is rarely, if ever, found sufficient to require the facial invalidation of an overbroad statute, then the effect could be very grave indeed. In my view, the principles set forth in Coates v. City of Cincinnati, are essential to the preservation and enforcement of the First Amendment guarantees. Since no subsequent development has persuaded me that the principles are ill-founded or that *Coates* was incorrectly decided, I would reverse the judgment of the District Court on the strength of that decision and hold ... the Oklahoma Merit Act unconstitutional on its face."

Brockett v. Spokane Arcades, Inc.

472 U.S. 491 (1985).

The court concluded that a state obscenity statute was overbroad because it used the term "lust" in defining obscene matter. (The definition included materials that appealed to "only normal sexual appetites," and were thus constitutionally protected.) The court decided, however, that the lower federal court had erred in declaring the statute invalid as a whole. On this issue, the court's opinion said:

"For its holding that in First Amendment cases an overbroad statute must be stricken down on its face, the Court of Appeals relied on that line of cases exemplified by Thornhill v. Alabama, 310 U.S. 88 (1940), and more recently by Village of Schaumburg v. Citizens for a Better Environment, 444 U.S. 620 (1980). In those cases, an individual whose own speech or expressive conduct may validly be prohibited or sanctioned is permitted to challenge a statute on its face because it also threatens others not before the court—those who desire to engage in legally protected expression but who may refrain from doing so rather than risk prosecution or undertake to have

---

[14] ... The dissent ... insists that Coates v. City of Cincinnati, 402 U.S. 611 (1971), must be taken as overruled. But we are unpersuaded that *Coates* stands as a barrier to a rule that would invalidate statutes for overbreadth only when the flaw is a substantial concern in the context of the statute as a whole. Our judgment is that the Oklahoma statute, when authoritative administrative constructions are accepted, is not invalid under such a rule.

the law declared partially invalid. If the overbreadth is 'substantial,'[12] the law may not be enforced against anyone, including the party before the court, until it is narrowed to reach only unprotected activity, whether by legislative action or by judicial construction or partial invalidation. Broadrick v. Oklahoma, 413 U.S. 601 (1973).

"It is otherwise where the parties challenging the statute are those who desire to engage in protected speech that the overbroad statute purports to punish, or who seek to publish both protected and unprotected material. There is then no want of a proper party to challenge the statute, no concern that an attack on the statute will be unduly delayed or protected speech discouraged. The statute may forthwith be declared invalid to the extent that it reaches too far, but otherwise left intact.

"The cases before us are ones governed by the normal rule that partial, rather than facial, invalidation is the required course. The Washington statute was faulted by the Court of Appeals only because it reached material that incited normal as well as unhealthy interest in sex, and appellees, or some of them, desiring to publish this sort of material, claimed that they faced punishment if they did so. Unless there are countervailing considerations, the Washington law should have been invalidated only insofar as the word 'lust' is to be understood as reaching protected materials.

. . .

"Partial invalidation would be improper if it were contrary to legislative intent in the sense that the legislature had passed an inseverable Act or would not have passed it had it known the challenged provision was invalid. . . . It would be frivolous to suggest, and no one does, that the Washington Legislature, if it could not proscribe materials that appealed to normal as well as abnormal sexual appetites, would have refrained from passing the moral nuisance statute. And it is quite evident that the remainder of the statute retains its effectiveness as a regulation of obscenity. In these circumstances, the issue of severability is no obstacle to partial invalidation, which is the course the Court of Appeals should have pursued."

Federal Court Injunctions Against Vague and Overbroad Statutes

It is accurate to say that laws are judged for vagueness and overbreadth on their "face" only in the sense, as Justice Stewart points out in *Coates,* that it is unnecessary to know the details of the defendant's conduct, or to determine whether it was constitutionally protected. It is a mistake to conclude that statutes are judged for vagueness and overbreadth only with reference to their literal statutory language. A statute may appear to be vague and overbroad, but those problems may disappear if judicial construction clarifies its prohibitions and limits its potentially overbroad applications. A good example is the Smith Act, considered at length in Section 1 of this chapter. Were it not for the limiting constructions given the statute in the *Yates, Scales* and *Noto* cases, its literal application would require a conclusion that it is overbroad. State courts, too, can remove potential issues of vagueness and overbreadth by a limiting construction of the statute involved. Thus, in reviewing a case that originated in a state court, the issue before the Supreme Court is whether the statute, as construed by the state courts, is vague or overbroad. (Notice that in *Herndon* the vagueness problem stemmed, in part, from the state court's construction and, in *Coates,* the state court had not construed the statute beyond its plain language.)

In any case in which issues of first amendment vagueness and overbreadth are raised there are difficult questions of degree—determining the degree of vagueness or overbreadth that will be fatal and deciding whether a party can raise the challenge

---

[12] The Court of Appeals erred in holding that the substantial overbreadth requirement is inapplicable where pure speech rather than conduct is at issue. . . .

that the statute is vague or overbroad as to other persons. Those problems are, however, further complicated when the challenges are raised in a federal court suit to enjoin enforcement of the law as opposed to Supreme Court review of a state criminal conviction. The first problem for the federal court is that it can only guess whether state courts would give an apparently vague or overbroad law a narrowing construction that would obviate the problem. That can be particularly troublesome when the law sought to be enjoined is newly enacted and has never been construed in the state courts. The second problem is to define standing to raise the challenges— obviously less of a problem where a defendant seeking Supreme Court review is attempting to overturn the very statutory provision under which he was convicted. Allowing a defendant in a state criminal action to enjoin a pending prosecution can create inordinate delay in the state criminal process or create a mechanism by which state court decisions on federal issues are reviewed and "reversed" by lower federal courts and not by the Supreme Court. On the other hand, permitting suit by any person who alleges a future intent to engage in behavior arguably within the statutory prohibition practically allows anyone to mount a vagueness or overbreadth challenge to a state law. Allowing anyone alleging a subjective "chill" to ask a federal court to strike down a state law on the basis that there are some hypothetical uncertainties or applications to protected speech produces litigation with many of the undesirable features of advisory opinions. The complex federal jurisdiction rules addressed to these problems were explored, in general terms, earlier in Chapter 3. They will be examined here with reference to their impact on litigation of vagueness and overbreadth challenges.

(1) **Postponing decision.** A technique for addressing the possibility that state courts might narrow the statute's apparent vagueness or overbreadth is for the federal court to stay the action before it, allowing the parties to obtain an "authoritative" state court construction of the law. In Baggett v. Bullitt, 377 U.S. 360 (1964), the Court invalidated, as impermissibly vague, a Washington loyalty oath for teachers requiring affirmation that the teacher was not a "subversive person." In Dombrowski v. Pfister, 380 U.S. 479 (1965), a Louisiana law requiring registration of "subversive organizations" was invalidated for vagueness and overbreadth. In both cases, the Court refused to postpone exercise of jurisdiction to allow state court interpretation. Portions of Justice Brennan's opinion in *Dombrowski* can be read as suggesting that abstention to clarify state law is never appropriate when the law is challenged on vagueness and overbreadth grounds. He emphasized that a major premise of vagueness and overbreadth doctrine was that such laws operated to chill constitutionally protected speech by those not "hardy enough to risk criminal prosecution." He further pointed out that the abstention process was time consuming and, in the intervening time, those affected remained subject to the statute's "chilling effect." Both opinions, however, also emphasized that the challenged laws presented a multitude of issues of interpretation that were not likely to be resolved in any single proceeding. Babbitt v. United Farm Workers Nat'l Union, 442 U.S. 289 (1979) held that abstention to allow state court interpretation is required where the uncertainty of a challenged statute concerns a single issue that can be resolved by state courts in a single proceeding.

(2) **Dismissal.** Justice Brennan's discussion in *Dombrowski* of the "chilling effect" of vague and overbroad statutes upon parties not before the court led lower federal courts to permit a proliferation of vagueness and overbreadth challenges to state criminal statutes. Younger v. Harris, 401 U.S. 37 (1971), substantially curbed that litigation. At issue in the case was the constitutional validity of the California criminal syndicalism law which had been upheld in Whitney v. California, 274 U.S. 357 (1927) (supra Section 1). Harris had been indicted under the act, and sued to enjoin his state prosecution. Other parties plaintiff were allowed to intervene—

Progressive Labor Party members who alleged that Harris' prosecution inhibited them from advocacy of Party programs, and a college instructor who claimed he was uncertain whether he could teach about Marxism. The lower federal courts enjoined Harris' prosecution, holding the law unconstitutional. The Supreme Court reversed, concluding that the federal injunction suit should have been dismissed. The intervenors had not alleged a credible threat they would be prosecuted, and as to them there was no "live controversy." Allowing Harris to sue presented the opposite problem—undue interference with a pending state criminal proceeding. Harris could raise his constitutional defense in the pending prosecution. More broadly, Justice Black's opinion for the Court stated: "Procedures for testing the constitutionality of a statute 'on its face' in the manner apparently contemplated by *Dombrowski,* and for then enjoining all action to enforce the statute until the State can obtain court approval for a modified version, are fundamentally at odds with the function of . . . federal courts in our constitutional plan." Among the difficulties, he listed the "speculative and amorphous nature of the required line-by-line analysis of detailed statutes [which] ordinarily results in a kind of case that is wholly unsatisfactory for deciding constitutional questions."

The seed of *Younger v. Harris* has grown into a luxuriant forest of rules. Barring suit by persons actually prosecuted and those not threatened with prosecution has left a narrow corridor for bringing federal court actions to determine the constitutionality of state criminal laws. Suit for declaratory judgment of unconstitutionality (as opposed to an injunction) is permitted where the plaintiff shows a credible threat of prosecution, but has not been prosecuted. Steffel v. Thompson, 415 U.S. 452 (1974). Further, a temporary injunction against prosecution *pendente lite* may be issued on a sufficient showing of irreparable harm and likely success on the merits. Doran v. Salem Inn, Inc., 422 U.S. 922 (1975). If a temporary injunction is not entered, and state prosecution is begun before "proceedings of substance on the merits" have occurred in the federal declaratory judgment action, the federal action must be dismissed. Hicks v. Miranda, 422 U.S. 332 (1975). If a federal declaratory judgment of unconstitutionality is issued, it is an open question whether subsequent state prosecutions can then be enjoined by the federal court. (Justices White and Rehnquist expressed polar positions on that issue in concurring opinions in Hicks v. Miranda.) The question may be particularly perplexing if the statute is declared unconstitutional for vagueness and overbreadth, but there is a possibility that state court construction of the statute in the subsequent state prosecution might narrow the statute's interpretation. Shapiro, *State Courts and Federal Declaratory Judgments,* 74 N.W.U.L.Rev. 759 (1979).

An interesting situation occurs when the defendant has been prosecuted in a state court, and the conviction has become final. The defendant wishes to continue the conduct that resulted in conviction, and, without seeking to set aside the past conviction, asks a federal court to bar future prosecution. In that situation, a federal court may enjoin future state criminal prosecutions. Since the federal plaintiff is willing to let the past criminal conviction stand, there is no interference with state criminal actions and, in form, the federal trial court is not exercising quasi-appellate review of a state court decision. Wooley v. Maynard, 430 U.S. 705 (1977); Carey v. Brown, 447 U.S. 455 (1980). Neither *Wooley* nor *Carey* was decided on vagueness or overbreadth grounds. The implications of those cases, however, for vagueness and overbreadth challenges should be noted. The past state conviction gives some concreteness to the federal litigation. It is known what the defendant has done and intends to do in the future. The particular features of the statute at issue are defined by the previous conviction. And, most significant, a state court has had a prior opportunity to construe the statute and narrow its interpretation.

United States v. Stevens

559 U.S. 460 (2010).

A purveyor of videos of pit bulls engaging in dogfights and attacking other animals was indicted for violating a federal criminal statute banning the commercial creation, sale, or possession of certain "depictions of animal cruelty," 18 U.S.C. § 48. The Court, in an opinion by Chief Justice Roberts for eight Justices, sustained his facial challenge to the law and affirmed dismissal of the indictment—without deciding whether a law more narrowly prohibiting what he had purveyed would be constitutional—because, as the Court construed it, the statute was "substantially overbroad." Congress enacted the statute primarily to ban "crush videos" (which predominantly involve women slowly crushing animals to death with bare feet or high heeled shoes to arouse viewers with a particular sexual fetish), and perhaps dogfight videos also. The Court interpreted the statutory definition of "a depiction of animal cruelty"—a depiction "in which a living animal is intentionally maimed, mutilated, tortured, wounded, or killed," if that conduct violates federal or state law where "the creation, sale, or possession takes place[,]" and which "exempts from prohibition any depiction 'that has serious religious, political, scientific, educational, journalistic, historical, or artistic value' "—to cover not only crush videos and animal fighting videos, but also depictions of ordinary hunting (where animals have been intentionally killed or wounded without added cruelty) if created, sold or possessed in jurisdictions like Washington, D.C., where hunting is illegal, or under circumstances where the killing is made illegal not because it is thought to be cruel, but for other reasons, such as to protect an endangered species, to regulate livestock slaughter to protect health, to license hunting or fishing, or to prevent accidents.

The Court perceived the statute as creating "a criminal prohibition of alarming breadth" for not requiring "that the depicted conduct be cruel" and because "many forms of speech . . . do not qualify for the serious-value exception[.]" The Court rebuffed the claim of the Executive Branch that it would apply the statute only to cases of "extreme cruelty," because "[w]e would not uphold an unconstitutional statute merely because the Government promised to use it responsibly" and this very "prosecution is itself evidence of the danger in putting faith in government representations of prosecutorial restraint[, for w]hen this legislation was enacted, the Executive Branch announced that it would interpret § 48 as covering only depictions 'of wanton cruelty to animals designed to appeal to a prurient interest in sex' [and n]o one suggests that the videos in this case fit that description."

The Chief Justice concluded his opinion as follows:

"Our construction of § 48 decides the constitutional question; the Government makes no effort to defend the constitutionality of § 48 as applied beyond crush videos and depictions of animal fighting. It argues that those particular depictions are intrinsically related to criminal conduct or are analogous to obscenity (if not themselves obscene), and that the ban on such speech is narrowly tailored to reinforce restrictions on the underlying conduct, prevent additional crime arising from the depictions, or safeguard public mores. But the Government nowhere attempts to extend these arguments to depictions of any other activities—depictions that are presumptively protected by the First Amendment but that remain subject to the criminal sanctions of § 48.

"Nor does the Government seriously contest that the presumptively impermissible applications of § 48 (properly construed) far outnumber any permissible ones. However 'growing' and 'lucrative' the markets for crush videos and dogfighting depictions might be, . . . they are dwarfed by the market for other depictions, such as hunting magazines and videos, that we have determined to be within the scope of § 48.

We therefore need not and do not decide whether a statute limited to crush videos or other depictions of extreme animal cruelty would be constitutional. We hold only that § 48 is not so limited but is instead substantially overbroad, and therefore invalid under the First Amendment."

Justice Alito's lone dissent objected that because the " 'strong medicine' of overbreadth invalidation need not and generally should not be administered when the statute under attack is unconstitutional as applied to the challenger before the court[,]" the decision should be vacated and remanded for the Court of Appeals "to decide whether the videos that respondent sold are constitutionally protected." And "[i]f the question of overbreadth is to be decided, . . . I do not think the present record supports the Court's conclusion that § 48 bans a substantial quantity of protected speech." Justice Alito would have held "that § 48 does not apply to depictions of hunting" in most instances and that in any event hunting depictions are exempted as "depictions that have 'serious' . . . 'scientific,' 'educational,' or 'historical' value." Pointing to legislative history, he had "not . . . the slightest doubt that Congress, in enacting § 48, had no intention of restricting the creation, sale, or possession of depictions of hunting." Justice Alito later concluded that "§ 48 may validly be applied to at least two broad real-world categories of expression covered by the statute: crush videos and dogfighting videos. Thus, the statute has a substantial core of constitutionally permissible applications." Hence, respondent Stevens had "not met his burden of demonstrating that any impermissible applications of the statute are 'substantial' in relation to its 'plainly legitimate sweep.' "

B. PRIOR RESTRAINT

Introduction. The historical introduction to this chapter referred to the English history of licensed presses and Blackstone's conclusion in 1765 that liberty of the press consisted in an absence of prior restraints upon publication, but imposed no limit on punishing the publisher after publication. (Section 1, Subsection A, 1.) As late as 1907, Justice Holmes, on first encountering the problem, repeated the Blackstone proposition that the Constitution forbade "all such *previous restraints* upon publication, as had been practiced by other governments" but not "the subsequent punishment of such as may be deemed contrary to the public welfare."[a] It is now obvious that the Constitution does impose serious limits on the punishment of speech and publications. The prior restraint concept is not obsolete, however. A person, whose publication or speech is not constitutionally protected from punishment, under a properly drawn criminal statute, can still complain if it is inhibited by an unconstitutional prior restraint.

The traditional system of prior restraint was an administrative licensing mechanism, with the publisher forbidden to publish without prior approval of an executive official. The Court has upheld administrative licensing systems, where official permission in advance has been required for expressive activities conducted on public property. (The problems posed by requirements for parade permits are discussed below, beginning at page 940.) The Court has sustained an administrative licensing system in only one context not involving use of public property. In Times Film Corp. v. City of Chicago, 365 U.S. 43 (1961), the Court concluded that a motion picture licensing ordinance was not invalid "on its face." The nation's existing motion picture licensing systems, however, did not survive the decision four years later in Freedman v. Maryland, 380 U.S. 51 (1965). The Court concluded that the motion

---

[a] Patterson v. Colorado, 205 U.S. 454, 462 (1907). It was not until 1919 that Holmes announced: "I wholly disagree with the argument . . . that the First Amendment left the common law as to seditious libel in force." Abrams v. United States, 250 U.S. 616, 630 (1919) (dissenting opinion).

picture licensing system under review was invalid because: (1) it did not require the administrative censor to seek judicial review if a permit was refused; (2) if the exhibitor sought judicial review, exhibition of the film was not permitted pending review; (3) there was no assurance of prompt judicial determination. The Court explained that there were important differences between judicial and administrative proceedings. "Unlike a prosecution for obscenity, a censorship proceeding puts the initial burden on the exhibitor or distributor. Because the censor's business is to censor, there inheres the danger that he may well be less responsive than a court— part of an independent branch of government—to the constitutionally protected interests in free expression."

The next case does not involve administrative censorship but a court injunction. *Near v. Minnesota,* the Court's seminal decision on prior restraint, equated injunctions with administrative censorship. Is an injunction any more "prior" than a criminal statute forbidding the same conduct?

Near v. Minnesota

283 U.S. 697, 51 S.Ct. 625, 75 L.Ed. 1357 (1931).

■ MR. CHIEF JUSTICE HUGHES delivered the opinion of the Court.

Chapter 285 of the Session Laws of Minnesota for the year 1925 provides for the abatement, as a public nuisance, of a "malicious, scandalous and defamatory newspaper, magazine or other periodical." . . .

. . .

Under this statute . . . the county attorney of Hennepin county brought this action to enjoin the publication of what was described as a "malicious, scandalous and defamatory newspaper, magazine or other periodical," known as The Saturday Press, published by the defendants in the city of Minneapolis. . . .

. . . [T]he articles charged, in substance, that a Jewish gangster was in control of gambling, bootlegging, and racketeering in Minneapolis, and that law enforcing officers and agencies were not energetically performing their duties. . . . There is no question but that the articles made serious accusations against the public officers named and others in connection with the prevalence of crimes and the failure to expose and punish them. . . .

. . . The court . . . found that the defendants through these publications "did engage in the business of regularly and customarily producing, publishing and circulating a malicious, scandalous and defamatory newspaper," and that "the said publication under said name of The Saturday Press, or any other name, constitutes a public nuisance under the laws of the State." Judgment was thereupon entered adjudging that "the newspaper, magazine and periodical known as The Saturday Press," as a public nuisance, "be and is hereby abated." The judgment perpetually enjoined the defendants "from producing, editing, publishing, circulating, having in their possession, selling or giving away any publication whatsoever which is a malicious, scandalous or defamatory newspaper, as defined by law," and also "from further conducting said nuisance under the name and title of said The Saturday Press or any other name or title."

[The judgment was affirmed by the State Supreme Court.]

This statute, for the suppression as a public nuisance of a newspaper or periodical, is unusual, if not unique, and raises questions of grave importance transcending the local interests involved in the particular action. It is no longer open to doubt that the liberty of the press, and of speech, is within the liberty safeguarded by the due process clause of the Fourteenth Amendment from invasion by state action. . . .

First. The statute is not aimed at the redress of individual or private wrongs. Remedies for libel remain available and unaffected. The statute, said the state court, "is not directed at threatened libel but at an existing business which, generally speaking, involves more than libel." It is aimed at the distribution of scandalous matter as "detrimental to public morals and to the general welfare," tending "to disturb the peace of the community" and "to provoke assaults and the commission of crime." . . .

Second. The statute is directed not simply at the circulation of scandalous and defamatory statements with regard to private citizens, but at the continued publication by newspapers and periodicals of charges against public officers of corruption, malfeasance in office, or serious neglect of duty. Such charges by their very nature create a public scandal. They are scandalous and defamatory within the meaning of the statute, which has its normal operation in relation to publications dealing prominently and chiefly with the alleged derelictions of public officers.

Third. The object of the statute is not punishment, in the ordinary sense, but suppression of the offending newspaper or periodical. The reason for the enactment, as the state court has said, is that prosecutions to enforce penal statutes for libel do not result in "efficient repression or suppression of the evils of scandal." . . .

This suppression is accomplished by enjoining publication and that restraint is the object and effect of the statute.

Fourth. The statute not only operates to suppress the offending newspaper or periodical, but to put the publisher under an effective censorship. When a newspaper or periodical is found to be "malicious, scandalous and defamatory," and is suppressed as such, resumption of publication is punishable as a contempt of court by fine or imprisonment. Thus where a newspaper or periodical has been suppressed because of the circulation of charges against public officers of official misconduct, it would seem to be clear that the renewal of the publication of such charges would constitute a contempt, and that the judgment would lay a permanent restraint upon the publisher, to escape which he must satisfy the court as to the character of a new publication. Whether he would be permitted again to publish matter deemed to be derogatory to the same or other public officers would depend upon the court's ruling. . . .

If we cut through mere details of procedure, the operation and effect of the statute in substance is that public authorities may bring the owner or publisher of a newspaper or periodical before a judge upon a charge of conducting a business of publishing scandalous and defamatory matter—in particular that the matter consists of charges against public officers of official dereliction—and unless the owner or publisher is able and disposed to bring competent evidence to satisfy the judge that the charges are true and are published with good motives and for justifiable ends, his newspaper or periodical is suppressed and further publication is made punishable as a contempt. This is of the essence of censorship.

The question is whether a statute authorizing such proceedings in restraint of publication is consistent with the conception of the liberty of the press as historically conceived and guaranteed. In determining the extent of the constitutional protection, it has been generally, if not universally, considered that it is the chief purpose of the guaranty to prevent previous restraints upon publication. . . .

. . .

The objection has . . . been made that the principle as to immunity from previous restraint is stated too broadly, if every such restraint is deemed to be prohibited. That is undoubtedly true; the protection even as to previous restraint is not absolutely unlimited. But the limitation has been recognized only in exceptional cases: "When a nation is at war many things that might be said in time of peace are such a hindrance to its effort that their utterance will not be endured so long as men fight and that no Court could regard them as protected by any constitutional right." Schenck v. United States, 249 U.S. 47, 52. No one would question but that a government might prevent actual obstruction to its recruiting service or the publication of the sailing dates of transports or the number and location of troops. On similar grounds, the primary requirements of decency may be enforced against obscene publications. The security of the community life may be protected against incitements to acts of violence and the overthrow by force of orderly government. . . . These limitations are not applicable here. Nor are we now concerned with questions as to the extent of authority to prevent publications in order to protect private rights according to the principles governing the exercise of the jurisdiction of courts of equity.

The exceptional nature of its limitations places in a strong light the general conception that liberty of the press, historically considered and taken up by the Federal Constitution, has meant, principally although not exclusively, immunity from previous restraints or censorship. . . .

. . .

The statute in question cannot be justified by reason of the fact that the publisher is permitted to show, before injunction issues, that the matter published is true and is published with good motives and for justifiable ends. . . .

. . .

For these reasons we hold the statute, so far as it authorized the proceedings in this action under clause (b) of section one, to be an infringement of the liberty of the press guaranteed by the Fourteenth Amendment. We should add that this decision rests upon the operation and effect of the statute, without regard to the question of the truth of the charges contained in the particular periodical. The fact that the public officers named in this case, and those associated with the charges of official dereliction, may be deemed to be impeccable, cannot affect the conclusion that the statute imposes an unconstitutional restraint upon publication.

Judgement reversed.

■ MR. JUSTICE BUTLER, dissenting.

. . .

The Court quotes Blackstone in support of its condemnation of the statute as imposing a previous restraint upon publication. But the *previous restraints* referred to by him subjected the press to the arbitrary will of an administrative officer. . . .

. . .

The Minnesota statute does not operate as a *previous* restraint on publication within the proper meaning of that phrase. It does not authorize administrative control in advance such as was formerly exercised by the licensers and censors but prescribes a remedy to be enforced by a suit in equity. In this case there was previous publication made in the course of the business of regularly producing malicious, scandalous and defamatory periodicals. The business and publications unquestionably constitute an abuse of the right of free press. The statute denounces the things done as a nuisance on the ground, as stated by the state supreme court, that they threaten morals, peace, and good order. There is no question of the power of the state to denounce such transgressions. The restraint authorized is only in respect of continuing to do what has been duly adjudged to constitute a nuisance. . . . It is fanciful to suggest similarity between the granting or enforcement of the decree authorized by this statute to prevent *further* publication of malicious, scandalous, and defamatory articles and the *previous restraint* upon the press by licensers as referred to by Blackstone and described in the history of the times to which he alludes.

. . .

The judgment should be affirmed.

■ MR. JUSTICE VAN DEVANTER, MR. JUSTICE MCREYNOLDS, and MR. JUSTICE SUTHERLAND concur in this opinion.

Injunctions and Prior Restraint

In Pittsburgh Press Co. v. Pittsburgh Commission on Human Relations, 413 U.S. 376, 389–390 (1973), the Court noted that not all injunctions against future publications were invalid prior restraints. "The special vice of a prior restraint is that communication will be suppressed, either directly or by inducing excessive caution in the speaker, before an adequate determination that it is protected by the First Amendment." The Court indicated that the challenged order—which required the newspaper to desist from segregating "help wanted" advertisements by gender—was not a prior restraint for two reasons: there was a continuing course of past conduct identical to that enjoined, making it unnecessary "to speculate as to the effect of publication"; the publication enjoined was clearly defined and not constitutionally protected.

A restraining order issued *ex parte,* prohibiting speech without notice or hearing, obviously can create substantial constitutional questions. E.g., Carroll v. President and Commissioners of Princess Anne, 393 U.S. 175 (1968) (*ex parte* order forbidding rally is unconstitutional where no showing that it was impossible to notify opposing parties and provide hearing); Fort Wayne Books, Inc. v. Indiana, 489 U.S. 46 (1989) (pre-trial seizure of adult bookstore under state racketeering law is unconstitutional prior restraint). If the injunction in *Near* had forbidden the defendants to publish any newspaper, the overbroad remedy might violate the first amendment.

In *Near,* does the constitutionality of the challenged injunction procedures depend on the question whether a contempt action for violation of the injunction would permit a defense that the alleged contempt was a constitutionally protected publication or exhibition? In Near v. Minnesota, Justice Butler's dissent made the point that in a contempt action the newspaper publisher would have available all defenses available in a criminal libel action. 283 U.S. at 730. Chief Justice Hughes' opinion did not challenge that assertion. If one assumes that a criminal libel law is constitutional, and that only publications that constituted criminal libel could be punished as contempt, should an injunction against future libelous publications still be characterized as a prior restraint?

See Blasi, *Toward a Theory of Prior Restraint: The Central Linkage,* 66 Minn.L.Rev. 11 (1981); Mayton, *Toward a Theory of First Amendment Process: Injunctions of Speech, Subsequent Punishment and the Costs of Prior Restraint Doctrine,* 67 Corn.L.Q. 245 (1982); Jeffries, *Rethinking Prior Restraint,* 92 Yale L.J. 409 (1983).

Parade and Demonstration Permit Systems

Despite traditional prior restraint law, systems requiring official permission in advance for parades and demonstrations have been upheld. In Cox v. New Hampshire, 312 U.S. 569 (1941), the Court sustained a licensing system for parades on public streets, designed to prevent traffic congestion and overlapping parades at the same time and place, and to give authorities notice in advance to afford opportunity for proper policing. A parade or demonstration permit ordinance is unconstitutional, however, if it allows the administrative official standardless discretion to deny permission, or if it authorizes denial on the basis of impermissible standards.[1] In Shuttlesworth v. Birmingham, 394 U.S. 147 (1969), for example, a parade ordinance was unconstitutional because it authorized denial of a permit if "the public welfare, peace, safety, health, decency, good order, morals, or convenience require that it be refused." A number of complex issues have arisen, however, with reference to the appropriate procedures for testing the constitutional validity of parade and demonstration permit ordinances and of individual decisions denying permits.

It is clear that if the ordinance is unconstitutional because it provides inadequate standards for granting or denial of permits, the defense is available in a prosecution for parading or demonstrating without a permit. The defendant need not have sought a permit, nor, if a permit were sought, have taken steps to review the official decision denying permission. The issue of the validity of the ordinance is open, too, whether or not permission could have been denied under a properly drafted provision.[2] The rationale has been that the unconstitutional ordinance is "void" and therefore it is appropriate to contest its validity without first seeking a permit under it. Lovell v. Griffin, Ga., 303 U.S. 444 (1938).

Suppose, however, that the ordinance is valid but the licensing official denies permission for unconstitutional reasons. Poulos v. New Hampshire, 345 U.S. 395 (1953), establishes that a state can require that the applicant seek review of the invalid denial of the permit under a valid ordinance. *Poulos* reasoned that the rationale for requiring permission in advance for a parade or demonstration allowed the state to insist that the disappointed applicant not ignore the official denial of permission, and to require challenge through appropriate procedures before the parade or demonstration is held. *Poulos* presents a real dilemma to the applicant unconstitutionally denied permission.[3] The ordinance in *Poulos* required the applicant to seek judicial review of the denial and precluded him from holding his planned meeting pending those judicial proceedings. Justice Reed's opinion in that case rejected the argument that judicial review would be so time-consuming as to make it impossible to hold the planned meeting, stating that while delay was "unfortunate," it

---

[1]   In Forsyth County v. Nationalist Movement, 505 U.S. 123 (1992), the Court did not resolve the question whether the first amendment limits the amount of any fee for a parade permit to a "nominal sum." The Court held invalid an ordinance that allowed the administrator to "adjust the amount to be paid [up to a maximum of $1,000 per day] in order to meet the expense incident to the administration of the ordinance and to the maintenance of public order in the matter licensed." The court concluded that the ordinance gave the administrator unbridled discretion to set fees, and that assessing the fee with reference to security costs would increase permit fees based on content, because the fee would include the projected cost of controlling hostile crowds.

[2]   In Kunz v. New York, 340 U.S. 290 (1951), for example, defendant's license application was denied because he had in the past ridiculed and denounced the religious beliefs of others, and there had been disorder. His conviction for holding a public worship meeting on the streets without a permit was reversed because the ordinance lacked standards for permit denials.

[3]   The dilemma is exacerbated if there is uncertainty concerning the constitutional validity of the underlying ordinance. In Cox v. New Hampshire, 312 U.S. 569 (1941), the parade permit ordinance under which the defendants were convicted was silent about the standards for granting or denying permits. The convictions were affirmed, however, because the New Hampshire Supreme Court interpreted the ordinance, on the defendants' appeal, to allow denial only upon considerations such as traffic congestion, overlapping parades, and risks of disorder. In Shuttlesworth v. Birmingham, Ala., 394 U.S. 147 (1969), the Court reversed a conviction for parading without a license despite a similar limiting construction of the ordinance under which the defendants were convicted. Given the language of the ordinance, and past administrative practice, it "would have taken extraordinary clairvoyance" for defendants to have foreseen, when they held their parade, the "remarkable job of plastic surgery" by the state court four years later.

was "a price citizens must pay for life in an orderly society." In Freedman v. Maryland, 380 U.S. 51 (1965), however, a motion picture censorship ordinance was held unconstitutional because it did not require the licensing official to go to court after denying a license, and did not provide for prompt judicial review. Southeastern Promotions v. Conrad, 420 U.S. 546 (1975), required the directors of a municipal auditorium to follow the *Freedman* procedures upon denial of permission to use the auditorium. Thomas v. Chicago Park District, 534 U.S. 316 (2002), held that *Freedman*'s requirement that licensing officials seek prompt judicial review was not applicable to content-neutral denial of parade and demonstration permits. ("Such a traditional exercise of authority does not raise the censorship concerns that prompted us to impose the extraordinary procedural safeguards on the film licensing process in *Freedman*.") On the other hand, in City of Littleton v. Z.J. Gifts, 541 U.S. 774 (2004), the Court concluded that an "adult business" licensing ordinance would need to provide assurance of prompt judicial review if the denial of the license was content-based. *Freedman*'s judicial review safeguard was meant to prevent "undue delay," and requires prompt judicial decision.

In Walker v. Birmingham, 388 U.S. 307 (1967), the Court reviewed the criminal contempt conviction of Black ministers who had been enjoined by a state court from holding a Good Friday march to protest racial discrimination. The Court's decision in Shuttlesworth v. Birmingham, note 3 supra, two years later made clear that the parade permit ordinance on which the injunction was based was unconstitutional, and that the clearly stated position of police commissioner Eugene "Bull" Conner, that no permit would be issued, rested on unconstitutional considerations. Moreover, the grant of an *ex parte* injunction, without notice or opportunity to participate in the proceedings, probably also violated the first amendment.[4] Alabama, however, was among the states following the rule that an injunction must be obeyed, even if erroneous, until it is set aside on appellate review.[5] Accordingly, the Alabama Supreme Court refused to consider constitutional attacks on the injunction or the underlying parade ordinance. The Supreme Court affirmed, by a vote of five to four. Justice Stewart's opinion for the Court said that the "case would arise in quite a different constitutional posture if the petitioners, before disobeying the injunction, had challenged it in the Alabama courts, and had been met with delay or frustration of their constitutional claims." In United States v. Ryan, 402 U.S. 530, 532 n. 4 (1971), the Court said: "Our holding [in Walker v. Birmingham] that the claims there sought to be asserted were not open on review of petitioners' contempt convictions was based [upon] the availability of review of those claims at an earlier stage."

3. SPEECH CONFLICTING WITH OTHER COMMUNITY VALUES: GOVERNMENT CONTROL OF THE CONTENT OF SPEECH

Introduction. Section 1 of this chapter examined the lengthy controversy concerning speech that advocates the commission of a crime, and speech advocating the violent overthrow of existing government. This section returns to the inquiry whether there are legitimate government interests that will justify punishing the speaker because of speech content. The four areas examined here—defamation and privacy, obscenity, fighting words and offensive speech, and commercial speech—have one thing in common. In the early 1940's, the Court stated categorically that they were outside the area of constitutional protection normally afforded by the first amendment.

---

[4]   Carroll v. President and Comm'rs of Princess Anne, 393 U.S. 175 (1968).

[5]   The rule is the same in the federal courts. United States v. United Mine Workers of America, 330 U.S. 258 (1947).

In Chaplinsky v. New Hampshire, 315 U.S. 568, 571–572 (1942), Justice Murphy's opinion for a unanimous court said:

"There are certain well-defined and narrowly limited classes of speech, the prevention and punishment of which has never been thought to raise any Constitutional problem. These include the lewd and obscene, the profane, the libelous, and the insulting or 'fighting' words—those which by their very utterance inflict injury or tend to incite an immediate breach of the peace. It has been well observed that such utterances are no essential part of any exposition of ideas, and are of such slight social value as a step to truth that any benefit that may be derived from them is clearly outweighed by the social interest in order and morality."

Barely more than a month later, in Valentine v. Chrestensen, 316 U.S. 52 (1942), the Court added "purely commercial advertising" to the list of subjects outside the realm of first amendment protection.

Definitional problems to one side (and definitional problems have been particularly serious in the obscenity field), the approach of *Chaplinsky* and *Valentine* has not proved enduring. Within these areas of expression, the Court has imposed significant first amendment barriers to government control of the content of expression. At the same time, the Court has recognized legitimate governmental interests in these cases that permit some control of content. The most important question to be asked is whether the Court has drawn the lines that define constitutionally protected speech content in the right places. A second question is whether the first amendment law that has crystallized in each of these four categories is consistent with that in the other three.

A. PROTECTION OF INDIVIDUAL REPUTATION AND PRIVACY

Beauharnais v. Illinois

343 U.S. 250 (1952).

An Illinois statute made criminal any publication which "portrays depravity, criminality, unchastity, or lack of virtue of a class of citizens, of any race, color, creed or religion which said publication . . . exposes the citizens of any race, color, creed or religion to contempt, derision, or obloquy or which is productive of breach of the peace or riots." Beauharnais was convicted under this statute for passing out leaflets in the form of a petition to the mayor and city council of Chicago "to halt the further encroachment, harassment and invasion of white people, their property, neighborhoods and persons, by the Negro." It also included a statement: "if persuasion and the need to prevent the white race from becoming mongrelized by the negro will not unite us, then the aggressions . . . rapes, robberies, knives, guns and marijuana of the negro, surely will." The Supreme Court upheld his conviction with four Justices dissenting. Justice Frankfurter, speaking for the court, examined in detail the status of libel laws in the states and referred to earlier statements to the effect that punishment for libel presents no constitutional problem. He then said: "[i]f an utterance directed at an individual may be the object of criminal sanctions, we cannot deny to a state power to punish the same utterance directed at a defined group, unless we can say this is a wilful and purposeless restriction unrelated to the peace and well-being of the state." After discussing problems in the cities he concluded that "we would deny experience to say that the Illinois legislature was without reason" in enacting the law.

At the end of his opinion he included the following paragraph: "Libelous utterances not being within the area of constitutionally protected speech, it is unnecessary, either for us or for the State courts, to consider the issues behind the phrase 'clear and present danger.' Certainly no one would contend that obscene speech, for example, may be punished only upon a showing of such circumstances. Libel, as we have seen, is in the same class."

Justice Black, in dissent, complained that the Court was degrading first amendment freedoms to the "rational basis" level. He concluded as follows: "To say that a legislative body can, with this Court's approval, make it a crime to petition for and publicly discuss proposed legislation seems as far-fetched to me as it would be to say that a valid law could be enacted to punish a candidate for President for telling the people his views. I think the First Amendment, with the Fourteenth, 'absolutely' forbids such laws without any 'ifs' or 'buts' or 'whereases.' Whatever the danger, if any, in such public discussions, it is a danger the Founders deemed outweighed by the danger incident to the stifling of thought and speech. The Court does not act on this view of the Founders. It calculates what it deems to be the danger of public discussion, holds the scales are tipped on the side of state suppression, and upholds state censorship. . . . If there be minority groups who hail this holding as their victory, they might consider the possible relevancy of this ancient remark: 'Another such victory and I am undone.' "

New York Times Co. v. Sullivan

376 U.S. 254, 84 S.Ct. 710, 11 L.Ed.2d 686 (1964).

■ MR. JUSTICE BRENNAN delivered the opinion of the Court.

We are required in this case to determine for the first time the extent to which the constitutional protections for speech and press limit a State's power to award damages in a libel action brought by a public official against critics of his official conduct.

Respondent L.B. Sullivan is one of the three elected Commissioners of the City of Montgomery, Alabama. He testified that he was "Commissioner of Public Affairs and the duties are supervision of the Police Department, Fire Department, Department of Cemetery and Department of Scales." He brought this civil libel action against the four individual petitioners, who are Negroes and Alabama clergymen, and against petitioner the New York Times Company, a New York corporation which publishes the New York Times, a daily newspaper. A jury in the Circuit Court of Montgomery County awarded him damages of $500,000, the full amount claimed, against all the petitioners, and the Supreme Court of Alabama affirmed. . . .

Respondent's complaint alleged that he had been libeled by statements in a full-page advertisement that was carried in the New York Times on March 29, 1960. Entitled "Heed Their Rising Voices," the advertisement [charged that peaceful demonstrations of Southern Negro students in behalf of their rights guaranteed by the Constitution] ". . . are being met by an unprecedented wave of terror by those who would deny and negate that document which the whole world looks upon as setting the pattern for modern freedom. . . ." Succeeding paragraphs purported to illustrate the "wave of terror" by describing certain alleged events. The text concluded with an appeal for funds for three purposes: support of the student movement, "the struggle for the right-to-vote," and the legal defense of Dr. Martin Luther King, Jr., leader of the movement, against a perjury indictment then pending in Montgomery. . . .

Of the 10 paragraphs of text in the advertisement, the third and a portion of the sixth were the basis of respondent's claim of libel. They read as follows:

Third paragraph:

"In Montgomery, Alabama, after students sang 'My Country, 'Tis of Thee' on the State Capitol steps, their leaders were expelled from school, and truckloads of police armed with shotguns and tear-gas ringed the Alabama State College Campus. When the entire student body protested to state authorities by refusing to re-register, their dining hall was padlocked in an attempt to starve them into submission."

Sixth paragraph:

"Again and again the Southern violators have answered Dr. King's peaceful protests with intimidation and violence. They have bombed his home almost killing his wife and child. They have assaulted his person. They have arrested him seven times— for 'speeding,' 'loitering' and similar 'offenses.' And now they have charged him with 'perjury'—a *felony* under which they could imprison him for *ten years.* . . ."

Although neither of these statements mentions respondent by name, he contended that the word "police" in the third paragraph referred to him as the Montgomery Commissioner who supervised the Police Department, so that he was being accused of "ringing" the campus with police. He further claimed that the paragraph would be read as imputing to the police, and hence to him, the padlocking of the dining hall in order to starve the students into submission. As to the sixth paragraph, he contended that since arrests are ordinarily made by the police, the statement "They have arrested [Dr. King] seven times" would be read as referring to him; he further contended that the "They" who did the arresting would be equated with the "They" who committed the other described acts and with the "Southern violators." . . .

It is uncontroverted that some of the statements contained in the two paragraphs were not accurate descriptions of events which occurred in Montgomery. Although Negro students staged a demonstration on the State Capitol steps, they sang the National Anthem and not "My Country, 'Tis of Thee." Although nine students were expelled by the State Board of Education, this was not for leading the demonstration at the Capitol, but for demanding service at a lunch counter in the Montgomery County Courthouse on another day. Not the entire student body, but most of it, had protested the expulsion, not by refusing to register, but by boycotting classes on a single day; virtually all the students did register for the ensuing semester. The campus dining hall was not padlocked on any occasion, and the only students who may have been barred from eating there were the few who had neither signed a preregistration application nor requested temporary meal tickets. Although the police were deployed near the campus in large numbers on three occasions, they did not at any time "ring" the campus, and they were not called to the campus in connection with the demonstration on the State Capitol steps, as the third paragraph implied. Dr. King had not been arrested seven times, but only four; and although he claimed to have been assaulted some years earlier in connection with his arrest for loitering outside a courtroom, one of the officers who made the arrest denied that there was such an assault.

On the premise that the charges in the sixth paragraph could be read as referring to him, respondent was allowed to prove that he had not participated in the events described. Although Dr. King's home had in fact been bombed twice when his wife and child were there, both of these occasions antedated respondent's tenure as Commissioner, and the police were not only not implicated in the bombings, but had made every effort to apprehend those who were. Three of Dr. King's four arrests took place before respondent became Commissioner. Although Dr. King had in fact been indicted (he was subsequently acquitted) on two counts of perjury, each of which carried a possible five-year sentence, respondent had nothing to do with procuring the indictment.

Respondent made no effort to prove that he suffered actual pecuniary loss as a result of the alleged libel. One of his witnesses, a former employer, testified that if he had believed the statements, he doubted whether he "would want to be associated with anybody who would be a party to such things that are stated in that ad," and that he would not re-employ respondent if he believed "that he allowed the Police Department to do the things that the paper say he did." But neither this witness nor any of the others testified that he had actually believed the statements in their supposed reference to respondent. . . .

The trial judge submitted the case to the jury under instructions that the statements in the advertisement were "libelous per se" and were not privileged, so that petitioners might be held liable if the jury found that they had published the advertisement and that the statements were made "of and concerning" respondent. . . .

. . .

. . . We reverse the judgment. We hold that the rule of law applied by the Alabama courts is constitutionally deficient for failure to provide the safeguards for freedom of speech and of the press that are required by the First and Fourteenth Amendments in a libel action brought by a public official against critics of his official conduct. We further hold that under the proper safeguards the evidence presented in this case is constitutionally insufficient to support the judgment for respondent.

. . .

Under Alabama law as applied in this case, a publication is "libelous per se" if the words "tend to injure a person . . . in his reputation" or to "bring [him] into public contempt"; the trial court stated that the standard was met if the words are such as to "injure him in his public office, or impute misconduct to him in his office, or want of official integrity, or want of fidelity to a public trust. . . ." The jury must find that the words were published "of and concerning" the plaintiff, but where the plaintiff is a public official his place in the governmental hierarchy is sufficient evidence to support a finding that his reputation has been affected by statements that reflect upon the agency of which he is in charge. Once "libel per se" has been established, the defendant has no defense as to stated facts unless he can persuade the jury that they were true in all their particulars. . . . Unless he can discharge the burden of proving truth, general damages are presumed, and may be awarded without proof of pecuniary injury. . . .

The question before us is whether this rule of liability, as applied to an action brought by a public official against critics of his official conduct, abridges the freedom of speech and of the press that is guaranteed by the First and Fourteenth Amendments.

Respondent relies heavily, as did the Alabama courts, on statements of this Court to the effect that the Constitution does not protect libelous publications. Those statements do not foreclose our inquiry here. None of the cases sustained the use of libel laws to impose sanctions upon expression critical of the official conduct of public officials. . . . Like insurrection, contempt, advocacy of unlawful acts, breach of the peace, obscenity, solicitation of legal business, and the various other formulae for the repression of expression that have been challenged in this Court, libel can claim no talismanic immunity from constitutional limitations. It must be measured by standards that satisfy the First Amendment.

The general proposition that freedom of expression upon public questions is secured by the First Amendment has long been settled by our decisions. The constitutional safeguard, we have said, "was fashioned to assure unfettered interchange of ideas for the bringing about of political and social changes desired by the people." Roth v. United States, 354 U.S. 476, 484. . . .

Thus we consider this case against the background of a profound national commitment to the principle that debate on public issues should be uninhibited, robust, and wide-open, and that it may well include vehement, caustic, and sometimes unpleasantly sharp attacks on government and public officials. See Terminiello v. Chicago, 337 U.S. 1, 4; De Jonge v. Oregon, 299 U.S. 353, 365. The present advertisement, as an expression of grievance and protest on one of the major public issues of our time, would seem clearly to qualify for the constitutional protection. The question is whether it forfeits that protection by the falsity of some of its factual statements and by its alleged defamation of respondent.

Authoritative interpretations of the First Amendment guarantees have consistently refused to recognize an exception for any test of truth—whether administered by judges, juries, or administrative officials—and especially not one that puts the burden of proving truth on the speaker. . . .

Injury to official reputation affords no more warrant for repressing speech that would otherwise be free than does factual error. Where judicial officers are involved, this Court has held that concern for the dignity and reputation of the courts does not justify the punishment as criminal contempt of criticism of the judge or his decision. Bridges v. California, 314 U.S. 252. . . .

If neither factual error nor defamatory content suffices to remove the constitutional shield from criticism of official conduct, the combination of the two elements is no less inadequate. This is the lesson to be drawn from the great controversy over the Sedition Act of 1798, . . . which first crystallized a national awareness of the central meaning of the First Amendment. . . .

Although the Sedition Act was never tested in this Court, the attack upon its validity has carried the day in the court of history. . . . These views reflect a broad consensus that the Act, because of the restraint it imposed upon criticism of government and public officials, was inconsistent with the First Amendment.

. . .

What a State may not constitutionally bring about by means of a criminal statute is likewise beyond the reach of its civil law of libel. The fear of damage awards under a rule such as that invoked by the Alabama courts here may be markedly more inhibiting than the fear of prosecution under a criminal statute. . . . The judgment awarded in this case—without the need for any proof of actual pecuniary loss—was one thousand times greater than the maximum fine provided by the Alabama criminal statute, and one hundred times greater than that provided by the Sedition Act. And since there is no double-jeopardy limitation applicable to civil lawsuits, this is not the only judgment that may be awarded against petitioners for the same publication. Whether or not a newspaper can survive a succession of such judgments, the pall of fear and timidity imposed upon those who would give voice to public criticism is an atmosphere in which the First Amendment freedoms cannot survive. Plainly the Alabama law of civil libel is "a form of regulation that creates hazards to protected freedoms markedly greater than those that attend reliance upon the criminal law." Bantam Books, Inc. v. Sullivan, 372 U.S. 58, 70.

The state rule of law is not saved by its allowance of the defense of truth. . . . Allowance of the defense of truth, with the burden of proving it on the defendant, does not mean that only false speech will be deterred. . . . Under such a rule, would-be critics of official conduct may be deterred from voicing their criticism, even though it is believed to be true and even though it is in fact true, because of doubt whether it can be proved in court or fear of the expense of having to do so. They tend to make only statements which "steer far wider of the unlawful zone." . . . The rule thus dampens the vigor and limits the variety of public debate. It is inconsistent with the First and Fourteenth Amendments.

The constitutional guarantees require, we think, a federal rule that prohibits a public official from recovering damages for a defamatory falsehood relating to his official conduct unless he proves that the statement was made with "actual malice"— that is, with knowledge that it was false or with reckless disregard of whether it was false or not. . . .

. . .

. . . We think the evidence against the Times supports at most a finding of negligence in failing to discover the misstatements, and is constitutionally insufficient to show the recklessness that is required for a finding of actual malice. . . .

We also think the evidence was constitutionally defective in another respect: it was incapable of supporting the jury's finding that the allegedly libelous statements were made "of and concerning" respondent. Respondent relies on the words of the advertisement and the testimony of six witnesses to establish a connection between it and himself. . . .

Reversed and remanded.

■ MR. JUSTICE BLACK, with whom MR. JUSTICE DOUGLAS joins, concurring.

. . . "Malice," even as defined by the Court, is an elusive, abstract concept, hard to prove and hard to disprove. The requirement that malice be proved provides at best an evanescent protection for the right critically to discuss public affairs and certainly does not measure up to the sturdy safeguard embodied in the First Amendment. Unlike the Court, therefore, I vote to reverse exclusively on the ground that the Times and the individual defendants had an absolute, unconditional constitutional right to publish in the Times advertisement their criticisms of the Montgomery agencies and officials. . . .

. . .

■ MR. JUSTICE GOLDBERG, with whom MR. JUSTICE DOUGLAS joins (concurring in the result).

. . .

In my view, the First and Fourteenth Amendments to the Constitution afford to the citizen and to the press an absolute, unconditional privilege to criticize official conduct despite the harm which may flow from excesses and abuses. . . .

New York Times *and "The Central Meaning of the First Amendment"*

The relationship of *New York Times* to the old law of seditious libel and its potential importance for the future is explored in Kalven, *The New York Times Case: A Note on "the Central Meaning of the First Amendment,"* 1964 Sup.Ct.Rev. 191, 209. Professor Kalven contended that freedom from prosecutions for seditious libel— freedom to criticize government—is essential to the existence of a free society. After careful examination he concluded that a major purpose of the opinion was to make it clear that the "central meaning" of the first amendment was that seditious libel cannot be sanctioned: "Although the total structure of the opinion is not without its difficulties, it seems to me to convey, however imperfectly, the following crucial syllogism: The central meaning of the Amendment is that seditious libel cannot be made the subject of government sanction. The Alabama rule on fair comment is closely akin to making seditious libel an offense. The Alabama rule therefore violated the central meaning of the Amendment."

Gertz v. Robert Welch, Inc.

418 U.S. 323, 94 S.Ct. 2997, 41 L.Ed.2d 789 (1974).

■ MR. JUSTICE POWELL delivered the opinion of the Court.

This Court has struggled for nearly a decade to define the proper accommodation between the law of defamation and the freedoms of speech and press protected by the First Amendment. With this decision we return to that effort. We granted certiorari to reconsider the extent of a publisher's constitutional privilege against liability for defamation of a private citizen. 410 U.S. 925 (1973).

I.

In 1968 a Chicago policeman named Nuccio shot and killed a youth named Nelson. The state authorities prosecuted Nuccio for the homicide and ultimately obtained a conviction for murder in the second degree. The Nelson family retained petitioner Elmer Gertz, a reputable attorney, to represent them in civil litigation against Nuccio.

Respondent publishes American Opinion, a monthly outlet for the views of the John Birch Society. Early in the 1960's the magazine began to warn of a nationwide conspiracy to discredit local law enforcement agencies and create in their stead a national police force capable of supporting a Communist dictatorship. As part of the continuing effort to alert the public to this assumed danger, the managing editor of American Opinion commissioned an article on the murder trial of Officer Nuccio. For this purpose he engaged a regular contributor to the magazine. In March of 1969 respondent published the resulting article under the title "FRAME-UP: Richard Nuccio And The War On Police." The article purports to demonstrate that the testimony against Nuccio at his criminal trial was false and that his prosecution was part of the Communist campaign against the police.

In his capacity as counsel for the Nelson family in the civil litigation, petitioner attended the coroner's inquest into the boy's death and initiated actions for damages, but he neither discussed Officer Nuccio with the press nor played any part in the criminal proceeding. Notwithstanding petitioner's remote connection with the prosecution of Nuccio, respondent's magazine portrayed him as an architect of the "frame-up." According to the article, the police file on petitioner took "a big, Irish cop to lift." The article stated that petitioner had been an official of the "Marxist League for Industrial Democracy, originally known as the Intercollegiate Socialist Society, which has advocated the violent seizure of our government." It labelled Gertz a "Leninist" and a "Communist-fronter." It also stated that Gertz had been an officer of the National Lawyers Guild, described as a Communist organization that "probably did more than any other outfit to plan the Communist attack on the Chicago police during the 1968 Democratic convention."

These statements contained serious inaccuracies. The implication that petitioner had a criminal record was false. Petitioner had been a member and officer of the National Lawyers Guild some 15 years earlier, but there was no evidence that he or that organization had taken any part in planning the 1968 demonstrations in Chicago. There was also no basis for the charge that petitioner was a "Leninist" or a "Communist-fronter." And he had never been a member of the "Marxist League for Industrial Democracy" or the "Intercollegiate Socialist Society."

The managing editor of American Opinion made no effort to verify or substantiate the charges against petitioner. Instead, he appended an editorial introduction stating that the author had "conducted extensive research into the Richard Nuccio case." And he included in the article a photograph of petitioner and wrote the caption that appeared under it: "Elmer Gertz of Red Guild harasses Nuccio." Respondent placed the issue of American Opinion containing the article on sale at newsstands throughout the country and distributed reprints of the article on the streets of Chicago.

Petitioner filed a diversity action for libel in the United States District Court for the Northern District of Illinois. . . .

. . .

. . . [T]he District Court concluded that the *New York Times* standard should govern this case even though petitioner was not a public official or public figure. . . .

Petitioner appealed to contest the applicability of the *New York Times* standard to this case. . . . The Court of Appeals . . . affirmed. . . . [W]e reverse.

II.

. . .

Three years after *New York Times,* a majority of the Court agreed to extend the constitutional privilege to defamatory criticism of "public figures." This extension was announced in Curtis Publishing Co. v. Butts and its companion Associated Press v. Walker, 388 U.S. 130, 162 (1967). The first case involved the Saturday Evening Post's charge that Coach Wally Butts of the University of Georgia had conspired with Coach Bear Bryant of the University of Alabama to fix a football game between their respective schools. *Walker* involved an erroneous Associated Press account of former Major General Edwin Walker's participation in a University of Mississippi campus riot. Because Butts was paid by a private alumni association and Walker had resigned from the Army, neither could be classified as a "public official" under *New York Times*. Although Mr. Justice Harlan announced the result in both cases, a majority of the Court agreed with Mr. Chief Justice Warren's conclusion that the *New York Times* test should apply to criticism of "public figures" as well as "public officials." The Court extended the constitutional privilege announced in that case to protect defamatory criticism of nonpublic persons who "are nevertheless intimately involved in the resolution of important public questions or, by reason of their fame, shape events in areas of concern to society at large." . . .

. . .

III.

We begin with the common ground. Under the First Amendment there is no such thing as a false idea. However pernicious an opinion may seem, we depend for its correction not on the conscience of judges and juries but on the competition of other ideas. But there is no constitutional value in false statements of fact. Neither the intentional lie nor the careless error materially advances society's interest in "uninhibited, robust, and wide-open" debate on public issues. . . .

Although the erroneous statement of fact is not worthy of constitutional protection, it is nevertheless inevitable in free debate. . . . And punishment of error runs the risk of inducing a cautious and restrictive exercise of the constitutionally guaranteed freedoms of speech and press. Our decisions recognize that a rule of strict liability that compels a publisher or broadcaster to guarantee the accuracy of his factual assertions may lead to intolerable self-censorship. Allowing the media to avoid liability only by proving the truth of all injurious statements does not accord adequate protection to First Amendment liberties. . . .

The need to avoid self-censorship by the news media is, however, not the only societal value at issue. If it were, this Court would have embraced long ago the view that publishers and broadcasters enjoy an unconditional and indefeasible immunity from liability for defamation. . . . Such a rule would indeed obviate the fear that the prospect of civil liability for injurious falsehood might dissuade a timorous press from the effective exercise of First Amendment freedoms. Yet absolute protection for the communications media requires a total sacrifice of the competing value served by the law of defamation.

The legitimate state interest underlying the law of libel is the compensation of individuals for the harm inflicted on them by defamatory falsehood. We would not lightly require the State to abandon this purpose. . . .

. . .

The *New York Times* standard defines the level of constitutional protection appropriate to the context of defamation of a public person. Those who, by reason of the notoriety of their achievements or the vigor and success with which they seek the public's attention, are properly classed as public figures and those who hold governmental office may recover for injury to reputation only on clear and convincing proof that the defamatory falsehood was made with knowledge of its falsity or with reckless disregard for the truth. This standard administers an extremely powerful antidote to the inducement to media self-censorship of the common law rule of strict liability for libel and slander. And it exacts a correspondingly high price from the victims of defamatory falsehood. . . . For the reasons stated below, we conclude that the state interest in compensating injury to the reputation of private individuals requires that a different rule should obtain with respect to them.

. . .

. . . [W]e have no difficulty in distinguishing among defamation plaintiffs. The first remedy of any victim of defamation is self-help—using available opportunities to contradict the lie or correct the error and thereby to minimize its adverse impact on reputation. Public officials and public figures usually enjoy significantly greater access to the channels of effective communication and hence have a more realistic opportunity to counteract false statements than private individuals normally enjoy. Private individuals are therefore more vulnerable to injury, and the state interest in protecting them is correspondingly greater.

More important than the likelihood that private individuals will lack effective opportunities for rebuttal, there is a compelling normative consideration underlying the distinction between public and private defamation plaintiffs. An individual who decides to seek governmental office must accept certain necessary consequences of that involvement in public affairs. He runs the risk of closer public scrutiny than might otherwise be the case. And society's interest in the officers of government is not strictly limited to the formal discharge of official duties. . . .

Those classed as public figures stand in a similar position. Hypothetically, it may be possible for someone to become a public figure through no purposeful action of his own, but the instances of truly involuntary public figures must be exceedingly rare. For the most part those who attain this status have assumed roles of especial prominence in the affairs of society. Some occupy positions of such persuasive power and influence that they are deemed public figures for all purposes. More commonly, those classed as public figures have thrust themselves to the forefront of particular public controversies in order to influence the resolution of the issues involved. In either event, they invite attention and comment.

Even if the foregoing generalities do not obtain in every instance, the communications media are entitled to act on the assumption that public officials and public figures have voluntarily exposed themselves to increased risk of injury from defamatory falsehood concerning them. No such assumption is justified with respect to a private individual. He has not accepted public office nor assumed an "influential role in ordering society." Curtis Publishing Co. v. Butts, 388 U.S., at 164 (Warren, C.J., concurring in result). He has relinquished no part of his interest in the protection of his own good name, and consequently he has a more compelling call on the courts for redress of injury inflicted by defamatory falsehood. Thus, private individuals are not only more vulnerable to injury than public officials and public figures; they are also more deserving of recovery.

For these reasons we conclude that the States should retain substantial latitude in their efforts to enforce a legal remedy for defamatory falsehood injurious to the reputation of a private individual. The extension of the *New York Times* test proposed by the *Rosenbloom* plurality would abridge this legitimate state interest to a degree that we find unacceptable. . . .

We hold that, so long as they do not impose liability without fault, the States may define for themselves the appropriate standard of liability for a publisher or broadcaster of defamatory falsehood injurious to a private individual. This approach provides a more equitable boundary between the competing concerns involved here. It recognizes the strength of the legitimate state interest in compensating private individuals for wrongful injury to reputation, yet shields the press and broadcast media from the rigors of strict liability for defamation. At least this conclusion obtains where, as here, the substance of the defamatory statement "makes substantial danger to reputation apparent." This phrase places in perspective the conclusion we announce today. Our inquiry would involve considerations somewhat different from those discussed above if a State purported to condition civil liability on a factual misstatement whose content did not warn a reasonably prudent editor or broadcaster of its defamatory potential. Cf. Time, Inc. v. Hill, 385 U.S. 374 (1967). Such a case is not now before us, and we intimate no view as to its proper resolution.

IV.

. . . For the reasons stated below, we hold that the States may not permit recovery of presumed or punitive damages, at least when liability is not based on a showing of knowledge of falsity or reckless disregard for the truth.

The common law of defamation is an oddity of tort law, for it allows recovery of purportedly compensatory damages without evidence of actual loss. Under the traditional rules pertaining to actions for libel, the existence of injury is presumed from the fact of publication. Juries may award substantial sums as compensation for supposed damage to reputation without any proof that such harm actually occurred. The largely uncontrolled discretion of juries to award damages where there is no loss unnecessarily compounds the potential of any system of liability for defamatory falsehood to inhibit the vigorous exercise of First Amendment freedoms. Additionally, the doctrine of presumed damages invites juries to punish unpopular opinion rather than to compensate individuals for injury sustained by the publication of a false fact. More to the point, the States have no substantial interest in securing for plaintiffs such as this petitioner gratuitous awards of money damages far in excess of any actual injury.

. . . It is necessary to restrict defamation plaintiffs who do not prove knowledge of falsity or reckless disregard for the truth to compensation for actual injury. We need not define "actual injury," as trial courts have wide experience in framing appropriate jury instructions in tort actions. Suffice it to say that actual injury is not limited to out-of-pocket loss. Indeed, the more customary types of actual harm inflicted by defamatory falsehood include impairment of reputation and standing in the community, personal humiliation, and mental anguish and suffering. Of course, juries must be limited by appropriate instructions, and all awards must be supported by competent evidence concerning the injury, although there need be no evidence which assigns an actual dollar value to the injury.

We also find no justification for allowing awards of punitive damages against publishers and broadcasters held liable under state-defined standards of liability for defamation. In most jurisdictions jury discretion over the amounts awarded is limited only by the gentle rule that they not be excessive. Consequently, juries assess punitive damages in wholly unpredictable amounts bearing no necessary relation to the actual harm caused. And they remain free to use their discretion selectively to punish expressions of unpopular views. Like the doctrine of presumed damages, jury discretion to award punitive damages unnecessarily exacerbates the danger of media self-censorship, but, unlike the former rule, punitive damages are wholly irrelevant to the state interest that justifies a negligence standard for private defamation actions. They are not compensation for injury. Instead, they are private fines levied by civil juries to punish reprehensible conduct and to deter its future occurrence. In short, the private defamation plaintiff who establishes liability under a less demanding standard than that stated by *New York Times* may recover only such damages as are sufficient to compensate him for actual injury.

V.

Notwithstanding our refusal to extend the *New York Times* privilege to defamation of private individuals, respondent contends that we should affirm the judgment below on the ground that petitioner is either a public official or a public figure. There is little basis for the former assertion. Several years prior to the present incident, petitioner had served briefly on housing committees appointed by the mayor of Chicago, but at the time of publication he had never held any remunerative governmental position. Respondent admits this but argues that petitioner's appearance at the coroner's inquest rendered him a "de facto public official." Our cases recognize no such concept. Respondent's suggestion would sweep all lawyers under the *New York Times* rule as officers of the court and distort the plain meaning of the "public official" category beyond all recognition. We decline to follow it.

Respondent's characterization of petitioner as a public figure raises a different question. That designation may rest on either of two alternative bases. In some instances an individual may achieve such pervasive fame or notoriety that he becomes a public figure for all purposes and in all contexts. More commonly, an individual voluntarily injects himself or is drawn into a particular public controversy and thereby becomes a public figure for a limited range of issues. In either case such persons assume special prominence in the resolution of public questions.

Petitioner has long been active in community and professional affairs. He has served as an officer of local civic groups and of various professional organizations, and he has published several books and articles on legal subjects. Although petitioner was consequently well-known in some circles, he had achieved no general fame or notoriety in the community. None of the prospective jurors called at the trial had ever heard of petitioner prior to this litigation, and respondent offered no proof that this response was atypical of the local population. We would not lightly assume that a citizen's participation in community and professional affairs rendered him a public figure for all purposes. Absent clear evidence of general fame or notoriety in the community, and pervasive involvement in the affairs of society, an individual should not be deemed a public personality for all aspects of his life. It is preferable to reduce the public figure question to a more meaningful context by looking to the nature and extent of an individual's participation in the particular controversy giving rise to the defamation.

In this context it is plain that petitioner was not a public figure. He played a minimal role at the coroner's inquest, and his participation related solely to his representation of a private client. He took no part in the criminal prosecution of Officer Nuccio. Moreover, he never discussed either the criminal or civil litigation with the press and was never quoted as having done so. He plainly did not thrust himself into the vortex of this public issue, nor did he engage the public's attention in an attempt to influence its outcome. We are persuaded that the trial court did not err in refusing to characterize petitioner as a public figure for the purpose of this litigation.

We therefore conclude that the *New York Times* standard is inapplicable to this case and that the trial court erred in entering judgment for respondent. Because the jury was allowed to impose liability without fault and was permitted to presume damages without proof of injury, a new trial is necessary. We reverse and remand for further proceedings in accord with this opinion.

It is so ordered.[a]

■ MR. JUSTICE DOUGLAS, dissenting.

The Court describes this case as a return to the struggle of "defin[ing] the proper accommodation between the law of defamation and the freedoms of speech and press protected by the First Amendment." It is indeed a struggle, once described by Mr. Justice Black as "the same quagmire" in which the Court "is now helplessly struggling in the field of obscenity." Curtis Publishing Co. v. Butts, 388 U.S. 130, 171 (concurring opinion). I would suggest that the struggle is a quite hopeless one, for, in light of the command of the First Amendment, no "accommodation" of its freedoms can be "proper" except those made by the Framers themselves.

. . .

■ MR. JUSTICE BRENNAN, dissenting.

. . . [W]e strike the proper accommodation between avoidance of media self-censorship and protection of individual reputations only when we require States to apply the . . . knowing-or-reckless-falsity standard in civil libel actions concerning media reports of the involvement of private individuals in events of public or general interest.

. . .

■ MR. JUSTICE WHITE, dissenting.

. . .

. . . As I see it, there are wholly insufficient grounds for scuttling the libel laws of the States in such wholesale fashion, to say nothing of deprecating the reputation interest of ordinary citizens and rendering them powerless to protect themselves. I do not suggest that the decision is illegitimate or beyond the bounds of judicial review, but it is an ill-considered exercise of the power entrusted to this Court, particularly when the Court has not had the benefit of briefs and argument addressed to most of the major issues which the Court now decides. I respectfully dissent.

. . .

---

[a] A concurrence by Justice Blackmun and a dissent by Chief Justice Burger are omitted.

Dun & Bradstreet, Inc. v. Greenmoss Builders, Inc.

472 U.S. 749, 105 S.Ct. 2939, 86 L.Ed.2d 593 (1985).

■ JUSTICE POWELL announced the judgment of the Court and delivered an opinion, in which JUSTICE REHNQUIST and JUSTICE O'CONNOR joined.

. . . The question presented in this case is whether [the] rule of *Gertz* applies when the false and defamatory statements do not involve matters of public concern.

I

Petitioner Dun & Bradstreet, a credit reporting agency, provides subscribers with financial and related information about businesses. All the information is confidential; under the terms of the subscription agreement the subscribers may not reveal it to anyone else. On July 26, 1976, petitioner sent a report to five subscribers indicating that respondent, a construction contractor, had filed a voluntary petition for bankruptcy. This report was false and grossly misrepresented respondent's assets and liabilities. . . .

. . .

Respondent then brought this defamation action in Vermont state court. It alleged that the false report had injured its reputation and sought both compensatory and punitive damages. . . .

After trial, the jury returned a verdict in favor of respondent and awarded $50,000 in compensatory or presumed damages and $300,000 in punitive damages. Petitioner moved for a new trial. . . . The trial court indicated some doubt as to whether *Gertz* applied to "nonmedia cases," but granted a new trial "[b]ecause of . . . dissatisfaction with its charge and . . . conviction that the interests of justice require[d]" it.

The Vermont Supreme Court reversed. . . . [T]he court held "that as a matter of federal constitutional law, the media protections outlined in *Gertz* are inapplicable to nonmedia defamation actions."

. . .

IV

We have never considered whether the *Gertz* balance obtains when the defamatory statements involve no issue of public concern. To make this determination, we must employ the approach approved in *Gertz* and balance the State's interest in compensating private individuals for injury to their reputation against the First Amendment interest in protecting this type of expression. This state interest is identical to the one weighed in *Gertz*. . . .

The First Amendment interest, on the other hand, is less important than the one weighed in *Gertz*. We have long recognized that not all speech is of equal First Amendment importance. It is speech on " 'matters of public concern' " that is "at the heart of the First Amendment's protection." . . . In contrast, speech on matters of purely private concern is of less First Amendment concern. . . . As a number of state courts, including the court below, have recognized, the role of the Constitution in regulating state libel law is far more limited when the concerns that activated *New York Times* and *Gertz* are absent. . . .

. . . [C]ourts for centuries have allowed juries to presume that some damage occurred from many defamatory utterances and publications. . . . This rule furthers the state interest in providing remedies for defamation by ensuring that those remedies are effective. In light of the reduced constitutional value of speech involving no matters of public concern, we hold that the state interest adequately supports awards of presumed and punitive damages—even absent a showing of "actual malice."

V

The only remaining issue is whether petitioner's credit report involved a matter of public concern. In a related context, we have held that "[w]hether . . . speech addresses a matter of public concern must be determined by [the expression's] content, form, and context . . . as revealed by the whole record." . . . These factors indicate that petitioner's credit report concerns no public issue. It was speech solely in the individual interest of the speaker and its specific business audience. . . . This particular interest warrants no special protection when—as in this case—the speech is wholly false and clearly damaging to the victim's business reputation. . . . Moreover, since the credit report was made available to only five subscribers, who, under the terms of the subscription agreement, could not disseminate it further, it cannot be said that the report involves any "strong interest in the free flow of commercial information." . . . There is simply no credible argument that this type of credit reporting requires special protection to ensure that "debate on public issues [will] be uninhibited, robust, and wide-open." . . .

In addition, the speech here, like advertising, is hardy and unlikely to be deterred by incidental state regulation. . . . It is solely motivated by the desire for profit, which, we have noted, is a force less likely to be deterred than others. Ibid. Arguably, the reporting here was also more objectively verifiable than speech deserving of greater protection. See ibid. In any case, the market provides a powerful incentive to a credit reporting agency to be accurate, since false credit reporting is of no use to creditors. Thus, any incremental "chilling" effect of libel suits would be of decreased significance.

VI

We conclude that permitting recovery of presumed and punitive damages in defamation cases absent a showing of "actual malice" does not violate the First Amendment when the defamatory statements do not involve matters of public concern. Accordingly, we affirm the judgment of the Vermont Supreme Court.

It is so ordered.

■ CHIEF JUSTICE BURGER, concurring in the judgment.

. . .

I continue to believe . . . that *Gertz* was ill-conceived, and therefore agree with Justice White that *Gertz* should be overruled. . . .

■ JUSTICE WHITE, concurring in the judgment.

. . .

. . . I remain convinced that *Gertz* was erroneously decided. I have also become convinced that the Court struck an improvident balance in the *New York Times* case between the public's interest in being fully informed about public officials and public affairs and the competing interest of those who have been defamed in vindicating their reputation.

. . .

The *New York Times* rule . . . countenances two evils: first, the stream of information about public officials and public affairs is polluted and often remains polluted by false information; and second, the reputation and professional life of the defeated plaintiff may be destroyed by falsehoods that might have been avoided with a reasonable effort to investigate the facts. In terms of the First Amendment and reputational interests at stake, these seem grossly perverse results.

. . .

I still believe the common-law rules should have been retained where plaintiff is not a public official or public figure. . . .

It is interesting that Justice Powell declines to follow the *Gertz* approach in this case. I had thought that the decision in *Gertz* was intended to reach cases that involve any false statements of fact injurious to reputation, whether the statement is made privately or publicly and whether or not it implicates a matter of public importance. Justice Powell, however, distinguishes *Gertz* as a case that involved a matter of public concern, an element absent here. Wisely, in my view, Justice Powell does not rest his application of a different rule here on a distinction drawn between media and nonmedia defendants. On that issue, I agree with Justice Brennan that the First Amendment gives no more protection to the press in defamation suits than it does to others exercising their freedom of speech. None of our cases affords such a distinction; to the contrary, the Court has rejected it at every turn. It should be rejected again, particularly in this context, since it makes no sense to give the most protection to those publishers who reach the most readers and therefore pollute the channels of communication with the most misinformation and do the most damage to private reputation. If *Gertz* is to be distinguished from this case, on the ground that it applies only where the allegedly false publication deals with a matter of general or public importance, then where the false publication does not deal with such a matter, the common-law rules would apply whether the defendant is a member of the media or other public disseminator or a nonmedia individual publishing privately. Although Justice Powell speaks only of the inapplicability of the *Gertz* rule with respect to presumed and punitive damages, it must be that the *Gertz* requirement of some kind of fault on the part of the defendant is also inapplicable in cases such as this.

. . .

■ JUSTICE BRENNAN, with whom JUSTICE MARSHALL, JUSTICE BLACKMUN and JUSTICE STEVENS join, dissenting.

. . .

II

The question presented here is narrow. Neither the parties nor the courts below have suggested that Respondent Greenmoss Builders should be required to show actual malice to obtain a judgment and actual compensatory damages. Nor do the parties question the requirement of *Gertz* that respondent must show fault to obtain a judgment and actual damages. The only question presented is whether a jury award of presumed and punitive damages based on less than a showing of actual malice is constitutionally permissible. *Gertz* provides a forthright negative answer. To preserve the jury verdict in this case, therefore, the opinions of Justice Powell and Justice White have cut away the protective mantle of *Gertz*.

A

Relying on the analysis of the Vermont Supreme Court, Respondent urged that this pruning be accomplished by restricting the applicability of *Gertz* to cases in which the defendant is a "media" entity. . . . First Amendment difficulties lurk in the definitional questions such an approach would generate. . . . Perhaps most importantly, the argument that *Gertz* should be limited to the media misapprehends our cases. We protect the press to ensure the vitality of First Amendment guarantees. This solicitude implies no endorsement of the principle that speakers other than the press deserve lesser First Amendment protection. . . .

. . . [A]t least six Members of this Court (the four who join this opinion and Justice White and The Chief Justice) agree today that, in the context of defamation law, the rights of the institutional media are no greater and no less than those enjoyed by other individuals or organizations engaged in the same activities.[10]

B

. . .

. . . The credit reporting at issue here surely involves a subject matter of sufficient public concern to require the comprehensive protections of *Gertz*. Were this speech appropriately characterized as a matter of only private concern, moreover, the elimination of the *Gertz* restrictions on presumed and punitive damages would still violate basic First Amendment requirements.

The credit reports of Dun & Bradstreet bear few of the earmarks of commercial speech that might be entitled to somewhat less rigorous protection. In *every* case in which we have permitted more extensive state regulation on the basis of a commercial speech rationale the speech being regulated was pure advertising—an offer to buy or sell goods and services or encouraging such buying and selling. Credit reports are not commercial advertisements for a good or service or a proposal to buy or sell such a product. . . .

Of course, the commercial context of Dun & Bradstreet's reports is relevant to the constitutional analysis. . . . The special harms caused by inaccurate credit reports, the lack of public sophistication about or access to such reports, and the fact that such reports by and large contain statements that are fairly readily susceptible of verification, all may justify appropriate regulation designed to prevent the social losses caused by false credit reports. And in the libel context, the States' regulatory interest in protecting reputation is served by rules permitting recovery for actual compensatory damages upon a showing of fault. Any further interest in deterring potential defamation through case-by-case judicial imposition of presumed and punitive damage awards on less than a showing of actual malice simply exacts too high a toll on First Amendment values. Accordingly, Greenmoss Builders should be permitted to recover for any actual damage it can show resulted from Dun & Bradstreet's negligently false credit report, but should be required to show actual malice to receive presumed or punitive damages. Because the jury was not instructed in accordance with these principles, we would reverse and remand for further proceedings not inconsistent with this opinion.

The Florida Star v. B.J.F.

491 U.S. 524, 109 S.Ct. 2603, 105 L.Ed.2d 443 (1989).

■ JUSTICE MARSHALL delivered the opinion of the Court.

Florida Stat. section 794.03 (1987) makes it unlawful to "print, publish, or broadcast . . . in any instrument of mass communication" the name of the victim of a sexual offense. Pursuant to this statute, appellant The Florida Star was found civilly liable for publishing the name of a rape victim which it had obtained from a publicly released police report. The issue presented here is whether this result comports with the First Amendment. We hold that it does not.

I

The Florida Star . . . serves . . . Jacksonville . . . and . . . [includes a] "Police Reports" section . . . contain[ing] brief articles describing local criminal incidents under police investigation.

---

[10] Justice Powell's opinion does not expressly reject the media-nonmedia distinction, but does expressly decline to apply that distinction to resolve this case.

On October 20, 1983, appellee B.J.F. reported to the . . . Sheriff's Department . . . that she had been robbed and sexually assaulted by an unknown assailant. The Department prepared a report on the incident which identified B.J.F. by her full name . . . [and] placed the report in its press room. The Department does not restrict access either to the press room or to the reports made available therein.

A Florida Star reporter-trainee sent to the press room copied the police report verbatim, including B.J.F.'s full name, on a blank duplicate of the Department's forms. A Florida Star reporter then prepared a one-paragraph article about the crime, derived entirely from the trainee's copy of the police report. The article included B.J.F.'s full name. It appeared in the "Robberies" subsection of the "Police Reports" section on October 29, 1983, one of fifty-four police blotter stories in that day's edition. The article read:

"[B.J.F.] reported on Thursday, October 20, she was crossing Brentwood Park, which is in the 500 block of Golfair Boulevard, enroute to her bus stop, when an unknown black man ran up behind the lady and placed a knife to her neck and told her not to yell. The suspect then undressed the lady and had sexual intercourse with her before fleeing the scene with her 60 cents, Timex watch and gold necklace. Patrol efforts have been suspended concerning this incident because of a lack of evidence."

In printing B.J.F.'s full name, The Florida Star violated its internal policy of not publishing the names of sexual offense victims.

. . . B.J.F. [sued] the Department and The Florida Star, alleging that [they] negligently violated section 794.03. . . .

. . .

. . . The jury awarded B.J.F. $75,000 in compensatory damages and $25,000 in punitive damages. . . .

The First District Court of Appeal affirmed . . . . The Supreme Court of Florida denied discretionary review.

. . . We . . . reverse.

II

The tension between the right which the First Amendment accords to a free press, on the one hand, and the protections which various statutes and common-law doctrines accord to personal privacy against the publication of truthful information, on the other, is a subject we have addressed several times in recent years. . . . [A]lthough our decisions have without exception upheld the press' right to publish, we have emphasized each time that we were resolving this conflict only as it arose in a discrete factual context.

The parties to this case frame their contentions in light of a trilogy of cases which have presented, in different contexts, the conflict between truthful reporting and state-protected privacy interests. In Cox Broadcasting Corp. v. Cohn, 420 U.S. 469 (1975), we found unconstitutional a civil damages award entered against a television station for broadcasting the name of a rape-murder victim which the station had obtained from courthouse records. In Oklahoma Publishing Co. v. District Court, 430 U.S. 308 (1977), we found unconstitutional a state court's pretrial order enjoining the media from publishing the name or photograph of an 11-year-old boy in connection with a juvenile proceeding involving that child which reporters had attended. Finally, in Smith v. Daily Mail Publishing Co., 443 U.S. 97 (1979), we found unconstitutional the indictment of two newspapers for violating a state statute forbidding newspapers to publish, without written approval of the juvenile court, the name of any youth charged as a juvenile offender. The papers had learned about a shooting by monitoring a police band radio frequency, and had obtained the name of the alleged juvenile assailant from witnesses, the police, and a local prosecutor.

. . .

We conclude that imposing damages on appellant for publishing B.J.F.'s name violates the First Amendment . . . Despite the strong resemblance this case bears to *Cox Broadcasting,* that case cannot fairly be read as controlling here. The name of the rape victim in that case was obtained from courthouse records that were open to public inspection, a fact which Justice White's opinion for the Court repeatedly noted. . . . Significantly, one of the reasons we gave in *Cox Broadcasting* for invalidating the challenged damages award was the important role the press plays in subjecting trials to public scrutiny and thereby helping guarantee their fairness. . . . That role is not directly compromised where, as here, the information in question comes from a police report prepared and disseminated at a time at which not only had no adversarial criminal proceedings begun, but no suspect had been identified.

Nor need we accept appellant's invitation to hold broadly that truthful publication may never be punished consistent with the First Amendment. Our cases have carefully eschewed reaching this ultimate question, mindful that the future may bring scenarios which prudence counsels our not resolving anticipatorily. . . . Indeed, in *Cox Broadcasting,* we pointedly refused to answer even the less sweeping question "whether truthful publications may ever be subjected to civil or criminal liability" for invading "an area of privacy" defined by the State. . . . Respecting the fact that press freedom and privacy rights are both "plainly rooted in the traditions and significant concerns of our society," we instead focused on the less sweeping issue of "whether the State may impose sanctions on the accurate publication of the name of a rape victim obtained from public records—more specifically, from judicial records which are maintained in connection with a public prosecution and which themselves are open to public inspection." . . . We continue to believe that the sensitivity and significance of the interests presented in clashes between First Amendment and privacy rights counsel relying on limited principles that sweep no more broadly than the appropriate context of the instant case.

In our view, this case is appropriately analyzed with reference to such a limited First Amendment principle. It is the one, in fact, which we articulated in *Daily Mail* in our synthesis of prior cases involving attempts to punish truthful publication:

"[I]f a newspaper lawfully obtains truthful information about a matter of public significance then state officials may not constitutionally punish publication of the information, absent a need to further a state interest of the highest order." 443 U.S., at 103.

According the press the ample protection provided by that principle is supported by at least three separate considerations. . . .

First, because the *Daily Mail* formulation only protects the publication of information which a newspaper has "lawfully obtain[ed]," . . . the government retains ample means of safeguarding significant interests upon which publication may impinge, including protecting a rape victim's anonymity. To the extent sensitive information rests in private hands, the government may under some circumstances forbid its nonconsensual acquisition, thereby bringing outside of the *Daily Mail* principle the publication of any information so acquired. To the extent sensitive information is in the government's custody, it has even greater power to forestall or mitigate the injury caused by its release. The government may classify certain information, establish and enforce procedures ensuring its redacted release, and extend a damages remedy against the government or its officials where the government's mishandling of sensitive information leads to its dissemination. Where information is entrusted to the government, a less drastic means than punishing truthful publication almost always exists for guarding against the dissemination of private facts. . . . [8]

. . . [Second,] punishing the press for its dissemination of information which is already publicly available is relatively unlikely to advance the interests in the service of which the State seeks to act. . . . [W]here the government has made certain information publicly available, it is highly anomalous to sanction persons other than the source of its release. . . . The *Daily Mail* formulation reflects the fact that it is a limited set of cases indeed where, despite the accessibility of the public to certain information, a meaningful public interest is served by restricting its further release by other entities, like the press. . . .

A third and final consideration is the "timidity and self-censorship" which may result from allowing the media to be punished for publishing certain truthful information. . . . *Cox Broadcasting* noted this concern with overdeterrence in the context of information made public through official court records, but the fear of excessive media self-suppression is applicable as well to other information released, without qualification, by the government. A contrary rule, depriving protection to those who rely on the government's implied representations of the lawfulness of dissemination, would force upon the media the onerous obligation of sifting through government press releases, reports, and pronouncements to prune out material arguably unlawful for publication. This situation could inhere even where the newspaper's sole object was to reproduce, with no substantial change, the government's rendition of the event in question.

Applied to the instant case, the *Daily Mail* principle clearly commands reversal. The first inquiry is whether the newspaper "lawfully obtain[ed] truthful information about a matter of public significance." . . . It is undisputed that the news article describing the assault on B.J.F. was accurate. In addition, appellant lawfully obtained B.J.F.'s name. Appellee's argument to the contrary is based on the fact that under Florida law, police reports which reveal the identity of the victim of a sexual offense are not among the matters of "public record" which the public, by law, is entitled to inspect. But the fact that state officials are not required to disclose such reports does not make it unlawful for a newspaper to receive them when furnished by the government. Nor does the fact that the Department apparently failed to fulfill its obligation under section 794.03 not to "cause or allow to be . . . published" the name of a sexual offense victim make the newspaper's ensuing receipt of this information unlawful. Even assuming the Constitution permitted a State to proscribe *receipt* of information, Florida has not taken this step. It is, clear, furthermore, that the news article concerned "a matter of public significance," . . . in the sense in which the *Daily Mail* synthesis of prior cases used that term. That is, the article generally, as opposed to the specific identity contained within it, involved a matter of paramount public import: the commission, and investigation, of a violent crime which had been reported to authorities. . . .

The second inquiry is whether imposing liability on appellant pursuant to section 794.03 serves "a need to further a state interest of the highest order." . . . Appellee argues that a rule punishing publication furthers three closely related interests: the privacy of victims of sexual offenses; the physical safety of such victims, who may be targeted for retaliation if their names become known to their assailants; and the goal of encouraging victims of such crimes to report these offenses without fear of exposure.

---

[8] The *Daily Mail* principle does not settle the issue of whether, in cases where information has been acquired *unlawfully* by a newspaper or by a source, government may ever punish not only the unlawful acquisition, but the ensuing publication as well. . . . We have no occasion to address it here.

At a time in which we are daily reminded of the tragic reality of rape, it is undeniable that these are highly significant interests, a fact underscored by the Florida Legislature's explicit attempt to protect these interests by enacting a criminal statute prohibiting much dissemination of victim identities. We accordingly do not rule out the possibility that, in a proper case, imposing civil sanctions for publication of the name of a rape victim might be so overwhelmingly necessary to advance these interests as to satisfy the Daily Mail standard. For three independent reasons, however, imposing liability for publication under the circumstances of this case is too precipitous a means of advancing these interests to convince us that there is a "need" within the meaning of the *Daily Mail* formulation for Florida to take this extreme step.

First[,] . . . B.J.F.'s identity would never have come to light were it not for the erroneous, if inadvertent, inclusion by the Department of her full name in an incident report made available in a press room open to the public. . . . Where, as here, the government has failed to police itself in disseminating information, it is clear under *Cox Broadcasting, Oklahoma Publishing,* and *Landmark Communications* that the imposition of damages against the press for its subsequent publication can hardly be said to be a narrowly tailored means of safeguarding anonymity. . . .

That appellant gained access to the information in question through a government news release makes it especially likely that, if liability were to be imposed, self-censorship would result. Reliance on a news release is a paradigmatically "routine newspaper reporting techniqu[e]." . . . The government's issuance of such a release, without qualification, can only convey to recipients that the government considered dissemination lawful, and indeed expected the recipients to disseminate the information further. Had appellant merely reproduced the news release prepared and released by the Department, imposing civil damages would surely violate the First Amendment. The fact that appellant converted the police report into a news story by adding the linguistic connecting tissue necessary to transform the report's facts into full sentences cannot change this result.

A second problem with Florida's imposition of liability for publication is the broad sweep of the negligence per se standard applied under the civil cause of action implied from section 794.03. Unlike claims based on the common law tort of invasion of privacy, . . . civil actions based on section 794.03 require no case-by-case findings that the disclosure of a fact about a person's private life was one that a reasonable person would find highly offensive. On the contrary, under the per se theory of negligence adopted by the courts below, liability follows automatically from publication. This is so regardless of whether the identity of the victim is already known throughout the community; whether the victim has voluntarily called public attention to the offense; or whether the identity of the victim has otherwise become a reasonable subject of public concern—because, perhaps, questions have arisen whether the victim fabricated an assault by a particular person. Nor is there a scienter requirement of any kind under section 794.03, engendering the perverse result that truthful publications challenged pursuant to this cause of action are less protected by the First Amendment than even the least protected defamatory falsehoods: those involving purely private figures, where liability is evaluated under a standard, usually applied by a jury, of ordinary negligence. See Gertz v. Robert Welch, Inc., 418 U.S. 323 (1974). . . .

Third, and finally, the facial underinclusiveness of section 794.03 raises serious doubts about whether Florida is, in fact, serving . . . the significant interests which appellee invokes . . . Section 794.03 prohibits the publication of identifying information only if this information appears in an "instrument of mass communication," a term the statute does not define. Section 794.03 does not prohibit the spread by other means of the identities of victims of sexual offenses. An individual who maliciously spreads word of the identity of a rape victim is thus not covered, despite the fact that the communication of such information to persons who live near, or work with, the victim may have consequences equally devastating as the exposure of her name to large numbers of strangers. . . .

When a State attempts the extraordinary measure of punishing truthful publication in the name of privacy, it must demonstrate its commitment to advancing this interest by applying its prohibition evenhandedly, to the smalltime disseminator as well as the media giant. Where important First Amendment interests are at stake, the mass scope of disclosure is not an acceptable surrogate for injury. A ban on disclosures effected by "instrument[s] of mass communication" simply cannot be defended on the ground that partial prohibitions may effect partial relief. . . . Without more careful and inclusive precautions against alternative forms of dissemination, we cannot conclude that Florida's selective ban on publication by the mass media satisfactorily accomplishes its stated purpose.

III

Our holding today is limited. We do not hold that truthful publication is automatically constitutionally protected, or that there is no zone of personal privacy within which the State may protect the individual from intrusion by the press, or even that a State may never punish publication of the name of a victim of a sexual offense. We hold only that where a newspaper publishes truthful information which it has lawfully obtained, punishment may lawfully be imposed, if at all, only when narrowly tailored to a state interest of the highest order, and that no such interest is satisfactorily served by imposing liability under section 794.03 to appellant under the facts of this case. The decision below is therefore

Reversed.

■ JUSTICE SCALIA concurring in part and concurring in the judgment.

I think it sufficient to decide this case to rely upon the third ground set forth in the Court's opinion: that a law cannot [justify] . . . a restriction upon truthful speech, when it leaves appreciable damage to that supposedly vital interest unprohibited. . . .

This law has every appearance of a prohibition that society is prepared to impose upon the press but not upon itself. . . .

■ JUSTICE WHITE, with whom THE CHIEF JUSTICE and JUSTICE O'CONNOR join, dissenting.

. . .

I

. . .

Cox Broadcasting stands for the proposition that the State cannot make the press its first line of defense in withholding private information from the public—it cannot ask the press to secrete private facts that the State makes no effort to safeguard in the first place. . . .

. . .

. . . [A]t issue in *Daily Mail* was the disclosure of the name of the perpetrator of an infamous murder of a 15-year-old student. . . . Surely the rights of those accused of crimes and those who are their victims must differ with respect to privacy concerns. . . .

Consequently, I cannot agree that *Cox Broadcasting,* or *Oklahoma Publishing,* or *Daily Mail* require—or even substantially support—the result reached by the Court today.

II

. . .

. . . Here, the "release" of information provided by the government was not, as the Court says, "without qualification." As the Star's own reporter conceded at trial, the crime incident report that inadvertently included B.J.F.'s name was posted in a room that contained signs making it clear that the names of rape victims were not matters of public record, and were not to be published. . . .

. . .

. . . [Second, p]ermitting liability under a negligence per se theory does not mean that defendants will be held liable without a showing of negligence, but rather, that the standard of care has been set by the legislature, instead of the courts. . . . [T]he legislature—reflecting popular sentiment—has determined that disclosure of the fact that a person was raped is categorically a revelation that reasonable people find offensive. And as for the Court's suggestion that the Florida courts' theory permits liability without regard for whether the victim's identity is already known, or whether she herself has made it known—these are facts that would surely enter into the calculation of damages in such a case. . . .

Third, the Court faults the Florida criminal statute for being underinclusive . . . But our cases which have struck down laws that limit or burden the press due to their underinclusiveness have involved situations where a legislature has singled out one segment of the news media or press for adverse treatment, . . . or singled out the press for adverse treatment when compared to other similarly situated enterprises. . . . Here, the Florida law evenhandedly covers all "instrument[s] of mass communication" no matter their form, media, content, nature or purpose. . . . Florida wanted to prevent the widespread distribution of rape victim's names, and therefore enacted a statute tailored almost as precisely as possible to achieving that end.

. . .

Consequently, neither the State's "dissemination" of B.J.F.'s name, nor the standard of liability imposed here, nor the underinclusiveness of Florida tort law require setting aside the verdict for B.J.F. . . . I turn, therefore, to the more general principles at issue here to see if they recommend the Court's result.

III

At issue in this case is whether there is any information about people, which—though true—may not be published in the press. By holding that only "a state interest of the highest order" permits the State to penalize the publication of truthful information, and by holding that protecting a rape victim's right to privacy is not among those state interests of the highest order, the Court accepts appellant's invitation to obliterate one of the most note-worthy legal inventions of the 20th-Century: the tort of the publication of private facts. . . . If the First Amendment prohibits wholly private persons (such as B.J.F.) from recovering for the publication of the fact that she was raped, I doubt that there remain any "private facts" which persons may assume will not be published in the newspapers, or broadcast on television.

Of course, the right to privacy is not absolute. Even the Article widely relied upon in cases vindicating privacy rights, Warren & Brandeis, The Right to Privacy, 4 Harv.L.Rev., at 193, recognized that this right inevitably conflicts with the public's right to know about matters of general concern—and that sometimes, the latter must trump the former. . . . Resolving this conflict is a difficult matter, and I do not fault the Court for attempting to strike an appropriate balance between the two, but rather, for according too little weight to B.J.F.'s side of the equation, and too much on the other.

. . .

Zacchini v. Scripps-Howard Broadcasting Co.

433 U.S. 562 (1977).

Hugo Zacchini was an entertainer, whose 15 second act consisted of being shot from a cannon into a net 200 feet away. A reporter for a local television station, attending the county fair where Zacchini was performing, was asked by Zacchini not to film his act. The reporter, however, returned the next day and videotaped the entire act. The tape, which ran 15 seconds, was shown on the 11:00 o'clock news that night. In the state trial court, Zacchini was awarded summary judgment in an action for appropriation of his "professional property." The Ohio Supreme Court reversed, relying on Time, Inc. v. Hill, 385 U.S. 374 (1967), for the proposition that the television station had a privilege to report the act as a newsworthy event. The Supreme Court reversed. The court's opinion, by Justice White, concluded that the Hill case was inapposite:

"Time, Inc. v. Hill, which was hotly contested and decided by a divided Court, involved an entirely different tort from the 'right of publicity' recognized by the Ohio Supreme Court. As the opinion reveals in Time, Inc. v. Hill, the Court was steeped in the literature of privacy law and was aware of the developing distinctions and nuances in this branch of the law. . . . The Court was aware that it was adjudicating a 'false light' privacy case involving a matter of public interest, not a case involving 'intrusion,' . . . 'appropriation' of a name or likeness for the purposes of trade, . . . or 'private details' about a non-newsworthy person or event. . . . It is also abundantly clear that Time, Inc. v. Hill did not involve a performer, a person with a name having commercial value, or any claim to a 'right of publicity.' This discrete kind of 'appropriation' case was plainly identified in the literature cited by the Court and had been adjudicated in the reported cases.

". . .

". . . Wherever the line in particular situations is to be drawn between media reports that are protected and those that are not, we are quite sure that the First and Fourteenth Amendments do not immunize the media when they broadcast a performer's entire act without his consent. The Constitution no more prevents a State from requiring respondent to compensate petitioner for broadcasting his act on television than it would privilege respondent to film and broadcast a copyrighted dramatic work without liability to the copyright owner. . . ."

Justice Powell's dissent, joined by Justices Brennan and Marshall, emphasized that the case involved a 15 second clip that was part of a routine daily news program.

"In my view the First Amendment commands a different analytical starting point from the one selected by the Court. Rather than begin with a quantitative analysis of the performer's behavior—is this or is this not his entire act—we should direct initial attention to the actions of the news media: what use did the station make of the film footage? When a film is used, as here, for a routine portion of a regular news program, I would hold that the First Amendment protects the station from a 'right of publicity' or 'appropriation' suit, absent a strong showing by the plaintiff that the news broadcast was a subterfuge or cover for private or commercial exploitation."

Justice Stevens, dissenting, would have remanded the case to the Ohio Supreme Court for clarification as to whether its decision denying liability rested on the constitutional ground.

B. CONTROL OF OBSCENITY AND PORNOGRAPHY

Paris Adult Theatre I v. Slaton

413 U.S. 49, 93 S.Ct. 2628, 37 L.Ed.2d 446 (1973).

■ MR. CHIEF JUSTICE BURGER delivered the opinion of the Court.

Petitioners are two Atlanta, Georgia, movie theaters and their owners and managers, operating in the style of "adult" theaters. . . . [R]espondents, the local state district attorney and the solicitor for the local state trial court, filed civil complaints in that court alleging that petitioners were exhibiting to the public for paid admission two allegedly obscene films . . .

Respondents' complaints, made on behalf of the State of Georgia, demanded that the two films be declared obscene and that petitioners be enjoined from exhibiting the films. . . .

. . . Certain photographs, . . . produced at trial, were stipulated to portray the single entrance to both Paris Adult Theatre I and Paris Adult Theatre II as it appeared at the time of the complaints. These photographs show a conventional, inoffensive theater entrance, without any pictures, but with signs indicating that the theaters exhibit "Atlanta's Finest Mature Feature Films." On the door itself is a sign saying: "Adult Theatre—You must be 21 and able to prove it. If viewing the nude body offends you, Please Do Not Enter."

. . . [T]he trial judge dismissed respondents' complaints. . . . On appeal, the Georgia Supreme Court unanimously reversed. . . .

. . .

II

We categorically disapprove the theory, apparently adopted by the trial judge, that obscene, pornographic films acquire constitutional immunity from state regulation simply because they are exhibited for consenting adults only. This holding was properly rejected by the Georgia Supreme Court. Although we have often pointedly recognized the high importance of the state interest in regulating the exposure of obscene materials to juveniles and unconsenting adults, . . . this Court has never declared these to be the only legitimate state interests permitting regulation of obscene material. . . .

In particular, we hold that there are legitimate state interests at stake in stemming the tide of commercialized obscenity, even assuming it is feasible to enforce effective safeguards against exposure to juveniles and to passersby. . . . These include the interest of the public in the quality of life and the total community environment, the tone of commerce in the great city centers, and, possibly, the public safety itself. . . . [T]here is at least an arguable correlation between obscene material and crime. Quite apart from sex crimes, however, there remains one problem of large proportions aptly described by Professor Bickel:

"It concerns the tone of the society, the mode, or to use terms that have perhaps greater currency, the style and quality of life, now and in the future. A man may be entitled to read an obscene book in his room, or expose himself indecently there. . . . We should protect his privacy. But if he demands a right to obtain the books and pictures he wants in the market, and to foregather in public places—discreet, if you will, but accessible to all—with others who share his tastes, *then to grant him his right is to affect the world about the rest of us, and to impinge on other privacies.* Even supposing that each of us can, if he wishes, effectively avert the eye and stop the ear (which, in truth, we cannot), what is commonly read and seen and heard and done intrudes upon us all, want it or not." 22 The Public Interest 25–26 (Winter 1971). (Emphasis added.) . . .

But, it is argued, there are no scientific data which conclusively demonstrate that exposure to obscene material adversely affects men and women or their society. . . . It is not for us to resolve empirical uncertainties underlying state legislation, save in the exceptional case where that legislation plainly impinges upon rights protected by the Constitution itself. . . . Although there is no conclusive proof of a connection between antisocial behavior and obscene material, the legislature of Georgia could quite reasonably determine that such a connection does or might exist. . . .

. . .

If we accept the unprovable assumption that a complete education requires the reading of certain books, . . . and the well nigh universal belief that good books, plays, and art lift the spirit, improve the mind, enrich the human personality, and develop character, can we then say that a state legislature may not act on the corollary assumption that commerce in obscene books, or public exhibitions focused on obscene conduct, have a tendency to exert a corrupting and debasing impact leading to antisocial behavior? . . . The sum of experience, including that of the past two decades, affords an ample basis for legislatures to conclude that a sensitive, key relationship of human existence, central to family life, community welfare, and the development of human personality, can be debased and distorted by crass commercial exploitation of sex. Nothing in the Constitution prohibits a State from reaching such a conclusion and acting on it legislatively simply because there is no conclusive evidence or empirical data.

It is argued that individual "free will" must govern, even in activities beyond the protection of the First Amendment and other constitutional guarantees of privacy, and that government cannot legitimately impede an individual's desire to see or acquire obscene plays, movies, and books. We do indeed base our society on certain assumptions that people have the capacity for free choice. Most exercises of individual free choice—those in politics, religion, and expression of ideas—are explicitly protected by the Constitution. Totally unlimited play for free will, however, is not allowed in our or any other society. . . .

. . .

It is asserted, however, that standards for evaluating state commercial regulations are inapposite in the present context, as state regulation of access by consenting adults to obscene material violates the constitutionally protected right to privacy enjoyed by petitioners' customers. . . . [I]t is unavailing to compare a theater, open to the public for a fee, with the private home of Stanley v. Georgia, [394 U.S.,] at 568, and the marital bedroom of Griswold v. Connecticut, supra, [381 U.S.,] at 485–486. . . .

. . .

. . . Where communication of ideas, protected by the First Amendment, is not involved, or the particular privacy of the home protected by *Stanley*, or any of the other "areas or zones" of constitutionally protected privacy, the mere fact that, as a consequence, some human "utterances" or "thoughts" may be incidentally affected does not bar the State from acting to protect legitimate state interests. . . .

Finally, petitioners argue that conduct which directly involves "consenting adults" only has, for that sole reason, a special claim to constitutional protection. Our Constitution establishes a broad range of conditions on the exercise of power by the States, but for us to say that our Constitution incorporates the proposition that conduct involving consenting adults only is always beyond state regulation, is a step we are unable to take. . . .

. . .

■ MR. JUSTICE BRENNAN, with whom MR. JUSTICE STEWART and MR. JUSTICE MARSHALL join, dissenting.

. . . I am convinced that the approach initiated 16 years ago in Roth v. United States, 354 U.S. 476 (1957), and culminating in the Court's decision today, cannot bring stability to this area of the law without jeopardizing fundamental First Amendment values, and I have concluded that the time has come to make a significant departure from that approach.

. . .

Our experience with the Roth approach has certainly taught us that the outright suppression of obscenity cannot be reconciled with the fundamental principles of the First and Fourteenth Amendments. . . . [W]e have failed to formulate a standard that sharply distinguishes protected from unprotected speech . . .

. . . [A]fter 16 years of experimentation and debate I am reluctantly forced to the conclusion that none of the available formulas, including the one announced today, can reduce the vagueness to a tolerable level while at the same time striking an acceptable balance between the protections of the First and Fourteenth Amendments, on the one hand, and on the other the asserted state interest in regulating the dissemination of certain sexually oriented materials. . . . Although we have assumed that obscenity does exist and that we "know it when [we] see it," Jacobellis v. Ohio, [378 U.S.] at 197 (Stewart, J., concurring), we are manifestly unable to describe it in advance except by reference to concepts so elusive that they fail to distinguish clearly between protected and unprotected speech.

. . .

The problems of fair notice and chilling protected speech are very grave standing alone. But it does not detract from their importance to recognize that a vague statute in this area creates a third, although admittedly more subtle, set of problems. These problems concern the institutional stress that inevitably results where the line separating protected from unprotected speech is excessively vague. . . .

. . . [A]lmost every case is "marginal." And since the "margin" marks the point of separation between protected and unprotected speech, we are left with a system in which almost every obscenity case presents a constitutional question of exceptional difficulty. . . .

. . .

The Court evidently recognizes that difficulties with the Roth approach necessitate a significant change of direction. But the Court does not describe its understanding of those difficulties, nor does it indicate how the restatement of the Memoirs test is in any way responsive to the problems that have arisen. In my view, the restatement leaves unresolved the very difficulties that compel our rejection of the underlying Roth approach, while at the same time contributing substantial difficulties of its own. The modification of the Memoirs test may prove sufficient to jeopardize the analytic underpinnings of the entire scheme. And today's restatement will likely have the effect, whether or not intended, of permitting far more sweeping suppression of sexually oriented expression, including expression that would almost surely be held protected under our current formulation.

. . .

In any case, even if the Court's approach left undamaged the conceptual framework of *Roth,* and even if it clearly barred the suppression of works with at least some social value, I would nevertheless be compelled to reject it. . . .

. . .

Ultimately, the reformulation must fail because it still leaves in this Court the responsibility of determining in each case whether the materials are protected by the First Amendment. . . .

. . .

. . . I have considered the view, urged so forcefully since 1957 by our Brothers Black and Douglas, that the First Amendment bars the suppression of any sexually oriented expression. That position would effect a sharp reduction, although perhaps not a total elimination, of the uncertainty that surrounds our current approach. Nevertheless, I am convinced that it would achieve that desirable goal only by stripping the States of power to an extent that cannot be justified by the commands of the Constitution, at least so long as there is available an alternative approach that strikes a better balance between the guarantee of free expression and the States' legitimate interests.

. . .

In short, while I cannot say that the interests of the State—apart from the question of juveniles and unconsenting adults—are trivial or nonexistent, I am compelled to conclude that these interests cannot justify the substantial damage to constitutional rights and to this Nation's judicial machinery that inevitably results from state efforts to bar the distribution even of unprotected material to consenting adults. . . . I would hold, therefore, that at least in the absence of distribution to juveniles or obtrusive exposure to unconsenting adults, the First and Fourteenth Amendments prohibit the State and Federal Governments from attempting wholly to suppress sexually oriented materials on the basis of their allegedly "obscene" contents. Nothing in this approach precludes those governments from taking action to serve what may be strong and legitimate interests through regulation of the manner of distribution of sexually oriented material.

. . . Difficult questions must still be faced, notably in the areas of distribution to juveniles and offensive exposure to unconsenting adults. Whatever the extent of state power to regulate in those areas, it should be clear that the view I espouse today would introduce a large measure of clarity to this troubled area, would reduce the institutional pressure on this Court and the rest of the State and Federal Judiciary, and would guarantee fuller freedom of expression while leaving room for the protection of legitimate governmental interests. . . .

■ MR. JUSTICE DOUGLAS, dissenting.

My Brother Brennan is to be commended for seeking a new path through the thicket which the Court entered when it undertook to sustain the constitutionality of obscenity laws and to place limits on their application. I have expressed on numerous occasions my disagreement with the basic decision that held that "obscenity" was not protected by the First Amendment. . . .

. . .

I applaud the effort of my Brother Brennan to forsake the low road which the Court has followed in this field. The new regime he would inaugurate is much closer than the old to the policy of abstention which the First Amendment proclaims. . . . I see no constitutional basis for fashioning a rule that makes a publisher, producer, bookseller, librarian, or movie house operator criminally responsible, when he fails to take affirmative steps to protect the consumer against literature, books, or movies offensive to those who temporarily occupy the seats of the mighty.

. . .

Miller v. California

413 U.S. 15, 93 S.Ct. 2607, 37 L.Ed.2d 419 (1973).

■ MR. CHIEF JUSTICE BURGER delivered the opinion of the Court.

This is one of a group of "obscenity-pornography" cases being reviewed by the Court in a re-examination of standards enunciated in earlier cases. . . .

Appellant conducted a mass mailing campaign to advertise the sale of illustrated books, euphemistically called "adult" material. After a jury trial, he was convicted of violating California Penal Code § 311.2(a), a misdemeanor, by knowingly distributing obscene matter,[1] and the Appellate Department, Superior Court of California, County of Orange, summarily affirmed the judgment without opinion. Appellant's conviction was specifically based on his conduct in causing five unsolicited advertising brochures to be sent through the mail in an envelope addressed to a restaurant in Newport Beach, California. The envelope was opened by the manager of the restaurant and his mother. They had not requested the brochures; they complained to the police.

. . .

The brochures advertise four books entitled "Intercourse," "Man-Woman," "Sex Orgies Illustrated," and "An Illustrated History of Pornography," and a film entitled "Marital Intercourse." While the brochures contain some descriptive printed material, primarily they consist of pictures and drawings very explicitly depicting men and women in groups of two or more engaging in a variety of sexual activities, with genitals often prominently displayed.

I

. . . This Court has recognized that the States have a legitimate interest in prohibiting dissemination or exhibition of obscene material when the mode of dissemination carries with it a significant danger of offending the sensibilities of unwilling recipients or of exposure to juveniles. . . . It is in this context that we are called on to define the standards which must be used to identify obscene material that a State may regulate without infringing on the First Amendment as applicable to the States through the Fourteenth Amendment.

. . . In Roth v. United States, 354 U.S. 476 (1957), the Court sustained a conviction under a federal statute punishing the mailing of "obscene, lewd, lascivious or filthy . . . " materials. The key to that holding was the Court's rejection of the claim that obscene materials were protected by the First Amendment. . . .

Nine years later, in Memoirs v. Massachusetts, 383 U.S. 413 (1966), the Court . . . articulated a new test of obscenity. The plurality held that under the *Roth* definition

---

[1]   At the time of the commission of the alleged offense, . . . § 311 of the California Penal Code read in relevant part:

"As used in this chapter:

"(a) 'Obscene' means that to the average person, applying contemporary standards, the predominant appeal of the matter, taken as a whole, is to prurient interest, i.e., a shameful or morbid interest in nudity, sex, or excretion, which goes substantially beyond customary limits of candor in description or representation of such matters and is matter which is utterly without redeeming social importance." . . .

"as elaborated in subsequent cases, three elements must coalesce: it must be established that (a) the dominant theme of the material taken as a whole appeals to a prurient interest in sex; (b) the material is patently offensive because it affronts contemporary community standards relating to the description or representation of sexual matters; and (c) the material is utterly without redeeming social value." . . .

While *Roth* presumed "obscenity" to be "utterly without redeeming social importance," *Memoirs* required that to prove obscenity it must be affirmatively established that the material is "utterly without redeeming social value." Thus, . . . the *Memoirs* plurality [required] the prosecution to prove a negative, i.e., that the material was "utterly without redeeming social value"—a burden virtually impossible to discharge under our criminal standards of proof. . . .

Apart from the initial formulation in the *Roth* case, no majority of the Court has at any given time been able to agree on a standard to determine what constitutes obscene, pornographic material subject to regulation under the States' police power. . . . [3] . . .

The case we now review was tried on the theory that the California Penal Code § 311 approximately incorporates the three-stage *Memoirs* test, supra. But now the *Memoirs* test has been abandoned as unworkable by its author, and no Member of the Court today supports the *Memoirs* formulation.

II

. . . [W]e now confine the permissible scope of [obscenity] regulation to works which depict or describe sexual conduct. That conduct must be specifically defined by the applicable state law, as written or authoritatively construed. A state offense must also be limited to works which, taken as a whole, appeal to the prurient interest in sex, which portray sexual conduct in a patently offensive way, and which, taken as a whole, do not have serious literary, artistic, political, or scientific value.

The basic guidelines for the trier of fact must be: (a) whether "the average person, applying contemporary community standards" would find that the work, taken as a whole, appeals to the prurient interest; (b) whether the work depicts or describes, in a patently offensive way, sexual conduct specifically defined by the applicable state law; and (c) whether the work, taken as a whole, lacks serious literary, artistic, political, or scientific value. We do not adopt as a constitutional standard the "utterly without redeeming social value" test of *Memoirs v. Massachusetts;* that concept has never commanded the adherence of more than three Justices at one time. If a state law that regulates obscene material is thus limited, as written or construed, the First Amendment values applicable to the States through the Fourteenth Amendment are adequately protected by the ultimate power of appellate courts to conduct an independent review of constitutional claims when necessary. . . .

. . . [A] few plain examples of what a state statute could define for regulation under part (b) of the standard announced in this opinion [are]:

(a) Patently offensive representations or descriptions of ultimate sexual acts, normal or perverted, actual or simulated.

(b) Patently offensive representations or descriptions of masturbation, excretory functions, and lewd exhibition of the genitals.

---

[3] In the absence of a majority view, this Court was compelled to embark on the practice of summarily reversing convictions for the dissemination of materials that at least five members of the Court, applying their separate tests, found to be protected by the First Amendment. Redrup v. New York, 386 U.S. 767 (1967). Thirty-one cases have been decided in this manner. . . . The *Redrup* procedure has cast us in the role of an unreviewable board of censorship for the 50 States, subjectively judging each piece of material brought before us.

. . . At a minimum, prurient, patently offensive depiction or description of sexual conduct must have serious literary, artistic, political, or scientific value to merit First Amendment protection. . . . For example, medical books . . . necessarily use graphic illustrations and descriptions of human anatomy. In resolving the inevitably sensitive questions of fact and law, we must continue to rely on the jury system . . .

. . .

Under the holdings announced today, no one will be subject to prosecution for the sale or exposure of obscene materials unless these materials depict or describe patently offensive "hard core" sexual conduct specifically defined by the regulating state law, as written or construed. We are satisfied that these specific prerequisites will provide fair notice . . .

III

Under a National Constitution, fundamental First Amendment limitations on the powers of the States do not vary from community to community, but this does not mean that there are, or should or can be, fixed, uniform national standards of precisely what appeals to the "prurient interest" or is "patently offensive." These are essentially questions of fact . . . When triers of fact are asked to decide whether "the average person, applying contemporary community standards" would consider certain materials "prurient," it would be unrealistic to require that the answer be based on some abstract formulation. . . . To require a State to structure obscenity proceedings around evidence of a national "community standard" would be an exercise in futility.

We conclude that neither the State's alleged failure to offer evidence of "national standards," nor the trial court's charge that the jury consider state community standards, were constitutional errors. . . .

. . . [T]he primary concern with requiring a jury to apply the standard of "the average person, applying contemporary community standards" is to be certain that, so far as material is not aimed at a deviant group, it will be judged by its impact on an average person, rather than a particularly susceptible or sensitive person—or indeed a totally insensitive one. . . . [T]he requirement that the jury evaluate the materials with reference to "contemporary standards of the State of California" serves this protective purpose and is constitutionally adequate.

. . .

■ Mr. Justice Douglas, dissenting.

. . .

My contention is that until a civil proceeding has placed a tract beyond the pale, no criminal prosecution should be sustained. . . .

. . .

If a specific book, play, paper, or motion picture has in a civil proceeding been condemned as obscene and review of that finding has been completed, and thereafter a person publishes, shows, or displays that particular book or film, then a vague law has been made specific. There would remain the underlying question whether the First Amendment allows an implied exception in the case of obscenity. I do not think it does . . . But at least a criminal prosecution brought at that juncture would not violate the time-honored void-for-vagueness test.

. . .

■ MR. JUSTICE BRENNAN, with whom MR. JUSTICE STEWART and MR. JUSTICE MARSHALL join, dissenting.

. . . [I]t is clear that under my dissent in *Paris Adult Theatre I,* the statute under which the prosecution was brought is unconstitutionally overbroad, and therefore invalid on its face. . . .

Jenkins v. Georgia

418 U.S. 153, 94 S.Ct. 2750, 41 L.Ed.2d 642 (1974).

■ MR. JUSTICE REHNQUIST delivered the opinion of the Court.

Appellant was convicted in Georgia of the crime of distributing obscene material. His conviction, in March 1972, was for showing the film "Carnal Knowledge" in a movie theater in Albany, Georgia. . . .

. . . We conclude here that the film "Carnal Knowledge" is not obscene under the constitutional standards announced in Miller v. California, 413 U.S. 15 (1973), and that the First and Fourteenth Amendments therefore require that the judgment of the Supreme Court of Georgia affirming appellant's conviction be reversed.

. . .

Miller states that the questions of what appeals to the "prurient interest" and what is "patently offensive" under the obscenity test which it formulates are "essentially questions of fact." . . .

But all of this does not lead us to agree with the Supreme Court of Georgia's apparent conclusion that the jury's verdict against appellant virtually precluded all further appellate review of appellant's assertion that his exhibition of the film was protected by the First and Fourteenth Amendments. Even though questions of appeal to the "prurient interest" or of patent offensiveness are "essentially questions of fact," it would be a serious misreading of *Miller* to conclude that juries have unbridled discretion in determining what is "patently offensive." . . . [W]e made it plain that under that holding "no one will be subject to prosecution for the sale or exposure of obscene materials unless these materials depict or describe patently offensive 'hard core' sexual conduct. . . ." . . .

We also took pains in *Miller* to "give a few plain examples of what a state statute could define for regulation under part (b) of the standard announced," that is, the requirement of patent offensiveness. . . . These examples include "representations or descriptions of ultimate sexual acts, normal or perverted, actual or simulated," and "representations or descriptions of masturbation, excretory functions, and lewd exhibition of the genitals." Ibid. While this did not purport to be an exhaustive catalog of what juries might find patently offensive, it was certainly intended to fix substantive constitutional limitations, deriving from the First Amendment, on the type of material subject to such a determination. It would be wholly at odds with this aspect of *Miller* to uphold an obscenity conviction based upon a defendant's depiction of a woman with a bare midriff, even though a properly charged jury unanimously agreed on a verdict of guilty.

Our own viewing of the film satisfies us that "Carnal Knowledge" could not be found under the *Miller* standards to depict sexual conduct in a patently offensive way. Nothing in the movie falls within either of the two examples given in *Miller* of material which may constitutionally be found to meet the "patently offensive" element of those standards, nor is there anything sufficiently similar to such material to justify similar treatment. While the subject matter of the picture is, in a broader sense, sex, and there are scenes in which sexual conduct including "ultimate sexual acts" is to be understood to be taking place, the camera does not focus on the bodies of the actors at such times. There is no exhibition whatever of the actors' genitals, lewd or otherwise, during these scenes. There are occasional scenes of nudity, but nudity alone is not enough to make material legally obscene under the *Miller* standards.

Appellant's showing of the film "Carnal Knowledge" is simply not the "public portrayal of hard core sexual conduct for its own sake, and for the ensuing commercial gain" which we said was punishable in *Miller* . . . We hold that the film could not, as a matter of constitutional law, be found to depict sexual conduct in a patently offensive way, and that it is therefore not outside the protection of the First and Fourteenth Amendments because it is obscene. . . .

■ MR. JUSTICE BRENNAN, with whom MR. JUSTICE STEWART and MR. JUSTICE MARSHALL join, concurring in the result.

. . . Today's decision confirms my observation in Paris Adult Theatre I v. Slaton . . . that the Court's new formulation does not extricate us from the mire of case-by-case determinations of obscenity. . . .

After the Court's decision today, there can be no doubt that *Miller* requires appellate courts—including this Court—to review independently the constitutional fact of obscenity. . . .

In order to make the review mandated by *Miller,* the Court was required to screen the film "Carnal Knowledge" and make an independent determination of obscenity *vel non.* . . .

. . .

■ MR. JUSTICE DOUGLAS, being of the view that any ban on obscenity is prohibited by the First Amendment, . . . concurs in the reversal of this conviction. . . .

Ashcroft v. The Free Speech Coalition

535 U.S. 234, 122 S.Ct. 1389, 152 L.Ed.2d 403 (2002).

■ JUSTICE KENNEDY delivered the opinion of the Court.

We consider in this case whether the Child Pornography Prevention Act of 1996 (CPPA), 18 U.S.C. § 2251 et seq., abridges the freedom of speech. The CPPA extends the federal prohibition against child pornography to sexually explicit images that appear to depict minors but were produced without using any real children. The statute prohibits, in specific circumstances, possessing or distributing these images, which may be created by using adults who look like minors or by using computer imaging. The new technology, according to Congress, makes it possible to create realistic images of children who do not exist. . . .

By prohibiting child pornography that does not depict an actual child, the statute goes beyond New York v. Ferber, 458 U.S. 747 (1982), which distinguished child pornography from other sexually explicit speech because of the State's interest in protecting the children exploited by the production process. . . . As a general rule, pornography can be banned only if obscene, but under *Ferber*, pornography showing minors can be proscribed whether or not the images are obscene under the definition set forth in Miller v. California. . . .

While we have not had occasion to consider the question, we may assume that the apparent age of persons engaged in sexual conduct is relevant to whether a depiction offends community standards. Pictures of young children engaged in certain acts might be obscene where similar depictions of adults, or perhaps even older adolescents, would not. The CPPA, however, is not directed at speech that is obscene

. . . Like the law in *Ferber*, the CPPA seeks to reach beyond obscenity, and it makes no attempt to conform to the *Miller* standard. For instance, the statute would reach visual depictions, such as movies, even if they have redeeming social value.

The principal question to be resolved, then, is whether the CPPA is constitutional where it proscribes a significant universe of speech that is neither obscene under *Miller* nor child pornography under *Ferber*.

I

Before 1996, Congress defined child pornography as the type of depictions at issue in *Ferber*, images made using actual minors. . . . The CPPA retains that prohibition at 18 U.S.C. § 2256(8)(A) and adds three other prohibited categories of speech, of which the first, § 2256(8)(B), and the third, § 2256(8)(D), are at issue in this case. Section 2256(8)(B) prohibits "any visual depiction, including any photograph, film, video, picture, or computer or computer-generated image or picture" that "is, or appears to be, of a minor engaging in sexually explicit conduct." The prohibition on "any visual depiction" does not depend at all on how the image is produced. The section captures a range of depictions, sometimes called "virtual child pornography," which include computer-generated images, as well as images produced by more traditional means. For instance, the literal terms of the statute embrace a Renaissance painting depicting a scene from classical mythology, a "picture" that "appears to be, of a minor engaging in sexually explicit conduct." The statute also prohibits Hollywood movies, filmed without any child actors, if a jury believes an actor "appears to be" a minor engaging in "actual or simulated . . . sexual intercourse." § 2256(2).

These images do not involve, let alone harm, any children in the production process; but Congress decided the materials threaten children in other, less direct, ways. Pedophiles might use the materials to encourage children to participate in sexual activity. . . . Furthermore, pedophiles might "whet their own sexual appetites" with the pornographic images, "thereby increasing the creation and distribution of child pornography and the sexual abuse and exploitation of actual children." . . . Under these rationales, harm flows from the content of the images, not from the means of their production. In addition, Congress identified another problem created by computer-generated images: Their existence can make it harder to prosecute pornographers who do use real minors. . . . As imaging technology improves, Congress found, it becomes more difficult to prove that a particular picture was produced using actual children. . . .

Section 2256(8)(C) prohibits a more common and lower tech means of creating virtual images, known as computer morphing. Rather than creating original images, pornographers can alter innocent pictures of real children so that the children appear to be engaged in sexual activity. Although morphed images may fall within the definition of virtual child pornography, they implicate the interests of real children and are in that sense closer to the images in *Ferber*. Respondents do not challenge this provision, and we do not consider it.

Respondents do challenge § 2256(8)(D). Like the text of the "appears to be" provision, the sweep of this provision is quite broad. Section 2256(8)(D) defines child pornography to include any sexually explicit image that was "advertised, promoted, presented, described, or distributed in such a manner that conveys the impression" it depicts "a minor engaging in sexually explicit conduct." One Committee Report identified the provision as directed at sexually explicit images pandered as child pornography. . . . The statute is not so limited in its reach, however, as it punishes even those possessors who took no part in pandering. Once a work has been described as child pornography, the taint remains on the speech in the hands of subsequent possessors, making possession unlawful even though the content otherwise would not be objectionable.

Fearing that the CPPA threatened the activities of its members, respondent Free Speech Coalition and others challenged the statute in . . . the Northern District of California. The Coalition, a California trade association for the adult-entertainment industry, alleged that its members did not use minors in their sexually explicit works, but they believed some of these materials might fall within the CPPA's expanded definition of child pornography. The other respondents are . . . the publisher of a book advocating the nudist lifestyle; . . . a painter of nudes; and . . . a photographer specializing in erotic images. Respondents alleged that the "appears to be" and "conveys the impression" provisions are overbroad and vague, chilling them from producing works protected by the First Amendment. The District Court disagreed and granted summary judgment to the Government. . . .

The Court of Appeals for the Ninth Circuit reversed. . . .

. . .

II

. . . The CPPA's penalties are . . . severe. A first offender may be imprisoned for 15 years. . . . A repeat offender faces . . . not less than 5 years and not more than 30 years . . . . With these severe penalties in force, few legitimate movie producers or book publishers, or few other speakers in any capacity, would risk distributing images in or near the uncertain reach of this law. The Constitution gives significant protection from overbroad laws that chill speech within the First Amendment's vast and privileged sphere. Under this principle, the CPPA is unconstitutional on its face if it prohibits a substantial amount of protected expression. . . .

. . .

. . . [S]peech may not be prohibited because it concerns subjects offending our sensibilities. . . .

. . . The freedom of speech . . . does not embrace . . . defamation, incitement, obscenity, and pornography produced with real children. . . . While these categories may be prohibited without violating the First Amendment, none of them includes the speech prohibited by the CPPA. . . .

. . . The CPPA applies to a picture in a psychology manual, as well as a movie depicting the horrors of sexual abuse. . . .

. . . The statute proscribes the visual depiction of an idea—that of teenagers engaging in sexual activity—that is a fact of modern society and has been a theme in art and literature throughout the ages. Under the CPPA, images are prohibited so long as the persons appear to be under 18 years of age. This is higher than the legal age for marriage in many States, as well as the age at which persons may consent to sexual relations. . . .

. . . Both themes—teenage sexual activity and the sexual abuse of children—have inspired countless literary works. William Shakespeare created the most famous pair of teenage lovers, one of whom is just 13 years of age. . . .

Contemporary movies pursue similar themes. . . .

. . . Whether or not [they] violate the CPPA, they explore themes within the wide sweep of the statute's prohibitions. If these films . . . contain a single graphic depiction of sexual activity within the statutory definition, the possessor of the film would be subject to severe punishment without inquiry into the work's redeeming value. This is inconsistent with an essential First Amendment rule: The artistic merit of a work does not depend on the presence of a single explicit scene. . . .

The Government . . . argu[es] that speech prohibited by the CPPA is virtually indistinguishable from child pornography, which may be banned without regard to whether it depicts works of value. . . . *Ferber* recognized that the State had an interest in stamping it out without regard to any judgment about its content. . . . The production of the work, not its content, was the target of the statute. The fact that a work contained serious literary, artistic, or other value did not excuse the harm it caused to its child participants. . . .

. . . First, as a permanent record of a child's abuse, the continued circulation itself would harm the child who had participated. Like a defamatory statement, each new publication of the speech would cause new injury to the child's reputation and emotional well-being. . . . Second, because the traffic in child pornography was an economic motive for its production, the State had an interest in closing the distribution network. . . . Under either rationale, the speech had what the Court in effect held was a proximate link to the crime from which it came.

Later, in Osborne v. Ohio, 495 U.S. 103 (1990), the Court ruled that these same interests justified a ban on the possession of pornography produced by using children. . . . It did not suggest that, absent this concern, other governmental interests would suffice.

. . . [T]he CPPA prohibits speech that records no crime and creates no victims by its production. Virtual child pornography is not "intrinsically related" to the sexual abuse of children, as were the materials in *Ferber*. . . . While the Government asserts that the images can lead to actual instances of child abuse, . . . the causal link is contingent and indirect. The harm does not necessarily follow from the speech, but depends upon some unquantified potential for subsequent criminal acts.

The Government says these indirect harms are sufficient because, as *Ferber* acknowledged, child pornography rarely can be valuable speech. . . . This argument, however, suffers from two flaws. First, *Ferber*'s judgment about child pornography was based upon how it was made, not on what it communicated. . . .

[S]econd[,] . . . *Ferber* did not hold that child pornography is by definition without value. On the contrary, the Court recognized some works in this category might have significant value, . . . but relied on virtual images—the very images prohibited by the CPPA—as an alternative and permissible means of expression. . . . *Ferber*, then, not only referred to the distinction between actual and virtual child pornography, it relied on it as a reason supporting its holding. *Ferber* provides no support for a statute that eliminates the distinction and makes the alternative mode criminal as well.

III

. . . The Government . . . argues that the CPPA is necessary because pedophiles may use virtual child pornography to seduce children. . . . The Government, of course, may punish adults who provide unsuitable materials to children, see Ginsberg v. New York, 390 U.S. 629 (1968), and it may enforce criminal penalties for unlawful solicitation. The precedents establish, however, that speech within the rights of adults to hear may not be silenced completely in an attempt to shield children from it. . . .

. . . The evil in question depends upon the actor's unlawful conduct, conduct defined as criminal quite apart from any link to the speech in question. This establishes that the speech ban is not narrowly drawn. The objective is to prohibit illegal conduct, but this restriction goes well beyond that interest by restricting the speech available to law-abiding adults.

The Government submits further that virtual child pornography whets the appetites of pedophiles and encourages them to engage in illegal conduct. . . . The mere tendency of speech to encourage unlawful acts is not a sufficient reason for banning it. . . .

. . . There is here no attempt, incitement, solicitation, or conspiracy. The Government has shown no more than a remote connection between speech that might encourage thoughts or impulses and any resulting child abuse. Without a significantly stronger, more direct connection, the Government may not prohibit speech on the ground that it may encourage pedophiles to engage in illegal conduct.

The Government next argues that its objective of eliminating the market for pornography produced using real children necessitates a prohibition on virtual images as well. Virtual images, the Government contends, are indistinguishable from real ones; they are part of the same market and are often exchanged. In this way, it is said, virtual images promote the trafficking in works produced through the exploitation of real children. The hypothesis is somewhat implausible. If virtual images were identical to illegal child pornography, the illegal images would be driven from the market by the indistinguishable substitutes. Few pornographers would risk prosecution by abusing real children if fictional, computerized images would suffice.

In the case of the material covered by *Ferber*, the creation of the speech is itself the crime of child abuse; the prohibition deters the crime by removing the profit motive. . . . [H]ere, there is no underlying crime at all. Even if the Government's market deterrence theory were persuasive in some contexts, it would not justify this statute.

Finally, the Government says that the possibility of producing images by using computer imaging makes it very difficult for it to prosecute those who produce pornography by using real children. Experts, we are told, may have difficulty in saying whether the pictures were made by using real children or by using computer imaging. The necessary solution, the argument runs, is to prohibit both kinds of images. The argument, in essence, is that protected speech may be banned as a means to ban unprotected speech. This analysis turns the First Amendment upside down.

The Government may not suppress lawful speech as the means to suppress unlawful speech. Protected speech does not become unprotected merely because it resembles the latter. The Constitution requires the reverse. . . . The overbreadth doctrine prohibits the Government from banning unprotected speech if a substantial amount of protected speech is prohibited or chilled in the process.

. . . [T]he Government would have us read the CPPA . . . as [just] a law shifting the burden to the accused to prove the speech is lawful. . . .

The Government raises serious constitutional difficulties by seeking to impose on the defendant the burden of proving his speech is not unlawful. . . . If the evidentiary issue is a serious problem for the Government, as it asserts, it will be at least as difficult for the innocent possessor. . . .

We need not decide, however, whether the Government could impose this burden on a speaker. . . . [H]ere the defense is incomplete and insufficient, even on its own terms. . . . [It] provides no protection to persons who produce speech by using computer imaging, or through other means that do not involve the use of adult actors who appear to be minors. . . . In these cases, the defendant can demonstrate no children were harmed in producing the images, yet the affirmative defense would not bar the prosecution. For this reason, the affirmative defense cannot save the statute, for it leaves unprotected a substantial amount of speech not tied to the Government's interest in distinguishing images produced using real children from virtual ones.

. . .

IV

Respondents challenge § 2256(8)(D) as well. This provision bans depictions of sexually explicit conduct that are "advertised, promoted, presented, described, or distributed in such a manner that conveys the impression that the material is or contains a visual depiction of a minor engaging in sexually explicit conduct." . . .

. . . The CPPA prohibits sexually explicit materials that "conve[y] the impression" they depict minors. While that phrase may sound like the "appears to be" prohibition in § 2256(8)(B), it requires little judgment about the content of the image. Under § 2256(8)(D), the work must be sexually explicit, but otherwise the content is irrelevant. Even if a film contains no sexually explicit scenes involving minors, it could be treated as child pornography if the title and trailers convey the impression that the scenes would be found in the movie. The determination turns on how the speech is presented, not on what is depicted. . . .

The Government does not offer a serious defense of this provision. . . . The materials, for instance, are not likely to be confused for child pornography in a criminal trial. The Court has recognized that pandering may be relevant, as an evidentiary matter, to the question whether particular materials are obscene. See Ginzburg v. United States, 383 U.S. 463, 474 (1966). . . .

. . . Section 2256(8)(D), however, prohibits a substantial amount of speech that falls outside Ginzburg's rationale. Materials falling within the proscription are tainted and unlawful in the hands of all who receive it, though they bear no responsibility for how it was marketed, sold, or described. The statute, furthermore, does not require that the context be part of an effort at "commercial exploitation." . . . § 2256(8)(D) is substantially overbroad. . . .

V

. . . [T]he prohibitions of §§ 2256(8)(B) and 2256(8)(D) are overbroad and unconstitutional. . . .

The judgment of the Court of Appeals is affirmed.

. . .

■ JUSTICE THOMAS, concurring in the judgment.

In my view, the Government's most persuasive [argument] is the prosecution rationale—that persons who possess and disseminate pornographic images of real children may escape conviction by claiming that the images are computer-generated, thereby raising a reasonable doubt as to their guilt. At this time, however, . . . the Government points to no case in which a defendant has been acquitted based on a "computer-generated images" defense. While this speculative interest cannot support the broad reach of the CPPA, technology may evolve to the point where it becomes impossible to enforce actual child pornography laws because the Government cannot prove that certain pornographic images are of real children. In the event this occurs, the Government should not be foreclosed from enacting a regulation of virtual child pornography that contains an appropriate affirmative defense or some other narrowly drawn restriction.

. . . [I]f technological advances thwart prosecution of "unlawful speech," the Government may well have a compelling interest in barring or otherwise regulating some narrow category of "lawful speech" in order to enforce effectively laws against pornography made through the abuse of real children. . . .

■ JUSTICE O'CONNOR, with whom THE CHIEF JUSTICE and JUSTICE SCALIA join as to Part II, concurring in the judgment in part and dissenting in part.

. . .

... I would strike down the prohibition of pornography that "appears to be" of minors only insofar as it is applied to the class of youthful-adult pornography.

I

... The Government ... requests that the Court exclude youthful-adult and virtual-child pornography from the protection of the First Amendment.

I agree with the Court's decision not to grant this request. ... The Court correctly concludes that the causal connection between pornographic images that "appear" to include minors and actual child abuse is not strong enough to justify withdrawing First Amendment protection for such speech.

I also agree with the Court's decision to strike down the CPPA's ban on material presented in a manner that "conveys the impression" that it contains pornographic depictions of actual children .... The Court concludes that § 2256(8)(D) is overbroad, but its reasoning also persuades me that the provision is not narrowly tailored. The provision therefore fails strict scrutiny. ...

Finally, I agree with the Court that the CPPA's ban on youthful-adult pornography is overbroad. ...

II

I disagree with the Court, however, that the CPPA's prohibition of virtual-child pornography is overbroad. ...

... [G]iven the rapid pace of advances in computer-graphics technology, the Government's concern is reasonable. ...

. . .

Reading the statute only to bar images that are virtually indistinguishable from actual children would not only assure that the ban on virtual-child pornography is narrowly tailored, but would also assuage any fears that the "appears to be ... of a minor" language is vague. ...

... Respondents provide no examples of films or other materials that are wholly computer-generated and contain images that "appea[r] to be ... of minors" engaging in indecent conduct, but that have serious value or do not facilitate child abuse. Their overbreadth challenge therefore fails.

III

. . .

... I would strike the "appears to be" provision only insofar as it is applied to the subset of cases involving youthful-adult pornography. ...

... Drawing a line around, and striking just, the CPPA's ban on youthful-child pornography ... preserves the CPPA's prohibition of the material that Congress found most dangerous to children.

. . .

■ CHIEF JUSTICE REHNQUIST, with whom JUSTICE SCALIA joins in part, dissenting.

I agree with Part II of Justice O'Connor's opinion. ... Congress has a compelling interest in ensuring the ability to enforce prohibitions of actual child pornography, and we should defer to its findings that rapidly advancing technology soon will make it all but impossible to do so. ...

I also agree with Justice O'Connor that serious First Amendment concerns would arise were the Government ever to prosecute someone for simple distribution or possession of a film with literary or artistic value .... I write separately, however, because the ... CPPA ... need not be construed to reach such materials.

. . .

Other than computer generated images that are virtually indistinguishable from real children engaged in sexually explicit conduct, the CPPA can be limited so as not to reach any material that was not already unprotected before the CPPA. . . .

Indeed, we should be loath to construe a statute as banning film portrayals of Shakespearian tragedies, without some indication—from text or legislative history—that such a result was intended. . . .

. . .

United States v. Williams

553 U.S. 285 (2008).

The Court rejected facial overbreadth and vagueness challenges to the PROTECT Act of 2003, 18 U.S.C. § 2252A(a)(3)(B), which Congress enacted in the wake of the Free Speech Coalition decision. Justice Scalia's majority opinion noted that the Act's criminal prohibition of "offers to provide and requests to obtain child pornography" (whether or not part of an intended commercial transaction) does not

"require the actual existence of child pornography. In this respect, it differs from the statutes in *Ferber*, *Osborne*, and *Free Speech Coalition*, which prohibited the possession or distribution of child pornography. Rather than targeting the underlying material, this statute bans the collateral speech that introduces such material into the child-pornography distribution network. Thus, an Internet user who solicits child pornography from an undercover agent violates the statute, even if the officer possesses no child pornography. Likewise, a person who advertises virtual child pornography as depicting actual children also falls within the reach of the statute."

Nonetheless, the Court held "that offers to provide or requests to obtain child pornography are categorically excluded from the First Amendment."

The opinion earlier had noted the following:

"The Act's express findings indicate that Congress was concerned that limiting the child-pornography prohibition to material that could be proved to feature actual children, as our decision in *Free Speech Coalition* required, would enable many child pornographers to evade conviction. . . . The emergence of new technology and the repeated retransmission of picture files over the Internet could make it nearly impossible to prove that a particular image was produced using real children—even though '[t]here is no substantial evidence that any of the child pornography images being trafficked today were made other than by the abuse of real children,' virtual imaging being prohibitively expensive."

The Court construed the statute (1) to contain a scienter requirement of "knowingly" pandering or soliciting child pornography; (2) using "speech that accompanies or seeks to induce a transfer of child pornography . . . from one person to another[;]" (3) where "the defendant must actually have held the subjective 'belief' that the material or purported material was child pornography" and the "statement or action must objectively manifest a belief that the material is child pornography" ("a mere belief, without an accompanying statement or action that would lead a reasonable person to understand that the defendant holds that belief, is insufficient"); (4) to require that the "defendant must 'intend' that the listener believe the material to be child pornography, and must select a manner of 'advertising, promoting, presenting, distributing, or soliciting' the material that he thinks will engender that belief—whether or not a reasonable person would think the same[;]" and (5) to confine "the definition of 'sexually explicit conduct' " to portrayals that "must cause a reasonable viewer to believe that the actors actually engaged in that conduct on camera. Critically, unlike in *Free Speech Coalition*, § 2252A(a)(3)(B)(ii)'s requirement of a 'visual depiction of an actual minor' makes clear that, although the sexual intercourse may be simulated, it must involve actual children (unless it is obscene). This change eliminates any possibility that virtual child pornography or sex between youthful-looking adult actors might be covered by the term 'simulated sexual intercourse.' "

So understood, the Court invoked "the principle that offers to give or receive what it is unlawful to possess have no social value and thus, like obscenity, enjoy no First Amendment protection." Nor did the Court think it "would be unconstitutional to punish someone for mistakenly distributing virtual child pornography as real child pornography. . . . Offers to deal in illegal products or otherwise engage in illegal activity do not acquire First Amendment protection when the offeror is mistaken about the factual predicate of his offer. The pandering and solicitation made unlawful by the Act are sorts of inchoate crimes—acts looking toward the commission of another crime, the delivery of child pornography. As with other inchoate crimes—attempt and conspiracy, for example—impossibility of completing the crime because the facts were not as the defendant believed is not a defense." As for the contention "that some advertisements for mainstream Hollywood movies that depict underage characters having sex violate the statute[,] . . . [t]he average person understands that sex scenes in mainstream movies use nonchild actors, depict sexual activity in a way that would not rise to the explicit level necessary under the statute, or, in most cases, both." Furthermore, the Court responded as follows to the suggestion "that the statute might cover documentary footage of atrocities being committed in foreign countries, such as soldiers raping young children":

"Perhaps so, if the material rises to the high level of explicitness that we have held is required. That sort of documentary footage could of course be the subject of an as-applied challenge. The courts presumably would weigh the educational interest in the dissemination of information about the atrocities against the government's interest in preventing the distribution of materials that constitute 'a permanent record' of the children's degradation whose dissemination increases 'the harm to the child.' *Ferber.* . . . Assuming that the constitutional balance would have to be struck in favor of the documentary, the existence of that exception would not establish that the statute is *substantially* overbroad. . . . In the vast majority of its applications, this statute raises no constitutional problems whatever.

"Finally, the dissent accuses us of silently overruling our prior decisions in *Ferber* and *Free Speech Coalition.* . . . According to the dissent, Congress has made an end-run around the First Amendment's protection of virtual child pornography by prohibiting proposals to transact in such images rather than prohibiting the images themselves. But an offer to provide or request to receive virtual child pornography is not prohibited by the statute. A crime is committed only when the speaker believes or intends the listener to believe that the subject of the proposed transaction depicts real children. . . . Simulated child pornography will be as available as ever, so long as it is offered and sought as such, and not as real child pornography. . . . Is Congress forbidden from punishing those who attempt to acquire what they believe to be national-security documents, but which are actually fakes? . . . There is no First Amendment exception from the general principle of criminal law that a person attempting to commit a crime need not be exonerated because he has a mistaken view of the facts."

In a concurring opinion, Justice Stevens, joined by Justice Breyer, emphasized "two interrelated considerations on which Justice Scalia finds it unnecessary to rely":

"First, I believe the result to be compelled by the principle that 'every reasonable construction must be resorted to, in order to save a statute from unconstitutionality,'. . . .

"Second, . . . [i]t is abundantly clear from the provision's legislative history that Congress' aim was to target materials advertised, promoted, presented, distributed, or solicited with a lascivious purpose—that is, with the intention of inciting sexual arousal. . . .

" . . .

". . . [I]n addition to the other limitations the Court properly concludes constrain the reach of the statute, the heightened scienter requirements . . . contain an element of lasciviousness.

"The dissent argues that the statute impermissibly undermines our First Amendment precedents insofar as it covers proposals to transact in constitutionally protected material. It is true that proof that a pornographic but not obscene representation did not depict real children would place that representation on the protected side of the line. But any constitutional concerns that might arise on that score are surely answered by the construction the Court gives the statute's operative provisions; that is, proposing a transaction in such material would not give rise to criminal liability under the statute unless the defendant actually believed, or intended to induce another to believe, that the material in question depicted real children.

"Accordingly, when material which is protected—particularly if it possesses serious literary, artistic, political, or scientific value—is advertised, promoted, presented, distributed, or solicited for some lawful and nonlascivious purpose, such conduct is not captured by the statutory prohibition. . . ."

The dissenting opinion of Justice Souter, joined by Justice Ginsburg, argued "that maintaining the First Amendment protection of expression we have previously held to cover fake child pornography requires a limit to the law's criminalization of pandering proposals." Although they agreed that proposals for transfers of pornography depicting actual children could be banned whether such depictions already existed or such depictions did not yet exist but were the subject of the proposal, they found no justification for banning the "common cases" of proposals for extant images containing fake child pornography or "when the inclusion of actual children is not established by the prosecution[.]" They found it "not enough just to say that the First Amendment does not protect proposals to commit crimes. For that rule rests on the assumption that the proposal is actually to commit a crime, not to do an act that may turn out to be no crime at all."

Emphasizing that under the First Amendment virtual pornography "is affirmatively protected, not merely allowed as a matter of course[,]" Justice Souter distinguished not only the acceptable prosecution of attempted drug deals that mistakenly involved baking powder and attempted murders that mistakenly involved blanks in a pistol, but also the prosecution of "the mistaken spy, who passes national security documents thinking they are classified and secret, when in fact they have been declassified and made subject to public inspection." He found "significant differences between the cases of security documents and pornography without real children":

"Where Government documents, blank cartridges, and baking powder are involved, deterrence can be promoted without compromising any other important policy, which is not true of criminalizing mistaken child pornography proposals. There are three dispositive differences. [F]irst, if the law can criminalize proposals for transactions in fake as well as true child pornography as if they were like attempts to sell cocaine that turned out to be baking powder, constitutional law will lose . . . the line between child pornography that may be suppressed and fake child pornography that falls within First Amendment protection. No one can seriously assume that after today's decision the Government will go on prosecuting defendants for selling child pornography (requiring a showing that a real child is pictured . . .); it will prosecute for merely proposing a pornography transaction manifesting or inducing the belief that a photo is real child pornography, free of any need to demonstrate that any extant underlying photo does show a real child. . . . And eliminating the need to prove a real child will be a loss of some consequence[,] . . . simply because there must be a line between what the Government may suppress and what it may not, and a segment of that line will be gone. This Court went to great pains to draw it in *Ferber* and *Free Speech Coalition*; it was worth drawing and it is worth respecting now in facing the attempt to end-run that line through the provisions of the Act.

"[S]econd[, unlike] . . . the deluded drug dealer [and] the mistaken spy[—where there is no concern that convictions will suppress lawful powder transactions or lawful uses of unclassified documents—]if the Act can effectively eliminate the real-child requirement when a proposal relates to extant material, a class of protected speech will disappear. True, what will be lost is short on merit, but intrinsic value is not the reason for protecting unpopular expression.

"Finally, if the Act stands when applied to identifiable, extant pornographic photographs, then in practical terms *Ferber* and *Free Speech Coalition* fall. They are left as empty as if the Court overruled them formally. . . .

"These differences should be dispositive. . . . We should hold that a transaction in what turns out to be fake pornography is better understood, not as an incomplete attempt to commit a crime, but as a completed series of intended acts that simply do not add up to a crime, owing to the privileged character of the material. . . .

". . . When, as here, a protected category of expression would inevitably be suppressed and its First Amendment safeguard left pointless, the Government has the burden to justify this damage to free speech."

The dissent "suppose[d] the holding can only be explained as an uncritical acceptance of a [Government] claim made both to Congress and to this Court . . . that a jury's appreciation of the mere possibility of simulated or virtual child pornography will prevent convictions for the real thing, by inevitably raising reasonable doubt about whether actual children are shown." That "claim needs to be taken with a grain of salt." If "convinced[,] . . . I would be willing to reexamine *Ferber*. Conditions can change, and if today's technology left no other effective way to stop professional and amateur pornographers from exploiting children there would be a fair claim that some degree of expressive protection had to yield to protect the children." But "neither Congress nor this Court has been given the citation to a single case in which a defendant's acquittal is reasonably attributable to that defense" and "the overwhelming majority of [child pornographers] plead guilty rather than try their luck before a jury with a virtual-child defense." Hence, "without some demonstration that juries have been rendering exploitation of children unpunishable, there is no excuse for cutting back on the First Amendment and no alternative to finding overbreadth in this Act."

United States v. Stevens

559 U.S. 460 (2010).

A purveyor of videos of pit bulls engaging in dogfights and attacking other animals was indicted for violating a federal criminal statute banning the commercial creation, sale, or possession of certain "depictions of animal cruelty," 18 U.S.C. § 48. The Court, in an opinion by Chief Justice Roberts for eight Justices, sustained his facial challenge to the law and affirmed dismissal of the indictment—without deciding whether a law more narrowly prohibiting what he had purveyed would be constitutional—because, as the Court construed it, the statute was "substantially overbroad."[a] The Court's opinion first rejected, however, the "Government's primary submission . . . that § 48 necessarily complies with the Constitution because the banned depictions of animal cruelty, as a class, are categorically unprotected by the First Amendment." The opinion said in pertinent part:

"The Government . . . contends that depictions of 'illegal acts of animal cruelty' that are 'made, sold, or possessed for commercial gain' necessarily 'lack expressive value,' and may accordingly 'be regulated as *unprotected* speech.' . . . The claim is not just that Congress may regulate depictions of animal cruelty subject to the First Amendment, but that these depictions are outside the reach of that Amendment altogether. . . .

"As the Government notes, the prohibition of animal cruelty itself has a long history in American law, starting with the early settlement of the Colonies. . . . But we are unaware of any similar tradition excluding *depictions* of animal cruelty from 'the freedom of speech' codified in the First Amendment, and the Government points us to none.

"The Government contends that 'historical evidence' about the reach of the First Amendment is not 'a necessary prerequisite for regulation today,' . . . and that categories of speech may be exempted from the First Amendment's protection without any long-settled tradition of subjecting that speech to regulation. Instead, the Government points to Congress's "legislative judgment that . . . depictions of animals being intentionally tortured and killed [are] of such minimal redeeming value as to render [them] unworthy of First Amendment protection," . . . and asks the Court to uphold the ban on the same basis. The Government thus proposes that a claim of categorical exclusion should be considered under a simple balancing test: 'Whether a given category of speech enjoys First Amendment protection depends upon a categorical balancing of the value of the speech against its societal costs.' Brief for United States. . . .

"As a free-floating test for First Amendment coverage, that sentence is startling and dangerous. The First Amendment's guarantee of free speech does not extend only to categories of speech that survive an ad hoc balancing of relative social costs and benefits. The First Amendment itself reflects a judgment by the American people that the benefits of its restrictions on the Government outweigh the costs. Our Constitution forecloses any attempt to revise that judgment simply on the basis that some speech is not worth it. . . .

"To be fair to the Government, its view did not emerge from a vacuum. As the Government correctly notes, this Court has often *described* historically unprotected categories of speech as being "of such slight social value as a step to truth that any benefit that may be derived from them is clearly outweighed by the social interest in order and morality." . . . In *New York v. Ferber,* 458 U.S. 747 (1982), we noted that within these categories of unprotected speech, 'the evil to be restricted so overwhelmingly outweighs the expressive interests, if any, at stake, that no process of case-by-case adjudication is required,' because 'the balance of competing interests is clearly struck,' . . . .

---

[a]   A report of this portion of the opinion is set forth, supra, p. 935.

"But such descriptions are just that—descriptive. They do not set forth a test that may be applied as a general matter to permit the Government to imprison any speaker so long as his speech is deemed valueless or unnecessary, or so long as an ad hoc calculus of costs and benefits tilts in a statute's favor.

"When we have identified categories of speech as fully outside the protection of the First Amendment, it has not been on the basis of a simple cost-benefit analysis. In *Ferber,* for example, we . . . noted that . . . New York had a compelling interest in protecting children from abuse, and that the value of using children in these works (as opposed to simulated conduct or adult actors) was *de minimis.* . . . But our decision did not rest on this 'balance of competing interests' alone. . . . We made clear that *Ferber* presented a special case: The market for child pornography was 'intrinsically related' to the underlying abuse, and was therefore 'an integral part of the production of such materials, an activity illegal throughout the Nation.' . . . As we noted, "[i]t rarely has been suggested that the constitutional freedom for speech and press extends its immunity to speech or writing used as an integral part of conduct in violation of a valid criminal statute." . . . *Ferber* thus grounded its analysis in a previously recognized, long-established category of unprotected speech, and our subsequent decisions have shared this understanding. . . .

"Our decisions in *Ferber* and other cases cannot be taken as establishing a freewheeling authority to declare new categories of speech outside the scope of the First Amendment. Maybe there are some categories of speech that have been historically unprotected, but have not yet been specifically identified or discussed as such in our case law. But if so, there is no evidence that 'depictions of animal cruelty' is among them. We need not foreclose the future recognition of such additional categories to reject the Government's highly manipulable balancing test as a means of identifying them."

Justice Alito's dissent rejected the overbreadth challenge and relied on *Ferber* to conclude that the First Amendment does not protect either crush videos (which predominantly involve women slowly crushing animals to death with bare feet or high heeled shoes to arouse viewers with a particular sexual fetish) or "depictions of brutal animal fights." His opinion said in part:

"It is undisputed that the *conduct* depicted in crush videos may constitutionally be prohibited. . . . But before the enactment of § 48, the underlying conduct depicted in crush videos was nearly impossible to prosecute. These videos . . . were made in secret, generally without a live audience, and 'the faces of the women inflicting the torture in the material often were not shown, nor could the location of the place where the cruelty was being inflicted or the date of the activity be ascertained from the depiction.'

". . . Crush videos present a highly unusual free speech issue because they are so closely linked with violent criminal conduct. The videos record the commission of violent criminal acts, and it appears that these crimes are committed for the sole purpose of creating the videos. In addition, as noted above, Congress was presented with compelling evidence that the only way of preventing these crimes was to target the sale of the videos. Under these circumstances, I cannot believe that the First Amendment commands Congress to step aside and allow the underlying crimes to continue.

". . . *Ferber* . . . held that child pornography is not protected speech, and . . . *Ferber*'s reasoning dictates a similar conclusion here.

"In *Ferber,* an important factor—I would say the most important factor—was that child pornography involves the commission of a crime that inflicts severe personal injury to the 'children who are made to engage in sexual conduct for commercial purposes.' . . . As later noted in *Ashcroft v. Free Speech Coalition,* . . . in *Ferber* '[t]he production of the work, not its content, was the target of the statute.' . . .

"Second, *Ferber* emphasized the fact that these underlying crimes could not be effectively combated without targeting the distribution of child pornography. . . .

"Third, the *Ferber* Court noted that the value of child pornography 'is exceedingly modest, if not *de minimis,'* and that any such value was 'overwhelmingly outweigh[ed]' by 'the evil to be restricted.' . . .

"All three of these characteristics are shared by § 48, as applied to crush videos. First, the conduct depicted in crush videos is criminal in every State and the District of Columbia. Thus, any crush video made in this country records the actual commission of a criminal act that inflicts severe physical injury and excruciating pain and ultimately results in death. Those who record the underlying criminal acts are likely to be criminally culpable, either as aiders and abettors or conspirators. And in the tight and secretive market for these videos, some who sell the videos or possess them with the intent to make a profit may be similarly culpable. . . . To the extent that § 48 reaches such persons, it surely does not violate the First Amendment.

"Second, the criminal acts shown in crush videos cannot be prevented without targeting the conduct prohibited by § 48—the creation, sale, and possession for sale of depictions of animal torture with the intention of realizing a commercial profit. The evidence presented to Congress posed a stark choice: Either ban the commercial exploitation of crush videos or tolerate a continuation of the criminal acts that they record. Faced with this evidence, Congress reasonably chose to target the lucrative crush video market.

"Finally, the harm caused by the underlying crimes vastly outweighs any minimal value that the depictions might conceivably be thought to possess. Section 48 reaches only the actual recording of acts of animal torture; the statute does not apply to verbal descriptions or to simulations. And, unlike the child pornography statute in *Ferber* or its federal counterpart, . . . § 48(b) provides an exception for depictions having any 'serious religious, political, scientific, educational, journalistic, historical, or artistic value.'

"It must be acknowledged that § 48 differs from a child pornography law in an important respect: preventing the abuse of children is certainly much more important than preventing the torture of the animals used in crush videos. . . . But while protecting children is unquestionably *more* important than protecting animals, the Government also has a compelling interest in preventing the torture depicted in crush videos.

. . .

"Section 48's ban on trafficking in crush videos also helps to enforce the criminal laws and to ensure that criminals do not profit from their crimes. . . . We have already judged that taking the profit out of crime is a compelling interest. . . .

". . . Applying the principles set forth in *Ferber,* I would hold that crush videos are not protected by the First Amendment.

"Application of the *Ferber* framework also supports the constitutionality of § 48 as applied to depictions of brutal animal fights. (For convenience, I will focus on videos of dogfights, which appear to be the most common type of animal fight videos.)

"First, such depictions, like crush videos, record the actual commission of a crime involving deadly violence. Dogfights are illegal in every State and the District of Columbia, . . . and under federal law constitute a felony punishable by imprisonment for up to five years. . . .

"Second, Congress had an ample basis for concluding that the crimes depicted in these videos cannot be effectively controlled without targeting the videos. Like crush videos and child pornography, dogfight videos are very often produced as part of a 'low-profile, clandestine industry,' and 'the need to market the resulting products requires a visible apparatus of distribution.' *Ferber*. . . .

. . .

"Third, depictions of dogfights that fall within § 48's reach have by definition no appreciable social value. As noted, § 48(b) exempts depictions having any appreciable social value, and thus the mere inclusion of a depiction of a live fight in a larger work that aims at communicating an idea or a message with a modicum of social value would not run afoul of the statute.

"Finally, the harm caused by the underlying criminal acts greatly outweighs any trifling value that the depictions might be thought to possess. . . .

"For these dogs, unlike the animals killed in crush videos, the suffering lasts for years rather than minutes. As with crush videos, moreover, the statutory ban on commerce in dogfighting videos is also supported by compelling governmental interests in effectively enforcing the Nation's criminal laws and preventing criminals from profiting from their illegal activities. . . .

"In sum, § 48 may validly be applied to . . . crush videos and dogfighting videos."

Brown v. Entertainment Merchants Association

564 U.S. 786, 131 S.Ct. 2729, 180 L.Ed.2d 708 (2011).

■ JUSTICE SCALIA delivered the opinion of the Court.

We consider whether a California law imposing restrictions on violent video games comports with the First Amendment.

I

California Assembly Bill 1179 (2005), Cal. Civ. Code Ann. §§ 1746–1746.5 (West 2009) (Act), prohibits the sale or rental of "violent video games" to minors, and requires their packaging to be labeled "18." The Act covers games "in which the range of options available to a player includes killing, maiming, dismembering, or sexually assaulting an image of a human being, if those acts are depicted" in a manner that "[a] reasonable person, considering the game as a whole, would find appeals to a deviant or morbid interest of minors," that is "patently offensive to prevailing standards in the community as to what is suitable for minors," and that "causes the game, as a whole, to lack serious literary, artistic, political, or scientific value for minors." § 1746(d)(1)(A). Violation of the Act is punishable by a civil fine of up to $1,000. § 1746.3.

Respondents, representing the video-game and software industries, [secured a permanent injunction in the lower courts against enforcement of the Act.]

II

California correctly acknowledges that video games qualify for First Amendment protection. The Free Speech Clause exists principally to protect discourse on public matters, but we have long recognized that it is difficult to distinguish politics from entertainment, and dangerous to try. "Everyone is familiar with instances of propaganda through fiction. What is one man's amusement, teaches another's doctrine." Winters v. New York, 333 U. S. 507, 510 (1948). Like the protected books, plays, and movies that preceded them, video games communicate ideas—and even social messages—through many familiar literary devices (such as characters, dialogue, plot, and music) and through features distinctive to the medium (such as the player's interaction with the virtual world). That suffices to confer First Amendment protection. . . .

. . .

Last Term, in *Stevens*, we held that new categories of unprotected speech may not be added to the list by a legislature that concludes certain speech is too harmful to be tolerated. . . .

. . . [W]ithout persuasive evidence that a novel restriction on content is part of a long (if heretofore unrecognized) tradition of proscription, a legislature may not revise the "judgment [of] the American people," embodied in the First Amendment, "that the benefits of its restrictions on the Government outweigh the costs." . . .

That holding controls this case. As in *Stevens*, California has tried to make violent-speech regulation look like obscenity regulation by appending a saving clause required for the latter. That does not suffice. Our cases have been clear that the obscenity exception to the First Amendment does not cover whatever a legislature finds shocking, but only depictions of "sexual conduct," *Miller*,. . . .

Stevens was not the first time we have encountered and rejected a State's attempt to shoehorn speech about violence into obscenity. In *Winters*, we considered a New York criminal statute "forbid[ding] the massing of stories of bloodshed and lust in such a way as to incite to crime against the person,". . . . Our opinion . . . concluded that the New York statute failed a heightened vagueness standard applicable to restrictions upon speech entitled to First Amendment protection . . . [and] made clear that violence is not part of the obscenity that the Constitution permits to be regulated. . . .

Because speech about violence is not obscene, it is of no consequence that California's statute mimics the New York statute regulating obscenity-for-minors that we upheld in Ginsberg v. New York, 390 U.S. 629 (1968). . . .

The California Act . . . does not adjust the boundaries of an existing category of unprotected speech to ensure that a definition designed for adults is not uncritically applied to children. California . . . wishes to create a wholly new category of content-based regulation that is permissible only for speech directed at children.

That is unprecedented and mistaken. "[M]inors are entitled to a significant measure of First Amendment protection, and only in relatively narrow and well-defined circumstances may government bar public dissemination of protected materials to them." Erznoznik v. Jacksonville, 422 U.S. 205, 212–213 (1975). . . . No doubt a State possesses legitimate power to protect children from harm, . . . but that does not include a free-floating power to restrict the ideas to which children may be exposed. "Speech that is neither obscene as to youths nor subject to some other legitimate proscription cannot be suppressed solely to protect the young from ideas or images that a legislative body thinks unsuitable for them." *Erznoznik*,. . . .

California's argument would fare better if there were a longstanding tradition in this country of specially restricting children's access to depictions of violence, but there is none. Certainly the *books* we give children to read—or read to them when they are younger—contain no shortage of gore. . . .

High-school reading lists are full of similar fare. . . .

This is not to say that minors' consumption of violent entertainment has never encountered resistance. In the1800's, dime novels depicting crime . . . were blamed in some quarters for juvenile delinquency. . . . When motion pictures came along, they became the villains instead. . . . Radio dramas were next, and then came comic books. . . . But efforts to convince Congress to restrict comic books failed. . . . And, of course, after comic books came television and music lyrics.

California claims that video games present special problems because they are "interactive," in that the player participates in the violent action on screen and determines its outcome. The latter feature is nothing new: Since at least . . . 1969, young readers of choose-your-own-adventure stories have been able to make decisions that determine the plot by following instructions about which page to turn to. . . . As for the argument that video games enable participation in the violent action, that seems to us more a matter of degree than of kind. As Judge Posner has observed, all literature is interactive. . . .

. . . Justice Alito recounts . . . disgusting video games in order to disgust us—but disgust is not a valid basis for restricting expression. . . . [I]ronically, Justice Alito's argument highlights the precise danger posed by the California Act: that the *ideas* expressed by speech—whether it be violence, or gore, or racism—and not its objective effects, may be the real reason for governmental proscription.

III

Because the Act imposes a restriction on the content of protected speech, it is invalid unless California can demonstrate that it passes strict scrutiny—that is, unless it is justified by a compelling government interest and is narrowly drawn to serve that interest. . . . The State must specifically identify an "actual problem" in need of solving, . . . and the curtailment of free speech must be actually necessary to the solution. . . . That is a demanding standard. "It is rare that a regulation restricting speech because of its content will ever be permissible." . . .

California cannot meet that standard. At the outset, it acknowledges that it cannot show a direct causal link between violent video games and harm to minors. Rather, relying upon . . . Turner Broadcasting System, Inc. v. FCC, 512 U.S. 622 (1994), the State claims that it need not produce such proof because the legislature can make a predictive judgment that such a link exists, based on competing psychological studies. But . . .[t]hat decision applied *intermediate scrutiny* to a content-neutral regulation. . . . California's burden is much higher, and because it bears the risk of uncertainty, . . . ambiguous proof will not suffice.

The State's evidence is not compelling. California relies primarily on . . . research . . . studies purport[ing] to show a connection between exposure to violent video games and harmful effects on children. These studies have been rejected by every court to consider them, and with good reason . . . . They show at best some correlation between exposure to violent entertainment and minuscule real-world effects, such as children's feeling more aggressive or making louder noises in the few minutes after playing a violent game than after playing a nonviolent game.

Even . . . those effects are both small and indistinguishable from effects produced by other media[:] . . . "about the same" as that produced by their exposure to violence on television. . . . And . . . the *same* effects have been found when children watch cartoons starring Bugs Bunny or the Road Runner, . . . or when they play video games like Sonic the Hedgehog that are rated "E" (appropriate for all ages), . . . or even when they "vie[w] a picture of a gun," . . . .

The Act is also seriously underinclusive in another respect—and a respect that renders irrelevant the contentions of the concurrence and the dissents that video games are qualitatively different from other portrayals of violence. The California Legislature is perfectly willing to leave this dangerous, mind-altering material in the hands of children so long as one parent (or even an aunt or uncle) says it's OK. . . .

California claims that the Act is justified in aid of parental authority: By requiring that the purchase of violent video games can be made only by adults, the Act ensures that parents can decide what games are appropriate.... But ... California cannot show that the Act's restrictions meet a substantial need of parents who wish to restrict their children's access to violent video games but cannot do so. The video-game industry has in place a voluntary rating system designed to inform consumers about the content of games [that] ... the Federal Trade Commission ... found ["outpaces the movie and music industries" .... This system does much to ensure that minors cannot purchase seriously violent games on their own, and that parents who care about the matter can readily evaluate the games their children bring home. Filling the remaining modest gap in concerned-parents' control can hardly be a compelling state interest.

And finally, the Act's purported aid to parental authority is vastly overinclusive. Not all of the children who are forbidden to purchase violent video games on their own have parents who *care* whether they purchase violent video games.... [T]he legislation's ... entire effect is only in support of what the State thinks parents *ought* to want. This is not the narrow tailoring to "assisting parents" that restriction of First Amendment rights requires.

. . .

■ JUSTICE ALITO, with whom THE CHIEF JUSTICE joins, concurring in the judgment.

... I ... agree with the Court that this particular law cannot be sustained [but] disagree ... with [its] approach ....

In the view of the Court, ... violent video games really present no serious problem. Spending hour upon hour controlling the actions of a character who guns down scores of innocent victims is not different in "kind" from reading a description of violence in a work of literature.

The Court is sure of this; I am not. There are reasons to suspect that the experience of playing violent video games just might be very different from reading a book, listening to the radio, or watching a movie or a television show.

I

Respondents ... ask us to strike down the California law on two grounds: The broad ground adopted by the Court and the narrower ground that the law's definition of "violent video game," ... is impermissibly vague.... Because I agree with the latter argument, I see no need to reach the broader First Amendment issues addressed by the Court.

. . .

The first important difference between the *Ginsberg* law and the California violent video game statute concerns their respective threshold requirements. [T]he *Ginsberg* law built upon the test for adult obscenity, ... which ... requires an obscenity statute to contain a threshold limitation that restricts the statute's coverage to specifically defined "hard core" depictions.... The *Miller* Court clearly viewed this threshold limitation as serving a vital notice function.

By contrast, the threshold requirement of the California law does not perform the narrowing function served by the limitation in *Miller*. At least when *Miller* was decided, depictions of "hard core" sexual conduct were not a common feature of mainstream entertainment. But nothing similar can be said about much of the conduct covered by the California law. It provides that a video game cannot qualify as "violent" unless "the range of options available to a player includes killing, maiming, dismembering, or sexually assaulting an image of a human being." § 1746(d)(1).

For better or worse, our society has long regarded many depictions of killing and maiming as suitable features of popular entertainment, including entertainment that is widely available to minors. The California law's threshold requirement would more closely resemble the limitation in *Miller* if it targeted a narrower class of graphic depictions.

Because of this feature of the California law's threshold test, the work of providing fair notice is left in large part to the three requirements that follow, but those elements are also not up to the task. . . . [T]he California Legislature could have made its own judgment regarding the kind and degree of violence that is acceptable in games played by minors (or by minors in particular age groups). Instead, the legislature relied on undefined societal or community standards.

One of the three elements . . . refers expressly to "prevailing standards in the community as to what is suitable for minors." § 1746(d)(1)(A)(ii). Another element points in the same direction, asking whether "[a] reasonable person, considering [a] game as a whole," would find that it "appeals to a *deviant* or *morbid* interest of minors." § 1746(d)(1)(A)(i) (emphasis added).

The terms "deviant" and "morbid" are not defined in the statute . . . . A "deviant or morbid interest" in violence . . . appears to be an interest that deviates from what is regarded—presumably in accordance with some generally accepted standard—as normal and healthy. Thus, the application of the California law is heavily dependent on the identification of generally accepted standards regarding the suitability of violent entertainment for minors.

. . .

There is a critical difference, however, between obscenity laws and laws regulating violence in entertainment. By the time of this Court's landmark obscenity cases in the 1960's, obscenity had long been prohibited, . . . and this experience had helped to shape certain generally accepted norms concerning expression related to sex.

There is no similar history regarding expression related to violence. As the Court notes, classic literature contains descriptions of great violence, and even children's stories sometimes depict very violent scenes. . . . [T]he prevalence of violent depictions in children's literature and entertainment creates numerous opportunities for reasonable people to disagree about which depictions may excite "deviant" or "morbid" impulses. . . .

Finally, the difficulty of ascertaining the community standards incorporated into the California law is compounded by the legislature's decision to lump all minors together. The California law draws no distinction between young children and adolescents who are nearing the age of majority.

. . .

. . . I conclude that the California violent video game law fails to provide the fair notice that the Constitution requires. . . . I would not express any view[, however,] on whether a properly drawn statute would or would not survive First Amendment scrutiny.

II

[Some of] my reasons for questioning the wisdom of the Court's approach . . . are touched upon by the dissents, and while I am not prepared at this time to go as far as either Justice Thomas or Justice Breyer, they raise valid concerns.

A

The Court is wrong in saying that the holding in *United States* v. *Stevens* . . . "controls this case." First, . . . *Stevens* struck down a law that broadly prohibited *any person* from creating, selling, or possessing depictions of animal cruelty for commercial gain. The California law involved here, by contrast, is limited to the sale or rental of violent video games *to minors*[;] imposes no restriction on the creation of violent video games, or on the possession of such games by anyone[; and] does not regulate the sale or rental of violent games by adults. And the California law does not prevent parents and certain other close relatives from buying or renting violent games for their children or other young relatives if they see fit.

Second, . . . [g]oing well beyond *Stevens*, the Court now holds that any law that attempts to prevent minors from purchasing violent video games must satisfy strict scrutiny . . . .

Third, *Stevens* expressly left open the possibility that a more narrowly drawn statute targeting depictions of animal cruelty might be compatible with the First Amendment. . . . In this case, the Court's sweeping opinion will likely be read by many . . . as suggesting that no regulation of minors' access to violent video games is allowed—at least without supporting evidence that may not be realistically obtainable given the nature of the phenomenon in question.

B

. . . [T]he California law reinforces parental decisionmaking in exactly the same way as the New York statute upheld in *Ginsberg*. Under both laws, minors are prevented from purchasing certain materials; and under both laws, parents are free to supply their children with these items if that is their wish.

. . .

C

. . .

Today's most advanced video games create realistic alternative worlds in which millions of players immerse themselves for hours on end. These games feature visual imagery and sounds that are strikingly realistic, and in the near future video-game graphics may be virtually indistinguishable from actual video footage. . . .

Persons who play video games also have an unprecedented ability to participate in the events that take place in the virtual worlds that these games create. . . .

. . .

In some of these games, the violence is astounding. . . .

It also appears that there is no antisocial theme too base for some in the video-game industry. . . .

. . .

. . . [O]nly an extraordinarily imaginative reader who reads a description of a killing in a literary work will experience that event as vividly as he might if he played the role of the killer in a video game. . . .

When all of the characteristics of video games are taken into account, there is certainly a reasonable basis for thinking that the experience of playing a video game may be quite different from the experience of reading a book, listening to a radio broadcast, or viewing a movie. And if this is so, then for at least some minors, the effects of playing violent video games may also be quite different. The Court acts prematurely in dismissing this possibility out of hand.

. . . I would not squelch legislative efforts to deal with what is perceived by some to be a significant and developing social problem. . . .

■ JUSTICE THOMAS, dissenting.

. . .

In my view, the "practices and beliefs held by the Founders" reveal another category of excluded speech: speech to minor children bypassing their parents. . . . The historical evidence shows that the founding generation believed parents had absolute authority over their minor children and expected parents to use that authority to direct the proper development of their children. It would be absurd to suggest that such a society understood "the freedom of speech" to include a right to speak to minors (or a corresponding right of minors to access speech) without going through the minors' parents. The founding generation would not have considered it an abridgment of "the freedom of speech" to support parental authority by restricting speech that bypasses minors' parents.

. . .

The California law . . . does not prohibit adults from buying or renting violent video games for a minor or prohibit minors from playing such games. The law also does not restrict a "minor's parent, grandparent, aunt, uncle, or legal guardian" from selling or renting him a violent video game. § 1746.1(c).

. . .

Under any of this Court's standards for a facial First Amendment challenge, this one must fail. . . . Even assuming that video games are speech, in most applications the California law does not implicate the First Amendment. All that the law does is prohibit the direct sale or rental of a violent video game to a minor by someone other than the minor's parent, grandparent, aunt, uncle, or legal guardian. . . . In the typical case, the only speech affected is speech that bypasses a minor's parent or guardian. Because such speech does not fall within "the freedom of speech" as originally understood, California's law does not ordinarily implicate the First Amendment and is not facially unconstitutional.

. . .

■ JUSTICE BREYER, dissenting.

. . .

A facial challenge . . . can succeed only if "a substantial number of its applications are unconstitutional, judged in relation to the statute's plainly legitimate sweep." *United States* v. *Stevens*, . . . (2010). . . . Moreover, it is more difficult to mount a facial First Amendment attack on a statute that seeks to regulate activity that involves action as well as speech. See Broadrick v. Oklahoma, 413 U.S. 601, 614–615 (1973). Hence, I shall focus here upon an area within which I believe the State can legitimately apply its statute, namely sales to minors under the age of 17 (the age cutoff used by the industry's own ratings system), of highly realistic violent video games, which a reasonable game maker would know meet the Act's criteria. . . . I shall assume that the number of instances in which the State will enforce the statute within that area is comparatively large, and that the number outside that area (for example, sales to 17-year-olds) is comparatively small. And the activity the statute regulates combines speech with action (a virtual form of target practice).

. . . I would apply both this Court's "vagueness" precedents and a strict form of First Amendment scrutiny. In doing so, the special First Amendment category I find relevant is . . . the category of "protection of children.". . .

The majority's claim that the California statute, if upheld, would create a "new categor[y] of unprotected speech," is overstated. No one here argues that depictions of violence, even extreme violence, *automatically* fall outside the First Amendment's protective scope as, for example, do obscenity and depictions of child pornography. . . .

. . .

II

In my view, California's statute provides "fair notice of what is prohibited," and consequently it is not impermissibly vague. . . .

. . . [T]he relevant comparison is not to adult obscenity cases but to *Ginsberg*, which dealt with "nudity," a category no more "narrow" than killing and maiming. And in any event, *narrowness* and *vagueness* do not necessarily have anything to do with one another. All that is required for vagueness purposes is that the terms "kill," "maim," and "dismember" give fair notice as to what they cover, which they do.

. . .

. . . As in *Miller* and *Ginsberg*, the California law clearly *protects* even the most violent games that possess serious literary, artistic, political, or scientific value. § 1746(d)(1)(A)(iii). And . . . here the industry itself has promulgated standards and created a review process, in which adults who "typically have experience with children" assess what games are inappropriate for minors. . . .

. . . Justice Alito argues that the *Miller* standard sufficed because there are "certain generally accepted norms concerning expression related to sex," whereas there are no similarly "accepted standards regarding the suitability of violent entertainment." But there is no evidence that is so. The Court relied on "community standards" in *Miller* precisely because of the difficulty of articulating "accepted norms" about depictions of sex. I can find no difference—historical or otherwise—that is *relevant* to the vagueness question. . . .

. . .

. . . And if there remain any vagueness problems, the state courts can cure them through interpretation. . . .

III

. . .

Like the majority, I believe that the California law must be "narrowly tailored" to further a "compelling interest," without there being a "less restrictive" alternative that would be "at least as effective." . . . I would not apply this strict standard "mechanically." . . . Rather, in applying it, I would evaluate the degree to which the statute injures speech-related interests, the nature of the potentially-justifying "compelling interests," the degree to which the statute furthers that interest, the nature and effectiveness of possible alternatives, and, in light of this evaluation, whether, overall, "the statute works speech related harm . . . out of proportion to the benefits that the statute seeks to provide." . . .

First Amendment standards applied in this way are difficult but not impossible to satisfy. . . .

. . .

A

California's law imposes no more than a modest restriction on expression. . . . All it prevents is a child or adolescent from buying, without a parent's assistance, a gruesomely violent video game of a kind that the industry *itself* tells us it wants to keep out of the hands of those under the age of 17.

Nor is the statute, if upheld, likely to create a precedent that would adversely affect other media, say films, or videos, or books. A typical video game involves a significant amount of physical activity. And pushing buttons that achieve an interactive, virtual form of target practice (using images of human beings as targets), while containing an expressive component, is not just like watching a typical movie.

B

The interest that California advances in support of the statute is compelling. . . . [I]t consists of both (1) the "basic" parental claim "to authority in their own household to direct the rearing of their children," which makes it proper to enact "laws designed to aid discharge of [parental] responsibility," and (2) the State's "independent interest in the well-being of its youth." *Ginsberg*, . . . And where these interests work in tandem, it is not fatally "underinclusive" for a State to advance its interests in protecting children against the special harms present in an interactive video game medium through a default rule that still allows parents to provide their children with what their parents wish.

. . .

[M]any scientific studies . . . support California's views. . . .

. . .

. . . [A]ssociations of public health professionals . . . have reviewed many of these studies and found a significant risk that violent video games, when compared with more passive media, are particularly likely to cause children harm.

. . .

Unlike the majority, I would find sufficient grounds in these studies and expert opinions for this Court to defer to an elected legislature's conclusion that the video games in question are particularly likely to harm children. . . .

C

I can find no "less restrictive" alternative to California's law that would be "at least as effective." . . . The majority points to a voluntary alternative: The industry tries to prevent those under 17 from buying extremely violent games by labeling those games with an "M" (Mature) and encouraging retailers to restrict their sales to those 17 and older. But this voluntary system has serious enforcement gaps.

. . .

IV

The upshot is that California's statute, as applied to its heartland of applications (*i.e.,* buyers under 17; extremely violent, realistic video games), imposes a restriction on speech that is modest at most. That restriction is justified by a compelling interest (supplementing parents' efforts to prevent their children from purchasing potentially harmful violent, interactive material). And there is no equally effective, less restrictive alternative. California's statute is consequently constitutional on its face—though litigants remain free to challenge the statute as applied in particular instances, including any effort by the State to apply it to minors aged 17.

I add that the majority's different conclusion creates a serious anomaly in First Amendment law. *Ginsberg* makes clear that a State can prohibit the sale to minors of depictions of nudity; today the Court makes clear that a State cannot prohibit the sale to minors of the most violent interactive video games. But what sense does it make to forbid selling to a 13-year-old boy a magazine with an image of a nude woman, while protecting a sale to that 13-year-old of an interactive video game in which he actively, but virtually, binds and gags the woman, then tortures and kills her? What kind of

First Amendment would permit the government to protect children by restricting sales of that extremely violent video game *only* when the woman—bound, gagged, tortured, and killed—is also topless?

This anomaly . . . disappears once one recognizes that extreme violence, where interactive, and *without literary, artistic, or similar justification*, can prove at least as, if not more, harmful to children as photographs of nudity. And the record here is more than adequate to support such a view. That is why I believe that *Ginsberg* controls the outcome here *a fortiori*. And it is why I believe California's law is constitutional on its face.

. . . In my view, the First Amendment does not disable government from helping parents make . . . a choice not to have their children buy extremely violent, interactive video games, which they more than reasonably fear pose only the risk of harm to those children.

For these reasons, I respectfully dissent.

Ashcroft v. American Civil Liberties Union

535 U.S. 564 (2002).

The advent of the Internet, and the proliferation of sexually explicit material on the World Wide Web, prompted Congress to seek to protect children from exposure to such material through legislation that repeatedly provoked first amendment challenges. In this case the Court held that the Child Online Protection Act's (COPA) use of "community standards" to identify "material that is harmful to minors" did "not by itself render the statute substantially overbroad for purposes of the First Amendment." For the Court, Justice Thomas described the background of the case this way:

"Congress first attempted to protect children from exposure to pornographic material on the Internet by enacting the Communications Decency Act of 1996 (CDA). . . . The CDA prohibited the knowing transmission over the Internet of obscene or indecent messages to any recipient under 18 years of age. . . . It also forbade any individual from knowingly sending over or displaying on the Internet certain 'patently offensive' material in a manner available to persons under 18 years of age. . . . The prohibition specifically extended to 'any comment, request, suggestion, proposal, image, or other communication that, in context, depict[ed] or describ[ed], in terms patently offensive as measured by contemporary community standards, sexual or excretory activities or organs.' . . .

"The CDA provided two affirmative defenses to those prosecuted under the statute. The first protected individuals who took 'good faith, reasonable, effective, and appropriate actions' to restrict minors from accessing obscene, indecent, and patently offensive material over the Internet. . . . The second shielded those who restricted minors from accessing such material 'by requiring use of a verified credit card, debit account, adult access code, or adult personal identification number.' . . .

"Notwithstanding these affirmative defenses, in Reno v. American Civil Liberties Union, [521 U.S. 844 (1997),] we held that the CDA's regulation of indecent transmissions, . . . and the display of patently offensive material, . . . ran afoul of the First Amendment. We concluded that 'the CDA lack[ed] the precision that the First Amendment requires when a statute regulates the content of speech' because, '[i]n order to deny minors access to potentially harmful speech, the CDA effectively suppress[ed] a large amount of speech that adults ha[d] a constitutional right to receive and to address to one another.' . . .

"Our holding was based on three crucial considerations. First, 'existing technology did not include any effective method for a sender to prevent minors from obtaining access to its communications on the Internet without also denying access to adults.' . . . Second, '[t]he breadth of the CDA's coverage [was] wholly unprecedented.' . . . 'Its open-ended prohibitions embrace[d],' not only commercial speech or commercial entities, but also 'all nonprofit entities and individuals posting indecent messages or displaying them on their own computers in the presence of minors.' *Ibid.* In addition, because the CDA did not define the terms 'indecent' and 'patently offensive,' the statute 'cover[ed] large amounts of nonpornographic material with serious educational or other value.' . . . As a result, regulated subject matter under the CDA extended to 'discussions about prison rape or safe sexual practices, artistic images that include nude subjects, and arguably the card catalog of the Carnegie Library.' . . . Third, we found that neither affirmative defense set forth in the CDA 'constitute[d] the sort of "narrow tailoring" that [would] save an otherwise patently invalid unconstitutional provision.' . . . Consequently, only the CDA's ban on the knowing transmission of obscene messages survived scrutiny because obscene speech enjoys no First Amendment protection. . . .

"After . . . *Reno* . . . , Congress . . . passed . . . COPA[, which] prohibits any person from 'knowingly and with knowledge of the character of the material, in interstate or foreign commerce by means of the World Wide Web, mak[ing] any communication for commercial purposes that is available to any minor and that includes any material that is harmful to minors.' 47 U.S.C. § 231(a)(1).

"Apparently responding to our objections to the breadth of the CDA's coverage, Congress limited the scope of COPA's coverage in at least three ways. First, while the CDA applied to communications over the Internet as a whole, including, for example, e-mail messages, COPA applies only to material displayed on the World Wide Web. Second, unlike the CDA, COPA covers only communications made 'for commercial purposes.' . . . And third, while the CDA prohibited 'indecent' and 'patently offensive' communications, COPA restricts only the narrower category of 'material that is harmful to minors.' . . .

"Drawing on the three-part test for obscenity set forth in *Miller v. California,* 413 U.S. 15 (1973), COPA defines 'material that is harmful to minors' as

'any communication, picture, image, graphic image file, article, recording, writing, or other matter of any kind that is obscene or that—

'(A) the average person, applying contemporary community standards, would find, taking the material as a whole and with respect to minors, is designed to appeal to, or is designed to pander to, the prurient interest;

'(B) depicts, describes, or represents, in a manner patently offensive with respect to minors, an actual or simulated sexual act or sexual contact, an actual or simulated normal or perverted sexual act, or a lewd exhibition of the genitals or post-pubescent female breast; and

'(C) taken as a whole, lacks serious literary, artistic, political, or scientific value for minors.' 47 U.S.C. § 231(e)(6).

"Like the CDA, COPA also provides affirmative defenses to those subject to prosecution under the statute. An individual may qualify for a defense if he, 'in good faith, has restricted access by minors to material that is harmful to minors—(A) by requiring the use of a credit card, debit account, adult access code, or adult personal identification number; (B) by accepting a digital certificate that verifies age; or (C) by any other reasonable measures that are feasible under available technology.'

§ 231(c)(1). Persons violating COPA are subject to both civil and criminal sanctions. . . ."

Various organizations with websites from which they derive some income, and on which they post sexually oriented material, including "resources on obstetrics, gynecology, and sexual health; visual art and poetry; resources designed for gays and lesbians; information about books and stock photographic images offered for sale; and online magazines[,]" sued, alleging "that, although they believed that the material on their Web sites was valuable for adults, they feared that they would be prosecuted under COPA because some of that material 'could be construed as "harmful to minors" in some communities.'" The District Court granted a preliminary injunction against enforcement of COPA, and the Third Circuit affirmed. The Supreme Court vacated and remanded the Court of Appeals' judgment, but not the preliminary injunction, because other issues remained in the case that the Supreme Court thought should be addressed initially in the lower courts.

With respect to whether COPA's use of community standards regarding minors was constitutionally permissible, there was no opinion to which a majority of the Court subscribed. Justice Thomas, joined by Chief Justice Rehnquist and Justices O'Connor and Scalia, first said this:

"Because juries would apply different standards across the country, and Web publishers currently lack the ability to limit access to their sites on a geographic basis, the Court of Appeals feared that COPA's 'community standards' component would effectively force all speakers on the Web to abide by the 'most puritan' community's standards.

"In evaluating the constitutionality of the CDA, this Court expressed a similar concern over that statute's use of community standards to identify patently offensive material on the Internet. We noted that 'the "community standards" criterion as applied to the Internet means that any communication available to a nationwide audience will be judged by the standards of the community most likely to be offended by the message.' *Reno,* . . .

"The CDA's use of community standards to identify patently offensive material, however, was particularly problematic in light of that statute's unprecedented breadth and vagueness. The statute covered communications depicting or describing 'sexual or excretory activities or organs' that were 'patently offensive as measured by contemporary community standards'—a standard somewhat similar to the second prong of *Miller*'s three-prong test. But the CDA did not include any limiting terms resembling *Miller*'s additional two prongs. . . . It neither contained any requirement that restricted material appeal to the prurient interest nor excluded from the scope of its coverage works with serious literary, artistic, political, or scientific value. . . . The tremendous breadth of the CDA magnified the impact caused by differences in community standards across the country, restricting Web publishers from openly displaying a significant amount of material that would have constituted protected speech in some communities across the country but run afoul of community standards in others.

"COPA, by contrast, does not appear to suffer from the same flaw because it applies to significantly less material than did the CDA and defines the harmful-to-minors material restricted by the statute in a manner parallel to the *Miller* definition of obscenity. To fall within the scope of COPA, works must not only 'depic[t], describ[e], or represen[t], in a manner patently offensive with respect to minors,' particular sexual acts or parts of the anatomy, they must also be designed to appeal to the prurient interest of minors and 'taken as a whole, lac[k] serious literary, artistic, political, or scientific value for minors.' . . .

"These additional two restrictions substantially limit the amount of material covered by the statute. Material appeals to the prurient interest, for instance, only if it is in some sense erotic. . . . Of even more significance, however, is COPA's exclusion of material with serious value for minors. . . . In *Reno,* we emphasized that the serious value 'requirement is particularly important because, unlike the "patently offensive" and "prurient interest" criteria, it is not judged by contemporary community standards.' "

Without the adherence of Justice O'Connor, Justice Thomas continued:

"When the scope of an obscenity statute's coverage is sufficiently narrowed by a 'serious value' prong and a 'prurient interest' prong, we have held that requiring a speaker disseminating material to a national audience to observe varying community standards does not violate the First Amendment. . . . Hamling v. United States, 418 U.S. 87 (1974). . . ."

Noting that *"Hamling's* holding was reaffirmed in Sable Communications of Cal., Inc. v. FCC, 492 U.S. 115 (1989)[,]" which upheld a prohibition on the use of telephones to make obscene or indecent communications for commercial purposes, Justice Thomas described *Sable's* rejection of a similar argument made by a "dial-a-porn" challenger: "[T]his Court once again rebuffed this attack on the use of community standards in a federal statute of national scope: 'There is no constitutional barrier under *Miller* to prohibiting communications that are obscene in some communities under local standards even though they are not obscene in others. *If Sable's audience is comprised of different communities with different local standards, Sable ultimately bears the burden of complying with the prohibition on obscene messages.*' . . . (emphasis added)." He continued:

"The Court of Appeals below concluded that *Hamling* and *Sable* 'are easily distinguished from the present case' because in both of those cases 'the defendants had the ability to control the distribution of controversial material with respect to the geographic communities into which they released it' whereas 'Web publishers have no such comparable control.' In neither *Hamling* nor *Sable,* however, was the speaker's ability to target the release of material into particular geographic areas integral to the legal analysis. . . .

"While Justice Kennedy and Justice Stevens question the applicability of this Court's community standards jurisprudence to the Internet, we do not believe that the medium's 'unique characteristics' justify adopting a different approach than that set forth in *Hamling* and *Sable.* If a publisher chooses to send its material into a particular community, this Court's jurisprudence teaches that it is the publisher's responsibility to abide by that community's standards. The publisher's burden does not change simply because it decides to distribute its material to every community in the Nation. . . . If a publisher wishes for its material to be judged only by the standards of particular communities, then it need only take the simple step of utilizing a medium that enables it to target the release of its material into those communities.

". . . [W]e have no reason to believe that the practical effect of varying community standards under COPA, given the statute's definition of 'material that is harmful to minors,' is significantly greater than the practical effect of varying community standards under federal obscenity statutes. . . . [I]f we were to hold COPA unconstitutional *because of* its use of community standards, federal obscenity statutes would likely also be unconstitutional as applied to the Web. . . .

". . . Because Congress has narrowed the range of content restricted by COPA in a manner analogous to *Miller's* definition of obscenity, we conclude . . . that any variance caused by the statute's reliance on community standards is not substantial enough to violate the First Amendment."

Justice O'Connor concurred in part and in the judgment:

"I agree with the plurality that even if obscenity on the Internet is defined in terms of local community standards, respondents have not shown that . . . COPA . . . is overbroad solely on the basis of the variation in the standards of different communities. . . .

". . .

"But respondents' failure to prove substantial overbreadth on a facial challenge in this case still leaves open the possibility that the use of local community standards will cause problems for regulation of obscenity on the Internet, for adults as well as children, in future cases. In an as-applied challenge, for instance, individual litigants may still dispute that the standards of a community more restrictive than theirs should apply to them. And in future facial challenges to regulation of obscenity on the Internet, litigants may make a more convincing case for substantial overbreadth. Where adult speech is concerned, for instance, there may in fact be a greater degree of disagreement about what is patently offensive or appeals to the prurient interest.

"Nor do I think such future cases can be resolved by application of the approach we took in *Hamling* . . . and *Sable.* . . . I agree with Justice Kennedy that, given Internet speakers' inability to control the geographic location of their audience, expecting them to bear the burden of controlling the recipients of their speech, as we did in *Hamling* and *Sable,* may be entirely too much to ask, and would potentially suppress an inordinate amount of expression. For these reasons, adoption of a national standard is necessary in my view for any reasonable regulation of Internet obscenity."

Justice Breyer also concurred in part and in the judgment, "believ[ing] that Congress intended the statutory word 'community' to refer to the Nation's adult community taken as a whole, not to geographically separate local areas." That "view of the statute avoids the need to examine the serious First Amendment problem that would otherwise exist. . . . To read the statute as adopting the community standards of every locality in the United States would provide the most puritan of communities with a heckler's Internet veto affecting the rest of the Nation. The technical difficulties associated with efforts to confine Internet material to particular geographic areas make the problem particularly serious." He did agree, however, "with much of the reasoning" of Justice Thomas' opinion, "insofar as it explains . . . that variation reflecting application of the same national standard by different local juries does not violate the First Amendment."

Justice Kennedy, joined by Justices Souter and Ginsburg, concurred only in the judgment. He wrote in part:

". . . Whether the national variation in community standards produces overbreadth requiring invalidation of COPA . . . depends on the breadth of COPA's coverage and on what community standards are being invoked. Only by identifying the universe of speech burdened by COPA is it possible to discern whether national variation in community standards renders the speech restriction overbroad. . . .

". . .

". . . Unlike Justice Thomas, . . . I would not assume that the Act is narrow enough to render the national variation in community standards unproblematic. Indeed, if the District Court correctly construed the statute across its other dimensions, then the variation in community standards might well justify enjoining enforcement of the Act. I would leave that question to the Court of Appeals in the first instance.

". . .

"It is true, as Justice Thomas points out, that requiring a speaker addressing a national audience to meet varying community standards does not always violate the First Amendment. See *Hamling* . . . ; *Sable* . . . These cases, however, are of limited utility in analyzing the one before us, because each mode of expression has its own unique characteristics. . . .

" . . .

"The economics and technology of Internet communication differ in important ways from those of telephones and mail. [I]t is easy and cheap to reach a worldwide audience on the Internet, but expensive if not impossible to reach a geographic subset. A Web publisher in a community where avant garde culture is the norm may have no desire to reach a national market; he may wish only to speak to his neighbors; nevertheless, if an eavesdropper in a more traditional, rural community chooses to listen in, there is nothing the publisher can do. As a practical matter, COPA makes the eavesdropper the arbiter of propriety on the Web. And it is no answer to say that the speaker should 'take the simple step of utilizing a [different] medium.' . . .

" . . .

" . . . [T]he Court of Appeals . . . may have been correct . . . to conclude that in practical effect COPA imposes the most puritanical community standard on the entire country. . . . The national variation in community standards constitutes a particular burden on Internet speech."

Justice Kennedy agreed with the Court, however, that "this observation *'by itself'*" did not "suffice[ ] to enjoin the Act. . . . We cannot know whether variation in community standards renders the Act substantially overbroad without first assessing the extent of the speech covered and the variations in community standards with respect to that speech." He concluded "that we cannot strike down the Act based merely on the phrase 'contemporary community standards[.]' "

Justice Stevens dissented, saying in part:

" . . . In its original form, the community standard provided a shield for communications that are offensive only to the least tolerant members of society. . . . In the context of the Internet, however, community standards become a sword, rather than a shield. If a prurient appeal is offensive in a puritan village, it may be a crime to post it on the World Wide Web.

" . . .

"We have . . . repeatedly rejected the position that the free speech rights of adults can be limited to what is acceptable for children. See . . . Butler v. Michigan, 352 U.S. 380, 383 (1957).

" . . . Like the . . . ban against selling adult books found impermissible in *Butler,* COPA seeks to limit protected speech that is not targeted at children, simply because it can be obtained by them while surfing the Web. . . .

"COPA not only restricts speech that is made available to the general public, it also covers a medium in which speech cannot be segregated to avoid communities where it is likely to be considered harmful to minors. . . .

"If the material were forwarded through the mails, as in *Hamling,* or over the telephone, as in *Sable,* the sender could avoid destinations with the most restrictive standards. . . . In light of this fundamental difference in technologies, the rules applicable to the mass mailing of an obscene montage or to obscene dial-a-porn should not be used to judge the legality of messages on the World Wide Web."

Justice Stevens was not persuaded by the emphasis placed by Justices Thomas and Kennedy on other provisions of COPA:

". . . These other provisions may reduce the absolute number of Web pages covered by the statute, but even the narrowest version of the statute abridges a substantial amount of protected speech that many communities would not find harmful to minors. Because Web speakers cannot limit access to those specific communities, the statute is substantially overbroad regardless of how its other provisions are construed."

Ashcroft v. American Civil Liberties Union (II)

542 U.S. 656 (2004).

On remand of the previous case, the District Court continued the preliminary injunction against the enforcement of COPA on the basis that the challengers were "likely to prevail" at trial because the Government had failed to show the absence of less restrictive alternatives to COPA. The Court of Appeals affirmed, as did the Supreme Court, which then remanded for trial.[a] Justice Kennedy's opinion for the Court concluded that the "Government has failed, at this point, to rebut the plaintiffs' contention that there are plausible less restrictive alternatives to the statute." He elaborated as follows:

". . . As the Government bears the burden of proof on the ultimate question of COPA's constitutionality, respondents must be deemed likely to prevail unless the Government has shown that respondents' proposed less restrictive alternatives are less effective than COPA. . . . [O]n this record there are a number of plausible, less restrictive alternatives to the statute.

"The primary alternative considered by the District Court was blocking and filtering software[, which] . . . is less restrictive than COPA, and, in addition, likely more effective as a means of restricting children's access to materials harmful to them. . . .

"Filters . . . impose selective restrictions on speech at the receiving end, not universal restrictions at the source. Under a filtering regime, adults without children may gain access to speech they have a right to see without having to identify themselves or provide their credit card information. Even adults with children may obtain access to the same speech on the same terms simply by turning off the filter on their home computers. Above all, promoting the use of filters does not condemn as criminal any category of speech, and so the potential chilling effect is eliminated, or at least much diminished. All of these things are true, moreover, regardless of how broadly or narrowly the definitions in COPA are construed.

"Filters also may well be more effective than COPA. First, a filter can prevent minors from seeing all pornography, not just pornography posted to the Web from America. . . . COPA does not prevent minors from having access to those foreign harmful materials. That alone makes it possible that filtering software might be more effective in serving Congress' goals. . . . It is not an answer to say that COPA reaches some amount of materials that are harmful to minors; the question is whether it would reach more of them than less restrictive alternatives. In addition, the District Court found that verification systems may be subject to evasion and circumvention, for example by minors who have their own credit cards. Finally, filters also may be more effective because they can be applied to all forms of Internet communication, including e-mail, not just communications available via the World Wide Web.

" . . .

---

[a] The Government lost again on the further remand, see ACLU v. Mukasey, 534 F.3d 181 (3rd Cir. 2008), and the Supreme Court denied certiorari on January 21, 2009.

"One argument to the contrary is worth mentioning— . . . that filtering software is not an available alternative because Congress may not require it to be used. That argument carries little weight, because Congress undoubtedly may act to encourage the use of filters. We have held that Congress can give strong incentives to schools and libraries to use them. It could also take steps to promote their development by industry, and their use by parents. It is incorrect, for that reason, to say that filters are part of the current regulatory status quo. . . . By enacting programs to promote use of filtering software, Congress could give parents that ability without subjecting protected speech to severe penalties.

"The closest precedent on the general point is . . . *Playboy Entertainment Group*[, which], like this case, involved a content-based restriction designed to protect minors from viewing harmful materials. The choice was between a blanket speech restriction and a more specific technological solution that was available to parents who chose to implement it. . . . Absent a showing that the proposed less restrictive alternative would not be as effective, we concluded, the more restrictive option preferred by Congress could not survive strict scrutiny. . . . In the instant case, too, the Government has failed to show, at this point, that the proposed less restrictive alternative will be less effective. . . ."

The majority also found "important practical reasons to let the injunction stand pending a full trial on the merits[,]" including changes in the "legal landscape" since "the District Court entered its findings[,]" including the report of "a congressionally appointed commission . . . that found that filters are more effective than verification screens" and "two further statutes that might qualify as less restrictive alternatives to COPA—a prohibition on misleading domain names, and a statute creating a minors-safe 'Dot Kids' domain."

Justice Stevens, joined by Justice Ginsburg, concurred, emphasizing "that, as far as the record reveals, encouraging deployment of user-based controls, such as filtering software, would serve Congress' interest in protecting minors from sexually explicit Internet materials as well or better than attempting to regulate the vast content of the World Wide Web at its source, and at a far less significant cost to First Amendment values."

Justice Scalia's dissent found strict scrutiny inappropriate for "the type of material covered by COPA" and reiterated his view that "[s]ince this business could, consistent with the First Amendment, be banned entirely, COPA's lesser restrictions raise no constitutional concern." Justice Breyer's dissent, joined by Chief Justice Rehnquist and Justice O'Connor, first argued that COPA "imposes a burden on protected speech that is no more than modest"; regulates "material that does not enjoy First Amendment protection, namely legally obscene material, and very little more"; and "does not censor the material it covers. Rather, it requires providers of the 'harmful to minors' material to restrict minors' access to it by verifying age . . . [through] using a credit card, adult personal identification number, or other similar technology." He continued:

". . . [D]espite strict requirements that identifying information be kept confidential, . . . the identification requirements inherent in age-screening may lead some users to fear embarrassment. Both monetary costs and potential embarrassment can deter potential viewers and, in that sense, the statute's requirements may restrict access to a site. But this Court has held that in the context of congressional efforts to protect children, restrictions of this kind do not automatically violate the Constitution. . . .

"In sum, the Act at most imposes a modest additional burden on adult access to legally obscene material, perhaps imposing a similar burden on access to some protected borderline obscene material as well."

Emphasizing that "[n]o one denies" that "protecting minors from exposure to commercial pornography" is a 'compelling interest,'" he addressed "whether the Act, given its restriction on adult access, significantly advances that interest." He argued that considering "the existence of 'blocking and filtering software' . . . as a 'less restrictive alternative' . . . is a misnomer":

". . . Conceptually speaking, the presence of filtering software is not an *alternative* legislative approach to the problem of protecting children from exposure to commercial pornography. Rather, it is part of the status quo, *i.e.,* the backdrop against which Congress enacted the present statute. It is always true, by definition, that the status quo is less restrictive than a new regulatory law. It is always less restrictive to do *nothing* than to do *something*. But 'doing nothing' does not address the problem Congress sought to address—namely that, despite the availability of filtering software, children were still being exposed to harmful material on the Internet.

"[T]he relevant constitutional question . . . posits a comparison of (a) a status quo that includes filtering software with (b) a change in that status quo that adds to it an age-verification screen requirement. . . .

". . . Filtering software, as presently available, does not solve the 'child protection' problem. It suffers from four serious inadequacies that prompted Congress to pass legislation instead of relying on its voluntary use." They are, first, that filtering still allows some pornographic material to pass through; second, that it costs around $40 to install, which not every family has; third, that its efficacy "depends upon parents willing to decide where their children will surf the Web and able to enforce that decision"—"not a reasonable possibility" for millions, given that many "children will spend afternoons and evenings with friends who may well have access to computers and more lenient parents"; and, fourth, that it blocks a great deal of valuable material.

American Booksellers Association, Inc. v. Hudnut

771 F.2d 323 (7th Cir.1985).

■ Before CUDAHY and EASTERBROOK, CIRCUIT JUDGES, and SWYGERT, SENIOR CIRCUIT JUDGE.

■ EASTERBROOK, CIRCUIT JUDGE.

Indianapolis enacted an ordinance defining "pornography" as a practice that discriminates against women. "Pornography" is to be redressed through the administrative and judicial methods used for other discrimination. The City's definition of "pornography" is considerably different from "obscenity," which the Supreme Court has held is not protected by the First Amendment.

To be "obscene" under Miller v. California, 413 U.S. 15 (1973), "a publication must, taken as a whole, appeal to the prurient interest, must contain patently offensive depictions or descriptions of specified sexual conduct, and on the whole have no serious literary, artistic, political, or scientific value." . . . Both offensiveness and an appeal to something other than "normal, healthy sexual desires" . . . are essential elements of "obscenity."

"Pornography" under the ordinance is "the graphic sexually explicit subordination of women, whether in pictures or in words, that also includes one or more of the following:

(1)   Women are presented as sexual objects who enjoy pain or humiliation; or

(2)   Women are presented as sexual objects who experience sexual pleasure in being raped; or

(3)   Women are presented as sexual objects tied up or cut up or mutilated or bruised or physically hurt, or as dismembered or truncated or fragmented or severed into body parts; or

(4)   Women are presented as being penetrated by objects or animals; or

(5)   Women are presented in scenarios of degradation, injury, abasement, torture, shown as filthy or inferior, bleeding, bruised, or hurt in a context that makes these conditions sexual; or

(6)   Women are presented as sexual objects for domination, conquest, violation, exploitation, possession, or use, or through postures or positions of servility or submission or display." . . .

The statute provides that the "use of men, children, or transsexuals in the place of women in paragraphs (1) through (6) above shall also constitute pornography under this section." The ordinance as passed in April 1984 defined "sexually explicit" to mean actual or simulated intercourse or the uncovered exhibition of the genitals, buttocks or anus. An amendment in June 1984 deleted this provision, leaving the term undefined.

The Indianapolis ordinance does not refer to the prurient interest, to offensiveness, or to the standards of the community. It demands attention to particular depictions, not to the work judged as a whole. It is irrelevant under the ordinance whether the work has literary, artistic, political, or scientific value. The City and many amici point to these omissions as virtues. They maintain that pornography influences attitudes, and the statute is a way to alter the socialization of men and women rather than to vindicate community standards of offensiveness. And as one of the principal drafters of the ordinance has asserted, "if a woman is subjected, why should it matter that the work has other value?" Catharine A. MacKinnon, Pornography, Civil Rights, and Speech, 20 Harv.Civ.Rts.—Civ.Lib.L.Rev. 1, 21 (1985).

Civil rights groups and feminists have entered this case as amici on both sides. Those supporting the ordinance say that it will play an important role in reducing the tendency of men to view women as sexual objects, a tendency that leads to both unacceptable attitudes and discrimination in the workplace and violence away from it. Those opposing the ordinance point out that much radical feminist literature is explicit and depicts women in ways forbidden by the ordinance and that the ordinance would reopen old battles. It is unclear how Indianapolis would treat works from James Joyce's *Ulysses* to Homer's *Iliad;* both depict women as submissive objects for conquest and domination.

We do not try to balance the arguments for and against an ordinance such as this. The ordinance discriminates on the ground of the content of the speech. Speech treating women in the approved way—in sexual encounters "premised on equality" (MacKinnon, supra, at 22)—is lawful no matter how sexually explicit. Speech treating women in the disapproved way—as submissive in matters sexual or as enjoying humiliation—is unlawful no matter how significant the literary, artistic, or political qualities of the work taken as a whole. The state may not ordain preferred viewpoints in this way. The Constitution forbids the state to declare one perspective right and silence opponents.

I

The ordinance contains four prohibitions. People may not "traffic" in pornography, "coerce" others into performing in pornographic works, or "force" pornography on anyone. Anyone injured by someone who has seen or read pornography has a right of action against the maker or seller.

Trafficking is defined in § 16–3(g)(4) as the "production, sale, exhibition, or distribution of pornography." The offense excludes exhibition in a public or educational library, but a "special display" in a library may be sex discrimination. Section 16–3(g)(4)(C) provides that the trafficking paragraph "shall not be construed to make isolated passages or isolated parts actionable."

"Coercion into pornographic performance" is defined in § 16–3(g)(5) as "[c]oercing, intimidating or fraudulently inducing any person . . . into performing for pornography. . . ." The ordinance specifies that proof of any of the following "shall not constitute a defense: I. That the person is a woman; . . . VI. That the person has previously posed for sexually explicit pictures . . . with anyone . . . ; . . . VIII. That the person actually consented to a use of the performance that is changed into pornography; . . . IX. That the person knew that the purpose of the acts or events in question was to make pornography; . . . XI. That the person signed a contract, or made statements affirming a willingness to cooperate in the production of pornography; XII. That no physical force, threats, or weapons were used in the making of the pornography; or XIII. That the person was paid or otherwise compensated."

"Forcing pornography on a person," according to § 16–3(g)(5), is the "forcing of pornography on any woman, man, child, or transsexual in any place of employment, in education, in a home, or in any public place." The statute does not define forcing, but one of its authors states that the definition reaches pornography shown to medical students as part of their education or given to language students for translation. MacKinnon, supra, at 40–41.

Section 16–3(g)(7) defines as a prohibited practice the "assault, physical attack, or injury of any woman, man, child, or transsexual in a way that is directly caused by specific pornography."

For purposes of all four offenses, it is generally "not . . . a defense that the respondent did not know or intend that the materials were pornography. . . ." Section 16–3(g)(8). But the ordinance provides that damages are unavailable in trafficking cases unless the complainant proves "that the respondent knew or had reason to know that the materials were pornography." It is a complete defense to a trafficking case that all of the materials in question were pornography only by virtue of category (6) of the definition of pornography. In cases of assault caused by pornography, those who seek damages from "a seller, exhibitor or distributor" must show that the defendant knew or had reason to know of the material's status as pornography. By implication, those who seek damages from an author need not show this.

A woman aggrieved by trafficking in pornography may file a complaint "as a woman acting against the subordination of women" with the office of equal opportunity. Section 16–17(b). A man, child, or transsexual also may protest trafficking "but must prove injury in the same way that a woman is injured. . . ." Ibid. Subsection (a) also provides, however, that "any person claiming to be aggrieved" by trafficking, coercion, forcing, or assault may complain against the "perpetrators." We need not decide whether § 16–17(b) qualifies the right of action in § 16–17(a).

. . .

The district court held the ordinance unconstitutional. . . .

II

The plaintiffs are a congeries of distributors and readers of books, magazines, and films. The American Booksellers Association comprises about 5,200 bookstores and chains. The Association for American Publishers includes most of the country's publishers. Video Shack, Inc., sells and rents video cassettes in Indianapolis. Kelly Bentley, a resident of Indianapolis, reads books and watches films. There are many more plaintiffs. Collectively the plaintiffs (or their members, whose interest they represent) make, sell, or read just about every kind of material that could be affected by the ordinance, from hard-core films to W.B. Yeats's poem "Leda and the Swan" (from the myth of Zeus in the form of a swan impregnating an apparently subordinate Leda), to the collected works of James Joyce, D.H. Lawrence, and John Cleland.

. . .

III

"If there is any fixed star in our constitutional constellation, it is that no official, high or petty, can prescribe what shall be orthodox in politics, nationalism, religion, or other matters of opinion or force citizens to confess by word or act their faith therein." West Virginia State Board of Education v. Barnette, 319 U.S. 624, 642 (1943). Under the First Amendment the government must leave to the people the evaluation of ideas. Bald or subtle, an idea is as powerful as the audience allows it to be. A belief may be pernicious—the beliefs of Nazis led to the death of millions, those of the Klan to the repression of millions. A pernicious belief may prevail. Totalitarian governments today rule much of the planet, practicing suppression of billions and spreading dogma that may enslave others. One of the things that separates our society from theirs is our absolute right to propagate opinions that the government finds wrong or even hateful.

. . .

Under the ordinance graphic sexually explicit speech is "pornography" or not depending on the perspective the author adopts. Speech that "subordinates" women and also, for example, presents women as enjoying pain, humiliation, or rape, or even simply presents women in "positions of servility or submission or display" is forbidden, no matter how great the literary or political value of the work taken as a whole. Speech that portrays women in positions of equality is lawful, no matter how graphic the sexual content. This is thought control. It establishes an "approved" view of women, of how they may react to sexual encounters, of how the sexes may relate to each other. Those who espouse the approved view may use sexual images; those who do not, may not.

Indianapolis justifies the ordinance on the ground that pornography affects thoughts. Men who see women depicted as subordinate are more likely to treat them so. Pornography is an aspect of dominance. It does not persuade people so much as change them. It works by socializing, by establishing the expected and the permissible. In this view pornography is not an idea; pornography is the injury. There is much to this perspective. Beliefs are also facts. People often act in accordance with the images and patterns they find around them. People raised in a religion tend to accept the tenets of that religion, often without independent examination. People taught from birth that black people are fit only for slavery rarely rebelled against that creed; beliefs coupled with the self-interest of the masters established a social structure that inflicted great harm while enduring for centuries. Words and images act at the level of the subconscious before they persuade at the level of the conscious. Even the truth has little chance unless a statement fits within the framework of beliefs that may never have been subjected to rational study.

Therefore we accept the premises of this legislation. Depictions of subordination tend to perpetuate subordination. The subordinate status of women in turn leads to affront and lower pay at work, insult and injury at home, battery and rape on the streets. In the language of the legislature, "[p]ornography is central in creating and maintaining sex as a basis of discrimination. Pornography is a systematic practice of exploitation and subordination based on sex which differentially harms women. The bigotry and contempt it produces, with the acts of aggression it fosters, harm women's opportunities for equality and rights [of all kinds]." Indianapolis Code § 16–1(a)(2).

Yet this simply demonstrates the power of pornography as speech. All of these unhappy effects depend on mental intermediation. Pornography affects how people see the world, their fellows, and social relations. If pornography is what pornography does, so is other speech. . . . The Alien and Sedition Acts passed during the administration of John Adams rested on a sincerely held belief that disrespect for the government leads to social collapse and revolution—a belief with support in the history of many nations. Most governments of the world act on this empirical regularity, suppressing critical speech. In the United States, however, the strength of the support for this belief is irrelevant. . . .

Racial bigotry, anti-semitism, violence on television, reporters' biases—these and many more influence the culture and shape our socialization. None is directly answerable by more speech, unless that speech too finds its place in the popular culture. Yet all is protected as speech, however insidious. Any other answer leaves the government in control of all of the institutions of culture, the great censor and director of which thoughts are good for us.

Sexual responses often are unthinking responses, and the association of sexual arousal with the subordination of women therefore may have a substantial effect. But almost all cultural stimuli provoke unconscious responses. Religious ceremonies condition their participants. Teachers convey messages by selecting what not to cover; the implicit message about what is off limits or unthinkable may be more powerful than the messages for which they present rational argument. Television scripts contain unarticulated assumptions. People may be conditioned in subtle ways. If the fact that speech plays a role in a process of conditioning were enough to permit governmental regulation, that would be the end of freedom of speech.

It is possible to interpret the claim that the pornography is the harm in a different way. Indianapolis emphasizes the injury that models in pornographic films and pictures may suffer. The record contains materials depicting sexual torture, penetration of women by red-hot irons and the like. These concerns have nothing to do with written materials subject to the statute, and physical injury can occur with or without the "subordination" of women. As we discuss in Part IV, a state may make injury in the course of producing a film unlawful independent of the viewpoint expressed in the film.

The more immediate point, however, is that the image of pain is not necessarily pain. In *Body Double,* a suspense film directed by Brian DePalma, a woman who has disrobed and presented a sexually explicit display is murdered by an intruder with a drill. The drill runs through the woman's body. The film is sexually explicit and a murder occurs—yet no one believes that the actress suffered pain or died. In *Barbarella* a character played by Jane Fonda is at times displayed in sexually explicit ways and at times shown "bleeding, bruised, [and] hurt in a context that makes these conditions sexual"—and again no one believes that Fonda was actually tortured to make the film. In *Carnal Knowledge* a woman grovels to please the sexual whims of a character played by Jack Nicholson; no one believes that there was a real sexual submission, and the Supreme Court held the film protected by the First Amendment. Jenkins v. Georgia, 418 U.S. 153 (1974). And this works both ways. The description of women's sexual domination of men in *Lysistrata* was not real dominance. Depictions may affect slavery, war, or sexual roles, but a book about slavery is not itself slavery, or a book about death by poison a murder.

Much of Indianapolis's argument rests on the belief that when speech is "unanswerable," and the metaphor that there is a "marketplace of ideas" does not apply, the First Amendment does not apply either. The metaphor is honored; Milton's *Aeropagitica* and John Stewart Mill's *On Liberty* defend freedom of speech on the ground that the truth will prevail, and many of the most important cases under the First Amendment recite this position. The Framers undoubtedly believed it. As a general matter it is true. But the Constitution does not make the dominance of truth a necessary condition of freedom of speech. To say that it does would be to confuse an outcome of free speech with a necessary condition for the application of the amendment.

A power to limit speech on the ground that truth has not yet prevailed and is not likely to prevail implies the power to declare truth. . . . If the government may declare the truth, why wait for the failure of speech? Under the First Amendment, however, . . . the government may not restrict speech on the ground that in a free exchange truth is not yet dominant.

. . .

We come, finally, to the argument that pornography is "low value" speech, that it is enough like obscenity that Indianapolis may prohibit it. Some cases hold that speech far removed from politics and other subjects at the core of the Framers' concerns may be subjected to special regulation. E.g., FCC v. Pacifica Foundation, 438 U.S. 726 (1978); Young v. American Mini Theatres, Inc., 427 U.S. 50, 67–70 (1976) (plurality opinion); Chaplinsky v. New Hampshire, 315 U.S. 568, 571–72 (1942). These cases do not sustain statutes that select among viewpoints, however. In *Pacifica* the FCC sought to keep vile language off the air during certain times. The Court held that it may; but the Court would not have sustained a regulation prohibiting scatological descriptions of Republicans but not scatological descriptions of Democrats, or any other form of selection among viewpoints. . . .

At all events, "pornography" is not low value speech within the meaning of these cases. Indianapolis seeks to prohibit certain speech because it believes this speech influences social relations and politics on a grand scale, that it controls attitudes at home and in the legislature. This precludes a characterization of the speech as low value. True, pornography and obscenity have sex in common. But Indianapolis left out of its definition any reference to literary, artistic, political, or scientific value. The ordinance applies to graphic sexually explicit subordination in works great and small.[3] The Court sometimes balances the value of speech against the costs of its restriction, but it does this by category of speech and not by the content of particular works. . . . Indianapolis has created an approved point of view and so loses the support of these cases.

Any rationale we could imagine in support of this ordinance could not be limited to sex discrimination. Free speech has been on balance an ally of those seeking change. Governments that want stasis start by restricting speech. Culture is a powerful force of continuity; Indianapolis paints pornography as part of the culture of power. Change in any complex system ultimately depends on the ability of outsiders to challenge

---

[3]   Indianapolis briefly argues that Beauharnais v. Illinois, 343 U.S. 250 (1952), which allowed a state to penalize "group libel," supports the ordinance. In Collin v. Smith, 578 F.2d at 1205, we concluded that cases such as *New York Times v. Sullivan* had so washed away the foundations of *Beauharnais* that it could not be considered authoritative. If we are wrong in this, however, the case still does not support the ordinance. It is not clear that depicting women as subordinate in sexually explicit ways, even combined with a depiction of pleasure in rape, would fit within the definition of a group libel. The well received film Swept Away used explicit sex, plus taking pleasure in rape, to make a political statement, not to defame. Work must be an insult or slur for its own sake to come within the ambit of *Beauharnais,* and a work need not be scurrilous at all to be "pornography" under the ordinance.

accepted views and the reigning institutions. Without a strong guarantee of freedom of speech, there is no effective right to challenge what is.

IV

The definition of "pornography" is unconstitutional. No construction or excision of particular terms could save it. The offense of trafficking in pornography necessarily falls with the definition. . . .

. . . The district court came to the same conclusion. Its judgment is therefore

Affirmed.[a]

C. CONTROL OF "FIGHTING WORDS" AND OFFENSIVE SPEECH

Cantwell v. Connecticut

310 U.S. 296 (1940).

Cantwell, a member of the Jehovah's Witnesses, was engaged in proselytizing in the streets of New Haven. He was convicted of a common law breach of the peace based on a showing that he stopped two men in the street, asked, and received, permission to play an Anti-Catholic phonograph record. Both listeners were incensed by the contents of the record and were tempted to strike Cantwell unless he went away. On being told to be on his way he left their presence. The court reversed his conviction. Justice Roberts, speaking for the court, said, in part:

"The offense known as breach of the peace embraces a great variety of conduct destroying or menacing public order and tranquility. It includes not only violent acts but acts and words likely to produce violence in others. No one would have the hardihood to suggest that the principle of freedom of speech sanctions incitement to riot or that religious liberty connotes the privilege to exhort others to physical attack upon those belonging to another sect. When clear and present danger of riot, disorder, interference with traffic upon the public streets, or other immediate threat to public safety, peace, or order, appears, the power of the state to prevent or punish is obvious. Equally obvious is it that a state may not unduly suppress free communication of views, religious or other, under the guise of conserving desirable conditions. Here we have a situation analogous to a conviction under a statute sweeping in a great variety of conduct under a general and indefinite characterization, and leaving to the executive and judicial branches too wide a discretion in its application.

". . .

"We find in the instant case no assault or threatening of bodily harm, no truculent bearing, no intentional discourtesy, no personal abuse. On the contrary, we find only an effort to persuade a willing listener to buy a book or to contribute money in the interest of what Cantwell, however misguided others may think him, conceived to be true religion.

". . .

"Although the contents of the record not unnaturally aroused animosity, we think that, in the absence of a statute narrowly drawn to define and punish specific conduct as constituting a clear and present danger to a substantial interest of the State, the petitioner's communication, considered in the light of the constitutional guarantees,

---

[a] A concurrence by Judge Swygert is omitted. The decision was summarily affirmed by the Supreme Court without argument or opinion. (Chief Justice Burger, and Justices Rehnquist and O'Connor dissented, stating that the case should be set for argument.) 475 U.S. 1001 (1986).

raised no such clear and present menace to public peace and order as to render him liable to conviction of the common law offense in question."

Chaplinsky v. New Hampshire

315 U.S. 568 (1942).

Defendant, a Jehovah's Witness, got into an altercation on a public sidewalk with the city marshal of Rochester, New Hampshire, and allegedly told the officer: "you are a God damned racketeer" and a "damned fascist." Defendant was convicted under a statute forbidding a person to address "any offensive, derisive or annoying word to any other person who is lawfully in any street or other public place." The statute was construed by the state court to ban only "such words, as ordinary men know, are likely to cause a fight," thus to prohibit "the face-to-face words plainly likely to cause a breach of the peace by the addressee." Justice Murphy's opinion for the Court stated that fighting words—"those which by their very utterance inflict injury or tend to incite an immediate breach of the peace"—were not protected by the Constitution. A unanimous Court sustained the conviction.

Cohen v. California

403 U.S. 15, 91 S.Ct. 1780, 29 L.Ed.2d 284 (1971).

[Defendant was convicted of violating a California statute that prohibited "maliciously and willfully disturb[ing] the peace or quiet of any neighborhood or person" by "offensive conduct." In a Los Angeles courthouse corridor he had worn a jacket bearing the plainly visible words "Fuck the Draft." Women and children were present in the corridor. He testified that he wore the jacket as a means of informing the public of the depth of his feelings against the Vietnam war and the draft. In affirming, the California Court of Appeals held that "offensive conduct" means "behavior which has a tendency to provoke *others* to acts of violence or to in turn disturb the peace"; it was "certainly reasonably foreseeable" that defendant's conduct might cause others to commit an act of violence against defendant or attempt to forcibly remove his jacket.]

■ MR. JUSTICE HARLAN delivered the opinion of the Court.

. . .

. . . [A]s it comes to us, this case cannot be said to fall within those relatively few categories of instances where prior decisions have established the power of government to deal more comprehensively with certain forms of individual expression simply upon a showing that such a form was employed. This is not, for example, an obscenity case. Whatever else may be necessary to give rise to the States' broader power to prohibit obscene expression, such expression must be, in some significant way, erotic. . . . It cannot plausibly be maintained that this vulgar allusion to the Selective Service System would conjure up such psychic stimulation in anyone likely to be confronted with Cohen's crudely defaced jacket.

This Court has also held that the States are free to ban the simple use, without a demonstration of additional justifying circumstances, of so-called "fighting words," those personally abusive epithets which, when addressed to the ordinary citizen, are, as a matter of common knowledge, inherently likely to provoke violent reaction. Chaplinsky v. New Hampshire. . . . While the four-letter word displayed by Cohen in relation to the draft is not uncommonly employed in a personally provocative fashion, in this instance it was clearly not "directed to the person of the hearer." Cantwell v. Connecticut . . . No individual actually or likely to be present could reasonably have regarded the words on appellant's jacket as a direct personal insult. Nor do we have here an instance of the exercise of the State's police power to prevent a speaker from intentionally provoking a given group to hostile reaction. Cf. Feiner v. New York, 340 U.S. 315 (1951); Terminiello v. Chicago, 337 U.S. 1 (1949). There is . . . no showing that anyone who saw Cohen was in fact violently aroused or that appellant intended such a result.

Finally, in arguments before this Court much has been made of the claim that Cohen's distasteful mode of expression was thrust upon unwilling or unsuspecting viewers, and that the State might therefore legitimately act as it did in order to protect the sensitive from otherwise unavoidable exposure to appellant's crude form of protest. Of course, the mere presumed presence of unwitting listeners or viewers does not serve automatically to justify curtailing all speech capable of giving offense. . . . While this Court has recognized that government may properly act in many situations to prohibit intrusion into the privacy of the home of unwelcome views and ideas which cannot be totally banned from the public dialogue, e.g., Rowan v. Post Office Dept., 397 U.S. 728 (1970), we have at the same time consistently stressed that "we are often 'captives' outside the sanctuary of the home and subject to objectionable speech." Id., at 738. The ability of government, consonant with the Constitution, to shut off discourse solely to protect others from hearing it is, in other words, dependent upon a showing that substantial privacy interests are being invaded in an essentially intolerable manner. Any broader view of this authority would effectively empower a majority to silence dissidents simply as a matter of personal predilections.

In this regard, persons confronted with Cohen's jacket were in a quite different posture than, say, those subjected to the raucous emissions of sound trucks blaring outside their residences. Those in the Los Angeles courthouse could effectively avoid further bombardment of their sensibilities simply by averting their eyes. And while it may be that one has a more substantial claim to a recognizable privacy interest when walking through a courthouse corridor than, for example, strolling through Central Park, surely it is nothing like the interest in being free from unwanted expression in the confines of one's own home. . . . Given the subtlety and complexity of the factors involved, if Cohen's "speech" was otherwise entitled to constitutional protection, we do not think the fact that some unwilling "listeners" in a public building may have been briefly exposed to it can serve to justify this breach of the peace conviction where, as here, there was no evidence that persons powerless to avoid appellant's conduct did in fact object to it, and where that portion of the statute upon which Cohen's conviction rests evinces no concern, either on its face or as construed by the California courts, with the special plight of the captive auditor, but, instead, indiscriminately sweeps within its prohibitions all "offensive conduct" that disturbs "any neighborhood or person."

Against this background, the issue flushed by this case stands out in bold relief. It is whether California can excise, as "offensive conduct," one particular scurrilous epithet from the public discourse, either upon the theory of the court below that its use is inherently likely to cause violent reaction or upon a more general assertion that the States, acting as guardians of public morality, may properly remove this offensive word from the public vocabulary.

The rationale of the California court is plainly untenable. . . . We have been shown no evidence that substantial numbers of citizens are standing ready to strike out physically at whoever may assault their sensibilities with execrations like that uttered by Cohen. . . .

Admittedly, it is not so obvious that the First and Fourteenth Amendments must be taken to disable the States from punishing public utterance of this unseemly expletive in order to maintain what they regard as a suitable level of discourse within the body politic. We think, however, that examination and reflection will reveal the shortcomings of a contrary viewpoint.

. . .

Against this perception of the constitutional policies involved, we discern certain more particularized considerations that peculiarly call for reversal of this conviction. First, the principle contended for by the State seems inherently boundless. How is one to distinguish this from any other offensive word? . . . For, while the particular four-letter word being litigated here is perhaps more distasteful than most others of its genre, it is nevertheless often true that one man's vulgarity is another's lyric. Indeed, we think it is largely because governmental officials cannot make principled distinctions in this area that the Constitution leaves matters of taste and style so largely to the individual.

Additionally, we cannot overlook the fact, because it is well illustrated by the episode involved here, that much linguistic expression serves a dual communicative function: it conveys not only ideas capable of relatively precise, detached explication, but otherwise inexpressible emotions as well. In fact, words are often chosen as much for their emotive as their cognitive force. . . .

Finally, and in the same vein, we cannot indulge the facile assumption that one can forbid particular words without also running a substantial risk of suppressing ideas in the process. Indeed, governments might soon seize upon the censorship of particular words as a convenient guise for banning the expression of unpopular views. . . .

It is, in sum, our judgment that, absent a more particularized and compelling reason for its actions, the State may not, consistently with the First and Fourteenth Amendments, make the simple public display here involved of this single four-letter expletive a criminal offense. . . .

Reversed.[a]

■ MR. JUSTICE BLACKMUN, with whom THE CHIEF JUSTICE and MR. JUSTICE BLACK join.

I dissent. . . .

Cohen's absurd and immature antic, in my view, was mainly conduct and little speech. . . .

Snyder v. Phelps

562 U.S. 443 (2011).

Snyder, the father of a marine killed in Iraq, secured a multi-million dollar jury verdict for intentional infliction of emotional distress (IIED), intrusion upon seclusion, and civil conspiracy, based on picketing—in three public locations not far from his son's funeral—by members of the Westboro Baptist Church, who held signs such as "God Hates the USA/Thank God for 9/11," "America is Doomed," "Don't Pray for the USA," "Thank God for IEDs," "Thank God for Dead Soldiers," "Pope in Hell," "Priests Rape Boys," "God Hates Fags," "You're Going to Hell," and "God Hates You." The Supreme Court overturned these tort liability judgments in an opinion by Chief Justice Roberts that provided free speech protection to the picketing in a "narrow" holding "limited by the particular facts before us." The Chief Justice described those facts as follows:

---

[a]   See Cohen, *A Look Back at* Cohen v. California, 34 U.C.L.A.L.Rev. 1595 (1987).

"The church had notified the authorities in advance of its intent to picket at the time of the funeral, and the picketers complied with police instructions in staging their demonstration. The picketing took place within a 10-by 25-foot plot of public land adjacent to a public street, behind a temporary fence. . . . That plot was approximately 1,000 feet from the church where the funeral was held. Several buildings separated the picket site from the church. . . . The Westboro picketers displayed their signs for about 30 minutes before the funeral began and sang hymns and recited Bible verses. None of the picketers entered church property or went to the cemetery. They did not yell or use profanity, and there was no violence associated with the picketing. . . .

"The funeral procession passed within 200 to 300 feet of the picket site. Although Snyder testified that he could see the tops of the picket signs as he drove to the funeral, he did not see what was written on the signs until later that night, while watching a news broadcast covering the event."

The Court's legal analysis stated in relevant part:

"To succeed on a claim for intentional infliction of emotional distress in Maryland, a plaintiff must demonstrate that the defendant intentionally or recklessly engaged in extreme and outrageous conduct that caused the plaintiff to suffer severe emotional distress. . . .

"Whether the First Amendment prohibits holding Westboro liable for its speech in this case turns largely on whether that speech is of public or private concern, as determined by all the circumstances of the case. . . .

". . . [W]here matters of purely private significance are at issue, First Amendment protections are often less rigorous[,] . . . because restricting speech on purely private matters does not implicate the same constitutional concerns as limiting speech on matters of public interest: '[T]here is no threat to the free and robust debate of public issues; there is no potential interference with a meaningful dialogue of ideas'; and the 'threat of liability' does not pose the risk of 'a reaction of self-censorship' on matters of public import. . . .

"We . . . have articulated some guiding . . . principles that accord broad protection to speech [on matters of public concern] to ensure that courts themselves do not become inadvertent censors.

"Speech deals with matters of public concern when it can 'be fairly considered as relating to any matter of political, social, or other concern to the community,' Connick, . . . or when it "is a subject of legitimate news interest; that is, a subject of general interest and of value and concern to the public,". . . . The arguably 'inappropriate or controversial character of a statement is irrelevant to the question whether it deals with a matter of public concern.' Rankin v. McPherson, 483 U.S. 378, 387 (1987).

". . .

"Deciding whether speech is of public or private concern requires us to examine the ' "content, form, and context" ' of that speech, ' "as revealed by the whole record." ' . . . In considering content, form, and context, no factor is dispositive, and it is necessary to evaluate all the circumstances of the speech, including what was said, where it was said, and how it was said.

"The 'content' of Westboro's signs plainly relates to broad issues of interest to society at large, rather than matters of 'purely private concern.' . . . While [the] messages [on the placards] may fall short of refined social or political commentary, the issues they highlight—the political and moral conduct of the United States and its citizens, the fate of our Nation, homosexuality in the military, and scandals involving the Catholic clergy—are matters of public import. The signs certainly convey Westboro's position on those issues, in a manner designed, unlike the private speech in

Dun & Bradstreet, to reach as broad a public audience as possible. And even if a few of the signs—such as 'You're Going to Hell' and 'God Hates You'—were viewed as containing messages related to Matthew Snyder or the Snyders specifically, that would not change the fact that the overall thrust and dominant theme of Westboro's demonstration spoke to broader public issues.

"Apart from the content of Westboro's signs, Snyder contends that the 'context' of the speech—its connection with his son's funeral—makes the speech a matter of private rather than public concern. The fact that Westboro spoke in connection with a funeral, however, cannot by itself transform the nature of Westboro's speech. . . .

". . . We are not concerned in this case that Westboro's speech on public matters was in any way contrived to insulate speech on a private matter from liability. Westboro had been actively engaged in speaking on the subjects addressed in its picketing long before it became aware of Matthew Snyder, and there can be no serious claim that Westboro's picketing did not represent its 'honestly believed' views on public issues. . . . There was no preexisting relationship or conflict between Westboro and Snyder that might suggest Westboro's speech on public matters was intended to mask an attack on Snyder over a private matter. . . .

". . .

"Westboro's choice to convey its views in conjunction with Matthew Snyder's funeral made the expression of those views particularly hurtful to many, especially to Matthew's father. The record makes clear that the applicable legal term—'emotional distress'—fails to capture fully the anguish Westboro's choice added to Mr. Snyder's already incalculable grief. But Westboro conducted its picketing peacefully on matters of public concern at a public place adjacent to a public street. Such space occupies a 'special position in terms of First Amendment protection.' . . .

". . . Westboro's choice of where and when to conduct its picketing is not beyond the Government's regulatory reach—it is 'subject to reasonable time, place, or manner restrictions' that are consistent with the standards announced in this Court's precedents. . . . Maryland now has a law imposing restrictions on funeral picketing, . . . as do 43 other States and the Federal Government. . . . To the extent these laws are content neutral, they raise very different questions from the tort verdict at issue in this case. . . .

". . .

"The record confirms that any distress occasioned by Westboro's picketing turned on the content and viewpoint of the message conveyed, rather than any interference with the funeral itself. A group of parishioners standing at the very spot where Westboro stood, holding signs that said 'God Bless America' and 'God Loves You,' would not have been subjected to liability. It was what Westboro said that exposed it to tort damages.

". . . Westboro's speech . . . cannot be restricted simply because it is upsetting or arouses contempt. . . .

"The jury here was instructed that it could hold Westboro liable for intentional infliction of emotional distress based on a finding that Westboro's picketing was 'outrageous.' 'Outrageousness,' however, is a highly malleable standard with 'an inherent subjectiveness about it which would allow a jury to impose liability on the basis of the jurors' tastes or views, or perhaps on the basis of their dislike of a particular expression.' . . . Such a risk is unacceptable; 'In public debate [we] must tolerate insulting, and even outrageous, speech in order to provide adequate "breathing space" to the freedoms protected by the First Amendment.' What Westboro said, in the whole context of how and where it chose to say it, is entitled to 'special protection' under the First Amendment, and that protection cannot be overcome by a jury finding that the picketing was outrageous.

"For all these reasons, the jury verdict imposing tort liability on Westboro for intentional infliction of emotional distress must be set aside."

With respect to the intrusion upon seclusion claim, Snyder argued "that even assuming Westboro's speech is entitled to First Amendment protection generally, the church is not immunized from liability . . . because Snyder was a member of a captive audience at his son's funeral." The Court disagreed, stating that "[a]s a general matter, we have applied the captive audience doctrine only sparingly to protect unwilling listeners from protected speech."

". . . Westboro stayed well away from the memorial service. Snyder could see no more than the tops of the signs when driving to the funeral. And there is no indication that the picketing in any way interfered with the funeral service itself. We decline to expand the captive audience doctrine to the circumstances presented here.

"Because we find that the First Amendment bars Snyder from recovery for intentional infliction of emotional distress or intrusion upon seclusion—the alleged unlawful activity Westboro conspired to accomplish—we must likewise hold that Snyder cannot recover for civil conspiracy based on those torts."

Justice Breyer's concurring opinion contained this observation:

"As I understand the Court's opinion, it does not hold or imply that the State is always powerless to provide private individuals with necessary protection. Rather, the Court has reviewed the underlying facts in detail . . . To uphold the application of state law in these circumstances would punish Westboro for seeking to communicate its views on matters of public concern without proportionately advancing the State's interest in protecting its citizens against severe emotional harm. Consequently, the First Amendment protects Westboro. As I read the Court's opinion, it holds no more."

Justice Alito's lone dissent objected that "our profound national commitment to free and open debate is not a license for the vicious verbal assault that occurred in this case" and that it does not follow from the need to protect robust, caustic public debate that the church members "may intentionally inflict severe emotional injury on private persons at a time of intense emotional sensitivity by launching vicious verbal attacks that make no contribution to public debate." He asserted that "although this Court has not decided the question, I think it is clear that the First Amendment does not entirely preclude liability for the intentional infliction of emotional distress by means of speech." He observed that Westboro has adopted a strategy of choosing outrageous occasions for its protests and has issued press releases in advance to ensure public attention. "This strategy works because it is expected that respondents' verbal assaults will wound the family and friends of the deceased and because the media is irresistibly drawn to the sight of persons who are visibly in grief. The more outrageous the funeral protest, the more publicity the Westboro Baptist Church is able to obtain." Moreover, because they "chose to stage their protest at Matthew Snyder's funeral and not at any of the other countless available venues, a reasonable person would have assumed that there was a connection between the messages on the placards and the deceased. And some of the "signs would most naturally have been understood as suggesting—falsely—that Matthew was gay." Justice Alito wrote further:

"[I]t is abundantly clear that respondents, going far beyond commentary on matters of public concern, specifically attacked Matthew Snyder because (1) he was a Catholic and (2) he was a member of the United States military. Both Matthew and petitioner were private figures, and this attack was not speech on a matter of public concern. While commentary on the Catholic Church or the United States military constitutes speech on matters of public concern, speech regarding Matthew Snyder's purely private conduct does not.

"...

"I have attempted to show [that] respondents' attack on Matthew was of central importance. But in any event, I fail to see why actionable speech should be immunized simply because it is interspersed with speech that is protected. The First Amendment allows recovery for defamatory statements that are interspersed with nondefamatory statements on matters of public concern, and there is no good reason why respondents' attack on Matthew Snyder and his family should be treated differently.

"...

"... To be sure, statements made on a public street may be less likely to satisfy the elements of the IIED tort than statements made on private property, but there is no reason why a public street in close proximity to the scene of a funeral should be regarded as a free-fire zone in which otherwise actionable verbal attacks are shielded from liability. If the First Amendment permits the States to protect their residents from the harm inflicted by such attacks—and the Court does not hold otherwise—then the location of the tort should not be dispositive. . . . Neither classic 'fighting words' nor defamatory statements are immunized when they occur in a public place, and there is no good reason to treat a verbal assault based on the conduct or character of a private figure like Matthew Snyder any differently.

"...

"... [F]unerals are unique events at which special protection against emotional assaults is in order. . . . Exploitation of a funeral for the purpose of attracting public attention 'intrudes upon their . . . grief,' . . . and may permanently stain their memories of the final moments before a loved one is laid to rest. Allowing family members to have a few hours of peace without harassment does not undermine public debate. I would therefore hold that, in this setting, the First Amendment permits a private figure to recover for the intentional infliction of emotional distress caused by speech on a matter of private concern."

City of Houston, Texas v. Hill

482 U.S. 451, 107 S.Ct. 2502, 96 L.Ed.2d 398 (1987).

■ JUSTICE BRENNAN delivered the opinion of the Court.

This case presents the question whether a municipal ordinance that makes it unlawful to interrupt a police officer in the performance of his or her duties is unconstitutionally overbroad under the First Amendment.

I

. . .

. . . Hill observed a friend, Charles Hill, intentionally stopping traffic on a busy street, evidently to enable a vehicle to enter traffic. Two Houston police officers, one . . . named Kelley, approached Charles and began speaking with him. . . . Hill began shouting at the officers "in an admitted attempt to divert Kelley's attention from Charles Hill." Hill first shouted: "Why don't you pick on somebody your own size?" After Officer Kelley responded: "Are you interrupting me in my official capacity as a Houston police officer?" Hill then shouted: "Yes, why don't you pick on somebody my size?" Hill was arrested under Houston Code of Ordinances section 34–11(a) for "wilfully or intentionally interrupting a city policeman . . . by verbal challenge during an investigation." Charles Hill was not arrested. Hill was . . .acquitted . . . .

Code of Ordinances, City of Houston, Texas, § 34–11(a) (1984) reads:

"Sec. 34–11. Assaulting or interfering with policemen.

"(a) It shall be unlawful for any person to assault, strike or in any manner oppose, molest, abuse or interrupt any policeman in the execution of his duty, or any person summoned to aid in making an arrest."

Following his acquittal . . . , Hill [sued] seeking (1) a declaratory judgment that § 34–11(a) was unconstitutional both on its face and as it had been applied to him . . .

At trial, Hill introduced records provided by the City regarding both the frequency with which arrests had been made for violation of the ordinance and the type of conduct with which those arrested had been charged. He also introduced evidence and testimony concerning the arrests of several reporters under the ordinance. Finally, Hill introduced evidence regarding his own experience with the ordinance, under which he has been arrested four times since 1975, but never convicted.

The District Court held that Hill's evidence did not demonstrate that the ordinance had been unconstitutionally applied. . . .

. . . [T]he Court of Appeals, by a vote of 8–7, [reversed]. . . .

. . .

. . . We . . . affirm.

II

. . .

The City's principal argument is that the ordinance does not inhibit the exposition of ideas, and that it bans "core criminal conduct" not protected by the First Amendment. In its view, the application of the ordinance to Hill illustrates that the police employ it only to prohibit such conduct, and not "as a subterfuge to control or dissuade free expression." Since the ordinance is "content-neutral," and since there is no evidence that the City has applied the ordinance to chill particular speakers or ideas, the City concludes that the ordinance is not substantially overbroad.

We disagree with the city's characterization for several reasons. First, the enforceable portion of the ordinance deals not with core criminal conduct, but with speech. As the city has conceded, the language in the ordinance making it unlawful for any person to "assault" or "strike" a police officer is preempted by the Texas Penal Code. . . . Accordingly, the enforceable portion of the ordinance makes it "unlawful for any person to . . . in any manner oppose, molest, abuse or interrupt any policeman in the execution of his duty," and thereby prohibits verbal interruptions of police officers.

Second, contrary to the city's contention, the First Amendment protects a significant amount of verbal criticism and challenge directed at police officers. "Speech is often provocative and challenging. . . . [But it] is nevertheless protected against censorship or punishment, unless shown likely to produce a clear and present danger of a serious substantive evil that rises far above public inconvenience, annoyance, or unrest." Terminiello v. Chicago, 337 U.S. 1, 4 (1949). In *Lewis v. City of New Orleans,* . . . a municipal ordinance . . . made it a crime " 'for any person wantonly to curse or revile or to use obscene or opprobrious language toward or with reference to any member of the city police while in the actual performance of his duty.' " . . . We . . . invalidated the ordinance as facially overbroad. . . . Moreover, in a concurring opinion in *Lewis,* Justice Powell suggested that even the "fighting words" exception recognized in Chaplinsky v. New Hampshire . . . might require a narrower application in cases involving words addressed to a police officer, because "a properly trained officer may reasonably be expected to 'exercise a higher degree of restraint' than the average citizen, and thus be less likely to respond belligerently to 'fighting words.' " . . .

The Houston ordinance is much more sweeping than the municipal ordinance struck down in *Lewis*. It is not limited to fighting words nor even to obscene or opprobrious language, but prohibits speech that "in any manner . . . interrupt[s]" an officer. The Constitution does not allow such speech to be made a crime. The freedom of individuals verbally to oppose or challenge police action without thereby risking arrest is one of the principal characteristics by which we distinguish a free nation from a police state.

The city argues, however, that even if the ordinance encompasses some protected speech, its sweeping nature is both inevitable and essential to maintain public order. The City recalls this Court's observation in Smith v. Goguen, 415 U.S. 566, 581 (1974):

"There are areas of human conduct where, by the nature of the problems presented, legislatures simply cannot establish standards with great precision. Control of the broad range of disorderly conduct that may inhibit a policeman in the performance of his official duties may be one such area requiring as it does an on-the-spot assessment of the need to keep order."

The city further suggests that its ordinance is comparable to the disorderly conduct statute upheld against a facial challenge in Colten v. Kentucky, 407 U.S. 104 (1972).

This Houston ordinance, however, is not narrowly tailored to prohibit only disorderly conduct or fighting words, and in no way resembles the law upheld in *Colten*. Although we appreciate the difficulties of drafting precise laws, we have repeatedly invalidated laws that provide the police with unfettered discretion to arrest individuals for words or conduct that annoy or offend them. . . . In *Lewis*, Justice Powell elaborated the basis for our concern with such sweeping, dragnet laws:

"This ordinance, as construed by the Louisiana Supreme Court, confers on police a virtually unrestrained power to arrest and charge persons with a violation. . . . The present type of ordinance tends to be invoked only where there is no other valid basis for arresting an objectionable or suspicious person. The opportunity for abuse, especially where a statute has received a virtually open-ended interpretation, is self-evident."

. . .

Houston's ordinance criminalizes a substantial amount of constitutionally protected speech, and accords the police unconstitutional discretion in enforcement. The ordinance's plain language is admittedly violated scores of times daily, yet only some individuals—those chosen by the police in their unguided discretion—are arrested. . . . We conclude that the ordinance is substantially overbroad, and that the Court of Appeals did not err in holding it facially invalid.

. . .

IV

Today's decision reflects the constitutional requirement that, in the face of verbal challenges to police action, officers and municipalities must respond with restraint. We are mindful that the preservation of liberty depends in part upon the maintenance of social order. . . . But the First Amendment recognizes, wisely we think, that a certain amount of expressive disorder not only is inevitable in a society committed to individual freedom, but must itself be protected if that freedom would survive. We therefore affirm the judgment of the Court of Appeals.

It is so ordered.[a]

■ JUSTICE BLACKMUN, concurring.

I join the Court's opinion and its judgment except that I do not agree with any implication—if one exists—that Gooding v. Wilson, 405 U.S. 518 (1972), and Lewis v. City of New Orleans, 415 U.S. 130 (1974), are good law in the context of their facts, or that they lend any real support to the judgment under review in this case. . . .

■ JUSTICE POWELL, with whom JUSTICE O'CONNOR joins, and with whom THE CHIEF JUSTICE joins as to Parts I and II, and JUSTICE SCALIA joins as to Parts II and III, concurring in the judgment in part and dissenting in part.

. . . In my view, the Court should not have reached the merits of the constitutional claims, but instead should have certified a question to the Texas Court of Criminal Appeals. . . . Finally, although I agree that the ordinance as interpreted by the Court violates the Fourteenth Amendment, I write separately because I cannot join the Court's reasoning.

. . .

III

. . .

A

. . . Lewis v. City of New Orleans, 415 U.S. 130 (1974), is clearly distinguishable. . . . On its face, the New Orleans ordinance criminalizes only the use of language. . . . By contrast, the ordinance presented in this case could be applied to activity that involves no element of speech or communication. For example, the ordinance evidently would punish individuals who—without saying a single word—obstructed an officer's access to the scene of an ongoing public disturbance, or indeed the scene of a crime. Accordingly, I cannot agree with the Court that this ordinance punishes only speech.

. . . I have no doubt that a municipality constitutionally may punish an individual who chooses to stand near a police officer and persistently attempt to engage the officer in conversation while the officer is directing traffic at a busy intersection. Similarly, an individual, by contentious and abusive speech, could interrupt an officer's investigation of possible criminal conduct. A person observing an officer pursuing a person suspected of a felony could run beside him in a public street shouting at the officer. Similar tactics could interrupt a policeman lawfully attempting to interrogate persons believed to be witnesses to a crime.

. . .

B

Despite the concerns expressed above, I nevertheless agree that the ambiguous terms of this ordinance "confe[r] on police a virtually unrestrained power to arrest and charge persons with a violation. . . ." . . . The record contains a sampling of complaints filed under the ordinance in 1981 and 1982. People have been charged with such crimes as "Failure to remain silent and stationary," "Remaining," "Refusing to remain silent," and "Talking." . . . Although some of these incidents may have involved unprotected conduct, the vagueness of these charges suggests that, with respect to this ordinance, Houston officials have not been acting with proper sensitivity to the constitutional rights of their citizens. . . . Accordingly, I agree with the Court that the Houston ordinance is unconstitutional.

---

[a] A concurring statement by Justice Scalia is omitted.

. . . In view of the difficulty of drafting precise language that never restrains speech and yet serves the public interest, the attempts of States and municipalities to draft laws of this type should be accorded some leeway. . . . [I]t should be possible for the present ordinance to be reframed in a way that would limit the present broad discretion of officers and at the same time protect substantially the city's legitimate interests. For example, the ordinance could make clear that it applies to speech only if the purpose of the speech were to interfere with the performance by a police officer of his lawful duties. . . .

    . . .

■ CHIEF JUSTICE REHNQUIST, dissenting.

I join Parts I and II of Justice Powell's opinion concurring in the judgment in part and dissenting in part. I do not agree, however, that the Houston ordinance, in the absence of an authoritative construction by the Texas courts, is unconstitutional. . . .

Virginia v. Black

538 U.S. 343, 123 S.Ct. 1536, 155 L.Ed.2d 535 (2003).

■ JUSTICE O'CONNOR announced the judgment of the Court and delivered the opinion of the Court with respect to Parts I, II, and III, and an opinion with respect to Parts IV and V, in which THE CHIEF JUSTICE, JUSTICE STEVENS, and JUSTICE BREYER join.

In this case we consider whether the Commonwealth of Virginia's statute banning cross burning with "an intent to intimidate a person or group of persons" violates the First Amendment. Va.Code Ann. § 18.2–423 (1996). We conclude that while a State, consistent with the First Amendment, may ban cross burning carried out with the intent to intimidate, the provision in the Virginia statute treating any cross burning as prima facie evidence of intent to intimidate renders the statute unconstitutional in its current form.

I

Respondents Barry Black, Richard Elliott, and Jonathan O'Mara were convicted separately of violating Virginia's cross-burning statute, § 18.2–423. That statute provides:

"It shall be unlawful for any person or persons, with the intent of intimidating any person or group of persons, to burn, or cause to be burned, a cross on the property of another, a highway or other public place. Any person who shall violate any provision of this section shall be guilty of a Class 6 felony.

"Any such burning of a cross shall be prima facie evidence of an intent to intimidate a person or group of persons."

On August 22, 1998, Barry Black led a Ku Klux Klan rally in Carroll County, Virginia. Twenty-five to thirty people attended this gathering, which occurred on private property with the permission of the owner, who was in attendance. The property was located on an open field just off . . . State Highway 690 . . . in Cana, Virginia.

When the sheriff . . . learned that a Klan rally was occurring in his county, he went to observe it from the side of the road. During the approximately one hour that the sheriff was present, about 40 to 50 cars passed the site, a "few" of which stopped to ask the sheriff what was happening on the property. Eight to ten houses were located in the vicinity of the rally. Rebecca Sechrist . . . "sat and watched to see wha[t][was] going on" from the lawn of her in-laws' house. She looked on as the Klan prepared for the gathering and subsequently conducted the rally itself. During the rally, Sechrist heard Klan members speak about "what they were" and "what they believed in." The speakers "talked real bad about the blacks and the Mexicans." One speaker told the assembled gathering that "he would love to take a .30/.30 and just random[ly] shoot the blacks." The speakers also talked about "President Clinton and Hillary Clinton," and about how their tax money "goes to . . . the black people." Sechrist testified that this language made her "very . . . scared."

At the conclusion of the rally, the crowd circled around a 25-to 30-foot cross . . . between 300 and 350 yards away from the road. According to the sheriff, the cross "then all of a sudden . . . went up in a flame." As the cross burned, the Klan played Amazing Grace over the loudspeakers. Sechrist stated that the cross burning made her feel "awful" and "terrible."

. . . The sheriff . . . entered the rally, and asked "who was responsible for burning the cross." . . . Black responded, "I guess I am because I'm the head of the rally." . . .

Black was charged with burning a cross with the intent of intimidating a person or group of persons, in violation of § 18.2–423. At his trial, the jury was instructed that "intent to intimidate means the motivation to intentionally put a person or a group of persons in fear of bodily harm. Such fear must arise from the willful conduct of the accused rather than from some mere temperamental timidity of the victim." The trial court also instructed the jury that "the burning of a cross by itself is sufficient evidence from which you may infer the required intent." . . . The Court of Appeals of Virginia affirmed Black's conviction.

On May 2, 1998, respondents Richard Elliott and Jonathan O'Mara, as well as a third individual, attempted to burn a cross on the yard of James Jubilee. Jubilee, an African-American, was Elliott's next-door neighbor in Virginia Beach, Virginia. Four months prior to the incident, Jubilee and his family had moved from California to Virginia Beach. Before the cross burning, Jubilee spoke to Elliott's mother to inquire about shots being fired from behind the Elliott home. Elliott's mother explained to Jubilee that her son shot firearms as a hobby, and that he used the backyard as a firing range.

On the night of May 2, respondents drove a truck onto Jubilee's property, planted a cross, and set it on fire. Their apparent motive was to "get back" at Jubilee for complaining about the shooting in the backyard. Respondents were not affiliated with the Klan. The next morning, as Jubilee was pulling his car out of the driveway, he noticed the partially burned cross approximately 20 feet from his house. After seeing the cross, Jubilee was "very nervous" because he "didn't know what would be the next phase," and because "a cross burned in your yard . . . tells you that it's just the first round."

Elliott and O'Mara were charged with attempted cross burning and conspiracy to commit cross burning. O'Mara pleaded guilty to both counts, reserving the right to challenge the constitutionality of the cross-burning statute. The judge sentenced O'Mara to 90 days in jail and fined him $2,500. The judge also suspended 45 days of the sentence and $1,000 of the fine.

At Elliott's trial, the judge originally ruled that the jury would be instructed "that the burning of a cross by itself is sufficient evidence from which you may infer the required intent." At trial, however, the court instructed the jury that the Commonwealth must prove that "the defendant intended to commit cross burning," that "the defendant did a direct act toward the commission of the cross burning," and that "the defendant had the intent of intimidating any person or group of persons." . . . The jury found Elliott guilty of attempted cross burning and acquitted him of conspiracy to commit cross burning. It sentenced Elliott to 90 days in jail and a $2,500 fine. The Court of Appeals of Virginia affirmed the convictions of both Elliott and O'Mara.

Each respondent appealed to the Supreme Court of Virginia, arguing that § 18.2–423 is facially unconstitutional. The Supreme Court of Virginia . . . held that the statute is unconstitutional on its face. It held that the Virginia cross-burning statute "is analytically indistinguishable from the ordinance found unconstitutional in *R.A.V.* [*v. St. Paul,* 505 U.S. 377 (1992)]." . . .

. . .

II

. . .

Often, the Klan used cross burnings as a tool of intimidation and a threat of impending violence. . . .

. . .

Throughout the history of the Klan, cross burnings have also remained potent symbols of shared group identity and ideology. . . .

At Klan gatherings across the country, cross burning became the climax of the rally or the initiation. . . .

. . . In short, a burning cross has remained a symbol of Klan ideology and of Klan unity.

. . . [W]hile cross burning sometimes carries no intimidating message, at other times the intimidating message is the *only* message conveyed. For example, when a cross burning is directed at a particular person not affiliated with the Klan, the burning cross often serves as a message of intimidation, designed to inspire in the victim a fear of bodily harm. Moreover, the history of violence associated with the Klan shows that the possibility of injury or death is not just hypothetical. The person who burns a cross directed at a particular person often is making a serious threat, meant to coerce the victim to comply with the Klan's wishes unless the victim is willing to risk the wrath of the Klan. Indeed, as the cases of respondents Elliott and O'Mara indicate, individuals without Klan affiliation who wish to threaten or menace another person sometimes use cross burning because of this association between a burning cross and violence.

In sum, while a burning cross does not inevitably convey a message of intimidation, often the cross burner intends that the recipients of the message fear for their lives. And when a cross burning is used to intimidate, few if any messages are more powerful.

III

A

. . .

. . . The First Amendment permits "restrictions upon the content of speech in a few limited areas, which are 'of such slight social value as a step to truth that any benefit that may be derived from them is clearly outweighed by the social interest in order and morality.'" R.A.V. v. City of St. Paul, *supra,* at 382–383, (quoting Chaplinsky v. New Hampshire, [315 U.S. 568] at 572).

. . . [T]he First Amendment . . . permits a State to ban a "true threat." . . . ("[T]hreats of violence are outside the First Amendment"); Madsen v. Women's Health Center, Inc., 512 U.S. 753 (1994); Schenck v. Pro-Choice Network of Western N. Y., 519 U.S. 357, 373 (1997).

"True threats" encompass those statements where the speaker means to communicate a serious expression of an intent to commit an act of unlawful violence to a particular individual or group of individuals.... The speaker need not actually intend to carry out the threat. Rather, a prohibition on true threats "protect[s] individuals from the fear of violence" and "from the disruption that fear engenders," in addition to protecting people "from the possibility that the threatened violence will occur." ... Intimidation in the constitutionally proscribable sense of the word is a type of true threat, where a speaker directs a threat to a person or group of persons with the intent of placing the victim in fear of bodily harm or death. Respondents do not contest that some cross burnings fit within this meaning of intimidating speech, and rightly so. As noted in Part II, *supra,* the history of cross burning in this country shows that cross burning is often intimidating, intended to create a pervasive fear in victims that they are a target of violence.

B

... It is true, as the Supreme Court of Virginia held, that the burning of a cross is symbolic expression. The reason why the Klan burns a cross at its rallies, or individuals place a burning cross on someone else's lawn, is that the burning cross represents the message that the speaker wishes to communicate. Individuals burn crosses as opposed to other means of communication because cross burning carries a message in an effective and dramatic manner.

The fact that cross burning is symbolic expression, however, does not resolve the constitutional question. The Supreme Court of Virginia relied upon R.A.V. v. City of St. Paul, *supra,* to conclude that once a statute discriminates on the basis of this type of content, the law is unconstitutional. We disagree.

In *R.A.V.,* we held that a local ordinance that banned certain symbolic conduct, including cross burning, when done with the knowledge that such conduct would " 'arouse anger, alarm or resentment in others on the basis of race, color, creed, religion or gender' " was unconstitutional ... We held that the ordinance did not pass constitutional muster because it discriminated on the basis of content by targeting only those individuals who "provoke violence" on a basis specified in the law.... The ordinance did not cover "[t]hose who wish to use 'fighting words' in connection with other ideas—to express hostility, for example, on the basis of political affiliation, union membership, or homosexuality." ... This content-based discrimination was unconstitutional because it allowed the city "to impose special prohibitions on those speakers who express views on disfavored subjects." ...

We did not hold in *R.A.V.* that the First Amendment prohibits *all* forms of content-based discrimination within a proscribable area of speech. Rather, we specifically stated that some types of content discrimination did not violate the First Amendment:

"When the basis for the content discrimination consists entirely of the very reason the entire class of speech at issue is proscribable, no significant danger of idea or viewpoint discrimination exists. Such a reason, having been adjudged neutral enough to support exclusion of the entire class of speech from First Amendment protection, is also neutral enough to form the basis of distinction within the class." ...

Indeed, we noted that it would be constitutional to ban only a particular type of threat: "[T]he Federal Government can criminalize only those threats of violence that are directed against the President ... since the reasons why threats of violence are outside the First Amendment ... have special force when applied to the person of the President." ... And a State may "choose to prohibit only that obscenity which is the most patently offensive *in its prurience—i.e.,* that which involves the most lascivious displays of sexual activity." ... Consequently, while the holding of *R.A.V.* does not permit a State to ban only obscenity based on "offensive *political* messages," or "only those threats against the President that mention his policy on aid to inner cities," the First Amendment permits content discrimination "based on the very reasons why the particular class of speech at issue . . . is proscribable," . . .

Similarly, Virginia's statute does not run afoul of the First Amendment insofar as it bans cross burning with intent to intimidate. Unlike the statute at issue in *R.A.V.*, the Virginia statute does not single out for opprobrium only that speech directed toward "one of the specified disfavored topics." . . . It does not matter whether an individual burns a cross with intent to intimidate because of the victim's race, gender, or religion, or because of the victim's "political affiliation, union membership, or homosexuality." Moreover, as a factual matter it is not true that cross burners direct their intimidating conduct solely to racial or religious minorities. . . . Indeed, in the case of Elliott and O'Mara, it is at least unclear whether the respondents burned a cross due to racial animus. . . .

The First Amendment permits Virginia to outlaw cross burnings done with the intent to intimidate because burning a cross is a particularly virulent form of intimidation. Instead of prohibiting all intimidating messages, Virginia may choose to regulate this subset of intimidating messages in light of cross burning's long and pernicious history as a signal of impending violence. Thus, just as a State may regulate only that obscenity which is the most obscene due to its prurient content, so too may a State choose to prohibit only those forms of intimidation that are most likely to inspire fear of bodily harm. A ban on cross burning carried out with the intent to intimidate is fully consistent with our holding in *R.A.V.* and is proscribable under the First Amendment.

IV

The Supreme Court of Virginia ruled in the alternative that Virginia's cross-burning statute was unconstitutionally overbroad due to its provision stating that "[a]ny such burning of a cross shall be prima facie evidence of an intent to intimidate a person or group of persons." . . . In this Court, as in the Supreme Court of Virginia, respondents do not argue that the prima facie evidence provision is unconstitutional as applied to any one of them. Rather, they contend that the provision is unconstitutional on its face.

The Supreme Court of Virginia has not ruled on the meaning of the prima facie evidence provision. It has, however, stated that "the act of burning a cross alone, with no evidence of intent to intimidate, will nonetheless suffice for arrest and prosecution and will insulate the Commonwealth from a motion to strike the evidence at the end of its case-in-chief." The jury in the case of Richard Elliott did not receive any instruction on the prima facie evidence provision, and the provision was not an issue in the case of Jonathan O'Mara because he pleaded guilty. The court in Barry Black's case, however, instructed the jury that the provision means: "The burning of a cross, by itself, is sufficient evidence from which you may infer the required intent." . . .

The prima facie evidence provision, as interpreted by the jury instruction, renders the statute unconstitutional. Because this jury instruction is the Model Jury Instruction, and because the Supreme Court of Virginia had the opportunity to expressly disavow the jury instruction, the jury instruction's construction of the prima facie provision "is a ruling on a question of state law that is as binding on us as though the precise words had been written into" the statute. . . . As construed by the jury instruction, the prima facie provision strips away the very reason why a State may ban cross burning with the intent to intimidate. The prima facie evidence provision permits a jury to convict in every cross-burning case in which defendants exercise their constitutional right not to put on a defense. And even where a defendant like

Black presents a defense, the prima facie evidence provision makes it more likely that the jury will find an intent to intimidate regardless of the particular facts of the case. The provision permits the Commonwealth to arrest, prosecute, and convict a person based solely on the fact of cross burning itself.

It is apparent that the provision as so interpreted " 'would create an unacceptable risk of the suppression of ideas.' " . . . The act of burning a cross may mean that a person is engaging in constitutionally proscribable intimidation. But that same act may mean only that the person is engaged in core political speech. The prima facie evidence provision in this statute blurs the line between these two meanings of a burning cross. As interpreted by the jury instruction, the provision chills constitutionally protected political speech because of the possibility that a State will prosecute—and potentially convict—somebody engaging only in lawful political speech at the core of what the First Amendment is designed to protect.

As the history of cross burning indicates, a burning cross is not always intended to intimidate. Rather, sometimes the cross burning is a statement of ideology, a symbol of group solidarity. It is a ritual used at Klan gatherings, and it is used to represent the Klan itself. . . . Indeed, occasionally a person who burns a cross does not intend to express either a statement of ideology or intimidation. Cross burnings have appeared in movies such as Mississippi Burning, and in plays such as the stage adaptation of Sir Walter Scott's The Lady of the Lake.

The prima facie provision makes no effort to distinguish among these different types of cross burnings. It does not distinguish between a cross burning done with the purpose of creating anger or resentment and a cross burning done with the purpose of threatening or intimidating a victim. It does not distinguish between a cross burning at a public rally or a cross burning on a neighbor's lawn. It does not treat the cross burning directed at an individual differently from the cross burning directed at a group of like-minded believers. . . . I agree with Justice Souter that the prima facie evidence provision can "skew jury deliberations toward conviction in cases where the evidence of intent to intimidate is relatively weak and arguably consistent with a solely ideological reason for burning."

. . . The prima facie evidence provision in this case ignores all of the contextual factors that are necessary to decide whether a particular cross burning is intended to intimidate. The First Amendment does not permit such a shortcut.

For these reasons, the prima facie evidence provision, as interpreted through the jury instruction and as applied in Barry Black's case, is unconstitutional on its face. . . . Unlike Justice Scalia, we refuse to speculate on whether *any* interpretation of the prima facie evidence provision would satisfy the First Amendment. Rather, all we hold is that because of the interpretation of the prima facie evidence provision given by the jury instruction, the provision makes the statute facially invalid at this point. We also recognize the theoretical possibility that the court, on remand, could interpret the provision in a manner different from that so far set forth in order to avoid the constitutional objections we have described. We leave open that possibility. We also leave open the possibility that the provision is severable, and if so, whether Elliott and O'Mara could be retried under § 18.2–423.

V

With respect to Barry Black, we agree with the Supreme Court of Virginia that his conviction cannot stand, and we affirm the judgment of the Supreme Court of Virginia. With respect to Elliott and O'Mara, we vacate the judgment of the Supreme Court of Virginia, and remand the case for further proceedings.[a]

---

[a]   A concurring opinion by Justice Stevens is omitted.

. . .

■ JUSTICE SCALIA, with whom JUSTICE THOMAS joins as to Parts I and II, concurring in part, concurring in the judgment in part, and dissenting in part.

I agree with the Court that, under . . . R.A.V. v. St. Paul, 505 U.S. 377 (1992), a State may, without infringing the First Amendment, prohibit cross burning carried out with the intent to intimidate. . . . I write separately, however, to describe what I believe to be the correct interpretation of § 18.2–423, and to explain why I believe there is no justification for the plurality's apparent decision to invalidate that provision on its face.

I

. . .

The established meaning in Virginia . . . of the term "prima facie evidence" . . . is evidence that suffices, on its own, to establish a particular fact. But . . . this is true only to the extent that the evidence goes unrebutted. . . .

. . .

. . . [T]he Virginia Supreme Court did not suggest . . . that a jury may . . . ignore any rebuttal evidence that has been presented and, solely on the basis of a showing that the defendant burned a cross, find that he intended to intimidate. Nor, crucially, did that court say that the presentation of prima facie evidence is always sufficient to get a case to a jury . . . . [P]resentation of evidence that a defendant burned a cross in public view is automatically sufficient, on its own, to support an inference that the defendant intended to intimidate *only until* the defendant comes forward with some evidence in rebuttal.

II

The question presented, then, is whether, given this understanding of the term "prima facie evidence," the cross-burning statute is constitutional. . . .

. . . [O]ur overbreadth jurisprudence has consistently . . . inquired whether individuals who engage in protected conduct can be *convicted* under a statute, not whether they might be subject to arrest and prosecution. . . .

. . .

. . . [T]he plurality cannot claim that improper convictions will result from the operation of the prima-facie-evidence provision *alone*. As the plurality concedes, the only persons who might impermissibly be convicted by reason of that provision are those who adopt a particular trial strategy, to wit, abstaining from the presentation of a defense.

. . .

Conceding (quite generously, in my view) that this class of persons exists, it cannot possibly give rise to a viable facial challenge . . . . For this Court has emphasized repeatedly that "where a statute regulates expressive conduct, the scope of the statute does not render it unconstitutional unless its overbreadth is not only real, but *substantial* as well, judged in relation to the statute's plainly legitimate sweep." Osborne v. Ohio, 495 U.S. 103, 112 (1990). . . .

. . .

. . . [T]he plurality holds out the possibility that the Virginia Supreme Court will offer some saving construction of the statute. It should go without saying that if a saving construction of § 18.2–423 is possible, then facial invalidation is inappropriate. . . .

III

. . . [B]ecause the Virginia Supreme Court has not yet offered an authoritative construction of § 18.2–423, I concur in the Court's decision to vacate and remand . . . with respect to respondents Elliott and O'Mara. I also agree that respondent Black's conviction cannot stand. . . . Because I believe the constitutional defect in Black's conviction is rooted in a jury instruction and not in the statute itself, I would not dismiss the indictment and would permit the Commonwealth to retry Black . . . .

■ JUSTICE SOUTER, with whom JUSTICE KENNEDY and JUSTICE GINSBURG join, concurring in the judgment in part and dissenting in part.

I agree with the majority that the Virginia statute makes a content-based distinction within the category of punishable intimidating or threatening expression, the very type of distinction we considered in R.A.V. v. St. Paul, 505 U.S. 377 (1992). I disagree that any exception should save Virginia's law from unconstitutionality under the holding in *R.A.V.* or any acceptable variation of it.

I

. . .

. . . *R.A.V.* . . . [identified] an exception for content discrimination on a basis that "consists entirely of the very reason the entire class of speech at issue is proscribable." *R.A.V., supra,* at 388, 112 S.Ct. 2538. This is the exception the majority speaks of here as covering statutes prohibiting "particularly virulent" proscribable expression.

I do not think that the Virginia statute qualifies for this virulence exception as *R.A.V.* explained it. . . .

II

. . . I . . . read *R.A.V.* . . . as covering prohibitions that are not clearly associated with a particular viewpoint, and that are consequently different from the Virginia statute. . . .

III

. . . [N]o content-based statute should survive even under a pragmatic recasting of *R.A.V.* without a high probability that no "official suppression of ideas is afoot," *R.A.V., supra,* at 390. I believe the prima facie evidence provision stands in the way of any finding of such a high probability here.

. . .

As I see the likely significance of the evidence provision, its primary effect is to skew jury deliberations toward conviction in cases where the evidence of intent to intimidate is relatively weak and arguably consistent with a solely ideological reason for burning. . . . In such a case, if the factfinder is aware of the prima facie evidence provision, as the jury was in respondent Black's case, the provision will have the practical effect of tilting the jury's thinking in favor of the prosecution. What is significant is not that the provision permits a factfinder's conclusion that the defendant acted with proscribable and punishable intent without any further indication, because some such indication will almost always be presented. What is significant is that the provision will encourage a factfinder to err on the side of a finding of intent to intimidate when the evidence of circumstances fails to point with any clarity either to the criminal intent or to the permissible one. . . .

To the extent the prima facie evidence provision skews prosecutions, then, it skews the statute toward suppressing ideas. . . .

. . .

■ JUSTICE THOMAS, dissenting.

In every culture, certain things acquire meaning well beyond what outsiders can comprehend. That goes for both the sacred . . . and the profane. I believe that cross burning is the paradigmatic example of the latter.

I

. . . I believe that the majority errs in imputing an expressive component to the activity in question. In my view, whatever expressive value cross burning has, the legislature simply wrote it out by banning only intimidating conduct undertaken by a particular means. A conclusion that the statute prohibiting cross burning with intent to intimidate sweeps beyond a prohibition on certain conduct into the zone of expression overlooks not only the words of the statute but also reality.

A

. . .

. . . [T]he association between acts of intimidating cross burning and violence is well documented in recent American history. . . .

. . . [A] burning cross is now widely viewed as a signal of impending terror and lawlessness. . . .

In our culture, cross burning has almost invariably meant lawlessness and understandably instills in its victims well-grounded fear of physical violence.

B

. . .

It strains credulity to suggest that a state legislature that adopted a litany of segregationist laws self-contradictorily intended to squelch the segregationist message. . . . The ban on cross burning with intent to intimidate demonstrates that even segregationists understood the difference between intimidating and terroristic conduct and racist expression. It is simply beyond belief that, in passing the statute now under review, the Virginia legislature was concerned with anything but penalizing conduct it must have viewed as particularly vicious.

Accordingly, this statute prohibits only conduct, not expression. And, just as one cannot burn down someone's house to make a political point and then seek refuge in the First Amendment, those who hate cannot terrorize and intimidate to make their point. In light of my conclusion that the statute here addresses only conduct, there is no need to analyze it under any of our First Amendment tests.

II

Even assuming that the statute implicates the First Amendment, . . . the fact that the statute permits a jury to draw an inference of intent to intimidate from the cross burning itself presents no constitutional problems. Therein lies my primary disagreement with the plurality.

. . .

. . . Virginia law still requires the jury to find the existence of each element, including intent to intimidate, beyond a reasonable doubt.

. . .

D. REGULATION OF COMMERCIAL SPEECH

Virginia State Board of Pharmacy v. Virginia Citizens Consumer Council, Inc.

425 U.S. 748, 96 S.Ct. 1817, 48 L.Ed.2d 346 (1976).

■ MR. JUSTICE BLACKMUN delivered the opinion of the Court.

The plaintiff-appellees in this case attack, as violative of the First and Fourteenth Amendments, that portion of § 54–524.35 of Va.Code Ann. (1974), which provides that a pharmacist licensed in Virginia is guilty of unprofessional conduct if he "(3) publishes, advertises or promotes, directly or indirectly, in any manner whatsoever, any amount, price, fee, premium, discount, rebate or credit terms . . . for any drugs which may be dispensed only by prescription." The three-judge District Court declared the quoted portion of the statute "void and of no effect,". . . .

I.

. . .

Inasmuch as only a licensed pharmacist may dispense prescription drugs in Virginia, . . . advertising or other affirmative dissemination of prescription drug price information is effectively forbidden in the State. . . . The prohibition does not extend to nonprescription drugs, but neither is it confined to prescriptions that the pharmacist compounds himself. Indeed, about 95% of all prescriptions now are filled with dosage forms prepared by the pharmaceutical manufacturer.

II.

. . .

The present . . . attack on the statute is one made not by one directly subject to its prohibition, that is, a pharmacist, but by prescription drug consumers who claim that they would greatly benefit if the prohibition were lifted and advertising freely allowed. The plaintiffs are an individual Virginia resident who suffers from diseases that require her to take prescription drugs on a daily basis, and two nonprofit organizations. Their claim is that the First Amendment entitles the user of prescription drugs to receive information that pharmacists wish to communicate to them through advertising and other promotional means, concerning the prices of such drugs.

Certainly that information may be of value. Drug prices in Virginia, for both prescription and nonprescription items, strikingly vary from outlet to outlet even within the same locality. . . .

III.

The question first arises whether, even assuming that First Amendment protection attaches to the flow of drug price information, it is a protection enjoyed by the appellees as recipients of the information, and not solely, if at all, by the advertisers themselves who seek to disseminate that information.

Freedom of speech presupposes a willing speaker. But where a speaker exists, as is the case here, the protection afforded is to the communication, to its source and to its recipients both. This is clear from the decided cases. In Lamont v. Postmaster General, 381 U.S. 301 (1965), the Court upheld the First Amendment rights of citizens to receive political publications sent from abroad. More recently, in Kleindienst v. Mandel, 408 U.S. 753, 762–763 (1972), we acknowledged that this Court has referred to a First Amendment right to "receive information and ideas," and that freedom of speech "necessarily protects the right to receive." And in Procunier v. Martinez, 416 U.S. 396, 408–409 (1974), where censorship of prison inmates' mail was under examination, we thought it unnecessary to assess the First Amendment rights of the inmates themselves, for it was reasoned that such censorship equally infringed the rights of noninmates to whom the correspondence was addressed. . . . If there is a right to advertise, there is a reciprocal right to receive the advertising, and it may be asserted by these appellees.

IV.

The appellants contend that the advertisement of prescription drug prices is outside the protection of the First Amendment because it is "commercial speech." There can be no question that in past decisions the Court has given some indication that commercial speech is unprotected. In Valentine v. Chrestensen, [316 U.S. 52 (1942)], the Court upheld a New York statute that prohibited the distribution of any "handbill, circular . . . or other advertising matter whatsoever in or upon any street." The Court concluded that, although the First Amendment would forbid the banning of all communication by handbill in the public thoroughfares, it imposed "no such restraint on government as respects purely commercial advertising." . . . Further support for a "commercial speech" exception to the First Amendment may perhaps be found in Breard v. Alexandria, 341 U.S. 622 (1951), where the Court upheld a conviction for violation of an ordinance prohibiting door-to-door solicitation of magazine subscriptions. The Court reasoned: "The selling . . . brings into the transaction a commercial feature," and it distinguished *Martin v. Struthers,* . . . where it had reversed a conviction for door-to-door distribution of leaflets publicizing a religious meeting, as a case involving "no element of the commercial." . . .

. . .

Last Term, in Bigelow v. Virginia, 421 U.S. 809 (1975), the notion of unprotected "commercial speech" all but passed from the scene. . . .

Some fragment of hope for the continuing validity of a "commercial speech" exception arguably might have persisted because of the subject matter of the advertisement in *Bigelow.* We noted that in announcing the availability of legal abortions in New York, the advertisement "did more than simply propose a commercial transaction. It contained factual material of clear 'public interest.' " . . .

Here, in contrast, the question whether there is a First Amendment exception for "commercial speech" is squarely before us. Our pharmacist does not wish to editorialize on any subject, cultural, philosophical, or political. He does not wish to report any particularly newsworthy fact, or to make generalized observations even about commercial matters. The "idea" he wishes to communicate is simply this: "I will sell you the X prescription drug at the Y price." Our question, then, is whether this communication is wholly outside the protection of the First Amendment.

V.

. . .

If there is a kind of commercial speech that lacks all First Amendment protection . . . it must be distinguished by its content. Yet the speech whose content deprives it of protection cannot simply be speech on a commercial subject. No one would contend that our pharmacist may be prevented from being heard on the subject of whether, in general, pharmaceutical prices should be regulated, or their advertisement forbidden. Nor can it be dispositive that a commercial advertisement is noneditorial, and merely reports a fact. Purely factual matter of public interest may claim protection. . . .

Our question is whether speech which does "no more than propose a commercial transaction," . . . is so removed from any "exposition of ideas," Chaplinsky v. New Hampshire . . . that it lacks all protection. Our answer is that it is not.

Focusing first on the individual parties to the transaction that is proposed in the commercial advertisement, we may assume that the advertiser's interest is a purely economic one. That hardly disqualifies him for protection under the First Amendment. . . .

As to the particular consumer's interest in the free flow of commercial information, that interest may be as keen, if not keener by far, than his interest in the day's most urgent political debate. Appellees' case in this respect is a convincing one. Those whom the suppression of prescription drug price information hits the hardest are the poor, the sick, and particularly the aged. A disproportionate amount of their income tends to be spent on prescription drugs; yet they are the least able to learn, by shopping from pharmacist to pharmacist, where their scarce dollars are best spent. When drug prices vary as strikingly as they do, information as to who is charging what becomes more than a convenience. It could mean the alleviation of physical pain or the enjoyment of basic necessities.

Generalizing, society also may have a strong interest in the free flow of commercial information. Even an individual advertisement, though entirely "commercial," may be of general public interest. . . . Obviously, not all commercial messages contain the same or even a very great public interest element. There are few to which such an element, however, could not be added. Our pharmacist, for example, could cast himself as a commentator on store-to-store disparities in drug prices, giving his own and those of a competitor as proof. We see little point in requiring him to do so, and little difference if he does not.

. . . So long as we preserve a predominantly free enterprise economy, the allocation of our resources in large measure will be made through numerous private economic decisions. It is a matter of public interest that those decisions, in the aggregate, be intelligent and well informed. To this end, the free flow of commercial information is indispensable. . . . And if it is indispensable to the proper allocation of resources in a free enterprise system, it is also indispensable to the formation of intelligent opinions as to how that system ought to be regulated or altered. Therefore, even if the First Amendment were thought to be primarily an instrument to enlighten public decisionmaking in a democracy, we could not say that the free flow of information does not serve that goal.

Arrayed against these substantial individual and societal interests are a number of justifications for the advertising ban. These have to do principally with maintaining a high degree of professionalism on the part of licensed pharmacists. . . .

Price advertising, it is argued, will place in jeopardy the pharmacist's expertise and, with it, the customer's health. It is claimed that the aggressive price competition that will result from unlimited advertising will make it impossible for the pharmacist to supply professional services in the compounding, handling, and dispensing of prescription drugs. . . . Price advertising, it is said, will reduce the pharmacist's status to that of a mere retailer.

The strength of these proffered justifications is greatly undermined by the fact that high professional standards, to a substantial extent, are guaranteed by the close regulation to which pharmacists in Virginia are subject. And this case concerns the retail sale by the pharmacist more than it does his professional standards. Surely, any pharmacist guilty of professional dereliction that actually endangers his customer will promptly lose his license. At the same time, we cannot discount the Board's justifications entirely. The Court regarded justifications of this type sufficient to sustain the advertising bans challenged on due process and equal protection grounds in Head v. New Mexico Board, supra; Williamson v. Lee Optical Co., supra; and Semler v. Dental Examiners, supra.

The challenge now made, however, is based on the First Amendment. This casts the Board's justifications in a different light. . . .

. . .

There is, of course, an alternative to this highly paternalistic approach. That alternative is to assume that this information is not in itself harmful, that people will perceive their own best interests if only they are well enough informed, and that the best means to that end is to open the channels of communication rather than to close them. If they are truly open, nothing prevents the "professional" pharmacist from marketing his own assertedly superior product, and contrasting it with that of the low-cost, high-volume prescription drug retailer. But the choice among these alternative approaches is not ours to make or the Virginia General Assembly's. It is precisely this kind of choice, between the dangers of suppressing information, and the dangers of its misuse if it is freely available, that the First Amendment makes for us. Virginia is free to require whatever professional standards it wishes of its pharmacists; it may subsidize them or protect them from competition in other ways. . . . But it may not do so by keeping the public in ignorance of the entirely lawful terms that competing pharmacists are offering. In this sense, the justifications Virginia has offered for suppressing the flow of prescription drug price information, far from persuading us that the flow is not protected by the First Amendment, have reinforced our view that it is. We so hold.

VI.

In concluding that commercial speech, like other varieties, is protected, we of course do not hold that it can never be regulated in any way. Some forms of commercial speech regulation are surely permissible. We mention a few only to make clear that they are not before us and therefore are not foreclosed by this case.

There is no claim, for example, that the prohibition on prescription drug price advertising is a mere time, place, and manner restriction. We have often approved restrictions of that kind provided that they are justified without reference to the content of the regulated speech, that they serve a significant governmental interest, and that in so doing they leave open ample alternative channels for communication of the information. . . . Whatever may be the proper bounds of time, place, and manner restrictions on commercial speech, they are plainly exceeded by this Virginia statute, which singles out speech of a particular content and seeks to prevent its dissemination completely.

Nor is there any claim that prescription drug price advertisements are forbidden because they are false or misleading in any way. Untruthful speech, commercial or otherwise, has never been protected for its own sake. . . . Obviously, much commercial speech is not provably false, or even wholly false, but only deceptive or misleading. We foresee no obstacle to a State's dealing effectively with this problem.[24] The First

---

[24] In concluding that commercial speech enjoys First Amendment protection, we have not held that it is wholly undifferentiable from other forms. There are commonsense differences between speech that does "no more than propose a commercial transaction" . . . and other varieties. Even if the differences do not justify the conclusion that commercial speech is valueless, and thus subject to complete suppression by the State, they nonetheless suggest that a different degree of protection is necessary to insure that the flow of truthful and legitimate commercial information is unimpaired. The truth of commercial speech, for example, may be more easily verifiable by its disseminator than, let us say, news reporting or political commentary, in that ordinarily the advertiser seeks to disseminate information about a specific product or service that he himself provides and presumably knows more about than anyone else. Also, commercial speech may be more durable than other kinds. Since

Amendment, as we construe it today, does not prohibit the State from insuring that the stream of commercial information flows cleanly as well as freely. . . .

Also, there is no claim that the transactions proposed in the forbidden advertisements are themselves illegal in any way. . . .

What is at issue is whether a State may completely suppress the dissemination of concededly truthful information about entirely lawful activity, fearful of that information's effect upon its disseminators and its recipients. Reserving other questions, we conclude that the answer to this one is in the negative.

The judgment of the District Court is affirmed.

It is so ordered.

■ MR. JUSTICE STEVENS took no part in the consideration or decision of this case.

■ MR. CHIEF JUSTICE BURGER, concurring.

. . . Our decision today . . . deals largely with the State's power to prohibit pharmacists from advertising the retail price of *prepackaged* drugs. . . . [Q]uite different factors would govern were we faced with a law regulating or even prohibiting advertising by the traditional learned professions of medicine or law. . . .

. . .

■ MR. JUSTICE STEWART, concurring.

. . .

. . . [T]he Court's decision calls into immediate question the constitutional legitimacy of every state and federal law regulating false or deceptive advertising. I write separately to explain why I think today's decision does not preclude such governmental regulation. . . .

. . .

■ MR. JUSTICE REHNQUIST, dissenting.

The logical consequences of the Court's decision in this case, a decision which elevates commercial intercourse between a seller hawking his wares and a buyer seeking to strike a bargain to the same plane as has been previously reserved for the free marketplace of ideas, are far reaching indeed. Under the Court's opinion the way will be open not only for dissemination of price information but for active promotion of prescription drugs, liquor, cigarettes and other products the use of which it has previously been thought desirable to discourage. Now, however, such promotion is protected by the First Amendment so long as it is not misleading or does not promote an illegal product or enterprise. In coming to this conclusion, the Court has overruled a legislative determination that such advertising should not be allowed and has done so on behalf of a consumer group which is not directly disadvantaged by the statute in question. This effort to reach a result which the Court obviously considers desirable is a troublesome one, for two reasons. It extends standing to raise First Amendment claims beyond the previous decisions of this Court. It also extends the protection of

---

advertising is the sine qua non of commercial profits, there is little likelihood of its being chilled by proper regulation and foregone entirely.

Attributes such as these, the greater objectivity and hardiness of commercial speech, may make it less necessary to tolerate inaccurate statements for fear of silencing the speaker. . . . They may also make it appropriate to require that a commercial message appear in such a form, or include such additional information, warnings and disclaimers, as are necessary to prevent its being deceptive. . . . They may also make inapplicable the prohibition against prior restraints. . . .

that Amendment to purely commercial endeavors which its most vigorous champions on this Court had thought to be beyond its pale.

. . .

Attorney Advertising

Chief Justice Burger's attempt, in his concurrence, to distinguish prohibitions on professional advertising, proved to be unavailing. In Bates v. State Bar of Arizona, 433 U.S. 350 (1977), the Court held 5–4 that lawyers could not be prohibited from advertising the price of "routine legal services." In subsequent cases, a number of other lines have been drawn. The Court has distinguished between commercial solicitation and solicitation of legal employment by advocacy organizations. Ohralik v. Ohio State Bar Ass'n, 436 U.S. 447 (1978), sustained discipline of an attorney for personal solicitation of contingent fee employment, while In re Primus, 436 U.S. 412 (1978), reversed discipline of an ACLU lawyer. The Court noted that Primus' letter (offering legal assistance to a woman who had been sterilized as a condition of receiving welfare) came within the "generous zone of First Amendment protection reserved for associational freedom." The Court has also distinguished between in-person solicitation, involved in the *Ohralik* decision, and solicitation by advertisement and letter. In Zauderer v. Office of Disciplinary Counsel, 471 U.S. 626 (1985), the Court struck down a categorical prohibition of attorney advertising containing information or advice about legal problems. In *Shapero v. Kentucky Bar Ass'n,* 486 U.S. 466 (1988), the Court held that a state rule, prohibiting attorney mailings of advertisements "precipitated by a specific event . . . involving or relating to the addressee," was invalid. Both newspaper and direct mail advertising posed less risk of "overreaching or undue influence" than in-person solicitation.

The Court distinguished *Shapero* in Florida Bar v. Went For It, Inc., 515 U.S. 618 (1995). *Shapero* had dealt with a rule imposing a ban on direct mail solicitation "whatever the time frame and whoever the recipient." Justice O'Connor's opinion for the Court concluded that a rule forbidding solicitation of accident victims during a 30-day period after the accident was constitutional. "The Bar has substantial interest both in protecting injured Floridians from invasive conduct by lawyers and in preventing the erosion of confidence in the profession that such repeated invasions have engendered. . . . The palliative devised by the Bar to address these harms is narrow both in scope and in duration." Justice Kennedy's dissent, joined by Justices Stevens, Souter and Ginsburg, argued that the rule prejudiced accident victims "to vindicate the State's purported desire for more dignity in the legal profession."

The Court has been divided on the question whether the contents of particular lawyer-advertisements were misleading. In *Zauderer,* a majority concluded that advertising a contingent fee was misleading because there was no disclosure that clients could be liable for significant litigation costs. In *Shapero,* a plurality concluded that a letter sent to persons against whom foreclosure suits had been filed could not be prohibited merely because it liberally used underscored, uppercase letters (e.g., "Call *NOW,* don't wait. . . . Remember it is *FREE* and there is *NO* charge for calling.") or contained subjective predictions of customer satisfaction (e.g., "It may surprise you what I may be able to do for you.") In Ibanez v. Florida Department of Business and Professional Regulation, Board of Accountancy, 512 U.S. 136 (1994), a lawyer was also a state-licensed Certified Public Accountant and was authorized to use the designation "Certified Financial Planner" by the Certified Financial Planner Board of Standards, a private organization. The Court held that she could not be disciplined for referring to those two credentials in her yellow pages listing, on her business cards, and on her law offices stationery, because neither was false or misleading.

The Court distinguished CPAs from attorneys in Edenfield v. Fane, 507 U.S. 761 (1993). As noted, the Court had held in *Ohralik* that in-person solicitation by attorneys could be prohibited. In *Edenfield*, the Court concluded that a ban on in-person solicitation by accountants violated the First Amendment. While lawyers are trained in the art of persuasion, accountants are trained to emphasize independence and objectivity. Moreover, an accountant's typical potential client is an experienced business executive. Therefore, CPA solicitation is not "inherently conducive to overreaching."[a]

Overbreadth and Commercial Speech

Justice Blackmun, for the Court, in Bates v. State Bar, 433 U.S. 350, 379–381 (1977):

"In the usual case involving a restraint on speech, a showing that the challenged rule served unconstitutionally to suppress speech would end our analysis. In the First Amendment context, the Court has permitted attacks on overly broad statutes without requiring that the person making the attack demonstrate that in fact his specific conduct was protected. . . . Having shown that the disciplinary rule interferes with protected speech, appellants ordinarily could expect to benefit regardless of the nature of their acts.

"The First Amendment overbreadth doctrine, however, represents a departure from the traditional rule that a person may not challenge a statute on the ground that it might be applied unconstitutionally in circumstances other than those before the court. . . . The reason for the special rule in First Amendment cases is apparent: an overbroad statute might serve to chill protected speech. First Amendment interests are fragile interests, and a person who contemplates protected activity might be discouraged by the *in terrorem* effect of the statute. . . . Indeed, such a person might choose not to speak because of uncertainty whether his claim of privilege would prevail if challenged. The use of overbreadth analysis reflects the conclusion that the possible harm to society from allowing unprotected speech to go unpunished is outweighed by the possibility that protected speech will be muted.

"But the justification for the application of overbreadth analysis applies weakly, if at all, in the ordinary commercial context. . . . Since advertising is linked to commercial well-being, it seems unlikely that such speech is particularly susceptible to being crushed by overbroad regulation. . . . Moreover, concerns for uncertainty in determining the scope of protection are reduced; the advertiser seeks to disseminate information about a product or service that he provides, and presumably he can determine more readily than others whether his speech is truthful and protected. Ibid. Since overbreadth has been described by this Court as 'strong medicine,' which 'has been employed . . . sparingly and only as a last resort,' Broadrick v. Oklahoma, . . . we decline to apply it to professional advertising, a context where it is not necessary to further its intended objective."

---

[a] In Tennessee Secondary School Athletic Association v. Brentwood Academy, 551 U.S. 291 (2007), the Court unanimously rejected a first amendment challenge to an interscholastic athletic association rule prohibiting high school coaches from recruiting middle school athletes. The principal opinion by Justice Stevens spoke only for a plurality of four Justices, however, insofar as it relied on *Ohralik* in reasoning that "the dangers of undue influence and overreaching that exist when a lawyer chases an ambulance are also present when a high school coach contacts an eighth grader." Five Justices subscribed to Justice Kennedy's separate position disagreeing "with the principal opinion's reliance on *Ohralik*[,]" which "the Court has declined to extend . . . beyond the attorney-client relationship." He objected that "[t]o allow free-standing state regulation of speech by coaches and other representatives of nonmember schools would be a dramatic expansion of *Ohralik* to a whole new field of endeavor." Accordingly, he declined to join any portion of the principal opinion "that suggests *Ohralik* is applicable here."

Central Hudson Gas & Electric Corp. v. Public Service Commission

447 U.S. 557, 100 S.Ct. 2343, 65 L.Ed.2d 341 (1980).

■ Mr. Justice Powell delivered the opinion of the Court.

This case presents the question whether a regulation of the Public Service Commission of the State of New York violates the First and Fourteenth Amendments because it completely bans promotional advertising by an electrical utility.

I.

In December 1973, the Commission, appellee here, ordered electric utilities in New York State to cease all advertising that "promot[es] the use of electricity." The order was based on the Commission's finding that "the interconnected utility system in New York State does not have sufficient fuel stocks or sources of supply to continue furnishing all customer demands for the 1973–1974 winter."

Three years later, when the fuel shortage had eased, the Commission requested comments from the public on its proposal to continue the ban on promotional advertising. Central Hudson Gas & Electric Corp., the appellant in this case, opposed the ban on First Amendment grounds. After reviewing the public comments, the Commission extended the prohibition . . .

The Policy Statement divided advertising expenses "into two broad categories: promotional—advertising intended to stimulate the purchase of utility services—and institutional and informational, a broad category inclusive of all advertising not clearly intended to promote sales." The Commission declared all promotional advertising contrary to the national policy of conserving energy. It acknowledged that the ban is not a perfect vehicle for conserving energy. For example, the Commission's order prohibits promotional advertising to develop consumption during periods when demand for electricity is low. By limiting growth in "off-peak" consumption, the ban limits the "beneficial side effects" of such growth in terms of more efficient use of existing powerplants. And since oil dealers are not under the Commission's jurisdiction and thus remain free to advertise, it was recognized that the ban can achieve only "piecemeal conservationism." Still, the Commission adopted the restriction because it was deemed likely to "result in some dampening of unnecessary growth" in energy consumption.

The Commission's order explicitly permitted "informational" advertising designed to encourage *shifts* of consumption" from peak demand times to periods of low electricity demand. Informational advertising would not seek to increase aggregate consumption, but would invite a leveling of demand throughout any given 24-hour period. The agency offered to review "specific proposals by the companies for specifically described [advertising] programs that meet these criteria."

. . .

Appellant challenged the order in state court, arguing that the Commission had restrained commercial speech in violation of the First and Fourteenth Amendments. The Commission's order was upheld by the trial court and at the intermediate appellate level. The New York Court of Appeals affirmed. . . . We . . . reverse.

II.

The Commission's order restricts only commercial speech, that is, expression related solely to the economic interests of the speaker and its audience. . . . In applying the First Amendment to this area, we have rejected the "highly paternalistic" view that government has complete power to suppress or regulate commercial speech. . . .

Nevertheless, our decisions have recognized "the 'commonsense' distinction between speech proposing a commercial transaction, which occurs in an area traditionally subject to government regulation and other varieties of speech." . . . [5] The Constitution therefore accords a lesser protection to commercial speech than to other constitutionally guaranteed expression. . . . The protection available for particular commercial expression turns on the nature both of the expression and of the governmental interests served by its regulation.

. . .

If the communication is neither misleading nor related to unlawful activity, the government's power is more circumscribed. The State must assert a substantial interest to be achieved by restrictions on commercial speech. Moreover, the regulatory technique must be in proportion to that interest. The limitation on expression must be designed carefully to achieve the State's goal. Compliance with this requirement may be measured by two criteria. First, the restriction must directly advance the state interest involved; the regulation may not be sustained if it provides only ineffective or remote support for the government's purpose. Second, if the governmental interest could be served as well by a more limited restriction on commercial speech, the excessive restrictions cannot survive. . . . [8]

. . .

In commercial speech cases, then, a four-part analysis has developed. At the outset, we must determine whether the expression is protected by the First Amendment. For commercial speech to come within that provision, it at least must concern lawful activity and not be misleading. Next, we ask whether the asserted governmental interest is substantial. If both inquiries yield positive answers, we must determine whether the regulation directly advances the governmental interest asserted, and whether it is not more extensive than is necessary to serve that interest.

III.

We now apply this four-step analysis for commercial speech to the Commission's arguments in support of its ban on promotional advertising.

A.

The Commission does not claim that the expression at issue either is inaccurate or relates to unlawful activity. Yet the New York Court of Appeals questioned whether Central Hudson's advertising is protected commercial speech. Because appellant holds a monopoly over the sale of electricity in its service area, the state court suggested that the Commission's order restricts no commercial speech of any worth. The court stated that advertising in a "noncompetitive market" could not improve the decisionmaking of

---

[5]   . . . [T]he concurring opinion of Mr. Justice Stevens views the Commission's order as suppressing more than commercial speech because it would outlaw, for example, advertising that promoted electricity consumption by touting the environmental benefits of such uses. Apparently the concurring opinion would accord full First Amendment protection to all promotional advertising that includes claims "relating to . . . questions frequently discussed and debated by our political leaders."

Although this approach responds to the serious issues surrounding our national energy policy as raised in this case, we think it would blur further the line the Court has sought to draw in commercial speech cases. It would grant broad constitutional protection to any advertising that links a product to a current public debate. But many, if not most, products may be tied to public concerns with the environment, energy, economic policy, or individual health and safety. . . .

[8]   This analysis is not an application of the "overbreadth" doctrine. . . .

In this case, the Commission's prohibition acts directly against the promotional activities of Central Hudson, and to the extent the limitations are unnecessary to serve the State's interest, they are invalid.

consumers. The court saw no constitutional problem with barring commercial speech that it viewed as conveying little useful information.

This reasoning falls short of establishing that appellant's advertising is not commercial speech protected by the First Amendment. Monopoly over the supply of a product provides no protection from competition with substitutes for that product. Electric utilities compete with suppliers of fuel oil and natural gas in several markets, such as those for home heating and industrial power. . . .

. . .

B.

. . . The Commission argues, and the New York court agreed, that the State's interest in conserving energy is sufficient to support suppression of advertising designed to increase consumption of electricity. In view of our country's dependence on energy resources beyond our control, no one can doubt the importance of energy conservation. Plainly, therefore, the state interest asserted is substantial.

. . .

C.

Next, we focus on the relationship between the State's interests and the advertising ban. . . .

. . .

There is an immediate connection between advertising and demand for electricity. Central Hudson would not contest the advertising ban unless it believed that promotion would increase its sales. Thus, we find a direct link between the state interest in conservation and the Commission's order.

D.

We come finally to the critical inquiry in this case: whether the Commission's complete suppression of speech ordinarily protected by the First Amendment is no more extensive than necessary to further the State's interest in energy conservation. The Commission's order reaches all promotional advertising, regardless of the impact of the touted service on overall energy use. But the energy conservation rationale, as important as it is, cannot justify suppressing information about electric devices or services that would cause no net increase in total energy use. In addition, no showing has been made that a more limited restriction on the content of promotional advertising would not serve adequately the State's interests.

Appellant insists that but for the ban, it would advertise products and services that use energy efficiently. These include the "heat pump," which both parties acknowledge to be a major improvement in electric heating, and the use of electric heat as a "back-up" to solar and other heat sources. Although the Commission has questioned the efficiency of electric heating before this Court, neither the Commission's Policy Statement nor its order denying rehearing made findings on this issue. In the absence of authoritative findings to the contrary, we must credit as within the realm of possibility the claim that electric heat can be an efficient alternative in some circumstances.

The Commission's order prevents appellant from promoting electric services that would reduce energy use by diverting demand from less efficient sources, or that would consume roughly the same amount of energy as do alternative sources. In neither situation would the utility's advertising endanger conservation or mislead the public. To the extent that the Commission's order suppresses speech that in no way impairs the State's interest in energy conservation, the Commission's order violates the First and Fourteenth Amendments and must be invalidated. . . .

The Commission also has not demonstrated that its interest in conservation cannot be protected adequately by more limited regulation of appellant's commercial expression. To further its policy of conservation, the Commission could attempt to restrict the format and content of Central Hudson's advertising. It might, for example, require that the advertisements include information about the relative efficiency and expense of the offered service, both under current conditions and for the foreseeable future. . . . In the absence of a showing that more limited speech regulation would be ineffective, we cannot approve the complete suppression of Central Hudson's advertising.

IV.

Our decision today in no way disparages the national interest in energy conservation. We accept without reservation the argument that conservation, as well as the development of alternative energy sources, is an imperative national goal. Administrative bodies empowered to regulate electric utilities have the authority—and indeed the duty—to take appropriate action to further this goal. When, however, such action involves the suppression of speech, the First and Fourteenth Amendments require that the restriction be no more extensive than is necessary to serve the state interest. In this case, the record before us fails to show that the total ban on promotional advertising meets this requirement.

Accordingly, the judgment of the New York Court of Appeals is reversed.

. . .

■ MR. JUSTICE BLACKMUN, with whom MR. JUSTICE BRENNAN joins, concurring in the judgment.

I agree with the Court that the Public Service Commission's ban on promotional advertising of electricity by public utilities is inconsistent with the First and Fourteenth Amendments. I concur only in the Court's judgment, however, because I believe the test now evolved and applied by the Court is not consistent with our prior cases and does not provide adequate protection for truthful, nonmisleading, noncoercive commercial speech.

. . .

I seriously doubt whether suppression of information concerning the availability and price of a legally offered product is ever a permissible way for the State to "dampen" demand for or use of the product. Even though "commercial" speech is involved, such a regulatory measure strikes at the heart of the First Amendment. This is because it is a covert attempt by the State to manipulate the choices of its citizens, not by persuasion or direct regulation, but by depriving the public of the information needed to make a free choice. . . .

. . .

It appears that the Court would permit the State to ban all direct advertising of air conditioning, assuming that a more limited restriction on such advertising would not effectively deter the public from cooling its homes. In my view, our cases do not support this type of suppression. If a governmental unit believes that use or overuse of air conditioning is a serious problem, it must attack that problem directly, by prohibiting air conditioning or regulating thermostat levels. . . .

■ MR. JUSTICE STEVENS, with whom MR. JUSTICE BRENNAN joins, concurring in the judgment.

Because "commercial speech" is afforded less constitutional protection than other forms of speech, it is important that the commercial speech concept not be defined too broadly lest speech deserving of greater constitutional protection be inadvertently suppressed. The issue in this case is whether New York's prohibition on the promotion of the use of electricity through advertising is a ban on nothing but commercial speech.

In my judgment one of the two definitions the Court uses in addressing that issue is too broad and the other may be somewhat too narrow. The Court first describes commercial speech as "expression related solely to the economic interests of the speaker and its audience." Although it is not entirely clear whether this definition uses the subject matter of the speech or the motivation of the speaker as the limiting factor, it seems clear to me that it encompasses speech that is entitled to the maximum protection afforded by the First Amendment. Neither a labor leader's exhortation to strike, nor an economist's dissertation on the money supply, should receive any lesser protection because the subject matter concerns only the economic interests of the audience. Nor should the economic motivation of a speaker qualify his constitutional protection; even Shakespeare may have been motivated by the prospect of pecuniary reward. Thus, the Court's first definition of commercial speech is unquestionably too broad.

The Court's second definition refers to " 'speech proposing a commercial transaction.' " A salesman's solicitation, a broker's offer, and a manufacturer's publication of a price list or the terms of his standard warranty would unquestionably fit within this concept. Presumably, the definition is intended to encompass advertising that advises possible buyers of the availability of specific products at specific prices and describes the advantages of purchasing such items. Perhaps it also extends to other communications that do little more than make the name of a product or a service more familiar to the general public. Whatever the precise contours of the concept, and perhaps it is too early to enunciate an exact formulation, I am persuaded that it should not include the entire range of communication that is embraced within the term "promotional advertising."

This case involves a governmental regulation that completely bans promotional advertising by an electric utility. This ban encompasses a great deal more than mere proposals to engage in certain kinds of commercial transactions. It prohibits all advocacy of the immediate or future use of electricity. It curtails expression by an informed and interested group of persons of their point of view on questions relating to the production and consumption of electrical energy—questions frequently discussed and debated by our political leaders. For example, an electric company's advocacy of the use of electric heat for environmental reasons, as opposed to wood-burning stoves, would seem to fall squarely within New York's promotional advertising ban and also within the bounds of maximum First Amendment protection. The breadth of the ban thus exceeds the boundaries of the commercial speech concept, however that concept may be defined.

The justification for the regulation is nothing more than the expressed fear that the audience may find the utility's message persuasive. Without the aid of any coercion, deception, or misinformation, truthful communication may persuade some citizens to consume more electricity than they otherwise would. I assume that such a consequence would be undesirable and that government may therefore prohibit and punish the unnecessary or excessive use of electricity. But if the perceived harm associated with greater electrical usage is not sufficiently serious to justify direct regulation, surely it does not constitute the kind of clear and present danger that can justify the suppression of speech.

In sum I concur in the result because I do not consider this to be a "commercial speech" case. Accordingly, I see no need to decide whether the Court's four-part analysis, adequately protects commercial speech—as properly defined—in the face of a blanket ban of the sort involved in this case.

■ MR. JUSTICE REHNQUIST, dissenting.

. . .

The Court's decision today fails to give due deference to [the] subordinate position of commercial speech. The Court in so doing returns to the bygone era of Lochner v. New York, 198 U.S. 45 (1905), in which it was common practice for this Court to strike down economic regulations adopted by a State based on the Court's own notions of the most appropriate means for the State to implement its considered policies.

. . . New York's order here is in my view more akin to an economic regulation to which virtually complete deference should be accorded by this Court.

I doubt there would be any question as to the constitutionality of New York's conservation effort if the Public Service Commission had chosen to raise the price of electricity, . . . to condition its sale on specified terms, . . . or to restrict its production. . . . In terms of constitutional values, I think that such controls are virtually indistinguishable from the State's ban on promotional advertising.

. . .

The Definition of Commercial Speech

The conventional definition of commercial speech is that it is speech "proposing a commercial transaction." Justice Powell's *Central Hudson* opinion also defines commercial speech as that "related solely to the economic interests of the speaker and its audience." Are there differences between those two definitions? In Bolger v. Youngs Drug Products Corp., 463 U.S. 60 (1983), the Court determined that "informational pamphlets" discussing the desirability of prophylactics in general and the manufacturer's products in particular were commercial speech even though they were linked to a public debate. On the other hand, the Court stated in Board of Trustees of the State University of New York v. Fox, 492 U.S. 469 (1989), that giving legal advice or medical consultation for a fee was not commercial speech—speech for a profit was not necessarily speech that proposes a commercial transaction.

Consider whether the speech involved in the following cases falls within the parameters of commercial speech doctrine. Dun & Bradstreet, Inc. v. Greenmoss Builders, Inc., 472 U.S. 749 (1985), p. 955, supra (commercial credit report); Lowe v. Securities and Exchange Commission, 472 U.S. 181 (1985) (newsletters containing investment advice and commentary); San Francisco Arts & Athletics, Inc. v. United States Olympic Committee, 483 U.S. 522 (1987) (federal statute granting Committee power to prohibit commercial and promotional uses of the word "Olympic"); City of Cincinnati v. Discovery Network, Inc., 507 U.S. 410 (1993) (free magazine, consisting primarily of promotional material relating to publisher's adult education program, also included information about current events of general interest; free magazine, consisting primarily of advertisements of real estate for sale, also included information about interest rates, market trends, and other real estate matters).

Charitable Solicitation

Constitutionally protected commercial speech is not limited to advertising. In Schaumburg v. Citizens for a Better Environment, 444 U.S. 620 (1980), the Court invalidated an ordinance that prohibited solicitation for charities that received less than 75 percent of the receipts. Riley v. National Federation of Blind of N.C., Inc., 487 U.S. 781 (1988), held that it was unconstitutional to require solicitors to disclose the percentage of funds raised that would go to charities before asking for money. (The Court concluded that there were "less burdensome" alternatives available, such as state publication of financial disclosure forms that professional fundraisers were required to file. See also Secretary of State of Maryland v. Joseph H. Munson Co., 467 U.S. 947 (1984).) Illinois v. Telemarketing Associates, Inc., 538 U.S. 600 (2003), involved a state court action for fraud that the state attorney general filed against a corporation which retained more than 85 percent of the gross receipts from its solicitation of contributions to a charity. In permitting the action to proceed, the Court emphasized that the defendant was charged with making affirmatively false or misleading representations that were not protected by the First Amendment. The Court's earlier cases would be relevant if the complaint merely had alleged that the defendant's fundraising campaign was fraudulent only because so little money went to the charity. In this case, however, the complaint alleged that the defendant's telemarketers made affirmatively false statements to potential donors, leading them to believe that a substantial portion of their contributions would reach the charity.

44 Liquormart, Inc. v. Rhode Island

517 U.S. 484, 116 S.Ct. 1495, 134 L.Ed.2d 711 (1996).

■ JUSTICE STEVENS announced the judgment of the Court and delivered the opinion of the Court with respect to Parts I, II, VII, and VIII, an opinion with respect to Parts III and V, in which JUSTICE KENNEDY, JUSTICE SOUTER, and JUSTICE GINSBURG join, an opinion with respect to Part VI, in which JUSTICE KENNEDY, JUSTICE THOMAS, and JUSTICE GINSBURG join, and an opinion with respect to Part IV, in which JUSTICE KENNEDY and JUSTICE GINSBURG join.

Last Term we held that a federal law abridging a brewer's right to provide the public with accurate information about the alcoholic content of malt beverages is unconstitutional. Rubin v. Coors Brewing Co., 514 U.S. 476, 491 (1995). We now hold that Rhode Island's statutory prohibition against advertisements that provide the public with accurate information about retail prices of alcoholic beverages is also invalid. . . .

I

[Two prohibitions were challenged. One prohibited vendors licensed in Rhode Island, and out-of-state manufacturers, wholesalers, and shippers, from "advertising in any manner whatsoever" the price of any alcoholic beverage offered for sale in the State, except for price tags or signs displayed with the merchandise within licensed premises and not visible from the street. The second categorically prohibited the state's news media from publishing or broadcasting any advertisements that "make reference to the price of any alcoholic beverages."]

II

Petitioners 44 Liquormart . . . and Peoples Super Liquor Stores, . . . licensed retailers of alcoholic beverages[,] . . . operate[, respectively,] a store in Rhode Island and . . . several stores in Massachusetts . . . patronized by Rhode Island residents. Peoples uses alcohol price advertising extensively in Massachusetts, where such advertising is permitted, but Rhode Island newspapers and other media outlets have refused to accept such ads.

[Enforcement proceedings against 44 Liquormart stemmed from an ad it placed in a Rhode Island newspaper that] did not state the price of any alcoholic beverages . . .[, but] did . . . state the low prices at which peanuts, potato chips, and Schweppes mixers were being offered, identify various brands of packaged liquor, and include the word "WOW" in large letters next to pictures of vodka and rum bottles. Based on the conclusion that the implied reference to bargain prices for liquor violated the statutory ban on price advertising, the Rhode Island Liquor Control Administrator assessed a $400 fine.

After paying the fine, 44 Liquormart, joined by Peoples, [sued,] ... seeking a declaratory judgment that the two statutes and the administrator's implementing regulations violate the First Amendment....

. . .

... [The District Court] concluded that the price advertising ban was unconstitutional....

The Court of Appeals reversed....

. . .

III

[In Central Hudson Gas & Elec. Corp. v. Public Serv. Comm'n of N. Y., 447 U.S. 557 (1980),] the majority explained that although the special nature of commercial speech may require less than strict review of its regulation, special concerns arise from "regulations that entirely suppress commercial speech in order to pursue a nonspeech-related policy." ... In those circumstances, "a ban on speech could screen from public view the underlying governmental policy." ... [T]he Court concluded that "special care" should attend the review of such blanket bans, and it pointedly remarked that "in recent years this Court has not approved a blanket ban on commercial speech unless the speech itself was flawed in some way, either because it was deceptive or related to unlawful activity." ...

IV

. . .

When a State regulates commercial messages to protect consumers from misleading, deceptive, or aggressive sales practices, or requires the disclosure of beneficial consumer information, the purpose of its regulation is consistent with the reasons for according constitutional protection to commercial speech and therefore justifies less than strict review. However, when a State entirely prohibits the dissemination of truthful, nonmisleading commercial messages for reasons unrelated to the preservation of a fair bargaining process, there is far less reason to depart from the rigorous review that the First Amendment generally demands.

. . .

The special dangers that attend complete bans on truthful, nonmisleading commercial speech cannot be explained away by appeals to the "commonsense distinctions" that exist between commercial and noncommercial speech.... Regulations that suppress the truth are no less troubling because they target objectively verifiable information, nor are they less effective because they aim at durable messages. As a result, neither the "greater objectivity" nor the "greater hardiness" of truthful, nonmisleading commercial speech justifies reviewing its complete suppression with added deference....

... [B]ans that target truthful, nonmisleading commercial messages ... often serve only to obscure an "underlying governmental policy" that could be implemented without regulating speech.... In this way, these ... bans not only hinder consumer choice, but also impede debate over central issues of public policy....

... [T]hey usually rest solely on the offensive assumption that the public will respond "irrationally" to the truth.... The First Amendment directs us to be especially skeptical of regulations that seek to keep people in the dark for what the government perceives to be their own good. That teaching applies equally to state attempts to deprive consumers of accurate information about their chosen products....

V

In this case, there is no question that Rhode Island's price advertising ban constitutes a blanket prohibition against truthful, nonmisleading speech about a lawful product. There is also no question that the ban serves an end unrelated to consumer protection. Accordingly, we must review the price advertising ban with "special care," *Central Hudson* . . . mindful that speech prohibitions of this type rarely survive constitutional review. . . .

The State argues that the price advertising prohibition should nevertheless be upheld because it directly advances the State's substantial interest in promoting temperance, and because it is no more extensive than necessary. . . .

. . . [T]he State bears the burden of showing not merely that its regulation will advance its interest, but also that it will do so "to a material degree." . . . [W]e must determine whether the State has shown that the price advertising ban will significantly reduce alcohol consumption.

We can agree that . . . a prohibition against price advertising . . . will tend to mitigate competition and maintain prices at a higher level than would prevail in a completely free market. . . . [W]e can even agree . . . that demand, and hence consumption . . . , is somewhat lower whenever a higher, noncompetitive price level prevails. However, without any findings of fact, or indeed any evidentiary support whatsoever, we cannot agree . . . that the price advertising ban will significantly advance the State's interest in promoting temperance.

. . . [T]he State has presented no evidence to suggest that its speech prohibition will significantly reduce market-wide consumption. Indeed, the District Court's . . . finding . . . is directly to the contrary. Moreover, the evidence suggests that the abusive drinker will probably not be deterred by a marginal price increase, and that the true alcoholic may simply reduce his purchases of other necessities.

In addition, as the District Court noted, the State has not identified what price level would lead to a significant reduction in alcohol consumption, nor has it identified the amount that it believes prices would decrease without the ban. Thus, the State's own showing reveals that any connection between the ban and a significant change in alcohol consumption would be purely fortuitous.

. . ..

The State also cannot satisfy the requirement that its restriction on speech be no more extensive than necessary. It is perfectly obvious that alternative forms of regulation that would not involve any restriction on speech would be more likely to achieve the State's goal of promoting temperance. As the State's own expert conceded, higher prices can be maintained either by direct regulation or by increased taxation. Per capita purchases could be limited as is the case with prescription drugs. Even educational campaigns focused on the problems of excessive, or even moderate, drinking might prove to be more effective.

As a result, even under the less than strict standard that generally applies in commercial speech cases, the State has failed to establish a "reasonable fit" between its abridgment of speech and its temperance goal. . . . It necessarily follows that the price advertising ban cannot survive the more stringent constitutional review that *Central Hudson* itself concluded was appropriate for the complete suppression of truthful, nonmisleading commercial speech. . . .

VI

. . . Relying on . . . Posadas de Puerto Rico Associates v. Tourism Co. of P. R., 478 U.S. 328 (1986), and United States v. Edge Broadcasting Co., 509 U.S. 418 (1993),

Rhode Island first argues that, because expert opinions as to the effectiveness of the price advertising ban "go both ways," the Court of Appeals correctly concluded that the ban constituted a "reasonable choice" by the legislature. The State next contends that precedent requires us to give particular deference to that legislative choice because the State could, if it chose, ban the sale of alcoholic beverages outright. . . . Finally, the State argues that deference is appropriate because alcoholic beverages are so-called "vice" products. . . .

The State's first argument fails . . .[, because] Rhode Island errs in concluding that *Edge* and *Posadas* establish the degree of deference that its decision to impose a price advertising ban warrants.

In *Edge*, we upheld a federal statute that permitted only those broadcasters located in States that had legalized lotteries to air lottery advertising. The statute was designed to regulate advertising about an activity that had been deemed illegal in the jurisdiction in which the broadcaster was located. . . . Here, by contrast, the commercial speech ban targets information about entirely lawful behavior.

Posadas is more directly relevant. There, a five-Member majority held that, under the *Central Hudson* test, it was "up to the legislature" to choose to reduce gambling by suppressing in-state casino advertising rather than engaging in educational speech. . . . Rhode Island argues that this logic demonstrates the constitutionality of its own decision to ban price advertising in lieu of raising taxes or employing some other less speech-restrictive means of promoting temperance.

The reasoning in *Posadas* does support the State's argument, but, on reflection, we are now persuaded that *Posadas* erroneously performed the First Amendment analysis. The casino advertising ban was designed to keep truthful, nonmisleading speech from members of the public for fear that they would be more likely to gamble if they received it. As a result, the advertising ban served to shield the State's antigambling policy from the public scrutiny that more direct, nonspeech regulation would draw. . . .

. . . The *Posadas* majority's conclusion . . . cannot be reconciled with the unbroken line of prior cases striking down similarly broad regulations on truthful, nonmisleading advertising when non-speech-related alternatives were available. . . .

Because the 5-to-4 decision in Posadas marked such a sharp break from our prior precedent, and because it concerned a constitutional question about which this Court is the final arbiter, we decline to give force to its highly deferential approach. Instead, . . . we conclude that a state legislature does not have the broad discretion to suppress truthful, nonmisleading information for paternalistic purposes that the *Posadas* majority was willing to tolerate. . . .

We also cannot accept the State's second contention, which is premised entirely on the "greater-includes-the-lesser" reasoning endorsed toward the end of the majority's opinion in *Posadas*. There, the majority stated that "the greater power to completely ban casino gambling necessarily includes the lesser power to ban advertising of casino gambling." . . .

In Rubin v. Coors Brewing Co., 514 U.S. 476 (1995), the United States advanced a similar argument as a basis for supporting a statutory prohibition against revealing the alcoholic content of malt beverages on product labels. We rejected the argument, noting that the statement in the *Posadas* opinion was made only after the majority had concluded that the Puerto Rican regulation "survived the *Central Hudson* test." . . . Further consideration persuades us that the "greater-includes-the-lesser" argument should be rejected for the additional and more important reason that it is inconsistent with both logic and well-settled doctrine.

... Contrary to the assumption made in *Posadas*, we think it quite clear that banning speech may sometimes prove far more intrusive than banning conduct.... [W]e reject the assumption that words are necessarily less vital to freedom than actions, or that logic somehow proves that the power to prohibit an activity is necessarily "greater" than the power to suppress speech about it.

As a matter of First Amendment doctrine, the *Posadas* syllogism is even less defensible. The text of the First Amendment ... directs that government may not suppress speech as easily as it may suppress conduct, and that speech restrictions cannot be treated as simply another means that the government may use to achieve its ends.

. . .

Thus, just as it is perfectly clear that Rhode Island could not ban all obscene liquor ads except those that advocated temperance, we think it equally clear that its power to ban the sale of liquor entirely does not include a power to censor all advertisements that contain accurate and nonmisleading information about the price of the product. As the entire Court apparently now agrees, the statements in the *Posadas* opinion on which Rhode Island relies are no longer persuasive.

Finally, we find unpersuasive the State's contention that, under *Posadas* and *Edge*, the price advertising ban should be upheld because it targets commercial speech that pertains to a "vice" activity.... Our decision last Term striking down an alcohol-related advertising restriction effectively rejected the very contention respondents now make....

Moreover, the scope of any "vice" exception to the protection afforded by the First Amendment would be difficult, if not impossible, to define. Almost any product that poses some threat to public health or public morals might reasonably be characterized by a state legislature as relating to "vice activity". Such characterization, however, is anomalous when applied to products such as alcoholic beverages, lottery tickets, or playing cards, that may be lawfully purchased on the open market. The recognition of such an exception would also have the unfortunate consequence of either allowing state legislatures to justify censorship by the simple expedient of placing the "vice" label on selected lawful activities, or requiring the federal courts to establish a federal common law of vice.... For these reasons, a "vice" label that is unaccompanied by a corresponding prohibition against the commercial behavior at issue fails to provide a principled justification for the regulation of commercial speech about that activity.

VII

[The Court concluded that the Twenty-first Amendment did not tilt the First Amendment analysis in the State's favor.]

VIII

... The judgment of the Court of Appeals is ... reversed.

It is so ordered.

■ JUSTICE SCALIA, concurring in part and concurring in the judgment.

... I will take my guidance as to what the Constitution forbids, with regard to a text as indeterminate as the First Amendment's preservation of "the freedom of speech," and where the core offense of suppressing particular political ideas is not at issue, from the long accepted practices of the American people....

The briefs and arguments of the parties in the present case provide no illumination on that point; understandably so, since both sides accepted *Central Hudson*....

Since I do not believe we have before us the wherewithal to declare *Central Hudson* wrong—or at least the wherewithal to say what ought to replace it—I must resolve this case in accord with our existing jurisprudence, which all except Justice Thomas agree would prohibit the challenged regulation. I am not disposed to develop new law, or reinforce old, on this issue, and accordingly I merely concur in the judgment of the Court. . . .

■ JUSTICE THOMAS, concurring in Parts I, II, VI, and VII, and concurring in the judgment.

In cases such as this, in which the government's asserted interest is to keep legal users of a product or service ignorant in order to manipulate their choices in the marketplace, the balancing test adopted in Central Hudson . . . should not be applied, in my view. Rather, such an "interest" is per se illegitimate and can no more justify regulation of "commercial" speech than it can justify regulation of "noncommercial" speech.

. . .

II

. . . Faulting the State for failing to show that its price advertising ban decreases alcohol consumption "significantly," as Justice Stevens does, seems to imply that if the State had been more successful at keeping consumers ignorant and thereby decreasing their consumption, then the restriction might have been upheld. This contradicts *Virginia Pharmacy Bd.*'s rationale for protecting "commercial" speech in the first instance.

. . . [T]he Court's . . . opinions would appear to commit the courts to striking down restrictions on speech whenever a direct regulation (i.e., a regulation involving no restriction on speech regarding lawful activity at all) would be an equally effective method of dampening demand by legal users. But it would seem that directly banning a product (or rationing it, taxing it, controlling its price, or otherwise restricting its sale in specific ways) would virtually always be at least as effective in discouraging consumption as merely restricting advertising regarding the product would be, and thus virtually all restrictions with such a purpose would fail the fourth prong of the *Central Hudson* test. . . .

The upshot of the application of the fourth prong in the opinions of Justice Stevens and of Justice O'Connor seems to be that the government may not, for the purpose of keeping would-be consumers ignorant and thus decreasing demand, restrict advertising regarding commercial transactions—or at least that it may not restrict advertising regarding commercial transactions except to the extent that it outlaws or otherwise directly restricts the same transactions within its own borders. I welcome this outcome; but, rather than "applying" the fourth prong of *Central Hudson* to reach the inevitable result that all or most such advertising restrictions must be struck down, I would [hold] that all attempts to dissuade legal choices by citizens by keeping them ignorant are impermissible.

. . .

■ JUSTICE O'CONNOR, with whom the CHIEF JUSTICE, JUSTICE SOUTER, and JUSTICE BREYER join, concurring in the judgment.

. . . I would resolve this case more narrowly, . . . by applying our established *Central Hudson* test . . . .

. . .

. . . Rhode Island's regulation fails the final prong; that is, its ban is more extensive than necessary to serve the State's interest.

. . .

. . . The State has other methods at its disposal . . . that would more directly accomplish [its] stated goal without intruding on sellers' ability to provide truthful, nonmisleading information to customers. Indeed, Rhode Island's own expert conceded that "the objective of lowering consumption of alcohol by banning price advertising could be accomplished by establishing minimum prices and/or by increasing sales taxes on alcoholic beverages." . . . The ready availability of such alternatives—at least some of which would far more effectively achieve Rhode Island's only professed goal, at comparatively small additional administrative cost—demonstrates that the fit between ends and means is not narrowly tailored. . . .

. . .

. . . The closer look that we have required since *Posadas* comports better with the purpose of the analysis set out in *Central Hudson*, by requiring the State to show that the speech restriction directly advances its interest and is narrowly tailored. Under such a closer look, Rhode Island's price-advertising ban clearly fails to pass muster.

. . .

Lorillard Tobacco Co. v. Reilly

533 U.S. 525 (2001).

Cigarette, smokeless tobacco, and cigar manufacturers and retailers claimed that regulations promulgated by the Massachusetts Attorney General restricting outdoor advertising, point-of-sale advertising, and certain sales practices for tobacco products violated the First Amendment and were pre-empted by the Federal Cigarette Labeling and Advertising Act (FCLAA). Their suit in the lower federal courts was mostly unsuccessful, but the Supreme Court found serious First Amendment violations and the majority said again—as it had in *Greater New Orleans Broadcasting, supra*—that *Central Hudson* sufficed to decide the free speech parts of the case, so there was no need to break new ground. Only the outdoor and point-of-sale advertising regulations *for cigarettes* were held to be pre-empted, so the Court undertook First Amendment review of everything else.

On that score, Justice O'Connor's majority opinion first noted the parties' agreement that the first two steps of *Central Hudson* were satisfied, in that the petitioners' speech was "entitled to First Amendment protection" and "the State's interest in preventing the use of tobacco products by minors" was sufficiently important (indeed, in the Court's view "substantial, and even compelling"). With respect to the outdoor advertising regulations prohibiting smokeless tobacco or cigar advertising within a 1,000-foot radius of a school or playground, Justice O'Connor first said this regarding the third step:

"In previous cases, we have acknowledged the theory that product advertising stimulates demand for products, while suppressed advertising may have the opposite effect. . . . The Attorney General cites numerous studies to support this theory in the case of tobacco products.

". . .

"Our review of the record reveals that the Attorney General has provided ample documentation of the problem with underage use of smokeless tobacco and cigars. In addition, we disagree with petitioners' claim that there is no evidence that preventing targeted campaigns and limiting youth exposure to advertising will decrease underage use of smokeless tobacco and cigars. On this record and in the posture of summary judgment, we are unable to conclude that the Attorney General's decision to regulate advertising of smokeless tobacco and cigars in an effort to combat the use of tobacco products by minors was based on mere 'speculation [and] conjecture.'. . ."

Then she wrote that "[w]hatever the strength of the Attorney General's evidence to justify the outdoor advertising regulations, however, we conclude that the regulations do not satisfy the fourth step of the *Central Hudson* analysis." Because "the Court of Appeals concluded that the regulations prohibit advertising in a substantial portion of the major metropolitan areas of Massachusetts"; because the "substantial geographical reach . . . is compounded by" the restriction's inclusion of "not only advertising located outside an establishment, but also advertising inside a store if that advertising is visible from outside the store"; and because the "regulations restrict advertisements of any size and the term advertisement also includes oral statements[,]" in "some geographical areas, these regulations would constitute nearly a complete ban on the communication of truthful information about smokeless tobacco and cigars to adult consumers. The breadth and scope of the regulations, and the process by which the Attorney General adopted the regulations, do not demonstrate a careful calculation of the speech interests involved." Justice O'Connor concluded that the "uniformly broad sweep of the geographical limitation demonstrates a lack of tailoring" and "the range of communications restricted seems unduly broad." She questioned "why a ban on oral communications is necessary to further the State's interest" and objected that "a ban on all signs of any size seems ill suited to target the problem of highly visible billboards, as opposed to smaller signs. To the extent that studies have identified particular advertising and promotion practices that appeal to youth, tailoring would involve targeting those practices while permitting others."

Because "the sale and use of tobacco products by adults is a legal activity[,] . . . [a]s the State protects children from tobacco advertisements, tobacco manufacturers and retailers and their adult consumers still have a protected interest in communication." Noting that "a retailer in Massachusetts may have no means of communicating to passersby on the street that it sells tobacco products because alternative forms of advertisement, like newspapers, do not allow that retailer to propose an instant transaction in the way that onsite advertising does[; and that t]he ban on any indoor advertising . . . visible from the outside also presents problems in establishments like convenience stores, which have unique security concerns that counsel in favor of full visibility of the store from the outside[,]" the Court "conclude[d] that the Attorney General has failed to show that the outdoor advertising regulations for smokeless tobacco and cigars are not more extensive than necessary to advance the State's substantial interest in preventing underage tobacco use." No remand was appropriate, "because the State had ample opportunity to develop a record with respect to tailoring, . . . and additional evidence would not alter the nature of the scheme before the Court."

The indoor, point-of-sale advertising restrictions for smokeless tobacco and cigars, which prohibited placing ads " 'lower than five feet from the floor of any retail establishment which is located within a one thousand foot radius of" any school or playground[,]" were held to "fail both the third and fourth steps of the *Central Hudson* analysis." The 5 foot rule did not seem to advance the goal, because "[n]ot all children are less than 5 feet tall, and those who are certainly have the ability to look up and take in their surroundings." The height restriction was not a "regulation of conduct . . . unrelated to expression[, but] an attempt to regulate directly the communicative impact of indoor advertising."

Finally, the regulations barring the use of self-service displays and requiring that tobacco products be placed out of the reach of all consumers in a location accessible only to salespersons, and the ban on "sampling or promotional giveaways of cigars or little cigars" were held to "withstand First Amendment scrutiny." Understood as requirements that "tobacco retailers . . . place tobacco products behind counters and require customers to have contact with a salesperson before they are able to handle a tobacco product[,]" the Court viewed the restrictions as "seek[ing] to regulate the placement of tobacco products for reasons unrelated to the communication of ideas" and "conclude[d] that the State has demonstrated a substantial interest in preventing access to tobacco products by minors and has adopted an appropriately narrow means of advancing that interest." Justice O'Connor elaborated:

". . . Unattended displays of tobacco products present an opportunity for access without the proper age verification required by law. Thus, the State prohibits self-service and other displays that would allow an individual to obtain tobacco products without direct contact with a salesperson. It is clear that the regulations leave open ample channels of communication. The regulations do not significantly impede adult access to tobacco products. Moreover, retailers have other means of exercising any cognizable speech interest in the presentation of their products. We presume that vendors may place empty tobacco packaging on open display, and display actual tobacco products so long as that display is only accessible to sales personnel. As for cigars, there is no indication in the regulations that a customer is unable to examine a cigar prior to purchase, so long as that examination takes place through a salesperson."

Justice Kennedy, joined by Justice Scalia, concurred in part and in the judgment, saying that the "obvious overbreadth of the outdoor advertising restrictions suffices to invalidate them under the fourth part of the test in *Central Hudson*" and thus

"there is no need to consider whether the restrictions satisfy the third part of the test, a proposition about which there is considerable doubt. Neither are we required to consider whether *Central Hudson* should be retained in the face of the substantial objections that can be made to it. My continuing concerns that the test gives insufficient protection to truthful, nonmisleading commercial speech require me to refrain from expressing agreement with the Court's application of the third part of *Central Hudson*."

Justice Thomas, also concurring in part and in the judgment, would have "subject[ed] all of the advertising restrictions to strict scrutiny and would [have held] that they violate the First Amendment." He reiterated his view that "an asserted government interest in keeping people ignorant by suppressing expression 'is per se illegitimate and can no more justify regulation of "commercial" speech than it can justify regulation of "noncommercial" speech.'" He argued that "[e]ven if Massachusetts has a valid interest in regulating speech directed at children—who, it argues, may be more easily misled, and to whom the sale of tobacco products is unlawful—it may not pursue that interest at the expense of the free speech rights of adults." Applying strict scrutiny, and "assuming that there is a compelling interest in reducing underage smoking, and that the ban on outdoor advertising promotes this interest, I doubt that the same is true of the ban on point-of-sale advertising below five feet. . . . Far from serving a compelling interest, the ban on displays below five feet seems to lack even a minimally rational relationship to any conceivable interest." He continued:

"There is also considerable reason to doubt that the restrictions on cigar and smokeless tobacco outdoor advertising promote any state interest. Outdoor advertising for cigars . . . is virtually nonexistent. . . . To the extent outdoor advertising exists, there is no evidence that it is targeted at youth or has a significant effect on youth. . . .

"Much the same is true of smokeless tobacco. . . .

"In any case, even assuming that the regulations advance a compelling state interest, they must be struck down because they are not narrowly tailored. . . .

"...

"... In addition to examining a narrower advertising ban, the State should have examined ways of advancing its interest that do not require limiting speech at all. Here, respondents had several alternatives. Most obviously, they could have directly regulated the conduct with which they were concerned.... Massachusetts already prohibits the sale of tobacco to minors, but it could take steps to enforce that prohibition more vigorously. It also could enact laws prohibiting the purchase, possession, or use of tobacco by minors. And, if its concern is that tobacco advertising communicates a message with which it disagrees, it could seek to counteract that message with "more speech, not enforced silence," Whitney v. California, 274 U.S. 357, 377 (1927) (Brandeis, J., concurring).

"...

"Respondents have identified no principle of law or logic that would preclude the imposition of restrictions on fast food and alcohol advertising similar to those they seek to impose on tobacco advertising. In effect, they seek a 'vice' exception to the First Amendment. No such exception exists.... If it did, it would have almost no limit...."

Justice Stevens, joined by Justices Ginsburg, Breyer and Souter, dissented from the Court's conclusion that the "FCLAA... precludes States and localities from regulating the location of cigarette advertising ..." As for the First Amendment questions, though they "agree[d] with the Court both that the outdoor advertising restrictions ... serve legitimate and important state interests and that the record does not indicate that the measures were properly tailored to serve those interests[,]" they would have "remand[ed] for trial on the[ir] constitutionality ...." Justice Stevens, in this joined only by Justices Ginsburg and Breyer, also would have upheld the point-of-sale advertising restrictions and the sales practice restrictions, because they did not "implicate significant First Amendment concerns[.]"

Although "shar[ing] the majority's concern as to whether the 1,000-foot rule unduly restricts the ability of cigarette manufacturers to convey lawful information to adult consumers[,]" he noted that "when calculating whether a child-directed location restriction goes too far in regulating adult speech, one crucial question is whether the regulatory scheme leaves available sufficient 'alternative avenues of communication.' ... Because I do not think the record contains sufficient information to enable us to answer that question, I would vacate the award of summary judgment upholding the 1,000-foot rule and remand for trial on that issue." He thought the Court "lack[ed] sufficient qualitative information as to the areas where cigarette advertising is prohibited and those where it is permitted" and "information as to other avenues of communication available to cigarette manufacturers and retailers."

On the subject of the sales practice and indoor advertising restrictions, Justice Stevens made "two brief points":

"First, ... the sales practice restrictions are best analyzed as regulating conduct, not speech.... [L]aws requiring that stores maintain items behind counters and prohibiting self-service displays fall squarely on the conduct side of the line.... I see nothing the least bit constitutionally problematic in requiring individuals to ask for the assistance of a salesclerk in order to examine or purchase a handgun, a bottle of penicillin, or a package of cigarettes.

"Second, ... [although] the regulation limiting tobacco advertising in certain retail establishments to the space five feet or more above the floor[, w]hen viewed in isolation, ... appears to target speech ..., I am ultimately persuaded that the provision is unobjectionable because it is little more than an adjunct to the other sales practice restrictions. As ... Massachusetts can properly legislate the placement of products and the nature of displays in its convenience stores, I would not draw a distinction between such restrictions and height restrictions on related product advertising. I would accord . . . some latitude in imposing restrictions that can have only the slightest impact on the ability of adults to purchase a poisonous product and may save some children from taking the first step on the road to addiction. "

Sorrell v. IMS Health, Inc.

564 U.S. 552 (2011).

It is common practice for pharmaceutical manufacturers to promote drugs to doctors through "detailers," who visit the doctors with drug samples and medical studies explaining the "details" and potential advantages of various prescription drugs. These salespeople can be more effective if they know a physician's prescription practices ("prescriber-identifying information"). Pharmacies, "as a matter of business routine and federal law, receive prescriber-identifying information when processing prescriptions[,]" and many of them "sell this information to 'data miners,' [who create reports and] lease [them] to pharmaceutical manufacturers subject to nondisclosure agreements." The detailers "use the reports to refine their marketing tactics and increase sales."Vermont, hoping to "safeguard medical privacy and diminish the likelihood that marketing will lead to prescription decisions not in the best interests of patients or the State"—predominantly in the form of too much prescribing of brand-name drugs that are costlier than generic drugs—enacted a statute, whose "central provision"—§ 4631(d)—prohibits pharmacies, health insurers, and similar entities, without the prescriber's consent, from either selling prescriber-identifying information or allowing prescriber-identifying information to be used for marketing purposes. It also "bars pharmaceutical manufacturers and pharmaceutical marketers from using prescriber-identifying information for marketing, again absent the prescriber's consent." In this suit, Vermont data miners, and an association of pharmaceutical manufacturers that produce brand-name drugs, successfully challenged § 4631(d) on First Amendment grounds.

Justice Kennedy's opinion for the Court viewed the statute as a "content-and speaker-based" restriction, because it "disfavors marketing, that is, speech with a particular content[, and it] disfavors specific speakers, namely pharmaceutical manufacturers." Under the statutory scheme, for example, "it appears that Vermont could supply academic organizations with prescriber-identifying information to use in countering the messages of brand-name pharmaceutical manufacturers and in promoting the prescription of generic drugs. But § 4631(d) leaves detailers no means of purchasing, acquiring, or using prescriber-identifying information." Because "the almost invariable rule is that detailing by pharmaceutical manufacturers is in support of brand-name drugs[,]" the statute "has the effect of preventing detailers—and only detailers—from communicating with physicians in an effective and informative manner." In fact, Vermont's "formal legislative findings" made clear that § 4631(d) was "designed . . . to target" brand-name drug manufacturers "and their messages for disfavored treatment[, taking] " 'its practical operation . . . even beyond mere content discrimination, to actual viewpoint discrimination.' " Consequently, "heightened judicial scrutiny is warranted[,]" and neither Vermont's contention that § 4631(d) "is a mere commercial regulation[,]" nor its contention that the information, having been "generated in compliance with a legal mandate," allowed it to be "considered a kind of governmental information[,]" could overcome the need for heightened scrutiny.

Moreover, "the outcome is the same whether a special commercial speech inquiry or a stricter form of judicial scrutiny is applied. See, e.g., Greater New Orleans Broadcasting Assn., Inc. v. United States, 527 U.S. 173, 184 (1999)." Even "[u]nder a commercial speech inquiry, it is the State's burden to justify its content-based law as consistent with the First Amendment. Thompson v. Western States Medical Center, 535 U.S. 357, 373 (2002). To sustain the targeted, content-based burden § 4631(d) imposes on protected expression, the State must show at least that the statute directly advances a substantial governmental interest and that the measure is drawn to achieve that interest. . . . *Central Hudson.* . . ."

The statute did not satisfy these criteria, Justice Kennedy concluded. Physicians might have "an interest in keeping their prescription decisions confidential[, b]ut § 4631(d) is not drawn to serve that interest"—largely because pharmacies could "share prescriber-identifying information with anyone for any reason" except if it was to be used "for marketing." Since "insurers, researchers, journalists, the State itself, and others [could] use the information[,] . . . Vermont made prescriber-identifying information available to an almost limitless audience." Protection of "doctors from 'harassing sales behaviors'" also was inadequate, partly because "[i]t is doubtful that concern for 'a few' physicians who may have 'felt coerced and harassed' by pharmaceutical marketers can sustain a broad content-based rule like § 4631(d)[,]" and partly because "the State offers no explanation why remedies other than content-based rules would be inadequate." Doctors could "simply decline to meet with detailers . . . who use prescriber-identifying information." As for Vermont's argument "that detailers' use of prescriber-identifying information undermines the doctor-patient relationship by allowing detailers to influence treatment decisions[,]" most fundamentally, "this asserted interest is contrary to basic First Amendment principles. . . . If pharmaceutical marketing affects treatment decisions, it does so because doctors find it persuasive. Absent circumstances far from those presented here, the fear that speech might persuade provides no lawful basis for quieting it. Brandenburg v. Ohio, 395 U.S. 444, 447 (1969) *(per curiam).*"

Finally, Justice Kennedy rejected Vermont's contention that the statute was justified as a means to "lower[ ] the costs of medical services and promot[e] public health[,]" because it is impermissible to seek to achieve these goals "by diminishing detailers' ability to influence prescription decisions." The " 'fear that people would make bad decisions if given truthful information' cannot justify content-based burdens on speech. *Thompson*, 535 U.S., at 374[,] . . . [and t]hese precepts apply with full force when the audience, in this case prescribing physicians, consists of 'sophisticated and experienced' consumers." Justice Kennedy also wrote this:

". . . [T]he State may not seek to remove a popular but disfavored product from the marketplace by prohibiting truthful, nonmisleading advertisements that contain impressive endorsements or catchy jingles. That the State finds expression too persuasive does not permit it to quiet the speech or to burden its messengers.

"The defect in Vermont's law is made clear by the fact that many listeners find detailing instructive. . . . There are divergent views regarding detailing and the prescription of brand-name drugs. Under the Constitution, resolution of that debate must result from free and uninhibited speech. . . .

". . . The State may not burden the speech of others in order to tilt public debate in a preferred direction. . . .

" . . .

"If Vermont's statute provided that prescriber-identifying information could not be sold or disclosed except in narrow circumstances then the State might have a stronger position. . . .

". . . The State has burdened a form of protected expression that it found too persuasive. At the same time, the State has left unburdened those speakers whose messages are in accord with its own views. This the State cannot do."

Justice Breyer dissented, joined by Justices Ginsburg and Kagan. He perceived the statute as "only . . . depriv[ing] pharmaceutical and data-mining companies of data, collected pursuant to the government's regulatory mandate, that could help pharmaceutical companies create better sales messages"—an "effect on expression . . . inextricably related to a lawful governmental effort to regulate a commercial enterprise" that did not warrant "a special 'heightened' standard of review[.]" In any event, he thought "the statute me[t] the First Amendment standard . . . previously applied . . . to . . . commercial speech."

As he often suggests, Justice Breyer "would ask whether [the] regulatory provisions work harm to First Amendment interests that is disproportionate to their furtherance of legitimate regulatory objectives." And he "would give significant weight to legitimate commercial regulatory objectives." His "reasons why the Court should review Vermont's law 'under the standard appropriate for the review of economic regulation,' not 'under a heightened standard appropriate for the review of First Amendment issues[,]'" included (1) that it "neither forbids nor requires anyone to say anything, to engage in any form of symbolic speech, or to endorse any particular point of view, whether ideological or related to the sale of a product[;]" (2) that "the statute's requirements form part of a traditional, comprehensive regulatory regime[;]" and (3) that "Vermont's statute is directed toward information that exists only by virtue of government regulation." He emphasized that "until today, this Court has *never* found that the *First Amendment* prohibits the government from restricting the use of information gathered pursuant to a regulatory mandate—whether the information rests in government files or has remained in the hands of the private firms that gathered it." He also said this:

"[N]either of these categories—'content-based' nor 'speaker-based'—has ever before justified greater scrutiny when regulatory activity affects commercial speech. . . . Regulatory programs necessarily draw distinctions on the basis of content. . . . Electricity regulators, for example, oversee company statements, pronouncements, and proposals, but only about electricity. . . . The Federal Reserve Board regulates the content of statements, advertising, loan proposals, and interest rate disclosures, but only when made by financial institutions. . . . And the FDA oversees the form and content of labeling, advertising, and sales proposals of drugs, but not of furniture. . . . Given the ubiquity of content-based regulatory categories, why should the 'content-based' nature of typical regulation require courts (other things being equal) to grant legislators and regulators *less* deference? . . .

"Nor, in the context of a regulatory program, is it unusual for particular rules to be 'speaker-based,' affecting only a class of entities, namely, the regulated firms. . . .

". . .

" . . . [S]tatutes, regulations, programs, and initiatives almost always reflect a point of view, for example, of the Congress and the administration that enacted them and ultimately the voters. And they often aim at, and target, particular firms that engage in practices about the merits of which the Government and the firms may disagree. . . .

"Nothing in Vermont's statute undermines the ability of persons opposing the State's policies to speak their mind or to pursue a different set of policy objectives through the democratic process. Whether Vermont's regulatory statute 'targets' drug companies (as opposed to affecting them unintentionally) must be beside the First Amendment point.

"... Because the imposition of 'heightened' scrutiny in such instances would significantly change the legislative/judicial balance, in a way that would significantly weaken the legislature's authority to regulate commerce and industry, I would not apply a 'heightened' First Amendment standard of review in this case."

In any event, Justice Breyer then added that "Vermont's statute survives application of *Central Hudson*'s 'intermediate' commercial speech standard as well as any more limited 'economic regulation' test." In his view, the "statute threatens only modest harm to commercial speech." He saw "no evidence" of "unjustified discrimination [permitting] 'pharmacies' to 'share prescriber-identifying information with anyone for any reason' (but marketing)" and "no evidentiary basis for the conclusion that ... individualized counterdetailing is widespread, or exists at all, in Vermont." The State's interests in public health and controlling health care costs are " 'substantial[,]' ... [a]nd ... 'neutral' in respect to speech." And "the record evidence is sufficient to permit a legislature to conclude that the statute 'directly advances' each of these objectives. The statute helps to focus sales discussions on an individual drug's safety, effectiveness, and cost, perhaps compared to other drugs (including generics).... [A] detailing message ... [may] divert[ ] attention from scientific research about a drug's safety and effectiveness, as well as its cost. This diversion comes at the expense of public health and the State's fiscal interests." He also found the record adequate to support "the State's privacy objective[,]" because "[r]egulatory rules in Vermont make clear that the confidentiality of an individual doctor's prescribing practices remains the norm [and e]xceptions ... are comparatively few." And there was "no indication" that this information was used "for counterdetailing efforts."

Nor could the "majority ... point to any adequately supported, similarly effective 'more limited restriction.' *Central Hudson*":

"... Closing the [doctor's] office door entirely has no similar tendency to lower costs (by focusing greater attention upon the comparative advantages and disadvantages of generic drug alternatives). And it would not protect the confidentiality of information already released to, say, data miners. In any event, physicians are unlikely to turn detailers away at the door, for those detailers, whether delivering a balanced or imbalanced message, are nonetheless providers of much useful information.... Forcing doctors to choose between targeted detailing and no detailing at all could therefore jeopardize the State's interest in promoting public health."

Justice Breyer also would have upheld the ban on the marketing use of prescriber-identifying information by pharmaceutical manufacturers and marketers, "basically for the [same] reasons"—that the prohibition "works no more than modest First Amendment harm; the prohibition is justified by the need to ensure unbiased sales presentations, prevent unnecessarily high drug costs, and protect the privacy of prescribing physicians. There is no obvious equally effective, more limited alternative."

E. REGULATION OF FALSE STATEMENTS OF FACT

United States v. Alvarez

567 U.S. 709, 132 S.Ct. 2537, 183 L.Ed.2d 574 (2012).

■ JUSTICE KENNEDY announced the judgment of the Court and delivered an opinion, in which THE CHIEF JUSTICE, JUSTICE GINSBURG, and JUSTICE SOTOMAYOR join.

[At his first public meeting as a member of the Three Valley Water District Board in Claremont, California, Alvarez lied when he said that he had received the

Congressional Medal of Honor.] For all the record shows, respondent's statements were but a pathetic attempt to gain respect that eluded him. The statements do not seem to have been made to secure employment or financial benefits or admission to privileges reserved for those who had earned the Medal.

Respondent was indicted under the Stolen Valor Act [of 2005, 18 U. S. C. § 704, which provides in pertinent part:

"(b) FALSE CLAIMS ABOUT RECEIPT OF MILITARY DECORATIONS OR MEDALS.—Whoever falsely represents himself or herself, verbally or in writing, to have been awarded any decoration or medal authorized by Congress for the Armed Forces of the United States . . . shall be fined under this title, imprisoned not more than six months, or both.

"(c) ENHANCED PENALTY FOR OFFENSES INVOLVING CONGRESSIONAL MEDAL OF HONOR.—"(1) IN GENERAL.—If a decoration or medal involved in an offense under subsection (a) or (b) is a Congressional Medal of Honor, in lieu of the punishment provided in that subsection, the offender shall be fined under this title, imprisoned not more than 1 year, or both."]

. . . The District Court . . . rejected his claim that the statute is invalid under the First Amendment. . . . The . . . Ninth Circuit . . . reversed . . . .

. . .

. . . [T]he statement that the speaker held the Medal was an intended, undoubted lie.

It is right and proper that Congress, over a century ago, established an award so the Nation can hold in its highest respect and esteem those who . . . have acted with extraordinary honor. And it should be uncontested that this is a legitimate Government objective, indeed a most valued national aspiration and purpose. . . . [H]owever. [f]undamental constitutional principles require that laws enacted to honor the brave must be consistent with the precepts of the Constitution for which they fought.

The Government contends the criminal prohibition is a proper means to further its purpose in creating and awarding the Medal. When content-based speech regulation is in question, however, exacting scrutiny is required. Statutes suppressing or restricting speech must be judged by the sometimes inconvenient principles of the First Amendment. By this measure, the statutory provisions under which respondent was convicted must be held invalid, and his conviction must be set aside.

I

. . .

Respondent challenges the statute as a content-based suppression of pure speech, speech not falling within any of the few categories of expression where content-based regulation is permissible. The Government defends the statute as necessary to preserve the integrity and purpose of the Medal, an integrity and purpose it contends are compromised and frustrated by the false statements the statute prohibits. It argues that false statements "have no First Amendment value in themselves," and thus "are protected only to the extent needed to avoid chilling fully protected speech." . . . Although the statute covers respondent's speech, the Government argues that it leaves breathing room for protected speech, for example speech which might criticize the idea of the Medal or the importance of the military. The Government's arguments cannot suffice to save the statute.

II

. . .

Absent from those few categories where the law allows content-based regulation of speech is any general exception to the First Amendment for false statements. This comports with the common understanding that some false statements are inevitable if there is to be an open and vigorous expression of views in public and private conversation . . . .

The Government disagrees[,] . . . cit[ing] language from some of this Court's precedents to support its contention that false statements have no value and hence no First Amendment protection. . . . These isolated statements in some earlier decisions do not support the Government's submission that false statements, as a general rule, are beyond constitutional protection. That conclusion would take the quoted language far from its proper context. For instance, the Court has stated "[f]alse statements of fact are particularly valueless [because] they interfere with the truth-seeking function of the marketplace of ideas," Hustler Magazine, Inc. v. Falwell, 485 U. S. 46, 52 (1988), and that false statements "are not protected by the First Amendment in the same manner as truthful statements," Brown v. Hartlage, 456 U. S. 45, 60–61 (1982). See also, *e.g., Virginia Bd. of Pharmacy, supra*, at 771 ("Untruthful speech, commercial or otherwise, has never been protected for its own sake"); Herbert v. Lando, 441 U. S. 153, 171 (1979) ("Spreading false information in and of itself carries no First Amendment credentials"); *Gertz, supra*, at 340 ("[T]here is no constitutional value in false statements of fact"); Garrison v. Louisiana, 379 U. S. 64, 75 (1964) ("[T]he knowingly false statement and the false statement made with reckless disregard of the truth, do not enjoy constitutional protection").

These quotations all derive from cases discussing defamation, fraud, or some other legally cognizable harm associated with a false statement, such as an invasion of privacy or the costs of vexatious litigation. . . . In those decisions the falsity of the speech at issue was not irrelevant to our analysis, but neither was it determinative. The Court has never endorsed the categorical rule the Government advances: that false statements receive no First Amendment protection. Our prior decisions have not confronted a measure, like the Stolen Valor Act, that targets falsity and nothing more.

Even when considering some instances of defamation and fraud, moreover, the Court has been careful to instruct that falsity alone may not suffice to bring the speech outside the First Amendment. The statement must be a knowing or reckless falsehood. . . .

The Government thus . . . seeks to convert a rule that limits liability even in defamation cases where the law permits recovery for tortious wrongs into a rule that expands liability in a different, far greater realm of discourse and expression. That inverts the rationale for the exception. The requirements of a knowing falsehood or reckless disregard for the truth as the condition for recovery in certain defamation cases exists to allow more speech, not less. A rule designed to tolerate certain speech ought not blossom to become a rationale for a rule restricting it.

The Government then gives three examples of regulations on false speech that courts generally have found permissible: first, the criminal prohibition of a false statement made to a Government official, 18 U. S. C. § 1001; second, laws punishing perjury; and third, prohibitions on the false representation that one is speaking as a Government official or on behalf of the Government, see, *e.g.,* § 912; § 709. These restrictions, however, do not establish a principle that all proscriptions of false statements are exempt from exacting First Amendment scrutiny.

. . . Section 1001's prohibition on false statements made to Government officials, in communications concerning official matters, does not lead to the broader proposition that false statements are unprotected when made to any person, at any time, in any context.

The same point can be made about what the Court has confirmed is the "unquestioned constitutionality of perjury statutes," both the federal statute, § 1623, and its state-law equivalents. United States v. Grayson, 438 U. S. 41, 54 (1978). . . . It is not simply because perjured statements are false that they lack First Amendment protection. Perjured testimony "is at war with justice" because it can cause a court to render a "judgment not resting on truth." In re Michael, 326 U. S. 224, 227 (1945). Perjury undermines the function and province of the law and threatens the integrity of judgments that are the basis of the legal system. . . . Unlike speech in other contexts, testimony under oath has the formality and gravity necessary to remind the witness that his or her statements will be the basis for official governmental action, action that often affects the rights and liberties of others. Sworn testimony is quite distinct from lies not spoken under oath and simply intended to puff up oneself.

Statutes that prohibit falsely representing that one is speaking on behalf of the Government, or that prohibit impersonating a Government officer, also protect the integrity of Government processes, quite apart from merely restricting false speech. Title 18 U. S. C. § 912, for example, prohibits impersonating an officer or employee of the United States. Even if that statute may not require proving an "actual financial or property loss" resulting from the deception, the statute is itself confined to "maintain[ing] the general good repute and dignity of . . . government . . . service itself." United States v. Lepowitch, 318 U. S. 702, 704 (1943) . . . . The same can be said for prohibitions on the unauthorized use of the names of federal agencies such as the Federal Bureau of Investigation in a manner calculated to convey that the communication is approved, see § 709, or using words such as "Federal" or "United States" in the collection of private debts in order to convey that the communication has official authorization, see § 712. These examples, to the extent that they implicate fraud or speech integral to criminal conduct, are inapplicable here.

As our law and tradition show, then, there are instances in which the falsity of speech bears upon whether it is protected. . . . But it also rejects the notion that false speech should be in a general category that is presumptively unprotected.

. . . [T]he Court has acknowledged that perhaps there exist "some categories of speech that have been historically unprotected . . . but have not yet been specifically identified or discussed . . . in our case law." . . . [H]owever, the Court must be presented with "persuasive evidence that a novel restriction on content is part of a long (if heretofore unrecognized) tradition of proscription," Brown v. Entertainment Merchants Assn., 564 U.S. ___, ___ (2011) (slip op., at 4). The Government has not demonstrated that false statements generally should constitute a new category of unprotected speech on this basis.

III

. . .

The Act by its plain terms applies to a false statement made at any time, in any place, to any person. It can be assumed that it would not apply to, say, a theatrical performance. . . . Still, the sweeping, quite unprecedented reach of the statute puts it in conflict with the First Amendment. Here the lie was made in a public meeting, but the statute would apply with equal force to personal, whispered conversations within a home. The statute seeks to control and suppress all false statements on this one subject in almost limitless times and settings. And it does so entirely without regard to whether the lie was made for the purpose of material gain. . . .

Permitting the government to decree this speech to be a criminal offense, whether shouted from the rooftops or made in a barely audible whisper, would endorse government authority to compile a list of subjects about which false statements are punishable. That governmental power has no clear limiting principle. . . . Where false claims are made to effect a fraud or secure moneys or other valuable considerations, say offers of employment, it is well established that the Government may restrict speech without affronting the First Amendment. See, *e.g., Virginia Bd. of Pharmacy*, 425 U. S., at 771 (noting that fraudulent speech generally falls outside the protections of the First Amendment). But the Stolen Valor Act is not so limited in its reach. Were the Court to hold that the interest in truthful discourse alone is sufficient to sustain a ban on speech, absent any evidence that the speech was used to gain a material advantage, it would give government a broad censorial power unprecedented in this Court's cases or in our constitutional tradition. The mere potential for the exercise of that power casts a chill, a chill the First Amendment cannot permit if free speech, thought, and discourse are to remain a foundation of our freedom.

IV

. . . [E]ven . . . within its own narrow sphere of operation, the Act cannot survive. In assessing content-based restrictions on protected speech, the Court . . . has applied the "most exacting scrutiny." . . . Although the objectives the Government seeks to further by the statute are not without significance, the Court must, and now does, find the Act does not satisfy exacting scrutiny.

The Government is correct when it states military medals "serve the important public function of recognizing and expressing gratitude for acts of heroism and sacrifice in military service," and also " 'foste[r] morale, mission accomplishment and esprit de corps' among service members." . . . In periods of war and peace alike public recognition of valor and noble sacrifice by men and women in uniform reinforces the pride and national resolve that the military relies upon to fulfill its mission.

These interests are related to the integrity of the military honors system in general, and the Congressional Medal of Honor in particular. . . . The Government's interest in protecting the integrity of the Medal of Honor is beyond question.

But to recite the Government's compelling interests is not to end the matter. The First Amendment requires that the Government's chosen restriction on the speech at issue be "actually necessary" to achieve its interest. *Entertainment Merchants Assn.,*. . . . There must be a direct causal link between the restriction imposed and the injury to be prevented. . . . The link between the Government's interest in protecting the integrity of the military honors system and the Act's restriction on the false claims of liars like respondent has not been shown. Although appearing to concede that "an isolated misrepresentation by itself would not tarnish the meaning of military honors," the Government asserts it is "common sense that false representations have the tendency to dilute the value and meaning of military awards," . . . . It must be acknowledged that when a pretender claims the Medal to be his own, the lie might harm the Government by demeaning the high purpose of the award, diminishing the honor it confirms, and creating the appearance that the Medal is awarded more often than is true. Furthermore, the lie may offend the true holders of the Medal. From one perspective it insults their bravery and high principles when falsehood puts them in the unworthy company of a pretender.

Yet these interests do not satisfy the Government's heavy burden when it seeks to regulate protected speech. . . . The Government points to no evidence to support its claim that the public's general perception of military awards is diluted by false claims such as those made by Alvarez. . . . As one of the Government's *amici* notes "there is nothing that charlatans such as Xavier Alvarez can do to stain [the Medal winners'] honor." Brief for Veterans of Foreign Wars of the United States et al. as *Amici Curiae* 1. This general proposition is sound, even if true holders of the Medal might experience anger and frustration.

The lack of a causal link between the Government's stated interest and the Act is not the only way in which the Act is not actually necessary to achieve the Government's stated interest. The Government has not shown, and cannot show, why counterspeech would not suffice to achieve its interest. The facts of this case indicate that the dynamics of free speech, of counterspeech, of refutation, can overcome the lie. Respondent lied at a public meeting. Even before the FBI began investigating him for his false statements "Alvarez was perceived as a phony," .... Once the lie was made public, he was ridiculed online, ... his actions were reported in the press, ... and a fellow board member called for his resignation .... There is good reason to believe that a similar fate would befall other false claimants.... Indeed, the outrage and contempt expressed for respondent's lies can serve to reawaken and reinforce the public's respect for the Medal, its recipients, and its high purpose. The acclaim that recipients of the Congressional Medal of Honor receive also casts doubt on the proposition that the public will be misled by the claims of charlatans or become cynical of those whose heroic deeds earned them the Medal by right. ...

The remedy for speech that is false is speech that is true. This is the ordinary course in a free society. The response to the unreasoned is the rational; to the uninformed, the enlightened; to the straight-out lie, the simple truth.... Freedom of speech and thought flows not from the beneficence of the state but from the inalienable rights of the person. And suppression of speech by the government can make exposure of falsity more difficult, not less so. Society has the right and civic duty to engage in open, dynamic, rational discourse. These ends are not well served when the government seeks to orchestrate public discussion through content-based mandates.

... [T]he Government responds that because "some military records have been lost ... some claims [are] unverifiable," .... This proves little, however; for without verifiable records, successful criminal prosecution under the Act would be more difficult in any event. So, in cases where public refutation will not serve the Government's interest, the Act will not either. In addition, the Government claims that "many [false claims] will remain unchallenged." ... The Government provides no support for the contention. And in any event, in order to show that public refutation is not an adequate alternative, the Government must demonstrate that unchallenged claims undermine the public's perception of the military and the integrity of its awards system. This showing has not been made.

It is a fair assumption that any true holders of the Medal who had heard of Alvarez's false claims would have been fully vindicated by the community's expression of outrage .... The same can be said for the Government's interest. The American people do not need the assistance of a government prosecution to express their high regard for the special place that military heroes hold in our tradition. ...

In addition, when the Government seeks to regulate protected speech, the restriction must be the "least restrictive means among available, effective alternatives." .... [A]t least one less speech-restrictive means ... could likely protect the integrity of the military awards system. A Government-created database could list Congressional Medal of Honor winners. Were a database accessible through the Internet, it would be easy to verify and expose false claims. It appears some private individuals have already created databases similar to this, ... and at least one database of past winners is online and fully searchable .... The Solicitor General responds that although Congress and the Department of Defense investigated the feasibility of establishing a database in 2008, the Government "concluded that such a database would be impracticable and insufficiently comprehensive." ... Without more explanation, it is difficult to assess the Government's claim, especially when at least one database of Congressional Medal of Honor winners already exists.

The Government may have responses to some of these criticisms, but there has been no clear showing of the necessity of the statute, the necessity required by exacting scrutiny.

* * *

. . . The Stolen Valor Act infringes upon speech protected by the First Amendment.

The judgment of the Court of Appeals is affirmed.

■ JUSTICE BREYER, with whom JUSTICE KAGAN joins, concurring in the judgment.

I agree with the plurality that the Stolen Valor Act of 2005 violates the First Amendment. But . . . I base that conclusion upon the fact that the statute works First Amendment harm, while the Government can achieve its legitimate objectives in less restrictive ways.

I

In determining whether a statute violates the First Amendment, this Court . . . has taken account of the seriousness of the speech-related harm the provision will likely cause, the nature and importance of the provision's countervailing objectives, the extent to which the provision will tend to achieve those objectives, and whether there are other, less restrictive ways of doing so. Ultimately the Court has had to determine whether the statute works speech-related harm that is out of proportion to its justifications.

. . .

As the dissent points out, "there are broad areas in which any attempt by the state to penalize purportedly false speech would present a grave and unacceptable danger of suppressing truthful speech." Laws restricting false statements about philosophy, religion, history, the social sciences, the arts, and the like raise such concerns, and in many contexts have called for strict scrutiny. But this case does not involve such a law. The dangers of suppressing valuable ideas are lower where, as here, the regulations concern false statements about easily verifiable facts that do not concern such subject matter. Such false factual statements are less likely than are true factual statements to make a valuable contribution to the marketplace of ideas. And the government often has good reasons to prohibit such false speech. . . . But its regulation can nonetheless threaten speech-related harms. Those circumstances lead me to apply what the Court has termed "intermediate scrutiny" here.

II

A

. . . I would read the statute favorably to the Government as criminalizing only false factual statements made with knowledge of their falsity and with the intent that they be taken as true. . . . As so interpreted the statute covers only lies. But although this interpretation diminishes the extent to which the statute endangers First Amendment values, it does not eliminate the threat.

[A]s the Government points out, . . . this Court has frequently said or implied that false factual statements enjoy little First Amendment protection. . . .

But these judicial statements cannot be read to mean "no protection at all." False factual statements can serve useful human objectives, for example: in social contexts, where they may prevent embarrassment, protect privacy, shield a person from prejudice, provide the sick with comfort, or preserve a child's innocence; in public contexts, where they may stop a panic or otherwise preserve calm in the face of danger; and even in technical, philosophical, and scientific contexts, where (as

Socrates' methods suggest) examination of a false statement (even if made deliberately to mislead) can promote a form of thought that ultimately helps realize the truth. . . . See, *e.g.,* . . . *New York Times Co., supra,* at 279, n. 19 ("Even a false statement may be deemed to make a valuable contribution to public debate, since it brings about 'the clearer perception and livelier impression of truth, produced by its collision with error' " (quoting J. Mill, On Liberty 15 (Blackwell ed. 1947))).

Moreover, . . . the threat of criminal prosecution for making a false statement can inhibit the speaker from making true statements, thereby "chilling" a kind of speech that lies at the First Amendment's heart. . . . Hence, the Court emphasizes *mens rea* requirements that provide "breathing room" for more valuable speech by reducing an honest speaker's fear that he may accidentally incur liability for speaking.

Further, the pervasiveness of false statements, made for better or for worse motives, made thoughtlessly or deliberately, made with or without accompanying harm, provides a weapon to a government broadly empowered to prosecute falsity without more. And those who are unpopular may fear that the government will use that weapon selectively, say by prosecuting a pacifist who supports his cause by (falsely) claiming to have been a war hero, while ignoring members of other political groups who might make similar false claims.

I also must concede that many statutes and common law doctrines make the utterance of certain kinds of false statements unlawful. Those prohibitions, however, tend to be narrower than the statute before us, in that they limit the scope of their application, sometimes by requiring proof of specific harm to identifiable victims; sometimes by specifying that the lies be made in contexts in which a tangible harm to others is especially likely to occur; and sometimes by limiting the prohibited lies to those that are particularly likely to produce harm.

Fraud statutes, for example, typically require proof of a misrepresentation that is material, upon which the victim relied, and which caused actual injury. . . . Defamation statutes focus upon statements of a kind that harm the reputation of another or deter third parties from association or dealing with the victim. . . . Torts involving the intentional infliction of emotional distress (like torts involving placing a victim in a false light) concern falsehoods that tend to cause harm to a specific victim of an emotional-, dignitary-, or privacy-related kind. . . .

Perjury statutes prohibit a particular set of false statements—those made under oath—while requiring a showing of materiality. . . . Statutes forbidding lying to a government official (not under oath) are typically limited to circumstances where a lie is likely to work particular and specific harm by interfering with the functioning of a government department, and those statutes also require a showing of materiality. . . .

Statutes prohibiting false claims of terrorist attacks, or other lies about the commission of crimes or catastrophes, require proof that substantial public harm be directly foreseeable, or, if not, involve false statements that are very likely to bring about that harm. . . .

Statutes forbidding impersonation of a public official typically focus on *acts* of impersonation, not mere speech, and may require a showing that, for example, someone was deceived into following a "course [of action] he would not have pursued but for the deceitful conduct." United States v. Lepowitch, 318 U. S. 702, 704 (1943). . . .

Statutes prohibiting trademark infringement present, perhaps, the closest analogy to the present statute. Trademarks identify the source of a good; and infringement causes harm by causing confusion among potential customers (about the source) and thereby diluting the value of the mark to its owner, to consumers, and to the economy. Similarly, a false claim of possession of a medal or other honor creates confusion about who is entitled to wear it, thus diluting its value to those who have earned it, to their families, and to their country. But trademark statutes are focused upon commercial and promotional activities that are likely to dilute the value of a mark. Indeed, they typically require a showing of likely confusion, a showing that tends to assure that the feared harm will in fact take place. . . .

. . . [F]ew statutes, if any, simply prohibit without limitation the telling of a lie, even a lie about one particular matter. Instead, in virtually all these instances limitations of context, requirements of proof of injury, and the like, narrow the statute to a subset of lies where specific harm is more likely to occur. The limitations help to make certain that the statute does not allow its threat of liability or criminal punishment to roam at large, discouraging or forbidding the telling of the lie in contexts where harm is unlikely or the need for the prohibition is small.

The statute before us lacks any such limiting features. . . . As written, it applies in family, social, or other private contexts, where lies will often cause little harm. It also applies in political contexts, where although such lies are more likely to cause harm, the risk of censorious selectivity by prosecutors is also high. Further, given the potential haziness of individual memory along with the large number of military awards covered . . . , there remains a risk of chilling that is not completely eliminated by *mens rea* requirements; a speaker might still be worried about being *prosecuted* for a careless false statement, even if he does not have the intent required to render him liable. And so the prohibition may be applied where it should not be applied, for example, to bar stool braggadocio or, in the political arena, subtly but selectively to speakers that the Government does not like. These considerations lead me to believe that the statute as written risks significant First Amendment harm.

B

Like both the plurality and the dissent, I believe the statute nonetheless has substantial justification. It seeks to protect the interests of those who have sacrificed their health and life for their country . . . by seeking to preserve intact the country's recognition of that sacrifice in the form of military honors. To permit those who have not earned those honors to claim otherwise dilutes the value of the awards. . . . Thus, the statute risks harming protected interests but only in order to achieve a substantial countervailing objective.

C

We must therefore ask whether it is possible substantially to achieve the Government's objective in less burdensome ways. In my view, the answer . . . is "yes." . . . [N]ot all military awards are alike. Congress might determine that some warrant greater protection than others. And a more finely tailored statute might . . . insist upon a showing that the false statement caused specific harm or at least was material, or focus its coverage on lies most likely to be harmful or on contexts where such lies are most likely to cause harm.

I recognize that in some contexts, particularly political contexts, such a narrowing will not always be easy to achieve. In the political arena a false statement is more likely to make a behavioral difference (say, by leading the listeners to vote for the speaker) but at the same time criminal prosecution is particularly dangerous (say, by radically changing a potential election result) and consequently can more easily result in censorship of speakers and their ideas. Thus, the statute may have to be significantly narrowed in its applications. Some lower courts have upheld the constitutionality of roughly comparable but narrowly tailored statutes in political contexts. See, *e.g.,* United We Stand America, Inc. v. United We Stand, America New York, Inc., 128 F. 3d 86, 93 (CA2 1997) (upholding against First Amendment challenge application of Lanham Act to a political organization); Treasurer of the Committee to Elect Gerald D. Lostracco v. Fox, 150 Mich. App. 617, 389 N. W. 2d 446 (1986) (upholding under First Amendment statute prohibiting campaign material falsely claiming that one is an incumbent). Without expressing any view on the validity of those cases, I would also note, like the plurality, that in this area more accurate information will normally counteract the lie. And an accurate, publicly available register of military awards, easily obtainable by political opponents, may well adequately protect the integrity of an award against those who would falsely claim to have earned it. And so it is likely that a more narrowly tailored statute combined with such information-disseminating devices will effectively serve Congress' end.

The Government has provided no convincing explanation as to why a more finely tailored statute would not work. . . . I find the statute as presently drafted works disproportionate constitutional harm. It consequently fails intermediate scrutiny, and so violates the First Amendment.

For these reasons, I concur in the Court's judgment.

■ JUSTICE ALITO, with whom JUSTICE SCALIA and JUSTICE THOMAS join, dissenting.

. . . The . . . Stolen Valor Act of . . . was enacted to stem an epidemic of false claims about military decorations. These lies, Congress reasonably concluded, were undermining our country's system of military honors and inflicting real harm on actual medal recipients and their families.

. . . Congress responded . . . by crafting a narrow statute that presents no threat to the freedom of speech. The statute reaches only knowingly false statements about hard facts directly within a speaker's personal knowledge. These lies have no value in and of themselves, and proscribing them does not chill any valuable speech.

By holding that the First Amendment nevertheless shields these lies, the Court breaks sharply from a long line of cases recognizing that the right to free speech does not protect false factual statements that inflict real harm and serve no legitimate interest. I would adhere to that principle and would thus uphold the constitutionality of this valuable law.

I

The Stolen Valor Act . . . [p]roperly construed . . . is limited in five significant respects. First, the Act applies to only a narrow category of false representations about objective facts that can almost always be proved or disproved with near certainty. Second, the Act concerns facts that are squarely within the speaker's personal knowledge. Third, as the Government maintains, . . . and both the plurality and the concurrence seemingly accept, a conviction under the Act requires proof beyond a reasonable doubt that the speaker actually knew that the representation was false. Fourth, the Act applies only to statements that could reasonably be interpreted as communicating actual facts; it does not reach dramatic performances, satire, parody, hyperbole, or the like. Finally, the Act is strictly viewpoint neutral. The false statements proscribed by the Act are highly unlikely to be tied to any particular political or ideological message. In the rare cases where that is not so, the Act applies equally to all false statements, whether they tend to disparage or commend the Government, the military, or the system of military honors.

The Stolen Valor Act follows a long tradition of efforts to protect our country's system of military honors. . . .

. . .

As Congress recognized, the lies proscribed by the Stolen Valor Act inflict substantial harm. In many instances, the harm is tangible in nature: Individuals often falsely represent themselves as award recipients in order to obtain financial or other material rewards, such as lucrative contracts and government benefits. . . . In other cases, the harm is less tangible, but nonetheless significant. The lies . . . tend to debase the distinctive honor of military awards. . . . And legitimate award recipients and their families have expressed the harm they endure when an imposter takes credit for heroic actions that he never performed. One Medal of Honor recipient described the feeling as a " 'slap in the face of veterans who have paid the price and earned their medals.' "

It is well recognized in trademark law that the proliferation of cheap imitations of luxury goods blurs the " 'signal' given out by the purchasers of the originals." . . . In much the same way, the proliferation of false claims about military awards blurs the signal given out by the actual awards by making them seem more common than they really are, and this diluting effect harms the military by hampering its efforts to foster morale and esprit de corps. . . .

Both the plurality and Justice Breyer argue that Congress could have preserved the integrity of military honors by means other than a criminal prohibition, but Congress had ample reason to believe that alternative approaches would not be adequate. . . .

[The database] remedy, unfortunately, will not work. The Department of Defense has explained that the most that it can do is to create a database of recipients of certain top military honors awarded since 2001. . . .

Because a sufficiently comprehensive database is not practicable, lies about military awards cannot be remedied by what the plurality calls "counterspeech." . . .

The plurality and the concurrence also suggest that Congress could protect the system of military honors by enacting a narrower statute. . . . But much damage is caused, both to real award recipients and to the system of military honors, by false statements that are not linked to any financial or other tangible reward. Unless even a small financial loss—say, a dollar given to a homeless man falsely claiming to be a decorated veteran—is more important in the eyes of the First Amendment than the damage caused to the very integrity of the military awards system, there is no basis for distinguishing between the Stolen Valor Act and the alternative statutes that the plurality and concurrence appear willing to sustain.

. . .

II

A

Time and again, this Court has recognized that as a general matter false factual statements possess no intrinsic First Amendment value. . . .

. . . [M]any kinds of false factual statements have long been proscribed without " 'rais[ing] any Constitutional problem.' " . . . Laws prohibiting fraud, perjury, and defamation, for example, were in existence when the First Amendment was adopted, and their constitutionality is now beyond question. . . .

We have also described as falling outside the First Amendment's protective shield certain false factual statements that were neither illegal nor tortious at the time of the Amendment's adoption. The right to freedom of speech has been held to permit recovery for the intentional infliction of emotional distress by means of a false statement, . . . even though that tort did not enter our law until the late 19th century . . . . And . . . the Court concluded that the free speech right allows recovery for the even more modern tort of false-light invasion of privacy . . . .

In line with these holdings, it has long been assumed that the First Amendment is not offended by prominent criminal statutes with no close common-law analog. The most well known of these is probably 18 U. S. C. § 1001, which makes it a crime to "knowingly and willfully" make any "materially false, fictitious, or fraudulent statement or representation" in "any matter within the jurisdiction of the executive, legislative, or judicial branch of the Government of the United States." Unlike perjury, § 1001 is not limited to statements made under oath or before an official government tribunal. Nor does it require any showing of "pecuniary or property loss to the government." United States v. Gilliland, 312 U. S. 86, 93 (1941). Instead, the statute is based on the need to protect "agencies from the perversion which *might* result from the deceptive practices described." . . .

. . . All told, there are more than 100 federal criminal statutes that punish false statements made in connection with areas of federal agency concern. . . .

These examples amply demonstrate that false statements of fact merit no First Amendment protection in their own right. It is true, as Justice Breyer notes, that many in our society either approve or condone certain discrete categories of false statements, including false statements made to prevent harm to innocent victims and so-called "white lies." But respondent's false claim to have received the Medal of Honor did not fall into any of these categories. His lie did not "prevent embarrassment, protect privacy, shield a person from prejudice, provide the sick with comfort, or preserve a child's innocence." Nor did his lie "stop a panic or otherwise preserve calm in the face of danger" or further philosophical or scientific debate. . . . Respondent's claim, like all those covered by the Stolen Valor Act, served no valid purpose.

. . .

. . . The lies covered by the Stolen Valor Act have no intrinsic value and thus merit no First Amendment protection unless their prohibition would chill other expression that falls within the Amendment's scope. I now turn to that question.

B

. . .

. . . [T]here are broad areas in which any attempt by the state to penalize purportedly false speech would present a grave and unacceptable danger of suppressing truthful speech. Laws restricting false statements about philosophy, religion, history, the social sciences, the arts, and other matters of public concern would present such a threat. The point is not that there is no such thing as truth or falsity in these areas or that the truth is always impossible to ascertain, but rather that it is perilous to permit the state to be the arbiter of truth.

Even where there is a wide scholarly consensus concerning a particular matter, the truth is served by allowing that consensus to be challenged without fear of reprisal. Today's accepted wisdom sometimes turns out to be mistaken. And in these contexts, "[e]ven a false statement may be deemed to make a valuable contribution to public debate, since it brings about 'the clearer perception and livelier impression of truth, produced by its collision with error.' " *Sullivan, supra,* at 279, n. 19 (quoting J. Mill, On Liberty 15 (R. McCallum ed. 1947)).

Allowing the state to proscribe false statements in these areas also opens the door for the state to use its power for political ends. . . .

In stark contrast to hypothetical laws prohibiting false statements about history, science, and similar matters, the Stolen Valor Act presents no risk at all that valuable speech will be suppressed. The speech punished by the Act is not only verifiably false and entirely lacking in intrinsic value, but it also fails to serve any instrumental purpose that the First Amendment might protect. Tellingly, when asked at oral argument what truthful speech the Stolen Valor Act might chill, even respondent's counsel conceded that the answer is none. . . .

C

Neither of the two opinions endorsed by Justices in the majority claims that the false statements covered by the Stolen Valor Act possess either intrinsic or instrumental value. Instead, those opinions appear to be based on the distinct concern that the Act suffers from overbreadth. . . . But to strike down a statute on the basis that it is overbroad, it is necessary to show that the statute's "overbreadth [is] *substantial*, not only in an absolute sense, but also relative to [its] plainly legitimate sweep." . . . The plurality and the concurrence do not even attempt to make this showing.

. . .

The Stolen Valor Act is a narrow law enacted to address an important problem, and it presents no threat to freedom of expression. I would sustain the constitutionality of the Act, and I therefore respectfully dissent.

4. RESTRICTIONS ON TIME, PLACE, OR MANNER OF EXPRESSION

The title of this section signals a shift in emphasis from controlling expression because of its content to restricting the time, place, or manner of expression. It is, however, a shift rather than a break in the analysis of freedom of speech. Time, place, or manner issues were prominent in some of the cases in the preceding sections. Issues of speech content are often central to time, place, or manner restrictions. A repetitive question is whether any consistent principle can be formulated where government restrictions of expression blend considerations of time, place, or manner with considerations of content.

A. THE TRADITIONAL PUBLIC FORUM: SPEECH ACTIVITIES IN STREETS AND PARKS

Schneider v. New Jersey, Town of Irvington
308 U.S. 147 (1939).

The Court had before it three cases involving city ordinances forbidding the distribution of handbills in the streets (and in one case in any public place). The cases involved convictions of persons distributing handbills giving notice of meetings on public issues in two cases and as an incident to labor picketing in the third. The Court reversed the convictions, holding that the cities could not forbid all distribution of handbills on public streets. Justice Roberts, speaking for the Court, said, in part:

"Municipal authorities, as trustees for the public, have the duty to keep their communities' streets open and available for movement of people and property, the primary purpose to which the streets are dedicated. So long as legislation to this end does not abridge the constitutional liberty of one rightfully upon the street to impart information through speech or the distribution of literature, it may lawfully regulate the conduct of those using the streets. For example, a person could not exercise this liberty by taking his stand in the middle of a crowded street, contrary to traffic regulations, and maintain his position to the stoppage of all traffic; a group of distributors could not insist upon a constitutional right to form a cordon across the street and to allow no pedestrian to pass who did not accept a tendered leaflet; nor does the guarantee of freedom of speech or of the press deprive a municipality of power to enact regulations against throwing literature broadcast in the streets. Prohibition of such conduct would not abridge the constitutional liberty since such activity bears no necessary relationship to the freedom to speak, write, print or distribute information or opinion.

. . .

"The motive of the legislation under attack in Numbers 13, 18 and 29 is held by the courts below to be the prevention of littering of the streets and, although the alleged offenders were not charged with themselves scattering paper in the streets, their convictions were sustained upon the theory that distribution by them encouraged or resulted in such littering. We are of opinion that the purpose to keep the streets clean and of good appearance is insufficient to justify an ordinance which prohibits a person rightfully on a public street from handing literature to one willing to receive it. Any burden imposed upon the city authorities in cleaning and caring for the streets as an indirect consequence of such distribution results from the constitutional protection of the freedom of speech and press. This constitutional protection does not deprive a city of all power to prevent street littering. There are obvious methods of preventing littering. Amongst these is the punishment of those who actually throw papers on the streets."

Minimum Access vs. Equal Access to the Public Forum

There are two famous quotations expressing polar positions. While sitting on the Massachusetts Supreme Judicial Court, Justice Holmes observed: "For the Legislature absolutely or conditionally to forbid public speaking in a highway or public park is no more an infringement of the rights of a member of the public than for the owner of a private house to forbid it in his house." Commonwealth v. Davis, 162 Mass. 510, 511, 39 N.E. 113 (1895), affirmed 167 U.S. 43, 47–48 (1897). Justice Roberts' plurality opinion in Hague v. C.I.O., 307 U.S. 496, 515–516 (1939) contains this often quoted dictum: "Wherever the title of streets and parks may rest, they have immemorially been held in trust for the use of the public and, time out of mind, have been used for purposes of assembly, communicating thoughts between citizens, and discussing public questions. Such use of the streets and public places has, from ancient times, been a part of the privileges, immunities, rights, and liberties of citizens."

No Supreme Court decision has confronted the constitutionality of a municipality's decision to reserve its streets entirely for traffic and its parks as facilities for quiet rest and relaxation. In that context, the issue may be more theoretical than real. The cases before the Court have either involved time, place, or manner restrictions that did not totally preclude use of parks and streets for expression, or restrictions that denied equal access to the public facilities involved. Does resolution of the debate whether all parks and streets could be closed to expression affect the results in those cases? Does Justice Roberts' opinion in *Schneider* implicitly rest on accepting his dictum in *Hague*?

For discussion of these issues see Kalven, *The Concept of the Public Forum: Cox v. Louisiana*, 1965 Sup.Ct.Rev. 1.

McCullen v. Coakley

573 U.S. ___, 134 S.Ct. 2518, 189 L.Ed.2d 502 (2014).

■ CHIEF JUSTICE ROBERTS delivered the opinion of the Court.

A Massachusetts statute makes it a crime to knowingly stand on a "public way or sidewalk" within 35 feet of an entrance or driveway to any place, other than a hospital, where abortions are performed.... Petitioners ... approach and talk to women outside such facilities, attempting to dissuade them from having abortions. The statute prevents petitioners from doing so near the facilities' entrances. The question presented is whether the statute violates the First Amendment.

I

A

[In 2000, Massachusetts passed a law] designed to address clashes between abortion opponents and advocates of abortion rights that were occurring outside clinics where abortions were performed. The Act established a defined area with an 18-foot radius around the entrances and driveways of such facilities. § 120E½(b). Anyone could enter that area, but once within it, no one (other than certain exempt individuals) could knowingly approach within six feet of another person—unless that person consented—"for the purpose of passing a leaflet or handbill to, displaying a sign to, or engaging in oral protest, education, or counseling with such other person." ... A separate provision subjected to criminal punishment anyone who "knowingly obstructs, detains, hinders, impedes or blocks another person's entry to or exit from a reproductive health care facility." § 120E½(e).

The statute was modeled on a similar Colorado law that this Court had upheld in *Hill* v. *Colorado*, 530 U.S. 703 (2000)....

By 2007, some Massachusetts legislators and law enforcement officials had come to regard the 2000 statute as inadequate. At legislative hearings, multiple witnesses recounted apparent violations of the law. [Among others, reports that prospective patients occasionally retreated from the clinics rather than try to make their way to the clinic entrances or parking lots, and that the six-foot no-approach zone was difficult to enforce, led the legislature to amend the statute,] replacing the six-foot no-approach zones (within the 18-foot area) with a 35-foot fixed buffer zone from which individuals are categorically excluded. The statute now provides:

"No person shall knowingly enter or remain on a public way or sidewalk adjacent to a reproductive health care facility within a radius of 35 feet of any portion of an entrance, exit or driveway of a reproductive healthcare facility or within the area within a rectangle created by extending the outside boundaries of any entrance, exit or driveway of a reproductive health care facility in straight lines to the point where such lines intersect the sideline of the street in front of such entrance, exit or driveway." Mass. Gen. Laws, ch. 266, § 120E½(b) (West 2012).

A "reproductive health care facility," ... is defined as "a place, other than within or upon the grounds of a hospital, where abortions are offered or performed." § 120E½(a).

The 35-foot buffer zone applies only "during a facility's business hours," and the area must be "clearly marked and posted." § 120E½(c). In practice, facilities typically mark the zones with painted arcs and posted signs on adjacent sidewalks and streets. A first violation ... is punishable by a fine of up to $500, up to three months in prison, or both, while a subsequent offense is punishable by a fine of between $500 and $5,000, up to two and a half years in prison, or both. § 120E½(d).

The Act exempts four classes of individuals: (1) "persons entering or leaving such facility"; (2) "employees or agents of such facility acting within the scope of their employment"; (3) "law enforcement, ambulance, firefighting, construction, utilities, public works and other municipal agents acting within the scope of their employment"; and (4) "persons using the public sidewalk or street right-of-way adjacent to such facility solely for the purpose of reaching a destination other than such facility." § 120E½(b)(1)–(4). The legislature also retained the separate provision from the 2000 version that proscribes the knowing obstruction of access to a facility. § 120E½(e).

B

Some of the individuals who stand outside Massachusetts abortion clinics are fairly described as protestors, who express their moral or religious opposition to abortion through signs and chants or, in some cases, more aggressive methods such as face-to-face confrontation. Petitioners take a different tack. They attempt to engage women approaching the clinics in what they call "sidewalk counseling," which involves offering information about alternatives to abortion and help pursuing those options. McCullen and the other petitioners consider it essential to maintain a caring demeanor, a calm tone of voice, and direct eye contact during these exchanges. Such interactions, petitioners believe, are a much more effective means of dissuading women from having abortions than confrontational methods such as shouting or brandishing signs, which in petitioners' view tend only to antagonize their intended audience. In unrefuted testimony, petitioners say they have collectively persuaded hundreds of women to forgo abortions.

The buffer zones have displaced petitioners from their previous positions outside the clinics. . . . [In Boston, the "upshot is that petitioners are effectively excluded from a 56-foot-wide expanse of the public sidewalk in front of the [Planned Parenthood] clinic." In Worcester and Springfield, because the clinics are "well back from the public street and sidewalks[,]" they "must now stand either some distance down the sidewalk from the private walkway and driveway or across the street."]

Petitioners at all three clinics claim that the buffer zones have considerably hampered their counseling efforts. Although they have managed to conduct some counseling and to distribute some literature outside the buffer zones—particularly at the Boston clinic—they say they have had many fewer conversations and distributed many fewer leaflets since the zones went into effect. . . .

The second statutory exemption allows clinic employees and agents acting within the scope of their employment to enter the buffer zones. Relying on this exemption, the Boston clinic uses "escorts" to greet women as they approach the clinic, accompanying them through the zones to the clinic entrance. Petitioners claim that the escorts sometimes thwart petitioners' attempts to communicate with patients by blocking petitioners from handing literature to patients, telling patients not to "pay any attention" or "listen to" petitioners, and disparaging petitioners as "crazy." . . .

C

[P]etitioners sued . . . to enjoin enforcement of the Act, alleging that it violates the First and Fourteenth Amendments, both on its face and as applied to them. [The District Court rejected their challenges and the First Circuit affirmed.]

II

By its very terms, the Massachusetts Act regulates access to "public way[s]" and "sidewalk[s]." . . . Such areas occupy a "special position in terms of First Amendment protection" because of their historic role as sites for discussion and debate. United States v. Grace, 461 U.S. 171, 180 (1983). . . .

It is no accident that public streets and sidewalks have developed as venues for the exchange of ideas. Even today, they remain one of the few places where a speaker can be confident that he is not simply preaching to the choir. With respect to other means of communication, an individual confronted with an uncomfortable message can always turn the page, change the channel, or leave the Web site. Not so on public streets and sidewalks. There, a listener often encounters speech he might otherwise tune out. In light of the First Amendment's purpose "to preserve an uninhibited marketplace of ideas in which truth will ultimately prevail," . . . this aspect of traditional public fora is a virtue, not a vice.

. . .

. . . [T]he guiding First Amendment principle that the "government has no power to restrict expression because of its message, its ideas, its subject matter, or its content" applies with full force in a traditional public forum. Police Dept. of Chicago v. Mosley, 408 U.S. 92, 95 (1972). As a general rule, in such a forum the government may not "selectively. . . shield the public from some kinds of speech on the ground that they are more offensive than others." Erznoznik v. Jacksonville, 422 U.S. 205, 209 (1975).

We have, however, afforded the government somewhat wider leeway to regulate features of speech unrelated to its content. "[E]ven in a public forum the government may impose reasonable restrictions on the time, place, or manner of protected speech, provided the restrictions 'are justified without reference to the content of the regulated speech, that they are narrowly tailored to serve a significant governmental interest, and that they leave open ample alternative channels for communication of the information.'" Ward [v. Rock Against Racism, 491 U.S. 781 (1989),] at 791 . . . .

. . .

III

Petitioners contend that the Act is not content neutral for two independent reasons: First, they argue that it discriminates against abortion-related speech because it establishes buffer zones only at clinics that perform abortions. Second, petitioners contend that the Act, by exempting clinic employees and agents, favors one viewpoint about abortion over the other. If either of these arguments is correct, then the Act must satisfy strict scrutiny—that is, it must be the least restrictive means of achieving a compelling state interest. . . . Respondents do not argue that the Act can survive this exacting standard.

. . .

A

. . . [P]etitioners argue [that] "virtually all speech affected by the Act is speech concerning abortion," thus rendering the Act content based. . . .

We disagree. To begin, the Act does not draw content based distinctions on its face. Contrast Boos v. Barry, 485 U.S. 312, 315 (1988) (ordinance prohibiting the display within 500 feet of a foreign embassy of any sign that tends to bring the foreign government into "'public odium'" or "'public disrepute'"); Carey v. Brown, 447 U.S. 455, 465 (1980) (statute prohibiting all residential picketing except "peaceful labor picketing"). The Act would be content based if it required "enforcement authorities" to "examine the content of the message that is conveyed to determine whether" a violation has occurred. . . . But it does not. Whether petitioners violate the Act "depends" not "on what they say," Humanitarian Law Project, . . . but simply on where they say it. Indeed, petitioners can violate the Act merely by standing in a buffer zone, without displaying a sign or uttering a word.

It is true, of course, that by limiting the buffer zones to abortion clinics, the Act has the "inevitable effect" of restricting abortion-related speech more than speech on other subjects. Brief for Petitioners 24 (quoting United States v. O'Brien, 391 U.S. 367, 384 (1968)). But a facially neutral law does not become content based simply because it may disproportionately affect speech on certain topics. On the contrary, "[a] regulation that serves purposes unrelated to the content of expression is deemed neutral, even if it has an incidental effect on some speakers or messages but not others." *Ward,.* . . . The question in such a case is whether the law is " 'justified without reference to the content of the regulated speech.' " . . .

The Massachusetts Act is. Its stated purpose is to "increase forthwith public safety at reproductive health care facilities." 2007 Mass. Acts p. 660. Respondents have articulated similar purposes before this Court—namely, "public safety, patient access to healthcare, and the unobstructed use of public sidewalks and roadways." . . .

We have previously deemed the foregoing concerns to be content neutral. . . . Obstructed access and congested sidewalks are problems no matter what caused them. A group of individuals can obstruct clinic access and clog sidewalks just as much when they loiter as when they protest abortion or counsel patients.

To be clear, the Act would not be content neutral if it were concerned with undesirable effects that arise from "the direct impact of speech on its audience" or "[l]isteners' reactions to speech." . . . If, for example, the speech outside Massachusetts abortion clinics caused offense or made listeners uncomfortable, such offense or discomfort would not give the Commonwealth a content-neutral justification to restrict the speech. All of the problems identified by the Commonwealth here, however, arise irrespective of any listener's reactions. Whether or not a single person reacts to abortion protestors' chants or petitioners' counseling, large crowds outside abortion clinics can still compromise public safety, impede access, and obstruct sidewalks.

Petitioners do not really dispute that the Commonwealth's interests in ensuring safety and preventing obstruction are, as a general matter, content neutral. But petitioners note that these interests "apply outside every building in the State that hosts any activity that might occasion protest or comment," not just abortion clinics. . . . By choosing to pursue these interests only at abortion clinics, petitioners argue, the Massachusetts Legislature evinced a purpose to "single[ ]out for regulation speech about one particular topic: abortion." . . .

We cannot infer such a purpose from the Act's limited scope. . . . The Massachusetts Legislature amended the Act in 2007 in response to a problem that was, in its experience, limited to abortion clinics. There was a record of crowding, obstruction, and even violence outside such clinics. There were apparently no similar recurring problems associated with other kinds of healthcare facilities, let alone with "every building in the State that hosts any activity that might occasion protest or comment." . . . In light of the limited nature of the problem, it was reasonable for the Massachusetts Legislature to enact a limited solution. When selecting among various options for combating a particular problem, legislatures should be encouraged to choose the one that restricts less speech, not more.

Justice Scalia objects that the statute does restrict more speech than necessary, because "only one [Massachusetts abortion clinic] is known to have been beset by the problems that the statute supposedly addresses." But there are no grounds for inferring content based discrimination here simply because the legislature acted with respect to abortion facilities generally rather than proceeding on a facility-by-facility basis. On these facts, the poor fit noted by Justice Scalia goes to the question of narrow tailoring, which we consider below.

B

Petitioners also argue that the Act is content based because [of . . .] the exemption allow[ing] clinic employees and agents—including the volunteers who "escort" patients arriving at the Boston clinic—to speak inside the buffer zones.

It is of course true that "an exemption from an otherwise permissible regulation of speech may represent a governmental 'attempt to give one side of a debatable public question an advantage in expressing its views to the people.' " City of Ladue v. Gilleo, 512 U.S. 43, 51 (1994) .... At least on the record before us, however, the statutory exemption for clinic employees and agents acting within the scope of their employment does not appear to be such an attempt.

... [T]he exemption cannot be regarded as simply a carve-out for the clinic escorts; it also covers employees such as the maintenance worker shoveling a snowy sidewalk or the security guard patrolling a clinic entrance . . . .

Given the need for an exemption for clinic employees, the "scope of their employment" qualification simply ensures that the exemption is limited to its purpose of allowing the employees to do their jobs. . . . There is no suggestion in the record that any of the clinics authorize their employees to speak about abortion in the buffer zones. The "scope of their employment" limitation thus seems designed to protect against exactly the sort of conduct that petitioners and Justice Scalia fear.

Petitioners did testify in this litigation about instances in which escorts at the Boston clinic had expressed views about abortion to the women they were accompanying, thwarted petitioners' attempts to speak and hand literature to the women, and disparaged petitioners in various ways. . . It is unclear from petitioners' testimony whether these alleged incidents occurred within the buffer zones. There is no viewpoint discrimination problem if the incidents occurred outside the zones because petitioners are equally free to say whatever they would like in that area.

Even assuming the incidents occurred inside the zones, the record does not suggest that they involved speech within the scope of the escorts' employment. If the speech was beyond the scope of their employment, then each of the alleged incidents would violate the Act's express terms. Petitioners' complaint would then be that the police were failing to *enforce* the Act equally against clinic escorts. . . . While such allegations might state a claim of official viewpoint discrimination, that would not go to the validity of the Act. In any event, petitioners nowhere allege selective enforcement.

It would be a very different question if it turned out that a clinic authorized escorts to speak about abortion inside the buffer zones. See Alito, J., (concurring in judgment). In that case, the escorts would not seem to be violating the Act because the speech would be within the scope of their employment. The Act's exemption for clinic employees would then facilitate speech on only one side of the abortion debate—a clear form of viewpoint discrimination that would support an as-applied challenge to the buffer zone at that clinic. But the record before us contains insufficient evidence to show that the exemption operates in this way at any of the clinics, perhaps because the clinics do not want to doom the Act by allowing their employees to speak about abortion within the buffer zones.[4]

We thus conclude that the Act is neither content nor viewpoint based and therefore need not be analyzed under strict scrutiny.

---

[4]   Of course we do not hold that "[s]peech restrictions favoring one viewpoint over another are not content based unless it can be shown that the favored viewpoint has actually been expressed." We instead apply an uncontroversial principle of constitutional adjudication: that a plaintiff generally cannot prevail on an *as-applied* challenge without showing that the law has in fact been (or is sufficiently likely to be) unconstitutionally *applied* to him. Specifically, when someone challenges a law as viewpoint discriminatory but it is not clear from the face of the law which speakers will be allowed to speak, he must show that he was prevented from speaking while someone espousing another viewpoint was permitted to do so. . . .

IV

Even though the Act is content neutral, it still must be "narrowly tailored to serve a significant governmental interest." . . . By demanding a close fit between ends and means, the tailoring requirement prevents the government from too readily "sacrific[ing] speech for efficiency." . . .

For a content-neutral time, place, or manner regulation to be narrowly tailored, it must not "burden substantially more speech than is necessary to further the government's legitimate interests." *Ward*, ...

As noted, respondents claim that the Act promotes "public safety, patient access to healthcare, and the unobstructed use of public sidewalks and roadways." . . . Petitioners do not dispute the significance of these interests. . . . The buffer zones clearly serve these interests.

At the same time, the buffer zones impose serious burdens on petitioners' speech. At each of the three Planned Parenthood clinics where petitioners attempt to counsel patients, the zones carve out a significant portion of the adjacent public sidewalks, pushing petitioners well back from the clinics' entrances and driveways. The zones thereby compromise petitioners' ability to initiate the close, personal conversations that they view as essential to "sidewalk counseling."

. . . Given these limitations, McCullen is often reduced to raising her voice at patients from outside the zone—a mode of communication sharply at odds with the compassionate message she wishes to convey. . . .

These burdens on petitioners' speech have clearly taken their toll, [drastically reducing the number of women they previously had persuaded not to terminate their pregnancies].

The buffer zones have also made it substantially more difficult for petitioners to distribute literature to arriving patients. . . . In short, the Act operates to deprive petitioners of their two primary methods of communicating with patients.

[W]hile the First Amendment does not guarantee a speaker the right to any particular form of expression, some forms—such as normal conversation and leafletting on a public sidewalk—have historically been more closely associated with the transmission of ideas than others.

In the context of petition campaigns, we have observed that "one-on-one communication" is "the most effective, fundamental, and perhaps economical avenue of political discourse." Meyer v. Grant, 486 U.S. 414, 424 (1988). See also *Schenck, supra*, at 377 (invalidating a "floating" buffer zone around people entering an abortion clinic partly on the ground that it prevented protestors "from communicating a message from a normal conversational distance or handing leaflets to people entering or leaving the clinics who are walking on the public sidewalks"). . . . When the government makes it more difficult to engage in these modes of communication, it imposes an especially significant First Amendment burden.

Respondents also emphasize that the Act does not prevent petitioners from engaging in various forms of "protest"—such as chanting slogans and displaying signs—outside the buffer zones. . . . That misses the point. Petitioners are not protestors. They seek not merely to express their opposition to abortion, but to inform women of various alternatives and to provide help in pursuing them. Petitioners believe that they can accomplish this objective only through personal, caring, consensual conversations. And for good reason: It is easier to ignore a strained voice or a waving hand than a direct greeting or an outstretched arm. While the record indicates that petitioners have been able to have a number of quiet conversations outside the buffer zones, respondents have not refuted petitioners' testimony that the conversations have been far less frequent and far less successful since the buffer zones were instituted. It is thus no answer to say that petitioners can still be "seen and heard" by women within the buffer zones. . . . If all that the women can see and hear are vociferous opponents of abortion, then the buffer zones have effectively stifled petitioners' message.

. . .

B

1

The buffer zones burden substantially more speech than necessary to achieve the Commonwealth's asserted interests. . . . [T]he Act is truly exceptional: Respondents and their *amici* identify no other State with a law that creates fixed buffer zones around abortion clinics.[6] That . . . raise[s] concern that the Commonwealth has too readily forgone options that could serve its interests just as well, without substantially burdening the kind of speech in which petitioners wish to engage.

That is the case here. The Commonwealth's interests include ensuring public safety outside abortion clinics, preventing harassment and intimidation of patients and clinic staff, and combating deliberate obstruction of clinic entrances. The Act itself contains a separate provision, subsection (e)—unchallenged by petitioners—that prohibits much of this conduct. That provision subjects to criminal punishment "[a]ny person who knowingly obstructs, detains, hinders, impedes or blocks another person's entry to or exit from a reproductive health care facility." . . . If Massachusetts determines that broader prohibitions along the same lines are necessary, it could enact legislation similar to the federal Freedom of Access to Clinic Entrances Act of 1994 (FACE Act), 18 U.S.C. § 248(a)(1), which subjects to both criminal and civil penalties anyone who "by force or threat of force or by physical obstruction, intentionally injures, intimidates or interferes with or attempts to injure, intimidate or interfere with any person because that person is or has been, or in order to intimidate such person or any other person or any class of persons from, obtaining or providing reproductive health services." Some dozen other States have done so. . . . If the Commonwealth is particularly concerned about harassment, it could also consider an ordinance such as the one adopted in New York City that not only prohibits obstructing access to a clinic, but also makes it a crime "to follow and harass another person within 15 feet of the premises of a reproductive health care facility." . . .[8]

The Commonwealth points to a substantial public safety risk created when protestors obstruct driveways leading to the clinics. . . . That is, however, an example of its failure to look to less intrusive means of addressing its concerns. Any such obstruction can readily be addressed through existing local ordinances. . .

All of the foregoing measures are, of course, in addition to available generic criminal statutes forbidding assault, breach of the peace, trespass, vandalism, and the like.

In addition, subsection (e) of the Act, the FACE Act, and the New York City anti-harassment ordinance are all enforceable not only through criminal prosecutions but also through public and private civil actions for injunctions and other equitable relief. . . . We have previously noted the First Amendment virtues of targeted injunctions as alternatives to broad, prophylactic measures. Such an injunction "regulates the activities, and perhaps the speech, of a group," but only "because of the

---

[6]   *Amici* do identify five localities with laws similar to the Act here. . . .

[8]   We do not "give [our] approval" to this or any of the other alternatives we discuss. We merely suggest that a law like the New York City ordinance could in principle constitute a permissible alternative. . . .

group's past *actions* in the context of a specific dispute between real parties." *Madsen*,. . . . Moreover, given the equitable nature of injunctive relief, courts can tailor a remedy to ensure that it restricts no more speech than necessary. See, *e.g., id.,* at 770; *Schenck*, 519 U.S., at 380–381. In short, injunctive relief focuses on the precise individuals and the precise conduct causing a particular problem. The Act, by contrast, categorically excludes nonexempt individuals from the buffer zones, unnecessarily sweeping in innocent individuals and their speech.

The Commonwealth also asserts an interest in preventing congestion in front of abortion clinics. According to respondents, even when individuals do not deliberately obstruct access to clinics, they can inadvertently do so simply by gathering in large numbers. But the Commonwealth could address that problem through more targeted means. Some localities, for example, have ordinances that require crowds blocking a clinic entrance to disperse when ordered to do so by the police, and that forbid the individuals to reassemble within a certain distance of the clinic for a certain period. . . .

And to the extent the Commonwealth argues that even these types of laws are ineffective, it has another problem. The portions of the record that respondents cite to support the anticongestion interest pertain mainly to one place at one time: the Boston Planned Parenthood clinic on Saturday mornings. . . . Respondents point us to no evidence that individuals regularly gather at other clinics, or at other times in Boston, in sufficiently large groups to obstruct access. For a problem shown to arise only once a week in one city at one clinic, creating 35-foot buffer zones at every clinic across the Commonwealth is hardly a narrowly tailored solution.

. . .

2

Respondents have but one reply: "We have tried other approaches, but they do not work." . . .

Although respondents claim that Massachusetts "tried other laws already on the books," they identify not a single prosecution brought under those laws within at least the last 17 years. And while they also claim that the Commonwealth "tried injunctions," . . . the last injunctions they cite date to the 1990s . . . . In short, the Commonwealth has not shown that it seriously undertook to address the problem with less intrusive tools readily available to it. Nor has it shown that it considered different methods that other jurisdictions have found effective.

Respondents contend that the alternatives we have discussed suffer from two defects: First, given the "widespread" nature of the problem, it is simply not "practicable" to rely on individual prosecutions and injunctions. . . . But far from being "widespread," the problem appears from the record to be limited principally to the Boston clinic on Saturday mornings. Moreover, by their own account, the police appear perfectly capable of singling out lawbreakers. The legislative testimony preceding the 2007 Act revealed substantial police and video monitoring at the clinics, especially when large gatherings were anticipated. Captain Evans testified that his officers are so familiar with the scene outside the Boston clinic that they "know all the players down there." . . . And Attorney General Coakley relied on video surveillance to show legislators conduct she thought was "clearly against the law." . . . If Commonwealth officials can compile an extensive record of obstruction and harassment to support their preferred legislation, we do not see why they cannot do the same to support injunctions and prosecutions against those who might deliberately flout the law.

The second supposed defect in the alternatives we have identified is that laws like subsection (e) of the Act and the federal FACE Act require a showing of intentional or deliberate obstruction, intimidation, or harassment, which is often difficult to prove. . . .

. . . To meet the requirement of narrow tailoring, the government must demonstrate that alternative measures that burden substantially less speech would fail to achieve the government's interests, not simply that the chosen route is easier. A painted line on the sidewalk is easy to enforce, but the prime objective of the First Amendment is not efficiency. In any case, we do not think that showing intentional obstruction is nearly so difficult in this context as respondents suggest. To determine whether a protestor intends to block access to a clinic, a police officer need only order him to move. If he refuses, then there is no question that his continued conduct is knowing or intentional.

For similar reasons, respondents' reliance on our decision in *Burson v. Freeman* is misplaced. There, we upheld a state statute that established 100-foot buffer zones outside polling places on election day within which no one could display or distribute campaign materials or solicit votes. 504 U.S., at 193–194. We approved the buffer zones as a valid prophylactic measure, noting that existing"[i]ntimidation and interference laws fall short of serving a State's compelling interests because they 'deal with only the most blatant and specific attempts' to impede elections." . . . Such laws were insufficient because "[v]oter intimidation and election fraud are . . . difficult to detect." . . . Obstruction of abortion clinics and harassment of patients, by contrast, are anything but subtle.

We also noted in *Burson* that under state law, "law enforcement officers generally are barred from the vicinity of the polls to avoid any appearance of coercion in the electoral process," with the result that "many acts of interference would go undetected." . . . Not so here. Again, the police maintain a significant presence outside Massachusetts abortion clinics. The buffer zones in *Burson* were justified because less restrictive measures were inadequate. Respondents have not shown that to be the case here.

. . .

■ JUSTICE SCALIA, with whom JUSTICE KENNEDY and JUSTICE THOMAS join, concurring in the judgment.

Today's opinion carries forward this Court's practice of giving abortion-rights advocates a pass when it comes to suppressing the free-speech rights of their opponents. There is an entirely separate, abridged edition of the First Amendment applicable to speech against abortion. See, *e.g.*, Hill v. Colorado, 530 U.S. 703 (2000); Madsen v. Women's Health Center, Inc., 512 U.S. 753 (1994).

. . .

I. The Court's Content-Neutrality Discussion Is Unnecessary

. . . Inasmuch as Part IV holds that the Act is unconstitutional because it does not survive the lesser level of scrutiny associated with content-neutral "time, place, and manner" regulations, there is no principled reason for the majority to decide whether the statute is subject to strict scrutiny.

. . .

II. The Statute Is Content Based and Fails Strict Scrutiny

. . .

A. Application to Abortion Clinics Only

. . .

. . . It blinks reality to say, as the majority does, that a blanket prohibition on the use of streets and sidewalks where speech on only one politically controversial topic is likely to occur—and where that speech can most effectively be communicated—is not content based. Would the Court exempt from strict scrutiny a law banning access to the streets and sidewalks surrounding the site of the Republican National Convention? Or those used annually to commemorate the 1965 Selma-to-Montgomery civil rights marches? Or those outside the Internal Revenue Service? Surely not.

The majority says, correctly enough, that a facially neutral speech restriction escapes strict scrutiny, even when it "may disproportionately affect speech on certain topics," so long as it is "justified without reference to the content of the regulated speech." But the cases in which the Court has previously found that standard satisfied—in particular, Renton v. Playtime Theatres, Inc., 475 U.S. 41 (1986), and Ward v. Rock Against Racism, 491 U.S. 781 (1989), both of which the majority cites—are a far cry from what confronts us here.

. . .

. . . The majority points only to the statute's stated purpose of increasing " 'public safety' " at abortion clinics and to the additional aims articulated by respondents before this Court—namely, protecting " 'patient access to healthcare . . . and the unobstructed use of public sidewalks and roadways.' " Really? Does a statute become "justified without reference to the content of the regulated speech" simply because the statute itself and those defending it in court *say* that it is? Every objective indication shows that the provision's primary purpose is to restrict speech that opposes abortion.

I begin . . . with the fact that the Act burdens only the public spaces outside abortion clinics. . . . [A]lthough the statute applies to all abortion clinics in Massachusetts, only one is known to have been beset by the problems that the statute supposedly addresses. The Court uses this striking fact . . . as a basis for concluding that the law is insufficiently "tailored" to safety and access concerns (Part IV) rather than as a basis for concluding that it is not *directed* to those concerns at all, but to the suppression of antiabortion speech. That is rather like invoking the eight missed human targets of a shooter who has killed one victim to prove, not that he is guilty of attempted mass murder, but that *he has bad aim*.

. . . Showing that a law that suppresses speech on a specific subject is so far reaching that it applies even when the asserted non-speech-related problems are not present is persuasive evidence that the law is content based. . . .

The structure of the Act also indicates that it rests on content-based concerns. The goals of "public safety, patient access to healthcare, and the unobstructed use of public sidewalks and roadways," . . . are already achieved by an earlier-enacted subsection of the statute, which provides criminal penalties for "[a]ny person who knowingly obstructs, detains, hinders, impedes or blocks another person's entry to or exit from a reproductive health care facility." § 120E½(e). As the majority recognizes, that provision is easy to enforce. Thus, the speech-free zones carved out by subsection (b) add nothing to safety and access; what they achieve, and what they were obviously designed to achieve, is the suppression of speech opposing abortion.

Further contradicting the Court's fanciful defense of the Act is the fact that subsection (b) was enacted as a more easily enforceable substitute for a prior provision. That provision did not exclude people entirely from the restricted areas around abortion clinics; rather, it forbade people in those areas to approach within six feet of another person *without that person's consent* "for the purpose of passing a leaflet or handbill to, displaying a sign to, or engaging in oral protest, education or counseling with such other person." § 120E½(b) . . . . As the majority acknowledges, that provision was "modeled on a . . . Colorado law that this Court had upheld in *Hill*." And in that case, the Court recognized that the statute in question was directed at the suppression of unwelcome speech, vindicating what *Hill* called "[t]he unwilling listener's interest in avoiding unwanted communication." . . . The Court held that interest to be content neutral. . . .

The provision at issue here was indisputably meant to serve the same interest in protecting citizens' supposed right to avoid speech that they would rather not hear. For that reason, we granted a second question for review in this case . . . : whether *Hill* should be cut back or cast aside. . . . The majority avoids that question by declaring the Act content neutral on other (entirely unpersuasive) grounds. In concluding that the statute is content based and therefore subject to strict scrutiny, I necessarily conclude that *Hill* should be overruled. . . . Protecting people from speech they do not want to hear is not a function that the First Amendment allows the government to undertake in the public streets and sidewalks.

. . . It . . . should be argued in the next case, that by stating that "the Act would not be content neutral if it were concerned with undesirable effects that arise from . . . '[l]isteners' reactions to speech,' " . . . and then holding the Act unconstitutional for being insufficiently tailored to safety and access concerns, the Court itself has *sub silentio* (and perhaps inadvertently) overruled *Hill*. The unavoidable implication of that holding is that protection against unwelcome speech cannot justify restrictions on the use of public streets and sidewalks.

B. Exemption for Abortion-Clinic Employees or Agents

. . .

It goes without saying that "[g]ranting waivers to favored speakers (or . . . denying them to disfavored speakers) would of course be unconstitutional." Thomas v. Chicago Park Dist., 534 U.S. 316, 325 (2002). . . .

Is there any serious doubt that *abortion-clinic employees or agents* "acting within the scope of their employment" near clinic entrances may—indeed, often will—speak in favor of abortion . . . ? Or speak in opposition to the message of abortion opponents—saying, for example, that "this is a safe facility" to rebut the statement that it is not? . . . The Court's contrary assumption is simply incredible. And the majority makes no attempt to establish the further necessary proposition that abortion-clinic employees and agents do not engage in nonspeech activities directed to the suppression of antiabortion speech by hampering the efforts of counselors to speak to prospective clients. Are we to believe that a clinic employee sent out to "escort" prospective clients into the building would not seek to prevent a counselor like Eleanor McCullen from communicating with them? . . .

. . . Whatever other activity is permitted, so long as the statute permits speech favorable to abortion rights while excluding antiabortion speech, it discriminates on the basis of viewpoint.

The Court takes the peculiar view that, so long as the clinics have not specifically authorized their employees to speak in favor of abortion (or, presumably, to impede antiabortion speech), there is no viewpoint discrimination. . . . [I]t is implausible that clinics would bar escorts from engaging in the sort of activity mentioned above. Moreover, a statute that forbids one side but not the other to convey its message does not become viewpoint neutral simply because the favored side chooses voluntarily to abstain from activity that the statute permits.

There is not a shadow of a doubt that the assigned or foreseeable conduct of a clinic employee or agent can include both speaking in favor of abortion rights and countering the speech of people like petitioners. See Alito, J., concurring in judgment. Indeed, as the majority acknowledges, the trial record includes testimony that escorts at the Boston clinic "expressed views about abortion to the women they were accompanying, thwarted petitioners' attempts to speak and hand literature to the women, and disparaged petitioners in various ways, "including by calling them " 'crazy.' " What a surprise! The Web site for the Planned Parenthood League of Massachusetts (which operates the three abortion facilities where petitioners attempt to counsel women), urges readers to "Become a Clinic Escort Volunteer" in order to "provide a safe space for patients by escorting them through protestors to the health center." . . . The dangers that the Web site attributes to "protestors" are related entirely to speech, not to safety or access. "Protestors," it reports, "hold signs, try to speak to patients entering the building, and distribute literature that can be misleading." . . . The "safe space" provided by escorts is protection from that speech.

. . . [T]he majority's opinion contends that . . . [s]peech restrictions favoring one viewpoint over another are not content based unless it can be shown that the favored viewpoint has actually been expressed. A city ordinance closing a park adjoining the Republican National Convention to all speakers except those whose remarks have been approved by the Republican National Committee is thus not subject to strict scrutiny unless it can be shown that someone has given committee-endorsed remarks. For this Court to suggest such a test is astonishing.

. . . Having determined that the Act is content based and does not withstand strict scrutiny, I need not pursue the inquiry conducted in Part IV of the Court's opinion—whether the statute is " 'narrowly tailored to serve a significant governmental interest.' " . . . [I]f I did, I suspect I would agree with the majority that the legislation is not narrowly tailored to advance the interests asserted by respondents. But I prefer not to take part in the assembling of an apparent but specious unanimity. . . .

. . .

The obvious purpose of the challenged [provision] is to "protect" prospective clients of abortion clinics from having to hear abortion-opposing speech on public streets and sidewalks. The provision is thus unconstitutional root and branch and cannot be saved, as the majority suggests, by limiting its application to the single facility that has experienced the safety and access problems to which it is quite obviously not addressed. I concur only in the judgment that the statute is unconstitutional under the First Amendment.

■ JUSTICE ALITO, concurring in the judgment.

. . . [T]he Massachusetts law discriminates on the basis of viewpoint . . . .

. . . [D]uring business hours, individuals who wish to counsel against abortion or to criticize the particular clinic may not do so within the buffer zone. If they engage in such conduct, they commit a crime. See § 120E½(d). By contrast, employees and agents of the clinic may enter the zone and engage in any conduct that falls within the scope of their employment. A clinic may direct or authorize an employee or agent, while within the zone, to express favorable views about abortion or the clinic, and if the employee exercises that authority, the employee's conduct is perfectly lawful. In short, petitioners and other critics of a clinic are silenced, while the clinic may authorize its employees to express speech in support of the clinic and its work.

. . .

It is clear on the face of the Massachusetts law that it discriminates based on viewpoint. Speech in favor of the clinic and its work by employees and agents is permitted; speech criticizing the clinic and its work is a crime. This is blatant viewpoint discrimination.

. . .

. . . I do not think that it is possible to reach a judgment about the intent of the Massachusetts Legislature without taking into account the fact that the law that the legislature enacted blatantly discriminates based on viewpoint. In light of this feature, as well as the overbreadth that the Court identifies, it cannot be said, based on the present record, that the law would be content neutral even if the exemption for clinic employees and agents were excised. However, if the law were truly content neutral, I would agree with the Court that the law would still be unconstitutional on the ground that it burdens more speech than is necessary to serve the Commonwealth's asserted interests.

B. THE NON-TRADITIONAL FORUM—SPEECH ACTIVITIES IN PUBLIC PROPERTY OTHER THAN PARKS AND STREETS

Adderley v. Florida
385 U.S. 39, 87 S.Ct. 242, 17 L.Ed.2d 149 (1966).

■ MR. JUSTICE BLACK delivered the opinion of the Court.

Petitioners . . . were convicted on a charge of "trespass with a malicious and mischievous intent" upon the premises of the county jail . . . Petitioners, apparently all students of the Florida A. & M. University in Tallahassee, had gone from the school to the jail about a mile away, along with many other students, to "demonstrate" at the jail their protests of arrests of other protesting students the day before, and perhaps to protest more generally against state and local policies and practices of racial segregation, including segregation of the jail. The county sheriff . . . tried to persuade the students to leave the jail grounds. When this did not work, he notified them that they must leave, that if they did not leave he would arrest them for trespassing, and that if they resisted he would charge them with that as well. Some of the students left but others, including petitioners, remained and they were arrested. On appeal the convictions were affirmed. . . .

Petitioners have insisted from the beginning of this case that it is controlled by and must be reversed because of our prior cases of Edwards v. South Carolina, 372 U.S. 229 . . . We cannot agree.

. . . In *Edwards,* the demonstrators went to the South Carolina State Capitol grounds to protest. In this case they went to the jail. Traditionally, state capitol grounds are open to the public. Jails, built for security purposes, are not. . . . More importantly, South Carolina sought to prosecute its State Capitol demonstrators by charging them with the common-law crime of breach of the peace. The South Carolina breach-of-the-peace statute was . . . struck down as being so broad and all-embracing as to jeopardize speech, press, assembly and petition, ...

The Florida trespass statute under which these petitioners were charged cannot be challenged on this ground. It is aimed at conduct of one limited kind, that is, for one person or persons to trespass upon the property of another with a malicious and mischievous intent. There is no lack of notice in this law, nothing to entrap or fool the unwary.

. . .

. . . [T]he jury was authorized to find that the State had proven every essential element of the crime. . . . That [leaves] only the question of whether conviction . . . unconstitutionally deprives petitioners of their rights to freedom of speech, press, assembly or petition. We hold it does not. The sheriff, as jail custodian, had power, as the state courts have here held, to direct that this large crowd of people get off the grounds. There is not a shred of evidence in this record that this power was exercised, or that its exercise was sanctioned by the lower courts, because the sheriff objected to what was being sung or said by the demonstrators or because he disagreed with the objectives of their protest. The record reveals that he objected only to their presence on that part of the jail grounds reserved for jail uses. There is no evidence at all that on any other occasion had similarly large groups of the public been permitted to gather on this portion of the jail grounds for any purpose. Nothing in the Constitution of the United States prevents Florida from even-handed enforcement of its general trespass statute against those refusing to obey the sheriff's order to remove themselves from what amounted to the curtilage of the jailhouse. The State, no less than a private owner of property, has power to preserve the property under its control for the use to which it is lawfully dedicated. For this reason there is no merit to the petitioners' argument that they had a constitutional right to stay on the property, over the jail custodian's objections, because this "area chosen for the peaceful civil rights demonstration was not only 'reasonable' but also particularly appropriate. . . ." Such an argument has as its major unarticulated premise the assumption that people who want to propagandize protests or views have a constitutional right to do so whenever and however and wherever they please. . . . The United States Constitution does not forbid a State to control the use of its own property for its own lawful nondiscriminatory purpose.

These judgments are affirmed.

■ MR. JUSTICE DOUGLAS, with whom THE CHIEF JUSTICE, MR. JUSTICE BRENNAN, and MR. JUSTICE FORTAS concur, dissenting.

. . .

The jailhouse, like an executive mansion, a legislative chamber, a courthouse, or the statehouse itself . . . is one of the seats of government whether it be the Tower of London, the Bastille, or a small county jail. And when it houses political prisoners or those who many think are unjustly held, it is an obvious center for protest. . . .

. . .

We do violence to the First Amendment when we permit this "petition for redress of grievances" to be turned into a trespass action. . . .

. . .

There may be some public places which are so clearly committed to other purposes that their use for the airing of grievances is anomalous. There may be some instances in which assemblies and petitions for redress of grievances are not consistent with other necessary purposes of public property. A noisy meeting may be out of keeping with the serenity of the statehouse or the quiet of the courthouse. . . . But this is quite different from saying that all public places are off limits to people with grievances. . . . And it is farther yet from saying that the "custodian" of the public property in his discretion can decide when public places shall be used for the communication of ideas, especially the constitutional right to assemble and petition for redress of grievances. . . .

Viewpoint-Neutral Rules Denying Access to Non-Traditional Public Fora

From the 1966 decision in *Adderley* until 1992 the Court consistently refused to classify any public property other than the parks and streets as a traditional public forum. Moreover, viewpoint-neutral rules restricting access to non-traditional public fora were nearly-consistently upheld under an approach that sustained those rules if reasonably consistent with the government's interest in preserving the property for non-speech uses. (The one extreme exception was Board of Airport Commrs. of Los Angeles v. Jews for Jesus, Inc., 482 U.S. 569 (1987), which struck down an airport rule forbidding "all First Amendment activities" in the terminal. The rule literally prohibited talking and reading.)

The cases include: Greer v. Spock, 424 U.S. 828 (1976) (regulation forbidding demonstrations and political speeches on military base); Heffron v. International Society for Krishna Consciousness, 452 U.S. 640 (1981) (state fair rule limiting sale or distribution of written materials to fixed locations); Perry Education Association v. Perry Local Educators' Association, 460 U.S. 37 (1983) (teachers' organization other than elected bargaining representative forbidden to use school mailboxes to communicate with teachers); Los Angeles v. Taxpayers for Vincent, 466 U.S. 789 (1984) (municipal ordinance forbids placing signs on public property); Cornelius v. NAACP Legal Defense and Educational Fund, 473 U.S. 788 (1985) (legal defense and advocacy organizations excluded from participating in federal employees' charity drive); Ward v. Rock Against Racism, 491 U.S. 781 (1989) (regulation of music volume at public amphitheater); United States v. Kokinda, 497 U.S. 720 (1990) (postal regulation forbids soliciting charitable contributions on postal premises).

International Society for Krishna Consciousness, Inc. v. Lee

505 U.S. 672, 112 S.Ct. 2701, 120 L.Ed.2d 541 (1992).

■ CHIEF JUSTICE REHNQUIST delivered the opinion of the Court.

In this case we consider whether an airport terminal operated by a public authority is a public forum and whether a regulation prohibiting solicitation in the interior of an airport terminal violates the First Amendment.

The relevant facts in this case are not in dispute. Petitioner International Society for Krishna Consciousness, Inc. (ISKCON) is a not-for-profit religious corporation whose members perform a ritual known as sankirtan. The ritual consists of " 'going into public places, disseminating religious literature and soliciting funds to support the religion.' " The primary purpose of this ritual is raising funds for the movement.

Respondent Walter Lee . . . was the police superintendent of the Port Authority of New York and New Jersey and was charged with enforcing the regulation at issue. The Port Authority owns and operates three major airports in the greater New York City area. . . .

        . . .

The Port Authority has adopted a regulation forbidding within the terminals the repetitive solicitation of money or distribution of literature. The regulation states:

"1. The following conduct is prohibited within the interior areas of buildings or structures at an air terminal if conducted by a person to or with passers-by in a continuous or repetitive manner:

"(a) The sale or distribution of any merchandise, including but not limited to jewelry, food stuffs, candles, flowers, badges and clothing.

"(b) The sale or distribution of flyers, brochures, pamphlets, books or any other printed or written material.

"(c) Solicitation and receipt of funds."

The regulation governs only the terminals; the Port Authority permits solicitation and distribution on the sidewalks outside the terminal buildings. The regulation effectively prohibits petitioner from performing sankirtan in the terminals. As a result, petitioner brought suit seeking declaratory and injunctive relief . . . [T]he District Court granted petitioner summary judgment.

The Court of Appeals affirmed in part and reversed in part. . . . Relying on our recent decision in United States v. Kokinda, 497 U.S. 720 (1990), a divided panel concluded that the terminals are not public fora. . . . The Court of Appeals then concluded that, presented with the issue, this Court would find that the ban on solicitation was reasonable, but the ban on distribution was not. Petitioner sought certiorari respecting the Court of Appeals' decision that the terminals are not public fora and upholding the solicitation ban. Respondent cross-petitioned respecting the court's holding striking down the distribution ban. . . . [3]

. . . Where the government is acting as a proprietor, managing its internal operations, rather than acting as lawmaker with the power to regulate or license, its action will not be subjected to the heightened review to which its actions as a lawmaker may be subject. . . . Thus, we have upheld a ban on political advertisements in city-operated transit vehicles, Lehman v. City of Shaker Heights, 418 U.S. 298 (1974), even though the city permitted other types of advertising on those vehicles. Similarly, we have permitted a school district to limit access to an internal mail system used to communicate with teachers employed by the district. Perry Education Assn. v. Perry Local Educators' Ass'n, 460 U.S. 37 (1983).

These cases reflect, either implicitly or explicitly, a "forum-based" approach for assessing restrictions that the government seeks to place on the use of its property. . . . Under this approach, regulation of speech on government property that has traditionally been available for public expression is subject to the highest scrutiny. Such regulations survive only if they are narrowly drawn to achieve a compelling state interest. . . . The second category of public property is the designated public forum, whether of a limited or unlimited character—property that the state has opened for expressive activity by part or all of the public. . . . Regulation of such property is subject to the same limitations as that governing a traditional public forum. . . . Finally, there is all remaining public property. Limitations on expressive activity conducted on this last category of property must survive only a much more limited review. The challenged regulation need only be reasonable, as long as the regulation is not an effort to suppress the speaker's activity due to disagreement with the speaker's view. . . .

The parties do not disagree that this is the proper framework. Rather, they disagree whether the airport terminals are public fora or nonpublic fora. They also disagree whether the regulation survives the "reasonableness" review governing nonpublic fora, should that prove the appropriate category. Like the Court of Appeals, we conclude that the terminals are nonpublic fora and that the regulation reasonably limits solicitation.

. . .

---

[3] We deal here only with ISKCON's petition raising the permissibility of solicitation. Respondent's cross-petition concerning the leafletting ban is disposed of in the companion case, Lee v. International Society for Krishna Consciousness, Inc.

... [A] traditional public forum is property that has as "a principal purpose ... the free exchange of ideas." ... Moreover, consistent with the notion that the government—like other property owners—"has power to preserve the property under its control for the use to which it is lawfully dedicated," ... the government does not create a public forum by inaction. Nor is a public forum created "whenever members of the public are permitted freely to visit a place owned or operated by the Government." ... The decision to create a public forum must instead be made "by intentionally opening a nontraditional forum for public discourse." ... Finally, we have recognized that the location of property also has bearing because separation from acknowledged public areas may serve to indicate that the separated property is a special enclave, subject to greater restriction. ...

... [T]he tradition of airport activity does not demonstrate that airports have historically been made available for speech activity. Nor can we say that these particular terminals, or airport terminals generally, have been intentionally opened by their operators to such activity; the frequent and continuing litigation evidencing the operators' objections belies any such claim. In short, there can be no argument that society's time-tested judgment, expressed through acquiescence in a continuing practice, has resolved the issue in petitioner's favor.

Petitioner attempts to circumvent the history and practice governing airport activity by pointing our attention to the variety of speech activity that it claims historically occurred at various "transportation nodes" such as rail stations, bus stations, wharves, and Ellis Island. Even if we were inclined to accept petitioner's historical account describing speech activity at these locations, an account respondent contests, we think that such evidence is of little import for two reasons. First, much of the evidence is irrelevant to public fora analysis, because sites such as bus and rail terminals traditionally have had private ownership. ... The development of privately owned parks that ban speech activity would not change the public fora status of publicly held parks. But the reverse is also true. The practices of privately held transportation centers do not bear on the government's regulatory authority over a publicly owned airport.

Second, the relevant unit for our inquiry is an airport, not "transportation nodes" generally. ... To make a category of "transportation nodes" ... would unjustifiably elide what may prove to be critical differences of which we should rightfully take account. The "security magnet," for example, is an airport commonplace that lacks a counterpart in bus terminals and train stations. And public access to air terminals is also not infrequently restricted—just last year the Federal Aviation Administration required airports for a 4-month period to limit access to areas normally publicly accessible. ... To blithely equate airports with other transportation centers, therefore, would be a mistake.

The differences among such facilities are unsurprising since ... airports are commercial establishments funded by users fees and designed to make a regulated profit, and where nearly all who visit do so for some travel related purpose. As commercial enterprises, airports must provide services attractive to the marketplace. In light of this, it cannot fairly be said that an airport terminal has as a principal purpose "promoting the free exchange of ideas." ... To the contrary, ... Port Authority management considers the purpose of the terminals to be the facilitation of passenger air travel, not the promotion of expression. ... Even if we look beyond the intent of the Port Authority to the manner in which the terminals have been operated, the terminals have never been dedicated (except under the threat of court order) to expression in the form sought to be exercised here: i.e., the solicitation of contributions and the distribution of literature.

The terminals here are far from atypical. Airport builders and managers focus their efforts on providing terminals that will contribute to efficient air travel. . . . Thus, we think that neither by tradition nor purpose can the terminals be described as satisfying the standards we have previously set out for identifying a public forum.

The restrictions here challenged, therefore, need only satisfy a requirement of reasonableness. . . . We have no doubt that under this standard the prohibition on solicitation passes muster.

We have on many prior occasions noted the disruptive effect that solicitation may have on business. . . . Passengers who wish to avoid the solicitor may have to alter their path, slowing both themselves and those around them. The result is that the normal flow of traffic is impeded. . . . This is especially so in an airport. . . .

In addition, face-to-face solicitation presents risks of duress that are an appropriate target of regulation. The skillful, and unprincipled, solicitor can target the most vulnerable, including those accompanying children or those suffering physical impairment and who cannot easily avoid the solicitation. . . . The unsavory solicitor can also commit fraud through concealment of his affiliation or through deliberate efforts to shortchange those who agree to purchase. . . . Compounding this problem is the fact that, in an airport, the targets of such activity frequently are on tight schedules. This in turn makes such visitors unlikely to stop and formally complain to airport authorities. As a result, the airport faces considerable difficulty in achieving its legitimate interest in monitoring solicitation activity to assure that travelers are not interfered with unduly.

The Port Authority has concluded that its interest in monitoring the activities can best be accomplished by limiting solicitation and distribution to the sidewalk areas outside the terminals. This sidewalk area is frequented by an overwhelming percentage of airport users. Thus the resulting access of those who would solicit the general public is quite complete. In turn we think it would be odd to conclude that the Port Authority's terminal regulation is unreasonable despite the Port Authority having otherwise assured access to an area universally traveled.

. . .

For the foregoing reasons, the judgment of the Court of Appeals sustaining the ban on solicitation in Port Authority terminals is

Affirmed.

■ JUSTICE O'CONNOR, concurring. . . .

In the decision below, the Court of Appeals upheld a ban on solicitation of funds within the airport terminals operated by the Port Authority of New York and New Jersey, but struck down a ban on the repetitive distribution of printed or written material within the terminals. I would affirm both parts of that judgment.

I . . . agree that publicly owned airports are not public fora. . . . I also agree with the Court that the Port Authority has not expressly opened its airports to the types of expression at issue here and therefore has not created a "limited" or "designated" public forum relevant to this case.

. . . That airports are not public fora, however, does not mean that the government can restrict speech in whatever way it likes. . . . For example, in Board of Airport Commrs. of Los Angeles v. Jews for Jesus, Inc., 482 U.S. 569 (1987), we unanimously struck down a regulation that prohibited "all First Amendment activities" in the Los Angeles International Airport (LAX) without even reaching the question whether airports were public fora. . . .

. . .

. . . In my view, the Port Authority is operating a shopping mall as well as an airport. The reasonableness inquiry, therefore, is not whether the restrictions on speech are "consistent with . . . preserving the property" for air travel, . . . but whether they are reasonably related to maintaining the multipurpose environment that the Port Authority has deliberately created.

Applying that standard, I agree with the Court . . . that the ban on solicitation is reasonable. . . .

In my view, however, the regulation banning leafletting . . . cannot be upheld as reasonable on this record. I therefore concur in the judgment . . . striking down that prohibition. . . . [I]t is difficult to point to any problems intrinsic to the act of leafletting that would make it naturally incompatible with a large, multipurpose forum such as those at issue here.

. . .

Moreover, the Port Authority has not offered any justifications or record evidence to support its ban on the distribution of pamphlets alone. Its argument is focused instead on the problems created when literature is distributed in conjunction with a solicitation plea. . . . Because I cannot see how peaceful pamphleteering is incompatible with the multipurpose environment of the Port Authority airports, I cannot accept that a total ban on that activity is reasonable without an explanation as to why such a restriction "preserv[es] the property" for the several uses to which it has been put. . . .

. . .

■ JUSTICE KENNEDY, with whom JUSTICE BLACKMUN, JUSTICE STEVENS, and JUSTICE SOUTER join as to Part I, concurring in the judgment.

While I concur in the judgment affirming in this case, my analysis differs in substantial respects from that of the Court. In my view the airport corridors and shopping areas outside of the passenger security zones, areas operated by the Port Authority, are public forums. . . . The Port Authority's blanket prohibition on the distribution or sale of literature . . . is invalid under the First and Fourteenth Amendments. The Port Authority's rule disallowing in-person solicitation of money for immediate payment, however, is in my view a narrow and valid regulation of the time, place, and manner of protected speech in this forum, or else is a valid regulation of the nonspeech element of expressive conduct. I would sustain the Port Authority's ban on solicitation and receipt of funds.

I

. . .

. . . The Court today holds that traditional public forums are limited to public property which have as " 'a principal purpose . . . the free exchange of ideas' "; and that this purpose must be evidenced by a long-standing historical practice of permitting speech. The Court also holds that designated forums consist of property which the government intends to open for public discourse. All other types of property are, in the Court's view, nonpublic forums. . . .

This analysis is flawed at its very beginning. It leaves the government with almost unlimited authority to restrict speech on its property by doing nothing more than articulating a non-speech-related purpose for the area, and it leaves almost no scope for the development of new public forums absent the rare approval of the government. . . .

. . .

The Court's approach is contrary to the underlying purposes of the public forum doctrine. . . . Public places are of necessity the locus for discussion of public issues, as well as protest against arbitrary government action. . . .

. . .

The effect of the Court's narrow view of the first category of public forums is compounded by its description of the second purported category, the so-called "designated" forum. The requirements for such a designation are so stringent that I cannot be certain whether the category has any content left at all. . . .

The Court's answer to these objections appears to be a recourse to history as justifying its recognition of streets, parks, and sidewalks, but apparently no other types of government property, as traditional public forums. The Court ignores the fact that the purpose of the public forum doctrine is to give effect to the broad command of the First Amendment to protect speech from governmental interference. The jurisprudence is rooted in historic practice, but it is not tied to a narrow textual command limiting the recognition of new forums. In my view the policies underlying the doctrine cannot be given effect unless we recognize that open, public spaces and thoroughfares which are suitable for discourse may be public forums, whatever their historical pedigree and without concern for a precise classification of the property. . . . In a country where most citizens travel by automobile, and parks all too often become locales for crime rather than social intercourse, our failure to recognize the possibility that new types of government property may be appropriate forums for speech will lead to a serious curtailment of our expressive activity.

One of the places left in our mobile society that is suitable for discourse is a metropolitan airport. It is of particular importance to recognize that such spaces are public forums because in these days an airport is one of the few government-owned spaces where many persons have extensive contact with other members of the public. Given that private spaces of similar character are not subject to the dictates of the First Amendment, . . . it is critical that we preserve these areas for protected speech. In my view, our public forum doctrine must recognize this reality, and allow the creation of public forums which do not fit within the narrow tradition of streets, sidewalks, and parks. . . .

I agree with the Court that government property of a type which by history and tradition has been available for speech activity must continue to be recognized as a public forum. In my view, however, constitutional protection is not confined to these properties alone. Under the proper circumstances I would accord public forum status to other forms of property, regardless of its ancient or contemporary origins and whether or not it fits within a narrow historic tradition. . . .

The second category of the Court's jurisprudence, the so-called designated forum, provides little, if any, additional protection for speech. Where government property does not satisfy the criteria of a public forum, the government retains the power to dedicate the property for speech, whether for all expressive activity or for limited purposes only. . . . [W]hen property has been designated for a particular expressive use, the government may choose to eliminate that designation. But this increases the need to protect speech in other places, where discourse may occur free of such restrictions. . . .

Under this analysis, it is evident that the public spaces of the Port Authority's airports are public forums. First, . . . the public spaces in the airports are broad, public thoroughfares full of people and lined with stores and other commercial activities. An airport corridor is of course not a street, but that is not the proper inquiry. The question is one of physical similarities, sufficient to suggest that the airport corridor should be a public forum for the same reasons that streets and sidewalks have been treated as public forums by the people who use them.

Second, the airport areas involved here are open to the public without restriction. . . . It is the very breadth and extent of the public's use of airports that makes it imperative to protect speech rights there. [I]f the Port Authority allows the uses and open access to airports that is shown on this record, it cannot argue that some vestigial power to change its practices bars the conclusion that its airports are public forums, any more than the power to bulldoze a park bars a finding that a public forum exists so long as the open use does.

Third, and perhaps most important, it is apparent from the record, and from the recent history of airports, that when adequate time, place, and manner regulations are in place, expressive activity is quite compatible with the uses of major airports. . . .

The danger of allowing the government to suppress speech is shown in the case now before us. A grant of plenary power allows the government to tilt the dialogue heard by the public, to exclude many, more marginal voices. The first challenged Port Authority regulation establishes a flat prohibition on "[t]he sale or distribution of flyers, brochures, pamphlets, books or any other printed or written material," if conducted within the airport terminal, "in a continuous or repetitive manner." . . . Justice O'Connor finds it void even under the standards applicable to government regulations in nonpublic forums. . . .

II

It is my view, however, that the Port Authority's ban on the "solicitation and receipt of funds" within its airport terminals should be upheld under the standards applicable to speech regulations in public forums. The regulation may be upheld as either a reasonable time, place, and manner restriction, or as a regulation directed at the nonspeech element of expressive conduct. The two standards have considerable overlap in a case like this one.

. . . The confluence of the two tests is well demonstrated by a case like this, where the government regulation at issue can be described with equal accuracy as a regulation of the manner of expression, or as a regulation of conduct with an expressive component.

I am in full agreement with the statement of the Court that solicitation is a form of protected speech. . . . If the Port Authority's solicitation regulation prohibited all speech which requested the contribution of funds, I would conclude that it was a direct, content-based restriction of speech in clear violation of the First Amendment. The Authority's regulation does not prohibit all solicitation, however; it prohibits the "solicitation and receipt of funds." I do not understand this regulation to prohibit all speech that solicits funds. It reaches only personal solicitations for immediate payment of money. . . . In other words, the regulation permits expression that solicits funds, but limits the manner of that expression to forms other than the immediate receipt of money.

So viewed, I believe the Port Authority's rule survives our test for speech restrictions in the public forum. In-person solicitation of funds, when combined with immediate receipt of that money, creates a risk of fraud and duress which is well recognized, and which is different in kind from other forms of expression or conduct. Travelers who are unfamiliar with the airport, perhaps even unfamiliar with this country, its customs and its language, are an easy prey for the money solicitor. . . . As the Court recounts, questionable practices associated with solicitation can include the targeting of vulnerable and easily coerced persons, misrepresentation of the solicitor's cause, and outright theft. . . .

. . .

Much of what I have said about the solicitation of funds may seem to apply to the sale of literature, but the differences between the two activities are of sufficient significance to require they be distinguished for constitutional purposes. . . . For one, the government interest in regulating the sales of literature is not as powerful as in the case of solicitation. . . . And perhaps most important, the flat ban on sales of literature leaves open fewer alternative channels of communication than the Port Authority's more limited prohibition on the solicitation and receipt of funds. . . . [T]he Port Authority's regulation allows no practical means for advocates and organizations to sell literature within the public forums which are its airports.

. . .

For these reasons I agree that the Court of Appeals should be affirmed in full in finding the Port Authority's ban on the distribution or sale of literature unconstitutional, but upholding the prohibition on solicitation and immediate receipt of funds.

■ JUSTICE SOUTER, with whom JUSTICE BLACKMUN and JUSTICE STEVENS join, concurring . . . and dissenting. . . .

I

I join in Part I of Justice Kennedy's opinion. . . .

. . .

I also agree with Justice Kennedy's statement of the public forum principle: we should classify as a public forum any piece of public property that is "suitable for discourse" in its physical character, where expressive activity is "compatible" with the use to which it has actually been put. . . .

II

From the Court's conclusion . . . sustaining the total ban on solicitation of money for immediate payment, I respectfully dissent. . . .

Even if I assume arguendo that the ban on the petitioners' activity at issue here is both content neutral and merely a restriction on the manner of communication, the regulation must be struck down for its failure to satisfy the requirements of narrow tailoring to further a significant state interest. . . .

. . . Since there is here no evidence of any type of coercive conduct, over and above the merely importunate character of the open and public solicitation, that might justify a ban, . . . the regulation cannot be sustained to avoid coercion.

As for fraud, our cases do not provide government with plenary authority to ban solicitation just because it could be fraudulent. . . . The evidence of fraudulent conduct here is virtually nonexistent. . . .

Even assuming a governmental interest adequate to justify some regulation, the present ban would fall when subjected to the requirement of narrow tailoring. . . .

Finally, I do not think the Port Authority's solicitation ban leaves open the "ample" channels of communication required of a valid content-neutral time, place and manner restriction. A distribution of preaddressed envelopes is unlikely to be much of an alternative. The practical reality of the regulation, which this Court can never ignore, is that it shuts off a uniquely powerful avenue of communication for organizations like the International Society for Krishna Consciousness, and may, in effect, completely prohibit unpopular and poorly funded groups from receiving funds in response to protected solicitation. . . .

. . .

Lee v. International Society for Krishna Consciousness, Inc.

505 U.S. 830 (1992).

In the companion case to International Society for Krishna Consciousness, Inc. v. Lee, the court affirmed the judgment of the court of appeals that the ban on distribution of literature is invalid under the First Amendment. The Court's per curiam opinion stated that affirmance was "[f]or the reasons expressed in the opinions of Justice O'Connor, Justice Kennedy, and Justice Souter in International Society for Kirshna Consciousness." Justice Rehnquist's dissent, joined by Justices White, Scalia and Thomas, also relied on his opinion in that case. He said, in addition:

"The risks and burdens posed by leafletting are quite similar to those posed by solicitation. The weary, harried, or hurried traveler may have no less desire and need to avoid the delays generated by having literature foisted upon him than he does to avoid delays from a financial solicitation. And while a busy passenger perhaps may succeed in fending off a leafletter with minimal disruption to himself by agreeing simply to take the proffered material, this does not completely ameliorate the dangers of congestion flowing from such leafletting. Others may choose not simply to accept the material but also to stop and engage the leafletter in debate, obstructing those who follow. Moreover, those who accept material may often simply drop it on the floor once out of the leafletter's range, creating an eyesore, a safety hazard, and additional clean-up work for airport staff."

CHAPTER 14

RELIGION AND THE CONSTITUTION

Introduction. This chapter deals with the first amendment's prohibitions of laws "respecting an establishment of religion" and of laws "prohibiting the free exercise thereof." As Justice Rutledge stated in his dissenting opinion in Everson v. Board of Educ., 330 U.S. 1, 40 (1947): "'establishment' and 'free exercise' were correlative and coextensive ideas, representing only different facets of the single great and fundamental freedom." A single ideal of government neutrality in matters of religion forbids both government aid to and government burdens on religious groups, religious activities, and individual religious beliefs.

Despite their common purpose, there has been an uneasy tension between applications of the free exercise and establishment clauses, caused by potential conflict between the two constitutional commands. Consider a common example. Suppose a state university permits a wide range of speakers on political or social issues to use a particular university facility without charge. If speakers engaged in religious conversion, worship, or advocacy are singled out and denied permission to speak, does this constitute discrimination against religion in violation of the free exercise clause? If religious speakers are permitted, is the state subsidizing religious worship in violation of the establishment clause?

A question, then, that runs throughout this chapter is whether there is any single, reconciling interpretation of the establishment and free exercise clauses. A prominent attempt at reconciliation is Kurland, *Of Church and State and the Supreme Court,* 29 U.Chi.L.Rev. 1 (1961), *Selected Essays* 699 (1963). Professor Kurland's hypothesis is criticized in Pfeffer, *Religion-Blind Government,* 15 Stan.L.Rev. 389 (1963).

1. THE ESTABLISHMENT CLAUSE

A. INTRODUCTION

Everson v. Board of Education

330 U.S. 1, 67 S.Ct. 504, 91 L.Ed. 711 (1947).

■ MR. JUSTICE BLACK delivered the opinion of the Court.

A New Jersey statute authorizes its local school districts to make rules and contracts for the transportation of children to and from schools. The appellee, a township board of education, acting pursuant to this statute authorized reimbursement to parents of money expended by them for the bus transportation of their children on regular busses operated by the public transportation system. Part of this money was for the payment of transportation of some children in the community to Catholic parochial schools. These church schools give their students, in addition to secular education, regular religious instruction conforming to the religious tenets and modes of worship of the Catholic Faith. The superintendent of these schools is a Catholic priest.

The appellant, in his capacity as a district taxpayer, filed suit in a state court challenging the right of the Board to reimburse parents of parochial school students.... The New Jersey Court of Errors and Appeals [held] that neither the statute nor the resolution passed pursuant to it was in conflict with the State constitution or the provisions of the Federal Constitution in issue....

The only contention here is that the state statute and the resolution, in so far as they authorized reimbursement to parents of children attending parochial schools, violate the Federal Constitution in these two respects, which to some extent, overlap. *First.* They authorize the State to take by taxation the private property of some and bestow it upon others, to be used for their own private purposes. This, it is alleged, violates the due process clause of the Fourteenth Amendment. *Second.* The statute and the resolution forced inhabitants to pay taxes to help support and maintain schools which are dedicated to, and which regularly teach, the Catholic Faith. This is alleged to be a use of state power to support church schools contrary to the prohibition of the First Amendment which the Fourteenth Amendment made applicable to the states.

First. ... It is much too late to argue that legislation intended to facilitate the opportunity of children to get a secular education serves no public purpose.... The same thing is no less true of legislation to reimburse needy parents, or all parents, for payment of the fares of their children so that they can ride in public busses to and from schools rather than run the risk of traffic and other hazards incident to walking or "hitchhiking." ...

. . .

Second. The New Jersey statute is challenged as a "law respecting an establishment of religion.". . . .

A large proportion of the early settlers of this country came here from Europe to escape the bondage of laws which compelled them to support and attend government favored churches....

These practices of the old world were transplanted to and began to thrive in the soil of the new America. The very charters granted by the English Crown to the individuals and companies designated to make the laws which would control the destinies of the colonials authorized these individuals and companies to erect religious establishments which all, whether believers or non-believers, would be required to support and attend....

These practices became so commonplace as to shock the freedom-loving colonials into a feeling of abhorrence. The imposition of taxes to pay ministers' salaries and to build and maintain churches and church property aroused their indignation. It was these feelings which found expression in the First Amendment. No one locality and no one group throughout the Colonies can rightly be given entire credit for having aroused the sentiment that culminated in adoption of the Bill of Rights' provisions embracing religious liberty. But Virginia, where the established church had achieved a dominant influence in political affairs and where many excesses attracted wide public attention, provided a great stimulus and able leadership for the movement. The people there, as elsewhere, reached the conviction that individual religious liberty could be achieved best under a government which was stripped of all power to tax, to support, or otherwise to assist any or all religions, or to interfere with the beliefs of any religious individual or group.

The movement toward this end reached its dramatic climax in Virginia in 1785–86 when the Virginia legislative body was about to renew Virginia's tax levy for the support of the established church. Thomas Jefferson and James Madison led the fight against this tax. Madison wrote his great Memorial and Remonstrance against the law. In it, he eloquently argued that a true religion did not need the support of law; that no person, either believer or non-believer, should be taxed to support a religious institution of any kind; that the best interest of a society required that the minds of men always be wholly free; and that cruel persecutions were the inevitable result of government-established religions. Madison's Remonstrance received strong support throughout Virginia, and the Assembly postponed consideration of the proposed tax measure until its next session. When the proposal came up for consideration at that session, it not only died in committee, but the Assembly enacted the famous "Virginia Bill for Religious Liberty" originally written by Thomas Jefferson. The preamble to that Bill stated among other things that

"Almighty God hath created the mind free; that all attempts to influence it by temporal punishments, or burthens, or by civil incapacitations, tend only to beget habits of hypocrisy and meanness, and are a departure from the plan of the Holy author of our religion who being Lord both of body and mind, yet chose not to propagate it by coercions on either . . . ; that to compel a man to furnish contributions of money for the propagation of opinions which he disbelieves, is sinful and tyrannical; that even the forcing him to support this or that teacher of his own religious persuasion, is depriving him of the comfortable liberty of giving his contributions to the particular pastor, whose morals he would make his pattern. . . ."

And the statute itself enacted

"That no man shall be compelled to frequent or support any religious worship, place, or ministry whatsoever, nor shall be enforced, restrained, molested, or burthened, in his body or goods, nor shall otherwise suffer on account of his religious opinions or belief. . . ."

This Court has previously recognized that the provisions of the First Amendment, in the drafting and adoption of which Madison and Jefferson played such leading roles, had the same objective and were intended to provide the same protection against governmental intrusion on religious liberty as the Virginia statute.[a] . . . Prior to the adoption of the Fourteenth Amendment, the First Amendment did not apply as a restraint against the states. Most of them did soon provide similar constitutional protections for religious liberty. But some states persisted for about half a century in imposing restraints upon the free exercise of religion and in discriminating against particular religious groups. . . .

The meaning and scope of the First Amendment, preventing establishment of religion or prohibiting the free exercise thereof, in the light of its history and the evils it was designed forever to suppress, have been several times elaborated by the decisions of this Court prior to the application of the First Amendment to the states by the Fourteenth. The broad meaning given the Amendment by these earlier cases has been accepted by this Court in its decisions concerning an individual's religious freedom rendered since the Fourteenth Amendment was interpreted to make the prohibitions of the First applicable to state action abridging religious freedom. There is every reason to give the same application and broad interpretation to the "establishment of religion" clause. . . .

The "establishment of religion" clause of the First Amendment means at least this: Neither a state nor the Federal Government can set up a church. Neither can pass laws which aid one religion, aid all religions, or prefer one religion over another.

---

[a] For a very different reading of the historical record, see Howe, *Religion and the Free Society: The Constitutional Question, Selected Essays* 780 (1963). Professor Howe, stressing that the Bill of Rights did not in its inception limit the states, argues that the prohibition on establishment was a "non-libertarian" limitation on national power. Compare Pfeffer, *Church, State, and Freedom* 134–143 (rev. ed. 1967).

Neither can force nor influence a person to go to or to remain away from church against his will or force him to profess a belief or disbelief in any religion. No person can be punished for entertaining or professing religious beliefs or disbeliefs, for church attendance or non-attendance. No tax in any amount, large or small, can be levied to support any religious activities or institutions, whatever they may be called, or whatever form they may adopt to teach or practice religion. Neither a state nor the Federal Government can, openly or secretly, participate in the affairs of any religious organizations or groups and vice versa. In the words of Jefferson, the clause against establishment of religion by law was intended to erect "a wall of separation between church and State." . . .

. . . New Jersey cannot consistently with the "establishment of religion" clause of the First Amendment contribute tax-raised funds to the support of an institution which teaches the tenets and faith of any church. On the other hand, other language of the amendment commands that New Jersey cannot hamper its citizens in the free exercise of their own religion. Consequently, it cannot exclude individual Catholics, Lutherans, Mohammedans, Baptists, Jews, Methodists, Non-believers, Presbyterians, or the members of any other faith, *because of their faith, or lack of it,* from receiving the benefits of public welfare legislation. While we do not mean to intimate that a state could not provide transportation only to children attending public schools, we must be careful, in protecting the citizens of New Jersey against state-established churches, to be sure that we do not inadvertently prohibit New Jersey from extending its general state law benefits to all its citizens without regard to their religious belief.

Measured by these standards, we cannot say that the First Amendment prohibits New Jersey from spending tax-raised funds to pay the bus fares of parochial school pupils as a part of a general program under which it pays the fares of pupils attending public and other schools. It is undoubtedly true that children are helped to get to church schools. There is even a possibility that some of the children might not be sent to the church schools if the parents were compelled to pay their children's bus fares out of their own pockets when transportation to a public school would have been paid for by the State. The same possibility exists where the state requires a local transit company to provide reduced fares to school children including those attending parochial schools, or where a municipally owned transportation system undertakes to carry all school children free of charge. Moreover, state-paid policemen, detailed to protect children going to and from church schools from the very real hazards of traffic, would serve much the same purpose and accomplish much the same result as state provisions intended to guarantee free transportation of a kind which the state deems to be best for the school children's welfare. And parents might refuse to risk their children to the serious danger of traffic accidents going to and from parochial schools, the approaches to which were not protected by policemen. Similarly, parents might be reluctant to permit their children to attend schools which the state had cut off from such general government services as ordinary police and fire protection, connections for sewage disposal, public highways and sidewalks. Of course, cutting off church schools from these services, so separate and so indisputably marked off from the religious function, would make it far more difficult for the schools to operate. But such is obviously not the purpose of the First Amendment. That Amendment requires the state to be a neutral in its relations with groups of religious believers and non-believers; it does not require the state to be their adversary. State power is no more to be used so as to handicap religions, than it is to favor them.

. . . [New Jersey's] legislation, as applied, does no more than provide a general program to help parents get their children, regardless of their religion, safely and expeditiously to and from accredited schools.

The First Amendment has erected a wall between church and state. That wall must be kept high and impregnable. We could not approve the slightest breach. New Jersey has not breached it here.

Affirmed.

■ MR. JUSTICE JACKSON [with whom MR. JUSTICE FRANKFURTER joined], dissenting.

. . . The Court's opinion marshals every argument in favor of state aid and puts the case in its most favorable light, but much of its reasoning confirms my conclusions that there are no good grounds upon which to support the present legislation. In fact, the undertones of the opinion, advocating complete and uncompromising separation of Church from State, seem utterly discordant with its conclusion yielding support to their commingling in educational matters. The case which irresistibly comes to mind as the most fitting precedent is that of Julia who, according to Byron's reports, "whispering 'I will ne'er consent,'—consented."

. . .

■ MR. JUSTICE RUTLEDGE, with whom MR. JUSTICE FRANKFURTER, MR. JUSTICE JACKSON and MR. JUSTICE BURTON agree, dissenting.

. . .

Two great drives are constantly in motion to abridge, in the name of education, the complete division of religion and civil authority which our forefathers made. One is to introduce religious education and observances into the public schools. The other, to obtain public funds for the aid and support of various private religious schools. . . . In my opinion both avenues were closed by the Constitution. Neither should be opened by this Court. The matter is not one of quantity, to be measured by the amount of money expended. Now as in Madison's day it is one of principle, to keep separate the separate spheres as the First Amendment drew them; to prevent the first experiment upon our liberties; and to keep the question from becoming entangled in corrosive precedents. We should not be less strict to keep strong and untarnished the one side of the shield of religious freedom than we have been of the other.

The judgment should be reversed.

Denominational Preferences

The Court was unanimous in *Everson* in the conclusion that the establishment clause forbids aid to all religions as well as aid to one religion. Still, in Larson v. Valente, 456 U.S. 228 (1982), the Court referred to the proposition that "one religious denomination cannot be officially preferred over another" as "the clearest command of the Establishment Clause." (The Court invalidated a charitable contribution statute that exempted from its requirements religious organizations that solicit less than 50 percent of their funds from nonmembers.)

The "Three-Part Lemon Test"

In cases decided after 1971, it is common to begin opinions concerning the establishment clause by reciting standards summarized in Chief Justice Burger's opinion for the Court in Lemon v. Kurtzman, 403 U.S. 602, 612–613 (1971). To be valid against attack under the establishment clause:

"First, the statute must have a secular legislative purpose; second, its principal or primary effect must be one that neither advances nor inhibits religion . . . ; finally, the statute must not foster 'an excessive government entanglement with religion.' "

Despite their apparent simplicity, the three "*Lemon* standards"—which will be examined time and again in the cases to follow—have substantial ambiguities and remain controversial.

Lamb's Chapel v. Center Moriches Union Free School District
508 U.S. 384 (1993).

The school district permitted the use of school property for "social, civic and recreational meetings" but did not allow student bible clubs to meet on school property. The Court concluded that precluding use of school property by bible clubs was a violation of the free speech clause. The Court answered an argument, that allowing use of school property for bible study would be an establishment, by stating that "this would not have been an establishment of religion under the three-part test articulated in Lemon v. Kurtzman." In a concurrence, Justice Scalia objected to the court's use of the Lemon test, arguing that it was

"[l]ike some ghoul in a late-night horror movie that repeatedly sits up in its grave and shuffles abroad, after being repeatedly killed and buried, *Lemon* stalks our Establishment Clause jurisprudence once again, frightening the little children and school attorneys of Center Moriches Union Free School District . . .

        " . . .

        " . . . It is there to scare us (and our audience) when we wish it to do so, but we can command it to return to the tomb at will. . . . When we wish to strike down a practice it forbids, we invoke it . . . ; when we wish to uphold a practice it forbids, we ignore it entirely . . . Such a docile and useful monster is worth keeping around, at least in a somnolent state; one never knows when one might need him."

Justice White's opinion for the Court responded to Justice Scalia in a footnote.

"While we are somewhat diverted by Justice Scalia's evening at the cinema, we return to the reality that there is a proper way to inter an established decision and *Lemon*, however frightening it might be to some, has not been overruled."

B. GOVERNMENT RELIGIOUS EXERCISES, CEREMONIES, DISPLAYS, AND PRACTICES

1. PUBLIC SCHOOLS

Zorach v. Clauson
343 U.S. 306, 72 S.Ct. 679, 96 L.Ed. 954 (1952).

■ MR. JUSTICE DOUGLAS delivered the opinion of the Court.

New York City has a program which permits its public schools to release students during the school day so that they may leave the school buildings and school grounds and go to religious centers for religious instruction or devotional exercises. A student is released on written request of his parents. Those not released stay in the classrooms. The churches make weekly reports to the schools, sending a list of children who have been released from public school but who have not reported for religious instruction.

This "released time" program involves neither religious instruction in public school classrooms nor the expenditure of public funds. All costs, including the application blanks, are paid by the religious organizations. The case is therefore unlike McCollum v. Board of Education, 333 U.S. 203, which involved a "released time" program from Illinois. In that case the classrooms were turned over to religious instructors. We accordingly held that the program violated the First Amendment which (by reason of the Fourteenth Amendment) prohibits the states from establishing religion or prohibiting its free exercise.

Appellants, who are taxpayers and residents of New York City and whose children attend its public schools, challenge the present law, contending it is in essence not different from the one involved in the *McCollum* case. Their argument, stated elaborately in various ways, reduces itself to this: the weight and influence of the school is put behind a program for religious instruction; public school teachers police it, keeping tab on students who are released; the classroom activities come to a halt while the students who are released for religious instruction are on leave; the school is a crutch on which the churches are leaning for support in their religious training; without the cooperation of the schools this "released time" program, like the one in the *McCollum* case, would be futile and ineffective. The New York Court of Appeals sustained the law against this claim of unconstitutionality.

The briefs and arguments are replete with data bearing on the merits of this type of "released time" program. . . . Those matters are of no concern here, since our problem reduces itself to whether New York by this system has either prohibited the "free exercise" of religion or has made a law "respecting an establishment of religion" within the meaning of the First Amendment.

It takes obtuse reasoning to inject any issue of the "free exercise" of religion into the present case. No one is forced to go to the religious classroom and no religious exercise or instruction is brought to the classrooms of the public schools. A student need not take religious instruction. He is left to his own desires as to the manner or time of his religious devotions, if any.

There is a suggestion that the system involves the use of coercion to get public school students into religious classrooms. There is no evidence in the record before us that supports that conclusion.[6] The present record indeed tells us that the school authorities are neutral in this regard and do no more than release students whose parents so request. If in fact coercion were used, if it were established that any one or more teachers were using their office to persuade or force students to take the religious instruction, a wholly different case would be presented.[7] Hence we put aside that claim of coercion both as respects the "free exercise" of religion and "an establishment of religion" within the meaning of the First Amendment.

Moreover, apart from that claim of coercion, we do not see how New York by this type of "released time" program has made a law respecting an establishment of religion within the meaning of the First Amendment. . . . There cannot be the slightest doubt that the First Amendment reflects the philosophy that Church and State should be separated. And so far as interference with the "free exercise" of religion and an "establishment" of religion are concerned, the separation must be complete and

---

[6]   Nor is there any indication that the public schools enforce attendance at religious schools by punishing absentees from the released time programs for truancy.

[7]   Appellants contend that they should have been allowed to prove that the system is in fact administered in a coercive manner. The New York Court of Appeals declined to grant a trial on this issue, noting, *inter alia,* that appellants had not properly raised their claim in the manner required by state practice. This independent state ground for decision precludes appellants from raising the issue of maladministration in this proceeding. . . .

The only allegation in the complaint that bears on the issue is that the operation of the program "has resulted and inevitably results in the exercise of pressure and coercion upon parents and children to secure attendance by the children for religious instruction." But this charge does not even implicate the school authorities. The New York Court of Appeals was therefore generous in labeling it a "conclusory" allegation. . . .

unequivocal. The First Amendment within the scope of its coverage permits no exception; the prohibition is absolute. The First Amendment, however, does not say that in every and all respects there shall be a separation of Church and State. Rather, it studiously defines the manner, the specific ways, in which there shall be no concert or union or dependency one on the other. That is the common sense of the matter. Otherwise the state and religion would be aliens to each other—hostile, suspicious, and even unfriendly. Churches could not be required to pay even property taxes. Municipalities would not be permitted to render police or fire protection to religious groups. Policemen who helped parishioners into their places of worship would violate the Constitution. Prayers in our legislative halls; the appeals to the Almighty in the messages of the Chief Executive; the proclamations making Thanksgiving Day a holiday; "so help me God" in our courtroom oaths—these and all other references to the Almighty that run through our laws, our public rituals, our ceremonies would be flouting the First Amendment. A fastidious atheist or agnostic could even object to the supplication with which the Court opens each session: "God save the United States and this Honorable Court."

We would have to press the concept of separation of Church and State to these extremes to condemn the present law on constitutional grounds. The nullification of this law would have wide and profound effects. A Catholic student applies to his teacher for permission to leave the school during hours on a Holy Day of Obligation to attend a mass. A Jewish student asks his teacher for permission to be excused for Yom Kippur. A Protestant wants the afternoon off for a family baptismal ceremony. In each case the teacher requires parental consent in writing. In each case the teacher, in order to make sure the student is not a truant, goes further and requires a report from the priest, the rabbi, or the minister. The teacher in other words cooperates in a religious program to the extent of making it possible for her students to participate in it. Whether she does it occasionally for a few students, regularly for one, or pursuant to a systematized program designed to further the religious needs of all the students does not alter the character of the act.

We are a religious people whose institutions presuppose a Supreme Being. We guarantee the freedom to worship as one chooses. We make room for as wide a variety of beliefs and creeds as the spiritual needs of man deem necessary. We sponsor an attitude on the part of government that shows no partiality to any one group and that lets each flourish according to the zeal of its adherents and the appeal of its dogma. When the state encourages religious instruction or cooperates with religious authorities by adjusting the schedule of public events to sectarian needs, it follows the best of our traditions. For it then respects the religious nature of our people and accommodates the public service to their spiritual needs. To hold that it may not would be to find in the Constitution a requirement that the government show a callous indifference to religious groups. That would be preferring those who believe in no religion over those who do believe. Government may not finance religious groups nor undertake religious instruction nor blend secular and sectarian education nor use secular institutions to force one or some religion on any person. But we find no constitutional requirement which makes it necessary for government to be hostile to religion and to throw its weight against efforts to widen the effective scope of religious influence. The government must be neutral when it comes to competition between sects. It may not thrust any sect on any person. It may not make a religious observance compulsory. It may not coerce anyone to attend church, to observe a religious holiday, or to take religious instruction. But it can close its doors or suspend its operations as to those who want to repair to their religious sanctuary for worship or instruction. No more than that is undertaken here.

. . .

In the *McCollum* case the classrooms were used for religious instruction and the force of the public school was used to promote that instruction. Here, as we have said, the public schools do no more than accommodate their schedules to a program of outside religious instruction. We follow the *McCollum* case. But we cannot expand it to cover the present released time program unless separation of Church and State means that public institutions can make no adjustments of their schedules to accommodate the religious needs of the people. We cannot read into the Bill of Rights such a philosophy of hostility to religion.

Affirmed.

■ MR. JUSTICE BLACK, dissenting.

. . . In considering whether a state has entered this forbidden field the question is not whether it has entered too far but whether it has entered at all. New York is manipulating its compulsory education laws to help religious sects get pupils. This is not separation but combination of Church and State. . . .

. . . [a]

■ MR. JUSTICE JACKSON, dissenting.

. . .

A number of Justices just short of a majority of the majority that promulgates today's passionate dialectics joined in answering them in McCollum v. Board of Education . . . The distinction attempted between that case and this is trivial, almost to the point of cynicism, magnifying its nonessential details and disparaging compulsion which was the underlying reason for invalidity. A reading of the Court's opinion in that case along with its opinion in this case will show such difference of overtones and undertones as to make clear that the *McCollum* case has passed like a storm in a teacup. The wall which the Court was professing to erect between Church and State has become even more warped and twisted than I expected. Today's judgment will be more interesting to students of psychology and of the judicial processes than to students of constitutional law.

Santa Fe Independent School District v. Doe

530 U.S. 290, 120 S.Ct. 2266, 147 L.Ed.2d 295 (2000).

■ JUSTICE STEVENS delivered the opinion of the Court.

Prior to 1995, the Santa Fe High School student who occupied the school's elective office of student council chaplain delivered a prayer over the public address system before each varsity football game for the entire season. This practice . . . was challenged in District Court . . . While these proceedings were pending in the District Court, the school district adopted a different policy that permits, but does not require, prayer initiated and led by a student at all home games. The District Court entered an order modifying that policy to permit only nonsectarian, nonproselytizing prayer. The Court of Appeals held that, even as modified by the District Court, the football prayer policy was invalid. . . .

I

. . .

Respondents commenced this action in April 1995 and moved for a temporary restraining order to prevent the District from violating the Establishment Clause at

---

[a] Justice Frankfurter's dissent, which emphasized his "agreement with Mr. Justice Jackson's dissent," is omitted.

the imminent graduation exercises. In their complaint the Does alleged that the District had engaged in several proselytizing practices, such as promoting attendance at a Baptist revival meeting, encouraging membership in religious clubs, chastising children who held minority religious beliefs, and distributing Gideon Bibles on school premises. They also alleged that the District allowed students to read Christian invocations and benedictions from the stage at graduation ceremonies, and to deliver overtly Christian prayers over the public address system at home football games.

[T]he District Court entered an interim order . . . With respect to the impending graduation, the order provided that "non-denominational prayer" consisting of " 'an invocation and/or benediction' " could be presented by a senior student or students selected by members of the graduating class. The text of the prayer was to be determined by the students, without scrutiny or preapproval by school officials. References to particular religious figures "such as Mohammed, Jesus, Buddha, or the like" would be permitted "as long as the general thrust of the prayer is non-proselytizing."

In response to that portion of the order, the District adopted a series of policies over several months dealing with prayer at school functions. The policies enacted in May and July for graduation ceremonies provided the format for the August and October policies for football games. The May policy provided:

"The board has chosen to permit the graduating senior class, with the advice and counsel of the senior class principal or designee, to elect by secret ballot to choose whether an invocation and benediction shall be part of the graduation exercise. If so chosen the class shall elect by secret ballot, from a list of student volunteers, students to deliver nonsectarian, nonproselytizing invocations and benedictions for the purpose of solemnizing their graduation ceremonies."

[T]he senior class . . . voted, by secret ballot, to include prayer at the high school graduation. In a second vote the class elected two seniors to deliver the invocation and benediction.

In July, the District enacted another policy eliminating the requirement that invocations and benedictions be "nonsectarian and nonproselytising," but also providing that if the District were to be enjoined from enforcing that policy, the May policy would automatically become effective.

The August policy, which was titled "Prayer at Football Games," was similar to the July policy for graduations. . . . Like the July policy, it contained two parts, an initial statement that omitted any requirement that the content of the invocation be "nonsectarian and nonproselytising," and a fallback provision that automatically added that limitation if the preferred policy should be enjoined. . . . [T]he district's high school students voted to . . . allow a student to say a prayer at football games. A week later, in a separate election, they selected a student "to deliver the prayer at varsity football games."

The final policy (October policy) is essentially the same as the August policy, though it omits the word "prayer" from its title, and refers to "messages" and "statements" as well as "invocations." It is the validity of that policy that is before us.

The District Court did enter an order precluding enforcement of the first, open-ended policy. Relying on our decision in Lee v. Weisman, 505 U.S. 577 (1992), it held that the school's "action must not 'coerce anyone to support or participate in' a religious exercise." Applying that test, it concluded that the graduation prayers appealed "to distinctively Christian beliefs," and that delivering a prayer "over the school's public address system prior to each football and baseball game coerces student participation in religious events." Both parties appealed, the District contending that the enjoined portion of the October policy was permissible and the Does contending that both alternatives violated the Establishment Clause. The Court of Appeals majority agreed with the Does.

. . .

We granted the District's petition for certiorari, limited to the following question: "Whether petitioner's policy permitting student-led, student-initiated prayer at football games violates the Establishment Clause." We conclude, as did the Court of Appeals, that it does.

II

. . . In Lee v. Weisman, 505 U.S. 577 (1992), we held that a prayer delivered by a rabbi at a middle school graduation ceremony violated that Clause. Although this case involves student prayer at a different type of school function, our analysis is properly guided by the principles that we endorsed in *Lee*. As we held in that case:

"The principle that government may accommodate the free exercise of religion does not supersede the fundamental limitations imposed by the Establishment Clause. It is beyond dispute that, at a minimum, the Constitution guarantees that government may not coerce anyone to support or participate in religion or its exercise, or otherwise act in a way which 'establishes a [state] religion or religious faith, or tends to do so.' " . . .

In this case the District first argues that this principle is inapplicable to its October policy because the messages are private student speech, not public speech. It reminds us that "there is a crucial difference between government speech endorsing religion, which the Establishment Clause forbids, and private speech endorsing religion, which the Free Speech and Free Exercise Clauses protect." Board of Ed. of Westside Community Schools (Dist. 66) v. Mergens, 496 U.S. 226, 250 (1990) (opinion of O'Connor, J.). We certainly agree with that distinction, but we are not persuaded that the pregame invocations should be regarded as "private speech."

These invocations are authorized by a government policy and take place on government property at government-sponsored school-related events. Of course, not every message delivered under such circumstances is the government's own. We have held, for example, that an individual's contribution to a government-created forum was not government speech. See Rosenberger v. Rector and Visitors of Univ. of Va., 515 U.S. 819 (1995). Although the District relies heavily on *Rosenberger* and similar cases involving such forums, it is clear that the pregame ceremony is not the type of forum discussed in those cases. The Santa Fe school officials simply do not "evince either 'by policy or by practice,' any intent to open the [pregame ceremony] to 'indiscriminate use,' . . . by the student body generally." . . . Rather, the school allows only one student, the same student for the entire season, to give the invocation. The statement or invocation, moreover, is subject to particular regulations that confine the content and topic of the student's message. . . .

Granting only one student access to the stage at a time does not, of course, necessarily preclude a finding that a school has created a limited public forum. Here, however, Santa Fe's student election system ensures that only those messages deemed "appropriate" under the District's policy may be delivered. That is, the majoritarian process implemented by the District guarantees, by definition, that minority candidates will never prevail and that their views will be effectively silenced.

Recently, in Board of Regents of Univ. of Wis. System v. Southworth, 529 U.S. 217 (2000), we explained why student elections that determine, by majority vote, which expressive activities shall receive or not receive school benefits are constitutionally problematic:

"To the extent the referendum substitutes majority determinations for viewpoint neutrality it would undermine the constitutional protection the program requires. The whole theory of viewpoint neutrality is that minority views are treated with the same respect as are majority views. Access to a public forum, for instance, does not depend upon majoritarian consent. That principle is controlling here."

Like the student referendum for funding in *Southworth*, this student election does nothing to protect minority views but rather places the students who hold such views at the mercy of the majority. . . .

In *Lee*, the school district made the related argument that its policy of endorsing only "civic or nonsectarian" prayer was acceptable because it minimized the intrusion on the audience as a whole. We rejected that claim by explaining that such a majoritarian policy "does not lessen the offense or isolation to the objectors. At best it narrows their number, at worst increases their sense of isolation and affront." Similarly, while Santa Fe's majoritarian election might ensure that most of the students are represented, it does nothing to protect the minority; indeed, it likely serves to intensify their offense.

Moreover, the District has failed to divorce itself from the religious content in the invocations. It has not succeeded in doing so, either by claiming that its policy is "one of neutrality rather than endorsement" or by characterizing the individual student as the "circuit-breaker" in the process. Contrary to the District's repeated assertions that it has adopted a "hands-off" approach to the pregame invocation, the realities of the situation plainly reveal that its policy involves both perceived and actual endorsement of religion. In this case, as we found in *Lee*, the "degree of school involvement" makes it clear that the pregame prayers bear "the imprint of the State and thus put school-age children who objected in an untenable position." . . .

The District has attempted to disentangle itself from the religious messages by developing the two-step student election process. The text of the October policy, however, exposes the extent of the school's entanglement. The elections take place at all only because the school "board has chosen to permit students to deliver a brief invocation and/or message." The elections thus "shall" be conducted "by the high school student council" and "[u]pon advice and direction of the high school principal." The decision whether to deliver a message is first made by majority vote of the entire student body, followed by a choice of the speaker in a separate, similar majority election. Even though the particular words used by the speaker are not determined by those votes, the policy mandates that the "statement or invocation" be "consistent with the goals and purposes of this policy," which are "to solemnize the event, to promote good sportsmanship and student safety, and to establish the appropriate environment for the competition."

In addition to involving the school in the selection of the speaker, the policy, by its terms, invites and encourages religious messages. The policy itself states that the purpose of the message is "to solemnize the event." A religious message is the most obvious method of solemnizing an event. Moreover, the requirements that the message "promote good citizenship" and "establish the appropriate environment for competition" further narrow the types of message deemed appropriate, suggesting that a solemn, yet nonreligious, message, such as commentary on United States foreign policy, would be prohibited. Indeed, the only type of message that is expressly endorsed in the text is an "invocation"—a term that primarily describes an appeal for divine assistance. In fact, as used in the past at Santa Fe High School, an "invocation" has always entailed a focused religious message. . . . [T]he students understood that the central question before them was whether prayer should be a part of the pregame ceremony. We recognize the important role that public worship plays in many communities, as well as the sincere desire to include public prayer as a part of various occasions so as to mark those occasions' significance. But such religious activity in public schools, as elsewhere, must comport with the First Amendment.

The actual or perceived endorsement of the message, moreover, is established by factors beyond just the text of the policy. Once the student speaker is selected and the message composed, the invocation is then delivered to a large audience assembled as part of a regularly scheduled, school-sponsored function conducted on school property. The message is broadcast over the school's public address system, which remains subject to the control of school officials. It is fair to assume that the pregame ceremony is clothed in the traditional indicia of school sporting events, which generally include not just the team, but also cheerleaders and band members dressed in uniforms sporting the school name and mascot. The school's name is likely written in large print across the field and on banners and flags. The crowd will certainly include many who display the school colors and insignia on their school T-shirts, jackets, or hats and who may also be waving signs displaying the school name. It is in a setting such as this that "[t]he board has chosen to permit" the elected student to rise and give the "statement or invocation."

In this context the members of the listening audience must perceive the pregame message as a public expression of the views of the majority of the student body delivered with the approval of the school administration. . . .

. . .

Most striking to us is the evolution of the current policy from the long-sanctioned office of "Student Chaplain" to the candidly titled "Prayer at Football Games" regulation. This history indicates that the District intended to preserve the practice of prayer before football games. The conclusion that the District viewed the October policy simply as a continuation of the previous policies is dramatically illustrated by the fact that the school did not conduct a new election, pursuant to the current policy, to replace the results of the previous election, which occurred under the former policy. Given these observations, and in light of the school's history of regular delivery of a student-led prayer at athletic events, it is reasonable to infer that the specific purpose of the policy was to preserve a popular "state-sponsored religious practice." . . .

School sponsorship of a religious message is impermissible because it sends the ancillary message to members of the audience who are nonadherents "that they are outsiders, not full members of the political community, and an accompanying message to adherents that they are insiders, favored members of the political community." . . . The delivery of such a message—over the school's public address system, by a speaker representing the student body, under the supervision of school faculty, and pursuant to a school policy that explicitly and implicitly encourages public prayer—is not properly characterized as "private" speech.

III

The District next argues that its football policy is distinguishable from the graduation prayer in *Lee* because it does not coerce students to participate in religious observances. Its argument has two parts: first, that there is no impermissible government coercion because the pregame messages are the product of student choices; and second, that there is really no coercion at all because attendance at an extracurricular event, unlike a graduation ceremony, is voluntary.

The reasons just discussed explaining why the alleged "circuit-breaker" mechanism of the dual elections and student speaker do not turn public speech into private speech also demonstrate why these mechanisms do not insulate the school from the coercive element of the final message. In fact, this aspect of the District's argument exposes anew the concerns that are created by the majoritarian election system. . . . [T]he issue resolved in the first election was "whether a student would deliver prayer at varsity football games," and the controversy in this case demonstrates that the views of the students are not unanimous on that issue.

One of the purposes served by the Establishment Clause is to remove debate over this kind of issue from governmental supervision or control. We explained in *Lee* that the "preservation and transmission of religious beliefs and worship is a responsibility and a choice committed to the private sphere." . . . The two student elections authorized by the policy, coupled with the debates that presumably must precede each, impermissibly invade that private sphere. The election mechanism, when considered in light of the history in which the policy in question evolved, reflects a device the District put in place that determines whether religious messages will be delivered at home football games. The mechanism encourages divisiveness along religious lines in a public school setting, a result at odds with the Establishment Clause. Although it is true that the ultimate choice of student speaker is "attributable to the students," the District's decision to hold the constitutionally problematic election is clearly "a choice attributable to the State,". . . .

The District further argues that attendance at the commencement ceremonies at issue in *Lee* "differs dramatically" from attendance at high school football games, which it contends "are of no more than passing interest to many students" and are "decidedly extracurricular," thus dissipating any coercion. Attendance at a high school football game, unlike showing up for class, is certainly not required in order to receive a diploma. Moreover, we may assume that the District is correct in arguing that the informal pressure to attend an athletic event is not as strong as a senior's desire to attend her own graduation ceremony.

There are some students, however, such as cheerleaders, members of the band, and, of course, the team members themselves, for whom seasonal commitments mandate their attendance, sometimes for class credit. The District also minimizes the importance to many students of attending and participating in extracurricular activities as part of a complete educational experience. As we noted in *Lee*, "[l]aw reaches past formalism." . . . To assert that high school students do not feel immense social pressure, or have a truly genuine desire, to be involved in the extracurricular event that is American high school football is "formalistic in the extreme." . . . We stressed in *Lee* the obvious observation that "adolescents are often susceptible to pressure from their peers towards conformity, and that the influence is strongest in matters of social convention." . . . High school home football games are traditional gatherings of a school community; they bring together students and faculty as well as friends and family from years present and past to root for a common cause. Undoubtedly, the games are not important to some students, and they voluntarily choose not to attend. For many others, however, the choice between whether to attend these games or to risk facing a personally offensive religious ritual is in no practical sense an easy one. The Constitution, moreover, demands that the school may not force this difficult choice upon these students for "[i]t is a tenet of the First Amendment that the State cannot require one of its citizens to forfeit his or her rights and benefits as the price of resisting conformance to state-sponsored religious practice." . . .

Even if we regard every high school student's decision to attend a home football game as purely voluntary, we are nevertheless persuaded that the delivery of a pregame prayer has the improper effect of coercing those present to participate in an act of religious worship. For "the government may no more use social pressure to enforce orthodoxy than it may use more direct means." As in *Lee*, "[w]hat to most believers may seem nothing more than a reasonable request that the nonbeliever respect their religious practices, in a school context may appear to the nonbeliever or dissenter to be an attempt to employ the machinery of the State to enforce a religious orthodoxy." . . . The constitutional command will not permit the District "to exact religious conformity from a student as the price" of joining her classmates at a varsity football game.

. . . [N]othing in the Constitution as interpreted by this Court prohibits any public school student from voluntarily praying at any time before, during, or after the schoolday. But the religious liberty protected by the Constitution is abridged when the State affirmatively sponsors the particular religious practice of prayer.

IV

Finally, the District argues repeatedly that the Does have made a premature facial challenge to the October policy that necessarily must fail. The District emphasizes, quite correctly, that until a student actually delivers a solemnizing message under the latest version of the policy, there can be no certainty that any of the statements or invocations will be religious. Thus, it concludes, the October policy necessarily survives a facial challenge.

This argument, however, assumes that we are concerned only with the serious constitutional injury that occurs when a student is forced to participate in an act of religious worship because she chooses to attend a school event. But the Constitution also requires that we keep in mind "the myriad, subtle ways in which Establishment Clause values can be eroded," . . . and that we guard against other different, yet equally important, constitutional injuries. One is the mere passage by the District of a policy that has the purpose and perception of government establishment of religion. Another is the implementation of a governmental electoral process that subjects the issue of prayer to a majoritarian vote.

. . .

The judgment of the Court of Appeals is, accordingly, affirmed.

It is so ordered.

■ CHIEF JUSTICE REHNQUIST, with whom JUSTICE SCALIA and JUSTICE THOMAS join, dissenting.

. . . [T]he tone of the Court's opinion . . . bristles with hostility to all things religious in public life. . . .

. . . [T]he fact that a policy might "operate unconstitutionally under some conceivable set of circumstances is insufficient to render it wholly invalid." . . . While there is an exception to this principle in the First Amendment overbreadth context because of our concern that people may refrain from speech out of fear of prosecution, . . . , there is no similar justification for Establishment Clause cases. No speech will be "chilled" by the existence of a government policy that might unconstitutionally endorse religion over nonreligion. Therefore, the question is not whether the district's policy may be applied in violation of the Establishment Clause, but whether it inevitably will be.

. . . The Court . . . applies the most rigid version of the oft-criticized test of Lemon v. Kurtzman, 403 U.S. 602 (1971).

Lemon has had a checkered career in the decisional law of this Court. . . .

Even if it were appropriate to apply the *Lemon* test here, the district's student-message policy should not be invalidated on its face. . . .

. . .

Elk Grove Unified School District v. Newdow

542 U.S. 1 (2004).

In 1954, Congress amended the Flag Salute, adding the words "under God." Under state law, each public school must begin the school day with appropriate patriotic exercises. The Elk Grove School District implemented the law by requiring the flag salute, permitting students who object on religious grounds to abstain. Plaintiff, whose daughter attends school in the district, brought suit seeking a declaration that the addition of the words "under God" in 1954 violated the Establishment Clause. Four Justices joined Justice Stevens' opinion for the Court, which concluded that plaintiff did not have standing to bring the action. (He was not the custodial parent, and his daughter did not object to saying the Pledge of Allegiance.) Justice Stevens referred to the "deeply rooted commitment 'not to pass on questions of constitutionality' unless adjudication of the constitutional issue is necessary." Chief Justice Rehnquist, joined by Justices O'Connor and Thomas, objected to dismissal of the case. Justice O'Connor also wrote that she would sustain the Pledge on the ground that it did not "make a person's religious beliefs relevant to his or her standing in the political community by conveying a message that religion or a particular religious belief is favored or preferred." Justice Thomas also addressed the merits, indicating that he, too, would sustain the Flag Salute. He would substantially rethink the Establishment Clause, however, to permit state "establishment," subject to a requirement that Congress not interfere with state establishments. (Justice Scalia did not participate in the decision.)

Edwards v. Aguillard

482 U.S. 578, 107 S.Ct. 2573, 96 L.Ed.2d 510 (1987).

■ JUSTICE BRENNAN delivered the opinion of the Court.

The question for decision is whether Louisiana's "Balanced Treatment for Creation-Science and Evolution-Science in Public School Instruction" Act (Creationism Act), La.Rev.Stat.Ann. §§ 17:286.1–17:286.7 (West 1982), is facially invalid as violative of the Establishment Clause of the First Amendment.

I

The Creationism Act forbids the teaching of the theory of evolution in public schools unless accompanied by instruction in "creation science." ... No school is required to teach evolution or creation science. If either is taught, however, the other must also be taught. Ibid. The theories of evolution and creation science are statutorily defined as "the scientific evidences for [creation or evolution] and inferences from those scientific evidences." ...

Appellees, who include parents of children attending Louisiana public schools, Louisiana teachers, and religious leaders, challenged the constitutionality of the Act in District Court ... The District Court granted [appellees'] motion for summary judgment ...

The Court of Appeals affirmed. ... We ... affirm.

II

The Establishment Clause forbids the enactment of any law "respecting an establishment of religion." The Court has applied a three-pronged test to determine whether legislation comports with the Establishment Clause. First, the legislature must have adopted the law with a secular purpose. Second, the statute's principal or primary effect must be one that neither advances nor inhibits religion. Third, the statute must not result in an excessive entanglement of government with religion. Lemon v. Kurtzman, ...[4] State action violates the Establishment Clause if it fails to satisfy any of these prongs.

---

[4] The *Lemon* test has been applied in all cases since its adoption in 1971, except in Marsh v. Chambers, 463 U.S. 783 (1983), where the Court held that the Nebraska Legislature's practice of opening a session with a prayer by a chaplain paid by the State did not violate the Establishment

. . .

The Court has been particularly vigilant in monitoring compliance with the Establishment Clause in elementary and secondary schools. . . . Students in such institutions are impressionable and their attendance is involuntary. . . . The State exerts great authority and coercive power through mandatory attendance requirements, and because of the students' emulation of teachers as role models and the children's susceptibility to peer pressure.[5] . . .

. . .

III

Lemon's first prong focuses on the purpose that animated adoption of the Act. . . . If the law was enacted for the purpose of endorsing religion, "no consideration of the second or third criteria [of *Lemon*] is necessary." . . . In this case, appellants have identified no clear secular purpose for the Louisiana Act.

True, the Act's stated purpose is to protect academic freedom. . . . This phrase might, in common parlance, be understood as referring to enhancing the freedom of teachers to teach what they will. The Court of Appeals, however, correctly concluded that the Act was not designed to further that goal. . . . Even if "academic freedom" is read to mean "teaching all of the evidence" with respect to the origin of human beings, the Act does not further this purpose. The goal of providing a more comprehensive science curriculum is not furthered either by outlawing the teaching of evolution or by requiring the teaching of creation science.

A

While the Court is normally deferential to a State's articulation of a secular purpose, it is required that the statement of such purpose be sincere and not a sham. . . .

It is clear from the legislative history that the purpose of the legislative sponsor, Senator Bill Keith, was to narrow the science curriculum. During the legislative hearings, Senator Keith stated: "My preference would be that neither [creationism nor evolution] be taught." Such a ban on teaching does not promote—indeed, it undermines—the provision of a comprehensive scientific education.

It is equally clear that requiring schools to teach creation science with evolution does not advance academic freedom. The Act does not grant teachers a flexibility that they did not already possess to supplant the present science curriculum with the presentation of theories, besides evolution, about the origin of life. Indeed, the Court of Appeals found that no law prohibited Louisiana public school teachers from teaching any scientific theory. . . .

. . .

Furthermore, the goal of basic "fairness" is hardly furthered by the Act's discriminatory preference for the teaching of creation science and against the teaching of evolution. While requiring that curriculum guides be developed for creation science,

---

Clause. The Court based its conclusion in that case on the historical acceptance of the practice. Such a historical approach is not useful in determining the proper roles of church and state in public schools, since free public education was virtually nonexistent at the time the Constitution was adopted. . . .

[5] The potential for undue influence is far less significant with regard to college students who voluntarily enroll in courses. "This distinction warrants a difference in constitutional results." Abington School Dist. v. Schempp, supra, at 253 (Brennan, J., concurring). Thus, for instance, the Court has not questioned the authority of state colleges and universities to offer courses on religion or theology. See Widmar v. Vincent, 454 U.S. 263, 271 (1981) (Powell, J.); id., at 281 (Stevens, J., concurring in judgment).

the Act says nothing of comparable guides for evolution. . . . Similarly, research services are supplied for creation science but not for evolution. . . . Only "creation scientists" can serve on the panel that supplies the resource services. . . . The Act forbids school boards to discriminate against anyone who "chooses to be a creation-scientist" or to teach "creationism," but fails to protect those who choose to teach evolution or any other noncreation science theory, or who refuse to teach creation science. . . .

If the Louisiana Legislature's purpose was solely to maximize the comprehensiveness and effectiveness of science instruction, it would have encouraged the teaching of all scientific theories about the origins of humankind. But under the Act's requirements, teachers who were once free to teach any and all facets of this subject are now unable to do so. Moreover, the Act fails even to ensure that creation science will be taught, but instead requires the teaching of this theory only when the theory of evolution is taught. Thus we agree with the Court of Appeals' conclusion that the Act does not serve to protect academic freedom, but has the distinctly different purpose of discrediting "evolution by counterbalancing its teaching at every turn with the teaching of creationism. . . ."

B

. . .

. . . [W]e need not be blind in this case to the legislature's preeminent religious purpose in enacting this statute. There is a historic and contemporaneous link between the teachings of certain religious denominations and the teaching of evolution. It was this link that concerned the Court in Epperson v. Arkansas, 393 U.S. 97 (1968), which also involved a facial challenge to a statute regulating the teaching of evolution. In that case, the Court reviewed an Arkansas statute that made it unlawful for an instructor to teach evolution or to use a textbook that referred to this scientific theory. Although the Arkansas anti-evolution law did not explicitly state its predominate religious purpose, the Court could not ignore that "[t]he statute was a product of the upsurge of 'fundamentalist' religious fervor" that has long viewed this particular scientific theory as contradicting the literal interpretation of the Bible. . . . After reviewing the history of anti-evolution statutes, the Court determined that "there can be no doubt that the motivation for the [Arkansas] law was the same [as other anti-evolution statutes]: to suppress the teaching of a theory which, it was thought, 'denied' the divine creation of man." . . . The Court found that there can be no legitimate state interest in protecting particular religions from scientific views "distasteful to them," . . . and concluded "that the First Amendment does not permit the State to require that teaching and learning must be tailored to the principles or prohibitions of any religious sect or dogma,". . . .

These same historic and contemporaneous antagonisms between the teachings of certain religious denominations and the teaching of evolution are present in this case. The preeminent purpose of the Louisiana Legislature was clearly to advance the religious viewpoint that a supernatural being created humankind. The term "creation science" was defined as embracing this particular religious doctrine by those responsible for the passage of the Creationism Act. Senator Keith's leading expert on creation science, Edward Boudreaux, testified at the legislative hearings that the theory of creation science included belief in the existence of a supernatural creator. Senator Keith also cited testimony from other experts to support the creation-science view that "a creator [was] responsible for the universe and everything in it." The legislative history therefore reveals that the term "creation science," as contemplated by the legislature that adopted this Act, embodies the religious belief that a supernatural creator was responsible for the creation of humankind.

Furthermore, it is not happenstance that the legislature required the teaching of a theory that coincided with this religious view. The legislative history documents that the Act's primary purpose was to change the science curriculum of public schools in order to provide persuasive advantage to a particular religious doctrine that rejects the factual basis of evolution in its entirety. . . .

In this case, the purpose of the Creationism Act was to restructure the science curriculum to conform with a particular religious viewpoint. Out of many possible science subjects taught in the public schools, the legislature chose to affect the teaching of the one scientific theory that historically has been opposed by certain religious sects. As in *Epperson,* the legislature passed the Act to give preference to those religious groups which have as one of their tenets the creation of humankind by a divine creator. The "overriding fact" that confronted the Court in *Epperson* was "that Arkansas' law selects from the body of knowledge a particular segment which it proscribes for the sole reason that it is deemed to conflict with . . . a particular interpretation of the Book of Genesis by a particular religious group." . . .

We do not imply that a legislature could never require that scientific critiques of prevailing scientific theories be taught. . . . [T]eaching a variety of scientific theories about the origins of humankind to schoolchildren might be validly done with the clear secular intent of enhancing the effectiveness of science instruction. But because the primary purpose of the Creationism Act is to endorse a particular religious doctrine, the Act furthers religion in violation of the Establishment Clause.

. . .

V

The Louisiana Creationism Act advances a religious doctrine by requiring either the banishment of the theory of evolution from public school classrooms or the presentation of a religious viewpoint that rejects evolution in its entirety. The Act violates the Establishment Clause of the First Amendment because it seeks to employ the symbolic and financial support of government to achieve a religious purpose. The judgment of the Court of Appeals therefore is

Affirmed.

■ JUSTICE POWELL, with whom JUSTICE O'CONNOR joins, concurring.

. . .

. . . The Establishment Clause is properly understood to prohibit the use of the Bible and other religious documents in public school education only when the purpose of the use is to advance a particular religious belief.

. . .

■ JUSTICE WHITE, concurring in the judgment.

As it comes to us, this is not a difficult case. . . .

. . .

Here, the District Judge, relying on the terms of the Act, discerned its purpose to be the furtherance of a religious belief, and a panel of the Court of Appeals agreed. Of those four judges, two are Louisianians. I would accept this view of the statute. Even if as an original matter I might have arrived at a different conclusion based on a reading of the statute and the record before us, I cannot say that the two courts below are so plainly wrong that they should be reversed. . . .

. . .

■ JUSTICE SCALIA, with whom THE CHIEF JUSTICE joins, dissenting.

Even if I agreed with the questionable premise that legislation can be invalidated under the Establishment Clause on the basis of its motivation alone, without regard to its effects, I would still find no justification for today's decision. . . . [T]he question of its constitutionality cannot rightly be disposed of on the gallop, by impugning the motives of its supporters.

I

. . . [T]he parties are sharply divided over what creation science consists of. Appellants insist that it is a collection of educationally valuable scientific data that has been censored from classrooms by an embarrassed scientific establishment. Appellees insist it is not science at all but thinly veiled religious doctrine. Both interpretations of the intended meaning of that phrase find considerable support in the legislative history.

. . .

II

. . .

B

. . .

In sum, even if one concedes, for the sake of argument, that a majority of the Louisiana Legislature voted for the Balanced Treatment Act partly in order to foster (rather than merely eliminate discrimination against) Christian fundamentalist beliefs, our cases establish that that alone would not suffice to invalidate the Act, so long as there was a genuine secular purpose as well. We have, moreover, no adequate basis for disbelieving the secular purpose set forth in the Act itself, or for concluding that it is a sham enacted to conceal the legislators' violation of their oaths of office. I am astonished by the Court's unprecedented readiness to reach such a conclusion, which I can only attribute to an intellectual predisposition created by the facts and the legend of Scopes v. State, 154 Tenn. 105, 289 S.W. 363 (1927)—an instinctive reaction that any governmentally imposed requirements bearing upon the teaching of evolution must be a manifestation of Christian fundamentalist repression. In this case, however, it seems to me the Court's position is the repressive one. The people of Louisiana, including those who are Christian fundamentalists, are quite entitled, as a secular matter, to have whatever scientific evidence there may be against evolution presented in their schools, just as Mr. Scopes was entitled to present whatever scientific evidence there was for it. . . .

. . .

Because I believe that the Balanced Treatment Act had a secular purpose, which is all the first component of the *Lemon* test requires, I would reverse the judgment of the Court of Appeals and remand for further consideration.

III

I have to this point assumed the validity of the *Lemon* "purpose" test. In fact, however, I think the pessimistic evaluation that The Chief Justice made of the totality of *Lemon* is particularly applicable to the "purpose" prong: it is "a constitutional theory [that] has no basis in the history of the amendment it seeks to interpret, is difficult to apply and yields unprincipled results. . . ." Wallace v. Jaffree, 472 U.S., at 112 (Rehnquist, J., dissenting).

. . .

Given the many hazards involved in assessing the subjective intent of governmental decisionmakers, the first prong of *Lemon* is defensible, I think, only if the text of the Establishment Clause demands it. That is surely not the case. . . . It is, in short, far from an inevitable reading of the Establishment Clause that it forbids all governmental action intended to advance religion; and if not inevitable, any reading with such untoward consequences must be wrong.

. . .

2. RELIGIOUS SPEECH AND DISPLAYS ON PUBLIC PROPERTY

Equal Access for Religious Speech on Public Property

Religious speakers denied access to public property have sought to compel access on free speech grounds, while the government-owner of the property has sought to justify denial of access on establishment grounds. In Widmar v. Vincent, 454 U.S. 263 (1981), a student group was denied permission to conduct meetings on state university facilities because of a policy denying use of university facilities "for purposes of religious worship or religious teaching." (The group was an organization of evangelical Christian students whose on-campus meetings, open to the public, included prayer, hymns, Bible commentary, and religious discussion.) The exclusion was held to violate the First Amendment's Free Speech Clause. The "discriminatory exclusion" was "content-based," and could only be justified if "necessary to serve a compelling state interest and . . . narrowly drawn to achieve that end." The exclusion was not necessary to serve the University's interest in maintaining separation of church and State because the religious group's benefit from access to the University's public forum was "incidental."

In Board of Education v. Mergens, 496 U.S. 226 (1990), students at a public secondary school were denied permission to form a Christian club "to read and discuss the Bible, to have fellowship, and to pray together" because school officials decided that a religious club at school would violate the Establishment Clause. The Court held that the school had violated a federal statute, the Equal Access Act, 20 U.S.C. §§ 4071–4074. The Act prohibits public secondary schools receiving federal funds, and maintaining a "limited public forum," from denying "equal access" to students on the basis of the content of their speech. By a vote of eight to one, but without a majority opinion, the Court held that the Equal Access Act did not violate the Establishment Clause. Justice O'Connor, joined by Chief Justice Rehnquist and Justices White and Blackmun, applied the three-part *Lemon* test. Granting equal access to secular and religious speech was a secular purpose; did not have the primary effect of advancing religion because high school students will understand that the school does not endorse speech it merely permits; did not involve excessive entanglement because the Act prohibits faculty from regularly attending, directing or controlling activities of religious student groups. Justice Kennedy, joined by Justice Scalia, said there was no Establishment Clause violation because religious groups were not given benefits to a degree that established a state religion, and students were not coerced to participate in religious activity.

In Lamb's Chapel v. Center Moriches Union Free School District, 508 U.S. 384 (1993), exclusion of a non-student's religious speech from a public secondary school was held to violate the Free Speech Clause. An evangelical church and its pastor were denied permission to use school facilities to show a six-part film series containing lectures concerning "Christian family values." The Court relied on *Widmar* for its conclusion that the school district's "posited fears of an Establishment Clause violation are unfounded."

McCreary County, Kentucky v. American Civil Liberties Union of Kentucky

545 U.S. 844, 125 S.Ct. 2722, 162 L.Ed.2d 729 (2005).

■ JUSTICE SOUTER delivered the opinion of the Court.

Executives of two counties posted a version of the Ten Commandments on the walls of their courthouses. After suits were filed charging violations of the Establishment Clause, the legislative body of each county adopted a resolution calling for a more extensive exhibit meant to show that the Commandments are Kentucky's "precedent legal code." The result in each instance was a modified display of the Commandments surrounded by texts containing religious references as their sole common element. After changing counsel, the counties revised the exhibits again by eliminating some documents, expanding the text set out in another, and adding some new ones.

The issues are whether a determination of the counties' purpose is a sound basis for ruling on the Establishment Clause complaints, and whether evaluation of the counties' claim of secular purpose for the ultimate displays may take their evolution into account. We hold that the counties' manifest objective may be dispositive of the constitutional enquiry, and that the development of the presentation should be considered when determining its purpose.

I

. . .

. . . Within a month [of respondents' filing a suit], . . . the legislative body of each County authorized a second, expanded display, by nearly identical resolutions reciting that the Ten Commandments are "the precedent legal code upon which the civil and criminal codes of . . . Kentucky are founded," . . . .

. . . [T]he Counties expanded the displays of the Ten Commandments in their locations . . . . In addition to the first display's large framed copy of the edited King James version of the Commandments, the second included eight other documents in smaller frames, each either having a religious theme or excerpted to highlight a religious element. The documents were the "endowed by their Creator" passage from the Declaration of Independence; the Preamble to the Constitution of Kentucky; the national motto, "In God We Trust"; a page from the Congressional Record of February 2, 1983, proclaiming the Year of the Bible and including a statement of the Ten Commandments; a proclamation by President Abraham Lincoln designating April 30, 1863, a National Day of Prayer and Humiliation; an excerpt from President Lincoln's "Reply to Loyal Colored People of Baltimore upon Presentation of a Bible," reading that "[t]he Bible is the best gift God has ever given to man"; a proclamation by President Reagan marking 1983 the Year of the Bible; and the Mayflower Compact.

. . . [T]he District Court entered a preliminary injunction . . . ordering that the "display . . . be removed from [each] County Courthouse IMMEDIATELY" . . . . As to governmental purpose, it concluded that the original display "lack[ed] any secular purpose" because the Commandments "are a distinctly religious document. . . ." The court found that the second version also "clearly lack[ed] a secular purpose" because the "Count[ies] narrowly tailored [their] selection of foundational documents to incorporate only those with specific references to Christianity."

The Counties . . . voluntarily dismissed [their appeal] after hiring new lawyers [and] installed another display in each courthouse, . . . consist[ing] of nine framed documents of equal size, one of them setting out the Ten Commandments explicitly identified as the "King James Version" at Exodus 20:3–17 and quoted at greater length than before. . . . Assembled with the Commandments are framed copies of the Magna Carta, the Declaration of Independence, the Bill of Rights, the lyrics of the Star Spangled Banner, the Mayflower Compact, the National Motto, the Preamble to the Kentucky Constitution, and a picture of Lady Justice. The collection is entitled "The Foundations of American Law and Government Display" and each document comes with a statement about its historical and legal significance. . . .

The ACLU moved to . . . enjoin the Counties' third display, and the Counties responded with several explanations for the new version, including desires "to demonstrate that the Ten Commandments were part of the foundation of American Law and Government" and "to educate the citizens of the county regarding some of the documents that played a significant role in the foundation of our system of law and government." . . . The court, however, took the objective of proclaiming the Commandments' foundational value as "a religious, rather than secular, purpose" under Stone v. Graham, 449 U.S. 39 (1980) . . . , and found that the assertion that the Counties' broader educational goals are secular "crumble[s] . . . upon an examination of the history of this litigation," . . . .

. . . [T]he trial court supplemented the injunction, and a divided panel of the . . . Sixth Circuit affirmed. . . .

We . . . now affirm.

II

Twenty-five years ago in a case prompted by posting the Ten Commandments in Kentucky's public schools, this Court recognized that the Commandments "are undeniably a sacred text in the Jewish and Christian faiths" and held that their display in public classrooms violated the First Amendment's bar against establishment of religion. . . . *Stone* found a predominantly religious purpose in the government's posting of the Commandments, given their prominence as " 'an instrument of religion,' " . . . The Counties . . . argu[e] that official purpose is unknowable and the search for it inherently vain. In the alternative, the Counties would . . . hav[e] us limit the scope of the purpose enquiry so severely that any trivial rationalization would suffice, under a standard oblivious to the history of religious government action like the progression of exhibits in this case.

A

Ever since Lemon v. Kurtzman . . . , looking to whether government action has "a secular legislative purpose" has been a common, albeit seldom dispositive, element of our cases. . . .

The touchstone for our analysis is the principle that the "First Amendment mandates governmental neutrality between religion and religion, and between religion and nonreligion." . . . When the government acts with the ostensible and predominant purpose of advancing religion, it violates that central Establishment Clause value of official religious neutrality, there being no neutrality when the government's ostensible object is to take sides. . . . By showing a purpose to favor religion, the government "sends the . . . message to . . . nonadherents 'that they are outsiders, not full members of the political community, and an accompanying message to adherents that they are insiders, favored members' " . . . .

. . .

B

. . . [T]he Counties ask us to abandon *Lemon*'s purpose test, or at least to truncate any enquiry into purpose here. Their first argument is that the very consideration of purpose is deceptive: according to them, true "purpose" is unknowable, and its search merely an excuse for courts to act selectively and unpredictably in picking out evidence of subjective intent. The assertions are as seismic as they are unconvincing.

Examination of purpose is a staple of statutory interpretation that makes up the daily fare of every appellate court in the country, . . . and governmental purpose is a key element of a good deal of constitutional doctrine, e.g., Washington v. Davis, 426 U.S. 229. . . .

. . . [S]crutinizing purpose does make practical sense . . . where an understanding of official objective emerges from readily discoverable fact, without any judicial psychoanalysis of a drafter's heart of hearts. . . .

The cases with findings of a predominantly religious purpose point to the straightforward nature of the test. . . . [I]n *Stone*, the Court held that the "[p]osting of religious texts on the wall serve[d] no . . . educational function," and found that if "the posted copies of the Ten Commandments [were] to have any effect at all, it [would] be to induce the schoolchildren to read, meditate upon, perhaps to venerate and obey, the Commandments." . . .

Nor is there any indication that the enquiry is rigged in practice to finding a religious purpose dominant every time a case is filed. In the past, the test has not been fatal very often, presumably because government does not generally act unconstitutionally, with the predominant purpose of advancing religion. . . . If someone in the government hides religious motive so well that the "'objective observer, acquainted with the text, legislative history, and implementation of the statute,'" . . . cannot see it, then without something more the government does not make a divisive announcement that in itself amounts to taking religious sides. A secret motive stirs up no strife and does nothing to make outsiders of nonadherents, and it suffices to wait and see whether such government action turns out to have . . . the illegitimate effect of advancing religion.

C

. . . [T]he Counties' alternative tack . . . would read the cases as if the purpose enquiry were so naive that any transparent claim to secularity would satisfy it, and they would cut context out of the enquiry, to the point of ignoring history, no matter what bearing it actually had on the significance of current circumstances. There is no precedent for the Counties' arguments, or reason supporting them.

. . .

. . . [T]he Counties are simply asking us to ignore perfectly probative evidence; they want an absentminded objective observer, not one presumed to be familiar with the history of the government's actions and competent to learn what history has to show. . . .

III

. . .

We take *Stone* as the initial legal benchmark, our only case dealing with the constitutionality of displaying the Commandments. *Stone* recognized that the Commandments are an "instrument of religion" and that . . . their isolated exhibition did not leave room even for an argument that secular education explained their being there. . . . But *Stone* did not purport to decide the constitutionality of every possible way the Commandments might be set out by the government, and under the Establishment Clause detail is key. . . .

A

The display rejected in *Stone* had two obvious similarities to the first one in the sequence here: both set out a text of the Commandments as distinct from any traditionally symbolic representation, and each stood alone, not part of an arguably secular display. *Stone* stressed the significance of integrating the Commandments into a secular scheme to forestall the broadcast of an otherwise clearly religious message, . . . and for good reason, the Commandments being a central point of reference in the religious and moral history of Jews and Christians. They proclaim the existence of a monotheistic god (no other gods). They regulate details of religious obligation (no graven images, no sabbath breaking, no vain oath swearing). And they unmistakably rest even the universally accepted prohibitions (as against murder, theft, and the like) on the sanction of the divinity proclaimed at the beginning of the text. . . . What is more, at the ceremony for posting the framed Commandments in Pulaski County, the county executive was accompanied by his pastor, who testified to the certainty of the existence of God. The reasonable observer could only think that the Counties meant to emphasize and celebrate the Commandments' religious message.

This is not to deny that the Commandments have had influence on civil or secular law . . . . The point is simply that the original text viewed in its entirety is an unmistakably religious statement dealing with religious obligations and with morality subject to religious sanction. When the government initiates an effort to place this statement alone in public view, a religious object is unmistakable.

B

. . .

In th[e] second display, unlike the first, the Commandments were not hung in isolation . . . . Instead, the second version was required to include the statement of the government's purpose expressly set out in the county resolutions, and underscored it by juxtaposing the Commandments to other documents with highlighted references to God as their sole common element. The display's unstinting focus was on religious passages, showing that the Counties were posting the Commandments precisely because of their sectarian content. That demonstration of the government's objective was enhanced by serial religious references and the accompanying resolution's claim about the embodiment of ethics in Christ. Together, the display and resolution presented an indisputable, and undisputed, showing of an impermissible purpose.

. . .

C

1

After the Counties changed lawyers, they mounted a third display, without a new resolution or repeal of the old one. The result was the "Foundations of American Law and Government" exhibit, which placed the Commandments in the company of other documents the Counties thought especially significant in the historical foundation of American government. . . . [T]he Counties cited several new purposes for the third version, including a desire "to educate the citizens of the county regarding some of the documents that played a significant role in the foundation of our system of law and government." . . .

[N]ew statements of purpose were presented only as a litigating position, there being no further authorizing action by the Counties' governing boards. . . . [T]he extraordinary resolutions for the second display passed just months earlier were not repealed or otherwise repudiated. Indeed, the sectarian spirit of the common resolution found enhanced expression in the third display, which quoted more of the purely religious language of the Commandments than the first two displays had done. . . .

. . .

2

. . . [W]e do not decide that the Counties' past actions forever taint any effort on their part to deal with the subject matter. We hold only that purpose needs to be taken seriously under the Establishment Clause and needs to be understood in light of context; an implausible claim that governmental purpose has changed should not carry the day in a court of law any more than in a head with common sense. . . .

Nor do we have occasion here to hold that a sacred text can never be integrated constitutionally into a governmental display on the subject of law, or American history. We do not forget, and in this litigation have frequently been reminded, that our own courtroom frieze was deliberately designed in the exercise of governmental authority so as to include the figure of Moses holding tablets exhibiting a portion of the Hebrew text of the later, secularly phrased Commandments; in the company of 17 other lawgivers, most of them secular figures, there is no risk that Moses would strike an observer as evidence that the National Government was violating neutrality in religion.

IV

. . .

The dissent . . . puts forward a limitation on the application of the neutrality principle, with citations to historical evidence said to show that the Framers understood the ban on establishment of religion as sufficiently narrow to allow the government to espouse submission to the divine will. The dissent identifies God as the God of monotheism, all of whose three principal strains (Jewish, Christian, and Muslim) acknowledge the religious importance of the Ten Commandments. On the dissent's view, it apparently follows that even rigorous espousal of a common element of this common monotheism, is consistent with the establishment ban.

But the dissent's argument for the original understanding is flawed from the outset by its failure to consider the full range of evidence showing what the Framers believed. The dissent is certainly correct in putting forward evidence that some of the Framers thought some endorsement of religion was compatible with the establishment ban. . . .

But the fact is that . . . there is also evidence supporting the proposition that the Framers intended the Establishment Clause to require governmental neutrality in matters of religion, including neutrality in statements acknowledging religion. The very language of the Establishment Clause represented a significant departure from early drafts that merely prohibited a single national religion, and, the final language instead "extended [the] prohibition to state support for 'religion' in general." . . .

The historical record, moreover, is complicated beyond the dissent's account by the writings and practices of figures no less influential than Thomas Jefferson and James Madison. Jefferson, for example, refused to issue Thanksgiving Proclamations because he believed that they violated the Constitution. . . .

The fair inference is that there was no common understanding about the limits of the establishment prohibition, and the dissent's conclusion that its narrower view was the original understanding, stretches the evidence beyond tensile capacity. What the evidence does show is a group of statesmen, like others before and after them, who proposed a guarantee with contours not wholly worked out, leaving the Establishment Clause with edges still to be determined. . . .

While the dissent fails to show a consistent original understanding from which to argue that the neutrality principle should be rejected, it does manage to deliver a surprise. As mentioned, the dissent says that the deity the Framers had in mind was the God of monotheism, with the consequence that government may espouse a tenet of

religious nature of the monument is clear to even the most casual passerby, the word "Lord" appears in all capital letters (as does the word "am"), so that the most eye-catching segment of the quotation is the declaration "I AM the LORD thy God." . . .

To drive the religious point home, and identify the message as religious to any viewer who failed to read the text, the engraved quotation is framed by religious symbols: two tablets with what appears to be ancient script on them, two Stars of David, and the superimposed Greek letters Chi and Rho as the familiar monogram of Christ. Nothing on the monument, in fact, detracts from its religious nature. . . .

. . .

Texas seeks to take advantage of the recognition that visual symbol and written text can manifest a secular purpose in secular company, when it argues that its monument . . . ought to be viewed as only 1 among 17 placed on the 22 acres surrounding the state capitol. Texas, indeed, says that the Capitol grounds are like a museum for a collection of exhibits, the kind of setting that several Members of the Court have said can render the exhibition of religious artifacts permissible, even though in other circumstances their display would be seen as meant to convey a religious message forbidden to the State. . . . So, for example, the Government of the United States does not violate the Establishment Clause by hanging Giotto's Madonna on the wall of the National Gallery.

But 17 monuments with no common appearance, history, or esthetic role scattered over 22 acres is not a museum, and anyone strolling around the lawn would surely take each memorial on its own terms without any dawning sense that some purpose held the miscellany together more coherently than fortuity and the edge of the grass. . . .

. . .

Finally, . . . I do not see a persuasive argument for constitutionality in the plurality's observation that Van Orden's lawsuit comes "[f]orty years after the monument's erection . . . ," an observation that echoes the State's contention that one fact cutting in its favor is that "the monument stood . . . in Austin . . . for some forty years without generating any controversy or litigation,". . . . It is not that I think the passage of time is necessarily irrelevant in Establishment Clause analysis. We have approved framing-era practices because they must originally have been understood as constitutionally permissible, . . . and we have recognized that Sunday laws have grown recognizably secular over time. . . . There is also an analogous argument, not yet evaluated, that ritualistic religious expression can become so numbing over time that its initial Establishment Clause violation becomes at some point too diminished for notice. But . . . the State's argument . . . seems to be that 40 years without a challenge shows that as a factual matter the religious expression is too tepid to provoke a serious reaction and constitute a violation. Perhaps, but . . . other explanations may do better in accounting for the late resort to the courts. Suing a State over religion puts nothing in a plaintiff's pocket and can take a great deal out, and even with volunteer litigators to supply time and energy, the risk of social ostracism can be powerfully deterrent. I doubt that a slow walk to the courthouse, even one that took 40 years, is much evidentiary help in applying the Establishment Clause.

I would reverse the judgment of the Court of Appeals.

Town of Greece v. Galloway

572 U.S. ___, 134 S.Ct. 1811, 188 L.Ed.2d 835 (2014).

■ JUSTICE KENNEDY delivered the opinion of the Court, except as to Part II-B.*

The Court must decide whether the town of Greece, New York, imposes an impermissible establishment of religion by opening its monthly board meetings with a prayer. It must be concluded, consistent with the Court's opinion in Marsh v. Chambers, 463 U.S. 783 (1983), that no violation of the Constitution has been shown.

I

[The practice of inviting a local member of the clergy to deliver an invocation at the front of the board of supervisors meeting room began in 1999 in this town of 94,000 near the border of the city of Rochester.]

The town followed an informal method for selecting prayer givers, all of whom were unpaid volunteers. A town employee would call the congregations listed in a local directory until she found a minister available for that month's meeting. The town eventually compiled a list of willing "board chaplains" who had accepted invitations and agreed to return in the future. The town at no point excluded or denied an opportunity to a would-be prayer giver. Its leaders maintained that a minister or layperson of any persuasion, including an atheist, could give the invocation. But nearly all of the congregations in town were Christian; and from 1999 to 2007, all of the participating ministers were too.

Greece neither reviewed the prayers in advance of the meetings nor provided guidance as to their tone or content, in the belief that exercising any degree of control over the prayers would infringe both the free exercise and speech rights of the ministers. . . . The town instead left the guest clergy free to compose their own devotions. The resulting prayers often sounded both civic and religious themes. . . . Some of the ministers spoke in a distinctly Christian idiom; and a minority invoked religious holidays, scripture, or doctrine . . . .

Respondents . . . attended town board meetings to speak about issues of local concern, and they objected that the prayers violated their religious or philosophical views. . . . After respondents complained that Christian themes pervaded the prayers, to the exclusion of citizens who did not share those beliefs, the town invited a Jewish layman and the chairman of the local Baha'i temple to deliver prayers. A Wiccan priestess who had read press reports about the prayer controversy requested, and was granted, an opportunity to give the invocation.

[Respondents sued,] . . . alleg[ing] that the town violated the . . . Establishment Clause by preferring Christians over other prayer givers and by sponsoring sectarian prayers, such as those given "in Jesus' name." . . . They did not seek an end to the prayer practice, but rather requested an injunction that would limit the town to "inclusive and ecumenical" prayers that referred only to a "generic God" and would not associate the government with any one faith or belief. . . .

The District Court on summary judgment upheld the prayer practice . . . .

. . .

The . . . Second Circuit reversed. . . . [T]he Court now reverses the judgment of the Court of Appeals.

---

* The Chief Justice and Justice Alito join this opinion in full. Justice Scalia and Justice Thomas join this opinion except as to Part II-B.

II

In *Marsh* v. *Chambers*, . . . the Court found no First Amendment violation in the Nebraska Legislature's practice of opening its sessions with a prayer delivered by a chaplain paid from state funds. The decision concluded that legislative prayer, while religious in nature, has long been understood as compatible with the Establishment Clause. As practiced by Congress since the framing of the Constitution, legislative prayer lends gravity to public business, reminds lawmakers to transcend petty differences in pursuit of a higher purpose, and expresses a common aspiration to a just and peaceful society. . . .

Marsh is sometimes described as "carving out an exception" to the Court's Establishment Clause jurisprudence, because it sustained legislative prayer without subjecting the practice to "any of the formal 'tests' that have traditionally structured" this inquiry. . . . The Court in *Marsh* found those tests unnecessary because history supported the conclusion that legislative invocations are compatible with the Establishment Clause. The First Congress made it an early item of business to appoint and pay official chaplains, and both the House and Senate have maintained the office virtually uninterrupted since that time. . . . When *Marsh* was decided, in 1983, legislative prayer had persisted in the Nebraska Legislature for more than a century, and the majority of the other States also had the same, consistent practice. . . . Although no information has been cited by the parties to indicate how many local legislative bodies open their meetings with prayer, this practice too has historical precedent. . . .

Yet *Marsh* must not be understood as permitting a practice that would amount to a constitutional violation if not for its historical foundation. . . . [Instead,] *Marsh* stands for the proposition that it is not necessary to define the precise boundary of the Establishment Clause where history shows that the specific practice is permitted. Any test the Court adopts must acknowledge a practice that was accepted by the Framers and has withstood the critical scrutiny of time and political change. . . . A test that would sweep away what has so long been settled would create new controversy and begin anew the very divisions along religious lines that the Establishment Clause seeks to prevent. See *Van Orden* v. *Perry*, . . . (Breyer, J., concurring in judgment).

The Court's inquiry, then, must be to determine whether the prayer practice in the town of Greece fits within the tradition long followed in Congress and the state legislatures. Respondents assert that [it] falls outside that tradition and transgresses the Establishment Clause for two independent but mutually reinforcing reasons. First, they argue that *Marsh* did not approve prayers containing sectarian language or themes, such as the prayers offered in Greece that referred to the "death, resurrection, and ascension of the Savior Jesus Christ," . . . and the "saving sacrifice of Jesus Christ on the cross," . . . . Second, they argue that the setting and conduct of the town board meetings create social pressures that force nonadherents to remain in the room or even feign participation in order to avoid offending the representatives who sponsor the prayer and will vote on matters citizens bring before the board. The sectarian content of the prayers compounds the subtle coercive pressures, they argue, because the nonbeliever who might tolerate ecumenical prayer is forced to do the same for prayer that might be inimical to his or her beliefs.

A

. . .

An insistence on nonsectarian or ecumenical prayer as a single, fixed standard is not consistent with the tradition of legislative prayer outlined in the Court's cases. . . . The Congress that drafted the First Amendment would have been accustomed to invocations containing explicitly religious themes of the sort respondents find objectionable. . . . The decidedly Christian nature of these prayers must not be dismissed as the relic of a time when our Nation was less pluralistic than it is today. Congress continues to permit its appointed and visiting chaplains to express themselves in a religious idiom. It acknowledges our growing diversity not by proscribing sectarian content but by welcoming ministers of many creeds. . . .

. . .

. . . *Marsh* nowhere suggested that the constitutionality of legislative prayer turns on the neutrality of its content. . . .

To hold that invocations must be nonsectarian would force the legislatures that sponsor prayers and the courts that are asked to decide these cases to act as supervisors and censors of religious speech, a rule that would involve government in religious matters to a far greater degree than is the case under the town's current practice of neither editing or approving prayers in advance nor criticizing their content after the fact. . . . Government may not mandate a civic religion that stifles any but the most generic reference to the sacred any more than it may prescribe a religious orthodoxy. . . .

. . . There is doubt, in any event, that consensus might be reached as to what qualifies as generic or nonsectarian. . . . Once it invites prayer into the public sphere, government must permit a prayer giver to address his or her own God or gods as conscience dictates, unfettered by what an administrator or judge considers to be nonsectarian.

In rejecting the suggestion that legislative prayer must be nonsectarian, the Court does not imply that no constraints remain on its content. . . . If the course and practice over time shows that the invocations denigrate nonbelievers or religious minorities, threaten damnation, or preach conversion, many present may consider the prayer to fall short of the desire to elevate the purpose of the occasion and to unite lawmakers in their common effort. That circumstance would present a different case than the one presently before the Court.

. . . Prayer that reflects beliefs specific to only some creeds can still serve to solemnize the occasion, so long as the practice over time is not "exploited to proselytize or advance any one, or to disparage any other, faith or belief." *Marsh*, ...

. . .

The prayers delivered in the town of Greece do not fall outside the tradition this Court has recognized. A number of the prayers did invoke the name of Jesus, the Heavenly Father, or the Holy Spirit, but they also invoked universal themes, as by celebrating the changing of the seasons or calling for a "spirit of cooperation" among town leaders. . . .

Respondents point to other invocations that disparaged those who did not accept the town's prayer practice. One guest minister characterized objectors as a "minority" who are "ignorant of the history of our country," . . . while another lamented that other towns did not have "God-fearing" leaders. . . . Although these two remarks strayed from the rationale set out in *Marsh*, they do not despoil a practice that on the whole reflects and embraces our tradition. Absent a pattern of prayers that over time denigrate, proselytize, or betray an impermissible government purpose, a challenge based solely on the content of a prayer will not likely establish a constitutional violation. . . .

Finally, the Court disagrees with the view taken by the Court of Appeals that the town of Greece contravened the Establishment Clause by inviting a predominantly Christian set of ministers to lead the prayer. The town made reasonable efforts to identify all of the congregations located within its borders and represented that it would welcome a prayer by any minister or layman who wished to give one. That nearly all of the congregations in town turned out to be Christian does not reflect an aversion or bias on the part of town leaders against minority faiths. So long as the town maintains a policy of nondiscrimination, the Constitution does not require it to search beyond its borders for non-Christian prayer givers in an effort to achieve religious balancing. . . .

B

Respondents further seek to distinguish the town's prayer practice from the tradition upheld in *Marsh* on the ground that it coerces participation by nonadherents. They and some *amici* contend that prayer conducted in the intimate setting of a town board meeting differs in fundamental ways from the invocations delivered in Congress and state legislatures, where the public remains segregated from legislative activity and may not address the body except by occasional invitation. Citizens attend town meetings, on the other hand, to accept awards; speak on matters of local importance; and petition the board for action that may affect their economic interests, such as the granting of permits, business licenses, and zoning variances. Respondents argue that the public may feel subtle pressure to participate in prayers that violate their beliefs in order to please the board members from whom they are about to seek a favorable ruling. In their view the fact that board members in small towns know many of their constituents by name only increases the pressure to conform.

. . . On the record in this case the Court is not persuaded that the town of Greece . . . compelled its citizens to engage in a religious observance. The inquiry remains a fact-sensitive one that considers both the setting in which the prayer arises and the audience to whom it is directed.

. . . As a practice that has long endured, legislative prayer has become part of our heritage and tradition, part of our expressive idiom, similar to the Pledge of Allegiance, inaugural prayer, or the recitation of "God save the United States and this honorable Court" at the opening of this Court's sessions. . . . It is presumed that the reasonable observer is acquainted with this tradition and understands that its purposes are to lend gravity to public proceedings and to acknowledge the place religion holds in the lives of many private citizens, not to afford government an opportunity to proselytize or force truant constituents into the pews. . . .

The principal audience for these invocations is not . . . the public but lawmakers themselves, who may find that a moment of prayer or quiet reflection sets the mind to a higher purpose and thereby eases the task of governing. . . . To be sure, many members of the public find these prayers meaningful and wish to join them. But their purpose is largely to accommodate the spiritual needs of lawmakers and connect them to a tradition dating to the time of the Framers. . . . The prayer is [also] an opportunity for them to show who and what they are without denying the right to dissent by those who disagree.

The analysis would be different if town board members directed the public to participate in the prayers, singled out dissidents for opprobrium, or indicated that their decisions might be influenced by a person's acquiescence in the prayer opportunity. . . . Respondents point to several occasions where audience members were asked to rise for the prayer. These requests, however, came not from town leaders but from the guest ministers, who presumably are accustomed to directing their congregations in this way and might have done so thinking the action was inclusive, not coercive. . . . Nothing in the record indicates that town leaders allocated benefits and burdens based on participation in the prayer, or that citizens were received differently depending on whether they joined the invocation or quietly declined. In no instance did town leaders signal disfavor toward nonparticipants or suggest that their stature in the community was in any way diminished. A practice that classified citizens based on their religious views would violate the Constitution, but that is not the case before this Court.

. . . Courts remain free to review the pattern of prayers over time to determine whether they comport with the tradition of solemn, respectful prayer approved in *Marsh*, or whether coercion is a real and substantial likelihood. But in the general course legislative bodies do not engage in impermissible coercion merely by exposing constituents to prayer they would rather not hear and in which they need not participate. . . .

. . . Nothing in the record suggests that members of the public are dissuaded from leaving the meeting room during the prayer, arriving late, or even, as happened here, making a later protest. . . . Should nonbelievers choose to exit the room during a prayer they find distasteful, their absence will not stand out as disrespectful or even noteworthy. And should they remain, their quiet acquiescence will not, in light of our traditions, be interpreted as an agreement with the words or ideas expressed. Neither choice represents an unconstitutional imposition as to mature adults . . . .

. . . The inclusion of a brief, ceremonial prayer as part of a larger exercise in civic recognition suggests that its purpose and effect are to acknowledge religious leaders and the institutions they represent rather than to exclude or coerce nonbelievers.

Ceremonial prayer is but a recognition that, since this Nation was founded and until the present day, many Americans deem that their own existence must be understood by precepts far beyond the authority of government to alter or define and that willing participation in civic affairs can be consistent with a brief acknowledgment of their belief in a higher power, always with due respect for those who adhere to other beliefs. . . .

* * *

The town of Greece does not violate the First Amendment by opening its meetings with prayer that comports with our tradition and does not coerce participation by nonadherents. . . .

■ JUSTICE ALITO, with whom JUSTICE SCALIA joins, concurring.

. . .

Apparently, all the houses of worship listed in the local Community Guide [from which a clerical employee in the town's office of constituent services compiled the list of clergy to offer prayers] were Christian churches. . . . There are no synagogues within the borders of the town . . . , but there are several not far away across the Rochester border. . . .

. . . [R]espondents do not claim that the list was attributable to religious bias or favoritism . . . .

. . .

. . . The prayer took place at the beginning of the meetings. . . .

. . . I do not understand this case to involve the constitutionality of a prayer prior to what may be characterized as an adjudicatory proceeding. The prayer preceded only the portion of the town board meeting that I view as essentially legislative. . . .

II

. . . [T]he narrow aspect of the principal dissent . . . is really quite niggling. . . .

A

First, the principal dissent writes, "[i]f the Town Board had let its chaplains know that they should speak in nonsectarian terms, common to diverse religious groups, then no one would have valid grounds for complaint." . . .

. . .

Not only is there no historical support for the proposition that only generic prayer is allowed, but as our country has become more diverse, composing a prayer that is acceptable to all members of the community who hold religious beliefs has become harder and harder. It was one thing to compose a prayer that is acceptable to both Christians and Jews; it is much harder to compose a prayer that is also acceptable to followers of Eastern religions that are now well represented in this country. Many local clergy may find the project daunting, if not impossible, and some may feel that they cannot in good faith deliver such a vague prayer.

. . .

B

If a town wants to avoid the problems associated with this first option, the principal dissent argues, it has another choice: It may "invit[e] clergy of many faiths."
. . .

If . . . such a rotating system would obviate any constitutional problems, then despite all its high rhetoric, the principal dissent's quarrel with the town of Greece really boils down to this: The town's clerical employees did a bad job in compiling the list of potential guest chaplains. For that is really the only difference between what the town did and what the principal dissent is willing to accept. The Greece clerical employee drew up her list using the town directory instead of a directory covering the entire greater Rochester area. . . . (I would view this case very differently if the omission of [the] synagogues [on the Rochester side of the border] were intentional.)

. . .

. . . Many local officials, puzzled by our often puzzling Establishment Clause jurisprudence and terrified of the legal fees that may result from a lawsuit claiming a constitutional violation, already think that the safest course is to ensure that local government is a religion-free zone. . . . [A] unit of local government should not be held to have violated the First Amendment simply because its procedure for lining up guest chaplains does not comply in all respects with what might be termed a "best practices" standard.

III

While the principal dissent, in the end, would demand no more than a small modification in the procedure that the town of Greece initially followed, . . . the logical thrust of many of its arguments is that prayer is *never* permissible prior to meetings of local government legislative bodies. . . .

The features of Greece meetings that the principal dissent highlights are by no means unusual. . . . [I]f prayer is not allowed at meetings with those characteristics, local government legislative bodies, unlike their national and state counterparts, cannot begin their meetings with a prayer. I see no sound basis for drawing such a distinction.

IV

The principal dissent claims to accept the Court's decision in *Marsh* v. *Chambers*, . . . but [its] acceptance . . . appears to be predicated on the view that the prayer at issue in that case was little more than a formality to which the legislators paid scant attention. The principal dissent describes this scene: A session of the state legislature begins with or without most members present; a strictly nonsectarian prayer is recited while some legislators remain seated; and few members of the public are exposed to the experience. This sort of perfunctory and hidden-away prayer, the principal dissent implies, is all that *Marsh* and the First Amendment can tolerate.

[To Justice Alito, *Marsh* and the congressional practice on which it was based were not nearly that narrow.]

V

. . . I am concerned that at least some readers will take [the dissent's] hypotheticals as a warning that . . . today's decision leads . . . to a country in which religious minorities are denied the equal benefits of citizenship.

Nothing could be further from the truth. All that the Court does today is to allow a town to follow a practice that we have previously held is permissible for Congress and state legislatures. In seeming to suggest otherwise, the principal dissent goes far astray.

■ JUSTICE THOMAS, with whom JUSTICE SCALIA joins as to Part II, concurring in part and concurring in the judgment.

Except for Part II-B, I join the opinion of the Court, which faithfully applies *Marsh* v. *Chambers*. . . . I write separately to reiterate my view that the Establishment Clause is "best understood as a federalism provision," . . . and to state my understanding of the proper "coercion" analysis.

I

. . . As I have explained before, the text and history of the Clause "resis[t] incorporation" against the States. . . . If the Establishment Clause is not incorporated, then it has no application here, where only municipal action is at issue.

. . .

II

Even if the Establishment Clause were properly incorporated against the States, the municipal prayers at issue in this case bear no resemblance to the coercive state establishments that existed at the founding. . . .

. . .

. . . At a minimum, there is no support for the proposition that the framers of the Fourteenth Amendment embraced wholly modern notions that the Establishment Clause is violated whenever the "reasonable observer" feels "subtle pressure," or perceives governmental "endors[ement]." . . . [W]hatever nonestablishment principles existed in 1868, they included no concern for the finer sensibilities of the "reasonable observer."

■ JUSTICE BREYER, dissenting.

As we all recognize, this is a "fact-sensitive" case. . . .

. . . In essence, the Court of Appeals merely held that the town must do more than it had previously done to try to make its prayer practices inclusive of other faiths. And it did not prescribe a single constitutionally required method for doing so.

In my view, the Court of Appeals' conclusion and its reasoning are convincing. Justice Kagan's dissent is consistent with that view, and I join it. I also here emphasize several factors that I believe underlie the conclusion that, on the particular facts of this case, the town's prayer practice violated the Establishment Clause.

First, Greece is a predominantly Christian town, but it is not exclusively so. A map . . . shows a Buddhist temple within the town and several Jewish synagogues just outside its borders. . . . Yet during the more than 120 monthly meetings at which prayers were delivered during the record period (from 1999 to 2010), only four prayers were delivered by non-Christians. And all of these occurred in 2008, shortly after the plaintiffs began complaining about the town's Christian prayer practice and nearly a decade after that practice had commenced.

. . . The inclusivity of the 2008 meetings, which contrasts starkly with the exclusively single-denomination prayers every year before and after, is commendable. But the Court of Appeals reasonably decided not to give controlling weight to that inclusivity, for it arose only in response to the complaints that presaged this litigation, and it did not continue into the following years.

Second, the town made no significant effort to inform the area's non-Christian houses of worship about the possibility of delivering an opening prayer. . . .

. . .

Third, . . . in a context where religious minorities exist and where more could easily have been done to include their participation, the town chose to do nothing. It could, for example, have posted its policy of permitting anyone to give an invocation on its website, . . . which provides dates and times of upcoming town board meetings along with minutes of prior meetings. It could have announced inclusive policies at the beginning of its board meetings, just before introducing the month's prayer giver. It could have provided information to those houses of worship of all faiths that lie just outside its borders and include citizens of Greece among their members. Given that the town could easily have made these or similar efforts but chose not to, the fact that all of the prayers (aside from the 2008 outliers) were given by adherents of a single religion reflects a lack of effort to include others. . . .

Fourth, the fact that the board meeting audience included citizens with business to conduct also contributes to the importance of making more of an effort to include members of other denominations. . . .

Fifth, . . . the Constitution does not forbid . . . efforts to explain to those who give the prayers the nature of the occasion and the audience.

The U.S. House of Representatives, for example, provides its guest chaplains with . . . guidelines . . . designed to encourage the sorts of prayer that are consistent with the purpose of an invocation for a government body in a religiously pluralistic Nation . . . . The town made no effort to promote a similarly inclusive prayer practice here.

. . . The question in this case is whether the prayer practice of the town of Greece, by doing too little to reflect the religious diversity of its citizens, did too much, even if unintentionally, to promote the "political division along religious lines" that "was one of the principal evils against which the First Amendment was intended to protect." . . .

. . . I conclude, like Justice Kagan, that the town of Greece failed to make reasonable efforts to include prayer givers of minority faiths, with the result that, although it is a community of several faiths, its prayer givers were almost exclusively persons of a single faith. . . .

. . .

■ JUSTICE KAGAN, with whom JUSTICE GINSBURG, JUSTICE BREYER, and JUSTICE SOTOMAYOR join, dissenting.

. . . [O]ur Constitution makes a commitment . . . that however . . . individuals worship, they will count as full and equal American citizens. . . .

I respectfully dissent from the Court's opinion because I think the Town of Greece's prayer practices violate that norm of religious equality . . . . I agree with the Court's decision in *Marsh* v. *Chambers* . . . . And I believe that pluralism and inclusion in a town hall can satisfy the constitutional requirement of neutrality; such a forum need not become a religion-free zone. But . . . [t]he practice at issue here differs from the one sustained in *Marsh* because Greece's town meetings involve participation by ordinary citizens, and the invocations given—directly to those citizens—were predominantly sectarian in content. Still more, Greece's Board did nothing to recognize religious diversity: In arranging for clergy members to open each meeting, the Town never sought (except briefly when this suit was filed) to involve, accommodate, or in any way reach out to adherents of non-Christian religions. So month in and month out for over a decade, prayers steeped in only one faith, addressed toward members of the public, commenced meetings to discuss local affairs and distribute government benefits. In my view, that practice does not square with the First Amendment's promise that every citizen, irrespective of her religion, owns an equal share in her government.

I

[Justice Kagan offered three "hypothetical scenarios in which sectarian prayer—taken straight from this case's record—infuses governmental activities"—(1) "a party in a case going to trial," where the judge "asks a minister to come to the front of the room, and instructs [those] present to rise for an opening prayer" that references Christian scripture, (2) an election official on election day asking everyone there to join him in similar prayer, and (3) "an immigrant attending a naturalization ceremony" told by a presiding official "that before administering the oath of allegiance, he would like a minister to pray for you and with you[,]" which also turned out to be in sectarian language.] I would hold that the government officials responsible for the above practices—that is, for prayer repeatedly invoking a single religion's beliefs in these settings—crossed a constitutional line. I have every confidence the Court would agree. . . .

. . . [I]f my hypotheticals involved the prayer of some other religion, the outcome would be exactly the same. . . . [T]he question would be why such government sponsored prayer of a single religion goes beyond the constitutional pale.

One glaring problem is that the government in all these hypotheticals has aligned itself with, and placed its imprimatur on, a particular religious creed. "The clearest command of the Establishment Clause," this Court has held, "is that one religious denomination cannot be officially preferred over another." *Larson* v. *Valente*, 456 U.S. 228, 244 (1982). . . . By authorizing and overseeing prayers associated with a single religion—to the exclusion of all others—the government officials in my hypothetical cases (whether federal, state, or local does not matter) have violated that foundational principle. They have embarked on a course of religious favoritism anathema to the First Amendment.

And making matters still worse: They have done so in a place where individuals come to interact with, and participate in, the institutions and processes of their government. A person goes to court, to the polls, to a naturalization ceremony—and a government official or his handpicked minister asks her, as the first order of official business, to stand and pray with others in a way conflicting with her own religious beliefs. Perhaps she feels sufficient pressure to go along—to rise, bow her head, and join in whatever others are saying: After all, she wants, very badly, what the judge or poll worker or immigration official has to offer. Or perhaps she is made of stronger mettle, and she opts not to participate in what she does not believe—indeed, what would, for her, be something like blasphemy. She then must make known her dissent from the common religious view, and place herself apart from other citizens, as well as from the officials responsible for the invocations. And so a civic function of some kind brings religious differences to the fore: That public proceeding becomes (whether intentionally or not) an instrument for dividing her from adherents to the community's majority religion, and for altering the very nature of her relationship with her government.

That is not the country we are, because that is not what our Constitution permits. Here, . . . all participate in the business of government not as Christians, Jews, Muslims (and more), but only as Americans—none of them different from any other for that civic purpose. Why not, then, at a town meeting?

II

. . . I agree with the majority that the issue here is "whether the prayer practice in the Town of Greece fits within the tradition long followed in Congress and the state legislatures."

Where I depart from the majority is in my reply to that question. The town hall here is a kind of hybrid. Greece's Board indeed has legislative functions, as Congress and state assemblies do—and that means some opening prayers are allowed there. But much as in my hypotheticals, the Board's meetings are also occasions for ordinary citizens to engage with and petition their government, often on highly individualized matters. That feature calls for Board members to exercise special care to ensure that the prayers offered are inclusive—that they respect each and every member of the community as an equal citizen. But the Board, and the clergy members it selected, made no such effort. Instead, the prayers given in Greece, addressed directly to the Town's citizenry, were *more* sectarian, and *less* inclusive, than anything this Court sustained in *Marsh*. For those reasons, the prayer in Greece departs from the legislative tradition that the majority takes as its benchmark.

. . .

Let's count the ways in which [the practice in Nebraska's unicameral legislature, upheld in *Marsh*, and the practice here] diverge. First, the governmental proceedings at which the prayers occur differ significantly in nature and purpose. The Nebraska Legislature's floor sessions—like those of the U.S. Congress and other state assemblies—are of, by, and for elected lawmakers. Members of the public take no part in those proceedings; any few who attend are spectators only, watching from a high-up visitors' gallery. (In that respect, note that neither the Nebraska Legislature nor the Congress calls for prayer when citizens themselves participate in a hearing—say, by giving testimony relevant to a bill or nomination.) Greece's town meetings, by contrast, revolve around ordinary members of the community. Each and every aspect of those sessions provides opportunities for Town residents to interact with public officials. And the most important parts enable those citizens to petition their government. In the Public Forum, they urge (or oppose) changes in the Board's policies and priorities; and then, in what are essentially adjudicatory hearings, they request the Board to grant (or deny) applications for various permits, licenses, and zoning variances. So the meetings, both by design and in operation, allow citizens to actively participate in the Town's governance—sharing concerns, airing grievances, and both shaping the community's policies and seeking their benefits.

Second . . . , the prayers in these two settings have different audiences. In the Nebraska Legislature, the chaplain spoke to, and only to, the elected representatives. . . . The same is true in the U.S. Congress and, I suspect, in every other state legislature. . . .

The very opposite is true in Greece: Contrary to the majority's characterization, the prayers there are directed squarely at the citizens. Remember that the chaplain of the month stands with his back to the Town Board; his real audience is the group he is facing—the 10 or so members of the public, perhaps including children. And he typically addresses those people, as even the majority observes, as though he is "directing [his] congregation." He almost always begins with some version of "Let us all pray together." . . . In essence, the chaplain leads, as the first part of a town meeting, a highly intimate (albeit relatively brief) prayer service, with the public serving as his congregation.

And third, the prayers themselves differ in their content and character. *Marsh* characterized the prayers in the Nebraska Legislature as "in the Judeo-Christian tradition," and stated, as a relevant (even if not dispositive) part of its analysis, that the chaplain had removed all explicitly Christian references at a senator's request. . . .

But no one can fairly read the prayers from Greece's Town meetings as anything other than explicitly Christian—constantly and exclusively so. . . . About two-thirds of the prayers given over this decade or so invoked "Jesus," "Christ," "Your Son," or "the Holy Spirit"; in the 18 months before the record closed, 85% included those references. . . . Many prayers contained elaborations of Christian doctrine or recitations of scripture. . . .

Still more, the prayers betray no understanding that the American community is today, as it long has been, a rich mosaic of religious faiths. . . . The monthly chaplains appear almost always to assume that everyone in the room is Christian . . . . The Town itself has never urged its chaplains to reach out to members of other faiths, or even to recall that they might be present. And accordingly, few chaplains have made any effort to be inclusive; none has thought even to assure attending members of the public that they need not participate in the prayer session. . . .

C

Those three differences, taken together, remove this case from the protective ambit of *Marsh* and the history on which it relied. To recap: *Marsh* upheld prayer addressed to legislators alone, in a proceeding in which citizens had no role—and even then, only when it did not "proselytize or advance" any single religion. . . . It was that legislative prayer practice (not every prayer in a body exercising any legislative function) that the Court found constitutional given its "unambiguous and unbroken history." . . . None of the history *Marsh* cited—and none the majority details today—supports calling on citizens to pray, in a manner consonant with only a single religion's beliefs, at a participatory public proceeding, having both legislative and adjudicative components. . . .

. . .

Everything about [the] situation [in Greece] infringes the First Amendment. . . . That the Town Board selects, month after month and year after year, prayer givers who will reliably speak in the voice of Christianity, and so places itself behind a single creed. That in offering those sectarian prayers, the Board's chosen clergy members repeatedly call on individuals, prior to participating in local governance, to join in a form of worship that may be at odds with their own beliefs. That the clergy thus put some residents to the unenviable choice of either pretending to pray like the majority or declining to join its communal activity, at the very moment of petitioning their elected leaders. That the practice thus divides the citizenry, creating one class that shares the Board's own evident religious beliefs and another (far smaller) class that does not. And that the practice also alters a dissenting citizen's relationship with her government, making her religious difference salient when she seeks only to engage her elected representatives as would any other citizen.

None of this means that Greece's town hall must be religion- or prayer-free. . . . What the circumstances here demand is the recognition that we are a pluralistic people too. When citizens of all faiths come to speak to each other and their elected representatives in a legislative session, the government must take especial care to ensure that the prayers they hear will seek to include, rather than serve to divide. No more is required—but that much is crucial—to treat every citizen, of whatever religion, as an equal participant in her government.

And contrary to the majority's (and Justice Alito's) view, that is not difficult to do. If the Town Board had let its chaplains know that they should speak in nonsectarian terms, common to diverse religious groups, then no one would have valid grounds for complaint. . . . Or if the Board preferred, it might have invited clergy of many faiths to serve as chaplains, as the majority notes that Congress does. . . .

But Greece could not do what it did: infuse a participatory government body with one (and only one) faith, so that month in and month out, the citizens appearing before it become partly defined by their creed—as those who share, and those who do not, the community's majority religious belief. . . .

III

How, then, does the majority go so far astray, allowing the Town of Greece to turn its assemblies for citizens into a forum for Christian prayer? The answer does not lie in first principles: I have no doubt that every member of this Court believes as firmly as I that our institutions of government belong equally to all, regardless of faith. Rather, the error reflects two kinds of blindness. First, the majority misapprehends the facts of this case, as distinct from those characterizing traditional legislative prayer. And second, the majority misjudges the essential meaning of the religious worship in Greece's town hall, along with its capacity to exclude and divide.

. . .

. . . The majority thus errs in assimilating the Board's prayer practice to that of Congress or the Nebraska Legislature. Unlike those models, the Board is determinedly—and relentlessly—noninclusive.

And the month in, month out sectarianism the Board chose for its meetings belies the majority's refrain that the prayers in Greece were "ceremonial" in nature. . . .

. . .

. . . When the citizens of this country approach their government, they do so only as Americans, not as members of one faith or another. And that means that even in a partly legislative body, they should not confront government-sponsored worship that divides them along religious lines. I believe, for all the reasons I have given, that the Town of Greece betrayed that promise. . . .

C. FINANCIAL AID TO CHURCH-RELATED SCHOOLS AND CHURCH-RELATED INSTRUCTION

1. ELEMENTARY AND SECONDARY SCHOOLS

Aid to Pupils and Their Parents

In *Everson* the Court upheld the provision of transportation of students to religious schools. In Board of Educ. v. Allen, 392 U.S. 236 (1968), the Court by a vote of 6 to 3 upheld a New York law providing for the loaning of text books free of charge to students in all private schools, including church schools. The Court decided that the state statute was valid because "no funds or books are furnished to parochial schools, and the financial benefit is to parents and children, not to schools. Perhaps free books make it more likely that some children choose to attend a sectarian school, but that was true of the state-paid bus fares in *Everson* and does not alone demonstrate an unconstitutional degree of support for a religious institution." Justice Black, who had written the *Everson* opinion, was one of the dissenters. He said: "[I]t is not difficult to distinguish books, which are the heart of any school, from bus fares, which provide a convenient and helpful general public transportation service."

Payments to Religious Schools

The *Allen* decision added fuel to the controversy whether direct government payments to religious elementary and secondary schools violated the establishment clause. In Lemon v. Kurtzman, 403 U.S. 602 (1971), however, the Court struck down a Pennsylvania statute authorizing reimbursement of nonpublic schools for part of the expenses of teachers' salaries, textbooks and instructional materials. A possible simple distinction between aid to religious schools and aid to parents and children, for expenses of attending religious schools, did not survive the next round of cases. In 1973, the Court concluded that direct grants to parents, to reimburse the costs of their children's attendance at nonpublic schools, were also invalid. Committee for Public Education and Religious Liberty v. Nyquist, 413 U.S. 756 (1973); Sloan v. Lemon, 413 U.S. 825 (1973).

Tax Exemptions, Deductions and Credits

In Walz v. Tax Commission of New York, 397 U.S. 664 (1970), the Court sustained the universal practice of exempting church property used for religious worship from the payment of real estate taxes. The Court concluded that the "unbroken practice" of according tax exemptions to churches had not led to an established church and had "operated affirmatively to help guarantee the free exercise of all forms of religious beliefs."

Two cases concerning tax treatment of parents' payments for the cost of religious education are in some tension. In Committee for Public Education & Religious Liberty v. Nyquist, 413 U.S. 756 (1973), the Court struck down a state law giving tax credits, whose amounts were determined by parental income, for each child attending a nonpublic school. The Court concluded that the tax credits were indistinguishable from direct tuition grants to parents—a practice also held invalid in *Nyquist*. In Mueller v. Allen, 463 U.S. 388 (1983), however, the Court sustained state income tax deductions for amounts spent on tuition, textbook, and transportation expenses of children attending elementary or secondary schools. The Court noted that the deduction was applicable to expenses for schooling of all children, including those attending public schools (although the most substantial benefit would flow to parents whose children attended schools charging tuition). Moreover, the tax benefit took the form of a deduction, rather than a fixed dollar credit.

The Court distinguished both Walz v. Tax Commission and Mueller v. Allen in Texas Monthly v. Bullock, 489 U.S. 1 (1989). The Court held that it was unconstitutional to exempt from a sales tax applicable to periodicals generally, sales of periodicals "published or distributed by a religious faith and that consist wholly of writings promulgating the teachings of the faith and books that consist wholly of writings sacred to a religious faith." Here, the exemption was equivalent to a subsidy amounting to state sponsorship of religious belief. In *Walz*, the tax exemption was within a broad class of charitable tax exemptions, and in *Mueller* the exemption was equally available to parents sending their children to nonsectarian schools.

Agostini v. Felton

521 U.S. 203, 117 S.Ct. 1997, 138 L.Ed.2d 391 (1997).

■ JUSTICE O'CONNOR delivered the opinion of the Court.

In Aguilar v. Felton, 473 U.S. 402 (1985), this Court held that the Establishment Clause of the First Amendment barred the city of New York from sending public school teachers into parochial schools to provide remedial education to disadvantaged children pursuant to a congressionally mandated program. On remand, the District Court . . . entered a permanent injunction . . . . Twelve years later, petitioners—the parties bound by that injunction—seek relief from its operation. Petitioners maintain that *Aguilar* cannot be squared with our intervening Establishment Clause jurisprudence and ask that we explicitly recognize [that] *Aguilar* is no longer good law. We agree . . . that *Aguilar* is not consistent with our subsequent Establishment Clause decisions and further conclude that, on the facts presented here, petitioners are entitled under Federal Rule of Civil Procedure 60(b)(5) to relief from the operation of the District Court's prospective injunction.

I

In 1965, Congress enacted Title I of the Elementary and Secondary Education Act of 1965, . . . 20 U.S.C. § 6301 et seq., to "provid[e] full educational opportunity to every child regardless of economic background." . . .

In 1978, six federal taxpayers—respondents here—sued the [New York City] Board [of Education] . . [for] declaratory and injunctive relief, claiming that the Board's Title I program violated the Establishment Clause. . . . The District Court granted summary judgment for the Board, but the . . . Second Circuit reversed. . . . [T]his Court affirmed on the ground that the Board's Title I program necessitated an "excessive entanglement of church and state in the administration of [Title I] benefits." . . . On remand, the District Court permanently enjoined the Board "from using public funds for any plan or program under [Title I] to the extent that it requires, authorizes or permits public school teachers and guidance counselors to provide teaching and counseling services on the premises of sectarian schools within New York City."

The Board, like other LEA's [Local Educational Agencies] across the United States, modified its Title I program so it could continue serving those students who attended private religious schools. Rather than offer Title I instruction to parochial school students at their schools, the Board reverted to its prior practice of providing instruction at public school sites, at leased sites, and in mobile instructional units (essentially vans converted into classrooms) parked near the sectarian school. The Board also offered computer-aided instruction, which could be provided "on premises" because it did not require public employees to be physically present on the premises of a religious school.

It is not disputed that the additional costs of complying with *Aguilar*'s mandate are significant. Since the 1986–1987 school year, the Board has spent over $100 million providing computer-aided instruction, leasing sites and mobile instructional units, and transporting students to those sites. . . . These "*Aguilar* costs" . . . reduce the amount of Title I money an LEA has available for remedial education, and LEA's have had to cut back on the number of students who receive Title I benefits. . . .

In October and December of 1995, petitioners—the Board and a new group of parents of parochial school students entitled to Title I services—filed motions in the District Court seeking relief under Federal Rule of Civil Procedure 60(b) from the permanent injunction entered by the District Court on remand from our decision in *Aguilar*. . . . Specifically, petitioners pointed to the statements of five Justices in Board of Ed. of Kiryas Joel Village School Dist. v. Grumet, 512 U.S. 687 (1994), calling for the overruling of *Aguilar*. The District Court denied the motion. . . . The . . . Second Circuit [affirmed.] We . . . reverse.

II

. . .

Petitioners point to three changes in the factual and legal landscape that they believe justify their claim for relief under Rule 60(b)(5). They first contend that the exorbitant costs of complying with the District Court's injunction constitute a significant factual development warranting modification of the injunction. Petitioners also argue that there have been two significant legal developments since *Aguilar* was decided: a majority of Justices have expressed their views that *Aguilar* should be reconsidered or overruled; and *Aguilar* has in any event been undermined by subsequent Establishment Clause decisions . . .

. . .

. . . [P]etitioners have failed to establish . . . significant change in factual conditions. . . .

. . . [T]he statements made by five Justices in *Kiryas Joel* do not, in themselves, furnish a basis for concluding that our Establishment Clause jurisprudence has changed. In *Kiryas Joel*, we considered the constitutionality of a New York law that carved out a public school district to coincide with the boundaries of the village of Kiryas Joel, which was an enclave of the Satmar Hasidic sect. Before the new district was created, Satmar children wishing to receive special educational services under the Individuals with Disabilities Education Act (IDEA) . . . could receive those services at public schools located outside the village. Because Satmar parents rarely permitted their children to attend those schools, New York created a new public school district within the boundaries of the village so that Satmar children could stay within the village but receive IDEA services on public school premises from publicly employed instructors. In the course of our opinion, we observed that New York had created the special school district in response to our decision in *Aguilar*, which had required New York to cease providing IDEA services to Satmar children on the premises of their private religious schools. . . . Five Justices joined opinions calling for reconsideration of *Aguilar*. [O'Connor, Kennedy, Scalia, Rehnquist and Thomas.] But the question of *Aguilar*'s propriety was not before us. The views of five Justices that the case should be reconsidered or overruled cannot be said to have effected a change in Establishment Clause law.

. . . [P]etitioners' ability to satisfy the prerequisites of Rulre 60(b)(5) hinges on whether our later Establishment Clause cases have so undermined *Aguilar* that it is no longer good law. . . .

III

A

In order to evaluate whether *Aguilar* has been eroded by our subsequent Establishment Clause cases, it is necessary to understand the rationale upon which *Aguilar*, as well as its companion case, School Dist. of Grand Rapids v. Ball, 473 U.S. 373 (1985), rested.

In *Ball*, the Court evaluated two programs implemented by the School District of Grand Rapids, Michigan. The district's Shared Time program, the one most analogous to Title I, provided remedial and "enrichment" classes, at public expense, to students attending nonpublic schools. The classes were taught during regular school hours by publicly employed teachers, using materials purchased with public funds, on the premises of nonpublic schools. The Shared Time courses were in subjects designed to supplement the "core curriculum" of the nonpublic schools. . . . Of the 41 nonpublic schools eligible for the program, 40 were " 'pervasively sectarian' " in character—that is, "the purpos[e] of [those] schools [was] to advance their particular religions." . . .

. . .

Distilled to essentials, the Court's conclusion that the Shared Time program in *Ball* had the impermissible effect of advancing religion rested on three assumptions: (i) any public employee who works on the premises of a religious school is presumed to inculcate religion in her work; (ii) the presence of public employees on private school premises creates a symbolic union between church and state; and (iii) any and all public aid that directly aids the educational function of religious schools impermissibly finances religious indoctrination, even if the aid reaches such schools as a consequence of private decisionmaking. Additionally, in *Aguilar* there was a fourth assumption: that New York City's Title I program necessitated an excessive government entanglement with religion because public employees who teach on the premises of religious schools must be closely monitored to ensure that they do not inculcate religion.

B

Our more recent cases have undermined the assumptions upon which *Ball* and *Aguilar* relied. . . .

1

. . . Our cases subsequent to *Aguilar* have . . . modified in two significant respects the approach we use to assess indoctrination. First, we have abandoned the presumption . . . that the placement of public employees on parochial school grounds inevitably results in the impermissible effect of state-sponsored indoctrination or constitutes a symbolic union between government and religion. In Zobrest v. Catalina Foothills School Dist., 509 U.S. 1 (1993), we examined whether the IDEA . . . was constitutional as applied to a deaf student who sought to bring his state-employed sign-language interpreter with him to his Roman Catholic high school. . . . Because the only *government* aid in *Zobrest* was the interpreter, who was herself not inculcating any religious messages, no *government* indoctrination took place and we were able to conclude that "the provision of such assistance [was] not barred by the Establishment Clause." . . . *Zobrest* therefore expressly rejected the notion—relied on in *Ball* and *Aguilar*—that, solely because of her presence on private school property, a public employee will be presumed to inculcate religion in the students. *Zobrest* also implicitly repudiated another assumption on which *Ball* and *Aguilar* turned: that the presence of a public employee on private school property creates an impermissible "symbolic link" between government and religion.

. . .

Second, we have departed from the rule relied on in *Ball* that all government aid that directly aids the educational function of religious schools is invalid. In Witters v. Washington Dept. of Servs. for Blind, 474 U.S. 481 (1986), we held that the Establishment Clause did not bar a State from issuing a vocational tuition grant to a blind person who wished to use the grant to attend a Christian college and become a pastor, missionary, or youth director. . . . In our view, this transaction was no different from a State's issuing a paycheck to one of its employees, knowing that the employee would donate part or all of the check to a religious institution. . . . Because the private school would not have provided an interpreter on its own, we also concluded that the aid in *Zobrest* did not indirectly finance religious education by "reliev[ing] the sectarian schoo[l] of costs [it] otherwise would have borne in educating [its] students."

Zobrest and *Witters* make clear that, under current law, the Shared Time program in *Ball* and New York City's Title I program in *Aguilar* will not, as a matter of law, be deemed to have the effect of advancing religion through indoctrination. Indeed, each of the premises upon which we relied in *Ball* to reach a contrary conclusion is no longer valid. . . .

. . .

What is most fatal to the argument that New York City's Title I program directly subsidizes religion is that it applies with equal force when those services are provided off-campus, and *Aguilar* implied that providing the services off-campus is entirely consistent with the Establishment Clause. . . .

. . .

3

We turn now to *Aguilar*'s conclusion that New York City's Title I program resulted in an excessive entanglement between church and state. . . . [T]he factors we use to assess whether an entanglement is "excessive" are similar to the factors we use to examine "effect." . . .

Not all entanglements, of course, have the effect of advancing or inhibiting religion. . . . Entanglement must be "excessive" before it runs afoul of the Establishment Clause. . . .

The pre-*Aguilar* Title I program does not result in an "excessive" entanglement that advances or inhibits religion. As discussed previously, the Court's finding of "excessive" entanglement in *Aguilar* rested on three grounds: (i) the program would require "pervasive monitoring by public authorities" to ensure that Title I employees did not inculcate religion; (ii) the program required "administrative cooperation" between the Board and parochial schools; and (iii) the program might increase the dangers of "political divisiveness." . . . Under our current understanding of the Establishment Clause, the last two considerations are insufficient by themselves to create an "excessive" entanglement. They are present no matter where Title I services are offered, and no court has held that Title I services cannot be offered off-campus. . . . Further, the assumption underlying the first consideration has been undermined. . . . [A]fter *Zobrest* we no longer presume that public employees will inculcate religion simply because they happen to be in a sectarian environment. . . .

. . . We . . . hold that a federally funded program providing supplemental, remedial instruction to disadvantaged children on a neutral basis is not invalid under the Establishment Clause when such instruction is given on the premises of sectarian schools by government employees pursuant to a program containing safeguards such as those present here. . . . Accordingly, we must acknowledge that *Aguilar*, as well as the portion of *Ball* addressing Grand Rapids' Shared Time program, are no longer good law.

. . .

■ JUSTICE SOUTER with whom JUSTICE STEVENS and JUSTICE GINSBURG join, and with whom JUSTICE BREYER joins as to Part II, dissenting.

In this novel proceeding, . . . [t]he result is . . . to authorize direct state aid to religious institutions on an unparalleled scale, in violation of the Establishment Clause's central prohibition against religious subsidies by the government.

I respectfully dissent.

  I

. . .

[I]f a line is to be drawn short of barring all state aid to religious schools for teaching standard subjects, the *Aguilar-Ball* line was a sensible one capable of principled adherence. . . .

. . .

. . . In *Zobrest* and *Witters*, . . . individual students were themselves applicants for individual benefits on a scale that could not amount to a systemic supplement. But under Title I, . . . [t]he aid . . . is not even formally aid to the individual students (and even formally individual aid must be seen as aid to a school system when so many individuals receive it that it becomes a significant feature of the system). . . .

In sum, nothing since *Ball* and *Aguilar* and before this case has eroded the distinction between "direct and substantial" and "indirect and incidental." That principled line is being breached only here and now. . . . [a]

Zelman v. Simmons-Harris

536 U.S. 639, 122 S.Ct. 2460, 153 L.Ed.2d 604 (2002).

■ CHIEF JUSTICE REHNQUIST delivered the opinion of the Court.

The State of Ohio has established a pilot program designed to provide educational choices to families with children who reside in the Cleveland City School District. The question presented is whether this program offends the Establishment Clause . . . . We hold that it does not.

There are more than 75,000 children enrolled in the Cleveland City School District. The majority . . . are from low-income and minority families. Few of these families enjoy the means to send their children to any school other than an inner-city public school. For more than a generation, however, Cleveland's public schools have been among the worst performing public schools in the Nation. . . .

It is against this backdrop that Ohio enacted . . . its Pilot Project Scholarship Program . . . The program provides financial assistance to families in any Ohio school district that is or has been "under federal court order requiring supervision and operational management of the district by the state superintendent.". . . . Cleveland is the only Ohio school district to fall within that category.

The program provides . . . to parents of children in a covered district . . . tuition aid for students in kindergarten through third grade, expanding each year through eighth grade, to attend a participating public or private school of their parent's choosing. . . . Second, the program provides tutorial aid for students who choose to remain enrolled in public school. . . .

The tuition aid portion of the program is designed to provide educational choices to parents who reside in a covered district. Any private school, whether religious or nonreligious, may participate in the program and accept program students so long as the school is located within the boundaries of a covered district and meets statewide educational standards. . . . Participating private schools must agree not to discriminate on the basis of race, religion, or ethnic background, or to "advocate or foster unlawful behavior or teach hatred of any person or group on the basis of race, ethnicity, national origin, or religion." . . . Any public school located in a school district

---

[a]   A dissenting opinion by Justice Ginsburg, joined by Justices Stevens, Souter and Breyer, is omitted.

adjacent to the covered district may also participate in the program. . . . Adjacent public schools are eligible to receive a $2,250 tuition grant for each program student accepted in addition to the full amount of per-pupil state funding attributable to each additional student. . . . [P]articipating schools . . . are required to accept students in accordance with rules and procedures established by the state superintendent. . . .

Tuition aid is distributed to parents according to financial need. . . . Where tuition aid is spent depends solely upon where parents who receive tuition aid choose to enroll their child. If parents choose a private school, checks are made payable to the parents who then endorse the checks over to the chosen school. . . .

[For t]he tutorial aid portion of the program . . . [, p]arents arrange for registered tutors . . . and then submit bills . . . for payment. . . . The number of tutorial assistance grants offered to students in a covered district must equal the number of tuition aid scholarships provided to students enrolled at participating private or adjacent public schools. . . .

The program has been in operation within the Cleveland City School District since the 1996–1997 school year. In the 1999–2000 school year, 56 private schools participated in the program, 46 (or 82%) of which had a religious affiliation. None of the public schools in districts adjacent to Cleveland have elected to participate. More than 3,700 students participated in the scholarship program, most of whom (96%) enrolled in religiously affiliated schools. Sixty percent of these students were from families at or below the poverty line. In the 1998–1999 school year, approximately 1,400 Cleveland public school students received tutorial aid. This number was expected to double during the 1999–2000 school year.

. . .

In July 1999, respondents [sued] to enjoin the . . . program on the ground that it violated the Establishment Clause . . . . [T]he District Court granted [them] summary judgment . . . . [A] divided panel of the Court of Appeals affirmed . . . . We . . . reverse . . . .

The Establishment Clause of the First Amendment, applied to the States through the Fourteenth Amendment, prevents a State from enacting laws that have the "purpose" or "effect" of advancing or inhibiting religion. *Agostini v. Felton,* 521 U. S. 203, 222–223 (1997) . . . There is no dispute that the program challenged here was enacted for the valid secular purpose of providing educational assistance to poor children in a demonstrably failing public school system. Thus, the question presented is whether the Ohio program nonetheless has the forbidden "effect" of advancing or inhibiting religion.

To answer that question, our decisions have drawn a consistent distinction between government programs that provide aid directly to religious schools . . . and programs of true private choice, in which government aid reaches religious schools only as a result of the genuine and independent choices of private individuals . . . While our jurisprudence with respect to the constitutionality of direct aid programs has "changed significantly" over the past two decades, . . . our jurisprudence with respect to true private choice programs has remained consistent and unbroken. Three times we have confronted Establishment Clause challenges to neutral government programs that provide aid directly to a broad class of individuals, who, in turn, direct the aid to religious schools or institutions of their own choosing. Three times we have rejected such challenges.

In Mueller [v. Allen, 463 U. S. 388 (1983)], we rejected an Establishment Clause challenge to a Minnesota program authorizing tax deductions for various educational expenses, including private school tuition costs, even though the great majority of the program's beneficiaries (96%) were parents of children in religious schools. . . . We . . .

found it irrelevant to the constitutional inquiry that the vast majority of beneficiaries were parents of children in religious schools . . . That the program was one of true private choice, with no evidence that the State deliberately skewed incentives toward religious schools, was sufficient for the program to survive scrutiny under the Establishment Clause.

In Witters [v. Washington Dept. of Servs. for Blind, 474 U. S. 481 (1986)], we used identical reasoning to reject an Establishment Clause challenge to a vocational scholarship program that provided tuition aid to a student studying at a religious institution to become a pastor. . . .

Five Members of the Court, in separate opinions, emphasized the general rule from *Mueller* that the amount of government aid channeled to religious institutions by individual aid recipients was not relevant to the constitutional inquiry. . . .

Finally, in Zobrest [v. Catalina Foothills School Dist., 509 U. S. 1 (1993)], we applied *Mueller* and *Witters* to reject an Establishment Clause challenge to a federal program that permitted sign-language interpreters to assist deaf children enrolled in religious schools. . . . [W]e stated that "government programs that neutrally provide benefits to a broad class of citizens defined without reference to religion are not readily subject to an Establishment Clause challenge." . . .

. . .

Mueller, *Witters*, and *Zobrest* thus make clear that where a government aid program is neutral with respect to religion, and provides assistance directly to a broad class of citizens who, in turn, direct government aid to religious schools wholly as a result of their own genuine and independent private choice, the program is not readily subject to challenge under the Establishment Clause. A program that shares these features permits government aid to reach religious institutions only by way of the deliberate choices of numerous individual recipients. The incidental advancement of a religious mission, or the perceived endorsement of a religious message, is reasonably attributable to the individual recipient, not to the government, whose role ends with the disbursement of benefits. . . . [W]e have never found a program of true private choice to offend the Establishment Clause.

We believe that the program challenged here is a program of true private choice, consistent with *Mueller*, *Witters*, and *Zobrest*, and thus constitutional. As was true in those cases, the Ohio program is neutral in all respects toward religion. It is part of a general and multifaceted undertaking by the State of Ohio to provide educational opportunities to the children of a failed school district. It confers educational assistance directly to a broad class of individuals defined without reference to religion, *i.e.*, any parent of a school-age child who resides in the Cleveland City School District. The program permits the participation of *all* schools within the district, religious or nonreligious. Adjacent public schools also may participate and have a financial incentive to do so. Program benefits are available to participating families on neutral terms, with no reference to religion. The only preference stated anywhere in the program is a preference for low-income families, who receive greater assistance and are given priority for admission at participating schools.

There are no "financial incentive[s]" that "ske[w]" the program toward religious schools. *Witters*,. . . . Such incentives "[are] not present . . . where the aid is allocated on the basis of neutral, secular criteria that neither favor nor disfavor religion, and is made available to both religious and secular beneficiaries on a nondiscriminatory basis." *Agostini*,. . . .

Respondents suggest that even without a financial incentive for parents to choose a religious school, the program creates a "public perception that the State is endorsing religious practices and beliefs." . . . But we have repeatedly recognized that no reasonable observer would think a neutral program of private choice, where state aid reaches religious schools solely as a result of the numerous independent decisions of private individuals, carries with it the *imprimatur* of government endorsement.... The argument is particularly misplaced here since "the reasonable observer in the endorsement inquiry must be deemed aware" of the "history and context" underlying a challenged program.... Any objective observer familiar with the full history and context of the Ohio program would reasonably view it as one aspect of a broader undertaking to assist poor children in failed schools, not as an endorsement of religious schooling in general.

There also is no evidence that the program fails to provide genuine opportunities for Cleveland parents to select secular educational options for their school-age children. Cleveland schoolchildren enjoy a range of educational choices: They may remain in public school as before, remain in public school with publicly funded tutoring aid, obtain a scholarship and choose a religious school, obtain a scholarship and choose a nonreligious private school, enroll in a community school, or enroll in a magnet school. That 46 of the 56 private schools now participating in the program are religious schools does not condemn it as a violation of the Establishment Clause. The Establishment Clause question is whether Ohio is coercing parents into sending their children to religious schools, and that question must be answered by evaluating *all* options Ohio provides Cleveland schoolchildren, only one of which is to obtain a program scholarship and then choose a religious school.

... It is true that 82% of Cleveland's participating private schools are religious schools, but it is also true that 81% of private schools in Ohio are religious schools. . . .

... The constitutionality of a neutral educational aid program simply does not turn on whether and why, in a particular area, at a particular time, most private schools are run by religious organizations, or most recipients choose to use the aid at a religious school. . . .

    . . .

Respondents finally claim that we should look to Committee for Public Ed. & Religious Liberty v. Nyquist, 413 U. S. 756 (1973), to decide these cases. We disagree for two reasons. First, the program in *Nyquist* was quite different from the program challenged here. *Nyquist* involved a New York program that gave a package of benefits exclusively to private schools and the parents of private school enrollees. Although the program was enacted for ostensibly secular purposes, ... we found that its "function" was "*unmistakably* to provide desired financial support for nonpublic, sectarian institutions,". . . . Its genesis, we said, was that private religious schools faced "increasingly grave fiscal problems." . . . The program thus provided direct money grants to religious schools. . . . It provided tax benefits "unrelated to the amount of money actually expended by any parent on tuition," ensuring a windfall to parents of children in religious schools. . . . It similarly provided tuition reimbursements designed explicitly to "offe[r] ... an incentive to parents to send their children to sectarian schools." . . . Indeed, the program flatly prohibited the participation of any public school, or parent of any public school enrollee. . . . Ohio's program shares none of these features.

Second, ... we expressly reserved judgment with respect to "a case involving some form of public assistance (*e.g.*, scholarships) made available generally without regard to the sectarian-nonsectarian, or public-nonpublic nature of the institution benefited." ... [W]e now hold that *Nyquist* does not govern neutral educational assistance programs that, like the program here, offer aid directly to a broad class of individual recipients defined without regard to religion.

In sum, the Ohio program is entirely neutral with respect to religion. It provides benefits directly to a wide spectrum of individuals, defined only by financial need and residence in a particular school district. It permits such individuals to exercise genuine choice among options public and private, secular and religious. The program is therefore a program of true private choice. In keeping with an unbroken line of decisions rejecting challenges to similar programs, we hold that the program does not offend the Establishment Clause.

. . .

■ JUSTICE O'CONNOR, concurring.

. . . I write separately for two reasons. First, although the Court takes an important step, I do not believe that today's decision . . . marks a dramatic break from the past. Second, given the emphasis the Court places on verifying that parents of voucher students in religious schools have exercised "true private choice," I think it is worth elaborating on the Court's conclusion that this inquiry should consider all reasonable educational alternatives to religious schools that are available to parents. . . .

I

These cases are different from prior indirect aid cases in part because a significant portion of the funds appropriated for the voucher program reach religious schools without restrictions on the use of these funds. The share of public resources that reach religious schools is not, however, as significant as respondents suggest. . . .

. . . [A]t most $8.2 million of public funds flowed to religious schools under the voucher program in 1999–2000. . . .

Although $8.2 million is no small sum, it pales in comparison to the amount of funds that federal, state, and local governments already provide religious institutions. Religious organizations may qualify for exemptions from the federal corporate income tax, . . . and property taxes in all 50 States, . . . [and] clergy qualify for a federal tax break on income used for housing expenses . . . In addition, the Federal Government provides individuals, corporations, trusts, and estates a tax deduction for charitable contributions to qualified religious groups . . . Finally, the Federal Government and certain state governments provide tax credits for educational expenses, many of which are spent on education at religious schools. . . .

. . .

. . . Federal dollars also reach religiously affiliated organizations through public health programs such as Medicare, . . . and Medicaid, . . . , through educational programs such as the Pell Grant program, . . . and the G. I. Bill of Rights, . . . and through child care programs such as the Child Care and Development Block Grant Program . . .

. . .

Against this background, the support that the Cleveland voucher program provides religious institutions is neither substantial nor atypical of existing government programs. . . .

II

Nor does today's decision signal a major departure from this Court's prior Establishment Clause jurisprudence. . . .

The Court's opinion . . . focuses on a narrow question related to the *Lemon* test: how to apply the primary effects prong in indirect aid cases? . . .

. . . What the Court clarifies in these cases is that the Establishment Clause . . . requires that state aid flowing to religious organizations through the hands of beneficiaries must do so only at the direction of those beneficiaries. Such a refinement of the *Lemon* test surely does not betray *Everson*.

III

There is little question in my mind that the Cleveland voucher program is neutral as between religious schools and nonreligious schools. . . .

I do not agree that the nonreligious schools have failed to provide Cleveland parents reasonable alternatives to religious schools in the voucher program. . . .

. . .

In my view the more significant finding in these cases is that Cleveland parents who use vouchers to send their children to religious private schools do so as a result of true private choice. . . .

I find the Court's answer to the question whether parents of students eligible for vouchers have a genuine choice between religious and nonreligious schools persuasive. . . .

. . .

Based on the reasoning in the Court's opinion, which is consistent with the realities of the Cleveland educational system, I am persuaded that the Cleveland voucher program affords parents of eligible children genuine nonreligious options and is consistent with the Establishment Clause.

■ JUSTICE THOMAS, concurring.

. . .

. . . I agree with the Court that Ohio's program easily passes muster under our stringent test, but, as a matter of first principles, I question whether this test should be applied to the States.

. . .

. . . When rights are incorporated against the States through the Fourteenth Amendment they should advance, not constrain, individual liberty.

. . . Thus, while the Federal Government may "make no law respecting an establishment of religion," the States may pass laws that include or touch on religious matters so long as these laws do not impede free exercise rights or any other individual religious liberty interest. . . .

. . . I can accept that the Fourteenth Amendment protects religious liberty rights. But I cannot accept its use to oppose neutral programs of school choice through the incorporation of the Establishment Clause. There would be a tragic irony in converting the Fourteenth Amendment's guarantee of individual liberty into a prohibition on the exercise of educational choice.

. . .

. . . [S]chool choice programs that involve religious schools appear unconstitutional only to those who would twist the Fourteenth Amendment against itself by expansively incorporating the Establishment Clause. Converting the Fourteenth Amendment from a guarantee of opportunity to an obstacle against education reform distorts our constitutional values and disserves those in the greatest need.

. . .

■ Justice Stevens, dissenting.

. . .

[T]he voluntary character of the private choice to prefer a parochial education over an education in the public school system seems to me quite irrelevant to the question whether the government's choice to pay for religious indoctrination is constitutionally permissible. Today, however, the Court seems to have decided that the mere fact that a family that cannot afford a private education wants its children educated in a parochial school is a sufficient justification for this use of public funds.

■ Justice Souter, with whom Justice Stevens, Justice Ginsburg, and Justice Breyer join, dissenting.

. . .

The applicability of the Establishment Clause to public funding of benefits to religious schools was settled in *Everson* . . . , which inaugurated the modern era of establishment doctrine. The Court stated the principle in words from which there was no dissent:

"No tax in any amount, large or small, can be levied to support any religious activities or institutions, whatever they may be called, or whatever form they may adopt to teach or practice religion." . . .

The Court has never in so many words repudiated this statement, let alone, in so many words, overruled *Everson*.

Today, however, the majority holds that the Establishment Clause is not offended by Ohio's Pilot Project Scholarship Program. . . . The money will thus pay for eligible students' instruction not only in secular subjects but in religion as well, in schools that can fairly be characterized as founded to teach religious doctrine and to imbue teaching in all subjects with a religious dimension . . .

. . . It is only by ignoring *Everson* that the majority can claim to rest on traditional law in its invocation of neutral aid provisions and private choice to sanction the Ohio law. It is, moreover, only by ignoring the meaning of neutrality and private choice themselves that the majority can even pretend to rest today's decision on those criteria.

I

. . . [D]octrinal bankruptcy has been reached today.

Viewed with the necessary generality, the cases can be categorized in three groups. In the period from 1947 to 1968, the basic principle of no aid to religion through school benefits was unquestioned. Thereafter for some 15 years, the Court termed its efforts as attempts to draw a line against aid that would be divertible to support the religious, as distinct from the secular, activity of an institutional beneficiary. Then, starting in 1983, concern with divertibility was gradually lost in favor of approving aid in amounts unlikely to afford substantial benefits to religious schools, when offered evenhandedly without regard to a recipient's religious character, and when channeled to a religious institution only by the genuinely free choice of some private individual. Now, the three stages are succeeded by a fourth, in which the substantial character of government aid is held to have no constitutional significance, and the espoused criteria of neutrality in offering aid, and private choice in directing it, are shown to be nothing but examples of verbal formalism.

. . .

. . . [I]t was not until today that substantiality of aid has clearly been rejected as irrelevant by a majority of this Court, just as it has not been until today that a majority, not a plurality, has held purely formal criteria to suffice for scrutinizing aid that ends up in the coffers of religious schools. . . .

II

Although it has taken half a century since *Everson* to reach the majority's twin standards of neutrality and free choice, the facts show that, in the majority's hands, even these criteria cannot convincingly legitimize the Ohio scheme.

A

. . . Today, . . . the majority employs the neutrality criterion in a way that renders it impossible to understand.

Neutrality in this sense refers, of course, to evenhandedness in setting eligibility as between potential religious and secular recipients of public money. . . . Thus, for example, the aid scheme in *Witters* provided an eligible recipient with a scholarship to be used at any institution within a practically unlimited universe of schools . . . ; it did not tend to provide more or less aid depending on which one the scholarship recipient chose, and there was no indication that the maximum scholarship amount would be insufficient at secular schools. . . .

In order to apply the neutrality test, then, it makes sense to . . . ask whether the voucher provisions . . . were written in a way that skewed the scheme toward benefitting religious schools.

This, however, is not what the majority asks. . . .

. . . If regular, public schools (which can get no voucher payments) "participate" in a voucher scheme with schools that can, and public expenditure is still predominantly on public schools, then the majority's reasoning would find neutrality in a scheme of vouchers available for private tuition in districts with no secular private schools at all. "Neutrality" as the majority employs the term is, literally, verbal and nothing more. . . .

. . .

B

The majority addresses the issue of choice the same way it addresses neutrality, by asking whether recipients or potential recipients of voucher aid have a choice of public schools among secular alternatives to religious schools. Again, however, the majority asks the wrong question and misapplies the criterion. The majority has confused choice in spending scholarships with choice from the entire menu of possible educational placements, most of them open to anyone willing to attend a public school. . . . When the choice test is transformed from where to spend the money to where to go to school, it is cut loose from its very purpose.

Defining choice as choice in spending the money or channeling the aid is, moreover, necessary if the choice criterion is to function as a limiting principle at all. . . .

. . .

. . . Although leaving the selection of alternatives for choice wide open, as the majority would, virtually guarantees the availability of a "choice" that will satisfy the criterion, limiting the choices to spending choices will not guarantee a negative result in every case. There may, after all, be cases in which a voucher recipient will have a real choice, with enough secular private school desks in relation to the number of religious ones, and a voucher amount high enough to meet secular private school tuition levels. . . .

It is not, of course, that I think even a genuine choice criterion is up to the task of the Establishment Clause when substantial state funds go to religious teaching; ... Part III, *infra*, shows that it is not. The point is simply that if the majority wishes to claim that choice is a criterion, it must define choice in a way that can function as a criterion with a practical capacity to screen something out.

. . .

III

... [E]ven if I assumed *arguendo* that the majority's formal criteria were satisfied on the facts, today's conclusion would be profoundly at odds with the Constitution....

A

The scale of the aid to religious schools approved today is unprecedented, both in the number of dollars and in the proportion of systemic school expenditure supported.... [I]n previous cases ..., the sheer quantity of aid, when delivered to a class of religious primary and secondary schools, was suspect on the theory that the greater the aid, the greater its proportion to a religious school's existing expenditures, and the greater the likelihood that public money was supporting religious as well as secular instruction....

On the other hand, the Court has found the gross amount unhelpful for Establishment Clause analysis when the aid afforded a benefit solely to one individual, however substantial as to him, but only an incidental benefit to the religious school at which the individual chose to spend the State's money.... The majority's reliance on the observations of five Members of the Court in *Witters* as to the irrelevance of substantiality of aid in that case is therefore beside the point in the matter before us, which involves considerable sums of public funds systematically distributed through thousands of students attending religious elementary and middle schools in the city of Cleveland.

. . .

B

... [E]very objective underlying the prohibition of religious establishment is betrayed by this scheme, but something has to be said about the enormity of the violation....

. . .

When government aid goes up, so does reliance on it; the only thing likely to go down is independence. If Justice Douglas in *Allen* was concerned with state agencies, influenced by powerful religious groups, choosing the textbooks that parochial schools would use, 392 U. S., at 265 (dissenting opinion), how much more is there reason to wonder when dependence will become great enough to give the State of Ohio an effective veto over basic decisions on the content of curriculums? A day will come when religious schools will learn what political leverage can do, just as Ohio's politicians are now getting a lesson in the leverage exercised by religion.

. . .

... [I]n the matter of educational aid the Establishment Clause has largely been read away. True, the majority has not approved vouchers for religious schools alone, or aid earmarked for religious instruction. But no scheme so clumsy will ever get before us, and in the cases that we may see, like these, the Establishment Clause is largely silenced.... I hope that a future Court will reconsider today's dramatic departure from basic Establishment Clause principle.

■ JUSTICE BREYER, with whom JUSTICE STEVENS and JUSTICE SOUTER join, dissenting.

. . . I write separately . . . to emphasize the risk that publicly financed voucher programs pose in terms of religiously based social conflict. I . . . believe that the Establishment Clause concern for protecting the Nation's social fabric from religious conflict poses an overriding obstacle to the implementation of this well-intentioned school voucher program. And . . . "parental choice" cannot significantly alleviate the constitutional problem.

I

. . . The Clauses reflect the Framers' vision of an American Nation free of the religious strife that had long plagued the nations of Europe. . . .

. . . [T]he Court's 20th century Establishment Clause cases—both those limiting the practice of religion in public schools and those limiting the public funding of private religious education—focused directly upon social conflict, potentially created when government becomes involved in religious education. . . .

. . .

The upshot is the development of constitutional doctrine that reads the Establishment Clause as avoiding religious strife, *not* by providing every religion with an *equal opportunity* (say, to secure state funding or to pray in the public schools), but by drawing fairly clear lines of *separation* between church and state—at least where the heartland of religious belief, such as primary religious education, is at issue.

II

. . .

[T]he voucher program here . . . insists that the religious school accept students of all religions. Does that criterion treat fairly groups whose religion forbids them to do so? The program also insists that no participating school "advocate or foster unlawful behavior or teach hatred of any person or group on the basis of race, ethnicity, national origin, or religion." . . .

How are state officials to adjudicate claims that one religion or another is advocating, for example, civil disobedience in response to unjust laws, the use of illegal drugs in a religious ceremony, or resort to force to call attention to what it views as an immoral social practice? What kind of public hearing will there be in response to claims that one religion or another is continuing to teach a view of history that casts members of other religions in the worst possible light? How will the public react to government funding for schools that take controversial religious positions on topics that are of current popular interest—say, the conflict in the Middle East or the war on terrorism? . . .

. . .

III

. . . [V]oucher programs differ . . . in both *kind* and *degree* from aid programs upheld in the past. They differ in kind because they direct financing to a core function of the church: the teaching of religious truths to young children.

. . . History suggests . . . that *government funding* of this kind . . . is far more contentious than providing funding for secular textbooks, computers, vocational training, or even funding for adults who wish to obtain a college education at a religious university. . . .

Vouchers also differ in *degree*. The aid programs recently upheld by the Court involved limited amounts of aid to religion. But the majority's analysis here appears to permit a considerable shift of taxpayer dollars from public secular schools to private religious schools. . . . [T]he secular aid upheld in *Mitchell* differs dramatically from the present case. Although it was conceivable that minor amounts of money could have, contrary to the statute, found their way to the religious activities of the recipients, . . . that case is at worst the camel's nose, while the litigation before us is the camel itself.

IV

. . . Parental choice cannot help the taxpayer who does not want to finance the religious education of children. It will not always help the parent who may see little real choice between inadequate nonsectarian public education and adequate education at a school whose religious teachings are contrary to his own. It will not satisfy religious minorities unable to participate because they are too few in number to support the creation of their own private schools. It will not satisfy groups whose religious beliefs preclude them from participating in a government-sponsored program, and who may well feel ignored as government funds primarily support the education of children in the doctrines of the dominant religions. And it does little to ameliorate the entanglement problems or the related problems of social division . . . Consequently, the fact that the parent may choose which school can cash the government's voucher check does not alleviate the Establishment Clause concerns associated with voucher programs.

. . .

2.   HIGHER EDUCATION

Tilton v. Richardson

403 U.S. 672 (1971).

The Higher Education Facilities Act of 1963 provided for federal grants to institutions of higher education for the construction of academic facilities. The Act provided that only facilities used for non-sectarian instruction would be financed and that the restriction to non-sectarian use would have to be observed for 20 years. The Court by a vote of 5 to 4, but without an opinion of the Court, sustained the application of the statute to grants made for buildings at four church-related colleges. The Court held invalid the portion of the Act that would have permitted religious uses of the buildings after 20 years.

Hunt v. McNair

413 U.S. 734 (1973).

South Carolina established an Educational Facilities Authority to assist through the issuance of revenue bonds higher educational institutions in constructing and financing buildings, facilities and site preparation, but not including any facility for sectarian instruction or religious worship. The Act was challenged here as applied to the issuance of bonds to finance the construction of dining hall facilities at a Baptist College. The Court upheld the statute, relying on Tilton v. Richardson. It said: "aid normally may be thought to have a primary effect of advancing religion when it flows to an institution in which religion is so pervasive that a substantial portion of its functions are subsumed in the religious mission or when it funds a specifically religious activity in an otherwise substantially secular setting." In this case the court relied on the fact that the college had no religious test for faculty or student body and that the Baptist percentage of the student body (60%) was about the same as the percentage of Baptists in the surrounding community.

2. THE FREE EXERCISE OF RELIGION

Sherbert v. Verner

374 U.S. 398, 83 S.Ct. 1790, 10 L.Ed.2d 965 (1963).

■ MR. JUSTICE BRENNAN delivered the opinion of the Court.

Appellant, a member of the Seventh-day Adventist Church was discharged by her South Carolina employer because she would not work on Saturday, the Sabbath Day of her faith. When she was unable to obtain other employment because from conscientious scruples she would not take Saturday work, she filed a claim for unemployment compensation benefits under the South Carolina Unemployment Compensation Act. . . . The appellee Employment Security Commission, in administrative proceedings under the statute, found that appellant's restriction upon her availability for Saturday work brought her within the provision disqualifying for benefits insured workers who fail, without good cause, to accept "suitable work when offered . . . by the employment office or the employer. . . ." The Commission's finding was sustained . . . by the South Carolina Supreme Court . . . [4] . . .

II.

. . .

Significantly South Carolina expressly saves the Sunday worshiper from having to make the kind of choice which we hold infringes the Sabbatarian's religious liberty. When in times of "national emergency" the textile plants are authorized by the State Commission of Labor to operate on Sunday, "no employee shall be required to work on Sunday . . . who is conscientiously opposed to Sunday work. . . ." The unconstitutionality of the disqualification of the Sabbatarian is thus compounded by the religious discrimination which South Carolina's general statutory scheme necessarily effects.

III.

We must next consider whether some compelling state interest enforced in the eligibility provisions of the South Carolina statute justifies the substantial infringement of appellant's First Amendment right. It is basic that no showing merely of a rational relationship to some colorable state interest would suffice; in this highly sensitive constitutional area, "[o]nly the gravest abuses, endangering paramount interests, give occasion for permissible limitation," . . . . No such abuse or danger has

---

[4]   It has been suggested that appellant is not within the class entitled to benefits under the South Carolina statute because her unemployment did not result from discharge or layoff due to lack of work. It is true that unavailability for work for some personal reasons not having to do with matters of conscience or religion has been held to be a basis of disqualification for benefits. But appellant claims that the Free Exercise Clause prevents the State from basing the denial of benefits upon the "personal reason" she gives for not working on Saturday. Where the consequence of disqualification so directly affects First Amendment rights, surely we should not conclude that every "personal reason" is a basis for disqualification in the absence of explicit language to that effect in the statute or decisions of the South Carolina Supreme Court. Nothing we have found in the statute or in the cited decisions, and certainly nothing in the South Carolina Court's opinion in this case so construes the statute. Indeed, the contrary seems to have been that court's basic assumption, for if the eligibility provisions were thus limited, it would have been unnecessary for the court to have decided appellant's constitutional challenge to the application of the statute under the Free Exercise Clause.

Likewise, the decision of the State Supreme Court does not rest upon a finding that appellant was disqualified for benefits because she had been "discharged for misconduct"—by reason of her Saturday absences—within the meaning of § 68–114(2). That ground was not adopted by the South Carolina Supreme Court, and the appellees do not urge in this Court that the disqualification rests upon that ground.

been advanced in the present case. The appellees suggest no more than a possibility that the filing of fraudulent claims by unscrupulous claimants feigning religious objections to Saturday work might not only dilute the unemployment compensation fund but also hinder the scheduling by employers of necessary Saturday work. But that possibility is not apposite here because no such objection appears to have been made before the South Carolina Supreme Court, and we are unwilling to assess the importance of an asserted state interest without the views of the state court. Nor, if the contention had been made below, would the record appear to sustain it; there is no proof whatever to warrant such fears of malingering or deceit as those which the respondents now advance. . . . [E]ven if the possibility of spurious claims did threaten to dilute the fund and disrupt the scheduling of work, it would plainly be incumbent upon the appellees to demonstrate that no alternative forms of regulation would combat such abuses without infringing First Amendment rights.

In these respects, then, the state interest asserted in the present case is wholly dissimilar to the interests which were found to justify the less direct burden upon religious practices in Braunfeld v. Brown, [366 U.S. 599 (1961)]. The Court recognized that the Sunday closing law which that decision sustained undoubtedly served "to make the practice of [the Orthodox Jewish merchants'] . . . religious beliefs more expensive," . . . But the statute was nevertheless saved by a countervailing factor which finds no equivalent in the instant case—a strong state interest in providing one uniform day of rest for all workers. That secular objective could be achieved, the Court found, only by declaring Sunday to be that day of rest. Requiring exemptions for Sabbatarians, while theoretically possible, appeared to present an administrative problem of such magnitude, or to afford the exempted class so great a competitive advantage, that such a requirement would have rendered the entire statutory scheme unworkable. In the present case no such justifications underlie the determination of the state court that appellant's religion makes her ineligible to receive benefits.

IV.

. . . [We do not] declare the existence of a constitutional right to unemployment benefits on the part of all persons whose religious convictions are the cause of their unemployment. This is not a case in which an employee's religious convictions serve to make him a nonproductive member of society. Finally, nothing we say today constrains the States to adopt any particular form or scheme of unemployment compensation. Our holding today is only that South Carolina may not constitutionally apply the eligibility provisions so as to constrain a worker to abandon his religious convictions respecting the day of rest. . . .

. . .

The judgment of the South Carolina Supreme Court is reversed and the case is remanded for further proceedings not inconsistent with this opinion.[a]

■ MR. JUSTICE STEWART, concurring in the result.

. . .

. . . I cannot agree that today's decision can stand consistently with Braunfeld v. Brown, supra. The Court says that there was a "less direct burden upon religious practices" in that case than in this. With all respect, I think the Court is mistaken, simply as a matter of fact. The *Braunfeld* case involved a state *criminal* statute. . . .

The impact upon the appellant's religious freedom in the present case is considerably less onerous. We deal here not with a criminal statute, but with the particularized administration of South Carolina's Unemployment Compensation Act.

---

[a]   A concurring opinion by Justice Douglas is omitted.

Even upon the unlikely assumption that the appellant could not find suitable non-Saturday employment, the appellant at the worst would be denied a maximum of 22 weeks of compensation payments. I agree with the Court that the possibility of that denial is enough to infringe upon the appellant's constitutional right to the free exercise of her religion. But it is clear to me that in order to reach this conclusion the Court must explicitly reject the reasoning of Braunfeld v. Brown. I think the *Braunfeld* case was wrongly decided and should be overruled, and accordingly I concur in the result reached by the Court in the case before us.

■ MR. JUSTICE HARLAN, whom MR. JUSTICE WHITE joins, dissenting.

. . .

South Carolina's Unemployment Compensation Law was enacted in 1936 in response to the grave social and economic problems that arose during the depression of that period. . . . Thus the purpose of the legislature was to tide people over, and to avoid social and economic chaos, during periods when *work was unavailable.* . . .

The South Carolina Supreme Court has uniformly applied this law in conformity with its clearly expressed purpose. It has consistently held that one is not "available for work" if his unemployment has resulted not from the inability of industry to provide a job but rather from personal circumstances, no matter how compelling. The reference to "involuntary unemployment" in the legislative statement of policy, whatever a sociologist, philosopher, or theologian might say, has been interpreted not to embrace such personal circumstances. . . . Thus in no proper sense can it be said that the State discriminated against the appellant on the basis of her religious beliefs or that she was denied benefits *because* she was a Seventh-day Adventist. She was denied benefits just as any other claimant would be denied benefits who was not "available for work" for personal reasons.[1]

. . . What the Court is holding is that if the State chooses to condition unemployment compensation on the applicant's availability for work, it is constitutionally compelled to *carve out an exception*—and to provide benefits—for those whose unavailability is due to their religious convictions.[2]

. . .

---

[1]   I am completely at a loss to understand note 4 of the Court's opinion. Certainly the Court is not basing today's decision on the unsupported supposition that *some* day, the South Carolina Supreme Court may conclude that there is *some personal* reason for unemployment that may not disqualify a claimant for relief. In any event, I submit it is perfectly clear that South Carolina would not compensate persons who became unemployed for *any* personal reason, as distinguished from layoffs or lack of work, since the State Supreme Court's decisions make it plain that such persons would not be regarded as "available for work" within the manifest meaning of the eligibility requirements. Nor can I understand what this Court means when it says that "if the eligibility provisions were thus limited, it would have been unnecessary for the [South Carolina] court to have decided appellant's constitutional challenge. . . ."

[2]   The Court does suggest, in a rather startling disclaimer, that its holding is limited in applicability to those whose religious convictions do not make them "nonproductive" members of society, noting that most of the Seventh-day Adventists in the Spartanburg area are employed. But surely this disclaimer cannot be taken seriously, for the Court cannot mean that the case would have come out differently if none of the Seventh-day Adventists in Spartanburg had been gainfully employed, or if the appellant's religion had prevented her from working on Tuesdays instead of Saturdays. Nor can the Court be suggesting that it will make a value judgment in each case as to whether a particular individual's religious convictions prevent him from being "productive." I can think of no more inappropriate function for this Court to perform.

Thomas v. Review Board of the Indiana Employment Security Division
450 U.S. 707 (1981).

Thomas, a Jehovah's Witness, quit his job because of religious opposition to participating in the production of armaments, when his employer transferred him to a department making turrets for military tanks. He was denied unemployment compensation. The Indiana Supreme Court upheld the denial, because the unemployment compensation statute denied compensation to employees "who quit work voluntarily for personal reasons" that were not objectively job-related. Relying on Sherbert v. Verner, the Supreme Court reversed.

The sole dissenter, Justice Rehnquist, contended that Sherbert v. Verner should be overruled. In a footnote, he argued that *Sherbert* was distinguishable from *Thomas* because the Indiana statute had been construed to make *every* personal subjective reason for refusing employment a basis for disqualification.

Wisconsin v. Yoder
406 U.S. 205, 92 S.Ct. 1526, 32 L.Ed.2d 15 (1972).

[Respondents Yoder, Yutzy and Miller were members of the Amish religious sect and residents of Wisconsin where it was required that children attend school until the age of 16. Because of their religion's tenets, they refused to send their children (ages 14 and 15) to school after completing the eighth grade. They believe that by sending their children to high school they would not only expose themselves to possible censure of their church community, but also endanger their own salvation and that of their children. It was agreed that respondents' religious beliefs were sincere. Those beliefs required members of the community to make their living by farming or closely related activities. High school, and higher education generally, was objected to because the values taught were in marked contrast with Amish values and way of life. Respondents were convicted of violating the Wisconsin compulsory attendance law; the Supreme Court of Wisconsin reversed the conviction, sustaining respondents' claim under the free exercise clause of the first amendment.]

■ MR. CHIEF JUSTICE BURGER delivered the opinion of the Court.

. . .

The essence of all that has been said and written on the subject is that only those interests of the highest order and those not otherwise served can overbalance legitimate claims to the free exercise of religion. We can accept it as settled, therefore, that however strong the State's interest in universal compulsory education, it is by no means absolute to the exclusion or subordination of all other interests. . . .

. . .

So long as compulsory education laws were confined to eight grades of elementary basic education imparted in a nearby rural schoolhouse, with a large proportion of students of the Amish faith, the Old Order Amish had little basis to fear that school attendance would expose their children to the worldly influence they reject. But modern compulsory secondary education in rural areas is now largely carried on in a consolidated school, often remote from the student's home and alien to his daily home life. . . . The conclusion is inescapable that secondary schooling, by exposing Amish children to worldly influences in terms of attitudes, goals and values contrary to beliefs, and by substantially interfering with the religious development of the Amish child and his integration into the way of life of the Amish faith community at the crucial adolescent state of development, contravenes the basic religious tenets and practice of the Amish faith, both as to the parent and the child. . . .

In sum, the unchallenged testimony of acknowledged experts in education and religious history, almost 300 years of consistent practice, and strong evidence of a sustained faith pervading and regulating respondents' entire mode of life support the claim that enforcement of the State's requirement of compulsory formal education after the eighth grade would gravely endanger if not destroy the free exercise of respondents' religious beliefs.

. . .

The State advances two primary arguments in support of its system of compulsory education. It notes, as Thomas Jefferson pointed out early in our history, that some degree of education is necessary to prepare citizens to participate effectively and intelligently in our open political system if we are to preserve freedom and independence. Further, education prepares individuals to be self-reliant and self-sufficient participants in society. We accept these propositions.

However, the evidence adduced by the Amish in this case is persuasively to the effect that an additional one or two years of formal high school for Amish children in place of their long established program of informal vocational education would do little to serve those interests. Respondents' experts testified at trial, without challenge, that the value of all education must be assessed in terms of its capacity to prepare the child for life. It is one thing to say that compulsory education for a year or two beyond the eighth grade may be necessary when its goal is the preparation of the child for life in modern society as the majority live, but it is quite another if the goal of education be viewed as the preparation of the child for life in the separated agrarian community that is the keystone of the Amish faith. See Meyer v. Nebraska, 262 U.S., at 400. . . .

Whatever their idiosyncrasies as seen by the majority, this record strongly shows that the Amish community has been a highly successful social unit within our society even if apart from the conventional "mainstream." Its members are productive and very law-abiding members of society; they reject public welfare in any of its usual modern forms. The Congress itself recognized their self-sufficiency by authorizing exemption of such groups as the Amish from the obligation to pay social security taxes.

It is neither fair nor correct to suggest that the Amish are opposed to education beyond the eighth grade level. What this record shows is that they are opposed to conventional formal education of the type provided by a certified high school because it comes at the child's crucial adolescent period of religious development. . . .

The State, however, supports its interest in providing an additional one or two years of compulsory high school education to Amish children because of the possibility that some such children will choose to leave the Amish community, and that if this occurs they will be ill-equipped for life. The State argues that if Amish children leave their church they should not be in the position of making their way in the world without the education available in the one or two additional years the State requires. However, on this record, that argument is highly speculative. There is no specific evidence of the loss of Amish adherents by attrition, nor is there any showing that upon leaving the Amish community Amish children, with their practical agricultural training and habits of industry and self-reliance would become burdens on society because of educational shortcomings. . . .

In these terms, Wisconsin's interest in compelling the school attendance of Amish children to age 16 emerges as somewhat less substantial than requiring such attendance for children generally. For, while agricultural employment is not totally outside the legitimate concerns of the child labor laws, employment of children under parental guidance and on the family farm from age 14 to age 16 is an ancient tradition which lies at the periphery of the objectives of such laws. There is no intimation that the Amish employment of their children on family farms is in any way deleterious to their health or that Amish parents exploit children at tender years. Any such inference would be contrary to the record before us. Moreover, employment of Amish children on the family farm does not present the undesirable economic aspects of eliminating jobs which might otherwise be held by adults. . . .

Contrary to the suggestion of the dissenting opinion of Mr. Justice Douglas, our holding today in no degree depends on the assertion of the religious interest of the child as contrasted with that of the parents. It is the parents who are subject to prosecution here for failing to cause their children to attend school, and it is their right of free exercise, not that of their children, that must determine Wisconsin's power to impose criminal penalties on the parent. . . .

Our holding in no way determines the proper resolution of possible competing interests of parents, children, and the State in an appropriate state court proceeding in which the power of the State is asserted on the theory that Amish parents are preventing their minor children from attending high school despite their expressed desires to the contrary. Recognition of the claim of the State in such a proceeding would, of course, call into question traditional concepts of parental control over the religious upbringing and education of their minor children recognized in this Court's past decisions. It is clear that such an intrusion by a State into family decisions in the area of religious training would give rise to grave questions of religious freedom comparable to those raised here and those presented in Pierce v. Society of Sisters. On this record we neither reach nor decide those issues. . . .

For the reasons stated we hold, with the Supreme Court of Wisconsin, that the First and Fourteenth Amendments prevent the State from compelling respondents to cause their children to attend formal high school to age 16. Our disposition of this case, however, in no way alters our recognition of the obvious fact that courts are not school boards or legislatures, and are ill-equipped to determine the "necessity" of discrete aspects of a State's program of compulsory education. . . .

Nothing we hold is intended to undermine the general applicability of the State's compulsory school attendance statutes or to limit the power of the State to promulgate reasonable standards that, while not impairing the free exercise of religion, provide for continuing agricultural vocational education under parental and church guidance by the Old Order Amish or others similarly situated. The States have had a long history of amicable and effective relationships with church-sponsored schools, and there is no basis for assuming that, in this related context, reasonable standards cannot be established concerning the content of the continuing vocational education of Amish children under parental guidance, provided always that state regulations are not inconsistent with what we have said in this opinion.

Affirmed.

■ MR. JUSTICE POWELL and MR. JUSTICE REHNQUIST took no part in the consideration or decision of this case.

■ MR. JUSTICE STEWART, with whom MR. JUSTICE BRENNAN joins, concurring.

. . .

This case in no way involves any questions regarding the right of the children of Amish parents to attend public high schools, or any other institutions of learning, if they wish to do so. As the Court points out, there is no suggestion whatever in the record that the religious beliefs of the children here concerned differ in any way from those of their parents. . . .

■ MR. JUSTICE WHITE, with whom MR. JUSTICE BRENNAN and MR. JUSTICE STEWART, join, concurring.

Cases such as this one inevitably call for a delicate balancing of important but conflicting interests. I join the opinion and judgment of the Court because I cannot say that the State's interest in requiring two more years of compulsory education in the ninth and tenth grades outweighs the importance of the concededly sincere Amish religious practice to the survival of that sect.

. . .

I join the Court because the sincerity of the Amish religious policy here is uncontested, because the potential adverse impact of the state requirement is great and because the State's valid interest in education has already been largely satisfied by the eight years the children have already spent in school.

■ MR. JUSTICE DOUGLAS, dissenting in part.

I agree with the Court that the religious scruples of the Amish are opposed to the education of their children beyond the grade schools, yet I disagree with the Court's conclusion that the matter is within the dispensation of parents alone. The Court's analysis assumes that the only interests at stake in the case are those of the Amish parents on the one hand, and those of the State on the other. The difficulty with this approach is that, despite the Court's claim, the parents are seeking to vindicate not only their own free exercise claims, but also those of their high-school-age children.

. . .

. . . Frieda Yoder has in fact testified that her own religious views are opposed to high-school education. I therefore join the judgment of the Court as to respondent Jonas Yoder. But Frieda Yoder's views may not be those of Vernon Yutzy or Barbara Miller. I must dissent, therefore, as to respondents Adin Yutzy and Wallace Miller as their motion to dismiss also raised the question of their children's religious liberty.

This issue has never been squarely presented before today. Our opinions are full of talk about the power of the parents over the child's education. See Pierce v. Society of Sisters, 268 U.S. 510; Meyer v. Nebraska, 262 U.S. 390. And we have in the past analyzed similar conflicts between parent and State with little regard for the views of the child. See Prince v. Massachusetts, 321 U.S. 158. Recent cases, however, have clearly held that the children themselves have constitutionally protectible interests. . . .

. . .

The views of the two children in question were not canvassed by the Wisconsin courts. The matter should be explicitly reserved so that new hearings can be held on remand of the case. . . .

Employment Division, Department of Human Resources of Oregon v. Smith

494 U.S. 872, 110 S.Ct. 1595, 108 L.Ed.2d 876 (1990).

■ JUSTICE SCALIA delivered the opinion of the Court.

This case requires us to decide whether the Free Exercise Clause of the First Amendment permits the State of Oregon to include religiously inspired peyote use within the reach of its general criminal prohibition on use of that drug, and thus permits the State to deny unemployment benefits to persons dismissed from their jobs because of such religiously inspired use.

I

Oregon law prohibits the knowing or intentional possession of a "controlled substance" . . . [including] the drug peyote, a hallucinogen derived from the plant Lophophpra williamsii Lemaire. . . .

Respondents Alfred Smith and Galen Black were fired from their jobs with a private drug rehabilitation organization because they ingested peyote for sacramental purposes at a ceremony of the Native American Church, of which both are members. When respondents applied to petitioner Employment Division for unemployment compensation, they were determined to be ineligible for benefits because they had been discharged for work-related "misconduct". . . .

. . . The Oregon Supreme Court reasoned . . . that the criminality of respondents' peyote use was irrelevant to resolution of their constitutional claim—since the purpose of the "misconduct" provision under which respondents had been disqualified was not to enforce the State's criminal laws but to preserve the financial integrity of the compensation fund, and since that purpose was inadequate to justify the burden that disqualification imposed on respondents' religious practice. . . .

Before this Court in 1987, petitioner continued to maintain that the illegality of respondents' peyote consumption was relevant to their constitutional claim. We agreed, concluding that "if a State has prohibited through its criminal laws certain kinds of religiously motivated conduct without violating the First Amendment, it certainly follows that it may impose the lesser burden of denying unemployment compensation benefits to persons who engage in that conduct." Employment Div., Dept. of Human Resources of Oregon v. Smith, 485 U.S. 660, 670 (1988) (*Smith I*). We noted, however, that the Oregon Supreme Court had not decided whether respondents' sacramental use of peyote was in fact proscribed by Oregon's controlled substance law, and that this issue was a matter of dispute between the parties. . . . [W]e vacated the judgment of the Oregon Supreme Court and remanded for further proceedings. . . .

On remand, the Oregon Supreme Court held that respondents' religiously inspired use of peyote fell within the prohibition of the Oregon statute . . . It then considered whether that prohibition was valid under the Free Exercise Clause, and concluded that it was not. The court therefore reaffirmed its previous ruling that the State could not deny unemployment benefits to respondents for having engaged in that practice.

. . .

II

Respondents' claim for relief rests on our decisions in Sherbert v. Verner, supra, Thomas v. Review Board, Indiana Employment Security Div., supra, and Hobbie v. Unemployment Appeals Comm'n of Florida, 480 U.S. 136 (1987) . . . As we observed in *Smith I,* however, the conduct at issue in those cases was not prohibited by law. We held that distinction to be critical, for "if Oregon does prohibit the religious use of peyote, and if that prohibition is consistent with the Federal Constitution, there is no federal right to engage in that conduct in Oregon," and "the State is free to withhold unemployment compensation from respondents for engaging in work-related misconduct, despite its religious motivation." . . . Now that the Oregon Supreme Court has confirmed that Oregon does prohibit the religious use of peyote, we proceed to consider whether that prohibition is permissible under the Free Exercise Clause.

A

. . . The free exercise of religion means, first and foremost, the right to believe and profess whatever religious doctrine one desires. Thus, the First Amendment obviously excludes all "governmental regulation of religious *beliefs* as such." . . . The government may not compel affirmation of religious belief, see Torcaso v. Watkins, 367 U.S. 488 (1961), punish the expression of religious doctrines it believes to be false, United States v. Ballard, 322 U.S. 78, 86–88 (1944), impose special disabilities on the basis of religious views or religious status, see McDaniel v. Paty, 435 U.S. 618 (1978); . . . or lend its power to one or the other side in controversies over religious authority or dogma, see Presbyterian Church v. Hull Church, 393 U.S. 440, 445–452 (1969); Kedroff v. St. Nicholas Cathedral, 344 U.S. 94, 95–119 (1952); Serbian Eastern Orthodox Diocese v. Milivojevich, 426 U.S. 696, 708–725 (1976).

But the "exercise of religion" often involves not only belief and profession but the performance of (or abstention from) physical acts: assembling with others for a worship service, participating in sacramental use of bread and wine, proselytizing, abstaining from certain foods or certain modes of transportation. It would be true, we think (though no case of ours has involved the point), that a state would be "prohibiting the free exercise [of religion]" if it sought to ban such acts or abstentions only when they are engaged in for religious reasons, or only because of the religious belief that they display. It would doubtless be unconstitutional, for example, to ban the casting of "statues that are to be used for worship purposes," or to prohibit bowing down before a golden calf.

Respondents in the present case, however, seek to carry the meaning of "prohibiting the free exercise [of religion]" one large step further. They contend that their religious motivation for using peyote places them beyond the reach of a criminal law that is not specifically directed at their religious practice, and that is concededly constitutional as applied to those who use the drug for other reasons. They assert, in other words, that "prohibiting the free exercise [of religion]" includes requiring any individual to observe a generally applicable law that requires (or forbids) the performance of an act that his religious belief forbids (or requires). As a textual matter, we do not think the words must be given that meaning. It is no more necessary to regard the collection of a general tax, for example, as "prohibiting the free exercise [of religion]" by those citizens who believe support of organized government to be sinful, than it is to regard the same tax as "abridging the freedom . . . of the press" of those publishing companies that must pay the tax as a condition of staying in business. . . .

. . . We have never held that an individual's religious beliefs excuse him from compliance with an otherwise valid law prohibiting conduct that the State is free to regulate. On the contrary, the record of more than a century of our free exercise jurisprudence contradicts that proposition. As described succinctly by Justice Frankfurter in Minersville School Dist. Bd. of Educ. v. Gobitis, 310 U.S. 586, 594–595 (1940):

"Conscientious scruples have not, in the course of the long struggle for religious toleration, relieved the individual from obedience to a general law not aimed at the promotion or restriction of religious beliefs. The mere possession of religious convictions which contradict the relevant concerns of a political society does not relieve the citizen from the discharge of political responsibilities . . . "

We first had occasion to assert that principle in Reynolds v. United States, 98 U.S. 145 (1879), where we rejected the claim that criminal laws against polygamy could not be constitutionally applied to those whose religion commanded the practice. "Laws," we said, "are made for the government of actions, and while they cannot interfere with mere religious belief and opinions, they may with practices. . . . Can a man excuse his practices to the contrary because of his religious belief? To permit this would be to make the professed doctrines of religious belief superior to the law of the land, and in effect to permit every citizen to become a law unto himself." . . .

Subsequent decisions have consistently held that the right of free exercise does not relieve an individual of the obligation to comply with a "valid and neutral law of general applicability on the ground that the law proscribes (or prescribes) conduct that his religion prescribes (or proscribes)." United States v. Lee, 455 U.S. 252, 263, n. 3 (1982) (Stevens, J., concurring in judgment). . . . In Prince v. Massachusetts, 321 U.S. 158 (1944), we held that a mother could be prosecuted under the child labor laws for using her children to dispense literature in the streets, her religious motivation notwithstanding. We found no constitutional infirmity in "excluding [these children] from doing there what no other children may do." . . . In Braunfeld v. Brown, 366 U.S. 599 (1961) (plurality opinion), we upheld Sunday-closing laws against the claim that they burdened the religious practices of persons whose religions compelled them to refrain from work on other days. In Gillette v. United States, 401 U.S. 437, 461 (1971), we sustained the military selective service system against the claim that it violated free exercise by conscripting persons who opposed a particular war on religious grounds.

Our most recent decision involving a neutral, generally applicable regulatory law that compelled activity forbidden by an individual's religion was United States v. Lee . . . There, an Amish employer, on behalf of himself and his employees, sought exemption from collection and payment of Social Security taxes on the ground that the Amish faith prohibited participation in governmental support programs. We rejected the claim that an exemption was constitutionally required. There would be no way, we observed, to distinguish the Amish believer's objection to Social Security taxes from the religious objections that others might have to the collection or use of other taxes. "If, for example, a religious adherent believes war is a sin, and if a certain percentage of the federal budget can be identified as devoted to war-related activities, such individuals would have a similarly valid claim to be exempt from paying that percentage of the income tax. The tax system could not function if denominations were allowed to challenge the tax system because tax payments were spent in a manner that violates their religious belief." . . .

The only decisions in which we have held that the First Amendment bars application of a neutral, generally applicable law to religiously motivated action have involved not the Free Exercise Clause alone, but the Free Exercise Clause in conjunction with other constitutional protections, such as freedom of speech and of the press, see Cantwell v. Connecticut, 310 U.S. at 304–307 (invalidating a licensing system for religious and charitable solicitations under which the administrator had discretion to deny a license to any cause he deemed nonreligious); Murdock v. Pennsylvania, 319 U.S. 105 (1943) (invalidating a flat tax on solicitation as applied to the dissemination of religious ideas); Follett v. McCormick, 321 U.S. 573 (1944) (same), or the right of parents, acknowledged in Pierce v. Society of Sisters, 268 U.S. 510 (1925), to direct the education of their children, see Wisconsin v. Yoder, 406 U.S. 205 (1972) (invalidating compulsory school-attendance laws as applied to Amish parents who refused on religious grounds to send their children to school).[1] Some of our cases prohibiting compelled expression, decided exclusively upon free speech grounds, have also involved freedom of religion, cf. Wooley v. Maynard, 430 U.S. 705 (1977) (invalidating compelled display of a license plate slogan that offended individual religious beliefs); West Virginia Board of Education v. Barnette, 319 U.S. 624 (1943) (invalidating compulsory flag salute statute challenged by religious objectors). And it

---

[1]   Both lines of cases have specifically adverted to the non-free exercise principle involved. . . . *Yoder* said that "the Court's holding in *Pierce* stands as a charter of the rights of parents to direct the religious upbringing of their children. And, when the interests of parenthood are combined with a free exercise claim of the nature revealed by this record, more than merely a 'reasonable relation to some purpose within the competency of the State is required to sustain the validity of the State's requirement under the First Amendment.' " . . .

is easy to envision a case in which a challenge on freedom of association grounds would likewise be reinforced by Free Exercise Clause concerns. Cf. Roberts v. United States Jaycees, 468 U.S. 609, 622 (1984) ("An individual's freedom to speak, to worship, and to petition the government for the redress of grievances could not be vigorously protected from interference by the State [if] a correlative freedom to engage in group effort toward those ends were not also guaranteed.").

The present case does not present such a hybrid situation, but a free exercise claim unconnected with any communicative activity or parental right. Respondents urge us to hold, quite simply, that when otherwise prohibitable conduct is accompanied by religious convictions, not only the convictions but the conduct itself must be free from governmental regulation. We have never held that, and decline to do so now. There being no contention that Oregon's drug law represents an attempt to regulate religious beliefs, the communication of religious beliefs, or the raising of one's children in those beliefs, the rule to which we have adhered ever since *Reynolds* plainly controls. . . .

B

Respondents argue that even though exemption from generally applicable criminal laws need not automatically be extended to religiously motivated actors, at least the claim for a religious exemption must be evaluated under the balancing test set forth in Sherbert v. Verner . . . We have never invalidated any governmental action on the basis of the *Sherbert* test except the denial of unemployment compensation. Although we have sometimes purported to apply the *Sherbert* test in contexts other than that, we have always found the test satisfied, see United States v. Lee, 455 U.S. 252 (1982); Gillette v. United States, 401 U.S. 437 (1971). In recent years we have abstained from applying the *Sherbert* test (outside the unemployment compensation field) at all. In Bowen v. Roy, 476 U.S. 693 (1986), we declined to apply *Sherbert* analysis to a federal statutory scheme that required benefit applicants and recipients to provide their Social Security numbers. The plaintiffs in that case asserted that it would violate their religious beliefs to obtain and provide a Social Security number for their daughter. We held the statute's application to the plaintiffs valid regardless of whether it was necessary to effectuate a compelling interest. . . . In Lyng v. Northwest Indian Cemetery Protective Assn., 485 U.S. 439 (1988), we declined to apply *Sherbert* analysis to the Government's logging and road construction activities on lands used for religious purposes by several Native American Tribes, even though it was undisputed that the activities "could have devastating effects on traditional Indian religious practices," . . . In Goldman v. Weinberger, 475 U.S. 503 (1986), we rejected application of the *Sherbert* test to military dress regulations that forbade the wearing of yarmulkes. In O'Lone v. Estate of Shabazz, 482 U.S. 342 (1987), we sustained, without mentioning the *Sherbert* test, a prison's refusal to excuse inmates from work requirements to attend worship services.

Even if we were inclined to breathe into *Sherbert* some life beyond the unemployment compensation field, we would not apply it to require exemptions from a generally applicable criminal law. The *Sherbert* test, it must be recalled, was developed in a context that lent itself to individualized governmental assessment of the reasons for the relevant conduct. As a plurality of the Court noted in *Roy,* a distinctive feature of unemployment compensation programs is that their eligibility criteria invite consideration of the particular circumstances behind an applicant's unemployment ... As the plurality pointed out in *Roy,* our decisions in the unemployment cases stand for the proposition that where the State has in place a system of individual exemptions, it may not refuse to extend that system to cases of "religious hardship" without compelling reason. . . .

Whether or not the decisions are that limited, they at least have nothing to do with an across-the-board criminal prohibition on a particular form of conduct. Although, as noted earlier, we have sometimes used the *Sherbert* test to analyze free exercise challenges to such laws, . . . we have never applied the test to invalidate one. We conclude today that the sounder approach, and the approach in accord with the vast majority of our precedents, is to hold the test inapplicable to such challenges. The government's ability to enforce generally applicable prohibitions of socially harmful conduct, like its ability to carry out other aspects of public policy, "cannot depend on measuring the effects of a governmental action on a religious objector's spiritual development." *Lyng,* supra, at 451. To make an individual's obligation to obey such a law contingent upon the law's coincidence with his religious beliefs, except where the State's interest is "compelling"—permitting him, by virtue of his beliefs, "to become a law unto himself," Reynolds v. United States, 98 U.S., at 167—contradicts both constitutional tradition and common sense.[2]

The "compelling government interest" requirement seems benign, because it is familiar from other fields. But using it as the standard that must be met before the government may accord different treatment on the basis of race, . . . or before the government may regulate the content of speech, . . . is not remotely comparable to using it for the purpose asserted here. What it produces in those other fields—equality of treatment, and an unrestricted flow of contending speech—are constitutional norms; what it would produce here—a private right to ignore generally applicable laws—is a constitutional anomaly.

Nor is it possible to limit the impact of respondents' proposal by requiring a "compelling state interest" only when the conduct prohibited is "central" to the individual's religion. . . . It is no more appropriate for judges to determine the "centrality" of religious beliefs before applying a "compelling interest" test in the free exercise field, than it would be for them to determine the "importance" of ideas before applying the "compelling interest" test in the free speech field. . . . Repeatedly and in many different contexts, we have warned that courts must not presume to determine the place of a particular belief in a religion or the plausibility of a religious claim. . . . [4]

If the "compelling interest" test is to be applied at all, then, it must be applied across the board, to all actions thought to be religiously commanded. Moreover, if "compelling interest" really means what it says (and watering it down here would subvert its rigor in the other fields where it is applied), many laws will not meet the test. Any society adopting such a system would be courting anarchy, but that danger increases in direct proportion to the society's diversity of religious beliefs, and its determination to coerce or suppress none of them. . . . The rule respondents favor would open the prospect of constitutionally required religious exemptions from civic obligations of almost every conceivable kind—ranging from compulsory military service, see, e.g., Gillette v. United States, 401 U.S. 437 (1971), to the payment of

---

[2]   Justice O'Connor seeks to distinguish Lyng v. Northwest Indian Cemetery Protective Assn., supra, and Bowen v. Roy, supra, on the ground that those cases involved the government's conduct of "its own internal affairs," . . . [I]t is hard to see any reason in principle or practicality why the government should have to tailor its health and safety laws to conform to the diversity of religious belief, but should not have to tailor its management of public lands, *Lyng,* supra, or its administration of welfare programs, *Roy,* supra.

[4]   . . . Justice O'Connor . . . agrees that "our determination . . . cannot, and should not, turn on the centrality of the particular religious practice at issue." . . . Earlier in her opinion, however, Justice O'Connor appears to contradict this, saying that the proper approach is "to determine whether the burden on the specific plaintiffs before us is constitutionally significant and whether the particular criminal interest asserted by the State before us is compelling." "Constitutionally significant burden" would seem to be "centrality" under another name. . . . There is no way out of the difficulty that, if general laws are to be subjected to a "religious practice" exception, *both* the importance of the law at issue *and* the centrality of the practice at issue must reasonably be considered. . . .

taxes, see, e.g., United States v. Lee, supra; to health and safety regulation such as manslaughter and child neglect laws, see, e.g., Funkhouser v. State, 763 P.2d 695 (Okla.Crim.App.1988), compulsory vaccination laws, see, e.g., Cude v. State, 237 Ark. 927, 377 S.W.2d 816 (1964), drug laws, see, e.g., Olsen v. Drug Enforcement Administration, 279 U.S.App.D.C. 1, 878 F.2d 1458 (1989), and traffic laws, see Cox v. New Hampshire, 312 U.S. 569 (1941); to social welfare legislation such as minimum wage laws, see Susan and Tony Alamo Foundation v. Secretary of Labor, 471 U.S. 290 (1985), child labor laws, see Prince v. Massachusetts, 321 U.S. 158 (1944), animal cruelty laws, see, e.g., Church of the Lukumi Babalu Aye Inc. v. City of Hialeah, 723 F.Supp. 1467 (S.D.Fla.1989), cf. State v. Massey, 229 N.C. 734, 51 S.E.2d 179, appeal dism'd, 336 U.S. 942 (1949), environmental protection laws, see United States v. Little, 638 F.Supp. 337 (D.Mont.1986), and laws providing for equality of opportunity for the races, see, e.g., Bob Jones University v. United States, 461 U.S. 574, 603–604 (1983). The First Amendment's protection of religious liberty does not require this.

Values that are protected against government interference through enshrinement in the Bill of Rights are not thereby banished from the political process. . . . [A] society that believes in the negative protection accorded to religious belief can be expected to be solicitous of that value in its legislation. . . . It is therefore not surprising that a number of States have made an exception to their drug laws for sacramental peyote use. But to say that a nondiscriminatory religious-practice exemption is permitted, or even that it is desirable, is not to say that it is constitutionally required, and that the appropriate occasions for its creation can be discerned by the courts. It may fairly be said that leaving accommodation to the political process will place at a relative disadvantage those religious practices that are not widely engaged in; but that unavoidable consequence of democratic government must be preferred to a system in which each conscience is a law unto itself or in which judges weigh the social importance of all laws against the centrality of all religious beliefs.

Because respondents' ingestion of peyote was prohibited under Oregon law, and because that prohibition is constitutional, Oregon may, consistent with the Free Exercise Clause, deny respondents unemployment compensation when their dismissal results from use of the drug. The decision of the Oregon Supreme Court is accordingly reversed.

It is so ordered.

■ JUSTICE O'CONNOR, with whom JUSTICE BRENNAN, JUSTICE MARSHALL, and JUSTICE BLACKMUN join as to Parts I and II, concurring in the judgment.*

Although I agree with the result the Court reaches in this case, I cannot join its opinion. In my view, today's holding dramatically departs from well-settled First Amendment jurisprudence, appears unnecessary to resolve the question presented, and is incompatible with our Nation's fundamental commitment to individual religious liberty.

. . .

II

The Court today extracts from our long history of free exercise precedents the single categorical rule that "if prohibiting the exercise of religion . . . is . . . merely the incidental effect of a generally applicable and otherwise valid provision, the First Amendment has not been offended." Indeed, the Court holds that where the law is a generally applicable criminal prohibition, our usual free exercise jurisprudence does not even apply. To reach this sweeping result, however, the Court must not only give a

---

* Although Justice Brennan, Justice Marshall, and Justice Blackmun join Parts I and II of the opinion, they do not concur in the judgment.

strained reading of the First Amendment but must also disregard our consistent application of free exercise doctrine to cases involving generally applicable regulations that burden religious conduct.

A

... Because the First Amendment does not distinguish between religious belief and religious conduct, conduct motivated by sincere religious belief, like the belief itself, must therefore be at least presumptively protected by the Free Exercise Clause.

The Court today, however, interprets the Clause to permit the government to prohibit, without justification, conduct mandated by an individual's religious beliefs, so long as that prohibition is generally applicable. But a law that prohibits certain conduct—conduct that happens to be an act of worship for someone—manifestly does prohibit that person's free exercise of his religion. A person who is barred from engaging in religiously motivated conduct is barred from freely exercising his religion. Moreover, that person is barred from freely exercising his religion regardless of whether the law prohibits the conduct only when engaged in for religious reasons, only by members of that religion, or by all persons. It is difficult to deny that a law that prohibits religiously motivated conduct, even if the law is generally applicable, does not at least implicate First Amendment concerns.

. . .

To say that a person's right to free exercise has been burdened, of course, does not mean that he has an absolute right to engage in the conduct. . . . [W]e have respected both the First Amendment's express textual mandate and the governmental interest in regulation of conduct by requiring the Government to justify any substantial burden on religiously motivated conduct by a compelling state interest and by means narrowly tailored to achieve that interest. . . .

The Court attempts to support its narrow reading of the Clause by claiming that "[w]e have never held that an individual's religious beliefs excuse him from compliance with an otherwise valid law prohibiting conduct that the State is free to regulate." But as the Court later notes, as it must, in cases such as *Cantwell* and *Yoder* we have in fact interpreted the Free Exercise Clause to forbid application of a generally applicable prohibition to religiously motivated conduct. . . .

The Court endeavors to escape from our decisions in *Cantwell* and *Yoder* by labeling them "hybrid" decisions, but there is no denying that both cases expressly relied on the Free Exercise Clause, . . . and that we have consistently regarded those cases as part of the mainstream of our free exercise jurisprudence. Moreover, in each of the other cases cited by the Court to support its categorical rule, we rejected the particular constitutional claims before us only after carefully weighing the competing interests. . . . That we rejected the free exercise claims in those cases hardly calls into question the applicability of First Amendment doctrine in the first place. Indeed, it is surely unusual to judge the vitality of a constitutional doctrine by looking to the win-loss record of the plaintiffs who happen to come before us.

B

. . .

In my view, . . . the essence of a free exercise claim is relief from a burden imposed by government on religious practices or beliefs, whether the burden is imposed directly through laws that prohibit or compel specific religious practices, or indirectly through laws that, in effect, make abandonment of one's own religion or conformity to the religious beliefs of others the price of an equal place in the civil community. . . .

Indeed, we have never distinguished between cases in which a State conditions receipt of a benefit on conduct prohibited by religious beliefs and cases in which a State affirmatively prohibits such conduct. The *Sherbert* compelling interest test applies in both kinds of cases. . . .

. . . Even if, as an empirical matter, a government's criminal laws might usually serve a compelling interest in health, safety, or public order, the First Amendment at least requires a case-by-case determination of the question, sensitive to the facts of each particular claim. . . . Given the range of conduct that a State might legitimately make criminal, we cannot assume, merely because a law carries criminal sanctions and is generally applicable, that the First Amendment never requires the State to grant a limited exemption for religiously motivated conduct.

. . .

Finally, the Court today suggests that the disfavoring of minority religions is an "unavoidable consequence" under our system of government and that accommodation of such religions must be left to the political process. In my view, however, the First Amendment was enacted precisely to protect the rights of those whose religious practices are not shared by the majority and may be viewed with hostility. The history of our free exercise doctrine amply demonstrates the harsh impact majoritarian rule has had on unpopular or emerging religious groups such as the Jehovah's Witnesses and the Amish. . . .

III

The Court's holding today not only misreads settled First Amendment precedent; it appears to be unnecessary to this case. I would reach the same result applying our established free exercise jurisprudence.

. . .

. . . [T]he critical question in this case is whether exempting respondents from the State's general criminal prohibition "will unduly interfere with fulfillment of the governmental interest." . . . Although the question is close, I would conclude that uniform application of Oregon's criminal prohibition is "essential to accomplish" its overriding interest in preventing the physical harm caused by the use of a . . . controlled substance. Oregon's criminal prohibition represents that State's judgment that the possession and use of controlled substances, even by only one person, is inherently harmful and dangerous. Because the health effects caused by the use of controlled substances exist regardless of the motivation of the user, the use of such substances, even for religious purposes, violates the very purpose of the laws that prohibit them. . . . Moreover, in view of the societal interest in preventing trafficking in controlled substances, uniform application of the criminal prohibition at issue is essential to the effectiveness of Oregon's stated interest in preventing any possession of peyote. . . .

For these reasons, I believe that granting a selective exemption in this case would seriously impair Oregon's compelling interest in prohibiting possession of peyote by its citizens. Under such circumstances, the Free Exercise Clause does not require the State to accommodate respondents' religiously motivated conduct. . . .

Respondents contend that any incompatibility is belied by the fact that the Federal Government and several States provide exemptions for the religious use of peyote . . . But other governments may surely choose to grant an exemption without Oregon, with its specific asserted interest in uniform application of its drug laws, being *required* to do so by the First Amendment. Respondents also note that the sacramental use of peyote is central to the tenets of the Native American Church, but I agree with the Court that . . . our determination of the constitutionality of Oregon's general criminal prohibition cannot, and should not, turn on the centrality of the particular religious practice at issue. This does not mean, of course, that courts may not make factual findings as to whether a claimant holds a sincerely held religious belief that conflicts with, and thus is burdened by, the challenged law. The distinction between questions of centrality and questions of sincerity and burden is admittedly fine, but it is one that is an established part of our free exercise doctrine. . . .

I would therefore adhere to our established free exercise jurisprudence and hold that the State in this case has a compelling interest in regulating peyote use by its citizens and that accommodating respondents' religiously motivated conduct "will unduly interfere with fulfillment of the governmental interest." *Lee,* 455 U.S., at 259. Accordingly, I concur in the judgment of the Court.

■ JUSTICE BLACKMUN, with whom JUSTICE BRENNAN and JUSTICE MARSHALL join, dissenting.

This Court over the years painstakingly has developed a consistent and exacting standard to test the constitutionality of a state statute that burdens the free exercise of religion. Such a statute may stand only if the law in general, and the State's refusal to allow a religious exemption in particular, are justified by a compelling interest that cannot be served by less restrictive means.

Until today, I thought this was a settled and inviolate principle of this Court's First Amendment jurisprudence. . . .

. . .

. . . I agree with Justice O'Connor's analysis of the applicable free exercise doctrine, and I join parts I and II of her opinion. As she points out, "the critical question in this case is whether exempting respondents from the State's general criminal prohibition 'will unduly interfere with fulfillment of the governmental interest.' " I do disagree, however, with her specific answer to that question.

. . . The State's asserted interest . . . amounts only to the symbolic preservation of an unenforced prohibition. . . .

. . .

The State proclaims an interest in protecting the health and safety of its citizens from the dangers of unlawful drugs. It offers, however, no evidence that the religious use of peyote has ever harmed anyone. The factual findings of other courts cast doubt on the State's assumption that religious use of peyote is harmful. . . .

The carefully circumscribed ritual context in which respondents used peyote is far removed from the irresponsible and unrestricted recreational use of unlawful drugs. The Native American Church's internal restrictions on, and supervision of, its members' use of peyote substantially obviate the State's health and safety concerns. . . .

. . .

Finally, the State argues that granting an exception for religious peyote use would erode its interest in the uniform, fair, and certain enforcement of its drug laws. The State fears that, if it grants an exemption for religious peyote use, a flood of other claims to religious exemptions will follow. It would then be placed in a dilemma, it says, between allowing a patchwork of exemptions that would hinder its law enforcement efforts, and risking a violation of the Establishment Clause by arbitrarily limiting its religious exemptions. This argument, however, could be made in almost any free exercise case. . . .

The State's apprehension of a flood of other religious claims is purely speculative. Almost half the States, and the Federal Government, have maintained an exemption for religious peyote use for many years, and apparently have not found themselves overwhelmed by claims to other religious exemptions. . . .

Finally, although I agree with Justice O'Connor that courts should refrain from delving into questions of whether, as a matter of religious doctrine, a particular practice is "central" to the religion, I do not think this means that the courts must turn a blind eye to the severe impact of a State's restrictions on the adherents of a minority religion. . . .

Respondents believe, and their sincerity has never been at issue, that the peyote plant embodies their deity, and eating it is an act of worship and communion. Without peyote, they could not enact the essential ritual of their religion. . . .

If Oregon can constitutionally prosecute them for this act of worship, they, like the Amish, may be "forced to migrate to some other and more tolerant region." *Yoder,* 406 U.S., at 218. This potentially devastating impact must be viewed in light of the federal policy—reached in reaction to many years of religious persecution and intolerance—of protecting the religious freedom of Native Americans. See American Indian Religious Freedom Act, 92 Stat. 469, 42 U.S.C. § 1996 ("it shall be the policy of the United States to protect and preserve for American Indians their inherent right of freedom to believe, express, and exercise the traditional religions . . . , including but not limited to access to sites, use and possession of sacred objects, and the freedom to worship through ceremonials and traditional rites"). Congress recognized that certain substances, such as peyote, "have religious significance because they are sacred, they have power, they heal, they are necessary to the exercise of the rites of the religion, they are necessary to the cultural integrity of the tribe, and, therefore, religious survival." H.R.Rep. No. 95–1308, p. 2 (1978).

The American Indian Religious Freedom Act, in itself, may not create rights enforceable against government action restricting religious freedom, but this Court must scrupulously apply its free exercise analysis to the religious claims of Native Americans, however unorthodox they may be. Otherwise, both the First Amendment and the stated policy of Congress will offer to Native Americans merely an unfulfilled and hollow promise.

. . .

For these reasons, I conclude that Oregon's interest in enforcing its drug laws against religious use of peyote is not sufficiently compelling to outweigh respondents' right to the free exercise of their religion. Since the State could not constitutionally enforce its criminal prohibition against respondents, the interests underlying the State's drug laws cannot justify its denial of unemployment benefits. . . .

I dissent.

Church of the Lukumi Babalu Aye, Inc. v. City of Hialeah
508 U.S. 520 (1993).

The church practices the Santeria religion, whose services include animal sacrifices. When the church proposed to build a house of worship in Hialeah, the city enacted ordinances that targeted the practice of animal sacrifice by the church. One ordinance provided that "[i]t shall be unlawful for any person, persons, corporations or associations to sacrifice any animal within the corporate limits of the city of Hialeah, Florida." "Sacrifice" was defined as "to unnecessarily kill, torment, torture, or mutilate an animal in a public or private ritual or ceremony not for the primary purpose of food consumption." The ordinance contained an exemption for slaughtering by "licensed establishment[s]" of animals "specifically raised for food purposes." The court held that the ordinances violated the free exercise clause since they were neither "neutral" nor "of general applicability." The ordinances were drafted so that "almost the only conduct subject to [them] is the religious exercise of Santeria church members." All of the asserted governmental purposes (protecting public health and preventing cruelty to animals) were only pursued in the context of Santeria religious practices. "A law that targets religious conduct for distinctive treatment or advances legitimate governmental interests only against conduct with a religious motivation will survive strict scrutiny only in rare cases."

Locke v. Davey

540 U.S. 712, 124 S.Ct. 1307, 158 L.Ed.2d 1 (2004).

■ CHIEF JUSTICE REHNQUIST delivered the opinion of the Court.

The State of Washington established the Promise Scholarship Program to assist academically gifted students with postsecondary education expenses. In accordance with the State Constitution, students may not use the scholarship at an institution where they are pursuing a degree in devotional theology. We hold that such an exclusion from an otherwise inclusive aid program does not violate the Free Exercise Clause of the First Amendment.

. . .

These two Clauses, the Establishment Clause and the Free Exercise Clause, are frequently in tension. . . . Yet we have long said that "there is room for play in the joints" between them. In other words, there are some state actions permitted by the Establishment Clause but not required by the Free Exercise Clause.

. . . [T]here is no doubt that the State could, consistent with the Federal Constitution, permit Promise Scholars to pursue a degree in devotional theology . . . and the State does not contend otherwise. The question before us, however, is whether Washington, pursuant to its own constitution, which has been authoritatively interpreted as prohibiting even indirectly funding religious instruction that will prepare students for the ministry, . . . can deny them such funding without violating the Free Exercise Clause.

Davey urges us to answer that question in the negative. He contends that under the rule we enunciated in *Church of Lukumi Babalu Aye, Inc. v. Hialeah,* . . . the program is presumptively unconstitutional because it is not facially neutral with respect to religion. We reject his claim of presumptive unconstitutionality, however; to do otherwise would extend the *Lukumi* line of cases well beyond not only their facts but their reasoning. In *Lukumi,* the city of Hialeah made it a crime to engage in certain kinds of animal slaughter. . . . In the present case, the State's disfavor of religion (if it can be called that) is of a far milder kind. It imposes neither criminal nor civil sanctions on any type of religious service or rite . . . [I]t does not require students to choose between their religious beliefs and receiving a government benefit. The State has merely chosen not to fund a distinct category of instruction.

. . . Because the Promise Scholarship Program funds training for all secular professions, Justice Scalia contends the State must also fund training for religious professions. But training for religious professions and training for secular professions are not fungible. Training someone to lead a congregation is an essentially religious endeavor. . . . [T]he subject of religion is one in which both the United States and state constitutions embody distinct views—in favor of free exercise, but opposed to establishment—that find no counterpart with respect to other callings or professions. That a State would deal differently with religious education for the ministry than with education for other callings is a product of these views, not evidence of hostility toward religion.

Even though the differently worded Washington Constitution draws a more stringent line than that drawn by the United States Constitution, the interest it seeks to further is scarcely novel. In fact, we can think of few areas in which a State's antiestablishment interests come more into play. Since the founding of our country, there have been popular uprisings against procuring taxpayer funds to support church leaders, which was one of the hallmarks of an "established" religion. . . .

Most States that sought to avoid an establishment of religion around the time of the founding placed in their constitutions formal prohibitions against using tax funds to support the ministry. . . . The plain text of these constitutional provisions prohibited *any* tax dollars from supporting the clergy. We have found nothing to indicate . . . that these provisions would not have applied so long as the State equally supported other professions or if the amount at stake was *de minimis*. That early state constitutions saw no problem in explicitly excluding *only* the ministry from receiving state dollars reinforces our conclusion that religious instruction is of a different ilk. . . .

Far from evincing the hostility toward religion which was manifest in *Lukumi,* we believe that the entirety of the Promise Scholarship Program goes a long way toward including religion in its benefits. The program permits students to attend pervasively religious schools, so long as they are accredited. . . . And under the Promise Scholarship Program's current guidelines, students are still eligible to take devotional theology courses. . . .

In short, we find neither in the history or text of Article I, § 11 of the Washington Constitution, nor in the operation of the Promise Scholarship Program, anything that suggests animus towards religion. Given the historic and substantial state interest at issue, we therefore cannot conclude that the denial of funding for vocational religious instruction alone is inherently constitutionally suspect.

Without a presumption of unconstitutionality, Davey's claim must fail. The State's interest in not funding the pursuit of devotional degrees is substantial and the exclusion of such funding places a relatively minor burden on Promise Scholars. If any room exists between the two Religion Clauses, it must be here. We need not venture further into this difficult area in order to uphold the Promise Scholarship Program as currently operated by the State of Washington.

. . .

■ JUSTICE SCALIA, with whom JUSTICE THOMAS joins, dissenting.

. . .

The Court does not dispute that the Free Exercise Clause places some constraints on public benefits programs, but finds none here, based on a principle of " 'play in the joints.' " I use the term "principle" loosely, for that is not so much a legal principle as a refusal to apply *any* principle when faced with competing constitutional directives. There is nothing anomalous about constitutional commands that abut. A municipality hiring public contractors may not discriminate *against* blacks or *in favor of* them; it cannot discriminate a little bit each way and then plead "play in the joints" when haled into court. If the Religion Clauses demand neutrality, we must enforce them, in hard cases as well as easy ones.

Even if "play in the joints" were a valid legal principle, surely it would apply only when it was a close call whether complying with one of the Religion Clauses would violate the other. . . . The establishment question *would not even be close,* as is evident from the fact that this Court's decision in *Witters v. Washington Dept. of Servs. for Blind,* 474 U.S. 481, was unanimous. Perhaps some formally neutral public benefits programs are so gerrymandered and devoid of plausible secular purpose that they might raise specters of state aid to religion, but an evenhanded Promise Scholarship Program is not among them.

In any case, the State already has all the play in the joints it needs. There are any number of ways it could respect both its unusually sensitive concern for the conscience of its taxpayers *and* the Federal Free Exercise Clause. It could make the scholarships redeemable only at public universities (where it sets the curriculum), or only for select courses of study. Either option would replace a program that facially discriminates against religion with one that just happens not to subsidize it. The State could also simply abandon the scholarship program altogether. If that seems a dear price to pay for freedom of conscience, it is only because the State has defined that freedom so broadly that it would be offended by a program with such an incidental, indirect religious effect.

. . .

[T]he interest to which the Court defers is not fear of a conceivable Establishment Clause violation, budget constraints, avoidance of endorsement, or substantive neutrality—none of these. It is a pure philosophical preference: the State's opinion that it would violate taxpayers' freedom of conscience *not* to discriminate against candidates for the ministry. This sort of protection of "freedom of conscience" has no logical limit and can justify the singling out of religion for exclusion from public programs in virtually any context. . . .

II

The Court makes no serious attempt to defend the program's neutrality, and instead identifies two features thought to render its discrimination less offensive. The first is the lightness of Davey's burden. The Court offers no authority for approving facial discrimination against religion simply because its material consequences are not severe. I might understand such a test if we were still in the business of reviewing facially neutral laws that merely happen to burden some individual's religious exercise, but we are not. . . . The Court has not required proof of "substantial" concrete harm with other forms of discrimination, see, *e.g., Brown v. Board of Education,* . . . and it should not do so here.

The other reason the Court thinks this particular facial discrimination less offensive is that the scholarship program was not motivated by animus toward religion. The Court does not explain why the legislature's motive matters, and I fail to see why it should. . . .

The Court has not approached other forms of discrimination this way. When we declared racial segregation unconstitutional, we did not ask whether the State had originally adopted the regime, not out of "animus" against blacks, but because of a well-meaning but misguided belief that the races would be better off apart. . . . We do sometimes look to legislative intent to smoke out more subtle instances of discrimination, but we do so as a *supplement* to the core guarantee of facially equal treatment, not as a replacement for it. . . .

There is no need to rely on analogies, however, because we have rejected the Court's methodology in this very context. In *McDaniel v. Paty,* 435 U.S. 618 (1978), we considered a Tennessee statute that disqualified clergy from participation in the state constitutional convention. That statute, like the one here, was based upon a state constitutional provision—a clause in the 1796 Tennessee Constitution that disqualified clergy from sitting in the legislature. The State defended the statute as an attempt to be faithful to its constitutional separation of church and state, and we accepted that claimed benevolent purpose as bona fide. . . . Nonetheless, because it did not justify facial discrimination against religion, we invalidated the restriction. . . .

. . .

Today's holding is limited to training the clergy, but its logic is readily extendible, and there are plenty of directions to go. What next? Will we deny priests and nuns their prescription-drug benefits on the ground that taxpayers' freedom of conscience forbids medicating the clergy at public expense? This may seem fanciful, but recall that France has proposed banning religious attire from schools, invoking interests in secularism no less benign than those the Court embraces today. . . .

■ JUSTICE THOMAS, dissenting.

I write separately to note that, in my view, the study of theology does not necessarily implicate religious devotion or faith. . . . [T]he statute itself does not define "theology." And the usual definition of the term "theology" is not limited to devotional studies. "Theology" is defined as "[t]he study of the nature of God and religious truth" and the "rational inquiry into religious questions." American Heritage Dictionary 1794 (4th ed.2000). . . . These definitions include the study of theology from a secular perspective as well as from a religious one.

. . .

The Religious Freedom Restoration Act

The Religious Freedom Restoration Act (PL 103–141; 42 U.S.C. § 2000bb), enacted in 1993, provides, in relevant part:

SEC. 2.   CONGRESSIONAL FINDINGS AND DECLARATION OF PURPOSES.

(a)   FINDINGS. The Congress finds that

(1)   the framers of the Constitution, recognizing free exercise of religion as an unalienable right, secured its protection in the First Amendment to the Constitution;

(2)   laws "neutral" toward religion may burden religious exercise as surely as laws intended to interfere with religious exercise;

(3)   governments should not substantially burden religious exercise without compelling justification;

(4)   in Employment Division v. Smith, 494 U.S. 872 (1990) the Supreme Court virtually eliminated the requirement that the government justify burdens on religious exercise imposed by laws neutral toward religion; and

(5)   the compelling interest test as set forth in prior Federal court rulings is a workable test for striking sensible balances between religious liberty and competing prior governmental interests.

(b)   PURPOSES. The purposes of this Act are

(1)   to restore the compelling interest test as set forth in Sherbert v. Verner, 374 U.S. 398 (1963) and Wisconsin v. Yoder, 406 U.S. 205 (1972) and to guarantee its application in all cases where free exercise of religion is substantially burdened; and

(2)   to provide a claim or defense to persons whose religious exercise is substantially burdened by government.

SEC. 3.   FREE EXERCISE OF RELIGION PROTECTED.

(a)   IN GENERAL. Government shall not substantially burden a person's exercise of religion even if the burden results from a rule of general applicability, except as provided in subsection (b).

(b)   EXCEPTION. Government may substantially burden a person's exercise of religion only if it demonstrates that application of the burden to the person

(1)   is in furtherance of a compelling governmental interest; and

(2) is the least restrictive means of furthering that compelling governmental interest.

(c) JUDICIAL RELIEF. A person whose religious exercise has been burdened in violation of this section may assert that violation as a claim or defense in a judicial proceeding and obtain appropriate relief against a government. Standing to assert a claim or defense under this section shall be governed by the general rules of standing under article III of the Constitution.

SEC. 5. DEFINITIONS.

As used in this Act

(1) the term "government" includes a branch, department, agency, instrumentality, and official (or other person acting under color of law) of the United States, a State, or a subdivision of a State;

(2) the term "State" includes the District of Columbia, the Commonwealth of Puerto Rico, and each territory and possession of the United States;

(3) the term "demonstrates" means meets the burdens of going forward with the evidence and of persuasion; and

(4) the term "exercise of religion" means the exercise of religion under the First Amendment to the Constitution.

SEC. 6. APPLICABILITY.

(a) IN GENERAL. This Act applies to all Federal and State law, and the implementation of that law, whether statutory or otherwise, and whether adopted before or after the enactment of this Act.

(b) RULE OF CONSTRUCTION. Federal statutory law adopted after the date of the enactment of this Act is subject to this Act unless such law explicitly excludes such application by reference to this Act.

(c) RELIGIOUS BELIEF UNAFFECTED. Nothing in this Act shall be construed to authorize any government to burden any religious belief.

City of Boerne v. Flores

521 U.S. 507, 117 S.Ct. 2157, 138 L.Ed.2d 624 (1997).

[The report of this case appears *supra*, at p. 841.]

Cutter v. Wilkinson

544 U.S. 709, 125 S.Ct. 2113, 161 L.Ed.2d 1020 (2005).

■ JUSTICE GINSBURG delivered the opinion of the Court.

Section 3 of the Religious Land Use and Institutionalized Persons Act of 2000 (RLUIPA), 114 Stat. 804, provides in part: "No government shall impose a substantial burden on the religious exercise of a person residing in or confined to an institution," unless the burden furthers "a compelling governmental interest," and does so by "the least restrictive means." Plaintiffs below, petitioners here, are current and former inmates of institutions operated by the Ohio Department of Rehabilitation and Correction and assert that they are adherents of "nonmainstream" religions: the Satanist, Wicca, and Asatru religions, and the Church of Jesus Christ Christian. They complain that Ohio prison officials (respondents here), in violation of RLUIPA, have failed to accommodate their religious exercise "in a variety of different ways, including retaliating and discriminating against them for exercising their nontraditional faiths, denying them access to religious literature, denying them the same opportunities for group worship that are granted to adherents of mainstream religions, forbidding them to adhere to the dress and appearance mandates of their religions, withholding religious ceremonial items that are substantially identical to those that the adherents of mainstream religions are permitted, and failing to provide a chaplain trained in their faith." . . .

In response to petitioners' complaints, respondent prison officials have mounted a facial challenge to the institutionalized-persons provision of RLUIPA; respondents contend, *inter alia*, that the Act improperly advances religion in violation of the First Amendment's Establishment Clause. The District Court denied respondents' motion to dismiss petitioners' complaints, but the Court of Appeals reversed that determination. The appeals court held, as the prison officials urged, that the portion of RLUIPA applicable to institutionalized persons . . . violates the Establishment Clause. We reverse the Court of Appeals' judgment.

"This Court has long recognized that the government may . . . accommodate religious practices . . . without violating the Establishment Clause." . . . § 3 of RLUIPA, we hold, does not, on its face, exceed the limits of permissible government accommodation of religious practices.

I

A

RLUIPA is the latest of long-running congressional efforts to accord religious exercise heightened protection from government-imposed burdens, consistent with this Court's precedents. Ten years before RLUIPA's enactment, the Court held, in Employment Div., Dept. of Human Resources of Ore. v. Smith, . . . that the First Amendment's Free Exercise Clause does not inhibit enforcement of otherwise valid laws of general application that incidentally burden religious conduct. In particular, we ruled that the Free Exercise Clause did not bar Oregon from enforcing its blanket ban on peyote possession with no allowance for sacramental use of the drug. Accordingly, the State could deny unemployment benefits to persons dismissed from their jobs because of their religiously inspired peyote use. The Court recognized, however, that the political branches could shield religious exercise through legislative accommodation, for example, by making an exception to proscriptive drug laws for sacramental peyote use. . . .

Responding to *Smith*, Congress enacted the Religious Freedom Restoration Act of 1993 (RFRA). . . . In *City of Boerne*, this Court invalidated RFRA as applied to States and their subdivisions, holding that the Act exceeded Congress' remedial powers under the Fourteenth Amendment.** . . . Congress again responded, this time by enacting RLUIPA. Less sweeping than RFRA, and invoking federal authority under the Spending and Commerce Clauses, RLUIPA targets two areas: Section 2 of the Act concerns land-use regulation . . . ; § 3 relates to religious exercise by institutionalized persons. . . . Section 3, at issue here, provides that "[n]o [state or local] government shall impose a substantial burden on the religious exercise of a person residing in or confined to an institution," unless the government shows that the burden furthers "a compelling governmental interest" and does so by "the least restrictive means." . . . The Act defines "religious exercise" to include "any exercise of religion, whether or not compelled by, or central to, a system of religious belief." . . . Section 3 applies when "the substantial burden [on religious exercise] is imposed in a program or activity that receives Federal financial assistance," or "the substantial burden affects, or removal of

---

** RFRA, Courts of Appeals have held, remains operative as to the Federal Government and federal territories and possessions. . . . This Court, however, has not had occasion to rule on the matter.

that substantial burden would affect, commerce with foreign nations, among the several States, or with Indian tribes." ... "A person may assert a violation of [RLUIPA] as a claim or defense in a judicial proceeding and obtain appropriate relief against a government." ...

Before enacting § 3, Congress documented, in hearings spanning three years, that "frivolous or arbitrary" barriers impeded institutionalized persons' religious exercise. . . . To secure redress for inmates who encountered undue barriers to their religious observances, Congress carried over from RFRA the "compelling governmental interest"/"least restrictive means" standard. . . .

B

Petitioners initially filed suit against respondents asserting claims under the First and Fourteenth Amendments. After RLUIPA's enactment, petitioners amended their complaints to include claims under § 3. Respondents moved to dismiss the statutory claims. . . .

. . . [T]he District Court rejected the argument that § 3 conflicts with the Establishment Clause. . . .

. . . [T]he Court of Appeals for the Sixth Circuit reversed[, . . . holding] that § 3 of RLUIPA "impermissibly advanc[es] religion by giving greater protection to religious rights than to other constitutionally protected rights." . . . Affording "religious prisoners rights superior to those of nonreligious prisoners," the court suggested, might "encourag[e] prisoners to become religious in order to enjoy greater rights." . . .

We granted certiorari to resolve the conflict among Courts of Appeals on the question whether RLUIPA's institutionalized-persons provision, § 3 of the Act, is consistent with the Establishment Clause of the First Amendment. . . . We now reverse the judgment of the Court of Appeals for the Sixth Circuit.

II

A

. . . While the two [Religion] Clauses express complementary values, they often exert conflicting pressures. *See* . . . *Walz* . . . ("The Court has struggled to find a neutral course between the two Religion Clauses, both of which are cast in absolute terms, and either of which, if expanded to a logical extreme, would tend to clash with the other.").

Our decisions recognize that "there is room for play in the joints" between the Clauses, . . . some space for legislative action neither compelled by the Free Exercise Clause nor prohibited by the Establishment Clause. . . . On its face, the Act qualifies as a permissible legislative accommodation of religion that is not barred by the Establishment Clause.

Foremost, we find RLUIPA's institutionalized-persons provision compatible with the Establishment Clause because it alleviates exceptional government-created burdens on private religious exercise. . . . Furthermore, the Act on its face does not founder on shoals our prior decisions have identified: Properly applying RLUIPA, courts must take adequate account of the burdens a requested accommodation may impose on nonbeneficiaries . . . and they must be satisfied that the Act's prescriptions are and will be administered neutrally among different faiths. . . .

. . . Section 3 covers state-run institutions—mental hospitals, prisons, and the like—in which the government exerts a degree of control unparalleled in civilian society and severely disabling to private religious exercise. . . . RLUIPA thus protects institutionalized persons who are unable freely to attend to their religious needs and are therefore dependent on the government's permission and accommodation for exercise of their religion.

. . . In Goldman v. Weinberger, 475 U.S. 503, we held that the Free Exercise Clause did not require the Air Force to exempt an Orthodox Jewish officer from uniform dress regulations so that he could wear a yarmulke indoors. In a military community, the Court observed, "there is simply not the same [individual] autonomy as there is in the larger civilian community." . . . Congress responded to *Goldman* by prescribing that "a member of the armed forces may wear an item of religious apparel while wearing the uniform," unless "the wearing of the item would interfere with the performance [of] military duties [or] the item of apparel is not neat and conservative." . . .

We do not read RLUIPA to elevate accommodation of religious observances over an institution's need to maintain order and safety. Our decisions indicate that an accommodation must be measured so that it does not override other significant interests. In *Caldor*, the Court struck down a Connecticut law that "arm[ed] Sabbath observers with an absolute and unqualified right not to work on whatever day they designate[d] as their Sabbath." . . . We held the law invalid under the Establishment Clause because it "unyielding[ly] weigh[ted]" the interests of Sabbatarians "over all other interests." . . .

We have no cause to believe that RLUIPA would not be applied in an appropriately balanced way, with particular sensitivity to security concerns. While the Act adopts a "compelling governmental interest" standard, . . . [l]awmakers supporting RLUIPA were mindful of the urgency of discipline, order, safety, and security in penal institutions. . . .

. . .

B

The Sixth Circuit misread our precedents to require invalidation of RLUIPA as "impermissibly advancing religion by giving greater protection to religious rights than to other constitutionally protected rights." . . . Our decision in *Amos* counsels otherwise. There, we upheld against an Establishment Clause challenge a provision exempting "religious organizations from Title VII's prohibition against discrimination in employment on the basis of religion." . . . Religious accommodations, we held, need not "come packaged with benefits to secular entities." . . .

Were the Court of Appeals' view the correct reading of our decisions, all manner of religious accommodations would fall. Congressional permission for members of the military to wear religious apparel while in uniform would fail. . . . Ohio could not, as it now does, accommodate "traditionally recognized" religions . . . : The State provides inmates with chaplains "but not with publicists or political consultants," and allows "prisoners to assemble for worship, but not for political rallies."

In upholding RLUIPA's institutionalized-persons provision, we emphasize that respondents "have raised a facial challenge to [the Act's] constitutionality, and have not contended that under the facts of any of [petitioners'] specific cases . . . [that] applying RLUIPA would produce unconstitutional results." . . .

. . .

■ JUSTICE THOMAS, concurring.

I join the opinion of the Court. I agree with the Court that the Religious Land Use and Institutionalized Persons Act of 2000 (RLUIPA) is constitutional under our modern Establishment Clause case law. I write to explain why a proper historical understanding of the Clause as a federalism provision leads to the same conclusion.

. . .

Burwell v. Hobby Lobby Stores, Inc.

573 U.S. ___, 134 S.Ct. 2751 (2014).

Finding it unnecessary to reach a First Amendment Free Exercise claim, a bare majority of the Court held that a proper interpretation of the Religious Freedom Restoration Act of 1993 (RFRA) did not allow regulations of the United States Department of Health and Human Services (HHS), adopted pursuant to the Patient Protection and Affordable Care Act of 2010 (ACA), to require closely held corporations to provide health insurance coverage for four FDA-approved contraceptives to which the family owners had sincere religious objections based on the fact that those contraceptives, unlike sixteen others, may operate after the fertilization of an egg. In doing so, Justice Alito's majority opinion understood RFRA, as amended by RLUIPA, "to provide very broad protection for religious liberty." From this starting point, the Court went on to hold that (1) closely held corporations are "persons" who can "exercise religion" within the coverage of RFRA, in significant part because that protects the religious liberty of the individual corporate owners; (2) the contraceptive mandate "substantially burdens" the exercise of religion; and (3) assuming, but not deciding, "that the interest in guaranteeing cost-free access to the four challenged contraceptive methods is compelling within the meaning of RFRA," RFRA's least-restrictive means standard was "not satisfied[,]" either because the Government itself reasonably could assume the cost of providing those contraceptives for employees who wanted them, or because HHS could provide to closely held corporations the same accommodation it had decided to provide for nonprofit corporations with religious objections—namely, having the group-health-insurance issuer exclude that coverage from the employer's plan and provide separate payments for contraceptive services for plan participants without imposing any cost-sharing requirements on the eligible organizations, its insurance plan, or its employee beneficiaries, thus requiring the issuer to bear the cost. In the majority's view, either alternative would be less restrictive of the religious liberty of the closely held corporate owners than the contraceptive mandate.[a]

There were four dissenters. Justice Ginsburg, joined by Justice Sotomayor, would have held that RFRA—particularly in light of the Woman's Health Amendment to the ACA that added minimum coverage requirements for preventive services specific to women's health, and in light of the Senate's rejection of a "so-called 'conscience amendment,' which would have enabled any employer or insurance provider to deny coverage based on its asserted 'religious beliefs or moral convictions' "—did not extend any protection to for-profit corporations claiming a religious exemption from a generally applicable law. Those two Justices faulted the Court for failing to distinguish between nonprofit religious organizations, which "exist to serve a community of believers," from for-profit corporations whose owners sincerely hold religious beliefs,

---

[a]   In a concurring opinion, Justice Kennedy thought it "important to confirm that a premise of the Court's opinion is its assumption that the HHS regulation here at issue furthers a legitimate and compelling interest in the health of female employees." He further explained his position as follows:

"Among the reasons the United States is so open, so tolerant, and so free is that no person may be restricted or demeaned by government in exercising his or her religion. Yet neither may that same exercise unduly restrict other persons, such as employees, in protecting their own interests, interests the law deems compelling. In these cases the means to reconcile those two priorities are at hand in the existing accommodation the Government has designed, identified, and used for circumstances closely parallel to those presented here. RFRA requires the Government to use this less restrictive means. As the Court explains, this existing model, designed precisely for this problem, might well suffice to distinguish the instant cases from many others in which it is more difficult and expensive to accommodate a governmental program to countless religious claims based on an alleged statutory right of free exercise."

because the for-profits operate in a work "community . . . embracing persons of diverse beliefs."

Justice Breyer and Justice Kagan thought it unnecessary to decide whether RFRA extended to for-profit corporations. Instead, they joined the remainder of Justice Ginsburg's dissent, which would have held in any event that "the connection between the families' religious objections and the contraceptive coverage requirement is too attenuated to rank as substantial"—largely because the linkage is "interrupted by independent decisionmakers (the woman and her health counselor) standing between the challenged government action and the religious exercise claimed to be infringed. Any decision to use contraceptives made by a woman covered under Hobby Lobby's . . . plan will not be propelled by the Government, it will be the woman's autonomous choice, informed by the physician she consults." They also joined that part of the dissent that affirmed the Government's compelling interests in helping women "avoid the health problems unintended pregnancies may visit on them and their children" and securing "benefits wholly unrelated to pregnancy, preventing certain cancers, menstrual disorders, and pelvic pain." Finally, all of the dissenters concluded that "none of the proffered alternatives would satisfactorily serve the compelling interest to which Congress responded.

APPENDIX

THE UNITED STATES SUPREME COURT

A Chart
1789–2017[*]

The following chart is designed to provide a means of identifying the composition of the Court at any specified date, and thereby to help the student follow the relationship between changes in the personnel and doctrines of the Court.

If the student is concerned with a decision bearing a date which approximates a change in the Court's personnel it will be necessary to consult the footnotes. These notes show, following the dates of birth and death, political affiliation, home state at the time of appointment, and each justice's dates of commission and termination of service. Of course, members do not always participate in decisions rendered during their term of service; the fact of participation must be independently verified. Large X's indicate vacancies.

---

[*] This chart was originally prepared by Paul Gay, and has been updated by the editors.

Washington 1789–1797	Adams 1797–1801	Jefferson 1801–1809	Madison 1809–1817

Jay[1] 1789– –1795	[2]	Ellsworth[10] 1796–1800	Marshall[13] 1801–		

Jay[1] 1789–   –1795 | [2] | **Ellsworth[10]** 1796–1800 | **Marshall[13]** 1801–

Rut-ledge[2] | **John-son[7]** | **Paterson[8]** 1793–   –1806 | **Livingston[15]** 1806–

Cushing[3] 1789–   –1810 | **Story[17]** 1811–

Wilson[4] 1789–   –1798 | **Washington[11]** 1798–

Blair[5] 1789–   –1796 | **Chase[9]** 1796–   –1811 | **Duvall[18]** 1811–

Iredell[6] 1790–   –1799 | **Moore[12]** 1799–   –1804 | **Johnson[14]** 1804–

Todd[16] 1807–

1. John Jay, 1745–1829. Fed., N.Y. 9-26-1789 to 6-29-1795.
2. John Rutledge, 1739–1800. Fed., S.C. 9-26-1789 to 3-5-1791. *Comm. C.J. 7-1-1795 (recess appoint.) pres. August term 1795, rejected by Senate 12-15-1795.*
3. William Cushing, 1732–1810. Fed., Mass. 9-27-1789 to 9-13-1810.
4. James Wilson, 1742–1798. Fed., Pa. 9-29-1789 to 8-21-1798.
5. John Blair, 1732–1800. Fed., Va. 9-30-1789 to 1-27-1796.
6. James Iredell, 1751–1799. Fed., N.C. 2-10-1790 to 10-20-1799.
7. Thomas Johnson, 1732–1819. Fed., Md. 11-7-1791 to 2-1-1793.
8. William Paterson, 1745–1806. Fed., N.J. 3-4-1793 to 9-9-1806.
9. Samuel Chase, 1741–1811. Fed., Md. 1-27-1796 to 6-19-1811.
10. Oliver Ellsworth, 1745–1807. Fed., Conn. 3-4-1796 to 12-15-1800.
11. Bushrod Washington, 1762–1829. Fed., Va. 12-20-1798 to 11-26-1829.
12. Alfred Moore, 1755–1810. Fed., N.C. 12-10-1799 to 1-26-1804.
13. John Marshall, 1755–1835. Fed., Va. 1-31-1801 to 7-6-1835.
14. William Johnson, 1771–1834. Rep., S.C. 3-26-1804 to 8-4-1834.
15. [Henry] Brockholst Livingston, 1757–1823. Rep., N.Y. 11-10-1806 to 3-18-1823.
16. Thomas Todd, 1765–1826. Rep., Ky. 3-3-1807 to 2-7-1826. *Post created by Congress by Act of February 24, 1807.*
17. Joseph Story, 1779–1845. Rep., Mass. 11-18-1811 to 9-10-1845.
18. Gabriel Duval[l], 1752–1844. Rep., Md. 11-18-1811 to 1-14-1835.

Monroe 1817–1825	J.Q. Adams 1825–1829	Jackson 1829–1837	Van Buren 1837–1841	Harrison 3/4–4/4 Tyler 1841–1845

Marshall		Taney[24]	
	–1835	1836–	

Livingston	Thompson[19]		N.[29]
–1823	1823–	–1843	

Story

Washington	Baldwin[22]		⊠
–1829	1830–	–1844	

Duvall		Barbour[25]	Daniel[28]
–1835	1836–	–1841	1841–

Johnson	Wayne[23]
–1834	1835–

Todd	Trimble[20]	McLean[21]
–1826	1826–1828	1829–

Catron[26]
1837–

McKinley[27]
1837–

19. Smith Thompson, 1768–1843. Rep., N.Y. 12-9-1823 to 12-18-1843.
20. Robert Trimble, 1777–1828. Rep., Ky. 5-9-1826 to 8-25-1828.
21. John McLean, 1785–1861. Dem./Rep., Ohio 3-7-1829 to 4-4-1861.
22. Henry Baldwin, 1780–1844. Dem., Pa. 1-6-1830 to 4-21-1844.
23. James Moore Wayne, 1790–1867. Dem., Ga. 1-9-1835 to 7-5-1867.
24. Roger Brooke Taney, 1777–1864. Dem., Md. 3-15-1836 to 10-12-1864.
25. Philip Pendleton Barbour, 1783–1841. Dem., Va. 3-15-1836 to 2-25-1841.
26. John Catron, ca. (1778–86) 1865. Dem., Tenn. 3-8-1837 to 5-30-1865. *Post created by Congress by Act of March 3, 1837 and abolished by Congress by Act of July 23, 1866.*
27. John McKinley, 1780–1852. Dem., Ky./Ala. 9-25-1837 to 7-19-1852. *Post created by Congress by Act of March 3, 1837.*
28. Peter Vivian Daniel, 1784–1860. Dem., Va. 3-3-1841 to 5-31-1860.
29. Samuel Nelson, 1792–1873. Dem., N.Y. 2-13-1845 to 11-28-1872.

Polk 1845–1849	Taylor 1849–1850 Fillmore 1850–1853	Pierce 1853–1857	Buchanan 1857–1861	Lincoln 1861– 4/15/1865	Johnson 1865–1869	Grant 1869–

Taney   –1864 | **Chase[39]** 1864–   –1873

Nelson   –1872

S. | **Woodbury[30]** 1845–   –1851 | **Curtis[32]** 1851–   –1857 | **Clifford[34]** 1858–

Grier[31] 1846–   –1870 | **S.[40]** 1870–

Daniel   –1860 | **Miller[36]** 1862–

Wayne   –1867 | **B.[41]** 1870–

McLean   –1861 | **Swayne[35]** 1862–

Catron   –1865*

McKinley   –1852 | **Campbell[33]** 1853–   –1861 | **Davis[37]** 1862–

Field[38] 1863–

30. Levi Woodbury, 1789–1851. Dem., N. H. 9-20-1845 to 9-4-1851.
31. Robert Cooper Grier, 1794–1870. Dem., Pa. 8-4-1846 to 1-31-1870.
32. Benjamin Robbins Curtis, 1809–1874. Whig, Mass. 12-20-1851 to 9-30-1857.
33. John Archibald Campbell, 1811–1889. Dem., Ala. 3-22-1853 to 4-30-1861.
34. Nathan Clifford, 1803–1881. Dem., Me. 1-12-1858 to 7-25-1881.
35. Noah Haynes Swayne, 1804–1884. Rep., Ohio 1-24-1862 to 1-24-1881.
36. Samuel Freeman Miller, 1816–1890. Rep., Iowa 7-16-1862 to 10-13-1890.
37. David Davis, 1815–1886. Rep./Dem., Ill. 12-8-1862 to 3-4-1877.
38. Stephen Johnson Field, 1816–1899. Dem., Cal. 3-10-1863 to 12-1-1897. *Post created by Congress by Act of March 3, 1863.*
39. Salmon Portland Chase, 1808–1873. Rep., Ohio 12-6-1864 to 5-7-1873.
40. William Strong, 1808–1895. Dem./Rep., Pa. 2-18-1870 to 12-14-1880.
41. Joseph P. Bradley, 1813–1892. Whig/Rep., N.J. 3-21-1870 to 1-22-1892.

* Post abolished by Congress by Act of July 23, 1866.

Grant –1877	Hayes 1877–1881	Garfield 3/4–9/19 Arthur 1881–1885	Cleveland 1885–1889	Harrison 1889–1893	Cleveland 1893–1897	McKinley 1897– 9/14/1901

Waite[43] 1874–   –1888 | **Fuller**[50] 1888–

Hunt[42] 1872–   –1882 | **Blatchford**[48] 1882–   –1893 | **White**[55] 1894–

Clifford   –1881 | **Gray**[47] 1881–

Strong   –1880 | **Woods**[45] 1880–   –1887 | **Lamar**[49] 1888 – 1893 | **Jackson**[54] 1893–1895 | **Peckham**[56] 1895–

Miller   –1890 | **Brown**[52] 1890–

Bradley   –1892 | **Shiras**[53] 1892–

Swayne   –1881 | **Matthews**[46] 1881–   –1889 | **Brewer**[51] 1889–

Davis   –1877 | **Harlan**[44] 1877–

Field   –1897 | **McKenna**[57] 1898–

42. Ward Hunt, 1810–1886. Rep., N.Y. 12-11-1872 to 1-27-1882.

43. Morrison Remick Waite, 1816–1888. Rep., Ohio 1-21-1874 to 3-23-1888.

44. John Marshall Harlan, 1833–1911. Rep., Ky. 11-29-1877 to 10-14-1911.

45. William Burnham Woods, 1824–1887. Rep., Ga. 12-21-1880 to 5-14-1887.

46. [Thomas] Stanley Matthews, 1824–1889. Rep., Ohio 5-12-1881 to 3-22-1889.

47. Horace Gray, 1828–1902. Rep., Mass. 12-20-1881 to 9-15-1902.

48. Samuel Blatchford, 1820–1893. Rep., N.Y. 3-22-1882 to 7-7-1893.

49. Lucius Quintus Cincinnatus Lamar, 1825–1893. Dem., Miss. 1-16-1888 to 1-23-1893.

50. Melville Weston Fuller, 1833–1910. Dem., Ill. 7-20-1888 to 7-4-1910.

51. David Josiah Brewer, 1837–1910. Rep., Kan. 12-18-1889 to 3-28-1910.

52. Henry Billings Brown, 1836–1913. Rep., Mich. 12-29-1890 to 5-28-1906.

53. George Shiras, 1832–1924. Rep., Pa. 7-26-1892 to 2-23-1903.

54. Howell Edmunds Jackson, 1832–1895. Whig/Dem., Tenn. 2-18-1893 to 8-8-1895.

55. Edward Douglass White, 1845–1921. Dem., La. Asso. Just. 2-19-1894 to 12-18-1910; C.J. 12-12-1910 to 5-19-1921.

56. Rufus Wheeler Peckham, 1838–1909. Dem., N.Y. 12-9-1895 to 10-24-1909.

57. Joseph McKenna, 1843–1926. Rep., Cal. 1-21-1898 to 1-5-1925.

T. Roosevelt 1901–1909	Taft 1909–1913	Wilson 1913–1921	Harding 1921– 8/2/23	Coolidge 1923–1929

| Fuller | White | | Taft[69] | |
| –1910 | 1910– | | –1921 | 1921– | –1930 |

| White | Van Devanter[63] |
| –1910 | 1910– |

| Gray | Holmes[58] |
| –1902 | 1902– |

| Peckham | Lurton[61] | McReynolds[66] |
| –1909 | 1909– | –1914 | 1914– |

| Brown | Moody[60] | Lamar[64] | Brandeis[67] |
| –1906 | 1906–1910 | 1910– | –1916 | 1916– |

| Shiras | Day[59] | | Butler[71] |
| –1903 | 1903– | –1922 | 1922– |

| Brewer | Hughes[62](To C.J.) | Clark[68] | Sutherland[70] |
| –1910 | 1910– | –1916 | 1916– | –1922 | 1922– |

| Harlan | Pitney[65] | | Sanford[72] |
| –1911 | 1912– | –1922 | 1923– |

| McKenna | | | Stone[73] |
| –1925 | 1925– |

58. Oliver Wendell Holmes, 1841–1935. Rep., Mass. 12-4-1902 to 1-12-1932.
59. William Rufus Day, 1849–1923. Rep., Ohio 2-23--1903 to 11-13-1922.
60. William Henry Moody, 1853–1917. Rep., Mass. 12-12-1906 to 11-20-1910.
61. Horace Harmon Lurton, 1844–1914. Dem., Tenn. 12-20-1909 to 7-12-1914.
62. Charles Evans Hughes, 1862–1948. Rep., N.Y. Asso. Just. 5-2-1910 to 6-10-1916; C.J. 2-13-1930 to 6-30-1941.
63. Willis Van Devanter, 1859–1941. Rep., Wyo. 12-16-1910 to 6-2-1937.
64. Joseph Rucker Lamar, 1857–1916. Dem., Ga. 12-17-1910 to 1-2-1916.
65. Mahlon Pitney, 1858–1924. Rep., N.J. 3-13-1912 to 12-31-1922.
66. James Clark McReynolds, 1862–1946. Dem., Tenn. 8-29-1914 to 1-31-1941.
67. Louis Dembitz Brandeis, 1856–1941. Dem., Mass. 6-1-1916 to 2-13-1939.
68. John Hessin Clarke, 1857–1945. Dem., Ohio 7-24-1916 to 9-18-1922.
69. William Howard Taft, 1857–1930. Rep., Conn. 6-30-1921 to 2-3-1930.
70. George Sutherland, 1862–1942. Rep., Utah 9-5-1922 to 1-17-1938.
71. Pierce Butler, 1866–1939. Dem., Minn. 12-21-1922 to 11-16-1939.
72. Edward Terry Sanford, 1865–1930. Rep., Tenn. 1-29-1923 to 3-8-1930.
73. Harlan Fiske Stone, 1872–1946. Rep., N.Y. Asso. Just. 2-5-1925 to 7-2-1941; C.J. 7-3-1941 to 4-22-1946.

Hoover 1929–1933	F.D. Roosevelt 1933–4/12/1945	Truman 1945–1953

T. –'30	Hughes 1930– –1941	Stone 1941–1946	Vinson[85] 1946– –1953

Van Devanter –1937	Black[76] 1937–

Holmes –1932	Cardozo[75] 1932– –1938	Frankfurter[78] 1939–

McReynolds –1941	B.[81] 1941–2	Rutledge[83] 1943– –1949	Minton[87] 1949–

Brandeis –1939	Douglas[79] 1939–

Butler –1939	Murphy[80] 1940– –1949	Clark[86] 1949–

Sutherland –1938	Reed[77] 1938–

S. –'30	Roberts[74] 1930– –1945	Burton[84] 1945–

Stone (To C.J.) –1941	Jackson[82] 1941–

74. Owen Josephus Roberts, 1875–1955. Rep., Pa. 5-20-1930 to 7-31-1945.
75. Benjamin Nathan Cardozo, 1870–1938. Dem., N.Y. 3-2-1932 to 7-9-1938.
76. Hugo Lafayette Black, 1886–1971. Dem., Ala. 8-18-1937 to 9-17-1971.
77. Stanley Forman Reed, 1884–1980. Dem., Ky. 1-27-1938 to 2-25-1957.
78. Felix Frankfurter, 1882–1965. Ind., Mass. 1-20-1939 to 8-28-1962.
79. William Orville Douglas, 1898–1980. Dem., Conn. 4-15-1939 to 11-12-1975.
80. Frank Murphy, 1890–1949. Dem., Mich. 1-18-1940 to 7-19-1949.
81. James Francis Byrnes, 1879–1972. Dem., S.C. 6-25-1941 to 10-3-1942.
82. Robert Hougwout Jackson, 1892–1954. Dem., N.Y. 7-11-1941 to 10-9-1954.
83. Wiley Blount Rutledge, 1894–1949. Dem., Iowa 2-11-1943 to 9-10-1949.
84. Harold Hitz Burton, 1888–1964. Rep., Ohio 9-22-1945 to 10-13-1958.
85. Frederick Moore Vinson, 1890–1953. Dem., Ky. 6-21-1946 to 9-8-1953.
86. Thomas Campbell Clark, 1899–1977. Dem., Texas 8-19-1949 to 6-12-1967.
87. Sherman Minton, 1890–1965. Dem., Ind. 10-5-1949 to 10-15-1956.

Eisenhower 1953–1961	Kennedy 1961–1963	Johnson 1963–1969	Nixon 1969–1974	Ford 1974–1977

Warren[88] 1953–			–1969	**Burger**[97] 1969–
Black			–1971	**Powell**[99] 1971–
Frankfurter –1962	**Goldberg**[94] 1962 – 1965	**Fortas**[95] 1965 – 1969	**Blackmun**[98] 1970–	
Minton –1956	**Brennan**[90] 1956–			
Douglas			–1975	**Stevens**[101] 1975–*
Clark –1967		**Marshall**[96] 1967–		
Reed –1957	**Whittaker**[91] 1957 – 1962	**White**[93] 1962–		
Burton –1958	**Stewart**[92] 1958–			
J. –'54	**Harlan**[89] 1954–		–1971	**Rehnquist**[100] 1971–

88. Earl Warren, 1891–1974, Rep., Cal. 10-2-1953 to 6-23-1969.
89. John Marshall Harlan, 1899–1971. Rep., N.Y. 3-17-1955 to 9-23-1971.
90. William Joseph Brennan, 1906–1997. Dem., N.J. 10-15-1956 to 7-20-1990.
91. Charles Evans Whittaker, 1901–1973. Rep., Mo. 3-19-1957 to 4-1-1962.
92. Potter Stewart, 1915–1985. Rep., Ohio 10-13-1958 to 7-7-1981.
93. Byron R. White, 1917–. Dem., Colo. 4-16-1962 to 6-28-1993.
94. Arthur Joseph Goldberg, 1908–1990. Dem., Ill. 10-1-1962 to 7-26-1965.
95. Abe Fortas, 1910–1982. Dem., Tenn. 10-4-1965 to 5-15-1969.
96. Thurgood Marshall, 1908–1993. Dem., N.Y. 10-2-1967 to 10-7-1991.
97. Warren Earl Burger, 1907–1995. Rep., Va. 6-23-1969 to 9-26-1986.
98. Harry Andrew Blackmun, 1908–1999. Rep., Minn. 5-14-1970 to 6-30-1994.
99. Lewis Franklin Powell, Jr., 1907–1998. Dem., Va. 12-19-1971 to 6-26-1987.
100. William Hubbs Rehnquist, 1924–2005. Rep., Ariz. Asso. Just. 12-15-1971 to 9-26-1986; C.J. 9-26-1986 to 9-3-2005.
101. John Paul Stevens, 1920–2010. Rep., Ill. 12-19-1975 to 6-29-2010.

Carter 1977–1981	Reagan 1981–1989	Bush 1989–1993	Clinton 1993–2001

Burger	**Rehnquist**		
	–1986 | 1986–		

Powell	**Kennedy**[104]		
	–1987 | 1988–		

Blackmun		**Breyer**[108]	
		–1994 | 1994–	

Brennan		**Souter**[105]	
		–1990 | 1990–	

Stevens

Marshall		**Thomas**[106]	
		–1991 | 1991–	

White		**Ginsburg**[107]	
		–1993 | 1993–	

Stewart	**O'Connor**[102]		
–1981	1981–		

Rehnquist	(To C.J.) | **Scalia**[103]		
	–1986 | 1986–		

102. Sandra Day O'Connor, 1930–. Rep., Ariz. 9-25-1981 to 1-31-2006.
103. Antonin Scalia, 1936–2016. Rep., Washington, D.C. 9-26-1986 to 2-13-2016.
104. Anthony M. Kennedy, 1936–. Rep., Cal. 2-18-1988 to —.
105. David H. Souter, 1939–. Rep., N.H. 10-19-1990 to 6-29-2009.
106. Clarence Thomas, 1945–. Rep., Washington, D.C. 10-23-1991 to —.
107. Ruth B. Ginsburg, 1933–. Dem., Washington, D.C. 8-10-1993 to —.
108. Stephen G. Breyer, 1938–. Dem., Mass. 8-14-1994 to —.

G.W. Bush 2001–2009	Obama 2009–2017	Trump 2017–

Rehnquist –2005	Roberts 2005–*	

Kennedy*

Breyer*

Souter[105] 1990– –2009	Sotomayor[111] 2009–*	

Stevens –2010	Kagan[112] 2010–*	

Thomas*

Ginsburg*

O'Connor –2006	Alito[110] 2006–*	

Scalia –2016		Gorsuch[113] 2017–*

109. John G. Roberts Jr., 1955–. Rep., Md. 9-29-2005 to —.
110. Samuel A. Alito Jr., 1950–. Rep., N.J. 1-30-2006 to —.
111. Sonia Sotomayor, 1954–. Ind., N.Y. 8-8-2009 to —.
112. Elena Kagan, 1960–. Dem., Mass. 8-7-2010 to —.
113. Neil M. Gorsuch, 1967–. Rep., Co. 4-11-2017 to —.

* This table represents the composition of the Court to April 12, 2017.

INDEX

References are to Pages